BANKING SYSTEMS

BANKING SYSTEMS

Edited by

BENJAMIN HAGGOTT BECKHART

PROFESSOR OF BANKING, COLUMBIA UNIVERSITY

1954

Columbia University Press, New York

LIBRARY OF CONGRESS CATALOG CARD NUMBER: 54-5012

PUBLISHED IN GREAT BRITAIN, CANADA, INDIA, AND PAKISTAN
BY GEOFFREY CUMBERLEGE, OXFORD UNIVERSITY PRESS
LONDON, TORONTO, BOMBAY, AND KARACHI

MANUFACTURED IN THE UNITED STATES OF AMERICA

PREFACE

A NUMBER OF YEARS AGO, the late H. Parker Willis and I edited a volume entitled *Foreign Banking Systems*.[1] Published in 1929, this study included chapters on the banking systems of sixteen countries.

The intervening years have brought about great changes in banking and credit structures. The breakdown of commercial banking systems in the depression years resulted not only in widespread government intervention but also in the adoption of far-reaching legislation. This legislation commonly took the form of separating commercial from investment banking and of establishing banking commissions with extensive supervisory powers.

The war and the succeeding years of uneasy peace brought about further revolutionary changes in banking. Central banks have been nationalized in most countries and commercial banks have suffered the same fate in a few. A host of new governmental credit institutions has been established; governments have undertaken to guarantee many types of loans. The objectives of monetary and credit policies have expanded in many nations to include the maintenance of low interest rates and full employment. The techniques of credit control have expanded to include a selective control of various types of credit and direct control over the individual loans of commercial banks.

In view of these and many other changes, the time seemed an opportune one to issue a successor volume to *Foreign Banking Systems*. This was made possible by a generous grant of funds on the part of the Merrill Foundation for Advancement of Financial Knowledge, Incorporated. Since the new volume is not simply a revision of the former one, and since it contains a chapter on the banking systems of the United States, it has been given the title *Banking Systems*.

This volume, like its predecessor, contains chapters on the banking systems of sixteen nations. In eleven instances the countries selected were those covered in the earlier study. In five instances they

[1] H. Parker Willis and B. H. Beckhart (eds.), *Foreign Banking Systems*, New York, Henry Holt & Co., 1929.

are different. The difference in choice permits the inclusion of a more diversified group of nations.

The countries selected include those with highly developed industrial organizations; those with relatively underdeveloped resources; those with small and large proportions of foreign trade; those with well-developed banking systems and those which are in the process of evolving a fully functioning credit system; those with extensive capital markets and those which must mobilize savings in other ways. A few of the nations have convertible currencies, the majority do not. Economic organizations span the whole range from free competitive enterprise to the totalitarian state capitalism of Russia.

The unifying theme in the various chapters is the way in which credit systems have adapted themselves to the economic organizations of the respective nations. The role of commercial banks, savings institutions, urban and rural mortgage credit institutions, cooperative banks and government credit institutions in financing the credit needs of each nation is set forth. Extended treatment is accorded the place of the central bank and its credit policies and objectives. Where money markets exist, they also are discussed. A final section includes an evaluation of the banking and credit structure. The manner in which other banking systems function enables one the better to understand his own banking system, to appreciate its merits and to recognize its shortcomings.

Before closing this brief preface, a tribute should be paid to the authors of the sixteen chapters, who with professional interest in the subject and scholarly devotion agreed to prepare the manuscripts.

Special mention should also be made of the meticulous care with which Miss Matilda L. Berg and Miss Virgene F. Leverenz of the Columbia University Press edited the manuscripts, making uniform the style and presentation, and of Miss M. C. Stralucke for the arduous secretarial work involved in a study of this character. Finally, the editor would like to pay a personal tribute to Mr. Charles G. Proffitt, Director of the Columbia University Press, who showed deep interest in the project from its inception.

BENJAMIN HAGGOTT BECKHART

New York, New York
September, 1953

CONTENTS

TABLES

THE NETHERLANDS

SWEDEN

CHART

BANKING SYSTEMS

AUSTRALIA

by Torleiv Hytten

VICE-CHANCELLOR, THE UNIVERSITY OF TASMANIA

THE AUSTRALIAN ECONOMY

AUSTRALIA is a country roughly the size of the United States, but there the analogy ends. Australia has on the whole a far warmer climate, with two fifths of its area in the tropics, and also a drier climate with an interior very largely desert. It is therefore absurd to compare Australia's small population of 8,250,000 with the huge population of the United States. As far as climate is concerned, northern Australia is far more like North Africa with its deserts and sparse population, while the southern and eastern coasts resemble the European shores of the Mediterranean. The result is that the population is concentrated on the eastern and southern coastal belts, with by far the greatest concentration on the coasts of southern Queensland, New South Wales, and Victoria, that is, the region of temperate climate on the eastern side of the Continent. In addition there are closely settled regions on the coasts of South Australia and Western Australia and in Tasmania. This close settlement, then, stretches over more than 3,500 miles of coast with a hinterland of not much more than 200

TORLEIV HYTTEN was born in Norway, February 17, 1890, and came to Australia in 1910. He was educated in schools in Norway and at the University of Tasmania, where he received the Master of Arts degree with First-Class Honors in Economics in 1928. He was made Knight, first class, Order of St. Olav (Norway), for services to that country during the Second World War; appointed Companion of the Order of St. Michael and St. George (British), 1953.

After working as a journalist for a number of years, Mr. Hytten was appointed Lecturer in Economics, University of Tasmania, Hobart, 1926; Professor of Economics, 1929–35; Economic Adviser to the Government of Tasmania, 1929–35; appointed Economic Adviser to the Bank of New South Wales, 1935, but had an earlier association

miles, and sometimes less. Beyond this are wheatlands, which gradually shade into sheep country toward the arid center. One of the difficulties of the inland areas is that not only is the rainfall sparse, but it is also rather erratic, and, as a large proportion of the area is tropical, evaporation makes a sparse rainfall useless.

The development of Australia has been and is conditioned by this limitation of close settlement to the coast, sparse population in the arid interior, and a general necessity for conserving meager supplies of water. It is also conditioned by long distances internally and still longer distances from the rest of the world, which makes for greater marketing difficulties than those faced by most other countries.

As one writer [1] has pointed out, these conditions have left Australia isolated in more than one sense. Many of her problems are peculiarly her own in that her natural conditions are so different from those of other civilized countries that she has had to solve many of her prob-

---

with the Bank from 1933 onward; and was made Vice-Chancellor of the University of Tasmania in 1949.

Mr. Hytten conducted cases for the Tasmanian Government for grants from the Commonwealth Government before the Commonwealth Public Accounts Committee in 1930 and 1931 and before the Commonwealth Grants Commission in 1933 and 1934. He was Chairman of the Tasmanian State Employment Council in 1932; a member of the Royal Commission inquiring into the Tasmanian State Hydro-Electric Undertaking, 1940–41; Chairman, Commonwealth Committee on Railways, 1951; Chairman, Tasmanian Committee on Parliamentary Deadlocks, 1951.

He has been a member of the Council of the Economic Society of Australia and New Zealand for a number of years and was President in 1951 and 1952. He is also a member of the Council of the Australian Institute of International Affairs; Chairman of the Australian Round Table Group (contributing articles to the Round Table Magazine, London); Chairman of the Australian National Committee of the International Chamber of Commerce, 1948; Vice-Chairman of the International Chamber of Commerce Monetary Relations Committee, Paris, 1948; member of the Australian Research Council and Fellow of the Australian and New Zealand Association for the Advancement of Science; Fellow of the Institute of Industrial Management; Australian member, Executive Council of the Association of Universities of the British Commonwealth, 1951.

Mr. Hytten has attended the following international conferences:

International Wool Conference, Berlin, 1935
International Chamber of Commerce Congress, Paris, 1935
Australian Delegate to the League of Nations Assembly, 1935
International Conference of Bank Economists, Eastbourne, England, 1937 and 1947
International Chamber of Commerce Congress, Berlin, 1937
Industrial Management Congress, Stockholm, 1947
Association of Universities of the British Commonwealth, Executive Meetings, Delhi and Madras, 1951
International Chamber of Commerce Congress, Vienna, 1953
Congress of the Universities of the British Commonwealth, Cambridge, 1953

Mr. Hytten's publications consist mainly of articles in economic and similar journals, principally on the economics of transport and on banking.

[1] Harris, H. L., *The Economic Resources of Australia* (Sydney, 1933).

lems for herself. She has had to develop her own strains of drought-resistant wheat, solve problems connected with the production of high-grade butter in a warm climate, and the carriage of perishable goods, notably meat, over far greater distances than any other country. These are only some of her special problems, and others, including the development of a huge arid interior, have to be faced in the near future.

The population is extraordinarily homogeneous. Not only is it entirely white, apart from the 70,000 aboriginal population, but it is also about 95 percent British. The standard of living is high, and may be compared to that of the United States in some respects and to that of Britain in others. Labor is highly organized. The process of organizing unskilled labor, which has been undertaken by the Congress of Industrial Organization in the United States in recent years, was almost completed in Australia at the beginning of this century, and the political Labour Party, which largely represents organized labor, has been a strong force in Australian politics for the last forty years. Consequently labor legislation is probably more advanced than in most countries, and Australia has led the world in legislation for the arbitration of industrial disputes.

Australia's oldest industry, the pastoral industry, is still the largest single industry. It produces some beef and mutton, but by far the most important product is wool, which ranges in value from 30 percent to more than 40 percent of total primary production according to the varying fortunes of weather and world prices, and from 15 percent to 20 percent of all production. Wheat growing and dairying are the next largest, and fruit growing is extensive, ranging from the tropical fruits of Queensland to apples and berry fruits in Tasmania. Mining is also important, the principal metals being silver-lead, copper, zinc, gold, tin, and iron. Coal is found in all the states, but the principal deposits are in New South Wales. This State has large deposits of high-grade coal, and Victoria depends in a large measure on deposits of lignite. Queensland produces a little coal, but has vast fields as yet undeveloped.

The power resources of Australia are in a great degree dependent on coal, and all states are in some degree dependent on the high-grade New South Wales coal. There is little opportunity for hydroelectric development, except in Tasmania, which depends almost entirely on hydroelectric power. Development in other states is insignificant, although the Commonwealth Government is now planning to develop a fairly large scheme in New South Wales. A search for mineral oil has gone on for some years, but so far without result. Uranium deposits in South Australia and the Northern Territory are being developed, and may become important if and when atomic power is adapted to peaceful pursuits.

Manufacturing industry is a comparatively new development in Australia. Until the First World War, and even after, Australia was still in the main a country of primary production. Protection for the few industries competing with imports had to be high, and was bitterly opposed by exporters of primary products and by economists. What manufacture existed was chiefly concerned with the processing of food. But the growing autarky of European countries and the precipitate fall in the prices of primary products from 1929 onwards brought a realization that the development of manufacture would spread risks, and might be worth while even if some protection were needed. That change of opinion has been justified. There has been a rapid growth in new industry and some improvement in the efficiency of the established industries. Australia has for some time had the cheapest steel in the world, and engineering, shipbuilding, and other industries have grown up around the steel industry. Because of labor shortages since the war, output of steel has been below capacity, and capacity is still short of the total steel requirements of the country, but the industry is in the process of expansion.

The development of woolen textiles was a natural outcome of raw wool production, and in recent years the products of Australian mills have been exported in considerable quantities. Cotton manufacture is still small, but there has been a tremendous development in rayon knitting and weaving since the war. Manufacturing industry may now on the whole be said to be reasonably efficient, and is responsible for more than half the total value of all production.

Owing to the long distances both within Australia and to the principal markets overseas, transport has always been a difficult problem. Good harbors and the fact that settlement has been in the more equable coastal climate have made shipping more important than railways. The railways are almost entirely government-owned, and would indeed not have been built by private enterprise. They have never paid, because they were built ahead of time, but they have served to force the pastoral and agricultural development of the areas which they traverse.

It would be rash to say that this has led to the many experiments in nationalized industry in Australia. This is rather due to the willingness of the Australian to experiment and to what Hancock [2] describes as a "credulous idealism." There have been many ill-fated experiments, and the banking system was only saved from nationalization by the complexity of the Commonwealth Constitution on appeal to the High Court; but many public utilities are government-owned, and will remain so. This is important in that it explains the large part played by public finance, and the relatively high public debt, a considerable portion of which was raised to develop public utilities.

With so much invested in a few large primary industries, the volume of foreign trade is naturally very high. It is difficult to make international comparisons, but Australian foreign trade per head is among the highest in the world. Wool is by far the most important export, accounting for nearly half the value of all exports, with wheat next and butter and milk products, meat, fruit, sugar, and non-ferrous metals playing a substantial part. By far the best customer is Britain, taking about 40 percent in recent years, while other British countries take about 20 percent, leaving foreign countries with about 40 percent. Of these, the United States and France are the largest single customers, with from 6 percent to 8 percent, each. Imports consist, in the main, of capital equipment and partly and wholly finished manufactured goods, while petroleum products also play a considerable part. Britain supplies more than 50 percent and other British countries another 20 percent. The largest foreign supplier is again the United States, with about 10 percent.

Financial accommodation naturally becomes an important factor in this large trade, more so as, on account of distance, the time between production and delivery abroad of Australian exports is rather longer than in other countries. The same applies to imports, for which Australian banks generally have to establish credits abroad.

CREDIT NEEDS

The historical growth of Australia gives the key to the development of the credit system. The early trials of a convict settlement with a chaotic coinage are not important. Banking began with the establishment in 1817 of the Bank of New South Wales, which is still the

[2] Hancock, W. K., *Australia* (1st Australian ed., Sydney, 1945), p. 229.

largest bank in Australia. It started with the modest capital of £20,000, issued its own notes, made loans on land, and discounted trade bills. There was a great development of banking from 1826 onwards, and this was given further impetus by the gold discoveries about 1850, which were followed by heavy British investment. But the most important fact was that, when gold petered out, men turned to the land and were allowed to purchase or lease Crown land at moderate prices. The settlers had to seek the assistance of financial institutions, and these developed credit facilities, granting loans with liens on flocks or advances on land and its improvement. The commercial banks took their share in this development, but in addition there came into being large land and pastoral companies undertaking the purchase or sale on commission of wool and other products and to an extent also the financing of their customers. A boom in the late 1880s culminated in an acute financial crisis in 1893; in the first five months of that year 15 banks with a total of 1,000 branches closed their doors. The outcome has been a sound and perhaps somewhat conservative banking policy, evidenced by the fact that despite the difficult period of the early 1930s there has been no failure of any commercial bank in nearly 60 years.

The need of the rural community for finance has always been important to the Australian banks. Farmers and pastoralists borrow both for capital purposes and on short term to finance crops. Of the total land area less than 10 percent is privately owned; the rest of the occupied area (54 percent) is Crown land held by occupiers on lease or license. This is pastoral country where holdings have to be extensive for flexible operation. There are large areas in the west of New South Wales and Queensland where land capable of grazing one sheep to 10 acres is "good sheep country," and one sheep to 20 acres is not uncommon. These areas are leased and cannot be alienated from the Crown. While, therefore, loans are made on land, the practice of lending against sheep or cattle grew up fairly early in the history of Australian banking. Both farmers and pastoralists are continually in need of capital for improvements; not only buildings, but fences—sometimes of large areas—to keep sheep and cattle in and to keep rabbits out, and dams to conserve water. Such long-term loans are usually against a mortgage or a lien on livestock (stock mortgage).

In addition to this, short-term finance is needed for working expenses to tide the farmer over the period he has to wait for payment for his main income, which in the case of wool and wheat growers comes only once a year. In a country like Australia with rather sharp vicissitudes caused alternately by drought, bush fires, and floods, in addition to price fluctuations in a farmer's one and only product, the tiding-over period may extend over some years. This is usually done by overdraft, nominally callable on demand. Primary industry is responsible for 25 percent of total bank loans, but this does not tell the whole story, as farmers and pastoralists also have resort to finance outside the banking system.

Commerce requires finance for the large foreign trade. Exporters, as, for instance, wool brokers, need finance between sales and shipment or even arrival abroad. Similarly, exporters of other primary products have a long time to wait before their produce reaches markets abroad, principally in Britain. However, a number of primary products are now marketed by the Commonwealth Government. With a few minor exceptions, wheat grown in Australia must be sold to the Commonwealth Government through the Australian Wheat Board. The marketing of meat, of which Australia is the world's second largest exporter, is on a similar basis owing to a contract with Great Britain, and butter, dried fruits, and sugar are also sold through official channels. Most other products are handled through private channels and require normal methods of finance. This financing may be done on open account, by bills of exchange or by banker's irrevocable letter of credit, the latter being the more usual in these days of exchange controls and other government restrictions, even when the seller has no doubt of the buyer's integrity. Apart from this the exporter generally requires credit temporarily between sales and shipment, usually through bank loans.

Importers need finance in the same way, and again the distance means finance for longer periods than in most countries. The usual method is letter of credit or bill of exchange. Finance is also required by local trade and trade between the states, usually by local bills of exchange or checks, the latter predominating. Working capital for traders is usually provided by bank advances, while fixed capital for offices, warehouses, shops, and plant is more usually provided outside the banking system.

The growing secondary industries of Australia require an increasing amount of capital. Fixed capital for the purchase of land, buildings, plant and machinery is usually raised on the stock exchange.

Since the war a great deal of this capital has come from abroad. The estimated inflow in 1948–49 was £164 million and in 1949–50 £250 million.[3] Capital-issues control imposed under the National Security Act during the war was reimposed in 1951. A company must secure the consent of the Treasury before making an issue of authorized capital exceeding £25,000 over a period of two years. The control includes any method of raising capital, whether by shares or debentures, or on mortgage.

Provision of short-term working capital for industry is the main function of the commercial banks, but their policy is flexible, and long-term finance to buy land, erect buildings and plant is often provided for undoubted customers on a nominal "call" basis. However, the central bank has power to give directions as to the classes and purposes for which advances may be made, and accordingly issues instructions from time to time.

Directions given by the central bank late in 1950 severely restricted the lending scope of the commercial banks, which were instructed to provide industry with only short-term variations in working funds. It was the intention of the central bank that fixed capital and the bulk of working capital should be sought outside the banking system, on the stock exchange or from private sources.

The building industry has been particularly active since the war, and has substantial need for credit. The industry has taken from 15 percent to 18 percent of all advances by commercial banks in recent years, in addition to which a great deal has been advanced by government institutions, savings banks, and insurance companies. Most of this is for home building, and some is advanced through building societies, while some is advanced directly to home purchasers. These latter are the most usual form of personal loan, but personal finance is also provided for other purposes.

Table 1 gives an analysis of advances by the commercial banks, including the trading sections of the Commonwealth Bank. It is, of course, no guide to total credit needs, since manufacturing, for instance, would raise a far greater proportion of its needs on the market, while primary industry is in part financed by other financial institutions.

Last but not least are the financial requirements of the Commonwealth and six state governments, little of which comes from the

[3] *White Paper on National Income, 1949–50* (Canberra, 1950).

TABLE 1
CLASSIFICATION OF BANK ADVANCES IN AUSTRALIA
EIGHT COMMERCIAL BANKS AND COMMONWEALTH BANK (TRADING SECTIONS)
(AMOUNTS IN MILLIONS OF AUSTRALIAN POUNDS)

	JUNE, 1949		JUNE, 1951	
	Amount	Percent of Total	Amount	Percent of Total
Business advances classified according to main industry of borrower				
Rural				
Sheep	42.6		43.0	
Cattle	9.4		10.9	
Wheat	14.7		14.9	
Sugar	4.7		6.9	
Fruit	5.3		6.6	
Dairying and pigs	28.1		36.5	
Other	7.9		10.2	
	112.7	25	129.0	21
Manufacturing	99.9	22	119.3	19
Transport, storage, communication	9.4	2	13.4	2
Finance and property				
Builders and contractors	9.3		15.7	
Building societies, etc.	15.0		27.2	
Other (insurance, etc.)	32.3		38.2	
	56.6	13	81.1	13
Commerce				
Retail trade	32.5		47.0	
Wholesale trade	30.3		42.3	
Total	62.8	14	89.3	15
Miscellaneous	27.3	6	39.4	6
Not elsewhere specified	2.8	1		
Total business advances	371.5	83	471.5	76
Advances to public authorities				
Government, semigovernment, and municipal bodies	8.5	2	18.7	3
Personal advances classified according to main purpose				
Building or purchasing home	46.7	10	94.6	15
Other	23.8	5	37.5	6
	70.5	15	132.1	21
Grand total	450.5	100	622.3	100

Source: Commonwealth Statistician, *Australian Banking Statistics* (Canberra, 1952).

banks. By far the greater part of the debt is the war debt of the Commonwealth Government, most of it due to the 1939–45 war. Table 2 shows the growth of the debt since 1939.

TABLE 2
PUBLIC DEBT OF AUSTRALIA, JUNE 30, 1939 AND 1951
(AMOUNTS IN MILLIONS OF AUSTRALIAN POUNDS)

Maturing in [a]	*1939*	*1951*
Australia	704	2,664
London	467	355
New York	44	42
	1,215	3,061

Source: Commonwealth Budget Papers 1939–40 and 1951–52.

[a] Loans maturing in London are expressed at face value, without adjustment on account of currency changes since the loans were floated. Thus the London debt should be increased by 25 percent to give local currency value, while the New York debt is recorded at $4.8665 = £A1, whereas the current rate is $2.24 = £A1.

CREDIT INSTRUMENTS

By far the most general credit instrument in Australia at the present time is the check. With the expansion of industry and commerce since the depression of the 1930s the use of current accounts and consequently of checks has grown considerably. Checks are generally used in settlement of accounts between businesses, to transfer funds from place to place, in increasing measure to pay household bills, and to some considerable extent in paying salaries and wages.

The Bills of Exchange Act of 1909 defines a check as "a bill of exchange drawn on a banker payable on demand." As a bill of exchange it is a negotiable document and is transferable by delivery and indorsement, which is necessary if drawn to the order of the payee. In general practice most checks are now drawn in favor of the payee "or bearer," and consequently indorsement is unnecessary. To avoid risk of loss or theft banks encourage their customers to cross their checks, which ensures that they may not be cashed but must be paid to the credit of a bank account and hence can be traced in the event of theft. By the addition of the words "not negotiable," the negotiable feature of the check is not destroyed but the holder of a check must ensure that the previous holder's title to the check is good. This is generally a more effective protection than indorsement, which may be forged, and is widely used on checks which are sent through the mail in settlement of accounts.

A form of instrument which has become very common in Australia is the bank check, that is a check drawn on a bank by itself. The bank check takes the place of the "marked" or "certified" check in use in other financial systems and common in Australia during the last century. Bank checks are usually employed to obviate the use of cash where large payments are required as between solicitors for settlement of conveyancing transactions, where the bank's check is regarded as good as legal tender, and is more convenient and safer to handle, for it is usually crossed as not negotiable. Bank checks are usually required by customers to effect payment for share scrip, bond warrants, bills of lading, and the like.

The bill of exchange, as such, is little used now in local trade, for most concerns do business either against cash or immediate settlement by check, or alternatively on open account. Some firms from traditional usage still draw bills of exchange on their debtors, but the banks rarely discount or negotiate them, and they are generally accepted only for collection. Finance of this type of transaction is provided by the banks mostly in the form of an overdraft for working expenses.

Bills of exchange are in wider use for the financing of overseas trade. In current practice, however, they are to a great extent drawn under letter of credit, and it is on that basis that they are negotiated by the banks. The bulk of export trade in the major commodities is financed by letter of credit established on account of the overseas buyer. In recent times much of this trade has been financed directly by remittance of cash from overseas, because of the expectation of an appreciation of the currency. Bills of exchange, generally drawn in sterling, are more widely used in connection with import trade. The same expectation of exchange revaluation has led to the popularity of "after sight" bills, so that conversion to sterling may be deferred to the last possible time. Much of this trade is also financed by letters of credit.

Letters of credit are also used to meet the needs of tourists, both locally and abroad. They may be issued addressed to a particular branch or bank or may be circulars addressed to many branches or correspondents. They usually authorize negotiation of the check or bill of the traveler drawn on his own branch or else on the head office or London office of the issuing bank.

Promissory notes are restricted in the main to hire purchase (installment credit) agreements and to some types of small personal loans granted by the banks. Promissory notes drawn in favor of a client are rarely discounted but are sometimes held, together with the hire purchase agreement as collateral security for overdraft accommodation to a hire purchase finance company.

BANKING AND CREDIT INSTITUTIONS IN AUSTRALIA

The varied credit needs that have been outlined have given rise to a variety of financial institutions, specializing to an extent in various fields, but generally overlapping in their functions. The large commercial banks, for instance, do almost any class of business also undertaken by more specialized institutions, such as the rural banks, savings banks, and pastoral finance companies. The central bank has divisions competing with practically every other type of financial institution. The large life insurance companies have not been included in the list given below. In the period up to the First World War these had a substantial investment in mortgage loans, but in the interwar period they changed their policy substantially and became large holders of government securities. Restrictions on the lending policy of commercial banks during and after the Second World War, coupled with the low interest rate offered on government bonds, has once more tempted them into the private investment field, again primarily lending on mortgage. It is as yet too early to say whether this is likely to be a permanent feature.

The principal credit institutions in Australia are outlined below.

1. The *Commonwealth Government Treasury,* which issues loans on its own behalf, as well as on behalf of the governments of the states.
2. *Commonwealth Bank of Australia,* which is the central bank, owned by the Government of the Commonwealth. It has two divisions:

Central Banking Division, to which is attached the Note Issue Department;

General Banking Division, with 436 branches. There are three sub-departments: The Industrial Finance Department, the Rural

Credits Department, and the Mortgage Bank Department. These departments are represented as required in the branches of the bank.

3. *Commercial Banks.* There are the following seven banks (number of branches in parentheses):

Bank of New South Wales	(655)
Commercial Banking Co. of Sydney Ltd.	(326)
National Bank of Australasia Ltd.	(436)
Commercial Bank of Australia Ltd.	(390)
Bank of Adelaide	(64)
English, Scottish and Australian Bank Ltd.	(257)
Australia and New Zealand Bank Ltd.	(553)

The first five of the banks have their head offices in Australia and the last two in London.

4. *Other Banks.*

Ballarat Banking Co. Ltd.

Brisbane Permanent Building and Banking Co. Ltd.

These are two joint stock banks operating only in their respective cities.

5. *Foreign Banks,* branches of which exist in Australia.

Comptoir National d'Escompte de Paris

Bank of New Zealand

Bank of China

These banks are mainly concerned with financing trade between Australia and their respective countries, and have only one office each in Australia.

6. *State Rural Banks.*

Rural Bank of New South Wales

State Bank of South Australia

Rural and Industries Bank of Western Australia

Agricultural Bank of Tasmania

Credit Foncier Department, State Savings Bank of Victoria

These five banks are created by and guaranteed by the state government concerned. They are restricted to the area of the state and have specialized in financing rural industry and to a limited extent city house building, though lately the Rural Bank of New South Wales has entered the general banking field.

7. *Merchant Banks.*

Anglo-Australian Corporation, Melbourne

Mainguard Ltd., Sydney

Charterhouse Investment Trust, London, with subsidiary companies registered in Melbourne and Sydney

These "merchant banks" are of very recent formation and at present appear to be acting more as investment houses. The Anglo-Australian Corporation is a subsidiary of Lazard Bros. of London. Mainguard Ltd. is a very recently formed Australian joint stock company.

8. *Savings Banks.*

Commonwealth Savings Bank, a section of the Commonwealth Bank operating in all states

State Savings Bank of Victoria, state-owned

Savings Bank of South Australia, state-owned

Hobart Savings Bank, trustee bank

Launceston Bank for Savings, trustee bank

9. *Pastoral and Land Finance Companies.* There are a number of these. They are important in extending rural credit, and in some cases almost act as the bankers of their customers.

In addition, there are other types of credit institutions of which the following are the more important: building and investment societies, co-operative credit associations, trustee executor and agency companies, insurance companies, friendly societies, and hire purchase companies. There are also the usual credit facilities to customers extended by both wholesale and retail traders.

COMMERCIAL BANKS

The outstanding feature in the history of Australian banking has been its continued concentration into a few large institutions with a large number of branches. At present there are seven principal private commercial banks with approximately 2,680 branches, in addition to which there are 436 branches operated by the trading section of the Commonwealth Bank. As mentioned in an earlier section, there was a considerable weeding out of the weaker banks in 1893. In 1914 there were 20 banks, and by 1925 these had been reduced to 15. Since then no commercial bank has failed, but there has been a continuous process of amalgamation, which still seems to be going on. On October 1, 1951, the greatest merger of all time in Australia took place between the Bank of Australasia and the Union Bank of Australia, two of the three banks controlled from London, with shareholders' funds amounting to 19 million pounds and deposits totaling 346 million pounds. The new bank is known as the Australia and New Zealand Bank Limited.

The network of branches of the eight principal commercial banks and the Commonwealth Bank extends over the main populated areas of the Commonwealth. Although the business of some banks is concentrated in one or two states, all important centers are served by branches of most of the banks.

The Australia and New Zealand Bank Limited, Bank of New South Wales, and Commercial Bank of Australia Limited, have extensive systems of branches in New Zealand, designed to provide normal banking facilities in that country as well as to finance trade between the two countries. Similarly the Bank of New South Wales has branches and agencies in Fiji, and that bank and the Commonwealth Bank have branches in New Guinea and Papua. All banks maintain offices in London in order to finance trade, clear foreign transactions, and assist tourists. To meet the needs of foreign trade, individual banks have built up a wide coverage of international correspondents, with whom various agency arrangements have been organized. Apart from the banks controlled from London, the Australian banks have no relations of proprietorship with banks in other countries.

The administration of the principal banks is concentrated in the person of the general manager, who is responsible to the board of directors for general policy. Senior appointments are made by the board on the recommendation of the general manager. Under the general manager the organization is devolved on a regional basis, either by state or by geographical and regional divisions within a state. These divisions are administered by inspectors or state managers who have wide powers over staff appointments and considerable discretion in authorizing lending within the general policy laid down by the head office in conformity with central bank advance policy. Branch managers are empowered to make loans up to varying amounts according to their status and experience and the type of business transacted at their branch.

The private banks operating in Australia were established by Royal Charter, by a special Act of Parliament, or under the general company law of the appropriate state. All are operated as limited liability companies, and their capital is issued in shares. In some cases there exists a reserve liability of shareholders equal to the subscribed amount of the shares, callable only on winding up; two private banks have an uncalled liability.

While the Commonwealth has powers to legislate in the matter of banking, there was no attempt to do so until 1945, apart from acts relating to the Commonwealth Bank, which will be dealt with later. But in that year a banking act was passed, subjecting the banks to Commonwealth law, which supersedes the laws of the states.

The Banking Act was the culmination of a long political controversy dating back to the depression of the early 1930s. There was during those years a natural weeding out of the less efficient in commerce and industry, and farmers and pastoralists were in particularly grave difficulties from the precipitous fall in the prices of food and raw material products. Although the banks provided extensive carry-on finance, there were naturally some bankruptcies and foreclosures, and the banks were subjected to a great deal of criticism. As the depression deepened, the Commonwealth Bank refused to grant the governments, both state and Federal, further accommodation until they put their finances in order. In the ensuing political crisis there was some agitation for the nationalization of the banks. As a result, a Royal Commission was appointed in 1936 to investigate the monetary and banking system of Australia and to suggest remedies. The Commission reported the following year and recommended a number of measures for greater control by the Commonwealth Bank, and the licensing of commercial banks. But it expressed the opinion that Australia would be best served by privately owned commercial banks controlled by the central bank. Then the war intervened and no action was taken until 1945.

The Banking Act and the Commonwealth Bank Act of 1945 put into operation a number of the recommendations of the Banking Commission, but went a great deal further in providing for detailed control of the banks. It provided for the licensing of banks, which had to be corporate bodies, and granted licenses to all the existing banks. One provision in the Commonwealth Bank Act made it compulsory for state and local government bodies to transfer their accounts to the Commonwealth Bank. The Melbourne City Council challenged this provision as unconstitutional and won its case, whereupon the Government introduced a bill to nationalize the banks. It was passed after a bitter controversy as the Banking Act of 1947. The stated objects of the act were:

a) the expansion of the banking business of the Commonwealth

Bank as a publicly-owned bank conducted in the interests of the people of Australia and not for private profit;

b) the taking over by the Commonwealth Bank of the banking business in Australia of private banks and the acquisition on just terms of property used in that business;

c) the prohibition of the carrying on of banking business in Australia by private banks.

It provided for the compulsory acquisition by the Commonwealth Bank of the shares held in Australia of private banks, or the taking over of the business of any private bank by negotiation. The act was immediately challenged by the banks as well as by the states of Victoria and South Australia, and its main provisions were declared *ultra vires* of the Constitution by the High Court of Australia. An election was fought in part on this issue in December, 1949, and the Labour Government was defeated. The incoming Liberal Government immediately introduced a bill repealing the act and making some amendments to the Commonwealth Bank Act of 1945.

However, the Banking Act of 1945 is not affected and still operates. Apart from the provisions already mentioned it makes general provision for government supervision and control.

In addition to the usual requirements of companies to publish their annual balance sheets, and the supervision and examination of the taxation authorities, the private banks are subject to several forms of government supervision and control. The Commonwealth Bank is charged with the duty of protecting the depositors of the other banks; it may at any time require a commercial bank to supply sworn information about its financial stability and in default may undertake investigation of its affairs. If "in the opinion of the Commonwealth Bank" a bank is likely to become unable to meet its obligations, the Commonwealth Bank may assume control and carry on its operations in order to safeguard the interests of depositors. So far, of course, this extreme step has not been necessary. The Commonwealth Bank is also empowered to request any information from another bank, except details of a particular customer's business. This power is given to enable the Commonwealth Bank to police its instructions on advance policy and exchange control.

The commercial banks are required to deposit in "Special Accounts" with the Commonwealth Bank "such amount as the Commonwealth Bank by notice in writing directs." This provides a continuation of what in the first place was a wartime anti-inflationary measure, as a result of which any deposits in excess of those held by the banks in September, 1939, were sterilized. Banks may make withdrawals only as permitted by the Commonwealth Bank. The commercial banks are also required to secure the consent in writing of the Commonwealth Bank to any purchase or subscription of government or other securities or company shares. By these means, and by its regulation of interest rates charged and allowed by commercial banks, the Commonwealth Bank is able effectively to control the earning capacity of the commercial banks.

The banking act also lays down the details of statistical information which the banks must provide about their business. Balance sheet and profit and loss account must be provided in a prescribed form for publication in the *Government Gazette*. Weekly statements of the main liability and asset items and totals of debits to customers' accounts must also be supplied for publication in the *Gazette* as an average for each month. Furthermore, the banks are obliged to give, but not for publication, details of the components of their income and expenditure, a weekly statement of their foreign currency holdings, and an analysis of advances and deposits grouped by main industrial categories, together with details of interest rates and the purpose for which advances are made. The Commonwealth Auditor-General has access at any time to the books of the banks and may undertake any investigation at the instruction of the Government.

Before the war, bank shareholders' funds were equivalent to about 20 percent of deposit liabilities to the public. The proportion varied with different institutions, being lowest (13.5 percent) in the case of the Bank of New South Wales and highest (31.6 percent) for the Bank of Adelaide. In the past decade, issued capital has been virtually unchanged, apart from amalgamations. Shareholders' funds have increased only slightly with the aggregation of undistributed profits; deposit liabilities, on the other hand, have expanded rapidly. The ratio of shareholders' funds to deposits has fallen to the vicinity of 6 percent.

These changes have occasioned no public discussion, and no increase in bank capital has been considered necessary in view of the high proportion of bank assets (41.5 percent of deposits in December, 1951) frozen in the Special Accounts with the central bank, bearing interest at ½ percent. Table 3 gives a comparison of shareholders' funds and deposit liabilities in 1939 and the latest available year.

Table 3
Bank Capital and Deposit Liabilities
(amounts in australian pounds)

Bank	*Paid-up Capital*	*Reserves and Profit and Loss Account*	*Total Share-holders' Funds*	*Deposit Liabilities*	*Total Sharehold-ers' Funds as Percent of Deposit Liabilities*
Bank of Australasia					
Oct. 16, 1939 [a]	4,500,000	4,712,106	9,212,106	40,921,527	22.5
Union Bank of Australasia Ltd.					
Aug. 31, 1939 [a, c]	4,000,000	5,007,351	9,007,351	38,743,598	23.2
Australia and New Zealand Bank Ltd.					
Sept. 29, 1951	10,667,500	8,535,305	19,202,805	345,629,443	5.6
Bank of Adelaide					
Sept. 30, 1939	1,250,000	1,030,841	2,280,841	7,201,011	31.6
Sept. 30, 1951	1,250,000	1,376,630	2,626,630	32,181,634	8.2
Bank of New South Wales					
Sept. 30, 1939	8,780,000	6,341,053	15,121,053	111,688,553	13.5
Sept. 30, 1951	8,780,000	7,218,869	15,998,869	451,658,519	3.6
Commercial Bank of Australia Ltd.					
June 30, 1939	4,117,350	2,365,910	6,483,260	31,006,658	20.9
June 30, 1951	4,117,350	2,549,509	6,666,859	158,296,016	4.2
The Commercial Banking Company of Sydney Ltd.					
June 30, 1939	4,739,012	4,429,199	9,168,211	53,713,812	17.1
June 30, 1951	4,739,012	4,998,220	9,737,232	192,283,031	5.1
The English, Scottish & Australian Bank Ltd.[a, b]					
June 30, 1939	3,000,000	3,614,367	6,614,367	36,816,506	17.9
June 30, 1951	3,000,000	3,237,769	6,237,769	110,227,412	5.7
The National Bank of Australasia Ltd.					
March 31, 1939	5,000,000	3,456,186	8,456,186	44,057,573	19.2
The Queensland National Bank Ltd.[c]					
June 30, 1939	1,750,000	881,557	2,631,557	11,928,098	22.1
The National Bank of Australasia Ltd.					
June 30, 1951	6,726,025	5,493,794	12,219,819	214,548,611	5.7

Source: Balance sheets of individual banks.

[a] Capital accounts of these banks are expressed in sterling currency and consequently should be regarded as 25 percent greater in Australian currency. Some parts of their deposit liabilities also are expressed in sterling. The balance sheet of Australia and New Zealand Bank Ltd. is now presented entirely in Australian currency; former reserves for currency depreciation have been attributed to the various capital and reserve accounts to enable them now to be quoted in Australian currency.

[b] The English, Scottish & Australian Bank Ltd. shareholders' funds were reduced in 1946 when £1,675,000 inscribed stock was repaid from liquid assets.

[c] Amalgamated with the National Bank of Australasia Ltd. in 1949.

A safeguard for depositors is provided in Section 15 (i) of the Banking Act of 1945. The section provides that: "except with the authority of the Commonwealth Bank, a bank shall hold assets (other than goodwill) in Australia of a value not less than the total amount of its deposit liabilities in Australia."

Although not specifically designed as reserve provisions, the special account requirements provide a flexible way of maintaining commercial bank reserves at a level determined by the central bank in accord with current circumstances.

Deposits are accepted by the commercial banks on current account payable on demand, but generally bearing no interest. As an act of grace, banks sometimes allow interest on the current accounts of charitable institutions. Rates allowed by one bank are 2 percent per annum on the average minimum monthly balance up to £2,000 and 1 percent on average amounts above that.

In addition, banks accept deposits for fixed terms which bear interest as follows: 3 months ½ percent, 6 months ¾ percent, 12 months 1 percent, 24 months 1½ percent for deposits up to £1,000 and 1 percent in excess. These deposits, which are almost peculiar to Australia, have an interesting feature. They rise strongly when trade is bad, and fall correspondingly in boom times. Thus during the depression of the early 1930s they reached nearly 70 percent of total deposits, while since the war they have dropped as low as 24 percent. The obvious reason is that in hard times liquid capital is safer with a good banking system than elsewhere.

There is also another factor contributing to the present low level of these deposits. In order to assist public purchases of government securities during the war, rates on interest-bearing deposits were successively reduced to the present level. In consequence, the relative importance of interest-bearing deposits, which the banks formerly sought quite keenly as a relatively fixed source of investible funds, has declined. Thus in June, 1939, deposits bearing interest of the commercial banks totaled £201 million and other deposits £120 million. In June, 1951, these figures were £250 million and 1,025 million pounds respectively. The changes in deposits are shown in Table 4.

Australian banks invest their funds almost entirely in advances to industry and Australian public securities. Both of these avenues of investment are now controlled by the Commonwealth Bank. The banks must have the central bank's permission to buy Treasury bills

TABLE 4
COMMERCIAL BANKS, AVERAGE DEPOSITS
QUARTER ENDED JUNE 30, SELECTED YEARS 1920–51
(AMOUNTS IN MILLIONS OF AUSTRALIAN POUNDS)

YEAR	NOT BEARING INTEREST		BEARING INTEREST		TOTAL
	Amount	Percent of Total	Amount	Percent of Total	Amount
1920	113	52.8	101	47.2	214
1925	108	43.9	138	56.1	246
1930	89	33.2	179	66.8	268
1935	107	36.6	185	63.4	292
1940	138	39.4	212	60.6	350
1945	364	61.8	225	38.2	589
1946	417	66.1	214	33.9	631
1947	451	69.0	203	31.0	654
1948	511	71.8	201	28.2	712
1949	608	73.7	217	26.3	825
1950	770	76.4	238	23.6	1,008
1951	1,025	80.4	250	19.6	1,275

Source: *Australasian Insurance and Banking Record* (Melbourne); *Commonwealth Statistician* (Canberra).

or bonds, and advances are controlled by regulations issued by the central bank.

The great change in the lending policy of Australian banks since the First World War is shown in Table 5. Until the depression of 1930 the ratio of cash and balances with the central bank to deposits was usually well above 20 percent, generally in the region of 24 percent. Sir Douglas Copland, writing in 1929 [4] pointed out that they got unduly low at 19 percent in the depression of 1924. But the introduction of Treasury bills in 1930 altered this position. Here was a fairly liquid investment, which could be rediscounted with the central bank, and which therefore made large cash holdings unnecessary; as a result these gradually dropped to about 11 percent in 1939.

The next factor to influence the ratio of cash holdings was the introduction of the Special Accounts in 1941. The effect of these was to lower advances fairly substantially while war inflation made for steadily mounting deposits. Before the war the ratio of advances to deposits was normally about 90 percent, and had been as high as 104 percent, but it dropped sharply to 35 percent in 1945, and is now 42 percent. While the special deposits cannot be withdrawn without

[4] Copland, D. B., "The Banking System of Australia," in Willis and Beckhart, *Foreign Banking Systems* (London, 1929).

TABLE 5
COMMERCIAL BANK DEPOSITS AND INVESTMENTS
AVERAGES, QUARTER ENDED JUNE 30, SELECTED YEARS 1920–51
(AMOUNTS IN MILLIONS OF AUSTRALIAN POUNDS)

Year	*Total Deposits*	*Advances and Bills Discounted*	*Advances in Percent of Deposits*	*Government Bonds*	*Treasury Bills*	*Special Accounts*	*Cash and Balances with Central Bank*	*Cash in Percent of Deposits*
1920	214	150	70.1	19			51	23.8
1925	246	195	79.3	10			50	20.3
1930	268	260	97.0	12	2		37	13.8
1935	292	252	86.3	23	24		38	13.0
1940	350	287	82.0	42	42		39	11.1
1945	589	206	35.0	109	55	240	36	6.1
1946	631	220	34.9	123	51	258	34	5.4
1947	654	284	43.4	81	21	279	36	5.5
1948	712	344	48.3	59	25	287	46	6.5
1949	825	377	45.7	63	14	383	43	5.2
1950	1,008	419	41.6	96	25	455	51	5.1
1951	1,275	503	39.5	92	48	567	60	4.7

Source: *Australasian Insurance and Banking Record; Commonwealth Statistician.*

consent of the central bank, it is possible to borrow against them, and the lower earning power has forced the banks to economize on cash reserves. Moreover, the monetary expansion has eased the pressure on cash resources. The cash ratio therefore dropped to 6 percent in 1947 and has since fallen to about 5 percent.

To all intents and purposes there is no such thing as a fixed commercial loan for a definite period in Australia. Practically all bank loans are on overdraft, nominally at call, but in practice providing long-term credit. There are only minor departures from this practice as far as the commercial banks are concerned, although other credit institutions do make loans for fixed periods.

The system in commercial banking is to mark on the customer's account a limit beyond which he is not allowed to draw. Interest is charged on the debit balance of his account and not on the full amount granted. Repayment, although nominally on demand, is made according to agreement with the bank, but the loan may be paid off more rapidly, if desired. This provides a very flexible system well suited to Australia, where so much primary production is very precarious; despite increasing industrialization, the fortunes of the whole community are liable to fluctuate with that of the farmer and pastoralist. The overdraft system has served well and is used even to provide fixed capital equipment of farmers and industrialists alike. The interest rate on overdrafts is controlled by the central bank. The maximum rate permissible was 4¾ percent until the end of 1947, when it was lowered to 4½ percent.

There has always been marked seasonal fluctuation in advances, with a high point in spring and early summer (September–November), and a low point about March, when most harvest and wool-clip payments have come in. In recent years monetary expansion has tended to conceal these seasonal fluctuations in demand for credit. In addition, scarcity of materials and labor has meant that farmers and pastoralists have not been able to do all the maintenance of fences, buildings and other plant, which they would normally do, and have reduced overdrafts or built up cash balances instead.

Apart from advances, the chief investments of the banks are in government and local authority securities, including Treasury bills. Practically no securities in companies are held by the banks on their own account. Holdings of securities have increased substantially in recent years, and show fairly wide fluctuations.

In lending policy, the banks are controlled by directions issued by the central bank from time to time. These generally are on broad lines, setting out the type of industry or commercial undertaking and the type of transaction within that industry or trade which the central bank wishes to restrict or to divert, for financing, outside the banks. For instance, it may direct that advances for home building be allowed up to certain amounts and for a certain period, but that the building of apartment houses or factories should not be financed through the banks. The banks themselves are left to interpret the directions, and only in doubtful cases need they consult the central bank. In such cases the reporting bank must not disclose the names of customers to the central bank, a necessary safeguard as the Commonwealth Bank is a competitor for general banking business. The system appears to work well enough, although there are complaints from the commercial banks as to undue restrictions to legitimate industrial expansion, and from the central bank that directions are not always strictly followed.

There is strong competition among the banks for business, but it has always been understood, although not strictly observed, that banks will not undercut one another in the matter of interest. Hence competition has generally been confined to services rendered to customers. With the maximum rate of interest now being controlled by the central bank, there is little room for differentiation and the maximum is tending to become the minimum.

There is a somewhat loose association of banks called the Associated Banks of Victoria, which discusses common problems and whose chairman usually acts as the mouthpiece of the Melbourne banks. But the association has little power, and the two Sydney banks are not members, although their Melbourne representatives usually attend meetings as observers.

The most important service of the commercial banks is the check service, which is used very extensively. By virtue of their extensive branch systems the Australian banks are able to clear most out-of-town items directly. In the cities, clearings are effected through the banks' clearinghouses, and the pooled settlement is then made through the banks' accounts with the central bank. The banks charge a small commission for inter-town checks, varying with the distance between centers.

The banks hold bonds and shares for safe custody on behalf of their clients, collecting bond interest and paying dividends to their customers' accounts. Small fees are charged for these services, and also as commission for making various payments authorized by clients.

In recent years the banks have extended services which were not formerly looked upon as part of their function. Several banks have travel departments, which not only look after the banking needs of travelers, but also render the services of a normal tourist bureau by booking passage and accommodations. The Bank of New South Wales originated this service in 1933, and its success may be judged from the fact that this bank now has 64 employees in travel departments in Australian and New Zealand cities and in London.

The same bank initiated an economic research service in 1931. Its Economic Department in Sydney, with branches in London and New Zealand, does research, gives advice to clients, and is responsible for a public quarterly bulletin as well as for an information service within the bank. It has also served as a training department for young university graduates in giving them virtually a post-graduate course in practical financial and industrial problems. These men were eagerly sought by Commonwealth Departments needing economists during the war, and their consequent promotion in the public service has in some cases been rapid, giving eloquent testimony of the soundness of their training. The National Bank followed, and now five of the eight banks have similar departments, although on a somewhat smaller scale. The National Bank was the first to inaugurate a public relations department separate from its economics staff; this policy has been adopted by other banks.

The relations between the banks and their employees are good. There is a bank officers' association, which is in the nature of a trade union and negotiates with the employers on matters of salaries and conditions of work, but the relations between the association and the banks have seldom been at all strained. On the contrary, the association was a strong supporter of banks in the political fight against nationalization, and bank staffs generally threw themselves eagerly into the campaign.

Recruitment is generally of boys and girls at matriculation standard, that is, at the age of 16 or 17. A general shortage of manpower since the beginning of the war has forced the banks to recruit younger people, who have not finished their secondary education. University graduates were not employed until economic research departments were instituted, but some of the banks now recruit graduates and encourage employees to embark on university courses by paying fees and as far as possible allowing time off for study. Bank officers are also encouraged to take accountancy examinations or to qualify as associates of the Australian Bankers' Institute, an examining body which requires training in accountancy, commercial law, banking practice, and elementary economics.

SAVINGS BANKS

The largest and most important savings bank is the Commonwealth Savings Bank of Australia. Established in 1912 as a separate institution under the direction of the Commonwealth Bank, it absorbed the state savings banks of Queensland and Tasmania. It holds more than 60 percent of all savings bank deposits.

In 1931 the State Savings Bank of New South Wales was forced to close its doors because of temporary difficulties. It was taken over by the Commonwealth Savings Bank, which in the same year also absorbed the Savings Bank of Western Australia. There is still a state savings bank in Victoria. South Australia has one and Tasmania two, all three governed by trustees and guaranteed by the respective state governments.

The Commonwealth Savings Bank has no subscribed capital. Apart from deposits its only reserve funds are accumulated profits, which, in 1950, were £6.3 million. Half of the annual profits are set aside in the reserve fund, and the other half is paid into the National Debt Sinking Fund for use in the redemption of the public debt.

At present the Commonwealth Savings Bank and the State Savings Bank of Victoria pay 2 percent on the first £500 and 1 percent thereafter up to £1,000, beyond which no interest is allowed. The other banks pay ¼ percent more, but have the same limitation as to amount. For small investors, savings bank deposits provide a useful investment at short call and show a higher return than the fixed deposits of the commercial banks. As agencies the Commonwealth Savings Bank uses post offices and stores in country centers. Total deposits of savings banks grew from £246 million in 1939 to £787 million in 1951.

Savings banks invest substantial amounts in government and local authority securities, but also place funds at fixed deposit with commercial banks. The Commonwealth Savings Bank lodges these funds with the General Banking Division of the Commonwealth Bank; other savings banks lodge them with the commercial banks.

The Commonwealth Savings Bank may also advance money to the Rural Credit Department, the Mortgage Bank Department, and the Industrial Finance Department of the Commonwealth Bank. The state savings banks lend money on mortgage through *credit foncier* departments. Thus an aggregation of small individual deposits is fed into the banking system to meet credit needs. The extent of holdings of government securities by savings banks could wield considerable influence on open-market operations by the central bank, but there is little evidence that this has occurred to any great extent.

RURAL CREDIT

Special types of organizations have been established, mainly to provide fixed loans for primary producers. The Rural Bank of New South Wales and the State Bank of South Australia are cases in point. Their funds are provided chiefly by state-guaranteed debentures, by advances by the states, or, to a small extent, by deposits from the public. These banks are controlled by commissioners appointed by the state government. In Victoria, the *credit foncier* department of the state savings bank uses funds provided by issues of debentures, some held by the savings bank, and some by the public. In Queensland, Western Australia, and Tasmania the corresponding institutions are in effect state government departments.

In addition, some state governments have set up departments to make advances to returned soldiers and others for the purpose of establishing and maintaining them on the land. These form no part of the banking system, although they provide credit which, if they did not exist, would have to be obtained from other sources.

The Commonwealth Bank has two departments for the provision of rural credit. One is the Mortgage Bank Department with a capital of £4 million provided out of the profits of the bank. The Commonwealth Bank itself may advance up to £1 million to the Mortgage Bank Department, which may also obtain advances from the Commonwealth Savings Bank and the Treasurer. The object of the department is to make long-term (from 5 to 41 years) loans up to £5,000, against mortgages on agricultural or pastoral land.

The other department of the Commonwealth Bank is the Rural Credits Department, which has a capital of £2 million. The Commonwealth Treasurer may lend the department, through the bank, an additional £3 million. The Commonwealth Bank itself may also make advances to the department. The department may make loans to producers upon the security of primary produce placed under the legal control of the bank, and to co-operative associations or marketing boards on other security associated with the production or marketing of primary products. Several boards have been set up by Commonwealth and state governments to cover the export of at least the major rural products, except wool. The term for advances is one year, but there is no limit as to amount.

Pastoral finance companies provide both short- and long-term capital to primary producers, mainly wool-growers. These are private joint stock companies, whose loan funds are provided by share and debenture capital and reserves. They supplement credit facilities offered by commercial banks. The financial operations of these firms complement their normal trading activities—mainly wool selling, livestock, and the sales of property, farm machinery, and other farm requisites. Pastoral finance companies usually accept deposits from their own customers, but not from the public. In general, their function is to advance to producers against later produce to be sold by them. The total amount of seasonal advances varies, but at peak times some firms must operate on overdraft with the commercial banks. Like the commercial banks, they charge interest on daily balances.

URBAN MORTGAGE AND CONSUMER CREDIT

Mortgage credit in towns and cities has been of growing importance since the war. The Australian likes to have his own house and garden and does not take as kindly to a rented apartment as do people in America or Europe. Nevertheless, large blocks of apartments are springing up in the larger cities. The considerable lag in house building, dating from the depression of the 1930s, had not been overtaken when the start of the Second World War all but stopped further building. Consequently, at the end of the war, there was a very substantial unsatisfied demand for housing, made more acute by the high marriage rate, immigration, and the general prosperity.

Mortgage credit is provided in a variety of ways. The commercial banks provide some, but there are also special institutions, such as building societies. Some of these have share capital; others, which are in the nature of co-operative societies, collect subscriptions that are virtually deposits on houses to be built. Some deposits are accepted, again usually in advance of a building loan being made to the depositor. These building societies rely to a large extent on accommodation from the commercial banks, which provide from 35 percent to 40 percent of their funds. They lend on long-term mortgage, loans being repayable with interest by regular installments. A certain amount of private finance is also provided directly by individuals, by trustee companies, and by firms of solicitors acting as trustees for estates or as agents of their clients. This type of business may grow with restrictions now imposed on commercial bank advances.

A growing amount of urban mortgage credit is provided by the states and by the Commonwealth Government. All states have housing commissions or similar bodies which build houses either for rent or for sale on long-term mortgage, also repayable by regular installments Special schemes cater for returned soldiers.

Credit for other purposes, such as the purchase of motor cars, furniture, and other durable consumer goods, is provided by so-called hire-purchase or cash-order companies. These rely partly on share capital and partly on advances from the commercial banks for their funds. Their loans are usually repayable with interest in weekly or monthly installments.

THE CENTRAL BANK

The Commonwealth Bank of Australia owes its peculiar structure to its origin; it was never intended by its founders to be a central bank.[5] It was established in 1912, under an act passed the previous year by a Labour Government, purely as a competitor with the commercial banks. This is at least the general view. Professor Giblin[6] has recently put the view that the first Governor, Sir Denison Miller, had central banking "as a distant objective." There has never been any statement to this effect, but it would explain the early policy of the Bank, which always avoided aggressive competition with the commercial banks.

It was the boast of the founders that the Bank was started without capital. The power given to raise £1 million of capital was never used. The Bank started with an advance of £10,000 from the Commonwealth Treasury, which was quickly repaid when, on opening for business, it took over the accounts of the Commonwealth Government with deposits amounting to more than £2.3 million. The Bank was not allowed to issue notes, a function which had been taken over by the Treasury from the private banks earlier. The Bank was originally managed by a governor appointed by the Government, but independent of political control, a provision which was successfully maintained.

In 1920 the first hesitant step was taken on the path to central banking functions. A Note Issue Department was established, and the Australian note issue was transferred from the Treasury to the control of the Bank through a notes board, with power to issue notes against a 25 percent gold cover. This was distinct from other depart-

[5] A good account of the origin and development of the Commonwealth Bank is to be found in the *Report of the Royal Commission on Monetary and Banking Systems* (Canberra, 1937).

[6] Giblin, L. F., *The Growth of a Central Bank* (Melbourne, 1951), p. 3.

ments of the Bank, which were still in the sole charge of the governor.

A new Commonwealth Bank Act of 1924 laid the real foundations for the development of central banking functions. The act created a board of directors consisting of the governor, the secretary to the Commonwealth Treasury, and six persons "who are or have been actively engaged in agriculture, commerce, finance or industry." The Note Issue Department was retained, but its management was transferred to the board of directors. The act gave authority to the Bank to fix and publish discount and rediscount rates (a power which was never used) and provided that the settlement of check clearing operations by the private banks should be made through the Commonwealth Bank. In 1925 a Rural Credits Department was established.

The act did not immediately result in the assumption of central banking powers by the Bank. The Commonwealth Bank moved rather cautiously, although its prestige by this time was very high. This was due in no small measure to the fact that although the Bank competed with the commercial banks, it had never been very aggressive, despite its complete freedom from taxation. The commercial banks opened accounts with it for clearing settlements, and from then on voluntarily kept the major portion of their cash reserves on deposit. Generally the commercial banks came more and more to look to the Commonwealth Bank for advice.

Then came the depression early in 1929. This difficult period strained the whole financial structure and was particularly trying for a rather inexperienced central bank. But friendly relations with the commercial banks paid dividends, and in spite of disputes and controversies, there was on the whole excellent cooperation.[7] One of the greatest difficulties was that of dwindling exchange reserves abroad. Early in 1930 the Commonwealth Bank took over the gold reserves of the commercial banks, which until then had been substantial, and later negotiated an Exchange Mobilization Agreement to conserve funds in London, where all foreign exchange funds were held.

Until then the Australian pound had traditionally been regarded as the equivalent of the pound sterling and had been tied rigidly to it, even when both currencies departed from gold. The Mobilization Agreement had the purpose of assisting government debt service abroad. The banks, now unable to meet in full the demands of im-

[7] *Report of the Royal Commission*, p. 72.

porters, began to ration their sales of foreign currencies. The result was the development of an open market at rates showing an increasing depreciation of the Australian currency. The banks had to follow or lose business. The climax came early in January, 1931, when the Bank of New South Wales announced a rate of £115 Australian to £100 sterling; before the end of the month the rate was raised to £130 Australian, the other banks following every step.

The Commonwealth Bank Board was never happy about the depreciation, but was powerless to prevent it. However, when the open market rate gradually declined to £125 Australian in November, 1931, the Board announced that it was taking control of foreign exchange and that it was prepared to buy and sell at that figure.

Throughout the period, the Commonwealth Bank Board maintained a generally deflationary policy. It strenuously opposed appeals by Commonwealth and state governments for increased loan funds for public works and to meet deficits, but eased its attitude a little after the so-called Premiers' Plan had effected a reduction in government expenditure, wages, and interest rates.

By the beginning of the war in 1939 the Commonwealth Bank had developed fully as a central bank. The commercial banks entered a voluntary agreement in 1941 to deposit in special accounts with the Commonwealth Bank at a low rate of interest any deposits in excess of those held at the beginning of the war. This was embodied in National Security Regulations later that year, and the Bank was also given power to take other anti-inflationary measures, including the control of interest rates, control of bank advances, control of the offering of Treasury bills to the banks. It had exercised exchange control since 1939.

The policy of the Bank was energetically directed to the purposes of total war; finance for anything that did not contribute to the war effort was severely curtailed. Interest rates were successively lowered. At the beginning of the war the rates on fixed deposits were 2 percent for three months and 2¾ percent for 12 months; by the end of 1945 they had been reduced to ½ percent and 1 percent, respectively. In the same period, the rate on Treasury bills was reduced from 1¾ percent to 1 percent, and on long-term bonds from 3⅞ percent to 3¼ percent. Since 1945 the interest rate on Treasury bills has been reduced to ¾ percent and that on long-term bonds to 3⅛ percent. By the end of 1951 the rate was rising again, and a loan raised in March, 1952, bore interest at the rate of 3⅞ percent. By June, 1952, the bond market showed a yield of 4¼ percent.

Foreign exchange was rationed severely to goods necessary for the war effort. During the war period Australia had an export surplus. As a result, reserves in London rose from £44 million sterling in 1939 to £167 million sterling in 1945. As part of the sterling area, Australia came within the range of the British Government's restrictions on the use of dollars in the sterling area's pool, and the Commonwealth Bank was merely left with the function of allocating the amount Australia was permitted to spend, which over the whole period amounted roughly to Australia's current dollar earnings.

Before the war ended the Labour Government introduced and passed the Commonwealth Bank Act of 1945 together with the Banking Act mentioned earlier. These two acts really codified the National Security Regulations, which until then had been regarded merely as war emergency measures. In introducing the legislation the Treasurer set out three main objects: to strengthen the central banking functions of the Bank; to ensure the expansion of its general banking business by active competition with the commercial banks; and to return control of the Bank to the governor, who would be responsible to the Treasurer, in order that the financial policy of the Bank would be in harmony with government policy. The general functions of the Bank are set out in section 8 of the act, which states:

> 8. It shall be the duty of the Commonwealth Bank within the limits of its powers, to pursue a monetary and banking policy directed to the greatest advantage of the people of Australia, and to exercise its powers under this Act and the Banking Act 1945 in such a manner as, in the opinion of the Bank, will best contribute to:
> (a) the stability of the currency of Australia;
> (b) the maintenance of full employment in Australia; and
> (c) the economic prosperity and welfare of the people of Australia.

This is a complete departure from the 1924 Act, which specifically sought to leave the Commonwealth Bank free of political control. It is in complete conformity with the policy of the Labour Party, which had looked with extreme disfavor upon the deflationary aspects of the policy of the Board during the depression; hence the specific instruction for a policy to maintain full employment.

The Act of 1945 formally constitutes the Bank as the central bank, with a capital of £4 million provided from the existing Capital and Reserve Fund for its central banking functions. Provision is made for increases in capital from the same fund. Of the profits of the central banking business, half will go to the National Debt Sinking Fund, and the other half will be divided equally between the Commonwealth Bank Reserve Fund and the Mortgage Bank Department, until the capital of the latter reaches £4 million.

A General Banking Division is set up to carry on the commercial business of the Bank, with accounts kept separate and distinct from the other accounts of the Bank. The capital of this division is £4 million provided from the Capital Reserve Fund and such other sums as may be transferred from the General Banking Division Reserve Fund, into which half the profits of the division are to be paid, the other half going to the National Debt Sinking Fund.

The Bank is specifically directed to expand this part of its business in a section (18) which states:

(1) It shall be the duty of the Bank, through the General Banking Division, to develop and expand its general banking business.
(2) The Bank . . . shall not refuse to conduct banking business for any person, by reason only of the fact that to conduct that business would have the effect of taking away business from another bank.

This was an entirely new departure, as in the past the Commonwealth Bank has never been an aggressive competitor with the commercial banks.

The Rural Credits Department, established in 1925, and the Mortgage Bank Department, established in 1943, are continued in their original form. Under the 1945 Act an Industrial Finance Department was set up with a capital of £4 million, half to be provided from the Special Reserve Account of the Note Issue Department and the other half to be transferred as required from other funds of the bank. The functions of this department, as stated in the act, are: to provide finance for the establishment and development of industrial undertakings and to provide advice on the operation of industrial undertakings. The department may lend money and purchase and sell shares or securities in industrial undertakings. Its profits are to be placed to the credit of a reserve fund within the department. A rather peculiar provision under this section of the act is that, although the general manager of the department is subject to the supervision of the governor, he is appointed by the Commonwealth Government, which also fixes his salary. Since its opening in January, 1946, the Industrial Finance Department has sought business energetically; its loans, advances, shares, and debentures at June 30, 1951, stood at nearly £23 million.

The management of the whole Bank was placed under the governor, who was assisted by an advisory council consisting of the secretary to the Department of the Treasury, the deputy governor of the Bank, an additional representative of the Treasury, and two officers of the Bank. The duty of the advisory council was to advise the governor on the monetary and banking policy of the Bank and on such other matters as were referred by the governor to the council. The governor was, in fact, responsible only to the Treasurer of the Commonwealth. The act provided that the Bank should from time to time inform the Treasurer of its monetary and banking policy and, in the event of any difference of opinion between the Bank and the Government, the Treasurer and the Bank should endeavor to reach agreement. If they were unable to reach agreement, the Treasurer had the option of informing the Bank that the Government accepted responsibility for the adoption by the Bank of a policy in accordance with the opinion of the Government, and the Bank then had to give effect to that policy.

When the bill was debated in the Commonwealth Parliament, these provisions caused such bitter opposition that the Leader of the Opposition promised to repeal them whenever a Liberal Government got into power. Accordingly, when a Liberal-Country Party Government was formed after elections held in December, 1949, the new Treasurer brought in a bill to amend the Act of 1945. The amendment was finally passed in 1951, following prolonged delay caused by a hostile senate. The new provisions of the act reconstitute the Commonwealth Bank Board to consist of the governor, the deputy governor, the secretary to the Treasury, and seven other members, of whom at least five must not be officers of the Bank or in the public service of the Commonwealth. This board is given power to determine the policy of the Bank and to ensure that effect is given by the Bank to the policy determined. Provision is made, however, for a close liaison with the Government and the Bank, in that the Bank must inform the Government of the policy of the Bank from time to time, and rather elaborate machinery is set up to resolve differences of opinion.

In the event of a difference of opinion, the Treasurer and the Board are directed to endeavor to reach an agreement; the Board must, if they fail, furnish the Treasurer with a statement in relation to the matter. The Treasurer may then submit a recommendation to the Governor-General, who, on the advice of his Ministers, may by order determine the policy to be adopted by the Bank. These provisions are very similar to those of the 1945 act, but a new condition is laid down that Parliament must be informed of what has taken place. The Treasurer must lay before each House of Parliament a copy of the order determining the policy to be followed by the Bank accompanied by statements by the Government and by the Board about the matter over which the difference of opinion has arisen. This provision is important in that it gives the public full knowledge of the circumstances. It is a safeguard in so far as any Commonwealth Government would, under these circumstances, hesitate to go against the opinion of the Board unless there is an extremely good cause for it.

The new Board was appointed in August, 1951. The five members appointed from outside the government service have wide experience in primary or secondary industry, but have had no experience in banking and finance.

The Commonwealth Bank Act of 1945 prescribes the form of the annual balance sheet of the Bank as a whole, of the General Banking Division, of each department of the Bank, and of the Savings Bank. The Central Banking Division publishes a weekly statement and the trading sections of the Bank render monthly returns on an aggregate basis which appear as part of the monthly banking averages published by the Commonwealth Statistician.

The form of presentation of the annual accounts, which are made up as at June 30, has remained unchanged since 1945, though a new department's accounts have been added.

The balance sheet of the Central Banking Division as at June 30, 1951, totals £873 million or £1,056 million if the Note Issue Department is added. The chief assets of the division are gold and balances abroad, £579 million, and government securities, £204 million, or £714 million and £351 million, respectively, if the holdings of the Note Issue Department are added. The chief liabilities of the Central Banking Division are the Special Accounts of the commercial banks, £552 million, and their other deposits, £30 million. The totals

TABLE 6

AGGREGATE BALANCE SHEET OF COMMONWEALTH BANK, INCLUDING CENTRAL BANKING AND COMMERCIAL BANKING ACTIVITIES BUT EXCLUDING SAVINGS BANK, JUNE 30, 1951

(AMOUNTS IN MILLIONS OF AUSTRALIAN POUNDS)

Liabilities	*Amount*	*Assets*	*Amount*
Capital	18	Gold and balances held abroad (including money at short call)	717
Reserve funds	4	Australian notes and coin	8
Special reserve: Premium on gold sold	5	Checks and bills of other banks	7
Notes on issue	275	Commonwealth Government securities (including Treasury bills)	308
Deposits, bills payable, and other liabilities (including provision for contingencies)	1,035	Securities of other governments and of local and semigovernmental authorities	94
		Bills receivable and remittances in transit	24
		Bank premises, at cost less amounts written off	2
		Loans, advances, bills discounted, and other assets (after deducting provision for debts considered bad or doubtful)	177
Total	1,337	Total	1,337

Note: Interdepartmental accounts totaling 19 million pounds have been offset.

of the balance sheets of the other departments give some idea of their relative importance. At June 30, 1950, the totals were (amounts in millions of Australian pounds):

Department	*Balance*
General Banking Division	157
Rural Credits Department	13
Mortgage Bank Department	5
Industrial Finance Department	24

The Commonwealth Savings Bank balance sheet as at June 30, 1951, totaled £554 million, with deposits at £533 million as the main liability, and Commonwealth Government securities (including Commonwealth Treasury bills) at £438 million as the main asset.

Most of the items in the various balance sheets are self-explanatory. It is perhaps worth mentioning that the central bank item "other assets" has a special significance in that it includes amounts lent back to the trading banks (current rate 3.5 percent) whenever the special account funds called in (at 0.5 percent) leave a bank temporarily short of free cash. At times this causes rather large variations in what might be regarded as a minor residual item.

The annual report of the Bank for 1949 indicated a reason for these variations. Its statement leaves no doubt that the Special Accounts are looked upon as the chief machinery for controlling the policy of the banking system in regard to advances. The statement points out that, although only 45 percent of the increase in the assets of the banks was called to Special Account between July, 1945, and July, 1948, industrial expansion made the position of some of the banks rather difficult. The Commonwealth Bank refused requests for releases from the Special Accounts, believing that this would lead to too rapid an expansion of advances (loans). On the other hand, according to the 1949 report, if there had been no alternative, the Bank's policy would have been "both rigid and drastic." As an alternative certain banks had therefore been granted short period loans at a rate of interest designed primarily to discourage reliance on this source of finance. The statement concludes by saying that these loans are designed as a temporary source of finance for the growing requirements of the economy by releases from the Special Accounts.

Another residual item among central bank liabilities—"Deposits, other (including provision for contingencies)" (Table 6, under Liabilities)—has grown to substantial proportions without any official explanation of what it covers. As deposits of trading banks are quoted separately, this item presumably covers government deposits, savings bank deposits, and perhaps some reserves.

Under Assets in Table 6, the heading "Gold and balances held abroad (including money at short call)" in the central bank and Note Issue Department account does not necessarily record the full foreign currency reserves of the central bank, as some quite liquid securities may be held overseas; these are also included (in Table 6, under Assets) in the item "Securities of other governments and of local and semigovernmental authorities."

The relatively small total shown in the balance sheet of the Rural Credits Department as at June 30 may give a false impression of the importance of this department in the financing of Australia's primary exports. Although "Loans, advances, etc." of this department were shown at £11 million at June 30, 1951, the turnover for the year reached £269 million.

For the benefit of those who might wish to make comparisons with the Bank's figures in the years preceding 1945, the Bank thoughtfully prepared two sets of balance sheets for June 30 in that year. These are to be found in the annual report for that year.

In terms of the Commonwealth Bank Act of 1945, the assets which the Note Issue Department may hold against its liability for notes issued are: gold; deposits with any bank; securities of the Government of the United Kingdom, or of the Commonwealth or one of its states. This represents a substantial relaxation from previous reserve requirements and, in conjunction with other sections of the 1945 Act which enable the Treasurer to determine Bank policy, means that the Commonwealth Government may increase the note issue at will by issuing its own securities, forcing the Bank to take them up and issue notes against them. Prior to the passing of the 1945 Act a reserve of gold or British Government securities was required.

It has been the practice of the Commonwealth Bank since 1946 to publish annually a figure of total international currency reserves of Australia held by all banks. In that year it also published figures for the war years which had not been released for security reasons.

TABLE 7

TOTAL INTERNATIONAL FUNDS OF AUSTRALIA

(AMOUNTS IN MILLIONS OF AUSTRALIAN POUNDS)

Date		*Amount*
Last Monday in June	1939	55·7
	1941	89.5
	1943	86.8
	1945	208.3
Last Wednesday in June	1947	198.7
	1948	273.5
	1949	451.7
	1950	650.1
	1951	843.0
Last Wednesday in December	1951	544.0

The central bank issues a weekly statement showing its assets and liabilities as at close of business each Wednesday, including its gold and balances held abroad. In the past, this item has comprised the largest part of total overseas reserves and is often taken as the main indicator of changes in the balance of payments; but its limitations should be recognized, especially in view of the large difference

(£124 million Australian) between it and the figure for total international funds of Australia in June, 1951.

TABLE 8
GOLD AND BALANCES HELD ABROAD BY THE CENTRAL BANK
(AMOUNTS IN MILLIONS OF AUSTRALIAN POUNDS)

Date	*Amount*
Last Wednesday in June, 1949	392
Last Wednesday in June, 1950	518
Last Wednesday in December, 1950	567
Last Wednesday in June, 1951	719
Last Wednesday in December, 1951	431

The larger figure of total international funds would include foreign balances of the trading banks, British securities held by the central bank, and possibly some fairly large transit items.

THE MONEY AND CAPITAL MARKETS

There is no open money market in Australia. What little exists is very elementary in organization. There is no commercial bill market, for the simple reason that commercial bills are scant in volume and appear to be gradually vanishing. Nor has there been any great demand for short-term investment at low rates of interest or the emergence of the very necessary middleman.[8] The discounting of Treasury bills is confined entirely to the commercial banks and the central bank. The bills are taken up by the Commonwealth Bank and sold to the commercial banks. There was an attempt by the Commonwealth Bank in 1936 to sell £1 million in Treasury bills to the public, but the Bank fixed the rate too low to make the offer attractive.[9] An open market cannot thrive unless it is permitted to fix its own rate.

There are two recent developments, however, which might foster a money market, although it would differ substantially from the older money markets of London and New York. One is the establishment of the "merchant banks" mentioned earlier. These have not yet developed sufficiently to make possible a forecast of their likely activities, and their growth may be hampered by the Banking Act of

[8] Bank of New South Wales, *Evidence before Royal Commission on Monetary and Banking Systems* (Sydney, 1936), pp. 44–45.

[9] *Ibid.*, p. 50.

1945, which provides that they must obtain a license before they can take deposits. The other concerns the nature of recent directives by the Commonwealth Bank, which could have the effect of driving away from the commercial banks sufficient business to create an outside market. Life insurance companies and other institutions with large funds at their disposal are already probing these possibilities.

The capital market has grown steadily over the last fifty years and rather rapidly since the Second World War. Among the largest investors are the insurance companies and trustee companies, and there is a steady growth of investment by the larger industrial concerns. There has been an enormous postwar rise in the price of wool, Australia's chief product, with the result that woolgrowers have had substantial amounts to invest. There has also been a substantial growth of investment from abroad. Some of this has been supplied by British and American industrial concerns erecting plants in Australia and some by private investors buying securities on the Australian market.

The largest borrowers are the Commonwealth and state governments. The former has borrowed principally for war purposes, and only a small portion of its debt is invested in public works, whereas the debt of the states is almost entirely for public works, including industrial undertakings such as railways and power plants. Government loans are raised by the Commonwealth Bank with the cooperation of the commercial banks and the stock exchanges. This method has proved extraordinarily cheap. During the First World War the flotation expenses were less than one third of 1 percent, and while no figures are available for the Second World War, the expenses are not likely to have been much higher.

Capital for private industry is raised through the stock exchanges, which are well developed in the largest cities. There are several experienced issuing houses, which have handled the growing volume of new industrial investment very well. Most overseas industrial enterprises in Australia look to Australians to take a share in the undertaking, which means some rather large capital issues in relation to the market. The stock exchanges also handle a large volume of dealings in government bonds. The merchant banks will undoubtedly find their place in the capital market. It is the intention of at least one of them to develop as an issuing house, and in the absence of a money market this seems a very likely form of development.

The capital market is now completely controlled. Bank lending is restricted by the directives issued by the central bank, which generally limit it to working capital, or rather to the portion of working capital which can be shown to be a fluctuating amount. A board has been set up to control capital issues, chiefly for rearmament purposes.

THE WORKING OF THE SYSTEM

One would say that a banking system which has stood up to varying fortunes without a bankruptcy for more than half a century has done well. Since the crisis of 1893 the Australian banking system has worked extremely smoothly. Although it has been charged with aiding the boom of the late twenties and with intensifying the depression, in making these charges the Royal Commission [10] admits that there were extenuating circumstances and that there surely was no foundation for the extreme view held in some quarters that the banking system had deliberately encouraged the boom and precipitated the crisis and depression.

The banks had no easy task either in damping down the boom or extending credit in the depression. The banks were certainly nervous of the boom, but it is not easy to apply the brake on lending when public optimism runs high and politicians talk of "boundless resources" crying for development. That was the atmosphere of the twenties. Nor is it easy to know what to do with marginal producers in a deep depression. No intelligent banker will force a sale on a depressed market, if there is any hope that the marginal producer will pull through. And bankers also know that a business or a farm is better run by its owner, who has some interest in it, than by a bank which has to put in a salaried manager. There naturally were foreclosures, but they were few and unavoidable. Actually there is evidence that the banks supported their clients strongly at least during the first eighteen months of the depression, as their advances rose steadily to the middle of 1930. After that they fell as a result of a tight cash position, and later continued to fall because there were no borrowers.

During the Second World War, the banks, this time more firmly led by the central bank, gave valuable assistance to the war effort by helping to divert resources to war production. They aided the raising of war loans, and even helped to organize the rationing system.

[10] *Report of the Royal Commission,* p. 218.

The central bank has grown in stature. Even if it has not achieved manhood it has at least cut its teeth. It now has all the powers necessary to control the most recalcitrant banking system; the chief danger of the future may be that its youthful exuberance will cause it to use a steam hammer to crack nuts.

One of the most dangerous provisions in the present Commonwealth Bank Act is that the central bank shall use its powers toward "the maintenance of full employment in Australia." Such a directive should never have been written into the constitution of a central bank. It is all the more dangerous in that "full employment" has been defined in a government White Paper [11] as a "tendency towards a shortage of men instead of a shortage of jobs." It is clear that such a definition, which must tend to a condition of over-full employment, can all too easily mean inflation, and the directive may therefore come into conflict with the other stated objectives of the Commonwealth Bank, namely the stability of the currency and "the welfare of the people of Australia."

Another obvious fault in the Commonwealth Bank Act is the directive to all-out competition with the commercial banks. It is most essential that if the Commonwealth Bank is to control a healthy banking system it must have the confidence of the commercial banks; this is clearly difficult if the central bank is to become their aggressive competitor. If it is desirable that a central bank, a public institution, should enter competition with private banks, the General Banking Division, which performs its commercial functions, ought to be entirely separated from the central bank.

Both these provisions of the act, as well as that of an unlimited note issue, would be less suspect, from the point of view of the commercial banks and the business community, with an assurance that the Commonwealth Bank was free from political control. Under the 1945 act there was no such assurance. The Treasurer could, without the knowledge of Parliament or the public, so impose his will on the Commonwealth Bank that the Bank might be made to serve the purposes of the political party in power. The 1951 amendment does provide some safeguard by means of open discussion of points of difference between the government and the Bank. The view that the government must have a final say is generally accepted in Australia

[11] *Full Employment in Australia.* White Paper presented to the Commonwealth Parliament by the Minister for Post-War Reconstruction (Canberra, 1945).

today. Economic difficulties similar to those of 1929–31 may well cause the pendulum to swing back, but meanwhile no political party holds a different view.

Some danger in the development of qualitative control of credit is implied in the central bank's power to control the policy concerning advances. Qualitative control is probably essential in order to fight a major war, and there is also something to be said for it in a postwar period during which scarce resources have to be allocated to the most essential needs of the community; but permanent controls of this kind can do infinite harm. The retention of the system beyond a period of emergency implies an omniscience in a central bank which it clearly cannot possess. Qualitative control is liable to introduce rigidities that may hamper healthy development in the whole economy.

With these reservations as to the 1945 act, one must come to the conclusion that Australia has been well served by its banking system. In a country with so much precarious primary production, a system consisting of a few large banks, with branches throughout the country, is ideal in that risks are so well spread that nothing but a general calamity can disturb it. The system has proved extremely flexible and capable of adapting itself to rapid and even violent changes of fortune. Recent bank mergers are designed to permit the development of special services and will no doubt intensify competition by offering these marginal services to customers. With a much stronger central bank, the system should be even better equipped to meet future crises, with the proviso that the central bank must be freed from any suspicion of political control.

ADDENDUM

In 1953 the Commonwealth Parliament passed an amending banking act. The principal feature was the introduction of a new system of special accounts. As previously, the act defines the maximum amount a bank may be required to hold in special account, and within that maximum the central bank determines from month to month the actual sum which each bank must hold. This consists of the sum in special account on October 10, 1952, plus 75 percent of any increase in deposits. The total that may be called must also be reduced by 75 percent of any fall in deposits. If this full amount is not called, an adjustment must be made in September each year so that a bank's uncalled liability does not exceed 10 percent of its average deposits in the preceding August. The object is to eliminate the possibility of a large uncalled liability such as might occur under the old formula.

The other main change from the Banking Act of 1945 was to remove central bank control over investments by banks in government and other securities, and in company shares. Section 15(i) of the 1945 act, requiring banks to hold assets in Australia at least equal to their deposit liabilities in Australia, now applies only to foreign banks toward which it was originally intended to be directed. Powers to determine selective loan policy, to fix interest rates, and to mobilize foreign currency reserves continue unaltered. Control of loan policy is still retained, but has virtually ceased to exist in practice.

An amending Commonwealth Bank act was also passed in 1953. The General Banking Division of the Bank was converted into a separate corporate body, the Commonwealth Trading Bank of Australia, which was made subject to central bank controls in the same way as the other trading banks. It is controlled by a general manager appointed by the government on the recommendation of the Commonwealth Bank Board, but he is subject to the direction of the governor and Board of the Commonwealth Bank. The position of the Trading Bank is similar to that of the Commonwealth Savings Bank; it is still part of the whole Commonwealth Bank.

REFERENCES

OFFICIAL SOURCES

Banking Act, 1945. Canberra, 1945.
Commonwealth Bank Act, 1945. Canberra, 1945.
Commonwealth Bureau of Census and Statistics. Finance Bulletin. Canberra. Annual.
—— National Income and Expenditure, 1949–50. Canberra, 1950.
—— Quarterly Summary of Australian Statistics. Canberra.
—— Year Book of the Commonwealth of Australia. Canberra.
Royal Commission on Monetary and Banking Systems in Australia. Report. Canberra, 1937.
Rural Reconstruction Commission. Fifth Report: Rural Credit. Canberra, 1945.

NONOFFICIAL SOURCES

Bank of New South Wales. Evidence before Royal Commission on Monetary and Banking Systems. Sydney, 1936.
Commonwealth Bank. Commonwealth Bank of Australia in the Second World War. Sydney, 1947.
Faulkiner, C. C. The Commonwealth Bank of Australia. Sydney, 1923.
Giblin, L. F. The Growth of a Central Bank. Melbourne, 1951.
Gifford, J. L. K., and J. V. Wood. Australian Banking. Brisbane, 1947.
Grattan, C. Hartley, ed. Australia. Berkeley, California, 1947.
Hancock, W. K. Australia. London, 1935. Sydney, 1945.
Harris, H. L. Economic Resources of Australia. Sydney, 1933.
Jauncey, L. C. Australia's Government Bank. London, 1934.
Plumptre, A. F. Wynne. Central Banking in the British Dominions. Toronto, 1940.
Taylor, Griffith. Australia in Its Physiographic and Economic Aspects. 4th ed. Oxford, 1925.
Teare, H. E. History, Theory and Practice of Australian Banking, Currency and Exchange, with Applications also to the Banking of New Zealand. Melbourne, 1926.

BRAZIL

by Alexandre Kafka

DIRECTOR OF RESEARCH, BRAZILIAN INSTITUTE OF ECONOMICS, FUNDAÇÃO GETÚLIO VARGAS, RIO DE JANEIRO

I. BACKGROUND OF THE FINANCIAL PROBLEMS OF BRAZIL

BRIEF SURVEY OF THE ECONOMY

BRAZIL'S average income is low. Its 53 million habitants produced in 1951 a national income of only 250,000 million cruzeiros. Output could increase rapidly if capital were available to develop Brazil's rich natural resources and the huge, sparsely populated areas of the interior. A high rate of population growth (over 25 percent between 1940 and 1950), however, requires a sizable rate of capital formation merely to maintain present living standards. Some aspects of national income are shown in Table 1.

We lack data to determine adequately the origin of income by sectors of activity. The absolute size of industry and its relative contribution to income are probably more important than in most less developed countries. As shown in Table 2 an overwhelming propor-

---

ALEXANDRE KAFKA, a Brazilian citizen, was born in Prague, in 1917. There he received his primary and secondary education and attended law school; he studied economics at the Graduate School of International Studies in Geneva, and at Balliol College, Oxford, where he received a B.A. (and M.A.). Since 1941 he has been Professor of Economics at the School of Sociology and Politics of the University of São Paulo (from which he is now on leave of absence). Since 1951 he has been Director of Research of the Brazilian Institute of Economics (Fundação Getúlio Vargas) and Economic and Financial Counselor to the Superintendency of Money and Credit in Rio de Janeiro. He has held other positions, among them those of economic adviser to the Federation of Industries of São Paulo and of Assistant Chief of the Latin American Division (South) of the International Monetary Fund.

The author is indebted to his colleagues of the University of Brazil, the Brazilian Institute of Economics, and the Superintendencia da Moeda e do Credito; and, in particular, to Professors Bulhoes, Gudin, Kingston, Lopes Rodrigues, Almeida Santos, and

tion of the gainfully occupied population is engaged in agriculture,[1] which yields a relatively much smaller share of national product, reflecting the specially low productivity in this sector.

The distribution of income not only by classes [2] but also by regions is very uneven. Nearly two thirds of the national income seems to accrue to the southern states (plus the Federal District),[3] which contain less than 40 percent of the population.[4] Not only do regions differ widely in wealth, but they differ also in their structure of production.

Dependence of national income on exports is far less pronounced than in many other semi-developed countries.[5] It is, however, substantial for the country as a whole, and particularly great for certain regions and subregions. As shown in Table 3, the share of coffee in the total value of exports is very large, particularly since the recent boom, which has more than restored the predepression coffee terms of trade.[6] A major part of imports is indispensable to the functioning of the economy; this was true even before import controls became really severe. A very high proportion of Brazil's exports finds a market in the United States, which is Brazil's main supply of imports.

Investments (and savings) are reasonably high in relation to national product (see Table 1).

RECENT TRENDS

For the country as a whole, real per capita income has undoubtedly been rising in the last few years; a good deal of the increase, however, has been due to the improvement in Brazil's terms of trade. Some of the rise in average real income is reflected in a population shift to

---

Oliveira Campos, as well as Messrs. Advincula da Cunha, Borges da Fonseca, Loeb, Van der Meiren, and Bastian Pinto for their help in preparing this paper. He has also had the advice of a number of experienced bankers, among whom are Deputy Adolfo Gentil, Luiz Camilo de Oliveira Neto, Francisco Alves dos Santos Filho, and Baron Saavedra. Professor Paul N. Rosenstein-Rodan has also made valuable suggestions. The author also wishes to thank Mr. Philip Glaessner for his constant help and encouragement, without which the present chapter could not have been written.

1 Mining is relatively unimportant.

2 See Jorge Kingston, *A Desigualdade na distribuição de rendas*, 1947, p. 79.

3 See *Revista Brasileira de Economia*, Year VI, No. 4, p. 102, and *Anuário Estatístico do Brasil*, 1952, p. 34.

4 *Ibid.*, p. 25.

5 In 1951 the production and distribution of export goods and services amounted to 32,514 million cruzeiros, out of a gross national product at market prices of 310,900 million cruzeiros; the proportion would be low, even considering the overvaluation of the cruzeiro.

6 See United Nations Document E/CN/12/217/Add. 2, March 26, 1952, p. 90.

TABLE 1

NATIONAL INCOME AND INVESTMENT, 1951

(AMOUNT IN 1,000 MILLIONS OF CRUZEIROS)

	Amount	Percent
Primary production, except mining, at factor cost	76.3	30.5
Other Sectors	175.0	69.5
Income from work	128.2	
Profits	34.7	
Interest	2.7	
Rent	7.4	
Income paid to foreign residents, net	−1.6	−0.6
National Income (net national product at factor cost)	249.7	100.0
Capital consumption allowances	14.9	
Indirect taxes minus subsidies	45.3	
Gross National Product (at market prices)	310.9	
Gross Domestic Investment	51.6	
Public investment	9.6	
Private investment	42.0	
Producers' durable equipment	21.9	
New construction	15.0	
Change in inventories	+5.1	
Net foreign investment	−6.9	

Source: Instituto Brasileiro de Economia.

Note: 1 Cr$ = 5.4 cents at parity; 2.0–2.7 cents in the "free market" rates.

TABLE 2

GAINFULLY OCCUPIED POPULATION, 10 YEARS OF AGE AND OLDER, 1950

(NUMBER IN THOUSANDS)

	Number	Percent of Total
Agriculture, livestock, vegetal extractive industries, and fisheries	10,934	61.5
Other activities	6,856	38.5
Mining	156	
Manufacturing	2,231	
Commerce and finance	1,074	
Transportation and communication	697	
Civil service and defense	512	
Services	1,673	
Social activities	434	
Liberal professions	79	
Total	17,790	100

Source: Instituto Brasileiro de Geografia e Estatística.

TABLE 3
FOREIGN TRADE, 1949–51
(AMOUNTS IN BILLIONS OF CRUZEIROS)

A. By Commodities

Exports	*1949*	*1950*	*1951*	*Imports*	*1949*	*1950*	*1951*
Total	20.1	24.9	32.5	Total	20.6	20.3	37.2
Food	13.7	18.7	22.5	Manufactures	11.8	10.8	22.2
Coffee	11.6	15.9	19.8	Coal, fuel, and lubricating oils	2.4	2.9	4.2
Raw materials	5.9	5.9	9.7	(Other) raw materials (and semi-manufactures)	2.8	2.9	6.0
Raw cotton	2.0	1.9	3.8	Food	3.6	3.5	4.6
Manufactures	0.5	0.3	0.3	Wheat and wheat flour	2.5	2.0	2.6
Textiles	0.4	0.2	0.2				

B. By Countries

Exports	*1949*	*1950*	*1951*	*Imports*	*1949*	*1950*	*1951*
Total	20.1	24.9	32.5	Total	20.6	20.3	37.2
The Americas	12.6	15.9	19.2	The Americas	13.7	12.0	23.5
United States	10.1	13.6	15.9	United States	8.8	7.0	15.6
Argentina	1.6	1.4	2.2	Argentina	2.2	2.0	3.3
Europe	6.7	7.9	11.8	Dutch Antilles	1.5	1.6	1.8
United Kingdom	1.7	2.1	3.2	Venezuela	0.2	0.3	1.1
France	0.4	1.2	1.6	Europe	6.7	8.0	12.7
Germany	0.3	0.3	1.6	United Kingdom	2.7	2.5	3.2
Other areas	0.8	1.1	1.5	Germany	0.1	0.4	2.1
				France	0.4	0.9	1.8
				Sweden	0.6	0.9	1.3
				Belgium, Luxemburg	0.9	1.2	1.2
				Other Areas	0.2	0.3	1.0

Source: Banco do Brasil S.A., *Relatório de 1951*, pp. 355 ff.; *Anuário Estatístico do Brasil*, 1951, p. 248 ff.; *Estatística do Comércio Exterior*, Dec., 1949; Jan. and Dec., 1951.
Note: Subtotals do not necessarily add up to totals, due to rounding.

the relatively wealthy South, while a good deal of the improvement—as in many developing countries—corresponds to a proportionate increase in the comparatively high wage non-agricultural labor force, to higher profits, and to a rise in the general level of real wages.

The growth of manufacturing, which received its first strong impetus in the First World War, continued in the twenties under the stimulus of a growing market and has been increasing rapidly since the great depression, particularly since the Second World War. Moreover, taking the last twenty years as a whole, it has been remarkably well balanced between consumer goods and basic industries. However, a relative lag in the development of basic utilities, such as railways, coastwise shipping, communication, fuel, and power-generating capacity, has tended to retard economic growth. Agricultural development has also been less rapid, particularly of export agriculture. Nevertheless, the improvement, from 1949 to 1951, in the terms of trade of the latter has tended to arrest the relative shrinkage of this sector. Both industrial and agricultural development have been concentrated in the south and the latter also, to a minor extent, in the west. These regions absorb part of the population growth of the stagnating north and northeast. In addition to earlier isolated action by the Federal government to establish a better balance between the various sectors of the economy and the various regions of the country, there is now under way a large-scale over-all development program which concentrates on basic utilities and industries, as well as on agriculture, and draws upon World Bank and Export-Import Bank loans, in addition to local funds.

Urban real estate investment seems to have been rather on the high side in relation to saving, especially if one considers the need for more basic investments. As important is the fact that the distribution of real estate investment has been very uneven. There has been an excessive development of high cost housing; and, furthermore, housing development has been extraordinarily concentrated in the metropolitan centers of the country.

While the early thirties were years of deflation there has since then been, with interruptions, an increasingly strong inflationary trend. Brazil's earlier inflation, while substantial, was very much slower.[7] Table 4 presents data of changes in the cost of living and money supply.

Since until recently the effective exchange rate had remained practically at the prewar level, it has been necessary to maintain increasingly severe exchange and import controls. The exchange and import control systems have come to serve the policy of industrialization at the expense of export agriculture. For some sectors of the latter and for some regions dependent on given export products, which have not been compensated for this policy by an improvement in world market

[7] The rate of inflation and price rise was unprecedented in the forties and very high in the thirties after 1932. The increase in the preceding century was tenfold, i.e., an annual rate, compounded, of less than 2.5 percent as against annual rates, compounded, of more than 10 percent over the last 20 years and nearly 16 percent over the last 10 years.

TABLE 4
INDICES OF COST OF LIVING AND OF MONEY SUPPLY PER CAPITA
(YEARLY AVERAGES)

Year	*Cost of Living* [a]	*Money Supply per Capita* [b]
1928	100	100
1930	90	77
1932	87	106 [c]
1933	86	101
1934	93	114
1936	112	128
1938	127	173
1940	138	167
1941	154	203
1945	333	488 [d]
1946	385	531
1947	500	589
1948	543	586
1949	535	637
1950	566	753
1951	614	923

[a] Figures for 1928–38 are from *Relatório,* Banco do Brasil, 1945, p. 268; those for 1938–51 are from *International Financial Statistics,* December, 1951, May, 1952.

[b] Money supply figures for 1928–44 are from *Relatório,* Banco do Brasil, 1941, 1945; those for 1944–51 are from *Conjuntura Econômica,* April, 1952. For data concerning population see *Anuário Estatístico,* 1951; and extrapolation and intrapolation.

[c] 1928–32: Inclusive of banks' deposits with Banco do Brasil; a corresponding adjustment was made in the figures so that the 1933 figure is linked up with the 1932 figure on the basis of figures excluding banks' deposits in both years.

[d] Up to 1944: End of year figures are used.

prices, temporary relief had, however, been found by barter deals, which at times took a form tantamount to regional devaluations on the export side. More recently a general readjustment of the exchange system has been initiated in the direction of depreciation, since the degree of overvaluation had become excessive.

CAUSES OF THE RECENT INFLATION

As in the case of some other primary producing countries it was, by a seeming paradox, the great depression which created new investment opportunities in Brazil and so gave a particular stimulus to the propensities to invest and spend. The crisis led to an increase in the relative profitability of products other than coffee,[8] and, in general, changed the terms of trade sharply and for a relatively long period against primary products and in favor of industry; the exchange rate and control systems, though introduced for balance of payments reasons, reinforced this tendency. Thus, a particularly favorable environment was created for accelerated diversification of the economy, and in particular—at a time when the internal market was already large enough to support it—for the more rapid growth of manufacturing, which implied a higher propensity to invest than had prevailed earlier. Actual investment for a large part of the thirties (and early forties) was undoubtedly hampered by the fall in the capacity to import [9] (and availability of imports) but this fall, after all, implied only a relative, not an absolute discouragement to investment incentives. It must also be remembered that Brazil's capacity to import apparently fell less in the great depression than that of many primary producing countries, while in some sections, already existing industrial capacity provided a substitute for imports. Also, expansionary monetary policy tended to maintain effective demand, investment, and investment incentives as such. Moreover, increased consciousness of dependence on foreign trade and of low living standards induced the government to favor industrialization and, particularly since the forties, to invest more itself.[10] All these tendencies were enormously stimulated by Brazil's experience in the Second World War. The shift of income from agriculture to industry, that is, from landowners to an urban entrepreneurial class, probably increased the national average and marginal propensity to save, but not as much as that to invest. Just as the period ending in the great depression, each of the earlier stages of Brazil's economic history had also been characterized by the dominance of one or two primary products each of which had in turn been dethroned (often more thoroughly than coffee). Always so far, however, another primary product had appeared to dominate the economy, for never before the 1930s had so many factors simultaneously

[8] The coffee valorization scheme tended to support the export price of coffee, but the farmer received a much lower average price, viz., the average of the export price and the—near zero—price paid by the National Coffee Department for the "sacrifice quota" (which was destroyed), which often reached more than a third of each farmer's crop. This feature of economic policy combined a maximum stimulus to abandonment of coffee with a maximum support to the capacity to import.

[9] See, e.g., *Economic Survey of Latin America,* 1949, p. 211.

[10] During the thirties, however, the government itself invested little, which probably affected unfavorably the investment output ratio in the forties.

fostered rapid diversification and, in particular, accelerated industrialization and thereby high investment incentives. Once started, this development has to some extent fed on itself and is by now firmly entrenched.[11]

These developments took place in an environment which had always been favorable to investment, by virtue of the opportunities offered by the country and the growth of population.[12] Moreover, a long history of inflation [13] and the appreciation of real property due to the rapid growth of cities have increasingly reinforced a traditional preference for holding savings in the form of real estate [14] and a corresponding reluctance to hold money or securities. This tends to make the decision to save largely dependent upon that to invest. Consequently, planned investment tends to fall short of planned savings more rarely than to exceed them, although they represent, apparently, a proportion of income which is by no means very low.

The existence of distinct economic regions probably is increasingly an independent and quasi-permanent factor making for a high national propensity to spend. Though interregional labor mobility is by no means low, an impracticably high degree would be necessary to make regional diversification of the economy contribute to stability. As things are, the regions suffering slumps or more protracted stagnation successfully demand compensatory government spending, while it is difficult to make compensatory cuts in official expenditures in other regions.

The fluctuations of foreign trade do little to limit the high propensity to spend. Good trade tends to expand income and with it increasingly the propensity to invest.[15] The high propensity to import does not normally permit the accumulation of reserves in good times. Consequently, bad trade means import restrictions but not deflation (just as, in the past, it often meant depreciation rather than deflation).

On the other hand, wages have so far, on the whole, followed (albeit rapidly) rather than led the cost of living. But they and social policy in general are becoming an autonomous factor making for a

[11] Albeit hardly in the precise way envisaged in recent theories of economic dynamics, which also explains why investment here was never discouraged by reaching the moving full employment ceiling.

[12] As is the case in many underdeveloped countries, once they have broken the "vicious circle of stagnation." See R. Nurkse, Lecture 1.

[13] The closed nature of corporations limits the extent to which stocks are available as a hedge against inflation.

[14] See Keynes, *General Theory*, Ch. XVII.

[15] See Kindleberger, *The Dollar Shortage*, especially p. 101.

higher propensity to spend. Certainly, the behavior of wages no longer permits inflation to yield an appreciably higher rate of real savings than would prevail under conditions of monetary stability.

The particular strength of inflation during the period under review and the fact that full employment [16] or at least very generalized bottlenecks [17] have prevailed in recent years in most regions of Brazil [18] with few interruptions, are largely the consequence of the changes in economic structure and incentives described in preceding paragraphs. Thus the recent inflation is somewhat different from the earlier one also in origin. As a result, principally, of the changes mentioned, the economy as a whole has recently shown an especially pronounced tendency to spend more than the value, at constant prices, of the total resources, domestic and foreign, available to it.[19] The amount of available resources has been affected unfavorably, among other causes, because, since the thirties, the inflow of new foreign capital has been small and at times negative, and particularly because the terms of trade have, until recently, been less favorable than before the great depression. Expansionary pressures similar to the ones mainly responsible for Brazil's earlier and milder inflation have also been present. Their effects have, indeed, at various times during the period under review overshadowed those of the basic changes mentioned above, though less so recently, when the effects of these basic changes have become especially pronounced. The expansionary pressures mentioned have included government deficits, forced balance of pay-

16 In the Keynesian sense: after 10 years of inflation it is unlikely that there remains any considerable extent of involuntary unemployment or underemployment.

17 These represent scarcities of skilled labor as well as equipment. The practical effects of such bottlenecks are the same as those of Keynesian full employment: the impossibility to increase production (in accordance with the structure of demand) merely by an increase in effective demand, at least without very sensible price increases. But the hypothesis of Keynesian full employment does not seem at all unlikely, since the bottlenecks hypothesis presupposes an extremely high degree of complementarity of unskilled labor and other factors of production in order to explain the price rises which have taken place in Brazil in recent years. Undoubtedly there are at all times regional pockets of unemployment and underemployment, which are due to a lack of effective demand from the regional points of view but from a wider point of view are not Keynesian at all but result from a non-adaptation of the distribution of labor to the structure of demand. They cannot, therefore, be cured by monetary expansion. In addition, there is also, without doubt, an appreciable amount of transitional unemployment, due to fairly rapidly changing structure of production, in a regional as well as structural sense. Finally there must also be some unemployment due to an insufficient "real" wage, i.e., low productivity as compared with the disutility of labor.

18 Including the most populous ones.

19 Such a tendency is characteristic of under and semi-developed countries. See Ragnar Nurkse, "The Problem of Capital Formation in Under Developed Countries," *Revista Brasileira de Economia,* No. 4, 1951.

ments surpluses during the late war and increases in world prices. Nevertheless, the most recent world market price rises have, as it were, ratified preceding inflation rather than created a new one.

The financial system has not resisted the propensity to overspend and has, indeed, become institutionally more liable to expansion than in earlier periods. These factors comprise a falling cash reserve proportion of the banking system as a whole (mainly in the thirties) and increased facilities for lending to banks by the "monetary authorities."

Obviously, the recent inflation has affected the relative attractiveness of different sectors of the economy in a way which has often contradicted the requirements of reasonably balanced economic growth. With notable exceptions, the loan and investment policy of the financial system has—not unnaturally—been governed by considerations of profitability rather than of social need. Tradition and certain institutional factors have also been important, however, and have influenced the banks in particular. The effects of inflation itself on the structure of loans and investments have often induced the authorities to allow resources required from the point of view of social need to be found by further credit expansion. At the cost of accelerating the inflation itself, its effects on the economic and social structure have in this way been somewhat mitigated.[20] Much government investment has been of this particular inflation-induced kind.

II. CREDIT NEEDS AND PROBLEMS

Brazil's economic development since the great depression has created new credit and capital needs, and at the same time, the conditions under which development has taken place have made more difficult the access of certain sectors to sources of credit and capital.

[20] There is some tendency for the direct effects on economic structure of inflation to be limited largely to those resulting directly from the changed composition of consumer demand, due to the shift in income brought about by inflation. Changes in relative profitability of more or less "roundabout" processes of production brought about by strong inflation in the face of a maximum limit for, or insufficient rise in, interest rates are apt to affect the structure of production less than would otherwise be the case due to the low planning "horizon." Furthermore, the prevalence of self-financing of firms implies that interest rates do allow for inflation correctly and, in practice, means that the working capital needs of existing production are apt to have first claim on a firm's resources, so that in the absence of strong shifts in income to entrepreneurs, long-term investments are limited by this fact alone. As we have seen, in recent years, the shift in income has been small, due to successful defense of its real wage by labor.

AGRICULTURE

During the last twenty years many sectors of agriculture have been less able than most other parts of the economy to rely on their own resources in providing their various capital requirements. In the 1930s this was largely due to the absolute competition of new investment outlets and the relative impoverishment of export agriculture through low world market prices, only partly offset by depreciation of the currency. Later on, inflation, combined with the fixed exchange rate, produced similar results that were only partly mitigated by rising world market prices. These conditions affected only certain sectors of export agriculture. On the other hand, many non-export sectors of agriculture have been affected indirectly by conditions in the export sectors, while the development of other non-export sectors has proceeded more rapidly than that of the respective credit facilities.

These problems have been much in the foreground in the last twenty years; they may become less pressing if the recent improvement in the terms of trade in favor of primary products should continue and if exchange policy should be appropriate.

Another important development that has given rise to new credit needs has been the division of the large coffee estates, particularly in the state of São Paulo. The problem of meeting the credit needs of the medium-sized and small farmers has, thus, become more acute.

The nature of Brazilian rural production creates a series of special problems in relation to the length of loans. The important perennial crops, coffee and cocoa, require considerable medium-term credit for planting but relatively little credit between crops.

The general problem of agricultural credit is connected with an urgent need for an increase in agricultural productivity. The flow of labor from agriculture to industry has produced the necessary incentives to make agriculture rely more upon capital equipment. The shortage of credit and capital at the disposal of agriculture has, however, to a large extent made it impossible to achieve this objective. It should also be noted that substantial investment in agriculture is needed merely to maintain agricultural productivity, because of the prevailing custom of "mining the soil," unless there is a sustained expansion of transport facilities designed to open up new lands. Again, migrant agriculture increases credit risks and creates special problems.

MANUFACTURING

As already noted, industry has been favored by economic developments and by the policy of the last two decades, and it has been able to undertake considerable expansion out of its own resources. Nevertheless, industry faces some very serious credit problems. Much of Brazilian industry consists of small firms, and the overwhelming majority of large firms which have adopted the corporate form of organization are closed corporations and do not care to appeal to outside equity capital. These firms have credit needs which could not be satisfied in the capital market, even if it were much larger than it is.

The weakness of this market presents a particularly serious problem for public utilities (see below) and for new firms which have to start with a relatively large initial capital.

PUBLIC UTILITIES

By reason of rate control and inflation, public utilities, particularly the small Brazilian-owned firms in the interior, have been far less able than other lines of activity to finance themselves out of earnings. This has increased their credit needs.

GOVERNMENT

The fact that certain sectors of basic importance are not always attractive (as public utilities, because of rate control and other factors) or accessible (as basic steel, because of large capital needs) to private initiative, either national or foreign, creates an exceptionally large need for credit for investment purposes on the part of government.

URBAN REAL ESTATE

Increasing urbanization and the rapid growth of population have created a severe shortage of low-cost urban housing. The freezing of old rents has contributed to the shortage, by leading often to the retention of unnecessarily large apartments with protected rents. (A part of real estate investment performs the socially important function of permitting the middle class to accumulate property, since it is the only inflation-proof type of investment easily accessible to it.)

TRADE

The size of Brazil and the deficient transportation and communications system mean that internal credit probably runs on the average for slightly longer periods than in more advanced countries. Moreover, the number of middlemen between the producer and retailer is perhaps somewhat larger than in more developed countries, giving rise to special credit problems.

Export trade requires special credit related to the financing of crop movements from the interior to the ports of exportation and to the (short-term) retention of stocks to avoid their dumping on foreign markets. Exports are mostly financed by sight letters of credit. A need for new types of import credit has arisen from changes in the channels of trade (increasing importance of United States in the period preceding the Second World War), since American exporters have never been willing to grant accommodation for periods as long as their European counterparts.

In recent years changes in import policy have created fluctuation in credit needs. Increases in export prices of staples and in the prices of imports, which are a preferred risk of banks, are also apt to change sharply the credit needs of these sectors, and the availability of credit to other sectors. This is one aspect of the way in which changes in the world markets are apt to upset the Brazilian economy.

CONSUMER CREDIT

Rising living standards in the cities have led to an increase in demand for consumer credit for durables and semi-durables.

SEASONAL VARIATIONS

There does not appear to be very pronounced seasonality in overall credit needs. Credit demand grows somewhat at and after harvest time until crops are actually sold. The credit needs between crops are considerable, however. There are also compensating seasonal variations in the credit needs of the various regions of Brazil, because the crops come at different times of the year.

REGIONAL CREDIT PROBLEMS

The various regions of Brazil have grown at different rates, on the basis of their different history and endowment with natural resources.

Since economic progress is apt to be cumulative, the credit needs of the poorer regions are particularly great if their lag in growth is to be reduced.

III. CREDIT INSTRUMENTS

In addition to the ordinary bill of exchange and promissory note,[21] the most important credit instrument in use in Brazil is the so-called "duplicata." [22] This is essentially a copy (hence the name "duplicata") of an invoice, which by law is given all the qualities of a bill of exchange. Due to its nature, however, it is necessarily a "real" bill and, hence, particularly safe and therefore a preferred credit instrument; it is, indeed, a criminal offense to issue a "duplicata" which does not represent a sale of merchandise. With few exceptions, a "duplicata" must by law be issued by the seller and accepted by the buyer, whenever a sale is made for credit of more than 30 days. This is so because the "duplicata" was originally instituted for purposes of sales tax control; the most common maturity is 90 to 120 days. It is customary, in certain states, for the larger firms not to accept "duplicatas" but only to confirm to the collecting banks that the "duplicata" drawn is in order.

The larger part of the movement of coffee and some other crops from the interior to the ports is financed by bills of exchange, because shipment is made on consignment. A good deal of agricultural and industrial working capital advances, as well as some interstate and intercity trade financing (where difficulties of communications hinder acceptance of bills), are on the other hand granted on the basis of promissory notes. Promissory notes or bills of exchange are often secured by negotiable way bills, bills of lading, warehouse receipts, or warrants.

Specialized agricultural and industrial credit is granted on the basis of a loan contract, or a promissory note secured by a crop, livestock, or equipment lien.[23] One significant fact should be noted, namely that crop mortgages cannot be constituted except by the landlord or with his consent and only after the crop has been planted. Brazilian

[21] Regulated by Law 2044 of 1908.

[22] Regulated by Law 187 of 1936.

[23] See Law 492 of 1937, decree-laws 228/38, 2612/40, and 4360/42 for the crop mortgage, decree-laws 1271/39, 1625/39, 4191/42, and 4312/42 for the equipment lien.

law also recognizes the crop mortgage bill; this is negotiable but is used to a minor extent.

Real estate is financed by ordinary mortgage credit and through the so-called "compromisso de compra e venda." [24] The latter is an installment sale. The buyer obtains immediate possession of the property and his future claim to ownership is valid against third parties; the seller retains ownership until payment of the final installment. The "compromisso" frequently coexists with a mortgage securing a loan granted to the seller of the property by a financing institution.

Negotiable mortgage certificates ("letras hipotecárias") may be issued by specially authorized banks as a means of financing their mortgage loans; [25] these are used only to a minor extent.

Brazilian law and practice pertaining to shares [26] differ from Anglo-Saxon law. Thus, bearer shares are permitted and in common use; all shares must have a par value and none may be issued below par value, and corporations may not deal in their own shares or hold "treasury stock"; all authorized capital must be issued. Debentures [27] (corporate bonds) are of small importance.

The Federal, state, and municipal governments issue bonds which are called either "obrigações" or "apólices" (there is, in practice, no difference between the two types). Also the Federal and some state governments issue Treasury bills (though most Treasury financing is done by open account loans obtained from the respective official banks). The Federal government issues special kinds of Treasury bills which exporters are obliged to accept in payment of 20 percent of the value of the exports realized by them. Some state governments also issue "bônus rotativos," non-interest bearing bills with a maturity of one year; payments to suppliers are sometimes made in these bills.

IV. SURVEY OF CREDIT INSTITUTIONS

Brazil has no central bank. Central banking functions are performed by the Treasury and a series of more or less autonomous departments. These include the principal official bank of the Federal government, the Banco do Brasil, as such, and a number of entities more or less closely associated with it. The Superintendency of Money

[24] Decree law 58 of 1937.

[25] Decrees 160A and 370 of 1890.

[26] Decree-law 2627 of 1944.

[27] Decree 177A of 1893.

and Credit was created in 1945 [28] to coordinate the activities of these departments, pending the creation of a central bank. The Banco do Brasil, besides being the government banker, is by far the country's largest bank. It is an agricultural and industrial, as well as a commercial bank. It accounts for over a quarter of all bank loans to business and individuals.

In spite of the increasing development of branch banking, there are a comparatively large number of independent deposit banks, including some owned by state governments, and two regional banks of the Federal government (for the Amazon and the Northeast), both with special funds and development features. Most of the other deposit banks carry on, formally and largely also in fact, a purely commercial type of business. A few of the deposit banks, however, specialize in urban mortgage credit and some of the state government banks have specialized agricultural or industrial credit departments, in addition to their commercial credit sections. Some cooperatives run small banking departments for their associates (and there is a small central bank for cooperatives, which promotes particularly the granting of rural credit through cooperatives). Very recently some investment banking, as well as quasi-investment-trust operations of banks, have begun to appear.

Commercial banks accept savings deposits. There are no private savings banks, but the Federal government and some state governments run savings bank systems. The savings banks accept checking deposits and perform some functions of industrial and mortgage banks. The National Development Bank created recently is so far mainly the administrator of the Federal government's development plan and funds. Thus, on the whole, there are few specialized banks and few facilities for specialized credit.

Financial institutions of importance include, in addition to banks, the Social Security System, the so-called capitalization companies, and the life insurance companies.

There is, practically, no money market. The capital market is still very limited. The finance of agricultural, urban real estate and consumer credit needs is still, to a large extent, carried on by private individuals and business firms.

Table 5 presents a consolidated balance sheet of the main financial institutions of Brazil.

[28] Decree-law 7293.

Table 5

Consolidated Balance Sheet of Principal Institutions of Brazilian Financial System, December 31, 1951

(AMOUNTS IN BILLIONS OF CRUZEIROS)

A. By Institutions [a]

Funds Obtained Outside System	*Amount*	*Funds Used Outside System*	*Amount*
Total	185.5	Total	185.5
Monetary authorities and banks	136.1	Monetary authorities and banks	143.4
Savings banks [b]	17.3	Savings banks [b]	14.5
Social Security System [c]	20.7	Social Security System [c]	17.4
Civil Servants Pensions Institute [c]	2.0	Civil Servants Pensions Institute [c]	1.8
Capitalization companies	3.1	Capitalization companies	3.0
Life insurance companies	3.0	Life insurance companies	2.8
Other insurance companies	3.4	Other insurance companies	2.6

B. By Sources and Uses of Funds

Sources	***Amount***	***Uses***	***Amount***
Total	185.5	Total	185.5
Cash and deposits	119.8	Loans, etc., to Federal Treasury [d]	31.4
Treasury deposits	3.2	Loans, etc., to other government agencies [e]	10.4
Other liabilities	35.1	Loans, etc., to business and individuals [f]	105.4
Sight and other exchange liabilities	7.7	Listed as	
Capital funds	19.7	To agriculture, etc.	13.1
		To industry	27.5
		To trade	35.8
		Unspecified and to other sectors	29.0
		Other uses, except	14.0
		Real estate holdings, and	13.1
		Gold and exchange assets	11.4

Note: Subtotals do not necessarily add up to totals, due to rounding.

[a] Discrepancies between the two columns of table 5*A* reflect funds which one part of the system supplies to, or obtains from, the other parts.

[b] Federal savings banks and São Paulo state system. Data for the latter refer to December 31, 1950.

[c] Excludes arrears of contributions, except of employers.

[d] Includes equivalent of note issue not covered by specified assets.

[e] State and municipal and autarquias of all kinds. The item is partly estimated.

[f] Includes "mixed companies."

V. COMMERCIAL BANKING

In addition to the official Banco do Brasil, which will be treated in a separate section, there are a considerable number of independent deposit banks, although branch banking is important. Banking offices are very unevenly distributed over the country. The importance of branches of foreign banks is relatively small and is declining.

As a result of inflation, and banks' attempts to spread the banking habit, deposits and loans have multiplied more than sixfold during the past ten years.

By reason of the intense demand for credit, a reflection of the strong propensity to spend, banks have in recent years been able to extend loans to the maximum extent they consider safe, although pursuing in the main a passive lending policy, i.e., accepting rather than seeking additional business. While there are some highly speculative banks, an overwhelming proportion of the banking system's assets is held by banks which are extremely conservative and sound. Their policy is governed by tradition and certain institutional factors, in addition to the relative attractiveness of different types of loans and investments and sectors of activity, which, as already noted, have been considerably influenced by inflation in a manner which has, of course, often contradicted the requirements of reasonably balanced economic growth.

Holdings of government bills and of bonds are extremely small. As already mentioned, the banks operate mainly, in form and largely also in fact, in discounts and short-term advances. As far as one can judge from the available data—and these must be used with care—trade is favored, while agriculture obtains direct bank credit with difficulty; industry occupies an intermediate position. Medium and long term credit for agriculture and industry are not available to the extent which might seem reasonable. Direct financing (or investment) in real estate has been limited.

Competition for deposits, for which banks pay high interest rates, is a reflection of the intense demand for resources and has become accentuated in recent years. For the first time in Brazil's history, banks have become substantially indebted to the monetary authorities.

Credit is apportioned among borrowers in the main by direct rationing rather than by use of interest rates. Loan rates are high in nominal terms, though not so much in real terms, considering inflation. As indicated earlier, there is practically no money or acceptance market and relatively little direct cooperation between banks. With few exceptions each bank constitutes a separate system operating with its own clientele of borrowers in a given region.

TYPES, NUMBER, AND DISTRIBUTION OF COMMERCIAL BANKS

As shown in Table 6 there are at present 403 (independent) banks (head offices) while the total number of bank offices, including head offices, branches, and correspondent offices of deposit banks, amounts to 3,000. In addition there are nearly 300 branch offices of the Banco do Brasil, several hundred branch offices of federal and state savings banks (which also hold checking deposits), and over 300 credit sections of cooperatives. Most banks have the bulk of their branches in their own states. The Banco do Brasil maintains foreign branches in Asunción and Montevidéo. The other banks have no branches abroad.

As is frequently the case in periods of strong inflation, the number of bank offices has increased extraordinarily during the past ten years, as the result of the growth of the economy and of increased competition of banks for each others' and the public's funds. This increase has taken the form of an increase more in the number of branches and correspondent offices than in the number of banks.

While the concentration of banking is far from negligible, it is very much less than in many countries with branch banking systems. Seventy-eight banks hold about 90 percent of the deposits of all deposit banks. The 15 largest domestic deposit banks hold nearly 40

TABLE 6
NUMBER OF DEPOSIT BANKS (EXCEPT BANCO DO BRASIL),[a] DECEMBER 31

	1941	*1945*	*1951*
Total	1,339	2,190	3,000
Domestic banks (All Offices)	1,259	2,151	2,958
Head offices	361	476	403
Branches and correspondents	898	1,681	2,555
Large banks			
Head offices	135	229	233
Branches	847 [b]	1,646 [b]	1,969
Correspondents	n.a. [c]	n.a.	571
Small banks			
Head offices	226	247	170
Branches	51	35	15
Branches of foreign banks	80	39	42

Source: Banco do Brasil, *Relatórios* 1941, 1945, 1951.

[a] Excludes investment companies and mortgage companies, which do not operate as deposit banks; in 1951, there were 16 head offices and 5 branches of investment companies, and one mortgage company.

[b] Includes correspondents.

[c] Not available.

percent. But no bank other than the Banco do Brasil has more than $250 million of deposits, and only five or six banks have more than $100 million. A few deposit banks have over 100 branches but none has more than 150.

The number of bank offices in the different regions varies widely in relation to population (Table 7). In the North it is as low as one office per 100,000 persons; it is much higher in the South, particularly in the capitals, and in some cities reaches one office per 10,000 persons. The distribution is, however, much more equal in relation to income. The increase in commercial bank offices has resulted in an appreciably improved distribution of bank offices. The Banco do Brasil plays an important role in bringing banking services to the poor and less developed regions of the North, Northeast, and Far West. Savings bank offices also contribute to a more even distribution of bank offices.

During the Second World War a considerable number of new banks were founded, many of them of an extremely speculative nature (many were organized to finance real estate speculation). The great majority of these banks were located in the Federal District and in the city of São Paulo. Since 1945 many of these banks have closed down, and, while the number of independent banks is still higher than before the war, it continues to decline—a tendency that is encouraged by the authorities.

The decline since the prewar period of the number of foreign bank branches reflects the compulsory closing of branches controlled by the former "Axis" countries during the late war. Since then, however, foreign banks have been permitted to open new branches.

As already mentioned, the credit operations of commercial banks in Brazil consist almost entirely, formally at least, of discounts and short-term working capital advances. Banks differ, of course, in the extent to which they finance different lines of activity. Some of the branches of the foreign banks, for example, specialize in the financing of import and export trade, and in the financing of foreign firms. Some domestic banks also engage in foreign trade finance; others specialize in the financing of one or more export products in the commercial stage, that is, from harvest until time of sale for exportation. Some banks also extend working capital advances to processors or to agricultural producers. Other banks finance mainly internal wholesale trade.

Few banks, and only one important one, specialize in urban mortgage credit. The banks owned by state governments sometimes

Table 7
Regional Distribution of Banking Offices, December 31, 1941, 1945, and 1951

Region	Banco do Brasil			Other Domestic Banks: Head Offices			Other Domestic Banks: Branches [a]			Branches of Foreign Banks			Federal Savings Banks Offices [b]	State Savings Banks Offices [c]	Banking Offices of Cooperatives			Investment Companies [d]
	1941	*1945*	*1951*	*1941*	*1945*	*1951*	*1941*	*1945*	*1951*	*1941*	*1945*	*1951*	*1951*	*1951*	*1941*	*1945*	*1951*	*1951*
Federal District	7	10	15	130	191	151	25	62	120	12	10	9	24		2	32	42	12 [j]
São Paulo	37	57	63	90	114	97	231	474	809	35	12	15	19 (5)	274 [h]	8	53	41	10
North	5	11	10	4	5	5		5	8	4	4	4	5 (12)		3	3	6	
North East	29	47	49	32	43	44	14	19	29	9	7	6	17 (43)		103	119	147	
East [e]	47	80	89	78	89	77	410	705	994 [g]	8	3	4	100 (69)	15 (+ 295) [i]	27	52	57	
South [f]	25	42	44	22	25	21	202	390	549 [g]	12	3	4	66 (16)		6	50	67	
Center West	7	13	15	5	9	2	16	35	46 [g]				5 (5)				3	

Sources: Banco do Brasil, *Relatórios*, 1941, 1945, 1951; Information obtained from Superintendencia da Moeda e do Crédito; *Revista das Caixas Econômicas*, 1951, p. 13; *Anuário Estatístico do Brasil*, 1951.

[a] Includes correspondents.

[b] As of July 31, 1951. Figures in parentheses represent postal savings agencies.

[c] São Paulo and Minas Gerais state systems.

[d] Includes only those investment companies doing no deposit banking business, and one mortgage company doing no deposit banking business.

[e] Excludes Federal District.

[f] Excludes São Paulo.

[g] One third are correspondents.

[h] As of December 31, 1950.

[i] As of December 31, 1948. Figures in parentheses are agencies attached to state tax collection offices.

[j] Includes one mortgage company and 5 branches of investment companies.

operate specialized rural credit departments in addition to their commercial credit functions. They also serve as their respective governments' fiscal agents. The Federal government owns a bank whose specific object is the development of the Amazon region and in particular the promotion of rubber production. A development bank for Northeast Brazil has recently been established.

The older banks, especially the large ones, are generally very conservative. Together with the sound younger banks, they account for an overwhelming proportion of the total loans and deposits of all commercial banks. In view of the wide latitude which legislation gives to banks in their choice of assets, and of the absence—until recently—of efficient inspection, the high degree of soundness of the system is impressive despite the existence of banks engaging in speculative operations. The old banks still represent the bulk of the large banks, though they are losing in relative position to some of the newer ones.

Some of the small banks in the interior perform an extremely useful function; their superior knowledge of local conditions enables them to grant credit to borrowers who, though perfectly sound, would be able to get loans from branches of larger banks only with great difficulty, if at all. Other small banks are pioneers in quasi-investment trust operations.

Each bank constitutes a separate system, operating with its own clientele of borrowers, generally only in one economic region. There are, of course, correspondent relationships between banks, and it is customary for certain large banks, within the legal limits, to lend to or to rediscount for one or two small ones.

LEGAL STATUS AND BANK INCORPORATION

The establishment of banks and of branches requires approval by the (Federal) Ministry of Finance, which decides upon the recommendation of the Superintendency of Money and Credit. The Ministry is free to deny authorization. Bank charters are granted for maximum periods of twenty years.

The larger banks and the majority of small ones are organized as share companies (Sociedades Anônimas). The liability of shareholders is limited to the value of their subscriptions, while directors may be held fully liable for losses caused intentionally or by negligence (law 1808/53). The law prescribes different sizes of minimum capital, according to the desire of a bank to have branches only in its home city, home state, or in other states of Brazil.[29] With two exceptions, commercial banks may engage in any type of banking operation including investment banking, may grant any type of credit including mortgage credit, and may hold any type of asset including real estate, shares, bonds, and so on. Consideration is, however, being given to a more restrictive interpretation of the present banking legislation. One of the exceptions mentioned above is the issuance of mortgage certificates ("letras hipotecárias"), which requires a special charter and a special capital set aside for the purpose.[30] There are only two or three such banks. Special permission is also required for banks to operate in foreign exchange. Its charter may, of course, limit a bank's activities but most charters afford great latitude (though, as we have mentioned, *formally* banks engage only in the classical type of operation).[31]

There are at present no restrictions as to the citizenship of the owners and shareholders of banks organized under Brazilian law and no legal obstacles to the establishment of branches of foreign banks and no restrictions on their operations. As we have seen, several foreign banks have recently been authorized to establish new branches. Legislation governing these branches [32] prescribes that a certain capital be ascribed to the Brazilian branch; that this capital should not be held against obligations of the bank incurred abroad, and that a foreign declaration of bankruptcy does not affect the Brazilian branch. Also foreign banks must have a resident representative with full powers to settle any questions arising out of the operations of the Brazilian branch.[33]

GOVERNMENT SUPERVISION AND CONTROL

Banking supervision operates at three levels. The Superintendencia through its Inspectorate General of Banks, has general respon-

29 The general banking law now before the Congress would prescribe a relationship of between 7 and 15 percent between capital accounts and deposits. See Decree 14.728 of 1921; decree-law 6419 of 1944; decree-law 8495 of 1945.

30 See Decrees 370 of 1890 and 14.728 of 1921.

31 Legislation regarding investment banks (Decree-law 7583 of 1945), specialized rural banks (Decree 24.691/34), and industrial banks (Decree 24.575/34) is on the statute books, but the latter two laws are apparently impracticable in their present form and there are no rural or industrial banks. Legislation now before the Congress would limit each bank to a given field: commercial operations, mortgage operations, rural credit, industrial credit, and so on.

32 Decree 14.728.

33 A bill now before the Congress would prohibit branches of foreign banks from accepting deposits; this idea has been proposed several times in the past 20 years. Other bills now before Congress establish a special relation between capital accounts and deposits for branches of foreign banks (the former to be 10–15 percent of the latter).

sibility for control of banks.[34] Foreign exchange operations are supervised by the Exchange Department of the Banco do Brasil; the fiscal affairs of banks are subject to supervision by the Ministry of Finance.

LIQUIDATION OF BANKS: MERGERS AND INTERVENTION

Banks in difficulties may request the Superintendencia to appoint an Administrator. The Superintendencia may do so also on its own initiative if a bank appears to be threatened by bankruptcy, or in order to assure the repayment of loans made to banks by the monetary authorities (See Section VII).[35] Under the same conditions, or if intervention by the Superintendencia has proved unable to stave off bankruptcy, either the bank, or the Superintendencia, or the Administrator, as the case may be, may propose the extrajudicial liquidation of the establishment.[36] Banks' charters can be canceled, theoretically, for general disobedience to banking law but in practice charters have only been canceled when a bank has become bankrupt or has been liquidated. Bank mergers were encouraged after the war, when certain temporary tax advantages were offered for the purpose; [37] however, few mergers took place (none involving two or more large banks), and the authorities have apparently not felt able to use any indirect power they may possess to encourage mergers. When many of the "shoe-string" banks founded during the Second World War collapsed after 1945, spectacular failures were averted through timely and sometimes overgenerous loans by the monetary authorities. The pronounced inflation of the past decade has, of course, helped to hide the initial unsoundness of many credits.[38]

INTERNAL ADMINISTRATION AND SERVICES

The administration of banks is in general centralized and bureaucratic. This applies as much to the running of each banking office as to the relations between head office and branches. Some banks, however, which operate in various regions, have resident regional directorates with fairly full powers.

The training of bank personnel including managers is entirely em-

[34] Created in 1951. No similar department existed between 1931 and 1951.

[35] Decree-laws 6.419 of 1944; 8495 of 1945.

[36] Decree-law 9228 of 1946 (Decrees 19.479 of 1930 and 19.654 of 1931) and Decree-law 9346 of 1946.

[37] Decree-law 9.229 of 1946.

[38] It is worthy of note that Brazilian banks also got through the 1930s with relatively few failures, due to emergency loans and the confidence of the public that the government would not let the banks fail.

pirical. Bank associations limit activities to negotiations with employees' unions and to the representing of banks' interests before the government.

Banks exchange information on general credit worthiness of customers and the credit *limits* they have granted to them, but not on the actual amounts of loans. Apart from their main activities, banks collect checks and bills of exchange, "duplicatas," and the like, for customers. Banks also advise clients on investments and will give other business information; on the other hand, there are no trustee departments.

COSTS, RECEIPTS, AND PROFITS

Information on bank costs and bank earnings is inadequate. The available data indicate that even for the more efficient banks operating costs (other than interest on deposits) are rather high (about 4 percent per year) in relation to total resources. Together with high interest rates on deposits, high operating cost means that there is a floor of between 7 percent and 9 percent below which loan rates cannot fall if banks are to make what is considered no more than a reasonable profit on capital.[39] Interest and operating costs as a percentage of resources fall as the size of the bank increases (measured by deposits). Declared bank profits in recent years have averaged better than 20 percent on capital and surplus; this is high but not exceptionally so in comparison with other branches of activity.[40] Declared profits as a percentage of capital and surplus rise as the size of the bank increases (measured by deposits). On the other hand, profits as well as gross receipts as a percentage of both loans and deposits are lower for large than for smaller banks. In recent years, profits of banks in relation to capital funds appear to have increased, partly because capital funds have not augmented in proportion to deposits. Real profits, however, also appear to have risen, less because of any marked increase in the spread between (1) loan rates and (2) cost as a percentage of loans, than as a consequence of the extension of the banking habit and hence of the proportion of deposits to national income.

BANK ASSETS

The assets of the commercial banks, segregated into various groups, are presented in Table 8.

39 On the causal chain, see p. 83–84.

40 See *Conjuntura Econômica,* September, 1950, November, 1951, February, 1952 (unpublished census data).

TABLE 8

ASSETS OF COMMERCIAL BANKS, DECEMBER 31, 1941 AND 1951

(AMOUNTS IN MILLIONS OF CRUZEIROS)

	1941					1951				
	DOMESTIC BANKS			BRANCHES OF FOREIGN BANKS	ALL COMMERCIAL BANKS	DOMESTIC BANKS			BRANCHES OF FOREIGN BANKS	ALL COMMERCIAL BANKS
	Large	*Small*	*All*			*Large*	*Small*	*All*		
Cash	n.a.[a]	n.a.	1,301	761	2,062	11,310	448	11,758	1,763	13,521
In vault	624	44	668	264	932	4,662	142	4,804	421	5,225
Deposit with Banco do Brasil	n.a.	n.a.	633	497	1,130	5,648	259	5,907	1,196	7,103
Deposit with Superintendency						1,000	47	1,047	146	1,193
Deposits with commercial banks and other cash [b]	n.a.	n.a.	448	34	482	364	8	372	157	529
Treasury bills [c]						292	4	296	98	394
Loans and discounts	8,020	599	8,619	1,659	10,278	54,275	1,949	56,224	5,165	61,389
Discounts	4,165	382	5,147	510	5,657	35,791	1,005	36,796	1,746	38,542
Current account loans	3,255	216	3,471	1,149	4,620	18,484	944	19,428	3,419	22,847
Government departments						2,310		2,310	11	2,321
Current account loans						1,195		1,195	9	1,209
Discounts						1,115		1,115	2	1,117
Autarquias						406		406	7	413
Current account loans						385		385	7	392
Discounts						21		21		21
Banks						258		258	26	284
Current account loans						197		197	26	223
Discounts						61		61		61
Trade						24,720	940	25,660	2,501	28,161
Current account loans						8,329	340	8,669	1,656	10,325
Discounts						16,391	600	16,991	845	17,836
Industry						16,232	624	16,856	2,472	19,328
Current account loans						6,124	420	6,544	1,609	8,153
Discounts						10,108	204	10,312	863	11,175
Agriculture						3,514	33	3,547	9	3,556
Current account loans						535	10	545	6	551
Discounts						2,979	23	3,002	3	3,005
Livestock						1,422	12	1,434	9	1,443
Current account loans						220	2	222	6	228
Discounts						1,202	10	1,212	3	1,215
Unclassified						5,412	340	5,752	131	5,883
Current account loans						1,497	171	1,668	100	7,768
Discounts						3,915	160	4,084	21	4,115

Mortgage loans	n.a.	n.a.	n.a.	n.a.	n.a.	2,376	154	2,530	12	2,542
Urban [d]						n.a.	n.a.	n.a.	n.a.	2,237
Rural [d]	n.a.	n.a.	n.a.	n.a.	n.a.	n.a.	n.a.	n.a.	n.a.	305
Investments [e]	n.a.	n.a.	n.a.	n.a.	n.a.	n.a.	n.a.	n.a.	n.a.	2,364
Federal bonds	n.a.	n.a.	n.a.	n.a.	n.a.	n.a.	n.a.	n.a.	n.a.	851
State and municipal banks	n.a.	n.a.	n.a.	n.a.	n.a.	n.a.	n.a.	n.a.	n.a.	875
Private securities	n.a.	n.a.	n.a.	n.a.	n.a.	n.a.	n.a.	n.a.	n.a.	638
Bills due	n.a.	n.a.	n.a.	n.a.	n.a.	507	37	544	26	570
Correspondents abroad	109	3	112	44	156	1,163	11	1,174	171	1,345
Real estate [e]	n.a.	n.a.	n.a.	n.a.	n.a.	n.a.	n.a.	n.a.	n.a.	2,236
Other accounts [f]						n.a.	n.a.	n.a.	n.a.	35,790
Total	n.a.	n.a.	n.a.	n.a.	n.a.	106,794	3,883	110,677	10,006	120,683
Compensation accounts [g]						76,923	1,348	78,271	11,711	89,982
Grand Total	24,653	1,334	25,987	6,991	32,978	183,717	5,231	188,948	21,717	210,665

Sources: 1941: *Movimento Bancário,* December, 1941 (mimeographed) and December, 1940–41, printed; 1951: *Mensário Estatístico,* No. 4, 1951, p. 19.

Notes: Subtotals do not necessarily add to totals, because of rounding.

[a] Not available.

[b] "Other cash" largely represents checks on other banks; it also includes tax stamps.

[c] Federal.

[d] Estimated on basis of data for 67 largest commercial banks, published in *Resenha Econômica Mensal* of Banco do Brasil in 1950 (various issues). In 1941 data probably included in current account loans.

[e] Estimated on basis of data for 67 largest commercial banks, pub- in *Conjuntura Econômica,* October, November, 1952.

[f] Mainly interagency accounts.

[g] Registration accounts.

Cash Reserves.—Brazilian banks are subject to two distinct cash reserve requirements. In the first place, since 1932, they are obliged to maintain in cash, or as a freely available deposit with the Banco do Brasil carrying 1 percent interest, 15 percent of their short-term deposits (deposits at sight and up to 90 days' notice) and 10 percent of their other deposits.[41] In the second place, since 1945, they have been obliged to maintain on *deposit,* with the Banco do Brasil, separately, without interest and for account of the Superintendencia, 8 percent of their short-term deposits and 4 percent of their long-term deposits. This second cash reserve may be varied upwards or downwards, by 75 percent, and is at present fixed at 4 percent and 3 percent; [42] under later legislation, it is considered part of the fixed reserve.[43] Consequently, *in theory,* the banks are subject only to the first cash reserve requirement. The authorities may also permit banks to carry up to 50 percent of their second reserve in Federal Bonds, which, though generally quoted at a substantial discount, are accepted at par for this purpose.[44] In practice, the second reserve does have some slight importance. In contrast to deposits made to satisfy the first cash reserve requirement, the second reserve may only be drawn upon by permission of the Superintendencia; it is thus, in a way, less "liquid" than the first reserve. A change in the second requirement may, therefore, to some extent, mean a change in total cash held, instead of meaning, simply, a change in the proportion of freely available and other deposits with the Banco do Brasil. On the average, banks maintain about 40 percent of their total cash reserves in the form of vault cash, the rest on deposit (freely available and for account of the Superintendencia) with the Banco do Brasil. In the metropolitan centers, and in the states where concentration of banking in large cities is particularly pronounced, vault cash is a smaller part of total cash reserves. In the interior, a larger part of cash reserves consists of vault cash due to impossibility or greater difficulty of drawing upon a local agency of the Banco do Brasil for notes. This situation arises from the fact that the Banco do Brasil, not being a central bank, cannot hold unissued notes, while issued notes, repre-

[41] Decree 21.499 of 1932. The original concept of short-term deposit included deposits at sight and up to 30 days' notice only. The change was made in 1946 and must be taken into account in interpreting the statistics. Deposits between 30 and 90 days' notice seem to represent less than 5 percent of all deposits. With certain exceptions, banks may not carry more vault cash than 20 percent of their deposits.

[42] Decree-law 7.293 of 1945.

[43] Decree-law 8.495 of 1945.

[44] Decree-law 9.140 of 1946.

senting either deposits or rediscounts, cost interest, so that it holds far too little vault cash.

The over-all average cash reserve at present is about 19 percent.[45] This is somewhat in excess of the legal minimum (even if the first and second cash reserves are totaled). It is low, however, if one considers the following facts: a secondary reserve and a money market are virtually lacking; rediscounts and emergency loans from the monetary authorities are not always speedily available; and banks, in general, do not want to depend upon aid unless it is absolutely necessary; also, in some cases, due to the relatively high average maturity of bills, the proportion of bills maturing daily is not large enough to give banks an appreciable degree of liquidity. Banks are, however, reluctant to hold much larger primary reserves because of the high interest rates paid on deposits and because of the intense demand for credit. Moreover, the fact that runs on and failures of banks have been rare, and the fact that the inflationary increase in deposits has continued almost without interruption, make banks less inclined to hold high reserves.

Cash ratios differ according to the character of the bank. Banks operating in foreign exchange hold higher reserves to enable them to buy exchange whenever it is made available, a consequence of exchange control. The desire to be independent of the monetary authorities applies particularly to branches of foreign banks, whose cash ratio averages at present 50 percent higher than that of the domestic banks and is comparable to the primary plus secondary reserve, which, for example, British banks would hold. Cash reserves also differ according to the economic region in which a bank or branch operates. Furthermore, as would be expected, total cash reserves are higher in the metropolitan centers and lower in the small townships of the interior, where unexpected withdrawals of deposits are exceptional. Reserves are only slightly in excess of legal requirements (except in the case of the foreign banks). Since the excess finds its origins in a real or imagined need, it does not indicate any significant capacity for credit expansion.

Domestic banks' total cash represents, on the whole, the same proportion of total deposits as in the average year prior to the Second World War,[46] though a slightly lower proportion of short-term de-

[45] Balance sheet figures on cash reserves must be taken with a grain of salt; window-dressing is known to exist.

[46] 1941, the year to which our statistics refer, was characterized by extraordinarily low cash reserves.

posits. It should be mentioned, however, that before the late war deposits of one commercial bank with another were relatively quite important as a secondary reserve.[47] During the past decade, cash reserves have increased for short periods when inflation has accelerated. When it has slowed down or vanished, reserves have been allowed to fall to enable banks to continue expanding loans, except when there was an expectation of genuine contraction. Also, cash has been allowed to fall when a particular boom (such as in coffee, recently) has made a special call on banks' reserves. The cash ratios of the branches of the foreign banks, though still relatively high, have fallen substantially since the prewar period, in response to the intense demand for credit.

Secondary Reserves—There is at present in Brazil no (independent) secondary reserve requirement. During the last few years some banks have started to hold small amounts of four months' Federal Treasury bills purchased from exporters, who are compelled to acquire them in part payment of their export proceeds. These bills are highly lucrative (they carry interest of 3 percent per annum, but are purchased by banks from exporters at discounts corresponding to a yield of 6–11 percent per annum). These bills are held in limited amounts even when the effective interest rate is high, because banks consider it better policy to accommodate their business clients, and because the bills mentioned are not normally rediscountable or acceptable as collateral for loans from the monetary authorities (though the latter procedure is permissible by law).

The monetary authorities could in no case sell Treasury bills directly to banks on a voluntary basis unless they were to pay interest somewhat near the lower limit of the discount cited above. This would be high compared to the rates paid on compulsory issues not only of bills but of bonds, and high when compared to the effective market rate of the latter. It would not necessarily be higher than the 6 percent rate at which the Federal government obtains current account loans from the Banco do Brasil—though it must be remembered that the Treasury shares in the Bank's profits. The relatively high interest rates which would have to be paid by the authorities are of course a consequence of the rates which banks pay on deposits (even more than the rates which banks can earn on other loans); it is the rate paid on de-

[47] Such interbank deposits have been prohibited since 1945, except for deposits arising out of correspondent relationship between banks situated in different localities.

posits which limits the sacrifice of interest which banks might be prepared to undergo in order to hold an asset of the type of the Treasury bills. Creation of a market in these bills would probably in any case take time and require considerable "moral suasion" or compulsion.

Discounts, Loans and Investments.—Types of assets. Bank investments in securities (other than short-term paper) are extremely small, between 3 and 4 percent of earning assets other than deposits with the Banco do Brasil.[48] This fact is due to the weakness of the securities markets (see Section IX). Nearly 40 percent of the investments represent Federal bonds, a similar percentage state bonds, the remainder private securities and a very few municipal bonds. Commercial banks' total holdings of Federal bonds have increased somewhat since they have become available as a substitute for cash under the second reserve requirement. State bonds are held mainly by the state-owned institutions.

Traditionally commercial banks in Brazil do not directly invest in real estate other than for their own use despite its profitable character, but some banks have at times, in recent years, been forced to accept real estate in payment of loans which have become frozen. Real estate holdings represent, on the average, 3 percent of earning assets. Some 4 percent of earning assets represents mortgage loans (see below), so that about 90 percent of the former consists of discounts of various kinds of paper and of current account loans.

Demand for credit and basic loan policy. As already mentioned, a strong demand for credit in recent years has enabled banks for the most part to pursue a passive lending policy, in the sense that they do not actively seek additional business. Competition has been limited, on the whole, to efforts by the "best" banks to attract the "best" firms as customers. Exceptions to "passivity" have occurred in periods when inflation has accelerated, and banks have had, temporarily, a plethora of funds, and, in the case of some banks, the planting season, when demand slackens after the harvest. The newer banks, however, have more often taken the initiative in persuading customers to borrow additional amounts.

The better banks investigate carefully the general credit worthiness and particularly the liquidity of their borrowers, and also to some extent the use to which borrowed funds will be put. These banks

[48] See *Resenha Econômica,* Year 4, No. 1, p. 66, and Table 8.

also, of course, limit loans to any one borrower to a certain proportion of his resources. Obviously, personal criteria are of importance in lending policies. It is not customary to force borrowers to undertake an annual "clean-up."

Each firm customarily deals with a number of banks; this arises from the fact that often a single bank is not large enough to satisfy all a customer's credit needs, and, conversely, the customer does not wish to be dependent on one bank alone. Cooperation between banks does not go to the point of setting a global credit limit for each borrower; rather, each bank sets a limit without taking into consideration the loans which the customer may obtain from other banks. This practice can thus lead sometimes to an overextension of credit even by otherwise conservative institutions.

Types and conditions of loans and discounts. Discounts represent about 60 percent of the earning assets of commercial banks. They consist largely of "duplicatas" (see Section III). There is also included, however, an appreciable proportion (it is not known how much) of ordinary bills of exchange and promissory notes. Promissory notes represent "legitimate" working capital advances as well as advances for other purposes. It is worth mentioning that in the case of some very reliable customers a bank will discount, that is, pay at face value less interest, on unaccepted "duplicatas." Maturities quite commonly go up to 120 days; discounts in any form are rarely granted for more than six months, at most eight months; renewals are rare, except for promissory notes in special cases (see below). Borrowers have a strong preference for having banks hold their bills to maturity, rather than rediscount them. It is customary for banks to agree with their customers on certain maximum limits to which they will be entitled to discount "duplicatas" or bills. These limits are not, however, considered as binding on the bank. The discount of promissory notes requires, in general, separate negotiation in each case.

Current account loans are made subject to either a six months' or one-year contract which is binding on the bank. A fee of between .25 percent and 1 percent of the amount contracted is paid, but interest is due only on the loan actually outstanding. The most common form is the current account loan against deposit of accepted and in some cases unaccepted "duplicatas" or bills. Advances against collateral represent generally 80 percent of the value of the paper deposited. There are, of course, current account loans not collateralled by trade paper. Acceptances [40] and overdrafts are traditionally very rare. The absence of the former is particularly interesting in view of the size of the country.

Preference for discounts. The preference of banks for discounts may be attributed to the absence of a binding loan contract and also to the fact that they are rediscountable. Moreover, since the collateral securing a current account loan is not the property of the bank, the latter, in case the drawee fails to pay, has not the quick relief against the borrower as it does when it actually *owns* a bill drawn by him. The difficulties which, in view of this fact, banks have experienced with current account loans which have become frozen during and after the years of war time speculation led, for some years, to a relative increase in discounts, as against loans.

The foreign banks have twice as many loans as discounts. These banks deal in much higher proportion than domestic banks with local subsidiaries of exceptionally large foreign firms, which guarantee their subsidiaries' credit. Also, like some domestic banks, their high proportion of import financing through opening of letters of credit abroad brings with it a higher proportion of advances rather than discounts.

There are also wide regional differences, in accordance with local conditions and custom, between the proportion of discounts and current account loans. In general, in the South discounts are a much higher proportion of assets (for example, more than 3 times as large as current account loans in Rio Grande do Sul) than in the North, where the former are often much larger. There are also regional differences in the types of paper discounted; we have mentioned the high proportion of promissory notes in some regions, for example, the South.

Aversion to medium-term and long-term credits. We have mentioned that only a few banks specialize in mortgage credit. This represents mainly urban real estate financing. Some credits represented by discounts of promissory notes or made on a current account basis are only nominally short term, but actually medium term, that is, granted on the understanding that they will be renewed.

[40] In the sense of banks' accepting bill drawn on customers in other localities.

There is a large field for medium or long-term credits to finance the needs of industry as well as urban real estate. The aversion of banks to such loans is largely traditional, arising in part from the fact that banks in Brazil almost never face a deficiency of credit demand on short-term account, a reflection of capital shortage.

It should also be mentioned that loan rates are in many cases so near the legal maximum that the loss in shiftability could not be compensated adequately by higher rates; this, however, is probably the least important reason, since, in a period of inflation, deposits rise continually and most goods are easily salable. There are also, of course, ways of circumventing the many laws—ways that do not contradict the letter of the law. More important is the fact that the size of the efficient unit in industry is often so large that fixed capital loans would in many cases tie up loans to one customer to an amount greater than banks consider safe. This is one aspect of the lack of "giant banks" and of the disproportion between the size of modern industry and the resources available to underdeveloped countries. So far as real estate is concerned, the market has been rather too speculative for loans by the more conservative banks.

Sectors of activity financed. Banks classify their loans according to the principal occupation of the borrower. The actual use to which funds are put may, of course, be quite different, and this makes it difficult to judge the effects of banks' loan structure on the country's economy. For the commercial banking system, as a whole, current account loans to commerce and discounts of commercial paper, including the finance of foreign trade (which is not listed separately) represent nearly 50 percent of total loans. The next most important category, representing over 30 percent, comprises loans and discounts to industry. In this connection, it should be noted that traders and processors handle much of the financing of farmers. Proportionately, rather little credit is granted directly to agriculture, and to livestock breeders by commercial banks (respectively 6–8 percent and about 3 percent of total loans). We shall return to the problem of agricultural and industrial credit in a later section. Loans to public entities represent mainly the activity of the state-owned banks. Interbank loans with trade paper as collateral [50] are permitted without limit; interbank rediscounts, together with rediscounts with the monetary

[50] Instruction 3 of the Superintendency.

authorities, are limited as a maximum to the capital funds of each rediscounting bank. As already mentioned, it is customary for some of the larger banks to rediscount or lend to some of the smaller ones. On the whole these operations are negligible.

We have no data to determine the proportions in which loans granted to various lines of activity have varied in recent years.

Seasonal trends. The statistics reveal only an extremely slight seasonal trend in over-all loans, that is, an increase after midyear (coffee harvest). There is a fairly pronounced seasonal decrease in agricultural loans in and following the coffee harvest months. Many banks finance agricultural processors and merchants, who in turn grant credit to agricultural producers during the planting season and in addition finance the harvesting and sale of the crops. Other banks, however, which do not engage in agriculture finance, experience a slackening of demand in this season. Corresponding to the movement of agricultural loans, there is a seasonal increase in loans in the interior during the planting season; after the harvest time there is a decrease of loans in the interior and an increase of loans in the commercial centers. The regional seasonals in loan demand to some extent offset one another.

Loan Rates.—The usury law [51] fixes maximum interest at 12 percent per annum inclusive of commissions. The loan rates of smaller banks are generally at this limit and in some cases above it. The loan rates of the larger banks are often lower. In general, these lower rates arise not from an absence of loan demand, but rather from the tradition—which the larger banks honor—that loan rates should maintain a certain relationship to deposit rates; also the costs of the larger banks (in relation to loans) are apt to be lower than those of the smaller ones. It should be remembered that, whereas the demand for funds influences loan rates to some extent directly, the above tradition means that its indirect influence via the rate paid on deposits is more important. This is so because the loan demand usually exceeds supply at the maximum permissible interest rates for loans and in any case is apt to be highly inelastic in respect to interest rates. It is thus the deposit rate or the maximum set for it which will influence the actual loan rate. The larger banks charge between 7 percent and 10 percent on their loans, though in cases of extreme stringency they will exceed

[51] Decree 22.626 of 1931.

their upper limit to newer customers; they do not go significantly below 7 percent because their costs and deposit rates will not permit them to do so. Loan rates are now, perhaps, slightly higher than before the war, reflecting an increased demand for funds (see Section I), greater competition for funds between banks, consequently higher rates paid on deposits, and relatively higher wage costs.

In general, rates are highest on overdrafts; discounts come next, while rates on current account loans secured by "duplicatas" are lowest. In the latter case, there are commission charges in addition to interest.

Regional Distribution of Loans.—There is very little redistribution or shifting of credit between or within regions (except for the seasonal shifts mentioned above). In view of the competition for deposits, banks feel that they must lend in each locality in proportion to the deposits they draw from it. Only the Banco do Brasil redistributes credit between regions on a substantial scale; funds obtained by it in the wealthy South are lent out to Minas Gerais and in the Northeast and West.

Foreign Assets.—Though foreign exchange holdings are relatively more important now than before the war, they form a very minor proportion of bank assets. This is due to the exchange regulations requiring banks to pass on to the Banco do Brasil, within 24 hours, any exchange not used by them in accordance with the established priorities.

Other Assets.—The other assets of the banks listed in the statistics represent mainly interagency accounts which banks report gross instead of net.

OWN RESOURCES AND LIABILITIES OF COMMERCIAL BANKS

Own Resources.—As shown in Table 9, the declared capital and reserves (surplus) of all commercial banks at present represent about 13 percent of the deposits. There are in addition undivided profits (not shown in consolidated balance sheets) which cannot be estimated precisely and presumably hidden reserves. The adequacy of the 13 percent ratio must be viewed in relation to the high proportion of "risk assets." As far as one can judge from the available data, banks' own resources now represent on the average a somewhat smaller

Table 9
Liabilities of Commercial Banks, December 31, 1941 and 1951
(AMOUNTS IN MILLIONS OF CRUZEIROS)

	1941					1951				
	DOMESTIC BANKS			BRANCHES OF FOREIGN BANKS	ALL COMMERCIAL BANKS	DOMESTIC BANKS			BRANCHES OF FOREIGN BANKS	ALL COMMERCIAL BANKS
	Large	*Small*	*All*			*Large*	*Small*	*All*		
Capital	1,039	94	1,121	161	1,282	5,379	406	5,785	451	6,242
Legal reserve [a]	452	28	480	73	553	928	27	955	51	1,006
Other reserves [a]						2,440	105	2,545	272	2,817
Deposits	8,433	511	8,944	2,045	10,989	60,712	2,162	62,874	6,229	69,103
At sight and short notice [b]	4,657	333	4,990	1,635	6,625	45,533	1,179	46,712	5,514	52,226
Government department	75		75	5	80	3,560	6	3,566	5	3,571
"Autarquias"	n.a.[e]	n.a.	n.a.	n.a.	n.a.	789		789	25	814
Banks [c]	143		143	48	191					
Public:	4,439	333	4,772	1,582	6,354	41,184	1,173	42,357	5,484	47,841
Unlimited at interest	3,303	215	3,518	1,085	4,603	18,386	710	19,096	2,913	22,009
Limited	607	16	623	129	752	10,007	218	10,225	648	10,873
Popular	340	5	345	25	370	8,014	160	8,174	87	8,261
Other	189	97	286	343	629	4,777	85	4,862	1,836	6,698
Time deposits	3,775	178	3,953	410	4,363	15,179	983	16,162	715	16,877
Government department	n.a.	n.a.	n.a.	n.a.		415	1	416		416
"Autarquias"	n.a.	n.a.	n.a.	n.a.	n.a.	1,370		1,370	21	1,391
Public	n.a.	n.a.	n.a.	n.a.	n.a.	13,394	982	14,376	694	15,070
Deposit certificates	n.a.	n.a.	n.a.	n.a.	n.a.	27	2	29		29
Monetary authorities (Loans and rediscounts)	n.a.	n.a.	n.a.	n.a.	314	n.a.	n.a.	n.a.	n.a.	6,465
Rediscount department	n.a.	n.a.	n.a.	n.a.	95	n.a.	n.a.	n.a.	n.a.	3,684
Banco do Brasil and Bank Loans Department	n.a.	n.a.	n.a.	n.a.	219	n.a.	n.a.	n.a.	n.a.	2,781
Correspondents abroad	41	3	44	53	97	370	4	374	143	517
Other accounts [d]						n.a.	n.a.	n.a.	n.a.	34,472
Total, I to VIII						106,794	3,883	110,677	10,006	120,683
Compensation accounts						76,923	1,348	78,271	11,711	89,982
Grand total	24,653	1,334	25,987	6,991	32,978	183,717	5,231	188,948	21,717	210,665

Sources: 1941: *Movimento Bancário,* December, 1941 (mimeographed) and December, 1940–41, printed; 1951: *Mensário Estatistico,* No. 4, 1951, p. 19.

Note: Subtotals do not necessarily add to totals, because of rounding.

[a] Surplus in United States terminology.

[b] Up to 90 days' notice, in 1951; up to 30 days' notice in 1941; the difference is about 5 percent of the public's deposits.

[c] Excludes transit items.

[d] Mainly interagency accounts.

[e] Not available.

proportion of deposits than before the war.[52] Wartime legislation and the practice of the monetary authorities have prevented a further reduction in capital by increasing minimum capital requirements.

The reduction in the capital ratio has affected all types of banks but particularly the domestic ones, whose declared capital funds in relation to deposits are now only slightly higher than those of the branches of foreign banks, whose own resources used to be relatively much lower.

There are regional differences in the proportion of own resources to deposits, explained mainly by the different rates of growth of the various regions. The smaller banks seem to have a higher proportion of capital funds in relation to deposits, partly because they have often not been able to increase their deposits as rapidly as the larger ones, partly because rediscount facilities—which they use more than the large banks—depend on the amount of capital funds.[53]

Deposits and Deposit Policy.—In contrast to their loan policy, Brazilian banks have in recent years actively sought to attract deposits to satisfy the increasing demand for funds by business. The proportion of sight and short-term deposits has increased in recent years and that of time deposits decreased.[54] The importance of deposits relative to paper money has also increased; deposits are relatively much more important in Brazil than in most Latin countries.

Short-term deposits [55] of the public now represent over two thirds of the total as against less than three fifths before the war. In view of inflation it is surprising that the change has not been larger. However, banks often grant depositors the privilege of withdrawing their time deposits at sight and pay particularly high interest rates on these deposits.

Among deposits at sight and short notice there has been a spectacular increase in the proportion of "popular" and "limited" deposits, that is, deposits carrying a maximum limit and paying higher

[52] A perfectly natural consequence of inflation, at least for the more conservative banks, since assets representing banks' own resources are not in general inflation-proof, and since *real* earnings will not rise unless the spread between deposit and loan rates increases sufficiently. The ownership of bank shares is more widely spread than that of most other shares, so that banks have a somewhat smaller possibility than other corporations to refrain from distributing profits.

[53] It is believed that, in the case of some of the small banks, capital figures are sometimes swelled artificially.

[54] Even if allowance is made for reclassification of certain deposits which now are included in sight deposits by means of Decree-law 8.495 of 1945.

[55] On a basis comparable to the prewar period.

rates of interest. The development of these special types of deposits reflects the increased availability of commercial bank offices and the increased interest in the "small man," as well as increased competition between banks for funds.

There are significant differences in the various economic regions in the proportion of short-term and long-term deposits explained by their different economic structure (such as the more even distribution of property in the South which makes for a relatively higher proportion of long-term deposits—that is, savings deposits). Where there is a relatively greater degree of commercial and industrial activity, as in São Paulo, commercial and, hence, short-term deposits represent a higher proportion of the total. There are indications of a very slight seasonal drop in deposits connected with the harvest and end-of-year shopping cash drain and the end-of-year main import season.

There are certain special privileges which in the case of bankruptcy protect popular deposits. Brazil has, however, no deposit guarantee system. This has undoubtedly contributed at times to an overgenerous attitude on the part of the government toward banks in difficulties. Very serious thought is being given to the establishment of some sort of deposit insurance; there are also some indications that at present the monetary authorities would pay off rapidly and to a very high proportion through the Banco do Brasil all the legitimate deposits of banks which they are forced to close.

Deposit Interest Rates.—A distinctive feature of the system is the high interest rates paid on deposits, including sight deposits. At present current account deposits may receive a maximum interest of 3 percent per annum; popular deposits (up to 100,000 cruzeiros) may receive 5 percent per annum; fixed-term deposits of one year may receive up to 6 percent.[56] There are important—traditional—regional differences in such ratios (Minas Gerais pays exceptionally high rates) and differences according to the category of bank.

High rates on deposits are not an innovation. Until the recent introduction of maximum limits, rates of interest that are paid on deposits were probably rising, as compared with the prewar period, due to increased competition of banks for funds.

Many of the larger banks pay lower rates than those listed above. They would have little objection to a general reduction in deposit interest rates and might quite possibly be expected also to reduce loan

[56] See Superintendency of Money and Credit, Instrução No. 56, 1953.

rates somewhat as a consequence. Strong opposition against a reduction in rates comes principally from the newer and smaller banks for whom high deposit rates are the means of overcoming competition of the superior service of the older and larger banks. The limits recently introduced have not, under these conditions, been substantially below customary rates. Lower rates would probably not affect substantially either the volume or the velocity of circulation of deposits. But, in theory, at any rate, there is nothing paradoxical about subsidizing people to hold money (rather than spending it) by paying interest on deposit currency, in a country where liquidity preference is as low as in Brazil.

We have already mentioned that the high interest rates paid on deposits influence the policy of banks: we shall return later to some of the effects of these high rates on monetary policy.

Indebtedness to Monetary Authorities.—One of the most important recent developments in the banking field is the increased indebtedness of the deposit banks to the monetary authorities which now amounts to more than 10 percent of their loans; from another point of view, this indebtedness amounts to more than 50 percent of total cash reserves; that is, the net cash reserves of banks as a whole are below the legal minimum. Before the war, indebtedness to monetary authorities was 3 percent of loans. A large part of the loans are of an emergency nature, mainly indebtedness by small institutions. Recently, however, rediscounts for other than emergency purposes have increased relatively and absolutely, a fact which affords the monetary authorities the possibility of using rediscounts as a means of influencing bank lending policies. Rediscounts are normally subject to a strong seasonal increase in the second half of the year, determined mainly by the coffee harvest when banks rediscount to expand loans for the movement of the harvest and also in part to compensate for a slight cash drain at harvest time.

Banks' earlier reluctance to borrow from the monetary authorities (despite the relatively low level of the rediscount rate) was partly due to a sound desire not to depend upon the authorities, and also due to the fact that the ability to borrow was relatively new, having existed (in the present form) only since the thirties. Although the amount of emergency loans which can be made to each bank (upon proof of loss of deposits and reserves) is unlimited, the total of rediscounts to which each bank is entitled without proof of need is limited, and before 1945 the limit was even narrower than it is today. Since a certain opprobrium attaches to emergency loans, banks are reluctant to use the better facilities, preferring to reserve them for limited emergencies. Moreover, since both rediscounts and emergency loans are granted by departments closely associated with the Banco do Brasil, which is also a competitor of commercial banks, the latter do not like to borrow from them and thus reveal their affairs to the Bank. Their reluctance is increased by the fact that clients do not like to have their paper leave the discounting bank; and banks cannot borrow against collateral of rediscountable paper (except for emergency loans and in the case of Treasury bills); thus, the rediscounted bill will be collected from the borrower by the Banco do Brasil. These considerations have affected particularly the larger banks, with the result that the small banks even now absorb an entirely disproportionate share of total loans to and rediscounts for banks by the monetary authorities. Apart from emergency borrowing, there have recently been other special factors making for increased borrowing by banks. These have also affected the larger banks. The strain on banks' resources resulting from the coffee boom has been a main factor, as banks have wanted to continue to lend to other sectors of activity in the same proportion as previously. Furthermore, the disinclination to borrow, characteristic of most of the best banks, has been worn down by time and by the favorable attitude toward borrowing on the part of the authorities, which have recently encouraged rediscounts of agricultural paper, especially to aid this sector.

VI. SAVINGS BANKS AND OTHER COLLECTIVE SAVINGS INSTITUTIONS

SALIENT FEATURES

Brazil's collective savings institutions consist of the savings banks, life insurance companies, capitalization companies, and the Social Security System. In addition, there are one or two mortgage banks, a few building societies, but they are of minor importance. Savings banks combine some of the features of commercial banks with those of pure savings institutions. Data with respect to these institutions are to be found in Table 10.

Complete up-to-date information on the development of these institutions is not available and there are no technically defensible

Table 10

Assets of Principal Financial Institutions, except Banks, Including All Insurance Companies, December 31, 1941 and 1945–51

(amounts in millions of cruzeiros)

	1941	*1945*	*1946*	*1947*	*1948*	*1949*	*1950*	*1951* [d]
Total assets	8,203	18,854	22,929	27,246	31,519	36,029	42,387	49,536
Public	6,570	15,430	18,727	22,496	25,606	29,213	33,827	40,089
Savings banks	3,766	7,960	10,271	11,947	12,180	13,493	15,260	17,281
Social security system,[a] except	2,593	6,820 [e]	7,632	9,553	11,228	14,290	16,843	20,703
Civil Servants' Pensions Institute (IPASE)	211	650	824	996	1,198	1,430	1,724	2,105
Private	1,633	3,242	4,202	4,965	5,913	6,816	8,560	9,447
Capitalization companies	429	1,018	1,260	1,581	1,917	2,264	2,697	3,080
Life insurance companies [b]	592	1,011	1,334	1,542	1,921	2,258	2,829	2,957
Other insurance companies [c]	612	1,395	1,608	1,842	2,075	2,282	3,034	3,410
Real estate holdings		1,908	2,369	3,253	4,759	6,489	8,272	10,452
Public		1,369	1,653	2,192	3,450	4,910	6,443	8,318
Savings banks	n.a.[f]	242	287	433	564	647	713	766
Social security system, except IPASE	55	867	1,052	1,384	2,414	3,667	5,044	6,828
IPASE	55	260	314	375	472	596	686	724
Private	234	539	716	1,061	1,309	1,579	1,829	2,134
Capitalization companies	42	166	280	425	547	714	815	906
Life insurance companies	95	147	250	292	362	416	465	579
Other insurance companies	97	226	286	344	400	449	549	649
Securities held		4,382	5,620	5,815	5,941	5,782	6,195	6,958
Public		3,321	4,401	4,527	4,568	4,575	4,499	5,148
Savings banks	n.a.	1,641	2,236	2,263	2,278	2,269	2,224	2,283
Social security system, except IPASE	966	1,656	2,141	2,240	2,264	2,279	2,247	2,836
IPASE		24	24	24	26	27	28	29
Private	626	1,061	1,219	1,288	1,373	1,207	1,696	1,810
Capitalization companies	156	249	271	292	315	368	444	455
Life insurance companies	272	501	567	572	620	369	712	721
Other insurance companies	198	311	381	424	438	470	540	634
Total loans		4,373	6,404	8,838	10,668	12,536	14,030	17,156

Public		3,687	5,528	7,738	9,155	10,658	11,433	14,508
Savings banks	1,500	2,679	4,117	5,350	6,176	7,109	8,498	9,842
Social security system,[a] except IPASE	n.a.	764	1,072	1,974	2,507	2,996	3,270	3,847
IPASE	99	244	339	414	472	553	665	819
Private	356	686	876	1,100	1,513	1,878	2,597	2,648
Capitalization companies	171	418	505	600	729	819	896	1,034
Life insurance companies	150	212	293	403	629	863	1,253	1,258
Other insurance companies	35	56	78	97	155	196	448	356
A. Mortgages loans								
Public								
Savings banks	709	1,397	2,252	3,206	3,795	4,294	4,915	6,776
Social security system, except IPASE	n.a.	n.a.	n.a.	n.a.	n.a.	n.a.	n.a.	n.a.
IPASE	19	97	171	217	282	387	539	642
Private								1,560
Capitalization companies	78	250	309	338	378	384	406	490
Life insurance companies	81	153	221	303	417	537	650	832
Other insurance companies	n.a.	n.a.	n.a.	n.a.	n.a.	n.a.	n.a.	238
B. Loans on life insurance and capitalization company policies								
Public								
Savings banks								
Social security system, except IPASE								
IPASE								
Private								924
Capitalization companies	93	166	193	255	342	427	469	393
Life insurance companies	65	65	71	92	205	316	589	414
Other insurance companies	n.a.	n.a.	n.a.	n.a.	n.a.	n.a.	n.a.	117

Source: *Anuário Estatístico do Brasil,* various years, and information obtained from the Instituto de Resseguros do Brasil, Ministry of Labour. IPASE.

[a] Excluding arrears of contributions, except those of employers.

[b] Includes only companies operating exclusively in life insurance.

[c] Includes companies operating in both life and other insurance.

[d] For the São Paulo State savings bank system, data refer to 1950.

[e] Partly estimated, taking known Fundo de Garantia (7240 million Cr$) = 92 percent of total assets, excluding compensation accounts.

[f] Not available.

estimates of the total annual savings. In recent years, institutional savings have increased greatly but on the whole have varied little in relation to national income or total savings. This is not surprising; rapid inflation, which discourages the placing of savings in forms which do not protect against loss of purchasing power of money, and longer term growth factors have tended to neutralize one another. More clearly than the loan and investment policy of the banks, that of the collective savings institutions reflects the way in which the price system has been affected by inflation. The most significant characteristic of the savings institutions under discussion is the large and ever-increasing extent to which their assets take the form of ownership of and loans against urban real estate, particularly that situated in the metropolitan centers. Their holdings of government and other securities, on the other hand, while showing some absolute increase, constitute a shrinking share of their portfolios. The main reason for this state of affairs is found in the appreciation of real estate holdings,[57] particularly during periods of rapid price inflation, but also as a result of increasing urbanization and the good yield and stable capital value of mortgage loans, as compared with the uncertain capital value of bonds, most of which have no effective maturity, and other securities. Under recent legislation [58] all these institutions may be obliged to contribute funds to the National Development Bank.

As an indication of the importance of the collective savings institutions, it should be noted that their assets are nearly equal to those of all industrial corporations and that the annual rate of growth of collective savings approaches that of corporate reinvestments.

SAVINGS BANKS

There are several official savings bank systems in Brazil, but no private savings banks. Commercial banks, as we have seen, accept savings deposits.

The Federal savings banks (Table 11) constitute the most important of the official savings bank systems. There are Federal savings banks in all states of the union. The system comprises 21 regional head offices in the state capitals and a net-work of 215 agencies and 150 postal savings agencies that make it the country's largest banking establishment. Each regional system enjoys a high degree of autonomy,

[57] As a result of which most of these institutions have extremely large hidden reserves.
[58] Law 1628 of 1952.

TABLE 11

BALANCE SHEET DATA OF SAVINGS BANKS IN RELATION TO THOSE OF COMMERCIAL BANKS,[a] DECEMBER 31, 1941 AND 1951

(AMOUNTS IN MILLIONS OF CRUZEIROS)

	1941				1951			
	Federal Savings Banks	*State Savings Banks*	*All Savings Banks*	*Commercial Banks*	*Federal Savings Banks*	*State[g] Savings Banks*	*All Savings Banks*	*Commercial Banks*
Total assets (excluding interagency accounts)	2,706	1,060	3,766	n.a.[e]	13,384	3,899	17,280	n.a.
Loans and discounts	1,500		1,500	10,278	9,440	402	9,842	63,931
Mortgage loans	710		710	n.a.	6,776	n.a.	n.a.	2,542[f]
Cash in vault	869 (Cash in vault, Deposits with banks, Deposits with Treasury)	1,039	1,908	932	183	22	205	5,285
Deposits with banks[b]				1,118	1,252	1,328	2,580	7,103[h]
Deposits with Treasury[c]					589		589	
Total investments[d]	437 (Total investments, Real estate, Other assets)	21	458	n.a.	631	1,653	2,284	2,364[f]
Real estate				n.a.	552	214	766	2,236
Other assets				n.a.	737	276	1,013	n.a.
Deposits	2,530	1,019	3,549	10,959	12,380	3,890	16,270	69,103
Popular	2,065	910	2,975	370	10,069	3,751	13,820	8,261

Sources: *Anuário Estatístico*, 1946–50; *Movimento Bancário*; *Resenha Econômica Mensal*, 1950–51; *Mensário Estatístico*; information obtained from Federal Savings Banks Council.

[a] Excludes State Savings Banks systems other than that of São Paulo.

[b] Including Banco do Brasil and Official Banks of State.

[c] Including Federal and State Treasuries.

[d] Including Federal and State bonds.

[e] Not available.

[f] Estimated.

[g] 1950.

[h] Banco do Brasil only.

but they are all subordinated to a Federal council, which coordinates broad policy subject to occasional directives by the Ministry of Finance.

The state savings banks systems, of which the most important is that of the State of São Paulo, also operate numerous agencies in the interior of their respective states. The state systems are completely independent of the Federal authorities.

The bulk of the savings bank deposits consist of the so-called popular deposits, that is, deposits which are limited in amount; they are withdrawable at sight and a large, but unknown, proportion of these deposits are accorded checking facilities. Savings bank deposits have amounted, in recent years, to some 25–30 percent of total deposits in commercial banks and about equal the time deposits. Interest rates paid by the savings banks are in line with those paid by commercial banks on popular deposits. Savings bank deposits are guaranteed respectively by the Federal and state governments.

As measured by total assets, savings banks, which before the war were the largest groups of collective savings institutions, still form the second largest subdivision among the latter, holding nearly 40 percent of their assets. These assets in recent years have been growing more slowly than those of the other collective savings institutions. The growth of savings bank deposits has been subject to two opposite tendencies; inflation has increased that part which represents monetary holdings of the respective depositors, and at the same time has decreased the part which represents genuine savings. The latter effect has predominated. Also, the deposits in savings banks are largely made by the salaried middle class, whose incomes have not kept pace with inflation in the same way as those of the depositors of commercial banks, which include a larger proportion of businessmen.

The Federal savings banks help finance Federal government operations by depositing their funds with the Treasury and by holding government bonds as well as the shares of mixed corporations. As already stated, however, they invest mainly in urban real estate mortgages, at times of the more expensive residential type, although some of their mortgage loans have helped to an important extent to finance the construction of workers' houses, while others furnish credit to industry. The Federal savings banks also make personal loans of various kinds principally to civil servants and act as pawnbrokers. In general each Federal savings bank employs its resources within its own region, except for that part on deposit with the Treasury.

The investment policy of the São Paulo state savings bank on the other hand is quite different, since that system is used almost exclusively to finance the activities of the state government. Practically all of its funds are either on deposit with the official state bank or invested in state securities.

THE SOCIAL SECURITY SYSTEM

The Social Security System at present covers some three million individuals; namely, all urban employees except domestic servants, and all civil servants. The system consists of 36 different institutions, of which 6 are large "Institutos" (covering industrial workers, commercial employees, bank employees, transport workers, the merchant marine, and civil servants on a national basis) and 30 Funds covering the employees of various public utilities and mining enterprises on a local basis. The Civil Servants' Pension Institute (IPASE) is considered part of the system, although it also carries voluntary private insurance of various kinds. The various institutions enjoy considerable autonomy but are subject to directives by a division of the Ministry of Labour.

The Social Security System is at present the most important holder of institutional savings (over 40 percent).[59] Since its institution in the thirties, it has been growing more rapidly than the savings banks or even the private savings institutes, having benefited by various increases in the percentage of contributions in relation to wages, and a growing urban labor force.

The system operates on the full reserve principle. Contributions are on a three-way basis, with the insured, their employers, and the Federal government [60] contributing equal percentages of each employee's insurable salary (the amount of the insurable salary is generally limited to Cr. 2,000.00 per month).

The Social Security institutions offer old age and disability payments, widows' pensions, medical care, and accident insurance. Cash benefits are based on the insurable salaries of the beneficiaries at the time these are pensioned; therefore, as a consequence of inflation, the

[59] Excluding contributions in arrears, except of employers.

[60] The Federal government has sometimes discharged its obligations by delivery of bonds or real estate, and at present owes a considerable debt to the system on which no interest is paid.

actuarial reserve is constantly in danger of falling below its theoretically necessary value. This fact and the difficulties experienced in the collection of contributions are largely responsible for the investment policy of the system, which, in accordance with the general considerations mentioned earlier, has concentrated on real estate holdings and mortgage loans, rather than securities. Holdings of securities consist to the extent of 60 percent of Federal government bonds; the remainder are shares of mixed corporations. The investment policy of the system has been guided also by the desire to enable its associates to become homeowners. The statutes of the institutions forming the system stress security and yield of investments along with social assistance; there is much less emphasis on the fact that investment policy should be in accordance with governmental economic policy.

PRIVATE COLLECTIVE SAVINGS INSTITUTIONS

Life insurance [61] and capitalization companies each represent about 7.5 percent of the total assets of all collective savings institutions. Their development has been relatively steady for the past ten years. Capitalization companies, common in Latin America, pay their policy holders a capital sum after a period of years against monthly premiums. The policies are partly amortized by drawings in a lottery, which adds to their attraction.

The security holdings of life insurance companies still constitute their largest single asset. In the aggregate, however, their investment in residential real estate, and in mortgage loans on residential real estate, are larger. In fact, their real estate holdings and mortgages are increasing far more rapidly than their security holdings.

Capitalization companies also invest mainly in real estate and mortgage loans but, with them, real estate is the principal item, mortgages come second, and securities are least important.

The security holdings of life insurance and capitalization companies include some 25 percent of shares of Brazilian corporations; the rest are Federal (and a few state) bonds, and some shares of mixed corporations. Mortgage loans include some long-term advances to industry, but represent mainly the financing of residential construction. Legislation prescribes the types of investment of capitalization [62] and insurance [63] companies. As we have seen, investment in common

[61] We do not include here companies operating in other branches than life insurance.
[62] Decree 22.456 of 1932. [63] Decree-law 2.063 of 1940.

stocks is permitted, that in urban real estate holdings, first mortgages on urban real estate, and government bonds is favored. Capitalization companies may also invest to a limited extent in rural real estate. The Ministry of Labour, Industry, and Commerce has powers to control the investment policy of these companies.

The year-end balance sheets of these companies show a high proportion of loans against policies; but apparently, this is quite a seasonal phenomenon.

VII. THE BANCO DO BRASIL AND CENTRAL BANKING

Over the past twenty years, Brazil has successively established a series of institutions, centering around the official Banco do Brasil, which together are functionally the equivalent of a central bank. While the performance of the present system has improved considerably in recent years, it retains a number of institutional drawbacks as compared with a single monetary authority; nevertheless, these cannot be considered as being responsible for difficulties of monetary policy.

The control powers of the "monetary authorities" are rather limited, both because important financial institutions escape their supervision altogether and because their powers over banks are restricted. In particular, under the present system a policy of expansion and especially that of offsetting a contraction is institutionally much easier to carry out than the reverse policy.

The various agencies performing central banking functions have been created independently over a long period of time, each in response to a particular problem. Their interrelationship is accordingly rather complicated.

A consolidated balance sheet of these different agencies is set forth in Table 12.

While monetary policy is of special importance in less developed countries, it is apt to encounter greater difficulties, and its practical scope is therefore apt to be rather more limited than in more advanced countries. Monetary policy cannot, normally, offset primary expansionary pressures arising, e.g., from government deficits or the balance of payments, except by reducing the rate of increase of domestic business assets held by the banking system—i.e., by reducing

TABLE 12

CONSOLIDATED BALANCE SHEET OF MONETARY AUTHORITIES, DECEMBER 31, 1941 AND 1951

(AMOUNTS IN MILLIONS OF CRUZEIROS)

	1941	1951
ASSETS		
Central Bank Account [b]		
Gold and exchange (net)	1,954	6,510
Loans to Government	8,569	31,144
Federal Treasury	6,890 [a]	26,149
Other	1,679	4,995
Loans to commercial banks	314	6,465
Loan to other accounts [b]		10,902
Total	10,867	55,021
Other Accounts		
Specialized credit	1,272	9,209
Rural	568	5,901
Industrial	686	3,308
Other loans and investments	1,107	15,752
Other accounts	709	2,701
Deposit with Central Bank account [b]	2,007	
Total	5,090	27,662
LIABILITIES		
Central Bank Account [b]		
Notes in circulation outside monetary authorities	6,240	33,686
In banks	932	5,225
Outside	5,308	28,461
Monetary deposits of public entities and banks	2,581	16,444
Public entities	1,763	8,471
Federal Treasury	n.a.[c]	3,186
Other	n.a.	5,285
Banks	1,118	7,973
Liabilities of exchange department, etc.[d]		3,619
Own resources	39 [a]	1,272
Liabilities to other accounts [b]	2,007	
Total	10,867	55,021
Other Accounts		
Sight deposits of the public	1,894	4,812
Compulsory deposits	287	2,437
Time deposits	780	991
Securities issued	76	98
Other liabilities	518	2,191
Own resources	1,535 [d]	6,251
Loan from Central Bank account [b]		10,902
Total	5,090	27,662
Notes in Banco do Brasil	406	1,632

Source: Balance sheets of Banco do Brasil and of Rediscount Department; Treasury Accounts; banking statistics.

[a] Partly estimated. [b] Residual account. [c] Not available.

[d] Liabilities of Exchange Department other than short-term exchange liabilities, including net liability to International Monetary Fund, i.e., after deduction of gold and cruzeiro subscriptions.

the rate of investment. This alone is likely to rule such a policy out of court as long as hastening (productive) investment is considered the primary goal of policy. For similar reasons, even secondary inflationary pressures are often difficult to combat by monetary means when primary expansion has not been resisted, as we shall see below. We shall also find that the scope of selective credit policy is extraordinarily limited. Under these conditions, special importance in promoting monetary stability attaches to flexible exchange and fiscal policies which can, within limits, offset certain primary inflationary pressures by increasing the rate of saving, and can also help to allocate resources in a desirable direction.

BRIEF SURVEY OF CENTRAL BANKING AGENCIES

1. First, among the central banking agencies, is the Treasury, which issues currency and holds the gold reserve.

2. Next is the Banco do Brasil which is the official bank of the Federal government. It is by far the country's largest bank. The Federal government holds the majority of the share capital, nominates the President, and nominates or elects all directors. The core of the bank is the General Credit Department, which combines commercial with certain central bank functions. This department receives deposits of the Federal government and of state and municipal governments, of banks and the public, and makes loans to the government, the public, and the banks, the latter both for its own account and for that of the Bank Loans Fund (see below). The General Credit Department's operations with the public make it the country's largest commercial bank, accounting (at the end of 1951) for about 25 percent of the loans of all commercial banks.

Two thirds as large as the operations of the General Credit Department with the public are those of the Agricultural and Industrial Credit Department, created to promote specialized credit. Its main sources of funds are advances by the General Credit Department and rediscounts. It also draws upon certain special types of deposits and places special bonds with the Social Security System.[64] Loans granted to the public in 1941 and 1951 are shown in Table 13.

Monetary legislation treats the two departments mentioned above (General Credit Department and Agricultural and Industrial Credit

[64] Deposits made by order of a court of law, certain deposits of the Social Security institutions, which are also obliged to take up special bonds ("bonus") issued by the department.

TABLE 13

BANCO DO BRASIL LOANS TO THE PUBLIC,[a] DECEMBER 31, 1941 AND 1951

(AMOUNTS IN MILLIONS OF CRUZEIROS)

Destination of Loan	*1941*	*1951*
Agricultural (including rural industries)	397	4,865
Livestock	357	3,230
Industry	834	8,178
Trade	664	7,593
Unclassified	117	870
Departmental Source of Loan		
General Credit Department [b]	1,553 [c]	15,093
Export-Import Department		433
Agricultural and Industrial Credit Department	816	9,210
Rural (including rural industries)	586	5,931
Industrial	230	3,279
Total	2,369	24,736

Source: Banco do Brasil, *Relatório,* 1941, 1951.

[a] Excludes securities.

[b] Long-term industrial loans granted by "Special Loans Agency" are included; the bulk of these loans was, however, transferred to the Agricultural and Industrial Credit Department in 1950.

[c] Including General Credit Department and Export-Import Department.

Department) in most respects not differently from other banks. This is not true of the remaining departments, which perform exclusively central banking functions. Consequently, the latter are listed separately below. The "Central Banking" departments are, however, legally part of the Bank, subject to general supervision by the president and management of the Bank and staffed for the most part by employees of the Bank. The heads of these departments are, however, all direct presidential appointees, and enjoy a high degree of autonomy *vis-à-vis* the president of the Bank and each other, depending upon their personality.

3. The Rediscount Department [65] and the Bank Loans Fund [66] together form Brazil's lender of last resort. Though legally distinct, both departments operate under the general supervision of the president of the Banco do Brasil, as representative of the Federal government, and share a director.

4. Still other central banking functions are undertaken by the

[65] Law 449 of 1937 as amended; the Rediscount Department operated between 1922 and 1924; and uninterruptedly since 1930.

[66] Decree 21.499 of 1932 as amended.

Exchange Department of the Banco do Brasil, which operates in the foreign exchange market and holds exchange reserves for account of the Treasury. Another such department is the Export-Import Department which controls exports and imports and also does some foreign trade financing.

5. Finally, the Superintendencia da Moeda e do Crédito,[67] created in 1945, is charged with the coordination and supervision of monetary and banking policy and is meant to prepare the way for the Central Bank. It comprises a policy-making council and an executive and advisory staff. The council is presided over by the Minister of Finance; its members are the President of the Banco do Brasil, the Director of the Rediscount Department and Bank Loans Fund, the Director of the Exchange Department, and an Executive Director (responsible for the staff). The Director of the Export-Import Department is a *de facto* member. The organization of the staff of the Superintendencia (apart from the Inspectorate of Banks) is still fluid; the dividing line between its executive functions and those of the other central bank agencies is only gradually becoming defined. At present, some tasks entrusted to the Superintendencia by law are discharged under contract by departments of the Banco do Brasil. The staff of the Superintendencia is almost exclusively drawn from the Bank, though the former is not itself a department nor subject to supervision by the management of the Bank.

While these various agencies can operate like a mixed central and commercial bank, such as the Banque de France, the structure of the Brazilian monetary authority creates a series of problems. A possible difficulty of coordination arises from the fact that each of the members of the policy-making council is also charged with executing certain aspects of policy. The fact that each of the members of the council can be dismissed *ad nutum* by the President of the Republic implies that the monetary authority is wholly subordinate to the Executive not only in policy formulation but also in its daily business. The fact mentioned may also be an obstacle to continuity not only in the execution but also in the formulation of policy. Despite these difficulties, the Superintendencia has been improving coordination and continuity of policy. This is particularly important, since the difficulty of coordination can especially become a factor making for excessive monetary expansion.

[67] Decree-law 7293 of 1945.

FUNCTIONS AND POWERS OF THE MONETARY AUTHORITIES

General Powers.—The powers of the Council comprise the determination of exchange, monetary and credit policy and control, as well as bank supervision; these powers are subject, however, to rather severe limitations.

While all banks including the General and the Agricultural and Industrial Credit Departments of the Banco do Brasil and other official banks are subject to the powers of the Superintendency, it exercises virtually no direct power over other financial institutions. Control of the Federal savings banks is vested in a council presided over by the Minister of Finance making possible a direct coordination with the Superintendency; but the Federal authorities have no influence on the policy of the state savings banks. Control over the Social Security System and the insurance and capitalization companies is exercised by departments of the Ministry of Labor, Industry and Commerce, which is not represented on the Council of the Superintendency. The only way in which the Council can influence the policy of these institutions, except through the President of the Republic, lies in the Finance Minister's power to exact from them a variable contribution to the National Development Bank.

International Monetary Relations.—Foreign exchange is acquired and held by the Exchange Department for Treasury account on the basis of Banco do Brasil loans to the Treasury. A part of convertible exchange holdings has been used to buy gold, which is held directly by the Treasury. The parity of the cruzeiro may be varied freely by the Executive [68] upon recommendation of the Council, and the latter may create multiple rates.

Through the Exchange Department, the Superintendency exercises ample powers of exchange control and guides the import license policy of the Export-Import Department.[69]

Note Issue.—Currency is issued exclusively by the Treasury. Paper money is issued under general legislation [70] only to the Rediscount Department and to the Bank Loans Fund of the Banco do Brasil,[71] with the approval of the Superintendencia. The issues which are made

68 Brazil is a member of the International Monetary Fund.

69 Brazil's exchange system is at present being overhauled completely.

70 Decree-law 4792 of 1942.

71 Coin is issued directly but only in exchange for paper.

under general legislation must be backed by a 25 percent gold or foreign exchange reserve.

In recent years most issues of currency have been the result of Treasury borrowings from the General Credit Department; this, in turn, has borrowed from the Rediscount Department, which has obtained currency from the Treasury. Every few years these mutual debts have been canceled by special legislation.[72] Under this procedure, most currency outstanding is a direct and sole responsibility of the Treasury and, as such, requires no backing of international reserves.[73]

Control Over Commercial Banks.—Rediscounts for and loans to commercial banks. As already mentioned, the monetary authorities lend to commercial banks through the Rediscount Department and through the Bank Loans Fund. The two entities are, however, in practice, largely a single one; the distinction is between the loans made rather than between the lending departments.

The Rediscount Department (in its operations with commercial banks) is designed to give seasonal elasticity to the currency and is regarded as the lender of last resort for limited emergencies. The Department's loans to each bank cannot, under law, exceed the borrowing bank's capital and surplus.[74] This limitation, however, has not always been strictly observed.

The Department discounts paper with a maximum maturity of one year (in case of agricultural loans) and has the power to lend against the collateral of Treasury bills although it has not done so (that is, to banks other than the Banco do Brasil); it cannot make advances against other collateral. The Department may charge interest up to the legal limit and may charge differential rates according to the region or the type of paper. In practice it generally charges commercial banks 6 percent, except for certain agricultural loans where the rate is 5.5 percent. It does not often use the interest rate even to force

72 Cancellation has been carried only to the extent that borrowings have been the result of deficits or gold purchases; the debt arising from exchange purchases which continue to be held by the Exchange Department is not canceled.

73 Central Banking legislation now before Congress would require a 25 percent international reserve against all sight liabilities.

74 This has been the limit since 1945. Prior to that it was half of capital and surplus and earlier yet there was an absolute limit for all rediscounts which could be granted by the Carteira. A bill is now before Congress which would permit wider limits for certain agricultural paper but would also restrict the normal limit.

banks to reduce the time for which they are indebted to the Department. The Department possesses a powerful weapon of control in that it may ration rediscounts, since it is not forced to lend up to the maximum legal limit; but it is reluctant to use this instrument by reason of its possible drastic effects.

The Bank Loans Fund is the ultimate emergency lender and can make advances to banks on the security of practically any type of asset. There are no limits to the loans which it can make to individual banks. Under the law, the Fund can make loans either for periods up to one year, on any eligible asset, or up to 5 years on the security of assets held by banks before 1947, the date of the latest legislation regarding the Fund, the duration of which is periodically extended. This fact, and the long periods for which loans may be (and are) made, reflect the fact that this agency was created (in 1932) to lend to banks whose assets had become frozen in the great depression, notably as a result of the agricultural debt moratoria. Irrespective of the period for which loans have been made—they have generally been granted for the longest periods possible—the banks are supposed to repay them, as and when their cash reserves increase with the return of deposits. In practice, this provision has not been easy to enforce. The Fund is severely limited in its use of the interest-rate weapon to discourage long-term borrowing. It cannot charge more than 10 percent, that is, less than the legal maximum and less than the rates charged by many banks.[75] Otherwise, it can only apply small fines and the generally too peremptory sanctions of closing the bank or of intervention in its credit policies.

The Rediscount Department and the Bank Loans Fund obtain currency from the Treasury, for which they pay 2 percent interest.

The administration of the Rediscount Department and of the Bank Loans Fund is centralized, though the branches of the Banco do Brasil act as their agents. Centralization brings with it frequent delays in the granting of rediscounts and even of emergency loans.

We have already referred [76] to the change in the banks' attitude toward the Rediscount Department. For the first time, this makes it

[75] As a *curiosum* we may mention that the check clearing system has become a vehicle of emergency loans, for banks. The system is run by the Banco do Brasil which at times meets clearing debts of banks in difficulties.

[76] See Section V, above, for material related to these paragraphs.

possible to influence the policy of the commercial banks directly rather than through the Banco do Brasil's operations with the public and government.

Open-market operations. While the monetary authorities possess limited possibilities of engaging in open-market operations, they have not made use of their powers. Even minor sales of bills or bonds to the market would be greatly upsetting, as the market is very thin, and, in consequence, sales of bills and bonds directly to banks would probably be a more practical method (as an alternative the banks might also be induced to constitute voluntary deposits with the monetary authorities). We have commented in an earlier section on the general difficulties and cost of increasing sales of Treasury bills to banks; the sale of bonds would be even more difficult (see Section IX) and costly.

Variation of cash reserve ratios. The power of the monetary authorities to vary the total cash reserve ratios of commercial banks is, as we have seen, extremely limited and somewhat uncertain in its effects. In any case, the high interest rates on deposits which Brazilian banks are allowed to pay are an obstacle to increasing their cash reserve ratios, because of the high cost of idle funds which these rates imply, unless the authorities were ready to pay adequate interest on the reserve deposits. Moreover, a change in average (rather than marginal) cash reserve ratios is a blunt weapon, as it affects banks irrespective of their liquidity position.

A further objection of banks to increases in the reserve requirement stems from the fact that these reserve deposits with the Banco do Brasil have usually been used to expand the Bank's loans, instead of being sterilized. To the extent that this is true it means that, for the banking system as a whole, the variation of reserves other than that in the form of ready cash of the commercial banks influences the distribution of loans between the Banco do Brasil and the other banks rather than the volume of loans. The latter depends only upon the size of the reserves of ready cash of all banks, including the Banco do Brasil. It must be remembered, however, that credit expansion by the Banco do Brasil frequently corresponds to needs which the authorities are resolved to meet in any case.

Direct Operations with the Public.—Through the Banco do Brasil the monetary authorities can directly vary the volume of loans to business. By virtue of the size of the Bank, this power is very great. Its use is, however, in practice easily available only for purposes of expansion or of counteracting contraction.[77] Many of the Bank's operations with business are made at the instance of government or represent special types of loans not available from other banks. It is naturally easier to expand loans to these sectors than to contract them. In any case it would be hard to make the Bank pursue a contractionary policy without imposing at the same time a similar policy on the commercial banks; but, as we have seen, the powers for these purposes are very limited and it would not be fair for the whole burden of contraction to fall exclusively, in the first instance, on the Banco do Brasil's customers, nor would it be practical in the long run, because the Bank would soon lose its ordinary business. The Banco do Brasil probably cannot even entirely avoid expanding its loans in situations which are already inflationary; it must often prevent inflation from prejudicing important sectors specially dependent upon its loans without at the same time prejudicing unfairly its other clients.

Although the Banco do Brasil is a government bank, its cash holdings[78] sometimes influence its operations with the public. To the extent that this is true it implies, as it were, a built-in tendency toward compensation of contractionary tendencies. A rise in the Bank's cash ratio (due to a government surplus or a payments deficit) may thus lead to expansion of the Bank's private loans. This is particularly true at times when the Bank is not in debt to the Rediscount Department. For reasons noted above the reverse process is not likely to take place when the Bank loses cash. The partly commercial nature of the Bank contributes to the expansionary bias.

The Banco do Brasil is often called upon to extend advances to state governments, to finance their investment programs or help them cover their current deficits.

The General and the Agricultural and Industrial Credit Departments of the Banco do Brasil have privileged but not automatic access to the Rediscount Department (the Bank can also call upon the Bank Loans Fund, although it is unlikely that it will ever be forced to do so). It is at least doubtful whether it is not subject to the same

77 The other official banks of the Federal government have only regional importance and are not at all used for purposes of monetary policy.

78 In recent years, the Bank's cash has varied between 6 percent and 8 percent of the total deposits. It is not subject to the first reserve requirement, only to the second one, which, however, it deposits with itself as agent for the Superintendencia.

legal maximum of rediscounts as other banks; and the management of the Rediscount Department or the Council of the Superintendency can certainly lay down rules as to the purposes for which they will allow the Bank to rediscount. However, since it is, today, inconceivable that the Bank might be permitted to default on its commitments, including loan contracts, the precise position of the Bank with respect to rediscounts depends very much on its management.

The Banco do Brasil enjoys by law a specially low rate for its rediscounts arising from loans made by its Agricultural and Industrial Credit Department and for loans against Treasury bills (the former are 2 percent lower than the rate for ordinary first class commercial paper, the latter is 3 percent).

Selective Credit Policy.—The monetary authorities have certain rather inadequate powers to influence the distribution of private bank credit. The available means include differential rediscount rates, the rationing of rediscounts, and the power to discriminate in setting the second reserve requirement. Through the Banco do Brasil, the monetary authorities can also channel credit into desired fields. As we have seen, however, it is difficult to do so without a net expansion.

The efficiency of selective credit measures remains particularly doubtful as the direct obstacles to their success are specially high. The obstacles are, of course, lack of control over ultimate loan destination, and, most important, the shiftability of borrowers' funds.[79] It must also be remembered that certain risks are not at all, or not at present, bankable. A further difficulty stems from the fact that selective credit policy not only is no substitute for quantitative control but seems to work well only along with a slight restriction of credit; [80] we have seen that this is difficult to bring about.

From the point of view of promoting balanced economic growth, it should be remembered that any type of rationing, including selective credit policy, probably works best in an emergency of limited duration, and not when it is a question of a long haul—like "economic development." In this case it seems safer to create directly the incentives which will enable the various sectors of the economy to attract

[79] A limit particularly important in Brazil, since it is usual for the same person to engage in many different lines of activity.

[80] See *Bulletin of the Oxford University Institute of Statistics,* Vol. XIV, Nos. 4–5, pp. 143–44.

loans in the desired proportions and to reserve selective credit control for those cases—they certainly exist—where the financial system shows a propensity to lend in a way which is contrary to the indications furnished by the price system.

Relations of the Monetary Authorities with the Federal Government.—Transactions of the monetary authorities with the Federal government have in general been by far the most important source of monetary and credit expansion. Such transactions comprise not only direct loans to central government departments but also loans to "autarquias" and to Federal government enterprises and sometimes price support purchases of commodities at the behest of the Federal government. Loans to the Federal government as such are granted by the General Credit Department, in the form of current account loans carrying interest at 6 percent or against 3 percent Treasury bills. Such loans are authorized each year in the budget, up to 20 percent of estimated revenue for the purpose of anticipating revenues. Nevertheless, they need not be repaid before borrowing begins against the subsequent budget. Other loans to the Federal government are based on special authorizations.

Other Powers.—In Section V we had occasion to note that the monetary authorities possess the usual powers of authorization, intervention, liquidation and inspection of banks. The power to fix maximum rates of interest to be paid upon deposits applies not only to banks but also to Federal and state savings banks. As we have seen, the use of this power would considerably ease the task of the monetary authorities in increasing the cash reserve ratio and in selling bills to banks.

Moral Suasion.—The close connection or even identity of the Central Bank agencies with the Banco do Brasil is considered by many banks to be an obstacle to close contact and greater confidence between the monetary authorities and the private banks. Recently, nevertheless, the Inspectorate of banks and the new interest of the monetary authorities in close relationship with the bank community have gone far in establishing relationships of mutual trust and confidence.

Clearance.—The monetary authorities, through the Banco do Brasil, administer clearing houses in 14 cities. There is, however, no intercity clearing. Remittances of funds between localities are largely effected through the branches of the Banco do Brasil.

VIII. SPECIALIZED CREDIT

While the short-term credit needs of trade and industry are reasonably well provided for by commercial banks and numerous institutions finance urban real estate, relatively much less credit is available to agriculture and to industry at medium-term and long-term. This is partly the reflection of the absence of a developed capital market, in which financial intermediaries could obtain funds for such loans, while commercial banks lack interest in such operations for a variety of reasons.

URBAN REAL ESTATE

Urban real estate is a preferred field of many individual investors, in addition to a few banks and the collective savings institutions discussed in Section VI.

Both the Social Security System and the Federal savings banks have made real estate credit available on relatively easy terms via mortgages; the former has done this also, in the case of housing developments which they start and sell off mostly during construction, via the "compromisso de compra e venda." Down-payments for finished houses or apartments purchased from these institutions have often been as low as 10–20 percent, interest rates 8 percent, and maturities 10–18 years. Mortgage credit from these institutions for purchases from other sellers has been available on similar terms. Capitalization and insurance companies have often granted credit with similar maturities, though with somewhat higher interest rates than the public savings institutions, and with higher down-payments. They have, however, sold apartments at the beginning of construction with down-payments as low as 10–20 percent.

Individual sellers of real estate generally finance sales through a "compromisso," granting credit for relatively short terms (rarely more than 5 years), generally with a 50 percent down-payment and interest rates of 10–12 percent. Private investors grant mortgage credit on similar terms. These conditions, of course, vary somewhat according as "money" is more or less plentiful. The relatively high down-payments demanded by private individuals and by capitalization and insurance companies in the case of mortgages, and in the case of individuals selling property, are, of course, a consequence of the expectation of the continuance of inflation. The fact that interest rates are higher for medium-term than for long-term real estate loans is explained by the different class of lenders who grant these credits.

A characteristic of the real estate market in recent years has been the spectacular increase in "condomínios" (cooperative apartment houses). Their financing has been undertaken by all the lenders mentioned. Much of this type of construction has been promoted by speculators who have sold off immediately, even before construction has begun.

Apart from the Social Security System, and the Federal savings banks, which have financed all types of housing projects, including those for workers, credit has been made available mostly for relatively more expensive types of housing; nevertheless, the capitalization and insurance companies have also financed some developments accessible to the lower middle class.

AGRICULTURAL CREDIT

In addition to short-term bank credit, Brazilian agriculture is largely financed by advances to producers granted by merchants, exporters and processors (cotton ginners, and others),[81] who in turn are financed by banks. Only the Banco do Brasil, through its agricultural and industrial credit department, and, on a much smaller scale, the similar departments of some of the state-owned banks offer types of credit adapted to the special needs of agriculture.

The total amount of rural credit outstanding on December 31, 1951, equaled about 16 percent of that year's gross value of rural production; about 66 percent of this amount represented agricultural credit and credit for primary processing of agricultural products (oil pressing, sugar), the rest, livestock credit. No less than 60 percent of the agricultural and 70 percent of the livestock credit was granted by the Banco do Brasil, mainly through its agricultural and industrial credit department but also through its general credit department. As we have seen (Section V) the commercial banks do not favor rural credit mainly for reasons already mentioned (in Section II, when discussing the special credit needs for agriculture); but also partly due to the recollection of the three rural "moratoria" and debt

[81] When the ultimate producer is a tenant, he will often be financed by his landlord, who in turn will be financed by a bank or merchant.

reductions (1933, 1938, and 1946—the latter for cattle only).[82] A large part of the Banco do Brasil's livestock loans represents advances which have become frozen under the latter "moratorium."

Agricultural and livestock credit grants by the commercial banks (except the state banks) are wholly short term (generally not more than for four months, largely against promissory notes); the credit of the Banco do Brasil is also mainly short term, but it covers a longer period (eight months or more), so that the Bank's borrowers are not obliged to renew their loans during the planting season (or production period) and are also protected against the need of distress sales. The Bank's loans are secured by a crop (or livestock) lien; in the case of agricultural loans, this means that the loan can be granted only after the crop has been planted; however, exceptions are increasingly made.

The agricultural credit of all banks favors cane sugar production, in addition to export products such as coffee, cotton, cocoa. Banks in many regions avoid financing cereals, because of the lack of storage and fumigation facilities.

In granting agricultural and livestock credit, the banks favor the large producers. Even the Banco do Brasil's rural loans to small producers are, in value terms, a very small proportion of the total. Absence of technical assistance and the relatively small development of cooperatives make it particularly difficult to grant credit to the small producer. However, efforts to extend greater credit facilities to small owners are being made; on the other hand tenants get practically no bank credit facilities at all because they are unable to offer sufficient guarantees.

Medium-term credit for improvement of properties is available, on a relatively small scale, from the Banco do Brasil, and, to an even smaller extent, from some of the state banks. Very little long-term credit is available from institutions. Property sales are financed on the basis of the "compromisso" by the seller.

Producers pay extremely high interest rates to merchants. Processors often obtain a special advantage through an option on the crops of the producers they have financed. Rates charged on agricultural credit by commercial banks are rarely below 12 percent. The

[82] Decree 22.626 of 1933; Decree-laws 1002, of 1938, and 1828 of 1939; and Decree-laws 9.599 and 9.686, as well as Law 8, all of 1946.

Banco do Brasil advances agricultural credit at 7 percent plus certain charges, which often considerably enhance the effective cost of its loans. Nevertheless, the Bank's agricultural operations are definitely conducted as a public service, at a loss.[83]

MEDIUM-TERM AND LONG-TERM INDUSTRIAL CREDIT

The agricultural and Industrial Credit Department of the Banco do Brasil is also an industrial bank. It grants medium-term and long-term loans for periods up to 10 years. The interest rate is, in general, 9 percent (never higher); the loans are secured by real estate or equipment mortgages. Some of the collective savings institutions grant medium-term or long-term industrial credit on a small scale. There are no other facilities for medium-term or long-term industrial credit except some formally short-term, but effectively long-term, advances granted by commercial banks.

The recently created National Bank for Economic Development is an autonomous government department ("autarquia"). It obtains its funds from a compulsory loan or from loans obtained from foreign financing institutions. It is so far mainly the administrator of the Federal government's own investment program. Its operations with private enterprises can include credits as well as giving the Federal government guarantee to their loans obtained from foreign financing institutions. Its loans to private enterprises must be in accordance with the Federal government general development program.

IX. THE MONEY AND CAPITAL MARKETS

THE MONEY MARKET

Apart from some slight beginnings of a rather special kind of market in Treasury bills, there is no bill or money market in Brazil. The reluctance of borrowers to have their business revealed (if their bills were traded) and the lack of bankers' acceptances impede the formation of the bill market. Moreover, banks would have the same qualms as in the case of Treasury bills about using their funds otherwise than to accommodate habitual clients (a reflection of the strength

[83] By decree 24.641 of 1934, a National Rural Credit Bank was authorized. It was never established, however, and the Banco do Brasil's Agricultural and Industrial Credit Department was organized in 1937.

of credit demand). There is no scope, as yet, for call money loans to the stock exchange. As already noted, the only link between banks, apart from correspondent relationships, are some relatively stable rediscount relationships between one or more small banks on the one hand, and a larger bank on the other.

The market in Treasury bills comprises banks and private persons and a few other institutional investors. The bills traded in it are exclusively the Treasury bills issued compulsorily to exporters. The market is very small. Probably no more than two billion cruzeiros of these bills have been outstanding at any one time, and the holdings of banks are no more than 20–25 percent of the total.

THE CAPITAL MARKET

The savings of private investors, and the undistributed profits of firms, which become available annually for investment, constitute fairly large amounts. But only a very small, though an increasing, part of these resources is available to the (primary) capital market, in the sense of a generally available pool of funds. The major part is available only for capital issues made to small groups or for reinvestment within the firm (or for direct investment by the individual savers). Similarly, only a few (though an increasing number of) new issues are made publicly.

The secondary market consists of six stock exchanges, of which only two, those at São Paulo and Rio, are important. In this market public securities are much more important than private issues. The turnover of government bonds has, in recent years, been influenced by the unloading of securities issued compulsorily (as in the war) or semicompulsorily (by state governments, to contractors, in lieu of payment). The turnover of shares on the stock exchange has increased in recent years, while corporate bonds are quite unimportant. Many transfers of shares, however, take place through the market only in form, but do not correspond to genuine public offers to buy and sell. They are made in order to keep the stock in the public view, or they represent private deals which are made through the stock exchange because, by law, all transfer of shares must be so made (Tables 14 and 15).

The monetary authorities do not operate at all in the securities market. Since commercial banks hold few securities, savings banks and other collective savings institutions are the principal institutional

TABLE 14
STOCK EXCHANGE TRANSACTIONS AT MARKET PRICES—ALL STOCK EXCHANGES
(AMOUNTS IN MILLIONS OF CRUZEIROS)

	1941	*1943*	*1945*	*1947*	*1948*	*1949*	*1950*	*1951*
Government bonds	934	1,089	1,312	948	1,218	1,596	1,745	1,763
Federal	407	366	814	586	406	388	568	493
State	432	591	435	312	775	1,169	1,131	1,224
Municipal	95	132	63	50	36	39	46	46
Shares and debentures [a]	233	660	529	677	677	591	843	1,090
Total	1,167	1,749	1,841	1,625	1,884	2,187	2,588	2,853

Source: *Anuário Estatístico*, 1945–51; *Relatório*, Banco do Brasil, 1951.
[a] Debentures negligible.

TABLE 15
STOCK EXCHANGE TURNOVER IN COMPARISON WITH REAL ESTATE TRANSFERS AND REGISTRATION OF MORTGAGES
(AMOUNTS IN BILLIONS OF CRUZEIROS)

	1941	*1943*	*1945*	*1947*	*1948*	*1949*	*1950*	*1951*
Stock exchange turnover (all stock exchanges)	1.2	1.7	1.8	1.6	1.9	2.2	2.6	2.9
Real estate transfers (Rio and São Paulo)								
Total	1.3	2.2	3.5	4.2	3.9	4.6	5.2	7.6 [a]
Sales	0.9	1.6	2.6	2.9	2.8	3.2	3.6	5.3 [a]
Mortgages (Rio and São Paulo)	0.9	0.6	1.5	3.1	2.5	2.9	3.4	4.4 [a]

Source: *Anuário Estatístico*, 1945–51; *Relatório*, Banco do Brasil, 1951. *Mensário Estatístico*, No. 7.
[a] Partly estimated.

investors operating in the market. Recently, there have appeared one or two issue houses. A few small banks have started a quasi-investment trust business. They accept deposits for investment in securities, crediting the deposit accounts with profits and dividends, and guaranteeing a minimum interest.

The principal factors which have hampered the creation of a larger market for public securities in recent years have been: inflation (which naturally renders unattractive any fixed-income investment that is not subject to capital appreciation); compulsory and semi-compulsory issues (which have disorganized the market); the lack of practically any redemption of matured issues; and bureaucratic difficulties connected with the *payment of interest*. The latter obstacles are about to be overcome. Undoubtedly, the high interest rates which the banks offer on deposits have not only contributed to maintaining high bond rates but have also stifled the development of the market by enabling banks to attract funds which might otherwise have gone to the securities market (in which the banks have not invested due to other pressing demands on their resources and to a tradition in favor of "self-liquidating" loans and bills). The relative importance of deposits and bonds outstanding makes any interest raising effect of the latter upon the former less likely.

During the last 10 years, bonds have yielded 7–8 percent interest. If the declining purchasing power of money is considered, real interest has, nevertheless, often been negative. Probably not more than 30 percent of all government bonds outstanding are held by institutions, though a somewhat larger proportion of Federal bonds is so held; the remaining securities are owned, despite their low or negative real yield, by individuals, whose savings are too small to permit other applications and who are dominated by "money illusion."

The market for debentures has been destroyed by inflation. The market for shares suffers from weakness, not only on the demand but also on the supply side. The supply of securities is low by reason of the prevalence of closed corporations.

The weakness of the capital market, partly due to a reluctance to issue securities to the public at large, tends to perpetuate internal financing and thus to prevent a dividend policy and a treatment of minority shareholders capable of attracting new stockholders, which, in turn, produces a weakness of the market on the demand side.

Government bonds have recently been issued largely by compulsion. During the war, the Federal government issued war bonds as a compulsory loan in proportion to each taxpayer's income tax. At present, the government is issuing non-transferable certificates which will be converted into bonds in five years, also as a compulsory loan on the basis of income tax collection. State governments have sometimes paid suppliers in bonds. The recourse to compulsory loans has reflected, of course, the limitations of the bond market. From the economic point of view there is nothing to recommend such loans as compared with taxes in a country where direct taxes are low and hence the disincentive effect of new taxation is quite limited, while the propensity to consume must be higher if the government obtains funds by issuing loans rather than by taxes (Table 16).

As indicated above, most private securities are subscribed by closed groups. But there is an increasing market among the public at large

TABLE 16
INTERNAL FUNDED DEBT, DECEMBER 31
(AMOUNTS IN BILLIONS OF CRUZEIROS)

	Federal	*State*	*Municipal*	*Total*
1941	6.0	5.4	0.3	11.7
1945	7.9	6.3	0.5	14.7
1946	10.0 [a]	6.6	0.6	17.2
1949	10.4	11.8	0.9	23.1
1950	10.4	12.4	1.0	23.8
1951	10.4	14.3	2.3	27.0

Source: *Anuário Estatístico do Brasil,* 1952, p. 555.

[a] Actual delivery of war bonds subscribed to as a compulsory loan during the war only started in 1945–46.

for shares of enterprises which have captured the public's fancy (petroleum); or, in some cases, potential future consumers have subscribed to power company issues. Issues of shares and, sometimes, of bonds for public subscription are made through a broker or more recently by issuing houses, which act merely as agents. There is no underwriting. In some cases the issuing companies have created for a short period a market for new issues.

X. CONCLUSION

The tendency to attempt to spend an amount greater than available resources, which has characterized the Brazilian economy in recent years, makes it particularly necessary that the monetary authorities provide more adequate means to limit credit expansion by the commercial banks and to control the financial system in general.

Equally important is the fact that many credit needs which are of basic importance, from the point of view of rapid capital formation and the creation of a more balanced economy, are not adequately met. Indeed, as we have mentioned, much of the constant pressure on resources, which is often responsible for an expansion of the monetary base, is the direct consequence of the discrepancy between the structure of credit and capital needs both by sectors of activity and by regions, and actual credit distribution; though much, of course, results from the attempt to invest and consume more than total available resources permit. To the discrepancy mentioned above the commercial banking system, which, as we have seen, is essentially remarkably sound, has contributed less than the other parts of the financial system.

One of the main discrepancies occurs with respect to agricultural credit in general. We have also seen that the medium-term and long-term credit and capital needs of industry, including those of public utilities and large-scale industries, are not adequately met. Government credit needs are at present met mainly by borrowing from the Banco do Brasil, which is not satisfactory, nor is it desirable that all funds for government investment be obtained from taxation. The credit needs of trade are adequately met by the commercial banking system which also grants considerable short-term working capital advances to industry. On the other hand, credit needs of low-cost housing construction are not adequately met, though otherwise real estate credit is widely granted, particularly in the metropolitan centers of the country.

A good deal of the discrepancy between credit and capital needs and the loan and investment structure of the financial system is due to inflation itself and the changes which it has wrought in the price structure. Better control of the volume of credit would solve part of this problem. Nevertheless, other difficulties arising from this discrepancy cannot be solved at all by financial policy alone, and still others can be solved adequately only by fiscal and exchange policy in conjunction with measures in the monetary field. There remains a wide field for monetary and banking policy, especially if aided by certain institutional changes, to make an effective contribution to the country's economic progress. We have commented, in the various preceding sections, on the aspects of Brazil's monetary and banking system, relevant to these policy problems. Very serious thought is at present being given to the reform of the country's monetary institutions.

REFERENCES

Bouças, Valentin F. A dívida externa do Brasil.
Bulhões, Otavio Gouveia de. O crédito seletivo. Rio de Janeiro, 1943.
Calmon, Pedro. História social do Brasil. 3 vols., São Paulo, 1940.
Calógeras, J. Pandiá. La Politique monetaire du Brésil. Rio de Janeiro, 1910.
Costa, Artur de Souza. Panorama financeiro e econômico da República. Rio de Janeiro, 1941.
Franco, Bernardo de Souza. Os bancos do Brasil, sua história, defeitos de organização atual e reforma no sistema bancário. Rio de Janeiro, 1848.
Freire, Felisbelo. História do Banco do Brasil. Rio de Janeiro, 1907.
Gudin, Eugenio. Princípios de economia monetária. 2 vols., Rio de Janeiro, 1947.

Inglês, de Souza Carlos. A anarquia monetária, suas consequências. São Paulo, 1924.

—— Restauração da moeda no Brasil. São Paulo, 1926.

Kingston, Jorge. "A sensibilidade do sistema bancário brasileiro," *Revista de Economia,* Ano VII, No. 3.

Lafer, Horacio. Os bancos e a reforma bancária no Brasil.

Lourenço, João de. A moeda nacional, 1941.

Macedo Soares, José Carlos de. O Banco do Brasil como banco central de emissão e redescontos. São Paulo, 1929.

Mortara, Alberto. "Il sistema bancário brasiliano," *Revista del Lavoro,* August, 1949.

Niemeyer, Otto E. Relatório apresentado ao Govêrno Federal do Brasil. Rio de Janeiro, 1931.

Sampaio, Aldo. Lições de economia circulatória e de economia repartitiva. São Paulo, 1944.

—— "El sistema monetário del Brasil," in *Sistemas monetários Latino Americanos.* Cordoba, 1943.

Simõnsen, Roberto C. A evolução industrial do Brasil. São Paulo, 1939.

Souza, Washington Luiz Pereira de. A reform a monetária e a estabilização no Brasil. Rio de Janeiro, 1929.

Taunay, Visconde de. O encilhamento. 3d ed. São Paulo.

Vergueiro, Abelardo Cesar. Carteira de redescontos. São Paulo, 1936.

Viana, Victor. O Banco do Brasil. Rio de Janeiro, 1926.

Vieira, Dorival Teixeira. "A evolução do sistema monetário brasileiro," *Revista de Administração,* April, 1947.

CANADA

by Donald Bailey Marsh

MC GILL UNIVERSITY, MONTREAL

THE CANADIAN BANKING SYSTEM, like its counterpart in other countries, has grown in response to national credit needs. In Canada, the more outstanding of these needs arise directly from the country's geographical contour and position. Canada's 14 million people live for the most part in a relatively narrow strip of land stretching for 3,987 miles along an international boundary line. This boundary line separates her from a powerful well-integrated economy, with depth as well as breadth—the United States of America.

In recent years, Canada has greatly increased the rate at which she

---

DONALD BAILEY MARSH received the degree of Bachelor of Arts from the University of New Brunswick in May, 1935, with first class honors in Philosophy and Economics. He received the degree of Master of Arts from Louisiana State University in June, 1936. In September, 1936, he entered the University of Illinois and completed work for the Ph.D. degree in May, 1940. Since receiving the doctorate, he has taught at Barnard College, Columbia University, the Columbia Graduate School, and (since 1947) at McGill University.

In addition to his teaching assignments at Barnard and Columbia, he was employed in tax research in connection with projects financed by the Columbia Council for Research in the Social Sciences; and he has prepared various memoranda for private business groups. In 1946 he was Rapporteur for the Committee on the Flow of Capital, U.S. Council of the International Chamber of Commerce. From 1945 to 1947 he was associated with Department of Financial and Business Research of the Chase National Bank. In 1947 he was appointed Professor of Economics, McGill University, and Economist, The Royal Bank of Canada. In 1952, he was appointed Director of Economic Research, The Royal Bank of Canada. In 1953 he was appointed Bronfman Professor of Economics, McGill University.

In addition to articles and reviews on a variety of economic subjects, he has written two books: *Taxes without Tears* (New York, 1945); and *World Trade and Investment* (New York, 1951).

The author is greatly indebted to a number of his colleagues at The Royal Bank of Canada, Head Office, who read all or part of the manuscript, answered many questions on Canadian banking procedure, and made a number of invaluable suggestions.

is developing the rich resources of her northland; and, in Alberta, the economic center of gravity has already shifted to a point well north of the United States border. But the forces that determined the present shape of Canada's banking structure are to be found in an earlier period. The problem of the future will be to adapt that structure, where necessary, to the changing needs of a rising industrial nation.

We shall be concerned first with Canada's peculiar credit needs, and the various devices and private institutions developed to meet them; second, with the chartered banking system; third, with the Bank of Canada; fourth, with certain other monetary and credit institutions, public and private; and, fifth, with the banking system in action during recent years.

INTRODUCTION

THE CANADIAN ECONOMY

A brief description of the Canadian economy can perhaps best be given by citing a few statistics of general interest and availability in most modern nations. In 1952, the value of Canada's gross national product was $23,011 million. The net balance-of-payments surplus on current account was $164 million; and the gross credits on current account were $5,581 million. In other words, exports of goods and services were over 24 percent of the gross national product. Gross domestic investment [1] was $4,416 million or over 19 percent of the gross national product. Consumer expenditure and government expenditure on goods and services were respectively $14,334 million and $4,216 million.[2]

The surplus on current account made necessary a net capital outflow; but the inflow of long-term investment during the year amounted to over $600 million. Balance in Canada's international accounts was effected by (1) a small increase in official reserves of gold and U.S. dollars ($80 million); (2) a much larger increase in Canadian-held U.S.

1 "Gross domestic investment" in Canada's national accounts includes "expenditures for new construction, new machinery and equipment, and changes in inventories of private and government business enterprise and private non-commercial institutions. Expenditures of persons for new housing (including major improvements and alterations) are also included." Dominion Bureau of Statistics, *National Accounts Income and Expenditure, 1926–1950* (Ottawa), p. 109.

2 Dominon Bureau of Statistics, *National Accounts Income and Expenditure, Revised Preliminary 1949–1952* (Ottawa, 1953), p. 16.

dollars, in the form of balances in American banks or of investment at short term or call in New York; and (3) an adjustment of the "leads and lags" occasioned by postponing Canadian-dollar payments and prepaying U.S. dollar payments, on the assumption that the premium on Canadian funds, which developed in early 1952, would in time decline or disappear. Thus foreign trade in goods and services and the investment of foreign capital were very large compared with the gross national product and, since Canadian investment, especially in plant and equipment, has a high import content, the importance of Canada's international transactions becomes clear.

The character of Canada's export trade also has a bearing on the nature of her economy and of her peculiar credit needs. In 1952, Canada's domestic exports amounted to $4,301.1 million. The leading exports were in the group "wood, wood products, and paper"—which made up almost a third of the total. Agricultural and vegetable products made up over a quarter of the total exports; nonferrous metals and products were a little less than a sixth, with animals and animal products and iron and products next in line but far less in amount. The export trade, thus biased in character toward foodstuffs and raw materials, was also biased in direction: of total exports, slightly over 54 percent went to the United States.

On the import side, "iron and products," largely manufactures, accounted for the largest share in 1952: $1,406.6 million out of $4,030.5 million altogether. Non-metallic minerals and products (for example, coal and oil) were about one sixth of the total, with agricultural and vegetable products ($489.2 million) and fibres, textiles and products ($359.4 million) next in line. Of total imports from all countries, 74 percent came from the United States.

Another important determinant of Canada's credit needs is not unrelated to the volume, character, and direction of her foreign trade. Canada is a great producer of food and raw materials. Aside from the great pulp and paper companies, food and raw-material production usually involves peculiar credit needs. For agriculture especially, loan payments must be adjusted to the growing season; and food and raw-material producers are as a rule unable to provide the kind of security that banks ordinarily require for the kind of credit accommodation needed. Nevertheless, credit for food and raw-material production is provided by Canadian banks, with the help of special credit machinery that will be discussed later.

Canadian manufacturing has grown rapidly, especially during and since the Second World War. The volume of manufacturing production in November, 1952, was 312.2 percent of its volume in the base period 1935–39. This rate of growth is approached or exceeded by a number of important components, such as electric power (241.3), primary iron and steel production (310.1), and transportation equipment (398.3). These figures may help to fill out the picture of a young, rapidly expanding industrial economy. However, the credit needs of industrial expansion provide a new test for the adaptability of Canada's banking system; and it is not surprising that, as we shall see, some of the traditional methods of financing show evidence of decline.

REVIEW OF CREDIT INSTRUMENTS IN USE

The most important credit instrument in use by Canadian banks is the promissory note. Its importance arises both from the active encouragement by the banks and from the fact that, even where other instruments are used, the promissory note may also be used as the ultimate promise to pay. On secured loans, the note may be accompanied by the personal guarantee of responsible persons, who may or may not be associated with the borrowing firms; by government or corporate securities as collateral; or by various types of assignments the most important of which are provided for under Sections 86 and 88 of the Bank Act.[3]

Loans under Section 86 are made against assignments of negotiable warehouse receipts and bills of lading. There is no basis for an accurate estimate, but we know these loans do not account for many advances by Canadian banks: a fair guess might be 1 to 2 percent of total advances.

Another type of assignment is of considerably more importance: the assignment of merchandise to the bank under Section 88. Such assignments are peculiar to Canadian banking and are a response to the credit needs of a growing country with a large output of primary products. Loans under Section 88 are made to a multitude of small borrowers whose credit worthiness may be hard to assess, and to large as well as small borrowers whose assets are mainly confined to the commodities on which the assignments are taken. Loans under

[3] 8 Geo. VI. c. 30. The general role of the Bank Act in the legal framework of Canadian banking will be considered later.

Section 88 may be made: (1) "to any wholesale purchaser or shipper of, or dealer in, products of agriculture, the forest, quarry and mine, or the sea, lakes and rivers, upon the security of such products"; (2) "to any person engaged in business as a manufacturer of any goods, wares and merchandise, upon the security of the goods, wares and merchandise manufactured by him or procured for such manufacture"; (3) "to any farmer" to finance the purchase of seed grain, fertilizer, or binder twine, on the security of these commodities and of the crop associated with them, or, under similar arrangements, to finance livestock raising, purchase of agricultural implements, purchase or installation of agricultural equipment or a farm electric system, and miscellaneous construction, repair, and improvements upon the security of agricultural implements; (4) "to any fisherman, upon the security of fishing vessels, fishing equipment and supplies or products of the sea, lakes and rivers. . . ."[4]

The credit instruments used in Section 88 loans are: (1) a general agreement required by the lending banks; (2) a special application and promise to give security; and (3) the actual assignment of the goods. The last instrument is required under the Bank Act;[5] and, in addition, a notice of intention to give Section 88 security must be "registered in the appropriate agency not more than three years immediately before the security is given."[6] The actual assignment of goods or property to the bank is accompanied by a promissory note and usually by an assignment of accounts receivable as added security.

With the growth and diversity of the national economy, the size of these loans may be expected in general to decline in relative, and even perhaps in absolute, amount. But this prospective decline must not be overemphasized or misinterpreted. First, in spite of growing industrialization, Section 88 security is likely to retain a fair share of its importance, owing to the ineligibility of general mortgage

[4] *Ibid.*, section 88 (1).

[5] *Ibid.* The second credit instrument is "required" indirectly: it does not appear in the text of the Bank Act, but it is mentioned in the particular assignment forms set out at the end of the act in schedules C and J in which the assignment is made "pursuant to the application for credit and promise to give security made by the undersigned to the [chartered] bank." The other schedules of similar import (D–I) refer to a loan or advance "for which the [chartered] bank holds the following notes. . . ."

[6] *Ibid.*, section 88 (4) (a). The "appropriate agency" in any province is the local office of the Bank of Canada. The office of the Clerk of the Territorial Court is the agency in the Yukon Territory; and the office of the Secretary of the Territorial Council in Ottawa is the agency for the Northwest Territories.

security under the Bank Act. Second, in spite of any relative, or even absolute, decline in quantity, Section 88 security is bound to retain its full importance for those borrowers to which it is still appropriate.

So far as actual figures on Section 88 security are concerned, estimates are extremely hard to make. Advances by branches to primary producers and small manufacturers in some areas may make up a very large proportion of total loans. Where loans on Section 88 security are made, the proportion in various branches ranges from a high of around 75 percent to as low as 3 percent; and many branches have no Section 88 loans at all. Again, as with Section 86 loans, there is no basis for an accurate estimate, but over-all advances by Canadian banks under Section 88 today may run to about $400–500 million, or to roughly 15 percent of total advances.

Trade paper as security (that is, collateral bills) takes the form of trade and bankers' acceptances. In addition to their use as collateral, these bills may finance trade through direct discounting. This use of trade acceptances is declining in domestic trade, but is still important in textiles, the needle trades, tobacco, and certain wholesale accounts (for example, in groceries). Bankers' acceptances are used infrequently to finance domestic trade owing to the lack of a developed acceptance market in Canada. Trade and bankers' acceptances still have their place in foreign trade, and drawings on open account or under letters of credit are ordinarily made on London or New York.

Where security is required at all, assignment of accounts receivable is not ordinarily relied upon as the sole security; but these assignments are ordinarily required as additional security under Section 88, and wherever the element of risk is such that primary security seems justified. The advantage of this procedure is obvious under Section 88, since the bank's original security, the assigned goods, must pass through sale into other hands. A general assignment of accounts receivable is not enforceable under Quebec law; but, the specific assignment of accounts receivable with notification to the debtor (the assignment of *existing* book debts) is enforceable. However, the added difficulty under Quebec law means that the practice of assigning accounts receivable is not as common or as useful in Quebec as in the other provinces. Outside Quebec the assignment of accounts receivable, in addition to or as part of its general role in supplying supplementary security, has become almost an integral part of Section 88 procedure.

The overdraft, though frowned on by the banks, is an important means of financing in some areas. The absence of a formal overdraft system makes the existence of *de facto* overdraft facilities depend to a large extent on the customer and the branch manager. The *de facto* system is especially likely to be unsatisfactory from the lending bank's point of view: (1) there is less control over borrowing; (2) there may be legal difficulty in proving the liability of the borrower; (3) there is extra routine, such as referring checks to the manager; (4) there is a loss of earnings to the bank when borrowers fail to maintain satisfactory credit balances; and (5) there is the further complication that the borrower's debt may become subject to outlawry at various dates corresponding to the dates at which he availed himself of overdraft credit. However, legal difficulties in fixing liability and in establishing outlawry dates are largely avoided in Canada by requiring the depositor's signature on a monthly verification of account in return for his canceled checks. Such a verification of an overdrawn account fixes the borrower's liability, and the date of the verification establishes the beginning of the outlawry period. With these safeguards, the *de facto* overdraft system continues, in spite of the banks' obvious preference for a promissory note or other formal evidence of debt.

Government paper issued by the provinces and by the Dominion Government form the basis of credits advanced to governments. A detailed discussion of these credit instruments appears in a later section.

A CATALOGUE OF CREDIT INSTITUTIONS

Canada's financial system consists of, first, a currency system with the central bank the sole bank of issue; second, a commercial banking system (the "chartered banks") under central-bank control; third, savings banks, some separate, some (and by far the most important) integrated as savings departments in the commercial banking system; fourth, a system of investment banks (called "dealers") to provide with some help from the chartered banks the longer term credit based on intermediate and long-term corporate securities; fifth, a rudimentary money market in short-term securities; sixth, a peripheral group of lenders (trust companies, insurance companies, small-loan companies, and credit unions) providing miscellaneous investment, credit, and banking services; and seventh, a number of governmental money and credit institutions in the fields of foreign exchange, industrial development, farm loans, housing loans, and export credit insurance.

These institutions, with minor differences, may be found in most Western nations. The spheres of influence accorded to these components of the financial structure reflect specific national conditions and are usually set by legislation. As we shall see later, Canadian legislation clearly delimits the role of the chartered banks; and overlapping with the conventional functions of other components in the financial structure is accordingly held to a minimum.

THE CHARTERED BANKS

This section is concerned with that part of Canada's financial structure which, in the United States for example, would be loosely analogous to the "commercial banking system." In Canada, this part of the financial structure is the preserve of the "chartered banks," so called because they operate under federal charter in accordance with the provisions of the Bank Act.[7] These chartered banks are, with minor exceptions,[8] the only private financial institutions that can legally use the word "bank" in their business name.

We shall be concerned first with the main characteristics of the chartered banking system with some attention to its origin and growth; and second, with the powers and prerogatives of the chartered banks as defined in the Bank Act.

[7] 8 Geo. VI. c. 30; Statutes of Canada 1944, c. 30.

[8] The exceptions are: The Post Office Savings Bank, two Quebec savings banks, and the Newfoundland Savings Bank. The Post Office Savings Bank, with branches in about 1,600 post offices throughout the Dominion, was established under the Post Office Act of 1867 (31 Vict. c. 10). It absorbed the Dominion Government Savings Bank in 1929. The two Quebec savings banks are: the Montreal City and District Savings Bank, founded in 1846; and La Banque d'Économie de Québec, founded as La Caisse d'Économie de Notre Dame de Québec in 1848. Both banks were federally chartered under the Quebec Savings Bank Act of 1871 (R.S.C. 1927, chapter 14), an act similar to the Bank Act and subject like that act to decennial revision. The Newfoundland Savings Bank was founded in 1834 as an agency of the Newfoundland Government and became part of Canada's banking system when Newfoundland joined Canada as the tenth province in 1949.

MAIN CHARACTERISTICS, ORIGIN AND GROWTH

The economic weight of the United States has greatly affected Canada's economic development. Through force of example, plus an inevitable similarity in the problems to be faced, Canada has become America's best customer: not only does Canada import American goods but she imports American institutions as well. But as far as current banking practice is concerned, the Canadian banking system seems to present a striking contrast. There are marks of Scottish and English origin that may be easily recognized for what they are; but, if we except a trend toward skyscrapers in bank architecture, there would seem to be scarcely anything derived from Canada's nearest neighbor.

As a matter of fact, Canada did import part of her banking structure from the United States, well over a century ago; but what she imported has no counterpart in the United States today. Canada's banking system shows marks of Scottish and English origin because Scottish and English precedent and experience influenced Alexander Hamilton; Hamilton's charter for the First Bank of the United States became the model for the earliest charters granted in Lower Canada; [9] and these charters in turn have in a continuous development become an integral part of Canada's Bank Act.

Canada's commercial banking system consists of eleven chartered banks with 3,923 branches in Canada.[10] This large number of branches rightly suggests a relatively high ratio of bank offices to population: there was a branch for every 3,796 of the Canadian population on October 31, 1953; [11] the corresponding figure for the United States was 7,875.[12] But the United States with its unit banking system [13] had many more separate banks per unit of population. The significant figure for the comparison of banking services is, of course, the number of bank offices. Comparative ratios of banks to population is an index of the degree of concentration and integration of banking corpora-

[9] Adam Shortt, "Origin of the Canadian Banking System," *Journal of the Canadian Bankers' Association*, IV (1896), pp. 1–19.

[10] Houston's *Bank Directory of Canada*, November, 1953, p. 3.

[11] That is 3,923 branches for a total of 14,000,000 persons as of Nov. 30, 1951.

[12] That is, 14,575 banks plus 5,520 branches and additional offices or a total of 20,095 for a total of 158,233,000 persons (including armed forces) as of Dec. 31, 1952. *Federal Reserve Bulletin*, May, 1953, p. 548.

[13] Except for some city-wide and state-wide branch systems where such are permitted.

tions. The degree of concentration for any given amount of banking services is bound to be higher in a branch banking system. This may be considered good or bad in principle; but it also has important effects on banking stability. Thus Canada survived the 1930s without a single bank failure, while the number of bank failures in the United States over the six-month period December 31, 1932, to June 30, 1933, was 3,876.[14]

The concentration of Canada's banking system into eleven banks with many branches is itself the product of a long process extending over a century and a half. As a substitute for any attempt at an adequate historical outline, we may say that the system passed through three main periods: germination,[15] proliferation, and concentration. After abortive attempts as early as 1792,[16] a charter was finally granted in 1820 to the Bank of New Brunswick in Saint John.[17] But the Bank of Montreal, which secured a charter from the Province of Lower Canada in 1822, had been conducting business as a private association (under the name of "Montreal Bank") since November 3, 1817.[18] There followed a period of general expansion during which, in spite of brief periods of recession, the number of banking corporations followed more or less a steady upward trend until 1885 and 1886

[14] Economic Policy Commission, American Bankers' Association, *Banking after the Crisis* (New York, 1934), p. 13. The figure actually records the drop in the "total number of reported banking institutions"; but presumably most of the drop represented bank failures.

[15] The seeds were of course Alexander Hamilton's ideas on banking probably brought to Canada by loyalist immigrants from the U.S. after the Revolutionary war. Shortt, "Origin of the Canadian Banking System," pp. 1–19.

[16] There is some difference of opinion regarding the activities of the Canada Bank. Breckenridge says: "The 'Canadian Banking Company' then (1792) organized by certain English firms and Montreal merchants, was not destined to survive its origin, although one at least of its 5 shilling notes which has been preserved (no. 6803) is proof that it exercised the function of issue." *The History of Banking in Canada* (Washington, D.C., 1910), p. 3. C. S. Howard comments that the note in question (which he reproduces) is unsigned except for registration and is dated more than two months before the bank's promoters issued a circular announcing their intention to found a bank. This as Mr. Howard points out does not of course preclude the issue of other notes subsequently, some specimens of which Sir Edmund Walker in an (uncited) article claims to have seen. See C. S. Howard, "Canadian Banks and Bank Notes: a Record," *Canadian Banker*, LVII (1950), pp. 30, 32–33.

[17] New Brunswick remained a separate colony until Confederation in 1867. The Bank of New Brunswick became part of the Bank of Nova Scotia in 1913.

[18] The Quebec Bank, which opened for business under similar circumstances in 1818, was also formally chartered in 1822 and continued in operation until 1917 when it became part of The Royal Bank of Canada. Another private association founded in 1818, the Bank of Canada, was also chartered in 1822 but had a short life, closing in 1831. The Bank of Upper Canada, at York, now Toronto, was chartered in 1821, and thus becomes the second bank actually chartered in British North America; it closed in 1866.

when the peak number of 41 was reached.[19] From that time the trend was as steadily downward until, through failure, winding up, or amalgamation, the number of separate banks had declined by 1931 to a mere ten. The number rose to eleven on March 31, 1953, when the Mercantile Bank of Canada received its charter. By October 9, 1953, a certificate permitting the bank to open for business had been granted by the Treasury Board (see "Incorporation" below), and December 7, 1953, was the date set for the opening in Montreal of the bank's main branch.

Table 1 shows the eleven chartered banks now operating, their total assets and number of branches in 1953, and the banks which, in the course of growth, the larger banks have absorbed. The dates of founding and of amalgamation shown for each of the banks thus absorbed reflect the rise and fall in the number of individual banks since 1817. Table 1 shows only the surviving eleven plus the banks that closed to become part of a larger system. Other liquidations and all the failures are excluded. Altogether 99 banks have been created in Canada since 1792, of which 39 have failed and 49 have been amalgamated or liquidated.

Of the 4,038 branches shown in Table 1, 115 are in foreign countries. The distribution by banks and countries appears in Table 2. In addition, Canadian banks are represented through correspondents in all important banking and commercial centers. Today Canada's banking system might with some fairness adopt the high-spirited slogans of both the great transportation systems: it not only "serves all Canada" [20] but "spans the world." [21]

19 The peak number of branches, 4,676, was recorded in 1920. By that time the number of separate banks had declined to 18. *The Canada Year Book* (Ottawa, 1950), p. 599.

20 Canadian National Railways.

21 Canadian Pacific Railways.

TABLE 1

THE ELEVEN CHARTERED BANKS (1953) AND THE BANKS ABSORBED BY THEM (1817–1953)[a]

Year Founded or Chartered	*Name of Bank*	*Head Office*	*Year Amalgamated*	*Total Assets (In Canadian dollars)*	*Number of Branches*
1817	Montreal Bank				
	became				
1822	BANK OF MONTREAL	Montreal		$2,361,090,936	603
1832	Commercial Bank of the Midland District				
	became				
	The Commercial Bank of Canada	Kingston	1867		
1835	Bank of the People	Toronto	1838		
1835	Bank of British North America	Montreal	1918		
1855	The Molsons Bank	Montreal	1923		
1857	Ontario Bank	Toronto	1906		
1864	The People's Bank of Halifax	Halifax	1905		
1864	People's Bank of New Brunswick	Fredericton, N.B.	1907		
1864	The Merchants Bank	Montreal			
	became				
1868	The Merchants Bank of Canada	Montreal	1922		
1869	The Exchange Bank of Yarmouth	Yarmouth, N.S.	1903		
1832	THE BANK OF NOVA SCOTIA	Halifax		946,432,863	415
1820	The Bank of New Brunswick	Saint John	1913		
1836	City Bank of Saint John	Saint John	1839		
1866	The Summerside Bank	Summerside, P.E.I.	1901		
1864	The Union Bank of Prince Edward Island	Charlottetown	1883		
1875	The Bank of Ottawa	Ottawa	1919		

1903	Metropolitan Bank	Toronto	1914		
1855	THE BANK OF TORONTO	Toronto		560,391,918	246
1861	La Banque Jacques Cartier became				
1900	LA BANQUE PROVINCIALE DU CANADA	Montreal		192,602,090	349
1864	The Merchants Bank became	Halifax			
1869	The Merchants Bank of Halifax became	Halifax			
1901	THE ROYAL BANK OF CANADA	Montreal		2,783,235,826	793
1818	The Quebec Bank	Quebec	1917		
1856	The Union Bank of Halifax	Halifax	1910		
1864	The Commercial Bank of Windsor	Windsor, N.S.	1902		
1865	The Union Bank of Lower Canada became	Quebec			
1886	The Union Bank of Canada	(Quebec, moved to Winnipeg, 1912)	1925		
1906	United Empire Bank	Toronto	1911		
1885	The Traders Bank of Canada	Toronto	1912		
1905	The Northern Bank became	Winnipeg	1908		
1908	The Northern-Crown Bank	Winnipeg	1918		
1904	The Crown Bank of Canada	Toronto	1908		
1867	THE CANADIAN BANK OF COMMERCE	Toronto		1,894,040,495	651
1825	The Halifax Banking Company	Halifax	1903		
1835	The Gore Bank	Hamilton	1868		

TABLE 1 (*Continued*)

Year Founded or Chartered	*Name of Bank*	*Head Office*	*Year Amalgamated*	*Total Assets (In Canadian dollars)*	*Number of Branches*
1860	The Eastern Townships Bank	Sherbrooke	1912		
1862	The Bank of British Columbia	Victoria, B.C.	1901		
1871	The Merchants Bank of Prince Edward Island	Charlottetown	1906		
1872	The Bank of Hamilton	Hamilton	1923		
1873	The St. Lawrence Bank became				
1876	The Standard Bank of Canada	Toronto	1928		
1882	The Western Bank of Canada	Oshawa	1909		
1905	The Sterling Bank of Canada	Toronto	1925		
1871	THE DOMINION BANK	Toronto		514,194,011	183
1874	La Banque d'Hochelaga became				
1924	BANQUE CANADIENNE NATIONALE	Montreal		508,861,522	560
1860	La Banque Nationale	Montreal	1924		
1875	IMPERIAL BANK OF CANADA	Toronto		604,002,760	234
1855	The Niagara District Bank	St. Catherine	1875		
1910	The Weyburn Security Bank	Weyburn, Sask.	1931		
1929	BARCLAYS BANK (CANADA)	Montreal		32,868,880	4
1953	THE MERCANTILE BANK OF CANADA	Montreal		[b]	[b]
Total assets and branches				$10,397,721,301	4,038

[a] For a more extended list, including the failures, see C. S. Howard, "Canadian Banks and Bank Notes: a Record," *Canadian Banker*, LVII (1950), 58–61. Assets figures are those of September 30, 1953; branches figures are those of October 31, 1953.

[b] Not open for business at date of writing (see text).

TABLE 2
DISTRIBUTION OF BRANCHES BY COUNTRY [a]

Bank	*Great Britain*	*United States*	*France*	*Cuba*	*British West Indies*	*Central and South America*	*Total*
The Royal Bank of Canada	2	1	1	18	24	23	69
The Bank of Nova Scotia	1	1	0	7	21	0	30
The Canadian Bank of Commerce	1	5	0	0	3	0	9
Bank of Montreal	2	2	0	0	0	0	4
The Dominion Bank	1	1	0	0	0	0	2
Banque Canadienne Nationale	0	0	1	0	0	0	1
Total	7	10	2	25	48	23	115

Source: *Houston's Bank Directory of Canada* (Toronto, December, 1953), pp. 3, 11–15.

[a] The following Canadian banks have no foreign branches: The Bank of Toronto, La Banque Provinciale du Canada, Barclays Bank (Canada), and Imperial Bank of Canada.

POWER AND PREROGATIVES OF THE CHARTERED BANKS

We are concerned at this point with what might be called the "static" side of Canadian banking—the legal foundation and administration of the chartered banks. The legal foundation of the chartered banking system is the Bank Act.[22] This act was originally passed in 1871 subject to revision every ten years, the last revision being that of August 15, 1944.[23] Since 1934, the Bank Act has contained clauses to reconcile it with the Bank of Canada Act,[24] which set up Canada's central bank in that year.

1. *Incorporation.*—All Canadian banks have the same charter: the current revision of the Bank Act itself. Thus the charters of all the banks run out on the same day every ten years and must be renewed through the decennial revision and enactment of the Act. The incorporation of any particular bank requires an Act of Incorporation giving the names of the applicants (who are made provisional directors of the new bank), the amount of capital stock, the name of the bank, and the location of the bank's head office. The minimum

[22] 8 Geo. VI; Statutes of Canada 1944, c. 30.

[23] The discrepancy in years occurs because (1) there were two temporary one-year extensions of the bank charters in 1911 and 1912 changing the "revision date" to 1913; and (2) there was a special extension of one year in 1933 making the "revision date" 1934, the year in which the Bank of Canada was set up.

[24] 24–25 Geo. V; Statutes of Canada 1934, c. 43.

capitalization is $500,000, divided into shares of $10 each, with not less than $250,000 paid up. Of the paid-up capital, $250,000 must be deposited with the Minister of Finance who then allows the provisional directors to call a meeting of the *bona fide* subscribers to the stock of the bank. At this meeting, directors (not less than five) are elected [25] and various bylaws are passed regarding date of annual meeting, vacancies on the board of directors, and the like. But the new bank cannot start operations until it gets a certificate from the Treasury Board.[26] Application for the certificate must wait on the election of directors by the shareholders and must contain a sworn statement listing all costs of incorporation and organization, paid or owed by the bank. If these costs appear reasonable to the Board, and if all the other requirements of the Bank Act have been met, the Board will issue the certificate and the Minister will repay without interest the money deposited with him.[27]

2. *Administration.*—Legally, as the Bank Act puts it, "the stock, property, affairs and concerns of the bank shall be managed by a board of directors." [28] Directors, of the authorized number,[29] are elected by the shareholders in the usual way at the annual meeting of the bank and are eligible for reelection from year to year. The directors in turn are required by the Act to elect one of their number as president along with one or more vice-presidents. They may also elect a chairman of the board and one honorary president. Officers of the

[25] Directors must own stock in the bank with a minimum paid-up subscription of $3,000 when the paid-up capital stock of the bank is $1,000,000 or less; $4,000 when paid-up capital stock is over $1,000,000 but not over $3,000,000; and $5,000 when paid-up capital stock is over $3,000,000. There are slightly lower requirements that may be applied to not more than one quarter the number of directors. A majority of the directors must be "natural born or naturalized subjects of Her Majesty and domiciled in Canada." 8 Geo. 20 (1–3).

[26] The Treasury Board was created in 1867. Its duties are in general to supervise the financial arrangements of government departments and to coordinate governmental monetary and fiscal policy. It consists of "the Minister of Finance and any five of the ministers belonging to the King's Privy Council for Canada, to be nominated from time to time by the Governor in Council." Rev. Stat. 23.S.9. The Board's composition, in July, 1951, was as follows: Hon. D. C. Abbott, Minister of Finance; Hon. J. G. Gardner, Minister of Agriculture; Hon. Alphonse Fournier, Minister of Public Works; Hon. Milton Gregg, Minister of Labour; Hon. Stuart Garson, Minister of Justice.

[27] 8 Geo. VI, c. 30, 17 (1). All this must be completed within a year of the passing of the Act of Incorporation, otherwise the Act of Incorporation becomes void and the bank must wind up its affairs. 8 Geo. VI, c. 30, 16 (1).

[28] 8 Geo. VI, c. 30, 19.

[29] *Ibid.*, 21 (1) (c). Fixed along with the size of the quorum by the shareholders through bylaws but not less than the minimum set by the Bank Act: five directors, with a quorum of three.

bank are the appointees of the directors, who ordinarily delegate this authority to their chief administrative officer, the general manager. The Act has no special restrictions on the power of the directors, themselves, or through the general manager or other authorized officer, to appoint "officers, clerks, and servants" as needed to carry on the business of the bank.[30]

The line of command within Canada's banks has evolved more or less (but not entirely) as one would expect from reading the Bank Act itself. Today the bank's chief executive officer is the president; its chief administrative officer is the general manager. The president has at times in the past been a director with outside interests who happened to be elected by his fellow directors to keep a watchful eye on bank management and policy in his spare time. Today there is only one "part-time" president in a Canadian bank. The others are all career men. Their first connection with the bank has been not as directors, but as members of the bank's staff.

The change over the last half century becomes especially clear when we compare the definition in the Canadian Bankers' Association Act with present practice. The act says "the chief executive officer of a member shall be its general manager or cashier, or in his absence the officer designated for the purpose by him, or in default of such designation the officer next in authority." [31] The classification "cashier" has disappeared from Canadian banking; and division of labor at the top, made necessary by growth, has split executive power on a rough line between policy and administration. Similarly the office of vice-president may be held by an outstanding director who is not a banker, or it may be held by a full-time banker who participates in day-by-day executive decisions. Since there may be more than one vice-president, the two characteristics of the office may be exemplified among the officers and directors of the same bank at the same time. For example, the office of "vice-president and general manager" clearly emphasizes the executive side; and the same emphasis may apply when a career banker carries the title of vice-president only, especially if he represents executive authority in an especially important center some distance from head office.

The rest of the "executive" category is made up of the assistant general managers, roughly analogous in number and function to executive vice-presidents in American banks. In addition, some ex-

[30] 8 Geo. VI, c. 30, 29 (1).

[31] 63–64 Vict., c. 93, 8.

ecutive functions devolve upon supervisors and others, at head office and in the various supervisory districts across the country.

The head-office function is essentially non-operating. It consists in creating policy directives, collecting or clearing information, and supervising performance. In a formal sense, no actual banking is done either at head office or in the district supervisors' departments which, within prescribed limits, perform the head-office function in various areas. Area supervision is done by the district supervisor, who reports to head office either directly or through an assistant general manager or vice-president in his own district.

It is the branch manager who is responsible for applying his own ideas, or ideas suggested by head office, to the actual job of attracting deposits and making profitable loans. Discretion granted to the branch manager in the making of loans depends upon the individual case and varies more or less directly with the size of the branch entrusted to him. Loans beyond a certain figure will require approval by his district supervisor, who in turn must refer loans beyond a certain size to head office for information or approval; head office then submits the larger loans in this group to the board of directors at their weekly meeting. Thus the head-office function is not to make loans, but, if necessary, to veto them. The positive side of banking rests for the most part with the branches.

A qualification is, however, in order regarding the investment of funds. A branch in a suburban district with few opportunities to make loans will find that it has "excess deposits"; and this condition may occur in some degree in many branches, even in business areas. Other branches may find that their opportunities to make sound loans exceed in various degrees their ability to get deposits from the public. Traditionally, head office has in effect shifted deposits (through appropriate bookkeeping entries) from areas having excess deposits to areas in need of loan funds, by borrowing from the former and lending to the latter at fixed rates of interest.[32] But in recent years, especially during the Second World War, excess deposits have become chronic, not only for the individual branches but for the bank as a whole. In fact, as many as 98 percent of the branches of a large bank may find themselves with some excess deposits. This has meant

[32] This bookkeeping does not of course deny the theoretical proposition that, given excess reserves of central-bank cash, the rate at which the bank as a whole receives deposits will depend in part upon the rate at which it is making loans.

that head office is a large net borrower from the branches; that is, instead of investing excess deposits indirectly, in business loans through its loans to "net-lending" branches, head office has been forced more and more to invest excess deposits directly in government and corporate securities. In this sense, then, head office through its investment department gets directly into operations which, if not "banking" in the traditional sense, do at least go beyond the head-office function as described above.

3. *Rights, Prohibitions, and Duties.*—There are certain things, specifically prescribed in the Bank Act, which banks are allowed to do. Certain other things, some commonly associated with banking elsewhere, are expressly prohibited. Finally, a certain routine is prescribed for the banks by the government as part of its regulating and supervising machinery.

a) *What the chartered banks may do.* Any chartered bank is expressly permitted by the Act to "open branches, agencies, and offices"; deal in gold and silver coin and bullion (subject, of course, to government policy); deal in, discount, and lend against bills of exchange, promissory notes, and other negotiable securities including those of municipal and other corporations, or against public securities issued by domestic and foreign governments; lend against lien or other notes and conditional sales contracts or similar instruments; and "engage in and carry on such business generally as appertains to the business of banking." [33]

b) *What the chartered banks may not do.* Canadian chartered banks are specifically forbidden to buy, sell, or barter goods, or engage in any trade or business; to purchase, deal in, or lend against, its own shares or the shares of any bank; to lend against mortgage or hypothecation of land, houses, or other immovable property, ships or other vessels, or on the security of "goods, wares and merchandise" (except, of course, as prescribed under sections 86 and 88 of the Bank Act); to lend more than $1,000 to any officer or employee of the bank without the approval of the directors and with that approval not more than $10,000; to lend more than 5 percent of the paid-up capital to any director, or to any company in which the president, general manager, or a director is a partner or shareholder, without the approval of two thirds of the directors present (the affected director must not be present or voting).[34]

[33] 8 Geo. VI, c. 30, 75 (1).

[34] *Ibid.*, 75(2) (a)–(f), (3).

Before 1934 any Canadian chartered bank could issue bank notes at its own discretion up to the amount of its paid-up capital, and issue any amount in excess of this, provided the notes were backed 100 percent by gold. In 1908 a seasonal excess issue up to 15 percent of paid-up capital was allowed to take care of extra demand during the crop season.[35]

The Bank Act revision of 1934 provided for a gradual curtailment by the banks of their note-issuing powers over a period of fifteen years. Finally by January 31, 1950, each bank was required to pay to the Bank of Canada an amount equal to the face value of its notes outstanding on that date; thereafter the Bank of Canada assumed responsibility for redemption.[36]

Canadian banks may still issue notes outside of Canada for circulation abroad in any British Dominion, colony, or possession in which the local government allows private bank-note issues. These notes are to be in denominations of £1 sterling or $5 or for multiples of these sums; and they are not to be issued in excess of 10 percent of the paid-up capital of the bank.[37] The only banks taking advantage of this provision today are The Royal Bank of Canada in the British West Indies and British Guiana, and The Bank of Nova Scotia and The Canadian Bank of Commerce in the British West Indies. Since the Second World War the issue has been greatly curtailed for a number of reasons. Increased taxes on circulation and the rising cost of printing notes in Canada for shipment to the islands have made the issues unprofitable. Moreover, in the Eastern group of the British West Indies [38] the right of issue has been rescinded by the local governments, with gradual retirement of outstanding issues beginning August 16, 1951. This leaves Jamaica, where the banks still have a small circulation; but, for the reasons already given, private issues have fallen, even without official action, until today local government notes supply all but a negligible part of the total circulation.

4. *Government Supervision.*—Government supervision of the chartered banks ranges in detail and rigor from the provision for a shareholders' audit to the signed monthly returns that must be sent to the Minister of Finance.

[35] This period, defined in the 1908 Act as from "October to January inclusive," became "September to February inclusive" in the 1912 Act.

[36] 8 Geo. VI, c. 30, 61 (6–8).

[37] *Ibid.*, (1) (a), (5).

[38] St. Kitts, Antigua, Dominica, Barbados, Grenada, Trinidad, and British Guiana.

The Bank Act attempts to safeguard the independence of the shareholders' audit of any bank's affairs. The detailed provisions do not concern us especially, but the auditors finally appointed by the shareholders are, in the last analysis, subject to the approval of the Minister of Finance.[39]

A more rigorous form of supervision is that exercised by the Inspector General of Banks. An inspection may be called at any time, but each bank must be inspected at least once a year. The Inspector General of Banks may in his inspection satisfy himself regarding the bank's compliance with the provisions of the Bank Act, the safety of its creditors and depositors, and the soundness of its financial position. He then reports his findings to the Minister of Finance. This inspection is, of course, in addition to the inspection of branches, without notice, by members of the bank's internal inspection staff.

In addition to inspections from time to time, a continuous check of bank operations is maintained through the signed annual, monthly, and special returns to the Minister of Finance. All returns furnished to the Minister by the banks are tabled in the House of Commons and many are subsequently published. In most cases the returns of all the banks are consolidated before tabling or publication.

The annual returns include, in addition to the material required in the annual report to the shareholders, a list of the names and addresses of shareholders, the number of shares held by each, and the amount, if any, still to be paid up; a "real estate" return giving details concerning the bank's "real and immovable property"; a list of directors and directorates; a statement of aggregate loans made in Canada by the bank, classified by industries and businesses of the borrowers; a statement of all deposits held by the bank in Canada classified as demand, and notice, deposits with the number and aggregate amount in each class of $1,000 or less, over $1,000 to $5,000, over $5,000 to $25,000, over $25,000 to $100,000, and of all deposits over $100,000; and a return of current operating earnings and expenses with supplementary information regarding dividends paid, provision for losses, and the like. Other annual returns (commonly called "unclaimed balances" returns) include a list of unclaimed dividends and deposit balances, and a list of unpaid checks, drafts, and bills, with details in both lists of the persons and branches concerned. Finally, an "interest rates" return, as of December 31, giving

[39] 8 Geo. VI, c. 30, 55 (1)–(6).

information regarding interest and discount rates charged by the bank, must be filed with the Minister of Finance. The contents of this return are determined by the regulations of the Treasury Board; and the general purpose is to enforce the provision in the Act that no bank may charge interest or discount in excess of 6 percent per annum.[40]

The monthly returns, filed within the first 28 days of each month, are essentially statements of the condition of the bank for the month preceding. This necessarily involves returns from the branches to head office giving details which can be consolidated into a statement of the bank's assets and liabilities at the end of the reported month. The special returns permit the Minister to require additional information without making necessary a change in the Act. So far as one can tell, the power has rarely, if ever, been used.

5. *Other Legal Requirements.*—Government supervision of the chartered banks entails other restrictions on the chartered banks' freedom of action. The most important of these concern legal reserves, and certain restrictions on loans and investments made by the banks.

a) *Legal reserves.* Chartered banks are required to hold not less than 5 percent of deposit liabilities payable in Canadian dollars in the form of cash reserves. These reserves must consist of deposits with the Bank of Canada and Bank of Canada notes held by the bank.[41] In addition, the chartered banks are required to maintain "with the Bank of Canada or elsewhere adequate reserves against liabilities elsewhere than in Canada."[42] Monthly returns showing the bank's Canadian-dollar position must be made to the Bank of Canada at the same time that the monthly statement of condition is sent to the Minister of Finance.[43] The banks must also "furnish such information as may be required by the Minister of Finance" concerning their deposit liabilities outside of Canada and the kind and amount of reserves held against them.[44]

As a matter of fact, the chartered banks maintain a conventional reserve in cash of approximately 10 percent against deposit liabilities in Canada. Reserves rarely fall below 10 percent; indeed, this figure is so well established that the monetary authority is likely to be upset by any marked deviation. Bank of Canada policy is formulated there-

[40] *Ibid.*, 91 (1)–(3).
[41] 8 Geo. V, c. 30, 59; 24–25 Geo. V, c. 43 as amended by 2 Geo. VI, c. 42, 13.
[42] 8 Geo. VI, c. 30, 59. [43] 2 Geo. VI, c. 42, 13. [44] 8 Geo. VI, c. 30, 59.

fore on the expectation, based on experience, that the chartered banks will maintain a cash reserve of 10 percent against their Canadian deposit liabilities.

b) *Secondary reserves.* In addition to the banks' primary or cash reserves, a large proportion of their total assets are, as financial prudence requires, carried in the form of quickly realizable obligations of business and government. These quick assets consist of various obligations of other banks in Canada and abroad, Dominion and provincial government direct and guaranteed securities, municipal and corporate and miscellaneous foreign securities, and call and short loans in Canada and abroad. On September 30, 1953, these primary plus secondary reserves (or "quick assets") for the banking system as a whole were 60.48 percent of total deposit liabilities and all other liabilities to the public.

c) *Inner reserves.* In addition to the reserves that appear on the bank's balance sheet, there are others set aside out of income as contingency reserves against losses on loans, bad or doubtful debts, depreciation in the value of assets other than bank premises, and the like. These are generally but inaccurately called "hidden reserves." Their amount is not known to the general public, but they are no secret to the Minister of Finance. Up to what the Minister of Finance defines to be the "reasonable requirements of the bank," these reserves may be set aside before taxes. Beyond this point further reserves may be set aside to any amount provided they represent transfers from income on which corporate-income taxes have been paid in full.[45]

6. *Check Clearance and Collection.*—Clearinghouse facilities are provided at thirty-four points throughout Canada by the Canadian Bankers' Association under the terms of its Charter, the Canadian Bankers' Association Act.[46] Usually once a day and only in the morning, banks at clearing points exchange local checks on each other through the clearinghouse. Out-of-town checks may also be included in these exchanges provided a commission at certain established rates is allowed to the receiving bank.[47]

[45] *Ibid.*, 56 (9).

[46] 63–64 Vict., c. 93.

[47] These rates are:

Checks not over $5,000: 5¢ per item regardless of amount, plus 0.1% of the daily total of the items cleared to each bank.

Checks over $5,000 but not over $25,000: 0.05%, with a minimum charge of $5 on each item.

Checks over $25,000: Commission charge subject to negotiation with a minimum of $14.50 on each item.

At non-clearing centers with more than one bank, local checks are exchanged by direct presentation among the banks, and out-of-town checks may be included provided again that the receiving bank is allowed a commission at the same rate as those established at the clearing center.

Ordinarily, clearing differences among Canadian banks are settled daily [48] by vouchers payable through the clearinghouse in the nearest of the five largest clearinghouse cities: Montreal, Ottawa, Toronto, Winnipeg, and Vancouver. Clearing differences in these clearing centers are settled daily by debit or credit entries in the account which each chartered bank must maintain with the Bank of Canada, Ottawa. These entries are made by the Bank of Canada on receiving telegraphic instruction from these central clearing points.

The amount of out-of-town checks cleared at any point is reduced because a branch of a given bank will usually exchange these checks by mail either with a branch of the same bank in the town on which the check was drawn or with a central clearing branch for the province in which the town is located.

THE BANK OF CANADA

Canada's central bank, the Bank of Canada, was established in 1934 under the Bank of Canada Act.[49] The decision to establish a central bank followed extended discussion and hearings. The Bank as finally set up followed closely the recommendations of the Royal Commission on Banking and Currency in Canada which reported in 1933.[50]

OWNERSHIP AND CONTROL

At first the Bank of Canada was a privately owned institution with a capital of $5,000,000, divided into 100,000 shares at a par value of $50 each. Shares were open to public subscription with the proviso that no shares could be held by other than British subjects resident in Canada and that no shares could be held directly or indirectly by

48 If there is no clearinghouse at a place where the clearing difference is less than $5,000 (or sometimes a higher or lower amount), daily settlement may be scrapped in favor of settlement weekly, or some other period, by local agreement among the banks.

49 24–25 Geo. V, c. 43.

50 *Report of the Royal Commission on Banking and Currency in Canada, 1933* (Ottawa, 1933).

a chartered bank or by any director, officer, or other employee of a chartered bank. The Minister had power to subscribe for any shares not sold in the public offering; but the issue was oversubscribed and the Bank was originally owned therefore entirely by private capital. The Bank's operations were divorced from the profit motive by limiting dividends to 4.5 percent per annum with excess profits to go first by a sliding scale formula to a rest fund. The excess profits above dividend and rest-fund requirements and, finally, after the rest fund reached $10,000,000, all profits above dividend requirements were to be paid to the Dominion Government.

In 1936 the Bank of Canada Act was amended [51] to secure government ownership of 51 percent of the capital stock through an increase in capitalization from the original $5,000,000 to $10,100,000, all the extra $5,100,000 in the form of Class "B" shares to be held by the Minister of Finance on behalf of the Dominion Government. The issue of public vs. private ownership was thus resolved by compromise, but there was no compromise on ultimate control: majority voting power and the selection of a majority of the directors were firmly in government hands.

In 1938, a further amendment [52] of the Bank of Canada Act brought about the complete nationalization of the Bank. The Bank was empowered by the government to buy all outstanding privately owned shares and thus to convert actual government control into complete government ownership as well.[53] As far as the mechanics of central banking are concerned, the 1938 amendment was, with government control assured, a matter of supreme indifference. But from a political point of view, various groups in and outside the party in power [54] with left-wing monetary notions were thus appeased. Each private shareholder was paid $59.20 for each Class "A" share registered in his name on July 15, 1938, plus accrued dividends; and the last vestige of private ownership disappeared from the capital account of Canada's central bank.[55]

[51] I Edward VIII, c. 22, 10.

[52] 2 Geo. VI, c. 42, 8, 9.

[53] This was effected by an exchange of 100,000 of the government-held Class "B" shares for the 100,000 privately held Class "A" shares redeemed by the Bank. The Class "B" shares were then canceled. This brought the Bank's capitalization back to its original $5,000,000 figure. The extra 2,000 Class "B" shares were surrendered to the Bank for cancellation along with an added $820,000 to reimburse the Bank for the premium of $9.20 per share paid upon repurchase to the holders of Class "A" shares.

[54] That is, the liberal party under the leadership of Mr. W. L. MacKenzie King.

[55] For a detailed discussion of the legislative history of the Bank of Canada see M. L. Stokes, *The Bank of Canada* (Toronto, 1939), Chaps. VII, VIII, X.

MANAGEMENT

Except that all directors of the Bank are now appointed by the government, the mechanics of the Bank's management remain as before nationalization. Management lies with the Board of Directors composed of a governor as chairman, a deputy governor, and twelve directors appointed for three-year terms by the Minister of Finance. The appointed directors are selected from diversified occupations, and none may be a director, officer, or employee of a chartered bank. Any shareholder of a chartered bank who is appointed director of the Bank of Canada must dispose of his chartered bank shares within three months of his appointment. The Deputy Minister of Finance, or an alternate nominated by the Minister, is an *ex officio* member of the Board of Directors but without the right to vote.[56]

Except when the Board is in session, its powers are delegated to an Executive Committee, composed of the governor, deputy governor, one director selected by the Board, and *ex officio* the Deputy Minister of Finance or his alternate, who sits, as on the Board of Directors, without the right to vote.[57] The insulation from direct government interference secured by an orthodox corporate structure is supplemented or perhaps balanced by a further power which the governor of the Bank holds over the Board of Directors itself. The governor, or, in his absence or incapacity, the deputy governor, may veto any decision of the Board of Directors or of the Executive Committee. The Minister of Finance must be informed of the veto within seven days; and the veto, along with the views of any director or member of the Executive Committee who wishes to be heard, must then be submitted by the Minister to the Governor in Council to be confirmed or disallowed.

WHAT THE BANK CAN DO

The Bank is empowered by the Act to buy and sell (1) gold and silver in coin or bullion, as well as nickel and bronze coin; (2) with certain limitations regarding maturities at the date of acquisition (noted later), securities issued or guaranteed by the Dominion of Canada or any province or by the United Kingdom, any British Dominion, the United States, or France.

Dominion and provincial securities with maturities of less than

[56] 24–25 Geo. V, c. 43, 5(1)(2), 9(1). [57] *Ibid.*, 13(1)(2)(4).

two years may be bought without limit. Where maturities exceed two years the Bank may not hold securities with a par value in excess of 50 percent of its outstanding note issue and deposit liabilities. Where maturities exceed ten years, the limit is a par value five times the paid-up capital and rest fund of the Bank.[58] Short-term securities of the United Kingdom, any British Dominion, or the United States may be bought without limit, but securities of the same countries with maturities beyond six months from acquisition by the Bank may not be bought if the par value of the Bank's holdings exceed one half its paid-up capital.[59]

In addition, the Bank may "buy and sell or rediscount bills of exchange and promissory notes endorsed by a chartered bank or issued in connection with the production or marketing of goods, wares, and merchandise as defined in the Bank Act." [60] Maturities for this type must not exceed 90 days; but transactions arising out of "section 88 paper" may run as long as 180 days. Where maturities exceed 90 days the Bank may by regulation limit its acquisitions to some fixed percentage of its total assets.[61]

The Bank may make loans to the chartered banks, the Quebec savings banks, the Dominion Government, or any provincial government. Loans to chartered banks may not run beyond six months. Loans beyond six months to the Dominion Government must not exceed one third of its estimated revenues for the fiscal year; and similar loans to the provinces must not exceed one quarter of their estimated total revenues for the same period. All these loans to governments must be repaid before the end of the borrowing government's fiscal year.[62]

The control implicit in central-bank rediscounting operations, especially in Canada, is made effective through open-market operations. For this purpose, the Bank may "buy and sell in the open market from or to any person, either in or outside Canada, securities, cable transfers, bankers' acceptances, and bills of exchange [subject to limitations already mentioned regarding types and maturities]." [63]

The "control" features of rediscounting and open-market operations are obvious enough in central-bank theory and experience; but the Bank is also empowered to accept Dominion and provincial gov-

[58] 24–25 Geo. V, c. 43, 21(1)(a)–(d).
[59] *Ibid.*, (e)(f).
[60] *Ibid.*, (g).
[61] *Ibid.*, (h).
[62] *Ibid.*, (i)–(k).
[63] *Ibid.*, (l).

ernment deposits,[64] and this, with its chartered-bank deposits,[65] gives the government, if not the Bank directly, additional power over chartered-bank cash. A shift of government deposits from the Bank of Canada to the chartered banks increases chartered-bank reserves and may therefore have a multiple-expansion effect on deposits. A shift of government deposits to the Bank of Canada decreases chartered-bank reserves and has a multiple-contraction effect on deposits.

WHAT THE BANK CANNOT DO

In contrast to the list of the Bank's powers, the list of prohibitions is brief. The Bank may not engage or have a direct interest in any trade or business; it may not buy its own stock or the stock of any other bank except the Bank for International Settlements, nor may it make loans on the security of bank stock; like the chartered banks it is forbidden to make advances on the security of real estate and immovables, except for additional security where the Bank's claims are endangered; it may not make unsecured loans, or accept deposits for a fixed term, or pay interest on deposits; and, finally, its renewal of maturing bills of exchange, promissory notes, etc., is limited to one, and then only "in special circumstances." [66]

MISCELLANEOUS DUTIES

The Bank of Canada, like other central banks, is required to act as fiscal agent for the Government of Canada, and may, by special agreement, do the same for the government of any province. The Bank may, and does, act also as agent for the Government of Canada in the management of the public debt.[67]

RESERVE REQUIREMENTS

As we have seen, the Bank now has the sole right of note issue.[68] Redemption of the Bank's notes in gold (400 oz. bars) was provided

[64] *Ibid.*, 21 (m). The Bank may also of course open accounts in other central banks or in the Bank for International Settlements and act in turn as depository or correspondent of these banks. *Ibid.*, (n).

[65] As mentioned earlier, required cash reserves against deposits and liabilities are 5 percent, to be held in currency or deposits in the Bank of Canada. Conventional reserves are approximately 10 percent.

[66] 24–25 Geo. V, c. 43, 22(a)–(f). The Bank may engage in some of these operations indirectly, through its wholly owned agency The Industrial Development Bank.

[67] *Ibid.*, 23 (2).

[68] *Ibid.*, 24(1).

for in the original Act; [69] but the Act also provided that the Governor in Council could "from time to time and for such period as he may deem desirable" suspend the Bank's obligation to redeem its currency in gold.[70] Gold payments were never in fact made by the Bank of Canada. The gold redemption clause in the Dominion Notes Act [71] had been suspended by an Order in Council, dated April 10, 1933, for one year.[72] Subsequent Orders in Council continued the suspension after the Dominion Notes Act was repealed (June 28, 1934) and sole note-issue power vested in the Bank of Canada.

Reserves against notes and deposit liabilities, formerly 25 percent in gold coin and bullion,[73] have not been required since May 1, 1940.[74] The Bank of Canada Act states: "The Bank shall . . . have the sole right to issue notes payable to bearer on demand and intended for circulation in Canada and may, subject to the provisions of section twenty-six of this Act [covering reserve requirements], issue such notes to any amount." [75] The suspension of the reserve requirement leaves the Bank with complete discretion regarding note issue and deposit liabilities.

OTHER MONETARY AND CREDIT INSTITUTIONS

There are a number of credit institutions whose function very closely approaches that of the chartered banks. For convenience, these may be divided into two main groups: (1) banks, "near-banks," and other lending institutions; and (2) instruments of government monetary and credit policy. The first group includes private and government-owned savings banks, along with credit unions, licensed small loans companies and moneylenders, trust companies, investment dealers, and insurance companies. The second group includes various "policy" institutions, all of which may perform some banking functions in the fields of foreign exchange, industrial, farm, and housing loans, and export credit.

69 *Ibid.*, 25(1).

70 *Ibid.*, 25(2).

71 R.S.C. 1927, c. 41, 4(3) as amended by 23–24 Geo. V, c. 12.

72 P.C. 664, April 10, 1933.

73 24–25 Geo. V, c. 43, 26(2).

74 An Order in Council, "The Exchange Fund Order" (P.C. 1734, 1940) relieved the Bank of the minimum reserve requirements at the same time that it transferred Bank of Canada gold and foreign exchange to the Exchange Fund Account administered by the Foreign Exchange Control Board.

75 24–25 Geo. V, c. 43, 24(1).

BANKS, NEAR-BANKS, AND OTHER LENDING INSTITUTIONS

In spite of the sharp legal distinctions drawn in the Bank Act and similar Dominion legislation, the banking function is exercised not only by the institutions specifically allowed to use the term "bank" in their corporate name, but by a host of other institutions which we have called "near-banks." The various savings banks, incorporated, like the Quebec savings banks, under Dominion law, are part of the legally defined realm of banking proper. So presumably are the Dominion Government's Post Office Savings Banks. Ontario's "Savings Offices," Alberta's "Treasury Branches," and the Newfoundland Savings Bank are the only corresponding institutions owned by the provinces; but, though they have been referred to in official literature as "Provincial Government Savings Banks," [76] they would seem to fall into a twilight zone between banking proper and the banking substitutes which we shall call "near-banks." Among the substitutes we include the credit unions, which have grown up in the last fifty years, and Canadian trust companies, licensed small loans companies, and licensed moneylenders. These institutions may be incorporated under Provincial law or they may be subject to regulations by special Dominion statute. Either way, they are beyond the purview of the Bank Act or similar statutes designed to regulate banking, even though they make loans and in many cases accept deposits subject to withdrawal by check.

1. *Savings Banks.*—The bulk of Canada's savings deposits are in the chartered banks. On September 30, 1953, chartered-bank savings deposits amounted to $5,226 million. Since these accounts, though formally "notice deposits," are conventionally subject to withdrawal by check, the Bank of Canada makes an estimate of average minimum quarterly balances to arrive at "true" savings deposits. This figure is added to non-personal notice deposits and published as "Inactive Chartered Bank Notice Deposits"; on September 30, 1953, these amounted to $4,371 million. The chartered banks are not allowed to call themselves savings banks, but they may operate and advertise their savings departments. Savings banks proper consist, as we have seen, of the Quebec savings banks, the Post Office Savings Banks, the "Treasury Branches" of Alberta, the "Savings Offices" of Ontario,

[76] *The Canada Year Book* (Ottawa, 1951), p. 1051.

and the Newfoundland Savings Bank.[77] On March 31, 1952, savings deposits in these institutions were approximately $340 million.

2. *Credit Unions.*—By far the most important of the near-banks are the credit unions. The first credit union in North America was organized on December 6, 1900, by Alphonse Desjardins at Lévis, Quebec. Other *caisses populaires* were soon founded in near-by Quebec towns; and, by the Co-operative Syndicates Act of 1906, the Quebec government provided for their incorporation. An attempt to secure similar legislation at the Dominion level failed in 1906–1907 when a bill passed by the House of Commons failed by one vote to pass in the Senate. However, the Co-operative Credit Associations Act providing for Dominion incorporation of credit unions received Royal assent on May 14, 1953. In 1922 Ontario followed Quebec in providing legislation for the incorporation of credit unions, and by 1939 all provinces had similar legislation on their books. By 1952 there were 3,335 credit unions in Canada, including Newfoundland, with 1,249,665 members and total assets of $424,564,711. Of these assets, loans to members against promissory notes were $106,367,836, loans against mortgages were $119,165,806, and the remaining large item, cash, was $55,913,807.[78]

A form of branch banking has been adopted by Canadian credit unions through their central credit unions. There are 23 central credit unions in Canada with 2,781 member credit unions.[79] In these central credit unions, surplus funds of the local credit unions are deposited for investment or for loans to other credit unions, cooperatives, school boards, municipalities, and similar borrowers. In this respect, the *caisses centrales* or *caisses regionales* in Quebec, and the central credit unions in other provinces, perform one of the functions of the head office in a chartered bank.

The central credit union also serves as a clearing center for checks drawn on its members. Here the central credit union makes use of the chartered banking machinery as well. Thus by agreement with a central credit union, say La Caisse Centrale Desjardins de Montréal,

[77] See note 8, above, for a discussion of the origin and legal history of the various kinds of savings banks.

[78] Department of Agriculture, *Credit Unions in Canada, 1952*, November, 1953, pp. 2, 14.

[79] *Ibid.*, p. 15. Figures for central credit unions include Newfoundland and Prince Edward Island, but these provinces did not report the number of member unions for 1950.

a chartered bank may negotiate checks drawn on the various affiliated *caisses populaires* subject to repurchases by La Caisse Centrale Desjardins de Montréal through a check drawn on its own account in the chartered bank. In some provinces, credit unions are given nonmember privileges in certain clearinghouse centers. This means that one of the chartered-bank members of the clearinghouse will represent a credit union and clear checks drawn on the union along with the chartered bank's own checks. Adjustment of the chartered bank's account with the credit union is then made by a debit to the credit union's account in the chartered bank.

3. *Licensed Small Loans Companies and Licensed Moneylenders.* —Small personal loans in Canada up to $500 are the concern of two groups of lenders licensed and regulated under the Small Loans Act of 1939: "licensed small loans companies," and "licensed money lenders." Both groups are regulated by the Superintendent of Insurance for Canada, who administers the act and reports yearly on their financial status to the Minister of Finance.

The four licensed small loans companies[80] are incorporated by special acts of parliament, the 55 licensed moneylenders are small corporations, partnerships, and individuals in the small-loan business. At the end of 1951 the licensed small loans companies had loans outstanding of $61,133,863 and total assets of $73,980,068. For the same years, the licensed moneylenders had small loans outstanding of $8,126,043 and total assets of $30,570,466. An item in the composite balance sheet of $20,980,983 representing "balances other than small loans" indicates that small loans are by no means the most important concern of the licensed moneylenders. The same item in the composite balance sheet of the licensed small loans companies was $8,933,116.[81] These other operations are not detailed in the published figure but are presumably loans over $500, including mortgage credit. The total of $69,259,906 extended by the licensed small loans companies and licensed moneylenders is probably a little less than the total for this type of credit extended by the chartered banking

[80] These are: Canadian Acceptance Company; Household Finance Corporation of Canada; Industrial Loan and Finance Corporation; and Personal Finance Company of Canada.

[81] Figures for small loans outstanding, etc., appear in *Report of the Superintendent of Insurance for Canada, Small Loans Companies and Money Lenders, for the Year Ended December 31, 1951* (Ottawa, 1953).

system;[82] but the chartered banks also finance small loans indirectly. In the small-loan business the chartered banks are wholesalers as well as retailers; the small loans companies and licensed moneylenders are retailers only. In December, 1951, the four licensed small loans companies owed $60,341,489, the fifty-five licensed moneylenders owed $21,397,938 under the heading "borrowed money."[83] Presumably all or the bulk of this total, $81,739,427, represented loans from the chartered banks.

4. *Loan and Trust Companies.*—Canadian loan and trust companies may be incorporated by the Dominion under the Loan Companies Act or the Trust Companies Act, respectively, or by special acts of provincial legislatures. Loan and trust companies incorporated by the Parliament of Canada and, by agreement, those incorporated by the legislatures of Nova Scotia, New Brunswick, and Manitoba are inspected by the Dominion Department of Insurance. Provincially incorporated trust companies other than those of Nova Scotia, New Brunswick, and Manitoba are directly under provincial authority; but they regularly make courtesy reports to the Department of Insurance so that Dominion-wide figures can be easily set up in summary form. At the end of 1951, total assets of the twenty trust companies incorporated by special act of Parliament or incorporated by the legislatures of Nova Scotia, New Brunswick, and Manitoba were $665,996,002. Total assets of the remaining provincially incorporated trust companies were $3,615,371,113. On the same date, total assets of the seven loan companies under Dominion supervision were $203,103,850; total assets for the remaining provincial companies were $147,268,620. Altogether the 48 Canadian loan and trust companies on December 31, 1951, had assets of $4,631,739,585.[84]

There are two reasons for classifying the loan and trust companies as "near-banks": (1) they are in the lending business; (2) certain trust companies accept deposits subject to withdrawal by check.

[82] There are no published figures for small loans ($500 or less) made by the chartered banks. An item, "personal loans," was $598.4 million in September, 1953, or about $96 million above December, 1952 (see Table 5). But this item is clearly dominated by loans to individuals for comparatively large amounts. An estimate of small loans based on the experience of one bank would put the small loans figure for all banks at about $60–$70 million.

[83] *Report of the Superintendent of Insurance . . . Small Loans Companies,* pp. 10, 42.

[84] *Report of the Superintendent of Insurance for Canada for the Year Ended December 31, 1951: Loan and Trust Companies* (Ottawa, 1953).

One aspect of loan and trust-company lending, mortgage credit, is as we have seen legally outside the purview of the Canadian chartered banks; but collateral loans at various terms and the purchase of bonds and debentures may approach very closely to some types of chartered-bank operations. Nevertheless, the slight relative importance of term lending by the chartered banks along with their legal inability to enter the field of mortgage credit make it possible to draw a fairly sharp line between the kind of loans made by loan and trust companies and the kind of loans made by the chartered banks.

The deposit business of the loan and trust companies approaches much more closely to what is generally understood as "banking." Legally the difference so far as trust companies are concerned is that banks are regarded as debtors to their depositors, even though the deposit liability carries with it certain safeguards that go beyond ordinary commercial debt; trust companies are regarded as the trustees for money deposited with them, even though many of their practical operations resemble the handling of ordinary deposit liabilities by the chartered banks.[85]

All deposits in loan and trust companies are savings deposits but, in Canada, this means that in practice they may in many cases be used as ordinary checking accounts. To the trust company, these savings deposits, though treated as ordinary liabilities in its balance sheet, must be invested in a limited list of securities, and these investments must be set aside and earmarked for the depositors. But to the ordinary depositor, who requires only a limited banking service, the only apparent difference in the service rendered by trust companies and banks in Canada are: (1) that trust companies allow a slightly higher rate of interest; and (2) that the "banking" hours of trust companies are longer and therefore more convenient.[86] These advantages, though locally important, are overwhelmed by the number and the convenient location of chartered-bank branch offices and

[85] See Winslow Benson, *Business Methods of Canadian Trust Companies* (Toronto, The Ryerson Press, 1949), pp. 8, 9.

[86] An even greater advantage from convenient banking hours is characteristic of savings-bank and credit-union competition with the chartered banks for the public's savings deposits. Here the offsetting advantages of the chartered banks are less in evidence. But, especially in Quebec where the credit-union movement is unusually strong owing to support by the Roman Catholic church, it is probable that many credit-union savings accounts represent a net increase in total savings. That is, in the absence of the credit-union movement, many depositors in credit unions would not be doing business with banks at all.

by the far greater range of banking services which each of these branches can supply.

5. *Stockbrokers and Investment Dealers.*—Stockbrokers in Canada are partnerships whose members are required by law to assume full personal responsibility for the obligations of the business. In the trading of corporate shares, usually as members of a recognized stock exchange, stockbrokers extend credit to clients against securities. These securities in turn are usually pledged to a chartered bank to cover the bank's call loans to brokers. Thus, again, the banks are in the position of wholesalers of credit, with the stockbrokers in this case taking care of credit at retail. This type of credit comes under central-bank control through the margin requirements fixed by agreement among the chartered banks, the exchanges, and the Bank of Canada. These requirements in turn affect the margin requirements set by the stock exchanges for their member brokers and applied by the brokers in making loans to clients.

Investment dealers are corporations with limited liability. They are often closely connected with brokerage houses and may have the same principals and very similar company names. These corporations underwrite and deal in government and corporate bonds and debentures. They may trade on their own account or on behalf of clients to whom they may extend credit in the ordinary course of business.

There is no exact counterpart in Canada of the "investment banker" in the United States; but the investment dealers provide the closest approach to it. There are no Dominion Government regulations covering investment dealers and the securities business generally. These matters are the concern of the provinces and legislation differs from province to province. Except for Ontario, the provinces do not provide any counterpart of the Federal Securities Exchange Commission (SEC) in the United States. Self-regulation takes the form of rules and regulations by the Investment Dealers Association of Canada. These rules and regulations are mainly concerned with ensuring uniform business practices and the financial solvency of members.

6. *Life Insurance Companies.*—Canadian life insurance companies and British companies operating in Canada are regulated, with like companies in other insurance fields, under the Canadian and British Insurance Companies Act of 1932.[87] Foreign life insurance companies,

[87] 22–23 Geo. V, c. 46, 1932.

and their counterparts in other insurance fields, are regulated by the Foreign Insurance Companies Act, 1932.[88]

Among lending institutions, life insurance companies in Canada are probably the furthest removed from chartered banking. They are the most important source of mortgage credit, a non-competitive field so far as the chartered banks are concerned. On December 31, 1951, the 52 (out of 83) life insurance companies making loans on real estate had $1,066,590,000 outstanding, out of a total for all lenders of $1,516,679,000.[89]

On December 31, 1951, the total assets of Canadian insurance companies were $4,888,658,312; of British companies, $155,002,189; and of foreign companies, $1,015,388,754. Of these total assets of $6,059,-049,255, real estate loans represented $1,102,665,124, policy loans $283,617,449, and bond and debenture holdings $4,017,471,808.[90] The heavy holdings of bonds and debentures in effect put the insurance companies into the term-lending field; but the relative insignificance of term lending by the chartered banks still leaves the life insurance companies in a largely non-competitive position so far as the activities of the chartered banks are concerned.

INSTRUMENTS OF GOVERNMENT MONETARY AND CREDIT POLICY

The Canadian government has established other agencies in the field of money and credit, some of which (for example, the Foreign Exchange Control Board) assist in matters of money and credit control, but most of which are designed to supply or encourage specific kinds of credit. We shall consider the Foreign Exchange Control Board, the Industrial Development Bank, Guaranteed Farm Improvement Loans, National Housing Loans, and Export Credits Insurance.

1. *The Foreign Exchange Control Board.*—The wartime Foreign Exchange Control Board was established by the Foreign Exchange Control Order of 1939 (under the War Measures Act).[91] Earlier, the

[88] *Ibid.*, c. 47, 1932.

[89] Central Mortgage and Housing Corporation, *Mortgage Lending in Canada* (Ottawa, 1953), p. 34. The other lending institutions included, with their outstanding mortgage loans, are: trust companies, $127,613,000; loan companies, $283,872,000; fraternal societies, including mutual benefit societies and pension fund associations, $32,998,000; and fire insurance companies, $5,606,000.

[90] *Abstract of Statements of Insurance Companies in Canada for the Year ended December 31, 1951* (Ottawa, 1952), p. 25A.

[91] Order in Council 2716, Sept. 15, 1939.

Exchange Fund Act of 1935 [92] had established the Special Exchange Fund Account for exchange stabilization purposes. The original funds of the Account represented the devaluation "profit" on the Bank of Canada's gold stock when the stock was revalued in January, 1934, at the "current market price" ($35 U.S. per ounce). This profit (approximately $50 million) [93] was credited by the Bank to the Special Exchange Fund Account held in the name of the Minister of Finance.

Originally, the Special Exchange Fund Account, like the British "Exchange Equalisation Account," had to work with a given supply of cash assets (gold) which could be changed in form through the purchase and sale of securities and foreign exchange, or changed in amount by profit and loss on transactions. But this period of self-contained operation ended with the Foreign Exchange Order of 1939.

The wartime Foreign Exchange Control Board inherited $83,876,-974.41, entirely in Canadian funds, from the Special Exchange Fund Account; and the Account henceforth became part of the control machinery under the administration of the Board. These original capital resources of the Board were increased in two ways: (1) through profits from exchange operations transferred to reserve ($49,321,-652.92 from September 15, 1939, to December 31, 1945); [94] and (2) through advances from the Dominion Government ($1,300 million as at December 31, 1945).[95] Net advances (minus repayments) amounted to $1,767,753,812 on December 31, 1951.[96]

The first of these advances ($325 million) was used to buy gold and foreign exchange (including $207 million of gold from the Bank of Canada) acquired under the Foreign Exchange Acquisition Order and the Exchange Fund Order.[97] Other advances were presumably used to buy the exchange resulting from heavy exports to the United States under the Hyde Park Declaration (April 20, 1941), and to buy gold from domestic producers. Since the war, net advances have varied directly with the gain or loss of gold and dollars or convertible exchange arising out of Canada's international transactions on current

92 25–26 Geo. V, c. 60. Assented to July 5, 1935.

93 Canada's gold reserves were $77 million in December, 1933, at the old parity; after revaluation (Jan. 31, 1934), they were $129.9 million. Board of Governors, Federal Reserve System, *Banking and Monetary Statistics,* pp. 545, 547.

94 Foreign Exchange Control Board, *Report to the Minister of Finance 1945* (Ottawa, 1946), p. 39.

95 *Ibid.*

96 *Ibid.,* 1950, p. 27.

97 Order in Council 1735, April 30, 1940, and Order in Council 1734, April 30, 1940.

and capital account, and inversely with the rise or fall of the Canadian dollar in terms of the currencies bought and sold by the board.

After the war, Canada's exchange control was put on a permanent basis through the Foreign Exchange Control Act of 1946.[98] The peacetime Foreign Exchange Control Board created by that act was in fact a continuation of the wartime Foreign Exchange Control Board. Its permanent personnel was supplied by officers of the Bank of Canada and its chairman was the Governor of the Bank.

From the beginning of wartime exchange control up to September, 1950, the chartered banks, described as "authorized dealers," acted merely as agents of the Foreign Exchange Control Board in buying and selling foreign exchange. That is, they bought and sold exchange on behalf of the Board in return for a fixed commission. Only in buying and selling foreign currency were the chartered banks free to take positions, or to marry purchases and sales, and then only at the prescribed rates, and presumably only in sufficient amounts to provide for ordinary till money. On September 30, 1950, the Canadian dollar was set free to find its own level in world markets; and henceforth the chartered banks, though they remained agents of the Board in implementing the controls that remained,[99] were allowed to buy and sell exchange on their own account and at their own risk.

On December 14, 1951, in an evening session of the House, the Minister of Finance announced the end of all remaining exchange controls effective the following day. The Foreign Exchange Control Act did not expire until 1953; but the regulations under the act were simply amended to exclude all classes of transactions from permit requirements. The Exchange Fund Account continued to operate under the Foreign Exchange Control Act until that act was repealed and a new Exchange Fund Act passed. This legislation had to be passed before the expiry of the Foreign Exchange Control Act; that is, not later than "sixty days after the commencement of the first session of Parliament commencing in the year 1953." [100] The new Currency,

98 10 Geo. VI, c. 53. Assented to Aug. 31, 1946; effective Jan. 1, 1947.

99 The statement issued Sept. 30, 1950, by the Honorable Douglas Abbott, Minister of Finance, contains the following paragraph on the duties of the banks: "Banks and other authorized agents will deal in foreign exchange as principals, but they will continue to act as official agents of the Foreign Exchange Control Board for the issue of permits and in other matters relating to exchange control. The general structure of exchange control remains unchanged, including control over securities transactions between residents and non-residents and control over payments of Canadian dollars to non-residents."

100 Department of External Affairs, *Canadian Weekly Bulletin*, Vol. VII.

Mint and Exchange Fund Act was given Royal assent on July 4, 1952 (1 Elizabeth II, c. 40).

2. *The Industrial Development Bank.*—The Industrial Development Bank was created in 1944 by the Industrial Development Bank Act.[101] Its purpose, as set forth in the preamble to that act, was

> to promote the economic welfare of Canada by increasing the effectiveness of monetary action through ensuring the availability of credit to industrial enterprises which may reasonably be expected to prove successful if a high level of national income and employment is maintained, by supplementing the activities of other lenders and by providing capital assistance to industry with particular consideration to the financing problems of small enterprises.

In effect this has meant the provision of loans by the Bank to borrowers who (1) want credit at longer term than the chartered banks are prepared to go; and (2) have too meager an earnings record to satisfy an insurance company.

The authorized capital of the Bank is $25 million divided into 250,000 shares of $100 each. All shares are subscribed by the Bank of Canada; and the Governor of the Bank of Canada is the President of the Industrial Development Bank.

Gross authorizations for loans and guarantees from the beginning of business on November 1, 1944, to September 30, 1952, were $80,833,595. Cancellations and reductions of authorizations, repayments and write-offs, and other reductions due to partial repayments and write-downs left net authorizations for September 30, 1952, at $40,742,701. Of these $33,629,575 were outstanding.[102]

The management of the Bank feels that the Bank performs a service beyond that reflected in its figures for loans and guarantees. This appears not only in its help to borrowers in difficulties but in making the way smoother for new enterprises seeking credit through private commercial channels. The willingness of the Industrial Development Bank to accommodate a new enterprise, through direct loan, guarantee of a private loan, or participation with a private lender, may make it easier for the enterprise in question to finance entirely through private lenders. On a number of occasions, however, the Industrial Development Bank has taken over accounts which the

[101] 8 Geo. VI, c. 44.

[102] Industrial Development Bank, *Annual Report to the Minister of Finance,* fiscal year 1952, p. 7.

chartered banks were unwilling or unable to accommodate. Advances or guarantees have been made to these enterprises under the Industrial Development Bank Act, Section 19, which corresponds to Section 88 of the Bank Act.[103]

3. *Farm Improvement and National Housing Loans.*—Certain loans for farm improvement and housing are eligible for government guarantee. The chartered banks are directly affected by the guarantee of farm improvement loans; mortgage lenders of various kinds are directly but not exclusively affected by the guarantee of loans for housing construction and improvement. Guarantees under the housing program are administered by a special government agency, the Central Mortgage and Housing Corporation.[104]

Farm Improvement loans eligible for guarantees are defined in the Farm Improvement Loans Act of 1944.[105] Eligible loans may not be for sums larger than $3,000 for each borrower, for terms longer than ten years, or at rates higher than 5 percent simple interest per year. The guarantee against loss is limited to 10 percent of the "aggregate principal amount" of the eligible farm improvement loans made by a chartered bank during each of three three-year periods from March 1, 1945, to February 28, 1954.[106] The period of guarantee, originally only three years, has been extended a further six years by two amendments; but the last amendment has a provision that cuts off guarantees on farm improvement loans made after the total for all banks during the period March 1, 1951, to February 28, 1954, goes beyond $200,000.

A bank making a guaranteed farm improvement loan over $2,000 with a repayment period longer than five years may, in spite of the Bank Act, take a mortgage on the borrower's farm or an assignment of the borrower's rights to a farm under an agreement of sale.[107]

In regard to National Housing loans the aim of the National Housing Act of 1944,[108] as stated in its preamble, is: "to promote construction of new houses, the repair and modernization of existing houses, the improvement of housing and living conditions and the expansion of employment in the postwar period." The act provides for loans to homeowners, landlords, and farmers, for new construc-

103 *Ibid.*, fiscal year 1950, p. 5.

104 Established under the Central Mortgage and Housing Corporation Act of 1945: 9–10 Geo. VI, c. 15.

105 8 Geo. VI, c. 41 (as amended by 11 Geo. VI, c. 34, and 11–12 Geo. VI, c. 9).

106 *Ibid.*, 3, 4.

107 *Ibid.*, 7.

108 8 Geo. VI, c. 46 (as amended by 9–10 Geo. VI, c. 26; 10 Geo. VI, c. 61; 11 Geo. VI, c. 40; 11–12 Geo. VI, c. 63; and 13 Geo. VI, c. 30).

tion, or for the improvement and extension of existing homes. Loans on new construction are made by the Central Mortgage and Housing Corporation jointly with "approved lending institutions" (life insurance, trust, and loan companies, approved by the Governor in Council). The joint loan to a homeowner, which is secured by a first mortgage on the property, must not be more than 80 percent of the value of the house; and of this not more than 25 percent will be advanced by the Central Mortgage and Housing Corporation. However, the Central Mortgage and Housing Corporation will make an additional loan of not more than one sixth of the joint loan, if the cost of the house to the homeowner seems to the Corporation to be "fair and reasonable." [109] Similar loans may be made to cooperatives.[110]

In addition to loans under the act, private builders of houses for sale may enter into contracts with the Corporation whereby houses built with the aid of housing loans shall sell at an agreed price. If a builder with a contract fails to sell a house within a year, the Corporation will buy the house at the price agreed on in the contract. Builders of rental housing may make similar contracts to guarantee for as much as 30 years an annual return up to 85 percent of the rental value maximum fixed by the Corporation for the first three years of operation.

Losses on joint loans are initially shared in the proportion which the Corporation's share bears to that of the approved lending institution, then the Corporation pays the lending institution an agreed amount on its losses within a given class of joint loans. Payments under the guarantee provision must not be greater than 15 percent of the lending institution's share of all joint loans within any given class of joint loans.[111]

The chartered banks enter the picture directly only where home-improvement and extension loans are made under the act.[112] These loans are made by chartered banks or by approved installment credit agencies.

In addition to certain formal requirements, guaranteed home-improvement loans must not be for amounts greater than $2,500 for a one-family house, or, in the case of multiple housing units, $2,500 for the first family unit and $1,200 for each additional unit. Guaran-

[109] *Ibid.*, Part I, 4(2)(c), (3). [110] *Ibid.*, Part I, 4(6).

[111] *Ibid.*, 4(2)(1). Classes of joint loans are defined by agreement between the Corporation and approved lending institutions.

[112] *Ibid.*, Part IV.

teed home-extension loans must not be for amounts greater than $3,750 for the first family unit added and $1,250 for each additional unit. Neither type of loan may run longer than five years, and the maximum term is three years for loans of $1,250 or less. The maximum interest rate allowed is 5 percent per year, unless the borrower is in default.

A chartered bank or an approved installment-credit agency making home-improvement or home-extension loans is guaranteed against loss up to five percent of their aggregate amount for that bank or installment agency.

From February 1, 1945, to December 31, 1952, net loans approved for all purposes under the National Housing Act of 1944 amounted to $1,034,005,000.[113]

4. *Export Credits Insurance.*—Export credit is guaranteed in Canada by the Export Credits Insurance Corporation, established in 1944 by the Export Credits Insurance Act.[114] The Corporation consists at any time of the current Deputy Minister of Trade and Commerce, the Deputy Minister of Finance, and the Governor of the Bank of Canada. The Board of Directors of the Corporation consists of the members and not more than four others appointed from time to time by the Governor in Council, one of whom is appointed General Manager of the Corporation. The Corporation's total authorized capital is $5,000,000, consisting of 50,000 shares at $100 each, all subscribed for by the Minister of Finance. In addition, as the subscription is paid up, an equal amount is paid in by the Minister to be credited to capital and surplus account.

The Export Credits Insurance Act is divided into two parts: Part I dealing with export credits insurance proper; and Part II dealing with loans to foreign governments and guarantees of foreign-government obligations to Canadian exporters. The Export Credits Insurance Corporation enters into the insurance contracts under Part I, and acts as agent for the Minister of Finance in making loans and guarantees under Part II.

The Corporation's total liability under insurance contracts must not be more than ten times its paid-up capital and surplus, except where the Governor in Council decides that contracts otherwise inap-

[113] Central Mortgage and Housing Corporation, *Annual Report to the Minister of Resources and Development*, 1952 (Ottawa, 1953), p. 51.

[114] 8 Geo. VI, c. 39; since amended by 10 Geo. VI, c. 49, and 11–12 Geo. VI, c. 17.

propriate in term and amount are in the national interest.[115] The maximum liability under these special contracts is $100,000,000. The Governor in Council may authorize the Minister of Finance to lend the Corporation amounts up to five times the paid-up capital and surplus of the Corporation; [116] and liabilities incurred from special contracts in the national interest are to be paid to the Corporation by the Minister of Finance. All receipts of the Corporation by way of payments for stock, paid-in capital and surplus, loans, or payments of special liabilities incurred in the national interest, come from unappropriated money in the Consolidated Revenue Fund.

From the beginning of the program to December 31, 1952, receipts from premiums were $1,589,847; operating expenses plus claims paid (less recoveries) were $1,702,788; and the deficit on operations was accordingly $112,941. This amount was lost on insured export sales amounting to $211,420,135.[117]

Guarantees outstanding under Part II of the act were limited at any time to $200,000,000; loans outstanding plus security purchases were similarly limited to $750,000,000. New loans and guarantees could not be made under the act after January 1, 1948. Total lines of credit actually established under the loan program amounted to $594.5 million, of which the larger part, $460.3 million, was still outstanding on March 31, 1953. Out of the $200,000,000 authorized, only $16.2 million in guarantees were actually given, over the period during which commitments could be made.[118]

THE BANKING SYSTEM IN ACTION

As in many other countries, Canada's chartered banks have been forced to adapt in recent years to a rapidly changing economic environment. What passed for postwar "normalcy" after the First World War lapsed into deep depression during the early 1930s; and the movement to recovery apparent in the late 1930s was soon caught up in the rush and pressure of the war economy. The peculiar problems

115 *Ibid.*, Sec. 14, 20a.

116 *Ibid.*, Sec. 15.

117 Export Credits Insurance Corporation, *Annual Report and Financial Statements*, Dec. 31, 1952, p. 6.

118 Canada, Department of Finance, Report on Operations under Part II of the Export Credits Insurance Act during the Fiscal Year 1948–49 (Ottawa, 1949), p. 2; *ibid.*, 1950–51, p. 3; and *ibid.*, 1952–53, p. 3.

of the period immediately following the Second World War brought with them further problems of adaptation, made all the more difficult after June, 1950, by the grim possibility that the most significant orientation of today's economy might be not "postwar" but "prewar."

DEPOSITS

Chartered-bank deposits are classified as either "demand" or "notice." [119] The legal distinction that accompanies this familiar classification is not reflected in any practical difference. Except for a small amount of deposit receipts outstanding, all deposits may function as checking accounts with no restriction on any form of withdrawal. In the average year, notice deposits are well over one half of total deposits; but, with the actual treatment accorded notice deposits, this does not guarantee any significant difference in liquidity requirements.[120]

There was at least a formal difference in treatment between notice and demand deposits, from the point of view of bank earnings, owing to the gentlemen's agreement of March, 1946, among the chartered banks limiting a chartered bank's holdings of Dominion Government bonds to 90 percent of its savings deposits, and its earnings on this investment to "a moderate profit margin" over the operating costs on savings deposits.[121]

This agreement was canceled on March 1, 1952, in recognition of the marked rise in bank loans and non-government security holdings relative to holdings of government bonds. At the time of cancellation, government bond holdings for all banks were only 56 percent of

[119] "Notice deposits," as classified by the Bank of Canada, are also referred to as "time deposits" by the chartered banks, and as "deposits payable after notice or on a fixed day" in the official return of the chartered banks to the Minister of Finance. They include personal savings deposits, against which the banks reserve but do not exercise the right to fifteen days notice of withdrawal, and non-personal notice deposits which pay an agreed rate of interest on special corporate deposits left with the bank for an agreed minimum length of time.

[120] The Bank of Canada's estimate of the "active notice deposits" runs a little over one sixth of total notice deposits. The active figure represents "chartered bank public notice deposits in Canada other than estimated aggregate quarterly minimum balances in personal savings accounts and non-personal notice deposits." Bank of Canada, *Statistical Summary*, February, 1952, p. 21, note 4.

[121] The formula was that total return from investment in government bonds less (1) the cost of handling the deposits including interest and overhead, and (2) the cost of investing the funds, must not be more than .30 percent of the funds so invested.

savings deposits, compared with 82 percent in 1946, and the agreed limit of 90 percent.[122]

The growth of deposits over recent years is shown in Table 3. Total deposits are now over three times prewar, and, except for minor fluctuations in certain months, have shown a continuous upward trend since the Second World War. One of the most notable increases over the 1930s is in government deposits. A shift of Dominion Government deposits from the chartered banks to the central bank means a direct reduction of chartered-bank cash reserves; a shift in the opposite direction means a direct increase in chartered-bank cash reserves. Thus the movement of these deposits has become an auxiliary method of control over chartered-bank cash and hence over the lending policies of the chartered banks.

TABLE 3

DEPOSITS IN CHARTERED BANKS, SELECTED YEARS 1929–52 (AVERAGE OF MONTH-END FIGURES)

(AMOUNTS IN MILLIONS OF CANADIAN DOLLARS)

Year	*Demand*	*Notice*	*Government of Canada and Provinces*	*Foreign*	*Total Deposits* [a]
1929	696	1,480	102	418	2,837
1932	486	1,376	82	312	2,322
1937	691	1,574	90	421	2,840
1948	2,259	3,972	355	817	7,567
1949	2,353	4,334	490	744	8,106
1950	2,563	4,548	380	731	8,449
1951	2,712	4,593	399	761	8,755
1952	2,932	4,811	333	824	9,167

Source: Dominion Bureau of Statistics, *Canadian Statistical Review*, 1953 Supplement, p. 136.

[a] Includes interbank deposits.

INVESTMENTS

The chartered banks are directly involved in the investment market as traders in bonds and debentures, and as substantial purchasers on their own account. Trading departments are operated in the principal cities; and markets for government issues, and sometimes for the more important municipal and corporate issues, are maintained. However, the Bank Act prohibits[123] the use of the bank's name in any

[122] Department of Finance, *Press Release*, March 1, 1952.

[123] 8 Geo. VI, c. 30, 161(2).

prospectus or advertisement for the sale of bonds, debentures, or shares of any kind other than those issued by or guaranteed as to principal and interest by the Dominion Government.

1. *Legal Restrictions.*—As we have seen, chartered banks are allowed to deal in and lend money on (among other things) stocks, bonds, debentures, and obligations of municipal and other corporations, whether secured by mortgage or otherwise, or of Dominion, provincial, British, foreign, and other public securities.[124] However, there is still the general prohibition (except under Sections 86 and 88 of the Bank Act) against making advances upon the security, mortgage, or hypothecation of any lands, tenements, or immovable property, or of any ships or other vessels, or upon the security of any goods, wares, and merchandise.[125] Applied to the investment portfolio, this is generally taken to mean that first mortgage bonds or debentures secured by a floating charge on assets may not be bought directly from the issuer; but that bonds or debentures of this sort may be bought from an investment dealer in the ordinary course of business.

2. *Other Restrictions.*—The legal restrictions on bank investment are not onerous; but, for obvious reasons, stocks are not an important factor in the banks' investment portfolios. Indeed, in all investments, including fixed-interest securities, liquidity takes precedence over yield. Funds available for investment by the chartered banks are determined by the excess of deposits over loans, less the required cash reserves; and the character of these deposits is of prime importance in formulating investment policy. Moreover, the treatment of notice deposits as ordinary checking accounts means that liquidity requirements are high for all deposits, and the banks are characteristically therefore in a short-term position.

3. *The Portfolio.*—During 1950, 22.3 percent of the chartered banks' total investment portfolios were in Dominion and provincial government short-term securities, 63.8 percent in longer-term governments (probably averaging 6 to 7 years), and only 13.9 percent in all other types. About one third of the short-term governments were in the form of Treasury Bills and Deposit Certificates. The absolute figures, from which these relatives may be calculated, appear in Table 4.

Until 1952 the banks' short-term government holdings included up to $450 million in 91-day Treasury Bills. These were turned over at

124 *Ibid.*, 75(1)(c).

125 *Ibid.*, 75(1)(d).

TABLE 4

INVESTMENT PORTFOLIO, LOAN PORTFOLIO, AND TOTAL ASSETS, CANADIAN CHARTERED BANKS, DECEMBER 31, SELECTED YEARS, 1929–51

(AMOUNTS IN MILLIONS OF CANADIAN DOLLARS)

	INVESTMENTS				LOANS				
Year	*Government of Canada*	*Provincial*	*Foreign Governments*	*Municipal and Corporate*	*Canada*	*Abroad*	*Cash in Canada* [a]	*Other Assets*	*Total Assets*
1929	297		151		1,787	496	228	562	3,521
1932	562		216		1,207	243	211	413	2,852
1937	1,111		59	242	938	226	250	456	3,281
1949	3,112	445	242	545	2,404	281	753	935	8,718
1950	3,079	416	193	599	2,910	347	810	1,143	9,496
1951	2,754	355	200	567	3,135	409	892	1,298	9,610
January	3,054	401	188	605	2,913	365	757	1,096	9,379
February	2,887	398	190	618	2,981	370	753	1,147	9,354
March	2,801	373	210	601	3,102	348	738	1,110	9,284
April	2,742	368	208	607	3,134	368	759	1,218	9,403
May	2,720	370	190	606	3,158	380	745	1,201	9,370
June	2,681	366	192	598	3,144	391	768	1,115	9,256
July	2,696	356	195	594	3,127	397	784	1,175	9,323
August	2,679	355	210	588	3,163	381	770	1,232	9,378
September	2,743	353	208	581	3,152	404	775	1,069	9,276
October	2,726	342	226	582	3,145	372	821	1,263	9,440
November	2,744	357	214	578	3,210	375	829	1,136	9,544
December	2,754	355	200	567	3,135	409	892	1,299	9,610

Source: Bank of Canada, *Statistical Summary*, January, 1952.

[a] Until March, 1935: gold and coin in Canada, Dominion notes and "free" central gold reserve deposits; after that date: Bank of Canada notes and deposits.

the rate of $75 million every two weeks. The Bank of Canada absorbed the unsold balance of each issue; and the precise amount held by the chartered banks was, therefore, unknown. In addition, the Bank of Canada bought and sold Treasury Bills between dates of issue at approximately the going rate.

Beginning January 29, 1953, tenders were called weekly on $50 million of Treasury Bills: $40 million in 91-day Bills and $5 million each in 182-day and 273-day Bills. This increased the total outstanding by April 24, 1953, from the original $450 million to $650 million. Once this amount was reached, tenders were reduced to $40 million per week: $35 million in 91-day Bills and $5 million in 273-day Bills. The new system provided 39 maturity dates instead of the previous six, and was intended to increase the attractiveness of Treasury Bills to banks and other investors.

Up to May, 1953, other short-term holdings were made up of Deposit Certificates and Treasury Notes. Deposit Certificates were issued for 6 months, and successive issues varied considerably in amount and in rate. For example:

Dated	*Maturity*	*Amount*	*Rate*
March 1, 1950	August 30, 1950	$100,000,000	0.750
August 30, 1950	February 28, 1951	300,000,000	0.875
February 28, 1951	August 29, 1951	200,000,000	1.000

On May 15, 1953, the $200 million in Deposit Certificates outstanding were retired, being replaced by the $200 million in additional Treasury Bills. Treasury Notes outstanding on December 31, 1953, amounted to $750,000,000, carried a rate of 2.25 percent, and all were held by the Bank of Canada.

During 1953, Bank of Canada holdings of short-term governments averaged about $1,400 million (January–October). Chartered bank holdings averaged a little over $1,000 million for the same period. On October 31, 1953, the Bank of Canada held $2,282 million in Dominion and provincial debt of all maturities, against $3,045 million held by the chartered banks.

4. *The Banks and the Bond Market.*—The figures just given are some indication of the Bank of Canada's importance in the bond market. The Bank can establish bids and offer prices, or withhold bids and offerings, and thus control fairly closely the general level of government-bond prices and hence the general level of interest rates.

But within the general environment created by Bank of Canada policy there is room for various degrees of competitive action depending in each case upon the type of security.

a) *Municipal and provincial securities.* The municipal and provincial bond market operates freely on a basis of competitive bidding for most new issues and of direct trading among chartered banks, investment dealers, and institutional buyers and sellers. The general practice in marketing new issues is for syndicates, composed of dealers and sometimes a chartered bank, to tender in competition with each other. For the larger cities and for the provinces, special syndicates of many dealers and as many as three banks are usually set up on a stand-by basis to handle any issue that would be too large for the smaller syndicate to handle.

The chartered banks participate in various syndicates, both as underwriting partners and as purchasers of some or all of the shorter-term debentures. Purchases by chartered banks are usually limited to maturities up to ten years, the time to maturity depending on portfolio requirements and the credit standing of the issuer. The banks may in this way have some influence on the bond market; for the price that the banks will pay for the "shorts" will have an important bearing on the syndicates' bid for the whole issue.

b) *Corporate securities.* Competitive bidding for corporate issues is less common than competitive bidding for municipal and provincial issues. The larger corporations generally have arrangements with an investment house for advice and assistance in obtaining capital requirements. The number of investment dealers taken into the underwriting groups will depend upon the amount involved. Again, when a serial issue is contemplated, the corporation's bankers will, as a matter of course, be given an opportunity to buy the "shorts." Small companies, with little or no experience in the raising of funds in the market, may make the initial approach to their bankers who, in turn, will take the matter to an investment house and the process will continue from there in the usual way.

c) *Loans.* The trend of chartered-bank loans in Canada [126] has been steadily upward since the Second World War. But the war years showed some decline relative to the best years in the 1930s; and even

[126] Includes current and call loans to borrowers in Canada including individuals, business firms, provincial and municipal governments, school districts, religious, educational, health and welfare institutions.

the postwar years show some decline compared with prewar years in the ratio of loans in Canada to total bank assets. The figures in Table 5 show the changes in the total amount of loans over selected years, the corresponding changes in total bank assets, bank loans as percentages of total bank assets in various years, and the distribution of loans among various types of private and governmental borrowers.

As Table 5 shows, by far the greater part of chartered-bank loans is made to individuals and private firms in agriculture and industry. These current loans are significant not only in their contribution to Canada's economy but, rightly or wrongly, their rapid rise during the last half of 1950 was blamed for at least part of the rise in inflationary pressure that followed the outbreak of war in Korea. We shall concentrate first on changes in the volume of loans and the short-run problem of inflation during post-Korean defense and rearmament; and, second, on the types of loans made and their long-run role in Canada's expanding economy.

Bank Loans and Inflation.—During 1950 total loans in Canada increased from $2,404 million to $2,910 million, or 21 percent. During the same period the cost of living index rose 10 points, from 161 to 171.1; and the wholesale price index rose 24 points, from 203.8 to 227.9.

The increase in the price indices and, to a large extent, the increase in bank loans were symptomatic of the "real" inflationary factors some of which are reflected also in certain other figures in the national accounts. For example, a large part of the increase in the gross national product from $16,383 million in 1949 to $17,693 million in 1950 took the form of increased inventories. Inventories increased by $785 million over the year, and made up the major part of a rise in gross home investment from $3,069 million to $3,908 million. Personal expenditure on consumer goods and services rose $663 million to $11,810 million for the year, and government expenditure on goods and services rose $205 million, to reach $2,333 million.

One deflationary factor during 1950 was an excess of merchandise and service imports over exports amounting to $316 million for the year. Nevertheless, the total effect of Canada's international transactions was to increase inflationary pressure: the current-account deficit of $316 million was overwhelmed by an inflow of capital, largely from the United States, amounting to over a billion dollars.

TABLE 5

CHARTERED BANK LOANS, SELECTED YEARS 1935–53

(AMOUNTS IN MILLIONS OF CANADIAN DOLLARS)

	OCTOBER 31			SEPTEMBER 30				
	1935	*1937*	*1945*	*1947*	*1950*	*1951*	*1952*	*1953*
Government and Other Public Services								
Provincial governments	26.8	26.4	11.5	20.6	23.6	24.9	6.3	10.6
Municipal governments and school districts	107.4	94.2	20.2	43.9	91.5	114.5	102.4	109.4
Religious, educational, health, and welfare institutions	16.1	16.4	6.4	13.5	33.1	45.9	43.3	47.1
Total	153.9	137.0	38.1	78.0	148.2	185.3	152.0	167.1
Financial								
Investment dealers and brokers call to 30 days	66.7	73.5	130.6	83.9	101.2	107.1	135.2	110.1
Trust, loan, mortgage, investment, and insurance companies, etc.	52.1	43.7	22.9	38.0	86.0	91.7	107.5	122.6
Total	118.8	117.2	153.5	121.9	187.2	198.8	242.7	232.7
Personal (total)	136.3	189.1	345.1	359.4	461.6	466.9	502.3	598.4
Agricultural, Industrial and Commercial								
Farmers	59.9	57.5	71.3	147.3	255.8	298.9	334.2	354.0
Industry	201.8	229.5	269.8	533.9	584.7	888.0	812.8	958.8
Public utilities, transportation, and communications	71.3	11.9	7.8	42.5	53.9	87.9	67.5	61.7
Construction contractors	24.1	32.1	47.4	93.9	122.7	151.8	158.7	175.0
Grain dealers and exporters	166.4	30.8	109.5	67.9	93.1	98.6	186.5	310.7
Installment finance companies	13.3	28.5	11.3	65.7	96.5	100.8	149.4	249.3
Merchandisers	115.9	130.2	157.6	359.9	436.1	542.9	484.0	595.8
Other business	17.1	16.8	28.0	67.8	135.5	133.8	139.0	179.4
Total	669.8	537.3	702.7	1,378.9	1,778.3	2,302.7	2,332.1	2,884.7
Total loans in Canada	1,067.6	980.6	1,139.5	1,938.2	2,575.3	3,153.7	3,229.1	3,882.9
Total assets of chartered banks	3,059.0	3,299.0	6,640.0	7,782.0	9,162.0	9,276.0	9,907.0	10,398.0
Loans as percentage of total assets	34.9	29.7	17.1	24.9	28.1	34.0	32.6	37.3

Source: Bank of Canada, *Statistical Summary,* December, 1950, pp. 207, 208; January, 1952, pp. 5, 6; October, 1953, pp. 163, 167.

As a result, Canada's official liquid reserves of gold and convertible exchange rose by $695 million; or, valued in U.S. dollars, Canada's reserves of gold and U.S. dollars rose $625 million to reach a total of $1,741.7 million at the end of 1950.

Government measures to reduce inflationary pressure through monetary and credit policy took two forms: (1) measures to reduce expenditures by business and consumers; and (2) measures to neutralize the effect of the capital inflow. Both kinds of anti-inflationary measures affected directly or indirectly the activities of Canada's chartered banks.

Domestic Policy.—On the domestic-policy side, three general lines of attack may be distinguished: a move to curtail expenditure on capital and consumption goods by making credit more expensive through *higher interest rates;* a move to check consumer expenditure on durable goods by the *direct curtailment of consumer credit;* and a reinforcement of both lines of attack through Bank of Canada policy.

1. The move to harden interest rates began as early as August, 1950, with the voluntary increase by the Bank of Canada of its rate on Treasury Bills. Later, on October 17, 1950, the Bank of Canada's rediscount rate, or "bank rate" was raised from 1.5 percent to 2 percent.[127] Both rises were important chiefly as indicators of Bank of Canada policy regarding the desired trend of interest rates in general. Bank rate, especially, had little direct significance, owing to the complete absence of chartered-bank borrowing or rediscounting with the Bank of Canada. However, the moderate firming of short-term rates was followed by a significant increase in long-term rates brought about by lowering the pegged price support in the government-bond market. During November, 1950, the long-term government bond market turned soft, and the Bank of Canada allowed the prices to slip so that the yield rose from around 2.75 percent to slightly over 3 percent by December 31. By August, 1951, prices had slipped further; and long-term governments were selling to yield 3.21 percent instead of the 2.75 percent yield ruling in August, 1950. The price of provincial-government and corporate securities followed the trend in government bonds, and yields rose accordingly. The change in yields over the period appears in Table 6.

[127] Bank rate had been 15 percent since Feb. 8, 1944. Before that date it had been 2.5 percent.

TABLE 6
COMPARISON OF BOND YIELDS, 1950–52

Bonds	August, 1950	February, 1951	April, 1951	August, 1951	January, 1952
	SELLING TO YIELD (IN PERCENT)				
Dominion of Canada (long term)	2.75	3.05	3.18	3.21	3.45
Provincial (Ontario and Quebec)	3.00	3.30	3.55	3.50	3.95
Municipal, top grade	3.35	3.60	4.10	4.10	4.30
Corporate	3.50–3.75	3.60–4.00	4.50–5.00	4.50–5.00	4.50–4.75

The rise in bond yields was reflected in a general firming of interest rates, including some of the loan rates of the chartered banks, but the banks' prime rate to corporations remained unchanged at 4.5 percent. The effect of a rise in the rate would have been to raise the cost of working capital to business; and, though probably not a significant deterrent to plant expansion, such a rise would raise the "cost of carrying stocks," that is, it would tend to discourage the holding of inventories against an expected price rise. However, even in the absence of any general rise in rates to borrowers, the Bank of Canada's rate policy did have a direct effect on the liquidity of the chartered banks and the public generally. The purchase of government bonds by the Bank of Canada at a pegged price above par meant that the Bank was forced to pump money into the market whenever the banks or the public chose to turn government bonds into cash. The large holdings of government bonds by the banks and the public were in effect completely liquid assets; and efforts to curb inflation were nullified because an attempt to reduce the money supply through high taxes relative to government expenditure could be offset by an increase in the money supply brought about by the sale of government securities to the Bank of Canada at the pegged price.

In other words, with a pegged price for government bonds (even though the "peg" was unofficial and slightly movable) the initiative in central-bank open-market operations lay with the public, not with the central bank; and, as cash tended to become scarce owing to the government's fiscal policy, the public replenished its cash by selling bonds to the central bank. Only with a removal of the peg could the initiative be returned to the central bank, so that open-market operations could be used to support rather than offset a deflationary fiscal policy. With the removal of the peg, two desired effects were achieved:

holders of government bonds were discouraged from selling, owing to the immediate capital loss they would suffer; and purchasers of government bonds on private account were encouraged to buy at the lower price and hold the bonds to maturity, in order to realize the new higher yield.

2. The direct control of consumer credit took the form of regulations issued October 25, 1950, by Order in Council under the Consumer Credit (Temporary Provisions) Act assented to September 15, 1950. The October regulations were revised on January 10, 1951, by an Order in Council under the same act revoking the October order and establishing more rigorous and detailed regulations effective February 1. A further revision was made by Order in Council, dated July 18, 1951, and effective August 1, revoking the January order and providing for even more rigorous restriction by plugging loopholes available through rental contracts and by requiring larger down payments and shorter periods of repayment for certain classes of goods. These controls were removed by an Order in Council effective May 6, 1952.[128]

In general, consumer goods were defined to be: (1) motor vehicles; (2) coupons, certificates and other documents entitling the holder to delivery of consumer goods; and (3) all goods not included in group 1 or group 2.

Loans and conditional sales contracts for the purchase of motor vehicles required a minimum down payment of 50 percent, with the balance payable in 12 months. Goods in groups 2 and 3 required a 33 1/3 percent down payment with the balance payable in 6 months for group 2 and 12 months for group 3. Minimum installments (except the last one, if the balance were smaller than the minimum) were $2.50 weekly or $10 monthly. Loans could not be made if the proceeds were to be used to buy, at retail, goods covered in the regulations or to make payments on these goods unless the regulations regarding maximum loan values and minimum payments and terms were met.

Certain goods were excepted under the regulations. The most important exceptions were books, mechanical and other aids to physical infirmity or disability, motor vehicles used for business purposes, and goods in group 3 used for business or by a religious, charitable, or educational institution.

Certain borrowers did not need to conform to the installment re-

[128] Hansard, May 5, 1952, p. 1855.

quirements under the regulations, provided the loan did not run beyond the period set for the class of goods bought. This exception applied to farmers, fishermen, and others engaged in extractive industry and, with certain stipulations, to others whose incomes vary seasonally over the year. The regulations on loans did not apply to borrowers who declared in writing that the proceeds would not be used to buy consumer goods; to loans made for agricultural purposes upon the security of agricultural equipment, implements, or a farm electric system as defined in the Bank Act and the Farm Improvement Loans Act; to loans secured wholly or partly by a mortgage on real property or secured by stocks, bonds, debentures, cash surrender value of insurance policies, or cash collateral; or to loans made by a pawnbroker on the security of the goods pawned.

3. In February, 1951, the Bank of Canada took the initiative in restricting bank credit by restricting chartered-bank cash, and by launching a program in cooperation with the chartered banks to limit advances so far as possible to "essential" industries and to limit total advances to the amount outstanding on a target date, fixed at February 28, 1951. The removal of consumer credit controls on May 6, 1952, was followed by the cancellation, effective May 20, of the credit restriction program of the chartered banking system, with the single exception of the higher margin requirements for carrying corporate stocks.

The restriction of chartered-bank cash is the natural counterpart of a higher interest-rate policy; but, for a short time at the beginning of the program, cash became especially short owing to the reluctance of the Bank of Canada to buy long-term government bonds from bank portfolios. That is, the Bank of Canada would buy bonds coming to the chartered banks from individuals, but it was clearly unwilling to "monetize" bank portfolios of long-term government bonds and thereby to increase chartered-bank cash reserves. This policy was an interesting and informal application of the 100 percent reserve principle; that is, bank assets were frozen by the sudden transformation of a large part of their liquid assets into illiquid and, in effect, non-negotiable securities. The policy was only temporary: short-term government securities were never turned down by the Bank of Canada, and the special treatment of long-term securities was apparently intended to last only until other credit restrictions began to have effect.

In fact, this special policy regarding long-term securities was made unnecessary not by other qualitative controls but by the incidental effect of the Bank's higher interest-rate policy. The price of long-term government securities fell until they were below their cost to the banks. This discouragement of chartered-bank selling from portfolio occurred at the same time that institutional investors, including the banks, were actually becoming interested in increasing their portfolios to take advantage of the higher yields. As a result large offerings to the Bank of Canada were no longer a problem, and normal operations in government securities could be resumed.

As we have seen, the chartered banks were required to restrict consumer loans to conform with the government's consumer credit regulations; but Bank of Canada policy on qualitative restrictions was first formulated in detail at one of its periodic discussions of credit conditions with the general managers of the chartered banks. In a meeting at Ottawa on February 14, 1951, the Governor of the Bank of Canada and the general managers of the chartered banks agreed on a policy to restrict chartered-bank loans and holdings of non-government securities to those outstanding on a target date set at February 28, 1951; but wheat loans and loans to purchase Canada Savings Bonds were excluded from the restrictions.

In its press statement of February 22, the Bank of Canada mentioned as "specific working rules":

> (1) . . . except in the case of small credits, the chartered banks will refrain from making term loans or purchasing corporate securities with a term of one year or longer.[129]
>
> (2) Margins of at least 50 percent will be required to carry corporation stocks, that is, collateral for such loans must be equal in value to not less than twice the amount of the loans. . . .
>
> (3) Margin requirements will be substantially increased in the case of bank loans on the security of instalment finance paper, and the total volume of bank credit for such purposes will not be increased.

For other types of loans, including commercial loans mainly for financing inventories and receivables, personal loans, and other categories, the general principle laid down was that "lending practices will be tightened whenever possible . . . in order to achieve the

[129] Previously it had been "suggested" by the Bank of Canada in February, 1948, that chartered banks cease to make term loans; but the "suggestion" was withdrawn in February, 1949. See Bank of Canada, *Annual Report 1949*, p. 7.

desired objective of avoiding further over-all increase in the banks' total loans and non-government investments."

Credits in general were restricted to one-year advances or less, with the exception of farm-improvement loans, veterans' loans, home extension loans, and oil and gas production loans. Loans for purchasing automobiles, establishing a new business or getting an interest in an established business, or purchasing real estate, were made for periods up to a year; but bank policy was one of discouragement. The same policy applied to loans for speculative building, or against stocks, bonds, or cash surrender value of life insurance. Contractors, stockbrokers, and bond dealers were accommodated as usual, on a short-term basis; but loans for increasing retail inventory, though considered on their individual merit, were generally discouraged. Loans to manufacturers and wholesalers were classed as "essential" or "non-essential." The general policy was: no loans to manufacturers or wholesalers of non-essentials above established authorized credits; no loans to manufacturers and wholesalers of essential goods to finance "excessive" inventories or to finance receivables beyond existing levels.

In August, 1951, total current loans were $3,162.9 million: a rise of $182 million above the target date, February 28. But the rate of rise was considerably slower than in 1950. The rise was attributed to an extra demand for credit to finance an unusually large carryover of wheat, to move the large 1951 crop, and to meet the increasing credit demands of the defense program.

International Policy.—A further threat to Canadian stability appeared during the summer of 1950 in the form of a flood of speculative capital from the United States. Canada's improving balance-of-payments position on current account encouraged the view that Canada's dollar was undervalued at $1.10 Canadian to $1.00 U.S., and would soon be raised to parity. As a result speculators hoping to make a quick profit used American dollars to buy Canadian government securities at the going rate; and even long-term investors in branch plants and subsidiary corporations in Canada made immediate transfers of funds that might otherwise have been spread over a longer period.

The resultant flood of American funds had to be purchased by the Foreign Exchange Control Board with Canadian dollars at the official rate of $1.10 Canadian to $1.00 U.S. The Bank of Canada sought to offset the inflationary effects of this inflow upon the money supply by selling short-term securities; and there was no need to support the long-term government-bond market owing to the demand for those bonds by foreign buyers.

TABLE 7
PRICE OF AMERICAN DOLLAR IN CANADIAN FUNDS

Business Days	*High*	*Low*	*Monthly Average*
1950			
October	107.00	104.56	105.34
November	104.84	103.25	104.03
December	106.00	104.59	105.31
1951			
January	105.94	104.75	105.17
February	105.38	104.41	104.92
March	105.25	104.44	104.73
April	106.81	104.94	105.99
May	106.94	105.38	106.37
June	107.31	106.63	106.94
July	106.63	105.33	106.05
August	105.94	105.09	105.56
September	105.75	105.19	105.56
October	105.50	104.19	105.08
November	104.78	103.50	104.35
December	103.88	101.19	102.56
1952			
January	101.13	100.00	100.48
February	100.69	100.00	100.11
March	100.00	98.38	99.60

Source: Bank of Canada, *Statistical Summary*, March, 1952, p. 43.

The dilemma faced by the government was essentially that, if the Canadian dollar were not revalued upward, there would be continued capital inflow and continued inflationary pressure as American dollars were bought in quantity by the Foreign Exchange Control Board; if the Canadian dollar were revalued, the capital flow would be reversed as speculators took their profits by selling their Canadian government securities, and repatriating American dollars amounting to their original investment plus a profit equal to the appreciation of Canadian exchange.

The dilemma was resolved on September 30, 1950, by setting the dollar free to find its level on the world market. The Canadian dollar rose until the premium on American funds was approximately 5 percent; and, as Table 7 shows, there it stayed with occasional peaks and lows for over a year. Moreover, the Bank of Canada's higher interest-rate policy broke the price of government bonds later in the year, so that, in the neighborhood of the ruling rate of exchange, the expected profit disappeared entirely. As a result the capital inflow was not reversed. Instead the net inflow of 1951, though smaller than that of 1950, continued high, amounting to $563 million for the year. During the last half of 1951, the Canadian dollar strengthened. On January 22, 1952, it reached par with the American dollar, and in succeeding months, as Table 7 shows, actually commanded a premium in American funds.

In the new foreign-exchange policy the chartered banks played their part by resuming their traditional prewar role of exchange dealers in the free market. Their earnings from foreign exchange were true "earnings": they had to be worked for. The work involved helping to make a market and therefore had a social purpose. All in all, then, the free market successfully resolved the government's dilemma, gave the users of the exchange market better accommodation, geared the banks' foreign exchange earnings to efficiency and public service. It would be hard to find a government policy with a better record for favorable results to all whom it was destined to affect.

The Banking System and Canada's Economic Development.—Some of the most valuable services rendered by any banking system, even in an expanding economy, are likely to lie in providing newly developed areas with unspectacular but very necessary services such as safeguarding depositors' funds, clearing and collecting checks, and providing safe-deposit boxes. But a picture of Canada's banking system in action should perhaps concentrate on services rendered to business through bank loans.

From Table 5 a brief calculation will show that a little over $2.5 billion in loans outstanding on September 30, 1950, were distributed approximately as follows: 5.5 percent to "government and other public services"; 7 percent to financial institutions such as investment dealers, brokers, and trust, loan, mortgage, investment, and insurance companies; 18 percent in personal loans; and 69 percent to agricultural, industrial, and commercial enterprises. Table 8 shows this 69 percent of total loans in more detail, and allows comparison with previous postwar years and with 1951–53.

Loans to farmers had almost tripled by 1951, and much greater increases occurred in certain types of industrial loans. The ninefold increase in petroleum loans reflects the discovery and development of important new fields in Alberta. The other gains over 1946 must be discounted in part owing to the abnormally low bank loans of the war period; nevertheless, a great part reflects expansion of plant, equipment, and working capital needs beyond any previous peacetime period.

Bank loans to industry consist primarily of short-term loans to provide working capital. Lending on longer term to corporations and other businesses for expanding plant and equipment has never developed in Canada to the extent that it has in the United States. Moreover, since the Second World War, term lending by the banks has not always enjoyed the blessing of the Bank of Canada.[130]

Oil and gas production loans were, as we have seen, exempted from the general rule banning term loans to business during the defense period. This exemption gave the banks freedom to continue their supply of credit to this important frontier of Canadian economic development. Here, again, the banking system has had to adapt itself to a new type of lending. Oil loans are generally made on the strength of oil in the ground, provided the company has at least one producing well. Usually there is an assignment of the proceeds of production of that well and subsequent successful wells, and loans are made for the drilling of new wells. When reports by geologists concerning the recoverable oil over the loan period are not too favorable, additional security may be taken; but the basic security is the assignment of the proceeds of production. This lending operation resembles loans under Section 88; but, with oil loans, the bank's security is underground, and the bank has to take the experts' word for it that some day, to the relief of both borrower and lender, the oil can be safely and profitably brought to the top. Loans for petroleum and its products at $56 million in 1953 were over five times what they were in 1949.

Much of the capital, both for oil production and for the great development in iron ore and other strategic metals, comes as it should from the sale of securities in the capital market. This is the non-inflationary method of economic development based on the savings of the people who buy shares in the enterprise. But the banks can take care of working capital needs, which vary greatly over short

[130] See p. 174 and note.

Table 8
Agricultural, Industrial, and Commercial Loans, 1946–53
(AMOUNTS IN MILLIONS OF CANADIAN DOLLARS)

Recipients	October 31		September 30					
	1946	*1947*	*1948*	*1949*	*1950*	*1951*	*1952*	*1953*
Farmers	109.8	147.3	161.9	184.4	255.8	298.9	334.2	354.0
Industry								
Chemicals and rubber products	5.9	14.4	27.0	25.3	29.2	54.3	30.3	43.4
Electrical apparatus and supplies	3.2	14.5	12.7	9.2	14.3	41.4	22.9	41.9
Food, beverages, and tobacco	74.2	105.1	130.9	117.0	122.5	172.0	168.4	162.8
Forest products	74.7	108.4	104.7	102.6	76.1	115.7	136.5	139.8
Furniture	7.6	12.3	12.7	13.1	16.2	19.8	14.4	17.6
Iron and steel products	46.4	88.6	73.2	75.2	53.4	97.5	95.6	124.5
Mining and mine products	13.7	17.0	18.9	21.9	26.0	33.4	48.0	62.0
Petroleum and products	3.4	9.0	6.4	10.6	22.9	31.0	32.8	55.6
Textiles, leather, and clothing	73.3	106.7	118.5	134.9	138.9	213.4	158.0	199.5
Transportation equipment	11.6	17.6	21.1	25.5	30.1	46.4	52.8	52.8
Other products	29.8	40.3	35.8	42.5	55.2	63.1	53.1	58.9
Total	343.6	533.9	561.8	577.9	584.7	888.0	812.8	958.8
Commercial								
Public utilities, transportation, and communication companies	15.9	42.5	36.3	34.5	53.9	87.9	67.5	61.7
Construction contractors	71.7	93.9	103.6	113.3	122.7	151.8	158.7	175.0
Grain dealers and exporters	67.7	67.9	103.3	190.1	93.1	98.6	186.5	310.7
Installment finance companies	28.3	65.7	53.1	74.6	96.5	100.8	149.4	249.3
Merchandisers	244.8	359.9	387.4	415.5	436.1	542.9	484.0	595.8
Other business	45.0	67.8	89.1	113.0	135.5	133.8	139.0	179.4
Total	473.4	697.7	772.8	941.0	937.8	1,115.7	1,185.1	1,571.9
Grand total	926.8	1,378.9	1,496.5	1,703.3	1,778.3	2,302.7	2,332.1	2,884.7

Source: Bank of Canada, *Statistical Summary*, December, 1950, pp. 207, 208; January, 1952, pp. 5, 6; October, 1953, p. 167. The table excludes personal loans, financial loans, and loans to government and other public services.

periods; and, as with the oil loans, they may provide longer term credit of a special kind where the period of production and the paying out of the loans are longer than average.

The forces that shaped the Canadian banking system are, as we have seen, to be found in an earlier period of Canadian economic growth and increasing political independence. Today the Canadian economy is in another phase of expansion. Canada's banks, conservative as they are and have to be, are playing an important part in this new chapter in Canadian economic history. The Canadian banking system has so far adapted itself to economic change without compromising in any way the safety of its depositors. It seems most probable that the banking system will continue to prove adaptable to the changing pattern of credit needs in Canada's expanding economy without fundamental changes in the banking structure itself.

ADDENDUM

Throughout this chapter frequent reference has been made to the general ineligibility of mortgage security against loans by the chartered banks. This was still true at the end of 1953; but, on September 30, 1953, the government circulated a proposal to allow the chartered banks to extend mortgage loans on new housing under a mortgage insurance scheme administered by the Central Mortgage and Housing Corporation. Implementing this proposal would mean amendment of the National Housing Act to widen the present definition of "lending institutions" so as to include the chartered banks and the Quebec savings banks, and to add provisions covering residential mortgage insurance similar to American procedure under the Federal Housing Authority. More important for the purposes of this chapter, the proposal involves amendment of the Bank Act and the Quebec Savings Bank Act sometime during the decennial revision year of 1954.

In its present form, the proposal is that the banks' liquidity will be maintained through mortgage insurance, payable on transfer of title to the Central Mortgage and Housing Corporation. Settlement, in the event of such foreclosure, will be made in cash at 98 percent of outstanding principal, approved borrowers' charges, foreclosure allowance, and interest arrears allowance.

The maintenance of bank liquidity on mortgages in good standing is not so clearly established; but it is proposed that Central Mortgage and Housing, within its own discretion, may buy mortgages outright, and that the Bank of Canada, also within its own discretion, may lend against mortgage security as it may against other collateral under the provisions of the Bank of Canada Act.

Considering the source of the proposal, it is extremely likely that, when the Bank Act is revised in 1954, mortgage security based on new residential housing will become eligible as collateral against loans by Canada's chartered banks.

REFERENCES

OFFICIAL SOURCES

Bank of Canada. Annual Reports to the Minister of Finance, 1935–1950.

Canada. Laws. Statutes. Acts Respecting Banks and Banking, 1871, 1881, 1890, 1900.

—— Central Mortgage and Housing Corporation. Annual Reports, 1946–1950.

—— Export Credits Insurance Corporation. Annual Reports and Financial Statements, 1945–1950.

—— Foreign Exchange Control Board. Annual Reports, 1945–1950.

—— Industrial Development Bank. Annual Reports, 1944–1950.

—— Report of the Royal Commission on Banking and Currency (1933). Ottawa.

NONOFFICIAL SOURCES

Allen, A. N. Commercial Legislation and Control. London, 1938. Section on Canada, pp. 103–32.

Beckhart, B. H. The Banking System of Canada. New York, 1929. Reprinted from *Foreign Banking Systems.*

Breckenridge, R. M. History of Banking in Canada. Washington, D.C., 1910.

Canadian Bankers' Association. Historical Outline of Canadian Banking Legislation and Some Features of the Present Working of the Canadian Banking System. Toronto, 1933.

Canadian Credit Men's Trust Association. Credit and Collections in Canada. Toronto, 1947.

Canadian Institute of International Affairs. The Canadian Economy and Its Problems. Toronto, 1934. Part II, pp. 189–318, is a symposium on central banking in Canada.

Chapman, John M. Branch Banking. New York, 1942. Chap. XIV, "Branch Banking in Canada."

Day, John Percival. Considerations on the Demand for a Central Bank in Canada. Toronto, 1933.
Hackett, W. T. G. A Background of Banking Theory. Toronto, 1945.
Holladay, James. The Canadian Banking System. Boston, 1938.
Howard, C. S. "Canadian Banks and Bank Notes: a Record," *Canadian Banker,* Vol. LVII (1950). Expanded reprint available from the author, The Royal Bank Building, Toronto 1, Ontario.
James, F. Cyril. The Economics of Money, Credit and Banking. 3d ed. New York, 1940. Chap. XXVII, "The Canadian Banking System," pp. 506–29, is by Philip Vineberg.
Jamieson, A. B. Chartered Banking in Canada. Toronto, 1953.
Marvin, Donald M. "The Bank of Canada," *Canadian Banker,* Vol. XLX (October, 1937).
National Monetary Commission. The Canadian Banking System, by Joseph French Johnson. Washington, D.C., 1910.
—— Interviews on Banking and Currency Systems of Canada. Washington, D.C., 1910.
Patterson, E. L. Stewart. Canadian Banking. Toronto, 1940.
Phillips, Paul. The Law of Banks and Banking in Canada. Toronto, 1941.
Plumtre, A. F. W. Central Banking in the British Dominions. Toronto, 1940.
Shortt, Adam. "The Early History of Canadian Banking," *Canadian Banker,* Vols. IV–V (1896–97).
—— "The History of Canadian Currency, Banking and Exchange," *Canadian Banker,* Vols. VII–XIV (1900–1906).
Stokes, Milton L. The Bank of Canada; the Development and Present Position of Central Banking in Canada. Toronto, 1939.

CUBA

by Philip J. Glaessner and G. Sterling Grumman

INTRODUCTION [1]

THE MAJOR FEATURES OF THE CUBAN ECONOMY

CUBA'S NATIONAL INCOME has averaged around two billion dollars in recent years. Since the population slightly exceeds five million, per capita income is doubtless the highest of any tropical country and does not compare unfavorably with that of some of the poorer Southern sections of the United States.

The distribution of income is sharply unequal between Havana and the provinces and between various social classes; the social inequalities are somewhat smaller, however, than in other areas of the Caribbean. The extent to which the agricultural population consists of wage earners is striking. Land ownership is very unequal, with owner-operators the exception.

Mr. Glaessner was educated at Cambridge University, England, and at Columbia University, New York. He has been an economist with the Federal Reserve Bank of New York since March, 1946. In September, 1948, Mr. Glaessner went to Brazil for a period of five months as one of the economists on the Joint Brazil–United States Technical Commission, whose report was published in the following year. In September, 1950, he went to Cuba as a member of the International Bank Survey Mission which wrote a report on the Cuban economy. During the period from September, 1951, to July, 1953, Mr. Glaessner was the chief economist of the American section of the Joint Brazil–United States Commission for Economic Development. Mr. Glaessner served in the United States Infantry in the last war. He is married and a resident of New York.

[1] The introduction to this chapter was prepared independently by Mr. Philip J. Glaessner. Mr. Grumman collaborated on this chapter while associated with the Federal Reserve Bank of New York, prior to his affiliation with J. P. Morgan & Co., Inc. The opinions expressed in this chapter are those of the authors, and do not reflect the views of their employers.

The island has an exceptionally fertile soil, most of it level. Nearly all major crops lend themselves well to mechanization. The climate is ideally suited for most tropical crops. Yet large areas of Cuba are not under cultivation, and agriculture is extensive rather than intensive.

The sizable unused resources of land are matched by idle capital and idle men. Seasonal unemployment has been an increasingly serious problem for many years. The sugar harvest lasts only three to four months, requiring a labor force many times that needed for sugar planting and maintenance of the sugar mills during the rest of the year. Practically all other crops also show strong seasonality that coincides with that of sugar.

While the size of permanent unemployment is difficult to estimate, the fact that it seems to be considerable, even during the present record sugar boom, is deeply disturbing. While population growth is not particularly rapid, it is estimated that the labor force is growing at the rate of 25,000 every year. There can be no doubt that in recent years employment opportunities have not increased to anything like the same extent.

Cuba remains the monocultural export economy *par excellence*. Exports have represented up to 40 percent of the national product of late, and sugar accounts for 90 percent of total exports, as shown in Table 1. The United States remains Cuba's most important trading partner, and the island has been the main Latin American beneficiary of offshore purchases by the Economic Cooperation Administration.

While the volume and value of Cuba's exports have reached record levels in the postwar period, the increase taking place has constituted little more than a recovery from the 1925–40 sugar depression. A sizable further expansion of the basic sugar industry appears most unlikely because of continued quota restrictions in the United States and even more severe restrictions in other areas. Thus Cuba, which as one of the world's cheapest large-scale producers of sugar has long played the game according to the rules of the international specialization of labor, now finds the rules changed against it.

Mr. Grumman received his B.S. degree from the Sheffield Scientific School at Yale University in 1942. From his graduation until the end of the war he was a volunteer in the American Field Service and served with the British Eighth Army in North Africa and Italy. In 1947 he entered the Columbia University School of International Affairs, where he concentrated in the field of international economics, and in 1949 received the M.I.A. degree. For the following three and a half years he was an economist in the Foreign Research Division of the Federal Reserve Bank of New York, and specialized in Latin American monetary and exchange problems. In January, 1953, he joined J. P. Morgan & Co., Inc.

Insufficient progress has been made in the direction of so adapting the economy that other industries can take over the role of sugar as a dynamic element in its growth. It should be noted, however, that after the imposition of a tariff by Cuba in 1927, the production of such foodstuffs as corn, rice, and beans expanded considerably, and that a sizable textile industry and a number of food-processing industries have been created.

The difficulties of diversification are deep-seated. Few foodstuffs or raw materials have been subject to as violent price fluctuations as sugar, and this in itself has created an economic climate blocking diversification. Enterprisers and investors, both Cuban and foreign, share the view that no real diversification of risk is possible in Cuba, since the fate of every venture is tied to the fortunes of sugar. At the same time, the spectacular intermittent capital gains that can be reaped through rapid fluctuations in the international sugar market block investment in other lines yielding steadier but more moderate profits.

TABLE 1

CUBAN GROSS NATIONAL PRODUCT, NATIONAL INCOME, AND FOREIGN TRADE, 1948

(AMOUNTS IN MILLIONS OF PESOS)

		Amount
Gross national product		
Consumption expenditures		1,512
Gross private domestic capital formation		188
Net investment abroad		85
Government purchases of goods and services		262
of which investments were	40	
Total gross national product		2,047
National income (at factor cost)		
Sugar sector		602
Non-sugar agriculture		202
Non-sugar industry and commerce		643
Other		370
Nonresidents' income		53
Total national income		1,870
Foreign trade items		
Exports		724
of which sugar exports were	649	
Imports		527
of which capital goods imports were	90	
of which imports of foods and beverages were	163	

Source: The International Bank for Reconstruction and Development, Findings and Recommendations of an Economic and Technical Mission, *Report on Cuba* (Washington, 1951), pp. 35, 510.

Available data on capital formation and savings show that, while savings in prosperous times reach impressive figures and have constituted as much as 12 percent of gross national product, little more than half of these savings has been matched by investments in productive facilities. About one sixth is going into real estate, while the rest has been invested abroad. Indeed, the extent to which the savings of this underemployed and semideveloped economy are exported is only understandable in the light of investors' lack of confidence in the island's economic future and the great investment opportunities in the neighboring United States.[2]

While the Cuban middle classes have shared the traditional Latin American preference for real estate investments, the severe mortgage moratoria of the depression years have permanently undermined their faith in real estate mortgages. This has acted as a brake on real estate investments. With the attractiveness of this avenue of new investment reduced, Cuban savings tend to go into liquid assets to an astonishing extent.

The reluctance of businessmen to start new ventures or extend their existing operations in Cuba has been further increased by the deplorable state of labor-management relations, which finds its major roots in the stagnation of the economy and corresponding unemployment to whose perpetuation it contributes. Wage levels and the extent of unionization throughout most sectors of the economy reflect specific conditions in the dominant sugar industry. The wage levels achieved there with government support make the non-sugar sector even less profitable than it would be otherwise. Resistance to mechanization is so strong that it has threatened to destroy the cigar industry, and endangers the position of other industries, including sugar itself. There is here a vicious circle, which the International Bank Mission to Cuba characterized as perhaps the master vicious circle impeding further Cuban development; in the absence of readily available alternative job opportunities, labor opposes the adoption of the very improvements that would lead to the creation of new jobs.

Reluctant capital and truculent labor have reached an impasse that is a major factor in blocking more rapid diversification of the economy. The island's recent relative prosperity is due not to new investment but to the bringing back into full production of all the

[2] A recent investigation shows that Cuban real estate holdings in southern Florida alone can be estimated at over 120 million dollars.

enormous capital plant created in the sugar industry (largely by foreign capital) during the first twenty-five years of the present century. Real per capita income is, even today, probably not higher than in the early 1920s.

Through such measures as increased protection along the lines already successfully tried for certain major food items, through more flexible wage arrangements, particularly in the non-sugar sectors, and through a vigorous but well-chosen policy of government investments and subsidies, Cuba can doubtless go a considerable way in the direction of absorbing her unemployed resources and adapting her economy to changed external circumstances. It is even possible that investors' fears concerning the impossibility of diversification of risks, when investing on the island, may be partially overcome.

There may, however, be no way in which, in today's world of international economic anarchy, a country of Cuba's limited size and population can altogether escape paying an economic price for its political and cultural sovereignty. Were Cuba part of a large and well-diversified economy, the solution for her problems, and in particular for that of mechanizing the production of her major crops, might well be that of many agricultural areas of the Southern United States, where farm mechanization is being followed by migration to the industrial centers farther north. With sizable migration not practical, Cuba may be likened to "Louisiana without Detroit."

In view of its considerable unemployed resources and the relative ease of securing imports from the neighboring United States, even during periods of shortage, it is not surprising that the price inflation in Cuba has been less than in most other Latin American countries. The Cuban public's strong liquidity preference and its willingness to invest in assets abroad have also been stabilizing factors.

CREDIT NEEDS

The sugar and foreign trade sectors naturally make considerable demands upon the credit facilities of Cuban institutions. However, a part of these needs is met by American institutions, especially the financing of the holding of sugar stocks in Cuba, the transit of sugar, and the holding of stocks in New York. Seasonal working capital needs of sugar mills are also, to some extent, financed by United States interests. This is explained by the fact that such a large proportion (about 47 percent) of the sugar mills is still in American hands.

The credit needs of the other sectors of the economy can appeal only to Cuban institutions. They are considerable for the second important export sector, tobacco. Equally important are the credit needs of non-export agriculture and of small local industries. The fact that so much of Cuban savings is invested abroad has intensified the need of local enterprise to rely upon credit institutions.

Seasonal changes in credit needs are particularly striking in Cuba. The income flow of the whole economy is closely bound up with the sugar harvest. While the sugar sector requires credit mainly during this period, producers in other sectors, and particularly consumers, including the sugar workers themselves, need substantial credit during the non-harvest season, when their income is low.

SURVEY OF CREDIT INSTITUTIONS

The heart of Cuba's present credit system is formed by 15 major banks, 6 of which are the branches of foreign banks. In addition, there are more than 40 small locally owned banks and the Banco de los Colonos, which concentrates in the field of advances to small and medium-sized sugar planters.

The new National Bank, which began operations in 1950, is the lender of last resort, the government banker, and, together with the Exchange Stabilization Fund, the holder of the country's centralized international reserves.

Most sectors of Cuba's agriculture, producing crops other than the two chief export crops, sugar and tobacco, and most small industrial establishments are not directly served by the banking system. Instead, mercantile credit meets their short-term credit needs inadequately and expensively. There are, as yet, very few cooperatives. In these fields, the recently activated state-owned Agricultural and Industrial Development Bank, working closely with the National Bank, has a great opportunity to supplement existing credit facilities.

Cuba's collective savings institutions are of considerable importance. There is a postal savings system, some 25 pension and retirement funds for wage earners and professional people, and 7 pension funds serving government employees. A surprisingly large number of Cuban and foreign-owned insurance companies operate on the island. Capitalization companies have become an important means of savings for the middle class, and the chief method for expanding home ownership.[3]

[3] Cf. pp. 202–3.

The market for private security issues is extremely limited, but a very promising activation of the government bond market has taken place in the last three years.

THE COMMERCIAL BANKS

The brief survey of the Cuban commercial banking system presented in this chapter focuses on the following salient features: (1) the predominance of large banks; (2) the recent growth of Cuban-owned banks; (3) the banks' very strong reserve position; (4) the passive role of commercial bank credit in Cuban business cycles; (5) the restricted nature of credit operations, as to both term and destination; and (6) the important part that the banks have recently played as purchasers and distributors of government obligations.

STRUCTURE

Commercial banks operating in Cuba fall into three distinct groups: the branches of the six foreign banks,[4] which account for just over half of total commercial bank assets; nine major Cuban-owned banks, with somewhat less than half of the total assets; and 41 minor banks, which hold only 6 percent of total assets. The present structure of the Cuban commercial banking system is in sharp contrast to that which prevailed during 1921–39, when foreign bank branches were completely dominant.

One of the significant consequences of the growth of the Cuban-owned banks in the last decade has been the partial reestablishment of the extensive network of branches that covered the island prior to the banking crisis of 1920. At that time there were 19 domestically owned banks with as many as 334 branches, in contrast to the 1930s when the total number of branches had shrunk to just over 50, nearly all owned by foreign banks. By the end of 1950, on the other hand, there were 56 banks with 155 branches, 121 of which were owned by domestic banks.

The recent growth of the Cuban-owned banking sector seems to have been due mainly to three developments: the great liquidity resulting from the war and postwar booms; the gradual shift from the dual monetary system to the peso system, which has tended to restrict

[4] The National City Bank of New York, The Chase National Bank of New York, The First National Bank of Boston, The Royal Bank of Canada, The Bank of Nova Scotia, and The Bank of China.

the business of foreign banks; and the creation of the National Bank, providing the Cuban-owned banks at long last with a lender of last resort. The emergence of Cuban-owned banks into a position of greater strength and importance constitutes one aspect of the gradual adaptation of the island's financial institutions to the changing character of its economy. It is a healthy development which has been welcomed by most foreign bankers.

LEGAL PROVISIONS

The establishment of new banks and branches requires the authorization of the Cuban National Bank. Existing banks were permitted to continue to operate by merely registering with the National Bank following its establishment. The law prescribes different capital minima for banks according to whether they wish to operate in the entire national territory or only in parts thereof. The capital and reserve of each bank must be at least 5 percent of its sight deposits. There are no restrictions as to the nationality of banks other than that the majority of directors of new banks must be Cuban nationals.

In addition to its wide powers of intervention in banking establishments, the National Bank may prescribe the maximum proportion of a bank's assets that may be invested abroad, and may set the maximum proportion that may be lent to the same person or firm. Furthermore, commercial banks are limited with respect to operations with their own directors and staff. They may not negotiate or lend against collateral of their own shares, or retain, for more than three years, real estate or chattels that they may have acquired as a consequence of credit liquidations.

INTERNAL ADMINISTRATION

In general, the internal administration of the major banks is highly centralized, and the powers of branch managers are often strictly circumscribed. The managers of the Cuban branches of foreign banks are in some cases given surprisingly little discretion by their head offices abroad—a consequence of the unfortunate experiences of these banks in their operations during the interwar period.

The major banks in Cuba, both foreign and Cuban-owned, are efficient and use up-to-date accounting methods and banking procedures. However, they are often grossly overstaffed, due to the difficulty of dismissing employees under the existing labor law and the strong unionization of bank employees.

RESERVE POSITION OF THE COMMERCIAL BANKS

During the last twelve years the fifteen major banks, whose operations account for the bulk of the banking business of the island, have been in a very liquid position. The ratio of cash in vaults to deposits has at all times exceeded 30 percent, and, during most of the war years, was well in excess of 50 percent—more than double the 25 percent reserve requirement in force since 1938. Since most Cuban-owned banks, as well as the foreign banks operating in Cuba, maintain very substantial net deposits with correspondents abroad, the ratio of readily available cash resources (including cash in vaults and net deposits abroad) to deposits is perhaps a more meaningful measure of the banks' liquidity than simply the ratio of vault cash to deposits. The readily available cash resources of the banks have fluctuated between 34 percent and 71 percent of total deposits. This strong reserve position is still being maintained; on September 30, 1951, the ratio of cash in vaults to deposits amounted to 36 percent and that of "readily available" cash resources to deposits to 44 percent, for the major banks, and, as can be seen in Table 2, the ratios were substantially the same for all groups of banks operating in Cuba.

The very strong reserve position of the banking system reflects certain fundamental characteristics of the Cuban economy. As stressed in the introduction to the present chapter, the prosperity of all economic activities in the island remains strikingly linked to the fate of sugar. Most bankers seem to feel that no real diversification of risk is possible. Moreover, only the sugar and commercial sectors of the economy are organized in such a way that their operations lend themselves to traditional commercial banking.

The instability of prices and national income during the interwar period and, in particular, the sugar collapse of 1920 taught Cuban bankers a lesson in conservatism which they have never forgotten. This is no less true of the foreign banks that suffered very substantial losses in the 1930s. The tendency of banks to maintain substantial liquid reserves because of the instability of the economy and the limited number of bankable risks was powerfully reinforced until 1950 by the absence of a lender of last resort.

By conservative management the Cuban banking system has been

TABLE 2

CONSOLIDATED BALANCE SHEET OF THE CUBAN BANKING SYSTEM, SEPTEMBER 30, 1951

(AMOUNTS IN MILLIONS OF PESOS)

	All Member Banks	*Six Foreign Banks*	*Cuban Banks*	*Fifteen Major Banks* [a]	*Nine Major Cuban Banks*	*Small Cuban Banks*
ASSETS						
Cuban pesos in vaults	53.7	18.8	34.9	49.0	30.2	4.7
United States dollars in vaults	14.8	8.7	6.1	13.8	5.1	1.0
Total cash in member bank vaults	68.5	27.5	41.0	62.8	35.3	5.7
Cuban pesos deposited with the National Bank	172.1	87.6	84.5	159.2	71.6	12.9
United States dollars deposited with the National Bank	24.6	13.7	11.0	23.8	10.1	0.8
Total deposits with the National Bank	196.7	101.3	95.5	183.0	81.7	13.7
Total cash reserves	265.3	128.8	136.5	245.9	117.0	19.4
Deposits with foreign correspondents and head offices abroad	62.7	39.7	23.0	61.2	21.5	1.5
Loans and discounts	328.3	171.7	156.6	305.7	134.0	22.6
Investments	76.6	21.0	55.6	74.1	53.1	2.5
Other assets	84.5	35.9	48.8	71.9	36.0	12.6
Total assets	817.4	397.1	420.5	758.8	361.7	58.6
LIABILITIES						
Cuban peso demand deposits (nonbank)	555.8	243.8	312.1	511.7	267.9	44.1
United States dollar demand deposits (nonbank)	88.6	52.7	35.5	86.1	33.4	2.5
Total demand deposits	644.4	296.5	347.6	597.8	301.3	46.6
Cuban peso savings deposits	16.6	50.0	26.7	74.7	24.7	1.9
United States dollar savings deposits	6.9	4.7	2.1	6.8	2.1	0.1
Total savings deposits	83.5	54.7	28.8	81.4	26.8	2.0
Interbank deposits	15.8	9.8	5.9	15.6	5.8	0.2
Total deposits	743.5	361.1	382.4	694.9	333.9	48.6
Other liabilities	30.3	19.1	11.4	26.2	7.1	4.1
Total liabilities	773.8	380.2	393.8	721.1	341.0	52.7
Capital and reserves	43.6	16.9	26.7	37.7	20.8	5.9
Total liabilities, capital, and reserves	817.4	397.1	420.5	758.8	361.7	58.6
Ratio of reserves to total deposits (nonbank)	36.4%	36.7%	36.3%	36.2%	35.7%	40.1%

Source: Banco Nacional de Cuba, *Estadísticas Monetarias y Bancarias*, September, 1951.

Note: Details may not add up to totals because of rounding.

[a] The nine large Cuban-owned banks that belong to the Havana Clearinghouse and the six foreign banks listed in footnote 4 on page 189.

able to enjoy a record of virtually perfect solvency since 1920. Alternatively, it could have been considerably more venturesome, but at the risk of periodic insolvency for the domestic banks and of substantial losses for the branches of foreign banks operating on the island. The banks chose the first alternative, and as a result have maintained a very strong reserve position.

PASSIVE ROLE OF COMMERCIAL BANK LENDING

The long-term tendency of Cuban commercial banks to hold large cash reserves is a reflection of the passive lending policy pursued by them since the 1920 sugar crash. The passive lending policy of the banks is well illustrated by the fact that throughout the last thirty years fluctuations in the volume of bank loans seem to have been substantially less pronounced than variations in the indices of over-all economic activity.

It is to be expected that a banking system that plays such a passive role should be subject to criticism for not taking an active part in promoting economic development and diversification and for not granting sufficient credit to achieve full employment. It should again be noted, however, that in the absence of a lender of last resort the pursuit of these ends would in the past have been tantamount to courting periodic insolvency.

Fluctuations in bank loans have nevertheless been considerable throughout the interwar period, reflecting the violent ups and downs of the Cuban economy. In the seventeen years following the sugar boom of 1920 bank loans fell to one fourth of their original level, while in the succeeding thirteen years they rose more than threefold and approached again the 1920 mark.

The increase has been more marked since the termination of the Second World War than in the previous decade, reflecting almost exclusively the large increase in loans made in pesos, which was a prelude to the establishment of a single currency system in Cuba. Peso loans now account for 90 percent of total bank loans, compared with 65 percent at the end of the war and 30 percent in 1937.

In addition to changes that reflect fluctuations in economic conditions abroad and especially in the foreign demand for sugar, there is a very pronounced seasonal variation in the level of bank credit. The seasonal low occurs in August and September, while loans reach a high level during the peak of the sugar harvest in April and May.

DISTRIBUTION OF LOANS

The conservatism of Cuban bankers and their preference for "self-liquidating" transactions is reflected in the overwhelming share of total loans that consists of commercial advances and of loans to the sugar industry. The best available indication of the destination of bank loans by economic sector is the breakdown according to the type of loan and the collateral used, as shown in Table 3. In the last twelve years sugar and commercial loans outstanding at the end of the year averaged 28 percent and 58 percent, respectively, of total loans, while loans secured by agricultural products other than sugar averaged only 3 percent. Production loans to industries other than the sugar industry have not accounted for more than a fraction of 1 percent.

It is likely that these statistics somewhat overstate the lack of balance in bank credit distribution. The International Bank Mission to Cuba found that, in certain provinces, substantial amounts of credit were being granted to cattlemen and rice growers in the form of promissory notes and overdrafts without collateral, and that some industrial establishments were able to secure accommodation to meet their working capital needs on the strength of personal guarantees. These advances are not recorded as cattle or industrial loans.

That the lack of balance in the distribution of loans is considerable is borne out, however, by the testimony of various bankers. Nearly all of them state that, in view of their experiences in the 1920s and 1930s, their lending operations center to an overwhelming extent on the granting of commercial and sugar loans. Several indicate that some small amount of credit is being extended to the manufacturing industry and to cattlemen, primarily on a personal credit basis. Loans to small, undercapitalized enterprises and to small agriculturalists are considered by bankers to involve risks that are too great for reputable commercial banks to shoulder, except with the help of an expensive inspection system.

The relative importance of loans to commercial businesses has increased substantially in the past decade, reflecting mainly the recent high levels of internal and external trade. Sugar loans, on the other hand, have suffered a relative decline since 1937. During the war and early postwar years this was partly due to bulk financing of the Cuban sugar crop by United States Government agencies, which relieved the Cuban banking system of part of the task of financing the carry-

TABLE 3
LOANS OF MAJOR BANKS OPERATING IN CUBA BY TYPES OF CREDIT, DECEMBER 31, 1937 AND 1949
(AMOUNTS IN THOUSANDS OF PESOS)

Type of Loan	AMOUNT 1937	AMOUNT 1949	PERCENTAGE OF TOTAL LOANS 1937	PERCENTAGE OF TOTAL LOANS 1949
Total loans	69,152	185,422	100.0	100.0
Sugar loans	31,793	32,374	46.0	17.5
Crop loans to planters	10,440	11,747	15.1	6.3
Loans to planters secured by mortgages	15,752	915	22.8	0.6
Production loans to mills	3,306	12,967	4.8	7.0
Secured by sugar	2,295	6,745	3.3	3.6
Loans secured by other agricultural products	567	5,822	0.8	3.1
Tobacco	108	275	0.2	0.1
Coffee	86	536	0.1	0.3
Rice	65	339	0.1	0.2
Cattle	171	56	0.2	
Other products	137	4,616	0.2	2.5
Production loans to industry (other than sugar)	423	400	0.6	0.2
Loans secured by securities and urban mortgages	12,967	18,085	18.8	9.8
Securities	8,087	15,688	11.7	8.4
Urban mortgages	4,880	2,397	7.1	1.4
Commercial loans [a]	23,402	128,741	33.8	69.4
Promissory notes	6,831	37,092	9.9	20.0
Trade paper	4,982	36,757	7.2	19.8
Overdrafts	9,729	35,450	14.0	19.1
Other loans	1,860	19,442	2.7	10.5

Source: Ministerio de Hacienda, Dirección General de Estadística, *Boletín de Estadísticas*, various issues.

[a] Bank loans to wholesalers, retailers, and foreign traders in the urban centers.

ing of sugar stocks. Another major factor in the decline was the mortgage moratoria of the thirties that virtually wiped out mortgage loans as a vehicle of sugar financing. Finally, the renewed prosperity of sugar growers has enabled many of them to get along without advances from the sugar mills, and the mills in turn have not had to borrow from banks as extensively as in earlier years.

In general, it may be said that financing the production, manufacture, storage and sale of sugar lends itself particularly well to a commercial banking system like that of Cuba, which operates largely in accordance with the doctrine of self-liquidating transactions. Moreover, a major portion of sugar loans are made to the sugar "centrales" which represent the greatest aggregation of capital on the island.

In the 1920s banks often granted loans against mortgages to small farmers, but with the advent of the mortgage moratoria of the 1930s and of 1940, this form of sugar crop financing was greatly reduced. It has been replaced by crop loans from sugar mills, which in turn borrow from commercial banks. While the lending policies of the mills have become more generous in the last few years, the small farmer who obtains an advance from the mill where he sells his crop often pays an implicit interest rate that is quite high. This seems to be particularly true in the case of some mills owned by Cuban family groups.

Another interesting aspect of Cuban sugar financing is the considerable extent to which American banks and the head offices of American sugar companies finance the cost of harvesting, processing, and warehousing sugar in Cuba, as well as the costs of shipping it to the United States and storing it there until it is sold. This assistance from United States banks or from the head offices of American-owned sugar companies releases funds for financing crop and processing expenditures in Cuba. In addition, Cuban subsidiaries have recently been retaining substantial portions of net profits to meet growing working capital needs.

Within the last decade a number of small banks have been established in provincial towns. With the big accounts and strongest risks adequately served by the existing foreign and large Cuban-owned banks, the small banks have catered to the needs of small merchants, manufacturers, and professional people, whose requirements for bank credit are very inadequately served by the large banks. It is significant that some of the managers of these banks have found that small merchants and professional groups are often better risks than larger enterprises. This view has received some confirmation in the findings of the Bank Examination Department of the National Bank.

STRUCTURE OF INTEREST RATES ON BANK LOANS

The structure of Cuban interest rates constitutes a curious mixture of low rates and sharp competition for prime risks, on the one hand, and relatively high rates together with a dearth of suppliers of less desirable credit risks, on the other. The large-scale, highly capitalized enterprises in the sugar industry can furnish exceptional guarantees as borrowers, while the large Cuban-owned banks as well as the branches of foreign banks are capable of offering very low rates to attract prime risks. Moreover the number of prime risks available in Cuba is comparatively small, and, as noted above, some sugar mills secure credit directly from New York banks.

Rates for first-class loans secured by sugar and for advances to large sugar mills range from 2.5 to 5.5 percent. Crop loans to large sugar planters carry rates of from 6 to 8 percent, while smaller planters are charged from 8 to 12 percent, the latter being the legal maximum interest rate. Interest rates on commercial loans vary from 4 percent for prime risks to the legal maximum in the case of small retailers in provincial towns.

While the cost of commercial bank credit to small farmers and industrial enterprises does not perhaps seem too exorbitant in view of the nature of Cuba's economy and the reputed conservatism of Cuban bankers, it must be noted that outside of the sugar and commercial sectors, bank credit is often of an unsuitable type or term, or else is unavailable at any interest rate.

FORMS AND TERMS OF BANK CREDIT

The propensity of Cuban banks for short-term, self-liquidating loans is natural in an economy subject to violent fluctuations, where long-range planning is difficult. As shown in Table 4, two thirds of all loans of the banking system are made for less than 90 days; less than 10 percent range from 90 to 180 days; while about one quarter are for periods longer than 180 days. It must be pointed out, however, that short-term advances are often made with provision for renewal. Recent experience shows that the creation of a lender of last resort may encourage banks to engage in some longer term operations. In fact, several Cuban-owned banks have recently made a number of working capital advances for periods of more than one year, and several foreign banks have granted industrial loans of two and three years' duration.

The legal forms of banking instruments in Cuba reflect the presence of American and Canadian institutions; Canadian influence may be noted in the wide use of the overdraft, and American practices are reflected in the use of trade acceptances. In general, the trade acceptance seems to be safer from the point of view of enforceability than the "pagaré" or promissory note. Since overdrafts are not ordinarily rediscountable under the new National Banking Law, banks have

TABLE 4
TYPE AND DURATION OF LOANS OF MAJOR BANKS OPERATING IN CUBA OUTSTANDING DECEMBER 31, 1949 [a]
(AMOUNTS IN THOUSANDS OF PESOS)

Type	*Up to 90 Days*	*90 to 180 Days*	*More than 180 Days*	*Total*
Total loans outstanding	122,748	14,224	48,451	185,423
Percentage of over-all total	66.2	7.7	26.1	100
Promissory notes	27,975	1,527	7,590	37,092
With collateral	5,026	438	6,348	11,812
Without collateral	22,949	1,089	1,242	25,280
Overdrafts	30,007	80	5,345	35,432
With collateral	4,888	80	3,557	8,525
Without collateral	25,119		1,788	26,907
Trade paper	34,957	968	832	36,757
With documents	1,669	13	14	1,696
Without documents	33,288	955	818	35,061
Loans secured by securities	3,582	456	11,628	15,666
Domestic	3,557	456	11,514	15,527
Foreign	25		114	139
Loans secured by commodities	8,746	201	2,986	11,933
Sugar and molasses	4,525		2,070	6,595
Tobacco	418			418
Coffee	502	34	8	544
Rice	325		14	339
Other domestic commodities	889	30	97	1,016
Other foreign commodities	2,087	137	797	3,021
Loans secured by cattle	19		37	56
Crop loans to sugar planters	1,251	6,903	3,593	11,747
Production loans to sugar mills	415	1,428	11,124	12,967
Production loans to other industries			400	400
Loans secured by mortgages	1,156	65	2,091	3,312
Urban	1,030	28	1,339	2,397
Rural	126	37	752	915
Other loans	14,640	2,595	2,826	20,061

Source: International Bank, *Report on Cuba*, p. 575.
[a] Excluding the Banco Popular.

an incentive to replace them with promissory notes or trade paper, although heavy stamp taxes on trade paper, exceeding moderate amounts, tend to discourage this.

The sugar "pignoración" is one of the most common types of short-term secured loans. This consists of an advance against a warehouse warrant that shows that sugar has been deposited in an approved warehouse, as evidenced by a receipt. The other two important forms of sugar loans are the crop lien advance to planters and the production loan to sugar mills, which usually takes the form of special contracts. Longer term loans are secured by mortgages or securities as well as by warehouse warrants.

INVESTMENT PORTFOLIOS

The investment portfolios of Cuban banks are very much smaller than in Anglo-Saxon countries. Recently, banks have held only 3.5 percent of their assets in the form of government bonds (both internal and external obligations), while other types of investment have been even less important. Only in the last three years have banks started to hold substantial amounts of internal government bonds. The lead in this movement has been taken by some of the aggressive, newer domestic banks, such as the Trust Company of Cuba, which have been active lately in promoting internal government bond issues.

Before 1949 the banks' investment portfolios consisted almost wholly of dollar obligations of the Cuban Government. The conservative Banco Gelats and the Cuban financial groups associated with it held, in the middle forties, about 25 percent of the outstanding external debt of the Cuban Government. This reflected the fact that, until recently, Cuban banks have had justifiably more confidence in the government's meeting its external obligations than in its treatment of its internal creditors.

Since the new National Bank is now willing to make a market for internal government bonds, the newer Cuban-owned banks have been prepared to increase very substantially their investments in new internal issues. Most of the foreign banks, on the other hand, did not take part in the 1949–50 placements of internal government debt, apparently because of a "wait and see" attitude on the part of their head offices abroad.

It has been noted within the last year that the branches of foreign banks have begun to hold sizable blocks of United States Government bonds as cover for the dollar deposits that they are still allowed to carry, even though the peso is now sole legal tender.

DEPOSITS

About 85 percent of the deposits of Cuban banks are demand deposits. Of these only about one seventh are dollar deposits, peso deposits having increased sharply in recent years. The ratio of savings to demand deposits is more than twice as large for foreign banks as for the domestic banks. Cuban banks do not pay interest on demand deposits, and only the smallest banks pay interest on savings deposits, the rates being 1 to 1.5 percent. However, savings deposits of up to 5,000 pesos have first claim on a bank's assets in case of liquidation. No bank may receive savings deposits of greater than 10,000 pesos from any one person.

COLLECTIVE SAVINGS INSTITUTIONS

While recently Cuban savings have probably been well in excess of 200 million pesos per annum, no more than about one fifth of this total seems to have taken the form of increases in savings deposits or of rises in the reserves of retirement funds, insurance, and capitalization companies. The preponderance of Cuban savings is reinvested in business enterprises, used to finance real estate operations as well as accumulated in idle balances or hoards both on the island and abroad. Collective savings institutions, nevertheless, are of growing importance for the savings of the middle class, and they offer virtually the only medium for the savings of wage earners. As investors, they play an important part in the government bond market, the market for private issues, and real estate operations.

In recent years, savings placed in government retirement funds have surpassed in importance savings deposits in commercial banks. Insurance companies continue to be the third most important collective savings institution, but capitalization companies have been rising rapidly in importance since the war. The Postal Savings System has become relatively less important.

RETIREMENT FUNDS

There are at present seven retirement and pension funds for government employees and about 25 social security funds for wage earners in the sugar industry, transportation systems, and manufacturing enterprises, and for professional groups such as physicians, lawyers, and architects—to mention only the most important. By far the largest fund is the Sugar Workers' Retirement Fund, whose reserves have been increasing at the rate of approximately $10 million a year, compared with an annual increase of $6 million to $8 million for all other funds together.

Most of the social security funds, with the notable exceptions of those serving the transportation and public utility sectors, were founded in the last ten years of sugar prosperity. They customarily offer retirement and death pensions, furnish medical assistance, and in some cases grant consumer loans to their members.

In operation, retirement funds in Cuba have encountered a number of serious problems. The older ones, such as the Transport Workers' Fund, have been near bankruptcy because of the failure of some of the bus and railroad companies to pay their contributions. In many cases, management has been ineffectual, and operating costs have been excessive as a result of political overstaffing. In administering the funds, there has been a general failure to relate contributions and benefits to actuarial reserve requirements. This failure has been particularly acute in the case of the Government Employees' Pension and Retirement Funds. These funds have repeatedly been forced to reduce their members' benefits—sometimes by as much as 35 percent —and delays in benefit payments have been common. The legislation creating many of the retirement funds limits the investment of reserves primarily to government bonds. In practice, the bulk of retirement funds' reserves during 1947 and 1948 was used to cover current government expenditures.

POSTAL SAVINGS SYSTEM

As noted in the section on commercial banks, the major banks operating in Cuba do not pay any interest on their savings deposits. Deposits with the Postal Savings System, on the other hand, carry a 4 percent return. Nevertheless, Postal Savings deposits are only 10 percent as large as savings deposits in the commercial banks, and the rate of growth has been very disappointing. This seems to have resulted from a lack of public confidence in the handling of government funds, as well as from the growth of capitalization companies which are attracting middle-class savings to an increasing extent.

Nearly half of the government-guaranteed Postal Savings deposits has been invested in government bonds which, until recently, consisted primarily of external debt issues. While most of the balance of Postal Savings deposits has been held as cash, the system has upon occasion made loans to government employees at modest interest rates. These advances, which are secured by attachment of salaries, proved of great benefit during the 1930s when government salary payments were often many months in arrears.

INSURANCE COMPANIES

Cuba is served by a surprisingly large number of foreign and Cuban-owned insurance companies. At the end of 1946, there were 63 Cuban and 64 foreign-owned insurance companies operating on the island. British and Canadian companies underwrite the bulk of life insurance, while Cuban institutions are dominant in the field of workers' compensation.

During the decade 1939 to 1949 total annual insurance premiums more than tripled, reflecting in part the rapid rise in group insurance as well as the increase in insurance carried by individuals. The reserves of insurance companies have been rising at the rate of $7 million to $8 million per year, and just as in commercial banking, Cuban-owned companies are conducting a growing share of the business.

Close to one third of aggregate reserves is now invested in Cuban securities, mostly government bonds. Mortgages account for another third, while most of the rest is retained at head offices or invested in foreign securities or real estate. In addition, some insurance companies have been an important source of funds for industrial enterprises and real estate operations, while others have financed public utility companies.

CAPITALIZATION COMPANIES

During the last ten years Cuban capitalization companies have grown to play an important role as savings institutions. The mixed capitalization contract that they have developed contains the familiar features used by capitalization companies in Mexico and other Latin American countries: provision for monthly payments; the option to obtain a policy loan after two or three years, usually at 6 percent interest; and a lottery feature enabling the winners to secure payment of the principal before the due date. In addition, the contract includes a mortgage loan agreement that enables the subscriber to purchase one of the houses constructed by his capitalization company. Homes are financed in part with funds subscribed under the capitalization contract and in part with mortgage loans from the company.

It has been estimated that in 1950 the technical reserves of capitalization companies exceeded 10 million pesos, and were increasing at the rate of 3 million to 4 million pesos a year. They had made mortgage loans totaling approximately 10 million pesos, and had constructed some 5,000 homes throughout the island. Capitalization companies can do much to foster middle and lower-class savings, especially if the new National Bank is successful in weeding out fraudulent concerns. The activities of capitalization companies are eventually to be supervised by the Bank Examination Department of the National Bank.

THE CENTRAL BANK

ORIGIN

The creation of a central bank was delayed for fifty years after Cuba attained independence. Until 1920 its absence was of little consequence, and the existing dollar system fitted Cuba's needs well, since the economy expanded without violent fluctuations. The 1921 sugar crisis, however, brought home dramatically the disadvantages of not having an independent currency and a lender of last resort. Most Cuban-owned banks were in consequence wiped out by the crisis. So far as the foreign banks were concerned, however, the absence of a central bank was not crucial, because they were able to draw on their home offices and, through them, on their own monetary authorities in case of need. Moreover, the Federal Reserve System in the twenties and early thirties maintained agencies on the island.

The protracted depression that started in Cuba in the middle twenties again brought to the foreground the necessity for establishing an independent currency and a central bank. The creation of a peso currency was initiated in the depression years when part of the dollars in circulation left the country and the government began to raise revenues in the form of seigniorage profits by coining silver. From the mid thirties until 1951 Cuba had two parallel currencies, the

United States dollar and the Cuban peso. The peso kept close to par with the dollar except for 1937–40 when it was at a discount, and for a short period during the war when it was at a premium.

The dual currency system was fully established by the late thirties, and the need for a central bank and a single peso-currency system was clearly indicated. It was not until December, 1948, however, that the National Bank Charter was finally passed into law, and the Cuban National Bank did not actually begin to operate until April 1, 1950, while the peso did not become sole legal tender until July 1, 1951.

FUNCTIONS AND POWERS OF THE MONETARY AUTHORITIES

In accordance with the structure and needs of the Cuban economy, the National Bank has, in addition to the normal functions, those of promoting more rapid diversification and development of the economy. It is also charged with the highly important task of advising the government in economic affairs. The quality of the management and staff of the Bank warrants the hope that it will be able to discharge this function exceptionally well.

The Bank's policy is formulated by a five-member council composed of a president named by the executive, a representative for foreign banks and one for Cuban banks, and the presidents of the Agricultural and Industrial Credit Bank, and the Stabilization Fund, who also are appointed by the executive. The Minister of the Treasury may attend meetings of the Council, but he does not have the right to vote.

The capital of the National Bank is subscribed by the government and the private banks, the former holding an absolute majority. The assembly of stockholders, in which the government is not represented, plays a relatively unimportant role in the direction of National Bank policy, its functions being restricted to discussing monetary and banking problems and voting on measures passed by the Council. The Council can override the assembly's objection by a vote of four out of five.

INTERNATIONAL RESERVES

The National Bank is the custodian of the country's centralized international reserves, and the Stabilization Fund, which was established in 1939 and under the new law is virtually an integral part of the National Bank, has control over exchange operations. The Fund acquires reserves by purchasing exchange from exporters, who are obliged to deliver up to 30 percent of their exchange proceeds as determined by the Fund. In an emergency when the nation's reserves are seriously threatened, the executive power may permit the Fund to raise compulsory deliveries of exchange to as high as 100 percent of export proceeds. The Stabilization Fund also has the authority to allocate exchange, should the need arise. Cuba's strong international reserve position makes compulsory deliveries of exchange unnecessary at the present time; they are maintained in order to keep intact the administrative machinery in case it should be needed in the future and to supply exchange to banks that do not normally receive enough to meet their needs.

LEGAL TENDER CURRENCY

The National Bank has the sole right to issue legal tender currency, which, together with the Bank's deposits, must be backed by a 25 percent reserve of gold and foreign exchange convertible into gold. On December 31, 1951, the Bank's holdings of gold and foreign exchange amounted to 431,561,293 pesos, 73 percent of its total note issue and deposit liabilities.

Although the United States dollar ceased to be legal tender on July 1, 1951, dollar deposits may be redeemed at the depositor's discretion in either pesos or dollars. If the depositor elects to receive them in dollars, the Cuban bank concerned has the option of paying either in dollars or in dollar drafts on New York banks. If redeemed in drafts, the funds are subject to the 2 percent export tax.

CREDIT CONTROL POWERS

The National Bank possesses all the traditional tools of credit control, including the power to change minimum reserve requirements, conduct open-market operations, rediscount commercial paper, change rediscount rates, and inspect the operations of banking institutions. In addition, its close relationship with the new Agricultural and Industrial Development Bank provides the National Bank with an important tool of qualitative credit control.

The National Bank has the authority to adjust the level reserve ratio within the limits of 12 to 40 percent against peso demand deposits and 8 to 40 percent against savings deposits. At present a 25 percent reserve continues to be required against commercial bank deposits. In the event of an excessive credit expansion, a reserve of up to 100 percent on any subsequent increases in demand deposits may be imposed. In the case of foreign currency deposits, the Bank may set reserves anywhere within the limits of 25 to 100 percent of deposits. Banks are obliged to keep four fifths of their legal reserves on deposit with the National Bank.

Open-market operations have not yet been extensively employed as a means of credit control. However, the National Bank's charter gives it the authority to purchase and sell government securities that have been outstanding for more than one year. It is also authorized to deal in securities that may have been outstanding for less than a year, provided such transactions are carried out during short periods of time and are undertaken purely as a measure of monetary policy. In addition, the Bank can conduct open-market operations in its own obligations or those of the Currency Stabilization Fund for the purpose of controlling credit.

The National Bank is permitted to rediscount commercial paper of from 90 to 270 days duration. The maturity depends upon the type of transaction. As shown in its balance sheet (presented in Table 5), it has not yet rediscounted commercial paper or made advances to member banks on any significant scale. This fact reflects in part the very large excess reserves of the commercial banks.

The Bank also exercises control over the transactions and credit policies of member banks through its power of inspection. It may inspect a member bank whenever it deems this necessary, and must do so at least once every year. Moreover, stockholding banks are obliged to submit balance sheets once every month.

The National Bank's control over the Agricultural and Industrial Development Bank [5] makes it possible for the former to directly expand or contract specialized credit at times when its contacts with commercial banks may be very limited. The relationship between the two banks also gives the National Bank an important control over the distribution of credit. Moreover, this direct relationship with the Agricultural and Industrial Development Bank may prevent a repetition of the unfortunate conflicts between the policies of central banks and those of specialized credit institutions that have been characteristic in other Latin American countries.

[5] Cf. pp. 212–14.

TABLE 5

BALANCE SHEET OF THE NATIONAL BANK OF CUBA, DECEMBER 31, 1951
(AMOUNTS IN MILLIONS OF PESOS)

	Amount [b]
Assets	
International reserves [a]	431.6
Advances to the Monetary Stabilization Fund	102.4
Gross centralized international reserves	534.0
Internal monetary reserves	40.3
Acceptances, rediscounts, and advances to member banks	9.5
Bonds of the Republic of Cuba	10.2
Other assets	4.4
Total assets	598.5
Liabilities	
United States dollar deposits of member banks	24.4
Other United States dollar deposits	3.6
Total international liabilities	28.0
Cuban peso deposits of member banks	142.0
Other Cuban peso deposits	27.6
Total Cuban peso deposits	169.6
Notes in circulation	393.6
Other liabilities	1.2
Total liabilities	592.4
Capital and reserves	6.1
Total liabilities and capital and reserves	598.5

Source: Banco Nacional de Cuba, *Balance Mensual*, December 31, 1951.

NOTE: The income of the National Bank of Cuba is derived primarily from the returns on its reserves deposited abroad or invested in foreign short-term securities. (The excess over the minimum reserve against the Bank's note issue and deposits may, under the law, be deposited abroad or placed in foreign short-term obligations or in securities for which there is a stable market.) The return on the Bank's investments in Cuban government securities accounted for less than one fifth of its total income in the fiscal year 1950–51, while all other forms of income amounted to about one seventh of the total. In the fiscal year ended June 30, 1951, total income was 2,237,441 pesos, while total expenditures were only 977,308.

[a] Including the 12,500,000 peso gold subscription to the International Monetary Fund.

[b] Details may not add up to totals because of rounding.

OPERATIONS WITH GOVERNMENT

The operations of the National Bank with the government are narrowly circumscribed. In addition to serving as fiscal agent, it may make advances to the government for one year only and in amounts not exceeding 8 percent of the government's average annual revenues of the preceding five years. As mentioned above, open-market operations cannot be undertaken with bonds that have not been outstanding for at least one year; open-market purchases of government securities that have been outstanding for a shorter period may only be carried out for the purpose of implementing monetary policy and must be included in the 8 percent limit on loans to the government. Obviously, open-market operations can indirectly enable the government to obtain much larger advances from the Bank, if, for example, the Bank is obliged to make stabilization purchases of older issues as new ones are offered.

The National Bank has taken an active part in restoring the market for government bonds, as evidenced by the crucial role that it performed in successfully floating the 1950 bond issues, described in a later section. Its present holdings of government bonds in the main reflect recent efforts to stabilize the market for long-term obligations, rather than attempts to control credit.

POLICIES AND PROGRAMS

It is as yet too early to evaluate fully the National Bank's policies and operations. So far, it has promoted successfully two relatively large bond issues, as noted above. It has also contributed to increasing the soundness of the Cuban banking system through its assistance to two small and one major Cuban bank.

The National Bank is assigned the important task of promoting long-term economic development and diversification and of smoothing out the violent fluctuations to which the economy is subject as a consequence of its dependence on sugar exports. The very presence of a lender of last resort may provide enough confidence to induce some banks to diversify their loan portfolios and expand their operations outside the metropolitan area of Havana. The National Bank's control over specialized credit through the Agricultural and Industrial Development Bank and its capacity to stimulate the markets for private and government securities are also important as ways of promoting economic development and diversification.

In formulating policy to minimize economic fluctuations, the Bank is faced with a basic conflict between internal and external stability. In countries like Cuba where internal fluctuations directly reflect variations in exchange balances rather than changes in domestic investment and consumption, central bank policy cannot be guided by changes in the reserve ratio, for this ratio tends to be largest at a time when credit should be restricted most and lowest in depressions when a bank should be pursuing a policy of easy credit. In periods of boom, reserves should be husbanded and credit curtailed, while in depressions accumulated reserves must be used to finance sizable import surpluses, and credit should be permitted to expand. Indeed, the effectiveness of anti-depression measures will rest largely on the central bank's success in absorbing liquidity, building up reserves, and restraining inflation during the period of high prosperity.

The task of the National Bank of Cuba in smoothing out cyclical fluctuations will be made more difficult by the almost religious belief in parity with the dollar, which limits the use of the exchange rate as an instrument of policy. Also, the importance of the sugar sector of the economy may easily, in depressions, force the Bank to engage in extensive financing of holdings of sugar stocks. This may not only accelerate unduly the depletion of reserves, but might also provide a deterrent to diversification.

AGRICULTURAL AND INDUSTRIAL CREDIT

AGRICULTURAL CREDIT

As already noted in the section on commercial banking, the only Cuban agricultural producers with relatively satisfactory access to bank credit are large sugar-cane planters, tobacco and rice growers, and cattlemen. Even these limited groups normally cannot secure medium-term or long-term loans from the banking system; and, since they at best constitute less than 25 percent of all farm units, the great mass of medium-scale and small-scale farmers who produce most non-export foodstuffs operate almost entirely without bank credit. In other words, the average small Cuban farmer has no way of obtaining bank credit to tide him over the period during which his crops are growing, to assist him in meeting his harvesting expenses, or to finance the storage of his crop so that he is not obliged to sell it immediately after the harvest when prices are at their yearly low. Nor can he command bank loans for the purchase of cattle or farm equipment or for carrying out improvements on his land. Moreover, with the existing strong aversion to mortgage lending as a result of mortgage moratoria, few agriculturists are able to acquire new farm land.

The causes for the reluctance of commercial banks to extend credit to most farmers are obvious. Small farmers are not considered safe bank risks, because their general level of education and technical competence is often low; a good many of them are squatters; and they have few modern implements. Most importantly, they produce non-export commodities, the prices of which fluctuate greatly because of the absence of proper marketing arrangements.

These factors not only make it impossible for most farmers to secure bank credit, but also lead to the imposition of onerous conditions by the processors, dealers, and local merchants, who extend mercantile credit to them. The system of mercantile credit has been well described in the recent report on Cuba by the International Bank's Economic and Technical Mission.

> Most Cuban farmers have little opportunity to obtain credit except from those who extend it as an incident to the purchase of their products or to the sale to them of merchandise. Control over the production and sale of farm products thus passes to a considerable extent to the creditor; and, in cases where merchandise credit is given, the farmer often loses the opportunity to buy where he can get the best bargain.[6]

The credit facilities available to rice and coffee growers provide two concrete examples of the way in which mercantile credit is extended. Rice millers and the big rice growers collect 10 percent a year on their loans to small rice growers and in addition they receive implicit interest in the form of higher prices obtainable for commodities sold to their debtors. Usually crop liens or mortgages are given as guarantees, and some of the lenders maintain an inspection system.

It is generally agreed that not more than 2 or 3 percent of the coffee growers are at present acceptable banking risks. The credit needs of the rest are very imperfectly supplied by wholesalers and processors in Santiago and in other urban centers. Explicit interest rates collected by these merchants range from 8 to 12 percent, while implicit charges often exceed 25 percent. There is normally an understanding that the borrower will sell his coffee to the lender, who usually pays from 10 to 30 percent under the price that could have been obtained if the grower were free to market his coffee competitively.

It is readily apparent that the existing mercantile credit system is wholly inadequate to meet the needs of Cuban agriculture. The

[6] International Bank for Reconstruction and Development, Findings and Recommendations of an Economic and Technical Mission, *Report on Cuba* (Washington, 1951), p. 591.

limited amounts of short-term credit thus made available cannot support a well-balanced farming program requiring the availability of medium-term and long-term credit. The absence of adequate credit outside of the sugar sector has had a tendency to freeze the *status quo* in agricultural production, thus inhibiting diversification.

The task of transforming non-sugar agricultural producers into acceptable banking risks and the promotion of old and new crops call for social action in the form of cooperatives or of a government institution not guided exclusively by profit considerations. Unfortunately, production and marketing cooperatives are virtually non-existent in the Cuban countryside; this may be due to the excessive individualism of the small farmer, to his isolation, his suspicion of all paper titles, or his distrust of all borrowing and lending operations, which results from his experience of abuse and extortion by the local merchants.

In an attempt to cope with the problem, the Cuban Government, under the leadership of the new National Bank, has created and set up an Agricultural and Industrial Development Bank, which started operations in October, 1951. The organization and main functions of this Bank are described in a subsequent section.

INDUSTRIAL CREDIT

In the industrial sector, just as in the non-sugar agriculture, there seems to exist a vicious circle which blocks the growth of smaller enterprises. The few large firms, often foreign-owned, are strongly capitalized and have little trouble in obtaining short-term credit and even term loans. In recent years their profits have been so substantial that they have been able to finance expansion by plowing back their earnings, so that they have not required much bank credit. Smaller industrial enterprises and new undertakings, on the other hand, are often undercapitalized and find it almost impossible to secure even working capital advances from the banks. One basic reason for their lack of capitalization is the restricted scope of their activities, which in turn is due in great part to their inability to secure credit. Their credit needs are further accentuated by the virtual absence of a Cuban capital market for private securities.

Most working capital advances extended to Cuban industrial enterprises run for only 90 days. In consequence, many industrial undertakings cannot work at full capacity during the dead season, when they should be building up stocks in preparation for the spurt in demand that comes with the sugar harvest. Thus, seasonal fluctuations in sugar lead to seasonality in industry and business generally.

The difficulty of securing credit is a particularly serious obstacle to the growth of new processing industries, such as canning, because in the absence of an active agricultural credit system the industrial producer is often forced to make advances to farmers, in order to secure his local supply of raw materials.

THE AGRICULTURAL AND INDUSTRIAL DEVELOPMENT BANK

Administration.—The Agricultural and Industrial Development Bank, which is an autonomous agency of the Cuban state, was established on December 20, 1950. The Bank is divided into an agricultural and an industrial division, each of which, in turn, contains a banking and a development subdivision. The Bank is governed by a board of five directors, two of whom are presidential nominees and two representatives of the National Bank, while the fifth, who acts as president, is appointed by the executive from candidates nominated by the other four directors. Through staggered appointments and long terms of office, the board of directors is given a measure of independence *vis-à-vis* the government similar to that enjoyed by the board of directors of the National Bank.

In addition to its representation on the board of directors, the National Bank has certain veto powers over the operation of the Agricultural and Industrial Development Bank, of which the most important relate to its annual budget and to sales and purchases of its bonds.

Capital Structure and Source of Funds.—The Bank has a capital of 15 million pesos, assigned in equal shares to the agricultural and industrial credit sections. In addition, it has a development fund of 10 million pesos, again divided equally between agriculture and industry. The capital has been subscribed in the form of government bonds, which the Bank may sell up to an annual amount equivalent to 10 percent of its capital and reserves.

In addition to its capital funds, the Bank can discount or rediscount agricultural and industrial short-term paper, and may issue its own bonds, secured by the portfolios of the two banking divisions. These bonds are tax exempt, are eligible for investment by retirement funds, and may be used as collateral on the same terms as government bonds.

The proceeds of rediscounting operations and bond issues may be used only by the banking subdivision; the funds available to the development subdivisions are limited to the 10 million pesos in the development fund and whatever profits may be allocated for development purposes.

The Bank's Operations.—The two banking subdivisions are given power to grant a wide variety of short-term, medium-term, and long-term loans, secured by various forms of collateral. The Agricultural Banking subdivision may grant loans either directly, through other banking institutions, or through rural credit associations. Short-term production loans, which may not run for more than 18 months and which may be secured by a wide variety of collateral, are extended to finance the raising of crops, expenditures on insecticides and fertilizer, purchases of cattle, and the warehousing and transportation of crops to markets. The Bank can make medium and long-term mortgage loans up to 25 years for permanent installations, repairs, irrigation, purchases of farm machinery, and the refinancing of previously incurred debt. Similarly, the Industrial Banking subdivision can make short-term advances up to 18 months, guaranteed by authorized securities. Its medium-term and long-term mortgage loans up to 25 years are for the purposes of purchasing equipment, financing construction and repairs, and refinancing previously incurred debts. This subdivision may, in addition, acquire industrial bonds and stocks that have been outstanding for at least a year.

A number of original provisions govern the operations of the development subdivisions, which need not be guided by considerations of short-term profits. The Agricultural Development subdivision is able to extend credit to rural credit associations, grant rehabilitation loans to small farmers, establish and direct research and experiment stations, provide agricultural extension services, and promote farm cooperatives. The Industrial Development subdivision can participate in the founding of new industrial enterprises, subscribing up to 50 percent of their capital. It may also grant loans for industrial development, and engage in research enterprises.

As the operations of the Agricultural and Industrial Development Bank date only from 1951, an evaluation of its practices is, of course, impossible. An aspect of its loan operations may, however, be foreshadowed by the fact that the cereal warehouses and meat cold-storage plants, constructed by the Cuban Government in recent years, have been turned over to the new Bank; this will afford the opportunity of giving crop support loans against warehousing receipts. The excellent choice of management for the new Bank and the fact that its staff contains some outstanding agronomists and technicians in the field of agricultural credit warrant hope for unspectacular but substantial progress in furnishing credit to neglected sectors of the Cuban economy.

Branches and Agencies of the Bank.—The Bank will serve the agricultural and industrial communities through a number of branches, rural credit associations, and local committees. Remote rural areas will be served wherever possible through credit associations, which will make loans to its members and rediscount these loans with the Bank. In areas where no credit associations exist, local committees called *patronatos* will be established as agencies of the Bank for the purpose of making loans to farmers. They will be composed of three members selected by the Bank and will work with a Bank-appointed agronomist with experience in agricultural and credit problems.

CONSUMPTION CREDIT TO WAGE EARNERS

The extreme seasonality of sugar production creates special consumer credit needs on the part of sugar workers and all those associated with the transportation and trading of sugar. A major part of the wages of these workers is earned and received during the four months of the sugar harvest, between January and May. Most workers spend their entire wages immediately on receipt, either to cover current expenditures or to repay debts contracted during the "dead season." [7] Until the next harvest they lead a hand-to-mouth existence, securing advances from local storekeepers by pledging their future earnings. Most of them are never wholly out of debt. Their credit worthiness being so low, the supply of credit so limited, and its cost consequently so great, only the most essential needs of life are purchased, and expenditures are postponed wherever possible until the harvest season. The consequent concentration of spending during the sugar season introduces strong seasonality not only into the retail-wholesale business, but also into the operation of most consumer goods industries on the island.

Although the practices of storekeepers at sugar mills have reportedly

[7] Cubans call the period between sugar harvests "tiempo muerto" (dead time).

improved greatly in the last few years, following the outlawing of the company store, the extent to which workers are still tied to one store through established credit relations, particularly in the sugar colonies, continues to invite abuses. Many Cuban shopkeepers persist in taking advantage of their situation by charging implicit interest rates of from 2 to 3.5 percent a month through unethical practices.

In an effort to protect sugar workers from such extortionistic practices, the Sugar Workers' Retirement Fund recently established a Sugar Workers' Loan Fund of 1.5 million pesos for the purpose of making advances for consumption. The Loan Fund makes personal advances to sugar workers at moderate interest rates and receives repayments through wage deductions at the mill. It should be noted, nevertheless, that earlier attempts to grant consumption credit in this way to the transportation workers were not very successful, partly owing, however, to the financial weakness of the Transportation Workers' Retirement Fund. Insufficient consideration seems to have been given, so far, to the feasibility of setting up some plan for compulsory savings which would force sugar workers to space their expenditures more wisely and evenly than at present.

MORTGAGE LENDING

In contrast to the limited amount of mortgage lending at the present time, there existed before the great depression a vigorous and highly developed market for real estate mortgages and mortgage bonds in Cuba, reflecting the traditional preference for investments in real property as well as the suitability of mortgages for sugar financing and their relatively high liquidity. During the 1930s, however, the mortgage market was seriously damaged by a series of moratorium decrees. In an effort to stem the epidemic of insolvencies following the collapse of sugar exports, interest rates on mortgage debts were reduced, and amortization periods for such loans were greatly extended.

Cuban investors have not yet recovered from the precedent established by the moratoria, and most institutional and private investors still fear the adoption of similar measures in the event of another severe depression. Notwithstanding these apprehensions, the last few years have witnessed a moderate revival in mortgage lending. Urban mortgage loans have been made at rates of interest varying from 8 to

12 percent for large transactions and as high as 18 percent a year for smaller ones. Mortgage lending on rural property, however, is still very limited.

The moratoria have stimulated new forms of real estate lending, designed to protect creditors against the disadvantages of possible future moratorium legislation. Under the "contracto de compra y venda," for example, title to the property is transferred to the lender under a trusteeship arrangement. The borrower is protected unless he fails to live up to the terms of the contract, and, in the event of a moratorium, the lender would possess the property without being obliged to foreclose.

Mortgage loans by insurance companies, banks, and capitalization companies are restricted primarily to modern construction in urban areas. In the case of residential real estate, individual homes are preferred to multiple units. Interest rates of 4 to 8 percent and maturities running to 16 years are common. Inflated real estate values, especially in Havana, have induced conservative policies, and most mortgage loans are not for more than half of the appraised value of the property. In the last ten years, capitalization companies have been playing an increasingly important role in the financing of residential construction, and by the end of 1950, as mentioned in an earlier section, had made advances of some 10 million pesos in mortgage loans to their members.

THE CAPITAL MARKET

As stressed in the introduction to the present chapter, savings have been quite substantial during the recent years of sugar prosperity. However, the portion of these savings that has been invested through the securities markets has remained very low. Cuban savings are largely invested abroad, hoarded, or plowed back into business enterprises.

THE PRIVATE SECURITY MARKET

There is virtually no market for private domestic securities in Cuba today. Institutional investors have placed only a small part of their assets in private securities, although some insurance companies have lately purchased the securities of certain major public utilities and industrial enterprises. The capital required to establish new private businesses or expand established ones, if it can be secured at all, is obtained from small groups of investors on a personal basis.

The market for outstanding securities leads a shadowy existence. Less than 60 securities are listed on the Havana Stock Exchange, of which only a few are widely owned and actively traded. Most sales and purchases are privately negotiated, since open bidding takes place during only 20 minutes of every trading day.

The weakness of the security market is another manifestation of the lack of confidence in the economic future of the country, which stems from the conviction that everything depends on sugar and that no real diversification of risk is at present possible. Cubans, moreover, are particularly skeptical of security investments because of the unfortunate experiences they have had on three occasions in the last thirty years: in 1920, when a number of large Cuban-owned banks, sugar companies, and trading firms collapsed; in 1929, when Cubans were caught in the New York stock market crash; and throughout the 1930s, when holders of mortgage bonds found that, as a result of the various moratoria, their capital had become frozen.

The development of a capital market has, furthermore, been inhibited by the absence of an adequate market mechanism. There have been almost no arrangements for underwriting new private issues, although recently commercial banks under the leadership of the new National Bank have cooperated in floating issues of government bonds. Moreover, because of the continued adherence to the old Spanish laws governing underwriting operations, excessive charges for these services have been customary, and underwriters have sometimes failed to deliver reasonable proportions of the proceeds of security sales. Other factors that have stemmed the growth of a capital market are political uncertainties, poor labor-management relations, and the well-known cases of victimization of minority stockholders by the majority.

Since the rudimentary state of Cuba's market for private securities finds its roots in some of the most basic obstacles to the country's further growth, no rapid improvement of present conditions can be expected. However, the Agricultural and Industrial Development Bank's Development Divison may provide a new source of capital to industrial firms and may gradually build up a market for their securities among the general public along the lines successfully followed by the Nacional Financiera in Mexico.

GOVERNMENT BOND MARKET

Until 1949 the market for internal government bonds was almost as limited as the market for private securities. However, there was always a good deal of trading in external government bonds because of the government's excellent servicing record. Just prior to the issues of 1949 and 1950 only 80 million pesos in bonds was outstanding, and only 10 percent of the bonds were internal issues. During the course of the Second World War the external debt was almost entirely repatriated, and the yield on these bonds steadily declined.

In 1949 and 1950 the market for internal debt obligations was activated by the flotation of three major issues, totaling 95 million pesos. The first offering, a 25 million-peso veteran bond issue, was not unsuccessful, but the 1950 issues, totaling 70 million pesos, were more widely subscribed by the public. Compared with subscriptions to the 1949 issue of less than 4 million pesos by 175 private investors, in 1950, in the case of the first issue of 45 million pesos, nearly 700 private investors subscribed approximately 14 million pesos, while the second issue of 25 million was mostly taken up by commercial banks. Collective savings institutions were thus obliged to absorb a much smaller proportion of the 1950 issues than of the 1949 veteran bonds.

The success of these issues is attributable to a combination of factors. The war and postwar sugar boom greatly increased the liquidity of Cuban individuals and institutional investors. A part of the liquid funds that were building up began to spill over into the government bond market in the early forties, leading to a continuous rise in the quotation of the external debt obligations of the Cuban Government on the Havana Stock Exchange, with the result that their yield declined from 7.2 percent in 1938 to less than 4 percent in 1950.

The newly established National Bank has been able to overcome the reluctance of the Cuban-owned commercial banks to act as purchasers and distributors of government bond issues. In floating the 1950 issues, the Bank formulated various provisions designed to protect the banks and to insure the proper use of the loan proceeds. Thus, the banks were assured that the National Bank would repurchase from them after one year any unsold portion of their commitments up to an aggregate total of 18 million pesos; they received a 1 percent commission on the bonds that they sold, and their officers were called upon to act as trustees of the loan. Moreover, the retirement funds agreed to subscribe to a major portion of the 1950 issues with the understanding that the National Bank would purchase from them a portion of their holdings of the 1949 veterans' issue. Finally, the National Bank stood ready to support the government bond market while the new issues were being floated, but only very limited support operations proved necessary.

At the end of 1950 the government's funded debt of about 175 million pesos, of which 102 million consisted of internal debt obligations, was fairly well distributed. More than one third was held by the collective savings institutions, another third was in the hands of the public, while the commercial banks held about 20 percent, the National Bank some 7 percent, and foreign investors the remainder.

There can be little doubt that the government should be able to place sizable new issues in the future if the funds raised so far are properly spent and service payments punctually met. Activation of the government bond market represents the first major achievement of the new National Bank.

CONCLUSION

Most Cuban credit institutions, with the exception of the newly created National Bank and the Agricultural and Industrial Development Bank, have developed in response to the credit needs of the sugar and foreign trade sectors that have dominated Cuba's economic life during the last half century. As might be expected, the commercial banking system serves these sectors well, in the sense that forms and terms of credit are well adapted to their special needs. Thus, we have noted the highly developed and flexible loan techniques for sugar financing and the varying forms of commercial credit extended by the banks operating in Cuba. It should also be stressed that, supplemented by loan funds from the United States, the Cuban banking system furnishes credit to prime risks at exceptionally low interest rates.

The emergence of Cuban-owned banks to a position of greater importance has tended to increase the availability of banking services throughout the island, but, so far, has not led to appreciable progress in meeting the credit needs of non-sugar agriculture and of industry, major parts of which continue to be completely dependent on mercantile credit. In general terms it may be said that the Cuban commercial banking system is as sound as can be expected in an economy so highly sensitive to changes in the world price of a single export.

The commercial banks can hardly be expected to contribute decisively to the structural transformation of the economy that is necessary in order to reduce unemployment, raise the standard of living, and minimize economic fluctuations. Because the fundamental obstacles to diversification are so formidable, only comprehensive measures on the part of the government in many fields and extensive changes of attitude on the part of all groups in Cuba can lead the country out of the economic impasse of the last 25 years. What is needed is an effort at adaptation not unlike that successfully carried out by Denmark in the nineteenth century, when it found that the basis of its foreign trade had been altered by events beyond its control.

The contribution that monetary policy can make to this transformation has been considerably enhanced recently. The new National Bank can introduce policies designed to stimulate wider use of the country's idle resources of labor, land, and capital. In so doing, it must try to avoid upsetting internal and external stability too greatly, lest the uncertainties and distortions resulting from price and exchange rate fluctuations outweigh its efforts to promote economic diversification and greater future economic stability.

The Agricultural and Industrial Development Bank, together with the National Bank, can play a very constructive role in inducing foreign and domestic entrepreneurs and investors to develop neglected sectors of the economy. Moreover, it can foster agricultural diversification by gradually freeing the small and medium-sized farmer from his dependency on onerous mercantile credit, by improving market conditions, and by assisting farmers to overcome their technical backwardness. The Agricultural and Industrial Credit Bank can also assist new industrial ventures to the point where they become acceptable bank risks and perhaps even appeal to private investors.

Opportunities for exercising effective monetary policy during cyclical fluctuations and in promoting economic development and diversification have been considerably expanded since the Second World War. In the past two years the island has acquired a new central bank, a development bank, and a currency system of its own, while it continues to enjoy a period of prosperity and high liquidity. Moreover, a market for domestic government bonds has emerged partly as a result of the development of collective savings institutions, but more especially because of the leadership provided by the new National Bank.

ADDENDUM

Since the completion of this chapter at the end of 1951 important political and economic changes have taken place in Cuba, but they have not materially changed the character of the country's financial system. The main political event, the change of government through the coup d'état of March, 1952, apparently left the autonomy of the National Bank unaffected.

In the economic sphere, the country has been faced with the problem of coping with the re-emergence of a sugar surplus, the result of the 1952 record crop of over 7 million long tons. In order to prevent a cumulative price decline in the world sugar market, the Cuban Government decided to set aside a quota of 1,750,000 tons of sugar to be sold in the United States during the next five years, and at the same time it established production limits of five million tons for 1953 and 1954. The commercial banks agreed to finance this retention of sugar by discounting participation certificates issued by the Cuban Sugar Stabilization Institute, and the National Bank stood ready to rediscount them. In practice, the banks acquired about 120 million pesos of these sugar obligations, while only 20 to 30 million were rediscounted.

As a result of these operations, the asset structures of both the National Bank and the commercial banks have shown marked changes. At the end of June, 1953, sugar financing accounted for about 40 percent of total member banks' assets, compared with less than 20 percent two years earlier. The commercial banks were nevertheless able to maintain a high degree of liquidity. At the end of July, 1953, the ratio of their cash reserves to total deposits stood at 35 percent—only one percentage point below the level of September, 1951, while total available cash resources still constituted 40 percent of deposits in spite of a sizable reduction in commercial banks' foreign assets.

The National Bank's active role in attempting to cushion the adverse effects of the sugar crisis is reflected in the increased importance of its domestic assets relative to its international reserves. On the one hand, the Bank's international reserves, which had reached a peak of 604 million pesos in July, 1951, were down to 525 million two years later after having declined to only 476 million in December, 1952. On the other hand, at the end of July, 1953, the National Bank's rediscounts and advances to member banks stood at 48.2 million pesos compared with 21.6 million a year before and 1.2 million in July, 1951, and short-term advances to the government totaled 16.3 million, while no such advances had been outstanding in July, 1951, or July, 1952. The Bank's portfolio of government bonds, finally, was barely greater in July, 1953, than two years before—reflecting its success in activating the Cuban bond market so that its role as investor in government bonds remains marginal. It is noteworthy that in spite of the increase in the National Bank's domestic assets, its international liquidity remained very great; at the end of July, 1953, the Bank's international assets amounted to 79 percent of its liabilities subject to minimum reserve requirements.

The sugar overproduction crisis and resulting fall in national income led to a decline in government revenues, while expenditures proved difficult to curtail. The resulting deficit was in small part financed by means of National Bank short-term advances, subject to the strict loan limits established under the National Bank Act. More important, however, was the issue of new long-term bonds with the result that by mid-1953 the Cuban Government's internal funded debt had more than doubled. The greater part of the new issues was placed with the public and the collective savings institutions, so that the percentage of the total debt held by the banking system amounted to less than one third in June, 1953, or about the same as in 1950.

Other important developments affecting Cuban commercial banking during the last two years have been the establishment of a deposit insurance system and the creation of a new semipublic financing institution. Under the deposit insurance scheme of September, 1952, deposits of less than 10,000 pesos are to be guaranteed by means of a 10 million-peso fund which is being formed through annual contributions of one million pesos by the National Bank and 100,000 pesos by the member banks.

The Financiera Nacional de Cuba was created in August, 1953, to promote and finance self-liquidating public works projects such as toll roads, waterworks, and so forth. The institution, which will issue its own bonds under government guarantee, has a capital of four million pesos, of which just over half has been subscribed by the National Bank and one sixth each by the insurance companies, capitalization companies, and most of the member banks. While the share subscription was voluntary for all except the National Bank, the stockholding entities are to be given preference in the agency's banking and insurance operations. The new institution, which is designed to supplement the work of the National Development Commission and the Agricultural and Industrial Credit Bank, will be administered by a board of seven members, of which the chairman is a political appointee, while four members represent the foreign and Cuban-owned member banks and the remaining two the insurance and capitalization companies. The Nacional Financiera may well become a useful tool for the greater diversification of the Cuban economy, the urgency of which has been underscored by the ending of the post-Korea sugar boom.

REFERENCES

OFFICIAL SOURCES

Banco Nacional de Cuba, Departamento de Investigaciones Económicas. *Estadísticas Monetarias y Bancarias,* June and July, 1951.

—— Memoria, December, 1949. Havana.

—— Memoria, 1949–50. Havana.

—— Que es y como opera el Banco Nacional de Cuba. Havana, 1950.

Ley número 13 de 23 de diciembre de 1948 (Law creating the National Bank of Cuba). *La Gaceta Oficial,* December 30, 1948.

Ley número 5 de 20 de diciembre de 1950 (Law of agricultural and industrial development of Cuba). *La Gaceta Oficial,* December 20, 1950.

Ministerio de Hacienda, Dirección General de Estadística. *Boletín de Estadísticas,* various issues.

NONOFFICIAL SOURCES

Alienes y Urosa, Julian. Características fundamentales de la economía cubana. Havana, 1950.

—— Economía de postguerra y desempleo. Havana, 1949.

—— "Evolución de la economía cubana en la postguerra," *El Trimestre Económica,* Vol. XVII, No. 2, April–June, 1950.

Cámara de Comercio de la República. Banco Nacional de Cuba. Havana, 1942.

Cuba Económica y Financiera, various issues.

Gutiérrez, Gustavo. Presente y futuro de la economía cubana. Havana, 1950.

Institute of International Finance. The Economic Position of Cuba. Bulletin No. 165, March 6, 1950.

International Bank for Reconstruction and Development. Findings and Recommendations of an Economic and Technical Mission. Report on Cuba. Washington, 1951.

Luis y Barrena, S. Informe técnico sobre el proyecto de ley creado El Banco Central de la República de Cuba y modificando el sistema monetario vigente. Havana, 1942.

Pazos y Roque, Felipe. Discurso pronunciado . . . para conmemorar el primer año de operaciones de Banco Nacional de Cuba. Havana, 1951.

Wallich, Henry C. Monetary Problems of an Export Economy. Cambridge, Mass., 1950.

FRANCE

by Henry Germain-Martin

BANQUE NATIONALE POUR LE COMMERCE ET L'INDUSTRIE

HISTORY OF THE FRENCH BANKING SYSTEM

FINANCIERS AND BANKERS BEFORE THE EIGHTEENTH CENTURY

THE FRENCH banking system at the present time presents a logical and harmonious structure, a result of legislation passed in 1941 and modified in 1945. To a certain extent these laws merely confirmed the organization which had developed progressively throughout history. In its earlier phases, however, banking in France was not organized and ordered as it is today.

Banking and credit first appeared in France with the expansion of trade in the Mediterranean area, beginning with the Knights Templars in the twelfth century. That monastic order became the banker of the Christian world during the Crusades, since the necessary transfer of funds could be made easily between the branches of the "Temple" scattered from Western Europe to the Middle East. The great wealth gathered by the Order was the envy of the kings who benefited from it, and the Order was finally dispersed following a suit brought against it in 1307 by Philippe-le-Bel.

The Church's prohibition of interest-bearing loans paralyzed bank-

---

HENRY GERMAIN-MARTIN. Docteur en droit (Sciences juridiques, Sciences politiques et économiques); Lauréat de l'Institut; Ancien chargé de cours à la Faculté de droit de Lille; Ancien Président de Chambre au Tribunal de Commerce de la Seine; Directeur du Département des Etudes Economiques et de Documentation Générale de la Banque Nationale pour le Commerce et l'Industrie; Professeur au Centre d'Etudes Supérieures de Banque: Cours de documentation et de méthode économiques, Cours d'histoire et d'organisation des banques. Chargé du Cours de gestion des entreprises à l'Ecole Nationale d'Administration.

ing operations for a long time but lost its effectiveness when the Popes themselves needed the help of bankers to administer their funds. Moreover, the daily necessities of trade led to many evasions of the canon law. In the Middle Ages the function of banks was more like that of modern investment banks than that of deposit banks. It was carried on by the great financiers, such as the Fuggers in Germany and the Medicis in Italy. Among them can be cited the French Jacques Coeur, banker to King Charles VII. The first bankers in France, however, were foreign-born. The Jewish and Lombardic names call to mind the liberalism with which they were admitted to French territory, as well as the restrictions to which they were subjected at other times. Their activity was mainly at the fairs, where devices for the settlement of accounts were developed. In order to simplify exchange, bankers created a money of account and in order to avoid the movement of funds, they used the bill of exchange which gradually became an instrument of credit. The Hundred Years War put an end to the big fairs, and banking transactions then started to develop in the larger cities.

The cost of the Crusades, and the exhaustion of the royal Treasury after Philippe-le-Bel, forced sovereigns to ask for private credits. The practice arose of anticipating revenues, and assigning taxes and discounting Treasury obligations. Colbert's attempt, at a later period, to put some order into royal finances had unfortunately no lasting effect. The state, burdened with heavier and heavier liabilities, still had to negotiate with tax collectors, with bankers and financiers.

At the end of the seventeenth century proposals were made for the creation of a state bank which would assume the service of the public debt and as compensation would be permitted to issue bank notes. Law's plan led in 1716 to the creation of the first public bank in France. That bank, based upon an extremely bold conception, was to be a deposit bank, an issuing bank, and a colonial company. The royal bills which had been issued at the end of Louis XIV's reign became bank notes secured by commercial transactions. Unfortunately, speculation led to bankruptcy, and all the king's efforts were unable to prevent the collapse, in 1720, of the bank notes and the shares of the company. The memory of Law's experience and the financial difficulties of the regime for a long time prevented the creation of a new bank. Not until 1776 was a Discount Office (Caisse d'Escompte) created by the minister Turgot. Intended to provide credit for trading, the Discount Office was later used by the state for its monetary transactions. The increasing number of *assignats* led to its disappearance in 1793. In spite of all that, the need for banking institutions was now clear. In the years following 1793 there were created the Office of Current Accounts (Caisse des Comptes Courants), the Discount Office for Trade (Caisse d'Escompte du Commerce), and the Commercial Banking Office (Comptoir Commercial), all these establishments giving a preview of the Bank of France which was organized in 1800 by Bonaparte.

THE DEVELOPMENT OF BANKING INSTITUTIONS AFTER 1800

Although granted an official status, the Bank of France was initially a privately owned company. It discounted bills freely and issued bank notes, but without an exclusive privilege. In 1806, state control of the bank appeared when the appointment of the Governor of the Bank was put into the hands of the executive, and in 1808 its business was defined by official statute.

Though the Bank of France encountered difficulties from time to time, it continued to expand, supported as it was by successive political regimes. It became a national institution and its preeminence was well established during the course of the nineteenth century. In fact the whole French banking system was expanding concurrently with general economic development, marked by the introduction of machines and building of railways which required an increased use of capital.

In the first half of the nineteenth century, banking continued as a personal affair, since Law's adventure had not encouraged the creation of new companies. A few bankers exercised financial leadership in Paris, most often in close cooperation with branches of their families in foreign cities. They formed the *Hautes Banques* (private banks) to which belonged mainly Jewish and Protestant families. In the provinces were a number of local banks, the oldest of them dating back to the eighteenth century but most of them to the Second Empire. The appearance of big commercial banks in the middle of the nineteenth century was closely associated with the movement initiated by Saint-Simon, who had many followers among businessmen. The English joint-stock banks served as models, once the broadening of the French corporation law was accomplished. The first bank to be created as a joint-stock corporation was the Comptoir National d'Escompte de la

Ville de Paris in 1848. It was then part of a system of 67 provincial offices, the capital of which was divided equally between the state, the local authorities, and the general public. The Paris Comptoir alone survived, becoming a privately owned company in 1854. The other big joint-stock banks which exist today appeared during the same period: the Crédit Industriel et Commercial in 1859, the Crédit Lyonnais in 1863, and the Société Générale in 1864. The founder of the Crédit Lyonnais, Henri Germain, elaborated the principle which became, in the second half of the nineteenth century, the basis of commercial banking. But the development did not proceed without setbacks. It is enough to recall the fate of the Crédit Mobilier, founded in 1852 by the brothers Pereire and liquidated in 1867 as a result of speculative transactions, or the fall of the Union Générale in 1882 and of the Comptoir d'Escompte de Paris in 1889. The Crédit Commercial de France was organized in 1894 and the Banque Nationale de Crédit in 1913.

Gradually the functions of the joint-stock banks became more specialized as opposed to those of the *banques d'affaires* (investment banks). Among the latter, the Banque de Paris et des Pays-Bas, founded in 1872, and the Banque de l'Union Parisienne, founded in 1904, were able to withstand several crises and to develop their financing business in the industrial field beyond the national frontiers. This specialization of banking activity has been maintained and prolonged into the twentieth century. Agricultural and small business credit have their own institutions. After the First World War, other institutions were organized to provide medium-term and foreign trade credit. Public and semi-public banks assumed more and more importance, both because of the new operations entrusted to them and because of the greater amount of funds administered by them. Thus they compensated for the deficiencies of the Paris money market which an excessive tax burden had deflected from its traditional activity, especially in the field of external loans. The current situation in banking in France is therefore strongly marked by specialization and by the opening of new fields of activity. At the same time concentration of the big joint-stock banks has not been without significance. With its structure thus strengthened, the French banking system has been in a position to face with confidence its various crises.

The repercussions of the crisis of 1929 were much less serious in

France than in some other countries. Because the commercial banking system was, indeed, not so closely tied to the investment operations of the economy, bank failures were less numerous and occurred most often in middle-sized or small banks. When there was danger that a first-class institution might fail, the government took action: the Banque Nationale de Crédit was reorganized in 1932 as the Banque Nationale pour le Commerce et l'Industrie; and the Banque d'Alsace-Lorraine was merged with the Crédit Industriel et Commercial. The crisis accentuated the movement toward a greater concentration of banking, and in addition to the bankruptcies taking place, many banks were wound up or reorganized. Just before the Second World War there were in France approximately 2,100 banks in the general sense of the word, with more than 9,000 offices, some of them open only part time. The six most important credit institutions had about 2,500 offices.[1]

RECENT STATE INTERVENTION AND NATIONALIZATION

Government intervention in banking activity is relatively new in France, whereas in many countries it is as old as the banking system itself. The first regulation of French banking dates back only to 1930; it listed a few disqualifications for becoming a banker but did not define the profession itself. Ever since the end of the nineteenth century, however, particularly after each of the main crises, many proposals have been advanced to protect savings. It was not until 1936 that the government created a Credit Commission, which conducted an inquiry and heard representatives of the different branches of activity concerned. There were no official conclusions, although control of the banking system was envisaged.

With the succession to power of the Vichy Government, it became necessary to include banks within the framework of the law of August 16, 1940, concerning the provisional organization of production. A temporary committee was created to prepare the definitive statutes of June 13 and 14, 1941, relating to the regulation and organization of the banking profession and of professions connected with it. First, these laws defined and classified enterprises in the field of banking or finance, each category being grouped into a professional association. Secondly, the new laws aimed to control and direct such enterprises through two bodies: the Permanent Committee on the Organi-

[1] Statistics of monetary and credit developments appear in the Statistical Appendix.

zation of Banks and Financial Houses, and the Bank Control Commission.

These bodies had a corporative nature: bankers themselves were to enforce discipline within their profession. The members of the Organization Committee were bankers appointed by the government, but the government was not to intervene in the control itself. The Bank Control Commission in 1941 also had a professional majority since it included two bankers, the Governor of the Bank of France, and the President of the Committee on the Organization of Banks, and only one civil servant, the Director of the Treasury in the Ministry of Finance. This corporative system governed the banking organization from 1941 to 1945. An attempt was made to prevent the creation of new banks and even of new branches, and every bank was forbidden to sell the stock or other interests it held in another bank.

New ideas came in when France was freed in 1945 and the era of nationalization in the banking sector began. The state wanted to be able to direct the distribution of credit and it became necessary to modify old laws and to define new concepts. On November 30, 1945, the National Constituent Assembly received the draft of a law for the nationalization of the Bank of France and the big banks and for the organization of the credit system. The law was voted almost without discussion on December 2, 1945. It was completed and modified by a law of May 17, 1946, relating to the organization of the credit system and by two decrees of May 28, 1946, regulating the activity of deposit banks, nationalized and nonnationalized. Thus was created a hierarchy, at the top of which was the Ministry of Finance and the Bank of France. The composition of the Bank Control Commission was modified, the Permanent Banking Organization Committee became the National Credit Council, and the Bankers Professional Association remained the link between the profession itself and these directing bodies.

The Bank of France and the four main credit establishments, the Crédit Lyonnais, the Société Générale, the Comptoir National d'Escompte and the Banque Nationale pour le Commerce et l'Industrie were declared nationalized as of January 1, 1946. Nationalization was effected by transfer to the state of the shares of the banks. The shareholders received in exchange amortizable bonds bearing a minimum rate of interest. None of the regional and local banks was nationalized owing to their lesser importance in the banking system, the "big four" having 57 percent of total deposits. The principal *banques d'affaires* were subjected only to a measure of control, for it would not have been possible to nationalize them without harm to their interests abroad. While the state absorbed the assets and liabilities of the nationalized banks, the banks have not lost all legal autonomy. The law stipulates that they remain enterprises having a commercial nature. They are subject to the general corporation law with the exception of the special dispositions of the decree of May 28, 1946. Their Boards of Directors are henceforth appointed by the Minister of National Economy, by the trade unions and by the Ministry of Finance, in order to represent the general interests of the nation. The powers of the general assemblies of shareholders are exercised by the Bank Control Commission.

The main characteristic of the 1945 legislation compared with that of 1941 is that the state has now at its disposal the means by which it can influence the distribution of credit. The basis of the banking organization laid during the war was kept in so far as it conformed with the new regulations. The 1941 texts were validated as "so-called laws." The professional relations of bankers with the new control bodies are no longer of the same nature. Of the three directing bodies created in 1941, only the Bankers Professional Association remained, to which affiliation is compulsory. It represents the profession and transmits to the banks the instructions regarding credit policy. The Permanent Banking Organization Committee has been replaced by a new body which has taken all its functions: the National Credit Council.[2] In this new structure the Bank of France has, fortunately, maintained its high position. Its relations with the Ministry of Finance, and especially with the Director of the Treasury, have become closer since nationalization.

THE PRIVATE INSTITUTIONS

PRINCIPLES OF CLASSIFICATION

The French banking structure may be envisaged in the distribution of demand deposits among the different types of banks. The reports of the National Credit Council give the figures for the end of each year.

[2] See pp. 288–92.

TABLE 1
DISTRIBUTION OF DEMAND DEPOSITS
(AMOUNTS IN BILLIONS OF FRANCS)

	1951	*1952*
Bank of France	69	61
Commercial banks [a]	1,439	1,449
Popular banks [a]	60	66
Agricultural banks [a]	116	135
Postal accounts	262	304
All demand deposits	1,946	2,015
Bank notes in circulation	1,883	2,124
Total	3,829	4,139

[a] Must be reduced by the amounts falling due for comparison with data in Statistical Appendix.

It will be seen that unlike some other countries, bank deposits in France are not much more important than the amount of notes in circulation. From the deposit figures tabulated above are excluded the balances of the current account of the Treasury, of various public institutions, of domestic interbank accounts, of foreign banks, and of the accounts arising from the operations of the Economic Cooperation Administration. The demand deposits held by commercial banks represent by far the most important part, especially when compared with those of specialized institutions such as the popular banks and the agricultural banks which carry on a credit business similar to that of the commercial banks. The postal accounts are savings deposits invested in Treasury obligations. Deposits in the savings banks, amounting to 689,300 million francs at the end of 1951, are for the most part used in long-term investments and are not listed with demand deposits.

The distribution of these holdings reveals several types of financial institutions, more or less public or private. As one penetrates still deeper into the financial organization of France, he will find it extremely difficult to devise a logical classification of banking and financial institutions. There is first a private sector, set apart originally by tradition and more recently by law. It is now under the supervision of the Bank Control Commission and includes commercial banks and investment institutions. The four nationalized banks are included here by reason of their commercial character. There is also a semipublic sector which includes institutions which have received from the state a special status and a few privileges, as, for example, the central banks of the French Union countries, which do not fit easily into any classification. In a broader sense, the semi-public sector includes also the institutions which have been created by the state to perform a particular banking service affected with the public interest. Some are specialized banks gathering up funds from the public and using them in transactions pertaining to real estate credit, agricultural credit, small business credit, and foreign trade credit. Others receive funds but carry on no other banking activities; such are the savings banks, the postal checking service and the municipal credit banks.

The third sector of banking activity is of a definitely public nature. Its institutions represent the government in all kinds of credit transactions. Among these, the Crédit National is set up as a corporation but has, by its management and its type of operations, a public character. The Caisse des Dépôts et Consignations and the Caisse Nationale des Marchés de l'Etat are, legally, public institutions. Finally, a few institutions have recently been created for the financing of reconstruction and equipment of important branches of industry; they are connected directly with the public treasury. These principles of classification are somewhat arbitrary but they are nevertheless necessary in order to group the institutions around different types of banking activities.

The law of June 13, 1941, undertook to define banking activities and to classify banking institutions. Until then, banking activities had never been defined and the code of commercial law mentioned them only indirectly by including among commercial transactions all exchange, banking, and brokerage transactions and all transactions made by the public banks. The law now defines banks as "financial firms or establishments, the usual function of which is to receive from the public, as deposits or otherwise, funds which they employ for their own account, either in discounts or in credit transactions, or in financial operations." The notion of "funds received from the public" is very important and it has been made more precise in Article 2 of the law. They are "the funds which a firm or a person receives in every form from or for the account of a third person, with the understanding that the funds will be returned." These definitions make it possible to distinguish the activities of commercial banks from those of financial houses or investment banks and to classify commercial banks according to the law of December 2, 1945, which marked a new stage of banking organization. Article 4 of that law divides all banks into the following categories: deposit banks, investment banks, and long-term and medium-term credit banks.

TABLE 2
TOTAL ASSETS OF REGISTERED BANKS, DECEMBER 31, 1951
(AMOUNTS IN MILLIONS OF FRANCS)

	Assets		Percent of Total	
8 Long-Term and Middle-Term Credit Banks		3,732		0.15
38 Investment Banks				
25 joint stock companies	300,475		12.2	
11 partnerships and personal companies	46,581		1.9	
2 banks specializing in precious metals	3,384		0.15	
Total		350,440		14.25
357 Deposit Banks				
4 nationalized commercial banks	1,141,734		45.7	
2 nonnationalized banks	126,595		5.1	
85 other Paris banks	92,180		3.7	
4 rediscount houses	86,327		3.5	
6 banks operating principally in French overseas territories or abroad	45,912		1.8	
15 French branches of foreign banks	73,370		3.0	
14 banks under foreign control	28,847		1.2	
22 regional banks	305,004		12.2	
186 local banks	56,636		2.3	
16 Algerian banks	167,509		6.7	
3 Saar banks	10,501		0.4	
Total		2,134,615		85.60
Grand total of all registered banks		2,488,787		100.00

THE COMMERCIAL OR DEPOSIT BANKS

Commercial banking is not very old in France, as indicated above, not developing until the last century. The nature of the funds—demand deposits—entrusted to them by their clientele determines their activity, the granting of short-term credit. Commercial banks must be careful to maintain liquidity, making only such loans as can be rapidly mobilized or turned into cash by resale or rediscounting. Today the large credit establishments are typically commercial banks in their business as well as in their structure.

Commercial banks vary greatly in size and importance. The six largest hold more than 50 percent of the aggregate resources of French banks and extend all over France. Some others operate in only one region or locality; others are centered in Paris, and lastly, some others represent foreign interests. Recent legislation has classified all as deposit or commercial banks, as opposed to the *banques d'affaires* or investment banks. According to the law of May 17, 1946, deposit banks are those which receive from the public deposits at sight or deposits with a term of not more than two years. Other restrictions have been provided on the use of the funds: a deposit bank may not have participations in any one enterprise to an amount greater than 10 percent of the capital of that enterprise, and the total amount of such participations may not exceed 75 percent of its own capital funds. Deposit banks, however, are not limited in participations in banks, financial establishments or building societies, if these appear necessary to their business. Deposit banks are also subject to the general regulations which affect the credit policy of all the banks.[3]

The nationalization law of 1945 separated the six large banks into two categories since the Crédit Lyonnais, the Société Générale, the Comptoir National d'Escompte and the Banque Nationale pour le Commerce et l'Industrie were nationalized, whereas the Crédit Industriel et Commercial and the Crédit Commercial de France were not. However, the structure of the first four establishments was different from that of the other two even before nationalization. They are really archetypes of credit establishments having numerous branches covering the whole national territory. They own more than half of all the bank offices and employed, on December 31, 1950, 61,823 people in France and in Algeria, or 56 percent of the total personnel of the registered banks (110,490).

The Crédit Industriel et Commercial has a structure (group banking) which is rather unusual in the French banking system. It groups a number of subsidiary companies which are mostly regional banks and extends their activity to the whole national territory. At the end of 1950, the C.I.C. had nearly 540 offices out of the 911 belonging to all the regional banks. That unusual structure enabled the C.I.C. to escape nationalization. As for the Crédit Commercial de France, it has but a limited business area: the Paris region, the southwest, and the

[3] See p. 292. Participations represent ownership of the capital stock of an enterprise.

main trading towns in France. It has close links with certain industrial groups. These two banks have only one twentieth of all the banking assets of France.

The four nationalized banks are all large and possess about one half of the total assets of French banks; but each of them has its own individuality.[4] The Crédit Lyonnais is preeminent among them: at the end of 1951, its total assets amounted to 373,368 million francs. While its traditions of caution have made it a model deposit bank, it has, however, quite a large portfolio of securities. Its officials are the spokesmen of the whole banking fraternity in dealings with the financial authorities.

The Société Générale, which comes second with total assets of 317,027 million francs at the end of 1951, was originally a larger institution than the Crédit Lyonnais. The latter was created as a local bank with a capital of 20 million francs, whereas the former was created under governmental auspices with a capital of 120 million francs. The Société Générale afterwards engaged in various industrial participations and the Crédit Lyonnais outpaced it by the end of the nineteenth century.

The Comptoir National d'Escompte de Paris is the oldest among the French credit establishments and was for a long time the most important of them. After a semi-crisis in 1889, which made necessary its reorganization, it became noted for the stability of its management. That position did not, however, preclude marked activity abroad and in the French overseas territory. At the end of 1951, the assets of the Comptoir National d'Escompte de Paris totaled 212,368 million francs and in that total the deposit accounts (as opposed to the current accounts) comprised a higher percentage than in any other bank.

Within a few years, the youngest among the credit establishments has caught up with and even outstripped its elders. This is the Banque Nationale pour le Commerce et l'Industrie, created in 1932, when the Banque Nationale de Crédit, itself created in 1913, was in need of exterior help. The new company has shown in its management as well as its methods a remarkable expansionary policy; first of all in France, then in French territories and abroad. Its assets at the end of 1951 amounted to 238,970 million francs and included a high figure for loans, in which the bank is very active.

[4] Moreover, they have subsidiaries and branches in various foreign countries and particularly in French overseas territories.

The organization of the nationalized banks, as required by law, leaves them their commercial character and permits them administrative autonomy. The fact of nationalization is evidenced primarily by the presence on the Boards of Directors of representatives of the principal economic and social groups. The combined balance sheets of the four nationalized banks give a good picture of the transactions performed by the deposit banks. It would not, however, be advisable to use only one date for such a study because of the monetary and financial evolution. Reference to two distinctive years—1938 and 1950—is given in the following table which will make possible, later on, interesting comparisons with the *banques d'affaires*:

TABLE 3
PERCENT DISTRIBUTION OF PRINCIPAL ITEMS IN AGGREGATE BALANCE SHEETS, DECEMBER 31, 1938 AND 1950

Items	*1938*	*1950*
Assets		
Cash due from Treasury and central banks	10.7	5.2
Balances with banks and correspondent institutions	12.0	6.2
Discounts	53.8	65.4
Loans and secured advances	14.2	15.6
Due from acceptances	2.1	3.3
Investments	0.2	0.2
Other	7.0	4.1
Total	100.0	100.0
Liabilities		
Checking accounts (mostly noncommercial)	31.1	26.2
Current accounts (mostly commercial)	35.4	46.3
Certificates of deposit and time accounts	2.4	2.5
Reserves	3.9	0.3
Capital	4.0	0.2
Other	23.2	24.5
Total	100.0	100.0

Because of continued inflation, the checking and current accounts represent more than 72 percent of the total balance sheet of 1950 as against 66 percent in 1938. The proportionate amount of certificates of deposit and time accounts, which fell just after the end of the war, has attained to previous level.

In spite of the capital increases that took place (mainly in 1942) the percentage of own funds and reserves has considerably decreased. The capital of the four biggest credit establishments increased from 1,600 million francs in 1938 to 2,675 in 1945 when they were nationalized. The capital of the whole banking system, at that time, was 10,482 million francs and it had risen to 28,000 million francs in 1950.

As a counterpart of their liabilities, the deposit banks employ funds in the following asset items: [5]

Discounts represent the major part of the loans and investments and account for nearly 65.4 percent of the aggregate balance sheet in 1950 as against 53.8 percent in 1938. They include Treasury and trade bills, the latter tending more and more to take the place of the former since the economic revival which has followed the end of the war. On December 31, 1950, the bills discounted included:

12.7 percent of Treasury and railway bills
2.8 percent of bills accepted by the Crédit National
49.9 percent of other bills

Loans and secured advances, which represent about 16 percent of the aggregate balance sheet, are somewhat more important than before the war.

Acceptances are also slightly more important than at that time, and their percentage in the balance sheet increased from 2.1 to 3.3 percent.

Shares and bonds are, as is proper in deposit banks, very low. So are the fixed assets (bank premises and so on).

The primary reserve which consists of the items "cash" (or till money) and "balances with banks and correspondent institutions" has considerably decreased in the aggregate balance sheet of the deposit banks. That comes from a desire to use more and more fully the whole of the banks' resources and it is to be noted that the portfolio is more easily marketable, or can be mobilized more easily, than before the war.

The accompanying table gives a comparative statement of the four nationalized credit establishments: [6]

[5] See Tables E, F, G, and H in the Statistical Appendix for an industrial distribution of loan totals.

[6] Deposit liabilities of banking institutions were defined by the law of June 13, 1941, and the definitions adopted were put into effect by the Commission de Contrôle des Banques in March, 1943.

Checking accounts are those used by the bulk of depositors in their personal affairs, in handling their savings and investment operations. They are built up principally through the deposit of funds (primary deposits) and are non-borrowing accounts. Though they are designated as checking accounts, the use of checks is not limited to these accounts, since checks are also employed by those having current accounts.

Current accounts are those opened by professional persons, merchants, agriculturalists, and industrialists to care for their credit needs. They reflect commercial operations and they are built up principally through the discounting of bills of exchange.

Other accounts include a miscellaneous group of deposits such as deposits due to correspondents (including the advances extended by the Bank of France for periods of 30 days against public securities and advances against securities; deposits due to affiliated concerns; items in the process of collection; deposits owing to stock brokers, dealers in securities and arbitrageurs; funds resulting from security subscriptions and sales; funds set side for the payment of securities and dividends; funds to be paid out (excluding acceptances); amounts owing to the branches and agencies of the head office.

TABLE 4

PRINCIPAL ITEMS FROM THE BALANCE SHEETS OF THE FOUR NATIONALIZED CREDIT ESTABLISHMENTS, DECEMBER 31, 1951

(AMOUNTS IN MILLIONS OF FRANCS)

Items	*Crédit Lyonnais*	*Société Générale*	*Banque Nationale pour le Commerce et l'Industrie*	*Comptoir National d'Escompte de Paris*
Assets				
Cash, due from the Treasury and central banks	18,824	16,729	11,133	16,568
Balances with banks and correspondent institutions	23,093	20,605	15,477	20,962
Discounts	252,452	212,940	163,573	124,492
Loans and secured advances	64,230	54,967	40,764	40,316
Other	14,769	11,786	8,023	10,030
Total	373,368	317,027	238,970	212,368
Liabilities				
Checking accounts	100,593	71,115	50,575	56,549
Current accounts	158,041	169,966	131,868	78,134
Other accounts	79,840	56,447	37,053	52,586
Certificates of deposit and time deposits	13,674	1,543	9,403	11,276
Other	21,220	17,956	10,071	13,823
Total	373,368	317,027	238,970	212,368

THE REGIONAL BANKS

The regional banks resemble the large commercial banks in many ways but their field of activity is more restricted. They are commercial banks with many branches which have been established for a long time in one region and are an integral part of its economy. They have little occasion to compete among themselves but they often compete with the large credit establishments. The assets of the 22 regional banks are very much smaller than those of the four big nationalized banks, that is, 12.2 percent as against 45.7 percent of the aggregate balance sheet of French banks at the end of 1951. The regional banks have sought for several decades to obtain through concentration the advantages of larger scale enterprises. Thus the Crédit Industriel et Commercial has control over half of the regional banks—among

---

Certificates of deposits and time deposits include deposits with fixed maturities in contradistinction to demand deposits. These are classified according to two maturities: those funds due in three months and those due in two years.

which are to be noted the Société Lyonnaise de Dépôts, the Crédit Industriel d'Alsace et de Lorraine and the Société Nancéienne.

Since 1942 this group has also included the Banque Transatlantique and its two subsidiaries, the Banque de Tunisie and the Banque Commerciale du Maroc. The Banque Transatlantique was considered, until 1948, as a *banque d'affaires* but is now registered as a deposit bank among the specialized banks of Paris.

Among the most important regional banks are: the Crédit du Nord, with a subsidiary in Belgium, the Société Marseillaise de Crédit with interests in North Africa and the Société Générale Alsacienne de Banque affiliated with the Société Générale. Of less magnitude are R. Varin-Bernier & Cie at Bar-le-Duc, the Banque de Bretagne at Rennes and the Banque Régionale du Centre at Roanne.

In a similar category belong some banks which have branches in North Africa only. The Bank Control Commission registers as deposit banks 16 Algerian banks which are supervised by the Algerian Credit Council. The most important of them is the Crédit Foncier d'Algérie et de Tunisie, founded in 1880, which does a business in mortgage loans, mainly in favor of agriculture. The Compagnie Algérienne de Crédit et de Banque has, since 1948, specialized in banking activity; it was previously part of a real estate business firm. The Banque Nationale pour le Commerce et l'Industrie created in 1940 a subsidiary in North Africa, the Banque Nationale pour le Commerce et l'Industrie (Afrique) which has rapidly expanded. The Banque Industrielle de l'Afrique du Nord, founded in 1919, is the investment subsidiary of the Banque de l'Algérie.

TABLE 5
ASSETS OF THE PRINCIPAL ALGERIAN BANKS
DECEMBER 31, 1951
(AMOUNTS IN MILLIONS OF FRANCS)

	Amount
Crédit Foncier d'Algérie et de Tunisie	58,967
Société Nouvelle de la Compagnie Algérienne	53,142
Banque Nationale pour le Commerce et l'Industrie (Afrique)	51,570
Banque Industrielle de l'Afrique du Nord (classed as a *banque d'affaires*)	7,975

LOCAL BANKS AND THE SPECIALIZED BANKS OF PARIS

Just as the regional banks have tended to extend their activity and to modify their structure on the model of the large credit establishments, so the local banks have often had to change themselves into regional banks in the effort to survive amid conditions which seem to have become more and more difficult. In the beginning of this century, there were more than 400 local banks. In 1951 the Bank Control Commission registered only 186 and their aggregate assets were only 2.3 percent of the total of French banks. They have very limited resources, sometimes only a few million francs, but they are thoroughly conversant with business and credit conditions at the places where they carry on their operations. Among the most important of them, each with assets above 1,000 million francs, are, in order of magnitude: the Banque Federative Rurale at Strasbourg; the Banque de Savoie at Chambéry; the Banque Laydernier et Cie at Annecy; the Banque J. Joire at Tourcoing; the Banque Nicolet et Lafanechére at Grenoble; the Banque Guilhot et Cie at Agen; the Banque Journal et Cie at Saint-Quentin; the Banque Dupuy, de Parseval et Cie at Sète; and the Banque Veuve Morin Pons et Cie at Lyons. Local banks which do business in the provinces and especially in the southern half of France perform as a rule all banking operations. The vitality of the local banks is confirmed by the fact that more than one third of them were created after the First World War, although some go back to the eighteenth century.

Houses of the same importance which are located in Paris have tended to specialize in satisfying the particular needs for credit arising in the Paris market. The 85 Paris banks represent nearly 3.7 percent of the aggregate bank assets at the end of 1951, that is, less than the regional banks but more than the other local banks. It is difficult to assess their importance by the size of their balance sheet, but among those which exceeded 3,000 million francs in 1951 were, in order of magnitude: De Neuflize Schlumberger et Cie; Vernes et Cie; la Banque Cotonnière; la Banque Transatlantique; la Banque Corporative du Bâtiment et des Travaux Publics; Lehideux et Cie; la Banque Parisienne de Crédit au Commerce et l'Industrie; Mallet Frères et Cie; and De Baecque, Beau, Lantin et Cie.

The classification of Paris banks is not easy because different and rather distinct functions can be assumed at the same time by the same house. Those private institutions, the *Hautes Banques,* played a very important part during the nineteenth century, both as investment banks and as commercial banks. They underwrote public issues in France as well as abroad. Their activity is today reduced to the amount of their own funds. The *Hautes Banques* which are now among the deposit banks of Paris have a Protestant origin: Vernes et Cie, De Neuflize Schlumberger et Cie, Mallet Frères et Cie, and M. M. Hottinguer et Cie. Their principal function is to administer private fortunes. Some of them, such as Mirabaud et Cie, are counted among the *banques d'affaires*, because of the importance of their participations in industrial shares.

The Jewish *Hautes Banques* are more likely to be *banques d'affaires*, with such houses as de Rothschild Frères and Lazard Frères et Cie, which are officially classified as such. The only deposit banks of this group are Heine et Cie, R. Meyer et Cie, and Dreyfus et Cie.

Besides the Protestant and Jewish groups, there is a Catholic *Haute Banque* which includes two important houses: Veuve Demachy et Cie and Lehideux et Cie. They are, like the previous ones, rather limited in scope, but they deal more with banking than with investment operations.

Among the specialized houses of the Paris market, a few are chiefly connected with money market operations. These are, in order of importance, the Compagnie Parisienne de Réescompte, the Banque d'Escompte, the Union d'Escompte, and the Banque Française d'Acceptation. The last, founded in 1929, in order to facilitate the financing of international transactions, was never able to expand very much because of the great depression.[7] The other houses, however, were stimulated by the wartime activity of the market for public bills. All the rediscount houses have not been classified by the Control Commission under the same heading. The Caisse Centrale de Réescompte and the Société Privée de Réescompte are considered as financial houses since both were founded by *banques d'affaires*. The money market in Paris is not as important as it is in some foreign places, and it is strictly regulated by the Bank of France.

Another type of specialization, an industrial type, occurs among a score of Paris banks. A few names will be enough to suggest this: Banque Cotonnière, Banque des Produits Alimentaires et Coloniaux, Banque des Travaux Publics, Crédit Sucrier et Commercial. These banks, which have been qualified as "corporative banks," are generally subsidiaries of the big *banques d'affaires*.

A final category of banks in Paris consists of those houses which are

[7] At the beginning of 1950 the Banque Française d'Acceptation merged with the Union Financière d'Entreprises Françaises et Etrangères to constitute the Union Française de Banques pour l'Acceptation et les Financements Exterieurs.

related to industrial or commercial banks in their origin and in their resources. They are classified as deposit banks and because of that they cannot take participations for more than 75 percent of their capital funds and those participations cannot be more than 10 percent of the capital funds of the enterprise in which they own shares. Among the main banks of this group are: Electro-Crédit, affiliated with the Compagnie Générale d'Electricité; the Union Maritime et Financière, affiliated with the shipowners' firm, Delmas-Vieljeux; the Banque Française d'Outre-Mer, doing business for Saint-Frères; Edilité-Crédit; de Charnacé et Cie; the Banque des Intérêts Français; Le Crédit Français; and Borgeaud et Cie.

Finally, among the *banques d'affaires*, are a few group banks such as Worms et Cie for shipbuilding yards; the Société Anonyme de Participation et d'Etudes, a subsidiary of Pont-à-Mousson; J. Danon et Cie, specialists in the coffee trade. The Société Industrielle et Financière de l'Amérique du Sud, linked with the business group Bemberg-Quilmes, may also be looked upon as a group bank, but it is partly a foreign bank, through its interests in Argentina.

THE FOREIGN BANKS IN FRANCE

In 1951, the official classification puts under this heading 15 banks having a branch in France and a head office abroad, as well as 13 having French charters but controlled by foreign interests. On a more general basis, the legislation of 1941 considers as foreign banks, wherever their head office, the banks which are directly or indirectly under the control of foreign persons. Those banks are subject to French laws regarding registration in the profession with all the conditions attached to that, especially as regards the amount of their capital. There is only one special obligation for foreign banks: they must keep in one of their French offices an accounting record of their transactions in French territory. The legal equality granted to foreign banks in France seems particularly favorable as compared to the legislative restrictions in many other countries.

Foreign banks were established in France mainly after the First World War. From 1914 to 1921 their number grew from 21 to 40. During the 1931 crisis, it decreased to 32. From 1939 to 1945, most of the banks were dormant, a dozen being placed under provisional management.

At present it is Anglo-Saxon banks for the most part which have subsidiaries in France. Those of the English banks—Barclays Bank Ltd., Lloyds and National Provincial Foreign Bank Ltd., Westminster Foreign Bank Ltd.—are somewhat more important than those of American banks—Morgan and Cie, Inc., the Chase National Bank, and the Guaranty Trust Company of New York.

Besides these main branches of foreign banks there are a few banks which have a French charter but are under foreign control, such as the Banque Jordaan, the Banca Commerciale Italiana, the Banque Commerciale pour l'Europe du Nord, the Mutuelle Industrielle, and the Banco di Roma. The Banque Belge pour l'Etranger, a subsidiary of the Société Générale de Belgique, was merged in 1948 in the Banque de l'Union Parisienne.

THE INVESTMENT BANKS (BANQUES D'AFFAIRES)

The distinction between commercial banks and investment banks has developed gradually in the course of financial history as a result of the differences in their resources: long-term funds require comparably long placements. This distinction is not, however, so sharp that there is no overlapping of function, and the two types of banks sometimes find themselves in competition. There is also a certain amount of cooperation between them, the commercial banks selling at their counters the securities which have been issued by the investment banks.

The distinct function of the investment banks as it has developed in practice was recognized by the law of May 17, 1946, Article 5:

> Investment banks are those whose principal activity is the undertaking and carrying out of participations in existing or new enterprises, and the opening of credits of any length for public or private enterprises which are benefiting, have benefited or will benefit by such participation. In such enterprises may be invested only their own funds or funds deposited with them for at least two years duration or to be withdrawn only upon previous notice.

The distinction between investment and commercial banks is to be found in the type of deposit which each may accept. The deposits which investment banks might accept were defined entirely too narrowly in the legislation initially adopted in 1945. In consequence, the article quoted above broadened the definition as follows:

> They [the investment banks] may open deposit accounts only for their own personnel, or for enterprises to which they have made loans or in which they have taken participations, or for persons or corporations acting

in their professional capacity, or for subscribers to stock in corporations in which they have participations.

The investment banks are therefore empowered to accept deposits in connection with their participations, but they may not accept individual deposits or open checking accounts except in very limited measure.

Under the new banking legislation the investment banks have retained a more flexible character than have the commercial banks. They escaped nationalization because of the nature of their activities, and are merely subject to governmental control under Article 11 of the law of December 2, 1945. Each investment bank organized as a corporation, if its total assets exceed 2,000 million francs, is subject to the supervision of a government Commissioner appointed by the Ministers of Finance and of Economic Affairs, with the approval of the National Credit Council. Like the auditors of the central bank and the commercial banks, these commissioners are organized into a committee, under the decree of February 15, 1949. Ten out of a total of 25 investment banks were subject to this type of supervision at the end of 1951. In each bank the Commissioner is assisted by a Control Committee consisting of: a representative of commercial and industrial organizations, a representative of the large labor unions, and a representative of the public and semi-public financial institutions. They are appointed by the Ministers of National Economy, of Labor and of Finance, respectively, from nominations of the organizations concerned.

The Commissioner has extensive powers. He attends all meetings of the Board of Directors and of the stockholders. He may see all documents. He may veto any decision which he considers to be contrary to the national interest, and may propose measures of general utility, especially in the carrying out of credit policy. The bank may appeal from the decision of the Commissioner to the National Credit Council, but it may not use the presence of the Commissioner as an excuse for avoiding any of its civil or criminal responsibilities. The independence of the Commissioner is assured by the fact that he cannot be sued except under very exceptional circumstances. In practice the supervision of the investment banks has worked very well. The persons chosen as commissioners have been able to serve the general interest which they were in duty bound to protect, without harming the interest of the bank which they were supervising.

A comparison of the balance sheets of the investment banks with those of the nationalized commercial banks indicates that the investment banks since 1938 have been extending their commercial banking functions and in some measure have become more like the latter.

TABLE 6

PERCENTAGE DISTRIBUTION OF ITEMS, DECEMBER 31, 1938 AND 1950

Items	PERCENT OF TOTAL 1938	1950
Assets		
Cash, deposits with Bank of France, and the Treasury	5.8	1.9
Deposits with other banks	18.8	11.2
Commercial bills	26.6	58.4
Loans and guaranteed advances	13.1	6.8
Acceptances	4.8	3.6
Investments	17.3	7.3
Other	13.6	10.8
Total	100.0	100.0
Liabilities		
Checking accounts	9.7	7.6
Current accounts	32.8	46.8
Certificates of deposit and time deposits	6.2	3.6
Other	33.3	33.4
Reserves	4.9	3.7
Capital	13.1	4.9
Total	100.0	100.0

Both personal checking accounts and current accounts have developed at the investment banks as at the commercial banks but more rapidly at the former. In 1950 they represented 54.4 percent of the liabilities of the investment banks, while at the commercial banks they totaled 72.5 percent. The corresponding percentages were in 1938 42.5 and 66.5 respectively.

The large proportion of capital to other liabilities has always been a distinguishing feature of the investment banks, but it has very markedly declined since 1938. Like the commercial banks, the investment banks have had to increase their capital; that of the Banque de Paris from 300 million francs in 1938 to 1,531 million francs in 1948 and to 2,755 million francs in 1949; that of the Union Parisienne from 200 million francs in 1938 to 1,000 million francs in 1950. Although the ratio of the capital and reserves of the investment banks to their total assets has declined recently, it still stood at 8.6 percent in 1950 as compared with 0.5 percent for the deposit banks. Unlike the deposit banks, the investment banks have few branches in the provinces, preferring to conduct their business in Paris where they are in contact with industry and finance. However, the Banque de Paris et des Pays-Bas has foreign branches and participates in foreign enterprise. It opened an office at Casablanca in December, 1950, and, with a group of French banks, established in Canada the Confederation Development Corporation. The investment banks are distinguished less by their size, which is often greater than that of a deposit bank, than by the composition of their assets. In recent years the investment banks have increased their holdings of commercial bills from 26.6 percent in 1938 to 58.4 percent in 1950, while their loans and advances have declined in the same period from 13.1 percent to 6.8 percent, about the same as the deposit banks. The investment banks hold a larger proportion of government securities and acceptances too play a larger part in the portfolios of investment banks than of deposit banks, in spite of the rising proportion at the latter. Holdings of industrial securities were formerly one of the characteristic features of an investment bank but these have fallen, in terms of total assets, from 17.3 percent in 1938 to 7.3 percent in 1950, a figure which is still much larger than that of the deposit banks. The cash and deposits with other banks has declined much more in the balance sheets of the investment banks than in that of the commercial banks, as a result of the increasing commercial activity of the former.

At the head of the group of investment banks proper stands the Banque de Paris et des Pays-Bas, distinguished for its long history dating from 1872 and for its continuous growth, and the Union Parisienne which was not established until 1904 but which has attained great importance. The Union Europèene Industrielle et Financière, established by the Schneider steel interests in 1920, was combined in 1942 with the Banque des Pays du Nord, and recently has taken over the control of the Crédit Foncier Colonial et de Banque. The Union des Mines, established by the big coal-mining companies in 1923, has expanded recently into new fields.

Some of the banks classified as *Hautes Banques* really belong among the investment banks. These are usually organized as partnerships under collective names such as de Rothschild Frères and Alexandre de Saint Phalle et Cie; or as limited partnerships like Lazard Frères et Cie, R. de Lubersac et Cie, Mirabaud et Cie, and Worms et Cie.[8]

[8] Mirabaud et Cie merged in the Banque de l'Union Parisienne in 1953.

The investment banks which are organized as partnerships are not required to publish their balance sheets, but their importance may be judged from the combined reports made available by the Bank Control Commission. In 1951 their assets amounted to 46,581 million francs, while those of the incorporated investment banks amounted to 300,475 million francs.

Among the investment banks may also be mentioned those which were established by industrial groups to prepare the financial operations which are then carried out with the aid of the banks which have branches. There are for example the Société de Participations et d'Etudes of the group Pont-à-Mousson; the Banque Parisienne pour l'Industrie, of the group Empain, and the Union Française de Crédit pour le Commerce et l'Industrie of the group Société Générale d'Enterprise. It should be remembered also that some of the incorporated banks already classified as deposit banks were actually established under the patronage of the investment banks. Thus the Banque de Paris et des Pays-Bas controls the Banque Cotonnière, the Banque des Produits Alimentaires et Coloniaux, and the Crédit Sucrier.

The incorporated investment banks have far-flung activities, both geographically and economically. This is exemplified by the Bank of Indo-China which is now considered the most important of all the investment banks. It was organized in 1875 with the right of note issue for Indo-China, New Caledonia and Somaliland, as well as for the French oceanic colonies. This privilege was repealed by the law of September 25, 1948, which provided for the establishment of a central bank of issue. This was founded in June, 1951, with representatives of France and the three associated Indo-China states.

The end of its note-issue privilege had the effect of somewhat reducing the assets of the Bank of Indo-China, but this was soon offset by an extension of its activities. Its capital was increased to 1,275 million francs in 1949. Working closely with the Banque de Paris et des Pays-Bas and the Banque Worms, it is concentrating on investment banking outside of continental France, and its network of offices covers not only the Far East but the entire world. Recently it has turned toward the Americas, with interests in the French Banking Corporation of New York, in the Crédit Foncier du Brésil, in the French and Italian Bank for South America, and in the recently established French Industrial and Financial Union which operates in

India. In 1949 a subsidiary, Banque de l'Indochine (South Africa) Ltd., was established in Johannesburg. The Bank of Indo-China is thus carrying on the great tradition of French investment banking in international affairs.

The French and Italian Bank for South America, although operating principally outside of France, has close connections with the French investment banks. It was established in 1910 with French and Italian capital, and has played an important part in the financing of trade between Europe and South America. Its capital was increased in 1950 from 625 to 1,125 million francs, held by an Italian-Swiss group through the Banca Commerciale Italiana and a French group which includes the Banque de Paris et des Pays-Bas and the Banque de l'Indochine.

MEDIUM-TERM AND LONG-TERM CREDIT BANKS

The majority of these banks were established by the big commercial banks in the years after the First World War, to fill a gap in the banking system of that period. Because of the need to maintain high liquidity, commercial banks could not provide capital funds for the modernization of industry and the rebuilding of equipment and inventory. For that reason they organized these specialized banks with large capital of their own, supplemented by borrowed funds. The issue of *bons de caisse* or notes maturing in two to five years was the principal form of borrowing, since this term corresponded to the credit granted.

At the close of the Second World War similar needs were present and were recognized by the new banking legislation. The law of May 17, 1946, which modified the law of December 2, 1945, defined the medium-term and long-term credit banks as follows:

> Medium- and long-term credit banks are those whose principal activity consists of granting credits of at least two years' term. They may not accept deposits for less than a two-year period without the authorization of the medium- and long-term credit committee of the National Credit Council. They are subject to the same limitations as the commercial banks regarding their participations.

There are 8 banks now classified in this group, with total assets of 3,732 million francs in 1951. The percentage distribution of their principal asset and liability items at the end of 1938 and 1950 is given in Table 7. In order of size they are:

la Société Anonyme de Crédit a l'Industrie Française (C.A.L.I.F.)
l'Union pour le Crédit a l'Industrie Nationale (U.C.I.N.A.)
l'Union Bancaire du Nord (U.B.N.)
l'Union de Banques Régionales pour le Crédit Industriel (U.B.R.C.I.)
la Société Auxiliare de Gestion et d'Avances (S.A.G.A.)
la Société Agenaise d'Avals et de Crédit
l'Association Financière pour le Commerce et l'Industrie
l'Omnium Financier pour l'Industrie Nationale (O.F.I.N.A.)

There are also some banks which grant medium-term credit without being classed among the specialized banks. Among these are l'Union Française d'Outre-Mer, founded in 1941 by the Banque Nationale pour le Commerce et l'Industrie, and the Caisse Centrale de Crédit à moyen terme, established in 1944 under the auspices of the Banque de Paris et des Pays-Bas.

TABLE 7
PERCENTAGE DISTRIBUTION OF ITEMS, MEDIUM-TERM AND LONG-TERM CREDIT BANKS, DECEMBER 31, 1938 AND 1950

Items	PERCENT OF TOTAL *1938*	*1950*
Assets		
Cash deposits with Bank of France and the Treasury	0.9	0.7
Deposits with other banks	5.6	3.8
Commercial bills	20.9	62.2
Loans and guaranteed advances	29.5	15.8
Acceptances	2.3	1.9
Investments	9.6	2.8
Other	31.2	12.8
Total	100.0	100.0
Liabilities		
Checking accounts	0.3	0.1
Current accounts	3.5	9.0
Certificates of deposit and time deposits	11.3	48.5
Reserves	7.8	6.9
Capital	43.3	15.6
Other	33.8	19.9
Total	100.0	100.0

Certain institutions devote themselves to the financing of installment sales. Le Crédit Mobilier et Industriel was established in 1919 under the name of the Société pour le Développement de la Vente à Crédit (S.O.V.A.C.) to finance sales for the automobile and other industries. La Diffusion Industrielle et Automobile par le Crédit (D.I.A.C.) was founded in 1924 to permit term payments for automobiles, material, and equipment manufactured by the Renault company. The Diffusion Industrielle Nationale (D.I.N.) plays the same role for the Peugeot automobile company.

The majority of the medium-term credit institutions have played a smaller part than had been hoped for them. Credit at medium-term had little development down to 1938. In recent years interest in it has been revived but it appears that the organization of special banks for the purpose, under private enterprise, is no longer an adequate solution. Public credit has been provided in this domain by the extension of the activity of agencies already in existence, such as the Crédit National and the Caisse des Marchés.[9]

The law of January 18, 1951, regarding the pledging of machines and equipment as security for such loans has renewed interest in medium-term credit, and several special institutions have been created with the aid of the large commercial banks. These include l'Union Française de Banques, la Compagnie Générale Française de Crédit, le Crédit Electrique, l'Union pour le Financement de l'industrie cinématographique, and la Société de cautions mutuelles des constructeurs français d'équipements mécaniques.

A law of May 24, 1951, designed to aid in the financing of naval construction resulted in the founding of a special credit institution, le Crédit Naval. Its capital amounts to 500 million francs and is divided up (in decreasing order) between: groups of construction, armament and insurance firms, the Caisse des Dépôts et Consignations, the Crédit Foncier de France, the Crédit National, and the Crédit Maritime et Fluvial. The Crédit Naval is classed as a medium- and long-term credit bank for it is authorized to make loans of five to fifteen years.

OTHER FINANCIAL INSTITUTIONS

The other financial institutions which were classified by the law of June 14, 1941, as belonging to the private banking sector include those enterprises and persons which, without being required to list themselves as banks, carry on the following banking operations:

serving as commission agents, broker or intermediary in the buying and selling of government and private issues and commercial bills;

[9] See pp. 267–72.

providing short- or medium-term credit or foreign exchange;
discounting, hypothecating or cashing commercial bills, checks or government issues.

Since these institutions are not permitted to accept deposits from the public, they are obliged to operate with their own or with specially designated funds. The regulations to which they are subject depend upon the extent of their operations. Usually they are required to register with the Bank Control Commission, after admission to the official list by the National Credit Council. Since July 1, 1950, a minimum capital of 2.5 million francs is required for incorporated or limited liability companies. This figure is reduced to 500,000 francs for single proprietors or partnerships.

As of December 31, 1951, 567 establishments were registered in France, Algeria, and the Saar:

TABLE 8
OTHER FINANCIAL INSTITUTIONS
(AMOUNTS IN MILLIONS OF FRANCS)

Institutions	*Number*	*Capital*
Finance companies	57	4,075
Installment credit companies	81	1,991
Discount companies and miscellaneous	113	2,528
Securities companies	316	734
Total	567	9,328

The finance companies are those which hold the funds of subsidiaries and sometimes act as holding companies, but do not accept deposits from the public. The installment credit companies are relatively less important because installment sales are little developed in France, and because they are subject to close supervision by the National Credit Council. The discount companies operate principally in the Paris money market. The term "miscellaneous," as used in the tabulation, indicates varied activities such as collection agencies for professional associations, companies specializing in certain financial services, groups of issuers of securities, and mutual indemnity societies. The securities companies form the most numerous group. At Paris three fourths of their activity is carried on by 20 of the 96 houses in that city. In the provinces their operations are more widely divided.

All these companies must belong to the Professional Association of Financial Enterprises and Establishments, which has functions similar to those of the Bankers Professional Association, but on a smaller scale. The Association transmits to the National Credit Council requests for admission to the list of financial enterprises and establishments; it enforces the regulations concerning the profession, and it organizes the relations and the representation of its members.

Other financial establishments which are auxiliaries of the banking and securities profession are subject simply to the formality of the "agreement." These are, for example, the brokers who place bank funds in the money market and the commission men who transmit orders for securities to the stock exchange dealers. Their membership in the Professional Association is voluntary, not compulsory. A still simpler form of control is exercised over certain financial establishments which manage the affairs of an estate or which have no dealings with outsiders; it consists simply of making a declaration as to their activity and carries only the obligation to conform to the regulations covering the operations carried out.

This survey of financial institutions as classified by the law of June 14, 1941, needs to be completed by some observations on the institutions concerned with security trading, which have themselves been the object of new legislative enactments. The situation in the security markets has raised a number of problems in recent years as the capital resources of the country declined. The Bourse itself is regulated by old laws which have been revised and enlarged by the Commercial Code and by the decrees of 1890 and 1898. The legislative edicts after 1940 were extended in 1942 and were ratified by the ordinance of October 18, 1945, which introduced important changes for the Bourse but did not alter the statute for brokers (*agents de change*). It did, however, for the first time give legal recognition to the profession of "over-the-counter" dealer (*courtiers*) with the privilege of handling securities not listed on the official Bourse. Formerly there had been only one organization for such dealers and stock exchange brokers. This new Association of Security Dealers is comparable to the Syndicate of Stock Exchange Brokers.

A more general institution superimposed upon the professional organizations is the Stock Exchange Committee, which forms part of the credit system. It includes four permanent members: the Governor of the Bank of France, the head of the Paris Brokers Association, a representative of the bankers, and a representative of security owners. In addition, the provincial security brokers and the "over-the-counter" security dealers may send representatives to discuss matters of concern to them. The Director of the Treasury acts as Treasury Commissioner. The Committee has wide power and may make individual or general decisions on everything which affects the organization of the market or the legal regulation of the members of the profession. It serves also as consultant of the government.

Among the new financial institutions should be mentioned the Central Fund for the Deposit and Clearing of Securities, created in 1941, and the National Investment Society created at the time of the "national solidarity" tax of 1945. The former acted as clearinghouse for brokers and banks and thus reduced the need for physical handling of all securities traded. Bearer shares were required to be deposited with it if they were not made nominative under the law of February 26, 1941. The volume of business often created delays, and numerous criticisms resulted in the final liquidation of the Central Fund by the law of July 5, 1949. It has been replaced by a new organization, the Interprofessional Society for the Clearing of Securities (S.I.C.O.V.A.M.) in which there is no obligation to deposit securities.

The second of the new organizations, the National Investment Society, was organized to handle the securities paid to the government as a part of the special tax of 1945, which necessitated large operations in the financial market. The initial capital, 2,000 million francs, was subscribed, 800 million by the large public credit institutions and 1,200 million by the state. The capital was increased to 3,800 million francs in 1950. This institution, which has a mixed public-private character, makes it possible for the government to mobilize its portfolio of securities. However, it does not perform functions analogous to those rendered by investment trusts in Great Britain and the United States.

SEMI-PUBLIC FINANCIAL INSTITUTIONS

SPECIALIZED BANKING INSTITUTIONS

The Crédit Foncier.—The Crédit Foncier was established in 1852 to grant loans on mortgages to property owners, to governmental units, and to the merchant marine. It is also authorized to finance the operations of a subsidiary, the Sous-Comptoir des Entrepreneurs, which makes loans to building constructors. The Crédit Foncier was organized as a private corporation, but is under the control of the state. Its activities are strictly regulated and its operations are subject to the approval of the Minister of Finance.

The essential function of the Crédit Foncier is to grant long-term credit on property with or without buildings and to finance the long-term credit needs of public bodies. The loans are amortized over periods of 10 to 75 years, with a usual maximum of 30 years, and occasional loans for periods as short as 1 to 9 years. Some mortgage credits are made on open account. The procedures followed by the Crédit Foncier brought it unquestioned success in the years which followed its creation. They corresponded to urgent needs which the commercial banks were not in a position to satisfy. After 1914 the creation of special financial institutions subsidized by the state, such as the Crédit Agricole, the passage of special laws for the construction industry, and general economic conditions, were less favorable to the Crédit Foncier. Its activity was reduced, although its issues of mortgage and municipal bonds, which provide the major part of its resources, have always been well received by the public. These obligations amounted to 105,999 million francs in 1951, when the capital was only 1,200 million francs.

Mortgage credit had been the principal activity of the Crédit Foncier up to 1914, but after that time mortgage credit was greatly exceeded by loans to governmental units. This movement was accentuated during the Second World War; mortgage loans rose from 6,300 million francs in 1938 to 29,128 millions in 1951, while loans to governmental units rose in the same period from 13,200 million to 93,081 millions. After the war, however, there was an increase in the volume of mortgage credit which grew out of the need for improving and maintaining existing buildings, and especially out of the need felt by many property owners to turn their assets into more liquid form for such purposes as tax payments. In the field of construction financing, the activity of the Crédit Foncier continued to be limited, because priority was given to the rebuilding of war-damaged property. The possibility of its participation in the financing of building construction was enlarged by the law of August 13, 1950, which permitted new loans to take the form either of medium- or long-term mortgage loans made by the Crédit Foncier itself, or of a mortgage credit account opened by the Sous-Comptoir des Entrepreneurs, the subsidiary which specialized in the building industry. Both agencies may participate in the financing of construction subsidized by the Fonds National d'Amélioration de l'Habitat. Such loans are made to property owners and to entrepreneurs, in the form of bills discounted by the Sous-Comptoir, and rediscounted by the Crédit Foncier, which may in turn present them for rediscount at the Bank of France.

Since 1946 therefore the activity of the Crédit Foncier has been extended not only in its former fields but also in the new duties entrusted to it. It enters more and more frequently into medium-term credit operations because of the new character of the credit needs of borrowers and the lack of sufficient credit at long term, but it has not, nevertheless, abandoned the monopoly which it enjoys in the field of long-term credit.

Agricultural Credit.—The credit needs of agriculture have a special character which has led to the establishment of specialized institutions. Ordinary banking operations do not correspond to the cycle of agricultural production nor to the habits of the rural populace. Farmers have more confidence in the small credit societies of their own group; agricultural credit is essentially mutual credit. State aid is not thereby excluded, since there is a traditional policy of aid to agriculture, with a private sector and a public sector.

There are first of all the private agricultural credit funds which have existed since the middle of the nineteenth century, inspired by the German agricultural associations based on the principles of Raiffeisen: mutual responsibility, moderate subscriptions, and low rates of interest. They have not asked for aid from the state, and thus escape its control. Their resources are quite limited, and their form varies from one region to another. Some of them have direct relations with important labor organizations. Others are simply rural credit funds like the famous Caisses Durand affiliated with the Union Central de Nantes. In Alsace-Lorraine they are associated with the Banque Fédérative Rurale de Strasbourg. Two of the larger groups account for most of the deposits: the Fédération Centrale de Crédit Agricole Mutuel, with 12,500 million francs, and the Union Rurale et Ouvrière Française, with 3,000 million francs. Altogether the private agricultural credit institutions had more than 2,400 offices in 1951.

The public sector of agricultural credit as it exists today is the result of successive acts of legislation. The law of November 5, 1894, regulated the formation of mutual credit societies among agricultural groups. Upon these societies the state superimposed regional societies by the law of March 31, 1899. Finally the law of August 5, 1920, subjected all organizations, regional or local, to the authority of a national society. The local societies do not accept deposits, and may make loans only to their members—farmers, unions, or agricultural cooperatives. Their purpose is to provide funds for current production expenses by means of short-term loans (less than 18 months) for the purchase of supplies or animals by means of medium-term loans (less than 15 years), and for the purchase or improvement of agricultural property by means of long-term loans. The regional societies have as members, not individual farmers, but the local societies of their region (usually those of one *département*). The uninvested funds of the local societies are deposited with the regional society which in turn deposits them with the Treasury, the Bank of France, or the Caisse Nationale de Crédit Agricole. The regional societies make decisions regarding the requests for loans transmitted by the local societies; they rediscount with endorsement the obligations offered, and in general they facilitate the operations of the members of the local societies.

The Caisse Nationale de Crédit Agricole is the keystone of the public agricultural credit system. It is under government control and its director is named by the Minister of Agriculture. It in turn exercises constant supervision over the regional societies, whose affiliation it may accept or refuse, whose directors it approves, and whose funds it handles. The important role of this institution is indicated on the one hand by the Treasury funds which it loans out, and on the other hand by the rediscounting of the short-term obligations of its member societies. The government advances to it funds destined for equipment loans at long term or for the financing of certain public welfare operations. These advances are periodically increased, for they are rapidly used up, especially in long-term investment loans. The Fonds National de Modernisation et d'Equipement provided 63,174 million francs for this purpose in 1951, in addition to the 31,200 million francs provided through direct loans by the government.

The capital funds of the agricultural credit institutions comprise a large amount which has greatly increased since 1938. In the regional societies the total has increased from 1,600 million francs at the end of 1938 to 28,000 millions in 1946, 91,000 millions in 1950, and 112,000 millions in 1951. This is the most rapid rate of growth among all the financial institutions. In addition to the capital funds, further resources are obtained by the issue of 5- to 20-year bonds floated by the Caisse Nationale. When the regional societies cannot make needed loans at short term out of their own funds they rediscount a part of their portfolio either with the Caisse Nationale or at a bank, particularly the Bank of France. During 1951 such rediscounts amounted to 190,036 millions of francs. Moreover, the Caisse Nationale stands ready also to rediscount the obligations of the regional societies for medium-term equipment loans.

By such devices the agricultural credit societies have been able to provide considerable support for agriculture, which has also been favored by special legislation. The total of agricultural credit on December 31, 1951, amounted to 121,000 millions out of the total bank credit of 1,654,000 million francs, not including the Bank of France. They have altogether 800,000 members, and the network of nearly 4,500 offices, belonging to 97 regional societies and 4,400 local societies, rivals in extent even that of the commercial banks. Agricultural credit is following a policy of expansion, while the commercial banks are being required to reduce their activities.

THE POPULAR BANKS

Another group of institutions which offers some competition to the commercial banks is the Crédit Populaire or Popular Bank system, organized by the law of March 13, 1917. It was designed to aid small business and industry which for lack of sufficient collateral was not able to obtain bank credit, by taking into account moral and psychological factors such as the honesty and ability of the borrower. To encourage the development of these banks the government grants them funds and exempts them from certain taxes. These advantages have permitted them to survive in spite of such difficulties as those of 1934 and 1936.

The Popular Banks are organized as cooperative societies with variable capital, and with a limit on their profits in order to provide reserves. They may make loans only for the business needs of their customers, augmenting the usual credit by rediscounts or by uncovered loans. During the Second World War they were given the task of making medium-term loans to former prisoners of war and to deportees and refugees, as well as individual loans to artisans.

These banks are subject to governmental control under the law of

July 24, 1929. The Popular Bank Syndical Chamber has the duty of protecting their rights and common interests, of exercising administrative, technical, and financial controls, and of taking all measures necessary to their proper functioning. In this Chamber, the Minister of Finance is represented by a Commissioner, and his control is carried out by Treasury finance inspectors. A central committee handles security operations. There is also a central fund for clearing and for handling payments.

The Popular Banks had at the end of 1950 a network of 53 main offices, 318 permanent agencies, and 414 part-time offices throughout France. There is a special organization for Algeria, with a central office and 8 banks which have developed rapidly in recent years. In the Saar the Popular Banks are particularly strong as a result of the saving habits of the people. At the end of 1951 the financial resources of the whole system included 2,612 million francs of capital and reserves, 796 millions as a loan fund for artisans, and 69,093 millions of deposits and drawing accounts, at sight and on time.

Although the Popular Banks have not grown quite as rapidly as the agricultural credit system, they have had a considerable increase since 1938. In spite of this the Syndical Chamber has been on guard to maintain a high liquidity ratio, and during the past several years the financial structure has been strengthened and some regional concentration achieved. In order to increase their working funds, the Popular Banks have made more and more use of the facilities offered by the large government agencies like the Caisse Nationale des Marchés and the Crédit National, in the form of guarantees, acceptances, and rediscounts.

The development of the Popular Banks is closely linked to the evolution of bank credit in France, even if it is not subject to the same regulation. In recent years these banks have concerned themselves especially with productive activities, following the directives of the National Credit Council. On the regional level they have encouraged the rediscounting of commercial paper by their clientele. The Popular Bank system seems to correspond to the needs of the French economy, since it has grown steadily as it has developed new branches of activity.

Complementing the Popular Banks are the mutual guarantee societies. They were started in 1917 but have expanded since the creation of the Caisse Nationale des Marchés in 1936. These societies arrange for mutual guarantees within a branch of industry, thus permitting the Caisse to provide loan funds to it. Since 1945 they have been especially concerned with the reequipment of metallurgical industries, with public works, and with transportation. On December 31, 1951, there were 164 of these mutual guarantee societies, with 36,186 million francs of guarantees outstanding.

Within the framework of the popular credit system should also be mentioned the Caisse Centrale de Crédit Hôtelier, Commercial et Industriel, formed in 1923 and made a part of the Syndical Chamber in 1945. Initially it handled credit operations for a specialized clientele of hotel and restaurant keepers and dispensers of soft drinks. Later its functions were broadened to include loans to commercial and industrial enterprises. Although it may make long-term loans, its principal role is that of making medium-term loans in order to aid in the formation and development of small commercial and industrial firms. The amount of each loan is limited to 3 million francs, and the maturity to ten years. This agency has grown rapidly since 1946, and at the end of 1951 it had 150 million francs of capital and reserves, and 5,488 million of loans outstanding. It has recently made medium-term and long-term loans to the tourist industries, with funds supplied by the government. At the end of 1951, the credits extended by the Caisse, in percent of total credits, were distributed as follows:

TABLE 9
CLASSIFICATION OF BORROWERS

	In percent of total loans
Hotels and tourist industries	70
Industrial enterprises	26
Commercial enterprises	4
	100

There are several other institutions which have objectives and resources similar to those of the popular credit banks. The Caisse Centrale de Crédit Cooperatif, established in 1938, functions as a union of cooperative societies. In addition to its own funds it disposes of several government grants and of the proceeds of debentures sold in the market, aggregating 2,087 million francs on December 31, 1951. It makes medium-term and long-term advances and equipment loans to producers' cooperatives, consumer cooperatives, and artisans' cooperatives; the total was 1,919 million francs at the end of 1951. It may also guarantee loans for the benefit of cooperatives so that they may borrow from the commercial banks.

Another similar institution is the Crédit Maritime Mutuel, organized in 1913 to aid the fishing and boatbuilding industries. Thirteen regional banks and 62 local banks, under the control of the Minister of Public Works, grant credit at short term and long term, principally from grants and subventions by the government. Since 1947 the agency has had the assistance of the Caisse Centrale de Crédit Cooperatif and its lending operations have increased up to a total of 2,699 million francs on December 31, 1951. It was reorganized under the law of December 13, 1950, to aid still further the development of deep-sea fishing, the modernization of the fishing fleet, and the extension of marine cooperatives.

There are also mutual guarantee societies dating back to 1867, which are similar to the private agricultural credit banks and most often formed by the same groups, but much less important. They are active among the middle classes, granting loans to small-business men, to artisans, and to individuals out of the funds deposited with them. In recent years, they have specialized and become proficient in granting medium-term credits. In 1951 there were 164 such societies, with 3,091 million francs in subscribed capital and members' funds.

FOREIGN CREDIT INSTITUTIONS

The revival of international trade after the Second World War and the needs of the French market led the National Credit Council in 1946 to concern itself with the financing of foreign trade. There had been in existence since 1920 the Banque Nationale Française du Commerce Extérieur, but this institution, although backed by the government, had been hindered in its development by the economic crisis of 1930. Under the decrees of June 1 and 2, 1946, in order to fulfill the requirements of the law of December 2, 1945, there was established the Banque Française du Commerce Extérieur and the Compagnie Française d'Assurance. The role of these two institutions was still further extended in 1949.

This bank for foreign trade operates under a special statute, with a capital of 500 million francs subscribed by the Bank of France, the Caisse des Dépôts et Consignations, the Crédit National, the Caisse Nationale de Crédit Agricole, and the nationalized banks. Its Board of Directors has 15 members named by the Ministers of National Economy and of Finance, and two government commissioners. It carries on all the operations necessary for the financing of imports and exports: short-term credits by discount or acceptance, medium-term credits, foreign exchange transactions, property and security transactions, and the like. The bank has no monopoly in this field; all banks may carry on such operations either for their own account or with its participation. With the Bank of France it maintains a central statistical office for foreign credit information, and with the Ministry of National Economy and the Centre National du Commerce Extérieur, an office for information on foreign trade.

The individual operations of the Banque Française du Commerce Extérieur need to be emphasized, because of the importance of international trade for France. Its credit rules have been adapted to the actual needs of foreign trade; they permit the relaxation of the usual rules of liquidity and they aid in keeping financing costs low. It has perfected a system of guarantees, some of which are unconditional guarantees against risk, while others guarantee only the liquidity or mobilization of the asset. In order to develop French foreign trade, new measures were adopted in 1949. The banking authorities arranged for increased rediscounts of export bills at the Bank of France, a lengthening of the maturity and a reduction in eligibility requirements. Export credits are no longer limited by the rediscount ceilings fixed for the commercial banks by the Bank of France. This privilege, formerly limited to bank acceptances, has been extended to promissory notes payable by exporters to their bankers if guaranteed by another bank, and especially if guaranteed by the Banque Française du Commerce Extérieur which most frequently uses this method of assistance. There has been arranged also a mobilization of bills arising from the prefinancing of orders or transactions with foreigners, provided the approval of the Bank of France is obtained. In 1950 the privilege of mobilizing such bills was extended to those running from two to five years. In this case the export must be guaranteed by credit insurance, and the Crédit National adds the fourth signature demanded by the Bank of France, in addition to that of the exporter, the banker and the Banque Française du Commerce Extérieur.

This reorganization of the financing of foreign trade seems to have had appreciable results, if one may judge by the increase in the assets of the Banque Française du Commerce Extérieur from 7,372 million francs in 1947, to 18,813 millions in 1948, 31,045 millions in 1949, 38,563 millions in 1950, and 66,702 millions in 1951.

The Compagnie Française d'Assurance pour le Commerce Extérieur, according to the decree of April 16, 1948, provides government insurance against catastrophes, political risks, and unusual monetary and commercial risks inherent in importing, exporting, or any kind of foreign trade. Under the law of July 5, 1949, insurance may be obtained also for the prefinancing of manufactures destined for export, and against fluctuations in foreign prices. A Commission des Garanties et du Crédit au Commerce Extérieur obtains on all these questions the opinions of representatives of the business and professions concerned.

SAVINGS BANKS AND POSTAL CHECKING SERVICE

The Savings Banks.—Within the aggregate of money market funds, those of the savings banks represent a large share, the investment of which is strictly regulated by legislation. There are two types of savings banks, the ordinary ones, with deposits amounting to 361,600 million francs in 1951, and the Caisse Nationale d'Epargne with deposits which amounted to 327,700 million francs in 1951.

The ordinary savings banks date from the beginning of the nineteenth century. They were organized on the initiative of individuals or more frequently of municipalities, but they were early recognized as useful public institutions and their functioning has been under national regulation since the initial statute of June 3, 1835, and the basic law of July 20, 1895. On the other hand, the Caisse Nationale d'Epargne is a government institution created by the law of April 9, 1881, and attached to the administration of Posts, Telegraph, and Telephones. It has a vast network of offices in 15,000 post offices, while the ordinary savings banks have only 600 offices.

The prestige of the banks, the ease of making and withdrawing deposits, and the relatively high interest paid to depositors have contributed to the success of the savings banks. They reach a group which has no contact with commercial banks, and they pay a higher rate of interest on deposits. The deposits, however, are not suitable for businessmen since the amount is limited by a ceiling (changed in accordance with monetary developments) which in 1950 was fixed at 300,000 francs for an individual and at 1,500,000 francs for philanthropic, insurance, or cooperative societies. Deposits are in practice payable on demand, although the ordinary savings banks may, in an emergency, limit withdrawals to a certain sum each fortnight.

The essential feature of savings bank legislation is the requirement that the banks redeposit with the Caisse des Dépôts et Consignations all funds except till cash and accounts with the Treasury and the Bank of France. The Caisse des Dépôts et Consignations in turn uses these funds to purchase French and foreign securities from a list approved by the Minister of Finance. These securities consist principally of government obligations, and constitute so large a volume that they may be an important factor in the management of the public debt and the bond market. The Caisse pays the savings banks interest on their deposits which is passed on to the depositors with a reduction of 1 percent. In 1949 depositors received 2.25 percent on their deposits; in 1950, 2.75 percent.

Since passage of the law of June 24, 1950, savings banks are no longer simple intermediaries for the Caisse des Dépôts et Consignations, but may make loans on their own account to local governments up to an amount equal to 50 percent of the excess of deposits over withdrawals. During the year 1951 they invested in this way about 30,000 million francs for the benefit of local regions.

Contact between the commercial banks and the savings banks is limited to the clearing of checks deposited at the savings banks. The savings banks may not draw checks except on the Caisse des Dépôts et Consignations, either for making payments or for meeting expenses.

Postal Checking Service.—This service was established in 1918, and, like the savings banks, it handles an increasing volume of funds. Its aim is to further the use of settlement by check, and within the framework of the post office, it provides a national clearinghouse for payments. It has become more and more important as a financial institution. At the end of 1951 individual holdings of postal checking funds amounted to 262,000 million francs in 2,759,000 different accounts, or to nearly 15.4 percent of the total of bank deposits, which was estimated at 1,707,000 millions. In 1938 the postal checking accounts had been only 4,000 million francs, or about 6 percent of the total of 66,000 millions at that time.

Operations are carried out either by a transfer order from one account to another, or by a check. The check may be crossed like a bank check, thus prohibiting payment into anything except another account. There are also postal travelers' checks, payable at sight at any post office, over a period of four months. Balances in postal checking accounts do not carry interest. Postal checking accounts have some advantages over bank accounts but they do not serve the same needs.

The postal checking service brings into the financial circulation of the country a considerable volume of funds, many of which arrive eventually at the commercial banks, as for example when bills are paid by postal check and deposited in bank accounts by the recipients. The functions of postal banks and commercial banks are complementary rather than competitive.

GOVERNMENT FINANCIAL INSTITUTIONS

THE CAISSE DES DÉPÔTS ET CONSIGNATIONS

This fund, established by the law of April 28, 1816, is the oldest of the governmental banking institutions and also the most powerful, for the greater part of governmental financial activity is connected with it. Originally its function was to receive funds under adjudication and deposits of certain public institutions and public officials, but its scope has been steadily widened. It is particularly important in that it manages the funds of the savings banks, of various private insurance agencies, and of the social security system. It is thus responsible for a volume of funds which approaches that of the deposits in the nationalized banks. At the end of 1951 the assets of the Caisse amounted to 997,000 million francs, as compared with a total of 2,164,000 millions for all French banks. This total increased by 116,000 millions in 1948, 87,000 millions in 1949, 160,000 millions in 1950, and 122,000 millions during 1951, varying principally with changes in the deposits of the savings banks which represent about 75 percent of its resources.

The Caisse puts more of its funds into investments and capital placements than into short-term operations. Although the long-term investments have decreased somewhat from the 86 percent which they represented in 1938, they still predominated at 69.2 percent in 1951. The Caisse has an obligation to obtain a return on funds invested for long periods as well as for the sight deposits of the savings banks.

Securities issued or guaranteed by the government offer both sufficient return and sufficient safety, and form also a means of carrying out a consistent policy in the bond market.

The security portfolio of the Caisse amounted to 344,000 million francs in 1951, of which 2,000 millions were in stocks and shares of foreign companies. The right to invest in industrial securities has not been much used by the Caisse, in spite of the broadened provisions of 1931. The Caisse plays an important role in the loans granted to public authorities, which amounted to 344,000 million francs in 1951. Of this amount 22,000 millions are in Treasury obligations payable semi-annually, and 139,000 millions in Treasury obligations payable annually. There are also loans to *départements,* municipalities, and government-owned institutions, to finance public works. Since it was entrusted with the management of the Caisse de Crédit aux Départements et aux Communes, the Caisse des Dépôts has been the most important agency in the financing of local governments, having provided them with 92,000 million francs as of the end of 1951. Another type of long-term investment is the advances made to the Treasury for carrying out various laws regarding social welfare. Thus the Caisse finances the construction of low-cost housing and rural electrification and assists in medium-term and long-term credit to agriculture. These operations amounted to 33,000 million francs at the end of 1950, and to 67,000 millions at the end of 1951, having increased by 34,000 millions for low-cost housing alone.

The Caisse devotes a fraction of its resources to demand and short-term loans, in order to provide the liquidity needed to meet its sight deposit obligations. In its balance sheet for 1951, cash represented 14,500 million francs, or 1.46 percent of the assets, while current accounts were 64,400 millions, or 6.47 percent of the liabilities. In the 1951 report, Treasury notes and short-term assets amounted to 227,200 million francs or to 22.84 percent of total assets.

The large volume of Treasury notes and of Crédit National acceptances in its portfolio makes the Caisse an important factor in the money market. It does not limit its activity to the management of government obligations but lends its support also to economic activities which require medium-term credit. This it accomplishes first of all through the banks, which have the privilege of discounting with a repurchase agreement at the Caisse part or all of the paper representing the loans made. Such paper must have two bank signatures, or one bank signature and one signature of a non-bank enterprise with a guarantee. This device, although instituted in 1931, had only limited use until after the war when it began to be increasingly used. The volume of outstanding authorizations to banks for medium-term loans rose from 5,600 million francs in 1948 and 50,300 millions in 1949, to 54,400 millions in 1951. Rediscounts in 1951 totaled 48,500 million francs.

It is not only the banks which obtain the aid of the Caisse in the granting of medium-term credit. The Crédit National also turns to the Caisse for aid in mobilizing the credits which it has granted to banks. The authorizations thus obtained from the Caisse amounted to 143,000 millions in 1950, of which only 29,600 millions were used; in 1951 the authorizations were 171,300 millions of which 81,500 millions were used. The Crédit Foncier, although a relative newcomer in the field of medium-term credit, also deals with the Caisse; it obtained 1,000 million francs in 1950, and 15,900 millions in 1951.

By its diverse and extensive activities the Caisse des Dépôts et Consignations has the appearance of a great governmental bank, although it does not always live up to that role in practice. Since its creation in 1816 it has assumed increasing responsibility, thanks to the flexibility of its unusual form of organization. It is managed by extremely competent and high authorities, through a Supervisory Committee which includes representatives of Parliament, the bank of issue, the Treasury, the cabinet, and the economic interests of the country. Its Director is appointed by the President of the Republic on the nomination of the Minister of Finance.

THE CRÉDIT NATIONAL

The Crédit National is an independent institution created by the law of October 10, 1919, to aid in the payment of war damages and the reconstruction of war-damaged enterprises. Its capital was subscribed half by the banks and half by different groups of industries. It also raises funds by the issue of bonds, but it is forbidden to accept deposits, discount bills (except medium-term), or deal in securities. As a corporation, it has a Board of Directors of eleven members, and holds an annual meeting of stockholders whose powers are like those of an ordinary corporation. It has no branches, but is represented outside of Paris by the Crédit Foncier. However, it is not completely independent, for the government has entrusted to it certain public services and has reserved for itself certain rights of direction and control, including the nomination of the President, who is director-general, and two other directors.

The settling of damages of the First World War was the most important part of the original task of the Crédit National. The total amounted to 64,000 million francs, and to raise this amount a series of bonds had to be issued. At the close of the Second World War the role of the Crédit National appeared even more important because of the amount of destruction and the cost of reconstruction, but the ability to borrow proved to be very limited. Bond issues of the Crédit National reached 75,000 millions in 1945, 1946, and 1950. In 1947 and 1948 it took over 57,000 million francs of issues put out by groups of war-damaged industries. Since 1949 it has also managed the Caisse Autonome de Reconstruction, created by the law of March 21, 1948, to handle the funds for reconstruction. It is the latter agency which now meets all the costs falling on the government for war damage and reconstruction, out of its own resources and, in case of need, out of Treasury advances. The costs of war damages involved 216,000 million francs in cash payments in 1950, plus 31,000 millions in securities; in 1951 these figures were 226,500 millions in cash payments and 35,700 millions in securities.

A new function was assigned to the Crédit National by the law of December 4, 1940: it accepts for the government the bills drawn on it by enterprises, creditors of the state, and pays the bills on maturity out of funds provided by the Treasury. These operations were of little importance until the end of the war, but after that they developed rapidly because the Treasury adopted the device of payment by draft. The maximum of such bills was reached in May, 1949, with 220,000 million francs, but fell off to 175,000 millions by the end of that year and to 147,000 millions by the end of 1950, as the Treasury made less use of such means of payment. In 1951 the Treasury made greater use of such bills, which rose to 202,700 million francs by the end of the year. The acceptances of the Crédit National are used in the money market like Treasury notes and are widely held by the banks. Of the 513,000 millions of government short obligations held by all banks at the end of 1951, 336,000 millions were Treasury notes and 177,000 millions were acceptances of the Crédit National.

The Crédit National aided the government also in the handling of Marshall Plan payments: controlling payments in dollars, recovering sums due from importers, and accounting for the counterpart funds authorized by the Americans. These operations amounted to 424,000 million francs in 1949, 620,000 millions in 1950 and 768,000 millions in 1951.

The Crédit National also handles various categories of advances of Treasury funds to special enterprises whose activity is protected or guaranteed by the government. Thus it discounts the bills issued by foreign governments or agencies in payment of exports guaranteed by government credit insurance (under the law of July 10, 1928); it makes loans to the French movie industry (under the law of May 19, 1941); it lends to enterprises which for some reason are cut off from the usual sources of credit (under the law of November 3, 1940), to producers' cooperatives and reconstruction enterprises (under the law of December 31, 1947), and to businessmen and industrialists of Alsace-Lorraine.

To such special operations were added in 1949 the loans made by the government out of the Fund for Modernization and Equipment, approved by the Investment Commission, in which the Crédit National acts as agent in preparing the documents, taking the guarantees, and collecting the interest and principal. The amount of such advances increased from 6,000 million francs at the end of 1949, to 26,000 millions at the end of 1950, and 44,830 millions at the end of 1951. In addition to these, the Crédit National makes direct loans at its own risk, for two to twenty years, to aid in the creation, the development or the reorganization of industrial and commercial enterprises which are deemed to be of general interest to the economy (under the law of March 23, 1941). The total of these direct loans increased sharply during recent years, rising from 32,000 million francs in 1949 to 82,816 millions in 1951. This great increase was due not only to the difficulty of obtaining new business capital in the market, but also to the fact that the government made available more funds through the Fund for Modernization and Equipment; this group of direct loans out of the Fund is, however, quite separate from the indirect loans mentioned above.

The Crédit National has been authorized since June, 1943, to discount or to buy with a repurchase agreement the bills representing medium-term credits made by the banks up to five years' maturity. In this way it aids the financing of industrial reequipment and modernization. Such nationalized industries as coal and electricity benefited first from this form of credit, which has now been extended to other essential sectors of the economy. The total of authorizations to rediscount rose from 5,000 million francs in 1945 to 175,000 millions in 1951, but the bills actually presented for rediscount were far below these figures.

The Crédit National itself has the privilege of rediscounting at the Caisse des Dépôts et Consignations (which is its principal source of funds), at the Bank of France, at the Bank of Algeria and Tunis, and more recently at the State Bank of Morocco. This privilege it exercised to the extent of 33,000 millions in 1950 and 90,000 millions in 1951, keeping in its own portfolio only about 7,000 million francs of bills. This action, it should be noted, has largely offset the credit restrictions practiced by the Bank of France since September, 1948.[10]

The activity of the Crédit National has been characterized by constant adaptation to the financial and economic needs of the country. Although it continues to be the direct auxiliary of the government in handling war damage and other public expense, its most important function has become that of a centralizing organization for medium-term credit.

THE CAISSE NATIONALE DES MARCHÉS DE L'ETAT

This agency was established by the law of August 19, 1936, to provide funds with which business men could produce goods ordered by the government. It is a governmental body with financial autonomy and administrative personality, managed by a Board of Directors of 12 members representing the principal financial institutions and different economic Ministries. Its field of operations has been recently extended to North Africa.

The Caisse does not provide funds directly for borrowers, but enables them to obtain bank credit more easily, in one of three ways:

1. Financing of government purchases may be aided by the Caisse, either before the production of the goods by a guarantee to the banker that the order for the goods is bona fide, or after the production of the goods, by a guarantee or by an acceptance. In either case the Caisse provides a third signature for the commercial bills, which makes them rediscountable by the lending bank at the Bank of France. It thus aids the producer who would be financially embarrassed by the usual delays in obtaining payment from the government, and also the

[10] See p. 295.

banker who is able to mobilize his resources. In the postwar period when government orders multiplied, the volume of Caisse authorizations rose from 10,800 million francs in 1946 to 53,300 millions in 1950 and to 111,200 millions in 1951. The authorizations actually used were in the same years 6,200 millions, 30,900 millions, and 61,430 millions respectively.

2. Financing of production may be aided by the Caisse by means of the *lettre d'agrément* authorized by the law of September 12, 1940. It is an official document addressed to the producer, inviting him to produce certain products currently needed. This letter assures him, when the goods are completed, of the aid of the Caisse in stocking or selling his products, and protects him from the risks of lowered prices or forced sales. The aid given by the Caisse takes the same form as in the financing of government purchases, either a guarantee or an acceptance. During the war the *lettre d'agrément* was used chiefly to finance the production of replacement and rationed goods, but it has since been extended to cover certain articles of general interest and even imports (under the ordinance of August 16, 1945). The advantages offered by this letter are much appreciated by industrialists, for whom it reduces the cost of their working capital. Although the holders of these letters are not required to use them at the Caisse itself, they do so in a majority of cases. These operations have grown since 1946 from 32,100 million francs of authorizations with a utilization of 6,900 millions, to a high point in 1949 of 47,100 millions of authorizations and 25,700 millions utilized. Since then the figures have declined somewhat, to 16,800 millions authorized and 12,000 millions utilized in 1951.

3. A third type of financing authorized for the Caisse by the law of August 19, 1936, was that granted to individuals, with a guarantee from their business or professional association. Before 1945 this type of credit was used chiefly by members of purchasing associations. After the war it aided in the reconstruction of economically essential industries like construction materials and mining equipment. Since 1949 it has been oriented toward the modernization of industry, especially the mechanical and metallurgical. The aid of the Caisse takes the form of an unconditional guarantee of the bills drawn to the order of their banker by the industry; these bills are then eligible for rediscount at the Bank of France. This type of credit, both medium-term and short-term, had a considerable growth until 1948 but has

declined since that time. From 1946 to 1949 the authorizations rose from 15,800 millions to 64,600 millions, then fell off to 43,000 millions in 1951. The corresponding figures for utilization rose from 10,700 millions in 1946 to 48,100 in 1949, and fell to 35,700 in 1951, when they represented only short-term operations.

In addition to the three main types of credit just described, the Caisse was also authorized to provide credit for the Caisse Nationale de l'Energie when the electrical industry was nationalized.[11] During 1949 short-term and medium-term credits were granted to this industry to the amount of 19,000 million francs. More recently the law of August 1, 1949, authorized the Caisse to guarantee, accept, or endorse the bills drawn by other nationalized industries, coal and railroads. At the end of 1950, 73,000 million francs of credit was authorized for these industries, of which 70,500 millions were actually utilized, mostly at medium term. The corresponding data for 1951 were 86,000 and 77,000 millions respectively.

The results achieved by the Caisse des Marchés de l'Etat indicate the increasing importance of its role. In 1939 the total of its outstanding authorizations was only 1,200 million francs, of which half was utilized. In 1951 the total authorizations had increased to 260,000 millions, and the utilizations to 186,000 millions, which were particularly important in the field of medium-term credits.

THE FINANCING OF RECONSTRUCTION AND EQUIPMENT

The problems raised by the financing of postwar reconstruction and equipment were of such magnitude that the government was obliged to create several specialized agencies. Some of these have a general role like that of the Commission des Investissements, which works closely with the Commissariat Général au Plan de Modernisation et d'Equipement and with the National Credit Council. Others have a more narrowly defined task of handling the credit for special sectors, like the Fonds de Modernisation et d'Equipement and the Caisse Autonome de la Reconstruction. All of them, whether general or special in their scope, function within the general directives laid down by the modernization and equipment plan.

The Commissariat for the setting up and execution of the plan was established by the decrees of January 3, 1946, and January 16, 1947, with a view to increase production and trade, to raise the

[11] See pp. 274–75.

productivity of labor, to provide full employment, and to raise the standard of living, and for these purposes to restore public and private equipment and tools damaged or destroyed by the war. The National Credit Council participated in working out the plan because of its concern with everything which touches on credit. In 1947 for example it made a study of the financing of projected investments, and after underlining the need for monetary reform, recommended the establishment of a special fund for this purpose to compensate for the insufficiency of funds available in the financial market. The result of its recommendation was the law of January 7, 1948, which created the Fonds de Modernisation et d'Equipement and at the same time levied a special tax to fight inflation, a part of which was turned over to the Fonds. The Fonds operates as a special account of the Treasury and its operations are authorized by the Minister of Finance on the advice of the Commissariat Général au Plan and of the Commission des Investissements. The funds with which it operates consist of one third of the special levy against inflation and one third of the proceeds of the bonds issued in connection with this levy, which was a kind of capital levy of January, 1948. Later the funds consisted largely of the counterpart funds in connection with American aid. Finally they included an advance made by the Treasury to balance the receipts and expenditures of the Fonds for each fiscal year. From 1948 to 1951 the total resources available to the Fonds amounted to 1,560,000 million francs, of which American aid accounted for 750,000 millions.

It is the duty of the Fonds to grant credit to enterprises, collectives and territories, which are making investments under the modernization and equipment plan. Direct loans are made to enterprises and government organizations which have been authorized to make expenditures for new construction. For other sectors of the economy, the loans are made indirectly through such intermediaries as the Caisse Nationale de Crédit Agricole and the Crédit Foncier for agricultural equipment; and through the Crédit National, the Caisse des Dépôts et Consignations, and the Crédit Hôtelier for the equipment of private industry.

In addition to the Fonds de Modernisation et d'Equipement, there was established under the law of March 21, 1948, the Caisse Autonome de la Reconstruction, which provides funds for the repair of war damages, within the scope of visiting legislation. Its funds are provided by the proceeds of bonds issued by groups of war-damaged enterprises (39,000 millions from 1945 to 1950), or issued by the Caisse itself (55,000 millions from 1945 to 1950), or are provided from special budgetary credits of the Treasury (878,000 millions from 1945 to 1950). In order to conserve its liquid resources, the law of April 8, 1949, provided that some of the payments for war damage might be made in the form of negotiable securities. This Caisse is managed by the Director of the Crédit National. Its Board of Directors includes among others the Governor of the Bank of France and a representative of the National Credit Council.

Another agency with much wider functions was set up by the decree of June 10, 1948, as the Commission des Investissements. Its mission is to maintain a balance between the demand and supply of capital funds. It follows all of the programs for investment either under the direction of, or with the indirect support of, the government. It must take care that the same policy is followed by all agencies which distribute or direct the various forms of medium-term and long-term credit. The Treasury, although it must maintain a fiscal equilibrium in the money and capital markets, does not have the facilities for carrying out such a task alone, since it involves close collaboration with the National Credit Council, the Commissariat Général au Plan de Modernisation et d'Equipement and other agencies charged with the distribution and utilization of investment funds. This collaboration is now assured by the Commission des Investissements, for which the Treasury supplies the staff. Under the joint presidency of the Ministers of Finance and of Economic Affairs, the commission includes also the Commissaire Général au Plan, the Governor of the Bank of France in his capacity of Vice-President of the National Credit Council, and the President Director-General of the Crédit National. The financial competence of this commission, which arises from the quality of its membership, has led the legislature to give it an essential role in the carrying out of plans for modernization and equipment. The appraisal of the credit demands addressed to the Fonds requires not only an appreciation of the economic importance of the particular project and its place in over-all planning, but also a study of its implications for larger financial policy. This is the task of the Commission des Investissements.

Still another agency created in the year 1948 was the Caisse Nationale de l'Energie, which was an extension of the powers of the earlier

Caisse Nationale d'Equipement de l'Electricité et du Gaz. This new Caisse, created at the time of nationalization of the electrical and gas industry, now extends its operations over the nationalized coal industry as well. It helps to equip establishments in these industries and also provides working capital in case of need. But its most important function is the reimbursement of the former owners, one of the largest and most complex tasks ever attempted in France. However, the Caisse has left to the usual banks and brokers all the other activities in relation to these issues: subscriptions, repayments, or payments of dividends. This Caisse is not comparable to other specialized government credit institutions like the Crédit National or the Crédit Hôtelier, since it acts only for the particular agencies to which it is attached. On the administrative level it is a public institution with financial autonomy; it is managed by a board of directors on which are representatives of the nationalized gas and electric and coal industries, of the government, and of banking.

THE BANK OF FRANCE

Organization.—The Bank of France was organized on January 18, 1800 (Nivôse 28, year VIII of the Revolutionary calendar) by a decree of the Consuls of the Republic. A corporation with perpetual charter, its stock was owned by individuals, not the government. A General Assembly of the 200 largest stockholders met once a year to choose the Council of 15 Regents and the three Auditors. Originally, the Bank was managed by a central committee of three members elected by the Regents from their own number, but after 1806 its Governors and the Vice-Governors were named by the Minister of Finance.

The chief function of the Bank had been originally the discount of commercial bills, and the issue of its own notes against them. The law of April 14, 1803, gave it a monopoly of the note issue, but only for Paris. In 1848, after the absorption of the note issue of the provincial banks, the monopoly was extended to all of France. Gradually during the course of the nineteenth century the Bank of France became a bankers' bank, a bank of rediscount, at which credit instruments could always be mobilized into cash. This special position of the Bank of France led eventually to the modification of the statute, which remained essentially unchanged for more than a century. The first stage in this process was a change in administration: the law of

July 24, 1936, followed by the decree of December 31 of that year, forced the opening of the General Assembly to all the stockholders, and a new General Council of 20 members was established. The actual power of the stockholders was, however, limited to the election of two members of this Council. The importance of the Council, which resembled a board of directors, was further limited by a law of November 24, 1940, which reduced the number of members to eleven; on December 5, 1944, the composition of the Council was again changed and the number of members set at fourteen.

The law of December 2, 1945, completed the transformation of the Bank begun in 1936, and nationalized it. On January 1, 1946, its shares became the property of the government and the shareholders were given in exchange government obligations, registered and negotiable, and redeemable over twenty years. The rate of exchange between the stock of the Bank of France and government bonds was calculated according to the liquidating value of the stock.

The present General Council of the Bank of France is made up of

Four members *ex officio*
- the Governor of the *Crédit Foncier*
- the Director of the *Caisse des Dépôts et Consignations*
- the Director of the *Crédit National*
- the Director of the *Caisse Nationale de Crédit Agricole*

Seven members appointed by the Minister of Finance on the nomination of the appropriate Ministers
- 2 representing commerce and metropolitan industry
- 5 others representing respectively agriculture, labor, colonies, foreign affairs and general economic interests

One member elected by secret ballot of employees of the Bank of France

The Councillors and the Auditors elected by the stockholders therefore ceased to function after December 31, 1945. The nationalization law (December 2, 1945) provided that the composition of the General Council, the payment of taxes and royalties, and other legal details would be modified and elaborated by further legislation, but none has so far been enacted. Since nationalization, the two Auditors elected by the General Assembly have ceased to exercise their function. The two Auditors who continue to act are chosen by the Ministry of Finance from the upper ranks of its personnel. They have the right to supervise all the operations of the Bank, and must approve all actions relating to the note issue, but in other matters have no powers other than those of an advisory character.

Initially a Discount Committee of 12 members was established. By the ordinance of April 13, 1945, the number was increased to 15 and the conditions of their appointment were set forth. Assisted by the members of the General Council, this Committee examines all paper presented for rediscount. An Auditing Committee, consisting of the members of the General Council and the Auditors, makes periodic examinations of the cash, the notes, the portfolio and the securities.

Although the nationalization law contained no provision for holding a final General Assembly, the General Council has continued the publication of the annual report of the Bank in the traditional form. In these reports it is apparent that the Bank of France has maintained its organization and its traditions in carrying out its new mission.

Functions.—The Bank of France has, without definite maturity, a monopoly of the note issue in all of France proper (the European or "metropolitan" area) according to the rules set in its statutes and the successive renewals of its charter in 1806, 1840, 1857, 1897, 1918, and 1945. Until 1928 the amount of the note issue was subject to a "ceiling" limitation, but that year a fractional reserve system was put into effect. The Bank of France was required to keep a reserve in gold coin or bullion equal to 35 percent of the notes in circulation and demand deposits. That requirement was abolished by a decree-law of September 1, 1939, and the ratio of reserve fell from 59 percent in 1939 to 3.3 percent in July, 1950, the lowest postwar level.[12]

In return for the privileges of its charter the Bank of France has certain obligations to the government:

to perform without charge certain fiscal operations for the Treasury, including all security transactions,
to provide for the general public such services as the cashing of government pay checks,
to pay to the Treasury a part of its profits computed on the basis of the rediscount rate and the note circulation,
to pay to the Treasury the profit arising from the redemption or retirement of notes in circulation.

The Bank of France also makes loans to the Treasury under terms which are subject to special Conventions between the Bank and the Treasury. These are of two kinds:

12 By the end of 1951, it amounted to 9.3 percent.

1) Permanent advances which do not bear interest. These are reported in the balance sheet of the Bank, and have amounted to 50,000 million francs since March 29, 1947.
2) Temporary advances which are subject to repayment by the Treasury but which in practice have been absorbed in the successive revaluations of the Bank's reserves. The latest revaluation was made under the law of August 4, 1950, at the rate of 393,396.50 francs per kilo of pure gold. At the end of 1951 there were two kinds of temporary advances still outstanding. One was the loan for the maintenance of the German Occupation troops in France, under Conventions from August 25, 1940, to July 20, 1944. The amount of these advances has remained at 426,000 million francs since the end of the war. The other temporary advances were made under Conventions entered into between September 29, 1938, and September 25, 1947; their maximum is fixed at 175,000 million francs.

The balance sheet of the Bank contains two other accounts which also represent advances to the state of more than 5,000 million francs each. The first is a negotiable Treasury note representing the indebtedness of the State to the Bank for the gold returned to the National Bank of Belgium in 1944. The second consists of negotiable notes of the Caisse Autonome d'Amortissement given to the Bank in place of the Treasury notes rediscounted during the war of 1914–1918 for the purpose of making loans to foreign governments (Convention of June 23, 1928) and as compensation for the loss suffered on a part of the foreign exchange holdings when certain foreign currencies were devalued (Convention of December 13, 1931).

Another account was opened on the books of the Bank to handle the advances made by the Bank for the Exchange Stabilization Fund of the Treasury, under the Convention of June 27, 1949. The account rose from 43,300 million francs at the end of 1949 to 131,000 million francs at the end of 1950, thus indicating the importance of the return flow of exchange by which France was benefiting. By the end of 1951 this account had fallen to 66,100 million francs. The favorable turn of the monetary situation in 1950 was evidenced also by the increase of the Bank's demand deposits abroad, which rose from 61,800 million francs in 1949 to 161,900 million francs in 1950. In 1951 they had fallen again to 22,000 million francs.

The foreign exchange reserves of the Bank still make up an important part of the cover for the money in circulation, although the metallic reserve is still extremely small in comparison with what it was formerly. The stock of gold which had reached 4,900 metric tons in 1932 had fallen almost continuously since that time to 2,407 tons in 1939, 968 tons in 1945 and 486 tons in 1951.

Central Banking Functions.—The Bank of France stands traditionally at the summit of the French banking system because of the rediscount operations which it carries out for the benefit of the other banks. These operations are subject not only to strict statutory regulation but also to the credit policies which over a long period have made the rate of discount the principal means of controlling the money market. Bills are not eligible for rediscount at the Bank of France unless they have less than 90 days maturity and bear three good names. The economic usefulness of the transaction which they represent is also examined.

The rate of rediscount proved insufficient to defend the gold reserve after the First World War, when the financial operations of the government were developing rapidly, when the banks were practicing new techniques in granting credit, and when, in the international field, the movement of capital was so influenced by high interest rates in other countries that exchange controls had to be instituted. The traditional rediscount policy had to be reenforced, especially after the crisis of 1930, by new techniques adapted from Anglo-Saxon practice.

The first of these new devices was the thirty-day loan to banks and other financial establishments as an aid in making their monthly settlements. These were authorized by a decision of the General Council of the Bank of France on February 21, 1935. The loans run from five to thirty days, at a rate usually equal to the rate of rediscount, and they are made for amounts equal to about 95 percent of the value of the collateral, which consists of the government obligations of not more than two years maturity, especially Treasury notes. The money market is thus made more flexible for both banks and Treasury. The amount of such loans has been limited, although the item on the balance sheet of the Bank of France which represents them fluctuates by 25,000 million francs at times.

The second of the new credit devices adopted by the Bank of France was the purchase and sale in the open market of short-term negotiable government obligations and of eligible private bills. These open-market operations, unlike the advances previously described, have shown a considerable increase, as the purposes for which they were used have been extended. Under the original legislation of June 28, 1938, it was "to affect the volume of credit and regulate the money market" that the Bank of France was authorized to go into the open market, under very strict limitations. Such operations were not to be used under any circumstances as a source of profit to the public treasury or the issuing agents. The securities in question were Treasury notes, the notes of the French nationalized railroads in minimum amounts of 100,000 francs and at maturities of less than two years, and bank acceptances in amounts of 50,000 francs and over, with 90 days to run and bearing three commercial signatures. Acceptances of the Crédit National drawn on the Treasury were later added to the list. In practice, open-market operations are carried on almost exclusively in Treasury notes whose absorption by the Bank of France is of great assistance to the Treasury in the management of the floating debt. These operations appear in the balance sheet of the Bank as "Negotiable securities purchased in France." Their total stood at 17,000 million francs in 1945 and had reached 137,000 millions in 1949. During 1950 it was relatively stable when the general growth of credit was halted for a time, but during the latter half of 1951 it rose again to reach 223,000 million francs at the close of the year.

In addition to the use of these two new credit devices, another significant change has taken place since 1948 in the relations between the Bank and the commercial banks. The latter now turn more frequently to the money market than to the Bank for funds with which to make their settlements. Therefore the central bank has extended its purchases (with and without repurchase agreements) to a new group of bills, first-class bankers' acceptances drawn to finance international trade, and bills carrying the unconditional guarantee of the Caisse Nationale des Marchés de l'Etat. This has had the effect of easing the credit restrictions of September, 1948, and was designed to stabilize the ordinary rediscount facilities of the banks. They may, of course, always turn to the money market to negotiate their Treasury notes, the acceptances of the Crédit National and all the bills arising from international trade, or to sell with a repurchase agreement the acceptances of the Caisse Nationale des Marchés de l'Etat and certain types of bills with unconditional guarantees.

The result of all these developments in the French money market is that since 1948 the discount portfolio of the Bank of France contains no public obligations, while open-market operations, traditionally carried on in government obligations, now are concerned with commercial bills. This situation did not become apparent in the reports of the Bank of France until 1950 when the portfolio began to be classified into the following items:

French bills discounted;
foreign bills discounted;
bills guaranteed by the *Office des Céréales;*
bills for the mobilization of medium-term credit.

The last item is the most interesting because of the importance of the financing of equipment which it reflects. The mobilization of medium-term credit has been carried on by the Bank of France, with the approval of the General Council given on May 11, 1944. This makes eligible for rediscount bills with not more than three months to run, if they were drawn by banks in order to mobilize loans of nine months to five years made for the purpose of enlarging or rehabilitating production equipment. These bills, which must have three signatures in addition to that of the borrower, are brought to the Bank of France by the Crédit National, the Crédit Foncier, or the Caisse des Dépôts et Consignations, which have themselves discounted them for the bankers who made the original loans. The bills are rediscounted by the Bank of France only if it approved the original loan; each loan application is studied individually in relation to the larger plan for reequipment of industry. Far more rediscounts are authorized than are made. At the end of 1950 the total of such rediscounts stood at only 57,000 million francs, although the earlier peak had been 100,000 millions. During 1951 the total rose rapidly reaching 133,000 million francs during the last quarter of the year.

The balance sheet item "French bills discounted" consists chiefly of trade acceptances payable in francs. It includes therefore predominantly commercial bills, with a few warrants, some bills drawn to mobilize short-term bank credit, and some guaranteed obligations or similar securities offered by debtors to the Treasury. This item was stable during 1950 but in 1951 rose from 335,000 million to 607,000 million francs, reflecting the central bank's aid to the economy. This was an amount equal to 36 percent of the volume of notes in circulation in October, 1951, at the moment when the credit policy had to be tightened anew because of the inflation.

The item in the balance sheet called "Foreign bills discounted" is comprised principally of documentary bills payable abroad, in foreign countries and in overseas French possessions. It is of relatively small importance in the Bank of France portfolio because of the disappearance of bills from the financing of international trade.

The item "Bills discounted for the Cereal Office" gives evidence of the financing of cereal inventories. The agricultural credit banks rediscount at the Bank of France the bills for crop loans which they have previously discounted for agricultural cooperatives. These operations vary widely with the seasons, the low point coming in the middle of the year.

The discount rates of the Bank of France are much less important in the money market than formerly, for present conditions in the money market are an outgrowth of the management of the public debt rather than of the economic situation. Short-term rates are a function of Treasury needs and a tendency to follow a cheap-money policy. However, the rules of monetary orthodoxy have not been entirely forgotten. On January 9, 1947, the Bank of France determined not to prolong the easy money policy which had carried the rediscount rate to a low point of 1.625 percent in January, 1945, and therefore raised it to 2.25 percent. However, government obligations and commercial bills arising from sales of goods were given a preferred rate of only 1.75 percent. This dual system was maintained during the two rate increases of October 9, 1947, and September 4, 1948, which brought the rates to 4.0 and 3.5 percent respectively. It was abandoned on September 30, 1948, when the discount of commercial bills was no longer in need of stimulation. After that time there was only one rate of 3 percent, but there was still a preferential rate for government obligations of less than three months' maturity, of 2.5 percent.

Along with this staggering of the discount rates, other new measures were taken. For one thing, the banks were "invited" to retain in their portfolios at least 95 percent of the Treasury securities which they held, and to devote to further purchases of such securities at least 20 percent of all increases in their deposits after that time. Secondly, the Bank of France set a maximum on the volume of rediscounts of each bank. These measures represented a new approach to the problem of credit control, the use of quantitative devices rather than qualitative. The Bank of France thus intervened much more directly than formerly, at the behest of the National Credit Council.[13]

During this phase of credit policy the restrictive effect of these over-

[13] See p. 288.

all measures was slightly offset by changes in the rate of discount. At the beginning of 1950 interest rates became of urgent concern because the economic situation seemed to be stabilized and a depression was feared. The new orientation of credit policy was confirmed by a lowering of the discount rate to 2.5 percent on June 8, 1950, but the principles established on September, 1948, nevertheless remained in force, and the rate of discount on government obligations of less than three months' maturity stayed at 2.5 percent. In the early autumn of 1951 the increasing demand for credit caused the Bank of France to raise the discount rate to 3 percent on October 11, and then to 4 percent on November 8.[14] The National Credit Council at the same time took steps to maintain the expansion of bank credit within the limits compatible with a sound currency: absolute insistence on the "floor" assigned to the banks for their holdings of government obligations, and fixing of new "ceilings" for discount operations, along with a strict supervision over credit and exchange operations. The changes in the rediscount rate were thus closely tied up with credit policy and represented only one control device among many. The supplementary powers granted to the Bank of France reinforced the traditional powers of control exercised by the Bank, and arose out of the new organization which is now a part of the banking law.

THE CONTROL OF BANKING AND CREDIT

The distribution of credit in France takes place through the banking mechanism which has already been described, but it is implemented and governed by principles laid down by several organizations established since 1945. These principles are expressed in directives which take into account various national interests—that of the public Treasury, that of the national economy and that of private finance. These directives represent a novel experiment in France, emanating as they do from the new institutions which were superimposed upon the banking system and which were created in two stages at two quite different epochs of banking history, 1941 and 1945.

L'Association Professionelle des Banques.—This association was created by the law of 1941 and continued by the legislation of

[14] On September 17, 1953, the discount rate was lowered to 3.5 percent.

1945–46. But long before that bankers had been organized into trade associations, of which the Union Syndicale des Banquiers de Paris et de la Province was the most important and may be considered the predecessor of the new association. Membership in the old societies was voluntary, but in the new Association it is obligatory. Its membership therefore includes every financial business classified as a bank (including foreign banks) by the National Credit Council acting through the Bank of France. The law provided specifically that no unlisted establishment might function as a bank, except for a few public agencies under special charters.

The organization of the Association is that laid down by the general statute of July 1, 1905, for such groups. It is directed by a Council of 20 members, with four representatives from each of the following:

nationalized banks,
incorporated banks of Paris,
other banks of Paris,
incorporated banks outside of Paris,
other banks outside of Paris.

Each year the Council forms an executive committee of seven members, one of whom handles the administrative and financial affairs under the direction of the president.

The Association has an important role which goes far beyond the maintenance of good relations among its members and the coordination of their activities. In the new set-up of credit, this role is essentially to act as liaison between the banks and the organs of control, the National Credit Council, and the Control Commission. The Association serves as consultant and as executor for the decisions taken by the control bodies. These decisions are transmitted by the Governor of the Bank of France to the President of the Association, who then communicates them to the membership.

The law gives to the Association a consultative role in inscribing the name of a bank on the official list; it transmits the request of the applying bank to the National Credit Council with a recommendation for action, and may do the same if the name of the bank is to be removed from the list. On the technical level, the Association is asked to study many questions regarding banking conditions, the concentration of banking, or the establishment of joint services. In this area it may be asked to carry out tasks such as the preparation and application of interbank agreements, on behalf of the Bank of France.

Its powers may even include disciplinary action, since the Bank Control Commission may, under the law of June 13, 1941, delegate to the Association (with the approval of the Minister of Finance) disciplinary measures to be taken in case of any infringement of the bank regulations, the instructions of the National Credit Council, or the agreements concluded among the banks. In practice the Association is not called upon for such action except in the case of minor infractions of banking charges, and even then an appeal may be made from its decision to the Control Commission.

The Association has as a final function the watching over of the interests of the banking profession, and may go to law wherever a bank is concerned. This right to sue any person who is carrying on any illegal banking activity is, however, shared with the Bank Control Commission.

The Bank Control Commission.—This was established in 1941 to ensure the enforcement of the new legislation, but its composition, like its function, has been steadily enlarged to take a prominent place in the general organization of credit. In addition to the Governor of the Bank of France, the president of the finance section of the Conseil d'Etat, the director of the Treasury from the Ministry of Finance, the director in charge of credit from the Ministry of Economic Affairs (or their alternates named by the Minister of Finance), the Commission has included since 1945 a representative of bank employees, nominated by their organizations and appointed by the Minister of Finance, and since 1950 a representative of the banks, nominated by the Association Professionelle des Banques and appointed by the Minister of Finance. Thus the most diverse interests may have a hearing before this high authority. The Bank Control Commission has jurisdiction in France, Algeria, and the Saar over all banks and financial establishments. Its powers include those of supervision, regulation, and discipline.

The first duty of the Commission is to supervise the application of banking regulations, and for this purpose to receive from each bank and financial establishment periodic reports of condition. It may demand additional information, if necessary, and take part in the inquiries conducted by the examiners of the Bank of France. Its supervisory powers are exercised primarily by means of the balance sheets sent in by each bank on a standard reporting form drawn up in March, 1943. The profit-and-loss account form was standardized in 1947. The publication of these statistics has added materially to the available monetary and banking information, and credit developments may now be measured with some exactitude.

One of the provisions of the banking law of 1941, which the Commission was charged with carrying out, was the progressive application of the new capital requirements for banks. By December 1, 1946, incorporated banks were to have a capital of 5 million francs, and partnerships or single owners a capital of one million francs; these figures were to be doubled if the bank had more than two permanent offices. This obligation was actually not fulfilled by all banks until April 1, 1948. Agencies of foreign banks have been "invited" to invest in France an amount equal to the equivalent capital of a French bank.

The supervisory and investigative powers of the Commission are more extensive than its powers of enforcement, and the first report of the Commission expressed the hope that stronger measures could be taken in the case of some bank activities which it could not approve. However, later reports were congratulatory on the "line of prudent policy" laid down for the banks.

The second group of powers entrusted to the Commission, those of regulation, give it the right to set the fundamental rules for the functioning of banks. Under the decree of May 28, 1946, the Commission may when necessary, on the proposition of the Bank of France, fix or modify the rules to be observed by the commercial banks in maintaining their solvency and their liquidity. There are many ratios which may be computed among various items of the balance sheet, but the Commission has so far concerned itself with only one, the liquidity ratio. Under the terms of the Commission's decision of February 11, 1948, deposit banks are required to maintain in their consolidated balance sheets a minimum of 60 percent of their short-term liabilities in the form of liquid and easily liquidated assets. The Commission showed moderation in setting a figure which was well below the general average for French banks. This is not considered to be an optimum figure, nor a figure applicable to all banks, but a limit below which a bank cannot fall without suffering a penalty. The Commission still has the right to make suggestions for improvement to individual banks, if the ratio is falling, even if it has not reached the 60 percent level. Appeal may be made by a bank which has suffered disciplinary action on this account in the same way as for other sanctions, i.e., to the Conseil d'Etat.

This device of setting a lower limit to the liquidity ratio has proven to be a strong addition to the control measures over bank credit, and a protection to the deposits of the public. It is a new and extremely flexible addition to measures of credit control.

An important part of the regulatory powers of the Commission was the classification of the banks provided by the new legislation. Although it was the National Credit Council which made the first general classification of banks and other financial institutions in France, the division within the three categories of banks was left to the Control Commission. Each agency was to act as a court of appeal from the decisions of the other, in regard to these classifications, an overlapping of powers which has given rise to a number of legal problems. As a result of these classifications it is known for the first time how many banks of each type are in existence in France—commercial banks, investment banks, and banks for medium-term and long-term credit.

Another function was entrusted to the Control Commission by the bank nationalization act of 1945. The Commission appoints a permanent auditor for each of the nationalized banks, who attends all meetings of the Board of Directors, examines all the documents of the bank, and prepares an annual report. Moreover, the Control Commission, assisted by three members of the National Credit Council, carries out all the duties of the former General Assembly of stockholders. It is also charged with the duty of standardizing the by-laws of the banks in accordance with the decree of May 28, 1946, regulating their activities.

The disciplinary powers of the Commission are exercised when an appeal is made to the Commission from a decision of the National Credit Council, usually by a bank which has been taken off the list or has been refused the privilege of inscription on the list. In addition, the Commission is constantly at work applying banking laws and rules and enforcing sanctions. It may give warnings to banking institutions and recommend their suspension or removal from the official list. It may impose fines and bring to court cases of illegal practice. In disciplinary matters, procedure is regulated by the decree of June 5, 1950. Appeal can be taken to the Conseil d'Etat, the highest tribunal for administrative questions in France.

Although the regulatory powers of the Commission applied primarily to the reorganization of the banking system which resulted from the legislation of 1941–45, it still plays an important part in the mechanism of credit control, and its supervisory and disciplinary powers are still important and have recently been extended. In 1950 it was given the task formerly assigned to the Commission de Vérification des Entreprises Publiques of preparing an annual report on the activity, the results, the administrative methods, the structure and the organization of the Bank of France, the Bank of Algeria and Tunis, the Bank of Madagascar, and all of the nationalized banks.

THE NATIONAL CREDIT COUNCIL

The National Credit Council was established by the bank nationalization law of 1945 for the purpose of controlling the nationalized banks and of establishing a general credit policy for the country. The management of the nationalized banks has already been described (see p. 229). General credit policy is determined by the government in the final analysis, but is put into operation through the National Credit Council, which prepares all the decisions regarding credit and money. The Council also has duties in connection with the regulation of banking and the settlement of disputes among banks.

On the Council are represented the principal economic interests of the country. They may be grouped into five classes, of which the first two are considered by the law as "active forces." These are as follows:

1. Ten representatives of borrowers. They are appointed by the Ministry of National Economy on the nomination of the Confédération Générale de l'Agriculture, the agricultural consumer cooperatives, groups of producer cooperatives, the Centre National du Commerce Extérieur, the Chambers of Commerce, the Chambers of Artisans, and the Maritime Chambers of Commerce.

2. Seven members representing the most representative workers' organizations. Three of these are appointed by the Minister of National Economy to represent workers in general; four are appointed by the Minister of Labor from the staffs and employees of the banks.

3. Seven members representing various Ministries of the Cabinet—National Economy, Industrial Production, Public Works and Transportation, Agriculture, Reconstruction and City Development, and Colonies—and the Commissariat au Plan de Modernisation et d'Equipement.

4. Seven members representing banks and financial institutions, appointed by the Minister of Finance. Three represent the nationalized banks, two the private banks. One represents the foreign trade financing institutions, and one the brokers of the Paris Stock Exchange.

5. Seven members representing the great public and semi-public financial institutions:

Director General of the *Caisse des Dépôts et Consignations,*
Governor of the *Crédit Foncier de France,*
President of the *Crédit National,*
Director-General of the *Caisse Nationale de Crédit Agricole,*
Director of the *Caisse Centrale de la France d'Outre-Mer,*
Director of the *Chambre Syndicale des Banques Populaires,*
Director of the postal checking accounts.

The Minister of Finance acts as President of the Council, and he may delegate his powers to the Governor of the Bank of France, who is Vice-President according to the law. The Director of the Treasury and the Director of Insurance, since the nationalization of insurance, also attend the meetings.

With so many members the Council is obliged to do much of its work through smaller committees. Originally there were four of these, but a fifth was later added to the number. The Deposit Committee suggests measures to encourage the use of deposits in commercial and savings banks, and measures for the amalgamation of banks [15] and their more efficient operation, especially in the handling of securities. The Committee on Short-Term Credit is responsible for general credit policy in the money market. The Committee on Medium-Term and Long-Term Credit is particularly important in this period of reconstruction and reequipment. The Committee on Foreign Trade aids in working out plans for imports and exports and their financing. The Committee on Banks and Financial Houses actively supervises these institutions.

The Council was given very broad powers. Some of these were temporary assignments relating to the nationalization of banks and to the organization of special forms of credit for long term and foreign trade financing. The permanent duties of the Council include first of all the regulation of the banking profession. It decides the right of a bank to be inscribed on the official list, although appeal from its decision may be carried to the Control Commission. It determines the principles on which branch offices may be opened. It sets interest rates and other charges on commercial banking operations, fixing upper limits for interest on deposits and lower limits for interest on loans. Charges on financial operations are not subject to regulation.

[15] In 1947 banks with more than 20 branches were requested to reduce the number by about 10 percent. This resulted in closing 280 out of the 3.549 bank offices. In a few cases, banks were permitted to open new offices.

Appeal from its decisions in such matters may be taken to the Conseil d'Etat as a court of last resort.

A second group of functions of the Council is consultative. It is permitted to express an opinion over a wide and diverse range of topics—the credit situation, the formation of savings and banking legislation. It is particularly concerned with the financing of reconstruction and foreign trade. Its directives regarding the distribution of credit are put into operation through the intermediary of the Bank of France.

A third group of functions may be called jurisdictional, as the Council is called upon to make many decisions for individual banks and for the whole group of banks. Decisions for individual banks may be made by the Council alone, but for general decisions the Council must secure the approval either of the Association Professionelle des Banques or of the Minister of Finance. This distinction is important, for it has happened that the Minister of Finance has approved a decision which had been rejected by the association of banks.

An important factor in the success with which the National Credit Council has functioned in the field of credit control has been the service for the centralization of banking risks, Centrale des Risques Bancaires, which was established at the very first session of the Council. Although the law had provided that the Council should receive copies of all directives issued by the various Ministries concerning the Modernization and Equipment Plan, and that the Control Commission and the Bank of France should transmit to it all the information and the documents it needed, it was clear that much more detailed information was required if any effective control were to be exercised over the money market. The service for the centralization of banking risks was therefore established at the Bank of France as a part of the discount department by the decision of March 7, 1946. All banks were ordered to report all business loans of 10 million francs or more, and all other loans of 5 million francs or more. The banking risks thus reported covered 45 percent of the outstanding bank loans, and had risen to 65 percent by the end of 1947.

When in 1948 the Council embarked on a policy of firmer credit control it was decided to open a series of local services for the centralization of banking risks at some of the branches of the Bank of France. At this time, March 23, 1948, the banks were instructed to report monthly instead of quarterly, under five heads, all their loans of 5 million francs and over for commercial credits, and of 2 million and over for other credits. As a result of these changes the central bank obtained information regarding more than 30,000 borrowers, who held 80 percent of the outstanding bank credit at the end of 1950. The information is available with an average delay of six weeks. Although only the banks and financial houses are obliged to report to the service for the centralization of banking risks, most of the big public and semi-public institutions voluntarily do the same. This group includes the Crédit National, the Crédit Foncier, the Crédit Agricole, and the Crédit Populaire.

This centralization of credit information makes possible an analysis of credit by branches of economic activity and permits the Council to adjust its intervention with far more delicacy. There is still a certain margin of uncertainty about the use of credit by various economic sectors. For this reason in October, 1947, when there was a strong inflationary expansion, the Council asked the principal banks to report the amount of their loans to enterprises with priority, and to those without priority, that is, to the enterprises which had been adjudged essential in the reconstruction, and to the others. The Council may also request the examiners of the Bank of France to make special reports on such matters. The Council is thus provided with unusual sources of information in aiding it to carry out its task.

The bankers who supply this detailed information to the service for the centralization of banking risks find it greatly to their advantage to have such reports available. It is possible for any banker to obtain information about any of his customers and their outstanding obligations and lines of credit. Although the mechanics of credit interchange is still not perfect, since it does not cover all types of credit and involves some delay, it forms a solid basis for decisions regarding credit to an individual enterprise, or credit policy as a whole.

It must be clear to anyone who has studied the operation of these three new organizations, the Association Professionelle des Banques, the Control Commission, and the National Credit Council, that they represent a radical departure from French banking tradition. Circumstances made it necessary for them to operate with the greatest circumspection, not only during the phase of postwar reconversion but also during the later years of apparent economic equilibrium, again menaced by the danger of inflation. From year to year the policy of credit control has been improved. The development of new devices has not meant the loss of flexibility. The new organisms have given proof of great vitality, and it can confidently be expected that they will be able to carry out the new tasks which the future will undoubtedly put upon them. Just how the control of credit has operated over the postwar period will provide further evidence on this point.

CREDIT POLICY IN THE POSTWAR PERIOD

Banking policy under the direction of the National Credit Council since 1946 must be considered in the light of the evolution of the economy in general and French finance in particular. In this section will be discussed the development of credit in the postwar period and the credit controls which have been imposed as a result.

The year 1946 was one of transition. Since the middle of 1945, when the war in Europe ended, there had been a great increase in money and bank credit. It was feared that much of the credit was for speculative purposes, but at the same time it was recognized that there was a real need to support with bank credit the increase in production and economic recovery. These contradictory forces made it necessary to have a credit policy extremely flexible and delicate, both in principle and in application.

At its first meeting in February, in addition to deciding upon the service for the centralization of banking risks already described, the Council decided to watch closely the relation between money and the level of production, and to restrain consumption credit. In a letter of February 7, 1946, the Governor of the Bank of France drew the attention of the banks to the difficulties created by granting credit for the financing of inventories at abnormally high levels. The wage increase of July 1, 1946, provoked a new warning at the very moment when the increase in deposits seemed to be slowing down. However, by October the situation was again causing alarm, and a new letter of October 29 urgently repeated the earlier instructions "in order to prevent bank credit from aiding producers and merchants to delay the delivery of merchandise beyond the normal periods of production and sale, and to carry on operations of stock-piling other than those ordered by the public authorities." Thus in less than a year the National Credit Council strengthened its position as it proceeded from inquiry, to recommendation, to orders.

During the course of the year 1946 the total of bank credit increased from 392,000 million to 600,000 million francs, or by 53 percent. These figures include loans to the government as well as to the private sector of the economy. At the beginning of the year the banks were supplying 87 percent of the total and the Bank of France only 13 percent, but by the end of the year the share of the Bank of France had risen to 21 percent. At the same time commercial loans had risen from 30 percent to 50 percent of total volume of commercial bank credit. Commenting on the situation in its report for the year, the Council said that this growth was evidence of a return to economic normalcy and was not in itself cause for anxiety, but it nevertheless called for the greatest vigilance in a period when psychological conditions might well lead to excess.

During the year 1947 the inflationary factors pent up during the war began to make themselves felt even more strongly than before. Unlike 1946, when the increase in loans had been almost exactly equaled by the increase in bank deposits, deposits in 1947 increased by only about half as much as the loans. The volume of money in circulation, however, which had increased by only as much as bank deposits during 1946, experienced in 1947 an increase almost double that of deposits, 189,000 million francs against 98,000 millions.

The National Credit Council began to take firmer steps to control credit very early in the year. As it stated in the second annual report covering 1947, "It was deemed advisable to enforce a policy adapted to the practical conditions of the moment, in the light of certain simple principles and concrete facts." The banks were therefore called upon to base their operations, not as in the past on the certainty of repayment, but on the double assurance that the funds were indispensable to the borrower and that their use would serve a real economic need. After January 9, 1947, every application for a new loan of an amount large enough to require reporting to the service for the centralization of banking risks had to be accompanied by a document justifying its use. For every loan, bringing the total of any individual borrower's advances and overdrafts over 30 millions (an amount later increased), the approval of the Bank of France was also necessary. On October 10, 1947, a further directive was issued to give preference to credit for productive activities which had been declared indispensable by the Commissariat Général au Plan—those for production and importation of essential foodstuffs and the key industries. In a letter of December 31, 1947, the Governor of the Bank of France reminded the banks that a policy of careful discrimination should be followed since this was the only policy that would enable them to meet the urgent demands of production and eliminate demands which were unjustified at such a time or could be met by other devices such as the liquidation of inventories, repatriation of foreign exchange holdings, or economies of management. Although these regulations appear very strict, they were applied in practice with great flexibility; every statement by the Council emphasized the importance of putting no obstacles in the way of increased production, and no limits were set to the total volume of credit.

The extreme seriousness of the problems raised by the depreciation of money during the war was becoming more and more apparent as general economic conditions became more stable. In its report covering the year 1947 the Council stated the objectives of its policy for the immediate future to be:

the restoration of confidence of savers and lenders in the long-range value of their holdings,
the return to tested and traditional practices for the investment of individual savings in channels most favorable to the modernization of equipment and the expansion of production and general well-being,
the progressive adaptation of bank resources—capital and deposits—to the new needs of economic evolution.

During the year 1948 the total of bank deposits and money in circulation rose from 1,661,000 million francs to 2,174,000 millions, an increase of 31 percent as compared with 30 percent in 1946 and 24 percent in 1947. In this year it was bank deposits which accounted for the major part of the increase, since they rose by 364,000 million francs, while money in circulation rose by only 72,000 millions. These changes were brought about by two factors which in part offset each other. First of all, a group of restrictive measures reduced the volume of liquid funds—the withdrawal from circulation of all 5,000 franc notes, on January 30, 1948, and the special tax against inflation coupled with a semi-forced loan. On the other hand, there were inflationary factors such as the increases in wages and prices. The participation of the banks in these developments is shown by the increase in business deposit accounts to 577,000 million francs in 1948, while personal checking accounts increased to only 320,000 millions.

In 1945 the two had been nearly the same, respectively 169,000 and 166,000 million francs.

During the first three quarters of 1948 the credit policy initiated in 1947 was continued with slight changes. The limit on loans which had to be approved by the Bank of France was raised on February 12 from 30 million to 50 million francs, and loans between these limits had only to be reported, not approved. This recognized not only the increase in prices which had taken place but also the upswing in production. Since rediscounts of commercial bills as well as of public obligations and guaranteed bills remained outside of this regulation, credit expansion was able to continue with little interruption. The National Credit Council soon became aware that certain enterprises whose economic activity could hardly be called essential were able to obtain from their suppliers the credit which the latter in turn obtained from their bankers. This was first observed in connection with firms in the cotton and leather industries. To prevent this, a special declaration was required for all discounts of commercial paper offered by the drawee instead of as usual by the drawer (March 24, 1948).

Although the Council was still acutely aware of the danger of inhibiting production by a too-strict credit policy, the steady increase in bank credit during 1948 created another danger, that of inflation. To prevent the use of credit merely as an insurance against forced sale of merchandise or against a change in the value of money, further and much stricter measures of control were instituted at the end of September. The Minister of Finance, acting as president of the National Credit Council, laid down the broad lines of this new policy, which was then worked out in detail by the Bank Control Commission and the Bank of France—instructions which were still in effect at the end of 1951. Banks could no longer extend credit to business by reducing their holdings of Treasury obligations; they were to maintain thenceforth a reserve of the latter equal to at least 95 percent of the amount they had been holding on September 30, 1948. At least 20 percent of the amount of any increase in their deposits after that date was to be invested in government obligations. The Bank of France was to set for each bank an upper limit to the total of its commercial discounts; however, this restriction might be alleviated according to circumstances. It was also tempered by the activity of the Bank of France in the open market and by the possibility of rediscounting at the Crédit National certain medium-term paper. The adoption of these quantitative measures did not mean the abandonment of the qualitative controls already in operation, but, if anything, their extension. After September 30, 1948, the Bank of France applied to commercial paper some of the methods of control to which it had formerly been exempt; for example, detailed supporting documents required in the case of advances were also required for discounts, but only when a discount raised the total of a firm's credits from all sources beyond 50 million francs.

The net result of bank activity during the year 1948 was an increase to 443,000 million francs in loans, of which 260,000 millions were discounts of commercial bills. However, banks no longer presented for discount Treasury bills and acceptances of the Crédit National at the Bank of France, but limited themselves almost entirely to the rediscount of commercial bills.

During 1949 general economic conditions were relatively favorable, with increasing supplies of materials available and a certain stability in prices. There were still, however, acute financial problems of which credit policy was obliged to take account. The building up of inventories, for example, required large amounts of working capital which necessitated increased bank credit. In what measure was the financing of inventories compatible with the credit restrictions of September, 1948? They had not been designed to prevent all increase in the volume of credit, and the increase, although somewhat restrained, had in fact not been negligible. During this year cash holdings increased by about 500,000 million francs, of which two thirds represented bank credit, the rest money in circulation.

Credit policy during this year was aimed at adapting the volume of loans to the level of activity and employment. Selective criteria were broadened, resulting in easier credit for certain lines, and encouraging business to seek wider markets, especially abroad. A series of priorities was established early in the year, and certain sectors of the economy were singled out for special attention. Bankers were urged to take particular care in making loans on butter inventories or cotton imports; further regulations, although without any upper limit, were issued for credit based on wool, weaving, wine and rum; credit to the leather industry was stabilized, and credit for cattle-fattening was forbidden.

The Governor of the Bank of France in a letter of August 31 reminded the banks that their first aim should be to satisfy justifiable needs of enterprises which were producing equipment and consumption goods efficiently, or which were carrying on or developing exports, especially to countries with "hard" currencies.

The constant preoccupation of credit policy during this year (1949) was the fight against inflation, which had already proceeded so far that the 2,713,000 million francs of existing cash holdings, if valued in 1938 francs, would have amounted to only 135,000 millions.[16] This figure compares with the 192,000 millions of cash assets actually held in France in 1938. Calculated in the same 1938 francs, the value of the bank deposits had also shown little change, although the velocity of circulation had increased. The relatively high level of interest rates made it seem probable that cash holdings had attained an equilibrium level at which they might be expected to remain stable.

For the first time in many years the increase in cash holdings had exceeded the increase in credit to business and government. The difference was represented by the increase in foreign exchange reserves of the Bank of France, since the inflow of capital from abroad tended to go to the central bank rather than to the commercial banks. During 1949 the increase in notes in circulation, 308,000 million francs, was greater than the increase in bank deposits, of 180,000 millions, thus reversing the trend of 1948, when deflationary measures had affected the balance. Within the totality of bank operations, however, various items showed a certain stability. The slowing down of lending produced a slowing down in the business deposit accounts: total loans of all banks and the Bank of France were 408,000 million francs in 1949 as compared with 443,000 millions in 1948. At the commercial banks the unsecured business loans increased very little while rediscounts continued to climb. Credit to the Treasury was of little importance.

In the early part of 1950 economic conditions appeared to be somewhat stabilized. Restrictive credit measures were slightly liberalized in response to the many complaints which had been made. Prior approval of the Bank of France was no longer necessary for loans of less than 100 million francs (the former limits had been 30 millions and then 50 millions). The maxima set for rediscounts at each bank

16 The Conseil National du Crédit defines cash holdings as:

(a) private current accounts with Bank of France (accounts of Treasury public bodies and banks excluded); (b) demand deposits with banking institutions; (c) private postal checking accounts; (d) private deposits with the Treasury; (e) bank notes in circulation. See Table A, Statistical Appendix, p. 302.

were progressively raised, and the total of all bank rediscounts which had stood at 187,000 million francs in September, 1948, rose to 250,000 millions in June, 1950. The Bank of France lowered its rate on rediscounts and advances. At the request of the bankers' professional association, the Bank of France requested the National Credit Council to reduce the commission charged for endorsement, and the interest charged on advances. The Council for the first time enforced credit conditions which up to then it had merely recommended. In addition to these general measures, the Bank of France decided to make loans to export industries up to five years if their operations were guaranteed by the government; to admit for rediscount the bills up to five years' maturity drawn for building construction if they met the usual conditions for medium-term credit; and to abrogate the last of the restrictive measures on agricultural credit.

The outbreak of war in Korea did not at once reverse this trend toward easier credit conditions. On August 3, 1950, the Council made a request to the Minister of Finance, preceded by a long declaration on economic conditions, asking for a revision of the rules for rediscounting and for an easing of the handling of Treasury notes. The epoch of credit restrictions seemed to have reached its end, but the request of the Council was refused on the grounds that the outbreak of hostilities justified the maintenance of measures for controlling and limiting credit. As a matter of fact, these measures were reinforced in the following year.

Although there was an important increase in credit during the last quarter of the year, the year as a whole showed less increase—328,000 million francs—than the preceding year with its increase to 408,000 millions. Money in circulation accounted for more of this increase than bank deposits, and made up 51 percent of the total cash holdings at the end of the year. On the asset side of the balance sheet, foreign exchange holdings were increasingly important and amounted to 195,000 million francs at the Bank of France, a figure nearly as large as the 222,000 million francs of credit outstanding. Treasury loans were lower than in the previous year, and accounted for only 54,000 millions of the 222,000 million francs.

The portfolios of the commercial banks increased less during 1950—260,000 million francs—than in 1949, when the increase had been 336,000 millions. The increase in the bill portfolio accounted for most of the change, as the unsecured advances changed very little. The increase (136,000 million francs) in bank deposits was not sufficient to provide new funds for lending, and the banks were obliged to turn to the Bank of France and other rediscount agencies. Especially at the end of the year they rediscounted medium-term bills at the Crédit National and the Caisse des Dépôts et Consignations.

The year 1951 was marked by renewed credit expansion which caused new fears of inflation. The volume of cash holdings increased rapidly during the first three quarters; the total of 3,120 million francs rose by 65,000 millions during the first quarter, by 130,000 millions during the second, and by 176,000 millions during the third. The same increase occurred during the fourth quarter, carrying the total for the end of the year to 3,667,000 million francs. About two thirds of this expansion occurred in holdings of bank notes rather than in bank deposits, reflecting the increasing need for currency as prices rose. A large part of the additional bank notes was issued as a result of the credit obtained at the Bank of France, either by means of rediscounts or through its open market operations. The discount portfolio of the Bank of France increased during the first three quarters of the year by 123,000 million francs, rising from 427,000 millions to 550,000 millions, or from 27 percent to 31 percent of the volume of notes in circulation; at the same time the discount portfolios of the four large nationalized banks increased by only 24,000 million francs, from 626,000 millions to 650,000 millions. Most of this increase in credit went to private borrowers. Treasury borrowing showed very little change. Government financing at this time was not of an alarming character, and the real inflationary danger lay in the volume of private borrowing at the Bank of France. Moreover, the foreign exchange reserves of the Bank, which had been increasing rapidly until March, 1951, began to decline after that date and by the end of September had fallen from 333,000 million francs to 270,000 millions, equal to only 15 percent of the note circulation, against 21 percent at the end of March. By the end of December, 1951, it had lost another 184,000 million francs.

This combination of menacing factors caused the National Credit Council at its meeting of October 4, 1951, to take a number of measures of which the most dramatic was an increase in the discount rate from 2.5 percent, at which it had stood since June 8, 1950, to 3 percent.

However, at the same time provision was made for supplementary credit to meet the needs of business arising from higher wages and prices. The Bank of France raised the ceiling limits on rediscounting, and provided that for short periods, with a slight increase over the discount rate, commercial bills might be brought to the Bank under a repurchase agreement. The limit on loans requiring the previous approval of the Bank of France was raised from 100 million francs to 500 millions, but commercial loans were required to submit to this rule as well as non-commercial loans.[17]

The regulation of September, 1948, which required banks to keep a certain proportion of government securities in their portfolios, was to be enforced more strictly thenceforth. The Bank Control Commission was to compute the ratio every day, instead of at periodic intervals as formerly; however, a certain flexibility was permitted in practice. These measures for the defense of the franc were complemented by foreign exchange regulations and by a further increase in the discount rate to 4 percent on November 8, 1951. This decision

[17] The regulations of January 9, 1947, and January 12, 1948, classified the credits granted by banks into two main categories:

1. The first category included those extended under a guarantee, discounts of public and commercial bills of exchange and documentary credits. In the granting of these credits, the lending bank retained freedom of action and did not have to seek the prior approval of the Bank of France.

2. The second category included all other credits, such as non-self-liquidating credits and credits of a financial character, whose liquidity depended upon rediscounts at the Bank of France and might lead to such rediscounts.

This distinction seemed to justify itself with respect to guaranteed obligations which seldom call for payment in cash, with respect to documentary credits which are always accompanied by documents attesting the underlying character of the transaction and with respect to government paper which the government could in any event place without limit in the portfolios of banks.

Moreover control over discounts of commercial paper in the immediate postwar period did not seem warranted by reason of the limited volume. When the volume did begin to rise after liberation, it represented at the outset a return to healthy commercial practices and did not carry the risk of inflation.

However, in 1948 the expansion in credit resulted from increases in commercial paper of such a character that it did seem to constitute a threat to the value of money. The increase in the amount of commercial paper was accompanied by an increase in the maturity of the drafts and did not correspond to the increase in production. These developments might well have justified bringing this type of paper under control, but in September, 1948, the monetary authorities decided otherwise, since they feared that to do so would paralyze business activity.

It was only in September, 1951, at the time of the outburst of new inflation that it was decided to subject discounts of commercial paper to control. Now such discounts along with non-self-liquidating paper and financial credits are included in the global limit of 500 million francs (cited in the text) requiring the prior approval of the Bank of France.

was made because of the deterioration in the balance sheet of the Bank of France.

The Governor of the Bank of France made a detailed explanation of credit policy in a letter sent to all bankers on December 21, 1951. After denouncing the speculation which was being carried on in certain sectors of the economy, he reminded the bankers that credit policy must not be turned aside from its economic role by those unwilling to cooperate in the stabilization of the monetary unit. The principles of priority which had been adopted helped those enterprises which were developing French production, improving technical methods and lowering prices for consumers. The Bank of France reaffirmed its classic conception of the rediscount rate as a device for providing credit during the period of production and distribution. It was the duty of the commercial banks to evaluate the loans offered to them.

The actual effect of the new credit rulings was to restrain the opening of new lines of credit, rather than the use of existing authorizations. During the last quarter of 1951, unlike the preceding quarters of the year, the increase in authorizations was less than the increase in utilization of credit lines. The new ceilings on rediscounts had been fixed so as to allow for the expected growth of the economy. During the first nine months of the year the average growth in loans had been 36,000 million francs; in October it reached 124,000 millions, in November 76,000 millions and in December 101,000 millions. The total of all credits utilized, as reported to the credit clearinghouse, showed an increase of 301,000 million francs for the last quarter of 1951, or almost twice that of the corresponding period of 1950.

However, the declining rate of increase in the bank note circulation gave rise to hopes that the inflationary upsurge was under control and that the new credit regulations were attaining their goal. This combination of quantitative and qualitative controls, combined with judicious flexibility in order to avoid strangling the economy, is well within the traditions of the Bank of France, which still stands at the service of the economy and the French franc.

Table A
Monetary Supply, 1945–52
(amounts in billions of francs)

Items	*1945* [a]	*1946*	*1947*	*1948*	*1949*	*1950*	*1951*	*1952*
Private current accounts with Bank of France	31	35	47	66	79	53	69	61
Demand deposits with other banks	355	510	608	946	1,115	1,240	1,428	1,637
Private postal checking accounts	43	62	85	143	187	209	262	304
Private deposits with the Treasury	7	10	15	17	22	28	33	31
Total deposits	436	617	755	1,172	1,403	1,530	1,792	2,033
Notes in circulation	577	732	921	993	1,301	1,590	1,883	2,124
Total of monetary supply	1,013	1,349	1,676	2,165	2,704	3,120	3,675	4,157

Sources: *Inventaire de la situation financière,* published by the Ministère des Finances; Reports of the Conseil National du Crédit.

[a] Data as of end of year.

Table B
Counterpart of Monetary Supply, 1945–52
(amounts in billions of francs)

Items	*1945* [a]	*1946*	*1947*	*1948*	*1949*	*1950*	*1951*	*1952*
Gold and foreign exchange [b]	130	95	65	65	154	467	279	236
Treasury debt								
Bank of France advances to the government [c]	455	566	720	763	768	705	742	802
Public obligations [d]	274	304	293	354	420	431	513	629
Treasury counterpart [e]	50	72	100	160	209	237	295	335
Credits to private sectors of the economy [f]	118	308	490	863	1,199	1,355	1,903	2,270
Total	1,027	1,345	1,668	2,205	2,750	3,195	3,732	4,272
To deduct [g]	14	4	8	40	46	75	57	115
Total of monetary supply	1,013	1,349	1,676	2,165	2,704	3,120	3,675	4,157

Sources: *Inventaire de la situation financière,* published by the Ministère des Finances; Reports of the Conseil National du Crédit.

[a] Data as of end of year.

[b] Items in Bank of France balance sheet: gold stock, foreign exchange reserves, advances to Exchange Stabilization Fund.

[c] Items in Bank of France balance sheet: negotiable Treasury notes, temporary and permanent advances to the Treasury, postal checking accounts.

[d] Treasury notes and acceptances of the Crédit National held by the Bank of France and other banks.

[e] Private postal checking accounts and private deposits with the Treasury. (These items are the counterparts of the same items in Table A.)

[f] Bank of France and other banks.

[g] Difference between the liabilities and assets of the banks which are not considered part of the monetary supply.

Table C

Banks, Public Finance, and Business Indexes, 1945–52

(AMOUNTS IN BILLIONS OF FRANCS)

Items	*1945* [a]	*1946*	*1947*	*1948*	*1949*	*1950*	*1951*	*1952*
Public obligations in bank portfolios [b]								
Bank of France	35	69	114	110	141	123	186	239
Other banks	239	235	179	244	279	308	327	390
Total	274	304	293	354	420	431	513	629
Credits to private sectors of the economy [c]								
Bank of France	17	58	92	205	352	452	826	944
Other banks	101	250	398	665	867	1,063	1,327	1,356
Total	118	308	490	870	1,219	1,515	2,153	2,300
Falling due (to deduct)				7	20	160	250	30
Total	118	308	490	863	1,199	1,355	1,903	2,270
Demand deposits								
Checking accounts	166	201	228	323	411	468	533	588
Current accounts	169	271	339	557	644	707	816	975
Other accounts	20	38	41	66	60	65	79	74
Total	355	510	608	946	1,115	1,240	1,428	1,637
Business indexes (1938 = 100)								
Wholesale prices	469	846	1,217	1,974	2,002	2,410	2,803	2,693
Retail prices	497	865	1,354	1,928	1,920	2,075	2,475	2,440
Industrial production (with construction)	67	92	93	121	126	131	144	143

Sources: *Inventaire de la situation financière,* published by Ministère des Finances; reports of the Conseil National du Crédit; business indexes of the Institut National de la Statistique.

[a] Data as of end of year.

[b] Treasury notes and acceptances of the Crédit National.

[c] Discount and loans. This total is overestimated on some dates and must be reduced by the amounts falling due.

Table D

Origin of the Credits to French Economy

(AMOUNTS IN BILLIONS OF FRANCS)

	December 1951	*December 1952*
Bank of France and Other Banks		
Loans and discount to enterprises	1,905	2,270
Crédit National and Caisse des Dépôts et Consignations		
Medium-term credit represented by bills	45	12
Other credits		
Medium-term and long-term loans granted directly by Crédit National and the Caisse Nationale de Crédit Agricole with funds of the Fonds de Modernisation et d'Equipement	232	309
Total	2,182	2,591

Source: Reports of the Conseil National du Crédit.

Table E
Distribution of the Credits to French Economy [a]
(amounts in billions of francs)

	December 1951	*December 1952*
Equipment		
Agriculture	120	157
Housing Act of 1950	17	61
Nationalized enterprises [b]	78	126
Industry and commerce	272	384
	487	728
Short-term credits		
Agriculture	147	204
Nationalized enterprises [b]	34	56
Industry and commerce	1,509	1,588
	1,690	1,848

Source: Reports of the Conseil National du Crédit.

[a] This distribution covers only those credits identified by the service for centralization of bank risks and by the statistics of public institutions.

[b] Charbonnages de France, Electricité de France, Gaz de France, Société Nationale des Chemins de Fer. The long-term credits do not include direct loans from the Fonds de Modernisation et d'Equipement: 123 billions in 1951, 135 billions in 1952.

The percentage of short-term credits is low compared with the activity of the nationalized enterprises which represented 10 to 15 percent of the national activity.

Table F
Equipment Credits, December 31, 1952 [a]
(amounts in billions of francs)

	Amounts
Coal, power, petroleum, and transport	166.2
Building, construction and public works	21.9
Iron metallurgy, ferrous and nonferrous metals, engineering	204.8
Textiles	17.0
Leather, paper, and wood	10.9
Chemicals and rubber	53.3
Manufacturing and marketing of foodstuffs	17.1
Nonspecialized trades	4.3
Housing Act of 1950	60.9
Miscellaneous business	14.1
Agricultural production	157.5
Total	728.0

Source: Reports of the Conseil National du Crédit.

[a] These credits concern the enlargement and modernization of equipment in industry, agriculture, and trade: medium-term credits granted by banks with their own resources and possibly completed with rediscount authorizations of public financial institutions; direct loans granted by public or semipublic institutions either with their own resources or with funds of the Fonds de Modernisation et d'Equipement.

Table G

Short-Term Credits, December 31, 1952

(amounts in billions of francs)

	Amounts
Industry and Trade [a]	
Coal, power, petroleum, and transport	137.7
Building, construction, and public works	87.3
Iron metallurgy, ferrous and nonferrous metals, engineering	405.1
Textiles	153.5
Leather, paper, and wood	82.4
Chemicals and rubber	124.0
Manufacturing and marketing of foodstuffs	149.7
Nonspecialized trades	76.0
Miscellaneous business	63.3
Total	1,279.0
Agriculture	
Cereals	153.5
Wines	11.8
Breeding	1.9
Other	36.8
Total	204.0

Source: Reports of the Conseil National du Crédit.

[a] Nationalized enterprises included.

Table H

Total Distribution of Short-Term and Medium-Term Credits, December 31, 1952

(amounts in billions of francs)

		Amount
Metallurgy		610.0
Engineering	337.2	
Iron	278.8	
Agricultural production		361.5
Chemicals		177.3
Textiles		170.3
Manufacturing and marketing of foodstuffs		166.9
Coal		112.4
Building and construction		109.2
Leather, paper, and wood		93.2
Nonspecialized trades		80.2
Miscellaneous business		77.6
Transport		75.4
Power		70.7
Housing		60.9
Petroleum and fuel		45.4
Total		2,211.0
Economy of the Saar Basin		50.0
Total		2,261.0

Source: Reports of the Conseil National du Crédit.

REFERENCES

This list brings up to date the list published in Robert J. Lemoine, *Foreign Banking Systems* (New York, Henry Holt and Co., 1929). Specialized works on the history of banking and banking operating techniques have been omitted from this brief bibliography.

HISTORY OF BANKING

Aureus. Banques et banquiers. Paris, Flammarion, 1939.
Bigo, R. Les Banques françaises au cours du XIXème siècle. Paris, Sirey, 1947.
Colling, A. La Prodigieuse Histoire de la Bourse. Paris, Société d'Editions économiques et financières, 1949.
Dauphin-Meunier, A. La Banque à travers les âges. 2 vols. Paris, Editions "Banque," 1937.
—— Histoire de la banque. Paris, Presses Universitaires, 1951.
Dillen, J. G. Van. History of the Principal Public Banks. The Hague, Nijhoff, 1934.
Dupont Ferrier, P. Le Marché financier à Paris sous le Second Empire. Thesis. Paris, Alcan, 1925.
Germain-Martin, H. Histoire économique et financière. Paris, Plon, 1927. L'Histoire de la nation française, Vol. X.
Hamel, J. Banques et opérations de banque, Vol. I. Paris, Rousseau, 1933.
Lacour Gayet, J. Histoire du commerce. Paris, S.P.I.D., 1950.
Pommery, L. Aperçu d'histoire économique contemporaine. 2 vols. Paris, Librairie de Médicis, 1952.
Ramon, G. Histoire de la Banque de France d'après les sources originales. Paris, Grasset, 1929.
Ripert, G. Aspects juridiques du capitalisme moderne. 2d ed. Paris, Librairie Générale de Droit, 1951.
Rist, Ch. Histoire des doctrines relatives au crédit et à la monnaie depuis John Law jusqu'à nos jours. 2d ed. Paris, Sirey, 1951.
Vergeot, J. B. Le Crédit comme stimulant et régulateur du crédit. La conception Saint-Simonienne. Thesis. Paris, 1918.

BANKING

Alheinc, R. H. La Banque au service des échanges. Paris, Presses Universitaires, 1946.
Ardant, H. Cours de technique bancaire français. Paris, Arts et Métiers, 1940–41.
—— Cours d'organisation et de fonctionnement des marchés financiers. Paris, Arts et Métiers, 1950–51.
—— Technique de la banque. Paris, Presses Universitaires, 1951.
Baldy, E. Les Banques d'affaires en France depuis 1900. Thesis. Paris, Pichon, 1922.

Banque et ses services, La. 12 vols. Paris, Editions "Banque," 1931–32.
Baudin, L. Le Crédit. Paris, Montaigne, 1934.
—— La Réforme du crédit. Paris, Librairie Générale de Droit, 1938.
Berthoud, J. Banque et opérations de banque. Institut d'Études Politiques, 1948–49.
Boulle, R. Les Grands Établissements de crédit devant la crise. Thesis. Paris, 1938.
—— Précis de technique bancaire, Vol. I: Caisse, Titres, Comptabilité. Paris, Marcel Rivière, 1952.
Cauboue, P. Various volumes in the series, Les Editions techniques et professionelles, published at Paris. These are, arranged by date: La Conduite des banques, 1931; Affaires de banque, 1932; Traité des opérations financières de banque, 1933; Les Variations du taux de l'escompte de 1921 à 1934, 1934; Le Rôle social des banques, 1934; Introduction à l'étude de la banque, 1935; La Pratique des opérations financières de banque, 1936; Philosophie de la banque, 1937; La Pratique de l'escompte, 1938; Les Variations du taux de l'escompte de 1935 à 1938, 1939.
—— Banque et problèmes bancaires du temps présent. Paris, Presses Universitaires, 1942.
—— La Pratique de la banque. Paris, Centre d'Information Interprofessionelle, 1943.
—— Technique des opérations de banque et de bourse. Paris, Editions Delmas, 1951.
Caullet, P. L'Aide à l'industrie et la liquidité des banques. Thesis. Lille, 1928.
Cluseau, E. La Réglementation des banques. Thesis. Toulouse, 1938.
Collas, H. La Banque de Paris et des Pays-Bas. Thesis. Dijon, 1908.
Collection Droit Social. L'Organisation professionnelle des banques. Paris, Librairie sociale et économique, 1942.
Daumain, J. Le Contrôle de l'Etat sur les banques privées. Thesis. Paris, 1937.
Dauphin-Meunier, A. La Banque (1919–1935). Paris, Gallimard, 1936.
—— La Banque de France. Paris, Gallimard, 1937.
David, P. Essai sur l'intervention de l'Etat dans le commerce de banque. Thesis. Lyon, 1937.
De fossé, G. La Gestion financière des entreprises. 2 vols. Paris, Presses Universitaires, 1952.
De Noe, J. F. L'Etat, le commerce de banque et la distribution du crédit. Thesis. Toulouse, 1939.
Distribution et Controle du Crédit. Paris, Armand Colin, 1952. A special number of the *Revue Economique* concerning the chief banking and financial institutions.
Dunod. Aide Mémoire Banque. Paris, Dunod, 1951.
Dupont, P. C. Le Contrôle des banques et la direction du crédit en France. Paris, Dunod, 1952.

Durand-Degeorges, M. Le Crédit industriel et commercial à moyen terme. Thesis. Paris, Librairie sociale et économique, 1942.
Escarra, J., R. Escarra, and J. Rault. Principes de droit commercial. Vol. VI: Banque et commerce de banque. Paris, Sirey, 1937.
Ferronnière, J. Les opèrations de banque. Paris, Dalloz, 1954.
François-Marsal, F. Encyclopédie de banque et de bourse. 5 vols. Paris, Crété, 1930–31.
Fruchaud, J. Banque 1950: Evolution des techniques bancaires de 1940 à 1950. Paris, Riber, 1950.
Gallie, L., and Edgar Faure. Banque et Bourse. Paris, Juris Classeur, 1935.
Germain-Martin, H. Banques d'émission. Paris, Les Cours de Droit, 1927.
—— Banques de dépôts. Paris, Les Cours de Droit, 1928.
Gougne, M. Tendance d'après-guerre des banques de dépôts. Thesis. Paris, Sirey, 1934.
Guenser, G. Le Marché monétaire français et son contrôle par la Banque de France. Paris, Sirey, 1938.
Hamel, J. Banque et opérations de banque, Vol. II. Paris, Rousseau, 1943.
International Banking Summer School (Paris, Sept., 1951). Le Financement des investissements. Paris, Association Professionnelle des Banques, 1952.
Laufenburger, H. Les Banques françaises. Paris, Sirey, 1940.
Lorin, J. La Politique des banques françaises de dépôts dans ses rapports avec le marché monétaire. Thesis. Paris, Presses Universitaires, 1923.
Merigot, J. C., and P. Coulbois. Le Franc 1938–1950. Paris, Librairie Générale de Droit et de Jurisprudence, 1950.
Ministère des Finances. Inventaire de la situation financière (1913–1946). Paris, Imprimerie Nationale, 1946.
—— Inventaire de la situation financière au ler Novembre 1949. Paris, Imprimerie Nationale, 1949.
—— Inventaire de la situation financière. Paris, Imprimerie Nationale, 1952.
Moreau-Neret. Les valeurs mobilières. 2 vols. Paris, Sirey, 1939.
Mouchotte. D. Problèmes français de crédit et de financement. Thesis. Paris, Librairie Générale de Droit, 1941.
Notes documentaires et études. Le Crédit en France avant et depuis la guerre. 2 fascicules. Paris, La Documentation Française, 1948.
Paves, L. La Banque et la Bourse. Paris, Dunod, 1950.
Penglaou, Ch. La Distribution du crédit aux entreprises commerciales, industrielles et agricolés en France. Paris, Sirey, 1939.
Petit, L., and de Veyrac. Le Crédit et l'organisation bancaire, Vol. VII of Traité d'économie politique by Truchy. Paris, Sirey, 1938.
Petit-Dutaillis, G. Le Risque du crédit bancaire. Paris, Riber, 1950.
Pirou, G. Le Crédit. 4th part of Vol. I of Traité d'économie politique by Pirou et Byé. Paris, Sirey, 1943.
Pose, A. La Monnaie et ses institutions. 2 vols. Paris, Presses Universitaires, 1942.

Problèmes actuels du Crédit, Les. Conférences de l'Ecole des Sciences Politiques. Paris, Alcan, 1930.
Rebotier, M. Les Participations bancaires à l'industrie. Thesis. Paris, Sirey, 1935.
Ripert, G. Traité élémentaire de droit commercial. 2d ed. Paris, Librairie Générale de Droit, 1951.
Saint-Germes, J. Bourse et banque. Paris, Librairie Générale de Droit, 1942.
Simon, Ph., and R. Cordier. Prècis de droit commercial et de contentieux bancaire. Paris, Editions La Revue Moderne, 1951.
Terrel, H., and H. Lejeune. Traité des opérations commerciales de banque. 8th ed. Paris, Masson, 1951.
Thery, A. Les grands établissements de crédit avant, pendant et après la guerre. Thesis. Paris, Librairie Générale de Droit, 1921.

SPECIALIZED INSTITUTIONS

Regional and Local Banks

Banques Regionales et Locales. Preface by H. Germain-Martin. Paris, Editions de la France Économique, 1922.
Charpenay, C. Les Banques régionalistes, leur vie, leur mort. Paris, Nouvelle revue critique, 1939.
Martin, J. La Situation actuelle des banques locales en France. Thesis. Paris, 1940.

Crédit Agricole

Caisse Nationale de Crédit Agricole. Rapport annuel.
Degon, M. Le Crédit agricole. Paris, Sirey, 1939.
Notes documentaires et études. Le crédit à l'agriculture. Jan., 1951.

Crédit Populaire

Aubert, J. Les organismes centraux du crédit populaire. Thesis. Paris, 1941.
Chambre Syndicale des Banques Populaires de France. Rapport annuel.
Chamley, P. Les banques populaires françaises. Thesis. Lyon, 1938.

Overseas Banks

Ministère de la France d'Outre-Mer. Documents et Statistiques. Vol. IV: La Monnaie et le crédit dans les territoires d'outre-mer. Paris, 1950.
—— Annuaire statistique de l'Union Française, 1938–1948. Chap. I.: Monnaie, crédit et prix. Paris, 1950.

Caisse des Dépôts et Consignations

Caisse des Dépôts et Consignations. Rapport annuel.
Solanet, P. La Caisse des Dépôts et Consignations. Thesis. Paris, 1942.

Savings Banks

Code des Caisses d'Epargne. Paris, Editions de l'épargne, 1949.

Laurent, R. Le Rôle des Caisses d'épargne dans la formation de l'épargne nationale. Paris, Editions de l'Epargne, 1947.
Lescure, J. L'Epargne en France. 2d ed. Paris, 1936.

Caisse Nationale des Marchés de l'Etat
Hirsch, J. Le Financement des marchés publics. Thesis. Paris, 1941.

Crédit National
Crédit National. Rapport annuel.
Prevost, F. Le Crédit National. Thesis. Paris, 1941.

Crédit Foncier
Crédit Foncier. Rapport annuel.
—— Plaquette du centenaire, 1852–1952.

REVIEWS

Banque. Monthly.
Banque et Bourse. Monthly.
Journal des Caisses d'Epargne.
Revue de Droit Bancaire. To 1936.
Revue Economique.
Revue Trimestrielle de Droit Commercial. Since 1948.
Revue D'Economie Politique. Yearly special number, *La France Economique* with an article on French banking.
Statistiques et Etudes Financières. This publication is the successor (since 1949) to the Bulletin de Statistique et de Législation Comparées.

ANNUAL REPORTS

Association Professionnelle des Banques. Since 1941.
Commission de Contrôle de Banque. 1946–1950.
Commission des Investissements. Since 1948.
Conseil National de Crédit. Since 1946.
Union Syndicale des Banquiers. To 1940.

SPECIAL REPORTS

VIème Congrès International de Science et de Technique Bancaire. Reports and discussions. Paris, Editions "Banque," 1937.
Commission du Crédit, 1937. Not published for sale.
Congrès des economistos de banque française. Evolution du crédit et controle des banques. Paris, Domat, 1935.

WESTERN GERMANY

by H. Irmler

LANDESZENTRALBANK VON NIEDERSACHSEN

STRUCTURE AND EVOLUTION OF THE GERMAN ECONOMY

GERMANY'S ECONOMIC STRUCTURE has undergone radical change as a result of the war. Roughly one quarter of the state territory as of the beginning of 1938 was dismembered. This area included in particular the territories east of the Oder-Neisse line, which constituted the agricultural surplus areas of Germany, although comparatively sparsely populated. The remaining area, some 355,000 square kilometers, was divided, as a result of the war, into two parts: (1) the Federal Republic of Germany and the Western Sectors of Berlin, with a total of some 50,000,000 inhabitants and 246,000 square kilometers; and (2) the Russian-occupied zone of Germany, including the Eastern Sector of Berlin, with 17,000,000 inhabitants and an area of 107,000 square kilometers. Owing to the tension between West and East, the economic relationship between these two parts has become looser and looser.[1]

H. IRMLER is a member of the Board of Managers of the Landeszentralbank von Niedersachsen in Hanover. Dr. Irmler was born in Leipzig in 1911. In 1930 he joined the Staff of a German credit bank. Having finished his studies (law and political science) he entered the service of the Deutsche Reichsbank, where he worked until the closing of the Reichsbank in the spring of 1948. Up to May, 1953, he worked with the Bank deutscher Länder in Frankfurt/Main as chief of the section on money and credit in the Research and Statistics Department.

Dr. Irmler wishes to acknowledge his indebtedness to Dr. Leonhard Gleske, member of the staff of the Research and Statistics Department of the Bank Deutscher Länder, for his assistance in preparing this study.

1 All the data in this chapter refer to the Federal Republic of Germany and, if so

The economic structure of the Federal Republic of Germany is in some ways similar to that of Great Britain. It is an essentially industrial country. Only about 24 percent of the labor force are engaged in agriculture and forestry, while 41 percent are occupied in industry and handicraft, both figures indicating the level of June 30, 1951. Of the national income in the year 1951, amounting to some DM 90,000 million, only about DM 10,800 million were derived from agriculture and forestry, while industry, handicrafts and trade accounted for DM 58,800 million. At the cessation of hostilities in 1945 the economic situation was characterized by a vast rate of destruction of both industrial and residential buildings, by disorganization of transport and communications, and by almost complete isolation from the rest of the world. Large investments were required in order to remedy at least the greatest ravages of war and to reactivate production. Comparatively small progress was achieved until 1948, the reason being that reconstruction was considerably impeded by the fact that an extraordinarily large volume of money had been inherited from the war years and that the supply of goods and services at the legal maximum prices then obtaining was by no means adequate to absorb this volume of money. This state of affairs, known as "repressed inflation," gradually resulted in money being rejected to an increasing extent, and consequently in a progressive disintegration of the economy and in a considerable decline in the population's willingness to work.

The currency reform, effected in June, 1948, by drastically reducing the volume of money from some RM 160,000 million to DM 13,500 million reestablished its value. Prices and wages retained their former level. At the same time most of the physical controls—which, it is true, during the last stage of the inflation had in reality existed only on paper—were abolished, thus permitting unrestricted expansion of the productive forces inherent in the economy. Industrial production in the Federal Republic, on a 1936 basis of 100, which amounted to 50 percent in 1946 and 54 percent in June, 1948, has increased to 170 percent by October, 1953. The net national product at market prices increased from DM 67,700 million in the first year after the currency reform to DM 116,000 million in 1952. The propor-

indicated, also to the Western Sectors of Berlin. A few observations on the economic and banking systems of the German Democratic Republic will be found at the end of this study.

tion used for investment purposes in 1951, 20 percent, considerably exceeded that of 1936, which was 17 percent.

In connection with this remarkable upward movement of industrial production it must not be forgotten that, as a result of the loss of the eastern territories and the repatriation of the Germans from these areas, and also owing to the constant influx of political refugees from the Soviet-occupied zone of Germany, the actual supply of goods and services to the population remained comparatively low, because the population residing in the territory of the German Federal Republic increased from 41,000,000 in 1936 to 50,000,000 by the end of 1951. The influx of refugees, who had to be integrated in the economic system, aggregates some 9,000,000 people. In spite of the great increase in production, the number of employed was augmented by only 2,000,000 after the currency reform, the comparatively small size of the increase being due to the simultaneous process of rationalization. On a per capita basis, industrial production in October, 1952, exceeded that of 1936 by 25 percent. At the same date the total number of employed workers, employees and civil servants in the Federal Republic, was 15,456,000, or approximately 4,200,000 more than in 1936 in the same territory.

Owing, in the main, to the influx of refugees and changes among the various age groups caused by the war, the social structure in the Federal Republic is still comparatively uneven. No less than about 10,000,000 people, including their dependents, or 20 percent of the entire population, live at public expense, receiving social pensions or relief payments. The structural unemployment resulting from these changes, which is in no way connected with unemployment due to a downward trend in economic activity, must be estimated at no less than 600,000 to 700,000. Even with a maximum of economic activity as was the case in the autumn of 1953, the number of unemployed in the Federal Republic never fell below 964,000, the figure for October of that year. At this time a considerable strain already became apparent in the labor market; in particular, there was a lack of specialized workers.

The comparatively great density of population in Germany (203 inhabitants per square kilometer), together with the resulting high degree of industrialization, makes the German economy largely dependent upon foreign countries. After the war foreign trade had to be reestablished. Despite a vast amount of foreign aid and a considerable increase in exports, an equilibrium in the balance of payments was not achieved before 1951.

TABLE 1
BALANCE OF PAYMENTS OF THE FEDERAL REPUBLIC OF GERMANY INCLUDING WEST BERLIN, 1949–52
(AMOUNTS IN MILLIONS OF DOLLARS)

	1949	*1950*	*1951*	*1952*
Balance of Payments Items (Net Balances, excluding Compensatory Items)				
Merchandise	− 943	−558	+370	+540
Services	− 78	− 67	−226	+ 22
Private unrequited remittances	+ 3	+ 7	+ 11	+ 11
Current capital payments	+ 8	+ 9	− 37	−135
Unascertainable items and errors in statistical ascertainment	− 25	− 34	− 67	+ 28
Total net balance	−1,035	−643	+ 51	+466
Compensating Movements in Capital, Gold and Foreign Exchange				
Total foreign aid (received +, given −)	+ 854	+491	+428	+114
Payments received out of former German balances in Sweden	+ 7			+ 2
Total net payments in gold and foreign exchange (paid +, received −)	+ 174	+152	−479	−582
Total net balance	+1,035	+643	− 51	−466

Source: Bank deutscher Länder, *Monthly Report*, August, 1953.

The most important industries in the Federal Republic are the textile industry and coal mining, each employing about 650,000 people. Other important branches are: the construction industry; the manufacturing of electrical equipment; chemicals; optical goods and precision instruments; woodworking; the leather and shoe industries; and the automotive industry. Some of these also export considerable products.

The rapid expansion of production after the currency reform was, in the first place, facilitated by the facts that great reserves of unused capacity were available and that in some cases destruction was found to be not quite so devastating after the ruins were cleared up, which was done mostly in the Reichsmark period. The funds invested during the first few years after Germany's collapse, and more particularly after the currency reform, therefore had a comparatively wide and rapid effect. Now it would seem, however, that the period of swift recovery of the economy has, in the main, come to an end. Considerable investment, chiefly in the industries producing basic materials and power, will therefore be necessary for a further increase in production.

As will be seen from Table 2, a considerable part of the investment was financed, not out of statistically recorded savings, but from short-term credits granted by banks, from private lending, and from retained earnings. This type of financing was found to be possible without jeopardizing financial stability, because, as has already been mentioned, large reserves of productive capacity were available for immediate utilization, while in addition the productivity of human labor was consistently increasing.

TABLE 2

THE FINANCING OF NET INVESTMENTS IN FIXED ASSETS IN THE AREA OF THE GERMAN FEDERAL REPUBLIC

(AMOUNTS IN MILLIONS OF DM)

Funds Provided	*1948–49*	*1950*	*1951*	*1952*
Public budget resources	3,320	2,910	4,280	5,155
Capital market resources	2,258	2,593	3,246	4,315
Counterpart funds	378	1,771	820	548
Total	5,956	7,274	8,346	10,018
Residual item [a] (calculated as difference)	7,644	4,526	7,029	6,632
Total				
Net capital investments in fixed assets	13,600	11,800	15,375	16,650

Sources: Bank deutscher Länder, *Report for the Year 1951* and *Monthly Report*, March, 1953.

[a] The present position, as regards the collection of statistical data, does not permit showing the sources from which the remaining net investments in fixed assets have been financed. Undoubtedly, a very considerable part has been provided by financing out of the internal resources of firms and companies. In addition to this the item includes investment credits granted otherwise than through banks or other institutional investors. The residual item also includes short-term bank credits applied directly or indirectly to the financing of investment in fixed assets.

STRUCTURE AND PROBLEMS OF GERMAN BANKING

Set-up of the Banking System.—Unlike the banking system in the Soviet-occupied zone of Germany, the banking system in the area of the German Federal Republic (the United States, British, and French zones of Germany) has not undergone any fundamental structural changes since the end of the war. The only changes of importance were the closing down of the former Reichsbank and the establishment of the present central banking system, as well as the limitation, in principle, of the network of branches of all banks, except the Deutsche Verkehrs-Kreditbank A. G. and except those credit institutions whose business activities are confined to the granting of credits at medium term and long term, to the Land (state) in which the institution's head office is located. This latter provision mainly affected the three big banks: the Deutsche Bank, Dresdner Bank, and Commerzbank. As a result of the Law on the Regional Scope of Credit Institutions, enacted on March 29, 1952, the provisions regarding the decentralization of the banks have been amended so that the area of the Federal Republic is now divided into only three banking regions instead of the former eleven regions. Each bank is permitted to maintain branches within the territory of one such region.[2]

Altogether some 13,000 to 14,000 credit institutions of all types exist in the Federal Republic of Germany. Out of this total, about 3,500, covering an estimated 90 percent of the entire balance sheet of all banks, are included in the monthly banking statistics of the central banking system. Those institutions not covered by the statistics (about 10,000) are the smallest establishments, especially rural credit cooperatives.

The largest group of banks rendering monthly returns is the credit banks, which includes 296 banks and bankers. Their balance sheet total was about DM 20,600 million at the end of September, 1953. Among the credit banks themselves, the 9 successor institutions to the three big Berlin banks are the most important, with a balance sheet total of DM 11,000 million. State, regional, and local banks account for another DM 7,400 million and the private bankers for some DM 2,200 million. The next large group are the savings banks, of which there are 869 in the Federal Republic. At the end of September, 1953, their balance sheet total amounted to about DM 14,900 million thus considerably exceeding that of the nine big banks. Contrary to many other countries, savings banks in Germany not only engage in savings business proper, but to an increasing extent operate also as credit banks, particularly in relation to smaller traders and manufacturers. The savings banks have central institutions of their own, in the form of 14 central giro institutions ("Girozentralen"),

[2] Detailed data on the central banking system and the successor institutions of the large banks will be found in the respective sections.

through which an important part of their cashless payment transactions is cleared. In addition, the central giro institutions also to a considerable extent operate as lenders, chiefly by means of public deposits. At the end of September, 1953, their balance sheet total amounted to some DM 8,500 million.

The third group is the credit cooperatives, urban and rural. The 737 urban credit cooperatives grant credits mainly to handicraft and small industrial firms. Their balance sheet total was DM 2,600 million in September, 1953. The more than 11,000 rural credit cooperatives had a balance sheet total of an estimated DM 2,500 million. The urban credit cooperatives, which are united in the German Association of Credit Cooperatives, have 12 central institutions of their own, through which they clear part of their payments. The rural credit cooperatives, which are united in the German Raiffeisen Association, clear payments through their 6 central institutions. Recently, the central institutions of credit cooperatives have been headed by the Deutsche Genossenschaftskasse in Frankfurt/Main, which is the head institution both of the urban and the rural credit cooperatives.

In addition to the credit banks, savings banks, and credit cooperatives, which entirely or partly engage in short-term credit transactions, there are special institutions granting credits at long term and a number of institutions engaging in specialized tasks. Among the institutions specializing in long-term loans, one must mention first the 37 mortgage banks and corporations chartered under public law granting credits against real estate, with an aggregate balance sheet total of DM 5,600 million for September, 1953. In addition, a number of important credit institutions specialize in the granting of long-term credits; among them are the Landwirtschaftliche Rentenbank, the Industriebank A. G., the Reconstruction Loan Corporation and the "Bank für Vertriebene und Geschädigte (Lastenausgleichsbank) A. G." details of which will be discussed later (p. 347).

Types of Credit.—These include credits on current account, acceptance credits, discount credits, and loans. The first three types are chiefly short-term credits, granted usually for a period of three months and not exceeding six months. Loans, on the other hand, comprise credits at medium terms (six months to four years) and credits at long term (four years and over). Credits on current account are granted by the banks in part in the form of personal credits without special guarantee and in part against guarantees in the form of goods and stocks or against registration of mortgages or land charges in respect of real estate or buildings. Together with bill credits they represent the most important form of working credits to industry and handicrafts. Credits on current account are granted in particular where no discountable trade bills are available—either because the credit is needed not only for financing the terms of payment to be granted to the purchaser but also for financing the process of production itself, or because the purchasers are unable to sign bills by way of payment or refuse to do so. As a rule, banks in Germany prefer to grant credits by discounting bills rather than against current account, the reason being that the Central Banks purchase trade bills bearing three good signatures and having a maturity not exceeding 90 days. Trade bills are the most important credit instrument enabling banks to obtain central bank money. In addition to credits on current account and bill credits, the acceptance credits should be mentioned; they serve chiefly to finance imports and exports and to that extent replace the reimbursement credits formerly granted by foreign banks, but which at present are available to German firms to a very limited extent only. Fluctuations in the volume of short-term credits and their breakdown by various types are shown in Table 3.

TABLE 3
TOTAL VOLUME OF SHORT-TERM CREDITS OUTSTANDING AT SELECTED DATES SINCE THE CURRENCY REFORM, CLASSIFIED BY TYPES OF CREDIT
(AMOUNTS IN MILLIONS OF DM)

		IN PERCENT OF THE TOTAL VOLUME OF SHORT-TERM CREDITS		
Year	*Volume of Short-Term Credits*	*Current Account*	*Acceptance Credits*	*Bill Credits*
1948 [a]	4,684	54.4		45.6
1949	9,848	46.6	20.9	32.5
1950	13,524	45.2	17.3	37.5
1951	16,088	43.4	10.2	46.4
1952	19,425	46.5	6.2	47.3

[a] Data as of December 31.

Credits at medium-term are granted comparatively rarely. They chiefly serve the intermediate financing of construction activity and also play a certain role in agriculture, where capital is turned over at a slower rate.

The banks in Germany granting long-term loans—savings banks, mortgage banks, corporations chartered under public law granting credit against real estate, and a few institutions specializing in long-term loans—give such credits mainly for investment purposes in industry, housing, and agriculture. Security is in most cases furnished by establishing mortgages and land charges. Long-term loans are also made to finance communal enterprises such as power stations, with the liability assumed by the communes. At the end of October, 1952, out of a total of DM 11,200 million of long-term loans by banks, DM 3,200 million were secured by mortgages or land charges, and DM 900 million by communal security.

Sources of Funds.—Taken as a whole, the banking system, of course, itself creates its deposits, and other liabilities to the public, by granting loans. The individual bank, however, obtains the resources for its loans mainly by accepting deposits. Banks specializing in long-term loans, or engaging in credit operations at long term as well as at short term, obtain the necessary funds by accepting savings deposits, and by selling mortgage bonds and communal bonds. Debentures at short term or medium term, which are used in some countries, particularly in Switzerland, are not issued by German banks.

In addition, the banking system in Germany is being used to a comparatively large extent for passing on public funds to specific borrowers or groups of borrowers. This practice chiefly concerns funds made available at reduced interest rates by the public authorities to groups of persons unable to put up sufficient security with the banks (for example expellees), or to housing, coal mining, and to the public utilities. By reason of the fact that prices are fixed, these activities cannot compete for scarce credit at the market price. The counterpart funds accruing in respect of Allied assistance and released for the purpose of granting investment credits play a special role in this connection.

Deposits comprise demand deposits and time deposits,[3] the latter consisting of monies placed for fixed periods, and monies at notice. A special form of deposits are the savings deposits.[4] Almost all banks,

[3] Time deposits are deposits subject to a period of notice, or agreed period to maturity, of 30 days or more.

[4] That is, deposits on accounts which are kept in accordance with the prescriptions of Article 22 and subsequent Articles of the Banking Law, and which are in particular characterized by the issue of a savings book, and by the fact that withdrawals without notice are limited to DM 1,000 per month.

excluding the special institutions granting long-term credits, accept all types of deposits; there is hardly any division of functions in this respect. Accordingly, in the matter of credit transactions, the department store bank granting turnover credits as well as investment credits has always predominated.

Payment Transactions.—In Germany, contrary to the usual practice in Great Britain and the United States, the most important role in cashless payment transactions is played by giro transactions (bank transfers), and not by check transactions. While no detailed statistical data are available, the proportion of check transactions is estimated at only 20 to 30 percent of total cashless payments. In the case of bank transfers, the banking account of the customer ordering the transfer is debited and the account of the beneficiary is credited. Such transfers of amounts to the debit of one account and to the credit of another can be effected both between the accounts maintained with one and the same bank and between accounts kept with different banks. In principle, the system of bank transfers may be compared with check transfers, except that the order is reversed. While in transmitting money by check the amount is first paid to the party presenting the check and then debited to the account of the drawer, in the case of bank transfers (giro transactions) the account of the remitter is debited first, while the bank of the remittee does not credit its customer's account until after having received the amount. For the purpose of effecting giro transactions, banks either use a network of branch establishments, as do the big banks, or they form so-called "giro systems," as is the case with savings banks and credit cooperatives. The "private giro systems" are modeled on the giro transactions of the former Reichsbank, which, in turn, had adapted the system, existing from the seventeenth century, of the Hamburger Bank. The Reichsbank was the first institution strictly to enforce the use of prescribed forms in its own system. At present the giro systems of the various groups of banks are restricted to the individual Länder; transfers beyond Land boundaries are effected exclusively by the Land Central Banks and the Bank deutscher Länder.

Until recently, the clearance of checks was restricted to places having a Land Central Bank or a branch of one, where there were clearinghouses or check clearing agencies to which the local banks submitted town checks. The Land Central Bank effects clearing between the individual banks by debiting or crediting the giro account balances maintained by the banks participating in check collection. Recently, however, a central check clearing system for interregional check collections, operating to some extent in a similar way as the clearing system of the Federal Reserve Banks, was established within the central banking system. The long delays in the collection of checks caused by the lack of appropriate facilities have thus been considerably reduced. The greater protection against the drawing of uncovered checks, resulting from the reduction of collection periods, will also contribute to an increased use of checks in Germany.

The Legal Basis of the Credit System.—The relation between the state and the banks was fundamentally changed by the banking crisis of 1931 and the resulting alterations in the economic structure. Increased state influence was reflected in the Reich Banking Law of December 5, 1934. By means of state supervision of the banks it was hoped to avoid, as far as possible, losses to trade and industry, banks' customers and shareholders, and to protect the economic system against functional disturbances in the field of payments and credit transactions. Prior to the banking crisis of the year 1931, only certain types of credit institutions were subject to state supervision: private banks of issue which at that time still existed; mortgage banks; building and loan associations; and, among the institutions under public law, savings banks, state banks, provincial banks, and so on. By the Banking Law of 1934, supervision over the banking system was entrusted to a "Reich Control Office" under the Reich Minister for Economics. The authority of this Office also included supervision of those credit institutions which *in addition* were subject to special Reich or state supervision. No change was made in the Banking Law after 1945. In keeping with the changed constitutional situation, supervisory authority, however, has been delegated to the Finance Ministers of the eleven Länder of Western Germany. These supervisory authorities coordinate their measures by means of a joint committee, the so-called Special Committee for Bank Supervision. While a revision of the law is under preparation, it has not yet made sufficient progress to be discussed, although it would appear that the most important provisions of the existing statute will be included in the new law without fundamental alteration.

Bank supervision includes the right of licensing new banks, the authority at any time to inspect the banks' books and balance sheets, and to demand information concerning all business transactions. The supervisory authorities may also make such audits as they deem necessary. Furthermore, the supervisory authorities may attend general meetings and sessions of the company boards and require the calling of such meetings and sessions. Moreover, they are to watch over observance of the regulations established by the law with respect to the granting of credit, liquidity, soundness, and profitableness.

Terms of Competition with Regard to Interest Rates.—Up to the end of the war, interest rates paid on bank deposits, uniform for all banks, were fixed by the central associations of banks, with the authoritative cooperation of the Reich Control Office for Banking. The agreements concerning interest and competition concluded by the banks' central organizations are still in force, but interest rates as such are established by competent authorities in the individual Länder. Credit institutions are obliged not to exceed specified maximum rates of interest on loans and deposits.

For the purpose of calculating interest, deposits are classified as follows: deposits payable on demand; deposits at notice; deposits placed for fixed periods; and savings deposits. In certain Länder of the German Federal Republic, rates of interest in some cases deviate slightly from those generally valid. The credit cooperatives and the private bankers are better off, inasmuch as the interest rates, which they may pay on deposits, are 0.25 percent higher than those of other credit institutions. By permitting this it is intended to maintain the ability of smaller banking institutions such as credit cooperatives and private bankers to compete, in obtaining deposits, with the big banks, which are more popular because of their supposed greater security.

Table 4 shows the level of interest rates paid on deposits since the currency reform and certain data of previous years.

In Germany there is no guarantee in respect to deposits similar to deposit insurance to be found in the United States. Nevertheless, depositors, at least those of larger institutions, may virtually count on not suffering any loss in the event of bank difficulties. Since such difficulties would spread to other banks, supporting syndicates would be formed, mostly under the management of highly respected banks, which would guarantee the deposits of the affected institutions.

Interest rates for loans are regulated in the same way as are interest rates on deposits and are closely connected with the discount rate of the central banking system. Fluctuations in the cost of credit charged to borrowers since 1948 are shown in Table 5.

TABLE 4

INTERESTS RATES PAID ON DEPOSITS, DECEMBER 31

(IN PERCENT PER ANNUM)

Deposits	1948	1949	1950	1951	1952	1953	Yearly Averages 1929[a]	Yearly Averages 1935[a]
Monies Payable on Demand								
On accounts free of turnover commission	1.00	1.00	1.00	1.00	1.00	0.75 –1.00	4.19	1.00
On accounts subject to turnover commission	1.50–2.00	1.50	1.50	2.50	1.50	1.25 –1.50	4.69	1.50
Savings Deposits								
With legal period of notice[b]	2.00–2.50	2.50	3.00	3.00	3.00	3.00		
With agreed period of notice:							5.68	3.08
6 months up to 12 months	2.50–3.00	3.00	3.50	3.50	3.50	3.50		
12 months upward	3.00–4.00	4.00	4.50	4.50	4.50	4.25 –4.50		
Monies at Notice								
1 month up to 3 months	2.00–2.375	2.25–2.375	3.25–3.50	3.25–3.50	2.75–3.00	2.00 –2.75		2.63
3 months up to 6 months	2.25–2.75	2.50–2.625	3.50–3.875	3.50–3.875	3.00–3.375	2.25 –3.00		3.08
6 months up to 12 months	2.50–3.00	2.75–2.875	4.25–4.375	4.25–4.375	3.75–3.875	3.125–3.750		3.58
12 months and over	3.00–4.00	3.00–3.75	4.75	4.75	4.25	3.50 –4.25		
Monies Placed for Fixed Periods:								
30 to 89 days	2.00–2.25	2.00–2.25	3.25–3.50	3.25–3.50	2.75–3.00	2.00 –2.75		2.63
90 to 179 days	2.25–2.50	2.25–2.50	3.50–3.875	3.50–3.875	3.00–3.375	2.25 –3.00		3.08
180 to 359 days	2.50–2.75	2.50–2.75	4.00–4.25	4.00–4.25	3.50–3.75	3.00 –3.50		3.58
360 days and over	3.00–3.50	3.25–3.50	4.625	4.625	4.125	3.75 –4.125		

[a] Source: *Statistical Yearbook for the German Reich, 1937*, pp. 402–3.

[b] Legal period of notice: up to DM 1,000, no notice required; for higher amounts, payments made only against 30 days' notice.

Table 5

Interest Rates Charged to Borrowers in the German Federal Republic, December 31

(in percent per annum)

Rates	*1948*	*1949*	*1950*	*1951*	*1952*	*1953*	Yearly Average *1929* [a]	Yearly Average *1935* [a]
Discount rate of the central banking system	5.00	4.00	6.00	6.00	4.50	3.5–4.5	7.11	4.00
Rate on advances of the central banking system	6.00	5.00	7.00	7.00	5.50	4.5–5.5	8.11	5.00
Charges for credits, including commission								
Credits on current account	9.0–9.5	8.0–8.5	10.0–10.5	10.4–10.5	8.9–9.0	8.0–9.0	10.20	6.58
Bill credits:								
DM 20,000 or more	6.5–7.5	6.0–7.0	8.0–8.7	8.0–8.7	6.5–7.2	5.5–7.2		
DM 5,000 up to DM 20,000	6.5–7.5	6.0–7.0	8.0–8.7	8.0–8.7	6.5–7.2	5.5–7.2		
DM 1,000 up to DM 5,000	7.0–8.0	6.5–7.0	8.5–9.0	8.5–9.0	7.0–7.5	6.0–7.5		
Under DM 1,000	7.5–9.0	7.0–8.0	9.0–10.0	9.0–10.0	7.5–8.5	6.5–8.5		
Acceptance credits	8.0–9.5	7.0–7.5	8.5–9.5	9.0–9.5	7.5–8.0	6.5–8.0		

[a] Source: *Statistical Yearbook for the German Reich, 1937*, pp. 402–3.

The Effects of the Currency Reform of 1948 on the Banks.—These were momentous, not only for the population in general, but for the banking system in particular. Prior to the currency reform most banks' balance sheet structure was essentially as follows: on the average, about 80 percent of the deposits were invested in treasury bills, treasury bonds, and loans of the Reich, while only a very small amount of credits were outstanding to trade and industry.[5] Business and private customers held large liquid funds in the form of bank balances. As mentioned before, in the spring of 1948 the money supply amounted to some RM 160,000 million or eight to nine times the estimated 1936 figure for the area of the German Federal Republic. The currency reform caused the surrender of all cash, which resulted in a considerable further increase in bank deposits. All bank deposits, except interbank which were wiped out, were converted in the ratio of RM 100 to DM 6.5, other claims and liabilities in the ratio of RM 10 to DM 1, and certain liabilities, mainly those of the Reich, were not converted at all. In consequence, the banks lost most of their assets, whereas almost all of their liabilities continued to exist to at least 6.5 percent of the former amount. They would therefore not have been able to establish an equilibrium in their revalued balance sheets unless by legislative measures they had been given the so-called "Equalization Claims on Public Authorities." These equalization claims actually are a "revaluation" of old Reich obligations, adapted to the need for establishing equilibrium in balance sheets in individual cases. As a rule, interest is paid on the equalization claims at 3 percent. Amortization of these claims has not so far been determined. Banks have to enter the claims in their balance sheet at par and may transfer them only to one another, in actual practice to the Central Bank. Calculation of the amount of the equalization claims to be allocated to a bank is based on its DM liabilities existing at the date of the currency reform, plus, as a rule, 7.5 percent of these liabilities as new "net worth," less the amount of the remaining assets convertible into Deutsche Marks. The sum total of the equalization claims of the Western German banks, excluding the central banking system, amounts to some DM 5,000 million. The Central Banking System itself received some DM 8,000 million Equalization Claims as a

[5] Cf. Dr. Eduard Wolf, "Geld- und Finanzprobleme der deutschen Nachkriegswirtschaft (Monetary and Financial Problems of the German Post-War Economy)," in *Die deutsche Wirtschaft zwei Jahre nach dem Zusammenbruch* (The German Economy Two Years after the Collapse), Berlin, 1947, p. 248, note.

counterweight against the creation of new money in the Currency Reform. The debtor of the claims is in each case that Land of the Federal Republic in which the banking institution in question has its domicile, and in case of the Bank deutscher Länder the Federal Government itself.

INDIVIDUAL GROUPS OF BANKS

CREDIT BANKS

For the most part, the German credit banks are "universal banks." They not only furnish short-term turnover credits to trade and industry, but also to a high degree are the traditional financiers of industry, in the placing of whose issues of shares and debentures they participate and for whose long-term investment needs they supply anticipatory credits. Actually, the disinclination on the part of the public to acquire securities has, to a certain extent, served to enhance the importance of the credit banks as sources of long-term finance for industrial enterprise.

The Three Big Banks, or Their "Successor Institutions."—As much as 55 percent of the business of the credit banks is handled by the three big banks known as the Deutsche Bank, the Dresdner Bank, and the Commerzbank, or by their 9 "successor institutions." Originating in the mid-nineteenth century, these banks represent an intensive process of concentration in banking which resulted from the growth of industry (especially of heavy industries), with the attendant tasks of financing, a growth which, in turn, favored large concentrations of industrial power. The critical years following 1929 marked an increase in bank concentration in that, through mergers, the number of big banks was reduced from five to three. A large number of provincial banking establishments which had suffered losses in the depression were absorbed.

At quite an early date the big banks began setting up, throughout Germany, a network of branches to attract the maximum amount of deposits. At the present moment these branches, agencies, and depositories number 352. In 1948, legislation introduced for the purpose of decentralizing the banking business brought about the dissolution of the centralized management of the big banks. The branch systems were turned into a total of 30 so-called "successor institutions" serving various regions and were forced to employ new titles which were not to be reminiscent of the names of the big banks. From the legal angle, the three big banks have not ceased to exist, since the "successor institutions" were not "refounded" in accordance with the terms of German Commercial Law. It was not until March, 1952, that special legislation set up three banking areas in Western Germany and permitted each bank to maintain branches within one of these areas. According to that law the three big banks established in September, 1952, with retroactive effect as from January 1, 1952, three legally independent successor institutions, each in the form of a corporation.

State, Regional, and Local Banks.—Besides the nine big banks and their branches, there have always existed a vast number of medium-sized credit banks with a total of almost 500 branches and depositories, which, while restricting themselves essentially to the more immediate vicinity of their domicile, nevertheless resemble the big banks in business operations. At present the monthly banking statistics of the Bank deutscher Länder and the Landeszentralbanken comprise 79 institutions of this kind appearing under the heading "State, Regional and Local Banks." This category handles approximately 33 percent of the business volume of all credit banks. Some of these regional banks have a branch network of considerable importance and may occasionally in their own area handle a greater volume of business than the "successor institutions." Quite a number, especially in South Germany, handle long-term mortgage bond transactions in addition to short-term loans. The regional commercial banks also include several public banks and, quite recently, credit institutions sponsored by trade unions and cooperative societies.

Private Bankers.—In former times the private banker enjoyed a very important position in banking, although in the last few decades the ever-increasing movement toward concentration has exercised an adverse effect on his influence and importance. Only a limited number of the 284 private bankers in Western Germany can claim any appreciable economic importance. Many of the smaller private bankers included in the above figure engage at the same time in non-banking transactions such as insurance brokerage and lottery collections. Rural private bankers occasionally concern themselves with trade in agricultural produce and building materials. As of the end of September, 1952, only 34 private bankers showed a balance sheet total of more than DM 10 million. Even so, there still exist certain quite important private banking establishments with a long tradition; most of these are in Hamburg, Düsseldorf, Frankfurt, Cologne, and Munich. The business volume of the 217 private bankers contained in the monthly banking statistics of the central banking system amounts to approximately 12 percent of that of all credit banks. By comparison with the big banks, private bankers are apt to be entrusted with rather small deposits on the average; they must therefore rely upon capital funds of their own. Generally speaking, private bankers do not maintain any branches, although one Bavarian private banking firm with 51 branches is a marked exception.

Corporate Forms.—The majority of German credit banks are chartered in corporate form as joint-stock companies. This applies to the nine big banks as well as to the vast majority of medium-sized and small credit banks, with the exception of enterprises operated in the form of partnerships, that is, enterprises which have one or more personally liable partners which do not issue shares. The shares of most banks chartered in this corporate form are quoted on the stock exchange. Besides the joint-stock banks and the private bankers there are a few limited liability companies and one private limited company, although these are mostly small institutions which by virtue of the business they handle are actually private bankers. Private bankers in Germany include all banks having one or more personally liable partners. State banks are as a rule constituted as corporations under public law.

Credit Business.—The credit banks concentrate mostly on short-term lending operations. Out of the total of credits outstanding on October 31, 1952, roughly 82 percent involved transactions with a term of not more than six months. The share of the credit banks in the total short-term credit volume is approximately 60 percent. However, it should be noted that in view of the special character of the German credit banks as department store or "universal banks," a certain percentage of current-account credits is in the nature of intermediate financing transactions, so that the actual repayment of these credits is dependent upon the ability of the borrower to refinance the loans upon the capital market.

Forms of Credit.—Current-account credits rank foremost among the various forms of credit. Table 7 shows the percentage distribution of the various forms of short-term credit granted by the credit banks (including, of course, the rediscounted bills shown in the balance sheet as "endorsement liabilities").

Table 6
Balance Sheet of the Credit Banks
December 31, 1952
(amounts in millions of DM)

Assets		*Amount*
Cash reserve and central bank balances		1,703
Balances at other credit institutions		1,213
Commercial bills		3,474
Treasury bills		86
Equalization claims		1,399
Loans		
Business and private customers	6,276	
Public authorities	88	
Credit institutions	292	
Total loans		6,656
Loans at long term		1,486
Transitory credits (on trust basis only)		245
Other assets		1,772
Total		18,034
Liabilities		
Deposits		
Credit institutions	2,320	
Business and private customers	8,506	
Public authorities	1,486	
Savings deposits	1,077	
Total deposits		13,389
Borrowed funds		2,045
Own acceptances in circulation		438
Transitory credits (on trust basis only)		245
Net worth		899
Other liabilities		1,018
Total		18,034
Endorsement liabilities on rediscounted bills	2,387	
Liabilities on account of guarantees	1,699	

Table 7
Percentage Distribution of Short-Term Credits Granted by the Credit Banks to the Non-Bank Customers
October 31, 1952

Form of Credit	*Big Banks*	*State, Regional and Local Credit Banks*	*Private Bankers*	*Total of Credit Banks*
Current account credits	45.5	49.7	40.8	46.1
Acceptance credits	7.0	9.0	14.3	8.6
Bill credits	47.5	41.3	44.9	45.3
Total	100.0	100.0	100.0	100.0

As will be noted, private bankers show the highest percentage in acceptance and bill credits, which is in part a result of the shortage of deposits referred to previously, which causes private bankers to resort in a higher degree to credits which can be rediscounted with the bank of issue.[6]

Changes during the Past Years.—In Germany, as in other countries, the system of war finance resulted in the fact that trade and industry found themselves indebted to the banks in a considerably reduced degree. The credit banks held state loans rather than industrial credits as their main asset, whereas trade and industry, as well as private individuals, owned substantial bank balances. Once these liquid funds had been essentially exterminated by the currency reform in 1948, the situation underwent radical change. Trade and industry were again forced to fall back upon bank credits in very high degree. During the first few years following the currency reform there was no risk of inflation in making available such credits, since productivity and turnover rose sharply, and at the same time there was a general tendency to replenish liquid funds; this meant that to a certain extent the expansion of credit was offset by a reduction in the velocity of circulation of money. Table 8 sets forth the reconstruction of the credit business of the credit banks after the currency reform.

Borrowers.—By far the greatest part of short-term loans were granted to trade and industry. In the case of industry, credits were granted especially to the iron-producing and iron-processing industry, the food and stimulants industry, and the textile and clothing industry.

An industrial classification of borrowers is given in Table 9, based on sample statistics obtained by the Bank deutscher Länder.

State Indebtedness.—The equalization claims against the public authorities should be looked upon as a residual item of wartime financing.[7] In the case of the credit banks, equalization claims represent a smaller share of assets than is the case of other groups of banks. For all banks these claims amount, on the average, to something like 12 percent of the balance sheet total; for the credit banks, they amount to only 8 percent of that total, but for rural credit cooperatives to 29 percent, and for savings banks to 23 percent. Essentially, these differ-

[6] In Germany it is permissible for financial institutions to rediscount bills with the central bank (cf. the section dealing with the Central Banking System).

[7] See pp. 325–26.

TABLE 8
THE CREDIT BUSINESS OF THE CREDIT BANKS 1948–52
(AMOUNTS IN MILLIONS OF DM)

Year	CURRENT ACCOUNT CREDITS: *Total*	*Acceptance Credits Only*	*Commercial Bills*	*Treasury Bills*	*Medium-Term*[a] *Loans*	*Long-Term*[b] *Loans*
1948[c]	1,655		1,266	1	10	
1949	3,913	1,623	1,955	18	229	
1950	4,980	1,904	3,240	44	191	607
1951	5,202	1,360	4,564	187	507	1,039
1952	5,895	971	5,507	86	561	1,588

[a] Terms varying between 6 months and 4 years.
[b] Terms exceeding 4 years.
[c] Data as of December 31.

TABLE 9
INDUSTRIAL CLASSIFICATION OF THE BORROWERS OF THE CREDIT BANKS
SEPTEMBER 30, 1952

	Successor Banks	*State, Regional, and Local Banks*	*Private Bankers*
	(AMOUNTS IN MILLIONS OF DM)		
Short-Term Credits to non-banking institutions (exclusive of treasury bills)	6,027	2,694	1,149
	PERCENTAGE DISTRIBUTION		
Agriculture, forestry, and fisheries	0.2	1.4	0.5
Mining, industries, and accessory plants	64.0	56.0	46.5
Handicraft	0.4	1.9	0.8
Building construction	0.2	0.4	0.6
Trade	32.3	34.0	47.3
Transport and communications	0.4	1.0	0.7
Miscellaneous	2.5	5.3	3.6
Total	100.0	100.0	100.0

ences are due to divergent developments in business operations between individual banks and banking groups since the currency reform.

The Deposit Business.—The credit banks hold more than half of all the deposits entrusted to German banks as a whole. Depositors include industrial undertakings, tradesmen, and private individuals. Public authorities maintain only small accounts with the credit banks; on September 30, 1952, only 11 percent of the total deposits held with credit banks were owned by public authorities.

The currency reform left the banks with few deposits, but since then deposit totals have gradually increased in considerable measure as a result of credit expansion. In consequence, they have at present attained a level which may be looked upon as normal for current production and prices. Table 10 shows the increase in deposits as from 1948 and their distribution among private enterprises and public authorities.

TABLE 10
DEMAND AND TIME DEPOSITS WITH CREDIT BANKS, 1948–52
(AMOUNTS IN MILLIONS OF DM)

	DEMAND DEPOSITS		TIME DEPOSITS	
Date	*Business and Private Customers*	*Public Authorities*	*Business and Private Customers*	*Public Authorities*
1948[a]	2,540	353	189	194
1949	3,365	406	608	333
1950	4,154	355	1,721	557
1951	5,036	326	2,488	746
1952 (November 30)	5,136	388	3,370	1,098

[a] Data as of December 31 except for 1952.

As shown by Table 11, time deposits have constantly increased as a proportion of total deposits.

In increasing measure, the credit banks have endeavored to gain a foothold in the savings business and during the past few years they have succeeded in this to a remarkable extent. Toward the end of 1952, 15 percent of total savings deposits were maintained with the credit banks as against some 6 percent in 1935.

TABLE 11
DEPOSIT DISTRIBUTION, 1948–52, NOT INCLUDING INTERBANK DEPOSITS
(AMOUNTS IN MILLIONS OF DM)

		IN PERCENT OF TOTAL DEPOSITS					
			TIME DEPOSITS AT A TERM OF				
Date	*Total Deposits*	*Demand Deposits*	*Up to 3 mos.*	*3–6 mos.*	*6–12 mos.*	*More than 12 mos.*	*Savings Deposits*
1948[a]	3,416	84.7		11.2			4.1
1949	5,023	75.1	8.3	4.3	3.4	2.7	6.2
1950	7,265	62.1	10.9	8.4	5.7	6.3	6.6
1951	9,291	57.7	11.5	11.6	6.2	5.5	7.5
1952 (November 30)	10,720	49.2	14.5	14.8	7.0	5.9	8.6

[a] Data as of December 31 except for 1952.

Relations to the Capital Market.—As already mentioned, the more important German credit banks, and especially the large banks, have always engaged both in short-term credit operations and in transactions in security underwriting and flotation. Short-term transactions were often related to the more hazardous business operations in the field of industrial finance. Industrial financing was often carried out in such a manner that short-term credits on current account were first granted and were subsequently consolidated by the issue of shares and bonds; thereupon the credits again disappeared from the banks' balance sheets. The major part of the industrial loans floated in Germany has been placed on the capital market with the assistance of the credit banks. Accordingly, these banks have always been deeply interested in the capital market. This interest extended not only to capital flotation, but also to protection against price fluctuations and to current servicing (payment of interest, issue of new coupon sheets, and so on).

Portfolio Securities.—The close connection with the long-term financial needs of private enterprises meant that, at times, the credit banks held a considerable volume of industrial loans and shares in their portfolios. This was particularly true in the period preceding the First World War. Between the two wars, security holdings of the credit banks declined considerably, with the exception, however, of loans to the Reich. At present, security holdings are of little importance in the balance sheets.

TABLE 12

THE SECURITY PORTFOLIO OF THE CREDIT BANKS, NOT INCLUDING LOANS TO THE REICH AND EQUALIZATION CLAIMS

(AMOUNTS IN MILLIONS OF RM OR DM)

Date	*Amount*	*Percent of Balance Sheet Total*
1913 [a]	1,077	6.6
1929	546	3.3
1932	444	4.2
1935	648	6.7
1937	737	7.1
1938 [b]	760	6.5
1950 [b]	138	1.1
1951	255	1.7
1952	581	3.3

[a] Data as of December 31.
[b] Relates exclusively to the area of the Federal Republic.

Amount of the Net Worth.—During the first few decades following their introduction, the net worth of the credit banks was large and played a considerable role in their lending activities. The ever-increasing importance of deposits resulted in a decrease of net worth in relation to balance sheet totals, and it finally became a "risk buffer" rather than an important source of funds. In considering the development of net worth over a longer period, one notices a constant absolute decrease, resulting mainly from the first and second inflations (1914–23 and 1938–48), twice involving an almost complete annihilation of the currency.

TABLE 13
NET WORTH OF THE CREDIT BANKS [a]
(AMOUNTS IN MILLIONS OF RM OR DM)

Year	*Amount*	*Percent of Balance Sheet Total*
1913	4,014	24.7
1929	1,356	8.1
1932	861	8.1
1935	789	8.2
1938	813	7.0
1950	456 [b]	4.0
1951	605	4.1

[a] Up to 1934; capital stock and legal reserves since 1945; paid-in capital plus reserves figure in the balance sheets, but after deduction of losses.
[b] Federal Republic only, including global adjustment of value.

The currency reform of June 20, 1948, again considerably curtailed the net worth of the credit banks, inasmuch as banks were generally allowed to enter as net worth in the balance sheets only 7.5 percent of liabilities remaining after the monetary cut. In the period since the currency reform, the credit banks have made substantial additions to their capital and reserves, a development which has been facilitated by tax concessions. In this connection, we should mention the establishment of what is technically known as "global adjustment of values" (valuation reserves), originally amounting to 1.5 percent of credits extended against bills discounted and guarantees, and to 3 percent of overdrafts and advances. In the case of private bankers these rates, owing to the special conditions prevailing for this group, have been fixed at 2.5 percent and 5 percent, respectively. The reserves accumulated in this way are in many cases considerably in excess of the net worth shown on the balance sheet. About half of the "global adjustment of value" may, according to a recent decision of the fiscal authorities, be added to the banks' own funds, while the balance continues to be carried as reserves.

Operating Costs and Bank Profits.—As may be seen from Tables 4 and 5, the present margin between interest granted on deposits and interest charged on loans is comparatively large. Nevertheless, the profits of the credit banks are not commensurately great. Some assets bring far lower interest yields than do credits against bills of exchange and loans on current account. Equalization claims, for instance, yield only 3 percent, and the minimum reserve requirements, the amounts of which are subject to variation, to be held in the form of balances with Land Central Banks, yield no interest. The average margin of profits calculated on the total of assets and liabilities is therefore appreciably lower than that existing simply between charges on loans and interest paid on deposits. It should furthermore be borne in mind that the interest margin must also cover costs of giro transactions, since banks effect such transactions mostly free of charge. The balance sheets and profit and loss accounts, however, show that bank earnings are quite good.

Personnel.—The training of personnel in the banks provides on principle for a three-year term of apprenticeship with subsequent examination. In the course of the past few decades, mechanized accounting procedures in the banks have permitted the majority of the different tasks to be performed by auxiliary personnel not requiring any special banking training or experience. Before the war, there existed a number of institutions and training courses financed by private banks, where students were trained in general and in special banking knowledge. With the exception of scientific banking institutions attached to some universities, and of savings banks schools, there are at present no institutions of this kind. The formation of a well-trained staff is therefore dependent upon the initiative of the individual banks.

Most bank employees are grouped in trade unions. The wage agreements concluded between the regional trade unions and the bank associations are valid for all employees, except higher rank officials.

Regionally, the credit banks have united in "communities of interest" or "associations of private banking" with the "Federal Union of the Associations of Private Banking" as the central institution. Tasks incumbent upon these associations include the representation of interests, cooperation in drafting legislation, assistance to members in problems connected with the banks. In addition, these bank associations are the opposite members of the trade unions in wage discussions.

SAVINGS INSTITUTIONS

Savings Banks.—Historically, communal savings banks have played a dominating role among savings institutions in Germany. These communal banks are incorporated under public law, operate on a non-profit basis, and are considered safe for the investment of trust funds. Towns, districts, and communes assume unlimited liability for savings bank deposits to an extent beyond the assets of the bank itself. In Western Germany there are at present 875 savings banks with a network of 8,000 main branches (operating in-payment and out-payment transactions and themselves keeping customers' accounts), sub-offices (operating in-payment and out-payment transactions, but not keeping accounts), and receiving offices (branch offices not making any out-payments). According to guarantors' liability, the savings banks may be classified as follows:

252 town savings banks
90 communal and local savings banks
363 district and regional savings banks
21 district and town savings banks
125 other public savings banks
(savings banks of local administrative unions)
13 private savings banks
11 other savings banks officially guaranteed

The first savings banks in Germany were founded as early as 1800, in Hamburg and Kiel, as private savings banks. The present form developed in the 19th century, when the communes began to engage in savings transactions. From the beginning, savings banks accumulated the deposits of broad groups of the population and engaged in credit transactions in the form of mortgage loans and of personal credits. In 1908 and 1909 they were authorized to engage in deposit and current account transactions and were also permitted to hold checking accounts. From that time they engaged in bank credit transactions and came to fulfill all the functions of a banker for those who previously had only been "savers." For the purpose of developing cashless payment transactions, the savings banks, which were already organized in regional associations, established central institutions of their own, namely the so-called Central Giro Institutions ("Girozentralen"), with which they maintain their liquid reserves excluding those which must be kept with the Land Central Banks, in accordance with the minimum reserve requirements introduced in 1948. In most of the Länder of the German Federal Republic, the Central Giro Institutions are at the same time provincial banks which grant long-term loans to communes and communal associations; to obtain the necessary funds, most of them issue bonds on the capital market. The savings banks of the Federal Republic are united in regional "Savings Bank and Giro Associations," the organization head of the latter being the "German Savings Bank and Giro Association."

At the present time it is characteristic of most savings banks that they engage both in savings and in short-term deposit transactions. Since the end of the First World War some of the savings banks, in particular the larger ones, have established important banking departments which scarcely differ from those of the credit banks. Savings deposits are in principle invested at long term or medium term, with due regard to an adequate degree of liquidity, while other deposits are loaned in the form of short-term credits on current account and in the form of bill credits.

In their credit operations, savings banks have to observe a number of provisions which are partly of statutory and partly of a legal character. The extending of loans against mortgages or land charges is restricted to 50 percent of savings deposits, while credits to municipalities granted by savings banks must not exceed 25 percent of all deposits. Limits are also fixed on the amount which may be granted to individual borrowers.

It is a characteristic feature of the present balance sheet position of savings banks that the "Equalization Claims on Public Authorities" (about DM 2,600 million) are the largest item on the asset side. Although this item has considerably declined as compared with the balance sheet total, namely from 70 percent of deposits at the end of 1948 to 22 percent at the end of December, 1952, nevertheless, at the latter date it equaled the volume both of short-term and long-term loans. At the end of 1950 mortgage loans amounted to 13 percent of the total assets of the savings banks. This proportion was about as low

TABLE 14
BALANCE SHEET OF THE SAVINGS BANKS
DECEMBER 31, 1952
(AMOUNTS IN MILLIONS OF DM)

Assets		*Amount*	*Liabilities*		*Amount*
Cash reserve and central bank balances		797	Deposits by:		
Balances at other credit institutions		1,295	Credit institutions	165	
Commercial bills		597	Business and private customers	3,103	
Treasury bills		109	Public authorities	1,713	
Equalization claims on public authorities		2,677	Savings deposits	4,850	9,837
Short-term loans			Borrowed funds and loans		953
Business and private customers	2,465		Own acceptances in circulation		17
Public authorities	114		Transitory credits		403
Credit institutions	22	2,607	Net worth [a]		375
Long-term loans		2,470	Other liabilities		671
Transitory credits		403	Total		12,190
Other assets		977			
Grand Total		12,190			
			Endorsement liabilities and rediscounted bills		172
			Liability on guarantees		142

[a] Including global adjustment of values.

as in 1924 after the first currency reform and has resulted from the almost complete destruction of savings, which so far have been newly formed only to a minor extent. As savings deposits again increased, the proportion of mortgage loans to balance sheet totals also grew, and the proportion of personal credits showed a corresponding decline.

The credits extended by savings banks are mostly loans to medium-sized and small firms and to handicraft industries. The average amount of the credits granted therefore is comparatively small, as may be seen in Table 16.

Together, savings banks and central giro institutions employ almost 32,000 officials and employees. The savings institutions have at their disposal a good training system in the form of savings banks' schools, training courses, and the like.

Postal Savings Bank.—The Postal Savings Bank has existed in Germany only since 1938, the model being the Austrian institution. All post offices and all postal check offices, postal agencies and subagencies engage in Postal Savings Bank service, even in the remotest parts of

TABLE 15
LOANS EXTENDED BY, AND DEPOSITS WITH, THE SAVINGS BANKS IN THE GERMAN FEDERAL REPUBLIC, 1926–52

Year	Bill and Current Account Credits	Loans at Long-Term	Securities (as from 1949, Equalization Claims)	Savings Deposits	Demand and Time Deposits
	AMOUNTS IN MILLIONS OF RM OR DM				
1926 [a]	1,579	740	354	2,159	780
1930	2,822	3,383	1,005	6,879	1,058
1936	2,380	4,408	2,629	8,967	1,351
1949	1,597	404	2,506	2,117	2,760
1950	2,294	1,300	2,508	2,778	3,403
1951	2,394	1,959	2,565	3,301	4,146
1952	3,302	2,740	2,677	4,850	4,980
	PERCENT OF TOTAL LOANS AND SECURITIES OR EQUALIZATION CLAIMS			PERCENT OF TOTAL DEPOSITS	
1926 [a]	59.0	27.8	13.2	73.5	26.5
1930	39.1	47.0	13.9	86.7	13.3
1936	25.3	46.8	27.9	86.9	13.1
1949	35.5	8.9	55.6	43.4	56.6
1950	37.6	21.3	41.1	45.0	55.0
1951	34.6	28.3	37.1	44.3	55.7
1952	37.9	31.4	30.7	46.4	53.6

[a] Data as of December 31.

TABLE 16
PERSONAL CREDITS GRANTED BY SAVINGS BANKS, CLASSIFIED ACCORDING TO SIZE OF THE INDIVIDUAL AMOUNTS LOANED, DECEMBER 31, 1952
(AMOUNTS IN MILLIONS OF DM)

Amount	Number of Items	Percent of Total Number	Total Amount	Percent of Total Amount
Under 1,000	752,800	66.55	242.4	7.53
1,001– 5,000	254,900	22.54	591.7	18.40
5,001– 10,000	60,500	5.34	413.9	12.86
10,001– 20,000	34,400	3.04	472.8	14.70
20,001– 50,000	20,800	1.84	619.9	19.27
50,001–100,000	5,500	0.48	365.8	11.37
100,001–200,000	1,700	0.15	228.0	7.09
200,001 and over	700	0.06	283.1	8.80
Grand totals	1,131,200	100.00	3,217.7	100.00

Source: The Working Union of German Savings Banks and Giro Associations.

the country. An account in this system is particularly advantageous in that deposits and withdrawals can be made anywhere.

The legal interest rate for deposits is 0.25 percent, lower than that granted for savings deposits at savings banks and other banks. In contrast with some other countries, the activity of the Postal Savings Bank in Germany is relatively small. At the end of 1952 deposits amounted to approximately DM 300 million or to only 4 percent of all savings deposits. In view of the fact that the number of postal savings accounts is about 3,000,000 the average credit balance of roughly DM 100 is small.

The funds on deposit in the postal savings accounts are managed, together with the funds in the postal check accounts, by the Federal Ministry of Post and Telecommunications. These funds are invested by a committee, on which the Bank deutscher Länder is represented. At least one third of the monies available, after deduction of the legal and other liquidity reserves, are used to purchase Treasury bills through the Bank deutscher Länder. The remaining two thirds are invested in fixed-interest-bearing securities eligible as security for advances by the Bank deutscher Länder, and in Treasury bonds. At least one half of these monies must be invested in securities or loans falling due within six months.

Building and Loan Associations.—These financial institutions use the savings funds of members to lend money to other members to enable them to obtain dwellings or houses of their own. In principle, the saver must have in his account about one fourth of the amount he needs; after waiting a certain period he obtains the remaining three quarters as a loan from the association. In addition, building and loan associations endeavor to obtain first mortgage money on the market, for instance from insurance companies.

There are 13 public and 18 private building and loan associations in Germany. Most of the former have been established as departments of central giro institutions; in some cases they are legal entities themselves. The private building and loan associations are, as a rule, formed by individual savers and, being non-profit organizations, they enjoy certain tax privileges. The business of the building and loan associations has increased since currency reform. In this field savers clearly see the purpose for which they are saving and, moreover, in many cases, it would not be possible for them to obtain building funds in any other way.

TABLE 17
LOANS AND DEPOSITS AT BUILDING AND LOAN ASSOCIATIONS, 1950–52
(AMOUNTS IN MILLIONS OF DM)

	LOANS			DEPOSITS AND BORROWED FUNDS	
Year	*Mortgages*	*Intermediate Credits*	*Equalization Claims*	*Savings Deposits*	*Borrowed Funds*
1950 December	217	190	50	502	35
1951 December	432	162	59	672	103
1952 December	601	109	62	942	77

Source: *Bank deutscher Länder, Monthly Report.*

CREDIT COOPERATIVES

In number the credit cooperatives constitute the largest single group of German banks. In business volume, however, they account for only about 10 percent of the balance sheet total of all banks. The total number of credit cooperatives is approximately 12,000, although in the monthly banking statistics of the Bank deutscher Länder and the Land Central Banks only about 2,360 of the larger cooperatives are included. The activities of the cooperatives are, for the most part, confined to serving artisans, small urban businesses, and the rural population.

Urban Credit Cooperatives.—For these, the name "Volksbank" (People's Bank) has been generally adopted. The initiator and founder of the urban cooperative movement was Schulze-Delitzsch, who lived in the mid-nineteenth-century; in consequence, some of these banks are called "Schulze-Delitzsch banks." In the German Federal Republic there are altogether over 700 people's banks with nearly 600 branches and receiving offices. On December 31, 1949, the number of members in the 667 people's banks included in the West German banking statistics was about 537,000. Of these members, 21.8 percent were independent handicraftsmen; 19.4 percent government and communal officials; 18.2 percent retail traders, wholesale traders, and other people engaged in trade or industry; 12.8 percent peasants, farmers, and tenant farmers; and the rest came from other occupations. The average value of the members' shares in the cooperatives varies, as among the individual Länder of the German Federal Republic, between DM 150 and DM 500. The guarantee sums, that is, the amounts which the members may have to pay in the event of the cooperative becoming insolvent, range from DM 200 to DM 900.

The borrowers were first traders (44 percent), followed by manufacturers (21.9 percent), while handicraftsmen, obtaining 18.6 percent of the credits granted, occupied third place. Most of the credits granted are small. At the end of 1949, no less than 84 percent of the entire volume of credits outstanding at the people's banks were individual amounts of less than DM 5,000.

TABLE 18
BALANCE SHEET OF THE URBAN CREDIT COOPERATIVES, DECEMBER 31, 1952
(AMOUNTS IN MILLIONS OF DM)

Assets		*Amount*
Cash reserve and central bank balances		166
Balances at other credit institutions		226
Commercial bills		154
Treasury bills		2
Equalization claims on public authorities		373
Short-term loans		
Business and private customers	906	
Public authorities	4	
Credit institutions	8	918
Long-term loans		97
Transitory credits		75
Other assets		191
Total		2,202

Liabilities		*Amount*
Deposits by:		
Credit institutions	30	
Business and private customers	871	
Public authorities	60	
Savings deposits	592	1,553
Borrowed funds and loans		228
Own acceptances in circulation		31
Net worth [a]		183
Transitory credits		75
Other liabilities		132
Total		2,202
Endorsement liabilities on rediscounted bills		223
Bills (drawn by the cooperatives themselves) in circulation		37
Liability on guarantees		77

[a] Including global adjustment of values.

Rural Credit Cooperatives.—These cooperatives, totaling some 11,000 in the area of the German Federal Republic, are the smallest group in the credit system. Members are chiefly farmers, but they include also small traders or manufacturers, handicraftsmen, and workmen. Almost every village has a rural credit cooperative, which does business under the title of "Rural Credit Association" or "Savings and Loan Bank"; in many cases the managers work without payment. The title of some of these cooperatives contains the word

"Raiffeisenkasse" ("Raiffeisen Bank"), so named for Friedrich Wilhelm Raiffeisen, the founder of the rural cooperative movement.

In principle, the rural credit cooperatives effect all banking transactions. The relative importance of the individual types of transaction, however, depends on the customers' requirements and their mode of payment. As a rule, farmers deposit only the money they have actually saved, while they make their current payments in cash. Therefore savings deposits account for a large proportion of the deposits at rural credit cooperatives, and demand deposits have a slow rate of turnover. Working credits to farmers run for a longer period than is the case at urban banks. Credits are granted exclusively to members of the cooperative, often without any guarantee by real property. Guarantee offered by one or two individual guarantors is in most cases deemed sufficient for securing credit, because all members are personally known to one another and consequently are frequently well informed of a borrower's financial position.

In addition to their banking transactions, most of the rural credit cooperatives trade in fertilizers and agricultural products. To that

TABLE 19
BALANCE SHEET OF THE RURAL CREDIT COOPERATIVES RENDERING MONTHLY REPORTS,[a] DECEMBER 31, 1952
(AMOUNTS IN MILLIONS OF DM)

Assets	*Amount*	*Liabilities*		*Amount*
Cash reserve and central bank balances	63	Deposits		
Balances at other credit institutions	131	Demand and time deposits	483	
Commercial bills	39	Savings deposits	519	1,002
Equalization claims on public authorities	365	Borrowed funds and loans		133
Short-term loans	471	Transitory credits		27
Long-term loans	71	Net worth		85 [b]
Transitory credits	27	Other liabilities		40
Other assets	120	Total		1,287
Total	1,287	Endorsement liabilities on rediscounted bills		32
		Bills (drawn by the cooperatives themselves) in circulation		4

[a] The monthly banking statistics cover approximately 55 percent of the total business volume of the rural credit cooperatives.

[b] Including global adjustment of values.

extent, they operate as agricultural purchase and sales cooperatives.

Central Institutions of Credit Cooperatives.—Both the urban and the rural credit cooperatives have formed regional unions, establishing central institutions of their own, which maintain a liquidity reserve for the individual credit cooperatives and through which payment transactions among the credit cooperatives are cleared. The urban credit cooperatives have twelve central institutions in the German Federal Republic, while the rural credit cooperatives have six. The central institutions of urban credit cooperatives, however, act almost exclusively as "banks of the people's banks," while the central institutions of rural credit cooperatives also engage in direct deposit and credit transactions, particularly in connection with the agricultural purchase and sales cooperatives. The central institutions of rural credit cooperatives as a rule are established as cooperatives; their members are the individual credit and commodity cooperatives. The central institutions of urban credit cooperatives are established either as cooperatives or as joint-stock companies.

The central lending institution of the credit cooperative system is the Deutsche Genossenschaftskasse (German Cooperative Bank) established in Frankfurt-am-Main under a law enacted on May 11, 1949. In practice, although not in a legal sense, it is the successor of the Deutsche Zentralgenossenschaftskasse Berlin (German Central Cooperative Bank Berlin), which was closed at the end of the war. The Deutsche Genossenschaftskasse is a corporation established under public law; the Federal Government holding shares of its capital. The task of this institution is to grant short-term and medium-term credits for the purpose of promoting the production and sales of agricultural produce, tools, and other equipment. Its depositors and borrowers are the central institutions of credit cooperatives and other important cooperative associations.

Associations of Credit Cooperatives.—The central association of the urban credit cooperatives is the Deutsche Genossenschaftsverband (Schulze-Delitzsch) e.V.—German Association of Credit Cooperatives (Schulze-Delitzsch), registered—which was reestablished on June 4, 1949. By the Cooperatives Law, the Deutsche Genossenschaftsverband is also an auditing association. Its affiliated members are the 14 regional cooperative auditing associations whose main task is the auditing of the member cooperatives.

The rural credit cooperatives are organized in a similar way. Their central association is the Deutsche Raiffeisenverband e.V. (German Raiffeisen Association, registered), with which 12 regional auditing associations are affiliated. Since the rural credit cooperatives do not have a sufficiently large clerically trained staff, it is the responsibility of the auditing associations to provide the rural cooperatives with directives and instructions, in many cases to keep their accounts, in special cases to train the so-called "accountants" of the small village banks and to assist the cooperatives in any way possible.

MORTGAGE BANKS AND REAL ESTATE CREDIT BANKS UNDER PUBLIC LAW

The business of the mortgage banks consists in granting mortgage loans on urban and rural real estate and in issuing bonds covering the mortgages acquired. The sum total of mortgage bonds in circulation must at all times be covered to the par value by mortgages aggregating at least the same amount and yielding the same rate of interest. The mortgages earmarked to cover the mortgage bonds must be entered by the mortgage banks on a register. For the protection of mortgage bond creditors, the bank supervisory authorities appoint state trustees who make sure that the statutory cover for the mortgage bonds is readily available at any time. The same applies to real estate credit banks established under public law.

In Western Germany, there exist 32 mortgage banks and real estate credit banks, 17 of which are private banks, and 15 are established under public law. Some of these banks also grant short-term credits and are consequently known as "mixed mortgage banks." Some of the mortgage banks established under public law were founded 200 years ago, whereas the bulk of the private mortgage banks, operating in most cases as joint-stock companies, did not come into existence until the beginning of the twentieth century.

The activity of private mortgage banks is not restricted to any defined area and hence extends throughout the Federal Republic. They advance urban and rural real estate credits, lending money on prewar constructions as well as on new housing projects. The resulting mixture of loans is considered a special safeguard for their mortgage bonds. In contrast, the public law institutions are assigned definite tasks. Some of them, known as "Landschaften" (rural real estate credit banks), provide mortgage credit in specific rural areas, while others further the construction of small housing units. Still another category, operating under the name of "Stadtschaften" (urban real estate credit banks), grants urban real estate credits, likewise limited to small areas and giving special emphasis to credits for the construction of small dwelling units.

In addition to those mortgage banks granting rural and urban real estate credits, there are four ship mortgage banks extending long-term credits to shipowners. The extension of funds takes place against the issue of bonds secured by a lien on the ships encumbered. The credit operations of this category of financial institutions are regulated by a law concerning ship mortgage banks in a fashion similar to the other mortgage banks.

Following the currency reform, all real estate credit institutions were obliged to reconstruct their mortgage bond business. The currency reform reduced the value of their mortgage bonds by the ratio of 10 to 1, so that the amount of mortgage bonds outstanding, including those issued since 1948, is relatively small.

As compared with an outstanding volume of mortgage bonds and communal bonds [8] of approximately RM 5,700 million prior to the currency reform in 1948 (Federal Area only), the total as of December, 1950, amounted to DM 1,400 million, and as of December, 1952, to DM 3,300 million. Of this latter figure, about DM 2,500 million were issued after the currency reform. The share of the mortgage banks and real estate credit institutions established under public law in the over-all circulation of mortgage bonds and communal bonds amounts to approximately 48 percent.

The remaining debtors issuing bonds are made up of the central giro institutions, of the banks known as "mixed mortgage banks" (engaging at the same time in short-term credit business and for this reason included in the group of the "state, regional and local banks"), and of some of the central institutions (for example, Deutsche Rentenbank-Kreditanstalt), which are still in existence legally, although no longer actively engaged in lending operations.

The liability item, "Funds borrowed at long-term" is larger than the banks' own bonds in circulation. Following the currency reform, mortgage banks were authorized by special legislation to procure additional funds for mortgage loans, by borrowing at long term without issuing bonds.

[8] "Communal bonds" (Kommunalobligationen) are bonds issued by institutions granting credit against real estate and covered by loans granted to municipalities or communes.

TABLE 20

BALANCE SHEET OF THE MORTGAGE BANKS AND REAL ESTATE CREDIT INSTITUTIONS ESTABLISHED UNDER PUBLIC LAW, DECEMBER 31, 1952

(AMOUNTS IN MILLIONS OF DM)

Assets	*Amount*	*Liabilities*	*Amount*
Cash on hand, balances with central banks and balances with other credit institutions	569	Funds borrowed at long term	1,853
Equalization claims	301	Banks' own bonds in circulation	1,459
Long-term loans	3,157	Transitory credits	315
Transitory credits	315	Net worth	287
Other assets	301	Other liabilities	729
Total	4,643	Total	4,643

CENTRAL BANKING INSTITUTIONS WITH SPECIAL TASKS

The Landwirtschaftliche Rentenbank.—Short-term credit requirements of agriculture are in the main met by the rural credit cooperatives and their central institutions. In addition, in the agricultural field, there is a need for credit which by its very nature can only be met by medium-term and long-term loans. To the extent that real estate credit institutions, especially the mortgage banks constituted under public law, are unable to meet this demand, it is incumbent upon the Landwirtschaftliche Rentenbank to furnish additional funds.

The economic basis for the activities of this bank, which was founded in 1949, takes the form of a land charge (as was the case with the Deutsche Rentenbank) with which all agricultural land is encumbered, and which is known as the "Rentenbank-Grundschuld." According to the law dated May 11, 1949, agriculture in general is required every year, and over a period of ten years, to make payments in the amount of 0.15 percent of the ratable value (assessed value) of agricultural real property. It is assumed that the total revenue for this charge will be in the neighborhood of DM 200 million. From these annual receipts the Landwirtschaftliche Rentenbank is required to turn over 50 percent, up to an aggregate total of DM 64 million, to the Deutsche Genossenschaftskasse (the central cooperative institution), toward the establishment of a reserve. The rest, about DM 36 million, will remain with the Landwirtschaftliche Rentenbank as a capital fund.

The Landwirtschaftliche Rentenbank, to which so far only a comparatively small portion of the proposed net worth has accrued, has been promised rediscount facilities by the central banking system for certain special credit transactions, principally the stockpiling of foodstuffs. It has also been able to lend long-term credits out of the counterpart funds destined for agriculture.

The Industriekreditbank A. G.—Founded in Düsseldorf on March 29, 1949, this serves to provide industrial enterprises with medium-term and long-term credits. Economically, although not juridically, this institution is the successor of the Deutsche Industriebank Berlin, which after the First World War extended a considerable volume of long-term credits, with a fair-sized net worth put up by industrial enterprises and with outside resources obtained through the issue of debentures. The reestablishment of this bank was due to the fact that credit banks proper should generally provide only short-term loans, and mortgage banks and savings banks are reluctant to extend long-term industrial loans because of the inherent risk. The capital stock, which in the case of the old Industriebank had amounted to RM 100 million and was strengthened by reserves amounting to as much as RM 537 million, at present amounts to DM 18 million contributed by industry as a whole. Although the bank is authorized to issue debentures, its activities so far have mainly consisted in assisting in lending a portion of the counterpart funds to industry by investigating and acting as a mediator in individual cases.

The Kreditanstalt für Wiederaufbau (Reconstruction Loan Corporation).—Provision of loans for the reconstruction of the economic system is one of the thorniest problems of postwar times. The Reconstruction Loan Corporation, established by a law dated November 5, 1948, was founded for this specific purpose and is intended to permit all branches of the economy to enter upon reconstruction projects by furnishing them with medium-term and long-term loans to the extent that other credit institutions are unable to lend the necessary funds.

The Reconstruction Loan Corporation is incorporated under public law with a capital of DM 1 million, half of which was supplied by the federal authorities, the other half furnished by the Länder. Moreover, DM 94 million out of the funds of the European Recovery Program were placed at its disposal, without interest and nonrepayable. These funds serve as a reserve. The loans extended by the

Reconstruction Loan Corporation are granted for medium-term and long-term periods against security; short-term credits are subject to the approval of the Bank deutscher Länder. As a rule, the Reconstruction Loan Corporation does not grant credits directly, but through the borrower's regular bank. The Corporation may issue debentures, borrow funds, accept DM accounts of the European Recovery Program and the Government Appropriation for Relief in Occupied Areas, and, in special cases, may also borrow short-term funds from the Bank deutscher Länder. The liabilities of the bank are limited to DM 8,000 million, while guarantees must not exceed DM 1,000 million.

On December 31, 1952, the Reconstruction Loan Corporation had outstanding credits to the amount of approximately DM 5,400 million. Out of this total, DM 3,400 million were financed out of counterpart funds. First among the credits granted by the Corporation are those furnished to the power industry and coal mining; next are those granted to "other industries" (partly through the Industriekreditbank A. G.); agriculture (mainly through the "Landwirtschaftliche Rentenbank"); and then to expellees (in cooperation with the Lastenausgleichsbank, Bonn), to transport enterprises of various kinds, to housing construction, and so on.

The Bank für Vertriebene und Geschädigte (Lastenausgleichsbank) A. G. (Expellees' Bank).—Since the end of the war, as already indicated, some 9,000,000 refugees have entered Western Germany and have had to be incorporated in its economic life. In order to permit the refugees to obtain necessary loans, which was frequently very difficult owing to lack of bankable security, a special bank for this purpose was founded in 1950. Called the "Vertriebenenbank," it has its seat in Bonn. From its capital, amounting to DM 3 million furnished by the Federal Government, the bank grants operating and investment credits, which are made available to refugee enterprises through other credit institutions. According to its by-laws the bank is entitled to issue bearer bonds, although as a result of the weak capital market it has functioned chiefly on the basis of the funds of the European Recovery Program and with loans from "Lastenausgleich," a levy for the equalization of values between property damaged by the war and property not thus damaged.

THE WESTERN GERMAN CENTRAL BANKING SYSTEM

STRUCTURE

The German central banking system was reorganized in the years 1946 through 1948. As a result, the former bank of issue, the Reichsbank, which like all other European central banks was a centrally directed institution, ceased operations. In the Russian-occupied zone, it was definitely closed, together with all commercial banks, immediately following surrender (May, 1945). In the three Western zones of occupation—the present area of the Federal Republic of Germany—however, the network of branches of the Reichsbank was maintained and converted into a new central banking organization. The Reichsbank itself continues to exist as a juridical entity, and trustees have been appointed for the administration of its assets and liabilities.

A "Two-Level System" (in outward appearance).—The reorganization has been given a "two-level structure." For each of the original eleven (since January 1, 1953, only nine) West German Länder, a Land Central Bank was formed as a corporation under public law.

In their respective business areas, these Land Central Banks operate as the "Bank of Banks" and as fiscal agent for their respective governments. They have taken over the premises, facilities, and official staff of the former Reichsbank offices, as well as a substantial part of their assets and liabilities, together with the liabilities of the giro system of those branches. The activity of each Land Central Bank is confined to the area of its Land.

The central institution of the nine Central Banks is the Bank deutscher Länder, located in Frankfurt-am-Main and created by law in March, 1948. The Bank deutscher Länder was set up with a capital of DM 100 million owned by the Land Central Banks.

Table 21 shows that the various Land Central Banks vary considerably in size, the reason being, of course, the difference in the area of the various Länder making up the Federal Republic.

A Uniform System (in practice).—Although the West German Central Banking System, in its outward appearance, gives the impression of a highly decentralized mechanism it may, in practice, be considered a centrally directed bank of issue. It is true that, legally, the Land Central Banks form independent entities. Nevertheless, the whole system is strongly anchored in the Bank deutscher Länder. The Board

TABLE 21
DOMICILE AND TOTAL CAPITAL OF THE LAND CENTRAL BANKS, SEPTEMBER 30, 1953
(AMOUNTS IN MILLIONS OF DM)

Land Central Bank	*Domicile*	*Capital Stock*	*Total Assets*
Of Bavaria	München (Munich)	50	598
Of Bremen	Bremen	10	95
Of Hesse	Frankfurt-am-Main	30	448
Of Baden-Württemberg	Stuttgart	50	546
Of Lower Saxony (Niedersachsen)	Hannover	40	314
Of North-Rhine Westphalia	Düsseldorf	65	1,113
Of Schleswig-Holstein	Kiel	10	184
Of the Freie und Hansestadt Hamburg	Hamburg	10	334
Of Rheinland-Palatinate	Mainz	20	183
	Total	285	3,815

of Directors of the Bank deutscher Länder, consisting (under its own chairman) of the presidents of the Land Central Banks and the president of the Board of Managers of the Bank deutscher Länder, lawfully decides the common banking policy and ensures that, to the maximum extent possible, this policy is followed in the different Länder. In order to carry out these duties, the Board of Directors must decide all questions relating to discount policy and the determination of minimum reserve requirements, must draw up directives relating to open-market policy and credit operations, and must make all important decisions in connection with monetary and credit policy. The Board of Directors, by law, are under specific prohibition to delegate their responsibility on fundamental questions relating to currency and credit policy (for instance to the Board of Managers of the Bank deutscher Länder). The resolutions adopted by the Board are carried out by the Direktorium der Bank deutscher Länder, the president of the Board of Managers being responsible to the Board of Directors for the execution of all decisions rendered by the latter, as well as for the general conduct of business. The Land Central Banks are bound to adhere to the resolutions passed by the Board of Directors of the Bank deutscher Länder, that is, resolutions practically rendered by their own presidents.

The over-all management of the Land Central Banks is controlled by their Boards of Directors (Verwaltungsräte der Landeszentralbanken), which latter also establish the principles governing the tasks of the Land Central Banks within the scope of the resolutions adopted by the Board of Directors (Zentralbankrat der Bank deutscher Länder) of the Bank deutscher Länder. The affairs of the Land Central Banks are conducted by a Board of Managers (Vorstand der Landeszentralbank), composed of the president, his deputy and the requisite number of members as set forth in the by-laws.

No Government Direction.—The central banking system is not subject to direct instructions by the government. Article I, Paragraph 3, of the law establishing the Bank deutscher Länder specifically stipulates that "except as otherwise provided herein or by law, the Bank shall not be subject to the instructions of any political body or public non-judicial agency." In accordance with Article II (revised), the Bank deutscher Länder is merely bound "to give due consideration to the general economic policy of the Federal Government and to support such policy within the scope of its tasks." Should the Federal Government hold that a resolution proposed by the Board of Directors of the Bank deutscher Länder (Zentralbankrat) is inconsistent with the general economic policy of the Federal Government, the government may demand suspension of the resolution for a period not exceeding eight days. Representatives of the government have no vote in meetings of the Board of Directors, although they may introduce motions.[9]

As in the case of the Bank deutscher Länder, the Land Central Banks are not subject to direct instructions from the Land Governments. Nevertheless the situation is somewhat different since the presidents of the Land Central Banks are appointed by the Prime Ministers of the respective Länder. Furthermore, the Land Central Banks are subject to the general supervision of their respective Land. Since the Länder governments are represented in the Boards of Directors of the Land Central Banks, they may exert a certain indirect influence on policy respecting matters not subject to resolutions of the Board of Directors of the Bank deutscher Länder. In their capacity as members of the Board of Directors of the Bank deutscher Länder, the presidents are not subject to any instruction by their own Boards of Directors with respect to opinion voiced and votes cast (Article VII, Paragraph 2, of the by-laws of the Bank deutscher Länder). It is in this capacity that they elect the president and the

[9] The above-mentioned revision of Article II of the law for establishing the Bank deutscher Länder has been substituted for the authority to issue instructions held by the former Allied Bank Commission.

members of the Board of Managers of the Bank deutscher Länder.

Functional Structure.—Within the framework of law the essential functions of the Land Central Banks are: to regulate the circulation of money and the supply of credit in their respective areas; to promote the solvency and liquidity of credit institutions; and to act as the sole fiscal agent of the Länder. In contrast, the Bank deutscher Länder holds the exclusive right of issuing bank notes within the area of the Federal Republic of Germany, and it promotes the solvency and liquidity of the member Land Central Banks. In its relations with the Federal Government, the Bank deutscher Länder serves as fiscal agent and assists the appropriate departments in the field of foreign exchange policy.

Consequently, the functions of the central banking system are distributed in such a way that normally the Bank deutscher Länder acts solely as the bank of the Land Central Banks (with the exception of its financial relations with the federal administration), whereas the Land Central Banks in turn act as central banks for the commercial banks located in their area (except for their financial relations with the Land Government). It is true that, in addition, the Land Central Banks also maintain accounts for private enterprises and private individuals, but they do not extend direct credits to the economy.[10] Just as the central banking system, considered as a whole, serves as the refinancing agency for the commercial banks, so does the Bank deutscher Länder, within the system, play the role of the lender toward the Land Central Banks. The Land Central Banks rediscount their bills with and borrow money from the Bank deutscher Länder at rates of discount which it has established. Moreover they maintain minimum reserves with the Bank deutscher Länder. In a similar fashion, the commercial banks obtain credit accommodation and maintain reserves with the Land Central Banks of their area. The relations between the Bank deutscher Länder and the Land Central Bank simulates the character of credit relations between independent institutions, whereas, in reality, the central banking system constitutes an organic unit. The reason is that the Bank deutscher Länder determines the credit policies of the Land Central Banks.

Permissible Transactions.—The law does not provide a specific

[10] A clause in the former Reichsbank Law applies solely to the areas of the three Land Central Banks of Rheinland-Palatinate, Baden and Württemberg-Hohenzollern, inasmuch as these institutions likewise extend direct credits to the economy.

"cover" for the bank notes [11] issued by the Bank deutscher Länder. Rather, the note cover is made up of all the earning assets of the bank, against which bank notes (or balances on giro account) are made available. The assurance of monetary stability lies in the careful handling of transactions allowed to the Bank deutscher Länder. In its practical consequence, this system of monetary control affords as much security as if the law prescribed the maintenance of a special cover (gold or foreign exchange) against the bank notes in circulation.

Comparatively narrow limits have been set by law on transactions permitted to the Bank deutscher Länder. The bank is authorized to purchase from, or to accept as collateral for advances to, the member Land Central Banks all those titles, such as bills of exchange, Treasury bonds, and securities, which the latter under the legal provisions for their establishment are authorized to purchase or to accept as collateral for advances. Furthermore, the Bank may grant to the Federal Republic of Germany advances to a limited extent, that is, the total of advances, together with the Treasury bills of the Federal Republic in circulation for which the Bank deutscher Länder has given a rediscount promise, shall not in the aggregate exceed DM 1,500 million. In addition the Bank deutscher Länder may purchase and sell (without limit), although only in the open market, bonds and Treasury bills issued by the Federal Republic.

The scope of credit transactions which the Land Central Banks are allowed to undertake with banks (in the French Zone also with private enterprise) is narrowly limited in the laws establishing the nine Land Central Banks. According to these laws (which are identical in context), the Land Central Banks may, in the main, purchase only such bills and checks as fall due within three months and represent prime commercial bills of exchange containing three solvent endorsements. In their relations with the respective Länder, the Land Central Banks may extend cash advances to their respective lands and, after having secured the consent of the Minister of Finance of the land, also to corporations established under public law, for the purpose of "bridging periodical cash deficits." These cash advances may be granted up to an amount not exceeding one fifth of the deposits with the respective Land Central Bank.

11 Initially the Bank deutscher Länder was vested with the authority to issue coins; however, the Federal Government in consideration of the Coinage Law promulgated in July, 1950, has claimed the right to issue coins for purposes of revenue. The Bank deutscher Länder's right of issue is now confined to bank notes.

Land Central Banks may purchase and sell Treasury bills issued by the Federal Government or by the Länder, with a maturity of not more than three months. In the open market, the Land Central Banks may engage in the purchase and sale of obligations issued by the Federal Government, by the Länder and by other corporations under public law, as well as of mortgage bonds and municipal bonds. Finally, they may grant interest-bearing loans for a period not exceeding three months against public capital issues, including equalization claims (also known as collateral loans).

Network of Branches.—According to practice in Continental Europe, the German Central Bank has always maintained a widespread network of branches. The present West German central banking system operates a total of 255 branches, 45 of which are branches with somewhat extended authority, directing the work of others subordinate to them. For many decades, banks throughout Germany have considered the central bank (formerly the Reichsbank, now the Land Central Banks) as a source of liquid funds, from which they obtained credits. Accordingly, an intimate contact has existed between financial institutions and the central bank branch operating in that area. This contact has been further strengthened by the monetary reform law (1948), requiring all financial institutions to establish minimum reserves with their respective Land Central Banks.

Credit Relations with the Commercial Banks.—In the aggregate, the commercial banks have, for a number of years, shown a relatively high indebtedness to the central banking system. Individually, the conditions obtaining in this respect are, however, apt to reveal substantial differences. Owing to the inflow of new deposits, or to a certain restraint in credit policy, a number of banks are always independent of the central bank and have free funds available to offer on the money markets. As a whole, since the end of 1950, the recourse of the banks to the central system has developed as shown in Table 22.

This dependence of the commercial banks gives to the central system a clearer view of the credit operations of the banks and a much greater influence on those operations than is possible in the case of completely independent banks.

Credit Policy.—As already mentioned, in shaping credit policy the central banking system has three means at its disposal: discount-rate policy; changes in minimum reserve requirements; and open-market policy. In addition, the system of necessity exerts consider-

TABLE 22
AMOUNTS BORROWED FROM, AND RESERVE BALANCES KEPT WITH, THE CENTRAL BANKING SYSTEM [a] BY COMMERCIAL BANKS IN THE AREA OF THE GERMAN FEDERAL REPUBLIC
(AMOUNTS IN MILLIONS OF DM)

Date	*Borrowings*	*Reserve Balance*	*Net Indebtedness* (Col. 1 less Col. 2)
1950 December 31	4,960	1,831	3,129
1951 March 31	4,740	1,675	3,065
June 30	4,411	1,777	2,634
September 30	4,618	1,833	2,785
December 31	5,306	2,628	2,678
1952 March 31	4,325	2,027	2,298
June 30	3,663	2,093	1,570
September 30	3,125	1,868	1,257
December 31	3,868	2,896	972
1953 June 30	2,463	2,254	209

[a] Excluding the Berlin Central Bank.

able influence on the policy of the commercial banks by moral suasion and, if need be, by imposing conditions in granting central bank credits to the commercial banks. Both actions have had a considerable share in the measures taken toward checking the price boom started by the Korean war. Upon instruction from the central system, the banks, in the course of a few months (March to May, 1951), reduced their short-term loans by some DM 800 million (equal to 6 percent of the short-term credit volume). Furthermore, during the first months of 1951 the central banking system issued certain guiding rules to the commercial banks, aimed at setting up fixed proportions between credits granted and net worth, as well as between liquid funds and liabilities. In 1952, the Board of Directors of the Bank deutscher Länder issued instructions to limit the rediscount facilities of the banks with their respective Land Central Banks.

Since the currency reform, the central system has repeatedly had recourse to the expedient of changes in rates of discount. Immediately following the currency reform, the rate of discount was fixed at 5 percent. In the course of the credit relaxations which proved necessary during 1949, the discount rate was twice lowered, from a high of 5 percent, in stages of 0.5 percent, to a final level of 4 percent. One year and three months later, after the Korean war had started, one of the measures adopted to check the excessive demand caused by the turn of political events was to raise the rate of discount from 4 percent to

6 percent and to raise the rate on advances from 5 percent to 7 percent. This rate of discount was the highest prevailing in Germany since 1931. As the Korean boom and the resulting consequences disappeared, the central system gradually lowered the discount rate, by 1 percent in May, 1952, and by 0.5 percent each in August, 1952, January, 1953, and June, 1953, thus reaching a rate of 3.5 percent. Special rates of discount are in effect for purchases of foreign bills of exchange (see Table 23, note *a*).

The interest rate charged by private banks to their customers is by tradition closely associated with the central bank's rate of discount. Consequently, changes in the rediscount rate directly affect the lending rates charges by the banks. The actual rates are established by the bank supervisory authorities of the individual Länder on the basis of the rediscount rate. As a rule, these rates represent the maximum; that is to say, lower rates may be applied.[12]

TABLE 23

CHANGES IN THE INTEREST RATES OF THE CENTRAL BANKING SYSTEM

Effective Date of Change	*Discount* [a]	*Advances*
July 1, 1948	5.0	6.0
May 27, 1949	4.5	5.5
July 14, 1949	4.0	5.0
October 27, 1950	6.0	7.0
May 29, 1952	5.0	6.0
August 21, 1952	4.5	5.5
January 8, 1953	4.0	5.0
June 11, 1953	3.5	4.5

[a] These are also the rates of interest against cash advances to public authorities. Pursuant to a resolution adopted on August 3, 1948, a uniform rate of discount of 3 percent was fixed for bills expressed in foreign currency. By a resolution adopted November 9–10, 1949, the Board of Directors, representing the central banking system, authorized the Board of Managers of the Bank deutscher Länder to fix variable rates for such bills, adjusted to the discount rates charged by foreign banks of issue. The same privilege applied to bills expressed in DM bearing a foreign acceptance (resolution of March 22–23, 1950), and for export drafts (resolution of November 15–16, 1950, and May 23–24, 1951).

Also the central banking system has repeatedly made use of its powers to vary minimum reserve requirements. The first change, a rise in reserve requirements against demand deposits from 10 to 15 percent, occurred in December, 1948, in order to mop up the embarrassingly large excess reserves of the commercial banks existing during the first months following currency reform. In the course of

[12] See Table 5.

1949 the minimum reserves of the banks were reduced. This action was taken for the same reasons that the rate of discount was lowered. As of September, 1949, all minimum reserve requirements with the exception of the rate on demand deposits at bank places (bank places are places at which there is a Land Central Bank or a branch of one) had been reduced to the legally admissible minimum. In the course of the credit restrictions which became necessary by reason of the impact of the Korean war, minimum reserve requirements were raised by an average of 50 percent. In May, 1952, reserve requirements were again lowered. Both the changes in the minimum reserve requirements and the breakdown for the individual groups of banks are shown in the following Tables 24 and 25. It should also be mentioned that the banks are required to pay, for reserve deficits, a special rate of interest fixed at 3 percent over and above the rates on advances.

TABLE 24
MINIMUM RESERVE REQUIREMENTS FOR COMMERCIAL BANKS IN PERCENT OF DEPOSITS [a]

	SIGHT DEPOSITS			
Date	*"Bank Places"*	*"Non-Bank Places"*	*Time Deposits*	*Savings Deposits*
July 1, 1948	10	10	5	5
December 1, 1948	15	10	5	5
June 1, 1949	12	9	5	5
September 1, 1949	10	8	4	4
October 1, 1950	15	12	8	4
May 1, 1952	15–10 [b]	12–8 [b]	8–5.5 [b]	4
September 1, 1952	12–9	10–8	7–5	4
February 1, 1953	11–8	9–8	7–5	4

[a] Legally permissible minimum and maximum rates are: 8–20 percent against sight deposits; 4–10 percent against time and savings deposits.

[b] Beginning in May, 1952, the banks were divided into certain categories, in accordance with the volume of their deposits. The larger the deposit volume, the higher the reserve requirement.

At the present time, the central banking system is hardly in a position to engage in open-market operations, owing to the lack of a functioning capital market.[13] Open-market transactions for regulating the money market are taking place mainly in Treasury bills of the Federal Government, of the Federal Railways, and the Länder (tenure 3 months), as well as in certain bills of public authorities, engaged in the financing of the storage of foodstuffs, especially grains and fodder.

[13] Cf. pp. 362–64.

TABLE 25
RESERVE BALANCES OF BANKS IN THE AREA OF THE GERMAN FEDERAL REPUBLIC, CLASSIFIED ACCORDING TO GROUPS OF BANKS, SEPTEMBER 30, 1953
(AMOUNTS IN MILLIONS OF DM)

Groups of Banks	*Legal Minimum Reserves (Reserve required)*	*Net Excess Reserves* [a]
Credit banks (Total)	1,068	23
Successor institutions to branches of former large banks	641	6
State, regional and local banks	336	12
Private bankers	91	5
Central giro institutions	222	4
Savings banks	712	8
Central institutions of rural credit cooperatives, and rural credit cooperatives	122	3
Central institutions of urban credit cooperatives	5	0.
Urban credit cooperatives	117	4
Other banks	189	11
Total	2,435	53

[a] The total by which reserves maintained fell short of the reserve requirement amounted to DM 3.0 million.

Foreign Exchange Control.—In Germany, free transactions in the foreign exchanges were discontinued as early as 1931. After the end of the war, foreign exchange legislation and control were taken over by the Allied powers and conducted by occupational agencies. In compliance with the law establishing the Bank deutscher Länder, which stipulated that the regulation of foreign exchange transactions is one of its responsibilities, the Military Governments granted to the Bank deutscher Länder legal authority in this field.[14] Since the autumn of 1949, the Bank deutscher Länder has to an increasing extent engaged in carrying out or regulating foreign exchange transactions and at present exercises complete control subject to supervision by the Federal Government. Pursuant to an authorization granted to it under Allied High Commission Law No. 33, the Bank deutscher Länder issued on September 1, 1950, a regulation concerning the declaration, delivery, and disposition of foreign exchange assets.

The Returns of the Central Banking System.—The Land Central Banks and the Bank deutscher Länder are bound by law to publish weekly returns. The returns are published on the 7th, 15th, 23d and

[14] General License No. 8 under Military Government Law 53.

last day of each month. In addition, the Bank deutscher Länder must publish a "combined return of the Bank deutscher Länder and the Land Central Banks" as of the last day of each month. As a result of the two-level structure of the central banking system, neither the return of the Bank deutscher Länder alone nor the returns of the Land Central Banks by themselves give a complete impression of the extent to which the economy has had recourse to central bank credit. Such an impression is only to be gained from the combined return, in which the mutual claims and liabilities between the Bank deutscher Länder and the Land Central Banks are eliminated as they are set off against each other. In consequence this return reflects the relations of the central banking system as a whole to the outside customers, that is, in the main to other banks and to the agencies of the occupying powers and of the German Federal Republic and the Länder. Therefore, it is not the weekly return of the Bank deutscher Länder, but the combined return of the Bank deutscher Länder and the Land Central Banks which has the same instructive value as the former Reichsbank return or the return of any other central bank. To demonstrate this, and also in order to supply an approximate impression of the present status of the central banking system, the combined return of the Bank deutscher Länder and the Land Central Banks as of September 30, 1953, is shown in Table 26.

TABLE 26

COMBINED RETURN OF THE BANK DEUTSCHER LÄNDER AND THE LAND CENTRAL BANKS, SEPTEMBER 30, 1953

(AMOUNTS IN THOUSANDS OF DM)

ASSETS

Gold		1,086,601
Credit balances in foreign currency		5,781,357
Foreign notes, coin, bills, and checks		359,459
Claims arising from settlement of foreign trade		5,647
Postal check balances		44,848
Inland bills of exchange and checks		2,165,477
Treasury bills and non-interest-bearing Treasury bonds issued by:		
The Federal Government and Federal administration	16,010	
The Länder	3,720	
Other public agencies	. . .	19,730
German subsidiary coins		99,222
Advances on the security of:		
Bills of exchange	29,800	
Equalization claims	132,397	
Other securities	1,582	163,779

TABLE 26 (*Continued*)

Advances and short-term credits to:			
The Federal Government and Federal administration		...	
The Länder		5,400	
Other public agencies		191,144	196,544
Securities			
Equalization claims		214,487	
Securities purchased on the open market		27,847	
Others		100,640	342,974
Participation of the Land Central Bank in the Bank deutscher Länder [a]			100,000
Claims on public authorities			
Equalization claims		5,442,566	
Non-interest-bearing bonds		622,271	6,064,837
Credit to Federal Government in respect of FMF and FBRD			183,098
Other assets			377,124
Grand total			16,990,697

LIABILITIES

Bank notes in circulation			11,277,259
Deposits			
Credit institutions (including Postal Check offices and Postal Savings Bank)		2,367,072	
Public authorities			
Allied agencies	638,899		
Federal Republic and Länder	541,333		
Communes and associations of communes	9,089		
Other public bodies	31,941	1,221,262	
Other depositors in Germany		164,281	
Foreign depositors		79,169	3,831,784
Liabilities arising from settlement of foreign trade			257,642
Capital stock			
Bank deutscher Länder		100,000	
Land Central Banks		285,000	385,000
Reserves, and amounts placed in reserve for specific liabilities			794,588
Items in course of settlement inside the central banking system			45,578
Other liabilities			398,846
Grand total			16,990,697

[a] Cf. Liabilities.

In addition to the publication of its returns the Bank deutscher Länder also issues monthly reports for the information of the public. In these the Bank states its opinion on monetary and economic developments and regularly presents all of the banking statistics collected jointly with the Land Central Banks.

MONEY MARKET

In Germany, contrary to Anglo-Saxon usage, the word "money market operations" has reference only to the clearing of central bank money between the banks and purchase or sale of so-called "money-market securities" by banks and other investors. It does not include the granting of short-term credits to non-bank customers. The securities which are negotiated on the money market are mainly Treasury bills and medium-term Treasury bonds [15] of the Federal Government, of the Federal Railways, or of the Länder, as well as bankers' acceptances and first-class commercial bills endorsed by banks. It is self-evident that the money market is comparatively restricted if the commercial banks as a whole do not have any excess reserves but are, on the contrary, indebted to the central bank to a greater or lesser extent. The most important lenders on the money market, besides a few large deposit banks, are certain public banks, such as the central giro institutions. The latter have to invest part of their funds in a liquid form, such funds in part consisting of liquid reserves of the affiliated savings banks and of credit balances maintained by public authorities. Certain public administrations, such as the Postal Administration and allied agencies, also place their short-term liquid funds on the money market. Thus, the equalization between banks holding excessive central bank reserves and banks requiring central bank money, as well as the investment of public funds available at short term, are effected through the money market.

As a result of regulations concerning the maintenance of minimum reserves, part of the clearance formerly effected between the banks through the money market was transferred to the central banking system. This is the case because the minimum reserve requirements are considered to be met if *on the monthly average* a balance on giro

[15] With a six months' or one year's term.

account amounting to the requirement is kept at the Land Central Bank. Many banks therefore, by discounting bills or by borrowing on security, in the course of the month build up certain excess reserves which they later use for meeting their end-of-month liabilities.

CAPITAL MARKET

It has not been possible for a fully functioning capital market to develop since currency reform. This is partly due to the fact that the public largely avoids investing its available funds in bonds or shares, preferring investment in plants, dwellings, or in liquid assets, mainly in savings deposits. Partly it is also due to the interest policy of the Government which, during the first years after the currency reforms, did not allow interest rates higher than 5 percent on mortgage bonds and 6.5 percent on industrial bonds.

It was not before November, 1952, that after months of discussion in the legislative bodies the "First Law for the Encouragement of the Capital Market" was passed.[16] The object of this law is, by means of tax concessions and a certain revision of the interest policy hitherto pursued, to make a decisive contribution toward overcoming the torpidity of the capital market. The tax saving may be considerable (depending upon the level of income) and may far exceed the nominal interest rate. In the future the interest earned on mortgage bonds and communal bonds, which mainly serves to provide funds for housing projects of a social character, will be freed from all taxation, and this will also apply to the greater part of outstanding issues. On the other hand, the earnings on most other securities will be subject to a capital yield tax of 30 percent, except where, for special reasons, this tax is fixed at 60 percent. In addition, the first holders of the securities will continue to have the benefit of the concessions allowed on capital accumulation agreements under Article 10 of the Income Tax Law.

Shares have been issued so far only to a comparatively small extent, and, as far as such issues have taken place, the shares were for the most part not offered to the general public but were purchased by interested circles. In many such cases, what actually took place was merely a conversion of "personal" companies into joint-stock companies. Sav-

[16] The following explanations are mainly based on the *Monthly Report* of the Bank deutscher Länder, November, 1952.

ings in a monetary form have been placed mainly with banks (on savings accounts) or at insurance companies and building and loan associations. This trend is in accordance with the liquidity preference of the public, which is manifesting itself in other West European countries as well.

If the capital market is to receive any appreciable degree of stimulation, it is quite insufficient to confine action merely to encouraging the market for securities bearing fixed interest rates. The market for dividend-bearing securities, which used to be even more important for the financing of industry than the market for fixed-interest-bearing obligations, is at present suffering from even greater prostration. One of the principal measures which ought to be taken is to reduce the rate of corporation tax on that part of the profits which is set aside for the payment of dividends. The present rate of this tax raises the cost of providing capital through share issues to a virtually prohibitive level. Unless relief on these lines is granted, the prospects of obtaining a better supply of capital will remain poor for a large section of industry, even in spite of the measures that have now been taken for the benefit of securities bearing fixed interest rates. The banks are not immediately prepared to fill the gap which is left by the failure of the share market to function. Since the currency reform the banks have granted a large amount of credits, which would normally have been anticipatory in their nature, but have in some cases become in practice long-term, owing to the impossibility of consolidating them by way of the capital market. The result is that the banks have become very cautious in granting new short-term credits for investment purposes. Consequently, although fresh savings have been showing a very gratifying growth since the last months of 1951, that fact in general has so far not been reflected in a corresponding increase in the amount of funds available for lending to industry for capital purposes.

THE BANKING SYSTEM IN WEST BERLIN

Contrary to what took place in the Western Zones of Occupation after the capitulation, all banks were closed in Berlin and in the Soviet Occupied Zone of Germany. According to the division of Berlin in a "Western" and an "Eastern" half (the latter comprising only about one quarter of the town), the Berlin banking system developed in different ways. In West Berlin the banking system was gradually adapted to the system existing in the Western Zones, that is, the present Federal Republic of Germany, while the East Berlin banking system was incorporated in the system of the Soviet Zone of Occupation.

COMMERCIAL BANKS

Reconstruction of the West Berlin banking system was not effected by reactivating the old institutions which had been closed, but by establishing new institutions. An institution under public law, the "Berliner Stadtkontor," was established as the largest institution for short-term credit transactions; it maintains numerous branches in the entire western area of the town. In 1950, it was transformed into a joint-stock company under the name of "Berliner Bank A. G." Gradually quite a number of joint-stock banks and private banking institutions were also established, some of which have close relations to banks in the German Federal Republic. There are also savings banks and people's banks in West Berlin. The Sparkasse der Stadt Berlin West (Savings Bank of West Berlin) and the Berliner Volksbank e.G.m.b.H. (People's Bank) maintain many branches and disbursing offices.

TABLE 27
BALANCE SHEET OF THE WEST BERLIN COMMERCIAL BANKS, DECEMBER 31, 1952
(AMOUNTS IN MILLIONS OF DM)

Assets		*Amount*
Cash reserve and central bank balances		136
Credit balances at other banks		117
Commercial bills		217
Berlin bonds		4
Equalization claims		222
Loans to:		
Business and private customers	380	
Public authorities	10	390
Long-term loans		589
Other assets		68
Total		1,743

Liabilities		*Amount*
Deposits		
Banks	134	
Business and private customers	489	
Public authorities	225	
Savings deposits	125	973
Borrowed funds and loans		596
Own acceptances in circulation		41
"Net worth"		55
Other liabilities		78
Total		1,743
Endorsement liabilities on rediscounted bills		118
Liability on guarantees		37

In Berlin the Berliner Bau- und Bodenbank (Berlin Building and Real Estate Bank) engages in medium-term loans, and the Berliner Industriebank A. G. (Berlin Industrial Bank) in long-term credit transactions. The latter in particular distributes the investment credits allocated to West Berlin from the counterpart funds of the European Recovery Program. Reactivation of the mortgage banks in Berlin has been contemplated, but not effected so far.

The volume of business which the West Berlin banking system has again reached is shown in Table 27, giving monthly statistics of West Berlin banks, excluding the Berliner Zentralbank.

CENTRAL BANK

In West Berlin the functions of a Central Bank are exercised by the Berliner Zentralbank which, like the Land Central Banks in the Federal Republic, is a corporation under public law. It does not, however, issue notes and coin of its own; the notes of the Bank deutscher Länder and the coins issued by the Federal Republic of Germany are legal tender in West Berlin. As to its organization and its scope of activities, the Berliner Zentralbank may be compared with the Land Central Banks of the German Federal Republic, although its position is in certain respects more independent. For instance, the Berliner Zentralbank is not obliged to adopt the resolutions of the Board of Directors of the Bank deutscher Länder, on which it is not formally represented. In practice, however, it voluntarily adopts most of these resolutions. The particular position of the Berliner Zentralbank within the central banking system is in keeping with the fact that West Berlin is a Land, *de facto,* but not *de jure,* of the Federal Republic of Germany.

In the same way as the Land Central Banks, the Berliner Zentralbank publishes weekly returns. Table 28 is the return as of September 30, 1953.

THE BANKING SYSTEM OF THE SOVIET-OCCUPIED ZONE OF GERMANY AND EAST BERLIN

In the Soviet-Occupied Zone of Germany and in East Berlin, the banking system has gradually been adapted to the model of the

TABLE 28

RETURN OF THE BERLINER ZENTRALBANK, SEPTEMBER 30, 1953

(AMOUNTS IN MILLIONS OF DM)

Assets	*Amount*	*Liabilities*	*Amount*
Cash reserve, and balances at the Bank deutscher Länder	128[a]	Deposits by:	
		Banks	64
		Public authorities	89
Bills and checks	27	Other creditors in West Berlin	3
Treasury bills of Land Berlin	...	Liabilities toward bank deutscher Länder in respect of advances on securities	...
Purchased equalization claims	156	ERP & GARIOA funds not yet called into use	25
Advances on security	2		
Cash advances	...	Counterpart funds of the Federal Government	50
Other assets	14		
Total	327	Capital stock	5
		Special funds	75
		Other liabilities	16
		Total	327
		Endorsement liabilities on rediscounted bills	18

[a] Including DM 14 million on ERP Special Account.

Russian organization of banking. As mentioned before, immediately after the capitulation of Germany in May, 1945, all banks in this zone were closed. In their place, new banking institutions under public law were established, a so-called "Landeskreditbank" (Land Credit Bank) in each of the five Länder of the Soviet Zone of Occupation. These five "Landeskreditbanken" replaced the former variety of joint-stock banks, private bankers, and banks incorporated under public law, engaging in short-term credit transactions. In addition to the "Landeskreditbanken," only the savings banks and credit cooperatives were permitted to operate. For the purpose of cash payments and transfers, the Postal Check Offices and the Postal Savings Bank Offices were reopened, and, in addition, in place of the deactivated Reichsbank a new central bank was established for each Land of the Soviet Zone of Occupation under the name of "Emissions- und Girobank" (Bank for Note Issue and Giro Transactions), the scope of activity of the latter banks roughly corresponding to that of the Land Central Banks in the Federal Republic of Germany. Early in 1950 the Deutsche Notenbank (German Bank of Issue) was established as the head institution of the five Emissions- und Girobanken.

In 1950 the process of concentration was further advanced in East German banking. The Deutsche Notenbank took over the five Emissions- und Girobanken and the five Landeskreditbanken with all their branches. Thus the Deutsche Notenbank virtually has a monopoly of short-term credit transactions in the Soviet-Occupied Zone of Germany. The only other banks engaging in short-term credit business are the savings banks and the cooperatives.

As a special bank for long-term loans the Deutsche Investitionsbank (German Investment Bank) was established as early as 1948. It is the only institution for the granting of investment credits.

Banking in the Soviet-Occupied Zone of Germany completely differs from what is implied by the term in Western countries. It is possible to understand its activities only by taking into account the economic system prevailing in Eastern Germany. It will be remembered that the economic system of Soviet Russia and its satellites, one of which virtually is the Soviet-Occupied Zone of Germany (German Democratic Republic), is organized on the principle of a central planned economy. The state plans and determines production, the distribution of the produced goods, and prices. In the same way the state regulates investments. Firms have to transfer to the central agency, the Deutsche Investitionsbank, the amounts they have written off in respect of depreciation, and from this agency they obtain funds for the investments they effect under the plan. Even short-term credits may be granted only for the purposes and in such amounts as scheduled in state planning. To this end the banks and their branches have to draw up and submit to the Deutsche Notenbank credit schedules. In agreement with competent state agencies, the Deutsche Notenbank adjusts these schedules. The credit institutions not only operate as distributing agencies for planned credits, but in accordance with the Russian model, they are responsible for currently controlling the utilization of the credits according to schedule. Thus the banking system in central planned economies in general has a purely technical function within the framework of state planning. It is itself not permitted to exert influence on production and investment. The banking system in the Soviet-Occupied Zone of Germany has already been largely assimilated to the requirements of a central planned economy.

SUMMARY

For some decades the structure of German banking has developed according to the special requirements of the German economy. Since the beginning of industrialization in the mid-nineteenth century, which enabled Germany to develop from an agrarian to an industrial country at a comparatively rapid rate, capital requirements have almost continuously exceeded the availability of real capital. Only in the years preceding the First World War was Germany beginning to overcome this continuous relative lack of capital. Under these circumstances, the operations of the banking system have centered on transactions with industry ever since the establishment of the joint-stock banks in the second half of the nineteenth century. The mixed or "universal" bank has always been predominant, that is, a bank which, on the one hand, received deposits and savings from and placed industrial bonds and shares with the population, while on the other hand, it granted to industry, in anticipation of the formation of savings, short-term credits even for investment purposes. In order to be able to receive savings from the population to as great an extent as possible and to utilize them for the granting of credits, the German banking system ramified to an extraordinarily great degree. Even the smallest village has at least a credit cooperative or a savings bank. In wide circles of population it is an established tradition to have comparatively little cash at home and instead to possess bank and savings bank balances or securities.

In addition to promoting the formation of savings inside the country, the German banks, and in particular the big banks, after the stabilization of 1924, succeeded in borrowing foreign monies to a considerable extent, or in effecting foreign loans for German industrial firms and public authorities. In retrospect, there can be no doubt that the banking system in a satisfactory fashion met the requirements arising from the particular economic structure of the country and from the rate of industrialization dictated by the growth of the population. In general, it has always been possible to satisfy the resulting credit requirements of the economy through the cooperation of all parts of the credit system.

Since the end of the Second World War, banking has developed in different directions in the two separated parts of Germany. This divergency in development affords an interesting example of the fact that the type of organization of a country's banking system is closely connected with the type of economic system and is in fact determined by the latter. The economic system of the Federal Republic of Germany is based on the principles of a market economy which, in all Western countries, are followed with an admixture of a greater or smaller degree of state planning. The banking system of Western Germany (the German Federal Republic) has therefore continued to develop along traditional lines. Essentially, the continuity of its development was not interrupted.

The banking system in the Soviet-Occupied Zone of Germany, in accordance with the principle of a central planned economy, has become an executive organ of state planning. In the Soviet Zone the banks are not banks in the meaning of the term as understood in the Western world. Accordingly, it was deemed appropriate in the Soviet-Occupied Zone of Germany to eliminate the traditional types of German banking. The banks' functions are merely technical in nature, namely, to meet the credit requirements resulting from the economic plan scheduled by the government, and to control the utilization of these credits according to schedule. Considerations of profitableness or credit worthiness are not the decisive factors in this type of credit operation.

The task with which the banking system of the Federal Republic has at present to cope is characterized by difficulties similar to those existing in greater or less degree in all countries of the world: by the necessity, on the one hand, to increase production greatly and for this purpose to finance to a growing extent essential investments, while, on the other hand, to take care not to jeopardize financial equilibrium. In Germany the problem was made even more complicated owing to the fact that a very large migration of population has had to be absorbed. This required the creation of a great number of new employment opportunities in order to remove the so-called structural unemployment. Thus, West German banking, under the management of the central banking system, had to harmonize the constant pressure for investments with the real resources available. Especially during the first year after the outbreak of the Korean war its task was rendered more difficult by extreme fluctuations in the propensity to spend, resulting from the inflation experienced by the population and from Germany's position as a buffer state; at the same time, its task was facilitated by the fact that everybody, including the government itself, is, on the basis of past experience, fully aware of the benefit of a stable currency as the precondition of any increase in production and prosperity.

REFERENCES

ABC des deutschen Bank- und Kreditwesens. Heppenheim, 1949. (New edition in preparation.)

Adler, Hans. "The Post-War Reorganization of the German Banking System." In: *Quarterly Journal of Economics,* Vol. LXIII, No. 3, August, 1949.

Bank deutscher Länder. *Geschäftsberichte.*

—— *Gesetze zur Neuordnung des Geldwesens.* Frankfurt-am-Main, 1950.

—— *Monatsberichte.*

Currency and Banking in Western Germany. New York, 1951.

Deutsche Bankwesen, Das. Aufbau, Aufgaben und Geschäfte der Banken, Sparkassen und Kreditgenossenschaften. Wiesbaden, 1951.

1. Eicke, Rudolf, "Die Arbeitsteilung im deutschen Kreditwesen," and "Spezialkreditinstitute."
2. Hoffmann, Josef, "Sparkassen und Girozentralen."
3. Hunscha, Kurt, "Die privaten Kreditbanken."
4. Lang, Johann, "Die Kreditgenossenschaften."
5. Schmidt, Willi, "Das westdeutsche Zentralbanksystem."
6. Tornier, Kurt, "Die Realkreditinstitute."

"German Banking" (Ludwig Markert). *Journal of the Institute of Bankers,* Vol. LXX, 1949.

"German Banking since the War." *The Banker's Magazine,* November, 1952.

"Grossbankenbilanz nach vierjähriger Pause." *Zeitschrift für das Gesamte Kreditwesen,* Vol. I, October, 1952.

Handbuch des gesamten Kreditwesens. Frankfurt-am-Main, 1949.

Hunscha. "Ausgleichsforderungen—Geschenk, Schuld oder Wertpapier." Frankfurt-am-Main, 1950.

Irmler, Heinrich. "Die Neuordnung des Zentralbankwesens in Deutschland." *Revue de la Faculté des Sciences Economiques et Sociales de l'Université d'Istanbul,* Vol. IX, No. 4.

Lanner, James. "Changes in the Structure of the German Banking System." *Economica,* May, 1951.

Löffelholz, Josef. Die Geschichte der Banken. *Die Bank,* Vol. I, 1950.

Neuer Ausschnitt des deutschen Bankwesens, Ein. Das Bilanzbild der Nachfolgebanken. Rhein-Main-Bank, Wirtschaftsberichte, September–October, 1952.

Neuordnung der Grossbanken, Die. Vorgeschichte und Bedeutung des Gesetzes über den Niederlassungsbereich von Kreditinstituten mit dem Gesetzestext vom 29.3.1952. Frankfurt-am-Main, 1952.

Obst, Georg. Geld-, Bank- und Börsenwesen. Stuttgart, 1951.

Rozumek. Das Kreditgeschäft im Bankbetriebe. Hamburg, 1951.

Schmidt, Willi. Bank deutscher Länder. Sonderauszug aus dem "Archiv für deutsche Wirtschaft und Kultur." Published by the German Economic and Cultural Documentation, Ltd., Düsseldorf.

Veit, Otto. Deutsche Geldpolitik. Frankfurt-am-Main, 1950.

—— "Die Verantwortung der Notenbank." *Weltwirtschaftliches Archiv*, Vol. 68, No. 2, 1952.

—— Die Zukunftsaufgabe der Landeszentralbanken. Wiesbaden, 1947.

"West German Bank Reform Achieved." *Statist*, December 13, 1952.

Wille, Karl. Die Etappen der Währungs- und Kreditpolitik der Reichsbank und des neuen deutschen Zentralbanksystems von 1923 bis Mitte 1952. Bonn, 1952.

INDIA

by Bal Krishna Madan

ECONOMIC ADVISER, RESERVE BANK OF INDIA, BOMBAY

THE ECONOMIC CONTEXT

THE REPUBLIC OF INDIA [1] is a predominantly agricultural country. With an area (1,300,000 square miles) equal to one third that of the United States, its population (362,000,000 according to the 1951 census) is nearly two and a half times as large. The pressure of population on the land is heavy and continues to grow at an annual rate of over 1 percent. The average agricultural holding is extremely small, varying from about 4 to 12 acres per cultivating family, and is mostly

---

BAL KRISHNA MADAN received an M.A. degree in Economics, 1933, a Ph.D. degree in 1938, Punjab University (first class first at all examinations); University Lecturer in Economics, Lahore, 1934–1937; Joint Secretary, Resources and Retrenchment Committee, Punjab Government, 1937–1939; Economic Adviser to Government, Punjab, 1940–1941; Director of Research, Reserve Bank of India, 1941–1945; Deputy Secretary, Indian Tariff Board, December 1945–1946; Alternate Executive Director, International Monetary Fund and International Bank for Reconstruction and Development, 1946–1948; Executive Director, International Monetary Fund, 1948–1950; Economic Adviser to the Reserve Bank of India, 1950–; Member (and Secretary), Punjab Board of Economic Enquiry, 1938–1940; Secretary, the Indian Delegation to the International Monetary Conference at Bretton Woods, 1944; Member, Agricultural Prices Committee of the Policy Committee on Agriculture, Government of India, 1945–1946; Official Member, Indian Legislative Assembly, 1946; Member, Assembly Committee on the Bretton Woods Agreements, 1946; Adviser, Indian Delegation to Commonwealth Finance Ministers' Conference, London, 1949; Adviser, Indian Delegation to ECOSOC, United Nations, 1948 and 1949; Member, Finance Commission, 1951–1952; Member, Taxation Enquiry Commission, 1953–; author of *India and Imperial Preference: A Study in Commercial Policy*, 1939; articles in economic journals and Reserve Bank of India publications.

Dr. Madan wishes to acknowledge the valuable assistance of his colleagues Dr. P. J. J. Pinto and Mr. M. Narasimham in the preparation of this article.

[1] The Republic of India consists of Part A States, comprising the former Indian Provinces and such of the former Indian States as are merged with them; Part B States, comprising the former Indian States, either singly or as Unions of States; and Part C States comprising centrally administered areas.

fragmented, which acts as a serious handicap for economic cultivation. The considerable diversity in the system of holding land ranges from the small owner-cultivator or peasant-proprietor, through tenancy of differing types and security of tenure and intermediaries of different grades, to non-cultivating and absentee landlords with big estates farmed with hired labor. Food crops account for 80 percent of the cultivated area and 70 percent of the total value of agricultural production; agricultural raw materials make up about 25 percent of agricultural production, while plantation crops like tea are also of some importance (5 percent). Altogether 70 percent of the population depends on agriculture for its main means of livelihood. Agriculture is small-scale, unorganized, and individualistic and is conducted with simple implements, though with a degree of traditional skill and elementary efficiency. Next comes the sizable sector represented by cottage and small-scale industries which has been slowly shrinking in the face of the advance of modern machine industries but is still far more important in the aggregate than the latter: 13.6 percent of the population depends upon industry, of which a little over 1 percent is accounted for by large-scale industry. For the rest, 6.2 percent of the population is engaged in trade, 3.8 percent in the professions and liberal arts, 3.2 percent in domestic service, and 2.7 percent in public services and administration.

India's foreign trade, large in the aggregate, forms about 10 percent of its internal trade. Since the Partition, the character of this trade has undergone a considerable shift. Exports today consist for the greater part of manufactured and semimanufactured articles and imports of raw materials and food in contrast with the position before the Second World War when India (undivided) was largely an exporter of primary products and importer of manufactures. The change reflects, in addition to the incidence of Partition on the country's economy, the secular trend toward the industrialization of the country.

The course of developments during the last decade—the war, the Partition, and their aftermath—as well as the programs of industrial expansion and economic development may be briefly noticed. The war imposed a tremendous strain on the economy and left a heavy accumulation of deferred demands, which led in the postwar period to serious balance of payments deficits and rapid depletion of the considerable foreign assets built up during the war itself. The Partition carried further a process, starting with the separation of Burma in 1937, which deprived the remaining (and main) body of India of the rich food and raw material producing areas, which were relatively sparsely populated. This, however, should not obscure the possibly more durable significance of the fact that India possesses a more diversified and semi-industrialized economy in contrast with the predominantly primary character of Pakistan's heritage.

An economic change of considerable import in the war and postwar periods has resulted from shifts in the distribution of incomes and wealth associated with the large and discrepant movements in prices and incomes, to the detriment of the middle-class and landless agricultural labor and to the advantage of large producers, agricultural and industrial, and, in particular, the commercial community. An important and spectacular manifestation of this change is to be found in the attrition of the lumps of traditional wealth of the princes and *zamindars* (big landlords), and the growth of a new-rich class in the course of the inflationary movement. This has tended to sap the sources of investment funds, while the savings of the new-rich class, born of the less productive enterprise to which inflation gives a fillip, seek further speculative and unproductive avenues of use with an eye to maintaining the snowball pace of easy gains. Difficult as it may be to reverse the process altogether, the investment market should improve as confidence in monetary stability is steadily reestablished and a return to reasonable expectations and normal incentives to productive enterprise takes place. The situation in this respect is not unlike that in several other countries, and signs of a steady revival of confidence are already evident. While the world inflationary movement enhances the difficulty of national stabilization measures, the budgetary picture shows an improvement during the last few years.

This then is the general picture at the beginning of a new phase in the development efforts of the state as embodied in a five-year plan prepared by the National Planning Commission for the period April, 1951, to March, 1956. One of the major tasks ahead is how to minimize the possible inflationary consequences of a sizable development program and to evolve a credit policy which subserves and promotes development without breeding fresh inflation.

CREDIT NEEDS

In the agricultural sector, the needs for credit refer, in the first place, to short-term finance for the operations of cultivation (like expenses on seed, agricultural labor, particularly for harvesting, and movement of crops) as well as for payment of land revenue and rent, so as to relieve the cultivator from the pressure to market his crops immediately. Long-term needs refer to the finance required for permanent improvements to the land, consolidation of holdings, acquisition of new land, or repayment of ancestral debt. Intermediate credit needs include the purchase of cattle and implements. While the security for short-term credit (usually repayable on sale of crops) is the person of the cultivator or the standing crops, that for longer term credit is mainly his land. In the rural areas, short-term and medium-term credit needs arise also in respect of the finance required by small-scale and cottage industries, for the purchase of raw materials and to cover working expenses as well as to meet living expenses between production and sale.

The industrial sector needs credit, both short-term and long-term, for working and block capital, respectively. Credit facilities are also required by the trade sector—by no means the least important—for purpose of distribution and by individuals for consumption.

An interesting feature is the impact of seasonal factors on the requirements of credit. During the busy season (November to May) the movement of crops from upcountry centers to the ports and to interior centers of consumption generates a demand for funds leading to tight conditions in the market. Conversely with the onset of the slack season (June to October) easier conditions set in.

CREDIT INSTRUMENTS

We may now describe briefly the types of credit instruments in vogue in India to meet these needs. The Indian Negotiable Instruments Act of 1881 refers to three such instruments. One is the *promissory note,* which is "an instrument in writing (not being a bank note or a currency note) containing an unconditional undertaking, signed by the maker, to pay a certain sum of money only to, or to the order of, a certain person or to the bearer of the instrument"; the making of a promissory note for the payment of money payable to bearer on demand is prohibited except by the Reserve Bank or the Central Government. Another instrument is the *bill of exchange* defined as "an instrument in writing containing an unconditional order, signed by the maker, directing a certain person to pay a certain sum of money only to, or to the order of, a certain person or to the bearer of the instrument." The third is the *check* which is defined as "a bill of exchange drawn on a specified banker and not expressed to be payable otherwise than on demand."

While these three instruments are recognized as negotiable by the Act, commercial usage has recognized many other credit instruments as negotiable. There are the indigenous *hundis,* equivalent to internal bills of exchange, broadly divided into *darsani* (sight) *hundis* which are payable on demand, and *muddati* (usance) *hundis* which are payable after a period of time; other types of *hundis* are those payable to the payee only (*dhanijog*), those payable to any respectable merchant or *shroff* (*shahjog*), those payable to any person or to his order (*firmanjog*), and those payable to the bearer (*dekhandar*). Apart from the above, there are also the familiar *bank draft, interest and dividend warrants* of companies and governments, and *letters of credit* which may be personal or commercial, general (circular) or special, revocable or irrevocable (confirmed), revolving or otherwise. There are also *treasury bills* which in India are sold both by the central and state governments through the offices of the Banking Department of the Reserve Bank of India. Other types of credit instruments are *securities, industrial and government.*

CREDIT INSTITUTIONS

At the base of the credit structure is the village moneylender. He lends for purposes of finance of consumption as well as for the productive requirements of agriculturists. Next comes the indigenous banker who combines moneylending and trading with banking functions by discounting *hundis* and otherwise financing industry and trade. Commercial banks which are organized on a joint-stock basis are confined mainly to the towns and cities; among these banks, the Imperial Bank of India occupies a unique position. The foreign joint-stock banks operating in the country are mainly the exchange banks whose primary purpose is to finance foreign trade, but in recent times they have tended to increase their domestic banking clientele. The credit needs of rural areas are partly met by the various cooperative banks and credit societies as well as land mortgage banks. Recently separate institutions have emerged to cater to the special credit needs of industry. The Industrial Finance Corporation of India is the result of the joint endeavor of the government, the Reserve Bank of India, the commercial banks, and the insurance companies. Certain state governments are setting up similar corporations in their respective areas. At the apex of the credit and banking structure in India is the Reserve Bank of India which is the central banking and monetary institution of the country.

Moneylender and Indigenous Banker.—We may begin with a description of those credit institutions of indigenous growth which have been catering to the needs of the population from ancient times, and still do to a very considerable extent, in what may be called "rural India."

The village moneylenders have been at their vocation for centuries, providing finance for the agriculturist and village artisan, and have formed an integral part of India's village economy. Their business technique and mode of keeping accounts are, on the whole, simple, though there is much diversity of practice as between classes of moneylenders, types of transactions, and parts of the country. Lending is based on mutual trust and a transaction is not seldom unwritten and unwitnessed. The security for short-term loans is often the person of the cultivator himself or the standing crops. It is hardly surprising, therefore, that the system has lent itself to abuse. The moneylender provides a neat illustration of the vicious circle of the peasant's poverty. Indigence is often the reason for borrowing from the moneylender for the expenses of marriages, funerals or other social needs in addition to, of course, productive purposes, and the exorbitant interest charges as well as the cultivator's own meager income make him increasingly unable to repay the loan, so that he sinks deeper into debt as the years go by. With the commercialization of agriculture, the farmer's needs for cash increased, while his ignorance of market conditions and ineptness at selling prevented him from realizing the full cash value of his crops. On the other hand, under the new laws of contract and transfer of property the moneylender's loans (which were now issued on the security of land and not, as formerly, on personal security) could be recorded, his claims were backed by the law, and in case of default the debtor's possessions could be attached and the debtor himself arrested or imprisoned. Small wonder then that the moneylender flourished as the green bay tree. Not only were large numbers of farmers dispossessed of their land, but several rural classes borrowed themselves into virtual serfdom. Agricultural debt increased rapidly during the phase of high and rising agricultural prices following the First World War when the improving credit of the agriculturist proved to be a double-edged weapon which he used to his own undoing. The volume of debt rose as directly as the agriculturist's prosperity which he cashed through the system of easy and uncontrolled credit, largely for consumption, made available by the moneylender. This phase was in turn followed by legislative action to prevent alienation of the farmer's land and to scale down indebtedness as well as to regulate the activities of moneylenders. A number of states enacted laws to institute systems of licensing and registration of moneylenders, to ensure the maintenance of proper accounts, to control the interest charged and suppress other usurious practices. Want of adequate data regarding moneylenders and imperfect knowledge of the law prevented the effective application of these regulatory measures in earlier stages. Recently, there has been an appreciable improvement in this respect; the laws have become more stringent and are better known. Consequently, the moneylender in many areas has been concentrating more and more on trade and gradually contracting or liquidating his moneylending operations. In contrast to the experience of the phase of high prices following the First World War, the recent period of high prices has not been accompanied by anything like a corresponding increase in agricultural indebtedness; the opportunity has in fact often been taken to use the higher capacity to repay and reduce debt.

The rates of interest charged by moneylenders vary widely from one part of the country to another, and are generally much higher than those of banks; there has been, however, a steady reduction during the last few decades, particularly wherever the growth of the co-operative movement has been marked.

Like the moneylender, the indigenous banker makes loans but unlike the moneylender he also receives deposits or deals in *hundis* or performs both these functions. He has usually a larger working capital. Whereas both the indigenous banker and moneylender advance partly with and partly without security, the former demands security more frequently than does the latter. It follows that repayments to the banker are more regular and the rates of interest charged by him are lower than in the case of the moneylender, who lends for heterogeneous purposes and incurs a bigger risk. As between the indigenous banker and the urban moneylender, the former finances trade and industry rather than consumption, the latter consumption rather than trade. In general, these two broad groups shade into each other, the difference between them being often of degree rather than of type.

Quite often banking is not the only occupation of the indigenous banker. Many bankers are also traders in their own right. The size of their business, too, does not conform to any uniform pattern. Their profession is looked upon not only as hereditary but is also largely confined to a few castes and communities, as the *Multanis, Shroffs,* and *Marwaris* in Northern and Central India, and in South India the Nattukottai *Chettis* and the *Brahmans* of Kalladaikurichi. While each of these has peculiarities, local or traditional in orgin, certain common features can be outlined. They accept deposits and perform other banking functions. The *Multanis,* however, are chary of extending their activities beyond banking; the *Marwaris,* on the other hand, have often large trading interests. The *Chettis* accept both fixed deposits and current accounts and in the years before the Second World War had quite a large volume of moneylending business in Burma, Thailand, and other areas in Southeast Asia.

The absence of formality and delay in conducting business and, springing from this, the easy accessibility and the special facilities he offers his customers have made the indigenous banker's (like the moneylender's) services sought after. His more flexible lending policy is facilitated by his closer personal knowledge of his clients giving him an advantage over his institutional counterparts with their more formal methods of working. Indeed in some respects he may be said to be a formidable competitor of the joint-stock banks, especially with his higher rates of interest on deposits and his easier requirements regarding security on advances.

The normal business of the indigenous banker is to finance trade. He indirectly finances agriculture through the agency of the village moneylender, who has recourse to the small town banker to supplement his often meager resources. The artisan and the small urban trader also resort to the indigenous banker, who makes advances either against any security or on personal credit. Though not a part, as yet, of the organized credit structure, the indigenous banker forms an important link between the Indian money market and the vast trading community. This aspect will be referred to later.

COMMERCIAL BANKING

To come now to a review of the present position of the organized Indian banking system, the commercial banks which form its most important constituent may be divided according to whether they are "scheduled" or not. To be scheduled (included in the Second Schedule to the Reserve Bank of India Act), a bank must (1) be incorporated, (2) have paid-up capital and reserves of at least Rs. 500,000 and (3) satisfy the Reserve Bank that its affairs are being conducted in a manner not detrimental to the interests of its depositors. At the end of 1952 there were 92 scheduled banks and 443 non-scheduled banks operating in the Indian Union. The total number of banking offices was 3,967, of which offices of scheduled banks were 2,646. The number of offices increased rapidly during the Second World War from 1,951 in 1939 to 5,335 in 1945 (undivided India). Not all this expansion was healthy; to some extent it "represented careless and even unscrupulous expansion of branches by banks having inadequate financial resources and following unsound methods of working." [2] It is not surprising, therefore, that in the postwar years there has been a contraction in banking offices and a few banks have gone into liquidation. The Restriction of Branches Ordinance (1946) attempted to check unhealthy branch expansion, and more recently the Banking Companies Act (1949) has entrusted the Reserve Bank of India with the task of sanctioning applications for the opening of new branches. There is a heavy concentration of banking offices in the principal cities of Bombay and Calcutta and to a smaller extent in Madras, as well as in the major trading centers in the upcountry areas, while large areas have remained deficient in banking facilities. A certain aversion to taking risks has contributed to this result. The practice seems rather to have been of a pioneer trying out a new area, to be

[2] *Report of the Rural Banking Enquiry Committee* (New Delhi, 1950), p. 23.

followed by a host of rivals in an attempt to claim a share of the business in the virgin territory. Not seldom it was left to the Imperial Bank of India to blaze the trail. The distribution at the close of 1952 of offices of joint-stock banks according to size of towns is shown in Table 1.

TABLE 1
DISTRIBUTION OF BANKING OFFICES BY SIZE OF TOWNS

Population of Towns	*No. of Towns*	*No. of Offices*
Over 100,000	79	1,406
100,000 to 50,000	95	489
50,000 to 10,000	721	1,462
10,000 to 5,000	327	332
Below 5,000	219	204
Unclassified	114	74
Total	1,555	3,967

The inadequacy of banking facilities for the country as a whole is indicated by the fact that there is at present one banking office for every 75,000 of the population.

SCHEDULED BANKS

Scheduled banks can be divided into three broad categories: the Imperial Bank of India which stands in a class by itself; the "exchange banks," all of them incorporated abroad; and other joint-stock banks.

Imperial Bank of India.—The Imperial Bank of India is the product of an amalgamation of the three "Presidency" Banks of Bengal, Bombay, and Madras, effected under the Imperial Bank of India Act, 1920. Constituted as a quasi-public institution to perform certain central banking functions till either it developed into a full-fledged central bank or a separate central banking institution came into being, it still bears traces of this origin. It is the sole agent of the Reserve Bank of India for Government Treasury business in those places where the Reserve Bank of India has no office; for this it receives remuneration in the form of an agreed rate of commission. The first bank to be set up on an all-India basis with three local Head Offices at Bombay, Calcutta, and Madras, it embarked upon a vigorous program of branch expansion in the twenties on government initiative [3] and had, at the end of December, 1952, a network of 410 branches in the Indian Union and 9 in Pakistan; it has, in addition,

[3] The Imperial Bank was obliged to open 100 offices in 5 years.

offices at London, Colombo, and Rangoon. Its contribution to the extension of banking facilities has been considerable, and in certain places an office of the Imperial Bank offers the only available banking facility. With deposits totaling over Rs. 2,000 million equal to nearly one fourth of total deposits of scheduled banks, it towers over all other Indian banks. Its position in the money market, where it has achieved for itself the role of an intermediate central banker, is preeminent, and today its *hundi* rate and the Imperial Bank Rate (the rate at which it is prepared to grant demand loans against government securities) more or less set the rate pattern in the Indian money market. Even after the setting up of the Reserve Bank of India, there were fears on the part of the other banks of privileges being accorded to the Imperial Bank; and these continued to be reflected in periodic demands for stricter regulation or nationalization of the bank.

The Exchange Banks.—These at present number 14, with 62 offices. The majority (7) are British, while America (2), the Netherlands (2), China (1), France (1), and Portugal (1) account for the rest. They constitute the oldest and in some ways the most closely knit sector in the Indian banking structure. The main concentration of their offices in India has been in the cities of Bombay and Calcutta and to a smaller extent in Delhi and Madras, their business being primarily concerned with the financing of foreign trade. In recent years, however, these banks have been opening up branches in upcountry centers as well. The larger resources of these banks and the cheaper terms offered by them have naturally attracted a large clientele and it is probably not wrong to say that a considerable part of their resources is used to finance internal trade. Since the Banking Companies Act of 1949 the same regulations are applicable to the exchange banks in respect of their Indian business as to the other banks. On the other hand, encouragement is also being given to Indian concerns to expand their foreign business. The Imperial Bank's foreign business is growing, and more recently some commercial banks have been extending their activities abroad, especially in the Far East.

Indian Joint-Stock Banks.—Indian joint-stock banks other than the Imperial Bank of India vary greatly in size, ranging from the largest banks such as the Central Bank of India, the Bank of India, and the Punjab National Bank with deposits of above Rs. 400 million each, to very small units among the non-scheduled banks. The development of regionalized branch concentration would indicate a tendency toward unit banking of the American type. In fact, it is perhaps not wrong to say that while there are a few large banks of an all-India importance, the majority of banking institutions restrict their operations to local areas and indeed to a specialized clientele.

BANKING LEGISLATION

Banking in India had been regulated through stray pieces of legislation before the passing of the Banking Companies Act of 1949. The Central Banking Enquiry Committee (1931) proposed a comprehensive Bank Act, and the Indian Companies Act (1913) was amended in 1936 with a separate chapter on banking. In 1946 ordinances were issued to control branch expansion and to allow inspection of banks by the Reserve Bank. It was not till 1949, however, that a comprehensive law to regulate banking activities was passed. This Act has defined banking as "the accepting, for the purpose of lending or investment, of deposits of money from the public, repayable on demand or otherwise, and withdrawable by cheque, draft, order or otherwise." Banks are now required to secure a license from the Reserve Bank of India for carrying on banking business. The Reserve Bank of India, before the grant of a license, has to satisfy itself that the banking company can meet its depositors' claims in full and that its affairs are being properly managed. Banks are prohibited from engaging in trading activities, but certain ancillary services usually provided by banks are permitted. The Act forbids the employment of managing agents and restricts certain other forms of employment. Other provisions of the Act deal with paid-up capital and reserves, cash reserves, restriction of advances, maintenance of percentage of assets, and opening of branches. While these regulations provide the framework within which banks have to operate, the actual mechanism of control is operated by the Reserve Bank. All banks are required to submit their accounts and balance sheets to the Reserve Bank within three months of the end of the period to which they refer. Also the Reserve Bank "at any time, may and on being directed so to do by the Central Government shall cause an inspection to be made by one or more of its officers of any banking company and its books and accounts." [4] The

[4] Bank inspections by the Reserve Bank had their origin in 1940 when, with the prior consent of the bank concerned, the Reserve Bank undertook to examine its books and ac-

Reserve Bank when directed to make an inspection by the Central Government shall, and in other cases may, report to the Central Government on any inspection made, and the Central Government, if it believes that the bank's affairs are being conducted in a way detrimental to the depositors' interests, may, after giving an opportunity to the bank concerned to make a representation, prohibit the bank from receiving fresh deposits, or ask the Reserve Bank to wind up the erring bank. The first use of this provision was recently made, when a scheduled bank was prohibited from receiving fresh deposits and went into liquidation in consequence. The Reserve Bank also generally gives advice to banks and cautions them with regard to particular aspects of their structure or business and helps them with technical advice or in other ways. It can, under the Act, on the request of the banks concerned, also assist, as intermediary or otherwise, in proposals for the amalgamation of such banks. Where the units are uneconomic, amalgamation on the right lines would undoubtedly be helpful. But numerous hurdles have to be surmounted before successful amalgamation can be brought about. Among them is the strong regional character of banks, which, however, need not seriously hamper amalgamation, as the recent fusion of four West Bengal banks into the United Bank of India shows.

BANK FAILURES

Smallness of size and inadequacy of resources, incompetent or dishonest management, mixed banking, speculation, and absence of central banking support have been among the causes accounting for bank failures, which by and large have not been too many or too frequent, except in the earlier phase of development of joint-stock banking in India. A degree of overextension of banking during the Second World War on the crest of the inflationary tide also added to the number of failures as did such a cataclysmic event as the partition of the country. More recently in 1948, following the suspension of payments by a scheduled bank, there was a minor banking crisis in Bengal. By and large, however, the record of joint-stock banking in India has

counts with a view to determining the real or exchangeable value of the bank's paid-up capital and reserves for the purpose of considering its eligibility for inclusion in the Second Schedule to the Reserve Bank of India Act. The purpose underlying the inspections by the Reserve Bank is being shifted from a mere quantitative assessment to a qualitative assessment of a bank's financial position, management and operations.

been one of continued, if somewhat uneven, progress, and has been generally free of major mishaps.

CAPITAL STRUCTURE

A not uncommon defect of the Indian banks was that several of them started on their career with capital which is altogether insignificant for the type of business and responsibilities which a bank is expected to undertake. While the Indian Companies Amendment Act of 1936 attempted to prevent the worst types of abuse by fixing the minimum capital requirement at Rs. 50,000, and a statutory accumulation of reserves so as to raise the owned funds by a further Rs. 50,000 in a short period, the Banking Companies Act of 1949 has gone further and related the capital requirement of banks to their territorial coverage. For banks incorporated outside India, the amount (equivalent to capital) to be kept deposited with the Reserve Bank depends on whether they have an office at Bombay or Calcutta or both. For other banks, the additional criterion employed is whether its places of business are situated in one state or more. The Act also lays down that the subscribed capital should not be less than one half of the authorized capital and that the paid-up capital should be at least one half of the subscribed capital. With regard to reserve funds, the Act prescribes that every banking company incorporated in India shall transfer at least 20 percent of its net profits, before any dividend is declared, to the reserve fund until the amount of the reserve fund equals the paid-up capital. Owing to heavy depreciation in the value of government securities in 1951 banks were granted exemptions from this provision in respect of profits earned during 1951 and 1952.

Of the total paid-up capital of Rs. 434 million for 76 scheduled and 443 non-scheduled banks, excluding those incorporated outside India, Rs. 337 million was accounted for by the scheduled banks; 14 of these had paid-up capital and reserves of over Rs. 10 million. The ratio of capital plus reserves to total deposits had been rather high in India before the Second World War. Since then the enormous increase in deposits has reduced that proportion. Table 2 brings out the trends clearly.

In the case of non-scheduled banks the ratio of capital to deposits

TABLE 2
CAPITAL RESOURCES OF INDIAN SCHEDULED BANKS (EXCLUDING IMPERIAL BANK), DECEMBER 31, 1939 AND 1943–52
(AMOUNTS IN MILLIONS OF RUPEES)

Year	(*1*) *Number of Banks*	(*2*) *Total Deposits*	(*3*) *Paid-up Capital*	(*4*) *Reserves*	(*5*) *Capital and Reserves per Bank*	(*6*) *Columns* (*3*) + (*4*) *as Percentage of* (*2*)
Undivided India						
1939	39	937	73	47	3.1	12.7
1943	57	3,245	166	71	4.2	7.3
1944	69	4,366	220	100	4.7	7.3
1945	75	5,428	267	120	5.2	7.1
Indian Union						
1946	77	6,112	289	144	5.6	7.1
1947	80	6,199	308	158	5.8	7.5
1948	78	5,949	313	195	6.5	8.5
1949	77	5,093	311	201	6.6	10.1
1950	74	5,227	302	203	6.8	9.7
1951	75	5,173	288	210	6.6	9.6
1952	75	5,095	281	203	6.5	9.5

has always been much higher. This, really, is not so much an indication of the adequacy of their capital fund position as of the smallness of their deposits; the difference in the character of their business probably also warrants a higher ratio.

Table 3 shows the phenomenal rise in bank deposits from 1939 to 1952. The growth of deposits, however, has not been uniform among the various classes of banks.

In contrast to the average annual increase of Rs. 1,146 million in deposits in the war and postwar periods (1939–47) deposits of banks were on the decline during the second half of 1948 and in 1949. This may be ascribed in the main to the heavy adverse balance of payments during that period. During 1950, bank deposits were steadily on the increase, but since 1951 they have been again moving down. In the case of scheduled banks demand deposits were more prominent, while the converse was true of the non-scheduled banks.

DEPOSITS

The survey of the ownership of deposits conducted by the Reserve Bank of India revealed that on December 31, 1952, total deposits in

TABLE 3

GROWTH IN DEPOSITS OF THE SEVERAL CLASSES OF BANKS, END OF YEAR

(AMOUNTS IN MILLIONS OF RUPEES)

	1939		1948		1950		1952		
Classes of Banks	*Deposits*	*Percent of total*	*Deposits*	*Percent of total*	*Deposits*	*Percent of total*	*Deposits*	*Percent of total*	*Increase, 1952 over 1939, in percent*
Imperial Bank of India	878	28.0	2,803	23.5	2,314	21.2	2,059	19.4	134.5
Major Indian scheduled banks [a]	745	23.7	3,170	26.6	2,894	26.5	2,904	27.3	289.8
Other Indian scheduled banks [b]	192	6.1	2,847	23.9	2,370	21.7	2,204	20.7	1,047.9
Exchange banks	742	23.6	1,602	13.5	1,704	15.6	1,753	16.5	136.3
Scheduled banks total	2,558	81.5	10,422	87.6	9,282	85.0	8,920	84.0	248.7
Nonscheduled banks	193 [c]	6.1	761	6.4	737	6.7	647	6.1	235.2
Cooperative banks with paid-up capital and reserves of Rs. 100,000 and over	388	12.4	720	6.0	904	8.3	1,057	9.9	172.4
Grand total	3,138	100.0	11,903	100.0	10,923	100.0	10,624	100.0	238.6

[a] Allahabad Bank, Bank of Baroda, Bank of India, Central Bank of India, and Punjab National Bank.

[b] Including one bank incorporated in Pakistan.

[c] Excluding banks with paid-up capital and reserves below Rs. 50,000.

India of scheduled banks (89) amounted to Rs. 8,144 million, of which demand deposits accounted for Rs. 4,277 million (52 percent of the total), time deposits for Rs. 2,500 million (31 percent) and savings deposits Rs. 1,367 million (17 percent). Just over half (52 percent) of demand deposits were owned by business concerns, a little less than one third (27 percent) were personal holdings and "others" (which includes deposits of clubs, charitable institutions, and the like, and deposits in accounts with balances below Rs. 500) accounted for the remaining 21 percent. A major part of time deposits (54 percent) was personal deposits, business held a little over a quarter (26 percent) and others accounted for the remaining 20 percent. Savings deposits were almost entirely (96 percent) personal.

TABLE 4
OWNERSHIP OF DEPOSITS IN 89 SCHEDULED BANKS, DECEMBER 31, 1952
(AMOUNTS IN MILLIONS OF RUPEES)

	DEMAND		SAVINGS		TIME	
Ownership	*Amount*	*Percent of total*	*Amount*	*Percent of total*	*Amount*	*Percent of total*
Business	2,243	52.5	18	1.3	652	26.1
Manufacturing	429	10.0				
Trading	1,129	26.4				
Transport	88	2.1				
Mining	41	1.0				
Plantations	57	1.3				
Financial						
Banks	299	7.0				
Others	201	4.7				
Personal	1,161	27.1	1,315	96.2	1,350	54.0
Others	774	18.1	34	2.5	485	19.4
Unclassified	99	2.3			14	0.5
Total	4,277	100.0	1,367	100.0	2,500	100.0

Banks in India normally pay interest on deposits; the rates vary with the period of time deposits, those on demand deposits being nominal. The Imperial Bank of India does not pay any interest on demand deposits. Table 5 indicates the interest allowed by the larger scheduled banks on the various types of deposits during 1952 in Bombay and Calcutta. The figures indicate the seasonal variations in interest rates.

The velocity of circulation of bank deposits in the postwar period has been around 9–13 as against the prewar figure of about 15.

Table 5
Interest Allowed by Larger Scheduled Banks[a] on Deposits During 1952
(RATE PER ANNUM)

Type of Deposit	BOMBAY								CALCUTTA							
	MARCH 1952		JUNE 1952		SEPTEMBER 1952		DECEMBER 1952		MARCH 1952		JUNE 1952		SEPTEMBER 1952		DECEMBER 1952	
	H	*L*	*H*	*L*	*H*	*L*	*H*	*L*	*H*	*L*	*H*	*L*	*H*	*L*	*H*	*L*
Call money	3.50	0.25	3.25	0.25	3.00	0.25	3.00	0.50	3.50	0.25	3.50	0.25	3.00	0.25	3.00	0.50
Current account	2.00	0.25	2.00	0.25	2.00	0.25	2.00	0.25	2.00	0.25	2.00	0.25	2.00	0.25	2.00	0.25
Savings bank	2.00	1.00	2.00	1.00	2.00	1.00	2.00	1.00	2.00	1.00	2.00	1.00	2.00	1.00	2.00	1.00
One month	3.25	1.38	3.25	1.38	3.00	1.50	3.25	1.50	3.00	1.38	3.00	1.38	3.00	1.50	3.25	1.50
3 months	3.25	1.50	3.25	1.50	3.25	1.50	3.25	1.50	3.00	1.50	3.25	1.50	3.25	1.50	3.25	1.50
6 months	3.25	0.75	3.50	1.50	3.50	1.25	3.00	1.50	3.25	0.75	3.25	0.75	3.25	1.00	3.25	1.00
1 year	3.25	1.50	3.50	1.50	4.00	0.75	3.75	0.75	3.25	1.25	3.50	1.50	3.50	1.50	3.75	1.50
2 years	3.00	2.00	3.25	2.00	3.25	2.00	3.50	2.00	3.00	2.00	3.25	2.00	3.25	2.00	3.50	2.00
3 years	3.00	2.50	3.50	2.50	3.50	2.50	3.75	2.50	3.00	2.50	3.50	2.50	3.50	2.50	3.75	2.50

H = Highest. L = Lowest.

[a] Fourteen banks with demand and time liabilities of Rs. 10 crores and above on December 26, 1952.

LOANS AND ADVANCES

The absence of a bill market in India has naturally meant that the proportion of bills purchased and discounted has always been small. The *hundi* however makes up partially for this.

The proportion of loans and advances to deposits does not appear to be much higher in India than elsewhere, as Table 6 shows.

TABLE 6
LOANS AND ADVANCES OF SCHEDULED BANKS, DECEMBER 31
(AMOUNTS IN MILLIONS OF RUPEES)

Year	*No. of Reporting Banks*	*Loans and Advances*	*Bills Purchased and Discounted*	*Ratio of (2) + (3) to Deposits*
Undivided India				
1939	59	1,510		59.0
1942	61	1,122		23.9
1945	91	3,403		34.7
Indian Union				
1946	94	4,220	497	44.3
1947	97	4,252	499	44.0
1948	95	4,421	490	47.1
1949	94	4,180	470	50.2
1950	91	4,404	650	54.5
1951	92	5,451	738	67.4
1952	91	4,740	608	60.0

During the early war years, advances declined as a result of the smaller volume of international trade, government's direct aid to industries helping the war effort, and certain governmental restrictions. Since 1942 and especially after the war, advances have been rapidly on the increase owing to increasing internal and external trade activity and rising prices.

The survey of bank advances conducted by the Reserve Bank as on December 31, 1952, shows that nearly half of the advances are commercial advances: advances to trade predominated and of this wholesale trade obtained the greater proportion; trade in "other goods" was financed to almost the same extent as agricultural commodities. Advances to industry accounted for more than one third of the total. Among the industries to which advances were granted, major industries like cotton, jute, and sugar figured prominently. Advances to agriculture in a predominantly agricultural country like India are

TABLE 7

DISTRIBUTION OF ADVANCES OF 88 SCHEDULED BANKS, DECEMBER 31, 1952

Borrower	Amount	Percent of Total Advances
A. ACCORDING TO PURPOSE		
Industry		
Cotton	475	9.3
Jute	141	2.8
Engineering	171	3.4
Sugar	275	5.4
Others	726	14.2
Total	1,788	35.1
Commerce	2,375	46.7
Agriculture	211	4.1
Personal and professional	396	7.8
All others	318	6.3
Total	5,088	100.0
B. ACCORDING TO SECURITY		
Secured		
Government and trustee securities	411	8.1
Bullion including gold and silver ornaments	137	2.7
Shares of joint stock companies	430	8.5
Merchandise	2,486	48.9
Real estate	211	4.1
Other securities	632	12.4
Total	4,307	84.6
Unsecured advances	781	15.4
Total	5,088	100.0

very small, even this limited amount of credit being extended mainly in respect of commercial crops rather than food crops. Personal and professional advances accounted for nearly 8 percent and "others" for 6 percent. A notable feature of bank advances in India is their seasonal pattern; this applies in particular to the operations of the Imperial Bank. They are generally highest about March or April when the busy season requirements for marketing and movement of crops reach their peak. Thereafter, they tend to decline and usually touch their low in August or September. Much the larger portion (85 percent) of all advances on December 31, 1952, was secured. An analysis of the advances according to security reveals that advances against merchandise, pledged or hypothecated, formed the largest single group, accounting for 49 percent; of these, those secured by non-agricultural commodities were larger than those secured by agricultural commodities. The amount of advances against food grains was comparatively small; governmental procurement and distribution of food grains with special financing arrangements accounted for this. Advances against government and trustee securities and those against shares of joint-stock companies amounted to about 8 percent each.

Interest rates charged by banks in India on loans and advances roughly vary inversely with the size of banks, and there are appreciable variations in rates among the different classes of banks; the usual rates for secured advances charged by the exchange banks during 1952 ranged between 3.0 percent and 6.5 percent, of the major Indian scheduled banks between 3.5 percent and 9 percent, and those of the smaller banks between 2 and 18.75 percent.

TABLE 8

RANGE OF USUAL INTEREST RATES, DECEMBER 31, 1952

Classes of Banks	*On Secured Advances*	*On Unsecured Advances*
Exchange banks	3.00– 6.50	4.00– 8.00
Major Indian scheduled banks	3.50– 9.00	4.50– 9.00
Other Indian scheduled banks	2.50–12.00	4.00–12.00
Nonscheduled banks	2.00–18.75	3.00–18.75

REGULATION OF ADVANCES

While on the subject of bank advances, it may be of interest to mention the legal restrictions on advances imposed by the Banking Companies Act of 1949. Under it, "no banking company can make any loans or advances on the security of its own shares, or grant unsecured loans or advances to any of its directors or to firms or private companies in which it or any of its directors is interested as a partner or a managing agent or to any individuals, firms or private companies in cases where any of the directors is a guarantor." A monthly return of all unsecured loans is to be submitted to the Reserve Bank; if on examining the returns the Bank considers that the grant of such loans is to the detriment of the interests of the depositors, it has power to prohibit or otherwise restrict the grant of a loan or direct the bank to secure the repayment of such loan. The Reserve Bank may also, under the Act, "determine the policy in relation to advances to be followed by banking companies generally or by any banking company in particular." The Reserve Bank, may, in particular, give directions which shall be binding on each banking company regarding the purposes for which an advance may or may not be made, the margins to be maintained in respect of secured advances and the rate of interest to be charged on advances. The Bank has not so far used these powers of general or selective credit control to any significant extent; it has exhorted banks to refrain from making speculative advances.

INVESTMENTS

A study of the investment portfolio of scheduled banks shows (as on December 31, 1952) an overwhelming preponderance (86 percent) of government securities, as much as Rs. 3,270 million being invested in them as against Rs. 527 million representing other investments, of which foreign investments accounted for Rs. 242 million.

TABLE 9
INVESTMENTS OF 88 SCHEDULED BANKS, DECEMBER 31, 1952
(AMOUNTS IN MILLIONS OF RUPEES)

	Amount	*Percent of Total*
Government securities maturing in:		
5 years	1,267	33.4
From 5 to 10 years	1,403	37.0
From 10 to 15 years	279	7.3
After 15 years	321	8.5
Total	3,270	86.2
Other investments		
Trustee securities	89	2.3
Fixed deposits	24	0.6
Shares and debentures	110	2.9
Other domestic investments	63	1.7
Foreign investments	242	6.4
Total	527	13.9
Grand total	3,797	100.0

The ratio of investments to deposits in the case of scheduled banks was 42 percent on December 31, 1952. During the war years the familiar phenomenon of high investments and low advances was witnessed in India. With the termination of the war, banks have reverted to a more normal pattern of assets distribution. To meet the increased demand for advances they have had recourse partly to disgorging their large holdings of government securities, particularly during the one and a half years ending December, 1949, when deposits also fell precipitously; besides, the banks reduced their balances with the Reserve Bank and adjusted their working to a lower cash ratio. Scheduled banks' holdings of government securities declined from Rs. 4,502 million in December, 1948, to Rs. 3,573 million in December, 1949. At the end of 1952 these holdings amounted to Rs. 3,270 million.

EARNINGS AND EXPENSES

At this point, the question of bank earnings and expenses may be touched upon. The gross earnings of banks had been rising during the years of the war. Net profits also rose till 1943, after which they have steadily declined, for while current earnings have increased, current expenses have risen to a larger extent. Table 10 gives the position with regard to earnings and expenses in the postwar period.

In 1952 the ratio of current operating expenses to total earnings was 77 percent in the case of Indian scheduled banks and 69 percent in the case of exchange banks. Net profits of exchange banks represented 30 percent of their total earnings in 1952 as compared with 22 percent for Indian scheduled banks.

Earnings from loans and bills constituted the most important item of earnings, accounting for about three fifths of total earnings in the case of Indian scheduled banks and nearly four fifths in the case of exchange banks. Earnings from government securities, which came next in importance, declined from 39 percent of total earnings in 1946 to 20 percent in 1952 in the case of Indian scheduled banks, reflecting the reduction in the banks' investment portfolios in the postwar period. The earnings of exchange banks from government securities were relatively small, about one tenth of their total earnings.

On the expenses side, establishment expenses and interest paid on deposits constitute the two major items. Establishment expenses rose considerably from about 27 percent of total earnings in 1946 to 37 percent in 1952 in the case of Indian scheduled banks; the sharp rise is largely the result of branch expansion and the increased emoluments of the staff consequent on the rise in the cost of living.

Despite the decline in net profits, allocations for bonus to staff and dividends to shareholders showed a continuous rise; the former, in the case of Indian scheduled banks, accounted for 14 percent of net profits in 1952 as against 8 percent in 1946, while the latter absorbed 35 percent in 1952 as compared with 23 percent in 1946.

TABLE 10

EARNINGS AND EXPENSES OF SCHEDULED BANKS, 1947–52

(AMOUNTS IN MILLIONS OF RUPEES)

	INDIAN SCHEDULED BANKS				EXCHANGE BANKS			
	1947	*1950*	*1951*	*1952*	*1949*	*1950*	*1951*	*1952*
Number of banks	69	71	72	73	15	15	15	14
Earnings	286	290	322	343	112	94	130	133
Expenses	203	218	239	263	66	59	72	92
Net current operating earnings	82	72	83	80	46	35	58	41
Net recovery (+) or depreciation (−)	+9	−6	−8	−6	—	−1	−3	−1
Net profit	92	66	75	74	46	33	55	40
	As Percentage of Earnings							
Earnings								
Bills and loans	51.7	52.2	56.4	59.1	61.9	67.3	67.9	77.7
Government securities	34.0	28.0	20.9	19.9	10.9	12.5	9.3	8.6
Other investments	1.4	2.9	3.1	3.1	0.6	0.8	0.6	1.0
Other earnings	12.9	16.9	19.6	17.9	26.6	19.5	22.2	12.7
	As Percentage of Earnings							
Expenses								
Establishment expenses	30.2	38.8	37.2	37.4	25.7	32.7	26.2	27.7
Interest on deposits	27.1	21.6	21.0	22.9	5.6	7.8	7.8	12.8
Interest on borrowings and other accounts	1.9	2.0	2.5	3.5	16.7	8.0	9.6	16.9
Other expenses	11.9	12.9	13.4	12.8	11.0	14.4	11.8	12.0
Net profit	32.2	22.7	23.3	21.7	40.7	35.5	42.6	29.8
	As Percentage of Net Profit							
Allocations								
Provision for taxes on profits	32.1	25.0	22.1	27.6	46.9	35.4	42.7	39.2
General reserves	8.4	9.7	7.9	8.4	5.2	5.7	5.4	4.9
Allocation to other special purposes	24.0	17.6	58.7	21.1	3.8	2.9	2.7	7.9
Dividend, bonus, etc., to shareholders	25.5	37.3	33.3	34.5				
Employees' share (bonus) in the profit	10.7	15.3	14.3	14.4	3.4	6.2	4.2	6.6

INDIGENOUS FORMS OF COOPERATIVE CREDIT

Before proceeding to a description of the cooperative movement itself, mention may be made of an indigenous form of cooperative credit societies, namely *Chit funds* and *Nidhis.* These institutions are peculiar to South India. *Chit funds* are cooperative ventures where a few people get together making periodical payments to one among themselves. A fixed number of periodical deposits are made with the promoter or a foreman and the total sum collected on each occasion is paid to one of them who is selected by a system of simple rotation or in an auction where he who bids the highest rate of interest is given the credit facility, a small commission being paid to the foreman for his services. There is no uniform rule regarding the nature of the security. The advance is expected to be repaid periodically and is to be spread over the duration of the chit which itself varies in different cases.

Nidhis are mutual loan societies many of which are registered under the Indian Companies Act. Deposits are received in the form of deposits proper or in the form of withdrawable share capital payable in monthly installments over a predetermined period. Credit against one's share capital is allowed and is usually available at low rates of interest, though in case of overdues the rates are raised. Loans are given mainly to help redeem old debts and to reduce the usurious rates of the moneylenders and are sometimes given to non-members as well. Both *Chit funds* and *Nidhis* have unfortunately been associated with a certain degree of suspicion. But there is no question that they have provided for savings and credit facilities.

THE COOPERATIVE MOVEMENT

Cooperative credit institutions in India date from 1904 when the first Cooperative Societies Act was passed. Later in 1912 there was another Act to place the movement on a more organized basis. The progress of the cooperative movement in India has not been uniform. While in the states of Madras and Bombay the movement has achieved a fair measure of success, it has not made a mark in others.

The greater proportion of cooperative societies are rural; and it was to serve the interest of the rural areas that the movement was first started. The structure of the movement is broadly federal. At the base is the primary society, composed of the residents of a particular area and usually constituted on the Raiffeisen model on the principle of unlimited liability. The agricultural society has a limited area of operation and its working capital is chiefly made up of entrance fees, share capital, reserve fund, deposits and loans. The deposits themselves are, however, not large. Probably because of the unlimited nature of the liability, the more well-to-do people in the villages have not been active cooperators because they feel that there is not enough security in a society which more often than not is composed of the needier sections of the community. The credit extended is mainly short-term and is very often granted on the personal security of the cultivator or against standing crops. The limit to borrowing is usually one half of the individual's assets.

At the next stage is the central bank. Usually this is a federation of primary societies in an area which may also have individual members. It is established generally in the urban areas, very often at the district headquarter town and thus has the facility of drawing upon outside capital. Its working capital consists of share capital, reserves, deposits and loans—the first two being "owned capital" as distinguished from "borrowed capital," the proportion being normally 1:8. Deposits are fixed, current, and savings, and loans are received from the Imperial Bank, other joint-stock banks and government, apart from the deposits of the primary societies. The share capital of the central bank is on the limited liability basis. Its work is characterized by a better standard of management than is true of primary societies, and its functions consist primarily in financing them. In Bombay and Madras the banks also conduct ordinary banking business such as discounting *hundis* and making advances against agricultural produce. In certain cases, there are "banking unions" whose functions are more or less similar to those of central banks.

In most states there is an apex institution—the State Co-operative Bank—to coordinate and centralize the work done by the central banks and the primary societies. These state banks have been able to attract funds to a much greater extent and to constitute a link between the cooperative movement and the joint-stock banks. Apart from granting financial accommodation to the central banks and through them to the primary societies, the state banks also undertake ordinary banking business and receive deposits from central banks and the public. State banks have also access to the Reserve Bank for rediscounting facilities at cheap rates.

While these institutions cater essentially to the short-term credit needs of rural areas, the long-term credit needs of agriculturists to repay old debt and to undertake investment on the land are served by the land mortgage banks. There are three main types of these banks: (1) the strictly cooperative type which is an association of borrowers who raise credit by issuing mortgage bonds, (2) the quasi-cooperative type which has a mixed membership of borrowers and non-borrowers with limited liability in which funds are provided also from share capital, and (3) the commercial type which works for profits. Funds are normally raised from debentures which are at times guaranteed by government and occasionally subscribed to in part by the Reserve Bank and, when made available for purposes of redemption of old debt or the like, are limited to a maximum amount—usually 50 percent of the value of the land. Deposits also are received, and thus the working capital consists of share capital, debentures, and deposits. The wartime rise in agricultural prices and land values helped the agriculturist to redeem his debts more by direct sale than by mortgage, and to that extent reduced the scope of operations of these banks.

Apart from the rural societies, there are also urban cooperative societies composed of consumers, small producers, and traders. These are mainly of four types: salary earners' societies; mill hands' societies; communal societies; and people's banks. These are sounder in structure than their rural counterparts, and are more efficient due probably to the nature of their membership and work.

In recent years, owing to the high prices of agricultural commodities, large numbers of agriculturists have been relatively better off and the cooperative banks have, therefore, been able to reduce the amount of loans overdue. In fact, the cooperative banks have been forging ahead of the nonscheduled banks as regards both the mobilization of savings through deposits and grant of fresh advances (Tables 3 and 11).

For as many as 212 towns and villages, these banks form the only source of banking facility. The larger cooperative banks, that is, those with capital and reserves of Rs. 100,000 or above, had at the end of 1952 aggregate deposits amounting to Rs. 1,057 million, while their advances totaled Rs. 829 million. This group includes not only the cooperative banks which provide short-term and medium-term finance, but the land mortgage banks which specialize in long-term finance. Over and above these larger cooperative banks, the smaller agricultural and nonagricultural cooperative credit societies (numbering over 100,000) had deposits totaling about Rs. 395 million and advances of about Rs. 696 million.

TABLE 11

LIABILITIES AND ASSETS OF COOPERATIVE BANKS, 1939 AND 1946–52

(AMOUNTS IN MILLIONS OF RUPEES)

Year	*Number of Reporting banks*	*Paid-up Capital and Reserves*	*Deposits*	*Cash*	*Investments*	*Loans*	*Number of Offices*
Undivided India							
1939	304	107	388	23	n.a.[a]	328	n.a.
Indian Union							
1946	285	113	578	66	262	309	506
1947	309	122	668	67	277	404	548
1948	323	131	720	86	292	434	597
1949	359	148	876	86	267	610	646
1950	391	166	904	118	302	613	733
1951	415	191	1,013	117	308	735	819
1952	445	207	1,057	114	303	829	872

[a] Not available.

SAVINGS INSTITUTIONS

Savings institutions, especially those of a public character, have been in existence in India for many years now, though the facilities are inadequate in view of the size of the country and the thin diffusion of savings in the economy.

The number of savings accounts with the commercial banks, most of which offered these facilities, on December 31, 1952, was more than two million. The total amount of savings deposits was nearly Rs. 1,437 million, which formed about one sixth of the total deposits of these banks.

No commercial banking institution, however, can rival the Post Office Savings Bank in the extent of its operations. On March 31, 1952, there were 11,027 post offices having savings bank facilities. Of these 223 were head post offices and about 6,500 were in rural areas. The total number of accounts was more than 4,400,000 and the balances totaled more than Rs. 1,998 million. The limit on the balance that can be held in a post office savings bank is Rs. 10,000; this limit has been set in order to restrict the advantage of the attractive rate of interest offered for the purpose of fostering the savings habit mainly to comparatively small savers. The work of the post offices in this regard includes, apart from the acceptance of savings deposits, the purchase and sale of government securities without charge, the issue of National Savings Certificates and offering insurance facilities to government employees.

Life assurance companies form an important group of institutions which help the promotion of savings. There are 163 life insurance companies registered in India. In addition more than 100 non-Indian concerns operate in the country. The Indian insurers mainly concern themselves with life business while the non-Indian concerns also conduct considerable general business. Insurance in India is governed by the Insurance Act of 1938 (as amended) and is supervised by a Controller of Insurance. During the war years the progress of insurance in India appears to have been rapid, partly owing to the wartime rise in prices and incomes which exaggerates the degree of real expansion. The net amount of life insurance business in India at the end of 1951 amounted to Rs. 6,770 million for more than three million policies insured with Indian companies and Rs. 1,159 million for nearly 230,000 policies with non-Indian companies. Over the past decade and a half the annual premium income has more than trebled while life funds have increased nearly five-fold, as will be seen from Table 12.

TABLE 12

GROWTH IN PREMIUM INCOME AND LIFE FUNDS WITH INDIAN INSURERS

(AMOUNTS IN MILLIONS OF RUPEES)

Year	*Annual Premium Income*	*Life Funds*
1937	96	448
1945	228	1,075
1946	256	1,166
1947	270	1,297
1948	276	1,504
1949	315	1,732
1950	316	1,815
1951	333	1,964

The pace of growth in the postwar years slowed down somewhat. Annual figures relating to new life insurance business show a contraction in the sums insured and the number of policies after the war and probably reflect the incidence of diminished savings, though there has been a welcome reversal of this trend recently. The loan policy of Indian insurance companies is governed by Section 27 of the Act of 1938 (as amended) which lays down that at least 50 percent of the adjusted liabilities should be invested in government and approved securities.

THE RESERVE BANK OF INDIA

Inaugurated on April 1, 1935, the Reserve Bank of India was organized as a shareholders' bank having a fully paid up share capital of Rs. 50 million divided into shares of Rs. 100 each. Except for shares of the nominal value of Rs. 220,000 which had been allotted to the Central Government to enable it to appoint Directors to the Central Board of Directors, the entire share capital was owned by private shareholders, with a maximum limit to the number of shares any individual could hold. Under the provisions of the Reserve Bank of India (Transfer to Public Ownership) Act of 1948, the Bank was nationalized, the Government of India acquiring the entire share capital of the Bank against compensation to shareholders.

The general superintendence of the affairs of the Bank vests in the Central Board of Directors nominated by the Central Government. The Central Board consists of a governor and two deputy governors, four directors, one each from the four Local Boards at Bombay, Calcutta, Delhi and Madras, one government official, and six other directors. The governor and the two deputy governors are the principal executives of the Bank with a five-year tenure of office. The functions of the local boards of the western, eastern, northern, and southern areas are advisory.

The Reserve Bank of India was constituted as a central bank "to regulate the issue of bank notes and the keeping of reserves with a view to securing monetary stability in India and generally to operate the currency and credit system of the country to its advantage."

The Reserve Bank has thus the sole right to issue bank notes in India,[5] which it does through the Issue Department, the assets of which are kept (following the model of the Bank of England) distinct from those of the Banking Department. These assets consist of gold coin, gold bullion, foreign securities, rupee coin, and rupee securities. The Act lays down that not less than 40 percent must consist of gold

[5] Under the India and Burma (Monetary Arrangement) Order, 1937, the Bank possessed this right in Burma also. This was interrupted during the war years and ceased in 1945. Following the creation of Pakistan and till the State Bank of Pakistan took over on July 1, 1948, the Reserve Bank had the sole right of note issue in that country also.

coin, gold bullion, and foreign securities, provided that gold coin and bullion do not fall below Rs. 400 million. Up to December 31, 1948, the Bank was authorized to hold only sterling securities, but the Act has been amended to enable the Bank to hold short-term securities payable in the currency of any country which is a member of the International Monetary Fund. In practice, however, the foreign assets of the Bank continue to be maintained mainly in sterling. With the previous sanction of the Central Government these assets may fall below 40 percent but a tax has to be paid on the deficiency. The Bank has, in fact, uniformly maintained a higher rate of reserve. During the latter part of the war, the repatriation of the sterling debt and the acquisition of sterling securities for transfer to the United Kingdom Government were reflected in a rise in the Bank's holdings of Government of India rupee securities, the statutory limits on the holdings of which in the Bank's Issue Department were removed.

TABLE 13

LIABILITIES AND ASSETS OF RESERVE BANK OF INDIA, JUNE 30

(AMOUNTS IN MILLIONS OF RUPEES)

	1939	*1942*	*1945*	*1948*	*1950*	*1952*
Liabilities						
Notes in circulation	1,846	4,472	11,375	13,204	11,685	11,295
Deposits of						
Central Government	87	141	2,780	2,843	1,407	1,173
Banks	166	646	802	1,032	524	567
Others	77	99	416	730	788	676
Assets						
Foreign assets	680	3,472	14,225	15,367	8,274	6,814
Rupee securities	447	1,305	793	1,787	5,287	5,516
Loans and advances	10	1	7	19	127	401
Total liabilities or assets	2,548	5,659	15,777	18,379	15,030	14,268

The liabilities of the Issue Department consist of notes held in the Banking Department (which figures as a cash asset in the balance sheet of the Banking Department) and notes in circulation, changes in which normally reflect the seasonal variations in requirements of currency, there being usually a large absorption of currency during the busy season for trade from November to April followed by a return of currency during the slack season.

The Reserve Bank's next important function is to regulate the banking and credit system of the country. Every scheduled bank has to maintain with the Reserve Bank a minimum balance equal to 5 percent of its demand liabilities and 2 percent of its time liabilities, failing which, penal interest at prescribed rates has to be paid. "The accumulation of these balances with the Reserve Bank places it in a position to use them freely in emergencies to support the scheduled banks whenever they seek its assistance as a lender of the last resort," [6] while the Bank can vary the cash holdings of banks to some extent by open-market operations. The Bank extends credit to scheduled banks and state cooperative banks through the grant of short-term accommodation against eligible securities and rediscount of eligible bills. To ensure that its credit facilities are rightly used, the Reserve Bank may call for such information or impose such conditions as it may consider necessary. Banks run on sound lines would normally receive ready assistance. Further, in an emergency the Reserve Bank can grant advances against such form of security as it considers reasonable in addition to those allowed normally. Rediscounting facilities are available with the Reserve Bank for bills of exchange and promissory notes drawn and payable in India and arising out of *bona fide* trade transactions bearing two or more good signatures (one of which shall be that of a scheduled bank) and maturing within 90 days from the date of such purchase or rediscount. Rules are also laid down regarding the eligibility for rediscount of bills drawn for other purposes, such as financing agriculture, and foreign bills, and for the purchase of government securities. Similar detailed requirements are laid down in respect of advances against trustee securities, bullion, and promissory notes supported by documents of title to goods.

The Bank grants certain remittance facilities on easy terms to scheduled banks and cooperative banks, as well as nonscheduled banks and indigenous bankers included in an approved list who are entitled to remit money by mail or telegraphic transfers between the accounts kept by its offices, branches, pay offices, and suboffices at any office, branch, or agency of the Reserve Bank of India.

The Bank extends the benefit of its advice and guidance also to those banks which are not scheduled. In times of emergency, the Reserve Bank is authorized to grant financial assistance to nonscheduled banks.

[6] Reserve Bank of India, *Functions and Working of the Reserve Bank of India* (Bombay, 1941), p. 8.

The Reserve Bank of India Act provides for assistance to agriculture on the usual central banking principles. Advances are made only through scheduled banks and state cooperative banks (and not directly) for a maximum period of 15 months. The Bank does not meet the long-term needs of agriculture. To make short-term credit more extensively available to agriculturists on reasonable terms, the Reserve Bank makes advances for the purpose of seasonal agricultural operations and marketing of crops at a concessional rate of 2 percent below the bank rate to state cooperative banks on condition that the benefit of the low rate is passed on to the ultimate borrower. While the Bank is not authorized to make long-term loans, it helps the land mortgage banks in floating their debentures, itself buying a fair proportion (up to 20 percent) of the new debenture issues, apart from granting them short-term accommodation in an emergency.

As the central bank of the country, the Bank carries on the banking transactions of the government and other operations including the provision of ways and means advances to the central and state governments and the management of their public debt. It may be noted that there have been no ways and means advances to the Government of India in the past few years; the government built up large cash balances during the war years which have been steadily drawn down. State governments maintain minimum cash balances with it and obtain ways and means advances for temporary requirements and also float loans through the Bank, which coordinates the borrowing operations of all governments. Its close connection with the banks and the money market and its position as the central bank enables the Reserve Bank to advise the various governments on financial and banking matters.

The balance sheets of the Banking Department of the Reserve Bank show no change in the amount of capital and reserves. Government deposits have been declining from the postwar peaks, partly owing to deficit budgets and limited public borrowing and partly to the transfer of a part of the deposits to Pakistan on Partition. Bankers' deposits comprise those lodged by the scheduled banks, cooperative banks, and those nonscheduled banks having accounts with the Reserve Bank. The generally easy money conditions in the prewar and war years were reflected in the fairly large balances of banks with the Reserve Bank. After the war, however, as a result of the uncertain economic conditions and a tightening of money conditions, large fluctuations have occurred in this item. The cash balances on the assets side of the Banking Department's balance sheet are influenced by various factors, more particularly government and bank deposits and the Bank's own investments, while the absence of a well-developed bill market, as the term is traditionally understood, has kept the figure of bills purchased and rediscounted at a low figure. The wartime increase in "Balances held abroad" (in cash and short-term securities, most of the latter being United Kingdom Treasury bills) has been followed by a reduction as a result of transfer to Pakistan of some portion and the adverse balance of payments position. "Investments" comprises rupee securities of the Government of India and the state governments, including those delivered by the Central Government to the Bank in respect of its reserve fund. In the postwar years, the support which the Bank had to extend to the government securities market at a time when commercial banks were liquidating their holdings of government securities has been reflected in the higher level of the Bank's investments. Thus the outstanding features in the balance sheets of the Issue and Banking Departments during the last twelve years or so are the phenomenal rise in note circulation and correspondingly the increase in sterling securities; the latter item has, however, been falling since the end of the war due to causes noted earlier.

The Bank also performs several ancillary functions, incidental to its position, such as providing remittance facilities to the public, regulating the clearing houses for the scheduled banks, and acting as the agency for the collection and dissemination of financial intelligence and statistics, mainly through its Department of Research and Statistics. In the Research Department the Bank has been building up a nucleus of trained economic personnel from which it has met not only its own expanding requirements and that of the Treasury branch of government, but of other organs engaged in the over-all planning of the country's economic and financial affairs.

The Reserve Bank has the duty of maintaining the external value of the rupee and, for this purpose, is required to sell and buy foreign exchange within the rates determined by the Central Government. Since the beginning of the Second World War, exchange control has been in force in India and is operated by the Reserve Bank.

We may now describe briefly the Bank's policy with regard to credit control. The Bank rate has been maintained at 3 percent since

1935. The easy money conditions which coincided with the inauguration of the Bank and continued through the war and early postwar years rendered resort to the Bank for financial accommodation largely unnecessary. The large portfolios of government securities accumulated by commercial banks during the war enabled them to acquire cash for increasing advances through sale of securities rather than through rediscounts with or loans from the Reserve Bank. This impaired still further the effectiveness of the Bank rate as an instrument of monetary policy. The Reserve Bank has no power to vary the reserve ratios of commercial banks. The large sector of indigenous bankers with considerable independent resources has also been outside the range of the Bank's direct control. The growing stringency of money conditions after the war changed the problem somewhat, and banks were approaching the Reserve Bank for financial accommodation against the pledge of government securities. However, banks continued to place greater reliance on the sale of government securities to meet their requirements of funds. With the revision of open-market policy in November, 1951, when the Reserve Bank stated that it would refrain from purchasing securities save in exceptional circumstances but that it would lend at the Bank rate, banks were forced to borrow from the Reserve Bank in greater measure. Simultaneously with this revision of policy, the Reserve Bank put up the Bank rate to 3½ percent and the higher rate was thus made more effective, especially because with the Imperial Bank also putting up its rate, it was no longer cheaper to borrow from that institution.

TABLE 14
ADVANCES BY THE RESERVE BANK OF INDIA TO SCHEDULED BANKS AND STATE COOPERATIVE BANKS
(AMOUNTS IN MILLIONS OF RUPEES)

Year	*Scheduled Banks*	*State Cooperative Banks*	*Total*
1937	7		7
1945	18		18
1946	247	3	250
1947	31		31
1948	220	12	232
1949	356	69	425
1950	137	54	191
1951	766	94	860
1952	2,457	111	2,568

The Bank's policy with regard to open-market operations may be briefly described. During the first four years of the Bank's working the scope of these operations was rather limited. After the war, a cheap money policy was pursued at a time when banks were reverting to a more normal pattern of assets distribution, liquidating, in the process, some of their holdings of government securities. With a view to relieving the abnormal stringency in the money market which developed particularly at times of heavy deficits in the balance of payments during 1948–49 and again during the phase of an upsurge in prices following the Korean War, the Reserve Bank, in pursuance of a policy of maintaining orderly conditions in the government bond market, was called upon to extend fairly substantial support to the gilt-edged market. The expansion of the cash balances of the commercial banks (and their consequent ability to expand credit) through these net purchases by the Reserve Bank has acted as a brake on the other anti-inflationary efforts of government in the postwar years. Recently and, in particular, after the change in the Bank's open markets operations policy in November, 1951 (referred to earlier), there has been considerably diminished support. Moreover, a steady and gradual rise in the interest rate pattern has been allowed to occur throughout the postwar period and has been particularly associated with the substantial relaxation of support to the government securities market.

DICHOTOMY OF THE INDIAN MONEY MARKET

The outstanding characteristic of the money market in India is its dichotomy into what may broadly be termed an organized market and an unorganized or bazaar market, with a divergence in the structure of interest rates. The organized market comprises the Reserve Bank, the Imperial Bank, the exchange banks, and the Indian joint-stock banks, while the bazaar market is made up of indigenous bankers. It is not quite correct to refer to the bazaar market as if it were homogeneous within itself; for, there are in fact, several bazaar markets corresponding to the various groups of indigenous bankers—the *Marwari,* the *Multani,* and the *Gujerati,* each with its own practices and its own rate structure. The position with regard to the bazaar markets becomes more complicated as quite often there is no clear demarcation in these markets between short-term and long-term finance, nor even between the purposes of finance, inasmuch as there is usually nothing on a *hundi* to indicate whether it is for financing trade or for providing financial accommodation, in other words, whether it is a genuine trade bill or financial paper.

The money market structure, loose as it is, is not entirely uncoordinated. The bazaar and the organized markets are not watertight. The indigenous bankers have dealings with the Imperial Bank and other commercial banks with whom they maintain accounts and to whom they go when a seasonal stringency of funds compels them to do so. The actual contact is provided through the finance broker who, by endorsing the *hundi* and taking it to the bank for rediscount, arranges for the accommodation to be made available. It is not unusual for bankers to insist that they will deal only with these brokers, who through their knowledge of both parties help to arrange the transaction. The banks are also known to fix the maximum amounts within which the brokers may deal. The brokers receive their remuneration from the indigenous banker. Recourse on the part of the indigenous money markets to the resources of the organized market takes place usually during the busy season. Normally, they depend on their own resources for business. The types of credit instruments vary, but the *muddati* (usance) *hundi* is probably the most popular instrument, though *darsani* (sight) *hundis* are also common when remittances have to be made. The seasonal hardening of rates applies perhaps with greater force to the bazaar market than to the organized sector.

In the days before the Reserve Bank was set up, the Imperial Bank had provided the main link between the two markets, though its status as a commercial bank did hamper a logical development of this role. As a commercial bank, it had also to look after its own interests and, consequently, despite the loan it was entitled to receive from the Paper Currency Department in order to relieve seasonal stringency in the money market, the Imperial Bank had not markedly succeeded in mitigating the seasonal fluctuations in interest rates. With the unification of control over currency and credit in the hands of the Reserve Bank, these seasonal variations were reduced substantially. The Reserve Bank, free from the suspicion with which the leadership of the Imperial Bank was looked upon by the other commercial banks, was also in a better position to achieve a degree of integration of the structure.

With a paucity of trade bills there is no discount market in India, though banks, especially the exchange banks, discount bills. Trade bills are usually carried until maturity (for example import bills) or rediscounted in London (for example export bills). The rediscounting facilities offered by the Reserve Bank, therefore, have not been taken advantage of to any great extent. The factors impeding the development of a bill market in India have been discussed several times in the past. The Central Banking Enquiry Committee felt that the high stamp duty in force, the lack of uniformity in drawing up bills as between different parts of the country, and doubts regarding their negotiability in the case of *hundis,* together with the preference for cash and the fact that there was no proper distinction between a trade bill and finance paper accounted for the lack of popularity of the bill as an instrument of credit. The Reserve Bank drew up a draft bill for the setting up of licensed warehouses, mainly with a view to developing agricultural paper. But the conditions for the development of a successful bill market, such as organized marketing facilities, and the framework of necessary intermediary institutions do not exist in India, where accommodation to trade still takes the form largely of grant of overdraft facilities.

Recently, with a view to creating a bill market in India, the Reserve Bank announced a scheme, in terms of which the Bank declared that it would make advances to scheduled banks in the form of demand loans against their promissory notes supported by usance bills or promissory notes of their constituents. For this purpose banks were permitted to convert a part of their lendings (to business, which were in the form of loans, cash credit, or overdrafts) into usance promissory notes for 90 days for lodging as collateral for advances. As an inducement to banks to popularize the bill as an instrument of credit, the Reserve Bank offered to make such advances at ½ percent below the Bank rate. As a further incentive the Bank agreed to bear half the cost of the stamp duty (which was already low at As. 2 per Rs. 1,000) incurred in converting demand bills into time bills. The minimum value of individual bills tendered was fixed at Rs. 100,000 each, while the minimum limit for a single advance which a bank might take at any one time was fixed at Rs. 2,500,000. The scheme has met with a measure of success, the gross advances availed of by banks during 1952 and 1953 (up to mid-December) amounting to Rs. 815 million and 658 million, respectively. Consequently, the scheme which had been initially restricted to banks having total deposits of Rs. 100 million and over was extended to banks having deposits of Rs. 50 million and over. Whatever the outcome of the attempts to develop a commercial bill market, there is much to be said for developing a sound market for Treasury bills, which are important credit instruments in the Indian money market. They have a currency of usually three months and enjoy rediscount facilities with the Reserve Bank. They are sold weekly by tender and provide an ideal outlet for short-term investment of the surplus funds with the banks, especially during the slack season. With the stringency that developed in the money market, Treasury bill sales to the public were suspended between December, 1949, and September, 1952.

THE CAPITAL MARKET

The rudimentary organization of the Indian capital market provides for the channelization of the savings of the community to meet the investment demands of trade, industry, and agriculture. The normal conception of a capital market consisting of issue houses, investment companies, professional promoters, or syndicates does not hold to any great extent in India. There are not many issue houses nor are there investment companies in any large number. The few institutions of this nature that do exist are of rather recent origin. There has, however, been a progressive widening of the field of institutional investment as reflected in an increase in the capital of joint-stock companies registered in the country from Rs. 760 million in 1913–14 to Rs. 2,904 million in 1938–39 and to Rs. 6,283 million in 1948–49. The amount of debentures of companies, which on the whole is much smaller than share capital, has also continued steadily to increase. The principal municipal corporations and Port Trusts have also issued debentures, which increased from Rs. 535 million to Rs. 731 million between 1939 and 1950.

A most important part of the capital market is, of course, the loans floated by government—central and state—the total amount of rupee loans outstanding having gone up from Rs. 4,529 million on March 31, 1939, to Rs. 14,842 million on March 31, 1953.

A somewhat peculiar method of obtaining funds for fixed capital in India (for example, in the cotton textile industry) has been the practice of long-term deposits obtained by certain companies. This has proved a fluctuating and uncertain source of capital and has tended to diminish considerably in importance.

The main purveyors of long-term capital to Indian business concerns have been the managing agents, an institution which is probably peculiar to this part of the world, and which historically has been the product of necessity. The managing agents are individuals or groups, who undertake to float a new venture out of their own resources and continue to manage the new concern's affairs. Thus their two main functions are company promotion and management. In connection with the former, the managing agents also undertake to carry out the preliminary investigation work involved. Having got the company going, the agents then proceed to offer public issues and perform the roles of issue houses or underwriters. Apart from assisting new concerns to obtain fixed capital (and it is usual for the managing agents themselves to own part of the share capital), they also help in obtaining working capital for their concerns. In return for this service, they are entrusted with the task of management, and it is not unusual to find the same firm of managing agents controlling many concerns in one industry, and even in several industries. Centralized management has brought with it economies of scale, but this has also meant that the defective operation of a managing agency in any of its fields would involve more than one company in difficulties, especially as interlocking of funds is common. This has not been the only disadvantage in the system. A desire to retain a controlling interest in the companies they manage has led some of the less scrupulous managing agencies to corner shares and adopt other malpractices. The system served the country well in the past, especially when managerial experience and technical skill were not easy to come by; but its future role will probably depend upon the extent to which official regulation helps to remove the defects in its working.

INDUSTRIAL FINANCE CORPORATION

The problem of providing adequate alternative sources of industrial finance has been engaging attention for many years now; and the German example of industrial *Konsortiums* stimulated interest in and a demand for industrial banks. The one or two early ventures in industrial banking proper did not, however, meet with success. In a small way the state has been helping industries by extending financial assistance to small-scale industries through State Aid to Industries Acts in the states (Provinces). A further development of this idea has recently borne fruit in the setting up of the Industrial Finance Corporation of India under a special statute in 1948. Aiming to provide finance through medium-term and long-term loans to public limited companies and cooperative institutions which could not obtain normal credit from banks or the capital market, the Corporation started with a paid-up capital of Rs. 50 million which was subscribed by the Central government, the Reserve Bank, the scheduled banks, the insurance companies, investment trusts, cooperative banks, and so on. The Corporation may issue bonds up to five times the value of its paid-up capital and reserves. Thus the lending capacity of the Corporation, if reserves equal the authorized capital of Rs. 100 million, would be Rs. 1,000 million. The Corporation provides financial assistance through loans or subscription to debentures of industrial concerns repayable within a period of 25 years, secured by sufficient pledge, hypothecation, or mortgage of tangible assets, or through guarantees of loans floated in the market repayable within 25 years. The Corporation may also underwrite the issue of stocks, shares, and debentures. The Corporation is, however, prohibited from subscribing directly to the shares or stocks of companies. As it tries to help in the provision of fixed capital, it is not expected to compete with the banks; they will concern themselves with the provision of working capital. Applications to the Corporation for loans are examined with reference to the importance of the industry in the national economy, the prospects of its success, the technical soundness of the scheme, and the financial position of the company itself. The Corporation's rate of interest compares very favorably with market rates. In the few years of the Corporation's life, a promising start has been made; on June 30, 1953, the amount of loans sanctioned in respect of 108 applications totaled Rs. 155 million. State governments also are setting up finance corporations closely modeled on the Industrial Finance Corporation of India to cater to the needs of smaller scale industries in their respective areas; five have already been formed, and some others are in process.

THE BANKING SYSTEM AND ECONOMIC PROGRESS

On the whole, the last two decades have witnessed steady progress in banking, though this has not been without some setbacks. An impetus to rapid development came during the Second World War, when inflation increased money incomes in the hands of the people. In the postwar period there has been a reaction, but this is rather in the nature of an inevitable corrective to the earlier expansion, which in some respects was indiscriminate. The adjustments now being accomplished, partly through recent legislation governing banking companies and the supervisory powers over banking companies given to the Central Bank, should enable the banking system to strengthen itself to play a larger role than in the past in the country's economic progress, without undue disturbance of economic stability. There is considerable scope and need for the expansion of sound banking institutions to mobilize the savings of the people for the great tasks of economic development that lie ahead.

The position today is that commercial banks are able to meet the demands of commerce and to a considerable extent the short-term needs of industry. But they do not cater to the long-term needs of industry and agriculture for funds, and their assistance, even short-term, to agricultural production has been negligible. The cooperative banks have attempted to fill the lacuna in the latter sphere, but only with a limited measure of success; the magnitude of their business, though on the increase, has been small relative to the requirements of agriculturists, but they have exercised, in combination with statutory restrictions, a moderating influence on interest rates in rural areas. The provision of long-term finance to agriculture through cooperative institutions is still woefully inadequate. The indigenous bankers continue to supply the credit needs of the greater proportion of internal trade, and moneylenders, though their sphere of activities is being gradually curtailed and their practices regulated, continue to be an important constituent of the money market in rural areas.

The problem of banking development in the future resolves itself into three major issues: the extension of banking and credit facilities; the coordination of the unorganized and organized sectors of the money and capital markets; and the development of sounder banking principles and traditions.

The inadequacy of banking offices in relation to the area of the country and its vast population leaves much to be desired. Banking facilities are particularly inadequate in Part B and Part C states and even in some of the Part A states. The task of promoting and mobilizing savings in the countryside no less than in the urban areas assumes special importance if investment for national economic development is to be sustained. As the Rural Banking Enquiry Committee, which reported in August, 1950, has recommended, there has to be a many-pronged drive to achieve this objective. The commercial and co-operative banks should extend their branches to the smaller towns and the larger villages, cooperative societies should be organized and strengthened particularly in the villages, while savings bank facilities should be made available by an increase in village post offices. The main reliance in this respect in the short run will probably have to be placed on the extension of branches of the cooperative banking institutions and of the Imperial Bank and the larger scheduled banks. The role of the Reserve Bank would be a vital one in the promotion of banking development; the Committee recommended that the Reserve Bank should establish its branches in the capitals of the more important states and assist the banking system generally, *inter alia,* by providing remittance and safe-custody facilities. The banking structure, as contemplated by the Committee, would consist of

(a) the Reserve Bank of India with a branch or office in each major province or State, (b) the Imperial Bank of India and other commercial banks extending their activities up to *taluka* (or *tehsil*) headquarters and other semi-urban centres, (c) the State and Central co-operative banks with their branches or affiliated primary co-operative banks and primary co-operative societies located in all towns or large villages or centrally situated villages, (d) State-owned or State-sponsored Agricultural Credit Corporations or agricultural banks or other suitable organizations, and (e) a chain of land mortgage banks for each region.

The increasing importance of cooperatives has been recognized; to increase their usefulness for providing short-term and medium-term finance for agriculture, the Rural Banking Enquiry Committee has recommended that the existing state cooperative banks should be strengthened and their scope enlarged, and where this is not possible a new State Agricultural Credit Corporation should be established; and for long-term finance, the Committee thought that land mortgage banks should be revitalized by assistance from the Reserve Bank and the several governments. By a recent amendment to the Reserve Bank Act, the period of accommodation for seasonal agricultural operations and marketing of crops by the Reserve Bank has been extended from 9 to 15 months. It may be mentioned here that in order to provide cheap agricultural finance, the Reserve Bank lends to state cooperative banks at a concessional rate of 2 percent below the Bank rate. The amount so far availed of has not been significant, owing largely to technical difficulties, to circumvent which several measures are now being considered.

Along with the extension of banking facilities, attention has to be given to the coordination of the different sectors of the existing structure. It has been noticed how there are in effect two systems in the country. To make the best use of the facilities that exist, it would be imperative to integrate the credit structure to a larger extent than has been possible hitherto. The extension of banking facilities through the opening up of branches of the Imperial Bank and other commercial banks and further increase in the scope of activities of cooperative societies should serve to strengthen the links between the indigenous system and the modern banking system. The earlier attempts of the Reserve Bank, soon after its establishment, to weld a unified pattern fell through. In return for the benefits of being part of the organized framework, it would only be fair to expect the indigenous bankers to confine themselves to banking activities proper and adopt modern methods of business.

> Until the vast portion of India's banking credit machinery, which is represented by the indigenous bankers, is put into gear with the relatively small machine of the modernised money market, with the Reserve Bank as its central control, it will be impossible for the Reserve Bank to exercise full control of currency and credit in India, which is understood as a function of a Central Bank in Western countries; and it will be equally impossible for the masses of the people who populate the country-side of India to get the full benefits of credit and banking facilities on reasonable terms, which a well organized banking system ought to give.[7]

Recently there have been growing signs of a recognition on the part of indigenous bankers that they should be prepared to accept a measure of regulation in the larger interests of the country. In this connection, the comprehensive survey of agricultural and rural finance

[7] Speech by Sir George Schuster, the then Finance Member of the Government of India, on the Reserve Bank of India Bill in the Legislative Assembly in 1933.

conducted under the auspices of the Bank is nearing completion and an integrated policy in regard to agricultural credit needs is expected to be devised in the light of the material provided by the survey.

Finally there is the need to develop sound banking principles and traditions of efficiency. It is a truism that the ultimate success a banking system is able to achieve is the result of the confidence it has built up for itself. This in its turn is dependent on the fundamental soundness of its working and of the principles followed. The Banking Companies Act of 1949 prevents the more flagrant abuses of banking principles arising as a result of the close connections between some banks and some prominent industrial and trading groups. The Banking Companies Act has also sought to improve the tone of the banking structure by providing for regular and systematic inspections of banks, by relating minimum capital requirements to the coverage of a bank's operations, and by prescribing that liquid assets (cash, gold, and unencumbered approved securities) should not be less than 20 percent of liabilities. The pressure of a larger number of small banks, often uneconomic in size and engaging in undesirable competition with each other, is also a point to be examined. Amalgamation of intrinsically sound banks, under the Reserve Bank's guidance, would go a long way to remedy this particular weakness. No less important than the safety of the system is its efficiency. The internal organization of banks in India conforms to the normal pattern elsewhere, that is, with head offices and branches, divided into various functional departments. Efficiency is sought to be promoted through a system of internal audit and branch inspections. In the long run, however, the efficiency of the banking system is the measure of those who run it, and, in this context, the importance of properly trained personnel to man the banks cannot be overemphasized. The Indian Institute of Bankers has contributed to providing the facilities for this training. With the extension of banking facilities envisaged, the demand for trained men is bound to increase. This would require a corresponding expansion in the scope of the work of institutions offering training in the theoretical and practical aspects of banking. The Reserve Bank has also given attention to this problem, and with this end in view sponsored in 1952 a scheme for the provision of training facilities for employees of cooperative banks. Measures are also expected to be taken for providing similar facilities for the employees of commercial banks.

Banking in India has so far concentrated more on financing trade, especially internal trade, rather than industry and agriculture. Finance for these branches of economic activity has its specialized requirements, and has, in the large, been left to private noncorporate forms of financing agencies like the managing agency system for industry and the indigenous bankers and moneylenders for agriculture. Development of institutional credit through industrial finance corporations for industry and cooperative societies and banks and land mortgage banks for the short-term and long-term requirements of agriculture has been slow and inadequate. The problem of improved financial facilities is integrally related to an improvement of the economics of industry and agriculture and making these branches of productive economic activity more efficient and credit-worthy. As it is, large sectors of economic enterprise work on a precarious margin of profit, whether because of faulty organization or management, lack of skill, or inadequacy of equipment; for any of these deficiencies, credit alone cannot provide a sufficient remedy. To attain any degree of real and sustained economic progress, an increase in the magnitude, range, and variety of institutional credit facilities to suit the manifold credit needs of different forms of economic enterprise has to go hand in hand with a comprehensive and concerted effort to deal with the many fundamental causes of economic backwardness and to activate the mainsprings of economic progress.

REFERENCES

OFFICIAL PUBLICATIONS

Reserve Bank of India

Reserve Bank of India Bulletin (Monthly).

Functions and Working of the Reserve Bank of India, 1941.

Report of the Central Board of Directors of the Reserve Bank of India (Annual).

Report on Currency and Finance (Annual).

Report on the Trend and Progress of Banking in India (Annual).

Review of the Co-operative Movement in India, 1939–40, 1939–46, and 1946–48.

Statistical Statements relating to the Co-operative Movement in India (Annual).

Statistical Tables relating to Banks in India (Annual).

Government of India

Annual Reports of the Industrial Finance Corporation.
The Banking Companies Act, 1949.
Central Banking Enquiry Committee Report, 1931.
Indian Insurance Year Book (Annual).
Provincial Banking Enquiry Committees Reports, 1929–30.
Reserve Bank of India Act, 1934.
Rural Banking Enquiry Committee Report, 1950.

OTHER PUBLICATIONS

Brij, Narain. A Plan for the Development of Indian Joint Stock Banks. Traders' Bank, Delhi, 1945.
Coyajee, J. C. Reserve Bank of India. Calcutta, The Book Company, 1935.
Dadachanji, E. E. Reserve Bank of India and the Money Market. Bombay, Butterworth & Co., 1931.
Das, N. Banking and Industrial Finance in India. Calcutta, Modern Publishing Syndicate, 1936.
Deshmukh, C. D. Central Banking in India, a Retrospect. Poona, Gokhale Institute of Politics and Economics, 1948.
Gubbay, M. S. M. Indigenous Indian Banking. Bombay, Taraporewala Sons & Co., 1928.
Gupta Om Prakash. Central Banking in India, 1773–1934. Hindustan Times Press, Delhi.
Hough, E. M. Co-operative Movement in India. London, P. S. King & Sons.
Jain, L. C. Indigenous Banking in India. London, Macmillan & Co., 1929.
Mani, P. D. S. Life Insurance in India. Bombay, Hindustan Advertisers, 1950.
Muranjan, S. K. Modern Banking in India. Bombay, Hind Kitabs Ltd., 1949.
Panandikar, S. G. Banking in India. Bombay, Longmans Green & Co., 1944.
Qureshi, A. I. The Future of the Co-operative Movement in India. Madras, Oxford University Press, 1947.
—— State Banks for India. London, Macmillan & Co., 1939.
Raj, K. N. The Monetary Policy of the Reserve Bank of India. Bombay, National Information and Publications Ltd., 1948.
Samant, and Mulky. Organisation and Finance of Industries in India. London, Longmans Green & Co., 1937.
Savkar, D. S. Banking and Finance in Bombay. Bombay, National Information and Publications Ltd., 1948.
—— Joint Stock Banking in India. Bombay, Popular Book Depot, 1938.
Sharma, K. K. Reserve Bank of India and Rural Credit. Delhi, Premier Publishing Co.

Shirras, Findlay. Indian Finance and Banking. London, Macmillan & Co., 1920.

Shroff, A. D. Study of the Reserve Bank Bill. Bombay, 1933.

Sitaram, P. S. Legal Decisions Affecting Bankers in India, 1920–47. Bombay, Thacker & Co. Ltd., 1947.

Tannan, M. L. Banking Law and Practice in India. Bombay, Thacker & Co. Ltd., 1944.

—— Regulation of Banks in India. Bombay, Taraporewala Sons & Co., 1931.

Tannan, M. L., and K. T. Shah. Indian Currency and Banking Problems. Bombay, R. G. & Son, 1917.

ITALY

by Antonello Gerbi

BANCA COMMERCIALE ITALIANA, MILAN

BRIEF REVIEW OF THE ITALIAN ECONOMY

FROM AN ECONOMIC point of view countries are usually classified as mainly agricultural, mineral, or industrial. Strictly speaking, Italy does not conform to any one of these three patterns. If Nature had intended her to be a big producer of cereals, fruit, or fibers, she would not have given Italy so many mountains, picturesque but rugged and steep, so much marshland, and so many arid areas. Of the 75,000,000 acres which form the territory of the Italian republic 13 percent is positively unproductive, 17 percent pasture, 18 percent forest and woods, and only 51 percent fit for sowing, wine growing, or for olives

---

ANTONELLO GERBI was born in 1904 in Florence. In 1925 he became Doctor of Law at Rome University; in 1927 he passed the barrister's examinations and was admitted to plead before the Milan Court of Appeal. From 1929 to 1931 he was Rockefeller Fellow (Division of Social and Economic Sciences), studying at Berlin University under Professor Friedrich Meinecke, at the London School of Economics under Harold Laski and others, and at the University of Vienna, under Professor A. F. Pribram. In 1933 he was nominated "libero docente" at Rome and attached in that capacity to Milan University. From 1935 to 1938 he gave courses in the history of political ideas. He was head of the Economic Research Department of the Banca Commerciale Italiana at Milan from 1932 to 1939. In 1938 he was sent on a mission to Peru, retained by the Banco Italiano—Lima, later (1942) the Banco de Crédito del Perú, to organize and direct the economic department (1939–1948). In 1948 on the invitation of the Banca Commerciale Italiana, he resumed his old job as director of the Economic Research Department at Milan. He has written *La Politica del Settecento* (Bari, 1928); *La Politica del Romanticismo* (Bari, 1932); *Il Peccato d'Adamo ed Eva, Storia dell' ipotesi di Beverland* (Milan, 1933); *El Perú en marcha. Ensayo de geografía económica* (Lima, 1941); *The Japanese in Peru* (New York, 1942); *Caminos del Perú. Historia y actualidad de las comunicaciones viales* (Lima, 1944); and *Viejas Polémicas sobre el nuevo mundo* (3d ed., Lima, 1946; Italian edition forthcoming); as well as several professional and technical pamphlets, handbooks, and reports, all unsigned.

or orchards. That is the picture today, after man has toiled for 25 centuries to redeem marshy ground, to water treeless plains, to harness rivers and deltas, to build upon mountainous slopes, or to cut out of rocks flights of terraces for vineyards and orchards, in an unceasing struggle to wrest cultivable space from a topography barren and frustrating. Nor is there any compensation for the dearth of arable land in the chemical composition of the humus or in the imaginary blessings of the climate. Only with great difficulty has production been maintained on a subsistence level, and then only by abundant use of fertilizers, by dint of hard work, and thanks to the skill of the Italian farmer, who is deeply rooted in and attached to his piece of land—in some regions also through a peculiar form of ownership. Mechanization is being introduced: some 80,000 tractors and 35,000 threshing machines are now in use.

The mineral resources are meager. Iron ore is scarce (found only on the island of Elba and in the Valley of Aosta) and so is coal. The same applies to non-ferrous metals, generally also most unsuitably located. The output of oil wells is insignificant. Only secondary products give returns of some significance, such as sulphur, mercury, marble, and of recent years natural gas. Obviously, Nature did not intend Italy to be an industrial country either.

Despite these handicaps, Italy has managed in the course of centuries to develop an agriculture and an industry of no mean dimensions and also, to a minor degree, a mining industry, thus providing a livelihood to a population which has grown rapidly from 27 millions in 1871 (when Italian unity was completed) to 38 millions in 1921 and 47 millions in 1951, leaving out of account the 10 million Italians who, in the meantime, have emigrated. It has all been done by exploiting to the utmost the scanty natural resources, above mentioned, and others created meanwhile, mainly hydroelectric power.

It has called, of course, for a rigid containment of consumption, for a constant encouragement of saving, almost to the point of sacrifice, as well as for finance and credit policies, careful and vigilant, bent on making full use of all available monetary means.

Today Italy produces nearly all the cereals required for home consumption and has become a large exporter of fruit, citrus products, vegetables, rice, hemp, and silk. Italian textile mills are equipped with 200,000 looms and 7,600,000 spindles, electricity plants with an installed power of 9,600,000 kilowatts; engineering works of worldwide repute and a comprehensive and varied industrial organization have turned out in 1952 goods worth 3,700,000 million lire, equal to one half of the net product of the whole private economy. Credit for this achievement goes to various contributing factors and, to no small extent, to the efficient and courageous national banking system. The history of Italian exchange dealers and moneylenders of the Middle Ages and Renaissance, the fact that Italy still possesses some of the oldest banking institutions in the world, the so oft-recalled traditions of Lombard Street, and the fact that, as in the musical vocabulary, so many Italian banking terms are still of universal currency, have perhaps overshadowed the more recent, remarkable if less glamorous performance of the present-day Italian banking institutions, none of which has had in these last 30 years the publicity, unenviable as it may have been, which on occasion of financial crashes or entanglements has brought banks in other countries so spectacularly into the limelight.

The ways and means of this development will be outlined in this paper. As we shall be dealing chiefly with the last few years, it might be pointed out at this stage that it was the banks which provided the finance required to build up Italy's basic economic structure (land and sea transport, communications, harbors, and the like) in cooperation, at times also in competition, with the state. Theirs was the channel through which foreign capital has come to the aid of the inadequate national resources; they helped exporters in the search of new outlets and facilitated the purchase of raw materials, of capital and consumption goods; they were also more than once of decisive help to the Treasury for its current and extraordinary needs and, last but not least, they managed to emerge structurally intact from times of war and inflation and from a situation which during the last war had split the country in two separate units, cut off from each other by the fluctuating front of military operations.

Their action in support of foreign trade also calls for special mention. A country so poor in primary products can pay for its imports only by reexporting as manufactures a large part of the goods imported and, naturally, part of its own agricultural output. The circumstances call for fluid and flexible export tactics, for a mass of sundry and fractional export contingents to all parts of the world, in an intense and unflinching effort to reach a maximum total. The aggregate volume of exports and imports now represents normally something like 20 percent of the gross national income. Most of the relative finance is provided by no more than half a dozen banks. Even in these times of complicated trade procedures their services seem to be highly appreciated both by their customers at home and by their correspondents abroad.

CREDIT NEEDS AND THE MEASURE OF THEIR SATISFACTION

In practically all productive fields credit requirements are higher than available resources. Italians are notoriously a frugal and thrifty people; a high proportion indeed of earnings goes into savings and yet it is not sufficient to cover current needs. Nor are there, as in other countries, potential sources of credit outside the banking system, such as insurance companies or *notaires* who, in other parts of the European continent, manage large private funds, or wholesale merchants capable of financing crops out of their own means. Hence the constant strain on the money and capital market and a cost of money unquestionably high, with its familiar train of embarrassing problems. Two of the chief repercussions are, first of all, the incidence of expensive banking accommodation on industrial costs, and secondly the burden on long-term finance for public works, housing, shipbuilding, and new electricity and telephone installations (new industrial plants being usually financed out of profits or by fresh issues of capital). For the banks it complicates the task of discriminating between credit takers through the customary differentiation in the matter of rates. The work of selecting debtors and supervising the utilization of credits granted consequently entails additional expenditure and absorbs a large part of the apparent wide margin between debit and credit rates. An adequate margin must be maintained and that, in its turn, prevents the banks from practicing in the matter of credit rates the liberality which might act as an incentive on the accumulation of deposits. It also compels them to keep debit rates on a level which is not conducive to a full utilization of facilities by all potential credit takers. In other words, it tends to restrict banking operations and to perpetuate a state of affairs in which credits are not fully used whilst banking services remain comparatively costly.

There is another side to the picture, less obvious, but more positive and more beneficial. The chief merit or justification of the high cost of money lies in the brake which it places on speculation and inflation, and in the priority which it gives to short-term business over operations calling for prolonged immobilization. It also helps to restrain tendencies to excessive liquidity.

The situation has, naturally, an effect also on the distribution of credit among the branches of the national economy. On the whole, and contrary to the criticism occasionally forthcoming from quarters perhaps not always unbiased, the Italian banking system caters quite effectively to the needs of the economy. There is some shortage of medium-term and long-term finance owing to the country's intrinsic poverty, also owing to its rapid demographic growth and the somewhat belated development of its financial market. Nonetheless it is a fact that the performance of the Italian banking system in regard to short-term accommodation has always come up to requirements, notwithstanding the comparatively modest structure and minor degree of elasticity of the money market; these two factors may have accentuated at times the pinch of a more severe selection of debtors or of an occasional brake on the normal flow of credit.

At the close of 1938 the whole Italian economy had at its disposal banking credits totaling some 35,000 million lire; from 1948 to 1952, during the five years of currency stability, the volume rose to 1,055,000, 1,378,000, 1,670,000, 1,980,000, and 2,404,000 millions, respectively; and it will probably be found that by the end of 1953 the latter figure had expanded by another 10 percent at least. It can be deduced that the volume of credit granted to the economy amounts practically to one quarter of the gross national income. If intervening currency adjustments are taken into account, the Italian banking system can rightly claim that its present contribution to the economy is appreciably higher than in prewar years. In fact, of the 35,000 millions of 1938 no less than 9,600 millions were to a large extent medium-term and long-term credits for building and kindred purposes to private customers and public bodies, and mainly granted by savings banks; at the end of 1952 that class of business accounted for only 264,000 millions, or barely twenty-seven times the prewar figure. There was a far greater expansion in the other branches of the economy, agriculture, industry, trade, public works and public services, agriculture alone with 683,900 millions against 7,400 millions in 1938, and industries and trades other than foodstuffs with 1,064,000 millions against 9,700 millions.

Long-term capital requirements are supplied primarily by a number of financial institutions (see pp. 478–92) whose activities have not, so far, kept pace with changed conditions. In 1938, in addition to the 35,000 millions of credits supplied by the banks to the economy, another 18,300 millions had been contributed from the aforesaid quarters: 8,800 millions by agencies for long-term industrial finance, 6,100 millions by mortgage banks and agencies for the financing of building activities, and 3,400 millions by others for agricultural development. By the end of 1952 this total had become 971,100 millions, divided into 697,000 millions from industrial finance institutions, 99,000 millions from mortgage banks and building finance agencies, and 175,200 millions for agricultural development. Whilst in 1938 these combined contributions accounted for above one third of the total of credit extended to the whole economy, by the end of 1952 the proportion had fallen to 28 percent. This bears out the contention that whatever deficiency there may be in the supply of credit is not due to a curtailment of current banking facilities, but must be sought in the domain of long-term loans for capital requirements.

Further and possibly even more striking evidence of the capacity of the Italian banking system to cope with present exigencies is provided by the remarkable growth of the number of clients during the 1948–52 period, a time of more subdued and guarded activity, of more cautious and restrained initiative, after the inflationary boom of the immediate postwar years. The number of credit takers kept on rising from year to year, from 1,570,000 at the end of 1948 to 1,950,000 in 1949, 2,258,000 at the end of 1950, and 2,603,000 at the end of 1952. Of these 2,603,000 one half are customers of the savings banks and of ancient institutions of the *Monte di Pegno* type, municipal agencies for private loans against some form of collateral. Of the rest a mere 100,000 (including, no doubt, all the leading Italian companies and firms) have been granted accommodation by one or the other of the three banks of national interest. This disposes of the insinuation that only "big people" have access to credit, allegedly denied to the "little man." It also shows that at the end of 1952 the average amount of credit to a customer was no higher than 923,000 lire, a comparatively low average due, of course, to the large number of small pawn-secured credits; incidentally it also gives an idea of the overhead charges which these small accounts entail for the banks, and helps to explain the necessity of keeping money rates at the present level. The fragmentation of credit does not affect the banks of national interest as much as other institutions; in their case the average amount of credit at the end of 1952 works out at some 7,000,000 lire against a bare 284,000 lire for the savings banks.

On the sources of corporate funds, fairly reliable figures are available as to the public issues of industrial shares and debentures:

(AMOUNTS IN BILLIONS OF LIRE)

Source	*1948*	*1949*	*1950*	*1951*	*1952*
Shares	86.1	89.6	65.5	81.4	107.0
Debentures	61.0	154.5	80.5	60.9	151.7

There is, however, a fairly widespread practice of self-finance or interlocking finance among companies forming part of single groups; in such cases the convenience of calling on the open market for fresh capital is often determined not only by the prospects of a satisfactory response, but also by the possibilities of internal finance; the above figures give, therefore, only a fractional and, in fact, fluctuating indication of the fresh capital invested from year to year.

For many years no figures have been published as to the actual destination of fresh capital issued; it can be taken that most of it has gone to the electricity, chemical and mining, engineering, and textile industries, whereas iron and steel, shipbuilding, and some branches of engineering have secured the necessary funds, for new plants or for current needs, through credits of the Istituto per la Ricostruzione Industriale (IRI) or through state subsidies.

TYPES OF CREDIT INSTRUMENTS IN USE

The credit instruments mostly in use are described below.

The *promissory note* (*pagherò cambiario*) corresponds practically to the Anglo-Saxon counterpart. It can be at sight or with fixed due date; it is subject to a progressive stamp duty which varies according to amount and duration, and is endorsable to order; in order to protect the holder in case of insolvency, certain legal formalities must be complied with (Royal Decree No. 1669, December 14, 1933).

The *bill of exchange* (*cambiale,* commonly known as *tratta*) is an order to pay and is subject to the same regulations as the promissory note; in fact, if and when accepted, it is equal to a promissory note (Royal Decree No. 1669, December 14, 1933).

The *check* (*assegno bancario,* also called *cheque*) is issued on a bank, to the drawer's own order or to the order of a third party, against the drawer's credit balance; it is also subject to stamp duty, but at the fixed rate of five lire apiece.

A *bank draft* (*vaglia cambiario* of the Bank of Italy or of the two former issuing banks, Banco di Napoli and Banco di Sicilia) is issued to order, generally endorsable, when not marked "not transferable." Those of the Bank of Italy are issued only against cash.

Credit certificates (*fedi di credito*) of the Banco di Napoli and Banco di Sicilia are special instruments inherited from the ancient traditions of these two banks; the certificates are the equivalent of bank drafts and endorsable with qualifying clauses (Royal Decree No. 1736, December 21, 1933).

Free bank drafts (*assegni bancari liberi*) are issued by authorized correspondents of the Bank of Italy, for account of the Bank of Italy. Like the Bank of Italy's own bank drafts, these are issued only against cash (Royal Decree No. 1736, December 21, 1933).

The *circular check* (*assegni circolari*) is a peculiar Italian instrument issued by a number of banks and institutions and backed by specific security, consisting of a 100 percent cover in government bonds. The check is endorsable (but may be "crossed") and is payable at sight at any branch of the issuing bank and with such of its correspondents with whom arrangements have been made to that effect (Royal Decree No. 1736, December 21, 1933).

Figures showing the circulation and relative importance of bank drafts, credit certificates, free bank drafts, and circular checks are given in Table 1, pp. 430–31.

Shares (*azioni*) are the usual equities, representative of fixed quotas in the share capital of limited liability companies. The issue of this type of stock is regulated by the Civil Code; in the past, shares could be issued either as bearer or registered stock, but under Royal Decree of October 25, 1941, all bearer shares had to be converted into registered shares. The existing legislation precludes the issue of shares with plural votes; those previously issued remain in force for the life of the issuing company. The total share capital of the existing

23,874 limited liability companies amounts to 1,865,000 million lire, and the total nominal amount listed at the stock exchanges to 789,000 millions with a present stock exchange value of about 1,500,000 millions.

Debentures or bonds (*obbligazioni*) are issued by industrial and commercial companies or by public institutions engaged in mortgage, land, building and agricultural finance, or by financial institutions in general. They bear interest at a fixed rate (at present, generally, between 6 percent and 7 percent for industrial issues, and from 4.5 to 6 percent for mortgage, building, and other types). The issue of debentures and bonds is regulated by the Civil Code and other special legislation; they may be in the shape of bearer or registered bonds.

Debentures issued by institutions of public right [1] carry a state guarantee which, in a subsidiary way, also covers a number of issues for mortgage and building finance; such issues are repayable on a graduated amortization plan (either by drawings or purchases on the market) over a period which varies from 10 to 50 years for mortgage and kindred credit, and from 10 to 30 years for other issues. Until December 31, 1949, they benefited by certain fiscal exemptions, which accounts for the large amounts issued in 1948 and 1949; the total at present outstanding is around 600,000 million lire.

Convertible debentures or bonds (*obbligazioni convertibili*) are a type of stock which, at the option of the holder, can be converted into shares, in whole or in part. This ensures a stable fixed income, plus, in some cases (debentures issued by IRI), a scaling up of the rate of interest, in proportion to the dividends paid on the share capital by the undertaking on whose behalf they have been issued. These bonds give the holder a twofold hedge against the risk of monetary devaluation. The present circulation amounts to about 59,000 million lire.

Government bonds (*cartelle di rendita statale*) include: consolidated (perpetual) or redeemable Government debts; debentures of

[1] There is no agreement among the jurists about the definition of "institutions of public right." Practically, they are those which were created by law as such, or acknowledged as such by law, if they already existed. Their main characteristics are: (a) no lucrative aims: the profits go to benevolent institutions, to the State or are ploughed back in the "patrimony" of the institution; (b) an activity of general interest; (c) the management is nominated by the Government, or at least the choice of the institution's organs must be ratified by an official supervisory authority. Among the most important are IMI, IRI, ICIPU, CCOP (see pp. 478–92) and, of course, the typical "credit institutions of public right" and the Bank of Italy (see pp. 492–507). The status of the savings banks is uncertain. Best American parallels: RFC, TVA and, from an institutional point of view, the Federal Reserve Banks.

TABLE 1
BANK DRAFTS AND CIRCULAR CHECKS IN CIRCULATION
DECEMBER 31, 1938 AND 1948–53
(AMOUNTS IN MILLIONS OF LIRE)

Year December 31	BANK OF ITALY: BANK DRAFTS Number	BANK OF ITALY: BANK DRAFTS Amount	BANK OF ITALY: FREE BANK DRAFTS Number	BANK OF ITALY: FREE BANK DRAFTS Amount	BANCO DI NAPOLI AND BANCO DI SICILIA: BANK DRAFTS, CREDIT CERTIFICATES, CHECKS ISSUED BY AUTHORIZED CORRESPONDENTS Number	BANCO DI NAPOLI AND BANCO DI SICILIA: BANK DRAFTS, CREDIT CERTIFICATES, CHECKS ISSUED BY AUTHORIZED CORRESPONDENTS Amount
1938	131,028	877	25,152	23	n.a.[a]	485
1948	310,042	15,674	108,588	1,267	1,021,963	27,736
1949	292,052	13,044	92,718	676	755,096	23,456
1950	162,000	13,472	67,000	884	776,000	24,534
1951	152,000	12,286	64,000	795	771,000	25,293
1952	156,000	14,512	56,000	524	539,000	25,442
1953						
May	157,000	12,016	53,000	464	497,000	20,806
June	157,000	12,040	53,000	466	476,000	21,824
July	166,000	13,899	54,000	525	523,000	29,515
August	159,000	11,890	53,000	493	528,000	23,808

Sources: *Bollettino del Servizio Studi Economici della Banca d'Italia* No. 7–8 (1950) and No. 5 (1953).
[a] Not available.
[b] Authorized by decree of February 11, 1943, to issue circular checks.

extinct railway companies taken over by the state; provincial and municipal bonds; and 5-year and 9-year Treasury bonds. They represent an aggregate of state and kindred funds of equal status with a circulation of about 1,077,000 million lire.

Ordinary Treasury bills (*Buoni del Tesoro ordinari*) are issued by the Treasury to bearer or to order, maturing in from one to twelve months and bearing an advance interest at progressive rates ranging from 2.75 to 4.50 percent. They are largely used by the banks for their compulsory reserves. The amount at present outstanding is over 931,000 million lire and constitutes about half of Italy's internal public debt.

Interest-bearing post office Bonds (*Buoni Postali fruttiferi*) are issued by the Post Office Savings Bank (that is, by the state). A bond of this kind has certain special features: it is a registered bond of no precise maturity; no fixed interest is paid at specific dates; the accumulated interest, calculated also on the interest accrued from year to

TABLE 1 (*Continued*)

AUTHORIZED BANKS		ISTITUTO DI CREDITO DELLE CASSE DI RISPARMIO ITALIANE		ISTITUTO CENTRALE DELLE BANCHE POPOLARI ITALIANE		TOTAL	
CIRCULAR CHECKS							
Number	*Amount*	*Number*	*Amount*	*Number*	*Amount*	*Number*	*Amount*
n.a.	955	137,265	140			n.a.	2,480
1,932,663	87,301	500,580	17,730	127,244 [b]	1,940	4,001,080	151,648
1,778,384	81,143	416,514	16,719	142,726	1,526	3,477,490	136,564
1,474,000	90,103	393,000	18,681	160,000	1,809	3,232,000	149,483
1,431,000	94,471	401,000	19,260	50,000	2,825	2,869,000	154,930
1,490,000	99,336	399,000	19,541	63,000	2,863	2,703,000	162,218
1,324,000	79,744	343,000	15,332	55,000	2,305	2,429,000	130,667
1,354,000	87,241	375,000	17,699	55,000	2,244	2,470,000	141,514
1,453,000	88,543	400,000	20,322	67,000	2,939	2,663,000	155,743
1,401,000	81,921	414,000	20,031	61,000	2,430	2,616,000	140,573

year, is paid together with the capital whenever the bond is presented for payment. The rate of interest rises from year to year during the life of the bond, at present from 3.75 percent for the first full year to a maximum of 5 percent after 15 years. These bonds represent nowadays by far the largest part of the deposits with the Post Office Savings Bank; at the end of October, 1953, the circulation totaled 978,400 million lire.

Documents of title to goods (*titoli di credito rappresentativi delle merci*) are substantially equivalent to international instruments of a similar nature. They include: bills of lading (*polizze di carico*) made out to bearer or to order, for sea transport, and, for land transport, duplicates of the railroad bill (*duplicato della lettera di vettura*) issued by the carrier; warehouse receipts (*fedi di deposito*) and letters of lien (*note di pegno*), which are issued by the general warehouses and which, whether or not they are attached to bills of exchange (documentary drafts), are eligible for loans on the security of the goods covered by the title.

BANKING AND CREDIT INSTITUTIONS

A catalogue of credit institutions can be compiled by following various criteria: according to their legal status, whether private or public, according to the sources of their means (deposits, notes, and bonds or debentures), and according to the nature of their operations (short, medium term, and long term). The Italian banking system does not fit very closely into any one of these classifications. However, the following tabulation attempts to group banks according to function.

	PRINCIPAL MEANS		
	Type	*Amounts in Millions of Lire*	*Date*
A. *Bank of Italy* (issuing bank and supreme controller of credit and circulation)	Note issue	1,307,500	September 30, 1953
B. *Commercial Banks*			
a) Ordinary credit banks of national interest			
(1) Banca Commerciale Italiana, Milan	Deposits	448,200	September 30, 1953
(2) Credito Italiano, Milan	Deposits	312,600	September 30, 1953
(3) Banco di Roma, Rome	Deposits	365,200	December 31, 1952
Total		1,060,200	December 31, 1952
b) Credit institutions of public right which also, and in some cases mainly, transact the same class of business as commercial banks; there are six of these			
(1) Banco di Napoli, Naples	Deposits	247,500	December 31, 1952
(2) Banco di Sicilia, Palermo	Deposits	152,900	December 31, 1952
(3) Banca Nazionale del Lavoro, Rome	Deposits	425,900	September 30, 1953
(4) Istituto Bancario San Paolo di Torino, Turin	Deposits	68,600	September 30, 1953
(5) Monte dei Paschi di Siena, Siena	Deposits	110,200	September 30, 1953
(6) Banco di Sardegna, Cagliari	Patrimony	2,709	December 31, 1952
Total	Deposits	966,900	December 31, 1952
c) Popular cooperative banks; on Dec. 31, 1952, they numbered 220, and the deposits of 122 of them amounted to about	Deposits	410,112	September 30, 1953
The most important of these banks are:			
(1) Banca Popolare di Novara, Novara	Deposits	175,400	September 30, 1953
(2) Banca Popolare di Milano, Milan	Deposits	54,300	September 30, 1953
They are grouped in the Istituto Centrale delle Banche Popolari Italiane with which they deposit their excess funds, and which issues circular checks on behalf of its minor associates. The Novara and Milan banks issue their own checks.			

	PRINCIPAL MEANS		
	Type	*Amounts in Millions of Lire*	*Date*
d) Smaller ordinary credit banks, numbering about 150 with total	Deposits	813,100	December 31, 1952
The most important are:			
(1) Banca d'America e d'Italia, Rome	Deposits	89,300	December 31, 1952
(2) Banca Nazionale dell'Agricoltura, Rome	Deposits	99,700	September 30, 1953
(3) Banco Ambrosiano, Milan	Deposits	74,300	September 30, 1953
e) Private banks and bankers [2]			
C. *Savings Banks*			
a) Ordinary savings banks: semi-public institutions with varying and elastic functions; altogether 81 with deposits totaling	Deposits	740,300	September 30, 1953
The most important are:			
(1) Cassa di Risparmio delle Provincie Lombarde, Milan	Deposits	163,900	September 30, 1953
(2) Cassa di Risparmio di Torino, Turin	Deposits	50,100	December 31, 1952
(3) Cassa di Risparmio di Verona, Vicenza e Belluno, Verona	Deposits	31,700	December 31, 1952
Practically all the savings banks are linked to a credit institution (Istituto di Credito delle Casse di Risparmio Italiane, Rome) which issues circular checks on behalf of its associates.			
b) Post Office Savings Bank for the gathering of savings mostly in rural regions, the monies so collected being administered by the Cassa Depositi e Prestiti	Deposits	1,080,900	September 30, 1953
D. *Mortgage Banks and Building Finance Institutions*			
The leading institutions of public right and the bigger savings banks (Provincie Lombarde and Bologna) run special departments for this type of finance which is also a specialty of a few other institutions:			
(1) Istituto Italiano di Credito Fondiario, Rome	Bonds	13,600	December 31, 1952
(2) Istituto di Credito Fondiario delle Venezie, Verona	Bonds	15,800	December 31, 1952
(3) Istituto di Credito Fondiario della Regione Tridentina, Trento	Bonds	1,900	December 31, 1952
(4) Credito Fondiario Sardo, Rome	Bonds	6,000	December 31, 1952
(5) Istituto Nazionale di Credito Edilizio, Rome	Bonds	10,700	December 31, 1952

[2] The private banks' deposits are included in the figure for the smaller ordinary credit banks.

	Principal Means		
	Type	*Amounts in Millions of Lire*	*Date*
E. *Institutions for Agricultural Credit* The main business is transacted by the agricultural departments of the leading savings banks, of the Banco di Napoli, Banco di Sicilia, and a few other institutions especially authorized. In Piedmont, Liguria, Tuscany, Central Italy, Sardinia, and for the province of Ferrara there are special institutions for agricultural credit, whose activities are supplemented by the Consorzio Nazionale per il Credito Agrario di Miglioramento, Rome	Aggregate means	107,900	December 31, 1952
This group has a background of smaller local and rural institutions which is, however, of very limited importance.			
F. *Financial Institutions for Medium and Long-term Industrial Finance*			
a) Of a public character:			
(1) Istituto per la Ricostruzione Industriale (IRI), which holds the control of the three banks of national interest and disposes of capital means of 120,000 millions, apart from other resources	Debentures outstanding, State subsidies, and creditors	191,400	December 31, 1952
(2) Istituto Mobiliare Italiano (IMI): grants credits up to 10 years and acts as intermediary for loans of the Export-Import Bank (U.S.A.) and under the Marshall Plan	Debentures outstanding: ordinary administration	129,700	December 31, 1952
	administration on behalf of government	295,900	December 31, 1952
(3) Consorzio di Credito per le Opere Pubbliche	Debentures outstanding (including dollar issues)	141,600	December 31, 1952

	PRINCIPAL MEANS		
	Type	*Amounts in Millions of Lire*	*Date*
(4) Istituto di Credito per le Imprese di Pubblica Utilità (ICIPU)	Debentures outstanding (including dollar and Swiss francs issues)	113,300	December 31, 1952
(5) Consorzio per Sovvenzioni su Valori Industriali, an appendix to the Bank of Italy	bonds outstanding and bills rediscounted	15,400	December 31, 1952
b) Of a private character:			
(1) Banca di Credito Finanziario (Mediobanca) whose capital is held by the 3 banks of national interest	Deposits	30,300	June 30, 1953
(2) Banca Centrale per il Credito Mobiliare (Centrobanca) whose capital is owned by the popular banks	Capital	300	December 31, 1952
(3) Ente Finanziamenti Industriali (EFI) formed by a number of industrial companies	Deposit certificates and current accounts	5,300	December 31, 1952
(4) Società Italiana per le Strade Ferrate Meridionali, converted into a holding company in 1906, after its network of railways had been taken over by the State, and now mainly engaged in electricity finance	Capital and reserves	23,700	December 31, 1952
G. *Regional institutions granting medium-term credits to medium and small enterprises*			
(1) Istituto di credito per il finanziamento alla media e piccola industria del Piemonte, Turin	Patrimony	300	September 30, 1953
(2) Istituto di credito per il finanziamento a medio termine alle medie e piccole industrie della Lombardia, Milan	Patrimony	600	September 30, 1953
(3) Istituto per l'esercizio del credito a medio e lungo termine nella regione Trentino Alto-Adige, Trent	Patrimony	1,500	September 30, 1953
(4) Istituto di credito per il finanziamento a medio termine alle medie			

	PRINCIPAL MEANS		
	Type	*Amounts in Millions of Lire*	*Date*
e piccole industrie dell'Umbria, Perugia	Patrimony	100	September 30, 1953
(5) Istituto di credito per il finanziamento a medio termine alle medie e piccole industrie delle Marche, Ancona	Patrimony	100	September 30, 1953
(6) Istituto di credito per il finanziamento a medio termine delle medie e piccole industrie del Lazio, Rome	Patrimony	200	September 30, 1953
(7) Istituto per lo sviluppo economico dell'Italia meridionale (ISVEIMER), Naples	Patrimony	1,000	August 31, 1953
(8) Istituto regionale per il finanziamento alle medie e piccole industrie in Sicilia (IRFIS), Palermo	Patrimony	2,120	August 31, 1953
(9) Credito industriale sardo (CIS), Cagliari		not yet known	
All these institutions are provided with additional funds by the Istituto centrale per il credito a medio termine a favore delle medie e piccole industrie (Mediocredito), Rome	Patrimony	60,000	September 30, 1953
H. *Cassa per il Credito alle Imprese Artigiane (Artigiancassa), Rome* Under its new statute, it may grant credits to artisans through the intermediary of a credit institution of public right (see above, B,*b*), a savings bank (see above, C), a popular cooperative bank (see above, B,*b*), and so forth.	Patrimony	5,500	September 30, 1953

The catalogue should be completed with a reference to the Italian branches of foreign banks (French and Argentinian) whose importance is, however, very limited and inclined to shrink further. The National City Bank of New York closed its Milan branch in 1939, and in 1950 Barclays Bank transferred its Italian subsidiary to the Banca Commerciale Italiana. It should be recorded that a few private commercial banks are under foreign (North American and Swiss) control.

COMMERCIAL BANKS

We have seen that commercial banking is the business of five separate groups of institutions. Those of the first two groups are by far the most important; they include all institutions of a national character and all the principal regional banks. The difference between them is that the three banks of "national interest" have a private ownership structure and are constituted as limited liability companies with a share capital. Of the six banks of a public character, two (Banco di Napoli and Banco di Sicilia) were previously issuing banks, another (Banca Nazionale del Lavoro) was founded and is still entirely owned by the state, and another (Banco di Sardegna) was also founded by the State to promote the island's economic development; the others are ancient foundations whose profits were used for public assistance and charity, and subsequently, in the course of centuries, turned into institutions of a predominant banking type. The institutions of the second group work with a fund of their own (the Banca Nazionale del Lavoro, with a capital entirely in the hands of the State) and operate in zones traditionally defined (except the Banca Nazionale del Lavoro whose activities cover the whole peninsula). It is true that they tend to expand beyond their original boundaries, in competition with the typical "national" banks and also among themselves, although not trespassing on their respective homelands. Thus the Banco di Napoli still holds a prior position in the southern parts of the peninsula, in what used to be the Kingdom of Naples, with the Banco di Sicilia in the front line on the island of Sicily and the Banco di San Paolo strongly entrenched in Piedmont and the Monte dei Paschi di Siena in Tuscany.

Classification as a member of the first group (credit banks of national interest) is restricted by law to banks with branches in at least 30 provinces (the republic of Italy numbers 90 provinces); every one of them is, in fact, established in some 120 places, including all the chief economic centers. Since industries are located chiefly in northern and central Italy, these chains of branches are not evenly distributed over the whole country. The overwhelming majority of the capital of these three banks is in the hands of a single shareholder, IRI; but they compete freely with each other, nonetheless, also in their endeavors to secure a foothold in such places as are not yet adequately served and for permits to open subsidiary agencies in the big centers in which they are already established.

There is certainly something strange, but also highly instructive, in an arrangement whereby one central bank holding company, IRI, far from moderating or coordinating the action of the several banks under its control, actually stimulates rivalry among them, restricting its control to internal administration, as if these three banks were independent subsidiaries operating in different countries. There is no gainsaying the fact that the policy has been to the advantage of the national economy and of the respective profit and loss accounts. The common legal bond has not prevented the three banks from preserving distinct personalities or from pursuing distinctive credit policies and, within given limits, separate programs of national and sectional expansion. The distinct personalities of the Banca Commerciale Italiana, Credito Italiano, and Banco di Roma are quite obvious to anyone with the slightest familiarity with Italian affairs.

The popular cooperative banks do not, in practice, differ very much from the foregoing; the banking law places them on the same footing as the credit institutions in general. They were originally established —the most important of them as far back as 1864–74—as cooperative banks, that is to say for the purpose of granting credit accommodation exclusively to their own shareholders and mostly on the security of their own shares. With the growth of deposits they found it necessary to look for credit takers outside this inner circle, outside the limits implied in the principle of mutuality, a departure from the original scope that provoked endless controversies at the time. Eventually they all adopted that course and ended by becoming ordinary local and regional banks. It widened their fields of activity considerably and, when their credit business actually exceeded the amount of their deposits, they turned to the bigger banks with whom they used currently to rediscount their holdings of commercial bills.

With this advent into the wider field of banking they became subject, of course, to the law of selection and survival which gradually eliminated those which did not fulfill any particular or useful purpose, complementary to the work done by the bigger banks, or those which had not, like the Banca Popolare di Novara or the Banca Popolare di Milano, developed into institutions of major caliber. At the beginning of the present century they numbered nearly 700; some time after the First World War their ranks had swollen to the record figure of 829, only to dwindle rapidly to 373 in 1935, and 220 in 1952. They are free to engage in banking business of every description. Constitutionally they differ from the other banks only in one respect: no single shareholder may hold more than 500,000 lire of shares or exercise more than one voting right, irrespective of the number of shares held. In practice, all of them, including the powerful Banca Popolare di Milano, confine their activities to their home province, but the biggest of all, the Banca Popolare di Novara, has a network of 80 branches and 160 subagencies, spread over 5 regions: Piedmont, Lombardy, Liguria, Venetia, and Latium; it also transacts a fairly active foreign business.

The category of smaller ordinary credit banks embraces about 150 institutions, mostly of a regional or purely local character. It comprises institutions with ancient traditions and wide circles of faithful customers; often they are deeply rooted in local affairs, very active, almost irreplaceable in the services which they perform. The bigger ones are no longer regional banks. The Banca d'America e d'Italia, connected with the Giannini group in the United States, has a network of branches which runs, horizontally, from Trieste on the Adriatic Sea to San Remo on the Mediterranean, and, vertically, from Turin in the upper north right down to Bari in the south. The Banca Nazionale dell'Agricoltura has about 100 branches and subagencies, mostly in agricultural and cattle breeding regions, but is also established in all the leading financial centers and has two offices in Germany, that country being once more the main outlet for Italian fruit and vegetable exports. The Banco Ambrosiano's head office and chief center of business is, of course, in Milan, the city of St. Ambrose, but it operates also outside the precincts of Lombardy, with establishments in the neighboring towns of Alessandria and Piacenza, and in five of Italy's chief financial centers, from Turin southwards to Rome.

These are the most conspicuous examples of a tendency to depart from the original pattern, to widen the erstwhile zone of action and sphere of clients (in this case mostly farmers, ecclesiastics, and importers from the United States) and to expand from the original local status into the wider arena of national banking. The group has given proof, unquestionably, of remarkable vitality and, at times, even of moderate expansive tendencies.

With the private banks the picture is just the reverse. Since 1938 their number has been halved, by liquidation, amalgamation, or conversion into limited liability companies. The survivors are mostly to be found in Milan and in a few other centers, and generally operate on behalf of restricted circles of wealthy private clients; they usually have a substantial sideline business, consisting mostly of mortgage finance and large advances against security (the smaller business of that type being the domain of the Monti di Pegno), also of stock exchange finance. Their legal status and the extreme discretion which surrounds their activities make it practically impossible to gauge the size of their operations. They serve a useful purpose in many ways, also as customers of the big banks and intermediaries between the latter and the less accessible circles of private clients.

NUMBER OF BRANCHES IN ITALY AND ABROAD

The commercial banks so far described have an aggregate network of 4,914 offices; the figure includes a number of agencies of the southern banks which do little else except receive deposits and should, therefore, rank as savings banks. The savings banks, in their turn, have 2,162 offices and subagencies, and their numbers grow from year to year. The smallest banks (*casse rurali e artigiane*), which are spread over the countryside and cater to the smaller tradesmen and artisans, have only about 703 offices and, in this case, the numbers tend to shrink. The whole Italian banking system has nearly 7,850 offices distributed in some 4,000 localities which means that about 50 percent of Italian municipalities have banking places.

The distribution is not, of course, always very even. All the places of some significance have more than one bank; a few of them appear, in fact, to be overbanked, owing to the invasion of outside institutions which, traditionally, belong to and operate in other, and in some cases rather distant, regions. On the other hand there is room for further expansion in the matter of local subagencies; that side of the general development has not always kept pace with the rapid growth of the larger centers. The opening of new branches is subject to a permit of the interministerial credit commission which applies rather restrictive principles: in 1950 it turned down about 500 out of 800 applications submitted, giving preference to the smaller banks and for such places as appeared to be inadequately served. In 1952, out of 292 applications, only 10 permits were granted, 8 of them to savings banks.

Foreign banking is an old Italian tradition, either through direct branches abroad or through participation in foreign institutions. It has always followed and promoted trade and emigration. Consequently the former pattern of foreign branches and affiliations has been profoundly affected, first by the financial crisis of the early thirties and subsequently by the Second World War. Those established in Austria, Poland, and Czechoslovakia had been closed or otherwise disposed of before 1938; at the outbreak of the Second World War the London and United States branches and some of the South American Associates were placed under official control; those in the Balkans were expropriated, and those in the former Italian colonies have lost practically all their business.

Expansion abroad has been the merit, almost exclusively, of the three banks of national interest, the spearhead being the Banca Commerciale Italiana, right from the beginning of the present century. The Credito Italiano followed suit; in the Balkans it had only one subsidiary, in Dalmatia, but in the Far East it created the Italian Bank of China. The Banco di Roma concentrated on the Levant (Syria, Palestine, Egypt, Turkey, and Malta), going so far as Iraq, with a branch at Baghdad and no less than 16 branches in Italian East Africa. Of the other banks the only one calling for special mention is the Banco di Napoli which had opened branches not only in the former Italian colonies, but also in New York and Buenos Aires, that is, in the centers which attracted the main currents of Italian emigration.

The present situation leaves the Banca Commerciale Italiana in the front rank in the matter of foreign banking with its two branches in Turkey (Istanbul and Izmir) and a number of associated banks: one across the Swiss border (in the Canton Ticino), one in France (with branches on the Riviera and in Marseilles), and others in Egypt (Cairo), in Lebanon (Beyreuth), and in Morocco (Casablanca). In addition, through the Banque Française et Italienne pour l'Amérique du Sud (in whose capital the Banque de Paris et des Pays-Bas and the Banque de l'Indochine are also interested), its influence extends to seven of the South American republics (Argentina, Brazil, Chile, Peru, Colombia, Uruguay, and Venezuela). The same bank has its own representatives in London, New York, Paris, and Frankfort.

The Credito Italiano has an affiliate in Egypt (in joint account with the Banco di Roma) and an associate in Belgium whose activities extend to the Argentine, Brazil and Uruguay; it also has six representative offices, including one in São Paulo and another in Bombay.

The Banco di Roma has branches of its own in Turkey, Lebanon, and in Egypt (the latter in joint account with the Credito Italiano) and affiliates in Switzerland (Canton Ticino), France, and Belgium, in addition to four representative offices in other countries.

GOVERNMENT SUPERVISION AND CONTROL: RESERVE REQUIREMENTS

The commercial banks, in fact all the banks, including the savings banks and other institutions, are governed by the Banking Law (Royal Decree March 12, 1936, No. 375) elaborated after the international financial crisis of the early thirties and based, similarly to banking reforms introduced elsewhere, on two fundamental principles:

1. The taking of deposits and the granting of credit are matters of public concern.

2. Financial credit is to be completely dissociated from ordinary credit.

The first of these two principles is embodied in a set of provisions whereby the creation of new credit institutions and subsequent admission to the special register are subject to official sanction. Supervision is exercised by a special body (instituted at the Bank of Italy), all other companies or firms being debarred from taking deposits except from their own directors, partners, officials, and employees. The privilege of taking deposits from the public is thus confined to specific institutions. The institutions eligible for that class of business are subject to a number of official controls and must conform to certain percentages and proportions between their capital and the monies they hold for account of third parties. The ratios of liquidity and of credits granted to customers are similarly governed by specific provisions. The whole set of rules and regulations is designed to ensure the safety of the funds entrusted to their care.

The second principle, as formulated, is the practical and legal enactment of a policy which the banks had then already adopted, in agreement with the higher authorities (Treasury and Central Bank), through a demobilization of assets which had become necessary at the height of the 1931–32 crisis. The three leading commercial banks (those now called "banks of national interest") and some minor institutions transferred all their holdings of shares and stocks, as well as their financial credits, to an institution created for the purpose (IRI) and, thereafter, confined their business to the field of ordinary credit in all its forms.

The principle is not formally enunciated in the Banking Law. The ordinary credit banks have continued to extend certain credit facilities at medium term, when called for by the normal cycle of production, and no objection has been raised by the supervisory organs except in such cases where excess might have been prejudicial to the banks concerned. The savings banks and the credit institutions of public right have continued to give credit also on long term, not necessarily always in connection with industrial activities, granting mortgage and similar credits or discounting state annuities, but always within the limits laid down by their own statutes. The banks of national interest themselves have, on occasion, been authorized to invest limited amounts on a long-term basis, particularly for purposes connected with the national defense. They are forbidden to engage in agricultural credits, except for the financing of "pool" consignments.

The same elasticity has been applied in regard to the minimum percentages for the compulsory security deposits. The necessity to depart from the original scheme arose with the devaluation of the lira by about 98 percent. Bank capital lagged far behind the nominal increase of all assets and liabilities. Now bank capital has increased and increased progressively, but, of course, at a slower pace than the expansion of deposits and credits.

The maximum credit to any single client had been fixed at one-fifth of the bank's own capital resources. With the deterioration of the currency a certain flexibility in the application of this regulation was felt to be desirable.[3] The banks still have to apply for official sanction to exceed this credit limit, but authority has been granted in 99 out of 100 cases; some 4,500 applications (for 821,000 million lire) and another 4,725 (for 936,000 millions) were sanctioned in 1951 and 1952 respectively. A new scheme is under consideration for fixing the limit of credit not only in proportion to the capital, but also to the deposits; the prospects are, however, still somewhat remote.

On the other hand, in August, 1947, new rules for the ratio of capital and deposits were issued to replace those previously in force. There had been frequent applications for permission to depart from the original terms. But for the necessity which arose in August–September, 1947, to curb inflation and to invest the Bank of Italy with wider powers of control over credit, nothing might have been done to establish a new regime. Theretofore, the credit institutions were under obligation to invest in government securities, to be lodged with the Bank of Italy, or to transfer to the latter in cash such quota of their deposits as exceeded a twentyfold (from March, 1946, onwards a

[3] Bank of Italy, *Annual Report 1949*, Rome, 1950, p. 269.

thirtyfold) amount of their capital resources; in other words, the capital was to represent 5 percent (later 3.33 percent) of the whole mass of deposits. Since October, 1947, the banks are required to invest in government securities or to transfer to the Bank of Italy 40 percent of the new deposits, until the funds so invested amount to 25 percent of their whole deposits. With the large increase of deposits since the end of 1947 the lower 25 percent ratio to be so invested or deposited has now become effective. In case of a falling-off of deposits the banks can, of course, immediately withdraw from the Bank of Italy or from the Treasury a corresponding amount of securities or cash. These compulsory deposits constitute a liquidity reserve which allows the credit institutions to keep cash on hand at a considerably lower level. As the latter bears practically no interest, whilst the funds deposited with the Bank of Italy give an appreciable return,[4] the whole arrangement is, ultimately, to the advantage of the banks.

The central bank has thus been provided with a considerable amount of money—more than 425,000 millions at the end of 1953—and also with a useful instrument for influencing the market. At one time, under the menace of credit stringency, it had been suggested that the compulsory ratio of 25 percent might be reduced to 22 percent. Nothing has been done so far, but it is not to be ruled out that, at some future date, the Bank of Italy may adopt tactics similar to those of the Federal Reserve system in regard to its member banks and change reserve requirements.

The history of the ratio for compulsory deposits reveals the growing inadequacy of the capital resources to the size of the services which the banks are called upon to perform. The proof lies in their balance sheets: in comparison with the prewar period credit and debit items have gone up from 50 to 60 times, capital resources only 8.5 times.

ADEQUACY OF CAPITAL FUNDS; ASSETS AND LIABILITIES

The process of bringing capital resources into line with requirements is still going on; fresh and substantial increases of capital may

[4] These deposits yielded an interest equal to the one-year ordinary Treasury bonds, less .25 percent. Ordinary Treasury bonds being then 5 percent bonds, the rate for compulsory deposits was calculated at 4.75 percent. Interest on the bonds having been reduced to 4.5 percent (April, 1949) and to 4 percent (May, 1952), paid in advance, equal, therefore, to 4.71 percent and 4.16 percent respectively, the rate on banking compulsory deposits was reduced to 4.25 percent (May, 1952). Thus, the return is the same whether banks keep compulsory deposits on current account with the Bank of Italy or invest them in ordinary Treasury bonds.

be anticipated over the next few years; this is possibly the only item of the balance sheets about which forecasts can be made with some degree of certainty. At the close of 1948 the ratio of capital resources to total liabilities had fallen to 1:90.[5] Some progress has been made since then, the aggregate capital resources of the commercial and kindred banks having gone up by nearly 200 percent, but their liabilities have grown too at almost the same pace: the ratio, therefore, has risen only to 1.6 percent.

The main observation that emerges from an examination of the changes which have taken place under the other chief headings is the stability of their proportional distribution. During 1948–51, the chief items (deposits, holdings of securities, and profit earnings) rose by about two thirds—a truly remarkable expansion over a limited period of three years; translated into percentages, the proportion to the total of the balance sheets at the end of 1951 is still, however, much the same as at the end of 1948. On the debit side fiduciary deposits (that is, savings) remain on a 28–29 percent level, with current accounts (that is, demand deposits of commerce and industry) almost unchanged at about 50 percent of total liabilities. The same holds good for the years 1951–53, during which total deposits rose by almost 50 percent. The distribution is less favorable than in prewar times when fiduciary deposits, generally more stable, were comparatively higher.

As regards deposits, the trend is upwards, but the increase has become effective (in real terms) only since 1948; that is, since currency stability has been maintained. Deposit fluctuations also show seasonal influences; these are pronounced in the later months of the year after the harvesting of the crops and tend to sag or fall in the early spring. It is difficult to state with accuracy the interest paid to depositors at the beginning of 1954. Since 1932 the maximum rate on deposits and current accounts has been regulated by legal provisions which originated from an agreement previously made among the banks and to which we shall revert at a later stage. The last change before 1954 goes back to February, 1945; it laid down a rate of .5 percent on sight accounts, with 1 percent on savings deposits, and 2 percent on time deposits of 6 months or longer. In practice the agreement was infringed very frequently, especially where substantial balances were concerned;

[5] "Total liabilities" include also capital resources, drafts in circulation, and sundry creditors: G. Menghini, "Considerazioni sul capitale delle aziende di credito italiane,' *Moneta e credito,* III, 4 (1950), 472–473.

TABLE 2

PRINCIPAL ITEMS FROM THE BALANCE SHEETS OF THE INSTITUTIONS OF PUBLIC RIGHT (5), BANKS OF NATIONAL INTEREST (3), ORDINARY CREDIT BANKS (150), AND POPULAR COOPERATIVE BANKS (122), DECEMBER 31, 1938–JUNE, 1953

(AMOUNTS IN BILLIONS OF LIRE)

	1938 [a]		1948		1949		1950		1951		1952		1953	
Assets	*Amount*	*Percent of Total*	*Amount*	*Percent of Total*	*Amount*	*Percent of Total*	*Amount*	*Percent of Total*	*Amount*	*Percent of Total*	*Amount*	*Percent of Total*	*Amount*	*Percent of Total*
Cash on hand and with other banks	9.3	11.2	293.4	16.3	430.2	19.2	431.8	16.2	552.0	16.9	646.8	16.6	582.6	14.6
Securities	17.0	20.5	336.1	18.7	354.8	15.9	467.6	17.5	566.3	17.3	670.0	17.2	720.2	18.1
Bills	18.3	22.0	290.8	16.2	415.2	18.6	479.5	18.0	560.5	17.1	737.3	19.0	781.5	19.6
Loans	12.4	14.9	489.1	27.2	599.9	26.9	711.2	26.6	865.1	26.4	1,088.3	28.0	1,140.7	28.6
Contango loans	1.6	1.9	45.5	2.5	40.2	1.8	47.2	1.8	63.5	1.9	88.8	2.3	95.8	2.4
Advances on securities	5.1	6.1	35.4	2.0	41.0	1.8	52.2	2.0	31.6	1.0	61.8	1.6	51.1	1.3
Foreign currencies and balances abroad			153.8	8.6	142.3	6.4	214.6	8.0	303.2	9.3	239.4	6.2	216.5	5.4
Total (with other items)	83.0	100.0	1,796.4	100.0	2,235.6	100.0	2,668.4	100.0	3,275.5	100.0	3,887.6	100.0	3,987.0	100.0
Liabilities [b]														
Capital and reserves	7.3	8.9	20.0	1.1	31.9	1.4	39.8	1.5	48.2	1.5	56.6	1.5	60.9	1.5
Deposits														
At sight	38.3	46.5	528.8	29.6	665.0	29.9	642.1	24.2	741.7	22.8	904.6	23.4	925.1	23.3
On term							129.2	4.9	171.8	5.3	246.3	6.4	290.8	7.3
Current accounts (clients and banks)	21.6	26.2	902.3	50.5	1,101.9	49.6	1,341.9	50.6	1,724.9	53.0	2,018.4	52.2	2,053.6	51.7
Contango liabilities	0.1	0.1	0.5		0.8		0.6		0.5		0.7		1.4	
Advances on securities	1.7	2.1	27.6	1.5	34.2	1.5	50.2	1.9	55.0	1.7	75.3	1.9	69.5	1.7
Checks outstanding	1.5	1.8	117.6	6.6	110.9	5.0	122.7	4.6	128.1	3.9	133.3	3.4	114.7	2.9
Total (with other items)	82.4	100.0	1,785.7	100.0	2,221.0	100.0	2,650.2	100.0	3,254.0	100.0	3,863.7	100.0	3,968.4	100.0

[a] The 1938 figures are not strictly comparable with those of post-war years.

[b] The difference between total asset and total liability items is accounted for mostly by the profits earned and by some bookkeeping adjustments.

nonetheless, and possibly for that very reason, it still acted in most cases as a brake. It was not swept away and replaced by a really free market, because competition for deposits, often prompted by reasons of prestige, in many cases pushed the rates above the limits which the law of supply and demand would have justified; in many instances the surplus remuneration was paid by indirect and concealed means.

The bigger banks were perfectly aware of the perils inherent in this practice and attempted more than once to reestablish a stricter discipline, but in these endeavors they came up against the state, which paid nearly 5 percent on Treasury bonds and on Post Office certificates, and against some of the major private concerns, which misused the authority to take deposits from their partners, directors, and employees and offered as much as 6 and 7 percent. There were thus far too many opportunities both for small savings and big money to reap more than the banks were prepared to pay under existing arrangements, and it could be done under conditions which offered practically equal guarantees of security and liquidity.

Eventually, at the end of 1953 and after prolonged negotiations, the banks reached a voluntary agreement, to come into force on February 1, 1954. This agreement was signed by banks whose aggregate deposits are 98 percent of the total deposits; the few abstentions reflect situations of a local and marginal importance. It is hoped that in a few months they will be solved, and the agreement made unanimous.

As is clear from Table 4, the rise applies mainly to the time accounts and deposits and to the current accounts. For the latter, the principle has been adopted, after a long struggle, to remunerate the bigger accounts with a higher rate, reaching 3 percent for the accounts of over 100 million lire. Besides, another new discrimination has been adopted: the accounts of public agencies with a balance of at least 500 million may receive up to 4 percent.

This agreement had the friendly blessing of the Bank of Italy, but no public or official sanction. The supervisory authorities adopted a policy of wait and see; before taking a definite attitude they want to watch how the agreement works.

There is no form of insurance of banking deposits, but there is a widespread feeling, fully justified by the experience of the last three decades, that the state would never allow any institution of importance to become insolvent. On the other hand there is an equally diffused notion that neither would the state allow any of the bigger industrial concerns to fail. The country's limited resources make it imperative that they should be marshalled to the fullest extent, even at a comparatively high cost.

Bank drafts and circular checks provide the banks with appreciable additional means, despite the government security cover to be furnished thereagainst to the extent of nearly 100 percent and notwithstanding the tendency which they evince of remaining stable on a 115,000–125,000 million lire level. The clearing is mostly done through the clearinghouses attached to each of the nine Italian stock exchanges; returns have risen rapidly from 5,600,000 million lire in 1948 to 8,500,000 million in 1950, and 12,466,000 million lire in 1952. The amount actually in circulation has remained, as said, practically unchanged; it follows, therefore, that the velocity of circulation is higher, with a shorter span of life of the single instruments; this can be explained by the fact that the habit of locking them up for hoarding purposes is dying out and also by greater monetary tension.

On the asset side cash in hand (including the compulsory deposits with the Bank of Italy) stands at about 16 percent of the total, with holdings of securities (mostly Treasury bills, including those lodged for compulsory deposits) at 17–18 percent. On the whole the front line of liquidity of the commercial banks remains, therefore, stable on a 33 percent level.

Commercial bills represent 17–18 percent, and credit balances another 26–28 percent of the credit side of the combined balance sheets, just the reverse of the prewar proportion, when the "bills" were one and a half times the "loans," a development unwelcome to the banks which insist as much as they can on having rediscountable bills from their borrowers.[6]

[6] "Bills" are mostly bills of exchange discounted by the banks; they represent real commercial transactions which have already taken place; they usually have a life of no more than 90 days; and they may be rediscounted at the Bank of Italy. "Loans" are advances to manufacturers and dealers; they finance cycles of production, agricultural and sales campaigns, etc. They may run up to one-year life. And, unless the debtor gives some collateral, or promissory notes ("foglio di smobilizzo"), they are a trifle less liquid than the "bills."

"Contango loans" are granted to brokers and speculators in the Stock Exchange, usually for the Stock Exchange term (no longer than 40 days), to finance the "riporti," i.e., the carry-over of Stock Exchange "positions" from one term to the following. Legally, they represent a spot purchase and a simultaneous re-sale for delivery at a future date.

"Advances on securities" are simply loans on collateral, *granted* by the banks to finance any productive activity; their length may vary considerably. On the *debit* side, "advances on securities" are advances *obtained* by the banks from the Bank of Italy, against collateral usually represented by Government obligations.

With the paucity of capital resources and the obligation to keep 25 percent of their deposits with the Bank of Italy, commercial banks have at times been called upon to make a supreme effort to satisfy the legitimate needs of their customers. Competition in this field is extremely keen, and the cases in which justified requirements have been left unsatisfied must be very few indeed, notwithstanding the occasional talk of "credit duress" in moments of hectic rises of prices or of hurried accumulation of sundry goods and merchandise.

The Bank of Italy publishes annually (in the past, semiannually) an analysis of the distribution of credit over the various branches of the economy. In their yearly reports some of the larger banks also give tables showing the percentage distribution of their credit among single trades. The changes in distribution can thus be followed, if not very closely, at least once a year and with an abundance of data and particulars. The classification embraces 18 of the main categories and about 80 of the smaller sections of the economy. The amounts of credit granted to each single category by separate groups of banks are divided into short term, medium term, and long term, with an indication of the number of borrowers for each separate class (see Table 3).

LOAN PORTFOLIO AS TO MATURITY AND TYPES OF INDUSTRIES

At the end of 1952 the credits granted by the commercial banks totaled 2,000,000 million lire, all of which, except some 19,000 millions, were intended to finance short-term operations. In the case of savings banks, medium-term and long-term operations accounted for about one quarter of the total then outstanding—108,000 million out of 406,000 million lire. This again bears witness to the fact that the commercial banks confine their assistance to operations of a short-term, self-liquidating nature, the bulk of finance operations being left to the specialized institutions. A comparison between the total credit granted and the respective value of production can be made only for a few groups; the conclusions to be drawn therefrom are of small significance, also because the figures all refer to a common date, December 31, which for some of them is a high water mark, and for others a low ebb of activity owing to different cycles of production.

Some significant trends may, however, be detected from Table 3. Thus, for instance, the percentage of credit granted to private customers is shown to be only about one half of what it was in prewar times. This class of business comprises an undefined variety of finance, largely for consumers' goods, but also for housing. Given the low

TABLE 3

DISTRIBUTION OF ALL LOANS GRANTED BY CREDIT INSTITUTIONS

(AMOUNTS IN BILLIONS OF LIRE)

Recipient	December 31, 1938: Credit Institutions: Short-Term Loans [a]	December 31, 1938: Credit Institutions: Medium- and Long-Term Loans [b]	December 31, 1938: Total	December 31, 1938: Financial Institutions	December 31, 1938: Total	December 31, 1948: Credit Institutions: Short-Term Loans	December 31, 1948: Credit Institutions: Medium- and Long-Term Loans	December 31, 1948: Total	December 31, 1948: Financial Institutions	December 31, 1948: Total
Individuals	3.2	0.9	4.1		4.1	57.1	12.5	69.6		69.6
Public bodies	1.6	3.9	5.5		5.5	29.0	16.9	45.9		45.9
Banks, stock exchange, finance and insurance companies	2.4	1.0	3.4	1.2	4.6	57.1	0.4	57.5	8.2	65.7
Transport and communications	0.5		0.5	0.5	1.0	23.6	0.4	24.0	23.7	47.7
Public works	2.8	2.1	4.9	5.5	10.4	75.2	8.9	84.1	44.0	128.1
Agriculture	2.6	0.4	3.0		3.0	87.2	1.6	88.8		88.8
Foodstuffs (industries and trades)	4.4		4.4	0.1	4.5	270.7	1.1	271.8	4.5	276.3
Industries and trades other than foodstuffs										
Iron, steel and engineering	3.5		3.5	0.7	4.2	105.8	0.6	106.4	79.5	185.9
Textiles and hides	2.8		2.8		2.8	133.5	0.7	134.2	3.3	137.5
Others	2.2		2.2	0.8	3.0	125.9	0.9	126.8	19.4	146.2
Retail trades and miscellaneous services	1.1	0.1	1.2		1.2	45.4	0.6	46.0	0.8	46.8
Total	27.1	8.4	35.5	8.8	44.3	1,010.5	44.6	1,055.1	183.4	1,238.5
Mortgage and building finance					6.1					24.0
Agricultural credit					3.4					113.0
Total					53.8					1,375.5

Recipient	December 31, 1949					December 31, 1950				
	Credit Institutions					Credit Institutions				
	Short-Term Loans	*Medium- and Long-Term Loans*	TOTAL	FINANCIAL INSTITUTIONS	TOTAL	*Short-Term Loans*	*Medium- and Long-Term Loans*	TOTAL	FINANCIAL INSTITUTIONS	TOTAL
Individuals	77.6	17.6	95.2		95.2	95.0	25.6	120.6		120.6
Public bodies	39.6	19.8	59.4		59.4	37.5	29.0	66.5		66.5
Banks, stock exchange, finance and insurance companies	63.9	2.5	66.4	7.4	73.8	83.1	0.4	83.5	7.5	91.0
Transport and communications	29.1	0.4	29.5	33.0	62.5	38.9	0.6	39.5	113.1	152.6
Public works	96.4	12.7	109.1	69.7	178.8	127.6	20.1	147.7	100.8	248.5
Agriculture	109.5	1.7	111.2		111.2	119.8	2.3	122.1		122.1
Foodstuffs (industries and trades)	327.3	1.1	328.4	7.8	336.2	366.9	1.7	368.6	10.6	379.2
Industries and trades other than foodstuffs										
Iron, steel and engineering	142.7	0.6	143.3	116.4	259.7	175.4	0.7	176.1	165.8	341.9
Textiles and hides	188.6	0.3	188.9	6.7	195.6	248.4	0.6	249.0	16.4	265.4
Others	179.8	1.4	181.2	32.5	213.7	218.2	1.4	219.6	56.9	276.5
Retail trades and miscellaneous services	65.3	0.3	65.6	1.1	66.7	77.0	0.5	77.5	0.3	77.8
Total	1,319.8	58.4	1,378.2	274.6	1,652.8	1,587.8	82.9	1,670.7	471.4	2,142.1
Mortgage and building finance					28.3					54.4
Agricultural credit					130.0					142.3
Total					1,811.1					2,338.8

TABLE 3 (*continued*).
DISTRIBUTION OF ALL LOANS GRANTED BY CREDIT INSTITUTIONS

	DECEMBER 31, 1951					DECEMBER 31, 1952					1938	1952
	CREDIT INSTITUTIONS					CREDIT INSTITUTIONS					CREDIT INSTITUTIONS	
	Short-Term Loans	*Long-Term Loans*	TOTAL	FINANCIAL INSTITUTIONS	TOTAL	*Short-Term Loans*	*Long-Term Loans*	TOTAL	FINANCIAL INSTITUTIONS	TOTAL	*Short-Term Loans Percent of Total*	*Short-Term Loans Percent of Total*
Individuals	106.5	30.1	136.6		136.6	123.2	35.1	158.3		158.3	11.8	5.4
Public bodies	62.4	40.0	102.4	3.8	106.2	56.9	49.7	106.6	3.8	110.4	5.9	2.5
Banks, stock exchange, finance and insurance companies	88.0	0.5	88.5	13.9	102.4	100.5	0.2	100.7	19.6	120.3	8.9	4.4
Transport and communications	49.5	0.6	50.1	87.6	137.7	62.2	1.7	63.9	105.6	169.5	1.8	2.7
Public works	159.3	26.8	186.1	149.5	335.6	213.4	30.6	244.0	209.2	453.2	10.3	9.4
Agriculture	159.4	2.7	162.1		162.1	135.1	3.7	138.8		138.8	9.6	5.9
Foodstuffs (industries and trades)	409.1	1.2	410.3	14.4	424.7	526.4	1.4	527.8	17.3	545.1	16.2	23.1
Industries and trades other than foodstuffs												
Iron, steel and engineering	219.4	0.5	219.9	191.2	411.1	302.1	0.6	302.7	208.9	511.6	12.9	13.3
Textiles and hides	264.7	0.6	265.3	25.9	291.2	321.0	1.0	322.0	30.7	352.7	10.3	14.2
Others	274.0	1.1	275.1	79.3	354.4	331.3	1.9	333.2	101.5	434.7	8.1	14.5
Retail trades and miscellaneous services	83.4	0.7	84.1	0.6	84.7	104.8	1.2	106.0	0.3	106.3	4.2	4.6
Total	1,875.7	104.8	1,980.5	566.2	2,546.7	2,276.9	127.1	2,404.0	696.9	3,100.9	100.0	100.0
Mortgage and building finance					74.3					99.0		
Agricultural credit					152.0					175.2		
Total					2,773.0					3,375.1		

[a] "Short-Term Loans" means usually those loans maturing within six months.

[b] "Medium-Term" loans means usually those maturing within five years.

standard of life in Italy and the difficulty of regaining at least the 1938 level, it is just as well that the resources of the banking system should not, as in 1938, be used too extensively to finance requirements of a more or less luxury nature, for the exclusive benefit of the privileged classes. There has been also a reduction in the percentage of credits to other banks, to financial companies and for stock exchange dealings, owing to the more subdued activities of the bourses and the smaller call for interbank credit. Credits to public bodies have fallen off too, proportionally even more so; already in 1938 this class of borrowers was turning to the savings banks and financial institutions, and now this has become the rule. These three categories of credit combined, not necessarily or directly connected with production, show a contraction from 26.6 percent to 12.3 percent of the total.

This diversion to other sources of credit has been to the advantage of agriculture, industry, and commerce, which the commercial banks have been able to accommodate more liberally. During the first postwar years there was a rise chiefly of credits for primary activities, mainly for agriculture and, to a minor extent, for mining. Subsequently, with the improvement of the food situation and the revival of foreign trade, credit has gone more and more to the secondary trades, especially textiles and hides, sea and land transport, and miscellaneous industries, usually to concerns of medium and smaller size which are, however, of quite remarkable importance in Italy. Among the percentage quotas which at the end of 1952 were still below the 1938 figure are to be found branches such as iron and steel, also engineering, all of them fully employed on the eve of war, and public works, including private housing schemes now largely financed by the savings banks and, in some regions, with the participation of foreign (Swiss) capital.

Without pretending that the present is an ideal distribution of credit, it can nevertheless be said to be preferable to the prewar pattern. It is a fact that nowadays the whole banking system assigns a far higher proportion of its resources to production cycles, agricultural credits, trade, and transport.

The flow of credit is also rhythmically better attuned to the alternating needs of crops and production cycles, apt to coincide and accumulate and to merge into each other; in fact, on the whole the utilization of credit shows no striking seasonal vagaries. If anything, it is subject to the incidence of tax installments (in February, April, and every second month thereafter), to the normal slowdown of economic activity during the summer holidays (August), and to the more intense Christmas shopping, when all staffs are given a cash bonus (the so-called "thirteenth month allowance"), largely responsible for the habitual 10 percent expansion in the circulation of the Bank of Italy. Even such subsidiary and minor ups and downs are often lost in the incidence of other special factors arising out of singular circumstances in particular branches or groups of concerns or of the temporary moods of the financial market.

When assessing the behavior of credit, one should finally take into account the tendency of a certain number of borrowers to use banking credit, chronically and exaggeratedly, for financial purposes; the practice has been severely censored and is being resisted by the banks, but is still a factor which deprives the monthly or quarterly credit figures for single branches of their true significance.

On the other hand the higher supervisory organ, that is, the Bank of Italy, cannot be said ever to have used its powers to influence either the direction or the qualitative selection of credit for the benefit of one or the other of the branches of the economy. Except for some general recommendations during the war to give preference to industries connected with national defense, the central bank has refrained from giving directives of the sort. Although repeatedly lectured by advocates of planning of various schools, it has consistently declined to usurp the functions of the credit institutions and to assume the role of supreme controller of the whole banking system. Even the so-called quantitative control has been exercised with discretion, and only by way of recommendations; for instance, in times of hoarding the Bank of Italy suggested that purchases of goods for that purpose should not be facilitated and that credit should not be given for speculative ends; its most categorical intervention is embodied in the set of provisions issued in August, 1947.

INTEREST CHARGES ON LOANS

The rate of interest charged to debtors is, naturally, linked to the rate offered for deposits. Both are governed by an agreement designed to prevent excesses; originally this was a voluntary agreement made in 1919 between the bigger banks, allowed to relax in 1929, reinforced and amplified in 1932 and on that occasion officially sanctioned by the Bank of Italy and by the government. Under the new banking law of 1936 it was the Bank of Italy which, in 1937, in agreement with the Bankers' Association, promulgated the new code and made it compulsory. The terms then laid down have been modified a dozen times (see Table 4) always upwards until the summer of 1947 (climax of the inflationary cycle), and thereafter downwards.

Some of the changes were independent of the fluctuations of the official discount rate; others, especially the more recent cuts, were adjustments to the concurrent movements of the official discount rate. Whilst the interest paid on deposits is fixed independently from other rates, the rates charged to borrowers are always related to those applied by the Bank of Italy with an extra 1 to 3.5 percent. Anyhow, they are minimum rates intended for first-class clients, others being charged higher rates which vary from case to case.

The practice of violating the "cartel" diminished the criticism leveled against the banks on account of the alleged "meager" remuneration offered to depositors. On the other hand loud laments are still heard from time to time concerning the "dearth" of banking money. The loudest complaints come from circles to whom the banks would give no credit whatever, in any case, and that tells its own tale.

Up to a few years ago it was quite the fashion also to criticize the banks not so much for the low interest paid on deposits or the high rates charged on loans, as for the "excessive" margin between the two. The argument was dropped after it was shown that the margin was justified by the cost of banking business, and that the banks did not draw excessive profits therefrom; eventually it also lost much of its substance with the practice of underhanded higher remuneration. The criticism now centers on the high rates charged for loans, that they weigh too heavily on the costs of production, stifle initiative, and place Italian industries in a condition of inferiority in respect of foreign competition.

It was not difficult for the banks to counter that argument. In years past rates charged on credit extensions have been even higher than now, and there was no tangible evidence of damage to the economy. The incidence of banking charges on production is very small. A policy of cheap money would perforce hamper the banks in the necessary discrimination in granting credits. The "high" cost of money helps to keep production cycles within minimum time limits and to check the temptation to use banking credit for financing investment operations. Besides, since 1947 the minimum rates have been

Table 4
Cartel Rates on Loans and Deposits
A. RATES ON LOANS

Type of Business	*April 1, 1937*	*June 1, 1937*	*July 16, 1938*	*Dec. 1, 1939*	*Oct. 4, 1940*	*June 21, 1940*	*March 16, 1942*	*Feb. 12, 1944*	*Sept. 11, 1944*	*June 1, 1945*	*June 1, 1946*	*Sept. 6, 1947*	*April 9, 1949*	*April 6, and April 15, 1950*
Unsecured credits														
On current account	4.50	6.00	6.50	7.00	7.00	7.50	7.50	8.00	7.50	8.00	8.00	9.50	8.50	7.50
Discount of promissory notes	4.50	5.50	5.75	6.00	6.00	6.50	6.50	7.00	6.50	6.50	6.50	8.00	7.00	6.25
Discount of finance bills	4.50	5.50	5.75	5.75	5.75	6.25	6.25	6.75	6.25	6.25	6.25	7.75	6.75	6.00
Secured advances and credits														
Against government and kindred securities	4.50	5.00	5.00	5.00	5.00	5.00	5.00	5.50	5.50	5.50	5.50	5.50	5.00	4.75
With a lien on cash deposits:														
On current account	4.50	5.50	5.50	6.00	6.00	6.00	6.00	6.00	5.50	6.00	6.00	7.50	6.50	5.75
Discount of promissory notes	4.50	5.50	5.50	5.50	5.50	5.50	5.50	5.50	5.00	5.00	5.00	6.50	5.50	5.00
With a lien on securities other than government and kindred securities, or goods, etc. on current account	4.50	5.50	6.00	6.25	6.25	6.75	6.75	7.25	6.75	7.25	7.25	8.75	7.75	7.00
Discount of promissory notes	4.50	5.50	5.50	5.75	5.75	6.25	6.25	6.75	6.25	6.25	6.25	7.75	6.75	6.25
Discount of Italian bills														
Not over 4 months	4.50	5.00	5.00	5.00	5.00	5.50	5.50	6.00	5.50	5.50	5.50	7.00	6.00	5.25
At 4 to 6 months	4.50	5.00	5.50	5.50	5.50	6.00	6.00	6.50	6.00	6.00	6.00	7.50	6.50	5.75
At 6 months and longer	4.50	5.00	6.00	6.00	6.00	6.50	6.50	7.00	6.50	6.50	6.50	8.00	7.00	6.25
Advances on agricultural products														
Discount of promissory notes					5.50	5.50	5.50	6.00	5.50	5.50	5.75 [a]	7.25	6.25	5.50
Temporary advances on current account							6.00	6.50	6.00	6.00	6.25 [a]	8.25	7.25	6.50
Official discount rate	4.50	4.50	4.50	4.50	4.50	4.50	4.50	4.50	4.00	4.00	4.00	5.50	4.50	4.00
Official debit rates on advances (on government and kindred securities)	4.50	4.50	4.50	4.50	4.50	4.50	4.50	4.50	4.50	4.50	4.50	4.50	4.00	4.00

TABLE 4 (*continued*)

CARTEL RATES ON LOANS AND DEPOSITS

B. RATES ON DEPOSITS

Type of Business	Oct. 1, 1932	Oct. 29, 1933	Oct. 31, 1933	Nov. 1, 1933	Feb. 1, 1934	Feb. 28, 1934	March 1, 1934	April 1, 1934	Oct. 1, 1944	Feb. 16, 1945	Feb. 1, 1954
Interest-Bearing Deposits											
Ordinary deposit accounts	2.50	2.50	2.50	2.00	2.00	2.00	1.50	1.50	1.00	0.50	0.50
Savings books at sight											
Small savings	3.00	3.00	3.00	2.75	2.75	2.75	2.75	2.50	2.00	1.50	1.50
Ordinary savings	2.75	2.75	2.75	2.75	2.25	2.25	2.25	2.00	1.50	1.00	1.25
Fixed term savings books											
At minimum 3 and less than 6 months	3.50	3.50	3.50	3.00	3.00	3.00	2.50	2.50	2.00	1.50	2.50
At 6 months or longer	4.00	4.00	4.00	3.50	3.50	3.50	3.00	3.00	2.50	2.00	3.25 [b]–4.00 [c]
Savings books at undefined due date but subject to reciprocal notice											
At minimum 3 and less than 6 months	3.50	3.50	3.50	3.00	3.00	3.00	2.50	2.50	2.00	1.50	2.50
At 6 months and longer	4.00	4.00	4.00	3.50	3.50	3.50	3.00	3.00	2.50	2.00	3.25
Interest-Bearing Bonds											
At minimum 3 and less than 6 months	3.50	3.50	3.50	3.00	3.00	3.00	2.50	2.50	2.00	1.50	2.50
At 6 months and longer	4.00	4.00	4.00	3.50	3.50	3.50	3.00	3.00	2.50	2.00	3.25 [b]–4.00 [c]
Current Accounts											
Accounts at sight	2.50	2.50	2.50	2.00	2.00	2.00	1.50	1.50	1.00	0.50	0.50–1.50–2.50–3.00 [d]
Reciprocal accounts	3.50	3.25	3.25	2.75	2.75	2.75	2.00	2.00	1.50	1.50	
Fixed accounts											
At minimum 3 and less than 6 months	3.50	3.50	3.00	3.00	3.00	2.50	2.50	2.50	2.00	1.50	2.50
At 6 months and longer	4.00	4.00	3.50	3.50	3.50	3.00	3.00	3.00	2.50	2.00	3.25 [b]–4.00 [c]
At undefined due date but subject to reciprocal notice of 90 days (60 days up to October 30, 1933)	3.50	3.50	3.00	3.00	3.00	2.50	2.50	2.50	2.00	1.50	2.50

[a] Beginning with the agricultural campaign 1946–47.
[b] At minimum six and less than twelve months.
[c] At twelve months and longer.
[d] The four rates apply respectively to accounts of less than 5 million, between 5 and 50 million, between 50 and 100 million, and over 100 million. The accounts held by public agencies, and with a yearly average balance of over 500 million, may benefit by a 4 percent rate.

cut by about one-fifth: they are now 1.5 to 2 percent lower, and with the concurrent increase of the rates on deposits the famous "spread" and profit margin has shrunk correspondingly. The shrinkage could take place thanks to the higher volume of business and the increase of incidental charges for commissions on sundry services, some of which are, on the other hand, very expensive. Except for a radical change in the conditions of the market, the present customer loan rates are not likely to undergo further reductions. This does not rule out the possibility that the average cost to the clients may yet be slightly reduced, either through an ever more severe selection of borrowers or through the borrowers availing themselves of other forms of credit accommodation, more economical and less burdened by incidental commissions.

INVESTMENT PORTFOLIO

With the transfer of ownership of all the former industrial participations to IRI (in 1931) the security holdings of the credit institutions were reduced to insignificant figures; in 1938 they still amounted to little more than 10,000 million lire with the savings banks holding a practically equal amount (9,300 millions). They were almost exclusively government bonds or obligations carrying a state guarantee. Holdings of shares were less than 700 million lire. At the end of June, 1953, the banks' holdings had gone up to 720,000 millions, but the composition had completely changed. Common stocks still represent but a trifling percentage of the whole; government or state-guaranteed obligations are more conspicuous, although only twelve times higher than before; by far the biggest rise has taken place in ordinary Treasury bills and in 9-year Treasury bonds issued from time to time to consolidate part of the outstanding series of ordinary Treasury bills.

The expansion of this type of Treasury bond is not altogether a spontaneous development; it started in earnest at the end of 1947 when the banks were placed under the obligation to lodge part of their own deposits in cash or ordinary Treasury bills with the Bank of Italy (see page 504). At current interest rates, it makes little difference to the banks whether these compulsory deposits be made in cash or in ordinary Treasury bills; it is a fact, nonetheless, that between the end of 1947 and the end of September, 1952, holdings of Treasury bills of the credit institutions had increased by 300,000 million lire to a total of almost 500,000 million lire, equal to about 60 percent of the aggregate security holdings of the banks and savings banks combined. Since then, the reduction of the rates on Treasury bills, and the heavy issues of other Government guaranteed bonds with a higher yield, have brought about a reduction in the holdings of the first—to less than 450,000 millions at the end of June, 1953—and an expansion of the other securities, to 480,000 millions.

Still more significant is the fact that at the end of September, 1951, and at the end of June, 1953, these holdings of Treasury bills accounted for nearly one half of the total amount outstanding (about 900,000 millions). The Treasury has not issued any long-term loan since 1946 and has covered its current needs almost entirely from the deposits at the Post Office Savings Bank and from issues of ordinary Treasury bills or 9-year Treasury bonds. This brings into clear focus the part played by the commercial banks. Equally clear is the influence which this investment—710,000 million lire of ordinary and medium-term Treasury bills and bonds—has had on the earnings of the banks and of the savings banks: the yield on one-year bills has never been less than 4.17 percent (actually 4.27 percent, if the issue premium is taken into account), or less than 2.30 percent on one-month to two-month bills. This explains why, in the case of the savings banks, the rise of their security holdings has been so much smaller: they are exempt from the obligation of compulsory deposits, in view of their long-established tradition to invest a good deal more than 25 percent of their deposits in government issues; the new regulation did not, therefore, call for a fresh and particular effort on their part. Before the war, savings banks held one half of the government issues held by all the credit institutions; at present they hold only between one sixth and one seventh.

As regards the capital market, the banks exercise practically the same functions as in the past, within the limits laid down by the banking reform. Debarred from subscribing to or underwriting issues, the commercial banks restrict themselves to the role of intermediaries, by cooperating in a technical way and receiving applications for issues of shares and debentures, also orders for dealings on the stock exchange which they carry out through the agency of stockbrokers.[7] In the case of the institutions of public right the rigidity of the system has been somewhat mitigated by exemptions for certain purposes and

[7] Public officials who hold the exclusive right of dealing on the stock exchanges.

by the creation of special departments which some of them have instituted for particular forms of finance credit (industrial, mining, films, hotels, and so on). For this class of business the banks of national interest have the Banca di Credito Finanziario (*Mediobanca*) which was established and is entirely owned by them (see pp. 490–91). Nonetheless, in times of depression or inactivity on the stock exchange, industrial companies may find it difficult to procure long-term capital. The formation of the Ente Finanziamenti Industriali (EFI)—which at the end of 1949 increased its capital to 2,000 million lire with the participation of a large number of front-rank industrial companies—is another instance of the endeavor to widen the possibilities of access to the capital market.

At present the only link between the commercial banks and the stock exchange is the *contango,* or carry-over accommodation, granted by the banks; in moments of intense activity they would thus be in a position to exercise some restraining influence on stock exchange trading; for the time being this is, however, little more than a theoretical possibility.

BANK COSTS

Before the war, the rule of thumb was one employee to one million lire deposits. In comparison with prewar times, deposits and current accounts stand now at 60:1 and expenditure on personnel at 140:1. The per capita cost has increased, of course, but the main cause of this increase of expenditure lies in the larger staffs now employed after the additions made for various reasons; some are of a social order (the return of employees called up for military service, the retention of those who were employed to replace them, and the compulsory quota of disabled war veterans); others are of a technical order (the huge increase in the number of accounts, the much heavier accountancy work now required, partly owing to currency devaluation, the multiplication of formalities for foreign business, and so on). Salaries now account for about 75 percent of the general expenses (on that side of the profit and loss accounts the interest paid to depositors amounts to only 15 per cent of the total; against 30 percent in 1938). The situation raises a serious problem in case the margin of profit should fall off still further.

Rationalization and mechanization of banking work have been of most effective help in limiting the inflation of personnel. Some of the major institutions with large networks of branches have adopted a system of centralized bookkeeping, at least group-wise. The Banca Commerciale Italiana has been a leader in that direction; the regional offices which it had established are now consolidated at Parma, a most suitably located center for the whole peninsula, where all the daily entries for the whole institution are registered, with an analysis of positions and risks for each branch of the institution and each sector of the national economy. The Parma *centro contabile* employs a staff of 700 and is equipped with the most up-to-date machinery, including a group of electronic selecting machines. But for this equipment twice the number of staff would be required, under conditions which would not afford the same possibilities of rapid and precise control.

BANKERS' ASSOCIATIONS

After the collapse of the corporative state and an interlude with an Interbanking Bureau, the banks formed the Italian Bankers' Association (Associazione Bancaria Italiana) which has a membership of 400; all the major banks and many of quite modest importance belong to it. It is governed by a board of some fifty members with a specific proportional representation of all the categories and groups of credit institutions. Its chief tasks are to study the technical and economic problems of banking, to safeguard the collective interests of the associated institutions, to cooperate with the authorities for the solution of problems arising in the matter of credit, to promote agreements between its associates (also for modifications of the cartel terms), and to arrange for publicity to encourage savings.

In a general way, the association acts as the banks' mouthpiece in their relations with the state administration and other professional organizations; when required, it formulates technical opinions on matters concerning credit. It also issues a monthly *Banking Review* which publishes papers on banking and financial technique and on economics, and organizes congresses like the International Credit Convention held in Rome in October, 1951. The financial contributions of the associated banks are apportioned to the size of the funds under their control (capital means, deposits, and current accounts).

The association does not deal with labor and staff matters which are the province of an autonomous association, the Associazione Sindacale fra le Aziende di Credito, to which nearly all the banks belong and which looks after their interests, especially in dealings with the bank employees associations and also in negotiations for collective labor contracts.[8]

SAVINGS INSTITUTIONS

ORDINARY SAVINGS BANKS

The study of this segment of the banking system can be confined to the so-called ordinary savings banks and to the Post Office Savings Bank, omitting life insurance companies, but not losing sight of the fact that savings deposits with the commercial banks represent a high quota of total savings.

Life insurance is still far behind the development attained in Anglo-Saxon countries. Currency devaluation was a grievous blow to this form of providence; in 1946 the premiums paid were less than six times the 1938 pre-devaluation figure: 6,900 million lire against 1,200 millions. In 1952 the figure had gone up to 37,000 millions, which is still only thirty times the 1938 total. Since the end of the war, the companies have made great strides, but chiefly in the number of new policies issued; at the end of 1949 there were already twice as many as in 1938. In most cases, the business is for small amounts placed in the more popular classes. Consequently, there has been a heavy proportional increase of administrative costs, whilst the total insured capital (800,000 million lire) is still far below the modest 1938 figure (25,000 million lire); tantamount to three fifths, if currency devaluation is taken into account. Premiums collected (1952) totaled about 37,000 million lire, again a modest figure when compared with the afflux of savings during that year to the commercial banks (235,000 millions), to the ordinary savings banks (90,000 millions) and to the Post Office Savings Bank (170,000 millions).

The Post Office Savings Bank holds about twice as much saving money as all the ordinary savings banks. The latter can, however, claim a fifty-year seniority and, in view of the variety of their activities, are of greater interest in a study of the banking system.

The savings banks are all institutions of public right. In many

[8] There is no national union of bank employees; some employees belong to no union at all; others are members of trade unions connected with one or the other of the Italian political parties.

cases, they were established for charity or kindred purposes or else took over the business of institutions for loans against sundry private or agricultural security. They do not pursue definite profit-making ends and do not distribute their profits, a high percentage of which goes to charity or social assistance (one third in the case of the Lombard Savings Bank).

The oldest—and that includes the most important—were formed in 1822–32; they multiplied rapidly, especially in central Italy; about 200 were in existence in 1925. Thereafter, and especially after legislation had been passed in 1927 to encourage mergers among the smaller ones, the number fell to 112 and continued to shrink up to the last war; there has been no great change since then; they now number about 85.

What is most surprising is that they should all have weathered so successfully the storms of devaluation, which on the one hand had an adverse effect on fixed interest investments and on the other hand provoked a steep rise in general expenses, particularly salaries, apart from a fatal impact on the formation of new savings. They have given proof of remarkable vitality and, since 1944, have opened no less than 400 new branches and sub agencies, their combined network being now 2,107 against 1,704. The expansion was helped by new provisions which, in the framework of the national effort for reconstruction, gave the savings banks a greater operative elasticity, aided by the fact that, as already mentioned, they are exempt from the obligation of making compulsory deposits for a given percentage of the monies they hold.

They have formed in Rome a central organization of their own, the Istituto di Credito delle Casse di Risparmio Italiane, which exercises a number of interesting functions on their behalf, principally the issue of circular checks for account of its associates (circulation at the end of August, 1953: 20,000 millions) and the discount of bills of exchange (about 40,000 millions).

Their deposits are largely made up of small savings from the urban centers (in the countryside the Post Office Savings Bank has a greater power of attraction). At the end of 1952 the combined holdings totaled some 685,000 million lire, 80 percent of which were in ordinary savings accounts (418,000 millions) or in term savings deposits (120,000 millions), the remaining 148,000 million lire being ordinary current accounts. Their deposits have not yet reached the 1938 level

(17,500 million lire which at present currency value would call for 900,000 millions); on the other hand, current accounts rose from 500 millions to 159,000 million lire (September, 1953); this is another indication of the slowness with which savings are being built up, but it also shows the extent to which the savings banks have managed to widen their spheres of activity. Deposits and current accounts represent practically the total of the funds at their disposal, implemented, sometimes, by advances obtained from the Bank of Italy, to the tune of some 25,000 millions.

Funds are invested chiefly in state bonds or government-guaranteed issues, with combined holdings at the end of June, 1953, of 210,000 millions, all of it in the aforesaid securities except for some 1,000 millions. The savings banks have the right—which they exercise although now on a reduced scale—to make advances to municipalities, provinces, and Land Redemption Syndicates, to discount state annuities, to advance monies on state bonds or government-guaranteed issues, or to civil servants and public officials on the security of one fifth of their salaries.[9]

The most important investment, outside securities, is nowadays of the ordinary banking business type: the discount of bills and finance paper for agricultural pools (for about 143,000 million lire), advances on current account with or without collateral (about 170,000 millions) and mortgage loans or advances. The latter type of finance is a speciality of the savings banks and has been developed to a point that makes them a primary factor in building and housing finance. It should be placed on record that the savings banks were among the first to provide funds for erecting popular dwellings by giving credit to building cooperatives and that, apart from financing cereal and other pools, they have been very active also in the matter of agricultural credit.

Their foreign business is practically nil. In the management of their affairs they exercise a caution that borders on bureaucracy;

[9] In Italy a public official is allowed to mortgage his salary to the extent of 20 percent. There is no special legal restriction to the savings banks lending activities. In practice, their customers are mainly "small people," retailers, artisans, farmers, shopkeepers, small manufacturers—with two important exceptions. The savings banks are prominent in financing the building industry, also in connection with mortgage lending; and they are a source of current finance for the local public bodies (municipalities, etc.). About 25 percent of their loans are medium and long-term (the commercial banks percentage is much lower); generally speaking, such loans are of a highly safe and low-yielding character.

TABLE 5

COMBINED BALANCE SHEET OF THE ORDINARY SAVINGS BANKS, DECEMBER 31, 1938 AND 1948–53
(AMOUNTS IN BILLIONS OF LIRE)

	1938		1948		1949		1950		1951		1952		JUNE, 1953	
Assets	*Amount*	*Percent*	*Amount*	*Percent*	*Amount*	*Percent*	*Amount*	*Percent*	*Amount*	*Percent*	*Amount*	*Percent*	*Amount*	*Percent*
Cash in hand and with other banks	1.9	7.5	53.3	12.6	63.9	11.8	70.4	11.0	85.5	11.7	121.7	13.6	127.5	13.8
Securities	8.7	34.1	111.4	26.3	132.5	24.4	152.1	23.8	159.7	21.9	194.9	21.8	210.4	22.7
Bills	1.2	4.7	72.1	17.0	97.9	18.0	104.0	16.3	115.2	15.8	136.0	15.3	143.3	15.5
Loans	0.8	3.1	65.8	15.5	80.7	14.9	88.9	13.9	105.4	14.4	127.1	14.3	136.0	14.7
Advances on stocks	0.7	2.7	5.0	1.2	6.3	1.2	6.4	1.0	7.3	1.0	8.4	0.9	7.7	0.8
Pawn and personal loans	7.3 [a]	28.6 [a]	9.9	2.5	16.5	3.0	20.3	3.2	22.2	3.0	23.0	2.6	24.6	2.7
Mortgage loans			37.9	8.9	49.4	9.1	72.5	11.4	93.6	12.8	112.5	12.6	123.3	13.3
Other items [b]	4.9	19.3	68.1	16.0	95.9	17.6	124.0	19.4	141.2	19.4	169.0	18.9	152.2	16.5
Total	25.5	100.0	423.5	100.0	543.1	100.0	638.6	100.0	730.1	100.0	892.6	100.0	925.0	100.0
Liabilities														
Patrimony and reserves	1.6	6.3	3.8	0.9	5.2	1.0	7.0	1.1	9.4	1.3	13.5	1.5	15.3	1.6
Deposits														
At sight	17.6 [c]	69.0 [c]	244.0	57.6	301.9	55.6	332.1	52.0	361.8	49.6	417.8	46.8	426.7	46.1
On term			31.1	7.3	48.6	8.9	68.8	10.8	88.8	12.2	120.0	13.4	142.2	15.4
Current accounts (clients and banks)	1.8	7.1	68.7	16.2	86.3	15.9	94.9	14.9	116.9	16.0	148.2	16.6	163.0	17.6
Advances on stocks	0.3	1.1	8.8	2.1	12.3	2.3	21.7	3.4	17.0	2.3	25.4	2.8	24.5	2.6
Checks outstanding			2.9	0.7	2.3	0.4	2.9	0.4	3.0	0.4	2.6	0.3	2.6	0.3
Other items	4.2	16.5	64.2	15.2	86.5	15.9	111.2	17.4	133.2	18.2	165.1	18.6	150.7	16.4
Total	25.5	100.0	423.5	100.0	543.1	100.0	638.6	100.0	730.1	100.0	892.6	100.0	925.0	100.0

[a] Includes "Pawn and personal loans" and "Mortgage loans."
[b] Excluding the items of same amount on the credit and debit side.
[c] Includes deposits "at sight" and "on term."

nevertheless, they constitute a vital and essential element profoundly rooted in the economy of the province or provinces in which they operate. Their personalities often reflect the characteristics, more or less dynamic or more or less traditionalistic, of those economies. Those established in the more modest provincial centers are for all intents and purposes small local banks. The biggest of all, the Cassa di Risparmio delle Provincie Lombarde, in size equal to one quarter of the whole sector, has grown into an institution with more than 200 agencies, thirty of which are outside Lombardy (in the Piedmontese provinces of Alessandria and Novara).

POST OFFICE SAVINGS BANKS (CASSA DEPOSITI E PRESTITI)

A Post Office savings bank is attached to each of the 12,000 post offices which makes this by far the largest organization for the gathering of savings, the ordinary savings banks having only 2,162 agencies in all. The system was set up in 1875 and up to the First World War served to implement the functions of the ordinary savings banks. Deposits were at first taken only on savings books; later two new instruments were introduced: in 1919 the Post Office current accounts and in 1924 the Post Office interest-bearing bonds. Interest is paid also on the current accounts,[10] but it is only in recent years that these have shown sign of expanding (from 1,000 million lire in 1938 to 277,000 millions in 1953).[11] The interest-bearing bonds met with immediate success and now account for eight tenths of the whole of the monies deposited with the Post Office. Their characteristics have already been explained (pp. 430–31). All that should be added is that, being a registered and non-transferable title, they effectively serve their anti-inflationary purpose. The fact that interest is added to the capital and is paid also on interest accrued so that the nominal amount doubles in the space of 18 years has made them extremely popular all over the countryside where people do not, as a rule, expect interest on small savings, but usually set them aside for special outlays (dowries, repairs to the home, replacement of agricultural machinery, and so forth).

The monies collected by the Post Office Savings Banks are administered by the Cassa Depositi e Prestiti. This is one of the central

[10] The rate has fluctuated between 1.5 and 2.5 percent; it is at present 1.5 percent but is computed on the lowest fortnightly balance, which makes it much lower.

[11] The increase is due possibly in part to the option or obligation of paying certain taxes, particularly the purchase tax, by means of Post Office transfers.

administrations of the State Treasury, originally modeled on the French Caisse des Dépôts et Consignations; nowadays, with the expansion of Post Office savings, it operates chiefly as a state bank—as a matter of fact, as the largest of all the state banks. It can secure additional funds through issues of one-year interest-bearing bonds at rates equal or very near to those of the one-year ordinary Treasury bills. The latest issue was made in 1950 for 1,000 million lire at 4.5 percent.

Under existing legislation, the Cassa Depositi e Prestiti can invest its funds in loans to municipalities, provinces, syndicates for land redemption and agricultural development, in land or agricultural credit bonds, state bonds or government-guaranteed issues or by placing them on current account with the Treasury. In the past, new money has practically all gone to the Treasury, the Cassa Depositi e Prestiti having become one of its chief and most regular purveyors. On the list of investments, loans to public bodies come second and at quite some distance behind; these loans are generally long-term loans, up to 35 and even 50 years, and are usually made on the security of government issues or credits against the state or of a lien on local taxes or supertaxes. The state has, in some cases, taken on itself part of the service cost of the loans. After the last war, municipalities have been authorized, exceptionally, to contract loans with the Cassa Depositi e Prestiti for the purpose of covering their deficits.

There are other minor investments such as advances to state administrations for certain public works (offices in Rome, schools abroad, railroads, and popular dwellings) and others, of still lesser importance as far as amounts are concerned but of some interest to the structure of the banking system, that is, the substantial participations (from one third to three fifths of the respective capital) in credit institutions pursuing similar ends: Consorzio per Sovvenzioni su Valori Industriali; Consorzio di Credito per le Opere Pubbliche; Istituto di Credito per le Imprese di Pubblica Utilità; and Istituto Mobiliare Italiano (p. 478).

The ordinary savings banks participate in institutions of this type only in nominal amounts, granting medium-term and long-term credit, but holding the majority of capital of the Bank of Italy. As a result thereof, the major part of the capital means of the bank of issue and of the more important financial institutions is "owned" by the banks which collect the small savings. Naturally, in this case possession does not mean control; on the contrary, it can be said that possession has been given to the savings banks in order to guarantee the independence of the financial institutions concerned and possibly also with the ulterior motive that popular feeling should closely associate the biggest of them with the defense of the currency, which is the main interest and main concern of small savers.

There are no private savings banks in Italy. The gathering in of savings is the business either of the post offices, practically *guichets* of the Treasury, or of the ordinary public institutions managed by boards of directors appointed by the government, provinces, and municipalities.

Although this group of institutions has lost some of its prewar importance, it still is decidedly a pillar of the banking system. The Italian habit and capacity for thrift are well known and have survived the ordeal of devaluation. The slower progress of the savings banks is explained more than anything else by the keener competition of the commercial banks, which are also allowed to take savings, and perhaps still more by the necessity after the war to rebuild other forms of savings, real and non-monetary, destroyed during the war: houses, cattle, equipment, and so forth. The only signs of diminished thrift are to be found in the increased expenditure on luxuries, for instance, tobacco, theater, cinemas, and betting, but in passing judgment on these weaknesses, the low average standard of life in this country should be taken into account; these so-called "luxuries" are to a large extent but a poor substitute for a whole set of comforts and amenities which in other countries are looked upon as part and parcel of the normal standard of life.

URBAN MORTGAGE CREDIT INSTITUTIONS

About a dozen institutions engage in urban mortgage building credit, apart from the ordinary short credit extended to the building trades by the commercial banks. It is divided into mortgage credit on premises already in use (for repair, improvement, and enlargement) on the security of the ground and buildings ("credito fondiazio"), and mortgage credit for new buildings on the security of the ground alone or, on occasion, also of the foundations ("credito edilizio").

The distinction is purely historical,[12] inasmuch as after the war, in order to facilitate the reconstruction of devastated cities, all institutions eligible for the first type of mortgage business ("credito fondiazio") were allowed to grant credit also for new buildings; the one and only institution whose business was and is still confined to new buildings ("credito edilizio") seems to find it a limitation to its expansion.

Mortgage business, in its turn, is divided into credit in urban centers and credit in rural areas; business in the latter category has fallen off, especially because of the calls for the reconstruction of damaged premises in the bombed cities; advances on rural property now amount to no more than one eighth of the aggregate advances made by all these institutions. Mortgage and building credit in the towns and in the countryside will therefore be dealt with jointly. It should, however, be kept in mind that the total includes loans (some 13,000 million lire at the end of 1953) in rural districts which, strictly speaking, should rank as agricultural and development finance.

The need for building credit is a very elastic element. On the one hand, there is a backlog of need for 5 million rooms which, at current costs, would call for an investment of some 2,800,000 million lire—under present circumstances and prospects, this is a positively astronomical figure. During the last years, a growing effort has been made. About 450,000 rooms were built in 1950, 650,000 in 1951, 800,000 in 1952, and no less than a million in 1953. The area and building cost per room also showed an upward tendency. The total investment rose therefore from 212,000 millions in 1950 to 342,000 in 1951, 444,000 in 1952, and 570,000 in 1953. During 1952 (the last year for which we have complete statistical data) the credits granted by institutions engaged in mortgage business totaled 154,000 million lire, half of which was provided by the specialized mortgage credit institutions.[13] As these advances are covered as a rule by mortgages for a maximum of half the value of the premises, it can be said by and large that over a third of the units have been erected for housing purposes with the benefit of this form of credit.

12 In compliance with the recommendation not to give too much space to the history of single institutions, we refrain from recounting the changes (at times quite substantial) which have taken place on this particular sector; the position here outlined is that created by the latest rearrangement under Law No. 474, July 29, 1949.

13 The other half was supplied by the Cassa Depositi e Prestiti (43,000 millions), by the savings banks (21,000 millions), and by the credit institutions of public right (4,000 millions).

At the end of the same year, the banks had loaned on a short-term basis to builders and building societies 136,000 million lire to implement their working capital. The performance of the building trades may appear to have been comparatively modest when compared with present needs, but has been comparatively high when viewed in the light of available financial resources; it can safely be stated that it has found all the necessary financial accommodation, despite the difficulties on the bond market.

Mortgage and building finance is the business of a dozen specialized banking institutions and of some state agencies. The latter operate directly on the market with funds obtained from various sources, United Nations Relief and Rehabilitation Association, European Recovery Program, or fiscal funds, all of them, ultimately, Treasury funds. The banking institutions procure the necessary funds through issues of bonds with uniform characteristics, the issues being subject to precise limits: the total amount outstanding at any one time must not exceed a twentyfold amount of their capital and reserves.[14]

The rate of interest varies, at the discretion of the issuing institution, from 3 to 5 percent but, for a number of years, market conditions have made it inadvisable to offer bonds at less than 5 percent; they are usually at least 10-year bonds, but may be issued up to 50 years' maturity. They may be placed on the market by the issuing institutions themselves, but generally they are handed over to the borrower who arranges the placing himself.[15] He has the option to reimburse the loan before maturity by repurchasing the bonds on the market.

The underlying mortgage guarantee of these bonds, usually real estate for a twofold value of the loan, is further enhanced by the standing of the issuing institutions. Some of the older series of bonds, converted more or less compulsorily into 4 percent issues in 1935, also carry a subsidiary state guarantee (not, however, the 5 percent issues), and these represent almost the whole of the present circulation.

[14] Tenfold until 1949. The restriction does not apply to four of the oldest institutions (Cassa di Risparmio delle Provincie Lombarde, Cassa di Risparmio di Bologna, Monte dei Paschi and Istituto di San Paolo), whose mortgage credit sections can issue bonds without limitations.

[15] One of the most important institutions grants credit up to 50 percent of the value of the premises, 33 percent in 25- to 30-year bonds and 17 percent in cash against mortgage bills of exchange maturing in from 5 to 6 years.

The institutions which specialize in this line of business are first of all the mortgage departments of the five institutions of public right (Banco di Napoli, Banco di Sicilia, Banca Nazionale del Lavoro, Monte dei Paschi and Banco di San Paolo) and the two biggest savings banks, Provincie Lombarde and Bologna, plus the Istituto Italiano di Credito Fondiario in Rome, the Credito Fondiario Sardo and the three institutions of the type which operate in Venetia: the Istituto di Credito Fondiario delle Venezie of Verona, the Istituto di Credito Fondiario della Regione Tridentina of Trento and the Cassa di Risparmio of Gorizia; and finally the Istituto Nazionale di Credito Edilizio of Rome.

The list must be completed with a reference to the Hotel and Tourism Credit department of the Banca Nazionale del Lavoro, not listed as such in current statistics, but which falls under this heading in view of its contribution to the rebuilding, reconditioning, and equipment of hotels, more particularly hotels of the first and second categories, which are of special interest to the tourist business. At the end of 1948 that department had reached its assigned ceiling; it had become too expensive to finance this class of business by issuing debentures; on the other hand, no less than 1,044 applications for a total of 42,000 million lire had accumulated by the end of 1949. Under Law No. 481 of July 19, 1949, the department was allocated 3,000 million out of the 8,000 million lire set aside for hotels and tourism out of ERP counterpart funds. It began using these funds only in the second half of 1950; in the meantime, it had found it possible to make another debenture issue and, at the close of 1952, the advances outstanding had already reached a total of 2,613 million lire, financed for a little more than half by ordinary means (issues of bonds having reached a total of 970 millions) and for 1,261 millions out of ERP funds obtained on terms which made it possible to grant special rates for this sort of credit.

The geographic zones of operations of these institutions are not strictly delimited. Three of them, the Istituto Italiano di Credito Fondiario, the Istituto Nazionale di Credito Edilizio and the Banca Nazionale del Lavoro operate over the whole national territory, whilst the Cassa di Risparmio delle Provincie Lombarde operates in the north, down to a line which stretches across the peninsula from La Spezia to Ancona. The others confine their business to their traditional boundaries or to those laid down in their statutes. Their bonds are quoted on various stock exchanges; present quotations show that the cost of this type of finance is fairly even throughout the country.

There is no great difference of policy between the institutions of public right or savings banks and the specialized institutions, except that the latter are perhaps inclined to favor popular dwellings and small estates. This is a business that does not appeal very much to private capital and of recent years the government has taken steps to provide the means required [16] by setting aside funds from American aid and others obtained at home in order to reduce the cost of housing schemes. At first, these government contributions were proportionate to the cost of construction and to the contributions of the employers and employees themselves (Fanfani plan), or granted by way of annuities over 30 or 35 years, at 4 to 4.5 percent, the higher rate applying to cooperative building societies (Tupini plan). Subsequently, the privileged treatment of the Tupini plan for owners of small apartments in small localities was made a general rule, and as much as 75 percent of the cost of the land and building was eventually advanced. These long-term plans call for grants running into hundred-thousands of millions; the actual cash disbursement is difficult to ascertain in view of the fact that not all the grants have been definitely assigned and are spread over a long period. For the loans directly granted by the state under the Aldisio plan, the savings banks usually act as intermediaries.

The total of advances granted by the 13 specialized institutions has followed a very characteristic trend. On the eve of war it was close on 6,000 million lire. As currency depreciation became more pronounced, it became easy for borrowers to repay their debts; concurrently, it brought about a demand out of all proportion for new loans of this kind, always in the hope that in the course of time these fresh liabilities might in their turn be repayable in debased paper currency. The tendency met with a decided resistance on the part of the institutions, with the result that by the end of 1945 their loans had fallen to 4,659 million lire. The total has gone up since then rather rapidly, but it should be remembered that the rise started from a very low level. At the end of 1950 the advances totaled 54,600 million lire and on June 30, 1953, 116,000 million lire. At the pres-

[16] The various plans are known under the names of the ministers who sponsored them as Fanfani, Tupini and Aldisio plans.

ent currency value the prewar figure would be equal to 300,000 million lire. The present indebtedness for mortgage and building finance is, therefore, considerably lower than in the past and there is consequently a wide margin for new commitments. Since the latter part of 1951 the market for these bonds has also improved appreciably; this again opens wider possibilities for fresh issues and at the same time makes repayment of earlier loans more expensive, although during the last months of 1953 the market was again rather dull. The yield on this type of security, issued by the leading institutions, varies from 5.8 percent to 7 percent, except—and this is a notable exception—in the case of the Istituto Nazionale di Credito Edilizio, whose bonds yield something like 8 percent.

AGRICULTURAL CREDIT INSTITUTIONS AND COOPERATIVE BANKS

The structure of agricultural credit is even more intricate than that of mortgage and building credit. It is divided into ordinary and development credit. Both usually extend beyond the time limits of an ordinary banking credit, up to five years for the "ordinary" agricultural credit destined to the purchase of machinery, and up to thirty years for the "development" credit. Also the former, therefore, is basically different from the usual commercial credit extended to farmers, owing to its longer duration and also to its particular nature, that is, to its underlying security, real and no longer purely personal, consisting generally of special liens or of a lien on movable goods (as cattle or crops). It may be extended by way of credit on current account or by discount of agrarian bills, practically akin to the ordinary bills of exchange, except that they must bear reference to the purpose of the loan.

The specific mention of the purpose of the loan is also an essential characteristic of development credit and distinguishes it from rural mortgage credit. The latter may be intended, of course, also for legitimate economic purposes, for instance in connection with the division of estates among various coheirs or copartners, or for the purchase of separate estates to be incorporated into organic units; it rests, however, on a specific real security and need not, therefore, concern itself with the use which the borrower is going to make of the money and still less with the question whether that use is going to be productive. Development credit must, on the other hand, be destined to productive ends—development of the property—or to social ends—formation of small farming estates.

The law of 1928 on agricultural credit distinguishes two categories of lenders: those expressly authorized by law to grant one or the other or both forms of argicultural credit and those to be expressly authorized by the competent authorities to undertake operations of the kind.

"Expressly authorized" institutions include (a) the Consorzio Nazionale per il Credito Agrario di Miglioramento, an institution of public right whose capital of about 1,100 million lire has been subscribed by the state together with 58 credit institutions, savings banks, and insurance companies. Its business is confined to development credit but extends over the whole national territory and thus implements the functions of (b) the regional institutions whose task it is to guide, coordinate and integrate the work done by local institutions, such as the Istituti Federali di Credito Agrario in Piedmont, Liguria, Tuscany, and Central Italy, and the Istituti di Credito Agrario in Sardinia and the province of Ferrara; these institutions have a different legal structure and confine their operations to their respective regions.

In three other important regions there are ramifications of the savings banks, more precisely the (c) Casse di Credito Agrario of the Istituto Federale delle Casse di Risparmio delle Venezie (Venetia), delle Provincie Lombarde (Lombardy) and of Bologna, and, for long-term development credit, the agrarian credit sections of the Istituto di Credito Fondiario per le Venezie. In the south there are (d) the agrarian credit sections of the Banco di Napoli and Banco di Sicilia, both for ordinary and for development credit. Finally, (e) the Banca Nazionale del Lavoro, authorized to engage in ordinary agrarian credit operations through its banking department (and since 1950 through its section, Credito alla Cooperazione) and to give development credit through its section, Credito Fondiario; this bank and, obviously, also the Banca Nazionale dell'Agricoltura rank as authorized institutions and may operate over the whole peninsula.

In general, the specialized institutions are not authorized to take deposits. Their means consist of their own capital resources, of special state advances and of rediscount facilities with the Bank of Italy.[17] Those authorized to give development credit—and this may be for as long as 30 years—are also allowed to issue debentures.

The second category, the banks which *may* be authorized to deal in agricultural credit, embraces a vast miscellany of organisms, savings banks, loan agencies, ordinary and cooperative credit institutions, agricultural associations and syndicates, also the National Union of War Veterans and, for development credit, the mortgage credit institutions and the Istituto Nazionale della Previdenza Sociale. When short of means for ordinary credit operations, they act as intermediaries either by transmitting their customers' applications to or by discounting their own bills with special institutions. In that case, they must not charge their customers more than 2 percent above the rate at which they have discounted their own bills. Otherwise, interest rates are practically free of limitations and vary from the 4.5 percent cartel minimum for the discount of agricultural bills to 7.75 percent for credits for cattle or machinery.

For agricultural development credit it is possible to obtain government aid for part of the interest charged on long-term loans or for works in mountainous regions; the allowance is 2.5 percent and is usually deducted from the interest charged (in this case, generally, at 6 to 7 percent. The cost of 5-year credit without state aid is about 7 percent.[18]

At the end of June, 1953, the aggregate balance sheets of the specialized institutions totaled 124,000 million lire of which only 6,000 millions represented capital resources and only 12,300 million debentures outstanding. The bulk of the liabilities (76,000 million) was indebtedness to mother institutions and banks.

On the asset side, 30,206 million lire represented investments in agricultural development; 4,191 millions, bills for agricultural

[17] This facility is used chiefly to finance agricultural pools, that is, total or part deliveries of certain crops to official bodies who provide for the marketing; this, obviously, has nothing to do with agricultural credit. The pool system, imposed by the government for economic and political ends, is not always very popular with the farmers. Since 1945, it has, however, been enforced for very few products (now only cereals, rice, hemp, and olive oil). It has now lost much of its compulsory character and serves no other purpose but to ensure remunerative prices to the farmers.

[18] Recently, also this sector has received aid out of the ERP lira fund: 1,200 millions was given to the agricultural credit institutions by way of 30-year advances at 5 percent, with another 1,500 millions at 4.5 percent to be used for loans for a maximum duration of 20 years.

development business; 41,508 millions, bills relating to ordinary credits; and 7,342 millions, bills for "pool" credits. On the whole, these are pretty low figures. Like the mortgage business, this branch is still far from having reached the prewar level in terms of monetary values. In 1938 the totals were 3,400 million lire for ordinary agricultural credit and 1,600 millions for development credit. The former, after a dizzy decline in 1943–44 (in the latter year down to 735 million lire) totaled 94,000 millions at the end of June, 1953, which, in terms of prewar lire, is tantamount to one half of the 1938 mark. The latter form of credit, with 36,000 millions, stood at less than one half of the 1938 level.

On the other hand, there has been a marked improvement in the type of business transacted. Of the 3,400 million lire in 1938 no less than 2,300 millions were advances on foodstuffs, 1,400 of these on agricultural pools. At the end of June, 1953, that business accounted for only 7,342 million lire—a negligible quota of the total of 102,000 millions. Ordinary credit had risen from 373 million lire to 54,300 millions (which is a seasonal peak) while credits for new purchases of cattle, machinery, and so forth, had grown from little more than 100 million lire to 25,000 millions. On these two crucial sectors there have been increases of 50 percent and 400 percent respectively. Development credit has been used nearly one half for rural buildings, the other half for new plantations, for the formation of small estates, and for irrigation works.

A sense of fairness impels us to mention also the Casse Comunali di Credito Agrario which grants loans in cash or bonds to farmers, and the Casse Rurali ed Artigiane; both are agencies of a cooperative type for credit to farmers and artisans. The two work together or separately but, with the impoverishment of the former and the constant reduction in number of the latter (from 3,540 in 1922 to less than 700 now), they are merely small units on the edge of the system.

The Banca Nazionale del Lavoro's section for Credito alla Cooperazione, which since 1950 has been authorized to grant agricultural credit, also complained that the funds at its disposal were inadequate. With its endowment fund of 500 million lire and another 500 millions in borrowed funds, plus the assistance of its mother concern, it had been able to give credits (by the end of 1950) to the extent of nearly 2,000 million lire, mostly to cooperative societies. In 1951 its means increased by 2,000 millions obtained from the Treasury and its activity

Table 6

Combined Balance Sheet of Institutions of Agricultural Credit, December 31, 1938 and 1948–53

(amounts in millions of lire)

Assets	*1938*	*1948*	*1949*	*1950*	*1951*	*1952*	June *1953*
Cash in hand and with other banks	45	1,089	3,192	1,550	4,943	14,834	15,734
Securities and participations	167	613	659	1,709	2,731	5,053	4,686
Bills							
Ordinary agricultural credit			16,982	19,049	24,348	32,877	41,508
Development agricultural credit	550 [a]	17,919 [a]	1,687	1,994	2,139	3,357	4,191
"Pool" bills	787	10,314	11,214	4,005	18,151	13,667	7,342
Loans	1,452	6,352	9,615	15,028	19,838	25,588	30,206
Current accounts for the "pool" financing			9,867	8,414	8,583	9,566	7,427
Other items	1,826 [b]	89,813 [b]	7,402	10,587	10,344	9,693	12,550
Total	4,827	126,100	60,618	62,336	91,077	114,635	123,644
Liabilities							
Patrimony	917	1,609	2,672	3,318	3,732	5,178	6,097
Government advances	208	171	164	1,234	1,735	2,453	5,220
Bonds outstanding	692	2,799	3,727	5,518	8,149	10,537	12,335
Current accounts indebtedness with mother-bank and associated institutes		26,525 [d]	41,899	38,932	62,058	76,725	76,110
Current accounts indebtedness for the "pool" financing	3,010 [c]		6,833	5,878	5,704	5,101	11,025
Other items		94,996	5,323	7,456	9,699	14,641	12,857
Total	4,827	126,100	60,618	62,336	91,077	114,635	123,644

[a] Includes "Ordinary agricultural credit" and "Development agricultural credit."

[b] Includes "Current accounts for the 'pool' financing" and "Other items."

[c] Includes "Current accounts with mother-banks and associated institutes," "Current accounts for the 'pool' financing," and "Other items."

[d] Includes "Current accounts with mother-banks and associated institutes" and "Current accounts for the 'pool' financing."

developed quickly. By the end of 1952 it had granted credits for more than 4,000 millions. A new allocation of 1,760 millions, inscribed in the budget for 1952–53 and 1953–54, should enable it to extend even more its operations. During the last years, that is after the Section was authorized to grant agricultural credit, the Section's more important customers became the agricultural cooperatives: their share among the beneficiaries rose from 1.5 percent (1949) to 8.9 percent (1950) and to about 50 percent in 1951–52.

GOVERNMENT CREDIT INSTITUTIONS

If we were to enumerate all the institutions over which the state has some measure of control, very few would be left out. On the sector of ordinary credit the state is the sole owner of the Banca Nazionale del Lavoro and, through IRI, of the three banks of national interest, that is to say, four of the Italian big five; with its right to appoint the administrative organs it has a large control also in the affairs of the fifth (Banco di Napoli) and of the other institutions of public right. In the sector of savings, the ordinary savings banks are under close government supervision; the Post Office Savings Bank is under direct state management. As to the Bank of Italy, its policy is, naturally, closely aligned to that of the Treasury.

The term "state credit institutions" does not as a rule apply to the banks aforementioned, but to the specialized institutions which were virtually initiated by the state and of which the state holds the entire or majority capital and elects the majority of the boards. "State credit institutions" are Istituto per la Ricostruzione Industriale (IRI), Istituto Mobiliare Italiano (IMI), Istituto di Credito per le Imprese di Pubblica Utilità (ICIPU), Consorzio Sovvenzioni Valori Industriali (CSVI), and Istituto Centrale per il Credito a Medio Termine a favore delle Medie e Piccole Industrie (Mediocredito), which are engaged in medium-term and long-term credit operations, are not allowed to take deposits from the public, and operate with funds procured by way of debenture issues or directly from the Treasury.

ISTITUTO RICOSTRUZIONE INDUSTRIALE (IRI)

This, by far the biggest of all, is a holding company much more than a credit institution.[19] It caters to the needs of the undertakings in

19 IRI has a Chairman, a Vice-Chairman, and a Board of Directors, composed of eleven members. The Chairman and Vice-Chairman are designated by the Prime Min-

whose capital it is already interested, thus acting as banker as well as partner. This is not to be construed as a qualification or limitation of its operations which are widespread and considerable. The undertakings controlled by IRI form a very important segment of the whole Italian economy, in fact, a decisive quota of some sectors (banks of national interest, shipbuilding, navigation, iron, steel, and heavy industries, also electricity and telephones).

IRI was founded in 1933 to take over the administration, the liquidation, or the restoration to private management of industrial participations previously held by the three leading commercial banks (Banca Commerciale Italiana, Credito Italiano, and Banco di Roma) and other smaller banks so that they could devote themselves exclusively to the business of ordinary credit. IRI's first task was to reorganize the companies previously controlled by the banks and to refund to the latter the cash value of their former holdings. This called for a heavy outlay of money, supplied by the Treasury by means of a long series of annuities discounted with the Bank of Italy.

Subsequently—and that stage is still in progress—IRI had to take over the functions previously exercised by the banks and supply the funds required by the industries now under its control. In more recent times, it had to provide also the means for reconstruction, modernization and conversion to peacetime work. With the devaluation of the currency, IRI's previous indebtedness to the Bank of Italy largely faded away, but fresh and substantial capital had now to be found to enable it to shoulder its new responsibilities; this capital was procured by means of debenture issues and, for a more important quota, of Treasury subsidies.

Already in 1936, IRI's capital structure could be considered technically sound; a reassessment of its holdings showed a surplus of more than 1,000 million lire. During the Second World War, however, almost all its industrial assets suffered very severe damage: at the end of hostilities the Italian mercantile fleet lay at the bottom of the sea, hydroelectrical and iron and steel plants had been bom-

---

ister and nominated by the President of the Republic. The eleven Directors are: three experts in finance and industry nominated for three years by the Premier (together with the Chairman and Vice-Chairman they form the executive Committee—"Comitato di Presidenza"); five *ex officio* high government officers (Budget Director, State Chief Accountant, and the heads of the ministerial departments of Industry, State Property, and Employment); three representatives of different ministries (Posts and Telegraphs, Shipping, Defense).

The yearly balance sheet is submitted to the Treasury and communicated to the Cabinet and to Parliament.

barded from the air and from the sea, factory equipment had been plundered by the Germans, and the peace treaty deprived armament factories and shipbuilding yards of their former foreign markets. The banks had lost their affiliations in the Balkans, but, on the whole, emerged without undue losses from the postwar crisis and, with their network of branches over the homeland intact, were able to cooperate with IRI in the general work of reconstruction and assistance to other companies of the group. In the last few years, IRI's activities broadened quickly, owing to mounting demands for renovation of iron and steel plants and for financial assistance to engineering works. These calls, of course, told heavily on IRI's own situation: at the end of 1950, against a capital provided by the Treasury of 60,000 million lire (plus a small reserve of little more than 2,000 millions) there were financial liabilities aggregating 73,000 millions, in addition to 15,000 millions on account of Treasury advances and 53,000 millions for debentures in circulation.

The assets were made up mainly of participations and advances for a total of 190,000 million lire; one half to engineering, 15 percent to navigation, 12 percent to electricity, 8 percent to iron and steel, and the balance spread over telephones, mining, chemical industries and banks—the latter, however, for only 3.7 percent of the whole.

In the course of the previous three years (1948–50) the financing required by the IRI industrial group had amounted to no less than 264,000 million lire, of which one half had been supplied by IRI itself, the balance being procured from other sources (Export-Import Bank and ERP advances, debenture issues, and bank credits). For its own contribution, IRI had, in its turn, called on various quarters, but of the 30,700 million lire which it had allocated in 1950 to a number of its borrowers nearly 75 percent had been obtained in the form of short-term advances [20] and only 20 percent by debenture issues; the rest out of small available funds and proceeds of liquidations.

The situation became even more strained by the end of June, 1951, IRI having in the meantime taken participations or made advances for another 20,000 million lire, mostly to navigation, iron, steel, and

[20] Originally, IRI was heavily indebted to the banks, whose participations it had taken over. This debt is practically extinguished, mostly through gradual and real payments, and for the rest through the devaluation of the lira. Now IRI borrows occasionally at short-term from the commercial banks, including those it controls. The sums involved are of a moderate size; and the terms are strictly those applied to any other customer.

engineering, by adding to its short-term and medium-term commitments. The situation called for an increase of capital which was raised from 60,000 million lire to 120,000 millions, under Law No. 940 of August 30, 1951, IRI being at the same time authorized to issue new debentures with a full state guarantee, up to 40,000 million lire.

IRI was now in a position to meet the financial calls of its group over a number of years either by issuing its own state-guaranteed debentures or by using its new capital resources. It could reduce its short-term debits and at the same time finance the modernization of the iron and steel industry and the building of new liners. These developments are reflected both in the balance sheet (see Table 7) and in the distribution of its participations and advances among the different sectors. Iron and steel went up from 8 to 17 percent and navigation from 15 to 17 percent, while engineering went down to 36 percent and the banks, the absolute figure remaining without change, from 3.7 to 2.6 percent. For many years, as far back as 1933, IRI had often issued debentures of the *participating* type, that is, debentures bearing interest at a rising rate, proportionate to the dividends which the companies concerned were paying on their share capital, also *mixed* debentures, convertible in whole or in part into shares of the respective companies.

For these operations IRI formed separate companies of which it holds the control and in which are centralized its participations on given sectors; the shares of these IRI subsidiaries are held also by the public and are quoted on the stock exchange. This brought into existence a set of IRI affiliates: FIN-MARE (1936) for navigation; FINSIDER (1937) for iron, steel, and engineering, and FIN-MECCANICA (1948) for engineering and shipbuilding. Finally, in 1952, another holding of the sort was formed, FINELETTRICA, grouping the IRI participation in the electricity industry.

Although, strictly speaking, not a member of the banking system, IRI is now, in fact, the major instrument for long-term economic plans and production policy. The directives for its policy are laid down by the Council of Ministers and its executive organs are appointed by government decree. Profits, after allocation of 20 percent to reserve and 15 percent to a fund for professional training and for social purposes, go to the Treasury in repayment of the capital funds which it supplied.

IRI is thus the center where economic policies are thrashed out.

TABLE 7
MAIN BALANCE SHEET ITEMS, ISTITUTO PER LA RICOSTRUZIONE INDUSTRIALE, DECEMBER 31, 1948–52
(AMOUNTS IN BILLIONS OF LIRE)

Assets	*1948*	*1949*	*1950*	*1951*	*1952*
Participations and credits					
Banking and financial institutions	2.5	6.8	7.0	7.1	7.1
Electricity companies	13.5	19.6	21.0	27.0	36.2
Telephone companies	3.5	6.7	7.9	10.3	12.2
Shipping companies	15.0	22.7	26.4	40.7	47.0
Iron and steel companies	12.5	12.9	14.7	22.3	47.8
Manufacturing concerns	74.5	82.2	87.6	94.5	99.3
Mining and chemical companies	6.5	7.1	7.9	9.2	11.7
Foreign companies and sundry	12.0	12.0	12.7	12.6	15.7
Total	140.0	170.0	185.2	223.7	277.0
Other assets	6.0	15.0	8.0	4.0	14.3
Total assets	146.0	185.0	193.2	227.7	291.3
Losses on manufacturing participations			10.4	17.1	22.5
Losses of previous years			0.1	0.1	0.2
Total	146.0	185.0	203.7	244.9	314.0
Capital Funds					
Endowment fund	60.0	60.0	60.0	100.0	120.0
Special reserve fund			2.3	2.5	2.6
Advances obtained from the Treasury	15.0	15.0	15.0	17.6	17.6
Reserves for losses on securities and participations	15.0	5.0			
Total	90.0	80.0	77.3	120.1	140.2
Liabilities					
Short- and medium-term debts	32.0	42.0	67.7	66.0	45.5
Long-term debts and bonds outstanding	20.0	55.0	58.7	58.8	128.3
Sundry debts and provisions	4.0	8.0			
Total	146.0	185.0	203.7	244.9	314.0

The erstwhile hope that it might "restore" reconstructed undertakings to the private economy (as it did during its first years of life) have now been almost abandoned. From time to time, however, a minority or marginal participation is sold back to private interests; e.g., lately, the ownership of a Liberal Turni newspaper was transferred to a group of business people. IRI's ultimate scope is still the subject of lively controversies: by some it is hailed as the predestined organ for progressive nationalization of the various sectors of the

Italian economy or as a supervisor or controller of the market; in other quarters there is an inclination to make it an ordinary administrator of state property. The more burning problem lies perhaps in the ultimate fate of other conspicuous shareholdings in possession of the state, although not administered by IRI.

ISTITUTO MOBILIARE ITALIANO (IMI)

When IMI was formed in 1931, it was generally considered the instrument for relieving the commercial banks of their industrial investments, for restoring liquidity in the banking system, and for providing the industries with the necessary financial aid.[21] The law had, however, fixed a 10-year duration for IMI's credit operations and this ruled out any possibility of a mandate of this size and nature. A special institution had to be created for that purpose and that is how IRI came into being little more than one year later.

In the past twenty years IMI has fulfilled a variety of tasks, for its own account and as trustee of state funds, by extending medium-term and long-term facilities to industries in many branches. Its capital is only 5,500 million lire, half of which is subscribed half by the Cassa Depositi e Prestiti and the rest by banks of public right, savings banks, private and government institutions. Capital resources have been implemented by issues of debentures. Until 1946 IMI was empowered to incur debenture indebtedness up to ten times its capital; the ceiling has since then been raised to fifteen times its combined capital and reserve.

Capital means and debenture issues are practically the only sources open to IMI for business on its own account. IMI debentures do not carry a state guarantee, but usually rest on a mortgage security; some series, including the most important, were issued in the market and are quoted on the stock exchange; others were placed privately, generally with institutions which had subscribed to IMI's capital. At the end of March, 1953, debentures outstanding totaled 133,000 million lire and credits granted were 136,000 million lire. The original

21 IMI has a Board of Directors of 19 members: (a) the chairman, designated by the Treasury and nominated by the President of the Republic; (b) seven members elected by the Secretary of the Treasury,—among high officers of his own department, and of the Ministries of Finance, Foreign Trade, Shipping, Public Works; (c) eleven members elected by the assembly of the institutions which subscribed the capital. IMI is under the supervision of the Inter-Ministerial Committee for Credit and Saving (see p. 493). Its balance sheets are submitted to the General Assembly of the institutions which subscribed the capital.

10-year time limit for credit extensions was raised in 1936 to 20 years. Both the upper 20-year limit and the lower 10-year limit were subject to exceptions and could be exceeded.

The bulk of the loans granted has gone to hydroelectric projects (43,000 million lire), telephones, shipbuilding, chemical industries, iron, steel and engineering; the last-named sector has taken a rather modest amount, having had the benefit and direct assistance of state funds managed by IMI (the Fondo Industrie Meccaniche, not to be confused with FIN-MECCANICA).

IMI's contribution to shipbuilding calls for special attention. It has been particularly active in this domain since 1940 when it took over the Istituto per il Credito Navale; its loans to shipbuilding yards have played a conspicuous part in the rebuilding of Italy's mercantile fleet. These loans and those to other industries in need of reconversion had, in many cases, state aid for the payment of interest and other facilities.

Under its statutes IMI was and still is authorized to take share capital participations, also to act as financial trustee for third parties and to issue debentures carrying the right to participate in the profits of industrial companies; in practice, IMI has never taken participations in or become a holder of common stock for its own account and is not, therefore, in a position to issue its own debentures against any such holdings. On paper, it has the option to do so, but that option is merely a formal illustration of original intents and purposes, still in abeyance. For the next few years, IMI will in all likelihood adhere to what has become a traditional policy and will go on covering its requirements by issuing debentures of the ordinary type, based solely on its own security.

Its elasticity and flexibility are evidenced by the manyfold functions successfully discharged, always adhering to the same method for procuring the necessary funds. Up to 1936 IMI applied itself first of all to strengthening the industrial concerns hit by the great depression. Between 1937 and the end of the war it helped to finance the so-called "autarchy" and the type of production more or less connected with defense. Since 1945 its program has broadened and become multifarious, directed to foster rehabilitation and the revival of economic life in general, always in close cooperation with the Bank of Italy whose territorial organization IMI uses for its administrative work.

TABLE 8
MAIN BALANCE SHEET ITEMS, ISTITUTO MOBILIARE ITALIANO, MARCH 31, 1948–53
(AMOUNTS IN MILLIONS OF LIRE)

Assets	*1948*	*1949*	*1950*	*1951*	*1952*	*1953*
Cash with banks and banking institutions	5,589	8,086	8,653	16,166	11,586	15,258
Securities	2,029	169	537	1,750	1,908	2,505
Loans	22,268	42,396	61,847	80,204	100,667	136,010
Other items	413	772	1,719	3,170	12,522	16,763
Operations with funds other than its own						
Credits in pounds sterling				58,486	86,350	94,380
Credits with Export-Import Bank funds	83,903	81,206	74,724	59,968	51,495	43,471
Credits with ERP funds		7,045	132,812	234,247	230,706	219,543
Credits with Treasury funds for reconstruction and reconversion of industrial plants	12,380	12,631	12,137	13,294	18,847	18,451
Credits out of the Fondo Industrie Meccaniche	86,374	82,783	72,397			
Credits for merchant marine reconstruction				3,821	3,768	3,398
Other items	7,644	2,171	8,321	14,839	20,035	20,231
Total	220,600	237,259	373,147	485,945	537,884	570,010
Capital Funds and Other Liabilities						
Capital paid and reserves	735	2,309	2,701	3,493	4,883	6,890
Debentures outstanding	20,287	35,543	58,399	76,123	95,028	133,033
Other items	8,588	12,300	8,968	12,043	22,602	26,149
Operations with funds other than its own						
Treasury funds	635	1,173	2,530	9,558	3,356	2,665
Pound sterling operations				58,486	86,350	94,380
Export-Import Bank funds	83,903	81,206	74,610	59,764	51,725	44,503
ERP funds		7,045	132,812	234,247	230,706	219,543
Treasury funds for reconstruction and reconversion of industrial plants	12,380	12,631	12,137	13,294	18,847	18,451
Fondo Industrie Meccaniche	86,374	82,783	72,397			
Merchant marine reconstruction				3,821	3,768	3,398
Other items	7,644	2,171	8,321	14,839	20,035	20,231
Profits	54	98	272	277	584	767
Total	220,600	237,259	373,147	485,945	537,884	570,010

Of particular interest are its postwar functions as trustee of funds received directly from the state or, through the Export-Import Bank and ECA, from the United States government. In addition to more than 35,000 million lire allocated for general reconstruction purposes and for shipbuilding, the Italian government has placed at IMI's disposal a fund of £50 million sterling for the purchase in the sterling area of machinery, equipment, tools, and sundry accessories. The operations carried out by IMI with funds other than its own are, consequently, connected in some way also with foreign exchange operations; they represent the utilization either of American credits or grants, or of Italian foreign exchange balances abroad. The size of this business has made IMI one of the biggest dealers on the foreign exchange market and has brought it, naturally, into close contact both with the Ufficio Italiano dei Cambi (exchange control) and with the bank of issue.

TABLE 9
IMI OPERATIONS WITH FUNDS OTHER THAN ITS OWN [a]
(AMOUNTS IN MILLIONS OF LIRE)

	1948	*1949*	*1950*	*1951*	*1952*
"Fondo Industria Meccanica," mostly to industries in trouble	34,056	43,604	46,700	53,800	36,700
Export-Import bank funds	24,347	53,883	53,700	44,800	35,300
Special reconversion operations	12,404	11,729	10,900	9,800	13,400
Merchant marine reconstruction			200	2,800	3,100
ERP operations		6,292	51,000	102,200	125,500
For the purchase of iron and steel machinery, and other capital goods			12,900	25,700	34,400
For purchases in the sterling area			37,900	65,800	84,200
Total	70,807	115,508	213,300	304,900	332,600

[a] All these figures are taken from the Bank of Italy yearly report. They include only operations really made, not the accountancy items brought on both sides of the balance sheet; they refer to the end of the calendar year. They do not coincide, therefore, with the balance sheet figures (Table 8).

At the end of 1952 the loans granted by IMI and still outstanding totaled about 460,000 million lire, nearly three quarters of which came out of funds other than its own: 125,500 millions out of dollars supplied by ECA; 34,400 millions out of lire counterpart funds; 35,300 millions under the $100 million credit opened by the Export-Import Bank; 84,200 millions out of the sterling placed at its disposal by the Italian Treasury; and 36,700 millions out of funds (in lire) provided by the Treasury as a measure of assistance to the mechanical industry.

These figures suggest that IMI's activities as a trustee and administrator have exceeded in the proportion of 3 to 1 the long-term and medium-term business transacted for its own account. When acting in that capacity, IMI clearly follows the same criteria and methods applied to the business done with its own funds, that is, out of the proceeds of its issues of debentures, or with the funds borrowed from the Italian government. Between the two classes of business there may be, at the most, slight technical differences inherent in the legal provisions by which they are governed, and the currencies may also be different (lire, dollars, or pounds sterling). On the other hand, the underlying policies for the allocation of credit follow the same lines and are dictated by the same spirit of fair and adequate distribution of funds.

CONSORZIO DI CREDITO PER LE OPERE PUBBLICHE AND ISTITUTO DI CREDITO PER LE IMPRESE DI PUBBLICA UTILITÀ

For longer term credit there are two other institutions of public right: the Consorzio di Credito per le Opere Pubbliche (founded in 1919) and the Istituto di Credito per le Imprese di Pubblica Utilità (ICIPU, founded in 1924). The former deals with public bodies, municipalities, provinces and development syndicates, the latter with private concerns. The former finances principally public works in general (roads, harbors, city power plants, popular dwellings, etc.), water and irrigation works, and agricultural development, whereas the latter specializes in electricity and telephones. Consorzio loans may run up to 50 years and are secured by annuities (which are a charge on the state) or by privileged claims on the proceeds of local taxes. ICIPU loans to telephones are generally at 10 to 20 years, those to electricity at 20 to 30 years, always secured by mortgages or by special liens.

Both are practically sections of one and the same institution. The Cassa Depositi e Prestiti was the chief subscriber to the capital of the Consorzio (2,040 millions) and of ICIPU (5,250 millions). They have a joint head office, also a joint Chairman, Vice-Chairman, General Manager, and some joint directors. ICIPU refunds to the Consorzio part of the joint general and administrative expenses.

Both procure necessary funds by issuing debentures and bonds on the Italian or on the foreign markets; only the Consorzio debentures carry a state guarantee; those issued by ICIPU are secured by a mortgage on the plants of the companies to whom the loans were made. At the end of 1952, the Consorzio's outstanding debentures totaled 141,600 million lire of which 22,253 millions had been placed abroad.[22] The electrification of the Italian State Railways (still in course of completion) is one of the outstanding ventures financed by the Consorzio.

At the same time ICIPU had bonds outstanding of 112,280 million lire of which 44,900 millions were foreign bonds. This comparatively high figure represents the lira equivalent, at present rates of exchange, of bonds issued between 1926 and 1930 in New York (and in Switzerland) by a number of Italian electricity companies, the service of which (as well as of the separate Consorzio and ICIPU issues) was suspended from 1940 to 1947 when ICIPU took over these liabilities and issued its own bonds against them. ICIPU has used the proceeds of its mortgage loans to finance the construction of electricity plants and, to a small extent, for the enlargement of telephone networks.

The balance sheets of these two institutions [23] are very compressed: on the debit side figure capital, reserve and bonds issued, on the credit side loans granted and other minor and temporary items. Both institutions are mere intermediaries, but very useful, between the subscribers to their issues of bonds on which they confer the prestige of their standing and patronage, and the parties for whose benefit the bonds are issued and to whom interest is charged at the same rates as those of the bonds (ranging from 4.5 to 6 percent) plus a small commission (for instance of .5 percent).

OTHER STATE-SPONSORED FINANCIAL INSTITUTIONS

A strictly legal classification would call for inclusion in this group of one more institution, the Consorzio Sovvenzioni su Valori Industriali. This was originally an appendage of the Bank of Italy, transformed into an autonomous section of IMI in 1936 (the chairmanship of IMI being on that occasion vested in the governor of the Bank of Italy), from which it was severed at the beginning of 1948 and once more attached to the Bank of Italy, as an autonomous section. (Under the same decree, the governor of the Bank of Italy relin-

22 Equivalent, at the present rate of exchange, of bonds circulating abroad, issued between 1926 and 1930 and converted into new bonds in 1947. Not all the bonds issued at home were offered for public subscription; some series were taken over by the Cassa Depositi e Prestiti, by semi-state institutions and by savings banks.

23 A third institution of the same type, Istituto per il Credito Navale, was founded in 1928 and incorporated into IMI in 1940 (see p. 481).

quished the chairmanship of IMI.) While this Consorzio looks rather like a survival and has only a marginal significance today, the last two financial institutions of this group are quite new and have a promising future before them. They are the Istituto Centrale per il Credito a Medio Termine a favore delle Medie e Piccole Industrie, shortly, Mediocredito, and the Cassa per il Credito alle Imprese Artigiane.

The first was founded (1952) as an institution of public right with the aim of financing, and thus supporting and widening, the activity of the regional institutes listed under "G" in our catalogue of banking and private institutions (see pp. 435–36). These regional institutions grant directly medium-term (up to ten years) credits to medium-sized and small enterprises, i.e., to those which have no more than 500 employees and no more than 1,500 million lire of capital invested. The central institution, Mediocredito, acts as a bankers' bank, rediscounting the bills discounted by the regional institutions and providing the latter with additional funds against the cession as a guarantee of the loans granted in any other form.

Besides the regional institutions, the following have been authorized to operate with i.e., to obtain funds from, the central institution: IMI, ICIPU, Banca di Credito Finanziario (Mediobanca), Banca Centrale di Credito Mobiliare (Centrobanca), EFI (Ente Finanziamenti Industriali), and the Banca del Lavoro, through its special section for credit to the medium-sized and small industries.

The central institution, Mediocredito, is not allowed to receive deposits. It may, however, obtain foreign loans and it may subscribe, alone or in a syndicate, bonds issued by the regional institutions or by the "authorized" institutions. So far the bulk of its resources is represented by its patrimony of 100,000 million lire, 15,000 having been conferred by the Treasury on the ordinary budget and 85,000 accruing from the reimbursement of the sterling loans granted by the Treasury through IMI. The duration of its credits cannot exceed two years even if the original operation had a longer term. Its activity began in April, 1953, and in less than six months more than 4,000 million lire had been utilized.

Finally, Mediocredito has been entrusted with another task: that of financing the medium-term credits granted by the above-mentioned institutions, both regional and national, to exporters of capital goods sold against a deferred or delayed payment. This type of operation, however, was not yet initiated in January, 1954.

The Cassa per il Credito alle Imprese Artigiane was originally founded (1947) to provide medium-term and short-term credit to the handicraftsmen—a form of economic activity which has in Italy a long tradition and a quite remarkable significance. After its recent (1952) reorganization, its resources consist in its patrimony of 5,500 million lire, of which 5,250 were provided from the State and 250 from the Savings Bank, the popular banks, and three institutions of public right. Also, the Cassa has the statutory possibility of placing loans abroad (the Government may guarantee these loans) and of issuing bonds. On the other hand, it cannot receive deposits.

After a first experimental period (May, 1949–July, 1952) during which the Cassa granted loans for 4,700 millions, the mechanism of its operations has been changed. It does not give any longer credit directly to the artisans, but it mobilizes the credits granted them by the following banks and institutions: the banks of public right, the Istituto Centrale delle Banche Popolari (Centrobanca), the Istituto di Credito delle Casse di Risparmio Italiane (Italcasse), the Savings Banks, the popular and cooperative banks, the Casse Rurali ed Artigiane, and the Credit Section of the Ente Nazionale dell'Artigianato e Piccole Industrie.

There are no fixed limits to the duration of the operations, but the Cassa cannot mobilize credits having a term longer than two years. An interesting feature is the contribution made by the Government toward the payment of interest on the loans granted. The contribution may oscillate between 1 percent and 3 percent to be deducted from the rates originally charged, and is defrayed out of a special fund of 1,500 millions (600 paid-up) provided by the Treasury. The artisans pay a maximum interest rate of 6 percent on the bills, 6.5 percent on the loans. The rediscount rate with the Cassa has been fixed at 4 percent.

On December 31, 1953, the Cassa had received applications for 1,023 million lire and granted credits for 374 millions.

PRIVATE FINANCIAL INSTITUTES

The Mediobanca, founded and owned by the three banks of national interest, is at present the most active and most important institution in the sector of medium-term credit. In addition to its own capital (3,000 million lire), it operates with monies received (chiefly through the agency of its three patrons) on savings or fixed deposit account from 1 to 3 years, bearing interest at rates ranging from 4 to 5 percent. In mid-1953 these funds amounted to more than 33,000 million lire, with a 32 percent liquidity, the other two thirds being invested in the form of credits, participations, and *Vor-Finanzierung* (pre-finance) of bond issues. Mediobanca has done an imposing volume of *Konsortial-Geschaeft* (syndicate business), especially between June 30, 1948, and June 30, 1951, acting as manager of syndicates for issues totaling 66,000 million lire (equal to 70–80 percent of the whole of the private bond issues quoted on Italian stock exchanges), apart from more than 12,000 million lire for semi-state bonds. During the two years between June, 1951, and June, 1953, the issue of private companies offered through Mediobanca reached 21,000 million lire, and the semi-state bonds 27,000 millions. This credit is widely distributed: chemical industries head the list, followed very closely by public utilities, textiles, and metallurgy, with navigation, foodstuffs, and housing as a much smaller contingent.[24]

Electricity figures for a comparatively low percentage; that industry must spread amortization of plants over a period much longer than five years, and for finance in that branch there is, in addition to ICIPU, another institution that has made a specialty of it for a long time, the Società Italiana per le Strade Ferrate Meridionali. The name is nowadays of purely historic interest; it goes back to the year 1862 when the company was established to build and run railroads. The network was taken over by the state in 1906. Compensation for the transfer of ownership provided the company with very substantial liquid means, invested in share capital participations and in the financing of undertakings created under its auspices or in which it is

24 Mediobanca is a young institution. It could not, straight from the start, perform all the functions which were performed by Banca Commerciale Italiana, Credito Italiano and Banco di Roma in several decades (1895–1931). But its beginnings were very promising. It was immediately clear that Mediobanca filled a gap, and the common consensus is that it filled it in a discreet and efficient way, and that its functions should now be widened.

As a fact, the creation of Mediobanca counteracted, not the prohibition against mixed banking, but some of the negative results of such a prohibition. Mediobanca is not a mixed bank. Rather, its mere existence is a homage paid to the principles of the 1931–33 banking reform.

But—and this is probably the most interesting aspect—Mediobanca is a proof that the private initiative may still do quite something in a field, which for almost twenty years had been a monopoly of the semi-public institutions. It has also proved the utility of a close cooperation between a medium-term credit institution and the large commercial banks. Nor have the latter banks engaged in any form of *mixed* banking: their risk is limited to the moderate size of their participations to the capital of Mediobanca.

otherwise interested. In other words, the company stands somewhere between a holding company and a *banque d'affaires.*

Its operations are financed first of all out of its considerable capital resources—capital, reserves, and book surpluses represent something like 24,000 million lire—and occasionally out of advances obtained on the security of its holdings. The bulk of its assets consists of securities for about 26,000 million lire and of credits, mostly to affiliated companies, for some 5,000 million. More than half of its participations are in electrical enterprises (some of which are practically under its sole control), the rest in chemical and cement industries, also in mortgage finance. The policy of the last years has been to diversify the assets, taking participations in many sectors outside the traditional ones, and including, for a small percentage, the mining, the oil-refining, the mechanical and the textile industries.

THE CENTRAL BANK AND ITS POLICY

ORGANIZATION AND INFLUENCE

Compared to some of the other Italian banks which can look back on a career of one or more centuries and to some of the central banks in other countries, the Bank of Italy is a relatively young institution. Established in 1893 as a limited liability company, it is only since 1926 that it has become the only bank of issue and since 1936 "the bank of the other banks," when transformed from a limited liability company into an institution of public right and deprived, at the same time, of the right of discounting bills directly from private customers.

In this case, youth has made for freedom from the yoke of traditional routines and of that freedom successive governors, from Stringher to Menichella, the present holder of office, have made wise and proper use. It is perhaps worthy of note that the present President of the Republic, Einaudi, was governor of the Bank from the end of 1944 to June, 1947. Such is the authority they have established that, although subject to Treasury supervision and although brought into more and more intimate cooperation with the Treasury, the Bank of Italy has never been merely an instrument of the Treasury; in matters of economic and credit policies its opinions have always carried great weight. Its position is enhanced by a rule under which the governor of the Bank of Italy by right attends all the meetings of the Comitato Interministeriale per il Credito e il Risparmio, the supreme state organ for money and currency policies, composed of the minister of the Treasury and four other ministers, the Bank being its agent for the preparatory work for the meetings and for the enforcement of deliberations.

The capital has remained at the low level of 300 million lire, divided into registered quotas of 1,000 lire apiece. With 178,000 quotas the savings banks hold the absolute majority, the balance being in the hands of institutions of public right and banks of national interest (altogether 75,500 quotas) and of various insurance and providence institutions (46,500 quotas). The "proprietors" of the Bank of Italy number 98; at the general meetings they have one vote for every one hundred quotas up to 500 quotas and, thereafter, one vote for every 500 quotas, but never more than 50 votes, even when serving as representatives of other participants at general meetings.

The powers of the general meeting are in any case very restricted in scope and do not go beyond approval of the balance sheet and election of auditors. The appointment or revocation of the governor, general manager, and general vice-manager is formally a privilege of the Superior Council, composed of the governor himself and of twelve directors elected at the general meetings of the participants held at the Bank's twelve main branches. These appointments and revocations must be sanctioned by a decree signed by the President of the Republic, on the recommendation of the President of the Council of Ministers and of the minister of the Treasury, after consultation with the whole Cabinet; in other words, they must be sanctioned jointly and severally by the whole government and by the head of the state, the executive power being thus fully responsible for the Bank's policy.

It may be questioned whether the Bank of Italy has had time to gain all the experience which other more venerable central banks may have accumulated. It has been shown, however, that in the midst of all the economic upheavals with the radical changes they have brought about in internal national structures and still more in international relationships, the experience gained in more placid decades and centuries is not always a decisive or potent asset; wisdom, energy, and tenacity often count more than age-long experience or a greater familiarity with cunning technicalities, now often out of date.

In the aftermath of war, with the currency and, as a matter of fact, the whole economy shattered by defeat and devastation, the action of the Bank of Italy in these last years must be acknowledged to have been satisfactory. The lira, bereft of cover and prestige, looked as if it were destined to share the fate of the German mark and the Austrian crown after the First World War; now it is one of the most stable and respected currencies. In September, 1949, at the time of sterling devaluation, the lira was devalued by only 8.5 percent. Throughout 1951, with sterling and the French franc under constant inflationary pressure, Italian prices kept practically stable with Italy's credit balance at the European Payments Union rising from month to month. This does not mean, obviously, that Italy is a richer country than Britain or France or that the quarters responsible for the Italian economy have accomplished great miracles, but it is a sign that, on the whole, the directives adopted and pursued were the right ones and that a proper balance between aims and means has been preserved. Even in 1952–53, although the balance in EPU became adverse and, under the pressure of a deficit in the balance of payments, the reserves suffered a moderate decrease, the prices kept steady, and the lira was quoted on the free markets at a shadow under the official parity.

The action of the Bank of Italy over these last few years deserves, therefore, a somewhat more detailed examination.

From a structural point of view, it would not be quite right to consider the Bank of Italy as the pivot of the Italian credit system; the credit system is very much decentralized, functionally and territorially, and the Bank of Italy does not stand in that center alone but in all surrounding centers and is the cohesive force of a system which is in appearance intricate and diversified.

THE BANK OF ITALY AS BANK OF ISSUE

First of all, but only since 1926, the Bank of Italy is the one and only bank of issue and stands, therefore, at the center of the money market.

The obligation to hold a 40 percent cover in gold and foreign currency for its circulation was repealed in 1935; there is no fixed ceiling for its circulation (this was abolished in 1928) and no legal reserve requirement. The only technical restraint lies in the tax which the Bank of Italy has to pay on its circulation, at the rate of one tenth of the current discount rate, with a minimum of .5 percent after deduction of its reserve. The notes issued for account of the Treasury are exempt from this tax. In 1950 the tax amounted to 1,733 million lire, a good deal less than the cost of printing the notes (2,325 million lire); in 1952 the figures were respectively 2,254 and 2,020 millions. The tax also is far from being a heavy burden on the bank, but it is still one of the chief benefits which the Treasury derives from the Bank of Italy.[25]

The exemption from the tax of notes issued for Treasury requirements is a residue of an ancient distinction between circulation "for trade" and circulation "for account of the state." It no longer applies except for the aforesaid fiscal assessment, but is still made by students when analyzing the causes of changes in circulation. In reality, with its position in the center of all centers, the Bank of Italy is suitably placed to balance and offset the impact of calls from diverse sources: when Treasury calls become more pressing it restricts credit to the private economy and, vice versa, when the Treasury has large liquid funds (at the beginning of the financial year or after a loan has been issued or substantial foreign aid has been received) it can broaden the basis of credit or buy more freely foreign exchange from exporters (through the Ufficio Italiano dei Cambi).

The other alternative, the necessity for the Bank to change its attitude toward the Treasury, is a less frequent occurrence; it has happened, however, in times of crisis, for instance on the first impact of sterling devaluation and of the outbreak of war in Korea.

Also in perfectly normal times the Bank of Italy plays a leveling role between the market and the Treasury, the most conspicuous instances being the alternating phases of expansion and contraction of the credit accommodation extended to the banks in even and in odd months: in February and every second month thereafter direct taxes are due for payment and the Treasury's cash tends to inflate, whilst the flow of deposits to the banks tends to slow down (if not actually to contract), and their cash position is subject to some tension.

THE BANK OF ITALY AS A BANKERS' BANK

This leads to an examination of the two other aspects of the Bank of Italy's central position. As the "bank of the banks" the Bank of Italy is debarred from discounting bills from private customers. This does not mean that it has completely withdrawn from the money market

[25] The profits also go to the Treasury, after payment of a dividend up to 10 percent (plus the profits derived from the investment of the reserve up to 4 percent); in 1952 the Treasury collected 135 million lire for its share of profits.

and that rediscount is its only weapon for ensuring the market liquidity. Nor does it, in fact, stand outside the market or away from it, being still allowed to make advances to private customers on the collateral of government and kindred securities. This permission was probably intended to ensure constant support for the State bond market but the effect has gone beyond that. The knowledge that advances on Treasury bonds can be obtained from the Bank of Italy at rates nominally lower, though in practice equal to the yield of the collateral, causes clients to keep their assets in Treasury bonds, which, in case of need, can be converted into cash almost without loss, rather than on deposit with the banks.

On the other hand, it would not suit the banks if the Bank of Italy were to raise its rate of interest on this type of advance, considering that this is the machinery through which the banks themselves procure additional funds in times of strain on their own cash position.[26] The fact that the Bank of Italy is allowed to deal with the public raises a conflict of interests; it would suit the banks, at least from a technical point of view, if the Bank of Italy were to apply two different rates, one much higher for the public and one much lower than the present one for the banks.

Rediscount alone is an instrument of limited efficiency for directing the market. As indicated, the banks find it more convenient to ask for advances on securities than to rediscount bills; the rates are the same, but whereas the Bank of Italy can discriminate between bills tendered for rediscount it cannot do so with government bonds offered as collateral for advances. Furthermore for many years the Bank of Italy's bill holdings have consisted chiefly of so-called "pool finance bills" for advances on crops and products subject to compulsory stock-piling (see p. 475); this type of finance, created for political ends and, therefore, ultimately a charge on the state, accounted for 84 percent of its whole bill portfolio at the end of 1949 and 79 percent at the end of 1950 (although at the latter date higher in absolute figures). At the end of 1952, the absolute figure was again higher and its percentage rose to 90 percent.

This leaves but a limited margin for influencing the market merely through rediscount operations or manipulations of the official dis-

[26] The banks are in the habit of keeping the bulk of their government and kindred securities with the local branches of the Bank of Italy (on "deposit") for advances thereon whenever the need arises.

Table 10
Main Balance Sheet Items, Bank of Italy
(amounts in billions of lire)

Assets	*1938* [a]	*1946*	*1947*	*1948*	*1949*	*1950*	*1951*	*1952*	*October, 1953*
Bills	3.7	44.0	137.2	128.9	170.8	191.7	180.4	206.2	241.2
Advances on securities and goods	3.7	13.1	34.2	51.7	59.9	89.4	92.9	122.4	90.6
State and state-guaranteed securities	0.8	37.8	37.5	39.3	37.7	36.9	34.5	32.1	30.1
Advances to the Treasury [b]	2.1	538.2	671.5	811.9	859.8	744.7	676.8	766.4	761.1
Foreign currencies held abroad		8.7	12.8	17.2	20.6	27.9	36.7	42.8	59.7
Sundry debtors (includes Exchange Office)	1.4	18.1	49.2	210.7	465.7	525.7	746.4	728.8	674.8
Liabilities									
Banknotes in circulation	18.9	505.0	788.1	963.0	1,048.2	1,048.5	1,291.8	1,381.4	1,300.0
Free deposits	0.8	59.1	52.5	68.0	110.7	123.4	75.1	59.5	50.9
Term deposits (includes compulsory bank reserves)	0.3	106.0	86.5	164.0	262.7	252.1	308.3	360.2	409.4
Sundry creditors	1.1	8.5	21.3	26.6	47.0	57.3	68.6	93.6	97.5
International aid (ERP counterpart funds)				58.2	159.5	35.0	36.5	12.3	15.0

[a] Data as of December 31 except for 1952.
[b] These include, besides the advances *strictu sensu*, the amount of the Allied Military lire redeemed by the Bank of Italy and the investment in Treasury bonds of the banks' compulsory deposits.

count rate. As it is, the whole bill portfolio of the Bank of Italy is of modest size and comprised only 11,000 million lire of ordinary bills at the end of 1949 and only 12,000 millions at the end of 1952; these are small percentages of the whole and still smaller percentages of the respective totals of credit granted by the banking system. As regards advances against securities, the advances granted to the public at the end of 1952 represented 13.7 percent of the whole amount outstanding; this is a comparatively high percentage, considering the basic difference between advances to the public and advances to the credit institutions, but of small significance in absolute figures: 17,000 million lire at the end of 1952.

THE BANK OF ITALY AS BANKER TO THE TREASURY

The third aspect of the Bank of Italy is in its functions as treasurer, occasionally also banker, to the Treasury, the Bank acts as state treasurer in the provinces and, in given circumstances, has also made substantial advances to the state. In the past, different laws authorized "temporary" and "extraordinary" advances to the state; during the last war and in the immediate postwar period the combined total soared up to 443,000 million lire and has remained frozen at that level after the measures taken for the defense of the lira at the end of August, 1947. However, since November, 1952, the Treasury has gradually and steadily reduced its debt for "temporary" advances (from 100,000 to 77,000 in September, 1953), as it took at its charge a growing amount of 50- and 100-lire notes. It is true that soon thereafter the state's credit ceiling with the Bank of Italy for current cash requirements was raised from its former 50,000 million lire limit to a figure undefined, not to exceed, however, 15 percent of budget expenditure. That ceiling has never been reached. Up to the middle of 1950 the Treasury's indebtedness to the Bank of Italy fluctuated between 60,000 million lire and 70,000 million lire, which is far below the legal limit. Since then the Treasury has been a creditor of the Bank of Italy, at first for small amounts and since April, 1951, for 60,000 million to 70,000 million lire.[27]

[27] The Treasury credit balance of 110,000 million lire at the end of January, 1952, is due to the proceeds of the Reconstruction Loan for the Flooded Areas. This balance decreased from month to month as the Treasury utilized the proceeds of the loan, and was reduced to 25,000 millions at the end of the year. It rose again to 116,500 millions in February, 1953, as the result of a new issue of nine-year Treasury bonds, and again dwindled during the year until, at the end of December, 1953, the Treasury was in debt to the Bank for 14,250 millions. Another Treasury bond issue, which is likely to yield about 200,000 millions, was offered in February, 1954.

Another claim on the Treasury that has remained unchanged since 1947 arises out of the military lire issue by the Allied armies (*amlire*) and bank notes issued for their account by the Bank of Italy, altogether 145,000 million lire which the Treasury now owes the Bank after it has withdrawn from circulation the notes issued by the Allied military authorities and replaced them with its own issues.

The last important credit claim on Treasury is the investment in securities, for the account of the Treasury, of the compulsory deposits lodged with the Bank of Italy by the credit institutions. In February, 1950, this was as high as 207,000 million lire, but has fallen off (to 152,000 millions in December, 1951), the credit institutions having probably found it more convenient themselves to invest in Treasury bills a larger quota of these compulsory deposits, rather than depositing actual cash. Since then, however, this item has gone up again to 230,000 millions toward the end of 1953.

It goes without saying that this is not the whole story of the Bank of Italy's relations with the Treasury, even if comments on minor miscellaneous services were added. We have seen that a large part of its bill portfolio, the quota relating to agricultural pools, ultimately serves to finance the state's economic policy and that the machinery for advances on securities is so devised as to operate as a prop for the market of government bonds. It should now be added that for its own account the Bank holds some 30,000 million lire of obligations issued or guaranteed by the state (about 9,000 million less than in 1948) and that it still carries on its balance sheet an amount of 1,773 million lire on account of gold requisitioned by the state during the First World War and transferred to London as collateral for credits obtained on that market.

Another and nowadays the most conspicuous asset item is to be found under the heading "sundry debtors," 90 percent of which consists of advances to the Ufficio Italiano dei Cambi, originating from and directly governed by the currency agreements between the state and other countries or by its trade policy. On the liability side there are figures, still conspicuous although less than in the past, on account of "international aid," i.e., the counterpart funds of ERP and Mutual Security Administration aid. The Bank of Italy is, therefore, linked to the Treasury by many closely interwoven ties; their inflationary and deflationary effects partly offset each other, until the ultimate residual factors, positive and negative, must be nicely balanced with the exigencies of the market and of productive activity.

Leaving aside operations of indirect finance, the Bank of Italy's credit to the Treasury amounts at present to some 800,000 million lire. It will suffice to compare this figure with that of the circulation, stable around 1,250,000 million lire all through 1952, to appreciate the extent and the primary importance of this relationship. From a purely technical and unrealistic point of view, it might be said that circulation is very largely covered by the Bank's credit to the Treasury and that the soundness of the lira rests ultimately on the fiscal potential of the Italian people—a corollary not altogether untenable or too far-fetched, even if one ignores other real guarantees, gold and foreign currencies, not to mention the credits to the private economy which, as seen before, are of comparatively small importance. It should be remembered that loans to the Treasury have remained almost unchanged since 1947, intervening fluctuations of circulation being brought about by other factors, principally by the building up of open and latent reserves and the increasing amount of credit given to a notably expanding production.

DEFENSE OF THE STABILITY OF THE LIRA

Since the autumn of 1947, the stability of the lira has been the main concern of the Bank of Italy. Its policy has come under severe criticism at home and abroad, from theoretical economists, exporters, labor unions, the ECA mission and, naturally, debtors in general. The rigidity applied to achieve that end may be explained chiefly by the very slender margin of safety for maneuvering. Critics often lose sight of the extent to which the lira has been devalued and of the low level at which the process was eventually stopped. Between 1914 and the first postwar period the currency lost about 85 percent of its purchasing power and the remaining 15 percent again lost another 98 percent between the years 1938 and 1947. In the space of little more than 30 years prices have risen at least 500 times according to official indexes and between 800 and 1,000 times according to the experience of consumers. A meal that could be had for one lira in 1913 now costs no less than 900 or 1,000 lire. The rise has not been uniform; rents and public services, for instance, have been blocked on much lower levels. On the whole, it cannot be denied that the fall in the value of the lira has been catastrophic (even if it has, incidentally, annulled the burden of the former public debt). On the other hand, it must be acknowledged that there is something almost miraculous and unprecedented in a currency that had lost 999 thousandths of its purchasing value in the course of one generation and yet managed to escape complete annihilation.

In its solicitude for the currency the Bank of Italy has always shown extreme caution. Expansion of the circulation has consistently been made to lag slightly behind the rising indexes of production and national income. Through alternating and typically seasonal fluctuations (stability during the first half year, a rising trend in the second half with a pronounced peak at the end of December), the circulation rose at the rate of about 190,000 million lire in 1948, 100,000 millions in 1949, 120,000 millions in 1950, 126,000 millions in 1951, 89,000 millions in 1952, and only 34,000 millions in 1953. At the end of that year it touched a 1,415,000 million lire high water mark, but is quite likely to recede seasonally by about 120,000 millions during the first two months of 1954.

The factor chiefly responsible for this expansion is the supply of lire to the Ufficio Italiano dei Cambi which purchases foreign currencies from exporters and sells them to importers. When the two sets of operations do not balance, the Ufficio Italiano dei Cambi calls on the Bank of Italy for fresh supplies of lire so that it may go on buying foreign exchange for which there is no adequate demand for imports and, vice versa, repays lire to the Bank of Italy when its sales of foreign currencies are higher than its purchases. The course of Italy's balance of payments in 1948–51 and the freezing of a part of some big Italian balances abroad brought about a situation in which the Ufficio Italiano dei Cambi has almost continually been called upon to buy more foreign exchange than it could dispose of and hence to call to an ever-growing extent on the Bank of Italy for lira supplies. The credit extended by the Bank of Italy to the Ufficio Italiano dei Cambi is not listed separately in its statements, but it is generally held to account for nine tenths of the "sundry debtors" item. At the end of 1947 that item figured for only 49,000 million lire, but rose progressively to 211,000 millions at the end of 1948, 466,000 millions at the end of 1949, 526,000 millions at the end of 1950 (after having touched 565,000 millions in August) and 741,000 millions at the end of 1951. It reached a "high" of 784,000 millions at the end of August, 1952. Since then, the trade balance deficit has caused a constant regression, to 678,000 millions at the end of September, 1953. In November,

1953, it stood at 683,000 millions. Against this the Ufficio Italiano dei Cambi holds sterling, dollars, Argentine pesos, also credit balances on clearing accounts and with the EPU. To a certain extent, the corresponding credit of the Bank of Italy is immobilized (not all foreign currencies being immediately realizable); at the same time, these figures give some indication of the currency reserve which Italy has managed to build up.

The Bank of Italy's own reserves appear under three headings: the "foreign currency balances held abroad," which have risen moderately up to 61,200 millions; the "gold deposited abroad" owed by the State and previously referred to, which still figures for 1,773 millions and only pro memoria; and the "gold in the vaults of the bank," still assessed at the 1936 price of 21,381 lire to the kilogram, that is, at 4,224 millions and now worth, at the present official price, 140,000 millions. It is not possible, therefore, to work out the precise total value of the currency reserves of the Bank of Italy. According to the statistics of the Federal Reserve System, American banks hold about $350 million for Italian account, $280 million on behalf of the Italian government and of Italian banks, the rest for private citizens. ECA calculated that in June, 1951, the gold and dollar reserves amounted to $538 million. The International Monetary Fund has put total reserves at the end of July, 1953, at $849 million (after a maximum of $1,062 million at the end of February, 1952).

The management of the currency reserves and the exchange control are specifically the business of the Ufficio Italiano dei Cambi, in close cooperation with the Bank of Italy whose governor is the chairman of the Ufficio's board of directors and which has supplied the Ufficio's capital fund of 100 million lire. The Ufficio is directly subject to the ministry of the Treasury which appoints the majority of its board and to whom the balance sheet has to be submitted after it has been approved by the board of directors. The Bank of Italy tends to operate only as an executive technical organ in the management of exchange control.

That is very much its attitude also in regard to the counterpart funds. The Bank administers these funds of ERP and provides for the necessary payments as and when single allotments have been sanctioned by Italian legislation and ECA (later MSA). The distribution of these funds has nothing to do with the credit policy of the Bank of Italy, but reflects only the government's directives in the matter of economic policy. Assignments aggregating nearly 780,000 million lire have been authorized between 1948 and 1953, mostly for railroads (137,000 millions), IMI–ERP loans (186,000 millions), agriculture and forests (82,400 millions), Cassa per il Mezzogiorno (94,000 millions),[28] and public works, particularly housing (181,000 millions), the balance being spread over a number of minor schemes.

On the other hand, the Bank of Italy plays a commanding part in the supervision of the whole credit system in its observance of banking law and agreements. It is to the Bank of Italy that applications for the opening of new banks or new branches must be addressed, as well as for increases of capital and for exceptions to the limits of credit or capital resources. These police powers, obviously, provide the Bank of Italy with another useful instrument for the exercise of control over the whole credit system, from the center or at least from inside.

POSTWAR CREDIT POLICIES OF THE BANK OF ITALY

A full analysis of the policies adopted by the Bank of Italy since the end of the war could not be made without passing in review the evolution of the whole Italian economy, discussing the difficult problems which had to be faced and commenting on a number of statistical series. Such an investigation would bring us far beyond the limits of the present study. On the other hand, the general directives of the Bank of Italy's policy are rather easy to discern, mainly because in the yearly report by the Governor, that policy is commented on and defended with an abundance of arguments and figures, defying comparison with the reports of almost any other central bank.

The postwar period may be conveniently divided in two phases: the first one, from the armistice (September 8, 1943) to September, 1947, when inflation was definitely stopped; the second, from September, 1947, to the present day, punctuated by the crisis of pound sterling devaluation (September, 1949) and the Korean war (for the period from the summer of 1950 to the summer of 1951).

During the first phase, the influence of the Bank of Italy was extremely restricted. The Bank had lost practically all its reserves, and it had to finance a huge and growing budget deficit. Inflation—which

[28] Cassa per il Mezzogiorno is a state agency, endowed with a yearly allocation of 100,000 million lire for twelve years, to promote the economic development of southern Italy. IBRD granted it a small dollar loan.

had been latent since 1938–39, but contained by price controls and wartime restrictions—exploded and after 1943 became the dominant and uncontrollable phenomenon of Italian economic life. The Bank's efforts to contain the inflationary process had the sole result of slowing it down, mainly because one of the first effects of inflation had been the loss of control of the monetary and credit markets by the Bank of Italy. The usual "weapons," the discount rate and control through the rediscount of bills and advances on securities, had almost completely lost their effectiveness. "Pool" financing (p. 475, note 17) and large advances to the Treasury forced a rapid increase in the money supply. Circulation increased by more than fourfold, from 175,000 to 800,000 million lire.

That does not mean that the Bank of Italy maintained a passive attitude before such dangerous developments. But its influence, rather than through customary technical instruments, was brought to bear through the Governor's moral authority (Mr. Einaudi) on the government (budget) on the one side, and on the other side on the banking system (credit allocation), which in the meantime had to bear the brunt of inflationary forces.

Measures adopted in the fall of 1947 marked a decisive turning point, both in the Bank of Italy's policies and in its capacity to implement them. Its program since then may be summed up in the words "defense of the lira," but it must be made clear at once that the defense of the lira has been planned and conducted with due consideration of a host of correlated factors: the necessary equilibrium in foreign trade and the balance of payments; the harmonization on the monetary market of Treasury needs with private needs; the promotion of investment within the limits of available savings, and the promotion of savings through the reestablishment of confidence in the lira and the strengthening of the country's productive equipment; and finally the desirability of keeping on parallel lines the growing production of capital and consumer goods.

Through emphasis on price stabilization, effective from the end of 1947, attained by the mechanism of compulsory banking reserves, the Bank of Italy gradually regained control of the market, and was again able to exercise control with full efficacy during critical periods. At the same time, the improvement of the Italian balance of payments and the cautious utilization of American aid enabled the Bank of Italy to rebuild its gold reserve, a reserve of moderate size in relation to the country's needs, but strong enough to cushion the repercussions of more than one international crisis. When the pound sterling was devalued by 30 percent, Italy was in a condition to limit to less than 9 percent lira devaluation, and to absorb without too great strain wide changes in international prices.

The "conservative" attitude of the Bank of Italy has been assailed several times, both in Italy and abroad. The Bank, however, has always replied to its critics that the gold and foreign currency reserves, far from having a mere subsidiary character in the frame of economic and financial reconstruction, exercise an essential stabilizing and progressive function. As disequilibria in foreign economic relations are bound to happen from time to time, even with exchange control, and speculative movements are quick to widen such disequilibria, the countries without adequate reserves see themselves driven to adopt countermeasures in the form of quantitative restrictions, import prohibitions, and the like. This gives to the regular flow of trade a jerky rhythm, provokes abnormal profits and losses, induces farmers and manufacturers to prefer the "protected" national markets, and sacrifices the blessings of the international division of labor. On the contrary, the Bank of Italy's reserves permitted it in 1951 to face the adverse trend in Italian balance of payments, without resorting to drastic measures of restricting purchases abroad, such as were adopted by Germany and later on by France and England.

On the other hand, the Bank of Italy has always turned down with the utmost energy all suggestions to utilize the reserves to face a deficit of a chronic character, because that would be tantamount to squandering them, and would forfeit Italy's credit standing abroad. The equilibrium in the balance of payments must be reached the hard way: through the increase of exports, both of goods and services, without rigid import restrictions. Accordingly, Italy gave her fullest support to EPU. From April, 1951, when for the first time Italy was a creditor in the European clearing, to December, 1951, the Bank of Italy advanced to the Italian Exchange Office no less than 170,000 million lire just to finance those growing credits (see p. 424).

Mostly through these operations, a notable liquidity appeared on the Italian market during the second half of 1951, in open contrast to the credit stringency, which characterized the first half. The Bank of Italy admits that during the spring there was "a sensation of hardship," but held that in that perilous circumstance it was "impossible to wear velvet gloves." As an aftermath of the Korean war, a speculative boom had started, which had to be brought under control "at any price." There was also the danger of a decrease in investments destined to the production of capital goods and to rearmament, and of a parallel increase in those destined to provide consumption goods. However, "the people had not become wealthier" as a consequence of the outbreak of hostilities in Korea, and the inadequacy of current incomes would have brought that abnormal demand to a rapid end.

When a new equilibrium was reached, toward the end of 1951, the danger still remained of a marked rise in prices as a result of the improvement of monetary liquidity and of a general feeling that things were going to be easier. The rise did not occur by reason of (a) a protracted fall in international prices; (b) the reaction of the consumers who chose to postpone their purchases; (c) the fact that the policies of trade liberalization and customs tariff reduction were abided by and in some cases pushed forward; (d) a Government Loan that absorbed some of the surplus purchasing power on the market. Anyway, had such a tendency to the rise in prices manifested itself, the Bank of Italy admonishes *post factum* that it would not have hesitated to request an increase in the official discount rate, and in the percentage of compulsory banking reserves, together with the adoption of the strictest criteria in the granting of credit.

This stern warning shows that the Bank of Italy persists in its policy of severity, and that it is satisfied with the results achieved. The Bank acknowledges that, to solve the fundamental problems of the national balance of payments and unemployment, it is necessary to "reconcile the reduction of the external deficit with an expansion of investment, preparing through the defence of the lira the conditions for an increase of our exports and a steadier savings formation."

Conditions were less dramatic, if not easier, in 1952 and 1953. The tension persisting on the monetary market under a "veil" of liquidity enabled the Bank of Italy to keep the inflationary forces well under control. The deficit in the balance of payments (drifting after the virtual end of the American grants from the dollar area to the European Payments Union) was faced in an orthodox way, by selling gold and foreign exchange. On the international markets the lira quotation registered a definite improvement.

CONSORZIO SOVVENZIONI SU VALORI INDUSTRIALI

The Consorzio Sovvenzioni su Valori Industriali, for all intents and purposes almost an appendage of the Bank of Italy, has played at other times quite a notable part in the sector of medium-term credit. Founded on the eve of the First World War to support the market for industrial securities, it carried on thereafter sundry "salvage" works until attached to IMI in 1936, as a special section. In 1945 it went back to the Bank of Italy, whose governor presides over its Central Management Committee and which, by way of rediscount, provides the Consorzio with the necessary funds for its activities. Another source is the issue of its own interest-bearing bonds and yet another, until 1943, the rediscount credit obtained from the Bank of International Settlements. The Consorzio's capital is small (200 millions), but it has amongst its patrons, in addition to the Bank of Italy, the institutions of public right, the Cassa Depositi e Prestiti, the more important savings banks and a "banking group" formed of nine banks, big and small, and the Società Italiana per le Strade Ferrate Meridionali.

Its credit operations consist of advances against bills issued on the collateral of industrial securities, mortgages on shipping, liens on manufactured or semi-finished goods and raw materials, or on the proceeds of bills discounted and warrants. For the moment, the Consorzio is marking time. At the end of 1952, loans outstanding amounted to 17,800 million lire, of which 14,100 millions had been financed by rediscount with the Bank of Italy and 615 millions by issues of interest-bearing bonds.

MONEY AND CAPITAL MARKETS

MONEY MARKET

A money market in the full sense of the term cannot be said to exist in Italy except in an embryonic stage. Ordinary Treasury bills are not offered by way of auction to the best bidders or at rates from time to time subtly adjusted to varying conditions of the moment; they are on tap at a fixed rate, unchanged from April 9, 1949 (previous fluctuations ranged within one half of one percent) to May 10,

1952, when they were reduced from 4.71 percent (for one-year bonds) to 4.17 percent. There is no day-to-day money market. Borrowing rates, as we have seen, are governed by the banking agreements. The official discount rate represents a minimum rate and the market is more responsive to increases than to cuts. Stock exchange finance, with the carry-over facilities given by the banks, is probably the best-organized sector. Their present investment under that heading amounts to some 95,000 million lire; the rates vary according to the size of the speculative positions to be carried over, but always within a limited range, from a minimum of 5 percent on government obligations to a maximum of 7 percent on first-grade industrials.

Although not of the importance of those in the bigger international centers, the Italian stock exchanges have nonetheless developed into active markets, adequate to present needs. There are ten of them. The Milan Bourse is by far the most active and most influential, the importance of the others being restricted to particular sectors: government bonds in Rome, insurance issues in Trieste, special mining stocks in Florence, shipping and sugar refineries in Genoa, and so forth. (With their performance in these last few years we have dealt on pp. 510–11.)

Their capacity of absorption is very largely influenced by the operations of the state, by its issues (of recent years only Treasury bonds) and by its fiscal policy. The so-called and at times hotly debated "nominatività" (the compulsory registration of stocks), introduced during the war and maintained thereafter for no other purpose than to prevent all-too-easy fiscal evasions, has become a bugbear and has created a psychosis of fiscal panic hardly propitious to new issues and to the market for common stocks. In recent times issues of shares have averaged from 70,000 million to 90,000 million lire per annum, which is only just the prewar level (if currency devaluation is taken into account), whereas demand for fresh capital is now unquestionably much higher than in 1938. In 1953, however, their issues reached 170,000 millions. On the other hand, it must be pointed out that only in the past few years have the companies started to pay comparatively high dividends. According to calculations made by the Bank of Italy, the average yield on industrial shares crashed from 5.11 percent in 1938 to 0.47 percent in 1946 and stayed on a 0.59 percent level in 1947, to bounce up again by stages to 6.56 percent in

1951 (6.19 percent in 1952).[29] During the years of inflation, common stock was looked upon as a refuge, regardless of profit, and is only now regaining its function and attraction as an instrument for financing new enterprises and for profit-making investment.

The discredit into which common stocks had fallen has not been of particular advantage to the bond market, despite the fact that bonds are exempt from registration. The big expansion of bond issues in 1949 was due to special fiscal privileges attaching to those which had been decided upon up to December 31 of that year; some of which were eventually issued in following years. This background of belated and "invisible" operations was, of course, a deterrent to other new issues to which the fiscal privileges did not apply and decidedly affected the flow of new business. It should be added that, with the peril of currency devaluation receding more and more, industrial companies have become more reluctant to enter into fresh debenture commitments. This is probably the reason why, apart from the more attractive dividends, the interest of investors now seems to converge on common stock more than on bond issues, the "fiscal terror" having been absorbed or surpassed by the fears created by the fiscal reform now in course (the Vanoni reform), which calls for declaration of income on common stocks and bonds alike.

The main factor of liquidity and capacity of absorption still lies in the operations of the Treasury. Against a yearly placing of private securities from 100,000 million lire to 200,000 millions between 1948 and 1953, the issues of one-year Treasury bills totaled 317,000 million lire in 1948, 150,000 millions in 1949, 29,000 millions in 1950, 52,000 millions in 1951, 75,000 millions in 1952, and only 14,000 millions in 1953. The lower issues during the last four years are mostly due to mass conversions of one-year bonds into nine-year Treasury bonds.

Altogether, 340,000 millions of nine-year Treasury bonds were placed in 1950–53. If we add to these figures the issues of mortgage bonds and those made by state-sponsored institutions (350,000 million lire over the six years), the prevalence of public over private issues will be thrown into yet clearer focus.

On the other hand, ordinary Treasury bills are not as a rule bought

29 It should be noted that the yield on debentures has throughout been decidedly higher than the yield on common stock, but now several first-class stocks pay dividends up to 8 or 9 percent.

for investment and do not absorb funds which would otherwise flow to the market. The bulk is taken by the banks which can use them also for their compulsory deposits with the Bank of Italy.

FINANCIAL MARKET

The banks are certainly the hard core of the money market, but have no direct influence on the financial market. As already explained, the ordinary credit institutions are not allowed to take share capital participations and cannot, consequently, participate in issue syndicates. No bank can operate directly on the stock exchange, stock dealings being a monopoly of public officials called *agenti di cambio* (stockbrokers). They receive, of course, a steady and large volume of orders from their customers, which they carry out through the agency of their habitual brokers; the bigger banks are allowed to keep an "observer" on the stock exchange, to supervise, in their clients' interest, the execution of their orders. Their offices and services are at the disposal of client companies for receiving applications to issues of bonds and common stock, whether these be offered to the public directly by the issuing company or through an underwriting syndicate (usually headed by a financial institution, for instance, Mediobanca). Their networks of branches and subagencies are extremely active when public loans are issued, that being, incidentally, an opportunity to test the degree of penetration of the bigger institutions into the various sectors of the economy and among the social classes; it is usually an occasion for intense competition.

The cost of flotation varies according to the issuer, also according to the size of the operation and the particular circumstances of the moment. As a rule, 1 percent is paid for commission and publicity on state issues and 2.5 to 3 percent on private issues.

Foreign participation in the Italian money and financial markets is nowadays of very secondary importance. The loan, previously referred to, by the Bank for International Settlements to the Consorzio Sovvenzioni su Valori Industriali is past history. The credit lines which foreign banks have opened to their Italian correspondents are used exclusively to finance foreign trade. Foreign bank balances with Italian banks are certainly much smaller than Italian bank balances with banks abroad, especially in the United States.[30]

[30] Foreign exchange restrictions have prevented movements of hot money which might at times have been attracted to Italy.

On the financial market the situation is just the reverse. No foreign bonds or shares are quoted on Italian stock exchanges whilst Italian bonds, issued before the war, are still listed in New York, London and Switzerland. Snia-Viscosa shares are quoted in London, Montecatini in Paris, and those of two public utilities companies (Soc. Adriatica di Elettricità and Soc. Meridionale di Elettricità) on the Swiss Stock Exchanges. There is also foreign capital, mainly Swiss, in electricity, textiles, and other Italian industries. The few foreign issues previously quoted in Italy disappeared as a result of the obligation imposed on holders to deliver them to the exchange monopoly. Foreign capital has of late shown renewed interest in Italian investments.

CONCLUSIONS

From this survey the Italian banking system emerges as a really efficient instrument for the gathering up of savings, down to the most minute sums, of whatever money may lie idle and unemployed, even if only temporarily. There is hardly any hoarding, except for some buying of gold coins and ingots, but on an infinitely smaller scale than, for instance, in France. Nor are there any great leakages in the system, except for the private funds on current account with industrial companies which, on principle, should take monies only from their partners or dependents; even this phenomenon, due to the higher rates offered, is not much more than an episode. Practically all savings and available funds go to the commercial banks, to the ordinary and Post Office savings banks or directly to the Treasury.

The apportionment of these funds between the Treasury and the private economy may be open to discussion; the measure in which the Treasury uses its share for current expenditure or for investment is, in its turn, much discussed, also on a political level. As regards the allocation of bank credit to the various branches of the private economy, it has not, in general, been the target of particular criticism; complaints are heard now and then that preference is given to one sphere over another or that greater liberality is shown to big borrowers than to smaller clients. On closer examination it will be found that this criticism has nothing to do with the actual distribution of ordinary credit, but arises from the oft-lamented shortage of capital, or that it is prompted by immobilizations or other effects of deficient business management, the commercial banks being in such cases expected to step in and retrieve the situation. The numerous financial institutions described in the preceding pages are of recent formation or at least much younger than the big commercial banks and looked as if they were destined to make good quickly the chronic scarcity of capital. As they were provided with quite sizable capital, at least at the start, and with the possibility of multiplying their means by issuing bonds, at times with a state guarantee or state contribution, they were bound to give the impression that it was going to be easy for them to quench the thirst for capital in their respective sectors. In a poor country, where the formation of capital is perforce a process hard and slow, their assignment should have been to promote and accelerate it or, with an instantaneous and concentrated effort, to implement it and take its place.

Up to the 1931 depression it had been left to the ordinary banks, more particularly to the bigger ones, to finance new industries, not merely by supplying the initial means but also by providing for subsequent requirements. Of this task they acquitted themselves, on the whole, most commendably, also by procuring foreign capital for the national industries and by following up their development in a spirit of close cooperation. With the great depression this function came to an abrupt end and whatever the merits earned by the financial institutions which stepped into the shoes of the ordinary banks, particularly for the reconstruction of plants destroyed or damaged during the war, they cannot be said to have shown quite the same flexibility or the same keenness of initiative, or the same capacity to forestall national or world-wide trends.[31] Hence the special interest that now attaches to the medium credit institutions which apply themselves to fill the gap between the ordinary credit banks and the government sponsored institutions.

The Italian banking system is, in fact, giving once more proof of its resiliency. There is hardly any big institution that has not modified its function in the course of its existence. Those whose life goes back

[31] Mixed banking was terminated in Italy as a result of the great depression. It fell a victim to that worldwide crisis. Participations and industrial long-term credits became frozen to such an extent, and the Stock Exchange fell to such low levels, that the banks found their liquidity seriously endangered, and saw no possibility of getting additional funds from the public. There was no run. But, after the example of the Credit-Anstalt, it was deemed advisable to prevent the possibility that a similar situation could arise in Italy too.

for centuries have undergone the most radical changes. Nonetheless, they preserve their distinct personalities and carry with ease and grace the weight of their traditions—including those dropped in the course of time—in the midst of a system heterogeneous in its seniorities, in its legal and structural aspects, which yet functions smoothly, without undue shocks or clashes. Liquidity and safety are ensured by the rigid regulations adopted in 1947 and enforced by the central bank. Absolute proof of the system's invulnerability can come only in the course of time. Similarly, only by following the trends of the economy and of prices during the coming months and years will it be possible to measure its success in avoiding inflation or deflation. All that can be said on the basis of recent experience is that the banking system has shown itself to be a docile and efficient instrument for the application of the directives of the Treasury and of the Bank of Italy and that, should anything go wrong, the fault may not be entirely its own.

REFERENCES

LEGAL AND STATISTICAL

The basic regulations which govern credit business in Italy are laid down in the Banking Law (Royal Decree of March 12, 1936, No. 375) and subsequent amendments. Of this law there are several editions; the best seems to be *La Legge Bancaria,* a coordinated text edited by the Italian Bankers Association, Rome, 1950.

A more complete collection of all legal provisions concerning banks and stock exchanges is given in *Codice della Banca, Borse e Valute,* published by Cesare Zuffi, Bologna.

Legal points bearing on banking are dealt with, in addition to the general legal journals, in the review *Banca, Borsa e Titoli di Credito,* published by Dr. A. Giuffrè, Milan.

The most important source for banking statistics is the *Bollettino* published every two months by the Ufficio Studi of the Bank of Italy. The Bank of Italy used to issue its statement every ten days, but now only once a month, generally toward the end of the following month. The main items are released a few days in advance in *Supplemento al Bollettino,* a fortnightly publication; the even numbers, published on the 25th of every month, give the Bank's situation and some figures relating to the budget and public debt; the odd numbers, published on the 10th of every month, give figures relating to savings, yields on stocks, and the situation of the credit institutions.

The banks must furnish the Bank of Italy a full statement every three months, but only the most important among them publish summaries in the press or in their own publications. Other figures and data and a full report on the financial markets are given in daily financial papers, such as *24 Ore* and *Il Sole* of Milan.

A fundamental survey of the whole situation is given in the yearly reports of the Bank of Italy, which are published usually in the month of May. Some of the most important commercial banks also give in their reports views and comments on the banking situation.

Elaborate statistics on the shares and bonds are to be found in: *Indici e dati relativi ad investimenti in titoli quotati nelle Borse italiane,* edited by Mediobanca (Banca di Credito Finanziario), with a text in four languages.

GENERAL AND SPECIFIC

Literature on the Italian banking system is plentiful on the historical, commemorative, and monographic side, very poor on the practical and scientific level. Some of the more recent studies are listed here.

Ballardini, Achille. Le Casse di Risparmio. Bologna, 1950.

Bresciani Turroni, Costantino. "Credit Policy and Unemployment in Italy," Banco di Roma, *Review of Economic Conditions in Italy,* May, 1949.

D'Albergo, Ernesto. Les banques italiennes. Paris, Recueil Sirey, 1940.

Di Nardi, Giuseppe. "L'Istituto d'Emissione" and "La Politica del Credito," which are Chapters II and X of Vol. IV, *Rapporto della Commissione Economica presso il Ministero della Costituente.* Rome, Istituto Poligrafico dello Stato, 1946.

Formentini, Paride. "Le Crédit Mobilier en Italie," *Bulletin de la Société Belge d'Etudes et d'Expansion,* No. 141 (1950).

Giussani, Camillo. "Le crédit à Moyen Terme en Italie," *Bulletin de la Société Belge d'Etudes et d'Expansion,* No. 156 (1953).

Lanzarone, Giuseppe. Il sistema bancario italiano. Turin, Einandi, 1948.

—— "The Italian Banking System," Banco di Roma, *Review of the Economic Conditions in Italy,* V, No. 6 (November, 1951), 485–509.

Parravicini, Giannino. L'ordinamento bancario e l'attività creditizia. Milan, Rizzoli, 1947.

For a useful guide to the interpretation of the Bank of Italy statements, see:

"La 'situazione' della Banca d'Italia," *Quaderni di studi e notizie,* Soc. Edison, VII, No. 108 (October, 1951), 619–25.

On the problems of agricultural credit, see:

"Banca e Credito Agrario," a special issue of the *Rassegna trimestrale dell'Istituto di Credito Agrario per la Sardegna,* II (1952).

For the distribution of the networks of branches, and deposits and credits in the provinces, see:

Ranieri, L. "Note geografiche sul'economia creditizia in Italia," *Rivista*

Internazionale di Scienze Sociali, XXI, No. 3 (July–September, 1949), 211–22 (with maps).
Schmidt, H. Das italienische Bankwesen. Schramberg, 1929.

Also of importance, although not exclusively concerned with banking problems are:

Foa, Bruno. Monetary Reconstruction in Italy. New York, 1947.
Lutz, Friedrich A., and Vera C. Lutz. Monetary and Foreign Exchange Policy in Italy. Princeton, 1950.

At the recent International Credit Conference, held in Rome, October, 1951, several papers were presented, which bear on our subject, among them:

Associazione Bancaria Italiana. La struttura del sistema bancario italiano in rapporto alla liquidità. English text available.
—— Ordinamento e problemi del credito agrario in Italia.
—— Il credito fondiario in Italia. French text available.
Bresciani Turroni, Costantino. Alcune considerazioni sulla politica monetaria e bancaria italiana dopo lo scoppio della guerra in Corea. English text available.
Dell'Amore, Giordano. La disciplina coattiva della liquidità bancaria.

Most of the studies of particular interest for the Italian banking system appear in periodicals:

Bancaria. Monthly organ of the Italian Bankers Association; contains studies of an economic-financial, statistical, legal, and fiscal character, with summaries in English and French.
Moneta e Credito. Published quarterly by the Banca Nazionale del Lavoro, with an English edition (Quarterly Review); contains theoretic studies on money, credit, and trends in Italy and in other countries.
Rivista Bancaria. Published quarterly by a committee of university professors; contains articles of a scientific character on economic, financial, statistical, and legal matters.

An indispensable work of reference is provided by the *Annuario delle Banche e Banchieri,* published by the Italian Bankers Association; last edition: Rome, 1951. On the Italian Bankers Association see also an article in Banco di Roma, *Review of the Economic Conditions in Italy,* IV, No. 6 (September, 1950), 386–95.

Much useful material will be found in the *Enciclopedia Bancaria,* published by Sperling & Kupfer, 2 vols., Milan, 1942; a new edition is in course of preparation. A copious bibliography is given under "Banca" in the *Enciclopedia Italiana.*

JAPAN

by Edna E. Ehrlich
and Frank M. Tamagna

INTRODUCTION

The Rise of Modern Japan.—In the course of the past century, Japan transformed an economy based almost exclusively on the utilization of land and labor into a modern industrial power characterized by vast accumulations of capital resources. When she opened her doors to the Western World at the middle of the nineteenth century, there already existed well-organized, enterprising mercantile groups possessed of administrative and managerial ability. This commercial class was offered a broader scope for its activities following the Restoration of 1868 through the elimination of the feudal system of authority, the breakdown of internal trade barriers, and the opening of international markets. It was, however, the rising productivity of agriculture, the discipline of an abundant labor force, the austerity of the people, and policies of monetary expansion that made possible the rapid economic growth that the country experienced during the

---

EDNA E. EHRLICH, M.A., Columbia University, 1944; Economist, head of the Far Eastern Unit, Foreign Research Division, Federal Reserve Bank of New York, from 1947 to present; Consultant, Department of Economic Affairs, United Nations, 1951.
FRANK M. TAMAGNA, LL.D., Ph.D.; Economist, Federal Reserve Bank of New York, 1940–46; Economist, Board of Governors of the Federal Reserve System, 1947–50; Chief, International Financial Operations and Policy Section, Board of Governors of the Federal Reserve System; Professorial Lecturer, School of Social Sciences and Public Affairs, American University; author of *Banking and Finance in China*, New York, 1942.
The authors wish to acknowledge the helpful suggestions received from members of the New York office of the Bank of Japan and from Mr. Reed Irvine of the Board of Governors of the Federal Reserve System. Needless to say, the authors alone are responsible for the opinions expressed and for any errors of fact that may remain.

century. In the following paragraphs the successive stages of Japan's industrial development are briefly described.

Up to the conclusion of the First World War, Japan concentrated on the developing of light consumer-goods industries and external trading facilities (especially shipping), and established an integrated financial system equipped to satisfy the varying and growing requirements of her economy. This period was also marked by a rise in agricultural production and a general improvement in the standards of living. These achievements were in part made possible by the rapid assimilation of foreign technology as well as by the importation of foreign capital in the forms of war indemnities, loans, and investments.

Following the First World War, and through the Second, Japan accelerated the growth and diversified the composition of her economic structure, through the creation at home of industries requiring higher technological skills and greater capital investments, and the development in dependent areas of new sources of raw materials. The period was further characterized by greater concentration of financial, industrial, and commercial companies engaged in activities of national interest. In 1937 the opening of hostilities with China committed Japan to the building of an economy capable of supporting modern armed forces; this helped bring into existence a totalitarian type of government which was to exercise tight controls over the entire economy.

Defeat in the Second World War left Japanese industry prostrate and faced with an uncertain future, while a spiraling postwar inflation led to the almost complete disintegration of the entire economic and financial structure. The successful application of a comprehensive economic stabilization program, which was adopted in 1949 at the urging of U.S. Minister Joseph M. Dodge, temporarily halted inflation and fostered the revival of production and trade. During the early years of this same period, the Japanese Government, under pressure from the Allied authorities, proceeded to deconcentrate the Zaibatsu (the monopolistic combines) and made attempts at injecting elements of competition and various fair trade practices into the domestic economy. Despite these moves, the institutions and companies that were formerly tied to the Zaibatsu or that were controlled by the government retained their importance and continued to conduct by far the largest proportion of business in their respective fields. In 1951, with the Allied occupation drawing to a close, the former Zaibatsu firms began to make plans for reintegration, some of which have since been carried out.

It is obviously impossible in this transitional phase to appraise the long-term effects of recent policies. A balance sheet may, however, be attempted on the basis of the existing conditions. On the liability side there remain the loss of foreign investments and dependent areas, and the interruption of trade with the Asiatic mainland which had provided Japan in the prewar period with much-needed imports and with assured markets for exports. On the asset side Japan has today a more diversified economy than at any time in the past. This has resulted partly from the reconversion of war industries and the re-establishment and expansion of civilian and export industries. Inflation itself—before it was halted—eliminated the burden of past indebtedness and made possible the revival and financing of activities, such as agriculture and small business, which had much to contribute to the country's prosperity.

Since the restoration of full sovereignty, in mid-1952, Japan has maintained her progress toward higher levels of production, with an overall increase in national income and a steady improvement of the standard of living. However, the continuation of American economic aid and other forms of extraordinary dollar payments has tended to conceal certain fundamental maladjustments in Japan's foreign trade and international payments—maladjustments which have been aggravated by domestic policies of monetary and credit expansion.

The Development of the Financial System.—As in other countries, banking business originated in Japan from the exchange and credit operations performed by merchants. The traditional Japanese practices were transformed into a modern institutional system with the passage of the National Bank Law in 1872. Most of Japan's leading banking institutions were founded during the next thirty years—the Dai-ichi Bank in 1872, the Mitsui Bank in 1876, the Yokohama Specie Bank in 1880, the Bank of Japan in 1882, the Mitsubishi and Sumitomo Banks in 1895, the Hypothec Bank of Japan in 1899, and the Industrial Bank of Japan in 1902. The beginnings of expansion abroad were marked by the establishment of the Bank of Taiwan in 1899 and the Bank of Chosen in 1909.

By the time of the First World War, Japan's financial system had already achieved a well-defined structure, and its general lines and composition changed but little thereafter. The decade of the twenties, however, constituted a most critical phase during which many small banks disappeared through liquidation or amalgamation with larger banks. The successive crises of that decade culminated in the panic of 1927, which involved a great number of large and small banks and forced the government to proclaim a general moratorium and the Bank of Japan to undertake emergency relief measures. These occurrences stimulated the passage of legislation making concentration of bank activities into fewer and larger institutions a matter of public policy.

After a brief and unsuccessful experiment with policies of deflation, in 1932 Japan was initiated by Minister of Finance Takahashi into the practice of exchange manipulation and budgetary deficits. Economic recovery was the major consideration in the earlier phases, but by the middle of the decade this gave way to concern with war preparedness. With the opening of hostilities in China and the outbreak of the Second World War, the Japanese Government imposed increasingly strict controls over the uses of bank credit, the internal flow of capital, and foreign financial transactions.

The establishment by Japan of a "Greater East Asia Co-prosperity Sphere," including the occupied parts of China and of Southeast Asia, brought into existence at the beginning of the forties a common currency area—the yen bloc—in which Japanese banks (especially the Yokohama Specie Bank and the Bank of Taiwan) formed the connecting links among the local banking systems, established under Japanese control and with Japanese financial participation. There was, at the same time, a mushroom growth in Japan of special institutions and organizations whose purposes were to provide the funds and administer the financial controls required by the war situation. Of central importance was the National Financial Control Association which, with the assistance of regional and specialized associations, controlled the amount and the distribution of credit and capital, and directed the operations of financial institutions in accordance with government policies.

The end of the Second World War resulted in the collapse of those institutions that were engaged primarily in the financing of foreign, colonial, and war activities, and the retrenchment of the banking system to the servicing of domestic and civilian needs. The transition, however, proved difficult and slow, particularly because in the early postwar years the government resorted to extremely inflationary techniques for meeting budgetary deficits and for financing both the extraordinary and current requirements of industry and commerce. There was, furthermore, widespread uncertainty among banking institutions as to their future position and their traditional business relations, in view of the much-discussed plans for deconcentration of the Zaibatsu. Financial stability and confidence were restored toward the close of the 1940s, however, when not only was the inflation halted, but the government adopted measures limited primarily to reconstituting the capital structure of the banks, and thus brought to an end the financial community's speculations regarding the possibility of major changes in the banking system. These developments were accompanied by a reorganization of the Bank of Japan, to make it a more effective body.

The Financial System in Mid-Century.—The successive phases of expansion, concentration, and retrenchment have left in existence, at the middle of the twentieth century, a well-organized and closely knit financial system. Its central organ is the Bank of Japan, which operates as a bank of issue, bankers' bank, and banker for the government, and whose Policy Board has responsibility (jointly with the Minister of Finance) for the formulation of general monetary and credit policies. Supervision of the banking system and other financial institutions is exercised by the Bank of Japan and the Minister of Finance.

General banking services are provided by 78 ordinary banks,[1] with a widespread branch system, for which the law makes no provision as to specialization of functions or distribution of activities. However, three of them (the Industrial Bank of Japan, the Hypothec Bank of Japan, and the Hokkaido Colonial Bank) are institutions that have historically their own specialized fields of activities. Another, the Bank of Tokyo, plays a leading role in foreign exchange transactions, which had been the specialized function of its predecessor, the Yokohama Specie Bank.

The Bank of Tokyo is also one of the eight ordinary banks that engage in both commercial banking and industrial financing on a nationwide scale. The other banks in this class are the institutions that were formerly tied to the biggest Zaibatsu groups (the Teikoku, Chiyoda, Osaka, and Fuji Banks),[2] and the more or less independent

[1] The number of ordinary banks had increased by mid-1953 to 82, as the result of the establishment of four additional provincial banks.

[2] By the beginning of 1954 three of these banks had reverted to the use of their prewar names. The Teikoku had again become the Mitsui Bank; the Chiyoda, the Mitsubishi Bank; and the Osaka, the Sumitomo Bank.

TABLE 1
STATISTICS OF FINANCIAL INSTITUTIONS
(AMOUNTS IN BILLIONS OF YEN)

	Number	*Number of Offices* [a]	*Capital and Reserves*	*Deposits*	*Loans, Advances and Discounts*	*Securities and Investments*
Bank of Japan	1	31	9	103	425	80
Ordinary banks [b]						
Specialized banks	3	239	10	119	222	12
Big banks	11	1,564	36	792	936	79
Local banks	58	3,398	16	414	346	69
Trust banks [c]	6	45	1	38	36	2
Total	78	5,246	64	1,364	1,539	162
Special government organs [d]	6	115	117	32	164	24
Mutual loan companies [e]	66	1,566	5	79	76	2
Credit cooperative associations [f]	650	853	4	67	47	3
Agricultural credit cooperatives [g]	13,003		10	138	55	3
Trust Fund Bureau [h]	1		1	293	146	128
Postal Savings System		15,091		178		

[a] Excluding the head offices.

[b] Details may not add up because of rounding.

[c] The asset and liability figures refer only to these institutions' banking accounts and exclude their trust accounts.

[d] Includes the Central Bank for Commercial and Industrial Cooperatives, the Central Cooperative Bank for Agriculture and Forestry, the People's Finance Corporation, the Reconversion Finance Bank, the Export Bank of Japan, and the Japan Development Bank. Asset and liability figures are approximate. The Reconversion Finance Bank, which was in the process of liquidation, accounts for 93,000 million yen of the capital item, and for 82,000 million yen of the loan item.

[e] Figures include 52,000 million yen of deposits and 30,000 million yen of loans made on the mutual system.

[f] Asset and liability figures are those of only 647 reporting associations.

[g] Asset and liability figures are those of only 12,405 reporting cooperatives.

[h] The figure in the capital and reserves column represents the Bureau's reserve funds.

Dai-ichi, Sanwa, and Kyowa banks. Sixty-one of the remaining banks are provincial institutions, providing general banking services on a regional basis. Some of them were formerly tied to smaller Zaibatsu; three of them (the Daiwa, Tokai, and Kobe banks) are sufficiently large to be classified in the Japanese statistics as "big" banks. The other six banks are institutions that have traditionally operated as trust companies. In addition to these 78 banks, there are branches in Japan of twelve foreign commercial banks.

Among other institutions engaged in financial operations are organs that are wholly or to a large extent government-owned and that have specific functions assigned by law. These include the Postal Savings System, central institutions (the Central Cooperative Bank for Agriculture and Forestry, and the Central Bank for Commercial and Industrial Cooperatives), specialized institutions (such as the Japan Development Bank and the Export–Import Bank of Japan), and government agencies (such as the Trust Fund Bureau of the Ministry of Finance). Finally, operating largely along traditional lines, are the private credit cooperatives, divided into urban and rural credit networks by their links with the two central institutions mentioned above, and the mutual loan companies (*mujin*) and mutual loan and savings banks. There are, in addition, institutions and organs of a nonbanking type that are characteristic of a modern capital market (such as insurance companies, securities dealers, and stock exchanges).

Data on the financial institutions by major groups as of September 30, 1951, are given in Table 1.

THE BANK OF JAPAN

Legal Status and Organization.—The Bank of Japan (Nippon Ginko) was established in 1882 under a thirty-year charter, which was extended in 1912 for another thirty years. Upon the termination of this second period, the original legislation was superseded by a new law (No. 67, of February 24, 1942) that governed both the Bank and Japan's currency system. With subsequent amendments, the most important of which was adopted in 1949, this law is still in existence.

The Law of 1942 established the Bank of Japan as a permanent institution, making its dissolution subject to special legislation. The Bank's capital was fixed at 100 million yen, of which 45 millions were represented by "subscription certificates" issued in 1942 in exchange for the stock originally held by the Bank's shareholders, and the remaining 55 millions were paid in by the government in 1948. The subscription certificates entitle their holders to participate in the profits of the Bank, but not in its administration.

The government has full authority with respect to the appointment of the Bank's executive officers and policy officials. The chief officers are the governor and vice-governor, who are appointed by the Cabinet for terms of five years. They are assisted in their duties by three or more executive directors, who are appointed by the Minister of Finance for terms of four years, and by advisors, who are appointed for terms of two years by the Minister of Finance from amongst persons engaged in finance and industry or men of learning and experience. The administrative acts of these officers are subject to the supervision of two or more auditors appointed by the Minister of Finance for terms of three years. Of special interest is the provision permitting the removal of any officer not only for inability to fulfill his functions or for contraventions of law, but also for acts detrimental to the public interest or "when deemed especially necessary for the attainment of the object of the Bank."

Under the 1942 law, formulation of the Bank's policies was made the function of an administrative board consisting of the governor, vice-governor, and directors. Final determination of policies, however, rested with the governor and the Minister of Finance, and the latter was empowered to direct the Bank to undertake any business or action "deemed especially necessary for the attainment of the object of the Bank." The amendment of 1949 abolished the administrative board and established instead a policy board with authority to formulate monetary and credit policies and to supervise the execution of such policies by the Bank officers. The creation of this body qualified the power vested in the Minister of Finance over the Bank as well as the authority of the governor within the Bank.

There are seven members on this new board; three are ex-officio (the governor of the Bank, a representative of the Ministry of Finance, and a representative of the Economic Counsel Board), and four are appointed by the Cabinet with the approval of the Diet for terms of four years—two persons experienced in financial affairs (one selected from the large city banks and the other from the provincial banks), one person experienced in commercial and industrial affairs, and one person experienced in agricultural problems. All proceedings of the board are decided by the majority vote of the appointed members and of the governor of the Bank, the two government representatives not having voting powers. The voting members elect a chairman who presides over the meetings and represents the board in its relations with other agencies. Since the first election in 1949 the chairman has been the governor of the Bank of Japan.

Another amendment to the law of the Bank of Japan, adopted in 1947, made provision for a Currency Issuance Deliberative Committee to deal with matters related to the currency issue and to make recommendations with respect to monetary policies. The functions of this committee were advisory only, and the Minister of Finance continued to remain responsible for final determination of the note issue limit and related matters. The committee failed to develop as an effective organ, and was abolished in 1952.

Other minor amendments were made in recent years with respect to the distribution of the Bank's earnings. The new provisions rescinded the Bank's exemption from the corporation, excess profit, and local taxes, and limited the payment of dividends to a maximum of 5 percent per annum on both the private and government shares of capital. Certain portions of the profits (after taxes and dividends) are allocated to reserves (for dividend purposes, to cover losses, and for other purposes approved by the Minister of Finance), and the net surplus (after such allocations) is paid by the Bank to the government.

Policies and Operations.—The Law of 1942 defines the functions of the Bank of Japan as including "the regulation of the currency, the control and facilitating of credit and finance, and the maintenance and fostering of the credit system, pursuant to the national policy, in order that the general economic activities might be adequately enhanced." The amendment of 1949 gives to the policy board the authority and power "to formulate, direct or supervise the execution by the Bank of Japan of . . . basic monetary, credit control and other bank policies pertaining to its contractual relations with other banking institutions so as to meet the requirements of the national economy." The board is required to make an annual report to the Diet (through the Minister of Finance) covering conditions of financial institutions, its own policy decisions, and recommended changes in legislation.

The Board is given authority in particular to determine:

1) rediscount rates and rates on advances by the Bank, as well as types of paper eligible for rediscount and advances, and other conditions of such operations;
2) open market policies with respect to timing of purchases and sales, types of securities and paper, and other conditions;

3) required ratios of reserves to be maintained by financial institutions having a contractual relationship with the Bank of Japan; [3]
4) maximum interest rates applicable by financial institutions on deposits and on loans and advances;
5) regulation of loans and investments by all financial institutions, as well as of the types, conditions, and margins of collateral securities on loans by financial institutions to security dealers;
6) any other matters pertaining to credit control and examination of financial institutions as may be entrusted to the Board by other laws or by contractual relationships.

The powers vested in the board had been previously exercised by either the governor or the Minister of Finance, in some cases with the advice of banking associations. As the board is a policy and not an administrative organ, its decisions continue to be executed by the governor with respect to acts and operations of the Bank, and to be enforced by the Minister of Finance with respect to orders and instructions to other financial institutions.

The law allows the Bank an extremely broad scope of activities. The Bank issues notes that are the sole currency and legal tender in Japan. All matters pertaining to the note issue are subject to the decision of the Minister of Finance, who sets quarterly the maximum amount of notes that the Bank may have outstanding, fixes the tax to be charged on excess notes outstanding beyond the fifteenth consecutive day, and determines the types and valuation of paper and securities eligible as monetary reserves. The law requires the Bank to maintain a reserve equivalent to the amount of the bank notes issued, but this reserve may include, in any ratio, commercial bills and notes and other kinds of paper, private and government advances, government bonds and corporate debentures, foreign balances, gold and silver.

The Bank is fiscal agent and banker for the government. It is required to manage Treasury funds and is authorized to make advances to the government up to any amount and without any collateral. It may also subscribe directly to government bonds or purchase them from the market. In the foreign field the Bank may buy and sell

[3] The provision for reserve requirements and the reference to "contractual relationship" were inserted with a view to the possible introduction of a system of legal reserve requirements against bank deposits.

foreign exchange, and is permitted to contribute capital funds to foreign financial institutions, make loans to such institutions and enter into clearing arrangements with them.

In the domestic private field the Bank is authorized to (a) discount commercial paper, bankers' acceptances, and other bills and notes; (b) purchase and sell commercial paper, bankers' acceptances and other bills and notes, government securities and other bonds, gold and silver; (c) make advances against collateral of bills and notes, government and other negotiable securities, gold and silver, and merchandise; (d) accept deposits and effect domestic transfers; (e) collect bills and notes, accept custody of articles of value, and conduct any other business incidental to its operations. Finally, the Bank may, with the permission of or upon instruction from the Minister of Finance, undertake any business necessary "for the maintenance and fostering of the credit system" or "for the attainment of the object of the Bank."

In the performance of its operations, the Bank has followed certain practices determined by custom as well as by law. While legal provisions do not place limitations on the circle of its customers, the Bank has traditionally developed its activities as banker for the government and for banking and other financial institutions.

Role in the Economy.—The establishment of the policy board in 1949 followed closely upon the inauguration of the Economic Stabilization Program. These events marked a significant change in the Bank of Japan's role in the national economy. Whereas until the spring of 1949 the Bank had followed an indecisive course in the presence of a surging inflation, thereafter it apparently became more fully aware of the influence that flexible monetary and credit policies could exert on the economy.

In the period between September, 1945, and March, 1949, the note issue of the Bank of Japan registered a sevenfold expansion; of this, some two thirds were accounted for by government financing (either through purchases of bonds or direct advances), while the remaining third could be traced to other types of financing. In the year and a half following the end of the war the Bank made its credit liberally available to financial institutions, which in turn extended loans to cover operating deficits of industries and inventory accumulations in all fields. In the following two years, these operations were largely undertaken by the government Reconversion Finance Bank, which obtained the necessary funds through sales of debentures to the Bank of Japan. Thus, the central bank's operations exerted a very strong and unchecked inflationary impact on the economy, despite the existence of selective and quantitative credit controls.

Throughout the postwar years the Bank appeared torn between the need to curb the expansion of the money supply and fear of throttling the reconstruction of the productive and distributive machinery of the economy. When the government deficits were brought to an abrupt halt in 1949 and provision was made for large-scale retirement of the government and government-guaranteed debt, the Bank became apprehensive lest the impact upon the economy be unduly severe. This attitude was strengthened by the general concern regarding the difficulties that faced Japan's export industries because of the establishment in April, 1949, of a single exchange rate, the recession that was taking place in the United States, and the Septem-

TABLE 2

ASSETS AND LIABILITIES OF THE BANK OF JAPAN

(AMOUNTS IN MILLIONS OF YEN)

	September 30 1945	*March 31 1949*	*June 30 1950*	*March 31 1951*
Assets				
Discounts		3,224	44,380	43,090
Advances	23,626 [a]	64,634	85,770	84,494
Loans for foreign exchange				280,175
Debentures	11,779 [b]	70,305		
Government bonds		134,894	136,009	136,855
Advances to the government		76,404	70,225	50,095
Cash (subsidiary coins)	32	630	974	523
Gold	501	501	501	501
Unpaid capital	55			
Miscellaneous accounts	21,649	52,604	31,478	37,560
Total	57,642	403,196	369,337	633,293
Liabilities				
Bank notes issued	41,426	312,547	311,185	396,307
Government deposits	11,148	48,349	28,211	190,666
Other deposits	3,308	23,100	6,952	11,687
Miscellaneous accounts	1,185	16,581	22,020	24,130
Capital subscribed	100	100	100	100
Reserve and surplus funds	112	208	869	7,098
Current earnings	363	2,311		3,305
Total	57,642	403,196	369,337	633,293

[a] This figure represents "Discounts" and "Advances," combined.

[b] This figure represents "Debentures" and "Government bonds," combined.

ber, 1949, devaluations of sterling and other currencies. Consequently, the Bank initiated a policy to counteract the possible adverse effects of retirement of the public debt and to stabilize the money supply. In order to induce dis-hoarding of currency and to increase bank funds, the Bank raised the interest rates that could be paid by financial institutions on time deposits. It then sought to increase the credit made available to the economy by easing its own rates, lowering the maximum rates on loans by other banks, and arranging to have part of the government deposits transferred from its own books to the accounts of certain large banks. It also assured financial institutions that it would provide accommodation in connection with operations related to desirable types of financing. Finally, it expanded the activities of the Accommodations Service Section, which it had established in 1947, to bring together two or more banks that could, by combining their resources, provide big enterprises with large loans unobtainable from a single institution.

This policy succeeded in its purpose of maintaining the volume of credit and currency practically unchanged in the period preceding the outbreak of hostilities in Korea, and thus softening the impact of a "super-balanced" budget. During the fifteen months from March, 1949, to June, 1950, there was a notable expansion in the Bank's loans and advances to financial institutions, although its aggregate assets showed a net contraction due to a reduction of the Bank's advances to the government and to the retirement (through government cash surplus) of Reconversion Finance Bank debentures from the portfolio of the Bank. In the note issue there was virtually no change; it was maintained stable throughout the period by net cash disbursements to the market from Treasury funds and bankers' deposits.

The outbreak of hostilities in Korea at the middle of 1950 resulted in a renewal of inflationary pressures in the Japanese economy. In the nine months between June, 1950, and March, 1951, the total assets of the Bank rose by 72 percent, an increase entirely reflected in the Bank's extension of advances to a government agency, the Foreign Exchange Control Board, for the purchase of incoming foreign exchange. On the liabilities side, the rise of currency in circulation (27 percent only) was checked by the favorable cash position of the Treasury, whose balances with the Bank rose almost sixfold.

As the Bank's figures indicate, the new inflationary pressures could be attributed primarily to the sudden improvement of Japan's balance of payments. While still the recipient of aid from the United States and maintaining stringent import restrictions, Japan gained unanticipated exchange earnings through a doubling of her exports, including the special procurement of goods and services by United Nations forces operating in Korea. This improvement in Japan's foreign accounts had an immediate monetary impact because the Bank of Japan both financed the Foreign Exchange Control Board's net acquisition of foreign balances, and also made its credit available to commercial banks for financing the greatly expanded volume of trade.

In order to restrain the inflationary pressures, in September, 1950, the government initiated measures to promote imports, which the Bank supported by extending financing facilities to importers at favorable terms. Moreover, in the domestic field the Bank adopted a cautious attitude with regard to all forms of financing: it raised (in December, 1950, and March, 1951) the rates applied on its advances in order to discourage borrowing by financial institutions; examined more strictly paper submitted for discount or advances; reduced the scope of its purchases of government bonds; raised interest rates on time deposits so as to promote the flow of savings to financial institutions; placed emphasis on the utilization of savings collected by the Postal Savings System and of funds raised through the sale of United States aid goods as non-inflationary sources for long-term investments; and issued warnings against the extension of credit for non-productive purposes and speculative uses. Despite the subsiding of demand and prices in international markets after March, 1951, the persistence of inflationary factors in the Japanese economy continued to require the application of restrictive measures by the Bank of Japan, including higher rediscount and interest rates.

The expansion of credit and other operations during the postwar period brought to the Bank additional earnings which far exceeded the increase in expenses. Part of these earnings were used to cover extraordinary expenses (including a housing program for Bank employees, the writing off of losses on overseas assets, and writing down of the value at which certain domestic assets, including government securities, were carried on its books). Nonetheless, despite the resumption of dividend payments (which had been suspended in the immediate postwar period) and larger payments to the government in the forms of taxes, dividends, and net surpluses, the Bank was in a position to set aside declared reserves at a rate much faster than its aggregate liabilities expanded.

The developments following the inauguration of the Dodge stabilization program in 1949 indicated the Bank of Japan's cognizance of the importance of monetary and credit measures as tools of economic stabilization, although various factors seemed to limit the actual scope of the Bank's activities. A tradition of direct financing of government deficits did not easily permit a shift to a flexible management of the public debt, which would involve both purchases and sales of securities with a view to market conditions rather than for the accommodation of the Treasury and financial institutions. The customary reliance on selective or qualitative controls proved of little effectiveness in checking inflationary pressures. The absence of reserve requirements and the inadequacy of other general or quantitative instruments of control made difficult the application of a sudden and sharp restraint on credit, such as the situation after mid-1950 seemed to require. However, the administrative action with respect to money rates and moral suasion which the Bank undertook in those months was perhaps more prompt and produced somewhat better results than in preceding years.

Reports and Information.—The Bank has customarily made public at regular intervals statements and reports covering its condition and operations, and has also made available a considerable amount of descriptive and statistical information on the Japanese economy. During the Second World War it restricted dissemination of some of this material and suspended the release of its publications in the English text. After the war, the Bank resumed the release in English of its semiannual reports, but it did not provide detailed data in its statements of condition and its profit and loss accounts until the issuance of its report for the six months ending September 30, 1949. The Bank also publishes in English the annual reports submitted by the policy board to the Diet.

Following the end of the war, the Statistical Department of the Bank resumed publication of the annual *Economic Statistics of Japan*, and began issuing an *Economic Statistics Monthly* which replaced the prewar monthly *Monetary Statistics of Japan* and gradually absorbed other statistical publications that had been appearing periodically or irregularly. In 1950 the Foreign Exchange Control Department of the Bank began to issue a *Foreign Exchange Statistics Monthly*. These annual and monthly publications provide current statistical information on financial institutions, as well as other financial and economic data. In addition to these publications, the Bank issues through its Economic Research Department a *Monthly Economic Review* which surveys current finance, trade, and other economic developments, and also contains statistical series and special articles. Finally, reference should be made to the voluminous *Statistical Year Book of Japan*, which the Bank brought out in 1948 jointly with the Ministry of Finance, and which presents hundreds of statistical series over a period extending from 1947 back to 1926.

COMMERCIAL BANKS

Banking Legislation.—The commercial or "ordinary" banks were still operating in 1953 under the Bank Law of March 20, 1927 (No. 21), although new legislation had been under consideration since 1950. The 1927 legislation deals primarily with the supervision of the banks, which is entrusted to the Minister of Finance. From 1937 until the end of the Second World War the Minister of Finance also exercised a very strict and detailed control over the operations of the banks and other financial institutions. Since the war, however, the banks have regained some of their internal autonomy; in so far as they have not, the Bank of Japan has had a growing role in decisions regarding their operations, although the Minister of Finance retains the responsibility for issuing the necessary regulations and instructions.

Banks are defined under the 1927 law as all concerns engaged in "the acceptance of deposits as a business or the acceptance of deposits together with the lending of money or the discounting of bills and notes, or the carrying on of exchange transactions"; their activities are limited to banking and accessory types of business. Banks are required to be incorporated and to have a minimum capital of 2 million yen if located in Tokyo and Osaka, or 1 million yen if located elsewhere. The Finance Minister's permission is required: to establish a new bank or bank office; to alter a bank's trade name or capital, or the location of any of its places of business; for a bank to amalgamate with another bank, or to discontinue business; and for certain other moves. The Minister of Finance has also broad power to take action on his own initiative. He can, for instance, order the suspension of business or the replacement of managers and auditors, or rescind the license of a bank, should the bank contravene any laws or regulations, or commit any act calculated to prejudice public welfare, or whenever such measures are deemed necessary because of the condition of the bank's affairs or property.

Banks are required to submit to the Minister of Finance semi-annual business reports for the periods ending September and March, to make public semi-annual balance sheets, and to prepare audit statements every three months. In addition, the Minister has the right at any time to order a bank to submit its business reports, audit statements, or other documents and records, and he can delegate Ministry officials to inspect and examine a bank's affairs and property.

All ordinary banks are also affected by the Law for Issuance of Debentures by Banks (No. 40) of March 31, 1950.[4] Prior to the enactment of this legislation which permitted all banks to issue debentures, the privilege had been restricted to a few financial institutions, including the three "special" banks which were concerned primarily with long-term lending. In authorizing all banks to issue debentures, the government hoped that this would lead to an increase in the long-term funds available to the banking system so as to enable it to expand its investments in corporate securities. In order to augment the amount of debentures that could be issued, under a formula limiting combined debenture and deposit liabilities to not more than twenty times a bank's net worth, the law provided for the issuance of preferred stocks which were to be subscribed by the United States Aid Counterpart Fund and were to bear dividends of 7.5 percent per annum, confer no voting rights, and be redeemed by the banks within ten years. A total of 6,000 million yen was allocated by the government out of the Fund for such subscriptions, and all but 800 million yen was almost immediately utilized to subscribe to preferred stocks issued by the three "special" banks and the two institutions that act as central banks for cooperative organizations. However, with the single exception of the Bank of Tokyo, none of the banks that had not traditionally issued debentures sought to exercise that newly-acquired privilege.

By erasing the operational distinction that had formerly existed between the long-term credit, debenture-issuing "special" banks and the short-term credit, deposit banks, the 1950 legislation eliminated

[4] This law was abrogated by the Long-Term Credit Bank Law of 1952. See page 553.

the need for the separate laws under which the former institutions had been individually chartered. These were therefore repealed and the three "special" banks were thenceforward subject to the same legislation as the ordinary banks.

Banking Organization.—The internal organization of Japanese banking institutions has been patterned generally upon French, German, and British lines; American influence has been felt only recently. Each banking institution is governed by a board of directors, consisting of from five to ten members elected by the general meeting of shareholders. The positions of board chairman and bank president are usually combined in one person, who is the legal representative of the institution and is entrusted with the executive direction of its business and operations. In some cases the board of directors also includes one or more managing directors, who are executive officers in charge of the most important activities and departments of the bank. Supervision and auditing of a bank's business and operations are exercised by three to five auditors, also elected by the general meeting of shareholders. One or more auditors are designated as executive auditors, receive fixed salaries, and attend to current operations; the others participate only in the regular audit held every three months.

Every sizable Japanese bank is organized into a head office and many branch offices. The head office usually includes two major sections—general administration, in charge of secretarial work, accounting, branch supervision, and research, and the business administration, in charge of domestic and foreign operations. Branch offices are subject to direct and strict supervision from the head office, which sends out examiners without advance notice to inspect books, and requires each branch to report regularly on its operations and condition and to have its position certified quarterly by auditors. Banking business is handled through several departments, among which the domestic, foreign exchange, foreign relations, savings, and (if the bank engages in trust business) trust departments are the most important.

Since the war the only formal ties among the banks have been the local associations that are organized into the National Federation of Bankers' Associations. In 1951 there were more than seventy of these local associations, each having as members the bank branches located in the district. The associations, which are prohibited by the Antimonopoly Law of 1947 from engaging in profit-making and cartel activities, have announced their objectives to be: liaison among member banks, investigation and research for the improvement and development of banking business, recommendations on banking matters to the government and other authorities, and the clearance of checks and bills accepted by member banks.

Banking Trends.—At the end of the fiscal year concluded March 31, 1951, Japan had 78 ordinary banks with 5,049 branches (excluding head offices), 93 subbranches, 68 agencies, and 13 outlying stations. In 1920, before the banking crises, there had been 1,987 separate banks; but liquidations, together with sweeping amalgamations that were encouraged by the government, reduced the number to 872 in 1930, to 351 in 1940, and then still further to 61 at the end of the war. The postwar rise to 78 was due primarily not to the establishment of new banks, of which there were only four, but to the absorption into the ordinary bank category of three former "special" banks, six former trust companies, and four former savings banks.

The ordinary banks'[5] aggregate assets or liabilities on March 31, 1951, were fifteen times the September 30, 1945, amount, and forty times the prewar level. Their paid-up capital and reserves totaled only 2 percent of their risk assets (total assets less cash, deposits with the Bank of Japan, and government obligations), about one tenth of the ratio maintained in the "normal" years of the early thirties.

The financial position of the banks was severely undermined early in the postwar period by the government's cancellation of its wartime guarantees, which had underlain most of the banks' advances to the munitions industries. The cancellation, which was enacted in October, 1946, was effected by the imposition of a 100 percent tax on all war indemnity claims against the government and against enterprises whose transactions had been backed by government guarantee. Thus, wherever a borrower's assets consisted largely of claims against the government or against such enterprises, the banks were left with uncollectible assets.

As soon as rumors of the government's intention to cancel its indemnities had reached the public (in August, 1946) it was necessary

[5] Although the old "special" banks shared the vicissitudes of the other banks during the postwar period, they retained their own peculiar characteristics and functions. They are therefore treated separately, and, except where otherwise indicated, the statistical data that follow on the ordinary banks exclude these three banks. On March 31, 1951, the total assets and liabilities of the former "special" banks amounted to 254,000 million yen.

to take immediate steps to protect the banks. The government at once froze a large part of the public's deposits, guaranteeing the remainder, and followed this up by ordering all banks to divide their assets and liabilities into "new" (good) and "old" (bad) accounts in accordance with detailed regulations, again guaranteeing any excess of "new" liabilities over "new" assets. Then, on October 18, the government enacted the Financial Institutions Reconstruction and Reorganization Law (No. 39), designating the manner of disposition of the "old" accounts (which was to be completed by 1948) and prescribing how the banks were to rehabilitate or reorganize themselves for future operation. The ordinary bank assets that were wiped out in the resulting reorganization program equaled almost one fifth of the total outstanding in September, 1945.

In March, 1949, the banks' assets, swollen by inflation, were five times the September, 1945, total, with three quarters of the increase taking the form or risk assets. The composition of the latter was greatly altered, however, unsecured loans having fallen from 88 percent of total credits to only 42 percent. Despite this improvement in the banks' credit portfolios, their liquidity position had deteriorated, with the ratio of reserves (cash, deposits with other banks, call loans, and government securities) to demand deposits having dropped from 96 to 57 percent.

The disinflationary impact of the stabilization program introduced in the spring of 1949 accentuated this situation. Holdings of government securities were liquidated in order to meet the demand for loans and advances from enterprises hard pressed to carry idle inventories and to provide for current needs, and during the fifteen months ended June, 1950, the ratio of reserves to demand deposits fell further to 42 percent. With the onset of the Korean War, there was a suddenly expanded industrial activity and a sharp rise in foreign trade which had again to be financed by the banks. By March, 1951, credits had been pushed up to a level equal to 82 percent of all deposits, and the ratio of reserves to demand deposits had dropped, after allowance for year-end window dressing, to about 36 percent. Obviously, the banking system was completely dependent for its continued operation upon the readiness of the central bank to make its credit facilities available at any time. In principle, however, this was merely an exacerbation of the usual situation in Japan where, because of the pressure of financing requirements and the limited availability of

Table 3
Aggregate Assets and Liabilities of All Ordinary Banks[a]
(amounts in millions of yen)

Assets	*September 30 1945*	*March 31 1949*	*June 30 1950*	*March 31 1951*
Cash, bills, and checks	4,019	95,235	116,297	208,639
Deposits with other financial institutions	4,490	17,997	19,448	21,364
Call loans	815	2,576	4,596	4,205
National government bonds	33,384	79,931	42,612	32,599
Other securities	7,700	33,985	61,477	100,610
Bills discounted	335	57,309	186,133	294,426
Secured loans	3,500	141,408	253,608	344,758
Unsecured loans	53,468	152,506	232,446	251,410
Overdrafts	2,756	5,874	9,292	8,523
Real estate and equipment	14,615 [b]	2,787	5,655	19,158
Other assets		37,697	72,653	572,731
Total	125,082	627,305	1,004,217	1,858,423
Liabilities				
Total deposits	103,414	505,999	789,631	1,097,290
Current deposits	11,253	141,094	181,486	305,206
Ordinary deposits	33,408	197,101	259,462	298,799
Time deposits	32,352	80,438	211,295	309,286
Deposits at notice	1,350 [c]	28,075	51,288	80,479
Installment savings		8,759	18,514	23,889
Government and government agency deposits		14,600 [e]	22,014	10,097
Special deposits	25,051 [d]		42,069	65,035
Other deposits		35,930	3,502	4,498
Borrowed money	13,735	53,397	101,715	103,721
Foreign exchange			213	255,431
Reserve for bad loans				9,118
Capital stock		12,949	13,882	14,712
Legal reserves	1,958 [f]	867	3,913	16,105
Current net income		1,218	11,379	6,581
Other liabilities	5,975	52,875	83,484	355,465
Total	125,082	627,305	1,004,217	1,858,423

[a] Excludes the three former "special" banks—the Industrial Bank of Japan, the Hypothec Bank of Japan, and the Hokkaido Colonial Bank.

[b] Includes "Other assets."

[c] Includes "Installment savings."

[d] Includes "Government and government agency deposits" and "Other deposits."

[e] Includes "Special deposits."

[f] Includes "Capital stock" and "Current net income."

funds, the banks tend customarily to operate with low reserves and to overextend their lending.

The banks showed very large profits in the years following the purging of their accounts. In the half year ended March 31, 1951, after allowance for depreciation reserves, the ratio of profits to paid-up capital was 53 percent, compared with 11 percent in the last half of 1937, and an average of 17 percent during the war. Fully 40 percent of the profits was transferred to "reserves for bad loans," an important form of concealed profits which are encouraged by the Minister of Finance as a means of accumulating more substantial reserves, and are deductible for tax purposes. Of the balance of the profits remaining after taxes, 74 percent was retained as surplus, in accordance with the Minister's postwar policy of having the banks build up their capital structure, and 19 percent was paid out in 10 percent dividends, a higher rate than had been paid at any time since the mid-thirties.

The "Big" Banks.—Looming in size over the rest of the ordinary banks are the so-called "big" banks. Most of these have branches throughout the country, whereas the "local" banks usually operate within only one or a few prefectures. Before the war there were seven big banks, of which all except the Sanwa Bank were controlled by large Zaibatsu groups. In mid-1941 these seven banks had 58 percent of the deposits, 66 percent of the discounts, loans, and advances, and 47 percent of the securities holdings of the 245 ordinary banks.

During the war the big banks became even more important, partly by the absorption of numerous smaller institutions, and partly because the larger institutions were favored in the financing of war production. At the end of 1945, loans to munitions industries ranged from 30 to 50 percent of the big banks' outstanding loans and investments, and these banks' share in the total discounts, loans, and advances held by all ordinary banks had risen to 83 percent. At the same time the big banks' securities holdings fell to 38 percent of the total. A large part of the wartime financing by the big banks was based on loans obtained from the Bank of Japan (such loans amounting at the end of 1945 to more than half of the latter's outstanding credits). Moreover, almost 50 percent of these loans consisted of "special" loans, that is, loans not backed by the normally required collateral; in contrast, only 18 percent of the loans obtained by all the other banks from the central bank constituted such "special" loans.

The very fact that loans to munitions industries comprised an exceedingly large share of the big banks' credit portfolios caused the cancellation of the government indemnities to affect those banks even more severely than the other ordinary banks. Nonetheless, since large financial institutions were considered essential for Japan's reconstruction, they were not required to undergo any structural changes but were permitted to carry out the same internal reorganization as the other banks. Measures were taken, however, to sever some of the ties between the big banks and the industrial, commercial, and other financial enterprises of the former Zaibatsu; these included the removal of officers who had exercised power on behalf of the Zaibatsu, the elimination of Zaibatsu ownership of bank stocks, the limitation of the amount of stock which one individual or company could hold in a financial institution, the elimination of interlocking directorates between financial institutions and other juridical persons, and the termination of contractual service arrangements or other alliances between financial institutions and industrial and commercial organizations.

It is questionable whether these measures actually achieved the purpose intended. One concrete reason for doubt is the apparent tendency of the big banks to continue to favor the larger concerns; although small enterprises account for more than half of Japan's industry, at the end of 1950 only 24 percent of the value of the big banks' outstanding loans constituted financing of enterprises capitalized at 3 million yen or less. In mid-1951 the Minister of Finance was constrained to urge the big banks to "make a more concrete display of their character as public utility enterprises" by not concentrating their loans to big enterprises; but despite such exhortations, and notwithstanding the establishment by the government at the end of 1950 of a fund for credit insurance on loans by financial institutions to small enterprises, the percentage of total loans to such enterprises had fallen by the end of 1951 to about 17 percent. Furthermore, activities of the big banks have recently been influenced by the new laws that modify much of the anti-monopoly legislation passed during the occupation.[6]

At the end of 1951 there were eleven banks classified as big banks. These included the six prewar big banks (the number having been reduced by one as the result of a merger), some of which had altered

[6] See section "Recent Developments and Policies," pp. 565–67.

their names at the government's request in order to remove the "taint" of Zaibatsuism—the Teikoku, Dai-ichi, Chiyoda (formerly Mitsubishi), Osaka (formerly Sumitomo), Fuji (formerly Yasuda), and Sanwa banks; the Bank of Tokyo, established in 1947 to take over the domestic assets and liabilities of the liquidated "special" Yokohama Specie Bank which had been predominant in the financing of foreign trade; the Kyowa Bank, formerly the giant Nippon Savings Bank which was reorganized as an ordinary bank; and the three largest of the provincial banks—the Daiwa (previously Nomura), Tokai, and Kobe banks.[7] On March 31, 1951, these eleven banks had 59 percent of the deposits, 55 percent of the discounts, loans, and advances, and 48 percent of the securities holdings of the ordinary banks. They also had 69 percent of the first-line reserves (cash, deposits with other banks, and call loans), but at the same time were responsible for 69 percent of all bank borrowing. The big banks also do most of the financing of foreign trade, ten of these banks (which excludes the Kyowa Bank) and two former "special" institutions, the Hypothec Bank and the Industrial Bank of Japan, being the only Japanese banks licensed as "foreign exchange banks" under the Foreign Exchange and Foreign Trade Control Law of 1950.

Bank Deposits.—Demand deposits with the ordinary banks were equal in March, 1951, to 55 percent of aggregate deposits, a high figure considering that until the end of the war the major part of the deposits had been in time and savings accounts. The traditionally large proportion of bank deposits at fixed terms reflects the fact that the Japanese people, rather than invest in securities, prefer to entrust their savings to banks or other financial institutions which in turn make direct loans to industry or invest in corporate debentures and government bonds. During the postwar inflation the rapid monetary depreciation caused a shift from fixed to demand deposits, and in March, 1949, the latter actually comprised two thirds of total deposits. Thereafter, however, the renewal of confidence in the currency's value brought a gradual relative increase in time and savings deposits.

Demand deposits are of two kinds: "current deposits," which are withdrawable upon demand and transferable by check or bill, and are maintained by business firms and individuals as a means of settling business transactions; and "ordinary deposits," also withdrawable upon demand but not transferable by check or bill. The third prin-

[7] See footnote 2, p. 521.

cipal type of deposit is the "time deposit," which is not withdrawable before the contractual term of three months or more has elapsed. In March, 1951, demand and time deposits together comprised more than four fifths of the ordinary banks' total deposits. The minor deposits are of several kinds, with varying terms, conditions and rates intended to attract funds of all sorts. Accounting for about 15 percent of total deposits in March, 1951, were (1) "installment savings," accumulated at intervals and in amounts agreed upon by bank and depositor; (2) "deposits at notice," withdrawable at any time upon giving advance notice (usually seven days); and (3) "special deposits," constituting various types of savings deposits that not only bear interest but are eligible for premium awards determined by lottery.

Interest rates on private deposits have been determined since the end of 1947 by the Bank of Japan; prior to then, rates had been fixed by the bank associations, but this practice was stopped after the Fair Trade Commission found it to be in violation of the Antimonopoly Law. The interest rates on deposits by government authorities are usually decided by special agreements with the banks.

Until 1944, rates differed not only with the type of deposit, but also with the "class" of bank, the leading banks in Tokyo and Osaka being designated "Class A" banks, and all other banks "Class B." In that year, interest rates on current deposits were abandoned, and the rates on ordinary and "at notice" deposits were consolidated at the rates for Class A banks. Until the fall of 1951 the rates for ordinary and "at notice" deposits were still the same as had been established back in 1939—1.8 and 2.2 percent, respectively, but on September 1 they were raised by 0.4 percent. These increases were part of an overall rise in deposit rates designed to promote savings in order to provide the overextended financial institutions with more funds and also to curb inflationary consumer spending. The rates for time deposits, which had been raised frequently during the intervening postwar years, were raised again on September 1 to 4 percent for three-month deposits, 5 percent for six-month deposits, and 6 percent for one-year deposits.

Bank Loans and Investments.—Like bank deposits, the Japanese instruments and procedures of credit also show certain peculiarities. Trade and bank acceptances are not commonly employed, except in the field of foreign commerce, and the practice of overdraft credit is negligible. The most important types of credit are the discounting of negotiable commercial paper, and advances against single-name bills. Frequently a second name is added to a bill as the personal guarantee of an officer of a company (usually when the enterprise is small and the officer has sizable personal assets); or a loan may be guaranteed by another commercial bank or by a governmental financial institution. A practice that has been used fairly extensively during the postwar period, particularly when the money market is tight, is the guar-

TABLE 4
LOANS AND DISCOUNTS BY TYPE OF SECURITY OF ALL ORDINARY BANKS,[a] MARCH 31, 1951
(AMOUNTS IN BILLIONS OF YEN)

Items	*Amount*	*Percent*
Secured loans		
Loans on real estate	60	7
Loans on stocks and bonds	18	2
Loans on guarantees	172	19
Other secured loans	94	10
Total	345	38
Unsecured loans (advances)	251	28
Overdrafts	9	1
Bills discounted		
Bank acceptances	2	[b]
Commercial bills	291	33
Documentary bills	1	[b]
Total	294	33
Grand total	899	100

[a] Excludes the three former "special" banks—the Industrial Bank of Japan, the Hypothec Bank of Japan, and the Hokkaido Colonial Bank.
[b] Less than 0.5 percent.

anteeing of loans secured by time deposits, i.e., loans to depositors who need immediate cash but are not permitted to withdraw their time deposits. This procedure is frowned upon by the Minister of Finance and the Bank of Japan, but it persists nonetheless. Also significant are loans on mortgage deeds, which provide working capital and long-term funds to industry and commerce.

About half of commercial bank credits go to manufacturing enterprises, with the textile industry receiving a far larger portion than any other industry. The wholesale and retail trades receive the major part of the rest of the banks' credits. At the end of March, 1951, about 10 percent of the outstanding aggregate credits were to provide capital funds to finance the purchase, maintenance, or repair of plant and equipment. The bulk, of course, was for operating purposes, that is, for procuring and carrying inventories and for the payment of wages, office expenses, and the rest.

TABLE 5
LOANS AND DISCOUNTS BY INDUSTRY OF ALL ORDINARY BANKS,[a]
MARCH 31, 1951
(AMOUNTS IN BILLIONS OF YEN)

Industry	*Amount*	*Percent*
Manufacturing		
Textiles	174	16.5
Chemicals	71	6.7
Primary metals	59	5.6
Food and kindred products	57	5.4
Transportation equipment	39	3.7
Electrical machinery and appliances	27	2.6
Other machinery	25	2.4
Others	118	11.2
Total	570	54.1
Wholesale and retail trade	269	25.5
Transportation, communications, and other public utilities	64	6.1
Mining	45	4.3
Construction	26	2.5
Finance and insurance	17	1.6
Service	15	1.4
Fisheries and aquaculture	14	1.3
Local public bodies	11	1.0
Forestry and hunting	4	0.4
Agriculture	3	0.3
Real estate	3	0.3
Others	12	1.1
Grand total	1,054	100.0

[a] Includes the three former "special" banks—the Industrial Bank of Japan, the Hypothec Bank of Japan, and the Hokkaido Colonial Bank.

The downward trend in interest charges which government policy had forced upon the banks during the war years was reversed as soon as the war ended. The peak was reached during 1949 when the average effective rate was as high as 10.2 percent per annum, more than double the rate at the end of 1945. Beginning in 1950, however, with the banks showing large and increasing profits, the Bank of Japan started to force rates lower in order to lessen industry's borrowing costs. In September, 1951, the average rate was 9.5 percent per annum, with loan rates ranging from 2.7 to 14.6 percent and discount rates from 5.1 to 14.6 percent.

Bank investments in securities are customarily small compared with other types of investments, and while in September, 1945, securities represented one third of bank assets, reflecting wartime investments in government bonds, by March, 1951, they had dropped to only 7 percent of total assets. During those postwar years there was a significant shift from government to non-government securities, and in 1951 the holdings of the latter were three times the size of the holdings of governments. Investments are primarily in industrial and commercial corporation debentures; holdings of corporate stocks and of other types of securities (such as local government bonds) are negligible. This predominance of debentures is to a large extent a consequence of the very limited market for stocks outside the financial institutions, and the resultant reliance by business instead on bank loans and the issuance of debentures for the capital they need for long-term investments.

Foreign Banks.—Early in 1952 twelve foreign banks had a total of thirty branches in Japan. There were three American banks (the National City Bank of New York, the Chase National Bank, and the Bank of America), two British banks (the Hongkong and Shanghai Banking Corporation, and the Chartered Bank of India, Australia and China), two Dutch banks (the Nederlandsch–Indische Handelsbank and the Nederlandsche Handel-Maatschappij), two Indian banks (the Mercantile Bank of India and the Bank of India), the Banque de l'Indochine, the Bank of China, and the Bank of Korea. Before the war only the British and Dutch banks, the National City Bank, and the Bank of China had branches in Japan.

Between 1945 and 1949 the responsibility of licensing foreign banks was assumed by SCAP (Supreme Commander for the Allied Powers representing the Allied Governments in control of Japan). At first these banks were restricted to activities required by the occupation but beginning in August, 1947, they were permitted also to engage in limited foreign trade transactions, and in mid-1948 the scope of their business was broadened still further. On December 28, 1949, the responsibility for licensing foreign banks was returned to the Minister of Finance. Since then foreign banks have been operating under Japanese regulations, and their business with Japanese nationals is no longer restricted. However, while they are permitted to engage in activities as broad as those of the domestic commercial banks, in practice they have been concerned principally with the financing of imports and exports between Japan and their respective countries. Hence, they are primarily foreign exchange banks, and their local banking business consists chiefly of deposit facilities and banking accommodations for foreign companies and their Japanese subsidiaries.

The foreign banks were still being regulated in 1952 by, specifically, Article 32 of the 1927 Bank Law and Ordinance No. 328 of November 15, 1927. Like the domestic banks, they are under the supervision of the Minister of Finance and a license must be obtained for each branch or other place of business before it can be established in Japan. Each such business place is considered a separate bank and is required to keep on deposit with the Trust Fund Bureau of the Ministry of Finance, as a guarantee, 100,000 yen in government bonds or other securities approved by the Minister of Finance.

OTHER FINANCIAL INSTITUTIONS

Savings Institutions.—Since 1949 there have been no private banks engaged solely in savings business, although prior to the 1927 banking crisis there had been as many as 661. By the end of the twenties, however, there were only 90 left, and by mid-1941 only 72, with total deposits equal to not quite one third the fixed and savings deposits in the ordinary banks. Beginning in May, 1943, the government, in an effort to increase the level of wartime savings, permitted the ordinary banks to open up savings departments, and, as a result of the ensuing wide-scale merging of savings banks with commercial banks, at the end of the war only four remained. These were eventually reorganized as ordinary banks, and the Nippon Savings Bank (which had been formed in May, 1945, by the consolidation of nine of the largest savings banks, and which had operated since then under the chairmanship of a member of the Yasuda Zaibatsu) became one of the big banks under the name Kyowa Bank.

The Postal Savings System, modeled after the British and Belgian systems, was established in 1875. It is regulated by the Postal Savings Bank Law (No. 23) of 1905, and remains an important channel for the collection of savings. The system operates through the widespread net of local post offices, and offers to even the poorest Japanese the facilities of a complete banking mechanism, rendering services on an almost microscopic scale. Individual or joint accounts can be maintained in the form of ordinary savings or fixed deposits for terms ranging from six months to ten years. In addition, since 1941 there has been available a fixed-savings certificate deposit under which certificates are issued, in a range of denominations, which mature in ten years but can be cashed after one year. The depositors are offered such special facilities as the collection of monthly savings installments by the postman, and free mail service for all correspondence relating to accounts. Although passbooks must be presented for each deposit or withdrawal, funds may be deposited at one office and withdrawn from another.

Because the system's depositors are from all spheres of the economy, the level of deposits responds rapidly to general economic trends and to seasonal and other influences. Thus in the spring of 1946 there was a steep rise, probably due to a belief that the capital levy and other taxes would hit postal savings less hard than bank deposits. Thereafter, there were heavy withdrawals until the middle of 1947, due to unemployment, lagging incomes, and higher living costs. In 1948 savings again began to mount rapidly, and on March 31, 1951, totaled 155,000 million yen, one third the time and savings deposits in the ordinary banks.

The offices of the Postal Savings System also handle the accounts and operations of the Postal Transfer System, which is modeled after the Austrian and German Postal Giro systems. Checking accounts are maintained into which cash or negotiable instruments can be paid, and from which depositors can withdraw cash upon demand. All post offices are authorized to accept cash deposits for these accounts and to meet cash withdrawals from them. They also issue postal and telegraphic money orders (domestic and foreign) payable to order, and postal notes for sums not exceeding twenty yen, payable to bearer or to order. These money orders and postal notes are sold to the general public against payment in cash, and to depositors against debits to their accounts. Distinctive features of the system are the facilities whereby a depositor can apply for a payment to be made by the debiting of his account and the crediting of another depositor's account (giro transfer), or for payment in cash from his deposit account to a non-depositor.

The transfer system is widely used and is patronized by persons from all classes of society, especially farmers, independent business firms, and professional men. It is also used by public bodies for the payment of pensions, annuities, and interest. No limitations are set upon the size of the checking accounts, but if an account rises above specified levels the interest rate may be lowered or interest payments suspended. In practice, depositors do not keep unduly large balances. Postal transfer accounts on March 31, 1951, totaled 2,500 million yen.

In addition to collecting savings and handling money transfers, the Postal Savings System acts as banking agent in selling to its depositors bonds of the national, prefectural, and municipal governments. It also conducts savings campaigns among the public, during which it sells special government bonds and savings certificates of small denominations.

A small portion of the people's savings is collected in trust accounts maintained with six *trust and banking companies* and the *trust departments* of eleven commercial banks. The trust and banking companies resulted from the 1948 reorganization of the trust companies; in this new form they are allowed to engage in ordinary banking business as well as in trust business. The companies operate under both the 1927 Bank Law and the Trust Business Law (No. 62) of 1922. Under the latter legislation only a privately incorporated company licensed by the Minister of Finance and with a minimum authorized capital of 1 million yen can conduct a trust business. One tenth of the capital must be deposited as a guarantee with the Trust Fund Bureau, and the investment of reserve funds is subject to certain restrictions. There is no clear definition of the proper functions of trust companies, but in general they are expected to act as trustees for the benefit of other parties and are authorized to accept in trust and administer money, real estate, leases, claims, and securities; to act as underwriters of bonds, debentures, and shares; and to perform other trust functions such as executing wills and marriage contracts, and auditing accounts of other enterprises.

In 1941 there were 26 trust companies, seven of which held over nine tenths of the aggregate accounts. These leading companies were all Zaibatsu-owned, and the funds they collected were used to help meet the financial requirements of the Zaibatsu industrial companies; therefore in 1941 one half of all the trust companies' assets consisted of loans. During the war most of the companies were absorbed by ordinary banks to which they were related; however, the business of eleven of these was continued in separate trust departments. More than four fifths of the aggregate trust accounts in 1951 of these departments and of the six remaining trust and banking companies was invested in loans and advances.

The Industrial Credit System.—Japan has a group of important governmental and semi-governmental institutions specializing in industrial financing. Dominant amongst these is the Industrial Bank of Japan, which for half a century operated as a "special" organ, but since 1950 has been administered under the Bank Law of 1927. The bank was established in 1902 under the Law of Incorporation of the Industrial Bank of Japan (No. 70) of 1900. Its operations are those of a hybrid institution—in its general banking activities it differs little from ordinary banks, but in its medium-term and long-term financing activities it resembles a mortgage institution. In addition it has the role of agent bank of the Central Bank for Commercial and Industrial Cooperatives. Although until 1950 the bank's shares had been completely privately owned, the government has always maintained very strict control over its policies.

The bank obtains the major part of its funds through the issuance of debentures, which in 1951 comprised just under half of its liabilities. It uses its funds, among other operations, to purchase government, prefectural and municipal bonds, corporate debentures, and such shares as are approved by the Minister of Finance; to make loans on the security of such bonds, debentures, or shares; to discount bills of exchange; to buy and sell bills of exchange and documentary drafts; and to make loans against mortgages on ships, industrial land and buildings, and certain residential land and buildings. (Fixed loans have a maximum term of five years, but certain types of loans are repayable on an installment basis, for which there is no time limit.) In March, 1951, 75 percent of the bank's assets consisted of loans and discounts. The bank also engages rather extensively, however, in foreign exchange business and in the guaranteeing of industrial and commercial loans and the acceptance of bills.

During the war the government ordered the bank to extend to vitally important industries any aid necessary, and guaranteed any resulting bank losses. It also raised the limit on the bank's debenture issue, and guaranteed both interest and principal. Thus until the end of the war the bank operated under the protection as well as the direction of the state. In 1942, moreover, in order to safeguard the stability of the bank, the government decided to relieve it of a large part of the burden of financing the munitions industries, and to that end created the short-lived Wartime Finance Bank, which concentrated on assisting those plants that obviously were not going to have any economic value after the war. Nevertheless at the end of the war 78 percent of the Industrial Bank's assets was in the form of loans on bills, mostly to munitions industries, and consequently when the government canceled its indemnities, the bank suffered a staggering blow. In the subsequent reorganization the bank issued a large amount of preferred stock financed through the United States Aid Counterpart Fund, so that the government now owns almost half of the capital of 1,950 million yen.

Just as the Wartime Finance Bank had been established to insulate the Industrial Bank from the more flagrantly risky war loans, so the Reconversion Finance Bank was established in January, 1947, to provide long-term rehabilitation funds to those essential industries that the banks considered poor credit risks. However, the activities of this institution grew so rapidly and were so extremely inflationary (because most of its funds were obtained through sales of debentures to the Bank of Japan) that the curbing of the bank's business was made an integral part of the 1949 stabilization program. (The bank was finally dissolved in January, 1952, and its outstanding assets and obligations were assumed by the Japan Development Bank.) To compensate for the drying-up of Reconversion Finance Bank credit, the Bank of Japan sought to increase the resources of the Industrial Bank for making long-term loans by encouraging subscriptions to the bank's debentures; to this effect, it lowered the rate charged on loans secured by such debentures, it increased the collateral value of the debentures, and with government cash surpluses it bought Reconversion Finance Bank debentures and government bonds from banks and insurance companies that in turn used the funds to acquire Industrial Bank debentures.

In 1951 about three fourths of the bank's loans was divided amongst six industries—machinery, textile, metal, chemical, mining and shipping. More than half of its loans was for equipment capital, and these comprised one third of the equipment capital loans extended by the entire banking system.[8]

The second of the industrial financing institutions is the Central Bank for Commercial and Industrial Cooperatives, created by Law

[8] See reference on page 553 to change in the Industrial Bank's formal status.

No. 14 of 1936, to coordinate the funds of the associations of small exporters, merchants and manufacturers that were set up under the Cooperative Association Law of 1900, and to provide them with credit facilities. The associations exercise certain supervisory and regulatory functions, establish cooperative manufacturing and warehousing facilities, and carry on banking activities on behalf of their members, granting short-term loans for seasonal business needs and intermediate term loans for the purchase of capital equipment and for the refunding of high-interest debts. Although their banking operations are encouraged by the government for social and political reasons—to free small merchants and producers from dependence upon the big concerns—credit from this source is still extremely limited, and most firms remain commercially and financially dependent upon larger enterprises which provide them with working capital and with credit facilities for marketing their products.

In 1951 a new Credit Association Law (No. 238) was passed which distinguishes between two classes of credit associations. The larger (mostly urban) associations are now referred to as *shinyo kinko,* which may be translated as credit associations. These remain under the supervision of the Finance Minister, and their minimum capital requirement has been raised to 10 million yen. In their dealings with members, who are restricted to employers of not more than 100 people, the associations may receive deposits (including installment savings); make loans, discount bills, and engage in other usual types of financing; and offer safekeeping facilities. Their business with nonmembers is limited to acceptance of deposits and granting of loans secured by deposits. At the end of 1951 these *shinyo kinko* comprised not quite half of the approximately 650 associations, but held more than 80 percent of total assets and liabilities.

The smaller (mostly rural) associations, which have remained predominantly craft associations, are now called *shinyo kumiai,* or credit cooperatives. Supervision has been transferred to the prefectural governors (except in the case of those cooperatives engaged in interprefectural business), and subscribed funds are required to amount to 3 percent of external liabilities. Membership is limited to those who employ not more than 20 people, if in the commerce or service fields, or not more than 100 people if in other businesses. The cooperatives may receive deposits from members and their relatives, and also from local public bodies and other non-profit making corporations; may make loans to and discount bills for members; and may make loans secured by deposits to relatives of members. Both the associations and the cooperatives may also conduct agency business.

The Central Bank for Commercial and Industrial Cooperatives is jointly capitalized at 500 million yen by the government and by the various associations and cooperatives and their federations, and is under the control of both the Minister of Finance and the Minister of International Trade and Industry. The bank is authorized to issue debentures; to receive money on deposit from the associations and federations, as well as from public agencies and other organizations of a non-commercial character; to make loans (for a maximum of five years, or for twenty years if repaid in installments) and grant overdrafts to the associations and federations; to discount their bills; to undertake banking and credit business relating to their commercial bills and domestic trade paper; and to act as their banker generally. (The bank is also the central financing organ for the mutual loans institutions, described in a later section, which grant loans to consumers and to very small enterprises.) Surplus funds are deposited with the Postal Savings System or with other banks that might be specified by the controlling ministers, invested in securities (primarily corporate debentures), or used for short-term loans to the associations and other of the bank's customers.

After the war the government created two more organs that fall into the industrial credit group—the Export–Import Bank of Japan, established under Law No. 268 of December 15, 1950, and the Japan Development Bank, established under Law No. 108 of March 31, 1951. Both are completely government owned and are under the supervision of the Minister of Finance.

The Export–Import Bank was originally established as the Export Bank, with the purpose of aiding Japan's export trade for a limited period of five years. The bank law was amended in 1952 and again in 1953, however, in order to broaden the bank's functions. In the last revision the five-year limitation on the bank's active business life was eliminated and the bank's capital increased to 21 billion yen, the sum provided partly out of the United States Aid Counterpart Fund and partly by a general budget allocation. At the end of 1953 the bank's resources also included a 3 billion yen loan from the Counterpart Fund, apparently obtained under the clause in the revised act that permits the bank to borrow funds from the government or from foreign financial institutions up to an amount which when added to the bank's guarantees will not exceed its capital and reserve funds.

The bank is expressly prohibited from competing with other financial institutions and is to make credit available only in those cases where ordinary banks find it difficult to provide adequate amounts on reasonable terms. It is expected normally to make loans jointly with ordinary banks, but if this should prove difficult, it may make loans independently. It is authorized: (1) to make loans to Japanese foreign traders for investment in foreign corporations or to Japanese manufacturers for the purchase of equipment required for their own enterprises in foreign countries, provided that such loans will contribute to the promotion of Japanese exports or to an advantageous shifting of the sources of imports; (2) to make loans to Japanese exporters or manufacturers of machinery and equipment (including ships and rolling stock) and, if necessary, of other goods for export; (3) if necessary, to advance funds for the export of machinery and equipment even before export contracts are concluded, and also to cover guarantees in connection with bids involving the export of machinery and equipment abroad; (4) to make loans to foreign governments, banks, or firms, to facilitate the purchase of Japanese exports; (5) to make loans to Japanese importers or manufacturers to finance stipulated imports that are considered essential to the economy; (6) to discount bills for banks in connection with all the above types of loans; and (7) to guarantee liabilities associated with any of the above transactions. The loans, discounted bills, and guaranteed liabilities may be for maximum terms of five years, although in special cases they may be extended for up to as long as ten years.

Like the Reconversion Finance Bank, the Japan Development Bank was established to promote Japan's economic reconstruction and industrial development. It is to make credits of a minimum term of one year available to important enterprises, when other financial institutions and security dealers consider the financing too risky or when funds are in short supply. In particular, the bank is: (1) to make loans for acquiring, improving, or repairing capital equipment; (2) to subscribe to corporate debentures issued for raising development funds; and (3) to loan funds or subscribe to debentures which would enable the repayment of development loans granted by ordinary banks or other financial institutions. In 1952 the bank law was amended to permit it also to borrow funds from the government, to underwrite obligations incurred by private firms for development activities, and to borrow from abroad. Such borrowings and guarantees are, as in the case of the Export–Import Bank, not to exceed the total of the bank's capital and reserves.

At the end of 1953 the capital of the bank totaled 17 billion yen, 10 billion from the United States Aid Counterpart Fund and 7 billion received under general budget allocation. However, its resources were many times greater as a result of its absorption in January, 1952, of the assets and liabilities of the Reconversion Finance Bank and in September and October, 1952, of the Counterpart Fund's loans to private enterprise. Most of the bank's activities so far have been in the form of direct loans to key industries. Toward the end of 1953, plans were under way to provide the bank with additional funds to enable it to take up a large part of the outstanding long-term loans of the ordinary banks in order to strengthen their position.

With the promulgation of the Long-Term Credit Bank Law, No. 187, on June 12, 1952, the way was paved for a new group of institutions that, in contrast to the above specialized institutions, could provide long-term credits to any sector of the economy. The law abrogates the 1950 Law for Issuance of Debentures by Banks, thus taking away from the ordinary banks the privilege of procuring funds through the issuance of financial debentures; those banks are expected to revert to their prewar emphasis on short-term lending. The long-term credit banks may be capitalized by government or private subscription, and must have a minimum capital of 500 million yen. They may issue debentures up to thirty times their capital and reserves during the first five years of their existence, and up to twenty times thereafter. They may provide funds for the purchase of equipment or for long-term working capital by making loans and by discounting or accepting bills, and may guarantee obligations arising in connection with such needs. They also may accept deposits from customers and from the national and local governments, and use such funds to extend short-term credits. It is intended, however, that these institutions emphasize their long-term credit function.

At the end of 1953 only two banks had been set up as long-term credit banks. One was the old Industrial Bank of Japan, which assumed this new status on December 1, 1952, with a capital of 2,770 million yen. In effect, this implied a return to the Industrial Bank's traditional emphasis on long-term lending, and the cessation of the short-term credit operations that it had assumed during the postwar years in addition to its usual activities. The second bank was the Long-Term Credit Bank of Japan, established also on December 1, 1952. This bank was opened with a paid-up capital of 1,500 million yen, half in ordinary stocks subscribed by most of the big and provincial banks, many business corporations, and other non-government investors, and half in preferential stocks subscribed by the government from the Counterpart Fund. The authorized capital is 2,250 million yen, with the preferential stocks (to which only the government can subscribe) limited to one third of the total. The Hypothec Bank of Japan and the Hokkaido Colonial Bank participated in the initial subscriptions in the amount of 37.5 million yen each, following their decision to continue as ordinary banks rather than to revert, as did the Industrial Bank, to their traditional concentration upon long-term lending. Most of the personnel for the new bank's operations came from these two institutions.

The Agricultural and Development Credit System.—Paralleling the industrial credit system is a group of banks that finance agricultural and developmental activities. Before the dissolution of the Empire in 1945 the system included a number of now defunct institutions engaged in the development of the colonial areas. The banks that remain continue to play a predominant role in the credit structure of the agricultural areas of Japan proper.

The central organ of the system is the Hypothec Bank of Japan, established for a period of 100 years under Law No. 82 of 1896. Since this special bank law was abrogated in 1950, the bank has been governed by the Bank Law of 1927; like the Industrial Bank, however, it continues to function much as it did before. Half of the bank's 2,000 million yen capital is now owned by the government as a result of Counterpart Fund financing of preferred stocks in 1950; prior to that time the ownership of the bank had been widely distributed. As in the case of the other special banks, the government has always exercised strict control over the Hypothec Bank's policies.

Under its special charter the bank had been permitted to obtain funds by floating debentures,[9] accepting deposits, and issuing savings certificates and bonds which represented a liability of the government but the proceeds of which were made available to the bank. (The bank is now regulated by the general bank law, therefore this last-

[9] Neither the Hypothec Bank nor the Hokkaido Colonial Bank now issues debentures.

mentioned activity is no longer permitted.) The funds thus obtained could be used to make mortgage loans of up to five years, or up to 50 years if repaid in annual installments; to make loans without security to local governments and other public bodies, to various cooperative associations, and to groups of at least five persons engaged in agriculture, industry, or fishery activities; and to acquire debentures issued by the Central Cooperative Bank for Agriculture and Forestry and certain other developmental institutions, as well as to make loans on the security of claims held by such institutions.

While the bank has traditionally aimed primarily at financing agricultural and subsidiary activities (including fishery and livestock raising), and residential lands and buildings, it has also engaged extensively in financing industrial activities, particularly those intended to promote or develop local resources, such as railways, electric power plants, and public works undertaken by local authorities.

In 1950, after the government had doubled the bank's capital, the Bank of Japan sought to facilitate an expansion of the Hypothec Bank's resources by encouraging subscriptions to its debentures. It therefore accorded the same favored treatment to those debentures (and to the debentures issued by the other institutions of the agricultural credit system) as it decided to give to the Industrial Bank debentures.

The Hokkaido Colonial Bank was established as a special bank in 1899 to facilitate the settlement of colonists and the exploitation of resources in the northernmost of the four large Japanese islands. In 1950 the bank was brought under the Bank Law of 1927 and its capital was increased from 500 million yen to 700 millions through financing by the Counterpart Fund, so that a substantial part of the capital is now owned by the government.

Funds are obtained through the issuance of debentures as well as by the acceptance of deposits. The bank makes loans on real estate mortgages; unsecured loans to public bodies and groups of real estate owners, farmers, manufacturers and fishermen; loans to companies organized to colonize and develop Hokkaido; and loans on the security of raw materials or goods necessary to industry. It also handles mortgage and real estate trusts. In recent years, the bank's ordinary banking activities have come to overshadow its mortgage functions.

The Central Cooperative Bank for Agriculture and Forestry was established in 1923, and is under the control of the Minister of Finance and the Minister of Agriculture and Forestry. It is similar in organization and functions to the Central Bank for Commercial and Industrial Cooperatives. Until 1943 the bank had been known as the Central Bank for Cooperative Associations, but in that year it was relieved of its responsibility as a central bank for the commercial and industrial associations, and its name was altered to better describe its functions as a pivotal financial organization for the agricultural, forestry and fishery associations only. These associations and their federations parallel in their own spheres the activities of the industrial and commercial associations. In their banking operations they are authorized to receive long and short-term deposits from members, public bodies, non-profit organizations, and local residents. Most of their loans are short term, but they also provide intermediate credits.

Some small amounts of the associations' idle funds are invested in securities, but the major part is deposited either with the prefectural federations (which in turn deposit their unused funds with the Central Cooperative Bank for Agriculture and Forestry), or directly with the latter institution. This concentration of idle resources facilitates the flow of funds from areas with surpluses to those in need of assistance. Additional funds are obtained by the bank from deposits by other public and non-profit organizations, and by the issuance of debentures. The bank uses its resources to provide the associations and federations with short-term credits for seasonal requirements and with intermediate credits for periods not exceeding five years; to discount bills and grant overdrafts; and to act generally as a banker for its clients. In the investment of idle funds it is restricted to the same types of assets as the Central Bank for Commercial and Industrial Cooperatives.

During the war years the bank's funds were largely diverted from the rural areas and used to finance munitions industries. The losses stemming from the cancellation of the government guarantees were consequently so large, and the implied losses for the farmers so great, the bank was allocated 3,800 million yen out of the total indemnities of 4,600 million yen granted by the government to financial institutions under the reorganization regulations of 1948. In 1951, after issuing 2,000 million yen of preferred stocks, financed through the Counterpart Fund, the bank's capital stood at 2,400 million yen.

Consumer Credit.—Consumer credit facilities were generally inadequate until 1938, when the Japanese Government intervened and established two special organs. The People's Bank facilitated the granting of low interest loans to medium-sized and small merchants and manufacturers, but also made loans to employees and workers with a view to meeting their special needs and stabilizing their living conditions. The bank was authorized to issue debentures, and although allowed to make small loans directly it generally operated indirectly by providing funds to other financial institutions for such loans or by compensating them for losses incurred on them. The second organ was the Pension Bank, which had the very limited purpose of providing small loans to pensioners, who were prohibited by law from giving their pension rights as security for loans and as a consequence had frequently been driven by dire necessity to loan sharks.

Both these institutions were dissolved in 1949, and those functions that were connected with the provision of small loans for business purposes were taken over by the People's Finance Corporation. This corporation, whose capital was raised in 1951 to 6,000 million yen, is also an organ of the Ministry of Finance, and is permitted to borrow funds from the government through budgetary appropriations. Although created to provide small loans to persons who "have the will of carrying on their business independently and have reasonable business plans" but are not able to obtain credit from other sources, more than a third of the corporation's loans outstanding in 1951 were for relief purposes. These credits were financed primarily by the "resuscitation loan fund," which was made available by the government for this particular purpose.

Another government organ providing funds to consumers is the Housing Loan Corporation, established in 1950. The corporation is to make loans only in cases where banks and other existing financial institutions find it difficult to undertake such financing, and the loans are to be granted only for structures which do not exceed prescribed size and cost. The authorized capital of the corporation was set at 5,000 million yen, but with the approval of the Minister of Finance it may be increased through budgetary subscription. The corporation may entrust the actual business connected with making loans to other financial institutions, paying them commissions for their services.

More significant sources of consumer credit are the pawn shops and the *mujins*. Most of the pawn shops are privately owned, but there are a number of public shops which are run by local public bodies and non-profit organizations in accordance with regulations issued in 1919. These shops are supervised by local authorities and are granted funds at a specially low interest rate by the Trust Fund Bureau.

The *mujin,* an institution peculiar to the Orient and having a legal standing since 1915, is a mutual loan society formed to help members of the local community through contributions of other members. The *mujins* are a source of petty funds for both unusual consumer needs and very small business enterprises. Some of them are the result of voluntary association; others, which are required to be joint-stock companies, are organized and operated on a business basis by individuals who enroll the participants. Funds are collected from the members of a group in installments over a fixed period of time, and distributed among the members by drawings, biddings, or similar means.

Beginning in 1945 the *mujins* were also permitted to receive deposits and make loans outside of their regular mutual business, such operations being facilitated by the Finance Minister's assigning the Central Bank for Commercial and Industrial Cooperatives to function as the central financial organ for the *mujins.*

In June, 1951, a new law was enacted with the aim of strengthening the *mujins'* standing and increasing the scope of their activities. Under this law the *mujins* are required to convert within three years into Mutual Loans and Savings Banks. As such, they will be under the supervision of the Minister of Finance, will be required to have a minimum capital of 20 million yen (or 30 million in large cities), and will be subject to reserve requirements and loan limitations. The Mutual Loans and Savings Banks, which numbered 66 at the end of 1952 (at which time only 4 *mujins* remained to be converted), will be allowed to conduct not only mutual business, but also many of the transactions that are undertaken by ordinary banks, with the important exception of drafts, checks, and other internal exchange.

THE CAPITAL MARKET

There is no broad investment market in Japan, nor are there elaborate intermediary and subsidiary organs such as are found in the United States or England. The market centers around the banks and other financial institutions, which are the largest purchasers of bonds and debentures. Investments in stocks have been largely restricted by corporate policies to closed and interlocking circles of investors, although postwar "deconcentration" policies brought about a sizable increase in the number of shareholders.

The Securities Market.—Japan's stock exchanges were first authorized in 1873. The number of registered stocks and the volume of transactions rose rapidly during the interwar period, simultaneously with the growing importance of corporate enterprise. In 1943 the government nationalized the securities market, and the eleven stock exchanges then in existence were made branches of the Japanese Securities Exchange. Operations of the Exchange were suspended at the end of the war and in 1947 the Exchange itself was placed in liquidation.

A new Securities and Exchange Law was passed in 1948, and amended in 1950. To carry out its provisions, a Securities and Exchange Commission was set up, composed of three persons of learning and experience, appointed for terms of three years by the Prime Minister with the consent of the Diet. The functions of the Commission include decisions upon matters of policy and supervision, and investigation of practices and operations related to the issuance of, and transactions in, securities.

The issuance and listing of corporate debentures and shares is subject to the filing with the Commission of a statement disclosing all information pertinent to the ownership and conditions of the company and to the nature and purpose of the proposed flotation. The Commission may refuse to permit the listing of securities on any exchange whenever it deems such listing unnecessary or inappropriate to the public interest, or whenever refusal is believed necessary for the protection of the investors. Issuers remain obligated for a period of three years for damages arising from misrepresentation or omission of pertinent facts.

Securities dealers are subject to license and are required to deposit a "business guaranty fund" as protection for their customers against non-fulfillment of obligations on securities transactions. The dealers' activities are supervised by the Commission, which may order any dealer to discontinue undesirable practices, to revise the evaluation of assets, or to suspend business dealings.

Securities dealers may associate to incorporate and become members of a securities exchange—provided that only one such exchange may be established in any one district as determined by the Commission. Every exchange is autonomously managed by a president assisted by directors and auditors, all elected by members; it raises revenues through membership fees and commission charges for securities transactions; and in order to maintain order in the securities market it may impose penalties on its members, restrict or suspend their transactions, or expel them.

The postwar suspension of transactions on the securities market came to an end in May, 1949, and nine securities exchanges were opened thereafter (Tokyo, Osaka, Nagoya, Kobe, Kyoto, Hiroshima, Fukuoka, Niigata, and Sapporo). These exchanges have a combined membership of about a thousand dealers, in general small-scale companies largely dependent on bank credit for their operations. Exceptions are the "big four" (Nomura, Yamaichi, Nikko, and Daiwa), each capitalized at 200 million yen as compared with the average capital of about 2.5 million yen for the other companies. The predominance of these four companies is particularly felt in Tokyo, where they handle between one half and two thirds of the total securities turnover. There is only one large company—the Japan Securities Financing Company, with a capital of 250 million yen—that makes it its principal business to extend loans to securities dealers and stock investors that ordinary banks find difficult to provide.

In addition to spot selling, three types of settlement are practiced: (a) the "one-day delivery," in which settlement is to be made at an agreed time on the very day of the transaction; (b) the "special delivery," allowing fifteen days for the completion of the transaction; and (c) the "ordinary delivery," requiring settlement within four days.

Distribution of Securities.—A significant phase of the securities market in the postwar period has been the redistribution of securities in pursuance to legislation for "deconcentration" of economic activities. A Securities Liquidation Coordinating Commission was set up in June, 1947, for the purpose of disposing of: (1) the securities of former Zaibatsu interests (Mitsui, Mitsubishi, Sumitomo, Yasuda, and others), title of which had been vested in the Holding Company Liquidation Commission, established in 1946; (2) the securities held by the Closed Institutions Liquidating Commission, which earlier in 1947 had been placed in charge of the liquidation of overseas and wartime special institutions; (3) the securities received by the government in payment of the extraordinary property tax of 1946; and (4) other securities transferred from the Bank of Japan and minor sources. The Coordinating Commission completed its work in June, 1951, by which time it had disposed of securities worth 14.3 billion yen, nearly one half by auction sales to the public and the remainder by sales to employees of the respective companies and by marketing through securities dealers.

It is impossible to appraise the effects of these operations from the standpoint of the deconcentration objective. According to a study made by the Securities and Exchange Commission, between 1945 and the end of 1949 the number of shares increased nearly fivefold and the number of shareholders rose approximately from one and one half million to four million, the increase being entirely accounted for by individual holders. On the other hand, dealers registered the largest gain in percentage distribution of the aggregate value of the securities by groups of holders. The increasing interest taken by individuals in stock may be attributed in part to specific factors—such as the special efforts made to dispose of shares among companies' employees, and the revaluation of companies' assets with resulting expectation of large dividends—and in part to the general inflationary boom prevailing in the economy. It is not improbable, however, that a significant portion of the redistributed shares were bought up by firms and individuals acting for the account of former Zaibatsu families.

Raising of New Capital.—Until 1949, Japanese enterprises took advantage of the favorable postwar market and readjusted their capital structure through the issuance of new shares; but with the return of more stable monetary conditions they returned to their traditional dependence on debentures for raising long-term funds. In 1950, ordinary banks absorbed nearly 90 percent of the new debentures, with the remainder distributed among special financial institutions, insurance companies, and individual and other investors.

Concern over securing a regular flow of long-term funds has given rise to institutional arrangements having the purpose of developing a broader and more stable capital market. At the end of 1949 the Bank of Japan took the initiative in setting up a Capital Issuance Council, securing the participation of the leading banks and securities companies, the Securities and Exchange Commission, and the Holding Company Liquidation Commission (then still in existence). The Council has set itself the task of surveying the market position monthly and estimating the amount of capital increase that may be effected each month. Although the Council operates informally, without legal basis or power, it may prove highly influential because of its membership.

The passage of the Securities Investment Trust Law in May, 1951, was intended to promote attempts to secure long-term funds along another line. The purpose of the law is to encourage investments by individuals through the establishment of an investment trust system whereby securities dealers will be allowed—under the supervision of the Securities and Exchange Commission—to place funds received from their customers for that purpose. With a view to protecting the customers, the law provides that the dealer issue to each customer a trust certificate representing the sum received, and enter in turn into a trust contract with a trust company which acts as depository of the stocks and bonds purchased on behalf of the certificate holders. The four big securities companies invited subscriptions to their trust certificates immediately upon the passage of the new law, and other dealers followed suit.

Insurance and Government Funds.—Apart from the banking system, insurance and government funds represent the most important institutional sources of capital in Japan.

Private insurance business is regulated by a law of 1939, which (a) subjects the establishment of any insurance company to license, and its activities to supervision, by the Minister of Commerce and Industry; (b) provides that property and life insurance may not be transacted by the same company; and (c) confines the investments of insurance companies to government securities, other securities eligible for trust investment, real estate, mortgage loans, loans to non-profit corporations, and bank deposits. Although life insurance is by far the most important, fire and marine insurance are well developed and other types of insurance are also available.

Non-life insurance business is carried out by some fifteen companies led by the Tokyo, the Osaka, the Sumitomo, and the Yasuda Fire and Marine Insurance companies. During 1950 non-life insurance companies increased their assets by about 6,000 million yen and at the middle of 1951 they showed aggregate assets of about 25,000 million yen, of which 30 percent was in deposits and trust accounts, nearly 25 percent in stocks, over 10 percent in real estate, and the remainder in loans, bonds, debentures, and miscellaneous investments.

In prewar years, Japan's life insurance business—in both private and public forms—ranked third in the world, after the United States and Great Britain; if population and national income are taken as the basis for comparison, it probably ranked first. Private companies are organized along both stockholding and mutual plan lines; all issue policies enabling their customers to participate in company profits. Five major companies (Japan, Meiji, Chiyoda, Imperial, and Dai-Ichi Life Insurance) dominate the field. In 1950 private life insurance companies added some 10,000 million yen to their assets and in the middle of 1951 they had total assets of about 35,000 million of which about one third was in loans, another third in stocks, one fifth in real estate, and the remainder in bonds, deposits, and miscellaneous accounts.

Perhaps the most widespread life insurance system of the world is represented by the Post Office Life Insurance and Postal Annuity, whose major objective is to offer popular policies of moderate face value. Policies are divided into four classes, namely: (1) straight life policies with various payment plans; (2) endowment policies; (3) annuities; and (4) special policies for children. In 1950 the assets of Post Office Insurance increased by some 16,000 million yen and in mid-1951 they amounted to about 45,000 millions. Only a small part of the funds was invested directly in government securities and loans to public organs or policy holders. The bulk was placed with the Trust Fund Bureau of the Ministry of Finance.

This Bureau, which has been in existence since 1877 (bearing the name, prior to 1950, of Deposits Funds Management Bureau), is administered as an autonomous agency under the supervision of the Ministry of Finance. Its main purpose is to manage the funds of the Postal Savings and Postal Transfer Systems, but it also handles various other public funds. Because of the great role played by the state in the savings and insurance fields, the Bureau is a central and most important organ of Japan's financial system. Its total funds in 1950 rose by 79,000 million yen reaching over 250,000 million yen; of this, more than one half represented postal savings and the remainder largely insurance funds (including postal insurance and social security funds). Under the Bureau's traditional investment policy (decided upon by a Committee on Investments which is presided over by the Minister of Finance and includes the governor of the Bank of Japan and other government officials and appointed members), loans have been extended mainly to special accounts of the national government and to local governmental authorities and non-profit institutions,

TABLE 6

ASSETS AND LIABILITIES OF THE TRUST FUND BUREAU

(AMOUNTS IN MILLIONS OF YEN)

	September 30 1945	*March 31 1949*	*June 30 1950*	*March 31 1951*
Assets				
National government bonds	35,523	70,742	73,277	87,385
Advances to government accounts	410	2,970	2,897	17,890
Local government bonds	2,742 [a]	923	483	405
Loans to local government agencies		40,010	83,148	103,340
Other securities	9,476 [b]	5,615	1,430	19,182
Other loans		1,196	21,092	11,627
Cash and deposits	311	1,295	18,642	16,136
Total	48,462	122,751	200,963	255,967
Liabilities				
Postal savings	40,693	86,434	137,855	157,858
Government insurance and postal pension	2,815	8,973	20,925	35,817
Social insurance	958	9,952	24,088	32,823
Other accounts	1,081	11,897	12,880	25,917
Reserve funds	2,915	5,495	5,215	3,550
Total	48,462	122,751	200,963	255,967

[a] Includes "Loans to local government agencies."

[b] Includes "Other loans."

and the bulk of the investments has been in government bonds. Recently a larger proportion of newly accrued funds has been used to purchase corporate and bank debentures; by this operation the Bureau has provided non-inflationary funds to the capital market.

As compared with the Bureau's permanent character and the financial resources it handles, other special funds of the government play a lesser role in the capital market. The most active in the past few years has been the United States Aid Counterpart Fund, representing the yen proceeds of United States aid goods sold in Japan. The receipts of this Fund amounted to some 100,000 million yen in the fiscal year 1950 and 150,000 millions in the fiscal year 1951. About one fourth of the receipts was used to retire government-guaranteed debentures of the Reconversion Finance Bank, and another third remained on deposit with the Bank of Japan or was invested in short-term government securities; the balance was used to rehabilitate the communications and railway systems and for investments in or loans to private enterprises in fields of public interest. Operations of this

Fund have been declining with the tapering-off of United States aid. In 1951 an amount of 10,000 million yen was paid in by the government as capital of the Japan Development Bank, which, upon obtaining repayment of loans made from this fund, is to reinvest or relend the proceeds.

Finally, the government makes other funds available for investments in various activities (such as agriculture, forestry, fishing) through "special accounts" of the budget, which are financed either through specific appropriations or transfers of funds from the general budget, or through borrowing from the Trust Fund Bureau.

RECENT DEVELOPMENTS AND POLICIES

Since the restoration of full sovereignty, in mid-1952, two fundamental trends have become apparent in Japan: (a) the gradual elimination of the measures adopted during the Allied occupation, and a re-establishment of centralized administrative controls and concentration of business activities; and (b) the reliance on government deficits and monetary and credit expansion, policies which have resulted in growing inflationary pressures on the domestic economy and in a progressive deterioration in the foreign trade and payments position, notwithstanding the extraordinary receipts from the special procurements of goods and services for United Nations forces and for other United Nations expenditures in Korea.

In the banking system, the first of these trends was evident in the new legislation formulated at the end of 1953. The major provisions of the proposed legislation were: (a) the abolition of the policy board of the Bank of Japan and its substitution by an advisory council within the Ministry of Finance; and (b) the restoration of the authority of the Ministry of Finance over the Bank of Japan and all other banking institutions. Additional provisions pointing towards a restoration of prewar conditions included a liberalization of the rules governing eligibility for all bank director positions, and the elimination of restrictions on banks' holdings of securities. Other provisions, whose main motivation apparently was the strengthening of the banking and credit system, were an increase in the capital requirements of banks, and the introduction of required reserves against bank deposits to be held in the form of government bonds.

In the field of monetary and credit policy, there was a steady expansion in the volume of credit and the money supply. Between March, 1951, and December, 1953, the assets/liabilities of the Bank of Japan rose by 30 percent, from 630 billion yen to 830 billion. This increase could be traced primarily to expanded bank financing of the government (through both direct advances and purchase of securities), which rose by 140 billion yen. Discounts and advances of the bank more than doubled during the period, increasing by 170 billion, but this was offset by a contraction of loans for foreign exchange from 280 billion yen to 90 billion—the latter movement largely a reflection of the country's deteriorating balance of payments. Over the same period the assets/liabilities of all the other banks rose from 2,110 billion yen to 4,050 billion, an expansion of more than 90 percent, with discounts increasing by 650 billion to a total of 970 billion, and advances by 830 billion to a total of 1,570 billion. The liquidity position of the banks was very much strained, the ratio of reserves to demand deposits at the end of 1953 being below 40 percent.

The Bank of Japan continued, despite these developments, to rely almost solely upon selective credit controls until late in 1953. During the same period it actually adjusted certain interest rates downward to favor the financing of certain domestic activities and imports. In September, 1953, the Bank made more severe its system of progressive penalty rates, with a view towards restraining excessive borrowing by the commercial banks. Under this system each bank was allowed a basic credit line; the lowest discount rates (5.84–6.57 percent) applied to the lower portion of such a credit line; higher rates (6.93–7.30 percent) applied to the full credit line; and still higher rates (7.66–9.13 percent) were applied to amounts beyond the credit line. The ranges of applicability of the various rates were thereafter revised from time to time in order to bring into operation progressively higher rates. The new system seems to have had some immediate effect in restraining the net expansion of loans and discounts. These measures of monetary restraint were supported by "moral suasion," with the Bank issuing statements indicating that it would be the Bank's policy to absorb the impact of governmental deficits and to bring about a reduction in domestic prices and costs so as to restore Japan's competitive position in world markets. In line with these statements, the Bank at the end of 1953 urged commercial banks and other institutions to be more cautious in their lending, and moved to restrict import financing while facilitating export financing.

The new policy of monetary restraint was brought about by the realization that it was necessary to arrest the rapid deterioration of Japan's international trade position. The country's foreign exchange resources, after reaching a peak in mid-1952 in the amount of 1,160 million dollars (in dollars and other currencies), fell to about one billion dollars by the middle of 1953. The decline was entirely in Japan's sterling holdings and in her credit balances in other currencies; her dollar holdings rose very moderately during that period, reflecting the receipts from special procurements by the United Nations. Although this development was in part attributable to import restrictions imposed by foreign countries, it was also a result of a certain loss of competitiveness by Japanese products in world markets. The latter was in turn a consequence of the upward pressure exerted on Japanese costs by monetary policy at a time when world prices were tending generally to decline. Japan was thus confronted with an urgent need for coordinating its economic and financial policies so as to achieve a more satisfactory position both internally and externally.

CONCLUSION

At the mid-point of the twentieth century, Japan's financial system includes a variety of institutions, government and private, national and local, some with general and some with specific functions in the various fields of the economy. The system appears to be fairly well adapted to the social, political and economic structure of the country, which combines traditional forms of local rural society with modern forms of commerce and industry that have been developed at the joint initiative of the government and private groups (the so-called Zaibatsu).

In the course of the past century, the creation of a Western type of state organization (including a large bureaucracy and strong armed forces) and the development of a modern and highly industrialized sector in the economy have given rise to new and expanding requirements for diversified types of financial facilities. These requirements have in turn contributed to the determination of the institutional and operational framework of the money and credit system. Financing of government activities by borrowing has become a most important and usual operation, and by means of it financial institutions have been enabled to obtain earning assets and yet maintain a liquid position. At the same time, because of the identification of the interests of the Zaibatsu groups with the national policies of the state, and also as a result of the Zaibatsu's close interrelationships with financial institutions of all types, the major industrial and commercial enterprises have been in the best position (next to the government) for mobilizing the savings of the nation to meet their current and long-term requirements.

This preferential position enjoyed by the state and by companies under government or Zaibatsu control has left other forms of economic activities dependent upon only marginal resources. Inadequacy of private capital resources and difficulties in obtaining bank credit appear to have been important factors contributing to the process of absorption, particularly during the interwar period, of small businesses and local banks by larger companies and institutions.

Financing of commerce has been the function primarily of ordinary banks. They have concentrated, however, on the financing of wholesale trade transactions and as a result the smaller firms and independent merchants have been forced usually to rely upon the credit made available to them by wholesalers and the facilities provided by cooperative or special organs. Although the financing of foreign trade has been hampered, particularly since 1930, this has been due to a shortage of exchange resources rather than to unavailability of domestic financing or inadequacy of banking facilities.

The different types of credit and other financial facilities required by the various sectors of agriculture have been provided and expanded by the government—from short-term financing of the movement of crops to long-term financing and refinancing of existing debt, and from collection of rural savings to transfer of funds among rural communities. Despite this assistance, agriculture built up a heavy debt burden in the twenties and early thirties, relief for which came thereafter only through subsidies and inflation.

The fact that financial institutions have developed largely as part of broader Zaibatsu groups, which were pursuing multifarious activities in widely differing fields, helps to explain the relative absence of specialization in banking and finance. These private institutions have been called upon to finance the various requirements, of long-term as well as of medium-term or short-term character, of the industrial and commercial companies within the same Zaibatsu group, and to provide them with other subsidiary financial facilities. On the other hand, the establishment of the few and significant specialized lending institutions, upon government initiative and under direct government control, has also assured financing of those needs of government-owned undertakings and private enterprises of national interest that have not been able to be satisfied by the large private banks. This direct integration of financial institutions with other forms of economic activities probably can be properly regarded as the outcome of the inadequacy of savings, which has led to a tendency to concentrate the available capital resources in order to aid industrial and colonial development. At the same time this trend has prevented the development of the autonomous forms of activities and the competitive practices that are general characteristics of the money and capital markets of the Western World.

The legislation promulgated in the early postwar years had two major objectives with respect to financial organizations—namely, to break the close ties between private financial institutions and the commercial and industrial enterprises belonging to the same Zaibatsu; and to eliminate the privileges and functional specialization of public institutions by placing them on the same basis as private institutions. While certain organizational changes resulted, there was hardly any modification in the fundamental composition of the financial system and in the framework of institution-customer relationships. More recently the Japanese Government has adopted several measures and is considering others that mean a reversion to the old technique of meeting specific financial problems by creating new public institutions, or expanding the scope of existing ones. This is but a symptom of the fact that the legislative and institutional reorganization of the early postwar period could not solve the traditional problem of scarcity of capital resources, which shaped Japan's financial system and policies in the past.

In fact, formal changes like those introduced in recent years can hardly be regarded as appropriate for altering a basic situation rooted in old necessities. The critical problem of the Japanese financial system remains the formation of a capital market appropriate to the high level of industrialization that has evolved. Some efforts have been made in this direction, but until a well-developed capital market actually appears, the various economic spheres will probably continue to compete for larger shares of the financial resources available through existing banking institutions—these being the principal if not the only sources of funds for both working capital and investment capital. The ability of these institutions to lend and invest and still maintain a liquid position will in turn continue to depend on the willingness of the central bank to make available its own credit facilities, a situation that has been for long characteristic in Japan and has led to the persistence of inflationary pressures. This problematic role of the central bank, as well as the integration under close private or government control of financial activities with other activities, can be understood only in the light of the combination of scarce capital resources and the accelerated process of economic development that has prevailed in Japan since the beginning of her Western course.

REFERENCES

OFFICIAL SOURCES

Statistical

Bank of Japan, Foreign Exchange Control Department. *Foreign Exchange Statistics Monthly.* Tokyo.

—— Statistics Department. Economic Statistics of Japan. Tokyo. Published annually.

—— *Economic Statistics Monthly.* Tokyo.

Economic Counsel Board. Japanese Economic Statistics, Section II—Foreign and Domestic Commerce. Tokyo. (Prior to November, 1951, published by the Supreme Commander for the Allied Powers, Economic and Scientific Section.)

Ministry of Finance, Research Section. *Quarterly Bulletin of Financial Statistics.* Tokyo.

Ministry of Finance and Bank of Japan. Statistical Year-Book of Finance and Economy of Japan. Tokyo, 1948.

General

Bank of Japan, Economic Research Department. *Monthly Economic Review.* Tokyo.

—— Policy Board. Annual Report. Tokyo.

Economic Stabilization Board. Monthy Economic Report. Tokyo.

Ministry of Finance, Banking Bureau. Draft of the Law Concerning Banks. Tokyo, November 11, 1950.

—— Draft of the Enforcement Law for the Law Concerning Banks. Tokyo, November 12, 1950.

—— Laws for Japanese Financial System. Tokyo, April, 1951.

Ministry of Finance, Financial Commissioner's Office. Guide to Economic Laws of Japan. Tokyo, 1950.

Ministry of Finance. The Banking System of Japan, by T. Otsuki. Tokyo, April, 1951.

United States Department of Commerce, Bureau of Foreign and Domestic Commerce. Japanese Banking, by Herbert M. Bratter. Washington, 1931.

United States Department of State. Report of the Mission on Japanese Combines, Part I, Analytical and Technical Data. Washington, 1946.

United States War Department. Army Service Forces, Manual M354-5. Civil Affairs Handbook, Money and Banking in Japan (prepared by the Federal Reserve Bank of New York and the Board of Governors of the Federal Reserve System). Washington, 1944.

—— Civil Affairs Information Guide, Pamphlet No. 31-4. Banking Accounting and Operations in Japan (prepared by the Foreign Economic Administration). Washington, 1945.

NONOFFICIAL SOURCES

Cohen, Jerome B. Japan's Economy in War and Reconstruction. Minneapolis, University of Minnesota Press, 1949.

Industrial Bank of Japan, The. *Survey of Japanese Finance and Industry.* Tokyo. Published monthly.

Oriental Economist, The. Tokyo. Published monthly.

Sarasas, Phra. Money and Banking in Japan. London, Heath Cranton Limited, 1940.

Takita, M. Development of Banking in Japan. Oita, Japan, Research Department of the Oita Commercial College, 1929.

MEXICO

by Margaret G. Myers

PROFESSOR OF ECONOMICS, VASSAR COLLEGE

ALTHOUGH Mexico was the first part of the North American continent to be settled by Europeans, and has a long history of artistic and intellectual achievement, its economic development can hardly be said to have begun until the revolution of 1910 broke the concentration of power and capital in the hands of lay and clerical landowners. Since that time progress has been impressive, and the standard of living has been slightly raised in spite of the rapid increase in population from 15,500,000 in 1910 to 25,500,000 in 1950. The national income for 1950 was estimated at 1,166 pesos per capita, or about $135.[1]

Agriculture has always been the principal activity of the country and still employs about 60 percent of the workers, who contribute only 15 percent of the national product. Their productivity is extremely low, because of the small size of their holdings, the aridity of the soil which requires irrigation in order to be cultivable, and the lack of fertilizer and machinery which necessitates allowing half the land to lie fallow each year. During the decade of the 1940s the situa-

---

MARGARET G. MYERS's writings include: *The New York Money Market: Origins and Development to 1913* (1931), *Paris as a Financial Center* (1935), and *Monetary Proposals for Social Reform* (1940). She is Professor of Economics at Vassar College.

The author would like to express her appreciation of the help so kindly given in the preparation of this material by bankers and public officials in Mexico, and especially by the Economics staff of the American Embassy in Mexico City.

1 Banco de Mexico, *Vigesimanovena asamblea general ordinario de accionistas* (Mexico, 1951), p. 13 (referred to hereafter as *Annual Report of the Bank of Mexico for 1951*).

Antonio Carrillo Flores, head of the Nacional Financiera, estimates that from 1938 to 1948 the per capita consumption of the principal foodstuffs increased as follows: maize, 90 kilos to 118 kilos; wheat, 25 kilos to 31 kilos; beans, 5.5 kilos to 8.7 kilos; sugar, 16 kilos to 21 kilos. *Revista de Economía,* September, 1950. (A kilo is 2.2 pounds.)

tion was greatly improved by numerous irrigation projects (13 percent of the federal budget was devoted to irrigation in 1947); by the opening of roads and railroads (the Pan-American highway through Mexico was completed in 1950); by improvements in animal breeds and seed grains; and by the campaigns against illiteracy and disease. As a result of these efforts the production of many commodities was greatly increased during the decade. Cotton tripled, sugar doubled, while corn, rice, wheat, beans, and chick peas showed gains which not only made Mexico self-sufficient for many foods, but in some cases produced a surplus for export.

Next to agriculture, mining has been the most important economic activity in Mexico, which is still the world's largest producer of silver and an important producer of lead, zinc, and copper. Before 1938 petroleum was largely exported; in that year the foreign owners were "expropriated" (most of their claims had been settled by 1947) and since that time the domestic consumption has increased until there is now very little available for export.

Manufacturing had a late start in Mexico but increased with great rapidity in the 1940s under the stimulus of war and the government policy of industrialization. Textiles are the oldest and one of the most important items of manufacture, but the emphasis in recent years has been shifted to primary products. Between 1940 and 1950 the iron and steel industry quadrupled its output of iron and ferrous alloys, and increased twentyfold its output of ingots and steel; the cement industry more than tripled its capacity, and the per capita consumption of electricity increased more than 30 percent. Chemical and fertilizer plants have been heavily subsidized by the government in order to increase the productivity of agriculture, without which there can be no sound industrialization.[2]

In the field of foreign trade Mexico is more fortunate than most Latin American countries, since her prosperity does not depend upon the exportation of any single commodity. She continues to export silver and other mining products, and in recent years has begun to export coffee, fruits, meat, and manufactured articles in volume. The tourist trade from the United States has been of increasing importance since the devaluation of the peso in 1948; the earnings of Mexican workers in the United States contribute in lesser degree. Imports consist largely of machinery, heavy consumer goods, and luxury items.

[2] *El Mercado de Valores*, Dec. 11, 1950.

Some raw materials for industry are imported, and in some years of drought in the 1940s it was necessary to import corn, wheat, and sugar.

The balance of trade ran heavily in favor of Mexico during the Second World War, and heavily against her for several years thereafter, as Mexicans resumed their purchases abroad. The government has used its tariff policy to further the industrialization program, admitting raw materials and machinery with little or no duty, and subjecting luxuries and competing manufactures like textiles to very high tariffs. During the balance-of-payments crisis in 1946 and 1947 certain luxury imports were prohibited altogether. Some controls have been exercised over exports also in recent years, and an export tax was levied after the devaluation of the peso in order to absorb devaluation profits of exporters.

Exchange controls have never been used in Mexico.[3] In an effort to stimulate sales of her goods in European countries with exchange difficulties, Mexico has made barter and trade agreements with Spain, Czechoslovakia, France, Belgium, England, Switzerland, and Italy.[4] Mexican officials recognize the desirability of eventual free trade, but insist that Mexico cannot afford that luxury until her infant industries are firmly established.

CURRENCY AND PRICES

Coin still plays a large part in the Mexican economy. It was not until 1945 that the volume of bank deposits exceeded the amount of coin and paper money in circulation. The standard coin is the silver peso, which until 1931, except for the years of revolution, was worth fifty United States cents. In that year Mexico abandoned the gold standard. The peso was devalued to 3.60 per dollar in 1933, to 4.85 per dollar in 1940, and to 8.65 to the dollar in 1949. Because of the rising price of silver since 1934, the larger silver coins have been abandoned in favor of paper currency. However, the Bank of Mexico has several times coined gold and silver and sold it to the public in the hope that it would be hoarded, thus reducing the danger of inflation.[5]

The process of inflation in Mexico can be traced in the index of wholesale prices of 210 articles, computed by the Bank of Mexico

3 R. Torres Gaitán, "La moneda," *Revista de economia continental*, Aug., 1946, p. 29.

4 *Annual Report of the Bank of Mexico for 1951*, p. 31.

5 Secretaría de Gobernación, *Seis años de actividad nacional* (Mexico, 1946), p. 330.

with 1939 as the base year. These index numbers apply only to prices in Mexico City; there are no comparable indices for the country as a whole.[6]

TABLE 1
INDEX OF WHOLESALE PRICES IN MEXICO CITY, 1939–50

Year	*210 Commodities*	*Consumers' Goods*	*Producers' Goods*
1939	100.0	100.0	100.0
1940	102.5	100.5	105.5
1941	109.3	106.1	114.0
1942	120.6	117.9	125.5
1943	145.7	147.7	142.7
1944	178.5	191.0	159.6
1945	198.7	218.8	168.5
1946	228.7	254.3	190.6
1947	242.3	264.0	209.1
1948	260.0	270.5	244.0
1949	284.8	281.6	289.8
1950	311.2	302.9	323.8

Against this rapid increase in wholesale prices can be set the less rapid increase in the index of production, as computed by the Bank of Mexico. This index, although admittedly unsatisfactory because of its limited coverage and out-of-date weighting, is the only one available. On a base of 1929 as 100, the index averaged 151 for 1945, and 192 for 1950. For manufacturing industry alone the index rose to 219 for 1945 and to 277 for 1950. It would probably have been higher if the weighting system had reflected the importance of recently developed industries.

BANKING AND CREDIT INSTITUTIONS

The development of financial institutions in Mexico has not yet caught up with the industrialization program and the shift from agriculture toward manufacture. The government has therefore organized a number of financial services (which in most countries are in the hands of private enterprise) and exercises a high degree of control over others. The Secretary of the Treasury is responsible not only for

[6] The list of commodities, but not their weights, is given in the 1947 report of the Bank of Mexico. Other details are given in *Primera reunion de técnicos sobre banca central* (Mexico, 1946).

the conduct of the government's financial affairs but also for the coordination and conduct of the institutions of the money market. Through the government's ownership of all or of a controlling interest of the stock, the Secretary of the Treasury controls many of the "national" banks; he names five of the nine directors of the Bank of Mexico, which stands at the top of the banking hierarchy, and appoints the head of the National Bank Commission, which examines and audits the reports of all banks. The Treasury itself maintains the staff which penalizes any infringement of the banking law reported by this commission. The Secretary of the Treasury also names the head of the Nacional Financiera, one of the most powerful agencies in the money market.

THE NATIONAL BANKS

Credit institutions owned partly or entirely by the government are termed national banks. The government has felt itself obliged to enter one banking field after another because of the failure of the private banking system to meet the credit needs of the country. Some of these national banks are small and limited in scope while two of them, the Bank of Mexico and the Nacional Financiera, are the two most important financial institutions of the country.

Among the smaller of these government institutions is the National Warehouses, organized in 1936 to provide bonded warehouses for business. There is a National Bank for Cooperatives, organized in 1941. The National Bank for the Army and the Navy was established in 1947. The National Bank for Motion Pictures was organized in 1947 from a *financiera* which was in difficulties; its capital of 10,000,000 pesos permits it to make loans covering 60 percent of the cost of production of the Mexican moving pictures which are a great source of national pride. The latest addition to the list of the national banks is the Nacional Monte de Piedad created in 1949 as a savings bank, from what was formerly the banking department of the national pawnshop.

The National Bank for Small Trade in the Federal District was established in 1942 as an ingenious attempt to provide, for the operators of street stands and market stalls, credit at less than the usurious rates charged by private lenders. Since many of these borrowers were unable to read or write, the bank arranged for the repayment of loans by means of stamps to be purchased daily and pasted in a book. That the bank met a genuine need was evidenced by the fact that during the year 1946 more than 25,000 loans were made, in amounts ranging from 40 to 200 pesos. Unfortunately the cost of providing these loans was high, and the bank's operations showed continual losses. The banking law revision of January 3, 1949, therefore followed the precedent set for the agricultural banks, and required that borrowers organize into cooperatives to obtain credit.[7]

Among the earliest of the national banks were those established for the purpose of providing much-needed credit for agriculture. The land reforms which accompanied the revolution of 1910 brought into existence a class of small independent farmers, as the *haciendas* were broken up and with them the economic system under which farming had been done for centuries. Relief from exploitation by absentee landlords was too often deprived of its advantages by the inability of the small farmers to get credit for equipment and supplies. In 1926 there was established the National Bank for Agricultural Credit, to make loans based on mortgages, and also several smaller (and short-lived) banks to provide credit for the *ejidos,* the small farms on communal land which could not be mortgaged.

These banks were notably unsuccessful, partly because they had insufficient capital, and partly because loans were often granted for political rather than for economic reasons. In 1930 the law was therefore revised, providing among other things that loans should no longer be made to individual farmers, but only to farmers organized into cooperatives. In 1935 the National Bank for Ejidal Credit was established with a similar provision. In spite of the revision of the law these banks have not been able to fill the need for agricultural credit. Their capital is still inadequate—about 200 million pesos for the former and 250 million pesos for the latter—and their losses since 1935 have amounted to more than 150 million pesos. It has been estimated that they provide only about one tenth of the total of agricultural credit outstanding, the rest coming from private individual lenders, since private banks have hardly touched this field.

On the constructive side, these banks have been able, even while charging interest of 8 and 9 percent to the cooperatives (which results in a rate of about 11 percent to the individual farmer) to reduce the

7 "El crédito al pequeño comercio," *Revista de Economía,* March 15, 1949.

cost far below the rate charged by private lenders, which may be 5 percent per month or even more. Moreover, the banks serve as channels through which government policy to aid agriculture in other ways can be carried out. They encourage the organization of farmers, assist them with warehousing, teach crop diversification and new methods, and help in the colonizing of new land.

The experience with agricultural credit, private and national, gives additional evidence that agriculture in Mexico needs far more than credit in order to be economically successful. The real problems are those created by the rapid growth of a population which is excessive in terms of the aridity and infertility of the soil. The need for improvement in the basic living conditions of large groups of the population was recognized by the establishment of the National Mortgage Bank for Public Works in 1933. This bank issues its own bonds at 6 to 8 percent interest. Private investors have bought very few of these bonds; they are mostly held by the Bank of Mexico or the commercial banks. Loans are made usually for 50 percent of the cost of the project, and are to be amortized in 15 or 20 years. The bank has provided credit primarily for federal projects such as road building (financed out of gasoline taxes), low cost housing, water supply, and electrification. It lends also to state and local governments if the project has been approved by the Department of Public Works; but these loans are often made without any specific income to provide for their repayment, and in many cases the local governments have not been able to meet the amortization schedule.[8] In 1950 the capital and reserves of the bank were 65.8 million pesos and its loans outstanding amounted to 422 million pesos.

A national bank which is not very large but has become increasingly important as an implement of governmental policy is the National Bank for Foreign Trade, established in 1937 with an authorized capital of 20 million pesos. This was later increased to 50 million pesos, of which 33.5 millions were paid in by 1950. The original function of the bank was that of financing Mexican exports, especially exports of agricultural commodities by small producers of such crops as rice, sugar, chick peas, and cotton. During the war the bank was entrusted also with the control of primary foodstuff imports, through its associate, Nacional Distribuidora. The bank helped to obtain for Mexico the food which had to be imported in the drought years, and

[8] *El Mercado de Valores*, April 16, 1951.

is concerned especially with the commodities judged essential in the industrialization program. The bank does not issue its own securities, but is permitted to rediscount with the Bank of Mexico large amounts of the paper which it has discounted for the agricultural credit and other banks.

THE BANK OF MEXICO

At the head of the financial hierarchy stands the Bank of Mexico, st of the national banks. Although organized in 1925, it was not until 1932 that it was given the monopoly of note issue, the usual first step in the creation of a modern central bank. The government at that time became owner of 51 percent of the stock, with the right to appoint five of its nine directors and exercise veto powers over its activities. It entrusted to the Bank the handling of the public funds and the public debt, forbade the Bank to make loans to individuals or private business firms, and required all commercial banks to become associated with it.

Although the Bank of Mexico is empowered to carry out the usual functions of a central bank, the traditional instruments of central bank policy are frequently rendered ineffective by the underdevelopment of the money market in Mexico. The rediscount rate, for example, has been little more than nominal. By 1941 the Bank had established its right to reject paper offered for rediscount, and was free of any legal limitations on the rate. However there was little occasion for an associated bank to rediscount during the early war period, since the favorable balance of payments during the war brought large amounts of funds into the banking system. And the occasional bank which was faced with a reserve deficiency preferred to pay the penalty on that deficiency (1 percent per month until 1949 and after that date 2 percent per month) rather than to rediscount at the central bank.

It may have been the futility of the rediscount rate which led the Bank of Mexico in 1941 to reduce the number of rates from three to two, with 4 percent charged on paper up to six months' maturity and 5 percent on paper of six to twelve months' maturity. In 1942 for the first time a single rate, 4.5 percent, was set for all types of paper.

To offset the anticipated inflation, it was further provided that in order to qualify for the rediscount privilege a bank must have 60 percent of its portfolio in "production" loans; in any case a bank would not be permitted to rediscount more than 10 percent of its commercial paper. The volume of rediscounts did not increase appreciably during this period.

When in 1943 the principle of a single rate was abandoned in order to give a preferential rate of 3 percent to agricultural paper, an increased volume of agricultural paper was presented for rediscount; but it came from other national banks rather than from the private banks. So unimportant had the rediscount rate become as an instrument of credit control that during the years when the Bank of Mexico was most preoccupied with the problem of preventing inflation, the discount rate was not altered, and was hardly even mentioned in the annual reports for 1945, 1946, and 1947. In September, 1948, it was announced that the private banks were to be permitted to rediscount only in emergency, and that the national banks which had been doing most of the rediscounting were no longer to be accommodated. Differential rates were again established, with 8 percent for commercial paper, 4.5 percent for industrial paper, and 3 percent for agricultural paper, but these rates were merely nominal.

Open-market operations, which are often used in order to force banks to rediscount and thus make the rate effective, are of little avail in a country like Mexico where the securities market is rudimentary. Although the Bank of Mexico has several times intervened in the market by operations which it referred to as "open market," the purpose in each case was to support a particular security in order to make it attractive to investors, rather than to release excess reserves. In December, 1941, for example, the Bank attempted to stabilize the price of government railroad bonds, but the only result was to leave the Bank the holder of large amounts of the issue. In April, 1947, the Bank agreed to repurchase at 99.5 many of the bonds issued by the Treasury for the financing of public works, but again this was an attempt to reassure investors and not to control the money market.

The device sometimes referred to in the United States as "moral suasion" has been used by the Bank of Mexico in recent years in the form of a "gentleman's agreement" among the banks to limit expansion. In March, 1943, the banks of the Federal District, under pressure from the Bank of Mexico, agreed to try to hold the total of their portfolios to the amount outstanding at the end of October, 1942; any increase was to be penalized by a corresponding increase in their reserve deposit with the Bank of Mexico. A few months later this penalty was softened by permitting cash on hand or government securities to be substituted for the increased reserve deposit. There was continual friction over the agreement, and the banks were accused of evading it by the device of shifting new loans from their head offices in Mexico City to their country branches or to affiliates which were not bound by the agreement. It was abandoned at the end of 1943, but a new agreement was made in May, 1944, with somewhat more liberal provisions. After further modification in January, 1946, the agreement was terminated altogether at the end of 1946. By that time the fear of inflation was giving way to fear of a postwar depression, and the reason for the agreement no longer existed.

Because of the ineffectiveness of the traditional instruments of money market control, the Bank of Mexico early in the war began to apply what it called "qualitative" controls. The Mexican concept of "qualitative" went much further than the classical idea of self-liquidating commercial paper, and included the classification of commercial paper according to the purpose for which it was made. A step in this direction had been taken as early as 1942 when the Bank ruled that the rediscount privilege was available only to an associated bank that had made 60 percent of its loans to production. However, the productive loans to industry, agriculture, and cattle raising continued to represent less than 60 percent of the total throughout the war years. The Bank therefore began to apply a new device which it believed to be particularly appropriate to the Mexican situation—flexible reserve requirements.

These were an extension of the requirements already in existence. The law of 1931 had adopted the principle of reserves against deposits to be held in the form of balances with the central bank, and had set the figure at 10 percent of demand deposits. This figure was modified frequently. When the war broke out a distinction was made for the first time between banks in the Federal District and those outside, and in 1943 the outside banks were further subdivided into banks in cities which had a branch of the Bank of Mexico, and banks in non-branch cities. This triple classification corresponds roughly to the classification of member banks in the United States into central reserve city, reserve city, and country banks.

During 1943 when the gentleman's agreement in Mexico City seemed to be having no result except to increase the amount of the loans made by the outside banks, the Bank of Mexico raised reserve requirements several times. By the end of that year they stood at 45, 30, and 30 percent, respectively, for the three classes of banks. The country banks' reserve balances could not keep pace with the increasing requirements. In spite of an absolute increase of 50 million pesos in their reserves, they showed a deficit of 30 million pesos by the end of the year. The same situation prevailed during 1944 and 1945. Reserve requirements were raised again until by the end of 1945 they stood at the then legal maximum of 50 percent of demand liabilities for the banks in the Federal District and in branch cities; for banks in non-branch cities they were 45 percent. Effective reserve requirements were raised still further by the ruling of the Secretary of the Treasury in April, 1945, that thenceforth the definition of demand liabilities was to be broadened. By the end of the following month this measure had increased the amount subject to reserve by about 130 million pesos, which reduced the excess of reserves of the Federal District banks by about 40 million pesos and increased the reserve deficit of the outside banks by about 60 million pesos. Loans continued to increase nevertheless, as the banks found it profitable to lend in spite of the high penalty rate on reserve deficiencies.[9]

When the war came to an end in 1945 it was generally believed in Mexico as in many other countries that the nature of the monetary problem had changed and that the imminent danger was deflation rather than inflation. The central banking authorities resolved therefore to continue to use flexible reserve requirements as an instrument of policy, but in the opposite direction of counteracting depression and unemployment by providing increased credit for rapid industrialization. In its report for the year 1946 the Bank of Mexico explained its decision by saying that the time had come "to subordinate purely monetary policy to the general economic policy" and to substitute for the "orthodox concepts of liquidity and solvency that of flexibility" of fiscal policy.

This emphasis upon flexibility continued to be the keynote of central bank and Treasury policy in the postwar years. On January 1,

[9] *Revista de Economía,* Nov. 15, 1949. Bank of Mexico Annual Reports.

1947,[10] reserve requirements were reduced to 45 and 40 percent, respectively, for the branch and non-branch city banks (leaving the requirement still at 50 percent for Federal District banks) and all banks were permitted a reserve deficiency up to 15 percent without the usual penalty, provided that the amount of the deficiency was invested in government securities. Banks in the Federal District were losing reserves rapidly during this period because of the increased importation of goods. Reserve requirements were further eased during 1947 by permitting 20 percent of the reserve to take the form of investment in government bonds. For the banks outside the Federal District a further deficiency of 10 percent, and later in the year of 25 percent, was permitted, if offset by new loans to agriculture and cattle raising.

Although the efforts of the monetary authorities to encourage production loans as compared with commercial loans did not produce any marked change in the ratio, the total of all loans increased during 1947. It was clear that there was little danger of deflation, and that there was still danger of inflation. The reserves of the Bank of Mexico, like those of the commercial banks in Mexico City, had been sharply reduced by the adverse balance of payments, and prices especially of production goods had been rising steadily. The government was unwilling to risk depression and unemployment in order to maintain the parity of the peso, and in the middle of 1948 abandoned its support. A year later the peso was stabilized at the new low rate of 8.65 to the dollar, and it became more important than ever for production to be increased if it was to keep pace with the increasing volume of circulating media.

The principle of flexible reserve requirements was therefore adapted to the effort to direct bank credit into production loans. In 1948 banks in the Federal District which were already permitted to count government or government-approved securities as part of their reserve (20 of the 50 percent of demand liabilities) were given the privilege of using private, instead of government, securities up to 10 percent.[11] Banks outside the Federal District were permitted to use government and private securities, as well as new loans to agriculture or cattle raising, as part of their required reserve; 25 of the total

[10] Bank of Mexico, *Circular 1041*, Dec. 12, 1946.

[11] This was an increase from the former 2.5 percent permitted in private securities. Government paper might take up 8.25 percent, with the remaining 1.25 percent in special securities to aid hotel construction.

45 percent, for banks in branch cities; 20 of the total 40 percent for banks in non-branch cities. Although the proportion of loans classified as production did not show any significant increase as a result of these changes in reserve requirements, the long-term loans and investments did increase somewhat more than short loans during 1949.

The danger of inflation was still acute. Prices were advancing more rapidly than production, and the favorable balance of payments following upon the devaluation of the peso was reflected in the increasing reserves of the Bank of Mexico and the commercial banks. The Bank of Mexico therefore took a more drastic step in the application of flexible reserves, and in its famous Circular 1108 directed that after September 30, 1949, all increases in demand liabilities of the deposit banks were to be subject to a 100 percent reserve requirement. There was, however, an important qualification: deficits in reserves up to 70 percent would be without penalty, provided that an equivalent sum was invested in equipment loans of one to two years' maturity, or in securities of two years' maturity, or in capital loans up to five years' maturity. The Circular did not change for any of the three groups of banks the reserve percentage for already existing deposits; this was already at 50 percent for banks in Mexico City, and at 45 and 40 percent for banks in branch and non-branch cities, respectively.

A provision in the General Banking Law limited the total of long loans for any bank to 20 percent of its demand liabilities. Since this remained in operation, it had the effect of putting a ceiling upon the extent to which the banks might take advantage of the escape clause in the new reserve requirement. The net result of the Circular was therefore to force the banks to invest up to the 20 percent limit in the longer loans; once up to that limit, increases in deposits would have to be offset by increased balances with the Bank of Mexico. During the first months after the imposition of the new requirement little effect was visible in the balance sheets of the banks. They had built up their deposits before September 30 to prepare for the imposition of the new requirement, and for several months thereafter their deposits were below the September level. Deposits rose only slowly during the first half of 1950, but with the outbreak of the Korean war increased rapidly during the latter half of that year.

In the meantime the protests of the banking community, and the difficulty of enforcing the elaborate details of the September, 1949,

Circular brought about a slight revision. For banks in Mexico City which already had the legal limit of 20 percent of demand liabilities invested in medium-term and long-term loans, the requirement after May, 1950, was that increases in deposits must be matched as follows:

30 percent by an increase in deposits at the Bank of Mexico;
20 percent by investment in productive activities, at medium term and long term;
20 percent by investment in securities, private or government;
30 percent (the remainder) unrestricted.

For banks outside the Federal District similar requirements were set, but 35 percent of the increase was left unrestricted for banks in branch cities, and 40 percent unrestricted for banks in non-branch cities.

As the expansion of bank credit continued, the requirements were revised again on January 12, 1951, in the direction of more severity. All banks whose deposits exceeded ten times their capital and reserves were required to deposit in the Bank of Mexico the full amount of increases in deposits after that date. Since deposits after January actually declined in amount, the date line was moved to June 15, 1951, by Circular 1185 of the Bank of Mexico.[12]

The system of flexible reserve requirements has thus been applied both as a device for preventing deflation and as a device for warding off inflation. Although it is difficult to evaluate its effect when so many other factors were influencing the money market, the monetary authorities have expressed their satisfaction with its usefulness, and believe that it is especially well adapted to a country like Mexico in which the money market is still insufficiently developed to permit open-market operations or even rediscounting to be used as an instrument of central bank policy.

The comparative balance sheets of the Bank of Mexico for 1945 and 1950 indicate some of the changes which have occurred in the policy of the central bank in recent years. The proportion of loans and discounts has fallen from 20 percent to 4 percent of total assets; while investments have risen from 25 percent to 39 percent of assets. These changes reflect the increasing pressure on the Bank of Mexico to aid the government in its program of industrialization. Of the total investments of the Bank of Mexico of 2,174 million pesos, more

[12] *El Mercado de Valores*, Sept. 10, 1951.

than 78 percent are long-term government securities. Since the total long-term debt of the Federal government at the end of 1950 was 2,850 million pesos, it is evident that the Bank of Mexico was holding a very large proportion, about 60 percent. Other national banks were

TABLE 2
BALANCE SHEET OF THE BANK OF MEXICO, DECEMBER 31
(AMOUNTS IN MILLIONS OF PESOS)

Assets	*1945*		*1950*	
Gold, silver, foreign exchange		1,801		2,836
Deposits with other banks		19		25
Loans and discounts		673		221
Loans to Federal government			8	
to national banks	231		16	
to private banks			2	
Rediscounts: 30 days	44		30	
90 days	76		90	
180 days	295		35	
360 days	26		40	
Investments		836		2,174
Federal government long term	331		1,709	
short term	345			
State and local government	18		9	
Bank bonds	95		184	
Bank stocks	15		22	
Industrial securities—mortgages	19		168	
Stock of Mexican companies	1		61	
Stock of foreign companies	3		21	
Other	9			
Other assets		89		364
Total assets		3,416		5,621
Liabilities				
Notes outstanding		1,731		2,798
Metallic issues		55		286
Bank deposits		1,235		1,668
Other sight deposits		64		147
Other obligations in domestic currency		47		39
Deposits and obligations in foreign currency		26		82
Other liabilities		87		339
Capital		50		50
Reserves		75		212
Earned surplus		46		
Total liabilities		3,416		5,621

Source: Annual Reports of the Bank of Mexico.

holding 92 million pesos, and private banks 301 million pesos, of the public debt, leaving a very small amount in the hands of individuals or non-banking corporations.

This monetization of the public debt has caused great concern among the monetary authorities of Mexico and they are quite aware of the inflationary danger which it presents. But they believe that international fund movements have had a greater influence on the price level than any domestic developments. In a study published in *El Mercado de Valores,* the weekly review of the Nacional Financiera, for July 7, 1951, it was pointed out that the rising price level in Mexico dated from 1935. The average annual increase in prices and in the circulating medium had been as follows:

1935–1940:	prices, 7.1 percent;	money, 21.3 percent
1941–1945:	prices, 20.5 percent;	money, 45.3 percent
1946–1949:	prices, 5.9 percent;	money, 10.3 percent
June, 1950–June, 1951:	prices, 30.9 percent;	money, 38.5 percent

On the basis of these figures, which indicate a slackening in the inflation during the years 1946–49 when the program of the government was very active, and an acceleration of the inflation only after the outbreak of the war in Korea when there was no sudden increase in government expenditures on public works, it was concluded that foreign factors had been predominant in the recent price increases.

NACIONAL FINANCIERA

Next to the Bank of Mexico itself, the most important of all the government-owned financial institutions is the Nacional Financiera, which has no counterpart in the United States unless it would be a combination of the Reconstruction Finance Corporation and the old J. P. Morgan and Company. At its origin in 1934 the primary function of the Nacional Financiera was to provide a market for national, state, and municipal bonds, but on its reorganization in 1941 it was given much broader powers in connection with the industrialization program. Its capital was increased in 1947 to 100 million pesos, at least 51 percent to be subscribed by the government and the rest by private and national banks.[13] In addition to its own capital it has at its disposal the funds obtained from two of its own issues. The *titulos*

[13] At the end of 1950 the Federal government owned 92 percent of the capital.

financieros, or finance bonds, pay interest of 3 to 6 percent, are issued in dollars as well as in pesos, have a maturity of five to twelve years, and are secured by mortgages and government obligations. These bonds have found little favor with the investing public, and in 1941 they were supplemented by *certificados de participación* which have been extremely popular. The participation certificates pay interest of 5 or 6 percent, are based on a specific security, and, although in some cases they have no maturity date, they are always sold with a repurchase agreement which makes them redeemable at par. More than 712 million pesos of these certificates were outstanding at the end of 1950, and what is more remarkable, more than two thirds of them were in the hands of non-bank private investors.

With the funds thus made available to it, the Nacional Financiera has become the most important element in the financing of the industrialization program. If an industry considered essential to the program has already been established but needs funds for expansion, the role of the Nacional Financiera may be limited to making short-term or medium-term loans, buying its stock or bonds, or assisting the flotation of its stock or bonds in the market. If an industry considered essential to the program has not yet been established, the Nacional Financiera will first attempt to interest private capital in the project and aid in its development with technical advice on engineering and financial problems, and with recommendations to the Treasury for tax exemption or tariff protection. If private capital cannot be obtained, the Nacional Financiera may itself start the enterprise, as it did in the case of the manufacture of sulphate of ammonia needed for fertilizer in carrying out the agricultural program. In any case, elaborate technical studies precede any action, and the research department prepares detailed reports as to location, markets, transportation facilities, comparative costs, and processes. It works closely with the department of industrial studies of the Bank of Mexico in order to prevent duplication of effort and ensure uniformity of policy.

The annual report of the agency for the year 1950 gives an indication of the wide extent of its activities. It assisted in establishing a factory for the industrial processing of maize, and one for the manufacture of sugar; it organized a shop to turn out 1,000 railroad cars per year, and another for the manufacture of trucks and tractors. It made loans for more efficient equipment to industries concerned with chemicals, petroleum, textiles, packing, sugar, cement, and coal.

It made loans also for the import and export of raw materials and equipment. It aided research in paper and pulp manufacture and in textile products. The total of loans outstanding at the end of the year 1950 was 822 million pesos, and the total of its investments in securities was 113 million pesos, a total for credit outstanding of 935 million pesos, which was exceeded only by the Bank of Mexico itself.

Because the operations of the Nacional Financiera in the securities market exceed those of any other individual or institution (not excepting the Bank of Mexico) the law of 1940 placed upon it the obligation to supervise and control the securities market. It should be noted that most securities transactions in Mexico take place outside the Stock Exchange [14] in over-the-counter transactions which are not reported to any agency. This fact makes all the more conspicuous the security transactions of the Nacional Financiera, which in 1947 for example totaled about 3,900 million pesos as compared with a total for the Stock Exchange of about 30 millions, or less than 1 percent as much. The total for all over-the-counter transactions was estimated for that year as between 12,000 million and 15,000 million pesos. Several times during the year the Nacional Financiera intervened in the market in order to support certain stocks and to provide credit so that others could support them.

In addition to its activities in industrial securities, the Nacional Financiera serves as agent for many governmental units in the marketing and retirement of their bonds. It acts as a sort of central bank for the private *financieras* by granting them secured loans which enable them to lend to industries. In recent years one of its most important activities has been as a clearinghouse for all foreign investment in Mexico, whether public or private. It is thus the agency in direct contact with the Bank for Reconstruction and Development and the Export-Import Bank of the United States,[15] as well as with commercial banks in the United States and other nations which are interested in placing funds in Mexico. It is hardly necessary to underline the enormous influence of the Nacional Financiera. It has contributed substantially to the process of industrialization upon which Mexico has been intent.

[14] See p. 602 below.

[15] Dealings with the International Monetary Fund were, however, still left to the Bank of Mexico.

PRIVATE BANKING SYSTEM

The private banking institutions are controlled by the General Banking Law. The first banking regulation was contained in the Commercial Code of 1884, which provided for a 5 percent tax on bank notes and forbade branches of foreign banks. In 1897 a separate Banking Law was enacted, defining the different types of financial institutions and setting the conditions under which they might be established and operated. At that time there were ten banks in existence, nine of which had the right of note issue. By 1900 the number of banks had increased to 34.[16] In 1951 there were in Mexico according to the *Boletín Estadístico* of the Comisión Nacional Bancaria, the following classes of financial institutions:

TABLE 3
CLASSES OF FINANCIAL INSTITUTIONS

Institution	*Main Offices*	*Branches*	*Agencies*
Commercial banks	107	326	171
Investment banks	93	4	1
Mortgage banks	20	2	6
Capitalization banks	16	2	20
Building and loan banks	5	8	
Trust companies	6		
Savings departments of commercial banks	83	246	131
Trust departments of commercial and investment banks	83	3	

In addition the law recognizes "auxiliary" financial institutions—the warehouses, the stock exchanges, the clearinghouses and the credit unions, which are also defined and regulated under the General Banking Law. All these institutions are very unevenly distributed over the country, with a tendency to concentration in the Federal District (Mexico City) and the industrial centers of the north.

THE COMMERCIAL BANKS

The oldest of the commercial banks now operating, and the third largest bank in the country, is the Banco de Londres y México or-

16 Ernesto Lobato López, *El crédito en México* (Mexico, 1945).

ganized in 1864 by British capital. The next bank in order of age, and the largest in size, is the Banco Nacional, organized in 1884 and permitted to retain the *Nacional* in its title although the government

TABLE 4

PRINCIPAL ACCOUNTS OF THE COMMERCIAL BANKS,[a] DECEMBER 31

(AMOUNTS IN MILLIONS OF PESOS)

Assets	*1945*		*1950*	
Cash items		1,529		2,022
Cash on hand	219		182	
Reserve with Bank of Mexico	1,179		1,558	
Other bank deposits	131		282	
Loans		1,069		2,177
To other banks	50		95	
To individuals: 30 days	35		54	
90 days	358		603	
180 days	512		1,064	
360 days	82		182	
over 360 days	32		179	
Investments		225		815
Federal government bonds	114		265	
Local government bonds	4		15	
Nacional Financiera participation certificates	30		104	
Bank bonds	11		198	
Bank of Mexico stock	18		22	
Other bank stock	30		61	
Mortgage bonds	4		12	
Stock of domestic corporations	10		111	
Other industrial securities	4		26	
Other assets		82		189
Total assets		2,904		5,203
Liabilities				
Demand deposits		1,854		3,265
Time deposits and savings accounts		389		602
Other obligations in domestic currency		275		596
Deposits and obligations in foreign currency		156		351
Capital		169		272
Reserves		32		69
Earned surplus		29		48
Total liabilities		2,904		5,203

[a] Compiled from the Annual Reports of the Bank of Mexico. Figures include accounts of savings departments of commercial banks.

owns no part of it. This bank with its network of branches throughout Mexico is said to control more than one fourth of the commercial bank assets of the country. The other large bank is the Banco de Comercio which has 18 affiliates in industrial centers, preferring affiliates to branches as a way of extending its influence. It probably controls another one fourth of the commercial banking assets. Foreign banks may have branches in Mexico subject to the general banking law of the country; in 1950 there was only one.

Since 1932 all commercial banks have been required to be associated with the Bank of Mexico by subscribing to its stock an amount equal to 6 percent of their capital, and by maintaining with the Bank of Mexico a deposit which constitutes the legal reserve. Since 1949 minimum capital for banks in the Federal District has been 3 million pesos (about $260,000) and for banks outside the Federal District, 1 million pesos. The law requires that under normal conditions liabilities of a bank must not exceed ten times the capital and reserves, but the Secretary of the Treasury has the power to increase this to fifteen times. This power he exercised during the war; however, the required ratio is now being stepped down gradually and in 1954 it will be back to ten.[17] The amount of the capital and surplus set a limit also to the amount of capital expenditure loans, loans for equipment and crops, and investment in bank stocks. An amount not greater than 40 percent of the capital and reserves may be invested in real estate or in securities based on real estate.

Another important limitation in the General Banking Law is that which sets 20 percent of demand liabilities as the ceiling for "production" loans and investments; that is, crop and equipment, or operating expense loans of between one and two years, capital expenditure credits of not more than five years, and investment in stocks or obligations of more than two years maturity. These crop and equipment loans are a typically Mexican response to the need for working capital. The *crédito de avío o habilitación* is usually a crop loan or an advance for agricultural supplies and professional tools, or wages, running for one or two years. The *crédito de refacción* provides funds for plant expansion and equipment, up to five years.

Although the law puts a ceiling on the amount of such loans, as if to emphasize the desirability of shorter loans in the commercial bank portfolio, the attitude of the Treasury and the Bank of Mexico in

[17] *El Mercado de Valores*, May 28, 1951.

recent years has been just the opposite. Banks have been criticized for making so few loans in the longer categories. In 1950 for example the loans of more than 360 days (the category which corresponds most nearly to the crop and equipment loan) amounted to only 178.7 million pesos out of total loans of 2,176.5 million pesos, or about 8 percent of all loans, and only about 4 percent of all liabilities.

The short paper which is preferred by the banks is less objectionable to the central banking authorities if it consists of promissory notes and trade acceptances based on merchandise transactions. The trade acceptance is widely used among merchants in Mexico, where the open book account is not customary. It may be held until maturity by the creditor and then placed with a bank for collection, or it may be discounted before maturity and placed in a bank portfolio. Mexican banks do not customarily rediscount such paper with the Bank of Mexico, even to meet reserve deficiencies.

The short paper which is most objectionable to the banking authorities is the "commercial" loan made for the financing of real estate or commodity speculation, with highly inflationary results. This type of loan was made in large amounts during the war and postwar periods. Bank loans were classified as "commercial" or "production" according to the name of the borrower. All loans made to retail and wholesale establishments, for example, were classified as commercial, and it was assumed that they were made for the purpose of financing speculation in inventories. Actually many of the loans so classified were providing funds for productive processes; it has been estimated that one third to one half of the loans were for the purpose of enabling merchants to grant credit to the small manufacturers or farmers who were supplying the market with goods. However, the term commercial, as applied to bank loans, has become a term of reproach in Mexico, and the efforts of the central bank have been directed toward increasing the proportion of production loans, even when this meant the lengthening of the loan maturity. The banks showed resistance to this pressure, and continued to give preference to the shorter loans at higher rates.

At the meeting of the Mexican Bankers' Association in April, 1950, the Secretary of the Treasury justified the government's attitude and attempted to meet the bankers' criticism by minimizing the danger of increasing long-term loans. He declared that many deposits in commercial banks were only nominally demand obligations, and that their low rate of velocity made them suitable for long-term investment. This would apply of course only to primary deposits, and not to those which arose from bank loans. He insisted that there was no danger to the individual bank, because the Bank of Mexico stood ready to aid any bank in difficulty, as it had done in the past.

The bankers still opposed the Treasury point of view but nevertheless the new reserve requirements were apparently of some assistance in keeping down the total of bank credit, and in increasing slightly the proportion of production loans. Until the middle of 1950 there was little change, either in the total of bank loans and deposits, or in the proportion of production loans. After the outbreak of the war in Korea however, the expanding market for Mexican minerals and other products brought a favorable balance of trade. During the last half of the year, checking deposits in private banks increased from slightly over 2,000 million pesos to slightly under 3,000 million pesos, or about 43 percent. During the same half year loans increased only 9 percent. The ratio of production loans to the total, which had been 54 percent in 1949, rose to 56 percent by December, 1950. Loans for more than 360 days showed the greatest rate of increase, although still small in absolute amount.

In the field of security investment, Mexican bankers have been extremely wary. This attitude stems less from the principle that commercial bank assets should be short term than from a lack of confidence in securities, especially in government securities. It is true that until recent years the government bond market was extremely limited in scope, but one of the difficulties in developing the market was the unwillingness of the banks to take part in it. In 1947 the Bank of Mexico began permitting government securities to count as part of the legal reserve, and in more recent years part of the additional reserve requirements have been permitted to be held in various types of government and government-approved obligations.[18] In 1945, only 8 percent of commercial bank assets were investments in securities; by 1950 they had increased to 16 percent.

The unwillingness of private commercial banks to venture into new fields of enterprise in Mexico was summarized by a writer on financial affairs, himself a banker: [19]

18 See p. 584.

19 Eduardo Villaseñor, *Ensayos Interamericanos* (Mexico, 1944), pp. 136–37 (translated by the author of this chapter).

In general the private banks have dedicated themselves, like the old banks under Diaz, to providing credit for the good, rich clients of well-known solvency, and the national banks have dedicated themselves to the new credit experiments which the new economic and social conditions in the country have made necessary. Thus as a consequence of the agricultural policy, the private banks have avoided credit to agriculture, and it is the national banks which have had to take care of this important sector of production.

The role which for the old banks was filled by their rich proprietor-customers is now played in the new era by the big industrialists. Thus it is quite customary for private banks not only to cling to their clients of high prestige and credit standing to the point of fighting over them among themselves, but also to turn themselves into what amounts to silent partners in their affairs, because the credit which ought to be in the form of first-class commercial paper is really in the form of equipment loans subject to frequent renewal.

Commerce has been served in the same way as industry by the private banks, that is, the good customers, the rich businessmen, absorb the greater amount of the credit, even to the point sometimes of becoming commission agents of credit for the small merchants who never succeed in getting loans directly from banks.

OTHER PRIVATE BANKING INSTITUTIONS

In addition to the commercial banks there are in Mexico several kinds of banking institutions designed to provide a channel for the long-term funds which are so vital to the industrialization program. Unfortunately most of these institutions are still in a rudimentary state. The volume of savings in the country is small and the institutions which handle such funds have too often used them for short-term loans at high rates of interest rather than for the much-needed long-term investments.

There are 83 savings banks in Mexico, with 246 branches and 131 agencies. They are departments of commercial banks rather than separate institutions, and are governed by Articles 18 to 25 inclusive of the General Banking Law. The capital for such a bank department located in Mexico City must be 250,000 pesos, and for one outside, 100,000 pesos; but any bank wishing to issue savings bonds or stamps must have a capital of 500,000 pesos wherever it is located. Total liabilities may not exceed twenty times the capital and reserves. An amount equal to 10 percent of deposits must be kept on deposit with other banks, and an additional 20 percent may be thus deposited or invested in loans and discounts of 90 to 360 days' maturity. These savings departments may make equipment and financing loans up to three years' maturity and invest in securities approved by the National Securities Commission. No individual may have an account of more than 40,000 pesos, nor draw out more than 500 pesos without previous notice. In 1950 these savings departments had 38 million pesos of capital and reserves, and about 450 million in deposits. They held about 100 million pesos in cash, had made loans of 240 million pesos and investments of 170 millions. Interest on savings deposits in 1950 was not to exceed 4.5 percent.[20]

Another group of banking institutions intended to function somewhat like investment banks are the *sociedades financieras*. Although authorized by the General Banking Law of 1932, they were not organized in any number until after 1941 when a revision of the law gave them wider powers. They may issue their own bonds, purchase and hold securities of other enterprises, and make loans ranging from six months' to thirty years' maturity, and, in a few special cases, of maturity less than six months. These companies were expected to provide capital funds for new industries, but they have not done so. Many of them were organized by a bank or a business enterprise in order to facilitate obtaining credit for itself, so that the *financieras* were in many cases mere affiliates of an established concern. Their bonds were largely held by the Bank of Mexico. Moreover a large part of the credit extended by them was at short maturity more appropriate to commercial than to investment banks.[21] At the end of 1950 for example, of their total assets of 917 million pesos, more than one fourth was in loans at less than 360 days, and only one fourth was invested in securities. Only a few of the *financieras* exercise their privilege of accepting sight and time deposits. Those which do are subject to a requirement of a 50 percent reserve to be held in the Bank of Mexico, on all deposits in existence on May 10, 1951; increases in deposits after that date are subject to a 100 percent reserve.

The general dissatisfaction with these societies produced in 1949 a new decree which raised the minimum capital from 500,000 pesos to 3,000,000 pesos for those in the Federal District, and 1,500,000

20 Comisión Nacional Bancaria, *Circular 340*, May 20, 1950.

21 *Carta mensual*, Aug.–Sept., 1949, p. 156. *Mercado de Valores*, May 3, 1948. Bank of Mexico, *Circular 1180*, May 10, 1951.

pesos for those outside.[22] This made it more difficult for them to be organized as subsidiaries to other firms. Some of the smaller *financieras* were unable to meet the increased capital requirement and went into liquidation, leaving only the stronger companies which were presumably better able to fulfill their function. By the end of 1950 the remaining *financieras* had capital and surplus of 280 million pesos and had sold 370 million pesos of their own bonds. Their total loans and investments amounted to 837 million pesos, making them an important factor in the Mexican money market.

Other institutions intended to function in the long-term market are the capitalization banks, which have been described as savings banks with a lottery feature. They were created by the laws of 1926 and 1932 amending the General Banking Law, and were empowered to sell annuities, various forms of certificates of deposit, and lottery bonds which have been very popular with investors. By 1950 there were 16 such banks with most of their business concentrated in Mexico City. They are required to have a minimum capital of 1,000,000 pesos, and to invest at least 30 percent of their liabilities in government issued or guaranteed securities. Although their growth has been relatively rapid since 1940, their total assets were only 416 million pesos in 1950. Even this amount had contributed little to the provision of long-term funds for industry, since the capitalization banks (like so many others) have shown a preference for the more profitable short loans, and have invested only one fourth of their total assets in securities. In an effort to make these banks more serviceable in the industrialization program, the Federal Executive has been empowered to issue general directives to capitalization banks and insurance companies as to type and purpose of investment, and as to limits on amounts invested.[23]

Although the mortgage is one of the most popular forms of investment in Mexico, the market for urban mortgages has not been formally organized. Before the revolution, mortgage credit was largely in the hands of the Church, but was costly and inadequate. After the revolution, when the government organized special banks for agricultural credit, the field of urban mortgages was still uncovered and was left to any of the existing financial institutions that might be interested. None of them has gone heavily into this sphere.

[22] *Diario oficial,* Dec. 31, 1950.

[23] *El Universal* (Mexico) May 12, 1950. *Diario Oficial*, Section 5, Dec. 30, 1950.

A special group of mortgage banks is authorized by the General Banking Law. There are now 20 of them, most in Mexico City. They issue their own bonds, and also guarantee a special kind of mortgage certificate known as *cedula,* which is purchased largely by private investors. Between 1940 and 1945 it has been estimated that they made loans amounting to 1,300 million pesos for private urban construction. Since that time they have expanded their activities but slightly, and in 1950 their total assets were only 190 million pesos, less than either the savings departments of commercial banks or the *financieras.*

There is another small group of financial institutions, the *sociedades fiduciarias* or trust companies. Their total assets in 1950 were only 41 million pesos, and 54 of the 93 companies were located in Mexico City. Their activities are so diversified that they have been called the "drugstores of the money market." Although primarily designed to handle trust funds and invest them in approved securities, they also make investments for their own account, made loans on real estate security until forbidden to do so in 1944, and still make short loans at high rates to borrowers whose standing is too poor to entitle them to loans at banks.[24]

THE NATIONAL BANK COMMISSION

All these private banking institutions are subject to the supervision of the National Bank Commission. It was established in 1924 as part of a general reorganization of the banking system, with six members nominated by the various financial institutions but appointed by the Secretary of the Treasury. The steadily increasing duties of this Commission devolve upon a staff which in 1950 numbered 120 inspectors in addition to the clerical and statistical force—a group quite inadequate to carry out the detailed annual inspections specified by the law. Therefore much of the "inspection" consists merely of close scrutiny of the written reports submitted by the banks, with the result that banks of good reputation function practically without supervision. If an irregularity is discovered, the bank is given 30 days in which to correct the difficulty; at the end of that time the Ministry of Finance is notified. It may impose a fine or go so far as to revoke the bank's charter. A bank which is unable to meet its commitments

[24] *El Mercado de Valores,* Jan. 19, Feb. 23, March 1, and April 5, 1948.

may declare itself bankrupt, or may be requested by the Commission to make such a declaration. In the latter case, another credit institution of good standing is named as assignee and given the task of liquidating the assets of the defaulting bank. This policy has reduced the problem of bank failures in Mexico to a minimum. There is no guarantee of deposits.

At times the Commission staff concentrates its efforts on a particular problem area. In recent years it has paid special attention to *financieras* unable to meet the increased capital requirements enacted by the law of 1949.

The statistical work of the Commission is published in the form of the bimonthly *Boletín Estadístico,* which gives information on the number and location of each type of financial institution, monthly summaries of the balance sheet items for each type, and monthly summaries of the balance-sheet items for the Bank of Mexico and for all national banks. Also included are the price index numbers computed by the Bank of Mexico, and the figures for check clearings.

MONEY AND CAPITAL MARKET

There are few private investors in Mexico. The great mass of the Mexican population is quite unable to save anything out of its meager income, and investment is entirely out of the question. Therefore capital funds which are not provided by the government are in large part provided by foreigners, and Mexico continues to be a capital-importing nation, as it has been throughout its history.

Some of this foreign investment takes the form of direct participation in Mexican industry. The Bank of Mexico estimated that by 1938 the total of such investment had reached about 2,000 million pesos, nearly one third of which was in transportation and communication, another third in public utilities, somewhat less than one third in mining, and the rest distributed among petroleum, industrial, commercial, and agricultural activities. By the end of 1949 the total in pesos (the peso had by then been devalued from 3.60 to 8.65 per dollar) had more than doubled, and the proportions invested in each type of enterprise had greatly changed. Nearly one fourth was in public utilities, another fourth in industry, something less than a fourth in mining, only one sixth in transportation and communication, and the remainder divided among commercial and agricultural enterprises. The foreign investment in petroleum had of course shrunk to less than 1 percent of the total.

Another form of capital importation into Mexico takes the form of purchase of securities by foreigners. No estimates are available for the amount of corporation securities held abroad. One Mexican public utility is listed on the New York Stock Exchange, the Industria Eléctrica de México.[25] Of the long-term government debt, about 782 million pesos of the total of 2,891 millions is payable in foreign currencies and part of this is probably held abroad.[26]

More important than holdings of Mexican government securities by foreign individuals have been the loans made in recent years to the Mexican government, channeled through the *Nacional Financiera*, by the Export-Import Bank of the United States and the International Bank for Reconstruction and Development. These loans amounted to about $200 million in the decade before 1950. In that year the rate of lending to Mexico was greatly accelerated. The International Bank for Reconstruction and Development loaned $26 million to the Mexican Light and Power Company, and $10 million to a consortium of eight banks for relending to small and medium-sized private enterprises. The Export-Import Bank opened lines of credit totaling more than $150 million for irrigation, transportation, and coke. In addition to these official loans, several private American banks made loans to the government of about $20 million for public works, as they had done in 1948 and 1949. These were the first private bank loans to the Mexican government in thirty years.[27]

Because all these foreign loans go through the Nacional Financiera, information about them is readily available. For funds invested by Mexicans in Mexico there is no such information. The total value of stocks and bonds issued by Mexican corporations is not known. Many small enterprises are not incorporated, and some of those which are incorporated raise funds outside of the organized money market. There is in Mexico nothing which corresponds closely to the investment banking house in the United States, so that even large corpora-

[25] Sanford A. Mosk, *Industrial Revolution in Mexico* (Berkeley and Los Angeles, 1950), p. 255.

[26] The Bank of Mexico reported holdings of 90 million pesos of the external debt in 1950.

[27] Annual Reports of the Bank of Mexico. *Mercado de Valores*, May 22, 1950. New York *Journal of Commerce*, Oct. 6, 1948.

tions do not find it easy to float new issues. It is known that in the bond market about 100 concerns offered more than 500 million pesos of bonds in the years 1942–46 inclusive, in industries representing metals, telephones, electricity, gas, cement, glass, textiles, paper, sugar, moving pictures, chemcials, and especially petroleum.[28]

Since private corporations issue relatively small amounts of securities in Mexico, the issues of the government and of the government-owned and controlled organizations are of unusual importance in the money market. The long-term debt of the Federal government is not large in per capita terms, especially when compared with that of other countries; at the end of 1950, for example, it was about $9 per capita, as compared with about $170 in the United States. But these figures are somewhat misleading since the Mexican Federal government is also responsible in the final analysis for much of the indebtedness of the various national banks and especially of the Nacional Financiera. The total of the fixed-interest securities issued by this agency and by the National Mortgage Bank, the finance companies and the savings departments of commercial banks was reported by the Bank of Mexico for 1950 as 1,644 million pesos. To this must be added the Federal and state government issues of 2,891 million pesos, making a total of 4,535 millions.

The organization of the capital market has lagged behind that of other financial institutions. Since 1907 there has been a stock exchange in Mexico City, but it was subject to no supervision over selection of members or listing of securities until 1916, when the Secretary of the Treasury was given nominal supervision. In 1928 the exchange was made subject to the National Bank Commission, and in 1948 it was put under the regulation of a National Securities Commission which had been established with representatives of the appropriate government departments, the Bank of Mexico, the National Bank Commission, the Nacional Financiera, the Bankers' Association, and the stock exchange itself. The National Securities Commission now controls the listing of securities on the exchange and decides on the eligibility of securities for purchase by the insurance companies and the banks. Unregistered securities may not be offered to the public until the company has filed with the National Securities Commission its financial statements and other information.[29]

28 *El Mercado de Valores*, June 27, 1949.

29 *Diario Oficial*, Sept. 11, 1946; March 10, 1947.

In spite of these reforms the stock exchange remains an almost insignificant element in the money market. In 1950 it was still housed in a small room, on the walls of which blackboards were used for the names of the listed securities. The members sat in rows before the desk of the presiding officer and made their offers to buy or sell as the list was read aloud; call boys chalked up the offers as they were made. A day described in the financial press as "unusually active" resulted in four completed transactions during the session which lasted less than an hour.[30] The total transactions at the exchange during the years 1947 to 1949 ranged from 10 million to 30 million pesos per year, while the transactions of the Nacional Financiera in the same period were running at 12,000 million to 15,000 million pesos annually.[31]

At the end of 1950, the stock exchange in Mexico City included these listings: *Stocks,* 8 mining, 77 industrials, 76 banks, 33 insurance companies, 6 finance companies; *Bonds,* 45 public issues, 37 financial institutions, 83 mortgage issues. For most companies there is no real advantage in listing their stocks and bonds on the exchange. There may even be a disadvantage for companies which do not wish to provide information to the National Securities Commission.[32]

The limited number of shares listed is one reason for the small volume of transactions carried on at the exchange. Another reason is the slightly higher cost of buying securities through a broker rather than over-the-counter through a bank. Perhaps the most compelling reason of all for most investors is the greater privacy of the over-the-counter market, which is subject to no regulation or control and makes no public record of its transactions. This is an important factor in a country in which evasion of income tax is said to be frequent.

Dissatisfaction with the stock exchange and the securities market is often expressed. Certain technical improvements have been suggested, and some have been made, with a view to speeding up clearing and payment. A new exchange was opened at Monterrey, the industrial center of the north, in 1950. But investors are still kept away by the small size of the exchange, its lack of liquidity, and the wide fluctuations of price which are characteristic of a limited market. The limitations of the capital market must not, however, be ascribed to the stock exchange. The exchange is rather the result than the cause

30 *El Universal,* May 25, 1950. 31 *El Mercado de Valores,* Aug. 1 and 15, 1949.
32 *El Mercado de Valores,* Aug. 29, 1949.

of the difficulties. Although technical improvements can and will be made in the functioning of the exchange, that factor alone will not provide a regular and ample flow of capital funds into Mexican industry.

Even the funds available for investment are not apt to find their way into securities. Small investors prefer savings deposits, and large investors often prefer real estate, or short loans at high rates of interest made to real estate operators or speculators in commodities. Although in recent years the *certificados de participación* of the Nacional Financiera have found favor, there is still a marked unwillingness on the part of many private and institutional investors to buy government bonds. In view of the credit record of the Mexican government in recent years there is no longer any reason for lack of confidence in its obligations. It is true that there is great antipathy to certain governmental policies among some of the wealthier groups of the population, and objection to the increasing interference of the government in economic life.[33] There is also, of course, the danger that inflation will reduce the real value of any fixed-income security, but that danger exists for non-governmental as well as for governmental obligations. It should be noted that there is in Mexico nothing which corresponds to the call loan made to brokers by banks to finance stock market speculation in the United States.

Several steps have been taken in recent years to attract small savings into investment channels. During 1950 the government carried on a campaign to popularize savings notes by issuing them in denominations of 12.50 pesos and up, with a lottery feature which offered ten times the cost of the note to the holder of the lucky number in the quarterly drawings. This campaign was intensified during 1951. In another approach to the same problem, there was authorized the establishment of a new type of brokerage house (*sociedad de inversión*) to carry on operations in securities.[34]

To a certain extent the lack of direct popular investment in securities is offset by the deposits of individuals in the financial institutions. At the end of 1950, private credit institutions, out of total assets of nearly 7,000 million pesos, had the following investments in securities:

[33] P. E. Reina Hermosillo, "El mercado de valores en México," *Revista de Economía*, Aug. 15, 1948. *El Mercado de Valores*, June 27, 1948.

[34] *Annual report of the Bank of Mexico for 1951*, pp. 12, 25. *Diario Official*, Jan. 4, 1951. *El Mercado de Valores*, Oct. 22, 1951.

460 millions in government obligations; 324 millions in bank obligations; 408 millions in industrial securities. This total of 1,192 million pesos of investments may be compared with their combined capital and surplus of 762 million pesos.[35]

In many countries insurance companies have become an important source of funds in the capital market; despite recent growth they have been of little importance in Mexico. Until 1935 the insurance business was almost entirely in the hands of foreign companies, and in that year only 40 percent of their investments were in Mexican securities, the rest in foreign issues. The revision of the law in 1935 tended to discourage foreign companies and to force all companies to invest more of their funds within the country. By 1949 there were 67 companies in operation, with total resources of 686 million pesos of which 39 millions were in mortgage loans and 60 millions in loans guaranteed by policies; 465 millions were technical reserves consisting of government and other securities. (In 1948 the government securities made up 78 millions of the total.) About 350,000 persons have life insurance coverage amounting to 1,800 million pesos. Property, fire, health, and other risk insurance was estimated at about 40,000 million pesos in 1949. Several changes[36] have been made in the laws governing the investments of insurance companies in recent years, designed to stimulate long loans for production.

In spite of all the efforts to encourage and even to force long-term investment, private funds are still grossly inadequate to meet the needs of the developing industrial economy. However this gap has been to a considerable extent filled by public investment. Sr. Carrillo Flores, head of the Nacional Financiera and an international authority on national income and investment, has estimated that between the years 1940 and 1948 the annual gross investment in Mexico increased from 685 million pesos to 1,300 million pesos, or from 11 percent to 14.5 percent of the national income. If these figures are put into terms of per capita real income, the investment increased from 35 to 54 pesos at the 1940 price level.[37] This is not a large amount in comparison with investments in other countries, but its rate of increase is remarkable and encouraging.

35 *Annual Report of the Bank of Mexico for 1951*, Tables 15 and 16.

36 *El Mercado de Valores*, Aug. 23, Sept. 6, Oct. 4, 1948. *Diario Oficial*, Dec. 30, 1950.

37 *El Mercado de Valores*, Dec. 12, 1950. Carillo Flores became Minister of Finance in 1952.

A factor which will play an important role in determining the direction of economic change in Mexico during the next few years is the amount and kind of inflation. As has been indicated, the central banking authorities are keenly aware of the problem and have directed all their forces to combat the tide of rising prices. When the outbreak of war in Korea increased the inflationary pressures, central bank policies were reinforced by other more direct devices. During the last quarter of 1950 the government increased the loans to agricultural banks in order to assure additional supplies of wheat and corn; forbade the export of basic foodstuffs or their conversion into alcohol until the domestic consumption demand was satisfied; canceled the general restrictions on imports which had been imposed in 1947 to protect the value of the peso, and provided special rediscount facilities for the importation of capital goods. In December a new law gave the government the authority to set maximum and minimum prices, to determine the use of commodities, to prevent the building up of inventories beyond one year's supply, and to regulate imports and exports to maintain domestic supplies.

During the early part of 1951 the provisions of this law were put into effect in several areas of the economy. Many prices were frozen, at both wholesale and retail levels, in foods, textiles, chemicals, paper, and automobiles. The National Price Commission was created to study prices and set rules for their regulation. In April, a Price Administration was set up within the Department of Economic Affairs. It had three branches, prices, distribution and priorities, and enforcement.[38]

In any country in which economic change is proceeding as rapidly as in Mexico, the institutions of the money market will be developing and changing. This is particularly true when as in Mexico there is a great deal of conscious planning in the financial sphere, planning in which many different agencies are taking part. In spite of the admitted limitations of the money market, enormous progress was made in the decade 1940 to 1950 and can be expected to continue. It is an advantage rather than a disadvantage that experimentation is going on, and that there is a flexibility which will permit adaptation to changing economic needs.

[38] *El Mercado de Valores*, Sept. 23, Dec. 18 and 25, 1950; Jan. 8, 15, 22, April 9, and Sept. 10, 1951.

REFERENCES

OFFICIAL SOURCES

Banco de Mexico. Asamblea General Ordinaria de Accionistas. Mexico, D. F. Annual, 1925–.

Comisión Nacional Bancaria. *Boletín Estadistico.* Mexico, D. F. Bimonthly.

Nacional Financiera. Asamblea General Ordinaria de Accionistas. Mexico, D. F. Annual, 1935–.

—— *El Mercado de Valores.* Mexico, D. F. Weekly.

Primera Reunion de Técnicos sobre Banca Central. Mexico, D. F., 1946.

Secretaria de Economía. *Revista de Estadística.* Mexico, D. F. Monthly.

Secretaria de Gobernación. Seis años de Actividad Nacional. Mexico, D. F., 1946.

Segunda Reunion de Técnicos de los Bancos Centrales del Continento Americano. Santiago, 1950.

UNOFFICIAL SOURCES

Asociación de Banqueros de México. Anuario Financiero. Mexico, D. F. Annual Carta Mensual. Mexico, D. F. Bimonthly.

Escuela Nacional de Economía. *Investigación Económica.* Mexico, D. F. Quarterly.

Lobato López, Ernesto. El Crédito en México, D. F., 1945.

Mosk, Sanford A. Industrial Revolution in Mexico. Berkeley and Los Angeles, 1950.

Revista de Economía. Mexico, D. F. Monthly.

Universal, El. Mexico, D. F. Daily.

Villaseñor, Eduardo. Ensayos Interamericanos. Mexico, D. F., 1944.

THE NETHERLANDS

by A. Batenburg, S. Brouwer, and D. W. Louman

INTRODUCTORY

IF IN LIMITED SPACE an idea is to be given of economic conditions in the Netherlands and of the role occupied therein by banking, a start may be made with the observation that originally trade and agriculture were the mainstays of the country's economy. Industry developed later; it did not receive a really strong stimulus for growth until the First World War forced the Netherlands to provide for its own needs, at a time when ample opportunities existed for export.

The second and even stronger impetus to industrialization followed the Second World War. This trend, apparent since 1945, developed

---

A. BATENBURG was born in Rotterdam in 1922. After the Second World War he became a teacher in economics and political science at various secondary schools. In 1948 he finished his university studies and passed with honors the final examinations of the Netherlands High School of Economics at Rotterdam. Immediately afterwards he entered the Nederlandsche Handel-Maatschappij, N.V. (Netherlands Trading Society) where he is chief of the Economic Research Bureau of the bank's Head Office at Amsterdam. In addition, he teaches the theory of money, banking and business cycles in the courses for the training of bank and stock-brokerage employees.

S. BROUWER, after having completed his economic studies, entered the practice of banking and finance. For about four years, he was with the Amsterdamsche Bank. He became a member of a stockbrokers' firm and after a period of about five years entered upon the duties of chief financial editor of one of the most important Netherlands daily newspapers. At the request of the management of the Amsterdamsche Bank, he returned in 1924, to establish an Economics Department. From 1924 to 1950 he was the manager of this Department. He is the author of various publications including a book publishd to commemorate the 75th anniversary of the Amsterdamsche Bank.

D. W. LOUMAN majored in economics at the University of Amsterdam. Having gained experience in private and public business, he entered the Economic Research Bureau of the Head Office of the Netherlands Trading Society in 1948.

from the slogans that work must be found for the ever increasing population and that the deficit of the balance of payments must be reduced and ultimately eliminated. Compared with the similar case in many other countries industrialization of the Netherlands encountered great difficulties. The country is poor in raw materials and the home market is of limited extent. Contact with other countries is for that reason a matter of utmost importance. In this respect the Netherlands is rich in experience. Extensive commercial ties have always existed with its immediate neighbors, as well as with its overseas territories, especially those in Asia.

At the present time the agrarian sector of the economy meets domestic needs to a considerable extent (although some cereals and fodder must still be imported). It also is of great importance in providing exports of the many products of agriculture, horticulture, and cattle breeding. In industrial activity, the metal industry, including shipbuilding, airplane and railway-car construction, and the textile industry now play leading roles. Foodstuffs and luxuries, the building trades and their allied fields, chemicals, the leather industry and mining are of great importance, too. In the postwar years foreign trade has expanded to full capacity; its importance is great. The same observation applies also to shipping.

Private enterprise plays a predominant role in the economic life of the Netherlands. There are various public-owned corporations, but these are mainly confined to public utilities. Owned by the state are the railroads, the postal, telegraph, and telephone services, and a large proportion of the collieries. The larger part of the capital of a blast furnace concern and of the Royal Dutch Airlines is also in government hands. Gasworks, electric power stations and streetcar lines are usually municipal or provincial enterprises.

As a rule industrial undertakings are financed from three sources: venture capital; long-term capital from third parties; and short-term capital, that is, credits for seasonal needs. The first two types of funds may be obtained by the larger concerns, the great majority of which are incorporated companies, from the open capital market. In view of the present-day scarcity of capital, the larger concerns also obtain private loans from institutional investors—savings banks, agricultural credit banks, life insurance companies, private pension funds and government funds—often through the intermediary of the commercial banks. Institutional investors as a rule are not yet inclined to supply venture capital, but there are plans aiming at the foundation of an institution backed by the State which would convert investments of the institutional investors into venture capital. Short-term credit is obtained from suppliers of goods as well as from commercial banks.

Smaller enterprises until a short time ago were almost fully dependent upon private means for capital funds. These enterprises cannot make use of the capital market by reason of the stipulation that the outstanding nominal amount of any security to be listed on the Amsterdam Stock Exchange must be at least Fl.500,000, and cannot obtain capital funds from commercial banks which generally grant credits to industry only if these are, in principle, of a short-term character. In consequence after the war a few specialized banking institutions were created with the cooperation of the government: (1) the Maatschappij tot Financiering van het Nationaal Herstel (called the Reconstruction Bank), which confines its activities to the granting of long-term credits to industrial enterprises; and (2) the Nederlandse Participatie Maatschappij, which participates in granting venture capital.

In the agrarian sector financing is easier than in the industrial, because the enterprises represented are preponderantly small and the farmer as a rule is also the owner of the durable goods employed in his business. Capital, therefore, is more easily acquired and, in case of insufficient means, the raising of money on mortgage often constitutes a way out of the difficulty. The farmer may apply to the agricultural credit banks, in the first instance, to cover his need for seasonal credits, and also, if necessary, for long-term credits.

Trading circles mainly operate with their own capital and with bank credit.

Whereas there are numerous points of contact between business areas, especially trade and industry and banking, the consumer but seldom has recourse to the banks. One of the reasons is that in the Netherlands the system of installment buying has never been popular.

The legal aspects of financing corporations by means of share capital are set forth in the chapter entitled "About Incorporations" of the Commercial Code. Since the amount of a corporation's capital must be fixed at the time of establishment, the Netherlands law does not recognize shares without par value. Of the capital fixed in the articles of association, at least one fifth must be subscribed. Bearer shares may be issued only if they have been fully paid up; if not fully paid shares must be registered. A shareholder cannot be freed from his obligation to pay the full amount of his shares. The only exception to this rule granted by the law is on behalf of bankers who acquire shares in order to sell them to the public. They may be allowed to pay less than the full amount of a bearer share, but not less than 94 percent. In addition to underwriting issues of shares or debentures, a bank may as an agent cooperate in the sale of securities, charging a commission for its services. Stock market prices in Holland are quoted in a percentage of the nominal value of the security.

Bonds and debentures are not subject to special rules in Netherlands law; they are regarded as ordinary instruments of indebtedness.

Short-term credit instruments include the bill of exchange, the promissory note, and the check, all of which form the subject matter of a series of articles in the Commercial Code. In recent years short-term financing has to an increasing extent taken the form of the current account credit. The granting of credit by a bill of exchange has the drawback that it is granted for a fixed period and for a fixed amount. A current-account credit with its daily compensation of debit and credit items is better adjusted to the needs of the business community.

The principal types of banking and credit institutions operating in the Netherlands may be classified in three groups according to the term for which the credit is extended.

1. Banks granting exclusively short-term or intermediate credit are:

The Netherlands Bank.

Deposit banks; only one bank, the Kas-Associatie at Amsterdam, has retained its original character.

Commodity banks, specializing in the granting of short-term credit to the wholesale trade in staple products.

Popular credit banks, that grant small credits to the "little man." The credits are extended for a few years and are repaid in installments. These banks comprise the pawnbrokers' shops, the municipal popular credit banks, and private money-lending banks.

Banks for installment business, financing the purchase of durable consumer goods such as automobiles and wireless sets.

2. Almost exclusively long-term credit is granted by:

Mortgage banks and ship-mortgage banks.

Building societies, comprised of a large number of persons who want to save in order to have a house of their own. Joint-saving offers a possibility for some of the savers to borrow enough to come into possession of a house within a rather short time. The institutions lend against a first mortgage only part of the building costs.

Banks for encumbered values, granting credits against the security of properties charged with periodical payments.

Industry banks; mention must be made of the Maatschappij tot Financiering van het Nationaal Herstel (Reconstruction Bank), and of the Nederlandse Participatie Maatschappij. Private enterprise, too, has taken the initiative, recently, in the establishment of a few institutions for the financing of industrial enterprises.

Banks for granting credit to public bodies; in particular to municipalities.

Investment-trusts.

Banks for granting advances to small trade.

3. Both long and short-term credit is granted by:

Commercial banks.

Agricultural credit banks.

Banks for the middle-class trade.

Savings banks.

Money-transfer services (not privately owned).

THE COMMERCIAL BANKS

In the Netherlands, commercial banks are classed as those institutions which either exclusively exercise an intermediary function in the effectuation of payments, or make it their business to receive money on deposit or on current account and to apply those funds to the granting of credits, mainly of short-term character, and to the granting of loans in the money market.[1] Some theorists rightly have raised objections to this official description of the concept "commercial bank," since in the Netherlands there are no institutions that exclusively exercise an intermediary function in the effectuation of payments. However, on the whole, the definition is acceptable because the two principal activities of a commercial bank—serving as an intermediary in effectuating payments and granting short-term

[1] Staatscourant, November 14–15, 1941, No. 223.

credits—are set forth.[2] In the latter activity, commercial banks are of special significance because they play an indirect part in the creation of money. The greater part of the commercial banks in the Netherlands belong to the so-called Netherlands Bankers Association. In 1953 this group comprised about 100 banks.

The object of the Netherlands Bankers Association is to promote all banking interests by holding meetings at which the members may exchange views, by furthering uniformity in the charges imposed by members, by mediating for the settlement of disputes affecting banking, by making scientific investigations in the field of banking, and by stimulating everything that may tend to further the prosperity of the country.

The large institutions among the members are known as the big five.[3] They are the Amsterdamsche Bank, the Incasso-Bank, the Nederlandsche Handel-Maatschappij (Netherlands Trading Society), the Rotterdamsche Bank, and De Twentsche Bank. The importance of these five banks is clearly illustrated by comparing balance-sheet items of this group with those of the 39 commercial banks published regularly by the Central Bureau of Statistics. The latter figures afford a sufficiently representative picture of the whole, as the balance-sheet figures of the other commercial banks constitute only about 10 percent of the similar data for all commercial banks operating in the Netherlands.

TABLE 1

BALANCE-SHEET ITEMS, DECEMBER 31, 1952

(AMOUNTS IN MILLIONS OF FLORINS)

Items	*39 Commercial Banks (Including the "Big Five")*	*The "Big Five"*	*Percentage Share of the "Big Five" in the Total*
Capital and reserves	791	345	44
Demand deposits	3,731	3,312	89
Time deposits	1,034	698	68
Treasury paper	3,670	2,846	78
Loans and advances	1,470	1,023	80

The figures for the big five include those of the banking business of the Nederlandsche Handel-Maatschappij in so far as this is carried on within the national boundaries. Although not apparent from its name—Netherlands Trading Society—this society is a bank. It was founded in 1824 on the initiative of King William I with the object of

[2] F. de Roos, *De Algemene Banken in Nederland* (Utrecht, 1949), pp. 20–21.

[3] *Ibid.*, pp. 23–24.

furthering the trade of the Netherlands with other countries and in particular with the Dutch overseas territories. Not until the turn of the century did the society shift its main emphasis to banking. Together with the Nationale Handelsbank and the Escompto Bank it belongs to that group of Dutch commercial banks that operate in Indonesia. The Nederlandsche Handel-Maatschappij furthermore has offices of its own in Japan, China, Hongkong, Malacca, Singapore, India, Pakistan, Burma, at Jeddah in Arabia, at Mombasa and Nairobi in Kenya, at Dar-es-Salaam in Tanganyika Territory, and in New York. In De Surinaamsche Bank the Nederlandsche Handel-Maatschappij has a subsidiary in Surinam, which is the bank of issue in Surinam. It has affiliated banks in London and Tangiers. Finally the Nederlandsche Handel-Maatschappij has a foothold in Uruguay in the allied Banco de Montevideo and in Curaçao and Aruba by its participation in Edwards, Henriquez and Companies' Bank, and in the Aruba Commercial Bank. The Nationale Handelsbank, too, has several offices in the Far East, in addition to those in Indonesia, namely in Japan and Siam. In 1953 it opened a branch office in Canada. Another Dutch Bank, the Hollandsche Bank-Unie, has branches in Israel, Turkey, and in South America (in Argentina, Brazil, Venezuela and Uruguay), and in the Dutch Antilles. The Nederlandsche Bank voor Zuid-Afrika possesses, apart from an office at Hamburg, an extensive network of establishments in South Africa. The banking business of these offices is carried on by a South African company created especially for this purpose: the Netherlands Bank of South Africa Ltd. Finally attention must be drawn to the Amsterdamsche Bank voor België, a subsidiary company, established at Antwerp, of the Amsterdamsche Bank. This Belgian subsidiary of one of our prominent banks located in the diamond center of Antwerp maintains the tradition of the head office, which itself renders great service to the diamond trade in Amsterdam.

The great importance of the big five in this country has been further accentuated by continued bank mergers and concentration. This process started about 1911, when the Rotterdamsche Bank absorbed one of the smaller credit institutions. Since then a series of small banks has been taken over by the larger ones, and this process goes on. Especially in the last few years the merger movement has again attracted much attention. The most important event was without doubt the merger of two large banks, namely the Amsterdamsche Bank and the

Incasso-Bank, which decided to unite their business, beginning January 1, 1948. The shares of the latter bank were taken over by the Amsterdamsche Bank, which now publishes one balance sheet and profit-and-loss account in which the figures of the Incasso-Bank are included. The all-important factor in the case of this merger was undoubtedly the desire to counteract the unfavorable influence of the present high level of bank costs, which have risen sharply since the Second World War. In so far as the merger of banks remains confined to the absorption of the small credit institutions by the big banks, the shift in the relative powers in the Dutch banking world will be of little importance. The situation will be different, however, if further mergers of the big banks take place along the lines of the merger between the Amsterdamsche Bank and the Incasso-Bank.

A special place among the commercial banks is occupied by the Nederlandsche Middenstandsbank, which in common with a large number of smaller credit institutions serves particular shopkeepers and other small commercial and industrial enterprises. A more detailed discussion of this institution will be found in the section on public and semi-public institutions (see p. 634).

One of the important functions of the commercial banks in the Netherlands is that of serving as an intermediary in the transfer of payments. The significance of commercial bank operations in this field has continually increased during the twentieth century even though full data to verify this statement are lacking. No figures are available as to the amount of money deposited with the commercial banks and with other institutions. Furthermore very little is known about the velocity of deposit circulation, and of course nothing about the velocity of the banknote circulation. Suffice it to say that in the postwar years deposit-money represented more than half the total monetary circulation (deposit-money and currency money together). By the end of 1952 this was just over 60 percent.

The check as a means of payment in the Netherlands is by no means as popular as in Anglo-Saxon countries. Professor F. de Roos in his often quoted book about the general (commercial) banks in the Netherlands points out that fiscal legislation in particular must be held responsible for the lack of popularity of the check.[4] In contrast to other transfers the check has been subject to a stamp duty, which

[4] *Ibid.*, p. 70.

was not abolished until 1943. Even the repeal of this legislation did not increase the popularity of the check.

Funds entrusted to commercial banks may be divided in current-account balances and time deposits. The latter are either fixed deposits or deposits subject to a fixed term of notice: the usual terms are 1, 3, 6 months or a year, and in general the agreed terms are observed. Time deposits may be repaid before the end of the term agreed, but in this case the depositor usually has to pay a small fine. Some banks give a certificate of deposit to the time depositor, which may be discounted or used as a security for a loan. Such certificates are not transferable. Banks may deviate from the usual terms and pay a special rate of interest, particularly on large amounts. Any guarantee of deposits, as known in the United States, does not exist in the Netherlands.

A very important change has occurred, especially during the Second World War, in the manner in which commercial banks invest the funds entrusted to them. The high cost of occupation, added to the fact that it was impossible to replace goods sold, gave rise to a plethora of money. As a result huge amounts flowed into the commercial banks for which practically no investment other than Treasury paper could be found. There has been little change in this situation even since the end of the war, a circumstance which is mainly to be ascribed to the monetary and budget policy pursued by the government. Since the devaluation of the guilder in September, 1949, however, and especially since the outbreak of the hostilities in Korea, loans and advances to private enterprise have reflected some growth. Notwithstanding, more than 64 percent of the total amount of outstanding Treasury paper at December 31, 1952, was held by the 39 commercial banks.

Treasury paper held by the banks may be classified as Treasury notes and Treasury bills, which are both issued by the Agent of the Ministry of Finance in denominations of Fl. 100,000, and Fl. 1,000,000. The maturity of the notes ascends from three months by steps of one month, up to twelve months. Treasury notes are freely dealt in on the money market, can be discounted, and are accepted as collateral by the Netherlands Bank. Treasury bills, too, are readily dealt in on the money market, and this paper also is accepted as collateral or can be discounted by the central bank, provided the remaining maturity does not exceed three months.

Table 2
Combined Statements of 39 Commercial Banks in the Neitherlands December 31, 1946–52
(AMOUNTS IN MILLIONS OF FLORINS)

ASSETS

	1950	*1951*	*1952*
Cash on hand, at The Netherlands Bank, at bankers' and Clearing Institutions [a]	141	188	131
Money on call	74	179	130
Netherlands Treasury Paper [b]	2,943	3,022	3,670
Other paper issued by public authorities with a maturity of not more than one year [c]	134	207	111
Balances with domestic banks	62	70	82
Balances with foreign banks	343	330	244
Bills discounted	40	40	50
Securities sold but not yet delivered	20	19	25
Short-term loans against securities	64	80	140
Loans to public bodies on current account	27	6	3
Loans to bankers	27	33	38
Loans to overseas offices	14	30	15
Debit balances of concerns in which the commercial banks participate	27	23	19
Debit balances of other debtors	1,004	1,205	1,162
Debtors on account of acceptances	31	34	29
Prepaid amounts	49	41	43
Loans to public bodies with a maturity of more than one year	20	3	36
Claims on overseas offices except those on current account	96	80	93
Stocks, bonds and syndicates	87	121	173
Participations [d]	62	85	109
Deposits against loan extensions	3	4	4
Investments by pension funds	2	2	3
Real estate, furniture, fixtures, and inventory	28	23	23
Total	5,298	5,825	6,330

LIABILITIES

	1950	*1951*	*1952*
Capital paid up and reserves	674	720	791
Pension funds	4	3	3
Time deposits	529	861	1,011
Savings accounts of affiliated Savings Banks	19	29	23

[a] This item consists of the balances of the banks: (1) with the central bank; (2) with institutions specializing in money market operations; (3) with the Giro-services. Also money on call is included under this item.

[b] Treasury notes (maturity from 1 to 12 months) and Treasury bills (maturity 3 and 5 years).

[c] Floating loans to the Bank for Netherlands Municipalities, to provinces, municipalities, and "polder" boards.

[d] Mainly participations in the capital of affiliated enterprises, and advances to them.

TABLE 2 (*Continued*)

	1950	*1951*	*1952*
Credit balances of banks	336	421	361
Credit balances of clients in guilders	2,819	2,945	3,443
Credit balances in foreign currencies	264	259	215
Bills of exchange debited to customers	127	109	120
Amounts owing	99	82	73
Securities purchased, but not yet received	16	23	19
Miscellaneous accounts	182	146	138
Overseas offices	153	35	52
Money borrowed on call	18	12	8
Other sums borrowed	42	124	40
Own acceptances	11	23	20
Acceptances by third parties [e]	20	11	9
Loan deposits of creditors	3	4	4
Total	5,298	5,825	6,330

[e] Bills of exchange, accepted by foreign banks on behalf of the home banks, in favor of foreign exporters.

Other credits granted by the commercial banks to public authorities consist mainly of floating loans to provinces, municipalities, and "polder" boards. These loans, which are granted against letters of indebtedness, are not transferable; their degree of liquidity is therefore lower than that of Treasury paper and consequently they bear a somewhat higher rate of interest.

From the survey of the balance-sheet figures of the 39 commercial banks given in Table 2 it is evident that these banks, thanks to their substantial holdings of Dutch Treasury paper, are in a liquid position. Particularly in 1950 and 1951 the volume of credits granted by the banks grew as a result of the rise in the prices of raw materials caused by the hostilities in Korea. At the same time an expansion of the Treasury paper holdings could be noted. In 1952 the Government's reduced need of resources was marked clearly by a decreased issue of Treasury notes, which was even discontinued altogether for some time.

Additionally, the interest on these investments was cut back a few times, as a consequence of which the banks began to add more Treasury bills to their portfolios. Since these bills have a longer period of currency than the Treasury notes, this development has led to a slight recession in the liquidity of the banks.

Table 3 gives a picture of the shifting from the amount of Treasury paper held by the five big banks to the total of credits granted to the private sector insofar as this is listed under the heading "debtors."

TABLE 3
PUBLIC AND PRIVATE CREDITS OF THE BIG FIVE
(AMOUNTS IN MILLIONS OF FLORINS)

	August 31 1949	*July 31 1951*	*December 31 1952*
Dutch Treasury paper	2,645	2,105	2,846
Private debtors	555	995	908

In the course of years, credit granted by the commercial banks to the business community has taken the form mainly of loans and advances. The bill of exchange has lost much of its importance.[5] Even in international payments the bill of exchange has given way to the much simpler telegraphic transfer which reduces the foreign exchange risk to a minimum. An important defect in the bill of exchange is that it is always expressed in a fixed amount and is related to a fixed term, whereas loans and advances both in tenure and in the size of the credit fit into the specific needs of the debtor. It is difficult, if not impossible, to compare the difference in cost to the borrower between loans and advances and credits granted by way of a bill of exchange. However there can be no doubt that the discount rate is lower than the interest rate on loans. As a rule interest charged on loans and advances is closely related to the discount rate on promissory notes or to the interest on the advances of the Netherlands Bank. The interest charged by the commercial banks on loans and advances customarily is from 1.5 to 2 percent higher than the rates fixed at the central bank.

Loans for the purchase of securities can be divided into "prolongation" credits, loans on securities, and advances on current account against securities. The difference between "prolongation" credits and loans on securities lies in the period for which the credit agreement runs. In prolongation credits, the period is one month, in the case of loans, three months. These two forms of credit are being superseded, however, by the granting of advances on current account against security collateral. In common with loans and advances granted to business enterprise, advances on current account extended for financing purchases of securities have the advantage that they adjust themselves more easily to the changing credit needs of security holders. It should be observed here that under the present regulations (see section

[5] *Ibid.*, pp. 30–33.

on the Netherlands Bank, pp. 638–48) no credit may now be extended for the purchase of securities on the stock market.

Before the First World War, public authorities exercised no control over the credit granting activities of the commercial banks.[6] There was no need for such control because the banks were at all times prepared to examine and adopt, in concert with the central bank, the policy required to ensure a sound monetary situation. The position of depositors was adequately protected by the conservative policy pursued by the banks. Special attention was always paid to the quality of each loan. Moreover, certain criteria existed in practice regarding the ratio between a bank's own means (capital plus reserves) and loans and advances. According to G. M. Verrijn Stuart, Director and Manager of the Amsterdamsche Bank N.V., balance-sheet figures in general justify the conclusion that a ratio of 1:3 between own means and the sum total of credits to commerce, industry, agriculture and transport, together with credits against securities and credits to public authorities other than those in the form of marketable Treasury paper is regarded as the upper limit in the expansion of these credits.[7] It should be remembered, however, that strict adherence to this standard can probably not be expected under changing monetary and economic conditions.

After the Second World War the freedom which commercial banks formerly enjoyed in granting credits became restricted, systems of credit control having been introduced. At first the system was qualitative in character, but from January 1, 1951, up to the end of the first quarter of 1952 it was quantitative.

As implied in the definition of "commercial banking," commercial banks in principle confine their credit granting activities to short-term loans. From this it follows that their contacts with the capital market do not include the granting of long-term investment credits. They adhere to the principle that the money entrusted to them, which is repayable at call or subject to relatively short-term notice (not as a rule exceeding one year), cannot be used for granting long-term credits to trade and industry.

During recent years this principle has been attacked from time to time on the score that it is incompatible with the need for long-term

[6] *Ibid.*, pp. 118–41.

[7] G. M. Verrijn Stuart, "Enkele opmerkingen over den omvang van het bankcrediet in Nederland," *Weerspiegelde Gedachten* (Haarlem, 1948), pp. 208–212.

financing, a need logically arising from the contemplated industrialization of the Netherlands. In recognition of this need for capital funds, commercial banks have participated in the organization of two institutions which grant long-term industrial credits (these are discussed later in the section dealing with public and semi-public credit institutions). In addition, large banks, in two instances, have founded a subsidiary for the purpose of participating in financing the capital of industrial concerns. However, neither the Nederlandsche Bedrijfsbank, which is closely related to the Nederlandsche Handel-Maatschappij, nor the Twentsche Investerings Maatschappij, a subsidiary of De Twentsche Bank, have grown into important institutions operating in this field. In consequence, whenever a commercial bank has a permanent interest in industrial concerns, this is an exception to the general rule.

As a matter of fact the relationships of the commercial banks with the capital market are quite different in character. First, commercial banks lend their services for the purchase and sale of securities for account of customers. They are entitled to do so because all commercial banks, in common, of course, with the stockbrokers, are members of the Stock Exchange. No sale or purchase of securities can take place but through the agency of a member of this Exchange. To an increasing extent stockbrokers are feeling the competition of commercial banks. The good reputation commercial banks have earned for themselves with the investing public and the services they can offer have enabled them to attract an ever-increasing portion of stock exchange transactions.

In the second place, commercial banks participate in the capital market in connection with the flotation of new security issues. Institutions specializing in the issuance of securities are unknown in the Netherlands, an absence explained by the fact that the issue market does not present a steady flow of business.[8] Prior to the First World War it was mainly the smaller banking institutions and stockbrokers who handled the issuance of stocks and bonds, but in recent years the large banks have handled an increasing share of the business.[9]

In the capital market a distinction must be made between syndicate and "guichet" issues. In the latter case, a bank acts only as agent, the

[8] D. C. Renooy, *De Nederlandse emissiemarkt van 1904 tot 1939* (Amsterdam, 1951), p. 9.

[9] *Ibid.*, pp. 201–2.

risk of the issue remaining for account of the enterprise that wants to raise the money. In the first case, the issue is usually "taken over" by a group of banks at a price, which under the existing Netherlands law must not be less than 94 percent of par. The minimum price of an issue to the public cannot be below par. The details of the Netherlands issue market and the part played by the banks is covered in a later section.

To make our story complete it should be mentioned that commercial banks also perform an agency function in the raising of private loans. However, in order to reduce the costs connected with such loans, an increasing number of borrowers try to establish direct contact with institutional investors.[10]

An idea of the importance in which various operations contribute to the gross profit of the commercial banks may be obtained from Table 4 which shows the combined results of four large commercial banks (Amsterdamsche Bank, Incasso-Bank, Rotterdamsche Bank, De

TABLE 4
EARNINGS OF FOUR LARGE COMMERCIAL BANKS FOR 1951 AND 1952
(AMOUNTS IN THOUSANDS OF FLORINS)

Item	*1951*	*1952*
Interest, discount on bills of exchange	68,140	70,795
Commissions and service fees	50,452	47,084
Securities, syndicates, participations	8,732	9,546
Gross profit	128,324	127,425
Expenses	65,063	66,445
Pension fund	5,361	5,488
Depreciation on premises	3,877	2,505
Total	74,301	74,438
Balance	54,023	52,987
Reserved for taxes	21,714	23,670
Net profit	32,309	29,317

Twentsche Bank) for the years 1951 and 1952. Interest and commission are obviously the principal sources of income. In fixing rates commercial banks are subject to a series of regulations agreed upon mutually concerning the minimum commissions and fees to be charged by the members for their services. These regulations cover transactions with customers, with other domestic banks, and with foreign banks. They contain a large number of minimum fees for various transactions. The handling of collections is governed by sep-

10 *Ibid.*, p. 209.

arate regulations, and transactions in foreign exchange are subject to the rules and regulations governing bill-broking. The seventy-odd licensed banks appointed by the central bank have established minimum fees, fixed according to rules, which are charged for handling foreign exchange licenses, for the purchase and sale of foreign exchange, for the conclusion of foreign exchange forward contracts, and so on. For the sake of completeness it should be added that as regards Stock Exchange transactions the banks are subject to the commission regulations fixed by the Stock Brokers' Association.

There is little or no cooperation between the banks in respect of research and publicity. The Economic Bureau of the Netherlands Bankers' Association acts as a center for research, and engages in studies of interest to foreign banking institutions. Research studies also are carried on in the economic departments of the large banks. The results of the work, however, remain for the most part reserved to the bank concerned.

Generally speaking, contact between the banks and their customers is of an individual character. Advertising takes the form of regularly published advertisements in the leading newspapers and in various publications. Weekly or fortnightly reviews of the Stock Exchange and folders or pamphlets giving information on subjects of current interest such as tax revisions and foreign exchange business are regularly issued. In recent years the banks have begun to play a more active part in establishing contacts between domestic and foreign importers and exporters and accordingly issue publications in this field too. The Nederlandsche Handel-Maatschappij, with its numerous overseas branches, carries on a rather extensive advertising campaign by means of the semi-annual publication of a "Survey of the Situation in the Field of Commerce in the Far East and Arabia" and of a regularly published "Countries Documentation," including reports containing economic and commercial data respecting various countries. The other leading banks are also quite active in this sphere. For instance the Amsterdamsche Bank distributes a publication entitled "Intermediary," containing a great variety of useful hints for all who are concerned with the international trade of the Netherlands.

Finally a few big banking institutions have publications of a more extensive character. The Amsterdamsche Bank—Incasso-Bank publishes a *Quarterly Review,* in which a survey is given of financial and economic conditions in the Netherlands, buttressed with statistical data. This survey is preceded by a leading article on a topical economic problem, written by an expert. A somewhat different publication is the *Quarterly Review* published by the Nederlandsche Handel-Maatschappij, which is partly devoted to the examination of a number of problems of general interest, partly to a survey of the economic development. The monthly review of the Hollandsche Bank-Unie contains, apart from a leading article, an interesting survey of the stock market. The Rotterdamsche Bank publishes monographs, at irregular intervals.

Generally speaking each bank takes care of the training of its own staff. Selected younger members of the staff are given the opportunity of following a written or oral banking course, both of which are organized by a foundation specially created for this purpose, to further the study of banking and stockbroking. This course of study covers all the important components of the banking business. The fees paid by the members of the staff are low, as bank management contributes the major share.

Trade unions in the Netherlands are of little importance among bank employees. The percentage of organized workers is about 30 percent. Nevertheless labor conditions have been fixed in a collective labor contract concluded by the employers' association on the one hand and various trade unions, except the communist tinged union, on the other. In addition to fixing a scale of minimum salaries, this contract contains stipulations respecting such items as appointment, duties of the employee, working time, holidays, and extraordinary leaves. Differences are submitted to arbitration. The collective labor contract governs the labor conditions of the employees who have not joined a trade union.

SAVINGS INSTITUTIONS

The most important group of savings institutions are the savings banks. To these in particular the "little man" applies when he wants to make provisions for the future and to receive a certain yield on his savings. In view of the great social significance of these institutions it is not surprising that alongside private savings banks the government, too, entered this field and in 1881 founded the Post Office Savings Bank, which is a separately managed savings bank and for which the state is responsible.

A large proportion of the private savings banks has joined the Netherlands Savings Banks Association, founded in 1907. This Association has the dual objects of promoting the interests of members of the Association which try to stimulate saving, and of improving and extending the system of private savings banks.[11] The importance of private savings banks and of the Post Office Savings Bank is apparent from Table 5, which gives the number of institutions and total deposits as of the end of each year shown.

TABLE 5
SAVINGS BANKS AND SAVINGS BANK DEPOSITS, 1946–51
(AMOUNTS IN MILLIONS OF FLORINS)

	NUMBER OF INSTITUTIONS		DEPOSITS		
End of Year	*Post Office Savings Bank*	*Private Savings Banks*	*Post Office Savings Bank*	*Private Savings Banks*	*Total*
1946	1,981	268	1,544	984	2,528
1947	1,994	264	1,514	1,024	2,538
1948	1,996	266	1,445	1,031	2,476
1949	2,013	270	1,440	1,104	2,544
1950	2,025	269	1,365	1,115	2,480
1951	2,030	266	1,298	1,096	2,394

These figures show that while total deposits with the Post Office Savings Bank largely exceed those with the private savings banks, the private total has shown a rise, in contrast to the government institution.

The money paid into the savings banks, which as a rule is repayable at short notice, is to a large extent invested in readily marketable securities (especially government bonds), in private loans which are almost exclusively granted to or guaranteed by public bodies, and in Treasury paper. Sometimes part of the funds are lent out on mortgage. The larger part of the savings funds received, consequently, benefits the predominantly non-risk-bearing sector of the capital market.

In addition to these two types of savings banks there are also the so-called "bank savings-banks," that is, savings banks which have close

[11] Gids voor de Nederlandse Spaarbanken, 1951.

relations with a commercial bank. There are only a few of these and in comparison with the savings banks proper their significance is not important.

The agricultural credit banks, too, which later will be separately discussed, are of considerable importance as savings institutions. According to the conclusive figures as of the end of 1951, their total deposits were even larger than those of the Post Office Savings Bank. Of the total amount entrusted to the private savings banks, the Post Office Savings Bank, and the agricultural credit banks, as at the end of 1951, nearly 40 percent was deposited with the agricultural credit banks, as compared with 28 percent with the private savings banks and 32 percent with the Post Office Savings Bank.

Institutions which do not differ greatly from savings banks are life insurance companies. These institutions are of great importance, not only because they attract a considerable volume of savings, but also because they are able to dispose of large amounts of capital which, as a result of the character of their obligations, are particularly suitable for comparatively long-term investment. They therefore exercise considerable influence on the capital market.

The insurance contracts concluded by the companies are of three types: ordinary insurance, annuity insurance, and popular insurance. Popular insurance is written in amounts under Fl. 500. In the nineteenth century, popular insurance was mainly in the hands of burial societies; by the end of the nineteenth century and in the earlier part of the twentieth it passed more and more into the hands of the large companies, better able to serve the interests of a large number of insured.

The number of policies at the end of 1952 totaled nearly 19,000,000, of which 3,500,000 took the form of ordinary and annuity insurance and 15,500,000 of popular insurance. Since the population of the Netherlands is about 10,500,000, it follows that there were about 1,800 life insurance policies to every 1,000 inhabitants.[12]

An idea of the magnitude of the insurance in force in the Netherlands is given in Table 6. Annuity insurance has been capitalized in the usual way by multiplying the yearly total of annuities by 10.

The total premium reserves as of the end of 1952 were 3,984 million florins.

Of late years annuity insurance has constituted a growing propor-

[12] *Verslag der Verzekeringskamer*, 1952, p. 44.

TABLE 6
AMOUNT OF INSURANCE WRITTEN BY LIFE INSURANCE COMPANIES, 1950–52
(AMOUNTS IN MILLIONS OF FLORINS)

	TOTAL AMOUNT			PERCENT OF TOTAL		
Type of Insurance	*1950*	*1951*	*1952*	*1950*	*1951*	*1952*
Ordinary life	6,118.4	6,772.2	7,418.8	43	42	42
Annuity	6,021.0	7,083.4	7,891.5	42	44	44
Popular insurance	2,191.4	2,286.4	2,409.6	15	14	14
Total	14,330.8	16,142.0	17,719.9	100	100	100

Source: *Verslag der Verzekeringskamer*, 1952, p. 10.

tion of the total. Dutch fiscal policy, which to a certain extent grants freedom from income tax for annuity premium payments in contradistinction to payments of premiums for ordinary insurance, contributes towards this trend.

Per capita insurance in force at the end of 1952 was 1,576 florins against 455 florins at the end of 1937.[13] Even despite the decreased purchasing power of the guilder this means a rise of 31 percent.

In comparison with the great importance of life insurance, the number of companies is rather small. At the end of 1952 there were 62 domestic life insurance concerns, among which 48 were limited liability companies and 9 mutual companies.[14] In addition there were a score of small enterprises confining themselves to popular insurance.

In order to engage in life insurance, a license from the Insurance Chamber is required; this is a supervisory agency set up by the Act on Life Insurance of 1922. The supervision is very detailed, so that the possibility of a company getting into difficulties is practically excluded and the interests of the insured are safeguarded.

The funds of the life insurance companies are invested at long term in real estate, mortgages, securities, and private and registered loans.

Under the heading "sundry investments" are included registered loans to the Government.

The extent to which life insurance is concerned with financing of industrial enterprises is relatively small, about 6 percent of total investments.

Among important institutions attracting savings and supplying funds to the capital market is the National Insurance Bank (Ryksver-

[13] *Ibid.*, p. 44. [14] *Ibid.*, p. 7.

TABLE 7
INVESTMENTS OF DOMESTIC LIFE INSURANCE COMPANIES, VALUE ACCORDING TO BALANCE SHEET, DECEMBER 31, 1952
(AMOUNTS IN BILLIONS OF FLORINS)

Investment	*Amount*	*Percent of Total*
Real estate	275.1	6.5
Mortgages	597.6	14.1
Securities	573.1	13.6
Loans by private contract	1,763.6	41.7
Sundry investments	1,019.9	24.1
Total	4,229.3	100.0

Source: *Verslag der Verzekeringskamer*, 1952, p. 36.

zekeringsbank). In its case, savings for the greater part are not voluntary but are imposed upon the employer, the employee, or both, by the various social insurance acts. This bank, established by the Workmen's Compensation Act of 1901, is a public institution for carrying out various social enactments, such as the Workmen's Compensation Act, the National Health Insurance Act, and the Old-Age Pensions Act and for administering the funds accumulating.

The largest fund according to the latest published annual report of the National Insurance Bank, viz., that for the year 1951, is the Health and Old-Age fund. The fund's investments at the end of 1951 amounted to Fl. 949 million.[15] By far the larger part of the invested amount, Fl. 847 million, was placed in loans to and bonds of the State of the Netherlands, of provinces, municipalities, and "polders," and of Indonesia. The remainder was placed at the disposal of private enterprises, building societies, and other agencies at a fixed rate of interest. In the case of the other funds, the Workmen's Compensation fund and the Old-Age fund B (voluntary old-age insurance), the investments amounted to Fl. 109 million and Fl. 167 million, respectively. These amounts too were invested in the same way as those of the Health and Old-Age fund. The Health and Old-Age fund and the Old-Age fund B participated also in the preference share capital of the "Society to Finance National Recovery" ("Reconstruction Bank").

In the aggregate the investments of all public insurance funds, those administered by the National Insurance Bank as well as those not administered by this bank, represented a nominal value, as at the

15 *Verslag Rijksverzekeringsbank*, 1951, p. 88a.

end of 1951, of Fl. 1,406 million, 9 percent of which was invested abroad.[16]

Pension funds, too, play an important role in the matter of forced savings, and consequently are of significance to the capital market. Unfortunately no aggregate data are available for private pension funds, which comprise a few thousand separate bodies.

Rules respecting the investments of the public insurance funds controlled by the National Insurance Bank, the deposits of the Post Office Savings Bank, the Civil Servants' Pension Fund, and the monies of the Postal Transfer System have been laid down in the Investment Act.[17] Under this act long-term investments must be confined to bonds of the State of the Netherlands, public authorities, the Dutch overseas territories, state or semi-state enterprises, mortgage bonds, mortgage loans, debentures of limited liability companies, and preferred shares of the "Society to Finance National Recovery." A Central Investment Council, set up by virtue of this act, decides what securities will be purchased.

MORTGAGE BANKS

Mortgage banks obtain the funds they require for their operations through the issue of mortgage bonds. They grant long-term credit against mortgages, mostly on urban real estate.

They are not the only suppliers of mortgage credit, institutional investors such as life insurance companies, and private money lenders too, play an important role in the market. Private money lenders often avail themselves of the services of a notary public, who may previously have arranged the transfer of the real estate. The mortgage banking business, consequently, fills only part of the need for mortgage credit, the extent of which cannot be measured owing to the lack of sufficient data.

The number of mortgage banks in the Netherlands, in proportion to that in surrounding countries, is rather large. On January 1, 1953, 32 mortgage banks were in operation. As a result of the less favorable situation their number has continued to decline during recent years,

[16] Central Bureau of Statistics, *Statistische en econometrische onderzoekingen, 4e kwartaal 1950* (Utrecht, 1950), p. 168.

[17] *Staatsblad*, No. 507, 1928; No. 685, 1935; No. 416, 1938.

through liquidation, merger with pension funds, and amalgamation of two or more banks.

Table 8 gives a survey of the own funds, borrowed money, and credits granted.[18]

TABLE 8
MORTGAGE BANK STATISTICS, 1946–49
(AMOUNTS IN BILLIONS OF FLORINS)

At the Close of	*Paid-up Capital*	*Reserves*	*Mortgage bonds Outstanding*	*Mortgages Outstanding*
1946	43.7	52.0	514.3	576.3
1947	44.6	51.9	524.0	579.1
1948	43.0	51.6	535.0	585.5
1949	42.8	50.7	561.9	610.9

The occupation of the country during the war brought with it a great abundance of money, resulting in many redemptions of mortgages. This tendency continued till the end of 1945. With the revival of activity in the building trades the demand for mortgage loans again began to increase. The mortgage banks have obtained their share of the increased business, especially in the private sector, which is a very important one. They have not as yet succeeded, however, in attaining their relative prewar importance.

THE AGRICULTURAL CREDIT BANKS

The neglect of agrarian credit by the commercial banks gave rise, at about the turn of the century, to the establishment of agricultural credit banks. These are similar in legal construction to cooperative societies and are adapted to the local agrarian sphere of the economy. They dispose of funds which have been entrusted to them as savings or balances in current account, lending them out to members either as working credits or medium-term and long-term credits for the purchase of durable equipment. Of recently increasing importance are the loans granted to local agricultural and horticultural associations, in particular to agricultural machinery cooperatives and to associations for the joint purchase of equipment and the joint processing and sale of agricultural products.

18 Jaarboekje Vakgroep Hypotheekbanken 1950, "Algemene Overzichten."

Agricultural credit banks possess many merits but also have certain disadvantages arising from their structure. An important difficulty is the frequent discrepancy between the amount and the nature of the money entrusted to these banks and the credits granted by them. Furthermore, in the absence of supervision agricultural credit banks are likely, by reason of the identity of interest with their customers, to relax loan standards. For these reasons they have established central institutions in the form of cooperative societies, with which excess funds may be deposited and from which credits may be obtained. The central institutions, in case of a shortage of their own funds, or in case they want to invest excess funds, have recourse to the money and capital markets. In addition to its functions as an investment and credit-granting association, the central institution also acts as a transfer agent and as a central bookkeeper for the agricultural credit banks; it also endeavors to help local associations in the granting of credit and keeps a proper check on their activities.

There are two such central institutions, namely the Coöperatieve Centrale Raiffeisenbank and the Coöperatieve Centrale Boerenleenbank, both founded in 1898. With the latter institution are affiliated agricultural credit banks which are predominately Roman Catholic. A very small number of banks has as yet not joined either institution.

Table 9 gives an idea of the size of the system of agricultural credit banks.

Alongside the agricultural credit banks, a few other banks operate in the agrarian sphere, most of which have been created by the above-mentioned central institutions. These banks confine their activities exclusively to the field of long-term credits; usually they are mortgage banks.

TABLE 9

SELECTED DATA OF THE AGRICULTURAL CREDIT BANKS, 1950–52

(AMOUNTS IN MILLIONS OF FLORINS)

At the Close of	*Number of Banks*	*Amount of Savings*	*Amount of Advances and Borrowings*	*Amount of Deposits on Current Account*
1950	1,314	1,573	476	247
1951	1,319	1,581	593	263
1952	1,320	1,716	652	306

PUBLIC AND SEMI-PUBLIC BANKS

The influence acquired by public authorities on banking through the taking over of the whole or part of the capital of existing banks or through the establishment or participation in the establishment of new banking institutions should not be under estimated. Mention must first be made of the Netherlands Bank; this is the central bank, the shares of which were acquired by the government in 1948. A review of this institution is included in a later section.

Two institutions created by public authorities are the Postal Check and Transfer Service, a government undertaking, and the Money-Transfer Office of the City of Amsterdam.[19] The object of both these institutions is to promote the system of effecting payments by deposit money. At the end of 1952 about 17 percent of the total deposit money in the Netherlands consisted of balances of customers with these two institutions. In contrast to the Postal Check and Transfer Service, which accepts only demand deposits, the Transfer Office of the City of Amsterdam accepts one-year time deposits, the only type of deposit to yield any interest. The Postal Check and Transfer Service extends credits mainly in the form of advances to the government and to the Postal, Telegraph and Telephone Service, and in the form of private loans to public authorities. The Amsterdam Transfer Service grants credits chiefly to municipal enterprises. The growth of the two services is shown in Tables 10 and 11.

At the headquarters of the Post Office Giro System are kept the books of those who have joined. These members (private individuals,

TABLE 10

POSTAL CHECK AND TRANSFER SERVICE

(NUMBERS IN THOUSANDS; AMOUNTS IN MILLIONS OF FLORINS)

At the End of the Year	*Number of Accounts*	*Current-Account Balances*
1920	33	95
1930	168	119
1940	392	463
1950	533	1,031
1952	571	1,288

19 Dr. F. de Roos, *De Algemene banken in Nederland* (Utrecht, 1949), pp. 9-11.

TABLE 11

MONEY-TRANSFER OFFICE OF THE CITY OF AMSTERDAM

(NUMBERS IN THOUSANDS; AMOUNTS IN MILLIONS OF FLORINS)

At the End of the Year	*Number of Accounts*	*Current-Account Balances*	*Time Deposits*
1920	10	5	
1930	43	30	10
1940	71	23	8
1950	77	39	11
1952	82	40	11

enterprises, municipalities, banks, etc.) customarily instruct the headquarters to debit their accounts in favor of other accounts (giro) or they may instruct the headquarters to pay amounts in cash to others, the latter not necessarily being members of the system. Instructions for both forms of payments, giro or cash, require special forms which are sent to the headquarters in special post-paid envelopes. Deposits to the credit of the accounts are accepted by post offices throughout the whole country. Payments in cash also are made by the post offices, on presentation of a check sent by the debtor to the creditor. A small fee is charged in case of deposits and payments in cash. Transfer by giro is free of charge. No interest is paid upon deposits. Commercial banks are members of the system, so that giro clearance can be made via the banks.

Since its reorganization in 1942, the Nederlandsche Middenstandsbank too can be qualified as a government institution.[20] Its principal customers are found among the middle classes, an economic category which is not easily defined. Its credit-granting operations are directed to retail dealers, small industrialists and artisans. Of chief importance are the normal business credits, which are granted for the account and risk of the bank itself. In some cases, however, credits are extended under a government guarantee. This applies to the so-called equipment credits granted to artisans, small industrialists, the railroads, transports, and the hotel industry to finance the improvement of their equipment. These credits are limited to Fl. 25,000 per item and must in principle be repaid within ten years. The government also guarantees the so-called special credits, which middle-class business may borrow to finance the strongly increased need of working capital. Other credits under government guarantee—for industrial enter-

[20] Dr. G. M. Verrijn Stuart, *Geld, crediet en bankwezen*, Vol. II ('s-Gravenhage, 1949), pp. 49–56.

prises only—are the Industrial credits; these are limited per item to Fl. 100,000 and to a maximum maturity of 10 years.

A new development which has proved to be of particular significance to Dutch banking was the establishment of the Maatschappij tot Financiering van het Nationaal Herstel N.V., commonly known as the "Herstelbank" (Reconstruction Bank), and the Nederlandse Participatie Maatschappij N.V. After the end of the Second World War in 1945, it was clear that large funds would be required to rehabilitate war-damaged industries, to expand existing enterprises and start new ones. A new source of funds had to be found, since it was by no means certain that sufficient means for these purposes would be available in the capital market, whilst commercial banks in principle refrained from granting investment credits. Consequently, the Reconstruction Bank was founded in 1945 by the government, the commercial banks, and a number of institutional investors. In its capital of Fl. 300 million the state participated to the extent of Fl. 151 million by buying all outstanding ordinary shares A and something over Fl. 17 million of the 3.5 percent preferred shares B. Moreover Fl. 75 million preferred shares B are held by government funds and Fl. 3 million of these shares are in possession of the government-owned Netherlands Bank. The commercial banks have participated in the preference share capital to a total of Fl. 25 million, and a number of life insurance companies and pension funds have an interest in the Reconstruction Bank represented by Fl. 4 million of these shares. The remaining Fl. 25 million of preferred stock were disposed of by a public issue. The preferred dividend of 3.5 percent per annum is guaranteed by the state. This short sketch of its capitalization shows the predominant interest acquired in the Reconstruction Bank by the state, a circumstance which classifies the Bank as a semi-government institution. In addition, the government has reserved the right to appoint the chairman-manager and the manager-secretary. While the Reconstruction Bank does not aim at profit-making, the management has always taken the view that the capital of the bank must be kept intact, so that exclusively investment credits are granted with strict adherence to sound economic criteria. Originally the bank was particularly concerned with the granting of loans to enterprises which received government contributions toward their war damage. Afterwards the emphasis was given to supplementary credits to enterprises that had suffered injury from the war, to credits to enterprises that wished to modernize or expand their equipment, and to the financing of new industrial concerns.

The volume of credits granted by the Reconstruction Bank, inclusive of the advances against later government contributions, is given in Table 12.

TABLE 12

CREDITS GRANTED BY THE RECONSTRUCTION BANK, DECEMBER 31, 1946–52
(AMOUNTS IN MILLIONS OF FLORINS)

Year	*Number of Enterprises*	*Loans Outstanding*	*Net Increase in Loans*
1946	68	50	50
1947	166	123	73
1948	232	206	83
1949	267	264	58
1950	296	257	7
1951	332	322	65
1952	329	326	4

During the time the Reconstruction Bank has been in operation, it developed that in some cases the risks involved in the granting of credits to projects that were of special importance to the economic life of the country were very great.[21] Difficulties of this kind arose in connection with:

1) a disproportion existing between equity and borrowed capital of an enterprise;

2) the nature of the business;

3) the aggregate interest which the Reconstruction Bank already possessed in certain industrial lines.

For those credits to which a more than normal risk is attached, the so-called "special financing" has been created. In such cases the state guarantees interest and principal of that part of the loan which, in view of sound business practices, would be inacceptable to the Herstelbank. On the part of the loan guaranteed by the state the debtor has to pay interest and redemption only in so far as profits permit. It is possible that these special loans may be wholly or partly remitted. As far as is known, the amount for which the Reconstruction Bank has had to have recourse to the government is small.

Although the granting of long-term loans constitutes the bank's main line of activity, it does happen on occasion that it participates

[21] Maatschappij tot Financiering van het Nationaal Herstel N.V., *Verslag over het boekjaar 1949* ('s-Gravenhage, 1950), p. 23.

in an enterprise. These participations at the end of 1952 amounted to about Fl. 29 million, divided into that part taken for the account of the Reconstruction Bank, and that part, the principal and dividend (up to 4 percent) of which has been guaranteed by the state.

In 1949 the Reconstruction Bank contracted a loan of $15 million from the International Bank for Reconstruction and Development to finance the purchase in hard-currency countries of capital goods by enterprises specified in the loan agreement. The state guaranteed the payment and the transfer of principal and interest. Afterwards this so-called "special projects loan" was reduced to $7.3 million at the end of 1952.

A further extension of the activities of the Reconstruction Bank occurred in 1950, and new projects are being developed.[22] The bank embarked on the financing of the export of goods manufactured in the Netherlands and of projects to be undertaken abroad by Dutch concerns, and has also granted facilities for the payment of installments due on the building of ships in Holland for foreign account. In a number of cases the Reconstruction Bank has granted loans jointly with ship-mortgage banks and commercial banks. A similar kind of export financing has taken place with respect to the construction of railroad materials for the account of foreign buyers. In 1952 this type of capital goods financing destined for export has been entrusted to a separate credit institution, formed in cooperation with the commercial banks, the so-called Export Financiering Maatschappij (Export Finance Corporation).

Although not a public or semi-public institution, mention should be made here also of the Nederlandse Participatie Maatschappij N.V., which in the matter of financing industrial enterprises is always bracketed with the Reconstruction Bank. The latter—as outlined above—specializes in the granting of long-term investment credits, whereas the Nederlandse Participatie Maatschappij invests its available means in shares listed on the stock exchange or directly in participations. In the latter case the company often has one or more seats on the board of directors and is therefore in a position to follow closely (and if necessary to influence) the course of affairs in the enterprises in which it is participating. Obviously the enterprises that rely upon the Nederlandse Participatie Maatschappij are losing their independence to a certain extent, and for this reason many are reluctant

22 *Ibid., 1950* ('s-Gravenhage, 1951), pp. 6–10.

to make use of its facilities. Nevertheless many applications are turned down because the Nederlandse Participatie Maatschappij participates only on a sound commercial basis. This is understandable in view of the fact that the government is not directly concerned with the operations of the Nederlandse Participatie Maatschappij. The capital of Fl. 25 million is in the hands of the groups of shareholders designated in Table 13.

TABLE 13
SHAREHOLDERS OF THE NEDERLANDSE PARTICIPATIE MAATSCHAPPIJ
(AMOUNTS IN THOUSANDS OF FLORINS)

Shareholder	*Amount*	*Percent of Total*
Life insurance companies	11,990	48
Pension funds and savings banks	2,170	9
Total	14,160	57
Commercial banks, Nederlandsche Middenstandsbank, and agricultural credit banks	3,555	14
Reconstruction Bank	7,285	29
Grand total	25,000	100

At the end of 1952, more than Fl. 20 million were invested in 64 enterprises.[23]

Mention should also be made of the Bank voor Nederlandsche Gemeenten (Bank for Netherlands Municipalities), one half of whose capital is in the hands of the central government and one half in the hands of other public authorities. The bank grants short-term and long-term loans to public authorities.

DE NEDERLANDSCHE BANK (THE NETHERLANDS BANK)

The Netherlands Bank is one of the oldest banks of issue. Authorization to issue banknotes was granted to it when it was organized in 1814 by sovereign decree of King William I. This charter has been constantly renewed, and under the Bank Act of 1948, containing new regulations affecting the statute of the institution, the Bank is once more entitled, this time to the exclusion of any other entity, to issue banknotes that have the quality of legal tender. This authorization is now no longer subject to expiration.

23 Nederlandse Participatie Maatschappij N.V., *Verslag over het boekjaar 1952* (Amsterdam, 1953).

In the same year, 1948, the private character of the Netherlands Bank came to an end. The act of April 23, 1948,[24] declared that the general interest required that the shares of the Bank be acquired by the Netherlands. There has been no serious conflict, at least not after the termination of the Second World War, between supporters and adversaries of the central bank as a public institution. The nationalization of the Bank was regarded as inevitable under modern conditions. The objections of the minority, which focused on the fact that the management of the Bank would no longer be able to maintain its independent position *vis-à-vis* the government, could not prevent the transfer of the shares to the state. An increasing degree of influence of the government on the central bank has become unavoidable.

The Bank Act of 1948,[25] which came into force simultaneously with the acquisition act, contains a description of the delegated tasks of the central bank. In addition to the authorization to issue banknotes, Article 15 of the act lists the following activities:

1. the issue of bank drafts on its branches and on its correspondents;
2. the receipt of money on current account from customers, the execution of orders to transfer and to pay, performance of collection services on behalf of customers, and the settling of debts with or between others;
3. the discount of:
   (a) bills of exchange and promissory notes with two or more jointly and severally liable parties and of no longer maturity than the usages of commerce imply;
   (b) treasury paper chargeable to the State;
   (c) debentures redeemable within six months under joint and several co-responsibility of the discounter;
4. the purchase and sale of:
   (a) bills of exchange, accepted by banks or bankers established in the Netherlands, with no longer maturity than the usages of commerce imply;
   (b) treasury paper chargeable to the State;
   (c) debentures listed on the Amsterdam Stock Exchange chargeable to, or as regards interest and redemption guaranteed by, the State;
5. the purchase and sale of mail and telegraphic transfers, checks, bills of exchange, other commercial paper, and treasury paper, all these payable abroad;
6. the making of advances by way of loans or on current account against the collateral of securities, commodities, dock warrants, coins, bullion and values as referred to under numbers 3, 4 and 5;

[24] *Staatsblad,* No. 1, 165. [25] *Ibid.,* No. 1, 166.

7. the trading in precious metals, the melting of the same into coins, and the assaying and refining of ores and metals;
8. the safekeeping of securities, valuable papers, commodities, dock warrants, deeds, jewelry and other objects of value.

It is expressly stated in the Bank Act that the Bank must not grant any uncovered loan or advance, though in contravention thereof, the act elsewhere contains the stipulation that the Bank, each time that the Minister of Finance considers this necessary for the temporary assistance of the Treasury, is obliged to make advances on current account to the state, represented by Treasury bills. Such advances are non-interest bearing, but their aggregate amount must not exceed Fl. 15 million.

The Bank, with the approval of the government and after the latter has sought the advice of the so-called Bank Council (the composition of which will be described later), may in the general interest perform other activities than those mentioned in the Bank Act.

The act contains, in addition to this enumeration of the activities of the central bank, a general description of its responsibilities. The relevant article, Article 9, is rendered here in full by reason of its importance in understanding clearly the functions of the Netherlands Central Bank.

1. It is the Bank's appointed task to regulate the value of the Dutch monetary unit in such a manner as is most serviceable for the prosperity of the country, at the same time stabilizing that value as much as possible;
2. The Bank is to take care of the circulation of money in the Netherlands, in so far as it consists of banknotes; to facilitate the monetary transfer service in the Netherlands, and to cooperate in bringing about a smooth course of payments to and from foreign countries;
3. The Bank is to supervise the credit system in accordance with the provisions of the law on credit control.

The main responsibility of the Netherlands Bank consists in regulating the value of the currency in the interest of the general public, in particular in endeavoring to stabilize that value.

In the last analysis the responsibility for monetary policy rests with the Minister of Finance. Therefore provision had to be made for the contingency that the views of the Minister might differ from those of the management of the Netherlands Bank. To prevent measures from being taken by the central bank which might counteract those of the Minister, the latter is entitled to provide the management with the necessary directives. Article 26 of the Bank Act stipulates that in cases where the Minister considers such action necessary for the coordination of monetary and fiscal policy—and after he has received the advice of the Bank Council—the Minister may give directives to the management of the Bank, which the management is obliged to follow. However, if the management objects, it may, within three days, give written notice to the Crown, which decides (in the person of the Minister of Finance) whether or not the directives shall be followed. It is obvious that a minister who has a deciding voice in a controversy in which he is himself a party does not possess unbiased vision.

The means at the disposal of the central bank for regulating the value of the currency are, besides the classic method of discount-rate policy, the use of open-market operations and the possibility of directly controlling the volume of credit in furtherance of Article 9 of the Bank Act. Discount-rate policy in the more recent past has lost much of its attractiveness and effectiveness. As long as the commercial banks in the Netherlands, thanks to their large holdings of easily marketable Treasury paper, are in a very liquid position, it is practically impossible for a discount policy to prove effective in the sense that the interest rates charged by commercial banks on loans and advances must rise simultaneously. As a matter of fact the automatic connection between the official and private rates of discount is no longer as close as formerly and therefore other means have been devised to enable the Netherlands Bank to perform its task in regulating the value of the currency.

The principal method of influencing the monetary supply in the postwar years, without doubt, has been direct interference of the central bank with the credit-granting activity of the private banks. As a result of the Unblocking Decree, which became operative in 1945 after the monetary purge of September of that year, a qualitative control of credit was established. In principle, every grant of credit was subject to a general license. Credits exceeding Fl. 50,000 were allowed only with special license; for other credits a general license granted to the banks was sufficient. This system of qualitative credit control was abandoned as of January 1, 1951, and was replaced by a system of quantitative control. The manner in which it was carried out showed that the purpose of qualitative credit control was to prevent the credit granted by the banks from having any adverse influence on the already unstable monetary situation in the Netherlands in the postwar years. Consequently, credits to finance investments and to finance purchases on the stock exchange were not allowed.

From January 1, 1951, to the end of the first quarter of 1952 the central bank fixed certain liquidity requirements to which commercial banks and agricultural credit institutions had to conform. The comparatively complicated system will not be analyzed here in detail, as the system has been abolished meantime. Under this plan, if liquidity requirements were not fully met, the further granting of credit did not become impossible, but was subject to onerous terms. The deficiency in liquid resources had to be met either by an advance on current account granted by the central bank, or by offering promissory notes for discount to the central bank. It was hoped by the management of the central bank that in this way its discount policy could once more be made effective.

Commercial banks raised serious objections to the manner in which the management of the Netherlands Bank had seen fit to interfere with the extension of credit. In fact the new control measures tended toward a restriction of business loans, while at the same time no guarantee was insured against any serious reduction in the amount of Treasury paper held by the commercial banks, which represented the credit these banks had granted to their largest debtor, the state. Moreover, the control measures imposed upon the commercial banks had discarded the old tradition of joint discussion between the management of the central bank and the representatives of the commercial banks in order to devise measures to maintain the soundness of the monetary and banking systems. As recently as 1946, relations between the central bank on the one hand and private banks on the other were defined in a gentleman's agreement concluded by the Netherlands Bank with individual commercial bankers and with the central boards of the agricultural credit institutions. This gentleman's agreement [26] contained the following stipulations:

1. the banks undertake to give the information required by the Netherlands Bank in exercising its supervision and to permit any investigation to be held in this connection;
2. the banks undertake to transmit, every year, a balance-sheet and a profit and loss account;
3. the banks undertake to transmit, once a month, statements respecting their business;

[26] De Nederlandsche Bank N.V., *Verslag over het boekjaar, 1944–45* (Amsterdam, 1946), pp. 12–13.

4. the banks undertake to notify the Netherlands Bank of the credits granted by them which exceed 5 per cent of the capital funds of the credit granting institution or which amount to Fl. 1 million or more;
5. the Netherlands Bank reserves to itself the right, when it perceives signs of some undesirable development, to consult with the bank in question;
6. the banks will inform the Netherlands Bank in proper time of planned reorganizations, voluntary liquidations and mergers, and of the purchase of stock in commercial banks;
7. admission to the membership of the commercial banking group shall not take place until after consultation between the Board of that group and the Netherlands Bank.

Early in 1952 the relation between the central bank and commercial (and other) banks was changed in a very important way, resulting from the fact that Parliament enacted legislation on the control of credit. Under the New Act the Government may control various activities of the commercial banks, the farmers' banks, the savings banks, and stockbrokers. The initial bill was strenuously opposed by these institutions, and a few details were changed as a result. The Government aimed at coordinating the credit policies of commercial and other banks with its own management of general economic and monetary conditions (policy control) on the one hand, and on the other at maintaining and fostering the liquidity and solvency of the banks (security control).

Policy control was opposed by the commercial and other banks in contradistinction to security control, although this latter type of control was considered superfluous. The legislation, being in the form of an enabling Act, does not prescribe detailed measures of control. After ministerial approval, however, the Netherlands Bank may in the future influence the total amount of credits outstanding either by quantitative or qualitative means. Quantitative control may take the form of fixing the ratio of liquid assets (or of specially defined parts of these assets) to the amount of deposits (or of specially defined parts of these deposits). Instructions may be given as to the maximum amount of loans and advances, and of investments (or of specially defined parts of these assets) which a bank may hold in relation to its capital funds as to the total amount of its deposits. The life of the Act has temporarily been fixed at three years, that is, up to the end of 1954.

One may obtain a better understanding of the business of the central bank from an explanation of the abridged balance sheet of the Netherlands Bank, published weekly. For purposes of illustration the abridged balance sheet of December 28, 1953, has been used in Table 14.

TABLE 14
ABRIDGED BALANCE SHEET OF THE NETHERLANDS BANK
DECEMBER 28, 1953
(AMOUNTS IN FLORINS)

ASSETS

		Amount
Bills of exchange, promissory notes, and debentures discounted		59.055
Bills of exchange, Treasury paper, and debentures purchased by the bank (Art. 15, sub. 4°. of the Bank Act, 1948)		none
Treasury paper taken over by the Bank from the State of the Netherlands pursuant to the agreement of February 26, 1947		216,600,005
Advances on current account against collateral		35.281,012
Advances to the state (Article 20 of the Bank Act, 1948)		none
Government debt by virtue of the agreement of February 26, 1947		1,000,000,000
Coin and bullion		
Gold coin and gold bullion	2,792,163,019	
Silver coin, etc.	15,852,280	2,808,015,298
Debts due to the bank and securities, expressed in foreign currency		1,607,847,909
Foreign currency		720,911
Debts due to the bank in guilders resulting from payment agreements		213,834,617
Investment of capital, reserves, pension fund, and provision fund		174,672,405
Premises and inventory		1,000,000
Miscellaneous accounts		38,414,381
Total		6,096,445,588
Total of Dutch Treasury paper in which guilder balances resulting from payment agreements have been invested		22,800,000

LIABILITIES

	Amount
Capital	20,000,000
Reserve fund	22,846,402
Special reserves	95,089,516
Pension fund	35,492,188
Provision fund on behalf of staff in temporary service	1,432,084

TABLE 14 (*Continued*)

Notes in circulation (old issues)		30,609,565
Notes in circulation (new issues)		3,329,665,225
Bank drafts		250
Balances on current account		
Treasury	736,068,012	
Treasury special account	1,001,818,592	
Balances of banks in the Netherlands	434,582,573	
Balances resulting from payment agreements	78,238,388	
Other balances of nonresidents	16,777,966	
Other balances	149,038,158	2,416,523,689
Creditors in foreign currency		99,341,455
Miscellaneous accounts		45,445,214
Total		6,096,445,588

Domestic extensions of credit by the central bank appear under the following items:

1. bills of exchange, promissory notes and debentures discounted;
2. advances on current account against collateral (inclusive of loans);
3. advances to the state (Article 20 of the Bank Act of 1948).

It will be noted that the Netherlands Bank grants credit mainly in the form of advances on current account, in respect to which the collateral consists predominantly of Treasury paper. If a credit from the central bank is needed for a very short period, an advance is preferred to the discounting of short-term paper, despite the fact that the rate of discount for bills and promissory notes is usually a little lower than the interest charged on advances. The bill of exchange is used to a much smaller extent than is Treasury paper, both in discounting and as a collateral for advances on current account. In recent years this is due partly to the fact that the bill of exchange has lost much of its importance as a credit instrument (noticeable also from the unimportant bill portfolios of the commercial banks), and partly to the fact that in discounting bills at least ten days' interest must be paid.

Advances to the state (Article 20 of the Bank Act of 1948) are concerned with the non-interest-bearing credit (Fl. 15 million as a maximum) mentioned above.

Explanation is required with respect to the following two items:

1. Treasury paper taken over by the Bank from the State of the Netherlands pursuant to the agreement of February 26, 1947;

2. Government debt by virtue of agreement of February 26, 1947.

Both items have reference to an agreement made between the government and the Netherlands Bank under which the former took over the debt in German Reichsmarks that was due to the central bank.[27] This Reichsmark asset which the Netherlands Bank carried on its books at the end of the Second World War represented the goods (and services) looted by the Germans in the years of occupation, and for which they had "paid" in their own currency, which, after the war, was practically worthless. In order to remove this item from the balance sheet of the central bank the government by virtue of an agreement took over these marks. The total amount involved was Fl. 4,324 million, part of which (Fl. 2,100 million) was settled with the Bank in the form of Treasury paper, and Fl. 1,500 million was retained by the Bank as a book-debt owed to it by the government. The remaining Fl. 724 million was settled in another way. The two items yield a moderate interest. Gradual redemptions have reduced both items by a sum amounting to about Fl. 2,400 million.

Some clue to the foreign exchange position of the central bank may be found in the following assets and liabilities:

Assets: (a) debts due to the bank and securities, expressed in foreign currency; (b) foreign currency; (c) debts due to the bank in guilders, resulting from payment agreements.

Liabilities: (a) balances in current account, resulting from payment agreements, and other balances of non-residents; (b) creditors in foreign currency.

In Table 14, the heading "Debts due to the Bank in guilders, resulting from payment agreements" comprises exclusively the debts due to the Bank resulting from those agreements stipulating that payments are to be effected only through a guilders account. Any debts owed by the Bank as a result of such agreements are entered on the liability side under the subheading "Balances resulting from payment agreements." At the bottom of the balance sheet a note has been added, indicating the extent to which guilder balances resulting from payment agreements have been invested in Dutch Treasury paper. The item "Debts due to the bank and securities, expressed in foreign currency" comprises the credit balance of our country in the European Payments Union. Weekly figures showing the composition of the

[27] *Ibid., 1946* (Amsterdam, 1947), pp. 51–52.

foreign exchange reserves of the Netherlands Bank, divided according to currencies, are lacking. The Netherlands Bank publishes the details of its foreign exchange reserves quarterly, broken down into generally convertible currencies, currencies convertible only within the EPU, and inconvertible currencies. Among the means which the Bank has at its disposal to meet foreign obligation, the asset "Gold coin and gold bullion" is, of course, of great significance.

The distinction between notes in circulation, of old and new issue, arises from the monetary purge that took place in September, 1945. The amount of old banknotes still in circulation is too small to be of any special consequence.

To the "Treasury special account" has been credited the countervalue in Dutch guilders of all grants received under the European Recovery Program and Mutual Security. After agreement was reached with the United States authorities, large amounts of the "special account" were released. These, together with the means available in our own country for the same purpose, were applied to the financing of various investments, such as the Zuider Zee and other land reclamation projects, the rebuilding of the island of Walcheren (which was devastated by floods in the last year of the war), house construction, development of agriculture, promotion of the tourist trade (for instance, through assistance in building and improving hotels), the erection of a block rolling-mill, a cold rolling-mill and a hot rolling-mill. Some money resultant from the "special account" has been used for the redemption of government debt.

Finally, a few facts will be included on the management of the Netherlands Bank. The governing board of the Bank consists of a president and a secretary, appointed by the government, as well as three (at least) or five (at most) directors. The governing board manages the affairs of the Bank. Control of the management of the Bank is exercised by a board of commissioners, consisting of twelve members appointed by the shareholders.

The government appoints a Royal Commissioner to supervise the actions of the central bank. The Royal Commissioner has a right to attend all meetings of shareholders and of the Board of Commissioners, including the joint meetings of the governing board and the Board of Commissioners. The governing board is bound to give the Royal Commissioner all and any desired information concerning the supervision of the Bank's operations. The Royal Commissioner is paid by the government.

The Royal Commissioner is also the chairman of the Bank Council, four members of which are appointed by and from the Board of Commissioners and twelve members by the government. These twelve members are appointed in such a way that trade (including transport), industry, and agriculture are each represented by two members, and the workmen's organizations and experts of the financial and banking community are each represented by three members. The president of the bank delivers to the Bank Council a report on the general economic and financial situation and the policy pursued by the Bank. Moreover, a consultation is held on any subjects brought up for discussion by one or more members in connection with the Bank's position and tasks. After consulting with the governing board, the Minister of Finance may take the advice of the Bank Council in matters which are of importance in the policies to be followed by the Bank, whilst the Bank Council is also authorized to advise the Minister in these matters on its own accord.

THE AMSTERDAM MONEY MARKET

Before the Second World War and especially during the third decade of this century Amsterdam was one of the most prominent financial centers of the world. The banker's acceptance, nationally and internationally, played an important part in this connection; special houses engaged in the acceptance business. In recent years a complete change has occurred in the character of the Amsterdam money market. The volume of bankers' acceptances has declined and although, in the very recent past, the amount was increased somewhat, the volume outstanding is still quite small. The place of the banker's acceptance has been taken by Dutch Treasury paper, divided between notes and bills. The former have a maturity of 3 to 12 months, graduating upwards by a month at a time; the latter are issued with a maturity of 3 years and 5 years.

After the war it was possible to take up any desired amount of Treasury paper at a stable discount rate with the Treasury Agent. However, this issuing policy has been readjusted since May, 1951, by gradually lowering the discount rates. This decrease in the discount rate on the Treasury paper of different term induced the commercial banks, in their function of principal institutes for the money market, to apply a shifting in the ratio between their Treasury note and Treasury bill holdings in favor of the latter, in order to maintain their interest revenues. After it appeared in 1953 that the government had ample funds at its disposal, the issue of Treasury notes was discontinued intermittently.

Transactions in Treasury paper are carried on through the medium of discount dealers, all of whom are members of the Association of Billbrokers and Discount Dealers. The seller pays a fixed commission dependent upon the maturity of the paper irrespective of whether the intermediary acts as *broker* or as *counterparty*.

The inventory of Treasury paper carried by a discount dealer is financed partly out of his own funds and partly by borrowing call money in the money market. One institution, which has preserved fairly completely the old character of joint-stock banks, lends its services in connection with the call loans, acting as a depositary of the Treasury paper that is pledged. A call money contract is drawn up in which it is stated that the Treasury paper "is transferred in ownership for security." The dealer, however, retains *the right of disposal.* The result is that the dealer can at all times swap the paper pledged, so that his freedom of action is not affected by the transfer of ownership.

If the dealer cannot get sufficient call money in the money market he is obliged to make use of the credit facilities of the Netherlands Bank. In this case, however, he is bound by various conditions. The Netherlands Bank lends money only against Treasury paper with a maturity of more than 105 days, and such loans must be repaid at the latest within 10 days. Only in case of extreme necessity does a dealer contract such loans.

The rate for call money is, if necessary, fixed daily by a committee of two bankers, the membership of which is filled in rotation by the banks. Borrowers have no voice in the establishment of the rates.

THE CAPITAL MARKET

Important structural changes have taken place in the capital market following the end of the Second World War, particularly with respect to the supply of capital. The fiscal policy pursued by the government brought about income equalization which resulted in an insufficiency of venture capital. The strongly progressive income tax severely reduced the saving capacity of the higher income brackets, which in many cases had already suffered serious economic impairment through the assessments imposed in the shape of the property-increment tax and a once-for-all capital levy. The pressure for social security, on the other hand, caused considerable savings to flow to life insurance companies, pension funds, savings banks, and various government funds, especially those into which obligatory and non-obligatory premiums are paid by virtue of several insurance acts. These institutional investors confine their investment activity chiefly to non-risk-bearing investments. Government funds may not be invested in common stocks, as they are bound by the regulations contained in the Investment Act of 1928; private institutional investors show but little, if any, interest in such investments.

For a long time efforts have been made in this country to find a solution for this problem and to determine how the savings now flowing in such considerable amounts to life insurance companies, pension funds, and the like, could be made available for the financing of venture-capital needs. As early as September, 1949, it was officially stated that plans to invest part of the savings accumulated with the institutional investors in common stocks were in an advanced stage of preparation.[28] Although on various occasions it was announced that plans in this direction had taken a more definite form, so far they have not materialized.

The public sector of the capital market may be divided into that market having to do with the securities already issued and dealt in on the stock exchange and that market having to do with new issues of stocks and bonds. At the Amsterdam Stock Exchange (the Rotterdam Stock Exchange has only limited local significance) dealings take place in both officially quoted and non-officially quoted stocks. The former quotations are printed daily in a Price List published by the Stock Exchange Association. Besides the quotations, the turnover of stocks is also given in the Price List.

Close relations exist between the Stock Exchange and the new issues

[28] Nota inzake de industrialisatie van Nederland, *Memorie van Toelichting betreffende Hoofdstuk X der Rijksbegroting voor 1950.*

market.[29] Developments on the stock exchange are among the factors conditioning the issuance of new securities. Newly issued securities may be admitted to the official list provided the subscribed nominal amount is at least Fl. 500,000. Although there is a fairly constant flow of new issues, the demand for fresh capital in this country is not large enough to warrant the organization of institutions that would specialize in this line of activity.[30] Prior to the First World War new issues were handled mainly by stockbrokers and by the banks, but now new issue flotations are mainly in the hands of large banking institutions. The smaller banks enter this field incidentally or apply themselves to the handling of issues that attract interest only in restricted circles as illustrated in the case of church loans.[31]

In the section dealing with commercial banks, mention was made of the fact that issues may be divided into "guichet" and syndicate issues. In the case of "guichet" issues the bank or banks concerned act only as agent between investors and the institution raising new capital, which itself must bear the risk of possible failure. In the case of syndicate issues, the securities are taken over by the syndicate, which offers them for public subscription. A certain margin is fixed between the acquisition price and the issuing price, the size of which may vary widely, dependent on the risk assumed by the syndicate. If the success of the issue is practically assured, the institution wishing to attract fresh means can, so to say, decree the size of the margin, which therefore will be quite small, but in other cases it may amount to 5 or 6 percent. The acquisition price of shares may not be lower than 94 percent of par; the issue price of the shares must be fixed at least at par.

There are no detailed statutory regulations on the issue of new securities. The Civil Code, however, contains special regulations on the responsibility pertaining to the contents of the prospectus.[32] The party issuing the securities has to pay the commission due to members of the Stock Exchange Association for their services. Additional costs include advertising expenses, the printing of prospectuses and securities, and the expense of listing on the stock exchange. The total of

[29] D. C. Renooy, *De Nederlandse emissiemarkt van 1904 tot 1939* (Amsterdam, 1951), pp. 13–14.

[30] *Ibid.*, p. 1.

[31] *Ibid.*, pp. 194–211.

[32] E. J. J. van der Heyden, *Handboek voor de Naamloze Vennootschap naar Nederlands recht* (Zwolle, 1950), pp. 124–43.

these expenses, however, as a rule constitutes only a small percentage of the amount of the issue. In conclusion the stamp duty of 0.012 percent on inland bonds (2 percent on foreign bonds) may be mentioned.

EVALUATIONS AND CONCLUSIONS

In the initial part of this section we presented a short outline on the development and present structure of the economic life of the Netherlands. This was followed by a discussion of the various types of banks in the Netherlands and of the role of these banks in financing business activity. We shall now try to evaluate the extent to which banking has adjusted itself to economic and financial developments in recent years, endeavoring to point out whether shortcomings exist and what possible lines of policy banking might follow.

The banking system of the Netherlands, aside from the specialized agricultural banks, still reflects in a predominant way the characteristics of its original function, that of the financier of domestic and international commerce.

The banks in the Netherlands, including all the larger ones, are, almost without exception, commercial banks. Specializing in the field of the financing of merchandise transactions, they have concentrated exclusively in the granting of short-term credits. Loans to industry too are a very important feature, but these likewise are confined to short-term credits.

The industrialization of the Netherlands has made considerable headway since World War II. Consequently the need for capital on the part of industrial enterprises, especially long-term capital, has greatly increased. This development has taken place at a time when, in any event, the business world would have required capital owing to the general rise of prices and its inability to build up reserves by reason of high taxation.

The capital market itself is unable to provide sufficient riskbearing capital. Over the past decade fiscal policy has resulted in an equalization of incomes. Large incomes, which are of particular importance in the supply of capital, have been reduced. In addition the supply of risk capital has been further adversely affected by the fact that those who might be inclined to furnish this are often not willing to assume the risks involved, by reason of the small gain remaining after taxes.

While savings in the form of insurance premium payments have greatly increased, institutional investors are generally averse to the use of their funds as risk bearing capital.

Commercial banks cannot help solve this problem. The type of deposits they hold confines their activity to short-term credits. Consequently a gap exists in the field of industry finance.

An effort to fill the gap was taken in the establishment of the Maatschappij tot Financiering van het Nationaal Herstel (Reconstruction Bank), whose purpose it is to grant long-term loans. Assistance by this bank is limited by the fact that its funds may not be used to finance those needs related to risk capital. In principle the Nederlandsche Participatie Maatschappij, likewise a post-war institution, might be able to furnish industry with risk-bearing capital, but the importance of this company too is as yet very limited.

At the present time institutional investors find sufficient opportunities for non-risk bearing investments of their funds outside of industry. But should this demand decline in the future, they will be compelled to invest their means, directly or indirectly, with industry. Should institutional investors have no experts who are acquainted with the problems connected with the financing of industrial enterprises, a new task may be reserved for the banking system. In that event the establishment of one or more industry-banks may provide the necessary intermediary.

REFERENCES

THE COMMERCIAL BANKS

Brouwer, S. Amsterdamsche Bank, De, 1871–1946. Amsterdam, 1946.

Harthoorn, P. C. Hoofdlijnen uit de ontwikkeling van het moderne bankwezen in Nederland voor de concentratie. Rotterdam, 1928.

Hirschfeld, H. M. Het ontstaan van het moderne bankwezen in Nederland. Rotterdam, 1922.

—— Nieuwe stroomingen in het Nederlandsche Bankwezen. Roermond, 1925.

Meijers, C. M. Een en ander over het bank- en effectenbedrijf. Amsterdam, 1930.

Nederlandsche Handel-Maatschappij, N.V., Quarterly Review, One hundred and Twenty-Five Years of Private Banking 1824–1949. Amsterdam, 1949.

—— Gedenkboek 1824–1924 van de. Amsterdam, 1924.
Nierop, H. A. van. Schets van het bankwezen. 3d ed. Haarlem, 1950.
Renooy, D. C. De Nederlandse emissiemarkt van 1904–1939. Amsterdam, 1951.
Roos, F. de. De algemene banken in Nederland. Utrecht, 1949.
Siebesma, P. Enige critische beschouwingen bij de bankwet van 1948. Franeker, 1949.
Verrijn Stuart, G. M. Geld-, crediet- en bankwezen. 's-Gravenhage, 1949.
—— "Enkele opmerkingen over de omvang van het bankcrediet in Nederland," *Weerspiegelde Gedachten*. Haarlem, 1948.
Westerman, W. M. De concentratie in het bankwezen, 2d ed. 's-Gravenhage, 1920.
Wijnand, J. H. Het Nederlandsche bankwezen. Amsterdam, 1944.

SAVINGS INSTITUTIONS

Savings Banks

Buning, J. R. A. De beleggingen der bijzondere spaarbanken in Nederland. Haarlem, 1941.
Centraal Bureau voor de Statistiek. Statistiek der spaarbanken.
Gids voor de Nederlandse spaarbanken.
Tinbergen, J. De betekenis van het sparen voor het herstel van de volkswelvaart. Amersfoort, 1950.
Verrijn Stuart, G. M. Bankpolitiek. 6th ed. 's-Gravenhage, 1949.
Verrijn Stuart, M. H. Spaarbank voor de stad Amsterdam, 1848–1948. Amsterdam, 1948.
Verslagen van de Nederlandse spaarbankbond.

Life Insurance Concerns

Grooten, J., and C. Dorsman. Levensverzekering; de Nederlandsche private Levensverzekeringonderneming en haar bedrijf. Wassenaar, 1924.
Holwerda, A. O. Spaarbank en levensverzekering. Is samenwerking mogelijk en gewenscht? Amersfoort, 1938.
Hommes, J. W. Het wezen en de technische opbouw van de levensverzekering. Amsterdam, 1950.
Huffnagel, G. E. Enkele opmerkingen over de sociaal-economische werkzaamheid van het Nederlandse levensverzekeringbedrijf. Utrecht, 1947.
Stigter, D. C. M., and A. G. Ploeg. Levensverzekering. 4th ed. 1949.
Verslagen der Verzekeringskamer.

National Insurance Bank

Boot, F. R. De financiering der sociale verzekering (fondsvorming of omslagstelsel). Amsterdam, 1947.
Centraal Bureau voor de Statistiek. Statistische en econometrische onderzoekingen, 4th quarter, 1950. Utrecht, 1950.
Heer, R. C. de. Beknopt overzicht van de financiële structuur van de Nederlandse sociale verzekering. Amsterdam, 1951.

Lindner, K. Vraagstukken van financiering en belegging in de sociale invaliditeits- en ouderdoms-verzekering. Deventer, 1938.
Rijksverzekeringsbank 1901–1941, Gedenkboek. Haarlem, 1941.
Verslagen omtrent de staat der Rijksverzekeringsbank en haar werkzaamheden.

MORTGAGE BANKS

Glasz, C. Hypotheekbanken en woningmarkt in Nederland. Haarlem, 1935.
Jaarboekje van de Vakgroep Hypotheekbanken.
Vliet, C. D. van. Het Nederlandsche hypotheekbankwezen. Amsterdam, 1939.
Vries, F. de. Concentratie in het hypotheekbankbedrijf. Economisch Statistische Berichten van 31 Dec. 1947.
Woud, J. van der. De hypotheekbank, haar wezen en haar waarde. Amsterdam, 1947.

AGRICULTURAL CREDIT BANKS

Balen, W. J. van. Groeizaam geld. Een indruk van de scheppende werking der boerenleenbanken in Nederland. Haarlem, 1938.
Coöperatieve Centrale Raiffeisenbank te Utrecht 1898–1948. Gedenkboek uitgegeven ter gelegenheid van het vijftigjarig bestaan. Utrecht, 1948.
Haastert, H. van, and G. W. M. Huysmans. Veertig jaren landbouwcrediet onder leiding der Coöperatieve Centrale Boerenleenbank, Eindhoven, 1898–1938. Eindhoven, 1938.
Jaarverslag Coöperatieve Centrale Boerenleenbank, Eindhoven.
Jaarverslag Coöperatieve Centrale Raiffeisenbank, Utrecht.

PUBLIC AND SEMI-PUBLIC BANKS

Berge, L. G. van den. Het giroverkeer in Nederland. 's-Gravenhage, 1939.
Janzen, H. J. M. Het middenstandsbankwezen in Nederland. 's-Hertogenbosch, 1923.
Knol, H. D. M. Middenstandsbanken en het onderzoek naar hare verhoudingen. Leiden, 1923.
Maatschappij tot Financiering van het Nationaal Herstel. Doel, werkwijze, statuten. 's-Gravenhage, 1948.
Postchèque- en Girodienst 25 jaar, 1918–1943. 's-Gravenhage, 1943.
Posthuma, J. F. "De economische betekenis van de Maatschappij tot Financiering van het Nationaal Herstel N.V." *De Economist,* 1947, blz. 1–22.
Roos, F. de. De algemene banken in Nederland. Utrecht, 1949.
Schras, G. J. De tegenwoordige grondslagen van het middenstandsbankwezen, 1931.
—— Na-oorlogse financieringsaspecten voor het middenstandsbedrijf. Amsterdam, 1946.
Verrijn Stuart, G. M. Geld-, crediet- en bankwezen. 's-Gravenhage, 1949.

DE NEDERLANDSCHE BANK N.V.

De Nederlandsche Bank N.V., te Amsterdam. Beschrijving van haren werkkring. 2d ed. Amsterdam, 1936.

Jaarverslagen van De Nederlandsche Bank N.V.

Jong, A.M. de. Geschiedenis van De Nederlandsche Bank. 2 vols. Haarlem, 1930.

Siebesma, P. Enige critische beschouwingen bij de bankwet van 1948. Franeker, 1949.

THE CAPITAL MARKET

Doesschate, J. F. ten, E. Tekenbroek, and H. J. Witteveen. Het vraagstuk der kapitaalschaarste in Nederland, meer in het bijzonder de schaarste aan risicodragend kapitaal. 's-Gravenhage, 1950.

Renooy, D. C. De Nederlandse emissiemarkt van 1904 tot 1939. Amsterdam, 1951.

Riemens, H. De financiële ontwikkeling van Nederland. Amsterdam, 1949.

Wijnand, J. H. De effectenbeurs; vroeger nu-straks. Amsterdam, 1943.

SWEDEN

by Lars-Erik Thunholm

ECONOMIC ADVISER, SVENSKA HANDELSBANKEN, STOCKHOLM

EVOLUTION OF THE SWEDISH BANKING AND CREDIT SYSTEM

THE MODERN banking and credit system of Sweden has evolved in response to the significant changes in the structure of the Swedish economy that have taken place in the course of the last century. While up to the middle of the nineteenth century the economy was mainly based on agriculture, in the latter half of the century it underwent a far-reaching process of industrialization based chiefly on the rich national resources of timber and iron ore. Already at the beginning of the twentieth century the evolution of extractive and manufacturing industries had reached a fairly high stage, but the process of industrialization has continued ever since. In recent decades the main accent has come to be put on more highly processed products such as pulp and paper, quality steels, and machinery.

The change wrought in Sweden's social structure by these economic developments is shown by available data on the occupational distribution of the population. In 1950, 40.8 percent of the working population were employed in industry, 23.6 percent in trade and transport, and 20.6 percent in agriculture, while the corresponding figures for 1870 had been 9.5, 3.0 and 51.6 percent. It should be

---

LARS-ERIK THUNHOLM was born in 1914. He was graduated from the Graduate School of Business, Stockholm, in 1937, and became Master of Political Sciences, Stockholm University, in 1941. He entered service of Svenska Handelsbanken, Stockholm, in 1938, and has been Economic Adviser to the Bank since 1946, and member of Board of Management since 1951. He has written several books and articles on money, banking, and international economics.

observed that these shifts in the population do not reflect an absolute decline in agricultural production; on the contrary, the flow of people from agriculture to industry and trade notwithstanding, there has been during this period a very considerable increase in the production of Swedish agriculture, thanks to improved farming methods and increased efficiency of agriculture.

This vast process of industrialization would not have been possible without the mobilization of substantial financial resources. Initially Sweden had no accumulated capital to divert to these purposes, but the financial problem was solved, thanks to the thrift of the population and to the gradual growth of a system of credit institutions able to collect existing savings where they could be found and channel these resources to the growing needs of industry and trade. In this way the establishment and growth of large-scale industrial enterprise was financed almost exclusively with domestic capital, whereas the huge financial needs of railway construction and town-building were originally covered to a large extent by capital imports from abroad. The leading role in the financing of industry in its earlier stages was played by the commercial banks, which not only supplied the necessary short-term funds for working capital purposes but also shouldered part of the enterprise risks through extensive long-term commitments. Alongside the commercial banking system, the savings and mortgage institutions assumed at a comparatively early stage a very important position in the credit system. The savings banking system, which has very old traditions in Sweden, played a decisive role in fostering thrift and collecting savings from all sources. The task of the mortgage credit institutions was chiefly that of financing the large-scale urbanization of the country which followed in the wake of industrialization. In the early stages this depended to a large extent on foreign capital; later the savings of the Swedish population had grown sufficiently large to supply an entirely domestic base for an efficient capital market.

These three main groups of banking institutions—commercial banks, savings institutions, and mortgage credit institutions—all developed very rapidly during the last decades of the nineteenth century and the first decades of the twentieth, and were, on the whole, able to meet in a smooth and efficient way the financial needs raised by the rapid development of the national economy. This process involved important changes in the structure of the Swedish credit market, and, in fact, the credit system that had evolved in the 1920s had very few resemblances with that of half a century earlier. Such structural changes have continued ever since, though in recent decades when the economy has entered into a phase of greater industrial maturity, these changes have perhaps not been as rapid or as far-reaching as during the earlier period of economic expansion.

THE CENTRAL BANK

History and Present Organization.—Central banking functions are exercised by the Sveriges Riksbank (National Bank of Sweden). This bank has a very long history. It was first established under private charter as far back as 1656, and it is particularly remarkable as the first note-issuing bank in Europe. However, in its early form the Bank had a very short career. An abuse of the note-issuing powers very soon caused great difficulties, and after a few years of existence the Bank was no longer able to meet its obligations. It was then reorganized under direct ownership of the state, and resumed in 1668 its activities as a state bank owned by and responsible to the Swedish Parliament. This status it has retained ever since.

In the course of its earlier history the functions of the Riksbank were mainly of a commercial banking character, and it developed only gradually into a central bank. It is true that during a large part of its earlier history, it enjoyed a monopoly of note issue in Sweden; later on, note-issuing activities were also assumed by the private commercial banks that were established from 1830 onwards. It was not until 1897 that the sole right of note issue was finally restored to the Riksbank. Changes in organization and activities brought about by new legislation adopted in 1897 marked a fundamental change in the Riksbank's position within the credit system. Up to this time, the Riksbank had carried on business on a large scale with the general public in competition with the private banks. Now it became a true central bank, firmly establishing its position of leadership among the credit institutions and gradually restricting its operations almost entirely to those of a central banking character.

The Riksbank is still owned by and supervised by Parliament, being thus formally independent of the government. The government is, however, represented on the Board of Governors, the Chairman being appointed by the government while the other six members are elected by Parliament. As a consequence of the strong increase of government influence over the economy, characteristic of developments in Sweden since the 1930s, the Riksbank's formal independence of the government has now lost all practical significance. Thus, the monetary policy pursued by the Riksbank has, in practice, become wholly subject to the desires and directives of the government.

Apart from the head office in Stockholm, the Riksbank maintains branch offices in 25 principal cities in Sweden. The Bank's capital accounts amounted at the end of 1952 to 135 million kronor.

Principal Functions.—The functions of the Riksbank do not differ very much from those of modern central banks in other countries. Essentially a bankers' bank and a "lender of last resort," the Riksbank also acts as banker to the Swedish Government. One of its primary functions is to regulate the supply of money and the level of interest rates on the credit market, for which purposes it exercises the regular powers of monetary policy, that is, discount rate policy, open-market operations, and the power to vary the cash reserve requirements imposed upon the commercial banks. The Riksbank's influence over the private banking system is comparatively strong, and it has at times been able effectively to supplement its monetary policy action by more or less informal recommendations to the commercial banks and to other credit institutions. Illustrative of this kind of recommendations is the "voluntary credit restraint" program that has been effective since the autumn of 1950, as an instrument in the anti-inflationary policy of the authorities.[1]

The note-issuing powers of the Riksbank have in the last two decades been subject to great changes. From 1873 to September, 1931, except for the period 1914–1924, the currency was on a gold standard, and under this system the right of the Riksbank to issue notes was governed by the size of its gold reserves. Even after the gold standard was suspended [2] the system of relating the note-issuing powers to the size of the gold reserve was retained for a considerable time. The minimum gold cover, however, was lowered several times, and since 1948 the note-issuing authority of the Riksbank has been entirely dissociated from the amount of its gold reserve. This does not mean that

[1] This program is further discussed below, p. 677.

[2] This was done by a temporary law which has since been successively renewed at certain intervals.

the Riksbank has been free to issue notes to an unlimited amount. There is still a legal "ceiling" on the note issue, which has from time to time been adjusted upwards, being at present 5,100 million kronor.

As a central bank the Riksbank holds the gold reserves of the country, and also its main foreign exchange assets. Since World War II the selling and buying of foreign exchange has been subject to a system of legal restrictions. In principle, all prospective buyers of foreign exchange must apply for a license from the Valutakontoret (The Foreign Exchange Office) which is virtually, though not formally, a department of the Riksbank.

Apart from these central banking functions, the Bank's activities also include a certain amount of ordinary lending; this, however, is on a very limited scale, being concerned mainly with some loans to state-owned or semi-official corporations and certain small loans out of special funds appropriated by the Parliament for certain purposes of a social character.

The Riksbank's offices in Stockholm and Göteborg act as clearing houses for the commercial banking systems, daily settlements being made in the banks' accounts with the Riksbank.

The official discount rate of the Riksbank, at present 2.75 percent, is traditionally taken as the basis for establishing rates on loans and deposits throughout the banking system. The commercial banks normally set their various interest rates in a certain pattern in relation to the official discount rate. There have been exceptions, however, when the commercial banks have adjusted or retained their rates, independently of a change in the official discount rate.

The rediscount rate of the Riksbank, applied to first-rate commercial bills rediscounted by the commercial banks, has traditionally been 0.5 percent lower than the official discount rate. In October, 1950, this preferential rate was abolished *pro tempore,* the rediscount rate being fixed at the same level as the official discount rate. In June, 1952, the Riksbank declared that it would in future apply a variable rediscount rate to be fixed independently of the official rate and with regard to the circumstances of each rediscounting operation. Apparently, the purpose of this deviation from traditional practice was to prevent any large-scale rediscounting on the part of commercial banks in the case of a further tightening-up of their liquidity position. It should be noted, however, that the rediscounting of bills by the commercial banks is nowadays a very rare practice; not since the early 1930s has there been any considerable rediscounting of bills with the Riksbank, except in a few periods of great strain, as during the first year of World War II.

Principal Assets and Liabilities.—The principal assets and liabilities of the Riksbank are shown in Table 1. As is evident from these figures, the main feature of postwar developments up to 1950 was a large decline in the gold and foreign exchange reserves, caused by a heavy deficit in Sweden's balance of international payments, mainly in the years 1946–48. The money-market effect of this decline, however, was largely offset by an increase in the Riksbank's holdings of government securities. The latter development, which was the result both of substantial Riksbank purchases in support of the bond market and of continuous government short-term borrowing from the Riksbank, has been the subject of much controversy in Sweden in recent years. The object of this policy has been to maintain cheap money in spite of the inflationary pressure prevailing in the country.

TABLE 1

PRINCIPAL ASSETS AND LIABILITIES OF THE RIKSBANK, END OF THE YEAR (AMOUNTS IN MILLIONS OF KRONOR)

	ASSETS			LIABILITIES		
Year	*Gold and Foreign Exchange Assets*	*Swedish Treasury Bills and Bonds*	*Loans and Discounts*	*Notes in Circulation*	*Government Balances*	*Commercial Bank Balances*
1938	2,076	106	50	1,061	418	428
1945	2,782	434	32	2,782	831	80
1949	1,190	3,184	138	3,287	467	361
1950	1,154	3,443	209	3,513	511	312
1951	2,378	2,821	247	4,090	528	522
1952	2,304	3,240	321	4,577	449	558

Critics have maintained that this policy has seriously aggravated the inflationary situation. In the summer of 1950 the Riksbank temporarily discontinued open-market purchases of bonds, and this led to a fall in bond prices, the yield on long-term government bonds being allowed to rise from 3 percent to around 3.5 percent. In order to adjust money market rates to this new level of long-term interest rates the Riksbank raised the official discount rate from 2.5 percent to 3 percent as of December 1, 1950. Already in the first months of 1951, however, the Riksbank had to resume bond purchases in order to defend the new 3.5 percent level, and the Bank also continued to take over substantial amounts of Treasury bills from the government. Later in 1951, however, the creation of funds through these channels was discontinued, the balance of payments having now swung very heavily in Sweden's favor and the consequent inflow of foreign exchange serving as an expansionary factor on the money market. Thus, in 1951 there was a net increase in the Riksbank's holdings of gold and foreign exchange assets to the amount of more than 1,200 million kronor. In 1952 and 1953 there were no major changes in the Riksbank's assets. The money market conditions became easier in the course of 1953, and the previous upward pressure on interest rates subsided.

COMMERCIAL BANKS

Structure of the Commercial Banking System.—The present number of commercial banks is 17. These institutions may be grouped in three different categories: (a) nation-wide banks; (b) regional banks, (c) local banks. The relative importance of these institutions in regard to assets and number of branches is shown in Table 2.

TABLE 2
STRUCTURE OF COMMERCIAL BANKING IN SWEDEN, DECEMBER 31, 1952
(AMOUNTS IN MILLIONS OF KRONOR)

	OFFICES		TOTAL ASSETS	
Bank	*Number*	*Percent*		*Percent*
Svenska Handelsbanken	305	29.7	3,681	27.2
Skandinaviska Banken	209	20.4	3,546	26.2
Stockholms Enskilda Bank	17	1.7	1,312	9.7
Göteborgs Bank	102	9.9	1,060	7.8
Sveriges Kreditbank	59	5.8	1,009	7.5
Total	692	67.5	10,608	78.4
Regional banks (9)	326	31.8	2,291	16.9
Local banks (3)	7	0.7	638	4.7
All commercial banks	1,025	100.0	13,537	100.0

The banks in the first group, comprising the five leading banking institutions in the country, have as their geographical field of activity practically the entire country. Moreover, they handle the bulk of banking transactions with foreign countries. The two largest banks, the Svenska Handelsbanken (head office: Stockholm) and the Skandinaviska Banken (head offices: Stockholm, Göteborg, and Malmö), have networks of branches covering practically the whole country, while the Göteborgs Bank has branches covering most of southern and central Sweden. The Stockholms Enskilda Bank, on the other hand, operates only in Stockholm and its vicinity. The fifth of the big banks in order of magnitude is the government-owned Sveriges Kreditbank (head office: Stockholm), organized in 1950, by merging two medium-sized commercial banks, in which the government had taken over substantial shareholdings a few decades ago.[3]

A very large proportion of the total banking resources of the country is concentrated in the hands of these big banks, which hold about 80 percent of the total assets of the commercial banking system and control 692 of the 1,025 bank branches in the country. This concentration of banking resources has not always been so pronounced. At the beginning of the present century the banking system still comprised a large number of small banks each serving a particular, more or less restricted area of the country. During the following decades, however, the structure of the system was very extensively remodeled through a far-reaching process of amalgamations, which between 1910 and 1930 reduced the number of banks from 80 to 30. This process must be viewed against the background of economic developments during this period. The increasingly rapid development and concentration of industrial enterprise called for a corresponding adaptation of the banking system. The large financial requirements of Swedish concerns and their need for specialized financial services necessitated the creation of large banks, able to mobilize resources on a broader basis. Toward the close of the 1920s the concentration of the banking system was largely completed; the decline in the number of banks has continued ever since, although at a slower rate, down to the present number of 17. Most of the mergers effected in recent years reflect the difficulties of some of the smaller banks in maintaining their earning capacity at a satisfactory level. They have therefore been tempted to sell their business to one of the large banks, which have often been willing to pay a high price for such an opportunity to round out their network of branches in some particular area of the country.[4]

3 These were the Jordbrukarbanken, practically the entire capital stock of which was owned by the government, and the Göteborgs Handelsbank, in which the government had a 50 percent holding. The Göteborgs Handelsbank had merged with the Skandinaviska Banken, and its business was divided between that bank and the Sveriges Kreditbank.

4 To offset the drawbacks of too large a concentration of banking resources some of the leading banks have gone very far in decentralizing lending activities, giving a fairly

In spite of this far-reaching concentration of resources in a few leading banks, the remaining regional banks still play a very important role in the banking system. Each such bank, within its particular area, is in a strong position, firmly entrenched in local traditions and ideally suited for serving the specific needs of its respective field. The largest institutions among this group also maintain offices in Stockholm and transact a certain volume of foreign business. The three largest regional banks are the Wermlands Enskilda Bank (head office: Karlstad), the Skånska Banken (head office: Malmö), and the Sundsvalls Enskilda Bank (head office: Sundsvall), the total assets of each ranging between 400 million and 425 million kronor (end of 1952). The Wermlands Enskilda Bank, founded in 1832, is the oldest commercial bank in Sweden still in existence.

Among the four local banks included in the third group of Table 2 there are two quite large institutions of a special character. One is the Inteckningsbanken in Stockholm (total assets 363 million kronor), which is a combined mortgage and commercial bank (see below, p. 687); the other is Sparbankernas Bank (total assets 232 million kronor), which, though formally a commercial bank, acts as a central bank for the savings banking system (see below, p. 683).

Legal Regulations.—The commercial banking system has for a very long time been subject to close government inspection and control, the object of which is primarily to safeguard the interests of the banks' creditors.[5] The first Bank Act regulating the activities of the commercial banks dates as far back as 1846; since then bank legislation has been broadened considerably with the enactment of each new Bank Act. The present Bank Act is dated 1911, but there have been a great many amendments. A proposal for a new Bank Act, embodying earlier amendments as well as giving certain new rules and regulations, was published early in 1952 and is expected to pass through the legislature in 1954.

All the commercial banks in Sweden are joint-stock companies operating under a government charter. The charter runs for ten years for each individual bank and then must be renewed. A new

wide margin of discretion to branch managers in credit matters. See H. Melin, "Some Aspects of Bank Organization," *Economic Conditions and Banking Problems* (Stockholm, 1950), p. 224.

5 The evolution of bank legislation in Sweden since the early 19th century is described in E. Browaldh, "The State and the Private Banking System," supplement to Svenska Handelsbanken's *Index*, September, 1946.

bank cannot be established without a charter, and amalgamations with other banks or the opening of new branches are, in principle, similarly subject to government approval. The Bank Act further prescribes certain minimum capital requirements and certain liquidity standards, prescribes which assets the banks may hold, and establishes certain rules for their lending activities.

In regard to capital requirements, the Act stipulates that no bank may have a capital less than a million kronor. Nowadays, this provision is of no practical importance, as most banks are of quite another order of magnitude. More important are certain rules which relate the right of the banks to accept deposits to the size of the capital accounts. These provisions are somewhat complicated and vary according to the size of the bank. The over-all rule for the bigger banks is that their deposits, after deduction of cash holdings and certain secondary reserve assets, may not exceed ten times the capital account. For the smaller banks the rules are somewhat more restrictive.

The Act further prescribes certain rules in regard to liquidity. Thus the banks must maintain cash holdings or certain defined secondary reserve assets which together amount to at least 25 percent of sight liabilities.

With respect to general activities, the Act enumerates the types of assets that may be held. This enumeration excludes real estate, except that required for bank premises, and, in principle, equity stocks. The latter prohibition was introduced in 1933. Before that, the banks had certain limited rights to acquire equities. This prohibition does not exclude banks from taking over the ownership of equities if that is necessary in case of the default of a borrower. In such cases, a bank must, however, sell these stocks as soon as it can do so without loss.

The loans granted by the banks must, in principle, be short-term. There is no provision in the Bank Act against long-term loans, but there are rules to this effect in the by-laws of the banks which are adapted to a standardized formula and must be approved by the government. The Bank Act, in addition, sets forth certain other rules for lending activities. Thus, a loan must in principle be secured by some collateral (mortgages, bonds, shares, commodities, or the like) or by the guarantee of a person other than the borrower. Unsecured loans may be given to business firms only in exceptional cases and also, of course, to the government and to municipalities.

The banks are further subject to government inspection. The duties of the Banking Inspectorate (Bank- och Fondinspektionen) include those of seeing that the banks conform to the Bank Act and to their by-laws, and generally of watching their activities with a view to safeguarding the interests of depositors. For this purpose the Inspectorate has a representative among the auditors of each bank, and makes regular examinations of bank portfolios.

In order to enable it to exercise its supervisory function, the Banking Inspectorate receives every month from each commercial bank a statement of the bank's assets and liabilities, drawn up on a form prescribed by the Inspectorate. These figures are published by the Inspectorate together with a summary of all the commercial banks' assets and liabilities.[6] This survey is sent to the press and is commented upon in the leading daily newspapers and also in the financial journals. A statement of the final accounts for the year is submitted annually in conjunction with the closing of the books. The annual statement of account is likewise published by the Inspectorate together with certain statistical tables illustrating commercial banking developments.

Bankers' Association.—The central organization of the Swedish commercial banks is the Svenska Bankföreningen ("Swedish Bankers Association") in Stockholm, which was formed in 1910. The aims of the association are twofold: (*a*) to represent the banks and express their views to the government and to other authorities and also to the public; and (*b*) to establish a certain uniformity in banking practice and in the terms and conditions of banking services.

In the latter respect there is an interbank agreement regarding the interest rates paid on various deposit accounts and also an agreement in regard to the charges for various banking services.

Deposits and Capital Resources.—The Swedish commercial banks may be described as *deposit* banks in the sense that their activities are principally based on deposits received from the public. It is true that as in all commercial banking systems the deposit business essentially plays a passive role. In consequence it is by the manner in which the banks invest or lend the money entrusted to them that their useful-

[6] *Uppgifter om bankerna*, published monthly by Kungl. Bank- och Fondinspektionen.

ness to the community is primarily judged. But it is equally true that this phase of their activities must necessarily be coordinated with and adapted to the development and structure of their deposits. The lending activities of Swedish commercial banks are basically very similar to those of commercial banks all over the world. There are certain specific features, however, that are characteristic of the activities of the Swedish banks in this field, and the structure of their deposits goes a long way toward explaining these peculiarities.

Deposits are received by the Swedish banks in four different forms: as checking accounts; short-term deposits (subject to withdrawal at 14 days' notice); time deposits (2–6 months' notice); and savings deposits. Checks may be drawn only against checking accounts. The difference between time and savings deposits is essentially that unlimited amounts are accepted on time deposit accounts and that, in principle, withdrawals can be made only after due notice,[7] whereas holdings on savings account are restricted by law to a maximum of 8,000 kronor per account, withdrawals being allowed on demand up to a maximum of 2,000 kronor per week. While check and short-term deposits to a very large extent represent the working balances and liquid reserves of industrial corporations and business firms, time deposits and savings accounts have traditionally been regarded as representing "true" savings lodged with the banks more or less permanently. In the course of the last two decades, however, there have been some modifications in this respect. The growing liquidity of firms and corporations has induced them to keep a high proportion of surplus funds as time deposits with the banks. Present rates paid by the banks in respect of various deposit accounts are shown in Table 3.

TABLE 3

DEPOSIT RATES PAID BY SWEDISH COMMERCIAL BANKS, DECEMBER 31, 1951

Type of Deposit	*Rate*
Check	0
Short-term (14 days notice)	0.75
Time	
2 months' notice	1.5
4 months' notice	2.5
6 months' notice	3.0 [a]
Savings	2.5

[a] Accepted only from noncorporate depositors.

[7] Upon the payment of a special fee exceptions from this rule are normally allowed.

A very remarkable predominance of time and savings deposits is typical of the structure of the deposits in the commercial banks. At the end of 1952 these accounts together represented about 75 percent of total deposits (see Table 4). Various reasons may be cited in explanation.

First, bank checks are not used as a means of payment (except by business firms over a certain size) so widely in Sweden as, for instance, in Great Britain or in the United States. This is largely a matter of tradition, but in recent decades this tradition has been strengthened by the creation and rapid growth of a very efficient postal check service, which now handles a considerable proportion of the transfer of funds throughout the country.

Secondly, the predominance of savings funds over transaction funds may be explained by the fact that the savings habits of the Swedish public are remarkably conservative. In spite of the fact that there are now well-organized bond and stock markets, savers still very largely prefer to hold their funds in bank accounts, either in a commercial bank or in a savings bank, instead of investing them in bonds or shares, even if the yield is thus lower than might otherwise be obtained.[8] (This also explains the rapid expansion of the savings bank system; see below, p. 680.) The Swedish saver looks to the banks for safety and liquidity. He knows that his money is safe with the banks, and he also knows that the money will be readily paid when he needs it.[9] Rather than incur the risks and inconvenience connected with investing his savings in bonds or shares, he prefers to lodge them with the banks and to let the banks take the trouble of investing the savings in a profitable way.

Thirdly, it is also of some significance that business firms and various non-profit institutions very often keep some of their financial reserves as time deposits with the commercial banks. As pointed out above, this practice has been growing in recent years.

Apart from funds on deposit, the activities of the commercial banks are also based, of course, on their own *capital resources*. Though these play a comparatively important part as a source of funds, as in most other banking systems in the world the proportion of capital accounts to total deposits—the "capital ratio"—has been decreasing during the

8 At the end of 1953 the 2.5 percent obtained on a savings account in a commercial bank compared with a yield of 3.5 percent on long-term government bonds.

9 There have been very few bank failures in Sweden, and in the instances when they have occurred a run upon a bank has been very rare.

last few decades. Thus the capital ratio was over 20 percent in the 1920s, while in 1952 it was around 11 percent. This is still, however, a relatively high capital ratio as compared with banking systems of many other countries. It should also be noted that the Swedish banks generally carry substantial hidden reserves in their assets, the valuation of which is traditionally very conservative, and that consequently their "true" capital position is considerably stronger than that shown by their published statements.

Distribution of Assets.—The distribution of the assets of commercial banks shows certain characteristic features that should be emphasized in comparison with other banking systems. The outstanding feature is the very high proportion of total assets made up of loans and discounts and the correspondingly low proportion held in investments and cash. This is clearly brought out in Table 4, which shows that at the end of 1952 loans and discounts accounted for no less than 72.2 percent of total assets, while investments amounted to 12.7 percent and cash holdings to only 7.4 percent.

The proportion of total assets made up of loans and discounts has always been comparatively high in the Swedish banks. There was some decline however in the 1930s and particularly during the Second World War, the percentage falling from 78.5 in 1929 to 71.9 in 1938 and further to a low of 64.0 in 1945. The counterpart of this development, which was due to a remarkable decline in the demand for bank credit on the part of industry and trade, was mainly an increase in the cash holdings of the banks in the 1930s, and a swelling of their investment portfolio in the war years. In the postwar years, however, there has been a very brisk demand for bank loans and the percentage of these assets in total assets has again increased substantially.

Investment portfolios consist mainly of Swedish Treasury bills and government bonds of comparatively short maturities. It is customary to regard this portfolio as a liquidity reserve rather than as an earning asset, the Swedish banks having practically always been unwilling to invest to any considerable extent in long-term bonds for income purposes. Thus in the 1930s, when the supply of short-term government bonds was very scarce and the government did not as a rule issue any Treasury bills, the banks simply let their surplus of loanable funds pile up as idle cash holdings. Even in the war years, when the banks were faced on the one hand by an inflationary expansion of deposits and on the other hand by a decline in credit demands on the part of

TABLE 4

PRINCIPAL ASSETS AND LIABILITIES OF SWEDISH COMMERCIAL BANKS, DECEMBER 31

(AMOUNTS IN MILLIONS OF KRONOR)

	ASSETS				LIABILITIES				TOTAL
YEAR	*Cash*	*Investments*	*Loans and Discounts*	*Other Assets*	*Demand Deposits*	*Time and Savings Deposits*	OTHER LIABILITIES	CAPITAL ACCOUNTS	ASSETS OR LIABILITIES
1929	128	162	4,423	924	659	2,822	1,330	826	5,637
1935	351	177	3,828	1,076	766	2,866	1,116	683	5,431
1938	601	190	4,338	902	1,152	3,108	1,022	749	6,031
1945	347	2,152	5,785	749	2,729	4,118	1,358	828	9,033
1949	686	1,271	8,035	925	2,021	6,378	1,510	1,008	10,917
1950	681	1,107	9,155	1,008	2,151	6,779	2,011	1,010	11,951
1951	936	1,849	10,122	1,138	2,626	7,887	2,420	1,111	14,044
1952	999	1,716	9,773	1,049	2,618	7,740	2,052	1,127	13,537
				PERCENT OF TOTAL ASSETS OR LIABILITIES					
1929	2.3	2.9	78.5	16.4	11.7	50.1	23.6	14.7	100.0
1935	6.5	3.2	70.5	19.8	14.1	52.8	20.5	12.6	100.0
1938	10.0	3.1	71.9	15.0	19.1	51.5	16.9	12.4	100.0
1945	3.8	23.8	64.0	8.4	30.2	45.6	15.0	9.2	100.0
1949	6.3	11.6	73.6	8.4	18.5	58.4	13.8	9.2	100.0
1950	5.7	9.3	76.6	8.5	18.0	56.7	16.8	8.5	100.0
1951	6.7	13.2	72.1	8.1	18.7	56.2	17.3	7.9	100.0
1952	7.4	12.7	72.2	7.7	19.3	57.2	15.2	8.3	100.0

the business community, and thus had to expand their holdings of government securities very heavily in order to maintain their earnings, these investments were mainly in Treasury bills and comparatively short-term government bonds. Thus, at the end of 1945 over 50 percent of the investment portfolio consisted of Treasury bills.

As may be seen in Table 4, there has been quite considerable fluctuation in the postwar years in the investment portfolio of the Swedish banks. Thus, from 23.8 percent of total assets in 1945 the holdings of Treasury bills and bonds declined to 9.3 percent in 1950. This reduction is, of course, explained by the considerable expansion of bank loans that took place in this period. At the end of the war the banks were inclined to regard their holdings of low-yield government securities as excessively large and were quite prepared to reduce these assets very substantially in order to meet credit demands from their customers. Since 1950 this tendency has been reversed. Partly spontaneously, partly in response to new legal liquidity rules the banks have again increased their holdings of short-term governments. At the end of 1952, these investments amounted to 1,716 million kronor or to 12.7 percent of total assets. Of this amount 866 million kronor were Treasury bills and the balance principally government bonds with comparatively short maturities.

Lending Activities.—All credit accommodation granted by the commercial banks is, in principle, of a short-term nature. In fact, such a rule is prescribed in the by-laws of the banks, the idea obviously being that the banks should avoid having their funds locked up in a way that could endanger their liquidity. It is not regarded as the business of a commercial bank to supply fixed capital to its customers. The emphasis must be on short-term, self-liquidating accommodation. The over-all rule is that bank credits may only be granted for a period of six months or, alternatively, at three months' notice. However, this principle applies in practice more to the legal form of a credit than to its real lifetime. Existing regulations do not preclude successive renewals, and thus loans that are short-term in form may actually remain outstanding for a very long period.

Credit accommodation is extended in four different forms: discounting of bills; loans; credits on current account; and documentary credits. The distribution of credits outstanding among these different categories is shown in Table 5.

TABLE 5

LOANS AND DISCOUNTS OF SWEDISH COMMERCIAL BANKS, DECEMBER 31

(AMOUNTS IN MILLIONS OF KRONOR)

Year	Bills Discounted [a]	Loans	Credits on Current Account	Documentary Credits	Total Loans [a]
1929	1,220	2.471	732		4.423
1938	1,163	2,705	470		4.338
1945	996	4.040	572	178	5.785
1949	1,820	5.053	921	241	8,035
1951	2,641	5,801	1,304	376	10,122
1952	2,431	5,674	1,455	213	9.773
		PERCENT OF TOTAL			
1929	27.6	55.9	16.5		100.0
1938	26.8	62.4	10.8		100.0
1945	17.2	69.8	9.9	3.1	100.0
1949	22.7	62.9	11.5	3.0	100.0
1951	26.1	57.3	12.9	3.7	100.0
1952	24.9	58.0	14.9	2.2	100.0

[a] Excluding foreign bills.

It should be noted that the discounting of domestic commercial bills still plays a very important role. At the end of 1952, the bill portfolio accounted for no less than 24.9 percent of the total. It is true that in the 1930s and the war years this percentage declined substantially, being only 17.2 percent in 1945, but in the postwar years the brisk demand for credit for commercial purposes has again raised the figure considerably. It is remarkable that the domestic trade bill has maintained its importance as a financial instrument far better in Sweden than in England and some Continental countries. In Sweden the discounting of trade bills is still a regular way of financing the sale of goods from manufacturer to wholesaler and from wholesaler to retailer. It is also of great importance in such special fields as the financing of the seasonal credit requirements of agriculture and the financing of the automobile trade.

The most important form of bank lending on the part of the commercial banks does not take the form of discounting bills but rather that of "loans," which are granted in a fixed amount and secured by such collateral as mortgages, bonds, and shares, or else guaranteed by one or several cosigners. At the end of 1952, such loans accounted for 58 percent of the total.

The "credits on current account," which accounted for 14.9 percent of total lending, take the form of an authorization for the customer to draw checks against the bank up to a certain amount. Interest will be debited for the actual credit utilized at any time, but above that the customer is charged 1 percent per annum on the whole amount of the credit authorized, whether utilized or not. Only the part of the credit utilized is included in the figures in Table 5.

Interest rates charged by the banks are normally fixed in relation to the official discount rate of the Riksbank, and are differentiated according to the type of collateral offered by the borrower. The typical rates charged at the end of 1953 are shown in Table 6.

TABLE 6

LOAN RATES CHARGED BY SWEDISH COMMERCIAL BANKS, DECEMBER 31, 1953

	At a Maximum of 3 Months Rate	*At a Term longer than 3 Months* [a] *Rate*
Discount Rate on Commercial Bills of Exchange	2.75	3.5
Loans		
On the security of Swedish Government bonds	3.0	3.5
On the security of other first-class bonds	3.25	4.0
On the security of mortgage on agricultural or urban real estate within 50 percent of value	3.5	4.0
On other security	4.5	5.0
Advances on current account	4.0 [b]	

[a] The higher interest rate is as a rule applicable on the renewal of a credit after the first 3-month period.

[b] Plus commission, as a rule 1 percent.

A classification of the loans and discounts of the commercial banks by the various activities of the borrowers is given, in summary, in Table 7. Such data are published regularly twice a year by the Svenska Bankföreningen.

Banks and Industry.—The relations between banks and industry have always been very close in Sweden, and at times the practice of supplying industrial customers with virtually long-term loans has been very common among the commercial banks. This was particularly so during the earlier stages of industrial expansion. In view of the public's disinclination to make direct investments in industrial enterprise, it would in fact have been impossible for Sweden to attain anything like her present state of industrial development had not the

TABLE 7
INDUSTRIAL CLASSIFICATION OF LOANS AND DISCOUNTS OF COMMERCIAL BANKS, NOVEMBER, 1953
(AMOUNTS IN MILLIONS OF KRONOR)

	Amount	*Percent*
Industry	2,108	22.1
Trade and services	2,179	22.9
Shipping companies, etc.	310	3.3
Insurance and finance	271	2.9
Municipal institutions	94	1.0
Agriculture	392	4.1
Building and constructional operations	871	9.2
Housing credits	2,326	24.4
Personal and sundry credits	966	10.1
Total	9,517	100.0

commercial banks adapted themselves to the function of financing to a large extent the capital requirements of industry. Credit accommodation has thus comprised not only the extension of short-term credits on a self-liquidating basis but also, in actual fact if not in form, the advancing of fixed capital on a long-term, or at least on a medium-term basis. That this has been possible without subjecting the banks to undue liquidity risks is very largely explained by the exceptional stability of the deposits lodged with them.

It should be stressed, however, that the relations between banks and industry in Sweden, though close, have never been as intimate as in some Continental countries, particularly in Central Europe. In principle, cooperation has taken the form of credits, not of direct ownership of industry.

It is true that bank ownership of industrial companies has occurred in many important instances, but in such cases this ownership has rather been forced upon the banks as a result of a default on loans extended. In such cases the efforts of the bank in question have then been directed at a reorganization of the former borrower's business in order to make it possible for the bank to divest itself of the ownership of the stock as rapidly as possible. There are several instances of successful operations of this nature. One of the most typical is the case of the Swedish Cellulose Corporation, the largest producer of pulp in Sweden. This corporation was organized in the 1920s by the Svenska Handelsbanken on the basis of a number of smaller pulp factories, which the bank had been forced to take over. After a long period of bank ownership, it was possible to sell this company in 1950 through a public issue on the stock market.

Bank holdings of equity stock reached their highest level in the early 1930s, as a consequence of the great depression. Thus—between 1929 and 1935—the share portfolio of the commercial banks rose from 98 million kronor to 355 million. Since then, the figure declined to 54 million kronor at the end of 1952.

The credit relations between banks and industry have been greatly facilitated by the fact that the banks have always maintained a very close contact with the bond market. In fact, most bond issues are handled by the commercial banks, which thus act as intermediaries between, on the one hand, industrial corporations, local authorities and other borrowers which desire to cover their requirements of long-term capital through bond issues and, on the other hand, the various financial institutions, such as insurance companies and savings banks, which account for the bulk of the supply of long-term capital. The services of the banks in this respect also include the underwriting of bond issues.[10] This broadens the basis of the cooperation between banks and industry, enabling the banks by degrees to unload their industrial loan portfolios through the medium of bond issues for the account of their industrial customers. In this way the capital handled by the banks is made to serve as a "revolving fund," although the process has been rather slow at times, particularly during the early stages of industrial expansion, when the bond market had not yet attained its present development.

In recent decades when Swedish industry attained a stage of greater maturity and considerable financial strength, the practice of virtually long-term commitments in industry on the part of the banks has no doubt grown less common. Nevertheless, as a general rule, the banks still stand ready to finance new and expanding industrial enterprise very extensively, and they therefore still play an important role in the continuing industrial development of the nation.

Postwar Credit Expansion.—Very strong inflationary tendencies have characterized the Swedish economy in the postwar period, and the authorities have been only partially successful in counteracting these tendencies. One of the symptoms of this inflationary development has been a strong upsurge in the demand for bank credit. In the

10 There are no special investment banks or issuing houses in Sweden.

absence of a truly restrictive monetary policy these demands have called forth a credit expansion of substantial proportions.

Inflationary developments were particularly strong in the years 1946–1947 and 1950–1951 with an intermittent period of stabilization in the years 1949–1950. This is reflected in the total loans, which rose from 5,785 million kronor at the end of 1945 to 7,989 million kronor at the end of 1947 (that is, by 38 percent in two years) and then remained stationary at this level for two years. Thus, as the end of 1949 total loans amounted to 8,035 million kronor. The new upsurge of inflation that set in toward the middle of 1950 then raised loans to a total of 10,122 million kronor at the end of 1951—a further increase of 26 percent in two years.

The increased demand for bank loans was partly a result of a substantial expansion in the real volume of production and trade. All through the postwar period real investment activities of business enterprise have been on a very high level, partly for the purpose of inventory accumulations and partly for expansion of plant and equipment. The result of this has been a sharp increase in industrial production. Thus in 1951 the volume of industrial production was about 25 percent higher than in 1946. This development was accompanied by a considerable inflationary pressure, resulting in a steep upward movement of prices and wages. Thus between 1946 and 1951 the cost of living rose by around 35 percent and there was in the same period an average increase of hourly wages of around 65 percent. While a certain increase in bank loans was indeed necessary to finance the higher volume of production and trade, there is no doubt that the credit expansion went too far and that a more restrictive lending policy on the part of the banks could have served to restrain the inflationary forces.

Such a policy would have been possible only on the basis of a restrictive Riksbank policy. In reality, however, the Riksbank, through its open-market purchases of bonds and through increasing its foreign exchange holdings (see above, pp. 662–63), continued to broaden the credit base of the banking system, and thus, in spite of the credit expansion, the banks maintained and even strengthened their liquidity position. Not until 1952, when the inflationary impulses originating in the balance of payments had already subsided, were effective measures taken against the credit expansion.

Cash Reserves.—The predominance of time and savings deposits explains why the banks traditionally have been able to keep their cash reserves at a relatively low level, compared, for instance, with the cash holdings of English or American banks. Though certain minimum standards are set by the law, the Swedish banks have never maintained any fixed or conventional "cash ratio," and in fact the relative size of cash holdings has varied greatly over the years. This is shown in Table 8, which relates cash holdings to total deposits. In the late 1920s the cash ratio was as low as around 3.5 percent, but in the 1930s it rose in some years as high as 15 or 16 percent. In the postwar period it has fluctuated between 5 and 9 percent. The Swedish banks' cash holdings at the end of 1952 amounted to 7.4 percent of total liabilities or to 9.6 percent of total deposits.

TABLE 8
CASH HOLDINGS RELATIVE TO DEPOSITS IN THE SWEDISH COMMERCIAL BANKS, DECEMBER 31
(AMOUNTS IN MILLIONS OF KRONOR)

Year	*Cash Holdings*	*Total Deposits*	*"Cash Ratio" (Percent)*
1925	126	3,494	3.6
1929	128	3,481	3.7
1935	351	3,632	9.7
1938	601	4,260	14.1
1945	347	6,846	5.1
1949	686	8,399	8.2
1952	999	10,358	9.6

The Bank Act requires that the banks shall maintain cash holdings or so-called "cash reserve assets" (mainly sight claims on other banks and holdings of Treasury bills and other government securities) which in the aggregate must represent at least 25 percent of their *sight* liabilities (mainly check deposits and the unutilized portion of credits granted).

In view of the fact that demand deposits are only a comparatively small part of total deposits, the liquidity requirements of the Bank Act are somewhat limited in scope. In recent years, however, efforts have been made by the authorities to regulate the liquidity of the banks more closely, principally with a view to controlling their lending activities. Thus, a provisional law was issued in 1950, which introduced special cash reserve requirements of a temporary nature, the object of these requirements being to restrain the lending capacity of the banks in view of the inflationary situation prevailing in Sweden.

The new compulsory reserve ratios were drawn up on the following formula:

1. For the five largest banks, cash holdings and "cash reserve assets" (mainly Treasury bills, government securities, and sight claims on other banks) together were to amount to 10 percent of *total* liabilities exclusive of savings deposits and contingent liabilities. For the medium-sized banks (those with a capital of between 10 million kronor and 50 million kronor) the corresponding ratio was fixed at 8 percent and for the small banks (capital below 10 million kronor) at 6 percent.

2. Not less than 40 percent of these obligatory ratios were to be held as cash holdings (till money plus sight deposits with the Riksbank) and at least 25 out of these 40 percent were to be held on deposit with the Riksbank. The five big banks thus had to keep 2.5 percent of total liabilities (exclusive of savings deposits and contingent liabilities) in non-interest-bearing accounts at the Riksbank.

In February, 1952, these new legal requirements were again suspended, following an agreement between the Riksbank and the commercial banks, through which the latter undertook, on a voluntary basis, to hold a still greater proportion of their liabilities in the form of liquid assets, and thus to refrain from further increasing their lending in a way that would aggravate the inflationary developments of the economy. However, the power to impose such reserve requirements (up to a maximum of 25 percent of liabilities) still remains in the form of an enabling act.

Qualitative Credit Control.—These efforts to control the *volume* of credit have been supplemented by certain attempts at a *qualitative* control of credit. Thus, in the autumn of 1950 a system of credit restrictions was adopted on the basis of a voluntary cooperation of the banks, through which the banks agreed to follow in their lending activities certain recommendations issued by the Riksbank. The guiding principles were the following:

1) Loans should be given primarily for supporting essential production and promoting export trade.

2) Banks should avoid credits for the finance of consumption.

3) Banks should avoid supporting through their loans any speculative activities.

4) Increased attention should be given to the security offered for loans and to the amortization period.

5) The banks should contact the Riksbank before undertaking the floating of any bond loans other than Government bonds.

These recommendations were renewed in February, 1952, when the new liquidity ratios were introduced, and are still in force at the beginning of 1954.[11]

Various Banking Services.—Apart from the deposit-receiving and lending functions, Swedish commercial banks, like commercial banks all over the world, place a great many other services at the disposal of their customers. The issuing of guarantees, the collection and transfer of funds and similar banking services are part of the functions of all Swedish banks. The leading banks maintain trust departments, and act as investment counsellors for their customers. An important function is the handling of public issues of bonds and stocks and the underwriting of bond issues. Moreover, most banks maintain stock exchange departments, which act as brokers on the Stock Exchange. In fact, around 75 percent of all transactions on the Stockholm Stock Exchange are handled by the stock exchange departments of the banks.

In view of the great importance of foreign trade in the national economy, foreign transactions are a very essential part of commercial banking. Ever since the Second World War, foreign exchange transactions have been subject to official restrictions. Under this system the leading commercial banks and also some of the smaller banks act as authorized dealers in foreign exchange. As such they buy and sell foreign currencies for their own account, but under the supervision of the Valutakontoret (see above, p. 661). In principle, a buyer of foreign exchange must have a license issued by the Valutakontoret. Exception is made for regular purchases of travelers' exchange, which the banks may sell within certain limits without requiring a license. The leading banks maintain direct relations with a wide network of correspondent banks all over the world, but no Swedish bank has branches abroad.

SAVINGS BANKS

The same factors that have made for a strong development of time and savings deposits in the commercial banks have also greatly fostered the growth of the savings bank system. The relative importance of commercial and savings banks as receivers of deposits from the Swedish public is shown in Table 9. It should be noted that the pro-

[11] For further details of the various credit control measures of a quantitative or a qualitative nature adopted in Sweden in recent years see L. E. Thunholm, "Monetary Policy in Sweden," *Quarterly Reveiw* of the Banca Nazionale del Lavoro, December, 1952.

Table 9
Total Deposits in Various Swedish Banking Institutions
(amounts in millions of kronor)

	1925		1935		1945		1952	
	Amount	*Percent*	*Amount*	*Percent*	*Amount*	*Percent*	*Amount*	*Percent*
Commercial banks	3,494	56.7	3,632	47.6	6,847	46.2	10,358	43.3
Savings banks	2,489	40.4	3,351	44.0	5,605	37.8	8,703	36.4
Post Office Savings Bank	165	2.7	497	6.5	1,422	9.6	2,638	11.0
Post Office check service	12	0.2	120	1.6	755	5.1	1,643	6.9
Agricultural credit associations	4	0.1	23	0.3	193	1.3	557	2.3
Total	6,164	100.0	7,623	100.0	14,822	100.0	23,899	100.0

portion of deposits with the commercial banks has been declining over a long period. In the last decade that is also true of the savings banks, while the Post Office Savings Bank and the "Postgiro" Service (see below, p. 684) have attracted a growing proportion of the funds available on the market.

The savings banks have developed concurrently with the commercial banks, the oldest institutions in this group dating from the 1820s. They are, however, totally different in structure. Most of the savings banks are very small institutions, each serving a strictly limited geographical area, such as a city, a town, a parish, or a county. The number is at present around 450, of which only a few have reached a magnitude comparable with the provincial commercial banks. Savings banks also differ from commercial banks in that they are non-profit institutions with no shareholders. Though they are private bodies, they are subject to a certain measure of official control, not only in the sense that they are regulated by a special law and controlled by a Savings Banks Inspectorate, but also in the sense that at least one third of the members of their governing boards must be appointed by state or local authorities.

Savings banks accept deposits only on savings account, and according to law they cannot accept more than 50,000 kronor per account. Their business is thus primarily to collect small or medium-sized savings. This fact limits the field in which they compete with commercial banks, though this competition is in fact very keen in regard to small savings, in which the commercial banks are also interested. Moreover, there has been a tendency for the bigger savings banks to try to attract not only private savings but also the surplus funds of local authorities, welfare organizations, and smaller industrial firms. In this they have been assisted by the fact that they normally pay a slightly higher rate of interest than do the commercial banks. Thus, at the end of 1953 the typical deposit rate in the savings banks system was 3 percent, as compared to 2.5 percent in commercial banks.

Most of the funds attracted by savings banks are invested either in bond holdings or in mortgage loans. At the end of 1951 total bond investments amounted to 822 million kronor, while total loans were 7,293 million kronor. Of the latter amount 5,985 million consisted of mortgage loans. In respect of such loans the savings banks serve both the urban real estate market and agriculture. They also give loans for other purposes, such as to local authorities, to small business firms, and to individuals.

Cooperation among the savings banks is highly developed. One result was the creation in 1942 of the Sparbankernas Bank, which is owned by the savings banks and acts as a sort of central bank for the entire savings banking system. Funds which the savings banks cannot for the moment invest in loans or securities or which they want to keep readily accessible, and which they formerly deposited with the commercial banks, are now deposited with their own bank, from which they may also in case of need obtain temporary advances. This bank also assists the savings banks in buying and selling bonds.

As shown in Table 9, the Post Office Savings Bank (established in 1884) has been growing very rapidly in the course of the last few decades. This is the result both of a very dynamic policy in trying to attract new customers and of the obvious advantages that the Bank is able to offer depositors. The government guarantee of deposits may have been influential in an earlier stage, but it is now not so important, as thanks to a time-honored tradition of safe banking, the Swedish public has come to consider all banks equally reliable. The primary advantage is rather to be found in the fact that through the very widespread network of post offices over the country, the Post Office Savings Bank affords facilities for the depositing and withdrawal of money over a much wider area than either the commercial banks or the other savings banks.

Savings deposits are also accepted by the Consumers' Cooperative Society, though of course only from its members. At the end of 1952 savings deposits lodged with the Kooperativa Förbundet (the Cooperative Wholesale Society) amounted to 190 million kronor, bearing interest at 3 percent. These funds are used entirely in the financing of the society's business operations.

SPECIALIZED CREDIT INSTITUTIONS

Apart from the commercial banks and the savings banks, both of which conduct many-sided activities, there are a great many credit institutions of a more specialized type, which engage in some particular kind of lending or serve some particular part of the credit market.

Many of these institutions have an official or semiofficial status or are supported by the government in one way or another. Though space does not permit of an extensive treatment of this network of specialized credit institutions, a short outline of their structure and functions is given below.

The "Postgiro" System.—It was noted above (p. 669) that the check as a means of payment has not gained the same currency in Sweden as in England or the United States. One of the reasons for this is the extensive use of post office services for payments within the country. For purposes of transfers there exists a special postal check service, centralized in the "Postgiro" Office, which was organized in 1925 and has since developed at a very rapid rate. Practically all business firms, official authorities and institutions, and a great many private persons hold accounts with this Office, and checks drawn on such accounts or payments made to them at the post offices are widely used to settle payments. Thus, for instance, practically all insurance companies collect the premium payments of their clients through the "Postgiro," and this is also the regular channel for such transactions as, for instance, the settling of gas, electricity, and telephone bills, the payment of doctors' and dentists' fees, and the disbursement of pensions.

Obviously, through these services the "Postgiro" Office offers strong competition to the commercial banks, and, in consequence, the bank check has not acquired the same popularity or widespread use. At the end of 1952 the accounts held with the "Postgiro" Office numbered 300,000 with a total balance of 1,643 million kronor. This is to be compared with the check deposits of the commercial banks, their number of accounts being 180,000 with a total balance of 2,341 million kronor. It should be emphasized, though, that the bulk of payment transfers through the Postal Check Service consists of payments in smaller amounts, while the transfer of larger amounts is mainly handled by commercial banks. No interest is paid on the "Postgiro" accounts, nor are there any service charges apart from postage.

The deposits with the "Postgiro" Office are mainly invested in Government securities and long-term loans to local authorities, and to some extent also in first-rate mortgage loans.

Mortgage Credit.—The mortgage loan market forms a very important part of the credit market in Sweden. For many years a considerable proportion of all mortgage loans, whether urban or rural, has been supplied by commercial banks, savings banks, and insurance companies, but there are also several groups of institutions specially organized for this kind of lending.

The traditional and still the regular way of financing a building project, whether residential or industrial, during the time of construction is through a short-term building loan from a commercial bank. When the building is completed the regular procedure is for the owner to secure a long-term mortgage loan from a mortgage association, an insurance company, or a savings bank, and to use the proceeds of this loan to pay back the short-term bank loan. It may happen, however, that continued financing, of a more or less permanent kind, remains wholly or partially with the commercial bank. This is very often true in the case of loans to finance industrial plant expansion but on occasion it has also been a common procedure in the case of residential buildings. Frequently the owner of the completed house may secure a long-term first mortgage loan (upper limit 60 percent of the assessed value of a house) from a mortgage institution and a secondary mortgage loan (normally covering the part of the assessed value that lies between 60 percent and 75 percent of the value) on a formally short-term basis from a commercial bank, or he may also obtain the first mortgage loan as a short-term commercial bank loan.

Particularly in periods of a surplus of loanable funds the Swedish commercial banks have competed very actively for housing loans. This was, for instance, the case in the latter half of the 1930s and during the war years, when the demand for credit on the part of industry and trade was rather sluggish. In the postwar years, however, the banks have been less interested in such loans. Still, at the end of 1953, no less than 24 percent of the total loan portfolio of the commercial banks consisted of housing loans.

Foreign observers have often been shocked at the very extensive commitments of the Swedish commercial banks in the mortgage loan market, and have been inclined to regard the habits of the Swedish banks in this respect as very dubious from a liquidity point of view. It should be observed, however, that, owing to the structure of the Swedish credit market, such mortgage loans have special liquidity characteristics, and that the banks, in fact, have always regarded them as more liquid than regular business loans. The reason for this is mainly the great number of credit institutions specializing in or primarily interested in mortgage lending and the consequent very active competition for mortgage loans, which in normal times makes these loans readily shiftable. Thus, as a rule, it is very easy for a commercial bank if it needs additional funds to shift a first-mortgage loan to a savings bank, an insurance company or a mortgage association, which normally are very eager to take over such loans. Only in times of exceptional strain in the credit markets have these institutions been somewhat slow to take over new mortgage loans, but then the Riksbank has traditionally intervened and eased conditions in the mortgage loan market, either through rediscounting such loans for the account of savings banks or through purchasing bonds of the special mortgage institutions.

The volume of outstanding urban mortgage loans (residential houses or office buildings) in various Swedish credit institutions at the end of 1949 is shown in Table 10. Quantitatively, the most important of these lenders are the savings banks, which account for about a third of the total amount. The loans given by the savings banks are either for a fixed period of 10 years with a fixed rate of interest, or short-term loans with a variable rate of interest.

TABLE 10
MORTGAGE LOANS OUTSTANDING IN VARIOUS CREDIT INSTITUTIONS, DECEMBER 31, 1930 AND 1949[a]
(AMOUNTS IN MILLIONS OF KRONOR)

	1930		1949	
Institution	*Amount*	*Percent*	*Amount*	*Percent*
Commercial banks[b]	750	20	2,650	20
Savings banks[b]	1,360	36	4,550	34
Post Office Savings Bank and "Postgiro"	110	3	182	1
Urban Mortgage Association	635	17	1,849	14
Housing Credit Association	13		293	2
Mortgage banks	210	6	803	6
Insurance companies	582	16	1,650[b]	13
Government lending agencies	59	2	1,276	10
Approximate total	3,700	100	13,250	100

[a] For some of the institutions listed in the table no exact statistics exist; the figures given are approximate estimates.
[b] Estimate.

The special mortgage credit institutions, which together account for about 20 percent of the total volume of mortgage loans outstanding, are of three kinds, namely the Urban Mortgage Associations, the Housing Credit Associations, and the Mortgage Banks.

The first two are organized on a similar pattern, being a type of cooperative loan association headed by a semi-official central institution. Thus, the central institution of the urban mortgage associations is the Konungariket Sveriges Stadshypotekskassa (The Urban Mortgage Bank of the Kingdom of Sweden). The mortgage associations give exclusively first-mortgage loans (upper limit 60 percent of assessed value) for a fixed period and with a fixed rate of interest.

The housing credit associations for which the Svenska Bostadskreditkassan (The Swedish Housing Credit Bank) acts as a central fund-raising institution provide exclusively loans against second mortgages on urban real estate. The upper limit of these loans is 75 percent of the assessed value and, contrary to what is normal in the case of first-mortgage loans, they must be amortized within a comparatively short period of years.

These two mortgage systems are cooperative undertakings in the sense that the borrowers are members of the associations and are responsible for their debts, but they have a semi-official character in so far as the respective central institution of each system is supplied with a guarantee capital by the state. Moreover, the respective chairmen of the institutions are appointed by the government. All loans are handled by the associations, which cover certain defined districts of the country, while the necessary funds are raised by the respective central institutions through the issue of bonds on the open market. These bonds, which are secured by the mortgages held by the associations, are regarded as gilt-edged securities in Sweden and are quoted practically on a par with government securities. The bulk of these bonds is normally purchased by the savings banks, the insurance companies, and various pension funds, endowments, and so on.

Similar to these mortgage institutions, though of far less importance, are a few private Mortgage Banks, which also raise funds through issuing their own bonds on the market. The most important of these is the Inteckningsbanken in Stockholm, mentioned above (p. 665) and the Göteborgs Intecknings-Garanti AB in Göteborg.

The very active competition from various institutions for available mortgage loans has tended to press down mortgage loan rates to a comparatively low level. The pattern of mortgage loan rates is closely related to interest yields on the bond market, the prices obtained for the bonds of the Urban Mortgage Bank being a decisive factor. The urban mortgage associations operate on a margin of costs of only 0.1 percent. A yield on mortgage bonds of 3.5 percent thus corresponds to an effective loan rate of 3.6 percent in the mortgage associations. This is the present (beginning of 1954) rate charged by the mortgage associations, while the rates charged by commercial banks, savings banks and insurance companies for first-mortgage loans vary between 3.5 percent and 3.75 percent. For second-mortgage loans the rate is about 0.5 percent higher than that for first-mortgage loans.

Agriculture Credit.—Commercial banks and savings banks have traditionally supplied a substantial portion of the credit accommodation needed by Swedish agriculture. In the case of commercial banks the accent is on short-term seasonal credits mainly in the form of the discounting of agricultural bills, but like the savings banks they also to some extent give mortgage loans of a more permanent kind to farmers.

There are also credit institutions especially organized to supply agricultural credit. The most important institutions for supplying long-term finance to agriculture are the Rural Mortgage Associations, which are organized on a plan similar to that of the urban mortgage system. Their central fund-raising organization is Sveriges Allmänna Hypoteksbank (The General Mortgage Bank of Sweden), a semi-official institution with a government guarantee capital. The associations give loans exclusively on the security of first mortgages on agricultural real estate.

The Agricultural Credit Associations, a comparatively new development in Sweden, are part of a very strong cooperative movement among Swedish farmers. There are some 600 agricultural credit associations which are grouped together under 10 central associations and a common central institution, the Svenska Jordbrukskreditkassan (The Swedish Agricultural Credit Bank). The agricultural credit associations conduct a general banking business in the agricultural field, receive deposits on various accounts similar to those of commercial banks (including check account), and supply credit to farmers in the form of loans, overdrafts, and the discounting of bills. The influence of the agricultural credit associations has grown very extensively during the two decades of their existence, and they now offer serious competition to the traditional lenders in the field of short-term agricultural loans—the commercial banks and the savings banks. At the end of 1952 the deposits with the agricultural credit associations totalled 556 million kronor, and the total loans and discounts amounted to 487 million kronor. The agricultural credit associations are supervised by the Bank- och Fondinspektionen (see above, p. 667).

Other Special Credit Institutions.—Among other credit institutions of a specialized character should be mentioned the Skeppshypotekskassan and Industrikredit. The Skeppshypotekskassan (The Ship Mortgage Bank) is a semi-official institution, organized on similar lines to the above-mentioned mortgage institutions. Its exclusive function is to extend loans to shipowners on the security of ship mortgages. The commercial banks also, of course, lend money to shipowners on such security, but they are not similarly able to grant fixed long-term loans. The loans of the Skeppshypotekskassan at the end of 1952 amounted to 87 million kronor.

AB Industrikredit (Industrial Credit Bank) was organized in 1934 jointly by the government and a few leading commercial banks for the purpose of giving medium- and long-term loans to industrial firms, in particular to such firms as are too small to have ready access to the bond market. The loans of this institution have never reached sizable proportions. At the end of 1952 total outstanding loans amounted to 46 million kronor.

GOVERNMENT LENDING AGENCIES

The Swedish Government has always taken a strong interest in the development of an efficient and comprehensive credit system. This has taken the form both of efforts to regulate the activities of the private credit institutions so as to prevent abuses and strengthen their ability to serve the needs of the community, and of efforts in case of need to supplement their activities through various government credit agencies. The latter is illustrated by the official support given to such institutions as the urban and rural mortgage systems and by the creation of such an institution as Industrikredit. Apart from such action, on various occasions government funds have been appropriated to official lending agencies, particularly in the agricultural and housing fields, but also to support small industry, shipping, educational activities, and other enterprises.

A few years ago, former government lending agencies for the support of agriculture were reorganized into a government credit guarantee system, credits for certain social purposes within agriculture now being extended under a government guarantee by the various credit institutions which serve the normal credit needs of agriculture. This has greatly facilitated these governmental credit activities and has avoided unnecessary duplication of personnel and technical services.

In the housing field, governmental credits are extended on a very large scale through the Bostadsstyrelsen (The Housing Board). The loans given by this institution cover, wholly or partially, the portion of production costs not financed by the regular credit institutions (for example, above 75 percent of the value of the house), the purpose being to facilitate the construction of houses and prevent a rise in the level of rents. The amount of government loans outstanding for such purposes is shown in Table 9.

CONCLUSION

The present banking and credit system in Sweden has evolved as the result of a fairly long continuous development, which at least in the case of commercial banks and savings banks goes back to the early decades of the nineteenth century. In the course of this evolution the structure of the system and the functions of its various institutions have changed a great deal. These changes have basically been the same as have been operative in most modern industrial countries, the leading theme being the need for a continuous adaptation of financial institutions to the changing financial requirements of the economy. However, there have been certain distinctive developments, characteristic of Sweden. In comparing the Swedish banking and credit system with the corresponding systems of other countries the following features of the Swedish system should perhaps be emphasized most particularly:

1. There is in Sweden a great multiplicity of various types of credit institutions, which have arisen more or less spontaneously in the evolution of the modern economy, in response to existing credit needs. Though there is, of course, a certain division of functions among these various institutions, they are not based on any common plan of

organization, and there is consequently in practice a great deal of overlapping of functions, which makes for very active competition among lenders on the credit market.

2. This competition is particularly active in the mortgage loan market. There are not only several specialized credit institutions for this kind of credit accommodation, but this market is also the favorite area of such institutions as savings banks, insurance companies and —in periods of easy credit conditions—of commercial banks. A consequence of this active competition for mortgage loans is a relatively low yield, that is, cheap costs to the borrower, and a relatively high degree of shiftability of such loans.

3. On the Swedish credit market savings funds are far more important, quantitatively, than transaction funds. This may to some extent be a reflection of the fact that the propensity to save is comparatively high among the Swedish population. This fact has made for a strong development of the system of savings banks and of insurance companies, and it also explains why the commercial banks have more time and savings deposits than checking deposits. The high proportion of slow-moving savings deposits has served to give the banking system a very stable structure, and may explain in part why there have been practically no bank failures in Sweden.

4. The many-sided activities of the commercial banks should also be stressed. These banks not only take care of the short-term credit needs of the business community but also serve very extensively real estate and agricultural credit needs. Some of their lending commitments are virtually—though not formally—of a long-term character, though this is a less important feature nowadays than it was a few decades ago. Commercial banks maintain close connections with the capital market through their capital issues activities and their stockbroking activities. In these respects, however, they act as intermediaries only, and do not participate in the ownership of industrial enterprise.

5. The Swedish Government has always kept a close watch on money market activities, striving to control the operations of the various private credit institutions through rather detailed banking laws and to supplement the activities of the private banking system through the creation of official lending institutions in order to meet unfilled credit needs.

REFERENCES

Brisman, S. Sveriges affärsbanker. 2 vols. Stockholm, 1924–1934. An historical treatment of the Swedish commercial banking system up to around 1900.

Cramer, C. R., and K. Å. Fredricsson. Svensk Fastighetskredit. Stockholm, 1942. An extensive treatment of the Swedish mortgage loan market and its institutions.

Gårdlund, T. Svensk industrifinansiering 1830–1913. Stockholm, 1947. An historical analysis of the finance of industry in its earlier stages.

Svenska Bankföreningen. Economic Conditions and Banking Problems. Stockholm, 1950. In English. A collection of papers presented at the 3d International Banking Summer School held at Saltsjöbaden, September, 1950.

Thunholm, L. E. Hur den svenska industrien finansierats. Stockholm, 1950. A survey of the finance of industry in Sweden.

—— Svenskt kreditväsen. 2d ed. Stockholm, 1952. A general survey of the Swedish banking and credit system.

—— "Monetary Policy in Sweden," *Quarterly Review* of the Banca Nazionale del Lavoro, December, 1952.

STATISTICAL SOURCES

Ekonomisk Revy. A review published by the Svenska Bankföreningen. Contains statistical information about the commercial banks and the credit system generally.

Index. A quarterly review published by the Svenska Handelsbanken. Gives current information about money and capital market conditions in Sweden; also in English.

Quarterly Review of the Skandinaviska Banken, The. Published also in English.

Svensk Sparbankstidskrift. A monthly review of the Svenska Sparbanksföreningen. Gives current statistical information about the savings banks and the capital market generally.

Sveriges Riksbanks Årsbok. A comprehensive yearbook published by the central bank, which gives all the relevant money and capital market statistics. The text is also given in English.

Uppgifter om bankerna. A monthly statistical bulletin, published by the Kungl. Bank- och Fondinspektionen. Gives detailed statistical information about the assets and liabilities of Swedish commercial banks.

SWITZERLAND

by Eugen Grossmann

PROFESSOR EMERITUS, UNIVERSITY OF ZURICH

THE ECONOMIC ENVIRONMENT

SWITZERLAND has to support a population of 4,700,000 on the relatively small area of 16,000 square miles, of which only 12,500 can be cultivated. The population density is about 290 per square mile. Since only 20 percent of all employed persons are engaged in agriculture and forestry, there has to be imported each year from 1,000 million to 1,500 million francs worth of food and cattle fodder, and about the same amount of raw materials. The funds to pay for these imports are obtained from the export trade, the tourist traffic, and international banking and insurance.

In Swiss agriculture, middle-sized and small-sized enterprises predominate. Of the 210,000 farms, 201,000 have an area of 50 acres or less, 8,000 have an area of 50 to 125 acres, and only about 600 have an area greater than 125 acres. These farms are mainly occupied with cattle raising and dairying, which accounts for 75 percent of the value produced by agriculture. Two thirds of this value, or 50 percent of the total, is derived from milk production, cattle fattening, and the export of purebred cattle. Pig raising accounts for 15 percent of the value produced by agriculture; other kinds of animals are of relatively small importance. The cultivation of cereals, vegetables, and fruits

---

EUGEN GROSSMANN was born December 11, 1879. He studied political economy in Zurich and Paris and was from 1904 to 1910 secretary of the Department of Finance and chief of the Statistical Office of the Canton of Zurich. From 1910 to 1914 he was manager of the Union of Swiss cities. From 1914 to 1946 he served as professor of public finance and statistics at the University of Zurich, and from 1918 to 1946 was expert of the Federal Department of Finance.

account for 5 or 6 percent each of the total value of all crops, and potato and wine production account for 3.5 percent each. Other branches of crop production have little importance.

The production of milk, cheese, potatoes and meat is sufficient for domestic consumption. But 66 percent to 70 percent of the consumption of cereals, 10 to 15 percent of vegetables, 60 percent of wine, and 70 percent to 75 percent of oils and fats have to be imported. Although the total production of food is not sufficient for domestic consumption there are some products which can be exported, notably cheese, fruits, and cattle. This group of products is not, however, of very great importance in the total of exports; in 1950 it comprised only 116 million francs in the total exports of 3,900 million francs.

It is largely by the export of industrial products that the Swiss economy obtains the food and raw materials which cannot be produced at home. In 1950 the gross export of industrial products amounted to 3,600 million francs. Since the import of such products amounted to only 1,600 million francs, the net exports were 2,000 million francs. The export of machinery brought in 863 million francs; of watches and small parts, 730 millions; of instruments and apparatus, 257 millions; of pharmaceutical products, 221 millions; of silk fabrics, 79 millions; and of cotton fabrics, 127 millions. Embroidery, which was a very important export product years ago, brought in only 66 million francs.

Swiss industry, like Swiss agriculture, consists largely of small and medium-sized enterprises. In 1949 the average number of workers in all factories was 43; in the watch industry the average was 43; in the chemical industry, 61; the silk industry, 110; and in the chocolate industry, 142. Of the 11,568 factories only 104 employed more than 500 workmen. These workers comprised 21 percent of the total number employed. On the other hand the capital equipment of the factories is large, averaging 3.6 horsepower for each workman. In recent years the use of hydroelectric power has become very important. In 1949 there were 291 hydroelectric plants with a capacity of 2,659,100 kilowatts. Their total output in the fiscal year 1948–49 was 9,880 million kilowatt hours of which 470 million were exported.

Switzerland has a very well-developed transport system. The whole railroad network measures 3,600 miles of which 3,400 are electrified. The navigation on lakes and rivers has little significance except for the tourist trade, but the freight traffic in the Rhine harbor at Basel is very important. In 1950, the cargo traffic in the Basel Rhine harbor reached a total turnover of 3,200,000 tons. Since the Second World War, Switzerland has possessed a small sea fleet. Motor vehicles also are playing an increasing part in Swiss life. In 1938 there were 124,000 vehicles and by 1950 their number had increased to 300,000. The telephone system is well developed.

A very important section of the economy is the tourist trade. In 1939 there were 10,000 hotels and inns in which 62,000 persons were employed. The revenue from the influx of foreign visitors normally runs into several hundred million francs a year. On the other hand the amount spent by Swiss nationals in travel and holiday expenses abroad may be estimated at about half this figure. The tourist trade is therefore important for Switzerland's balance of payments.

The banks and insurance companies also have important international connections. The 75 insurance companies collected, in 1948, premiums amounting to 1,700 million francs, of which 510 million francs represented reinsurance. Of the total damage and accident insurance, 54 percent was written for foreigners; of life insurance, 8 percent; and of reinsurance, 90 percent. Although there is no recent information about the international business of the Swiss banks, it is clear that domestic business alone could not provide enough scope for the 389 banks which, in 1950, had 2,400 million francs of capital and 27,300 millions of assets. An estimate made by President Bachmann of the National Bank in 1930, when credit extended to foreigners was approaching its peak, set the total foreign investments of the eight large banks at 3,200 million francs. This was offset by foreign deposits in the same banks of 1,400 million francs, leaving the net credit outstanding abroad at 1,800 millions or about 30 percent of the assets of those banks. It is evident that the banking and insurance business of Switzerland is an important factor in its balance of payments. Also worthy of note in this connection is the large volume of foreign securities owned by the Swiss people.

CREDIT NEEDS

Since the price of land is very high the credit needs of agriculture also run high. The total debt of Swiss farmers was estimated, in 1949, at 5,800 million francs, an amount equal to 46 percent of their invested capital of 12,300 million francs. Of the 5,800 million francs of indebtedness, the mortgage debt amounted to 5,000 million francs. All other debts accounted for the relatively small sum of 770 million francs.

The capital levy of 1945 provided some information about the credit needs of industry. According to these statistics, the assets of persons engaged in industry and trade amounted to 6,000 million francs. The liabilities were 1,994 millions of which 1,384 millions were represented by mortgages. Thus, for persons engaged in industry and trade, credit provided one third of their assets. The debts of persons in the hostelry business were 398 million francs, against assets of 795 million francs, or about 50 percent. In commercial establishments the indebtedness amounted only to one third, that is 877 million francs of debt against 2,732 millions of assets.

It is also worthy of note that the 1,927 million francs of debts were reported by gainfully employed individuals at the time of the capital levy in 1945, and that they consisted principally—1,613 million francs—of mortgage credit. The rest of their debts amounted to only 300 million francs against total assets of 9,670 millions.

The debts of individuals in all trades amounted to 8,600 million francs, of which 6,900 millions consisted of mortgages as contrasted with total assets of 36,200 millions. This sum includes agricultural debt to a very small amount, since about two thirds of the farmers possess so small a fortune that they were free from the capital levy and made no report.

Corporations of all kinds had assets of 38,400 million francs. Their debts were 27,700 million francs of which 2,200 millions were covered by mortgages. The biggest part of these debts, 21,300 million francs, was owed by the joint-stock companies. But the amount of the debts varies with each type of business. Naturally, they are very high in case of the banks, 91 percent; in insurance, 94 percent; and in the hotel trade, 75 percent; as against 44 percent in industrial joint-stock companies.

The whole private debt of persons and corporations, according to the statistics of the capital levy, amounted to 36,300 million francs. To this sum must be added the debts of the public authorities such as the Confederation, federal railways, cantons, and communes, amounting to about 13,000 million francs, so that the grand total is about 50,000 million francs.

The public debt is mainly consolidated into long-term bonds. In 1950 the debt of the Confederation, exclusive of the federal railways, was made up of 6,100 million francs of consolidated debt, 260 millions of floating debt and 1,300 millions of other debt, which consists mainly of Treasury bills. The cantons at the end of 1949 had a small floating debt of 177 million francs against 1,981 million francs of consolidated debt. In towns of over 10,000 population, the relation was even more favorable: 51 million francs of floating debt and 1,369 millions of consolidated debt. It should also be mentioned that the debts of the cantons and communes are in several cases more or less covered by productive assets such as forests, state banks, electricity plants, and gas works.

CREDIT INSTRUMENTS

The mortgage is of course the most common form of credit instrument in the Swiss banking system. In 1950, the banks had 11,914 million francs invested in mortgages, or 43.5 percent of their assets. Their security holdings were of relatively less importance, amounting to 2,754 million francs, of which 83.4 percent was in domestic obligations, 6.8 percent in domestic stocks, 8.7 percent in foreign obligations, and 1.1 percent in foreign stocks.

Although the banks are the principal lenders on mortgages, other lenders play a considerable role in this field and hold about one fourth of all the mortgages. In 1945, according to the statistics of the capital levy in that year, there were 81,000 taxpayers who owned 2,200 million francs in mortgages. At the end of 1948 the insurance companies owned mortgages amounting to 1,400 million francs. To these figures must be added the mortgages held by cantons and municipalities of 400–500 million francs. The total of non-bank mortgage credit outstanding was estimated at about 4,000 million francs at the end of 1950, in addition to the 12,000 million francs of mortgage loans of banks. It should be noted, however, that this total of 16,000 million francs is considerably less than the estimate of 24,000 million francs made by the National Bank for the same year, 1950, as the total of mortgage indebtedness.

Call loans and time loans are relatively important. Such credit is usually granted only on collateral security. At the end of 1950 call loans amounted to 4,200 million francs, of which 3,300 million francs were collateral and of this amount 1,400 millions were covered by mortgages. Most of the time loans were also covered; 996 millions by mortgages, 600 millions by other security, leaving only 152 millions uncovered out of the total of 1,748 million francs. These figures do not include the loans made to public bodies such as cantons and communes, which amounted to 846 million francs at the end of 1950.

The bill of exchange is of little importance in the Swiss banking system. At the end of 1950 there were in the portfolios of all the Swiss banks only 2,482 million francs of such bills, or 9.1 percent of their assets. If from this total is deducted the 1,086 million francs which represent bills of the Confederation, the cantons and the communes, the total for bills of exchange originating in commerce is only 1,396 million francs.

The assets and liabilities of all banks, as of the end of 1950, are shown in Table 1.

TABLE 1

ASSETS AND LIABILITIES OF ALL BANKS, DECEMBER 31, 1950

(AMOUNTS IN MILLIONS OF SWISS FRANCS)

Assets	*Amount*	*Percent of Total*
Cash on hand and due from other banks	2,922.8	10.6
Bills of exchange	2,482.1	9.1
Call loans	4,204.5	15.3
Time loans	1,747.6	6.4
Loans to public corporations	846.4	3.1
Mortgage credits	11,913.7	43.5
Securities	2,754.1	10.1
Other assets	514.0	1.9
Total	27,385.2	100.0
Liabilities		
Demand deposits	5,985.9	21.9
Due to banks	1,422.0	5.2
Savings deposits	9,262.1	33.8
Other time deposits	1,526.9	5.6
Fixed deposits (obligations)	4,503.4	16.4
Bonds outstanding	553.2	2.0
Loans from central mortgage banks	1,094.8	4.0
Other liabilities	629.6	2.3
Capital	1,538.4	5.6
Reserves	868.9	3.2
Total	27,385.2	100.0

To describe briefly certain of the items: "Savings deposits" (*Spareinlagen*) represents the savings of the middle-class individual, who makes deposits up to an amount often limited by the bank to 5,000 francs, and receives interest somewhat higher than that on other kinds of deposits. Withdrawals from such accounts are usually restricted in both time and amount.

The "Other time deposits" include the savings deposits recorded in the *Einlageheft,* and the accounts entered in the deposit book (*Depositenheft*), which resemble credit accounts. Both of these are usually unlimited in amount and unrestricted in time and amount of withdrawal. The difference between savings books and deposit books is largely a matter of technical banking procedure relating to such matters as the amount that may be deposited, the manner of withdrawals, and the rate of interest. Time deposits are not used by large commercial firms, but are often used by retail business and small traders. A third category of account included under this head is the medium-term and long-term deposit (*Kreditoren auf Zeit*) made for a fixed period of two months to two years, with interest fixed by mutual agreement. No book is issued to the depositor, but simply a certificate. These funds come from trade and industrial firms seeking temporary investment and are often sought by the banks as an aid in "window-dressing" over the end of a year.

The item which appears on the balance sheet as "Fixed deposits (obligations)"—*Kassenobligationen*—is one of the most interesting and important, since it is characteristic of the Swiss banking system and peculiar to it. These are short-term bonds running from 3 to 8 years and bearing coupons payable half-yearly. They are usually issued in round amounts of 500, 1,000, 5,000 or more francs, usually to bearer; they are transferable and therefore can be used as security for loans, but they are not quoted on the stock exchange. They can be cashed at the offices of the bank at the option of the holder.

The banks issue these obligations as a way of providing themselves with medium-term funds, staggering maturities so that liquidity can be assured and conversion maintained. The only legal regulation in regard to them is the necessity, for banks with total assets of more than 20 million francs, of reporting to the National Bank any increase in the interest offered. The object of this provision is to obviate any substantial or abrupt change. Otherwise, the rate of interest is governed by the maturity of the obligation and the state of the money and capital markets. The National Bank has no actual right of veto over an increase in the interest rate, but can call attention to the fact that central banking authorities do not regard the change as desirable. The banks usually follow the course indicated by the National Bank, and, in place of an increase in interest rates, may reduce the period for which the bonds are to run.

At the end of 1950 a rate of 2.5 percent applied to obligations with a life of 5 to 8 years. All the banks together had 4,500 million francs of bonds outstanding, an amount equal to 16 percent of their total assets. At the large banks these obligations amounted to only 10 percent of assets; at cantonal banks they amounted to 20 percent, and at local banks to 24 percent of all assets. By this device the Swiss banks are able to raise funds in a manner which is unknown in other countries.

BANKING SYSTEM

ORIGINS OF THE BANKING SYSTEM

The outstanding feature of Swiss banking is the lack of specialization. Considerable insight into the present situation can be obtained from a study of the origins of Swiss banking institutions. Private banks have been in existence since the beginning of the eighteenth century, but their banking operations were often mixed with other business such as forwarding and transportation. In 1755 the government of Zurich founded an institution for investing the liquid funds of the state in, for example, loans to foreign countries. It was first called the Staatliche Zinskommission, but was later named Leu and Company, from the name of its first chairman. In 1854 it was changed into a joint-stock company.

For some time after the foundation of this bank, no other credit institutions were established except savings banks with a philanthropic purpose. Ribbon and braid manufacturers in Basel founded savings banks for factory workers at the end of the eighteenth century, and at the same time in Bern, Basel, and Geneva savings banks for workers and domestic servants were founded. By 1835 there were approximately 100 of these philanthropic savings banks. Philanthropic motives were also present in the establishment of some cantonal banks founded after 1834 primarily to provide credit for farmers and small traders.

After 1850, under the influence of the brothers Pereire who founded the Crédit Mobilier in France, commercial banks were established in Geneva, Zurich, Basel, St. Gall, and Winterthur. These banks (which are still in existence or have been amalgamated with other banks), as well as the various local banks founded about the same time, provided credit for commerce and industry. Some of them also combined with their banking transactions a forwarding, insurance, warehouse, or even a coal business for a time.

In spite of the credit provided by these banks and the cantonal banks, the small traders and farmers found their credit needs still unsatisfied and began to found cooperative credit societies on the model of the Schulze-Delitzsch societies in Germany. In 1869 there was founded in Bern the Schweizerische Volksbank which has grown to be one of the largest banks in Switzerland. After 1887, farmers also began to found cooperative credit institutions after the model of the Raiffeisen banks in Germany, and these banks have grown rapidly in the last few decades. Other cooperative banks have been founded for special purposes. In 1911 the association of Swiss cooperative societies founded a bank of its own. In 1927 the trade unions and cooperative societies together founded the Genossenschaftliche Zentralbank. After 1931 several building societies were founded to finance housing, but these never became very important. Proposals for a special bank to finance exports have never been realized because of the opposition of the large banks.

PREDOMINANCE OF MIXED BANKING

Although these banks were organized to serve special needs, Swiss banking, on the whole, has been characterized from the earliest times by wide versatility. The early combination of banking with other kinds of business has disappeared, but there is still a tendency towards a mixed or department-store banking. Thus the bigger banks not only grant commercial credits but also cooperate in the issuance of securities. In fact, in some banks the security portfolio amounts to 10 or 11 percent of assets. At the end of 1950 the security portfolio of all the banks together amounted to 10.1 percent of assets, mostly in the form of obligations and mortgage bonds. Mortgage credit is granted by all banks. In the large commercial banks mortgages comprise only 6.6

percent of the assets, while in the savings banks the proportion is 70 percent of assets, and in the mortgage banks, 72 percent.

The English type of deposit bank is almost unknown in Switzerland. All banks grant all kinds of credit, except that the savings and mortgage banks do not make call loans or discount bills of exchange. Competition is therefore keen, and, in view of the large number of banks, results in a low rate of profit. In 1950 the rate of return on capital and reserves varied from 4.9 percent in the case of the savings banks to 5.0 percent for local banks, 5.2 percent for cantonal banks, 6.2 percent for the large commercial banks and 8.0 percent for the loan banks. The present structure (1950) of the Swiss banking system is shown in Table 2.[1]

TABLE 2
STRUCTURE OF SWISS BANKING

Type	*Number*	*Number of Branches*	*Percent of all Banking Assets*
Large commercial banks	5	182	29.1
Cantonal banks	27	1,067	38.5
Other local banks	86	315	6.7
Mortgage banks	87	470	11.6
Savings banks	117	364	8.2
Cooperative banks	924		3.6
Other banks	65		2.3
Total	1,311	2,398	100.0

Many of these banks have branches only in their own commune or canton; others have branches throughout Switzerland. There are six branches of Swiss banks abroad—three in England, two in the United States, and one in the Argentine. In banking as in industry and agriculture, the middle-sized and small banks predominate. Of the 1,311 banks listed above, 659 had total assets of 1 million francs or less; 373 had assets of 1 to 5 million francs; 268 banks had assets of 5 million to 500 million francs; 6 banks had assets of 500 to 1,000 million francs, and only 5 banks were larger.[2] There are also 90 private banks which are not included in the table.

CONCENTRATION AND AMALGAMATION

During the first decades of the twentieth century, concentration and amalgamation reduced the number of banks. In 1906 there were 9

1 The tabulation does not include the Schweizerische Nationalbank and its assets of 6,600 million francs.

2 See p. 705.

large banks; in 1921, there were 8; in 1933 there were 7; and by 1945 there were only 5. Of the four which disappeared, only one went into bankruptcy; the others were amalgamated with the remaining banks. The number of cantonal banks has remained at 27 since about 1930, but these have absorbed a number of the small local banks during the last twenty years. The large banks have also absorbed many small banks. The rate of concentration has slowed down somewhat since 1930. Between 1906 and 1929 a total of 96 banks disappeared, while in the two decades between 1930 and 1950, only 22 banks disappeared.

PROFESSIONAL ORGANIZATIONS

Swiss bankers have a variety of professional organizations. The Association of Large Banks was founded in 1897, and the Association of Cantonal Banks in 1909. They cooperate by agreements regarding interest and commissions, the issue of securities, and the quotas for such issues. As a general organization for all the banks, the Schweizerische Bankiervereinigung was founded in 1911. Since 1934 there has been also an organization of private bankers. Most local banks are also members of the Association of Local and Savings Banks.

THE COMMERCIAL BANKS

Only the five large banks are commercial banks in the true sense of the word. With the exception of Leu and Company, they were all founded during the second half of the nineteenth century. From the very beginning they played an active part in international finance, but their greatest expansion came after 1920 when political and monetary disturbances in the rest of the world brought to Switzerland large amounts of foreign funds and forced the banks to look abroad to find investment outlets. By 1931 it was estimated that one third of their outstanding loans were foreign.

These large banks did not escape the catastrophes, political and economic, of the years after 1930. Only one of them failed—the Banque Suisse d'Escompte—but five of them found their capital impaired. Only the Schweizerischer Bankverein of Basel and the Schweizerische Kreditanstalt of Zurich remained completely intact. Although the number of banks had been reduced to five by the end of 1950, their total assets had reached a new high point, as shown in the balance sheet presented in Table 3.

TABLE 3
PRINCIPAL BALANCE SHEET ITEMS OF FIVE LARGE BANKS
(AMOUNTS IN MILLIONS OF SWISS FRANCS)

Assets	*Amount*	*Percent of Total*
Cash on hand and due from other banks	1,804	23
Call loans	1,995	25
Time loans	556	7
Bills of exchange	1,902	24
Securities	929	12
Loans to public corporations	126	1
Mortgage credits	525	6
Other assets	140	2
Total	7,977	100
Liabilities		
Sight deposits	3,905	49
Savings deposits	846	11
Other time deposits	436	5
Fixed deposits (obligations)	782	10
Due to bankers	1,004	13
Other equities	345	4
Capital	475	6
Reserves	184	2
Total	7,977	100

The call loans of the large commercial banks are quite different from the call loans on securities made by banks in the United States. In Switzerland nearly one fourth of these loans were on mortgage security, and about two thirds were advanced against collateral security. They are extended to finance business rather than security speculation. The portfolio of bills of exchange increased from 446 million francs in 1938 to 1,902 millions in 1950. This great increase was caused mainly by the fact that in 1950 large amounts were loaned on short-term to government bodies, especially to the Confederation. In the large banks 45 percent of the portfolio of bills consisted of Treasury bills.

The security portfolio of these banks also increased after 1938, rising from 293 million francs in that year to a peak of 1,357 millions in 1945 and then falling off to 929 millions in 1950. It was made up as follows in 1950:

Securities	*Amount in Millions of Swiss Francs*
Swiss obligations and mortgage bonds	385
Foreign bonds	239
Foreign stocks	22
Swiss stocks	87
Obligations of Swiss banks, trust companies and others	196
Total	929

The large banks play an important role in the issuing of securities, foreign as well as domestic. In the issue of government obligations and securities of small local enterprises the large banks are joined by the cantonal banks and the local commercial banks. In some cases the banks organize special corporations to place securities in the hands of the public; these may function either as investment trusts or as trust companies. In other cases the banks merely open lists of shares to be signed at the bank counter by subscribers.

On the liability side of the balance sheet, the capital of these banks did not change very much between 1938 and 1950. Two of the five banks have capital stock outstanding of more than 100 million francs; two others have between 50 and 100 millions, and the smallest has a capital of 20 million francs. Checking accounts and sight deposits more than doubled in the same period, increasing from 1,616 million francs in 1938 to 3,905 million francs in 1950. Savings deposits increased less rapidly, from 537 million francs to 846 millions. These increases were brought about by inflation, the general prosperity within the country, and by the influx of funds from foreign countries. The fixed deposit obligations of the banks increased very little.

The total assets of these five banks, which represent 29.1 percent of all Swiss banking assets, were in 1950 divided as follows:

Bank	*Assets in Millions of Swiss Francs*
Schweizerischer Bankverein	2,670
Schweizerische Kreditanstalt	2,265
Schweizerische Bankgesellschaft	1,698
Schweizerische Volksbank	1,099
Leu and Company	243

Three of the banks have their head office in Zurich, the others in Basel and Bern. Four of them employ more than 1,000 persons each and altogether they employ 9,923 of the total 20,486 bank personnel of the country.

THE CANTONAL BANKS AND THE LOCAL COMMERCIAL BANKS

The commercial banking business is carried on not only by the five large banks described above, but also by two groups which are not strictly commercial banks. These are the 27 cantonal banks (with 1,067 branches) and the local banks, which do a mixed banking business. The total number of these banks did not change between 1930 and 1950 but some smaller banks were absorbed by them during that period. The largest is the Zürcher Kantonalbank with assets of 2,033 million francs in 1950, which make it the equal in size of the "large" banks. The next five banks in order of size in Vaud, Bern, St. Gall, Lucerne, and Thurgau, had, in 1950, total assets ranging from 500 million to 800 million francs; all the others had smaller total assets and some had less than 100 million francs. Altogether they represent 38.5 percent of the total banking assets of the country. Three of these banks in the cantons of Zug and Vaud are organized as joint-stock companies, but the others are owned by the governments of their cantons, so that about one third of the bank capital of Switzerland is government-owned. The cantonal banks employ about one fourth of the banking personnel of the country.

The balance sheet for the cantonal banks illustrates their mixed type of business. The principal items at the end of 1950 are shown in Table 4.

It is evident from these figures that loans on mortgages are the most important asset of the cantonal banks, making up 59 percent of the total. In three of these banks (in Bern, Zurich, and Vaud) the proportion is 73 percent; for all others it is only 52 percent. Because of a larger proportion of urban property used as security at the cantonal banks, the interest charged on such loans averaged 3.53 percent, a trifle higher than the average rate charged by the savings banks (3.52 percent). The rate was, however, a trifle lower than the average of 3.56 percent charged by the special mortgage banks.

The call loans made by the cantonal banks resemble those made by the large banks; 60 percent of the call loans are secured by mortgages, most of the rest by securities. The total of these loans is nearly double the figure of 554 million francs in 1938. Nearly half (46 percent) of the bills of exchange held by the cantonal banks consisted of obliga-

TABLE 4
BALANCE SHEET FOR THE CANTONAL BANKS, DECEMBER 31, 1950
(AMOUNTS IN MILLIONS OF SWISS FRANCS)

Assets		*Amount*	*Percent of Total*
Bills of exchange		411	4
Cash on hand and due from banks		395	4
Call loans		1,045	10
Loans		727	7
Loans to public corporations		523	5
Mortgages		6,247	59
Securities			
Foreign	0.2		
Swiss stocks	46.0		
Swiss bonds	965.0	1,011	10
Other assets		177	1
Total		10,536	100
Liabilities			
Demand deposits		1,147	11
Due to banks		195	2
Other time deposits		841	8
Savings deposits		4,085	39
Fixed deposits (obligations) and debentures		2,604	25
Loans from the Central Mortgage Bank		518	5
Other liabilities		172	1
Capital		646	6
Reserves		328	3
Total		10,536	100

tions of the Treasury. This figure of 411 million francs represents a sharp increase over the 130 million francs of bills held in 1938. The volume of securities held in 1950 was greater than the 769 million francs held in 1938, but represented a substantial decline from the peak figure of 1,392 million francs in 1945.

On the liability side of the balance sheet the greatest increases since 1938 have occurred in savings accounts, which showed a growth of about 1,000 million francs, and in checking accounts and sight deposits with a growth of about half that amount. Mortgage bonds increased by only 200 million francs,[3] and the banks' own debentures declined slightly from 473 million to 469 million francs. The public preferred short investments during those uneasy years.

[3] Issued by the two central mortgage banks.

LOCAL BANKS

Another group of banks which do a mixed banking business consists of 86 local banks with 171 branches. They are small, and only two of them have a capital of more than 15 million francs. In spite of their number their assets represent only 6.7 percent of total banking assets. They employ 1,347 persons. The principal items in their combined statements at the end of 1950 appear in Table 5:

TABLE 5
COMBINED STATEMENTS OF LOCAL BANKS, DECEMBER 31, 1950
(AMOUNTS IN MILLIONS OF SWISS FRANCS)

Assets	*Amount*	*Percent of Total*
Cash on hand and due from banks	114	7
Call loans	576	31
Bills of exchange	95	5
Time loans	151	8
Loans to public corporations	23	1
Mortgage credits	619	34
Securities	197	11
Other assets	51	3
Total	1,826	100
Liabilities		
Demand deposits	290	16
Due to banks	63	4
Time and savings deposits	734	40
Fixed deposits (obligations)	276	15
Loans from central mortgage banks	132	7
Other liabilities	153	8
Capital	128	7
Reserves	50	3
Total	1,826	100

Of the call loans, 42.9 percent were secured by mortgages and 43.5 percent by other collateral.

Of the three groups of banks which do a commercial banking business, the large banks show the highest rate of net profit, 6.20 percent of own capital and reserves in 1950. The cantonal banks had a net profit of 5.24 percent, and the local banks 5.01 percent.

TRUST COMPANIES AND INVESTMENT TRUSTS

Trust companies, somewhat similar to American and British investment trusts, were founded by the large Swiss banks about 1870 when capital was needed for the building of railways. Later (about 1890) other similar corporations were organized to provide funds for the electrical industry. This development reached its height about 1930. In 1931 there were 48 of these corporations with capital and reserves of 997 million francs and total assets of 1,946 million francs; in 1938 there were 40 corporations with capital of 523 million francs and total assets of only 987 million francs; in 1950 there were only 31 with a capital of 367 million francs and total assets of 659 million francs. This shows clearly the effects of the depression in world economy.

About three quarters of the capital now provided by these trusts is for the electrical industry. Two thirds of their assets consist of securities and direct participations. The portfolio of securities contains 83 percent shares and 17 percent bonds. The activity of these corporations in the export of capital is indicated by the fact that foreign securities comprise 65 percent and Swiss securities only 35 percent of the portfolio. This capital export not only has great importance for the Swiss balance of payments, in that interest and dividends brought in from foreign countries make payment for imported goods possible, but also brings to the Swiss machine industry many orders from abroad.

The banks also furthered the foundation of true investment trusts, in so far as their clients wished it, in order to distribute the risk of investment in different countries and in different branches of the economy. The first such institution was established in Geneva in 1849, as the Société civile d'emploi de fonds. In 1950 there were about 45 investment trusts in Switzerland.

SAVINGS INSTITUTIONS

In 1825 there existed 44 of these institutions and by 1918 their number had risen to 1,400. In that year depositors numbered 2,700,-

000 and deposits amounted to 2,600 million francs. Since 1918 no statistics have been published about the small institutions such as factory savings banks and school savings banks, but in the statistics published by the National Bank, one can follow year by year the development of savings banks proper. In 1950 there existed 117 specialized savings banks, although other types of banks also accepted savings deposits. At the end of 1950, savings deposits were held by the following institutions:

TABLE 6
SAVINGS BANK STATISTICS, DECEMBER 31, 1950
(AMOUNTS IN MILLIONS OF SWISS FRANCS)

Institution	*Number of Accounts*	*Amount of Deposits*
Cantonal banks	2,401,840	3,920.8
Savings banks	928,414	1,716.7
Mortgage banks	655,015	1,124.7
Cooperative loan banks	404,156	599.2
Other local banks	368,471	565.6
Large banks	280,086	301.5
All other banks	4,718	6.4
Total	5,042,700	8,234.9

It is evident that most savings depositors prefer the cantonal banks and the savings banks proper. The cantonal banks have the advantage of the protective guarantee of the government, while other institutions have a guarantee, in case of bankruptcy, only to the amount of 5,000 francs on a single deposit.

The 117 savings banks have relatively little capital of their own. In 1950 their capital and reserves amounted to 156 million francs as against total liabilities of 2,200 million francs. The largest part of the liabilities consists of savings deposits—1,700 million francs—and cash obligations—215 million francs. Other liabilities do not play an important role. The assets of the savings banks are composed mainly (70 percent) of mortgages and about 14 percent of securities. The resultant lack of liquidity often has serious consequences and was one of the reasons for the enactment of the Federal Banking Law of 1934, which will be described later.

The interest paid by the savings banks is stabilized among the different banks as much as possible. In consequence of the liquidity of the capital market in the last two decades, rates have declined. About

1930 they were between 4 percent and 4.3 percent, but in the period of the depression they sank very quickly. In 1939 they averaged 2.8 percent and in 1950 about 2.6 percent.

The saving propensity of the Swiss people, as far as can be judged by the development of the savings banks, has not diminished in recent years, in spite of the low interest and the depreciation of money. The number of savings books was nearly two million in 1908 and five million in 1950, while the savings deposits amounted to 1,600 million francs in 1908 and to 8,200 million francs in 1950. This increase was much greater than the increase occurring in the population and the depreciation taking place in the value of money.

In order to arrive at the full amount of savings, there should be added to the savings deposits the time deposits without special protection.[4] At the end of 1950 there were 402,945 deposit books of this kind, of which 251,031 were issued by the large banks and only 70,786 by the cantonal banks. The time deposits of the same year amounted to 1,027 million francs of which more than half—545 million francs—were in the large banks, 268 millions in the local banks and 164 millions in the cantonal banks.

It should be noted that in Switzerland the "man in the street" owns securities. The statistics of the capital levy of 1945 show that among those possessing from 5,000 to 25,000 francs of capital assets there were, besides the 80,000 holders of savings deposits, 25,000 holders of debentures, and nearly 10,000 holders of shares. Of their total assets of 793 million francs reported by this middle income group, only 499 million francs were in savings deposits.

MORTGAGE CREDIT INSTITUTIONS

Corresponding to the generally unspecialized character of banking, there are only a few pure mortgage credit institutions, and nearly all banks extend some mortgage credit. At the end of 1950, bank mortgage loans amounted to 11,900 million francs; their distribution is shown in Table 7.

About 52.4 percent of all mortgage credit was extended by the cantonal banks; then follow the mortgage credit banks with 19.3 percent, and the savings banks with 13.1 percent. Those three categories

[4] See p. 699.

TABLE 7
MORTGAGE CREDITS
(AMOUNTS IN MILLIONS OF SWISS FRANCS)

Institution	*Amount*	*Percent of Total*
Cantonal banks	6,247	52.4
Savings banks	1,571	13.2
Cooperative credit associations	621	5.2
Local banks		
Mortgage credit institutions	2,300	19.3
Other local banks	619	5.2
Large banks	524	4.4
Other banks	32	0.3
Total	11,914	100.0

together hold 85 percent of all mortgages. It is worthy of note that even the large banks, which are primarily commercial banks, invested 500 million francs in mortgages. On the other hand, the 87 mortgage credit institutions did not invest all the capital at their disposal in mortgages. In 1950 their total assets amounted to 3,173 million francs of which 2,300 millions were invested in mortgages, while one third was in securities, call loans, and the like.

Mortgage credit institutions are not specialized by locale as urban and rural. Three or four of the 87 institutions operate exclusively in urban mortgage credit, while the main part of the business of the 50 banks in country districts is rural mortgage credit. The rest of the banks carry on their affairs in both town and country.

Long term agricultural credit is organized according to the farmers' needs. Before the First World War, farmers asked for federal participation in mortgage credit, either in the form of a federal mortgage bank or through aid extended by the central bank. Both forms were impracticable. The cantonal banks opposed the establishment of a federal mortgage bank, and aid from the central bank was impossible. Later, the Confederation tried to further agricultural credit by other measures: for example, in 1921 it introduced a coupon tax for shares and obligations, the aim of which was to channel investments from the securities market to the mortgage market. In 1930 there were founded two central mortgage institutions: The Pfandbriefzentrale der schweizerischen Kantonalbanken and the Pfandbriefbank der schweizerischen Hypothekarinstitute, both of which are joint-stock companies. The capital of the former was subscribed by the cantonal banks and, of the latter, by the local mortgage credit institutions. In 1950, in loans to member banks, the Pfandbriefzentrale extended 505 million francs, the Pfandbriefbank 579 millions. There has been up to now no need to establish special banks to make soil improvement and conservation loans, since the Confederation and the cantons have given subsidies for this purpose. Cantonal and local banks have also given credit for such improvements.

Farmers have complained from early times of the high interest charged them. In some of the agricultural cantons usury laws dating from the Middle Ages are still in existence. The practical significance of these restrictions is not very important because the actual rate of interest is below the legal maximum. In fact the rate of interest on mortgages has fallen rapidly in the last three decades. In 1921 the important cantonal banks demanded an average interest of 5.5 percent on a first mortgage; in 1930 it was 4.95 percent; following the depression, it was cut in 1939 to 3.75 percent; in 1950 there was an average rate of 3.55 percent on the total of all mortgage debts including second mortgages. But the amount of agricultural debt is so high that, in spite of these low rates of interest, debt is burdensome and the farmers still complain.

The Farmers Union estimated the total debt of agriculture for 1949 at 5,700 million francs; that is equal to 46 percent of the capital of 12,300 million francs invested in agriculture. Therefore the reduction of agricultural debt is a very important problem. Some of the banks try to reduce these debts by requiring from their debtors the repayment of a certain percentage of the debt annually. In addition, the Confederation enacted in 1940 a federal law which, upon implementation by the cantons, required the amortization of all agricultural debt in a period of 20 years to 25 years. The law attempted also to prevent high agricultural debt through prescriptions concerning the right of inheritance. By 1952 only six cantons (including the largest, Zurich and Bern) had enacted the legislation necessary to require debt amortization.

COOPERATIVE BANKS

The first experiments in organizing credit on the basis of cooperation were made by workmen and small shopkeepers. In 1869 the Schweizerische Volksbank was established on the model of the

Schulze-Delitzsch cooperatives in Germany to facilitate short-term credit. This institution was popular with many borrowers in the lower middle class, because share ownership gave a claim to credit which, under certain circumstances, could amount to three times the value of the share. The bank developed very rapidly. At the height of its success in 1930, it had 100,000 members with shares outstanding of 189 million francs; its total assets of 1,500 million francs put it in a class with the large commercial banks. But the magnitude of its business, which extended even to other countries, proved fatal to the Schweizerische Volksbank. About 1930 it had to be reorganized and was obliged to limit its activity. At the end of 1950, assets amounted to 1,000 million francs, while the balance sheets of the three large banks ranged from 1,700 million to 2,600 million francs.

Cooperative short-term credit has less importance for the lower middle income class in Switzerland than in other countries. The reason is that cantonal banks and a great number of local banks give short-term credit to the man in the street and thereby make cooperative credit unnecessary. They also extend short-term credit to farmers. After 1880 there was an effort to found cooperative societies to further rural credit. In 1887 several of these were established in the canton of Bern, based on the Raiffeisen system. In 1902, 25 of these banks were joined in an association which served them as a central institution for clearing accounts. At the end of 1950 this association contained 912 local Raiffeisen banks, and there were 12 similar institutions in Vaud canton. The balance sheet of all these banks then amounted to 983 million francs. Their own capital and reserves amounted only to 52 million francs against 922 million francs of liabilities, of which 623 million francs were deposits and 181 million francs were fixed deposits (obligations).[5] Because of the relatively small demand for short-term agricultural credit, Raiffeisen banks quite often make mortgage loans.

Swiss labor possesses several credit institutions in the form of cooperative societies. Since 1911 the association of Swiss cooperative societies located in Basel has had its own banking department for members. Later, some local cooperative societies began to accept deposits from their members. When labor banks started to increase in the United States and Germany about the year 1920, Swiss labor began to follow this example. In 1927 the association of cooperative societies

[5] See p. 699.

TABLE 8
COOPERATIVE RURAL CREDIT SOCIETIES
(AMOUNTS IN MILLIONS OF SWISS FRANCS)

Assets	*Amount*	*Percent of Total Assets*
Cash on hand	11	1
Mortgage loans	621	63
Time loans	41	4
Call loans secured by mortgages	38	4
Other call loans	38	4
Loans to governmental units	55	6
Securities	10	1
Deposits due from banks	157	16
Other assets	12	1
Total	983	100

and the federation of trade unions founded the Bank der Genossenschaften und Gewerkschaften, which changed its name in the following year to Genossenschaftliche Zentralbank. Since then this bank has become more and more important. In 1950 its total assets amounted to 267 million francs with capital stock of 20.6 million francs and reserves of 5.3 million francs. The assets were composed mainly of mortgages and securities. The bank refused to finance any enterprise involved in politics or labor difficulties.

CENTRAL BANKING

The reason for the late establishment of a central bank in Switzerland lies in the federal character of the government. An article added to the Constitution in 1891 gave the Confederation the right to establish a central bank with a monopoly of note issue, but there was so much difference of opinion about the legal form which the bank should take and about the place where it should be located that it was not until 1907 that the Schweizerische Nationalbank really began to function, and 36 other banks stopped issuing notes.

The Swiss National Bank is a joint-stock company with an authorized capital of 50 million francs of which only half has been paid in. At the end of 1950 the cantons and cantonal banks owned 55 percent of the stock, and the other 45 percent was divided among nearly 6,900 private shareholders, some of whom owned no more than 5 shares. The Board of Directors consists of 40 members, of whom 25 are nominated by the Confederation, and 15 are elected by the shareholders in general meeting. Close supervision and control of the Bank is exercised by the Board of Delegates (Bankausschuss) which consists of seven members nominated by the Board of Directors. The highest managing and executive authority of the National Bank is the Board of General Managers (Direktorium), consisting of three members, who are nominated by the Federal Council on the recommendation of the Board of Directors. The Federal Council elects from among its members the Chairman and the Vice-Chairman. Since a majority of the Bank's executive authorities are chosen by the Federal Council it follows that the Federal Government exercises a considerable influence on the Bank. It has also to approve the annual accounts and report. Thus the National Bank, although created in the form of a corporation, must be described as a mixed economic organization.

The main task of the central bank, according to the original wording of Article 39 of the Constitution, was to regulate the circulation of money and to facilitate payments. The law has been amended several times since 1905 and was in process of revision in 1950. The notes issued by the central bank must be covered by at least 40 percent in metal (formerly gold and silver, now only gold) and 60 percent in Swiss bills of exchange, checks, and bonds, or in foreign bills or checks, or in call or Lombard loans. Under the law of 1905, the notes were convertible into gold and silver. When the First World War broke out, conversion was suspended and the notes were declared to be legal tender. It was not until the federal law of December 20, 1929, that redemption was resumed. At the same time the bank was given the choice of redeeming its notes in gold coin, gold bars, or gold exchange. This arrangement was to operate until such time as other countries should resume redemption of their notes in gold coin. This moment never arrived. Switzerland devalued its currency on September 26, 1936, and redemption was again suspended, with the notes again declared legal tender. Switzerland like all other countries has not been able to resume convertibility of her notes. Until 1951 it was, under the existing provisions of the Constitution, possible to suspend note conversion only in the emergency of war, and the suspension after 1936 was a matter of emergency regulation. In April, 1951, however, in a national referendum, a revision of the Constitution was accepted which made it possible for conversion to be suspended also in times of monetary disturbance. In any case notes must, under the terms of the Constitution, be covered by gold and short-term assets. In this connection the duties of the bank of issue have been newly defined: it has the principal duty of controlling the monetary circulation of the country, facilitating payments and implementing a policy which will serve the general interests of the country in so far as credit and currency are concerned.

The total circulation of bank notes had never averaged more than 1,500 million francs up to 1939, but since that time it has grown so rapidly that by 1950 it averaged 4,200 million francs. The increase in bank clearings has also been rapid in recent years, and in 1950 the total amounted to 62,000 million francs, with an additional 1,500 million francs of intrabank clearings.

Although the banking law prescribed a gold reserve of 40 percent for notes issued by the National Bank, the actual holdings of gold increased even more rapidly than the volume of notes outstanding, and the ratio of gold to notes had risen to 128 percent by 1950. The volume of gold held by the central bank had been about 170 million francs in 1913 (not including the 23 million francs of silver which was then legal reserve). By 1920 the gold holdings had increased to 534 million francs, and by 1930 to 607 millions. A great increase during the next two years brought the total to 2,546 million francs in 1932. In 1945 the bank held 4,691 million francs and, in 1950, 6,179 million francs of gold. The dollar currencies held by the central bank did not increase as rapidly as the gold, and in 1950 amounted to only 298 million francs.

Rediscount operations of the central bank are nowadays of little importance. Between the years 1931 and 1950 its portfolio of bills varied from a yearly average of 6.2 million francs to a high point of 119 million francs in 1948. The rate of rediscount varied from 2 to 6 percent between 1907 and 1936, with 41 changes, but since 1936 it has remained constant at 1.5 percent. The National Bank also buys Treasury bills, but in most years has had less than 50 million francs invested in this form. In 1940 its holdings of the bills reached a high point of 143 million francs and in 1945 it held 112 million francs.

Loans on security collateral (Lombard loans) have never been an important item in the portfolio of the National Bank. Between 1931 and 1950 the total of such loans reached a high point of 88 million francs in 1935 and a low point of 17 million francs in 1943. The rate on such loans had been changed forty times between 1907 and 1936, between 3 and 7 percent; since 1936 it has remained stable at 2.5 percent.

The small volume of credit provided for the economy by the National Bank makes it difficult for the bank to exercise any control over business conditions through its rediscount or loan rate. There has been some pressure of public opinion on the bank to carry on open-market operations, but the present law sets narrow limits to such activity. The bank is permitted only to buy and sell gold, foreign exchange, Treasury bills, and easily convertible debentures. For the purchase of bonds with more than three months' maturity, the bank may use only its own capital. The project of April 21, 1953, for a new bank law, which is now under consideration, would give the bank the right to buy and sell federal and cantonal bonds and mortgage bonds of the central mortgage banks, without a limitation on the amount, but with the maturity of the debentures limited to two years.

The narrow limits imposed on the rediscount and open-market policy of the central bank do not prevent it from exercising an influence on the economy. On the contrary, its regulation of foreign exchange gives it great influence because of the importance of foreign trade, international banking and insurance, and tourist traffic. The National Bank is still of the opinion that stability of the foreign exchanges is the most desirable situation for the Swiss economy. After the First World War when dollar exchange rose from its prewar parity of 5.18 francs per dollar to 6.48 francs in December, 1920, with a depression in the export and the tourist trades, the bank made every effort to return to gold parity, and succeeded in doing so by the end of 1924. By means of its foreign exchange operations it maintained the gold position of the franc until 1936, when the government was forced to devalue by 30 percent. Since that time the bank has maintained the franc at that level, although it had the power to permit variation between 190 and 215 milligrams of gold, as compared with the former level of 290 milligrams. Switzerland refused to follow the example of other nations which devalued in 1949 in order to obtain an export advantage in foreign trade. By keeping its currency at a constant rate with gold, Switzerland has suffered no disadvantage.

An important function of the National Bank in recent years has been its control over the export of capital. Because of the public opposition to the large volume of foreign loans being made by Swiss banks, the National Bank attempted in 1925 to regulate such issues by means of a gentlemen's agreement with the large banks which were the most active in this field. In 1934 a change in the banking law made it obligatory for banks to inform the National Bank when they were planning an issue of foreign securities on the Swiss market, or when they were purchasing securities or making loans abroad of more than 10 million francs in amount or more than 12 months' maturity. The National Bank had the right, after examining the proposal, to set the conditions under which the operation could be carried out, or even to veto it if the state of the money market made it inadvisable. The Bank had, however, no jurisdiction over the terms of credit or the collateral for the loan; its function was to protect borrowers at home from an increase in the rate of interest because of such foreign issues.

Although in general the policies of the central bank have been approved by the public, since the depression of 1921 a constant fight has been waged against the bank by the group which calls itself the Free Economy Association. These followers of Silvio Gesell, known originally as the Free Land, Free Money Association, have agitated constantly for the abolition of fixed rates of exchange, gold parity, and gold cover for notes. During the long depression after 1930 they succeeded in sending representatives to the federal parliament and to some of the cantonal parliaments. They claimed credit for the devaluation of 1936 although the government had quite different reasons for taking such a step. During the inflation which followed the Second World War, the Free Money party tried to get a governmental promise that the purchasing power of money would be stabilized, and proposed a new article for the Constitution which would oblige the National Bank to regulate the circulation of money so as to provide full employment and stabilize the index number of the cost of living. The realistic populace refused to accept these rather Utopian proposals, and in the plebiscite of April 15, 1951, they were rejected by a vote of 622,000 to 88,000. It seems quite improbable that in the future this party will have any influence in Switzerland.

THE STATE AND THE BANKS

Intervention of the state in the field of banking can take many forms—legal chartering and control of private banks, financial aid to banks in distress, or the establishment of state banks. Since Switzerland adheres to the principle of freedom of trade in banking as in other economic activities, a government charter is not necessary in order to establish a bank. Only foreign banks which wish to establish a branch in Switzerland are obliged to obtain permission from the Confederation. However, the law does restrict the use of the name *bank* to corporations which comply with the general banking law, and does not permit a bank which wishes to carry on a commercial banking business to take the form of a cooperative enterprise. This last restriction was added to the banking law after the Schweizerische Volksbank, a large bank organized as a cooperative, had got into difficulties which required government intervention. The banking law requires also that the statute of each bank give a clear description of its functions and the methods of operation and control. Some bankruptcies have been caused in recent decades because banks attempted to carry on activities for which their form of organization was not suited.

Legal control over banking has been primarily concerned with the protection of depositors and especially of savings depositors. The canton Bern enacted such a law in 1847, and eleven other cantons followed this example, which was made possible by an article of the civil law permitting cantons to guarantee the assets of savings banks. The cantons also protect depositors by requiring regular publication of reports, by setting standards for liquidity, and by making periodic inspections.

Some of the legislation regarding banking has been directed rather at the control of the capital market than at the protection of the bank depositor. One of the first enactments of this type was that which created the Coupon Tax in 1921, designed to turn investors from securities to mortgages by levying special taxes on income from securities. Another effort to encourage investment in mortgages was made by the federal law of 1930 which limited the issue of mortgage bonds to two institutions, the central mortgage bank of the cantonal banks, and the central bank of the mortgage banks.[6] The bonds were to have maturities of ten to forty years, and the mortgages which secured the bonds were to be issued to an amount not exceeding two thirds of the market value of agricultural property, or three fourths of the value of urban property. It was hoped that by controlling the mortgage

[6] See p. 712.

bonds more strictly, they would become more popular as investments.

The effect of the depression of the 1930s brought about the enactment of the federal bank and savings banks law of November 8, 1934. This law made relatively little change in the provisions regarding savings: such deposits up to 5,000 francs were given a prior lien on assets in case of bank failure, and the cantons were required to provide certain pledges for savings deposits in their own territory up to 5,000 francs.

Most of the provisions of this law related to commercial banking, and went much further in the direction of control than previous legislation. The Federal Government had always been unwilling to take responsibility for the details of bank operation, since it did not want to be blamed in case of their failure. But the experience during the depression showed that in times of difficulty state financial help was often necessary, and it was hoped that if controls were set up in advance, some of the crises might be avoided. The text of the law therefore included for the first time provisions regarding the proportion of the banks' own capital to liabilities, and to general provisions for protecting bank creditors from loss. In cantonal and cooperative banks the capital must equal at least 5 percent of the mortgage credits and 10 percent of the liabilities. The purpose of this provision was to prevent mortgage banks from operating with too large a proportion of borrowed funds. Five percent of the net profit must be carried to reserves every year until reserves amount to 20 percent of capital.

The detailed regulation of liquidity was left to the Executive Order of February 25, 1935, which included the following:

> Against short-term liabilities there must be held a reserve in current and in liquid assets. Liquid assets include currency and deposits with the central bank; current assets include foreign exchange, call loans, coupons payable in 30 days and debentures eligible for rediscount by the central bank.
>
> Short-term liabilities are defined as demand, time and savings deposits, notes and debentures payable in 30 days.
>
> The total of current and liquid assets must be equal to at least 25 per cent of the short-term liabilities. If the ratio of short to total liabilities is high, this reserve ratio may be increased to a maximum of 50 per cent. Total liquid assets must be 2.5 to 5 per cent of short-term liabilities.

The actual situation with respect to these requirements was extremely good in the year 1950. For the different types of banks the required and actual reserves were as given in Table 9.

TABLE 9
PERCENT OF LIQUID AND CURRENT ASSETS

	TO SHORT-TERM LIABILITIES		TO TOTAL LIABILITIES	
Type of Bank	*Required*	*Actual*	*Required*	*Actual*
Large banks	42.6	81.1	30.1	57.3
Cantonal banks	29.7	76.3	6.3	16.2
Savings banks	25.3	116.3	3.8	17.5
Mortgage banks	25.9	61.7	3.6	8.5
Other local banks	31.9	73.5	8.5	19.6

These figures are for all banks in each category. Some of the individual banks were below the prescribed limits.

The law relies heavily on publicity for banking control in other respects. Each bank is required to publish its balance sheet once a year; banks with more than 20 million francs of assets must publish a balance sheet semiannually, and banks with 100 million francs of assets and above must publish quarterly reports. These latter banks must also send a monthly report to the National Bank for its own information but not for publication. Banks are required to have their accounts audited annually by an independent agency approved by the government. This agency must check the statutory and other requirements for each bank and report at once to the Federal Bank Commission if any impropriety is noted. Banks are permitted to postpone the demands of their depositors under certain conditions, if there is any danger of a run.

A second method by which the state intervenes in the field of banking is the rendering of financial aid to banks in distress. Before 1930, this happened only a few times, but after that year the occasions on which help was necessary were more frequent. A federal Farmers' Aid Fund (Bauernhilfskassen) set up in 1932, which gave to the cantons a yearly sum of 3 million francs to provide low-cost credit to farmers, was utilized to help rural banks in difficulties when farmers were unable to repay bank loans. As the crisis worsened, further intervention was necessary. In 1933 the Banque Suisse d'Escompte and the Schweizerische Volksbank were subjected to runs and the government came to their aid. Despite state aid to the Banque Suisse d'Escompte by a deposit of 20 million francs, the bank failed. In the case of the Schweizerische Volksbank the government took over 100 million francs of its capital stock, saving the bank but losing half of the sum. Two other banks, the cantonal banks of Bern and Neuchatel (closely affiliated with the hotel and the watch industries), were in difficulty and had to be assisted by the cantons and by the National Bank. A Federal Loan Bank was established in 1932 with government funds to assist banks which were in temporary difficulty, but few claims were made upon its aid.

The third way in which the state may intervene in the field of banking is by the establishment of banks with government funds. There have been many proposals that the National Bank should be owned by the Federal Government; one such proposal was rejected by a plebiscite in 1897. Although many of the cantonal banks are owned wholly or in part by their governments, nationalization of the central bank is an issue less popular now than formerly, and the Labor Party does not favor it. Most of the 43 municipal banks are very small, and nearly all are savings banks. Only a few have assets of more than 10 million francs, and in 1950 they had altogether only 381 million francs of assets, or 1.4 percent of all the banking assets of the country. About 1910 the Association of Swiss Towns discussed a proposal for establishing a large municipal bank to provide cheaper credit, but the plan was not carried out as it would not have been possible for it to raise sufficient capital.

Similar plans to organize a postal savings bank were also without effect. The private savings banks have such a dense network of branches over the country that other facilities are unnecessary except perhaps in the very distant mountain villages. The cantonal and regional banks fear the competition of a postal savings bank.

Postal checking accounts form a kind of state bank which is extremely popular in Switzerland. Holders of these giro accounts had 1,125 million francs on deposit at the end of 1950. The funds are in part redeposited with the Confederation Treasury (416 million francs in 1950) and the Treasury had borrowed another 132 million francs from the bank.

A federal bank for mortgage credit has been discussed but never established. Another type of federal bank for the making of security loans is still in existence but is utilized only at critical times. Founded in 1914 as the Darlehenskasse der Schweizerischen Eidgenossenschaft (Loan Fund of the Swiss Federation) its purpose was to make loans to enterprises which had suffered during the war. In 1924 the bank was closed but reopened in 1932. Its capital or guarantee fund of 100 million francs which should have been provided, 25 percent by private enterprise and 75 percent by the Confederation, was never paid in, but it made loans which reached a maximum of 89 million francs in 1935.

MONEY AND CAPITAL MARKET

The money and capital markets in Switzerland have always been influenced by general business conditions, and political events. When the Franco-Prussian War broke out in 1870, there was a certain amount of panic in the population. Because of the slight development of central banking, there was a crisis on the money market; the short-term credit system broke down and interest rates rose to 6 percent. Again in 1914, when the First World War broke out, the discount rate of the National Bank was raised within four days from 3.5 percent to 6 percent. The National Bank took a number of measures to stop the run on the banks, and among them called on the banks to limit payment on deposit accounts to 200 francs and on savings accounts to 50 francs.

The effects of the approaching Second World War were limited mainly to a withdrawal of foreign capital from Switzerland. The war was expected and caused no excitement. The circulation of bank notes increased considerably because of the currency needed by soldiers. It rose by 23 percent between August 15 and September 2, 1939, to 2,079 million francs, while in the same period the postal checking accounts diminished 10 percent. The discount rate of the National Bank remained at 1.5 percent and the Lombard rate at 2.5 percent; only the open-market rate increased from 1 percent to 1.25 percent.

Besides the foreign political events which influenced the capital and money markets there have also been political events in Switzerland which caused difficulty. Disturbances at the end of 1918 caused the discount rate of the National Bank on October 3 to be increased from 4.5 to 5 percent and the rate for advances against securities from 5 to 5.5 percent. At the end of 1922 there was a certain stringency on the money market and people feared that the proposal of the Labor Party for a capital levy would be approved by the plebiscite. The official discount and security loan rate did not increase, but the market rate mounted from 1.13 percent in October, 1922, to 1.83 percent in November and 2.29 percent in December.

In the summer of 1935 there were additional difficulties when the

Labor Party submitted another proposal to the plebiscite, which would have involved excessive outlays by the state. The market rate increased then from 1.50 percent on an average in March to 2.78 percent in July and the National Bank was forced to raise the bank rate from 2 to 2.5 percent and the security loan rate from 2.5 to 3.5 percent.

Apart from these political events, the situation of the money and capital markets is the result of business conditions. The supply of funds consists primarily of loans by banks to their clients. Ever since the central bank began to publish bank statistics, the total of bank liabilities has grown with few interruptions. In 1906 they amounted to 4,917 million francs and in 1920 to 11,282 million francs. Then in 1922 they fell to 10,878 million francs. In the favorable business conditions between 1924 and 1930 they grew again to 17,956 million francs. In the following years of depression they fell to 14,862 million francs in 1935. Since 1939 the liabilities have mounted year by year until they reached, in 1950, the sum of 24,350 million francs.

The capital funds of the banks increased from 956 million francs in 1906 to 2,407 million francs in 1950, with only one interruption, a decrease of 500 million francs between the years 1932 and 1940. The total of the banks' liabilities and capital has therefore grown from 5,873 million francs in 1906 to 26,757 million francs in 1950. But the increase is not so great if we consider the depreciation of the franc. Expressed in the 1914 value of money, 26,700 million francs amount to only 13,000 million francs.

In addition to the banks, there are also insurance companies, public corporations and private persons which extend credit. The security investments of the insurance companies have increased in recent years, and stood at 2,544 million francs in 1950. Their holdings of mortgages have shown a slight decline and amounted to 1,409 million francs. There is some tendency on the part of insurance companies to invest in real estate directly, in order to obtain a higher return and to protect themselves against possible depreciation of the franc. These investments amounted in 1950 to 286 million francs. A new factor in the capital market is the Federal Old Age and Dependents' Insurance, founded in 1947. This institution, at the end of 1950, had invested 1,300 million francs in the capital market.

International transactions have great importance on the money and capital markets of Switzerland. In the years before 1890 Switzerland imported, principally from France, more capital than was exported.

At the beginning of the twentieth century there began a capital exchange consisting of capital imports from France and capital exports mainly to Germany. Kellenberger [7] estimated the average capital export over the years 1911–13 at 164 million francs. During the war period between 1914 and 1920, capital exports surpassed imports by 1,400 million francs. From 1921 to 1923 there was, mainly because of the high trade deficit, a net capital inflow of 451 million francs. The prosperity between 1924 and 1930 produced a continual surplus of capital export, amounting to a total of 2,400 million francs. Although each year in the depression between 1931 and 1936 did not reflect a surplus of capital import, the whole period showed a surplus of about 2,000 million francs. In 1937 and 1939 there was again an export surplus, but in 1938 an import surplus, and the three years together had an export surplus of 423 million francs.

For a time after 1939 there are no precise figures for international capital transactions. However the fact that capital imports surpassed exports between 1939 and 1950 is evidenced by the increased holdings of gold and foreign exchange from 2,600 to 6,200 million francs. Since the deficit in the balance of trade was, in spite of higher exports, larger than before the war, and invisible exports such as tourist traffic brought in less during the war, the growth of gold and foreign exchange holdings can be explained only by an inflow of capital from abroad.

This invasion of "hot money" was considered undesirable by the central bank because of its inflationary implications. Therefore measures were taken to discourage foreign capital by limiting the acceptance of dollars resulting from exports, by refusing dollars resulting from the liquidation of investments, and by suspending interest on foreign deposits according to a gentlemen's agreement of 1950. For a time gold was paid out to the public with the hope that it would be hoarded. The Confederation also accepted gold from the central bank. At the end of 1946, its stock of gold amounted to 1,200 million francs.

The ease of the money market, caused by the influx of foreign capital, the return of Swiss capital, and favorable business conditions, is reflected in the clearing accounts of the central bank. Until 1930 these accounts never reached a yearly average of 200 million francs.

[7] Ed. Kellenberger, *Kapitalexport und Zahlungsbilanz* (Berne, 1939–42), I, 17, 124, 155, 245, 307 and II, 87, 245, 364.

But in the years between 1930 and 1932 they rose from 168 million to 1,075 million francs. In 1938 they amounted to 1,700 million francs and in 1950 to 1,500 million francs.

The effects of the favorable business conditions were also evidenced by the volume of postal giro transactions. From 489 million francs at the end of 1938 they rose to 1,100 million francs at the end of 1950.

The capacity of the capital market can be measured by statistics of capital issues. While the demand for new money, that is, the value of issues after deducting conversions, amounted to an average of 293 million francs from 1931 to 1939 on inland debentures, it averaged, in the years 1940 to 1945, 960 million francs and fell to 544 million francs for the years 1946 to 1950. The issue of foreign debentures played also a certain role, especially in the period of prosperity from 1926 to 1930 when an annual average of 196 million francs of foreign debentures were floated on the capital market. In the years 1931 to 1939, foreign debentures amounted to a yearly average of only 55 million francs and in the years 1940 to 1946 this form of capital export disappeared. It is only since 1947 that foreign debentures have again been issued in the Swiss market. In 1947 to 1949 they ranged from 50 million to 60 million francs and in 1950 they surpassed 210 million francs, the level of the years 1926 to 1930.

In normal times the issue of shares plays an important role in the capital market. Statistics of the capital of joint-stock companies are not a good measure of the amount of equity shares sold, because they include also the increase of capital which is not provided by the market. The capital of the joint-stock companies grew steadily between 1902 and 1931 from 1,800 to 9,000 million francs. In consequence of liquidations and reductions of capital it sank until by 1941 it was only 6,800 million francs, but by 1950 it had grown again to 8,600 million francs.

In the last century, and especially in the last 20 years, the rate of interest has fallen because of the strong development of savings and the influx of hot money. Although neither the central bank nor the government has followed a policy of cheap money, the situation of the market has brought about a low level of interest rates. Since 1936 the discount rate of the central bank has remained at the low level of 1.5 percent. The same stability at a very low level can be noted in the market rate. Between 1907 and 1936 this rate fluctuated frequently between a high of 4.69 percent in 1919 and a low point of 1.44 percent in 1931. Since 1937 the variations have not been important. By an agreement among the banks the market rate was fixed at 1 percent until September, 1939, and thereafter—with a short interruption in 1940 when it amounted to 1.5 percent—at 1.25 percent. This rate (1.25 percent) was continued until October, 1947, and then increased to 1.375 percent. In 1948 it rose, in consequence of a certain stringency in the market, to 1.75 percent, but has been stabilized since July, 1949, at 1.5 percent. Call money in Zurich fluctuated in 1950 on a monthly average between 0.75 percent and 1.56 percent.

The rate of interest for savings has shown great stability. Between 1830 and 1863 the average rate in the five largest cantons fluctuated between 3.70 percent and 4 percent. In the following two decades it was a little higher, but about 1883 sank to 3.95 and in 1896 went as low as 3.40 percent. In 1912 it increased again to 4 and in 1921 reached 4.55 percent. But since that time it has fallen almost steadily, especially in the depression years when it fell from 4.10 percent in 1930 to 3 percent in 1935. The improvement of business after that time did little to improve the situation of the saver. On the contrary, the rate of interest sank to 2.41 in 1947. In the following year it rose a little to 2.46 but in 1950 sank again to 2.38 percent. The rate of interest on deposits which are not considered savings is even lower. In 1950 it amounted to 2.07 and at the large banks only to 1.86 percent.

The rate of interest on fixed deposit obligations which, in the years around 1870, fluctuated between 4 and 4.5 percent, sank in the depression years after 1880 to 3.31 percent (1895). Until 1910 it was between 3.75 and 4.10 percent. Then came a period which raised the rate to 5.55 percent by 1920. This rate fell in 1950 to 2.5 percent.

Interest on first mortgages fluctuated in the years 1850 to 1885 between 4 and 5 percent. Then it began to slide and about 1893 fell below 4 percent rising again to 4 percent after 1899. After the First World War the rate averaged between 5 and 5.5 percent. Since 1931 it has fallen again and is now stabilized at 3.5 percent.

The yield on issues of the Confederation and the federal railways is calculated and published by the central bank. For such securities the yield fluctuated in the years 1900 to 1913 between 3.48 and 4.17 percent and rose in consequence of the First World War to an average for 1920 of 7 percent. With some interruptions it declined after that to 2.67 percent in 1950.

CONCLUSION

In general one may say that the organization of Swiss credit, as it has been developed in the last 100 years, has corresponded to economic needs. The three groups of credit institutions, the cantonal banks, the large banks, and the local banks, form a peaceful triumvirate providing credit for the economy. There is neither too great a disunion nor too great a concentration of the credit system. Even the people in small towns have a choice of several different banks if they wish to invest money or borrow.

A favorable element is the reciprocal influence of cantonal and large banks. As the cantonal banks have no monopoly they fear the competition of the private banks. Their tendency to give credit to farmers below cost, and to cover the deficit by profit on commercial transactions, is kept in check by the competition of the large banks which are not influenced by such political considerations. On the other hand, the competition of the cantonal banks limits the gains of the large banks. The cantonal banks undercut the large banks only on agricultural mortgage credit, which does not interest the large banks, but the large banks resent the freedom from property and income taxes of the cantonal banks. This objection is quite justified from the legal point of view, but its economic significance is less important. It is true that for the large banks the income tax is very high and in 1950 they had to pay 15 million francs or nearly 40 percent of their net profit of 40 million francs.[8] But the cantonal banks have also to pay taxes to a modest extent, especially municipal taxes on real estate. In 1950 these amounted to 4 million francs on a net profit of 50 million francs or 9 percent. Moreover, in 1950 the cantonal banks had to give 14,-300,000 francs to the exchequer in the form of profit participations. Together with the taxes already noted, the cantonal banks had to pay 19 million francs or 39 percent of their net profit, which makes it clear that they have little advantage over the large banks.

The volume of credit provided by the banks is satisfactory. Not only have domestic credit needs always been covered but the banks have been able to give credit to foreign countries. The banks also have available large amounts of deposits made by foreigners. Capital ex-

[8] The tax on the banks' capital, which has to be paid whether there is a net profit or not, is not a matter of importance since the income tax is today much more important.

port has never limited the volume of credit available in Switzerland. The farmers never objected to capital exports as such, but they complained sometimes that capital export tended to raise the cost of mortgage credit. This, however, was a narrow point of view. They forgot that a country like Switzerland, which was forced into international exchange in commodities and tourist trade, could not remain self-sufficient in capital exchange.

As regards the safety of investments, bank depositors cannot complain for they have suffered few losses, even in the last four decades of disturbance. A great number of local banks have had to be aided or have had to close, but only one of the large banks, the Banque Suisse d'Escompte, caused a loss to depositors. Another large bank, the Schweizerische Volksbank, and some of the cantonal banks were saved by the intervention of the State.

The banks do not wish to assume the direction of economic life, nor could they do so. The most important obligation of the central bank is the stabilization of the foreign exchanges, because the possibility of influencing the money market by credit operations is limited. This is the reason why the central bank opposed the devaluation of the Swiss franc in 1936. The bank was of the opinion that such a change should be made only if it was inevitable. The central bank uses its influence in the continual interest of the Swiss economy as a whole.

Neither the commercial banks nor the cantonal banks took any positive action to hinder the inflation during the two wars, nor to hinder or further the deflation in the period of depression after 1930. They had evidence that the rise and fall of prices were influenced by world events. At home the army needed large amounts of goods and currency and, of course, the banks could not limit such demands. It might have been possible for them to restrict some of the investment in industry, but a great part of this was financed by industry's own capital and was motivated by the desire to reduce income taxes. Thus the restriction of credit would not have had much effect. To cut down credit for the building of houses and factories, banks and insurance companies made an agreement in 1951 to limit mortgage credits to 70 percent of the cost of houses and to 50 percent of the cost of industrial buildings. That will probably have a restrictive effect, but the high level of prices and salaries will only fall as the prosperity of the export industry comes to an end and full employment disappears.

REFERENCES

Allizé, F. L'organisation des banques en Suisse. Paris, 1923.
—— Bankwesen, das schweizerische. Bearbeitet von der Volkswirtschaftlichen und Statistischen Abteilung der Nationalbank. Zürich, 1906–50.
Bebié, R. Die Abwertung des Schweizerfrankens. Ursachen, Durchführung und erste Auswirkungen. Zürich, 1939.
Binder, H. Untersuchung über Arbeitsteilung, Arbeitsvereinigung und Arbeitsgemeinschaft im schweizerischen Bankwesen. Zürich, 1931.
Bodmer, M. Zur Tätigkeit und Stellung der Privatbankiers in der Schweiz. Zürich, 1934.
Burckhardt, C. F. W. Zur Geschichte der Privatbankiers in der Schweiz. Zürich, 1914.
Bussinger, P. Das gesetzliche Zinsfussmaximum in der Schweiz. Berne, 1929.
Düblin, J. Die Finanzierungs- und Kapitalanlagegesellschaften der schweizerischen Grossbanken. Basel, 1937.
—— Geld- und Kreditsystem der Schweiz. Festgabe für G. Bachmann. Zürich, 1944.
Düblin, J., ed. Handbuch der Schweizerischen Volkswirtschaft. Herausgegeben von der Schweizerischen Gesellschaft für Statistik und Volkswirtschaft. 2 vols. Berne, 1939. Articles: Abwertung, Banken, Bankgesetz, Bankenkonzentration, Bankensanierungen, Bankenverbände, Banknoten, Bankpolitik, Darlehenskasse der Schweizerischen Eidgenossenschaft, Grossbanken, Hypothekarkredit, Kantonalbanken, Kapitalbewegungen (internationale), Kapitalmarkt, Kommunalbanken, Kredit (landwirtschaftlicher), Kredit (öffentlicher), Kredit-(Diskonto-) politik, Kreditversicherung, Lokalbanken, Nationalbank, Notenbanken, Privatbankiers, Stillhalteabkommen, Treuhandgesellschaften und Revisionsverbände, Währungs-(Devison-) politik, Zahlungsmittelumlauf, Zahlungsverkehr (bargeldloser).
Höweler, Kr. Der Geld- und Kapitalmarkt der Schweiz. Berlin, 1927.
Hügi, V. Oekonomische Eigenarten im schweizerischen Bankgewerbe. Berne, 1927.
Jenne, W. Die Spar- und Leihkassen der Schweiz. Zürich, 1914.
Jöhr, A. Die schweizerischen Notenbanken 1826–1913. 2 vols. Zürich, 1915.
—— Die schweizerischen Grossbanken und Privatbankiers. Zürich, 1940.
Kellenberger, E. Kapitalexport und Zahlungsbilanz. 3 vols. Berne, 1939.
Keller, Th. Das Verhältnis der Banken zur Industrie unter besonderer Berücksichtigung der Schweiz. St. Gall, 1937.
Kurz, H., and G. Bachmann. Die schweizerischen Grossbanken. Zürich, 1928.
Läpple, V. Das schweizerische Emissionsgeschäft. Innsbruck, 1923.
Linder, A. Die schweizerischen Grossbanken. Berne, 1927.

Meier, W. Die Emission ausländischer Anleihen in der Schweiz. Zürich, 1931.

Meisterhans, E. Die Raiffeisenschen Kreditgenossenschaften in der Schweiz. Weida in Thüringen, 1923.

Mollet, W. Schweizerische Investmenttrusts. Solothurn, 1942.

Montalivet, R. Le Mouvement de concentration des banques suisses. Fribourg, 1913.

Moos, R. von. Die korporative Organisation des Bankgewerbes in der Schweiz (Bankenverbände). Zürich, 1922.

Perrelet, B. La Banque nationale suisse. Geneva, 1907.

Pestalozzi, A. Die Frage der Liquidität unter besonderer Berücksichtigung der schweizerischen Banken, 1935–1940. Zürich, 1943.

Rossy, P., and R. Reimann. Schweizerisches Bankgesetz. Kommentar. Zürich, 1935.

Schmid, W. Kleingewerbliche Kreditinstitute in der Schweiz. Weinfelden, 1923.

Schwander, W. Das schweizerische Bankgesetz unter spezieller Berücksichtigung seiner wirtschaftlich wichtigen Bestimmungen. Zürich, 1943.

Specker, M. Die Konzentrationsbewegung im schweizerischen Bankgewerbe in den Jahren 1918 bis 1938. Wetzikon, 1948.

Stampfli, A. Die schweizerischen Kantonalbanken. Zürich, 1914.

Stauffacher, W. Der schweizerische Kapitalexport unter besonderer Berücksichtigung der Kriegs und Nachkriegsperiode. Glaris, 1929.

Sulzer, W. Die Rolle des Wechsels im Kreditwesen und Zahlungsverkeher der Schweiz. Zürich, 1934.

Urech, W. Die staatliche Beaufsichtigung der Banken in der Schweiz. Aarau, 1944.

Viret, C., S. Schweizer, and E. Ackermann. Les Banques suisses. Enquête sur les changements de structure du credit et de la banque 1914–1938, publiée sous la direction de H. Laufenburger. Vol. II. Paris, 1940.

Welti, R. Die kurzfristigen Vorschüsse der Nationalbank an den Bund während des Weltkrieges und in der Nachkriegszeit. Winterthur, 1932.

Wenzel, E. Die deutschen Stillhalteabkommen und ihre Auswirkungen auf die schweizerischen Banken. Zürich, 1940.

Wetter, E. Die Lokal- und Mittelbanken der Schweiz. Zürich, 1914.

—— Bankkrisen und Bankkatastrophen der letzten Jahre in der Schweiz. Zürich, 1918.

UNION OF SOVIET SOCIALIST REPUBLICS

by Gregory Grossman

UNIVERSITY OF CALIFORNIA

INTRODUCTION

THE SOVIET ECONOMY is a money-using economy in very much the same sense as is, say, the American economy. True, in the USSR, important institutional differences condition the direction and character of money flows; but the fundamental characteristics of money—medium of exchange, unit of account, and store of value—are clearly present. In the early post-revolutionary years, the period of so-called War Communism, the attempt to operate a virtually moneyless economy resulted in failure and taught its hard lesson. On the other hand, the professed goal of an economy of unlimited abundance in which "economizing," and therefore money, would not be necessary, is too remote in time for serious discussion. The Soviet economy of our day is explicitly based on principles of remuneration for effort, careful (though not always rational) cost accounting, and consumer choice—all requiring the use of money for effective operation. There is, therefore, need for well-developed institutions for the safekeeping and

---

GREGORY GROSSMAN received his B.S. and M.A. degrees at the University of California (Berkeley), and his Ph.D. degree in economics at Harvard University. He served as economist in the Office of Intelligence Research, United States Department of State, and later as economist on the staff of the Board of Governors of the Federal Reserve System. At present he is Assistant Professor of Economics at the University of California (Berkeley). The author wishes to acknowledge gratefully the assistance in the preparation of this essay received from the Russian Research Center, Harvard University, where he held a Graduate Student Fellowship.

transfer of existing means of payment and for the creation of new means of payment; in short, there is need for a banking system. However, in addition to its purely financial and monetary functions, the Soviet banking system plays a no less significant role as one of the chief instrumentalities of the state for supervision, control, and enforcement. This function has come to be known as "control by the ruble."

The banking system of the USSR is geared to the economic needs and the institutional conditions of the country. A few prefatory remarks on the specific features and salient magnitudes of the Soviet economy are therefore in order. However, it must be realized that for at least a decade the flow of current information on the Soviet economy has been extremely small in amount, and ambiguous and frequently doubtful in character. Quantitative information of an aggregative nature has been particularly scarce and suspect, although during the early 1930s the Soviet Union not only collected, thanks to the planned and centralized character of the economy, but also published remarkably ample statistical information.

Out of a total population estimated at just over 200,000,000 persons, some 40,000,000 (at the beginning of 1952) were workers and employees primarily in establishments of a non-agricultural type, and (with the exception of a small number employed by cooperative establishments) directly employed by the state. No private employment is permitted. The remainder of the active population, except for full-time students and military and paramilitary personnel, consists of peasants, virtually all of whom are organized into "collective farms" (*kolkhozy*), in which they are nominally cooperating members rather than wage earners. The bulk of money income is earned in the non-agricultural sector; much of the output of agriculture is consumed within the household or kolkhoz in which it is produced, without the interposition of money. There is much inequality in money incomes; in 1950 the mean (considering basic wage or salary and supplementary pay, but only of workers and employees) was probably about 7,500 rubles.

The typical economic enterprise in the non-agricultural sector is organized internally along lines not unlike those of similar enterprises in capitalist countries, with a managerial hierarchy and with a director (manager) at the top. Organizationally, such an enterprise is a subdivision—several steps removed—of a ministry which is responsible for the operation of a certain functional (and, more infrequently, also geographical) sector of the economy. The enterprise must follow a centrally assigned plan prescribing its minimum performance and financial results. Material costs, wage rates, and product prices are fixed, and the enterprise is expected to make as large a profit as possible in view of the given and unalterable cost-price data. Theoretically, profit is maximized by efficient operation. Wages are largely on a piece-work basis, and the personnel, especially the senior personnel, are rewarded for above-plan production and above-plan profits.

The bulk of agricultural production is carried on by peasants working for their respective kolkhozy, and by the same peasants working on their own behalf on individual household plots with such livestock and simple equipment as they are permitted to retain. So-called machine-tractor stations (MTS) perform mechanized work for groups of kolkhozy and at the same time serve as additional instruments of state control over the nominally (but hardly actually) autonomous collective farms. Only very few peasants still remain outside the kolkhozy, but a substantial amount of agricultural production is also carried on by state-owned "state farms" (*sovkhozy*) employing wage labor.

All economic activity—current production as well as investment—is intended to be governed by detailed and rigid quinquennial, annual, and quarterly plans, broken down territorially and by ministry and enterprise, under the general supervision and guidance of the State Planning Commission (*Gosplan*) and its regional offices. The key elements of the plans are, of course, subject to political dictation by the Soviet regime. One characteristic feature of the Soviet economy is the coexistence of a number of parallel vertical lines of authority and responsibility for economic affairs: production (ministerial), governmental (administrative), financial (especially, banking), trade union, planning, party, and secret police. They all are to some extent concerned with spurring production and uncovering laxity and violation of economic regulations; and, although all are organs of the same monolithic regime, the multiplicity of lines of authority tends to enhance control by the regime and disperse power except at the very top. But there is considerable evidence that a fair degree of noncompliance with the numerous detailed and restrictive economic regulations goes on in the face of the elaborate control machinery, and one may even surmise that some of the creditable performance of the Soviet economy has been possible as much because of as despite the petty (and occasionally not so petty) violations of regulations.

Choice of occupation and employment is severely impaired by the industrial mobilization of youths and by a system of labor books and passports, not to mention the forced-labor element. But rationing of consumer goods (with the one exception of allocation of critically inadequate urban housing space) has been absent since December, 1947, so that consumer choice obtains in the retail market. However, consumers cannot through the exercise of their preferences determine the allocation of resources, and even less can they collectively dictate through the market what proportion of the country's resources shall be devoted to consumption and what proportion to non-consumption, such as investment, defense, and so forth. All important decisions with regard to the allocation of resources are made in a centralized fashion by the regime and are defined and coordinated by the planning machinery. This is not to say that these decisions may not be to some extent frustrated by the psychological resistances of the population and by the miscalculations of the planners themselves.

Since the beginning of the period of the Five-Year Plans in 1928, the dominant policy has been one of extremely rapid economic development, especially industrialization (with a strong emphasis on heavy industry), urbanization, mechanization of agriculture and commercialization of agricultural output, and general autarky. The course has not been an even one, but has been retarded or deflected by the collectivization crisis, political purges, and (since the late 1930s) by preparation for war and war itself. Nonetheless, the Soviet economy has reached a place second only to that of the United States in terms of over-all output; its national product and industrial output are each approximately one fourth to one third of the corresponding American magnitude. Whether the average Soviet consumer can be said to have been substantially better off in 1950 than in 1928, that is just before the Plan era, is, to say the least, very doubtful.

MONETARY STABILITY AND FINANCIAL ORGANIZATION

It may be readily seen that under conditions of such rapid economic development the problem of monetary stability and financial organization had to become of paramount importance. The fundamental adaptation of fiscal and financial institutions to the needs of the existing economic regimen was carried out in the reforms of 1930 and 1931, and not many significant changes have been introduced subsequently. The banking system in particular derives its present structure and functions from these reforms. The bulk of the funds used to finance the large investment activity as well as other activities of a non-consumption nature are channeled through the budget of the state, and by far the most important source of these funds has been the taxation of consumption (the so-called turnover tax).[1] This method of taxation obviously raises the level of retail prices (including tax) to a great degree, but despite strong efforts to "hold the line" against inflation, costs rose very greatly too, being led by a rise in annual wages (and salaries) of some sixfold between 1928 and 1940, and about twelvefold between 1928 and 1950. The attendant increase in currency (including coin) in circulation is shown in Table 1; the author has estimated [2] currency in circulation at the start of 1941 at about 18,000 million rubles, and the amount in circulation at the beginning of 1950, after the currency conversion of 1947, may be placed at about 42,000 million rubles.[3]

TABLE 1

CURRENCY IN CIRCULATION, JANUARY 1, 1929–37

(AMOUNTS IN MILLIONS OF RUBLES)

Year	*Amount*	*Year*	*Amount*
1929	2,100	1934	6,860
1930	2,860	1935	7,730
1931	4,360	1936	9,710
1932	5,670	1937	11,260
1933	8,410		

Source: League of Nations, Economic Intelligence Service, *Money and Banking* (2 vols., Geneva, 1938), II, 183.

1 The composition of taxes, 1928 through 1952, can be conveniently seen in Tables 2 and 5 of F. D. Holzman, "The Soviet Budget, 1928–1952," *National Tax Journal,* VI (1953), 235–37, and "The Burden of Soviet Taxation," *The American Economic Review,* XLIII (1953), 548–71.

2 Estimated from scattered references to various major items of the balance sheet of the Gosbank.

3 Estimated as follows: Currency in circulation at the beginning of 1937 was 11,260 million rubles (Table 1); total income of the population (including transfer receipts) in 1937 was estimated by Professor Bergson to have been 192,900 million rubles, of which 39,000 million was in kind (Abram Bergson, *Soviet National Income and Product in 1937* [New York, 1953], Table I, 18). This leaves 153,900 million rubles as *money* income, and a ratio of 13.7:1 to currency in circulation at the beginning of the year. There seems to have been no serious repressed inflation in either 1937 or 1950, and no sub-

In its essence, the organizational structure of the Soviet banking system is a simple one, paralleling closely the functional subdivision of financial tasks:

1. Note issue, commercial banking services to economic entities and to the state treasury, and financial relations with foreign countries are performed by the State Bank (Gosbank).

2. Long-term investment of funds is undertaken by the four so-called special banks, each serving its own sector of the economy.

3. Banking and similar services to individuals are furnished by the network of savings banks.

"Control by the ruble" is exercised by the Gosbank and by the special banks in their everyday contact with the activity of economic enterprises (on which more below). The whole banking structure is now state-owned and is under the Ministry of Finance.

THE GOSBANK

The State Bank of the USSR (Gosudarstvennyi Bank SSSR, or Gosbank) performs some of the usual central banking functions, chiefly note issue, acts as fiscal agent for the government, and is for all practical purposes the only commercial bank. As of January 1, 1948, the apparatus of the Gosbank consisted of the head office (*pravlenie*) in Moscow, 107 regional offices (*kontory*) and 67 regional suboffices (*subkontory*), and 4,457 local branches.[4] In addition, there are numerous field offices attached to the armed forces, collection and disbursement offices subordinate to the regional offices and to the branches, and other minor units.

On June 4, 1946, the Bank returned into the structure of the Ministry of Finance, after having been directly under the Council of Ministers of the USSR for eight years. It is governed by a Board, the chairman of which is *ex officio* Deputy Minister of Finance. The nominal capital—a rather meaningless figure—is 600 million rubles. In 1947, it had more than a million clients, including 269,000 enterprises

---

stantial change in modes of income payment in the meantime. The income velocity of currency circulation can therefore be assumed to have been roughly the same in both years. Professor Holzman has estimated money income in 1950 to have amounted to 573,200 million rubles ("The Burden of Soviet Taxation," Table I, 557), which suggests an amount of currency in circulation at the beginning of the year of about 41,800 million rubles.

[4] F. D. Livshits, *Bankovaia statistika* (Moscow, 1948), p. 98.

and economic organizations, 223,000 collective farms,[5] the remaining half a million clients being presumably governmental administrative (budgetary) entities, and various organizations such as trade union and party locals.

The balance sheet of the Gosbank has not been published since 1937,[6] but it is known to consist of the following elements:

Assets: precious metals, chiefly gold; claims against the Ministry of Finance for precious metals purchased on the Ministry's account; cash in vault; foreign exchange; short-term loans to economic enterprises;

Liabilities and net worth: "clearing accounts" of economic enterprises; "current accounts" of collective farms, governmental (budgetary) entities, non-economic organizations, and of other financial institutions (special banks, savings banks); bank notes in circulation; treasury notes and coin placed in circulation on behalf of the Ministry of Finance; capital and surplus. The so-called clearing accounts (*raschetnye scheta*) are deposits maintained by economic enterprises and organizations, that is, entities operated on a commercial (*khozraschet*) basis, with the exception of collective farms. We use the term *enterprise* hereafter to denote an entity which maintains a clearing account with the Gosbank. Each enterprise must have only one clearing account with the Gosbank; over this account it has power of disposal within narrow limits imposed by the planning system and under the continuous supervision of the Bank. Enterprises also maintain special accounts for the deposit of certain segregated funds, as for capital repairs (*kapital'nyi remont*) or for eventual transfer to parent organizations. Clearing accounts draw interest at the rate of 1.5 percent per annum.

All other entities, including collective farms, maintain so-called current accounts (*tekushchie scheta*), which differ from clearing accounts in some detailed aspects of their utilization (especially in the event of insolvency) and in the interest rates paid on them. Current accounts owned by collective farms and savings banks draw 3.5 percent interest; other accounts draw 1.5 percent, while those of budgetary entities do not draw any interest.

A new charter was apparently issued to the Gosbank in 1950; it is not known what, if any, substantive changes were involved.[7]

[5] *Ibid.*, p. 103.

[6] League of Nations, Economic Intelligence Service, *Money and Banking* (2 vols., Geneva, 1938), II, 183.

[7] See Ia. E. Rubinshtein, *Denezhnye raschety sotsialisticheskikh predpriiatii* (Moscow, 1950), p. 9.

CLEARING OPERATIONS AND PAYMENTS INSTRUMENTS

Payments between individuals, and between the state on the one side and individuals on the other, are effected in the Soviet Union almost invariably by means of currency, while payments between different economic and administrative organs of the state (including the cooperative sector) exceeding a low minimum figure [8] are required by law to pass through the clearing system of the Gosbank. More will be said on the significance of this strict dichotomy in connection with the control functions of the banking system.

The conduct of clearing operations for the whole state and cooperative sector of the economy constitutes one of the major functions of the Gosbank, which it performs by means of techniques quite similar to those in use in other advanced banking systems. But since there is only one commercial bank, a developed system of interbranch clearing within the Gosbank system takes the place of interbank clearing typical of other countries. The particular type of payments instrument employed by the Bank's clients is prescribed by regulations and seems to be less at the discretion of the parties concerned than in other advanced countries.

Ordinary checks are much less in use, even between enterprises, in the Soviet Union than in the United States, and, in so far as used, Soviet checks are not only non-negotiable, but also non-assignable. This is probably explainable by the fact that checks, and especially assignable checks, are less amenable to strict "control by the ruble" than the other means of payment. Certification of checks is practiced, and a peculiar variant of the certified check is the "limited" checkbook (*limitirovannaia chekovaia knizhka*). In the latter instance, the Bank certifies the checkbook for a certain maximum amount *in toto*. At the time of payment, the representative of the payee marks on the stub of the book the amount of the "limit" which has been drawn upon. These books seem to be employed chiefly for payments covering transportation services, and the prior certification feature is another instance of bank control over economic activity. However, enterprises may obtain credit from the Gosbank for the purpose of "carrying" a supply of limited checkbooks.

[8] All payments between enterprises exceeding 1,000 rubles in amount must be made through the Gosbank clearing system; payments of sums under 100 rubles must be made in currency; payment of sums between 100 and 1,000 rubles are made in either form, depending on the transaction. (One thousand rubles is a very small amount for inter-enterprise transactions these days.)

Over 70 percent of the clearing turnover handled by the Gosbank takes the so-called "acceptance" form (*aktsept*)[9] which resembles somewhat the trade acceptance in use in Western economies. The seller draws up a "demand for payment" against the buyer and presents it with accompanying documents to his branch of the Gosbank, which in turn forwards the papers to the buyer's branch of the Bank for acceptance and payment by the buyer. The so-called negative acceptance is generally in use, whereby the buyer's branch of the Gosbank automatically debits the buyer's clearing account unless the latter stops payment within a specified period after receipt of the documents. In the event that the buyer refuses to honor the demand for payment, which he may do under circumstances specified by law, his branch of the Gosbank may dispose of the shipment as it sees fit. The buyer may also exercise the right of "partial acceptance" and to dispute the remainder of the demand for payment.

A method of effecting payments between enterprises in much less frequent use than the acceptance is the so-called letter of credit (*akkreditiv*), although here the resemblance to the corresponding instrument in the West is somewhat more remote than in the case of the acceptance. It amounts, in effect, to a prepayment by the buyer for the commodity to be shipped by the seller. Some 3 percent of the clearing volume of the Gosbank is said to take this form.

A specific Soviet institution for the clearing of payments between enterprises is the so-called mutual clearing office (*biuro vzaimnykh raschetov* or *BVR*). These offices are affiliated with, but separate from, the Gosbank. Their memberships consist of enterprises making frequent mutual payments, and their function is to offset mutual claims of member enterprises.[10] The BVR's maintain deposits with the Gosbank for periodic settlement of credit and debit balances of member enterprises. Although considerable effort is apparently being devoted to extending and elaborating the BVR network, the advantages of this technique over the usual Gosbank clearing apparatus do not seem to be clear.

OPERATIONS AS FISCAL AGENT

The Gosbank acts as virtually the sole fiscal agent for all levels of government,[11] handling the flow of budgetary receipts and expendi-

[9] Rubinshtein, *Denezhnye raschety*, p. 33.

[10] See G. A. Shvarts, *Beznalichnye vzaimnye raschety v SSSR* (Moscow, 1946), *passim*.

[11] In the absence of Gosbank facilities near by, certain local soviets on the lowest levels are permitted to keep their funds with savings banks.

tures and safe-keeping the accumulated liquid funds of the treasury. Because of the Soviet practice of budgeting larger receipts than expenditures—an anti-inflationary measure—the deposits of the state treasury (Ministry of Finance) with the Gosbank tend to grow and may constitute one of the largest items on the liability side of the Bank's balance sheet.

SHORT-TERM CREDIT

The Gosbank is virtually the only source of short-term credit in the Soviet economy. As of January 1, 1941, it accounted for almost 99 percent of legitimate short-term credit outstanding; the other 1 percent was extended by the banks for long-term investment under special circumstances (see below). The extension of credit in any form by one enterprise to another is strictly proscribed in order to strengthen the control functions of the banking system. However, judging by the continual discussion of the problem of enforcing this prohibition, inter-enterprise credit seems to persist in various open and covert forms.

It is important to note that the Gosbank—just like any commercial bank in any country—creates *new* purchasing power in the process of extending credit. It does so by increasing the clearing account balance of the borrowing enterprise by the amount of the loan. Eventually, as the credit is drawn against, and as wages and salaries are paid out in successive stages of production, an additional amount of currency enters into circulation. Thus, the extension of short-term credit by the Gosbank has a direct bearing on the money supply in the Soviet economy, whether we subsume under "money" both currency and bank deposits or currency alone. Thus, just as in capitalist economies, the problem of inflation control—one of the most serious problems in the Soviet economy—is to a large extent a problem of credit control. The role of the Soviet banking system in the anti-inflationary struggle is discussed later at greater length. There is no legal limit to the volume of credit which the Gosbank may create, other than that imposed indirectly by the minimum backing requirements for bank notes. On the other hand, bank credit must be seen as an integral part of the over-all financial plan for the economy, although it is usually precisely this element of the financial plan which has to bear the brunt of adjustment in the event of divergence between plan and reality.

Under the Soviet approach to finance, short-term credit is ordinarily to be employed for the financing of working capital only. Fixed capital requirements are to be met from other sources, as discussed below in connection with banks for long-term investment. Table 2 shows

TABLE 2
SHORT-TERM LOANS BY THE GOSBANK TO THE SOVIET ECONOMY, JANUARY 1, 1933–53
(IN MILLIONS OF RUBLES)

Year	Amounts Outstanding	Year	Amounts Outstanding
1933	10,500	1938	40,700
1934	14,200	1939	44,900
1935	17,200	1940	47,900
1936	26,700	1941	55,000
1937	34,800	1953	203,000

Sources: League of Nations, *Money and Banking* (1938), II, 183; Ia. Golev, "Razvitie sovetskogo kredita," *Sovetskie finansy za XXX let* (Moscow, 1947), p. 127; V. Gerashchenko, "Gosbank v 1940 g.," *Den'gi i kredit*, 1939, No. 11–12, p. 12; *Pravda*, August 6, 1953.

the growth in short-term credit extended by the Gosbank over the years 1933–53. It must be borne in mind that this expansion was associated with an inflation in costs and prices, so that the real magnitudes underlying the financial expansion must have increased at a considerably slower rate. Before the Second World War, over 40 percent of the aggregate working capital of economic enterprises was financed by the Bank's short-term credit; however, the average duration of a loan was only about a month.

The theory governing Soviet short-term credit transactions is a rather simple one. Each state-owned enterprise is endowed by the treasury with its minimum annual working capital requirements (*normativ*). This endowment forms part of the "charter fund" of the enterprise, on which it pays no interest to the treasury, but which is subject to return to the treasury should changing circumstances justify a lower working capital requirement. Should there be, on the other hand, an increase in the minimum working capital needs of the enterprise, its charter fund is correspondingly increased either by additional grants from the treasury or by allowing the enterprise to retain a part of its current profits. The minimum working capital requirements are generally scrutinized in extreme detail by the control organs of the state and are based on elaborate "norms" worked out for each constituent element of current assets. The problem is generally presented as one of "accelerating the turnover of working capital," and periodic drives are conducted aimed at speeding up the turnover by a certain number of days. These drives invariably run up against the resistance of managers to reduce inventories, which is quite understandable considering the permanent sellers' market typical of the Soviet economy, the inflationary experience of the past, and the fact that no interest is charged on the portion of working capital which corresponds to the charter fund of the enterprise.

The role of the Gosbank in financing [12] the working capital needs of enterprises is theoretically limited to providing the resources necessary to carry inventories and other current assets over and above the minimum levels, i.e., to finance requirements raised by temporary, seasonal, and extraordinary conditions, as well as to finance goods en route. In certain exceptional, but important, cases to be discussed later the Gosbank also provides working capital which would ordinarily be a part of the charter fund of the enterprise. It may be pointed out here that Soviet accounting and auditing practice seems to attach extraordinary importance to associating specific items on the liability side of the balance sheet of an enterprise with specific items on the assets side; this again is part of the strict "control by the ruble."

Gosbank loans are extended to finance particular transactions, are usually secured by the corresponding assets of the enterprise, and are of a fixed and relatively short duration. The Bank charges 4 percent interest per annum on most loans, 2 percent on loans against documents covering goods in transit, and 1 percent on loans to collective farms. Overdue loans are charged 6 percent. The financial plan attempts to foresee for each quarter the credit requirements of enterprises; for each enterprise and for each major type of loan it assigns so-called credit limits which are not to be exceeded during the quarter. The Gosbank is equally responsible with the enterprise for adherence to this rule.

Almost half of the short-term lending of the Gosbank prior to the Second World War—postwar data are not available—was to finance the seasonal accumulation of inventories.[13] As might be expected,

[12] In Soviet usage "financing" (*finansirovanie*) refers exclusively to the appropriation of funds by the state to an enterprise on a non-returnable basis, while "credit extension" (*kreditovanie*) refers to the lending of funds for a definite period. In this chapter the usual English-language terminology is employed.

[13] M. Usoskin, *Osnovy kreditnogo dela* (Moscow, 1946), p. 155.

much of this financing is directly connected with the annual cycle of agricultural production; but, contrary to possible expectation, by far the most important class of agricultural producers—the collective farms (*kolkhozy*)—are allotted very little credit by the state. The loans extended to the kolkhozy are chiefly to purchase materials (fertilizer, seed, insecticides, and small tools) from the outside, rather than to "carry" their membership. In fact, the major job of financing the agricultural production cycle is undertaken by the kolkhozy and their membership themselves. This attitude of the state is, of course, very much in line with the general policy of stressing non-agricultural development as against the peasant economy. On the other hand, state farms (*sovkhozy*), which are state-owned and are operated as ordinary economic enterprises, seem to have considerable recourse to seasonal financing by the Gosbank. Agriculture as a whole accounted for only 4 percent of the total of Gosbank short-term credit outstanding as of January 1, 1941 (see Table 3), despite the fact that nearly half of the population was still deriving its livelihood from agricultural production; however, it is likely that at this date loans to agriculture must have been at their seasonal trough. Table 4 shows the seasonal pattern of Gosback loans to the sovkhozy.

The annual rhythm of agricultural production does, however, markedly govern the seasonal pattern of Gosbank short-term financ-

TABLE 3
GOSBANK SHORT-TERM LOANS OUTSTANDING, BY BRANCHES OF THE ECONOMY, 1933, 1938, AND 1941
(AMOUNTS IN MILLIONS OF RUBLES)

Branch of the Economy	*Jan. 1, 1933*	*Jan. 1, 1938*	*Jan. 1, 1941*
Heavy industry	900	4,700	10,000
Light and textile industries	700	6,600	9,100
Food-processing industry	1,700	8,500	10,700
Procurement of agricultural products	1,600	2,800	3,300
Forestry industry	500	1,300	2,500
Transportation	400	1,400	1,500
Agriculture	1,400	1,700	2,200
Domestic trade	2,300	10,700	11,100
Foreign trade	300	400	900
Local small-scale industry and industrial cooperatives	500	800	1,400
Other	200	1,800	2,300
Total	10,500	40,700	55,000

Source: Ia. Golev, "Razvitie sovetskogo kredita," p. 127.

TABLE 4
SEASONAL PATTERN OF WORKING CAPITAL IN SOVKHOZY, 1945
(AMOUNTS IN THOUSANDS OF RUBLES)

Date	All "Normed" [a] Working Capital	FINANCED BY GOSBANK LOANS: Amount	Percent of All "Normed" Working Capital	Percent of Loans Outstanding as of Jan. 1, 1945
January 1, 1945	1,309,700	144,200	11.0	100.0
April 1, 1945	1,442,100	183,200	12.7	127.0
July 1, 1945	1,670,400	350,400	21.0	243.0
October 1, 1945	1,646,200	294,000	17.9	204.0
January 1, 1946	1,497,000	199,400	13.3	138.0

Source: S. I. Nedelin, *Organizatsiia finansov sovkhoza* (Moscow, 1947), p. 57.
[a] "Normed" working capital refers to the aggregate of items of working capital for which specific inventory "norms" are centrally established (probably most working capital). Figures refer to sovkhozy of all-union significance under the People's Commissariat of Sovkhozy.

ing after agricultural output leaves agriculture proper and passes through the successive stages of processing and distribution: procurement, manufacturing, and wholesale and retail trade. At each stage the Gosbank undertakes the financing of at least a part of the seasonal accumulations of inventories and goods in process, and "carries" them until they pass into the next stage, and so on until purchase by the final consumer. Other seasonal short-term financing by the Gosbank is governed by natural production conditions in other sectors of the economy (including forestry and fishing), as well as by the need to stockpile fuel and materials for the long and severe winters.

Another important class of Gosbank short-term loans are those extended for the purpose of financing goods en route (or, as usually termed, loans against documents en route). Their importance rose from 18 percent of all Gosbank loans outstanding in 1933 and 1935 to 24 percent in 1939 and 32 percent in 1941 (January 1 figures throughout).[14] This type of loan is generally extended in conjunction with the acceptance form of effecting payments between enterprises (see above). The shipper (seller) submits to his branch of the Gosbank a "demand for payment" and the accompanying documents and receives a loan against these documents pending collection of the amount due from the buyer.

Although in principle the Gosbank is expected to finance only the

[14] *Ibid.*, p. 142, and Ia. Golev, "Razvitie sovetskogo kredita," *Sovetskie finansy za XXX let* (Moscow, 1947), p. 128.

working capital requirements above a constant minimum amount, certain important exceptions to this principle have been introduced for the sake of extending the Bank's "control by the ruble." It was found that some enterprises, chiefly in trade and in heavy industry, experienced little variation in working capital requirements, and thus were able to escape the control and supervisory functions of the Gosbank. The credit activity of the Gosbank was therefore extended (beginning in 1936 in trade, and in 1939 in heavy industry) to providing a part of the permanent working capital requirements of such enterprises on the basis of so-called "sharing" (*dolevoe uchastie*), according to which the Bank's credit finances a fixed fraction of every purchase of materials and supplies by the enterprise, as well as the formation of goods in process and finished products. In this way the Bank is able to maintain a constant watch over the day-to-day activity of such enterprises. This development probably in part explains the much higher relative significance of heavy industry in Gosbank financing in 1941 as compared with 1938 and 1933, as shown in Table 3.

A *credit plan* is drawn up quarterly by the Gosbank. The plan anticipates in detail the loan requirements over the next quarter in accordance with the general economic plan, and collates them with the anticipated movement in the resources at the bank's disposal, such as changes in deposits and in net worth (as a result of net earnings during the quarter). Lastly, the amount of note issue (or retirement) required to bring the two sides of the plan into agreement is determined. After confirmation by the Council of Ministers the credit plan becomes a directive governing the operations of the Gosbank for the quarter. On its basis, maximum lines of credit (credit limits) are apportioned by individual enterprises in accordance with their own quarterly plans and by individual branches of the Bank.

THE CASH PLAN; CURRENCY ISSUE

While the credit plan anticipates the movement in this element of the Bank's balance sheet over the quarter, the *cash plan,* drawn up quarterly and monthly, forecasts the *gross* inflow and outflow of currency into and from the Gosbank system. State-owned and cooperative enterprises are permitted to hold in their tills no more than the minimum amounts of currency; all amounts in excess of the minimum must be deposited with the Gosbank. Thus, the Bank's cash plan in effect presents an approximation to an account of the gross transactions between the population on the one hand, and the state (in both its economic and administrative roles) and cooperative entities on the other.[15] The difference between the two sides of the cash plan, of course, represents the net change in currency in circulation outside the Gosbank and should correspond (for an identical period) to the net change in the same item as arrived at by the credit plan.

By far the largest item on the inflow side of the cash plan, accounting for as much as 80 percent of the total inflow, is the receipts of retail trade enterprises; this item of course contains the very large turnover tax revenue. Other items on the inflow side include receipts for various services sold to the population, direct taxes, and proceeds from loans. On the outflow side, wage and salary payments account for up to 90 percent of cash outflow from the Gosbank, while other items include payments for agricultural deliveries to collective farms, pensions and assistance payments, service on loans and savings accounts.

Soviet currency consists of bank notes issued by the Gosbank, and treasury notes and subsidiary coin issued by it on behalf of the Ministry of Finance.[16] A law dating back to 1922, which is apparently still valid, requires that bank notes have a minimum 25 percent backing of precious metals (in fact, primarily gold) and foreign exchange; it is doubtful that this restraining provision is observed in times of financial emergency, such as the recent war. There is no formal backing for treasury notes, but the amount of these in circulation is not to exceed that of bank notes—a provision of little practical import, since treasury notes constitute the smaller denominations which have been steadily declining in relative significance with the progressive inflation of price levels. All Soviet currency is in fact inconvertible.

FOREIGN OPERATIONS

The exclusive right to deal in foreign exchange is vested in the Gosbank. However, a certain range of transactions has been delegated by it to the Bank for Foreign Trade of the USSR (*Vneshtorgbank*),

[15] A full accounting of such transactions is drawn up by the State Planning Commission (*Gosplan*) in the form of the so-called "balance of money incomes and expenditures of the population"; see also Joseph S. Berliner, "Monetary Planning in the USSR," *American Slavic and East European Review*, IX (1950), 237–54.

[16] Following the monetary reform of December, 1947, banknotes in denominations of 10, 25, 50, and 100 rubles, and treasury notes in denominations of 1, 3, and 5 rubles have been in circulation. Subsidiary coins of nickel and bronze (which were not affected by the reform) are in denominations of 1, 2, 3, 5, 10, 15, and 20 kopeks; some silver and copper coins, issued for a number of years after the 1924 monetary reform, are still in circulation.

chiefly exchange dealings with foreign visitors and diplomatic missions. The Gosbank itself buys foreign exchange from, and sells it to, the enterprises of the Ministry of Foreign Trade at fixed rates of exchange [17] in connection with their export-import operations. The Gosbank has a network of correspondents in commercial centers abroad, and performs all the other usual functions in connection with the financing of foreign economic relations. It also extends short-term credit (in rubles) to enterprises of the Ministry of Foreign Trade for their working capital needs. A considerable Soviet-owned and Soviet-controlled network of banking institutions has grown up in areas under Soviet domination and occupation after the war.

BANKS FOR LONG-TERM INVESTMENT

Practically all of the funds for long-term investment in the Soviet economy are funneled through four financial institutions, usually referred to as the *special banks,* each serving exclusively one or more branches of the economy. At present, they are:

The Industrial Bank (*Prombank*), financing investment in industry (including power production and mining), transportation, and communication;

The Agricultural Bank (*Sel'khozbank*);

The Bank for the Financing of Capital Construction in Trade and in the Cooperative Sector (*Torgbank*); and

The Central Bank for the Financing of Communal and Dwelling Construction (*Tsekombank*), and the system of communal banks affiliated with it.

The name "bank" fits ill the nature of their activity. They are only secondarily lending institutions; primarily they are agencies for the *disbursement* of investment funds, mainly from budgetary sources. They are also the chief agencies of the state for control over the timely and orderly carrying out of the huge investment program under the Five-Year Plans. The great bulk of the annual gross investment in the Soviet economy is within the bounds of state-owned enterprise. The

[17] The official rate of exchange for the ruble has been 4 rubles per one U.S. dollar since March 1, 1950; rates for other currencies are computed in proportion to their value against the U.S. dollar. These rates are arbitrary and for purposes of internal accounting only, and hardly express anything like a "purchasing power parity," as has been pointed out in the introductory section to this chapter.

corresponding funds originate to a large extent with the treasury, while the remainder is financed from what is called the "own means of enterprises," that is, from retained current profits and current depreciation allowances. These funds always pass through the system of special banks, under whose close supervision they are disbursed. The cooperative sector of the economy, including here the kolkhozy as well, finances the relatively small amount of investment within its bounds from its own net accumulation (including increments to the so-called "indivisible funds," that is, capital, of the kolkhozy), and out of long-term loans extended by the special banks. It is in the last instance (as well as in a few additional minor cases) that the special banks pose as lending institutions. The recipients of these loans are expected to pay an interest charge, and the loans bear definite maturities. The *lending* resources of the special banks are periodically augmented by budgetary appropriation.

The special banks have two additional lending functions. They (and not the Gosbank) extend *short-term* credit to enterprises engaged chiefly in construction—this activity being related to the role of the special banks in disbursing investment funds in general—and to certain communal and local enterprises. Secondly, they make loans to *individuals* for a few narrowly delimited purposes. Individuals are permitted to own homes for their immediate use, as well as some livestock—these being the two major types of nonliquid assets in private ownership in the USSR. Accordingly, the special banks finance the construction (or reconstruction) and purchase of homes and the acquisition of cattle by individuals, but at least in the instance of the financing of homeownership the lending terms (except for the low interest rates) would not be considered very liberal by American standards.[18] (Apart from these instances there are no known institutional facilities for consumer credit in the USSR. The reasons may be in part historical, but mainly relate to the policy of the regime to stress investment and military preparedness as against consumption.)

The special banks have no right of note issue and no commercial deposits in the usual sense of the term are maintained with them. In

18 The terms vary according to type of borrower, but in general they are: for the acquisition of homes, up to 10,000 rubles for a maximum of 10 years at 2–3 percent per annum; for the purchase of cattle, up to 3,000 rubles to a family for a maximum of 3 years at 3 percent per annum. It is doubtful that 10,000 rubles goes far toward the acquisition of even a modest home; in any event a minimum downpayment of 20 percent is required for the purchase of a home.

fact, they keep their funds on deposit with the Gosbank. Thus, unlike the Gosbank, they cannot create new money and are limited to disbursing or lending out existing means of payment placed at their disposal.

SAVINGS BANKS

The institutions described thus far provide financial services to collective entities: the state and economic enterprises owned by it; the cooperatives; and the collective farms. In contrast, the farflung network of savings banks renders a limited range of banking services to the population, that is, to individual Soviet citizens.[19]

The chief of these services is the safe-keeping of individual savings in the form of time deposits (with a minimum duration of six months), demand (savings) deposits, and—less developed—individual checking deposits. The deposits earn 5, 3, and 3 percent interest per annum, respectively; the client may, if he prefers, forego the interest and make a lottery deposit with the chance of winning up to double his account. However, savings deposits occupy a relatively modest place in the Soviet economy. Their total value just after the monetary reform of December, 1947, was 12,800 million rubles; it rose to 22,500 million by January 1, 1952. Thus, savings have been increasing at the rate of less than 2,500 million rubles a year, which is just a fraction of one percent of total annual personal money income. Savings deposits grow slowly, despite the large "real" savings (that is, investment) in the Soviet economy. The reasons are these: the Soviet state prefers to raise the bulk of the funds for the financing of capital investment and other state requirements by means of taxation and quasi-compulsory bond sales, leaving relatively little free cash for voluntary savings; the low standard of living is unfavorable to large voluntary savings; the comprehensive social security system reduces the individual's compulsion to save; and much of the voluntary saving, especially in the rural areas, occurs in the form of currency hoarding.

Mention may be made at this point of the liquid assets at the dis-

19 There are minor exceptions to this general division of functions. Collective farms and local governmental units, especially in remote localities, may, at their choice, keep their current funds on deposit with savings banks. On the other hand, since 1942, individuals have been permitted to maintain deposits of over 3,000 rubles with the Gosbank and they may also obtain loans for the construction of homes from communal banks.

posal of the Soviet population. These assets consist almost entirely of three kinds: currency in the possession of individuals—probably the largest part of all currency in circulation, which was estimated [20] at about 40,000 million rubles at the beginning of 1950, and may have

TABLE 5
SAVINGS BANK DEPOSITS, JANUARY 1, 1928–29 AND 1933–52
(AMOUNTS IN MILLIONS OF RUBLES)

Year	*Deposits*	*Year*	*Deposits*
1928	200	1942	5,000
1929	300	1943	4,400
1933	1,000	1944	4,400
1934	1,200	1945	5,200
1935	1,600	1946	8,500 [a]
1936	2,500	1947	12,000 [a]
1937	3,500	1948	12,800
1938	4,500	1949	14,300 [b]
1939	6,500	1950	17,000 [a]
1940	7,100	1951	18,500
1941	7,300 [c]	1952	22,500 [a]

Sources: Alexander Baykov and G. R. Barker, "Financial Developments in the USSR," *Bulletins on Soviet Economic Development,* No. 3, 1950, Table X, p. 18; *Pravda,* March 8, 1951, and March 7, 1952.

[a] Approximate figure. [b] Budgetary estimates. [c] 6.8 on outbreak of war.

reached 45–50,000 million by 1952; savings deposits to the amount of 22,500 million rubles as of January 1, 1952; and government bonds. No statistics on the amount of government bonds outstanding since the monetary reform of 1947 have been made public, but the amount may be placed very roughly at 175,000 million rubles at the start of 1952.

However, the "liquidity" of the preponderant part of these assets—namely government bonds—is open to serious doubt. Only a minor issue, amount outstanding unknown, is redeemable on demand; other bonds cannot be cashed before they are drawn for redemption or mature twenty years from date of issue. The privilege to borrow from savings banks up to 30 percent of the face value of the bonds, which was introduced in March, 1937, was suspended at the beginning of the Second World War, and has not been reestablished as far as is known.[21] Although purchase of the bonds is nominally voluntary, in fact such strong pressure is applied on the population at the time of

20 See note 3.
21 A. M. Aleksandrov, *Finansy i kredit SSSR* (Moscow, 1948), p. 188.

the drives that the bulk of the purchases must be regarded as forced purchases. The failure to restore the privilege to borrow against the bonds supports this view. If for these reasons bond holdings are not included among the liquid assets of the population, the ratio of such assets to the total of money incomes can be placed at roughly 1:10.

The assets of the savings bank system, above their minimum cash needs, are invested in special state bonds.

Another (if not more) important function of the savings banks is the sale of bonds to the population during the annual loan drives, and the carrying out of service payments on the state debt. Other activities of the savings banks include the issue of money orders, collection of party and other dues, collection of fees for communal services and of direct taxes, and similar services to the population.

THE BANKING SYSTEM DURING AND AFTER THE SECOND WORLD WAR

The focal position of the banking system (and especially of the Gosbank) in the Soviet economy and its role as a chief instrument of centralized control assured it an important place in the economic effort of the war years (1941–45) as well as during the early postwar period.[22] From the economic point of view, this whole period may be subdivided into three stages: conversion of the economy from a war-preparedness basis to a total war footing—June, 1941, to the first part of 1942; conduct of the war economy; and, beginning with the first part of 1943, reconstruction in the liberated areas and, eventually, reconversion from the war economy. The second stage, of course, overlapped the first and third stages.

Consideration will be given first to the Gosbank. During the initial stage—that of conversion to an all-out war effort after the German attack—the Bank stood ready to meet in full the extraordinary financial needs of the moment. Specifically, it extended large loans to various enterprises: (*a*) for purposes of making lump-sum payments to personnel called into the armed forces; (*b*) for the dismantling, transfer, reinstallation and restocking of the hundreds of plants

[22] In addition to postwar Soviet publications cited in the Bibliography, see also on this subject, N. Voznesenskii, *The Economy of the USSR during World War II* (Washington, 1948), pp. 78–83, and M. Atlas, "Kreditnaia sistema SSSR v gody velikoi otechestvennoi voiny," *Sovetskie finansy*, 1945, No. 6–7, pp. 12–17.

evacuated eastward; (*c*) for the redistribution of resources in favor of industries working for the war effort; (*d*) for the organization of local facilities of consumer supply, such as the so-called departments of workers' supply (*ORS*) within enterprises. The Bank's lending authority was unlimited with respect to (*a*) and (*b*), a very unusual latitude of action under the Soviet planning system. Furthermore, credit facilities were extended to enterprises in financial difficulties for reasons such as the loss of assets in occupied areas, misdirection of goods, decline in efficiency of operation, and the numerous other facets of the chaotic situation of that period.

Although there was a substantial counter-tendency during the early war years for the volume of credit to contract as physical inventories were drawn down and as the production of consumer goods declined sharply, it is surprising to encounter the claim that the Gosbank's outstanding credit to economic enterprises not only declined at first, but did not regain its prewar level until 1944.[23] This is the more surprising since the velocity of "clearing accounts," that is, the ratio of total transactions to the average level of the accounts, declined to as little as half the prewar figure.[24] As a result of the confused situation, the Gosbank experienced considerable difficulties with respect to its payments-clearing operations. Another difficulty, peculiar to Soviet conditions, arose from the fact that many enterprises and their respective branches of the Gosbank were frequently evacuated to different localities, causing a temporary rupture in the close supervision and control which the Gosbank exercises over enterprises under the Soviet system of "control by the ruble."

After the initial period came to an end in the first part of 1942, financial activity of the Gosbank became primarily directed at extending liberal credit assistance to war industries and rendering services to the armed forces. A large network of field offices attached to units of the army and navy was established by the Gosbank; it acted as the "cashier" of the armed forces and administered the savings of military personnel.

The third stage in the wartime activity of the Gosbank began in the early part of 1943 with the start of reconstruction in the liberated

23 Atlas, "Kreditnaia sistema," p. 14. This statement may refer to the total *after* the writing off of credits which had become uncollectible as a result of war and occupation; but even if this interpretation is accepted, war-induced credit expansion up to 1944 would seem quite modest in view of the magnitude of the requirements.

24 Golev, "Razvitie," p. 133.

areas. The Bank extended large credits in order to reconstitute the working capital of reconstruction enterprises, including that part of working capital which (under Soviet practice) would have been ordinarily supplied from non-bank sources, for example, out of the state budget. Collection of old debts was greatly relaxed.

The machinery of control by the ruble was, of course, harnessed for the prosecution of the war effort. There are numerous explicit as well as indirect indications that the tightness of the Bank's controls was considerably relaxed during the war years. This was inevitable, because cost considerations were subordinated to the all-important task of war production, and because fluid and confused conditions prevailed for much of the time.

The rigid relationship between the Gosbank and its customers, and the reliance upon minute administrative directives, may have hindered rapid adjustment to the wartime situation. The very fact that an enterprise was to deal with only one branch of the Gosbank created difficulities for evacuated enterprises. It seems, though, that the central authorities were not slow in issuing new directives in response to the new situation. Whether the directives were realistic and effective is another question. It is clear that the Gosbank was given very much greater latitude of action in meeting the extraordinary financial needs of enterprises than it enjoyed before or since in peacetime. This liberalization of Gosbank credit facilities took a corresponding burden off the treasury and, incidentally, made the budget accounts look much better balanced than would otherwise have been the case.

Lastly, the wartime role of the Gosbank as the bank of issue should be reported. It is well known now that the Soviet war effort (and probably also the reconstruction program) was financed to a considerable extent by means of currency issue.[25] It is claimed that currency circulation increased 2.4 times during the (first?) three years of the war.[26] But the conversion of ten old rubles into one new ruble at the time of the monetary reform of December, 1947—when the actual wage level had almost doubled in comparison with 1940—suggests a considerable further currency expansion by that date. However, it need not necessarily mean that the amount of currency in circulation immediately prior to the reform was excessive to the full

[25] See Voznesenskii, *The Economy of the USSR*, pp. 79 and 82, and the Decree on the carrying out of the monetary reform of December, 1947 (*Pravda*, Dec. 15, 1947).

[26] Voznesenskii, *The Economy of the USSR*, p. 82.

extent of the 10 to 1 conversion ratio, as the government might well have desired to err on the "safe" side.[27]

It is not quite clear through what precise fiscal or financial channels the additional amounts of currency were thrown into circulation. Officially, budgetary receipts during the four and a half years (mid-1941 to 1945) roughly corresponding to the duration of hostilities fell short of budgetary expenditures by from 33,000 million to 36,000 million rubles. According to Soviet usage, receipts are inclusive of proceeds from borrowing, gifts, and foreign aid. But for the six and a half years from the beginning of hostilities until the monetary reform (mid-1941 to 1947) total receipts slightly *exceeded* total expenditures: receipts were 1,732,000 million rubles and total expenditures were 1,722,000 million rubles. Unless the whole of the currency expansion during this period was accounted for by Gosbank credit to economic enterprises—which seems unlikely despite the temporary liberalization of credit policy—budgetary receipts as officially stated must have included inflationary sources of financing, such as borrowing from the Gosbank. There is no explicit reference to such borrowing in Soviet sources. At the beginning of the war, however, the treasury drew on its large deposits with the Gosbank, which had accumulated as a result of budgetary surpluses over a number of years. Moreover, idle deposits of enterprises and special banks with the Gosbank were taken over by the treasury. These funds are said to have exceeded 20,000 million rubles.[28] Their utilization undoubtedly resulted in a practically equivalent amount of currency being placed in circulation. It is not clear whether the funds appear, in whole or in part, under the budgetary receipts for the corresponding years.

The role played by the other banks during the war is reported briefly below. The special banks, whose main function is disbursement of state funds going into investment in fixed capital, reduced

[27] The monetary reform of Dec. 14, 1947, involved the following measures: currency was converted at the rate of 10 rubles of the old kind to one ruble of the new issue; savings deposits were reduced on a sliding scale, namely, amounts up to 3,000 rubles were not affected at all, amounts in excess of 3,000 rubles and not exceeding 10,000 rubles were cut down by one third, and amounts in excess of 10,000 rubles were cut down by one half; government bonds outstanding were converted into a new issue (with an interest rate of 2 percent instead of 4 percent) at one third their former face value, although with exceptions with regard to the issues of 1947 (full face-value conversion) and 1938 (one fifth face-value conversion); deposits of cooperatives and kolkhozy with the Gosbank were cut down by 20 percent; other liquid assets were not affected.

[28] See Atlas, "Kreditnaia sistema," p. 15; and E. Ia. Atlas, and others, *Denezhnoe obrashchenie i kredit SSSR* (Moscow, 1947), pp. 241–42.

the volume of their activity when military needs forced a sharp curtailment of investment, but they later resumed their importance as reconstruction took on large proportions. The savings banks faced the important task of attempting to absorb some of the swollen currency holdings of the population. Their sales of state bonds increased greatly, and they also administered the wartime state goods lotteries and collected voluntary gifts from the population. Much less successful were their attempts to attract savings deposits. Despite the fact that withdrawals of deposits made before the war were limited to 200 rubles a month (withdrawals of wartime deposits not so restricted), the total of savings deposits fell sharply at the outset, possibly in part due to loss of the occupied areas, and did not recover to the prewar level (6,800 million rubles) until the middle of 1945. After that, the figure climbed rapidly, reaching about 14,000 million rubles just before the monetary reform.

The savings banks were also assigned the task of administering the blocked accounts deposited by enterprises in favor of individual workers and employees as compensation for leave not taken during the war years. The total of such accounts reached 10,300 million rubles by the end of the war, when they were converted into special (3 percent) certificates, one fourth of the value of which was to be redeemable at annual intervals beginning April 1, 1946. However, only two annual payments were made before the monetary reform, when the residual amounts were converted, with a loss of two thirds of the face value, into bonds of the new (2 percent) Conversion Loan of 1948.

CONTROL BY THE RUBLE

The Soviet economy is not only a socialist economy, in the sense that its most important sectors are in the ownership of the state and of cooperative bodies, and a planned economy, in the sense that its course of development is consciously channeled by central authority toward predetermined goals, but it is also an extremely centrally administered economy, in that administrative regulation by central authority has to a large extent supplanted the operation of the market mechanism. To Soviet planners, steeped in an unbending Marxist approach to value, demand is not (with supply) a codeterminant of value. Only socially necessary labor time is said to determine value.

Given this position, it follows that the expression of demand through the market need not be especially heeded in the making of economic decisions, and rigid centralized administration of the economy can be adopted without conflict with economic precepts. It might be pointed out that in the view of a growing number of non-Soviet writers on the economic theory of socialism, state-ownership and planning are not inevitably wed to centralized administration of the economy, but are compatible, and desirably so, with a meaningful market mechanism.[29]

But, having substituted highly centralized dictatorial direction of the economy for the price mechanism, and having repressed the profit motive of the entrepreneur, the Soviet regime necessarily imposed a myriad of amazingly complex, detailed, and rigid laws and administrative regulations in order to channel the day-to-day actions of managers. The regulations are not to be transgressed, upon threat of severe penalty, regardless of the actual profitability of alternative courses of action. It is true that, after a series of grave errors, the regime has finally recognized the impossibility of completely suppressing self-interest as the determinant of an individual's economic behavior, and has given it limited outlet—such as piecework rates and bonuses—within the very rigid framework of the planning system. But the pursuit of self-interest is not to determine what shall be done with the economic resources, only how well the minutely assigned tasks shall be performed. A gigantic and evergrowing structure of control, supervision, inspection, and checking attempts to ensure that the minutest regulations are observed, that unsanctioned self-interest is suppressed, and that economic activity proceeds undeflected and unretarded along its charted course.

The Soviet banking system, because of its focal position in the economy, is a most important instrument of control—the term is used in its broad Soviet sense, which includes inspection, supervision, and constraint. As has been pointed out above, the banking system is only one of a number of such instruments. Others of note are: The Ministry of State Control of the USSR; the Control and Audit Administration of the Ministry of Finance of the USSR; various units of the State Planning Commission; higher level offices of the various

29 See, for instance, Oskar Lange and Fred M. Taylor, *On the Economic Theory of Socialism* (Minneapolis, 1938); Abba P. Lerner, *The Economics of Control* (New York, 1944); Abram Bergson, "Socialism," in Howard S. Ellis (ed.), *A Survey of Contemporary Economics* (Philadelphia, 1948).

economic ministries; and, of course, the Party, the trade unions, and the security organs of the state. To a considerable extent the control functions of these entities duplicate, and conflict with one another, and there is a fair amount of mutual checking.

In the Soviet framework, the control functions of the banks at least equal in importance the strictly monetary and financial functions. In order to facilitate control by the ruble, enterprises are forbidden to extend credit to each other, making them completely dependent upon the banking system for financial assistance. Their clearing accounts are kept to a minimum—before the war they were, on the average, sufficient for only four days' expenses. All payments (other than for wages and salaries) in excess of 1,000 rubles must be made through the Gosbank clearing system. Enterprises must deposit their currency receipts daily at the Gosbank, retaining only a minimum amount in the till. Each enterprise must deal with one, and only one, branch of the Gosbank (or in certain exceptional instances with one of the special banks) for clearing its payments and for borrowing for working capital needs, and with only one designated special bank for long-term financing. These requirements establish a constant and localized contact between the enterprise and the banking system; the primary control function of the Gosbank is to see to it that they are fully complied with.

Nominally, an enterprise has power of disposal over its clearing account at the Gosbank, but actually the Bank may refuse to release the funds if it deems that any regulation is being violated thereby. With respect to certain types of expenditure the Bank exercises a particularly close and continuous control, the most important of which is the disbursement of wages and salaries—usually in currency rather than by check. A cardinal feature of the Soviet planning system is the allocation to each enterprise of a fixed maximum sum for a given period as its wages fund, in effect, representing that part of the economy's manpower resources which has been deemed to be necessary and sufficient for the carrying out of the production program of the enterprise. Payment of wages and salaries in excess of this amount is *prima facie* indication of managerial inefficiency, unless accompanied by at least proportional overfulfillment of the production goal. The Gosbank is forbidden to release money for wage payment except in strict harmony with the enterprise's wages fund, making allowance for the degree of fulfillment of its production plan.

Temporary overdisbursement of up to 10 percent is permissible, provided that the enterprise undertakes to mend its ways and to bring wage payment back into line with actual output. The Gosbank is charged with exercising a similarly strict control over the timely transfer of funds from the clearing accounts to depreciation reserves.

Another aspect of control by the rule on the part of the Gosbank is through its short-term credit activity. Prior to extending credit the bank is expected to examine the working capital position of the enterprise and its output in relation to its planned assignment. The Bank may refuse credit should it uncover excessive working capital or other irregularities, in spite of the fact that resort to credit may have been anticipated by the financial plan of the enterprise. Supervision is exercised throughout the duration of the credit to assure its prompt and full repayment. As already mentioned, enterprises in certain branches of the economy which by the nature of their work do not have seasonal or other temporary needs for additional working capital have nevertheless been required to resort to bank credit on a continuous "sharing" basis, with the express purpose of strengthening the Bank's control over their activity.

In a similar fashion, the special banks exercise minute supervision over the utilization of the funds disbursed or lent out by them, so as to insure that: only approved capital projects are undertaken; price lists are followed; investment projects are completed and commissioned on time; investment funds are not diverted to other uses; and the numerous other regulations are complied with.

Direct administrative controls have a way of proliferating in number and mounting in cost of enforcement. There are always new loopholes to be plugged, and those who control must be themselves controlled. The effort to forestall unauthorized private gain conflicts with the requirement for flexibility in the day-to-day operations of management, so that literal observance of the endless directives and proscriptions may in itself hinder the attainment of planned targets. The secret of success for the individual manager may then lie in the art of "getting away" with infractions of regulations despite (or, partly, thanks to) the complex control apparatus. But patriotic zeal is hardly the chief motive in all cases of infraction; despite the threat of extremely severe punishment, the lure of private gain, spurred by the low standard of living, asserts itself and leads to "side deals," private profit, and graft.

How effective is the banking system, or for that matter any of the agencies of control of the state, in enforcing the letter of regulations? No data are, of course, available, but the frequent exposés in the Soviet press of individual cases of "anti-state" activity leave no doubt of the prevalence of violations. One wonders how many cases remain unpublicized, or even undiscovered, for every one that is turned into a public warning. Even more impressive are the stories of former eyewitnesses who speak of graft and illicit private profit pervading the whole economic organism.

BANKING AND PLANNING

It is important to emphasize once again that the banking system of the Soviet Union is not an autonomous entity free to pursue its own policies within a certain legal framework, as banking systems may be in major capitalist countries. Nor is there anything resembling autonomous central bank policy. Instead, the whole banking system, and not in the least the Gosbank itself, must be viewed as an executive and controlling arm of the over-all planning-operating economic apparatus of the state. The total amount of credit to be extended within the next period is determined virtually to the last ruble by the credit plan. Access to bank credit by a particular enterprise is provided for (up to a specified maximum sum) by its own plan, that plan, of course, having been approved by higher authority and integrated into the plan for the whole economy. Therefore, resort to bank credit is virtually automatic, provided the necessary administrative-economic criteria are met by the borrowing enterprise. These criteria refer chiefly to compliance with the plan assigned to the enterprise; credit-worthiness, in the strict financial sense, is not a major criterion in this connection. In brief, the decision which a Soviet banker is called upon to make before extending a loan to an enterprise is not based upon the economic success of the venture to be financed—that decision is made by the central planners—but whether the loan will further the precise execution of the plan. Thus, the control function of the bank is necessarily prior to its lending function.

The fact that banks in the USSR are primarily agents of control by the state over the economy furnishes an explanation of the very existence of bank credit in the Soviet Union. Were it not so, there would be no need for banks as lending institutions. For were it not for the bank's "control by the ruble," each Soviet enterprise could be endowed by the state with sufficient assets to undertake the execution of its plan despite seasonal and temporary variation in working capital requirements. Under this alternative arrangement there would generally be no need for short-term credit and banks would be mere offices for clearing payments and agencies for the disbursement of state grants. (Presumably, savings banks would still exist, though, to serve the needs of the population; also, some commercial banking, but on a small scale, would still be necessary to finance the cooperative sector.) As it is, however, because the enterprise is endowed by the state with a minimum of liquid assets and must therefore replenish working capital in order to execute its plan, the enterprise is forced to submit continually to the bank's control.

It is not surprising therefore that, in the transition of the satellite economies after the Second World War to socialist planned economies patterned after the Soviet model, reform of the banking system has been one of the first steps. The banking reforms in the satellite countries have almost invariably reproduced the Soviet banking structure: a single central-commercial bank like the Gosbank, several banks for long-term investment like the Soviet special banks, and a network of savings banks to serve the population. The reason for this development lies, of course, in the facilities for control over the economy which such a banking structure offers, coupled with the relative ease with which financial institutions can be taken over. Furthermore, Soviet principles and techniques governing intra-enterprise finances and financial relations between enterprises have been transplanted to the socialized sectors of the satellite countries. One now reads of the "control by the zloty" and the "control by the koruna," and so forth, in addition to the "control by the ruble."

Strictly speaking, there is no central banking, in the usual sense of the term, in the Soviet Union. The Gosbank exercises certain functions which have come to be considered as attributes of central banks, such as the exclusive right of note issue and—a more recent characteristic of some central banks—the virtually exclusive administration of foreign exchange. But it is at the same time practically the only commercial bank in the country, and therefore the most distinguishing attribute of central banking, the safe-keeping and management of the reserves of the country's commercial banking system, loses meaning in its case. Nor can one speak of monetary *management* by the Gosbank in the conventional sense of the term, that is, in the sense of influence over the total money supply through the cost of credit and the volume of the reserves of the banking system. This sort of monetary management, which essentially relies on the market mechanism for the achievement of its ends, would of course be out of place in the economy of the USSR as it is planned and directed—even if there were other commercial banks to keep reserves with the Gosbank. Instead, there is monetary *planning*—the planning of currency circulation as an integral part of over-all financial planning. It is primarily the responsibility of the planning authorities and not of the Gosbank itself. The particular role of the Gosbank in this respect—in addition to mere periodic forecasting of currency circulation—lies in its control over the execution of the financial plan of each enterprise and in furnishing credit in accordance with that plan. On the whole, a very strong, but passive role, and certainly not an independent one.

THE PROBLEM OF INFLATION

One of the chief directions in which the control activities of the banking system, and of the Gosbank especially, are directed is the prevention of currency issue in excess of the amount foreseen by the plan. The nature of the credit plan, and of the cash plan dovetailed with it, has been mentioned above. But the credit plan for the whole economy is supposedly a mere summation of the credit plans for individual sectors and enterprises. It follows that currency circulation will not transcend its planned limits if each economic unit adheres strictly to its financial plan, and, one might add, if no major errors are committed in the course of planning. In theory, therefore, given proper planning, the prevention of inflation rests on strict "financial discipline" for managers, and on a vigilant enforcement of it on the part of the banks.

Crucial in this connection is the clear dichotomy drawn in Soviet practice between money in currency form and money in the form of current and clearing accounts of enterprises with the Gosbank. The former (with insignificant exceptions) is the money of the population, that is, the means of payment used in transactions between the state and the individual and between individuals. Wages and salaries and other incomes of individuals are paid by the state in currency. Given temporarily fixed retail prices, excessive accumulation of currency in the hands of the population leads to the usual situation of repressed inflation: loss of labor incentives, inefficient and inequitable distribution of consumers' goods, and so forth. The other variety of money—not usually called "money" in Soviet literature—in the form of current and clearing accounts with Gosbank is reserved for effecting payments within the state sector; its excessive increase presumably does not present the authorities with similar problems of inflation, since undue accumulations of liquid funds held by enterprises are periodically excised by the treasury and since actions of managers are seriously constrained by the requirements and directives of the plan. (In fact, however, the actions of managers are probably not entirely insensitive to an inflationary situation.) The control duties of the Gosbank are conspicuously stringent at the very points where bank money is transformed into currency, as in the provision of currency for the payment of wages and salaries, and where currency is absorbed back into the body of state enterprise, as in the collection of receipts of retail stores. By a meticulous supervision of these channels of outflow and inflow of currency, the state attempts to keep the amount of currency in circulation within the bounds foreseen by the plan.

During the prewar years, Soviet authorities, despite avowed intentions to the contrary, were ineffective in preventing the overissue of currency, in large part probably because the control machinery over the outflow and inflow of cash was not yet sufficiently developed. It was found difficult in those years to keep income payments, chiefly wages and salaries, within planned bounds. The Gosbank was not endowed with far-reaching power over the payment of wages by enterprises until 1939. Competition by managers for scarce skilled labor, failure of labor efficiency to rise to anticipated levels, premature upgrading, payroll "padding," and other causes were constantly pushing the wage bill above its planned limit. The official wage level followed suit, recognizing the *de facto* increases, and thus adjusting itself (though with a lag) to the existing money supply. Between 1928 and 1940 the average annual wage and salary increased almost sixfold, with no commensurate rise in productivity even claimed by official sources. The year 1937, the last year of the Second Five-Year Plan, provides an interesting case in point. Originally, the Plan foresaw an average wage (or salary) of 1,755 rubles for that year. The *annual* plan for 1937 revised the figure upward to 2,976 rubles. The *realized* figure was 3,047 rubles, despite the underfulfillment of the targets (in terms of "constant" prices) for both national income and the gross output of industry.

Since the targets for the output of consumers' goods were typically not fully met in those years, and since prices remained temporarily fixed, the return flow of currency from the population to the state frequently fell short of the anticipated amounts. The inevitable result was a rapid increase in currency in circulation, as has been shown in Table 1. The experience of the First Five-Year Plan is particularly illustrative: Currency in circulation amounted to 1,970,000,000 rubles on October 1, 1928, the starting date of the First Plan period; it was anticipated to increase up to 2,900 million or 3,220 million rubles at the end of the five years (by October 1, 1933), but instead actually reached 8,410 million rubles by January 1, 1933.

The extensive issue of currency during the war years and the ensuing currency conversion in 1947 have already been mentioned. It is noteworthy that (judging from the extremely scanty information available) the line against inflation seems to have been held quite successfully since 1947, when the monetary overhang may be presumed to have been completely wiped out by the currency conversion. There is no evidence that average wages have risen substantially, if at all, since then, and there are no known indications of a repressed inflationary situation. If this impression is a correct one, credit must be given to (*a*) determined disinflationary planning, and (*b*) tight financial control by the banking system (and other authorities). The chief disinflationary[30] feature of postwar planning has apparently been the setting of retail prices high enough to yield large budgetary surpluses[31] to reabsorb into the state sector a great part of the currency outlay (to the population) caused by the steady increase in bank credit. Thus, presumably, the growth of currency in circulation is planned to stay within the limits warranted by the general growth of the market economy. In addition, the control functions of the banks, at least with respect to payroll disbursement, are apparently being conducted with sufficient success to sustain the planned disinflationary measures.

30 The term "disinflationary" is here to be understood in the sense of preventing an undue expansion in currency in circulation rather than in the sense of preventing a high (retail) price level.

31 In Soviet practice, receipts from the sale of bonds to the population (and to savings institutions serving the population) are considered a part of budgetary receipts for purposes of determining the budgetary surplus. This is a valid approach for purposes of dealing with the inflation problem, since the sale of bonds to the population returns currency to the state sector no less than does outright taxation.

The Role of the Interest Rate.—As has been mentioned above, Soviet banks charge (rather moderate) interest on the short-term and long-term loans made by them. It will be recalled that long-term loans are made only to cooperative enterprises and, occasionally, to individuals, but not to state-owned enterprises. However, state-owned enterprises do not pay or impute any interest on the "charter funds" with which they are endowed by the state to cover their requirements for fixed capital and a minimum of working capital. Although the payment of interest by one socialist entity to another seems to stand in conflict with Marxist economic doctrine, the practice of charging interest by banks is explained on pragmatic grounds. On the one hand, the revenue from interest charges provides banks (especially the Gosbank) with operating income. On the other hand, and probably of greater significance as a reason for the practice, interest charges on the borrowed portion of working capital stimulate managers to a more prudent husbanding of the resources of the enterprise. Yet, the effectiveness of the last point may be seriously doubted. The interest charges are quite low in view of the almost perpetual sellers' market in which the Soviet economy operates and of the inflationary experience of the past; these considerations undoubtedly have created a substantial bias in the minds of Soviet managers in favor of accumulating ample (and frequently illegally large) inventories. The periodic concerted drives staged by the regime to "liberate" excessive holdings of inventories by enterprises bear witness to this conclusion. It remains to be seen whether the determined anti-inflationary efforts of the Soviet authorities since 1947 will bear fruit in terms of lessening the propensity of managers to hoard material assets.[32]

It has also been mentioned above that savings banks pay 3 percent and 5 percent interest on the deposits of the population, depending on the type of deposit. It may be doubted that this premium is of major importance in eliciting the growth of savings deposits. Both the low standard of living and the comprehensive social security program of the government militate against voluntary savings in the first place, while the fluctuations in the purchasing power of the ruble in the recent memory of the population must swamp whatever appeal the

[32] The problem of *imputing* a scarcity price (e.g., interest) to fixed capital in the process of economic planning (as apparently was, and possibly is still being, practiced by some of the Soviet planners) has been the subject of considerable discussion in Soviet economic and engineering literature in recent years. See G. Grossman, "Scarce Capital and Soviet Doctrine," *The Quarterly Journal of Economics*, LXVII (1953), 311–43.

earning of interest on savings deposits may have. The continual increases in consumers' prices during the prewar years of the Plan period and the wartime experience culminating in a partial loss of deposits in savings banks during the monetary reform of 1947 must have had an adverse effect on voluntary saving, far outweighing the attraction of interest payments. However, the periodic reduction in consumers' prices since 1947 may be having a favorable effect on the attractiveness of postponing consumption and must have added considerably more to the purchasing power of savings deposits than the interest earnings for the same years. Nevertheless, there is no evidence of any considerably increased tendency by the population after 1947 to accumulate savings deposits relative to disposable money incomes. (Subscriptions to the annual bond drives cannot be regarded as a form of voluntary saving, as has been pointed out above.) In any event, voluntary savings constitute a minute source of new investment funds in the USSR. The rate of real savings in the Soviet economy—which of course is, and has for some time been, very high—is a matter of political decision by the regime and is enforced by it, chiefly through taxation. It is obvious that, given the low standard of living, no rate of interest (within the bounds of reason) paid by savings banks or by government bonds could elicit that amount of savings from the population on a voluntary basis.

REFERENCES

SOVIET SOURCES

The transliteration of Russian names and titles follows the usage of the Library of Congress

Aleksandrov, A. M. Finansy i kredit SSSR. Moscow, 1948.

Atlas, E. Ia., and others. Denezhnoe obrashchenie i kredit SSSR. Moscow, 1947.

Batyrev, V. M., and B. K. Sitnin. Finansovaia i kreditnaia sistema SSSR. Moscow, 1945.

Boguslavskii, M., Ia. Greben', and A. Proselkov. Operativnaia tekhnika i uchet v Gosbanke SSSR. Moscow, 1946.

Boguslavskii, M. V., and A. A. Proselkov. Uchet i operativnaia tekhnika v Gosbanke. Moscow, 1950.

D'iachenko, V. P., and others. Finansy i kredit SSSR. Moscow, 1940.

Finansovoe pravo. Moscow, 1946.

Finansy SSSR za XXX let. Moscow, 1947.

Livshits, F. D. Bankovaia statistika. Moscow, 1948.
Rubinshtein, Ia. E. Denezhnye raschety sotsialisticheskikh predpriiatii. Moscow, 1950.
Shvarts, G. A. Beznalichnye vzaimnye raschety v SSSR. Moscow, 1946.
Usoskin, M. Osnovy kreditnogo dela. Moscow, 1946.
Valler, L. B. Sberegatel'nye kassy v SSSR. Moscow, 1946.

NON-SOVIET SOURCES

Ames, Edward. "Banking in the Soviet Union." *Federal Reserve Bulletin*, XXXVIII (1952), 351–58.
Arnold, Arthur Z. Banks, Credit, and Money in Soviet Russia. New York, 1937.
Bareau, P. "Banking in Soviet Russia." *Journal of the Institute of Bankers*, LXIII, No. 2 (1942), 83–93.
Baykov, Alexander. The Development of the Soviet Economic System. Cambridge, 1946. Chaps. II, VI, and XIX.
Berliner, Joseph S. "Monetary Planning in the USSR." *The American Slavic and East European Review*, IX (1950), 237–54.
Davies, R. W. "Short-term Credit in the USSR." *Soviet Studies*, V (1953), 18–31.
Dobb, Maurice. Soviet Economic Development since 1917. London, 1948. Chap. XIV.
Hubbard, L. E. Soviet Money and Finance. London, 1936.
League of Nations, Economic Intelligence Service. Commercial Banks 1929, 1929–1934. Geneva, 1935. Pages 117–21.
London, University of, School of Slavonic and East European Studies. Monograph No. 4–5: Banking and Credit in the Soviet Union. London 1935.
Reddaway, W. B. The Russian Financial System. London, 1935.
Schwartz, Harry. Russia's Soviet Economy. New York, 1950. Chap. XII.

UNITED KINGDOM OF GREAT BRITAIN AND NORTHERN IRELAND

by John Edwin Wadsworth

MANAGER, INTELLIGENCE DEPARTMENT, MIDLAND BANK LIMITED, LONDON, ENGLAND

THE BACKGROUND

FOR GENERATIONS past the people of the United Kingdom have been actively engaged in trading at home and overseas, and their livelihood depends on this commerce. Two-fifths of the 22 million persons in civil employment are occupied in manufacturing industries, producing goods for home needs and for sale abroad. Although special encouragement of farming has raised the level of home food production, the densely populated British Isles are far from being self-supporting, a high proportion of the food consumed being imported, as well as most of the raw materials required for large-scale industrial production. With long experience in overseas trade, London became the center for international finance. Despite the losses of war and the

---

JOHN EDWIN WADSWORTH is a graduate of the University of London, a fellow of the Institute of Bankers, and a fellow of the Royal Statistical Society. He entered the service of the Midland Bank in 1920. After experience at several branches in London and in industrial centers and at the Head Office, including some years in the Intelligence Department, he was appointed Assistant Manager at a London branch. In 1945 he returned to the Intelligence Department as assistant manager, becoming the manager two years later. His publications include: *A Hundred Years of Joint Stock Banking* (with W. F. Crick), London, 1936, the official history of the Midland Bank; *Counter Defensive* (the war story of the Midland Bank), London, 1946; and many articles, mainly in banking journals.

strains of postwar developments, more than half the total of international payments for world trade and other items are still made in sterling,[1] and the provision of capital for other countries has been resumed, though restricted in range and amount. The varied and complex credit requirements of this highly developed commercial community are met by the banking system, which furnishes the services essential for the maintenance of internal and external trade, though the setting for its activities has been transformed by war and postwar developments, and the monetary system is now regulated in ways which differ from those of prewar years.[2]

A fundamental change in Britain's monetary arrangements had been made earlier, a new attitude toward financial matters evolving with the departure from gold in 1931. The Exchange Equalisation Account was established to steady the external value of sterling, and minor measures were adopted for regulating overseas borrowing. But the clearest expression of the fresh attitude was the acceptance of the idea that monetary policy should be directed toward promoting healthy business conditions at home, even though this policy might involve variations in the external value of the currency. As a consequence, the responsibility for monetary policy naturally moved from the central bank to the government, a position confirmed in statutory form in 1946, when the Bank of England passed into public ownership. With the new approach in financial matters, the authorities reduced the general level of interest rates by expanding the resources of the commercial banks and by enlarging the supply of investment funds. The success of the operation encouraged the tendency to replace interest rates by more direct methods of financial control. Associated with this development was the "qualitative" regulation of capital investment, later embodied in postwar legislation in the Borrowing (Control and Guarantees) Act of 1946.

The "borrowing" act, together with the Exchange Control Act of 1947,[3] constituted "streamlined" legislation giving general control to the authorities, to be exercised in detail through statutory "Orders." In the main the Orders have continued the methods of regulation devised during the war. At the outbreak of hostilities, the existing meas-

1 European Recovery Programme Information Office, note on sterling and the proposed European Payments Union, March 20, 1950, p. 2.

2 The preexisting system is vividly portrayed in the report of the Committee on Finance and Industry (Macmillan Report), 1931, Cmd. 3897.

3 10 & 11 Geo. 6, c. 14.

ures of intervention in monetary affairs were merged into far-reaching controls of external and internal financial conditions. Overseas transactions became subject to strict exchange control, which, broadly speaking, operated by segregating from the rest of the world what was defined as the "sterling area"—this consisted of the members of the British Commonwealth, except Canada, and various other countries from time to time.[4] In this way a number of countries, which for many years had held balances in London and based their currencies on sterling, became an administrative unit throughout which sterling moved freely, while transactions with other countries were strictly regulated. Individual member countries of the sterling area all operated exchange control systems on similar lines. In postwar legislation the member countries were renamed the "scheduled territories," but the old, descriptive title is still the one more often used.

An important part of these developments consisted of the "dollar pool," into which the hard currency earnings of all member countries were channeled, for allocation by the authorities in London in the interests of the sterling area as a whole. For many years the central reserve for the United Kingdom and other sterling area countries had been held in London, and this became—and still remains—part of the exchange control arrangements, being operated through the Exchange Equalisation Account. Following Britain's concentration on war production, contributions to the dollar pool came largely from other member countries of the sterling area, Britain in turn providing sterling credited to accounts in London of their residents. Britain's outlays for military activities and purchases in such member countries were usually paid for by additions to sterling accumulated in London, thus increasing this form of debt which came to be known as the "sterling balances." Whereas before the war sterling held in London for accounts of overseas countries and organizations was estimated to amount to £800 million, at the end of the war the total exceeded £3,600 million and by June, 1953, it was nearly £4,200 million.[5] The "sterling balances" in London are, in fact, mainly holdings of Treasury bills and other government securities, and deposits with London

[4] The other member countries in December, 1953, were: Irish Republic; British Colonies, Trust Territories, Protectorates and Protected States; other Commonwealth countries, including Southern Rhodesia but excluding Canada; Burma; Iceland; Iraq; Jordan; Libya.

[5] On June 30, 1953, the "sterling liabilities" of the United Kingdom amounted to £3,607 million, and in addition liabilities of this kind held by non-territorial organizations were £566 million.

banks, which do not appear as part of the government's external debt. They are formally payable on demand or at short notice, but by arrangements with the individual countries restraint is exercised over the rate of using them or they are divided into those available for current use (on No. 1 account) and those which are temporarily blocked (on No. 2 account). Despite this mounting overseas indebtedness and the using up of reserves and overseas capital assets which were collected out of private hands, the financial requirements for the war effort could not have been met by Britain had it not been for the introduction of Lend-Lease and Mutual Aid arrangements granted by the United States and Canada.

Within the United Kingdom strict control was exercised over the capital market and investment. Private expenditure was curtailed by rationing and shortages, as well as by heavy taxation. The banks, too, were required to confine advances to those relating to wartime needs. In these ways the funds created by government spending in excess of revenue were guided back to official hands, directly by subscriptions to new government securities, or indirectly through increased deposits with the commercial or savings banks. Thus as the deposits of the commercial banks increased, the additional resources were necessarily invested in government securities. Notwithstanding the fact that nearly one half of wartime expenditure was met out of taxation, the national debt rapidly increased, the total rising from about £7,400 million to £22,400 million during hostilities and standing at over £26,000 million from March, 1953. A large part of war and postwar borrowing has been in the form of short-term "floating" debt, and a new government security was devised—the Treasury deposit receipt—to supplement Treasury bills, which for many years had been the principal instrument for government borrowing of this kind. In prewar years the proportion of floating debt was about one eighth of the total, but by 1945 it was more than one quarter and it remained around that proportion until the funding of Treasury bills in November, 1951. In this way, and also because the general level of interest rates was kept low during the war and early postwar years, the charge for interest on the national debt was held down. With government expenditure of great magnitude, over a period when production was mainly for war purposes, the internal purchasing power of the pound declined, despite the efficiency of wartime controls: wholesale prices in 1946 were 73 percent above the level of 1938, while food subsidies, which were arranged to check the rise in living costs, were running at high levels.[6]

At the end of hostilities Britain was confronted with grave difficulties: her external and internal debts were greatly enlarged, her external assets and reserves were depleted, property and equipment in many areas had been heavily damaged, while arrears in depreciation were general and stocks had run down. As a nation Britain had changed from a creditor to a debtor position on capital account. For a time the situation was relieved by lines of credit from the United States and from Canada ($3,750 million and $1,250 million respectively), as well as by substantial gifts from several Commonwealth countries. Despite this assistance, and a comparatively swift recovery in output, throughout the postwar period Britain has been confronted with the problems of pressure on her external balance of payments and of arresting inflationary trends at home. The severity of her struggle has been revealed by three monetary crises, resulting in the withdrawal of the "convertibility" of sterling only a few weeks after it was introduced in 1947, the devaluation of 1949 and the return to more orthodox monetary measures towards the end of 1951.

Throughout the war years rates of exchange for sterling were fixed by the authorities and held rigid by strict exchange control. Expenditures in hard currencies were arranged through the dollar pool. After hostilities ended, the rate for sterling was continued at the wartime level of $4.03 to the £, and this was the parity arranged later under the rules of the International Monetary Fund, of which Britain became a member. One of the terms of the Anglo-American loan agreement was that within a year after the credit became available sterling for current use should be made freely convertible into dollars and the dollar pool abandoned. The time permitted proved far too short, for when convertibility was attempted, in July, 1947, the problem of sterling balances was outstanding, and, as may be seen from Table 1, the external deficit on the sterling area's current account was running at a high level and was mounting in respect of dollar trade. The dollar credits were rapidly used and resources of the International Monetary Fund drawn upon, but the drain on the central reserves continued until arrested by the withdrawal of sterling convertibility. Britain was thus obliged to reimpose restrictions on current

[6] They amounted to £410 million in the financial year to March, 1952; by March, 1953, annual outgoings were reduced to £220 million.

payments overseas, and her external liabilities were augmented by the loans absorbed in the vain effort to maintain convertibility. To aid the situation imports were curtailed and further expansion of exports pressed, especially to the dollar areas.

With the help of these measures and the additional impetus to recovery, again provided by the United States through Marshall Aid, Britain's external situation showed marked recovery. By 1949 the United Kingdom's balance of trade, taken as a whole, was virtually in equilibrium, except for one section (Table 1). A large deficit persisted in trade with the dollar countries. A buyers' market was then becoming more general; exports were adversely affected by a minor setback in business conditions in the United States, where prices tended to decline, though still moving upwards in the United Kingdom. As the belief that sterling was overvalued became widespread, the sterling area reserves of gold and dollars, never large enough in postwar years, fell rapidly. The outward drain was eventually arrested by devaluation of sterling by about 30 percent in terms of dollars. The new rate of $2.80 was quickly followed by a general realignment of currencies, the various countries acting in consultation with the International Monetary Fund. Altogether, countries accounting for three fifths of the aggregate value of world trade at the time adjusted their parities. In respect of well over one third of the aggregate, the change was by about 30 percent.

In home conditions the risk of inflationary developments could never be ignored: production increased, but the additional supplies were diverted as far as possible into the export trade; restraints upon imports were maintained and made more exacting. Government expenditure continued to run at a high level, partly on subsidies to contain price increases but also to provide for measures of social improvement. As during hostilities, so in the immediate postwar years, inflationary forces were held back mainly by physical controls, and the position was eased by loans and gifts from abroad, as well as the deficit on the balance of overseas trade. Nevertheless, for a time the government's policy, with the prospective financial requirements for reconversion and nationalization, was directed to lowering still further the level of interest rates, even though this added to inflationary forces.

Almost immediately after the end of hostilities the rate on Treasury deposit receipts was reduced from 1.125 percent, at which it had stood from their introduction, to 0.625 percent, and correspondingly for

Treasury bills it fell to a little over 0.5 percent. At the same time rates on deposit accounts at the commercial banks were lowered, and on current accounts interest payments for credit balances ceased. Every opportunity was taken to bring down the yield on long-term government securities, sometimes with the aid of resources accumulating in the hands of official bodies, particularly the savings banks and social insurance funds.[7] In addition to holdings of this kind, the government debt held by the issue department of the Bank of England could also be varied from time to time to conform with official policy. Altogether, probably about one fifth [8] of the total marketable government debt remains subject to official influence, but use of these holdings has always been restrained by various limitations and the extent to which long-term trends in prices can be affected is uncertain. For a time the yield on government securities with no fixed date for redemption fell as low as 2.5 percent, but as the process of holding down interest rates developed, it was found to involve a persistent expansion in commercial bank deposits. As the opinion gained ground that rates were being pressed down too far, investors preferred to keep funds in bank balances, while the banks in turn enlarged their holdings in floating debt and government securities, thus leading to "monetization of debt."

After the end of hostilities, relaxations in rationing and allocations became possible and, with developing inflationary trends, the remaining physical controls were less effective, while savings were falling short of investment requirements. Thus at the end of 1946 official support of prices of government securities ceased and the rise in bank deposits was checked. Moreover, following the convertibility crisis of 1947, the remedy adopted was to arrange for a budget surplus as a means of absorbing excessive purchasing power, with restraint on wage increases and voluntary limitation of the rate of dividend payments. This, then, represented a major change in policy to "disinflation," as it was described, which was followed with added strictness at the time of devaluation. It is noteworthy that at this stage no attempt was made to apply the traditional remedy of a sharp rise in interest rates.

7 Investment of savings banks deposits and the surplus resources of social insurance funds is in the hands of Commissioners for Reduction of the National Debt who comprise the Chancellor of the Exchequer, the Governor and Deputy Governor of the Bank of England, the Speaker of the House of Commons, the Lord Chief Justice, the Master of the Rolls, and the Accountant-General of the Supreme Court.

8 "The Size and Shape of the National Debt," *Midland Bank Review*, February, 1950, p. 3.

With the withdrawal of government support, the yield on government securities without a final date for redemption rose to over 3 percent, and in March, 1951, it was approaching 4 percent, but on short-term government borrowing rates were still held at the levels established in 1945, and the Bank rate then remained unchanged at 2 percent.

As government requirements for bank credit declined under the policy of disinflation, another development came to the fore. Businesses which had used up reserves accumulated during the war years were finding themselves short of working funds, especially as increasing commercial activity and rising prices called for larger resources. Some trades were reverting from government to private hands and stocks were higher. At the same time, taxation on profits and private incomes made it difficult to set aside adequate sums for capital purposes. In consequence, business firms turned to commercial banks for assistance and bank advances increased, though still conforming to government policy. The lessened demands made by government finance on the banks in conditions of disinflation did not bring down the level of deposits, which remained high to meet the enlarged requirements for advances.

After devaluation, recovery in the central reserves of the sterling area at first was marked, and during 1950, as Table 1 shows, a substantial surplus was earned by the sterling area on current balance of payments with the dollar area as well as with the world as a whole. Hence it was found possible for Marshall Aid for the United Kingdom to be suspended from the beginning of 1951, when the aggregate amount allotted to Britain had reached $2,694 million. In these conditions, and with sterling being still more widely used in international trade, some steps in the direction of convertibility were arranged, partly through the extension of the Transferable Account System [9] within Britain's own exchange control, but also through participation in international arrangements. Besides being a member of the International Monetary Fund and International Bank for Reconstruction and Development, Britain has also joined the European Payments Union, set up by the Organization for European Economic Co-operation to replace and extend the machinery of the intra-European payments schemes. In the Union, Britain participates on behalf of the rest of the sterling area, except Iceland, a country which is a member

[9] Residents of any Transferable Account country may make payments in sterling for direct current transactions to residents in other Transferable Account countries.

in its own right. Under the scheme, the sterling balances held by other members of the Union at June 30, 1950, were made available for the settlement of their deficits with the Union, the United States guaranteeing Britain against any loss of gold arising from this use of the balances.

It seemed that after five years Britain had reached independence of aid from abroad, but the improved situation was short-lived. Hostilities in Korea brought wide fluctuations in world prices of primary commodities and sharp variations in buying for stocks on government and private account. In the first half of 1951 the terms of trade turned swiftly against Britain, but imports were still increasing, partly to meet rearmament demands and restocking. In the monthly settlements of the European Payments Union, Britain became a debtor from September, 1951, onwards, and the strain on her current balance of payments led holders of sterling abroad to suppose that the external value of the pound might not be maintained. Britain's reserves began to run down rapidly, and they were further reduced at the end of the year by the first repayments of the American loan and of the Canadian credit, the terms of these facilities calling for $138.7 million (United States) and $37.7 million (Canadian) then and for each of the next 49 years. By March, 1952, most of the additions to Britain's reserves since the year of devaluation had been drained away.

In this situation imports were again curtailed and payments abroad restricted in various ways, while steps were taken to stimulate exports still further. The aim, in which Commonwealth countries agreed to participate, was to restore equilibrium between the sterling area and the rest of the world by the second half of 1952. By far the most noteworthy change, however, was the resumption of control, by the Bank of England and the Treasury, over the volume of bank cash and the return to the use of interest rate policy as a major instrument in monetary affairs. At the beginning of November, 1951, Bank rate was raised to 2.5 percent, and a special rate, of 2 percent, was introduced at which the Bank of England would provide loans to the money market against Treasury bills. The movement was carried further in March when Bank rate rose to 4 percent and the new special rate to 3.5 percent. Other rates moved upwards, the yield on government securities without a fixed date for redemption then running well above 4 percent. At the time of the first change in the Bank rate, Treasury bills to a total of about £1,000 million, roughly half of them held by the banks, were converted into one-, two- and three-year serial funding stocks. About the same total of government securities was dealt with when the one-year series approached maturity, with other government obligations of longer term, and as before the banks followed the wishes of the authorities in supporting the operation. The reduction in the liquidity of bank assets, with measures for restricting the supply of bank cash, tended to curtail the lending power of the banking system, though further short-term government borrowing soon restored the banks' holdings of Treasury bills. Meanwhile, the higher level of Bank rate brought about increases in the rate of interest allowed on deposit accounts and in the rates charged to borrowers.

A third change took place in September, 1953, when Bank rate was "unified" at 3.5 percent with the special rate for loans from the Bank of England to the money market, leading to greater flexibility in money market rates. Shortly afterwards, a third postwar conversion operation showed that market conditions were to rule over a still wider field, for this time the banks were left free to participate in the conversion, or to take up new stock as seemed best to them; the operation proved to be a success. The return to orthodoxy in monetary matters was thus confirmed, but at the same time the selective regulation of bank advances, as developed in war and postwar years, was continued and intensified.

Following this great change in monetary arrangements the amount of the central reserves has recovered, and prices generally have been stable. In addition, funds from the United States for defense expenditure have been made available through the Mutual Security Agency. Since the introduction of the new policy a number of terminal markets for commodities have been reopened and the banks have been granted greater freedom in their dealings in foreign currencies, though transactions remain subject to exchange control. Despite this improvement, while demands upon Britain's output continue to be pressed from so many directions at once—for defense, for exports, for equipment, and for consumption, to say nothing of the deferred claims upon production represented by the sterling balances—the possibility of inflationary trends recurring has always to be borne in mind, as well as the fact that the amount of gold and dollar reserves is still low in relation to the volume of transactions they have to support.

TABLE 1
BALANCE OF PAYMENTS AND RESERVES,
UNITED KINGDOM AND REST OF STERLING AREA, 1947, 1949–53
(AMOUNTS IN MILLIONS OF POUNDS STERLING)

A. UNITED KINGDOM

	1947	1949[a]	1950	1951	1952	First half 1953[b]
Balance of payments, deficit (−) or surplus (+), on current account with:						
All countries	−443	+ 31	+298	−410	+269	+ 81
Dollar area	−510	−296	− 80	−426	−161	+ 34
Net gold and dollar receipts and payments in respect of:						
Rest of sterling area	−222	+ 14	+269	+181	+109	+ 79
Other transactions	−292	− 66	+118	−162	−122	+ 73
Loans and grants received	+872	+345	+268	+ 63	− 1	
Net change in reserves	−152	− 3	+575	−344	−175	+186

B. STERLING AREA

(AMOUNTS IN MILLIONS OF UNITED STATES DOLLARS)

	1947	1949[a]	1950	1951	1952	First half 1953[b]
Gold and dollar reserves at end of period	2,079	1,688	3,300	2,335	1,846	2,367[c]

[a] Sterling was devalued from $4.03 to $2.80 to the £ on September 19, 1949.
[b] Provisional figures.
[c] On January 31, 1954, the total stood at $2,543 million.

COMMERCIAL BANKS IN THE UNITED KINGDOM

In all the stress of war and postwar developments the structure of British banking has shown little change, though operating methods have been adapted to meet the fresh requirements of internal and external commerce. The banks, enjoying complete public confidence, function through a closely coordinated system, and for well over half a century checks drawn on them have constituted the principal means of settlement and remittance. The whole financial organization of the United Kingdom centers on London, and there, with the Bank of England at the hub, are to be found the head offices of the largest banks; important branches of other banks, including those operating in overseas countries; the discount houses; merchant banks or acceptance houses; insurance concerns; the Stock Exchange and other financial markets. Interrelationships between City organizations are closely woven on a traditional pattern, and the London money market, with banks and discount houses as its most active constituents, is sensitive to conditions at home and abroad, while in some respects the various elements in "the City" work together as an entity.

Most of the banks have been established for at least a hundred years, and many can trace their history much farther back through generations of private bankers.[10] Structural simplification of the banking system has resulted from the amalgamation movement which, over the past century, has gathered individual local banks into a few undertakings, principal among them being five large banks, all with country-wide branch systems. The "Big Five" are together responsible for approximately three quarters of the banking resources of the United Kingdom, and for about the same proportion of branch offices. In addition, some of them own the share capital of banks in Scotland and Northern Ireland, which are their "affiliated" companies, and own or have large interests in banks operating abroad. Other substantial banks have head offices in Liverpool and Manchester, while Scotland and Ireland have indigenous banks, including those affiliated with English undertakings. Consolidation in banking was checked in 1918, when, to remove anxieties concerning the possible emergence of a banking monopoly,[11] the banks agreed to submit proposals for further amalgamations to the Treasury for approval, and for the past thirty years alterations in the banking structure have been few and relatively limited in scope.

In Table 2 the London clearing banks and other groups into which the banks fall are indicated: information on current activities of

TABLE 2
BANKS IN THE UNITED KINGDOM, END OF 1953 [a]
(AMOUNTS IN MILLIONS OF POUNDS STERLING)

	Number of Branches	*Capital, Reserves, etc.*	*Deposits*	*Notes*
England and Wales				
Barclays	2,094	36	1,389	
Lloyds	1,710	32	1,206	
Midland	2,121	31	1,444	
National Provincial	1,350	22	871	
Westminster	1,104	20	854	
Total, Big Five	8,379	141	5,764	

10 House histories of many of the large banks have been published; see Bibliography.
11 Report of the Treasury Committee on Bank Amalgamations, 1918, Cmd. 9052.

TABLE 2 (*Continued*)

	Number of Branches	*Capital, Reserves, etc.*	*Deposits*	*Notes*
Coutts [b]	6	2	53	
District	539	7	252	
Glyn, Mills [c]	2	2	71	
Martins	593	10	331	
National [d]	26	3	79	1
Williams Deacon's [c]	212	4	143	
Total, London Clearing	9,757	168	6,694	1
Other [e]	10	2	40	
Total, England and Wales	9,767	170	6,734	1
Scotland				
Affiliated with English banks, as indicated:				
British Linen (Barclays)	201	4	84	10
Clydesdale & North of Scotland (Midland)	353	6	167	20
National Bank of Scotland (Lloyds)	200	4	97	11
Total, affiliated banks	754	14	348	41
Bank of Scotland	238	8	94	12
Commercial Bank of Scotland	326	7	125	16
Royal Bank of Scotland	230	9	140	11
Union Bank of Scotland	202	4	75	9
Total, Scotland	1,750	42	782	89
Northern Ireland				
Affiliated with English banks, as indicated:				
Belfast Banking (Midland)	86	2	38	1
Ulster (Westminster)	93	3	49	2
Total, affiliated banks	179	5	87	3
Other	199	12	264	5
Total, Northern Ireland [f]	378	17	351	8
Total, United Kingdom	11,923 [g]	229	7,867	98

[a] December 31, 1953, for banks in England and Northern Ireland, and nearest date for banks in Scotland.

[b] Affiliated to National Provincial Bank.

[c] Affiliated to Royal Bank of Scotland.

[d] English branches only. The National Bank also has 217 branches in the Republic of Ireland and 11 branches in Northern Ireland, from which notes are issued. Total deposits and notes are quoted as these are not distinguished geographically.

[e] Grindlays, Hoare, Isle of Man Bank.

[f] Including Northern Ireland branches of banks with head offices in Republic of Ireland. These banks have, in addition, 779 branches in the Republic of Ireland, and the Ulster Bank has 94. Deposits and note issues are quoted in total as these are not distinguished geographically. One bank, the Royal Bank of Ireland, has no branches in Northern Ireland.

[g] Including offices in England of the Scottish banks (25) and of the Irish banks (3).

British banks is not comprehensive, but regularly published figures generally relate to the eleven banks which are members of the London Clearing House. The other sections in the table are distinguished because Scotland has its own body of law and the banking system in some ways differs from that of England and Wales, as also does that of Northern Ireland, notably because in those areas the commercial banks still issue notes, just as does the Isle of Man Bank.[12] But these issues are only of historical significance. Nearly half of the resources of all banks in Scotland are in the hands of banks affiliated with English institutions, while part of the cash reserves of the independent banks is held in London, and two of the three indigenous banks in Northern Ireland are affiliated with English banks. In all essentials the banks throughout the United Kingdom provide a similar kind of banking service. They are often referred to as the joint stock banks, a term which corresponds with commercial banks as now generally used.

By far the principal activity of the commercial banks is to maintain the system of payment and transmission of funds through the check system. Customers' balances in aggregate make up "Deposits" or, as they are formally described in the balance sheet, "Current, deposit and other accounts." They comprise current accounts, upon which checks are drawn, and deposit accounts which are subject to notice of withdrawal, usually of 21 days, and receive interest.[13] The figures in Table 3 show that, whereas in prewar years total deposits were roughly equally divided between current and deposit accounts, during the postwar period current accounts have represented about two thirds of the total, a change attributable to several influences, including the lessened attraction of deposit accounts when interest allowances were low. There are always checks in course of collection, and individual banks will hold checks on other banks and have balances with them. When considering the aggregate figures of the banks these transit items—usually between 3 percent and 4 percent of total deposits—can be deducted to eliminate duplication (see Table 3), thus giving a figure for "net deposits," but clearly this refinement cannot be made in the figures for one bank. Each individual bank

12 Notes are also issued by the local authority in Guernsey.

13 Among deposit accounts are "home safe" accounts for encouraging thrift and receiving specially favorable rates of interest for limited amounts, while "other accounts" include internal accounts of the banks themselves.

when assessing the proportion of various assets to resources, for example the ratio of cash to deposits, necessarily works upon its own total for gross deposits.

The aggregate figures for net deposits are subject to seasonal fluctuations,[14] but apart from these and occasional special influences, the reasons for changes in the volume of deposits are to be sought in the effects of war and postwar finance, government policy, the balance of external transactions, and the activities of the banks themselves. Besides providing for the distribution and transmission of money, mainly in the form of bank deposits, the banking system is also a channel through which money is brought into being. Taking the banking system as a whole, bank advances, as they are used, necessarily reappear as bank deposits, and government borrowing from the banks likewise adds to the volume of bank deposits. But the initiative in adding to the supply of money does not rest with the commercial banks. Their strict adherence to the cash ratio places the control of the volume of deposits in the hands of the Bank of England. For example, as a result of war and postwar government finance, net deposits were more than doubled during the war years, the rise continuing until steadied after 1947, as Table 3 shows, at about two and three-quarter times the 1938 figure. From then on, however, the authorities, while themselves making somewhat lessened demands upon banks for short-term borrowing, nevertheless have allowed the level of deposits to be maintained or increased, following the rise in advances, without further adjustments in other assets. After Bank rate was raised in November, 1951, and the funding of Treasury bills took place, the central bank could influence the credit policies of the commercial banks through the level of interest rates and by way of liquidity ratios (see pp. 787–88).

The individual banks, as business rivals, each endeavor to increase the share they hold of aggregate deposits, though they do not compete through rates of interest offered for them. During hostilities the banks agreed not to attract deposits from one another by higher rates, and in postwar years this arrangement has continued; from early postwar years until November, 1951, the maximum rate for deposit accounts was 0.5 percent (subject to 14 days' notice of withdrawal), and it has

14 In particular, deposits tend to fall in the early months of the year as tax payments draw down credit balances. An index computed by Lloyds Bank shows the movement in deposits free of seasonal influences.

varied with Bank rate, standing at 1.75 percent at 21 days' notice at the end of 1953. No interest at all is allowed on credit balances on current accounts. Competition is therefore expressed largely in lending activities, and in services offered and charges for them, as well as through advertisements and other public relations activities, which have been extended in postwar years. Each of the principal banks has more than a thousand branches and two have over two thousand, there being one bank office for about every 3,000 adult persons in Great Britain.

A widespread use of checks has been encouraged by codified legislation,[15] by the early development of the simple device of "crossing" checks,[16] and still more by the clearing system, which furnishes a reliable and speedy method of handling them. In 1953, £345 million items passed through the London Clearing House, representing in aggregate value over £123,000 million; in addition, provincial centers have their own clearing arrangements, some with a local clearing house, while substantial quantities of checks paid in for collection are drawn on branches of the receiving bank and are handled through its own organizations.[17] Settlements of clearing balances are made by transfers between the accounts of the commercial banks at the Bank of England and so affect the cash position of individual banks.

LIQUID ASSETS

In the disposition of the assets of the banks the effects of war and postwar finance have been striking, while a remarkable change took place with the funding of Treasury bills in November, 1951. If the assets are arranged as in Table 3, it is at once apparent how considerable is the proportion of resources employed, directly or indirectly, in government finance, the "public sector" absorbing two thirds of the total for net deposits. "Cash" consists, in part, of balances held by the commercial banks with the Bank of England, and, in somewhat smaller part, of Bank of England notes and coins in the tills. Cash represents finance for the government because resources of the Bank of England are in the main lent to the authorities, directly or in-

15 Bills of Exchange Act, 1882, 45 & 46 Vict., c. 61, and amending legislation.

16 By drawing two parallel lines across the face of a check it becomes a "crossed check" which has to be paid to a banker and is therefore usually presented through the clearing. It cannot ordinarily be cashed across the counter by the holder, and this represents an effective safeguard for checks sent by post.

17 To judge from stamp duty paid (each check ordinarily is stamped twopence), the number of checks issued in 1952 was at least 767 million.

TABLE 3

LONDON CLEARING BANKS, LIABILITIES AND ASSETS,[a] NOVEMBER 30, 1938, 1945, AND 1949–53

(AMOUNTS IN MILLIONS OF POUNDS STERLING)

	1938	*1947*	*1949*	*1950*	*1951*	*1952*	*1953*
Current accounts	1,255	3,781	3,977	4,109	4,118	3,949	4,080
Deposit and other accounts	1,013	1,986	2,089	2,142	2,071	2,234	2,339
Total deposits	2,268	5,767	6,066	6,251	6,189	6,183	6,419
Less checks in course of collection, etc.	59	184	202	221	215	209	225
"Net" deposits	2,209	5,583	5,864	6,030	5,974	5,974	6,194
"Cash"	237	487	497	502	517	503	520
"Cash" as percent of total deposits (cash ratio)	10.5	8.5	8.2	8.0	8.4	8.1	8.1
Money at call and short notice	155	483	553	555	570	524	478
Bills (mainly Treasury bills)	272	799	1,215	1,445	901	1,142	1,354
Treasury deposit receipts		1,195	688	477	108		
Liquid items (including Treasury deposit receipts)	664	2,964	2,953	2,979	2,096	2,169	2,352
Liquid items as percent of total deposits (liquidity ratio)	29.3	51.4	48.7	47.7	33.9	35.1	36.6
Investments (mainly government securities	644	1,500	1,517	1,514	2,033	2,138	2,245
Total, mainly government finance	1,308	4,464	4,470	4,493	4,129	4,307	4,597
Advances	972	1,199	1,478	1,618	1,927	1,746	1,678
Advances as percent of total deposits	42.8	20.8	24.4	25.9	31.1	28.2	26.1

[a] Omitting various items, particularly capital, reserves, and other amounts which change infrequently, as well as those with contra entries.

directly, while the cover for the note issue consists of government securities. By an arrangement made in December, 1946, the ratio of cash to gross deposits in individual banks is maintained on a regular day-to-day basis of 8 percent and is published for figures struck on the same day in each month by all the clearing banks. In this way "window dressing," as formerly practiced by some of the banks, no longer confuses the figures, while the mechanics of banking control are made the more precise.[18] No interest is earned by the commercial banks on their deposits with the Bank of England; like cash, these are therefore unremunerative.

[18] Macmillan Report, 1931, Cmd. 3897, describes the part formerly played by window dressing of the cash ratio in monetary arrangements.

Money at call and short notice, the next most liquid asset of the banks, again provides finance for the government. It is comprised mainly of loans made at call or for a few days to the money market (that is, to discount houses for carrying bills, mostly Treasury bills) and government bonds; but also, in part, of similar advances to Stock Exchange firms. As the commercial banks do not rediscount the bills they have bought, either with the Bank of England or with other banks, money market loans represent their day-to-day link with the central bank. It is through this channel that they have indirect access to the funds of the central bank, though sometimes the Bank of England buys bills from the commercial banks to preserve more orderly money market conditions.

Treasury bills constitute a method of short-term borrowing which the government has used for many years. The bills, which are repayable in 91 days, are either offered for tender once a week or issued to government departments and similar bodies having spare funds "through the tap," that is, direct from the Treasury. The bills held by the commercial banks consist mainly [19] of Treasury bills, commonly forming part of the issue made by tender. Actually, however, the London clearing banks obtain their holdings from the discount houses; individual banks select bills at least seven days old and of varying maturity dates to suit their future daily requirements. Treasury bills are readily salable on the London money market, where they are highly liquid through the facilities made available by the Bank of England.

Treasury deposit receipts were introduced during the war years as a new form of floating debt, which the banks took up from week to week in amounts determined primarily by Exchequer requirements. These receipts constituted a principal item in bank assets during the war years and were, in effect, advances to the government for periods of six months. In postwar years they were made available for periods of 154, 182, and 210 days. Unlike Treasury bills, Treasury deposit receipts (TDR's) could not be negotiated or transferred, but formally they could be discounted before maturity at the Bank of England at Bank rate (a facility which would have meant a loss to the holding bank and was not used), or they could be offered in payment for subscriptions to new government securities, subscriptions made for

[19] In November, 1953, about 96 percent of total bill holdings of the London clearing banks were Treasury bills.

a bank's own portfolio, or on behalf of its customers. In postwar years, when the only government securities on offer for long periods have been for advance tax payments and small savings,[20] TDR's became virtually loans for fixed periods to the government. Thus they were theoretically less liquid than Treasury bills, for, besides their longer term, TDR's were a purely banking security, whereas Treasury bills are held also by government departments, discount houses, overseas monetary institutions, and similar bodies. With the government's switch to the use of Treasury bills for short-term borrowing and subsequent suspension of the issue of TDR's this security made a last appearance in the monthly figures of the clearing banks in February, 1952.

With the expansion of government short-term borrowing, the banks' interests in floating debt had become larger. Whereas in 1938 bills accounted for little more than one tenth of net deposits of the clearing banks, in November, 1950, the proportion was nearly one quarter, or about one third if TDR's were included, and in consequence the position of the banks was more liquid. At the same time bank assets were less remunerative, for short-term rates were then controlled at a low level. Loans to the money market were made at annual rates ranging between 0.5 percent and 1.5 percent, while the banks bought Treasury bills at 0.5 percent. Following the changes in Bank rate in November, 1951, and again in March, 1952, rates increased and became more flexible, prime bank bills in November, 1953, earning from 1.75 percent to 2.25 percent and Treasury bills over 2 percent. In November, 1951, also, the funding of Treasury bills redistributed bank assets by increasing investments and reducing holdings of floating debt. This was of importance in monetary technique because in prewar years the banks maintained a conventional proportion of "liquid assets" of around 30 percent, known as the "liquidity ratio." Since the early war years the liquidity ratio had been well above the conventional level, and, counting Treasury deposit receipts among liquid assets, this condition of high liquidity persisted into the postwar period, as may be seen in Table 3. In November, 1951, however, the liquidity ratio was brought down to around 30 percent. This tended to curtail the lending power of the banks because, unless deposits increased, a rise in advances would involve sales of invest-

20 Tax Reserve Certificates, which were introduced in the war years and are designed to be used for tax payments so that sums can be conveniently accumulated as profits are earned; Defence Bonds and Savings Certificates. See p. 802.

ments to restore the liquidity ratio. Liquid assets comprise cash, money at call and short notice, and bills (mainly Treasury bills), all of which are subject to the influence of the authorities. Thus the liquidity ratio, though observed with more flexibility than the cash ratio, presents another method whereby the central bank is able to affect the banking situation.

RISK ASSETS

Investments of the banks consist almost entirely of British government securities. Before the outbreak of war the banks' holdings of government securities absorbed rather more than one quarter of total deposits, and until November, 1951, they were still around the same proportion of the much larger total. Since then, with the additions from the funding of Treasury bills they have accounted for over one third. As yields rose over the postwar period market prices of government securities fell, and, although bank investments in general consist of short-term or medium-term issues having smaller swings in prices, the downward trend must have required substantial writing down at balance sheet dates, when investments are valued "at or below market prices." Accordingly, in June, 1952, four of the five largest banks decided that investments should no longer be written down out of profits or by transfers from inner reserves. Instead, they were valued at or under cost and below redemption price; because at June, 1952, market prices were below these book values, the statements for each bank concerned also gave the aggregate value at market prices. In subsequent half-yearly banking figures the revised method of valuation has been used, although, as has been stated, market prices of investments have been in excess of book values. Liquidity requirements are higher when investments, as risk assets, are vulnerable to movements in interest rates. Of wider significance is the fact that the banking system holds about one quarter of all marketable government securities.[21]

By contrast with the greater claim on bank resources made by government finance, the proportion used for the private sector has been lower (see the percentage figures in Table 3). "Advances to customers and other accounts," as they appear in the balance sheet, in prewar conditions constituted nearly half the net deposits of the banks, but

21 "The Size and Shape of the National Debt," *Midland Bank Review*, February, 1950, p. 3.

in November, 1953, it was still little more than one quarter, though this represented substantial recovery from the level of about one sixth, when private business activities were restricted during hostilities. Nevertheless, bank advances provide a principal means of private and business finance for short periods. Sometimes this financing is in the form of overdrafts (more usual outside London), whereby the borrower conducts his account in debit to the amount required from day to day within an agreed limit; sometimes it is in the form of loans, when the borrowing is for the full amount on a separate account, as is customary in London. Overdrafts and loans are not separately distinguished in bank balance sheets, but with loans a credit balance is also maintained on current account, and to this extent both sides of the bank balance sheet may be inflated. Overdraft limits, which represent the amount the bank has arranged to lend on overdraft, as distinct from the amount outstanding at the time, are not published; it would, indeed, be difficult to place a precise figure on some understandings of this kind.

Bank advances are formally repayable on demand, though usually they run for six months and can be renewed, and therefore in commerce and industry they are fairly strictly confined to assisting in the provision of working capital, and in private borrowing for temporary facilities. Mortgage business is left largely to building societies and insurance undertakings and finance for fixed capital to other organizations. Moreover, the commercial banks do not directly provide hire-purchase (installment) finance, though—subject to Treasury guidance—they lend to undertakings specially equipped to do so. Advances are often supported by the deposit of collateral security, or by a personal guarantee, but they are also made on the strength of a balance sheet or on the reputation of the borrower. For many years the discounting of bills of exchange has been of comparatively small importance as a method of borrowing from the banks in internal trade; the promissory note as a bank security is uncommon. In war and post-war years bank advances have been subject to regulation by the authorities in conforming with the general direction of credit, and recent movements in the totals, as well as the regular classification of advances by industries, are discussed below as part of the qualitative control of credit. In addition to ordinary advances, the banks perform a number of services which involve a credit risk, for example in providing documentary credits and acceptances, in handling securities or documents, in participating in guarantees for due performance of contracts, and in providing indemnities of various kinds.

In arranging their assets the banks maintain a cash ratio of 8 percent of deposit liabilities and have co-operated with the authorities in providing short-term government finances. In other respects, however, the distribution of assets is in their own hands, and is directed to utilizing their resources profitably, in so far as this is consistent with safeguarding liquidity, in providing short-term government finances, avoiding undue capital losses, and complying with official guidance on bank lending. In practice the large banks tend to follow a similar pattern in their assets structure. The cash ratio has been proved by long experience, and—by convention—liquid assets, comprising cash, bills and money at call, are together maintained at not less than 30 percent of total deposits, representing the "liquidity ratio." The proportion of advances to deposits, however, is still well below that of prewar years, and for investments it is somewhat higher. Risk assets, comprising advances and investments together, represented 61 percent of total deposits in November, 1953; in prewar years the percentage was around 70.

A number of ancillary services are undertaken by the banks on behalf of customers, including safe custody of valuables, safe deposit facilities, payment of regular outgoings (such as rent and insurance premiums), and arrangements for a customer's check to be cashed at another town. By means of "trader's credits" one check can be used as an omnibus payment for several amounts to be separately credited to accounts at various banks and branches. "Home safes" are issued for savings accounts, and "night safes" are installed at branch banks for use of traders after business hours. Facilities are provided for stock exchange transactions on behalf of customers and dividends can be paid direct to a bank for the credit of a customer's account. Inquiries as to the financial standing of business undertakings and individuals are made as required. As for generations past, the bank manager acts as general adviser on many problems, not all of them financial, brought to the bank parlor for his consideration. Probably the most rapidly extending additional services, however, are those concerned with executor and trustee work and overseas business.

The commercial banks conduct executor and trustee business through departments or through subsidiary companies. Activities of this kind grew rapidly after the First World War, not only because large numbers of private individuals appointed banks as executors and trustees, but also because the banks acted as trustees for corporate bodies, and especially for unit trusts, many of which were formed at that period. Further expansion occurred during and after the Second World War, and it is noteworthy that in postwar years several new offices have been opened by the banks to deal with executor and trustee work.

OVERSEAS BUSINESS

The overseas business of the commercial banks, like their trustee activities, began to extend in the early years of this century, entering a field where, until then, the London merchant banks and specialized institutions, which are still of importance in international banking, had been unchallenged. As a general rule the commercial banks deal with other banks established abroad, and not directly with traders in another country, thus acting as sterling bankers for overseas banks and as agents on a reciprocal basis. In this way the widespread branch systems in the United Kingdom and comprehensive financial services of London are made available to banks abroad and visitors to this country, while the London banks and their customers have the benefit of the knowledge and experience of correspondent banks operating on their own territory. Some of the large joint-stock banks participate in banks operating overseas, but interests of this kind are more extensive in countries of the British Commonwealth than elsewhere.[22] Indeed, some British banks have relinquished part of their direct participations of this kind, while the Midland Bank as a matter of policy does not have any branches or interests in subsidiary companies abroad. Representatives of English banks in the United States and in South America are there to foster the business of the home bank.

Credits are arranged, in general, to cover exports from the United

[22] Barclays Bank has a controlling interest in the separate bank, Barclays Bank (Dominion, Colonial and Overseas), which in turn owns Barclays Overseas Development Corporation. Other subsidiary companies are Barclays Bank (Canada); Barclays Trust Company of Canada; and Barclays Bank (France). Lloyds Bank and National Provincial Bank own jointly Lloyds and National Provincial Foreign Bank Limited, and both have an interest in the Bank of British West Africa Limited. In addition, Lloyds Bank, Eastern Department, operates branches on the Indian continent, and Lloyds Bank is associated with the Bank of London and South America Limited and the National Bank of New Zealand Limited. Westminster Bank owns the Westminster Foreign Bank Limited and also has an interest in the Bank of British West Africa Limited.

Kingdom, or imports into it, and in respect of the movement of goods from one foreign country to another (goods which never touch Britain's shores), a form of international finance which is recovering the importance it enjoyed in prewar years. By opening a confirmed credit, which is irrevocable unless the beneficiary consents, the London bank is in effect granting accommodation; and when, as often occurs, banks outside the sterling area request this facility, sanction from the Exchange Control authorities is required and is commonly granted for ordinary trading purposes. Frequently sums are segregated in the London accounts of banks covering confirmed credits established on their instructions. In addition to credits, the shipment of goods is financed in various other ways, particularly by bills, negotiated or sent for collection by sellers of goods, a method of finance which has advantages for buyers.

As part of their activities in overseas business the commercial banks undertake heavy duties in the work of exchange control,[23] in addition to conducting transactions within the limits it imposes. British banks are "authorised agents" for the Treasury and are responsible for the day-to-day scrutiny of all transactions involving payments to and from other countries. Such transactions arise at branches of the banks in all parts of the country, and the exchange control forms on which they are presented are authorized there or sent to central departments in London for attention. An important change towards the end of 1951 was the reopening—on a restricted basis—of the foreign exchange market in London, which had virtually ceased to operate at the outbreak of hostilities. In the autumn of 1950 a narrowly limited freedom in dealings in Canadian dollars had been restored, and in the following spring authorized banks were permitted to buy and sell foreign notes and coins at market rates. In December, 1951, dealings for approved transactions in all those foreign currencies for which the Bank of England fixed rates were permitted between authorized banks, provided spot rates were kept within a range of rates set by the Bank of England. For spot transactions official rates were announced roughly 0.75 percent on either side of parity, that is, within the limits of 1 percent, up or down, prescribed by the rules of the International Monetary Fund. No official rates were applied to forward transactions. Since reopening the range of transactions in the market has been extended, the most significant addition being the introduction, in

[23] In accordance with the Exchange Control Act; see p. 770.

May, 1953, of arbitrage operations with various European countries in respect of spot and forward dealings in their currencies.

In the market in its postwar form the exchange control system as a whole continues to operate as before, and all foreign currency transactions by residents have to be related to current trade or other approved purposes. The authorized banks each have quotas, agreed with the Bank of England, setting limits to the amounts of the various foreign currencies they may hold as cover for forward commitments and for general transactions. Authorized brokers receive from the banks a fee for their services, and the banks charge their customers a commission, ranging from 0.125 percent to .031 percent in accordance with the amount of the transaction. In addition, with fluctuating rates the skillful dealer may make a "turn" on foreign exchange transactions.

Specialized departments deal with the servicing of securities held for owners abroad, with shipping requirements and—of special importance in postwar years—providing of trade information for customers in England seeking to expand their overseas business or for businessmen in other countries wishing to find a market in the United Kingdom.

Some idea of the volume of overseas business conducted by the commercial banks may be gathered from the balance sheet items for "Acceptances and confirmed credits," and for "Contracts for the forward sale of foreign currencies," which have risen in postwar years, but these do no more than reflect the position on the day when the balance sheet is made up. A more striking indication of the work involved is given by the fact that in 1948 one bank alone employed about a thousand persons on overseas business, and two years later it was dealing with exchange control forms at a rate of nearly a million a year.[24] London banks compete actively for foreign business by way of service and facilities, but rates of interest on credit balances are subject to the general maximum; in November, 1953, it was 1.75 percent a year at 21 days' notice, while for many overseas transactions uniform scales of charges, agreed upon between the principal banks, have been applied.[25] Earnings on the great volume of business

[24] The Midland Bank, Chairman's Annual Statement to Shareholders, January, 1951. H. H. Thackstone, *Current Financial Problems and the City of London,* p. 123.

[25] "The New Overseas Charges Agreement," *The Banker,* May, 1948, p. 110, where the principal charges are mentioned. In July, 1951, charges were raised, the minimum acceptance commission increasing from 0.75 to 1.2 percent.

make in aggregate a substantial contribution to Britain's invisible exports.

MANAGEMENT AND PROFITS

Notwithstanding the high proportion of their resources used in government finance and the work carried out for the authorities, the banks are commercial undertakings conducting business in active competition among themselves for profit on behalf of shareholders. Some consultation among them takes place at the Committee of London Clearing Bankers, through which the wishes of the Bank of England and the Treasury are communicated; the British Bankers' Association is a wider organization concerned with more general matters. The individual banks are registered as companies with limited liability, their capital being widely distributed among large numbers of shareholders,[26] and for most banks part of the uncalled capital may be called up only in the event of liquidation, thus constituting a "reserved liability." The boards of directors consist of men distinguished in public and business life; in some of the banks the principal executive officers are on the board of directors. As a rule the directors meet weekly or fortnightly, though committees for special purposes may be called more often, while the chairmen usually give full-time attendance at their banks. Day-to-day management of the individual banks is in the hands of the principal executive officers, sometimes acting together in a committee of management; in some banks considerable regional authority is vested in local boards or executives, whereas in others decisions are closely centralized in the head office.[27]

It is usual for employees to remain in the service of the same bank throughout their working lives, and the highest executive posts are open to every male entrant. With the extension of the use of bookkeeping machines, the proportion of women employed has increased: in 1950, of the total of 90,000 employed in banking in Great Britain, about 30 percent were women. During the war and postwar years individual banks have introduced schools for training new entrants and for more advanced studies. Largely because of an uneven rate of

[26] Of the 73,000 shareholders of the Midland Bank over one half own £100 or less of nominal paid-up capital of the Bank, and of the aggregate capital more than two thirds is owned by shareholders with £300 nominal or less (Annual Report, Midland Bank, December, 1950).

[27] G. E. Milward and others, *Large-Scale Organisation* (London, 1950), has chapters describing the organization of the Bank of England (by F. W. R. Laverack) and the Midland Bank (by H. L. Rouse).

entry in the interwar and war years, the age distribution of the staffs of banks is unsatisfactory. For most banks, staff representation takes place mainly through internal staff "associations"; the National Union of Bank Employees, affiliated with the Trades Union Congress, is recognized by only one of the principal banks. Two strikes of bank officials have occurred in Ireland, the first, in mid-1946 in Northern Ireland, lasting for nearly five weeks, and the second, at the end of 1950 in the Republic of Ireland, extending over seven weeks.

Some light on the activities of the commercial banks is shed by the regular classification of advances and by occasional observations in the chairmen's "statements" which accompany the annual accounts. These "statements," however, have wider importance, since they are generally read as an informed commentary on current economic conditions. In addition, the principal banks publish quarterly reviews, which are studied in government, academic, and business circles at home and abroad. The standard maintained by these publications indicates the use of economic and statistical departments within the banks, though it seems probable that the development of such activities has still to bring its full contribution to the banking service.

Little information is available on bank earnings and expenses. Dividends, after being lowered slightly by most banks in the depression of the thirties, were raised a little by some banks in 1952 and after. Meanwhile, published reserve funds have been enlarged and are now commonly at about the same figure as paid-up capital, but in addition the banks have the benefit of substantial "inner reserves," hidden by understatement of assets in the balance sheet. Even so, with the growth of deposits and business, the banks' own funds constitute a far smaller proportion of the total of banking commitments. At the end of 1938 the paid-up capital and published reserves of the London Clearing Banks amounted to 138.6 million or 6.3 percent of net deposits; by 1945 the percentage had fallen to 3.1 and by 1952 to 2.5, notwithstanding the fact that over the whole period the total for the banks' own funds increased to £160 million. The resources at the disposal of the banks are much larger than before the Second World War, but bank advances, which earn comparatively high rates, represent a lower proportion of assets. The average rate earned on advances is not known, though it has risen from the low level of the cheap money period, particularly as Bank rate has moved upwards. Terms for a bank advance might be expressed as "1 percent over

Bank rate, minimum 5 percent"; both the margin and minimum rate would vary in accordance with the standing of the borrower and nature of the advance. The other main source of earnings consists of service charges applied on current accounts, either as a percentage on turnover or at an amount for "commission" periodically assessed in relation to the activity of the account and credit balance maintained. If the "free balance" regularly standing at the credit of the account is large enough, then no charge will be made. Here again, no information as to the amount or average rate of service charge is published by the banks, but they probably range from the long-established 0.125 percent of turnover for comparatively small accounts to a few pence percent where the turnover is large. It seems probable that in recent years service charges have been rising and have been more widely applied, bringing a larger proportion to the total of bank earnings. Meanwhile, expenses of all kinds, in particular staff costs for salaries and pensions, are higher and seem to be moving upwards. With the rise in Bank rate, higher interest has been allowed on deposit accounts, thus adding to the working costs of the banks.

In various ways a more careful assessment of banking costs has been evident during postwar years. Since 1924 the principal banks had acted for one another's customers as required without interbank charges, but recently this system has changed, and in July, 1950, the two largest banks introduced a standard scale of charges for agency work on behalf of other banks, applied on an interbank basis and not as direct charges to members of the public. In all these developments affecting bank profits, where the balance rests between favorable and unfavorable influences is known only to individual bank managements, but the indications are that earnings have been increased in several directions to keep pace with rising costs.

QUALITATIVE CONTROL OF CREDIT

An important influence on the distribution of bank assets has been exercised through the "qualitative" control of credit, representing an entirely new development of the war and postwar years. New capital issues, bank advances, and other forms of borrowing have been permitted or proscribed in accordance with the purposes for which they are intended to be used, wartime regulations being continued in the

Borrowing (Control and Guarantees) Act of 1946 (9 & 10 Geo. 6, c. 58). In addition, for several years the Local Authorities Loans Act of 1945 (8 & 9 Geo. 6, c. 18) required all new borrowing by local authorities to be made from an official body—the Public Works Loan Commissioners—though short-term borrowing, including bank overdrafts, was permitted, for current temporary purposes, to the extent of one half the annual revenue of the borrowing authority. The Act was allowed to lapse at the close of 1952. Then again, the Exchange Control Act of 1947 debars the banks from lending, without official permission, to any undertakings within the sterling area which are controlled from outside that area, though generally speaking approval is given for advances and other credits for ordinary trading purposes.

One part of the main "borrowing" Act gives the Treasury power to guarantee loans, up to a maximum of £50 million in a year, if judged "expedient in the public interest for the purpose of facilitating the reconstruction of an industry or part of an industry in Great Britain," but this facility has not been used. The other part of the Act authorizes the Treasury to issue Orders regulating in Great Britain all borrowing exceeding £10,000 in any period of twelve months by one undertaking (a limit lifted by the first Order under the Act to £50,000). Regulations may also be made concerning the raising of money by the issue of shares or debentures for any amount by any corporate body (including unit trusts), or issues by any government other than the government of the United Kingdom. All transactions subject to regulation require approval by the Treasury, which acts through the Capital Issues Committee (CIC), a body of seven members experienced in finance and industry, appointed by the Treasury to act in an advisory capacity.[28]

Apart from borrowings by a local authority, to which special rules applied the legislation exempted from regulation borrowing for any amount from a bank in the ordinary course of the borrower's business. Sums received by a bank or discount house on current or deposit account also were not subject to control. Moreover, all unsecured borrowing repayable within six months was excluded, as well as borrowing for payment of death duties, or borrowing by building societies, industrial and provident societies of ordinary type. But even for borrow-

[28] At the outbreak of the Second World War the CIC replaced the Foreign Transactions Advisory Committee, which had been set up in 1936 to advise the Treasury on new capital issues affecting foreign exchanges. Members of the CIC usually meet weekly, but a permanent secretariat is available on all business days.

ing falling within these exemptions, nonstatutory guidance had to be taken into account.

Besides the first Order (SRO 945, 1947) in May, 1947, which made more explicit regulations already in being, only one other has since been issued, two years later (SRO 755, 1949), which had the effect of allowing bonus issues [29] up to £50,000 in any one year for one undertaking. In practice, therefore, regulation has followed the memorandum of guidance (Cmd. 6645) issued to the CIC prior to the Act by the government, which required new capital issues to be made "according to their relative importance in the general national interest, having regard, particularly, to current Government policy in respect of physical investment," and to be brought to the capital market in such a way as to avoid congested conditions. In greater detail the memorandum indicated that some types of issue would be favored, such as those for production for export, for industries in areas where unemployment was relatively high and for the production of raw materials or for essential services. Sympathetic consideration would be given where new capital was required by undertakings which had suffered from war damage or from enforced wartime changes. Issues for the distributive trades were to be restricted, as were those for the extension of hire-purchase facilities, while issues for finance companies, investment trusts, and unit trusts and entertainments would not normally be allowed.

The banks, too, as during hostilities, were brought into the program, a letter from the Chancellor of the Exchequer requesting [30] them to look to the memorandum for general guidance in their lending policy. But the letter also added that unduly large advances should not be made for personal needs, that facilities should not be provided for the speculative buying or holding of securities or stocks of commodities, and that the exemption for bank advances made in the "ordinary course" of the borrower's business should be strictly interpreted.

Fresh instructions to the CIC have modified the original guidance, as part of the government's endeavors to steer capital and credit

[29] These were issues to existing shareholders in the issuing company, either free of subscription, as bonus issues, or at a cost below the market price, the difference constituting a "bonus element." In postwar years they have been subject to various restrictions.

[30] In postwar years compulsive powers have been in the background under the Bank of England Act; see p. 813.

in accordance with the country's needs. For example, after the convertibility crisis in August, 1947, a special memorandum (Cmd. 7281) was issued to the CIC in the following December, with the object of ensuring that capital investment was in harmony with the government's efforts to redirect programs of development in order to promote exports. Once again the banks were required to conform to the fresh instructions, and were also asked to see that advances were not granted for the speculative buying or holding of "real property." Finance for hire purchase, especially in respect of consumer goods, was not to be increased. The next change occurred in April, 1949, when the pressure on sterling was becoming marked, the fresh memorandum to the CIC [31] drawing attention to the need to favor proposals for increasing basic production, for enlarging exports to hard currency sources, or saving imports from them, and for technical improvements leading to reductions in cost.

The attention of the banks was directed to the revisions made in April, 1949, in instructions to the CIC; in October, although no fresh guidance had been sent to the CIC, a further letter was addressed to the banks, and on this occasion it was published.[32] The letter emphasized the necessity for "every possible step to be taken to restrain inflationary tendencies" and asked the banks in their general policy to "use every endeavour to ensure that inflationary pressures are held in check." In the following December the CIC was formally requested [33] to observe strictly the guidance offered in the previous April. The next amendment occurred in April, 1951, when, with the changing situation resulting from requirements of rearmament, an additional memorandum was addressed to the CIC,[34] requiring first priority in new issues of capital to be given to defense projects. When issuing the memorandum the Chancellor of the Exchequer stated that he relied upon the banks to maintain restraint in their credit policy and repeated the forms of lending which on previous occasions had been mentioned as undesirable. Shortly afterwards, a letter from him formally requested the banks to observe in their lending policy the revised principles of guidance sent to the

[31] Hansard, April 14, 1949, Vol. 463, No. 102, col. 262.
[32] *Ibid.*, Oct. 26, 1949, Vol. 468, No. 171, col. 1352.
[33] *Ibid.*, Dec. 15, 1949, Vol. 470, No. 207, col. 295.
[34] *Ibid.*, April 17, 1951, Vol. 486, No. 88, col. 152.

CIC, and again stressed the importance of checking inflationary pressure. After the inauguration of the new monetary policy further instructions were addressed to the CIC in December, 1951,[35] requiring all applications to be submitted to a "very strict and searching scrutiny." The banks, too, were requested to "intensify their efforts to restrict credit to essential purposes" and to ensure that the highest priority was given to defense projects and exporting industries. Borrowing for agricultural expansion was later included in the priority classification. Early in 1952 further direct restrictions were placed on finance for hire-purchase trading. Issues by investment trusts and unit trusts were allowed after mid-1953, and later in the year restrictions on the terms of some credits, which had been applied in 1951, were lifted.

In practice the banks individually decide whether a particular advance is contrary to government policy, and in consequence, even though acceptable as a banking proposal, requires specific Treasury sanction. In case of doubt, guidance may be sought from the Bank of England. Despite possibilities of inconsistencies in interpretation, the classification of bank advances by industries,[36] which has been published every three months on the existing pattern since 1946, indicates that government policy is being generally observed. A fairly steady rise in the total in postwar years, no doubt attributable in part to increasing business activity and the rise in prices, was checked after 1951. When the categories are grouped as in Table 4 it is seen that advances for agriculture, manufacturing industries and essential services grew more rapidly than the total for all classified advances, while in the group for personal and professional advances the rate of increase was less rapid. Moreover, advances by the banks to the Finance Corporation for Industry and to the Industrial and Commercial Finance Corporation, which represent indirect assistance for industry (see pp. 808–11), are understood to be included under the heading "Other financial." On several occasions Chancellors of the Exchequer have expressed satisfaction with the cooperation received from the banks in the regulation of advances.[37]

35 Hansard, Dec. 7, 1951, Vol. 494, No. 27, col. 328.

36 The analysis, which covers all member banks of the British Bankers' Association (see p. 794), is based on the business of the borrower, and not, except in the category for personal and professional items, on the purpose of the advance.

37 See for example, Hansard, Nov. 14, 1950, Vol. 480, No. 11, col. 133, and April 10, 1951, Vol. 486, No. 83, col. 842.

TABLE 4

CLASSIFICATION OF BANK ADVANCES IN GREAT BRITAIN, NOVEMBER, 1947, 1949, AND 1951–53

(AMOUNTS IN MILLIONS OF POUNDS STERLING)

Category	*1947*	*1949*	*1951*	*1952*	*1953*	*1953 Index (1947 = 100)*
Agriculture and fishing	95.9	145.6	197.4	194.5	203.0	212
Mining and quarrying:						
Coal mining	8.0	5.3	3.0	1.8	1.6	20
Quarrying, etc.	3.8	3.9	4.7	4.5	4.3	113
Total	11.8	9.2	7.7	6.3	5.9	50
Manufacturing industries:						
Chemicals	17.9	17.7	39.3	34.0	25.4	142
Iron and steel and allied trades	14.5	24.5	17.6	35.2	57.3	395
Non-ferrous metals	2.7	4.0	5.4	4.0	4.4	163
Engineering, etc.	95.4	96.3	126.7	157.3	137.2	144
Cotton	6.3	7.7	13.8	14.6	11.5	183
Wool	10.9	11.3	28.8	16.9	27.3	250
Other textiles	16.8	25.1	61.3	43.0	40.8	243
Leather and rubber	7.0	9.5	22.0	15.1	14.9	213
Food, drink and tobacco	80.0	110.3	164.4	137.2	133.2	167
Unclassified industry and trade	59.0	83.8	135.4	110.2	103.0	175
Total	310.5	390.2	614.7	567.5	555.0	179
Building and contracting:						
Builders and contractors	58.3	62.3	70.1	61.3	58.6	101
Building materials	11.3	12.5	20.7	17.3	16.6	147
Total	69.6	74.8	90.8	78.6	75.2	108
Services:						
Retail trade	113.9	166.2	213.8	174.2	166.2	146
Entertainment	26.6	32.3	26.9	22.6	20.4	77
Public utilities	11.6	42.4	94.3	96.9	41.7	359
Transport and communications	12.1	15.7	17.3	20.2	19.1	158
Shipping and shipbuilding	20.0	15.6	13.5	11.4	17.6	88
Churches, charities, hospitals, etc.	18.2	10.3	13.3	13.1	13.1	72
Total	202.4	282.5	379.1	338.4	278.1	137
Local Government Authorities	83.4	85.9	87.5	80.6	83.5	100
Finance:						
Stockbrokers	4.0	5.8	7.2	5.3	6.9	172
Other financial	99.9	131.3	195.7	167.0	172.0	172
Total	103.9	137.1	202.9	172.3	178.9	172
Personal and professional	341.6	407.3	435.9	377.3	360.9	106
Total classified advances	1,219.0	1,532.5	2,016.2	1,815.4	1,740.7	143
November, 1947 = 100	100	126	165	149	143	

SAVINGS INSTITUTIONS

Savings of persons with comparatively small resources reached high levels during the war years, partly because of the general wish to support the efforts of the armed forces, but also because opportunities for spending were restricted at a time when wage distributions and other incomes were comparatively high. In postwar years new savings have fallen away and net dis-saving has occurred; the authorities are endeavoring to arrest this downward trend. Special facilities for small savings are provided by the Trustee Savings banks and the Post Office Savings Bank, as well as by two government securities, the Savings Certificate, introduced during the First World War, and the Defence Bond, inaugurated during the Second. Concerning these four channels for savings, together known as "national savings," information is published weekly of additions and withdrawals. Other channels for savings are, however, also important, particularly those provided by building societies, cooperative and friendly societies, and insurance undertakings, though for these only annual figures are available. Most forms of savings offer comparatively high rates of interest and some of them are encouraged by exemption in whole or in part from income tax. Associated with these privileges, limitations are usually placed on the amounts any one person may hold in savings of these kinds. An idea of the relative importance of the different forms of savings, with changes in the figures in postwar years, is provided by Table 5.

Among the savings organizations not under government control are the Yorkshire Penny Bank, of which the whole of the share capital is held by a group of seven commercial banks, and the Birmingham Municipal Bank, which is the only bank in Britain to be established by a local authority. Building societies collect savings funds by offering their own shares or in the form of deposits, upon which interest is paid at rates well above those for commercial bank deposits, with the income tax borne by the societies under special arrangements with the tax authorities. These societies lend their funds to members for buying houses and also assist in financing builders through a system known as "builders' pools," which developed rapidly after the First World War. Investments in shares in building societies and also deposits are usually withdrawable at notice of a month or less. Thus the societies

TABLE 5
AMOUNTS HELD IN DIFFERENT FORMS OF SAVINGS, 1938, 1947, 1949, AND 1951–53
(AMOUNTS IN MILLIONS OF POUNDS STERLING)

	1938	*1947*	*1949*	*1951*	*1952*	*1953*
Savings certificates	517	2,001	2,137	2,170	2,213	2,256
Defence bonds, etc.[a]	203	1,320	1,167	1.121	1,068	1,013
Trustee	228	695	826	914	941	950
Post Office	486	2,001	1,994	1,926	1,873	1,802
Total for national savings (March 31)	1,434	5,997	6,102	6,131	6,095	6,021
Yorkshire Penny Bank (December 31)	39	93	96	94	94	94
Birmingham Municipal Bank (March 31)	27	78	83	85	85	85
Building societies (December 31)	704	882	1,057	1,265	1,375	n.a.[b]
Friendly societies (December 31)	168	240	248	258	n.a.	n.a.[b]
Co-operative societies (December 31)	187	311	308	297	292	n.a.[b]
CWS Bank (early January)	227	249	224	184	180	n.a.[b]
Trades unions (December 31)	20	51	59	66	68	n.a.[b]
Industrial life assurance (premiums) (December 31)	72	112	124	133	138	n.a.[b]
Other savings societies (December 31)	113	211	242	270	n.a.[b]	n.a.[b]

[a] Includes about 200 million pounds of other securities.
[b] Not available.

have developed a method of borrowing at short term to lend on long-term mortgages. The figures in Table 5 include investments and deposits for about 800 separate societies in the latest year with a total of approximately 3 million shareholders and depositors. A rather slow trend towards amalgamation has been reducing the number of societies recently.

Friendly societies are associations for mutual insurance against sickness or death or for similar ends; the figures in the table cover societies and clubs with an aggregate of about 10,000,000 members. Co-operative societies operate retail shops throughout the country with a membership somewhat higher than that of friendly societies. The members invest in shares, leave deposits in their local societies or make loans to them, and the figures in the table include resources of this kind. The Co-operative Wholesale Society (CWS) trades on behalf of the retail and manufacturing societies and also operates a banking department, with accounts of other cooperative societies, trade unions, similar organizations, and individuals. The CWS Bank, as it is called, does not seek accounts from other trading and commercial organizations, but in recent years has extended its field by attracting accounts from several local authorities. It is able to offer rather more attractive terms largely because it does not, through its own organization, provide a complete banking service, but, like the building societies, friendly societies, and other savings institutions, relies upon the commercial banks for check clearings, cash, and similar services. The reduction in deposits of the CWS Bank since 1947 is attributed largely to withdrawals by co-operative societies in need of working capital. The figures for trade unions represent the aggregate funds of those organizations, while industrial life assurance consists of insurance where small sums as premiums are collected weekly or at other short intervals by agents.

The table does not cover all forms of savings; for example, it does not include "home safe" accounts or other savings deposits in the joint-stock banks, or compulsory savings by way of postwar credits under wartime income tax arrangements, in which a total of nearly 581 million pounds was outstanding, although since the end of hostilities about £170 million has been repaid. On the other hand, it is not possible to determine the exact proportion of those investments recorded—particularly in life insurance, defense bonds, building societies, and the CWS Bank—that should rightly be included in the figures for "small" savings. Then again, savings in one form may reappear in another, for example, trade union funds may be held in the CWS Bank or in savings banks, and duplication of this kind cannot be eliminated.

Trustee savings banks are subject to official examination and are required to pass their deposits to the National Debt Commissioners for investment, depositors being guaranteed repayment by the government. The banks, which are non-profit-making institutions with strong local attachments, have vigorously sought fresh savings in recent years by advertisement and by opening new branches, the number of which is still increasing. Nearly 450 have been established since the end of hostilities, making 1,210 offices in all belonging to 85 banks in the United Kingdom, a development aided by postwar legislation [38] which authorized savings banks with surplus funds to make

[38] Savings Bank Act 1949, 12 & 13 Geo. 6, c. 13.

grants to assist the progress of other banks. An individual may have an account in both a Trustee savings bank and the Post Office, where facilities for saving are similar. Deposits of as little as one shilling may be made, but in both kinds of bank deposits by one account-holder are restricted to £500 in a year and to £3,000 in total. In both, again, the long-established rate of interest allowed on ordinary deposits is 2.5 percent a year, which is subject to income tax, although this is not deducted at source.

Savings Certificates are essentially, though not exclusively, a security for the individual; they have been issued in units varying between 10s. and £1 in denomination, each series being offered on favorable terms compared with the yield on other government securities at the time. Interest on savings certificates is not liable to United Kingdom income tax, a privilege which distinguishes them from other government securities as well as from savings bank deposits, but unlike ordinary government securities, they cannot be bought or sold on the Stock Exchange. Another peculiarity is that no interest is payable to the holder until his certificate is converted into cash; interest is then paid in accordance with a scale of stated amounts over defined periods. In the official totals for the national debt the original capital sum subscribed for savings certificates is included, but not the interest payable, which is charged in the government's accounts only at the time when the capital sum is refunded. The yield on savings certificates held for their full term was brought down to little more than 2.5 percent in the eighth issue of November, 1947, while for the £1 issue, begun in January, 1943, the yield was only 28 shillings per £100. Thus during the war years every encouragement for small savings was offered except higher rates of interest, whereas in the latest issue (the ninth, begun in February, 1951), the return has been increased to slightly over 3 percent, free of tax, as a means of checking the tendency for savings to decline. The maximum holding of one individual in all issues of savings certificates would normally represent an original cash investment of about £1,500.

At the outbreak of the Second World War, many individuals already held the maximum amount then permitted in savings certificates, and accordingly the Defence Bond was introduced. Investments in Defence Bonds may be made in multiples of £5 and various issues have been available in recent years at 2.5 percent, with a small premium on redemption. In a series begun in February, 1951, the rate of interest was increased from 2.5 percent to 3 percent on bonds redeemable at par in ten years. The individual holding of these issues was restricted to £3,500, but for a new series issued in September, 1952, the limit was reduced to £1,000. These new defense bonds bear interest at 3.5 percent and will be repaid at £103 for each £100 if held for ten years, as well as enjoying somewhat easier facilities for repayment before maturity, which in the old bonds required six months' notice. By contrast with savings certificates, interest on defense bonds is paid at regular intervals and is subject to income tax, which is not deducted at source. The bonds are not a stock exchange security, as ordinarily understood, though they are transferable.

In a year-by-year comparison, as shown in Table 5, it appears that net national savings were maintained down to March, 1951; but, in fact, from 1946 onwards a net dis-saving would have occurred had it not been for accrued interest on national savings certificates, which has been added to the official figures and in recent years has provided an automatic increase by about £100 million a year. Apart from the removal of the wartime stimulus, several influences have tended to reduce the volume of saving in postwar years including the greater quantities of goods available in the shops and the higher level of prices. Although the rate of inflow has declined, especially in respect of savings certificates and defense bonds, the aggregate amount standing to the credit of holders of national savings is still much larger, in relation to total personal incomes, than in prewar years. In 1938 the aggregate for accumulated national savings was less than half the total amount distributed during the year in wages, salaries, and pay of the armed forces, while for 1952 the proportion was about three quarters. From the higher proportion of earnings now going into national savings, side by side with substantial withdrawals, it may be supposed that current savings are mainly for short periods, such as for holidays, as distinct from savings for a "rainy day."

In the management of the public debt, national savings are distinguished from other forms of savings[39] in that they represent direct loans to the government, which taken together account for more than one fifth of the total national debt. But the interest paid on national savings is relatively high, and the traditional allowance of 2.5 percent

[39] Particularly from building societies which employ investments in their shares and deposits mainly in mortgages for house purchase.

on savings bank deposits, which has obtained for so many years, constitutes an element of rigidity in the structure of interest rates. For other forms of national savings some flexibility in rates remains, as witness the offer of better terms for savings certificates and defense bonds early in 1951, and again, for defense bonds, in mid-1952, in the hope of attracting additional resources and so withholding spending power. Throughout the postwar period small savings have been regarded as one of the elements in general financial conditions needing official attention and, as the Chancellor of the Exchequer has observed,[40] the rearmament program "makes it all the more necessary that there should be the greatest possible volume of savings," for "it was an essential part of the policy of combating inflation and preventing increases in prices" that there should be "the maximum amount of savings."

GOVERNMENT-SPONSORED AND OTHER SPECIAL CREDIT FACILITIES

In the postwar period new institutions have been established by the government, or with official encouragement or support, designed to provide credit facilities in circumstances where they are not forthcoming under private auspices. During the interwar years efforts of this kind were made to aid farming, to close the "Macmillan gap," [41] to stimulate exports, and to promote industry in areas prone to suffer from a high level of unemployment (now known as the Development Areas), as well as to assist in the reorganization of old-established industries. Some of these schemes have continued, while others have been replaced by fresh organizations; in postwar years government assistance has been made available to the film industry. These arrangements are to be distinguished from government outlay on projects primarily for social objectives, for example, subsidy payments, especially on food; finance for the establishment of new towns or for colonial development; [42] or the general facilities for government

40 Hansard, Jan. 30, 1951, Vol. 483, No. 40, col. 728.

41 Cmd. 3879, where it was stated: "It has been represented to us that great difficulty is experienced by the smaller and medium-sized business in raising the capital which they from time to time require, even when the security offered is perfectly sound. To provide adequate machinery for raising long-dated capital in amounts ranging from small sums up to say £200,000 or more, always presents difficulties."

42 The New Towns Act 1946, 9 & 10 Geo. 6, c. 68; Overseas Resources Development Act 1948, 11 & 12 Geo. 6, c. 15.

guarantees.[43] The new institutions, though established under official auspices, conduct operations comparable to those of ordinary business and in further extension of facilities commonly arranged by private undertakings. Finance for some of the newly established organizations has been provided by the commercial banks and insurance undertakings.

The principal official organization for providing agricultural credit is the Agricultural Mortgage Corporation Limited, which was established in 1928 with an interest-free loan of £650,000 from the government, and one director appointed by the Treasury. The capital, now amounting to £750,000, is provided by the nine principal commercial banks in England and Wales,[44] but the Corporation raises funds primarily by issuing debentures, the amount outstanding at March, 1953, being £27 million. Advances are available to enable borrowers to buy farms or to improve them, and loans for the purchase of agricultural or horticultural properties are offered up to two thirds of their value, the advances being secured by a first mortgage of the property and repayable by equal yearly or half-yearly installments over a period of not more than sixty years.

Issues of debentures have been at rates in accordance with market conditions, the most recent, in August, 1952, yielding over 4.5 percent. The interest rate charged by the Corporation for both mortgage and improvement loans ranged from 3.5 percent in 1949 to 6 percent in 1952, and at the close of 1953 it stood at 5 percent. In recent years the business of the Corporation has grown steadily, the Chairman[45] having described the geographical distribution of loans as widespread over England and Wales, with an average amount of loan outstanding of under £3,300. Between 1938 and 1953 loans on first mortgage rose by £15 million to £24 million.

As hostilities drew to a close, two important new finance companies were formed with official encouragement, the Industrial and Commercial Finance Corporation (ICFC) for helping smaller companies, and the Finance Corporation for Industry for assisting major industries, both being established in March, 1945. To take first the aid for small companies, the ICFC has an authorized capital of £15 million of which one half has been paid up, subscribed by the

[43] See p. 796.

[44] A separate institution, the Scottish Agricultural Securities Corporation operates on similar lines in Scotland.

[45] Chairman's speech, Annual General Meeting of the Corporation, May, 1950.

commercial banks of England and Scotland, with a token subscription by the Bank of England. The Corporation may borrow to the extent of £30 million from its shareholders, with their consent, the subscribing banks providing loans in agreed proportions, while the eight directors are nominated by the commercial banks, and the first Chairman by the Bank of England.

The ICFC is generally concerned with providing sums of from £5,000 to £200,000 through lending operations which are complementary to those of the commercial banks. In ordinary circumstances, the amount required is not large enough to justify the expense of a public issue, and the assistance of the ICFC may be by loans, often partly unsecured, or by subscribing equity capital, when the ICFC may appoint a member to the board of directors of the borrowing company.[46] Charges made to borrowers comprise a "coverage" fee, and the interest on the advance at rates which depend upon the degree of risk and "follow the prevailing rates for permanent capital and long-term loans." [47] Usually loans are repayable by equal installments over a period of about twenty years. During eight years of life the business of the ICFC has expanded, advances and investments having reached in total £26.3 million by March, 1953. At the end of 1953 the ICFC had within three years opened branches in Birmingham, in Manchester, and in Edinburgh.

The Finance Corporation for Industry (FCI), which was also established in 1945, has as its main object the provision of medium-term or long-term capital, which cannot be obtained through the capital market or in other ways, for the reorganization and reequipment of major industries and the creation of new enterprises. The capital of £25 million, of which only £500,000 is paid up, is subscribed mainly by insurance and investment trust undertakings, but the principal source of funds is provided by an arrangement to borrow up to £100 million from the commercial banks. The type of business undertaken by the FCI implies advances in substantial amounts, and generally the minimum sum which will be considered is £200,000.

At first the business of the FCI was slow in getting under way, but in recent years advances have rapidly expanded, partly as a consequence of the nationalization of the iron and steel industry, the FCI

[46] For details of methods of finance see "The 'ICFC'—a New Factor in Industrial Finance," *Midland Bank Review*, November, 1946.

[47] Annual Report of I.C.F.C., March, 1950.

having provided resources for development under an agreement with the government at the time of transfer of the industry to public ownership. In March, 1953, advances to the FCI from bankers were nearly £62 million, largely used to finance iron and steel undertakings. Other industries assisted have included the development of oil wells and plants, diesel engines, chemical products, and textiles.

The policy of the FCI was described by the Chairman as being "to make advances at the finest rate of interest possible during the period while the factory, plant and other requirements are being erected and installed and the enterprise is being brought to the productive stage." Most projects supported by the FCI are not expected to come into production on a substantial scale for from three to five years, and then a few years may be required before the public can be expected to provide capital, but the FCI, while nursing enterprises for a small return, holds a stake in future profits by rights of conversion of advances into preference shares or equities.

A quite novel application of government finance has been aid for the film industry in postwar years. The National Film Finance Corporation was established by special legislation [48] in March, 1949, to take over the National Film Finance Company Limited, itself a government-sponsored body incorporated six months previously. The purpose of the Corporation, with a chairman, director, and other members all appointed by the Board of Trade, is to support film production in Britain, which after several setbacks has been unable to attract adequate capital from the public. The Corporation is empowered to arrange loans for periods of not longer than five years, the resources for such loans being provided by advances to the Corporation from the Board of Trade up to a total of £6 million, and by other lenders to the extent of a further £2 million.

The Corporation is required to repay advances and interest on them to the Board of Trade, the rate of interest beginning at 2 percent and rising to 3 percent. On March 31, 1953, the outstanding amount borrowed from the Board of Trade was £5.5 million. The rate of interest charged to borrowers in early years ranged from 4 percent to 5 percent, and had been "kept low in order not to add to costs of production." In fact, "the rate charged to producing companies has not

[48] Cinematograph Film Production (Special Loans) Acts, 1949, 1950, and 1952; 12 & 13 Geo. 6, c. 20; 14 Geo. 6, c. 18; 15 & 16 Geo. 6 and 1 Eliz. 2, c. 20.

usually been commensurate with risk," and substantial provisions have been set aside for meeting losses.[49]

Development Areas did not need assistance in war conditions, but when hostilities ended measures of financial aid were resumed, though now of wider scope than previously. New legislation [50] empowered the Treasury to assist industrial undertakings in the Development Areas by making annual grants for various purposes or by making loans where, although prospects for the undertaking were considered to be satisfactory, capital could not be obtained on suitable terms. The Board of Trade was also authorized to make loans to trading or industrial estate companies, which organize estates where factories are built, some for leasing in whole or in part to manufacturers. By 1952, loans from the Board of Trade to a number of industrial undertakings amounted in aggregate to less than £3 million.

Encouragement and financial support for export trade has been extended in postwar years through the work of the Export Credits Guarantee Department. The Department was opened shortly after the First World War to provide guarantees in connection with the export of goods, mainly produced in the United Kingdom, in the form of insurance against risk of loss through insolvency of the foreign buyer and adverse developments outside the control of the exporters concerned. The business of the ECGD at first increased fairly steadily, but since the end of hostilities the rate of growth has been rapid, the limit for the total for outstanding commitments having been raised on several occasions in postwar years to reach £900 million.[51] In 1953 the number of exporters holding policies was over 3,000, while the business guaranteed amounted to more than £400 million.

About thirty types of policies are available. The risks covered have been enlarged to include shortage or delay in sterling remittances from the buyer's country owing to exchange restrictions and other causes, or to insure against failure of remittances by reason of hostilities and civil disturbances in the buyer's country or cancellation of export licenses from the United Kingdom. Specialized types of guarantees for trade in the dollar areas cover part (normally half) of the expenditure

[49] National Film Finance Corporation Annual Report and Statement of Accounts for the year ended March 31, 1950. Cmd. 7927.

[50] Distribution of Industry Acts, 1945, 8 & 9 Geo. 6, c. 36; 1950, 14 Geo. 6, c. 8.

[51] Export Guarantees Acts, 1949, 12 & 13 Geo. 6, c. 14; 1952, 15 & 16 Geo. 6 and 1 Eliz. 2, c. 21.

lost on advertising and sales promotion, while in 1949 joint venture policies were introduced by which the Export Credits Guarantee Department enters into limited joint trading partnerships, for periods of from four to seven years. In most policies traders are themselves required to carry part of the risk, and rates of premium are assessed separately for each country and type of policy.

Until the end of 1952, long-term borrowing by local authorities was diverted from the capital market and funds were provided direct from the Exchequer on the terms available for government credit. During the year to March, 1951, total advances from the Public Works Loan Commissioners to local authorities exceeded £335 million, two thirds of the total being for housing.[52] In recent years the rate for borrowing by local authorities has been raised to reach, in 1952, 4.25 percent for loans for over fifteen years, though it fell back to 4 percent after Bank rate changed in the autumn of 1953.

Credit institutions promoted or supported by the government usually provide facilities at comparatively low levels of interest and other charges, despite the fact that they are generally financing enterprises which cannot attract funds from private sources. As, however, the new institutions seek to operate at a profit, or at least without loss over a period of years, it has still to be seen whether these aims can be served. In the past special credit facilities, sometimes provided with government assistance, have been set up to meet the difficulties of farmers or industrialists, or to steer economic activity towards particular areas or particular ends, but the scope of such facilities has been widened. Early in 1953 the Estate Duties Investment Trust was established, with a capital of £1 million subscribed by insurance and investment trust companies and by the ICFC, which manages the undertaking. The purpose of EDITH, as the new finance company is called, is to provide funds to meet estate duties where assets consist of shares in private companies. Somewhat similar organizations have since been established by groups of merchant banks and insurance undertakings. Merchant banks, in association with the FCI, formed Air Finance Limited in the autumn of 1953 as a private company to assist manufacturers of aircraft and aero engines to develop exports by offering extended credit terms, in suitable conditions, to overseas customers. A capital of just over £1 million has been subscribed partly

[52] The Public Works Loans Act 1953 (2 Eliz. 2, c. 6) provides for a further £500 million to be issued in loans from the Public Works Loan Commissioners to local authorities until fresh legislation is passed.

by the sponsors and partly by leading firms in the aircraft industry, while the FCI is to make available £10 million in loan facilities to the new undertaking. The Commonwealth Development Finance Company Limited was established early in 1953, with capital subscribed in part by the Bank of England, to aid projects for increasing the resources of the Commonwealth and strengthening the balance of payments situation of the sterling area.

THE BANK OF ENGLAND

The Bank of England, as the central bank, has been directly involved in the financial changes of war and postwar years. In 1946 it passed into public ownership, but this brought few changes in methods or scope of operation. The fundamental development, by which entire responsibility for monetary policy shifted from the central bank to the Treasury, had occurred long before—at the time of the departure from gold. The shift was confirmed by the necessity for complete Treasury direction of war finance, and during hostilities old ways were modified and new ones devised to meet the financial needs of the time. In essence, then, nationalization constituted formal recognition of a situation of several years' standing. But the Bank of England Act of 1946, besides exchanging the capital stock of the Bank of England into government stock, granted to the Treasury statutory powers over the Bank and also gave the Bank some authority over various activities of the commercial banks. Under the Act, the Crown now appoints the Governor, Deputy Governor, and all the directors of the Bank of England, and the Treasury has authority "from time to time to give such directions to the Bank as, after consultation with the Governor of the Bank, they think necessary in the public interest."

As to the commercial banks, the Act of 1946 provides that "the Bank, if they think it necessary in the public interest, may request information from and make recommendations to bankers, and may, if so authorized by the Treasury, issue directions to any banker for the purpose of securing that effect is given to any such request or recommendation." Thus the door is wide open for any request or recommendation which the Bank of England believes to be in the public interest, though the authority of the Treasury is necessary before a "directive" may be issued. Two other modifications of these extensive powers are made: no request or recommendation may be addressed to a banker concerning the affairs of any particular customer of his; and no direction may be made without prior consultation with the banker concerned, who will have the right to make representations to the Treasury. As explained by the Chancellor of the Exchequer at the time, the Act was designed to enable the government to establish priorities for the disposal of short-term credit in harmony with priorities arranged under other legislation for long-term capital.

No indication has been given that these compulsory powers of request, recommendation, or direction over the central bank or over the commercial banks have ever been exercised, the preexisting practice of consultation having continued to be effective. The Bank of England, with the authority of two hundred and fifty years of leadership in the banking system, has developed the method of influencing other banks and organizations by moral "suasion," and has in this way reinforced the policy followed at any particular moment, as well as initiated or supported improvements in the practices and structure of City organizations. In a similar way, the long-established framework of statute and tradition continues to provide the Bank with the setting for its operations, though both statute and tradition have been adapted to meet the needs and new duties and obligations resulting from war and postwar developments. Thus the accounts of the nationalized Bank are still in the form laid down over a century ago,[53] being divided between the two main sections: the Issue Department, for notes issued; and the Banking Department. The Bank continues to use the London discount market as the channel for regulating monetary conditions, though its relationships with the discount market have changed and the functions of that part of the City have been extended.

In recent years the duties of exchange control, of international financial arrangements, of regulation of new capital issues and bank borrowing, of dealing with the greatly enlarged public debt and with the extended scope of government transactions, have all brought to the Bank additional responsibilities and burdens.[54] Nevertheless, as a central bank the principal duty of the Bank of England is to carry

[53] The Bank Charter Act 1844, 7 & 8 Vict., c. 32.

[54] G. E. Milward and others, *Large-Scale Organisation* (London, 1950), has chapters describing the organization of the Bank of England (by F. W. R. Laverack) and the Midland Bank (by H. L. Rouse).

out, through the banking system, the monetary policy of the government; it is the note-issuing authority, the banker for the government and the commercial banks, and the ultimate source of funds for the discount market and monetary system. These several activities will be examined in detail, although in addition to them the Bank continues to conduct a small but diminishing amount of ordinary banking business. It does not compete with the commercial banks and has only eight provincial branches, all mainly concerned with central bank matters.

NOTE ISSUE AND THE BANK RETURN

To take first the note-issuing arrangements, the Bank provides the notes in circulation, which reach the public through the branch systems of the commercial banks. The note issue has been regulated by legislation which since the Bank Charter Act of 1844 has authorized the issue of notes against gold to any amount stated (the amount is, however, subject to variation by the Treasury from time to time at the request of the Bank). The notes issued against securities are known as the Fiduciary Issue; by the Currency and Bank Notes Act, 1939 (2 & 3 Geo. 6, c. 7) the fiduciary issue was restricted to a total of £300 million, but during the war this amount was increased rapidly under emergency regulations. By legislation introduced in November, 1953, it is proposed to establish the limit of the fiduciary issue at £1,575 million, the figure at which it stood at that time.[55] Profits of the note issue are passed over to the Exchange Equalisation Account. Bank of England notes, which are legal payment for any debt, are not payable in gold; holders of bank notes of five-pound denomination [56] merely have a right to exchange them for notes of one pound and ten shillings. As cover for note issues, gold now represents a relatively trifling sum of under £400,000, but it is significant that for this purpose the gold is revalued each week at the market price,[57] which in recent years

55 The Currency and Bank Notes Bill, presented in 1953, proposed a fiduciary issue of £1,575 million, which may be varied by the Treasury on the recommendation of the Bank of England. The new amount may not continue in force for longer than six months, unless renewed directions are issued from the Treasury. If the revised amount is greater than the fiduciary issue as specified in the statute, then it may not continue in force for more than two years except by a Treasury Order, which has to be sanctioned by both Houses of Parliament.

56 Notes of higher denomination than £5 ceased to be legal tender in 1945 (Annual Report, Bank of England, 1947) because they were believed to be facilitating "black market" and other irregular cash transactions.

57 2 & 3 Geo. 6, c. 7, sec. 2.

has been the price corresponding in sterling to the United States price of gold in dollars.

A main source of information concerning the activities of the Bank of England, including the position of the note issue, is provided by the Bank Return, which consists of a weekly statement of the main balance sheet items. A copy of a recent issue is presented in Table 6, with the figures rounded to thousands, and with slight stylistic modifications. As will be seen, assets held against the note issue consist almost entirely of British government securities, including "Government Debt" representing the original loan to the government in the Bank's formative years, but consisting mainly of "Other Government Securities," that is, British government paper: the comparatively small item for "Other Securities" comprises bonds of borrowers of high credit such as Commonwealth governments. These, with token coin, make the backing for the "Fiduciary Issue," and when the small amount of gold is added the total for "Notes Issued" is reached.

"Notes Issued" are, however, divided between those "In Circulation" and those "In Banking Department," and these last appear as a contra item in that part of the Return. They represent the portion of the note issue available for circulation if required; should the amount be unusually high and rising, then the fiduciary issue is likely to be reduced, while if it is low and falling, an increase is to be expected. In the Banking Department section of the Return, "Capital" represents the amount subscribed and paid up by shareholders and now held by the Treasury; "Rest" represents undistributed profits in past years and thus corresponds with a reserve that nowadays shows comparatively slight variations. The entries mentioned so far have dealt with the mechanics of the note issue and relics of the capital structure, but the remaining items are of significance on a wider field.

"Public Deposits" comprise "Public Accounts" (which are the balances on accounts of government departments, varying in accordance with the receipts and expenditure of the government for current purposes or for capital items) and, as a transitory item, the "Treasury Special Account." [58] "Other Deposits" are divided between "Bankers" and "Other Accounts," this last being simply balances of overseas

[58] H. M. Treasury Special Account was opened in 1948 under the provisions of the Economic Co-operation Agreement as a bookkeeping entry showing the sterling equivalent of goods supplied to Britain under the Economic Recovery Programme. After the decision to suspend Marshall Aid to the United Kingdom, in December, 1950, the amount standing to the credit of the account fell to low levels, but it has since risen with the receipt of Mutual Security funds.

central banks and governments, which are subject to change as a result of external transactions, as well as those of the few private customers of the Bank. The important subsection is that of "Bankers": these represent the balances of the commercial banks, and, since they are

TABLE 6

AN ACCOUNT IN THE BANK OF ENGLAND FOR THE WEEK ENDING WEDNESDAY, NOVEMBER 25, 1953

(AMOUNTS IN THOUSANDS OF POUNDS STERLING)

ISSUE DEPARTMENT

Liabilities	*Amount*	*Assets*	*Amount*
Notes issued:		Government debt	11,015
In circulation	1,549,909	Other Government securities	1,560,713
In banking department	25,448	Other securities	761
		Coin other than gold coin	2,511
		Amount of fiduciary issue	1,575,000
		Gold coin and bullion (@24s./8 per oz. fine)	357
Total	1,575,357		1,575,357

BANKING DEPARTMENT

Capital		14,553	Government securities		347,917
Rest		3,393	Other securities:		
Public deposits:			Discounts and advances	7,627	
Public accounts (including Exchequer, savings banks, Commissioners of National Debt, and dividend accounts)	10,364		Securities	15,021	22,648
H.M. Treasury Special account	11,484	21,848	Notes		25,448
Other deposits:			Coin		2,439
Bankers	288,751				
Other accounts	69,907	358,658			
Total		398,452			398,452

regarded by the commercial banks as part of their cash reserves, they constitute a vital link in the chain of monetary regulation to which reference is made below. A change in the amount of "Public Accounts" may be associated with one in the opposite direction in the subsection of "Other Deposits" for "Bankers" balances. For example, when the government receives payment for taxes in checks drawn on the commercial banks, these checks are credited to swell the total for "Public Accounts," and, when cleared, reduce the item for "Bankers" balances. But other changes will also be taking place, and in a fluid situation it is rarely possible to follow through any particular development. Nevertheless, the Bank of England can, and usually will, prevent movements of this nature from affecting the monetary situation by restoring "Bankers" balances through "open market operations," that is, by buying securities and adding to its assets in the form of "Government Securities."

As in the Issue Department, so in the Banking Department, the principal asset consists of "Government Securities," here comprising government bonds and Treasury bills, and sometimes including direct loans to the government known as Ways and Means Advances. It is the item for "Government Securities" which fluctuates when the Bank carries out open market operations, or deals through the "back door" (as described later), with a view to influencing monetary conditions. "Other Securities" are made up of "Discounts and Advances" and "Securities," the first comprising not only bills bought or loans extended on behalf of the Bank's ordinary customers, but also—and much more important—bills rediscounted at the Bank by discount houses and advances made to them at their request. Discount market transactions are of special significance, for it is essential to the working of the monetary system that the discount market has access to the resources of the central bank. "Securities" are miscellaneous securities, of other governments or of commercial undertakings, held by the Bank in the course of its business, but also including parcels of commercial bills bought by the Bank from the discount market as a regular arrangement, on the Bank's initiative.

REGULATION OF THE MONETARY SITUATION

When examining the individual items of the Bank Return, those relating to the note issue can be looked upon, apart from long-term developments, as convenient arrangements for dealing with the small change of the community.[59] At the Bank of England, the commercial banks either draw out or pay in notes, to correspond with public demand; the aggregate for "Bankers" balances varies accordingly. It is to "Bankers" balances (under "Other Deposits") on the one hand, and "Government Securities" and "Discounts and Advances" on the other, that particular attention needs to be paid in week-by-week

[59] As may be seen by comparing the amount of notes in circulation (Table 6) with the aggregate for deposits of the London clearing banks (Table 3).

interpretation, since all three reflect activities in the regulation of credit by the central bank. "Bankers" balances at the Bank of England are directly related to the level of deposits held by the commercial banks, since these banks maintain their cash on a basis of 8 percent of the aggregate of their customers' deposits, and "cash" consists in part of their balances with the Bank of England. The Bank of England, by open market operations, that is, by buying or selling securities (out of the item "Government Securities") can change the volume of "Bankers" balances; if it buys securities, these balances expand; if it sells, they contract.[60] Meanwhile, other monetary developments will occur, but any change in "Bankers" balances, if continued, will be reflected in movements in the level of deposits of commercial banks several times as great through the gearing of the 8 percent cash ratio.

In this pattern the significance of movements in the item labeled "Discounts and Advances" arises out of the peculiar position in Britain's banking system of the discount houses, as providing channels for the interchange of banking funds and the means whereby the resources of the central bank are made available to the commercial banks. Because the Bank of England will always lend to the discount market, though it may be at a penalty rate, it constitutes a lender of last resort, and calls of the commercial banks on the discount houses will always be met. The traditional means whereby the Bank of England influences the credit situation are thus three: by Bank rate movements; by open-market policy, including relations with the discount market; and by letting its wishes be known, that is, by "suasion."

In November, 1951, Bank rate was restored to its position as a main regulating element in the money market. Since the departure from gold the use of Bank rate had been in abeyance. It had been brought down to 2 percent, at which level it remained and was ineffective except for a short-lived rise at the outbreak of the Second World War. When the Bank rate was raised in November, 1951, after twenty years of desuetude, it represented, as under the gold standard, the minimum rate at which the Bank of England would discount approved commercial bills. At the same time a new rate was introduced at which the Bank of England would provide loans to the money market against

60 When the Bank *buys* securities it pays for them by a check drawn on itself. This check then passes to the credit of an account at a commercial bank and so increases the commercial bank's balance at the Bank of England. Conversely, when the Bank *sells* securities, it receives payment for them by a check which draws down a commercial bank's balance.

Treasury bills, representing by far the greater volume of bill business in the market. This special rate was announced at 2 percent when Bank rate was raised to 2.5 percent, and it became 3.5 percent when Bank rate moved up to 4 percent in March, 1952.

The third change, in September, 1953, was described by the Bank of England as one in which the Special rate and Bank rate were "unified" at 3.5 percent, a unification which would "allow more freedom in the day-to-day operation of the market, and . . . facilitate the flexible use of Bank rate in either direction as circumstances may require." The issue of an explanatory announcement was an unprecedented step, but by contrast other developments at this time represented a move in the direction of orthodox Bank rate policy, quite apart from the return from a plural version to the employment of one Bank rate. Whereas previous postwar changes had been advised to Parliament by the Chancellor of the Exchequer, this latest move was announced, following traditional practice, by the Bank of England after a meeting of the Court of Directors on a Thursday morning. Still more significant, the move was followed by greater flexibility and competition in money market rates and by a conversion operation, with the offer of a new government security, on this occasion the commercial banks being left free to accept the offer or take up the new stock in accordance with their own judgments.

In these ways the trend towards orthodoxy in monetary matters became more clearly marked, but it was still far different from the orthodoxy of Bank rate policy as practiced under the gold standard regime. For one thing, in the new conditions selective regulation of credit was maintained in full rigor, for another exchange control was continued and for a third the special arrangements with the discount market for ensuring the smooth flow of bank cash were kept in use. True, the central bank no longer automatically added to cash reserves, at no additional cost to the money market, whatever amounts were needed to provide for a growth in bank deposits. Instead, in various occasions of monetary stringency the money market was obliged to borrow from the Bank of England at Bank rate or at the special rate for Treasury bills when it was in force. As these were above the rates earned on bills discounted they imposed a penalty upon those seeking assistance in this way. As under the gold standard system, it became part of the order of things for the market to be, on occasion, "in the Bank," though since 1951 the central bank has operated in such a way as to render such conditions infrequent. Nevertheless, the ever-present possibility of the need to borrow at the Bank has meant that the rates at which bills are discounted have moved in conformity with Bank rate, as may be seen in Table 8. In addition, the rates which the banks allow on deposit accounts and charge for advances have been varied, as well as rates charged by the government to local authorities and by lenders generally. The yield on stock exchange securities, too, has responded.

With the return to regulation of the monetary system through Bank rate policy the new techniques practiced since the abandonment of gold, and developed in war and postwar years, have been retained as refinements added to open market operations. From the outbreak of hostilities until November, 1951, the discount market had been accorded all the funds it needed from the Bank of England through the "back door," that is, from the discount house which acts as the Bank's market agent, at about the same terms as were offered by the commercial banks, while the discount houses could take the initiative by bringing Treasury bills for discount in this way whenever supplies of funds were inadequate. The "special buyer," as the Bank's market agent is called, was always ready to buy bills from the discount houses at market rates, and, if the market had none of suitable tenor available, he would obtain them directly from the commercial banks, the process then being described as "indirect assistance." The banks, having increased their cash resources by selling bills to the authorities, would then lend their spare funds to the discount market and so relieve the situation. In these ways the money market was always supplied, without a penalty rate, with resources required to maintain, on the basis of 8 percent, whatever level of deposits at the commercial banks had resulted from government policy and monetary developments.

Since the change in monetary arrangements in November, 1951, the situation has been quite different, but the new techniques have been continued. Although at times the money market was obliged to borrow at extra cost when credit supplies were scarce, more often "the special buyer" has operated and "indirect assistance" has been available to bring relief when fortuitous movements of funds have brought temporary strain to the market. These highly developed open-market operations are often associated with changes in the volume of Treasury bills, a security which bulks so largely in the liquid assets of the commercial banks. Since commercial banks watch their "liquidity ratios," though not as closely as they do their cash ratios, the availability or scarcity of Treasury bills can affect the level of bank deposits. The government no longer uses TDR's, though the machinery remains in being for reissue of them; when TDR's and Treasury bills were running together government borrowing on short term could be adjusted between the two methods to bring about smooth working of the financial system, adding to the complexities of management of the national debt.[61]

EXTERNAL TRANSACTIONS

Among the duties of the Bank of England which have developed in recent years have been those it undertakes as agent for the Treasury, especially in the handling of the Exchange Equalisation Account (EEA) and in exchange control. The Exchange Equalisation Account is conducted as a department of the Treasury, and the large transactions in which it is engaged do not appear directly in the Bank Return, nor are they published elsewhere. The amount provided by the government for the Account, in the form of Treasury bills, began at £175 million in 1932, but by the outbreak of the Second World War this had risen to £575 million and the EEA used its sterling resources to take over the gold stock of the Bank of England. During the war the main purpose of the EEA was changed in that it became the custodian of the dollar pool, dealing with the gold, dollars, and other currency reserves of the sterling area; and so it has continued. As the central reserves of the sterling area increase, the EEA needs additional sterling resources to pay for the inflow, and during 1950 two further amounts of £300 million each were added, with a like sum in May, 1951, bringing the amount placed by the government at the disposal of the Account to £1,475 million. As reserves have run down the amount has been reduced, standing at £675 million in March, 1953. In addition, the total funds of the EEA are raised by profits from the note issue and vary according to profits or losses from gold and currency transaction. It has been stated by the Chancellor of the Ex-

[61] An analysis of the mechanics of control is given in "The Volume of Bank Deposits," *Midland Bank Review*, November, 1950.

chequer that the bulk of the reserves of the sterling area are held in gold.[62]

Various items in the Bank Return are affected by operations through the EEA and so is the general monetary situation. Deposits held by the commercial banks are likely to increase when the EEA is a net recipient of foreign currencies, because the Account pays for them in sterling obtained from the sale of Treasury bills. Conversely, when the EEA is losing foreign currencies, deposits in the hands of commercial banks are more likely to fall, but since the EEA uses spare sterling resources to buy Treasury bills, this action, in turn, tends to restore the cash ratios of the commercial banks. Although the consequences on the monetary situation may be offset by other developments, the present position is that the EEA, with its much larger resources and heavier responsibilities, has come to play a quite different part in monetary arrangements from the comparatively simple role of steadying the external value of sterling for which it was established.

In the same way that transactions on external account through the EEA affect the volume of commercial bank deposits, so also do receipts of Marshall Aid and changes in sterling balances or transfers under payments agreements with other countries, including the European Payments Union. The first impact of these operations often occurs in movements in holdings of Treasury bills. For example, if Treasury bills are taken up by holders in other countries as a short-term investment, this will reduce government requirements for short-term finance from the banking system.

As the representative of the Treasury in the conduct of exchange control, the Bank of England acts through the branch systems of the commercial banks and, although in postwar conditions additional responsibilities have been undertaken by the commercial banks, these duties remain a heavy burden at the central bank. Advisory functions in the regulation of bank borrowing also bring new tasks for the Bank of England, while the work of handling the long-term public debt, with the volume of securities it now embraces, has greatly increased. In the background are statistical and economic investigations always being undertaken at the Bank of England, an occasional publication[63]

[62] Hansard, Feb. 6, 1951, Vol. 483, No. 45, col. 1540.

[63] For example, *United Kingdom Overseas Investments 1938 to 1948;* 1948 and 1949, Bank of England, 1950 and 1951.

giving some indication of the nature of work of this kind. The Annual Report of the Bank of England is, however, a slight document as compared with those issued by central banks in some other countries, while no regular bulletin is published by the Bank.

THE LONDON MONEY MARKET

In the City of London other banks and institutions are engaged in providing facilities for short-term credit besides those already described, and some arrange new capital issues and long-term finance. The activities of discount houses, of merchant banks or acceptance houses, of banks or branches of banks operating abroad, of specialized institutions for providing hire-purchase facilities, of issuing houses and of the Stock Exchange—all contribute to meeting long-term and short-term financial requirements. Their operations, with those of the Bank of England, commercial banks, insurance and other financial organizations, and some large commercial undertakings, provide an active money market for the employment and provision of funds on widely varied terms and conditions. In some ways the businesses of the various institutions march together, for example, banks of all kinds and discount houses accept deposits, while new capital issues are arranged by the merchant banks as well as by issuing houses and stockbrokers. Lenders' fields of activity tend to be specialized by trades, countries, or methods of finance. All participants in the money market are engaged in credit arrangements and are subject to the general regulation of the CIC: in other ways their businesses have changed as a result of war and postwar finance, but their complex activities are mentioned below only in outline as giving some indication of the part they play in banking arrangements.

THE DISCOUNT HOUSES

The traditional and distinctive function of the London discount market as an intermediary for banking funds has been discussed, but it remains to consider the discount houses themselves and recent changes in their methods and activities, especially their dealings in short-term government bonds. Of the twelve discount houses,[64] nine

[64] The London discount houses, with the paid-up capital, together with reserves, if published (given in parentheses in pounds sterling, 000,000 omitted) in 1952–53 were:

publish balance sheets; their figures are combined in Table 7 to show the relationships between the principal items. Although the full extent of the resources of the discount market are not known, it is, very broadly speaking, usual for the portfolio of a discount house to be about thirty times the capital and reserves, published and unpublished, while, within that portfolio and proportion, "investments," that is short-term government bonds, are held in the ratio of approximately eight times the capital resources.[65]

TABLE 7
COMBINED FIGURES OF NINE DISCOUNT HOUSES, 1952–53[a]
(AMOUNTS IN MILLIONS OF POUNDS STERLING)

Liabilities	*Amount*	*Assets*	*Amount*
Capital, reserves, etc.	29	Cash and bank balances	10
Borrowings, deposits, etc.	964	Bills	703
		Investments	280
Total	993		993

Bills rediscounted (excluding Treasury bills), £57,000,000

[a] From balance sheets issued at various dates between December 31, 1952, and September 30, 1953.

In essence discount houses dispose of large resources which they borrow for short periods, usually of a few days, and employ in dealing in bills and bonds. The commercial banks provide a main source of loans to the discount houses and buy Treasury bills from them. When the use of commercial bills declined during the interwar years, the number of discount houses fell and the market became mainly concerned with Treasury bills. Following upon competition in discount rates, agreements or understandings were reached between the discount houses and the clearing banks, which in the war and postwar years have become more precise and far-reaching. As a consequence the clearing banks do not tender directly for Treasury bills but instead meet their requirements from the discount market, buying bills with maturity dates to suit the pattern of their expected future needs

Alexanders Discount (4); National Discount (5.6); Union Discount (8.7)—usually known as the three "companies"—Allen Harvey and Ross (1.3); Cater Brightwen (2.7); Gillett Brothers Discount (2); Jessel Toynbee (1.4); King and Shaxson (1); Smith St. Aubyn (1.5); Clive Discount (1); Ryders Discount (2); Seccombe, Marshall and Campion (0.5)—known as the "special buyer." All are companies, but the last three do not publish balance sheets.

[65] The total portfolio of nearly £1,000 million is about four times the prewar level. W. T. C. King, "The London Discount Market," *Current Financial Problems and the City of London* (London, 1948).

for cash, while the discount houses tender at an agreed price—the "syndicate" tender. Tenders outside the syndicate are made by various overseas and other banks, including clearing banks acting in behalf of their customers. Despite this regulation by consent, the policies of the individual discount houses differ considerably. Some are associated with merchant banks, others with particular trades using bill finance, while others again are more active in government bonds. So, also, rediscount commitments are likely to be higher with houses dealing in commercial bills, which are endorsed when sold, than they are with houses mainly handling Treasury bills, which are not generally endorsed.

With the introduction of TDR's during hostilities, a direct channel was opened for a time between the commercial banks and the Bank of England, as this short-term government borrowing did not employ the discount market at all, and, while continuing to handle Treasury bills, the discount houses turned to a rapid development of government bond business. War finance brought a flow of government securities, many of them of medium-term, on offer to the public for long periods at a time, and a larger market was required than could be provided by the usual Stock Exchange facilities. In prewar years, bond dealing by discount houses was not extensively practiced, but in the new conditions the authorities encouraged activities of this kind, provided that the bonds had not more than five years to run to final date of redemption, and that dealings were prudently conducted within the agreed relationship to resources, in general not more than eight times as large. Official encouragement was also given to concentration into stronger units, and discount houses were further reduced in numbers, by retirements, or by amalgamations. In bond dealings, if the established conditions are observed, it is understood that the Bank of England will lend to discount houses against bonds if they need assistance, while the commercial banks accept bonds as cover for money market loans, though at a higher rate than when bills are the security. In early postwar years, when transactions in government securities were particularly heavy, the resources of the discount houses were engaged to the full, and, as a consequence, they enlarged their resources by inviting public subscriptions to fresh capital, with the ready consent of the CIC, and a new discount company was established.

With Bank rate at 3.5 percent, commercial bank loans to discount houses are made at 1.75 percent per annum against Treasury bills and at 2.125 percent against bonds. In turn the agreed price at which the discount houses tender corresponded, in November, 1953, to an annual rate of about 2.1 percent for Treasury bills. With bonds the market might obtain a larger margin, as well as profits from switches out of one government security into another, though dealings incur the risk of capital losses from fluctuations in security prices. As may be seen in Table 8, money market rates have varied with changes in Bank rate, as also have yields on long-term government securities. Like other money market rates, the "tender" rate for Treasury bills is associated with Bank rate; discount houses may have to borrow at the penalty rate to balance their books, and changes in Bank rate thus lead to variations in their earnings.

TABLE 8
SELECTED RATES AND YIELDS

	YEARLY AVERAGES						MONTHLY AVERAGES		
	1938	*1947*	*1949*	*1950*	*1951*	*1952*	*Apr. 1952*	*May 1953*	*Nov. 1953*
Bank rate	2.0	2.0	2.0	2.0	2.5 [a]	4.0 [a]	4.0	4	3.5 [a]
Bank of England special rate for loans against Treasury bills					2.0 [a]	3.5 [a]	3.5	3.5	(3.5 [a])
Government									
Long-term (consols 2.5 percent, no final date of redemption)	3.38	2.76	3.30	3.54	3.78	4.23	4.15	4.12	3.86
Short-term (Treasury bills, 91 days)	.61	.51	.52	.51	.57	2.15	2.35	2.38	2.10
Fine Bank Bills [b]									
3 months	.63	.53	.63	.69	.91	2.72	3.00	3.00	2.19
6 months	.74	.59	.79	.88	1.03	3.17	3.50	3.50	2.44

[a] Bank rate raised on November 8, 1951, when special rate was introduced, and again on March 12, 1952. Unification of the two rates occurred on September 17, 1953.

[b] Bills accepted by or bearing the name of a bank or acceptance house.

In addition to the Bank of England and commercial banks, lenders to the discount market include merchant banks, foreign banks, insurance companies, and one or two large commercial undertakings. Not far short of a hundred sources of funds are available. In general, loans are divided into those at call, or day-to-day money, and those at short notice, described as "fixtures." Day-to-day money is usually received from the banks each morning or "called"; that is, withdrawn by them after they have made assessment of their cash position in the daily "view." Further funds may become available and be offered to the market as the day's work goes on.

With the government's return to use of Treasury bills, the discount houses have become more active in providing short-term government finance. A further development in the cheap money period of postwar years was the use of bill finance by commercial enterprises, including some large undertakings, in addition to bank advances or in substitution for them, partly to assist in carrying the stocks at enhanced prices and partly to provide working capital.[66] The discount houses, therefore, resumed, to some extent, their role of contributing to the finance of trade at home and abroad, though commercial bills probably accounted for little more than one tenth of their portfolios.[67] They are also active in financing the floating debt. Above all, they remain as the essential intermediaries in the banking system, trading on a much larger scale than in prewar years and providing the means for achieving the flexibility and smoothness which are essential to a well-ordered, short-term capital market.

THE MERCHANT BANKS AND OTHER INSTITUTIONS

Most of the merchant banks are old-established partnerships or private companies, and, although few of them publish balance sheets, they are much smaller in organization and resources than the great joint-stock banks. Yet their activities in international trade for generations past have made their names familiar in all parts of the trading world.[68]

For a century and more they have arranged credits for overseas trade and finance, accepting the bills drawn under these transactions, so that they have become known by the alternative title of "acceptance houses." They also issue and service bonds and loans on the London

[66] The commercial banks, however, limit the amount of general "finance bills" which they will buy from the discount market, or refuse to take them, preferring to deal in bills clearly arising out of specified commercial transactions. (Annual Report, Gillett Brothers Discount, February, 1951.)

[67] "Lombard Street's £1,000 Millions," *The Banker,* August, 1950.

[68] Some merchant banks are listed here. Paid-up capital and reserves, where these are published, are indicated in parentheses in pounds sterling (000,000 omitted): Baring Brothers (3.1); B. W. Blydenstein and Company (0.1); Wm. Brandt's Sons and Company; Brown Shipley (0.8); Erlangers (2.1); Guinness Mahon; Hambros Bank (5.4); S. Japhet and Company (1.3); Kleinwort and Sons (2.5); Lazard Brothers (2.3); Samuel Montagu and Company (1.3); Morgan Grenfell (1.5); Ralli Brothers (9.3); N. M. Rothschild and Sons; M. Samuel and Company (2.0); J. Henry Schroder and Company.

market for overseas borrowers and in the past thirty years have become active in new issues for home industries. In acceptance business, the merchant banks, though competitors in some fields, differ from the joint-stock banks in the range and type of business they undertake. Thus a characteristic of the merchant banks is that they tend to specialize in the financial business of particular countries and trades, while they also arrange advances against merchandise by acceptance credits, a type of finance which is increasing as trading in commodities is restored to private hands. Some merchant banks are interested in bill finance for home industries and for hire purchase.

Hire-purchase and installment trading in Britain covers a wide range of goods and is financed partly by specialized undertakings[69] and partly by retail traders who arrange, out of their own resources, for payments on deferred terms on their sales. The specialized hire-purchase finance companies, with capital subscribed by shareholders, enlarge their resources by attracting deposits, and by arranging short-term borrowing from banks, including merchant banks and discount houses, such advances being sometimes secured by the deposit of parcels of bills or promissory notes of buyers under hire-purchase and credit-sale agreements. During hostilities, the volume of hire-purchase trading was sharply reduced, and check trading[70] was discouraged. Beginning in 1949 it was permitted on a limited scale, fully in 1953. In general, hire-purchase trading has expanded rapidly although new capital and bank advances have been restricted. Thus the postwar growth of hire-purchase trading has been financed largely out of the existing resources of specialized undertakings and of retail traders.

A quite new credit institution has been formed to finance the building of ships in the United Kingdom. The Ship Mortgage Finance Company was established in March, 1951, with a subscribed capital of £1,000,000, of which one quarter was provided by the Shipbuilding Conference and the remainder by several insurance companies and other City interests. Further finance will be obtained by debenture stock issued by the Company to an amount not exceeding ten times

[69] Some hire-purchase finance undertakings are as follows, with paid-up capital and reserves, as published, indicated in parentheses in pounds sterling (000,000 omitted): Bowmaker (1.4); British Wagon Company (1.7); Forward Trust (0.4); Mercantile Credit Company (1.2); Midland Counties Motor Finance (0.5); Olds Discount Company (1.4); United Dominions Trust (4.5).

[70] A form of installment trading whereby "checks" in round amounts are sold on weekly terms and can be used at specified shops, commonly for buying clothing.

the issued capital and reserves. It is intended that, generally speaking, loans will be made by the Company up to half the value or cost of ships built in the United Kingdom, the loans to run for a maximum period of ten years, with a normal term of five or six years. Besides members from shipping interests, the board of directors includes the chairman of the ICFC.

LONG-TERM CAPITAL

In the provision of long-term capital the merchant banks have sponsored the establishment of investment trusts, and have representatives on the boards of some of them. They also arrange a substantial proportion of new capital issues, particularly those for larger undertakings. Several merchant banks are members of the Issuing Houses Association. New issues of capital are also arranged by about 25 issuing houses, who tend to deal with issues of smaller size, as well as by finance companies and by stockbrokers. The new issues are made by (1) publication of a prospectus inviting the public to subscribe, (2) by an offer for sale, (3) by "placing" or (4) by "introduction," the last three being various ways in which the whole of the issue of shares is in the first instance subscribed by an issuing house or finance company, and then resold to the public at a slightly higher price, methods which have advantages for small and comparatively little-known companies. Another way of raising capital consists of issues restricted to existing shareholders in the company at a price below current market levels for corresponding shares, that is with a "bonus element." [71] A recent survey indicates that among issues of securities in postwar years, less than a quarter of the aggregate amount subscribed was obtained by prospectus and offer for sale and well under one third by "placing" and "introduction"; the remainder were issued to shareholders. Again measured by aggregate amount, stockbrokers arranged well over one third of all new industrial securities, whichever method of issuing was used, merchant banks less than a third and other issuing houses and finance companies the remainder.[72]

Stockbrokers on the London Stock Exchange deal with orders from

71 These were issues to existing shareholders in the issuing company, either free of subscription, as bonus issues, or at a cost below the market price, the difference constituting the "bonus element." In postwar years they have been subject to various restrictions.

72 F. W. Paish, "The London New Issue Market," *Economica*, February, 1951. The period covered is from April, 1946, to December, 1949.

the public and make bargains with jobbers, who are principals, buying and selling securities at prices providing a difference, a "jobber's turn," as profit. The stockbrokers, as agents, receive a commission on transactions from the buyer or seller, and when the order arrives through a bank the commission is shared, the bank receiving one third. The banks themselves do not have representatives as members of the Stock Exchange, but use a variety of brokers for their own and their customers' transactions, representing in total a substantial volume of business. Nor do the commercial banks underwrite issues to the public; they simply act as bankers in handling the money subscribed.

Among securities dealt in on the Stock Exchange, the proportion of government and government-guaranteed securities has greatly increased as a result of war and postwar financial developments, including nationalization of large sections of industry, and a number of influences have both restrained the volume of new capital issues and directed the nature and flow of them. Quite apart from regulation by the CIC, investment transactions have been discouraged by the policy of dividend limitation, by the increase in stamp duties on share transactions from 1 percent to 2 percent *ad valorem* in 1947,[73] and by weight and incidence of company and personal taxation. According to a regularly published series of statistics,[74] in 1953 the total for new capital issues, excluding government borrowing, was over £396 million, or more than three times the amount for 1938. Over one half of the year's total, however, was for borrowing by the nationalized electricity and gas industries, but even including sums for nationalized bodies, the annual average amount of new money raised in postwar years is no more than £255 million as compared with about £135 million in the eight years immediately before the war; after allowing for price changes and postwar restocking this represents a smaller rate of addition to real resources.

"Dividend limitation" was inaugurated toward the end of 1947, when the Chancellor of the Exchequer requested business undertakings to refrain from increasing the dividends they distributed, and from time to time the request was renewed. It was reinforced by a

[73] Finance Act, 1947, 10 & 11 Geo. 6, c. 35.

[74] The figures, compiled by the Midland Bank, are based upon prices of issue and, besides excluding all borrowings by the British government, also omit shares issued to vendors, capitalization of reserves, other issues which add nothing to capital resources, and private placings for which no market quotation has been obtained.

discriminatory profits tax, while an excess profits levy was introduced into the budget of 1952. At the time the government was satisfied with the way in which limitation of dividends had been observed,[75] even though, as a consequence, yields on investments were sometimes out of accord with the financial experience of the company concerned. In the postwar period, also, companies have raised funds on a substantial scale by way of notes, or loan stock (usually unsecured and running for periods of from five to twenty years), which have been issued to shareholders or to a small group of insurance undertakings or other institutional investors. By thus obtaining capital without using the new issue market, a saving in expenses is made. Moreover, by raising money by loans instead of by equity capital, taxation costs are reduced because of a peculiarity in British company taxation arrangements.[76]

Quite apart from regulation and technical adjustments, deep-seated causes are changing the sources of capital funds for investment. The flow of investment funds runs to a much larger extent through government and institutional channels; in recent years the main source of finance for capital investment at home has been provision made by commercial undertakings for depreciation and reserves, with profits "ploughed back" into the business. Personal saving seems to be lower and more often directed into investments through life insurance undertakings.

CHANGES IN BANKING ACTIVITIES

Since the end of hostilities, Britain's financial policy has been adjusted to meet the difficulties in general economic conditions which have strained the balance of payments. In the background, however, was the declared intention to maintain a high level of employment[77] while avoiding inflation, and to incorporate monetary policy in these broad objectives, notwithstanding the subsequent agreement under the rules of the International Monetary Fund to observe a fixed rate of

75 Hansard, Jan. 30, 1951, Vol. 483, No. 40, col. 726.

76 Interest on debt is allowed as a deduction from earnings before the taxable profit is determined; on undistributed profits the tax rate, now 2.5 percent, has been below that on distributed profits, now at a rate of 22.5 percent. In addition, by the Finance Act, 1952, an "excess profits levy" was applied, which basically absorbed 30 percent of the amount by which profits from Jan. 1, 1952 exceeded those of recent years.

77 Cmd. 6527 (1944), para. 59.

exchange for sterling. Whether these aims will in the end prove compatible has still to be seen. On two occasions when the choice had to be made, home conditions were put first: sterling returned to inconvertibility and was devalued. With the resort to more orthodox monetary measures in November, 1951, another way of attacking the postwar financial problem is being tested. Despite the policy of disinflation, the internal value of the pound has fallen in the postwar period by about as much as during the war years. On the basis of consumer expenditure, the purchasing power of the pound was diminished by about one third between 1939 and 1945. By the year 1953 it had decreased by a third of the 1945 value. The value of the pound sterling has thus declined at home and abroad, but where and how it is available are also of great importance. In the absence of convertibility, this has rested largely upon banking arrangements and the administration of exchange control. The banks, inescapably bound up with general financial developments, have maintained through their services the means of payment at home and contributed to the growing use of sterling abroad, based upon the complementary trading requirements of Britain, other sterling area countries, and the world as a whole.

In the process, however, the banks have experienced a changed emphasis in their activities, which can be traced back at least half a century, but which has become more marked in war and postwar conditions. While the resources of the banks have been greatly enlarged since prewar days, two thirds of the funds at their disposal are required for government finance. Advances, despite the postwar increase, are below the proportion of assets held by the banks in prewar years; the lag is attributable not only to war and postwar finance and the influence of qualitative control, but also to the working out of long-term developments. A downward trend in the demand for bank advances was noticeable in the years before the outbreak of the Second World War, as self-finance for industry became more general.

The additional deposits have been more actively employed since the end of hostilities [78] and have called for services, particularly in

[78] Information is not available to measure the velocity of movement of bank deposits satisfactorily, since statistics of check clearings are not comprehensive and are subject to special influences (see p. 782). The comment in the text is based on a number of indications, including the statement in the Midland Bank Annual Report for 1951 (p. 10) that during 1951 turnover on current accounts rose by 16 percent and the number of checks paid or collected for customers increased by 6 percent.

the form of check clearings, which have become more costly to provide. While the banks are traders in money, gaining profits from the difference between the price they pay in interest for deposits and that earned on advances or other assets, they are also providers of the money supply with associated services, which now include comparatively expensive efforts on government account, as, for example, in respect of exchange control. In recent years, a narrower band of borrowers has been available to provide revenue, while services have been called for more extensively by the greater numbers of users of credit balances. Hence the tendency for increasing attention to be paid to service charges.[79] With the changed emphasis in activities, the banks, as large-scale business organizations, are conscious of the increasing claims made by the tasks of administration, as distinct from lending technique, upon the time and efforts of those concerned.

Throughout the stress of recent years the banking system has again displayed the capacity for adaptation and the tough resilience which it has shown for over a century. In the past the main developments were structural, the banks joining together to form country-wide organizations required to meet the needs of large units in industry and trade. In more recent years the changes have been in method and in attitude: fresh ways have been found for employing long-practiced techniques, and at the same time the demands made by government finance and by official regulations have been fulfilled. In home financial arrangements, control over the volume of deposit as well as the qualitative direction of credit alike take place without involving the statutory powers now at the disposal of the authorities. As regards external transactions, it is through the banks that the day-to-day scrutiny of foreign currency requirements is made for exchange control purposes, and it is largely by the development of their overseas connections that sterling is so widely used in international trade. The process of adaptation and of grafting new functions on to long-established organizations goes on, but the banks remain individual business undertakings, actively competing with one another. Side by side with their new activities the ordinary but essential banking services are continued along lines familiar to traders at home and abroad in the otherwise strange and sometimes disconcerting setting of the postwar world.

[79] "Bank Profits and Salaries," *The Banker*, February, 1951, p. 87.

REFERENCES

A more extensive bibliography will be found in "Banking Literature and the Sources of Banking Information" by Irene Shrigley, included in "Current Financial Problems and the City of London"—see below.

GOVERNMENT PUBLICATIONS

Acts of Parliament

Bank of England, 1946, 9 & 10 Geo. 6, c.27.
Borrowing (Control and Guarantees), 1946, 9 & 10 Geo. 6, c.58; with Statutory Rules and Orders 945, 1947; 755, 1949.
Currency and Bank Notes, 1928, 18 & 19 Geo. 5, c.13; 1939, 2 & 3 Geo. 6, c.7.
Currency and Bank Notes Bill, 1953.
Exchange Control, 1947, 10 & 11 Geo. 6, c.14.

White Papers

Capital Issues Committee, Memorandum of Guidance to, 1945, Cmd. 6645; 1947, Cmd. 7281.
Economic Survey, yearly 1947–53, Cmd. 7046, 7344, 7647, 7915, 8195, 8509, 8800.
Employment Policy, 1944, Cmd. 6527.
European Payments Union, Agreement for Establishment of, 1950, Cmd. 8064.
European Payments Union, Documents relating to, 1950, S.O. 63–117.
National Income and Expenditure, 1938–46, Cmd. 7099; Blue Book, 1946–52.
United Kingdom Balance of Payments, 1946–53, Cmd. 8976.
United States and United Kingdom, Financial Agreement between, 1945, Cmd. 6708.

Other

Finance and Industry, Report of Committee on, 1931, Cmd. 3879.
Statistics, Monthly Digest of, H.M.S.O.

BANKING HISTORY

In addition to the entries listed below, house histories of a number of banks are privately printed.
Bankers' Magazine. "Money and Banking in the Twentieth Century." Several issues during 1950.
Clapham, Sir J. The Bank of England. 2 vols. London, 1944.
Crick, W. F., and J. E. Wadsworth. A Hundred Years of Joint Stock Banking. London, 1936.

Gregory, T. E. Select Statutes, Documents and Reports Relating to British Banking 1893–1928. 2 vols. London, 1929.
—— Westminster Bank through a Century. London, 1936.
King, W. T. C. History of the London Discount Market. London, 1936.
Rait, R. S. History of the Union Bank of Scotland. Glasgow, 1930.
Sykes, J. Amalgamation Movement in English Banking. London, 1925.
Wadsworth, J. E. Counter Defensive. London, 1946.

BANKING SYSTEM AND THEORY

Bagehot, W. Lombard Street. 14th ed. London, 1915.
Balogh, T. Studies in Financial Organization. London, 1947.
Bareau, P. Future Prospects for the Sterling Area. Institute of Bankers, London, 1949.
Braithwaite, J. B. The Work of the Stock Exchange. Institute of Bankers, London, 1951.
Crick, W. F. Origin and Development of Sterling Area. Institute of Bankers, London, 1948.
—— The Sterling Area during and after the War. Institute of Bankers, London, 1948.
Crowther, G. An Outline of Money. Rev. ed. London, 1948.
Dacey, W. Manning. British Banking Mechanism. London, 1951.
—— "Cheap Money Technique." *Lloyds Bank Review*, London, January, 1947.
Economic Conditions and Banking Problems: a symposium. International Banking School, Saltsjöbaden. The Swedish Banking Association, Stockholm, 1950.
Feaveryear, E. A. The Pound Sterling. London, 1931.
Foreign Trade, Pattern and Finance of: a symposium. Institute of Bankers, London, 1949.
Grant, A. T. K. A Study of the Capital Market in Post-War Britain. London, 1937.
Green, J. M. S. The Capital Market. Institute of Bankers, London, 1951.
Hallowell, Burton C. A Study of British Interest Rates. Privately issued by Connecticut General Life Insurance Company, Hartford, Conn., 1951.
Hobson, O. How the City Works. London, 1934.
King, W. T. C. "Gilt-edged and the Volume of Money." *The Banker*, London, October, 1946; and, in subsequent issues, regular analyses of movements in bank deposits.
London, Current Financial Problems of the City of. A symposium. Institute of Bankers, London, 1948.
Milward, G. E., and others. Large-Scale Organisation. London, 1950. Chapters by F. W. R. Laverack, "The Bank of England," and by H. L. Rouse, "Midland Bank."
Paish, F. W. "The London New Issue Market." *Economica*, London, February, 1951.
Sayers, R. S. Modern Banking. 3d ed. London, 1951.

—— Central Banking, British Banking To-day. Institute of Bankers, London, 1953.
Thackstone, H. H. Current Financial Problems of the City of London (above). p. 123.
Truptil, R. J. British Banks and the London Money Market. London, 1936.
Tyser, G. The Work of an Issuing House. Institute of Bankers, London, 1951.
Wadsworth, J. E. Banking Funds and Government Policy in Britain. 2 vols. International Credit Conference, Rome, 1953.
—— The Commercial Banks. Institute of Bankers, London, 1953.

REVIEWS, ETC.

Annual "Statements" of chairmen of principal banks.

Banker.

Bankers' Magazine.

Economist.

Journal of Institute of Bankers.

Quarterly publications by various banks, e.g., Barclays, District, Glyn Mills, Lloyds, Midland, National Provincial, Westminster.

UNITED STATES

by J. Brooke Willis

COMMERCIAL BANKING

THE COMMERCIAL banking system of the United States possesses certain distinctive features. These are the large number of banks of small size, the duality of government supervision, the restricted development of branch banking, and the partial separation of "commercial" from "investment" banking.

American commercial banks have been said to engage in "department store banking." While they furnish a wide range of services, their principal activity is the lending and investing of money obtained through the receipt of demand and time deposits. In addition to ordinary deposit banking, commercial banks maintain "safe deposit," or storage facilities, and may act in various fiduciary capacities, notably as a trustee, executor, administrator, and guardian of estates; registrar of stocks and bonds; and receiver. However, in the exercise of trust powers all assets held in a fiduciary capacity must be segregated from the general assets of the bank and kept in a separate set of books and records.

The directors of national banks are authorized to exercise "all such incidental powers as shall be necessary to carry on the business of banking; by discounting and negotiating promissory notes, drafts, bills of exchange, and other evidences of debt; by receiving deposits; by buying and selling exchange, coin and bullion; by loaning money

---

J. BROOKE WILLIS is Associate Professor of Banking, Graduate School of Business, Columbia University; Consulting Economist, The Chase National Bank; author of *The Functions of the Commercial Banking System*, New York, 1943.

on personal security." [1] National banks are also authorized to purchase "investment securities" (bonds, but not stocks) for their own account. However, they are not allowed to underwrite issues of securities (governmental securities excepted), nor to invest any of their funds in the capital stock or the obligations of companies engaged in underwriting securities.

Institutions which receive deposits payable on demand and which undertake to transfer them on order of the depositor by check to third parties must comply with the banking laws. Mutual savings banks are a separate class of institution with limited and specialized powers which receive notice deposits of individuals but do not provide checking facilities. However, "commercial" banks also engage in savings banking through the receipt of "time" deposits, but are not required to segregate assets against these deposits.

Broadly speaking, commercial banks serve as a depositary of the country's liquid resources, provide a mechanism for the prompt transfer and clearance of money claims, and furnish direct credit accommodation to various classes of borrowers through the deposit account mechanism. The credit activities of commercial banks not only serve the working capital requirements of business and agriculture but also now extend to the financing of fixed capital needs and real estate. However, banks are not allowed to acquire ownership equities in business concerns, either for income or control, nor are they allowed, as noted above, to underwrite the open market flotation of corporate securities. It is in this sense that "commercial banking" has been separated from "investment" banking.[2]

Trust institutions are organized either as banks with trust departments or trust companies with banking departments. At the present time, nearly 3,000 banks perform trust functions and about one half of these are national banks.[3] The largest share of the business is handled by state-chartered member banks and by a comparatively few large institutions. The amount of funds placed in trust accounts

[1] *Federal Laws Affecting National Banks,* compiled by the Comptroller of the Currency, January 1, 1950, U.S.R.S. sec. 5136.

[2] For a concise description of the functions of commercial banks since 1913 see Joint Committee on the Economic Report, 82d Congress, 2d Sess., *Monetary Policy and the Management of the Public Debt,* Part 1, February, 1952, pp. 519–44. An account of the changing character of the credit activities of commercial banks is found in Neil H. Jacoby and R. J. Saulnier, *Business Finance and Banking,* National Bureau of Economic Research, 1947, and J. Brooke Willis, *The Functions of Commercial Banks,* New York, Kings Crown Press, 1942, Ch. VII.

[3] *Monetary Policy and the Management of the Public Debt,* Part 1, p. 542.

administered by banks and trust companies has been estimated at $50 billion.[4]

The foreign activities of the commercial banks are carried out through a small number of banks in the financial centers which, in turn, have established foreign branches, hold investments in international banking corporations, and maintain correspondent relationships with banks abroad. Ordinarily banks rely upon either foreign branch or correspondent relationships.

In addition to giving the member banks specific authority to accept drafts or bills of exchange growing out of transactions involving the importation or exportation of goods, the Federal Reserve Act authorized member banks having a capital and surplus of at least $1,000,000 to establish branches in foreign countries and also to invest a limited amount of their capital in any state-chartered international banking corporation subject to certain restrictions. After World War I the Edge Act authorized federal chartering of corporations to engage in international banking under regulations of the Federal Reserve Board.

The first foreign branch of a national bank, the National City Bank, was authorized on September 2, 1914. At present four national banks and three state member banks have more than ninety branches in twenty-three foreign countries. Three corporations chartered under state law have been organized and, in addition, two corporations are in operation under federal charter (Edge Act), the Chase Bank (affiliate of the Chase National Bank) and the Bank of America of New York (affiliate of Bank of America National Trust and Savings Association of San Francisco).[5]

ORGANIZATION

Number of Banks.—On December 30, 1951, the commercial banking system was comprised of 14,132 unit banks, that is, separate corporate entities with about 5,264 branches, in all, 19,396 offices.[6] The typical bank is small in size, having deposits between $1 million and $5 million as indicated by Table 1.

[4] *Trusts and Estates,* January, 1947, pp. 95–96.

[5] Paper delivered by M. S. Szymczak, Member Board of Governors of the Federal Reserve System, "The International Role of the Federal Reserve System," January 16, 1950.

[6] *Annual Report of the Federal Deposit Insurance Corporation,* 1951, Table 101, pp. 128–29.

TABLE 1

DISTRIBUTION OF INSURED COMMERCIAL BANKS ACCORDING TO SIZE OF DEPOSITS, SEPTEMBER 30, 1949

(IN PERCENT OF TOTALS)

Banks with Deposits of	*Number of Banks*	*Deposit Liabilities*
$250,000 or less	0.6	0.01
$250,000 to $1,000,000	18.2	1.1
$1,000,000 to $5,000,000	55.4	12.0
$5,000,000 to $25,000,000	20.6	18.4
$25,000,000 to $100,000,000	3.7	15.6
Over $100,000,000	1.5	52.9
	100.0	100.0

Source: *Annual Report of the Federal Deposit Insurance Corporation,* 1949, pp. 62–63.

Table 1 shows that 74.2 percent of the insured banks had deposits of less than $5 million while 94.8 percent had deposits of less than $100 million. Although most of the banks are fairly small in size, a few are very large and, indeed, embody the great bulk of the banking resources of the country. At the present time there are three banks each of which holds deposits of more than $5 billion. The largest bank, The Bank of America, N.T.S.A., held on June 30, 1952, $6,881,-410,177 of deposits; this was followed by the National City Bank of New York with $5,541,640, 663, and The Chase National Bank with $5,236,752,682. Eighteen banks had deposits exceeding $1 billion each, with combined deposits of nearly $44 billion as compared with total deposits in the banking system amounting to $162 billion.[7] The combined deposits of the 100 largest banks was $75 billion.

As would be expected, the majority of the banks are situated in places of small population as shown in Table 2.

Nearly one third of the insured banks were in places of population of less than 1,000. Less than 3 percent were in cities having a population of 500,000 or more; this group held about a third of all accounts and nearly half of all deposits.[8]

The average number of persons served per banking office has risen from approximately 3,500 in the year 1920 to 7,900 in 1950. This increase resulted, on the one hand, from the drastic decline in the number of banks and banking offices in 1922–32 and, on the other hand, from the growth in population. Of course, the population per banking

[7] *American Banker,* July 11, 1952.

[8] The concentration is exaggerated by the fact that in Table 2 all accounts and deposits in all offices of a bank are tabulated according to the population of the head office city.

TABLE 2
DISTRIBUTION OF INSURED COMMERCIAL BANKS ACCORDING TO POPULATION OF LOCALITY, SEPTEMBER 30, 1949
(IN PERCENT OF TOTALS)

Banks in Centers with Population in 1940 of	*Number of Banks*	*Number of Deposit Accounts*	*Amount of Deposits*
Less than 1,000	31.4	5.7	3.5
1,000 to 5,000	34.9	13.4	8.5
5,000 to 25,000	19.6	17.3	11.8
25,000 to 100,000	6.9	14.5	11.3
100,000 to 500,000	4.3	16.9	18.1
500,000 or more	2.9	32.2	46.8
Total	100.0	100.0	100.0

Source: *Annual Report of the Federal Deposit Insurance Corporation*, 1949, p. 66.

office varies widely. At one extreme are South Dakota, Kansas, Iowa, and Nebraska, which approximated 3,000 persons per banking office in 1950; at the other extreme are Florida, Massachusetts, Connecticut, and Alabama which averaged 12,000. Differences in density of population, stage of economic development, transportation and communication facilities appear to be a more important cause of variations than are the statutory restrictions upon branch banking.[9]

The present number of banks is only about half the number in the peak year 1922 when there were roughly 30,000, as shown in Chart I. This radical reduction is attributed to a variety of factors. During the 1920s the failure rate was extremely high, the result of too many banks, bad management, and inadequate diversification of risks. By 1929 the number of banks had decreased from the 1922 peak by about 4,000, as a result of suspensions, consolidations, and absorptions. In the severe economic recession of 1930–33, about 9,000 banks suspended operations, and an additional 2,300 disappeared as the result of consolidations and absorptions culminating in the banking "holiday" of March, 1933.[10] Following the reorganization of the structure

[9] *Monetary Policy and Management of the Public Debt* (82d Cong., 2d Sess.), Part 1, p. 572; answer of the Chairman of the Board of Governors of the Federal Reserve System to Question 57(a). The Board's answer presents detailed tables showing the number of banking offices and population by states and counties for selected years.

[10] A detailed description of the changes in the number and character of banking facilities since the establishment of the Federal Reserve System was recently given by the supervisory authorities in answer to a Congressional questionnaire. See *Monetary Policy and the Management of the Public Debt,* Part 1, pp. 544–57 and 570–602, and Part 2, pp. 925–32; see also Caroline H. Cagle and Raymond C. Kolb, "New Commercial Banking Offices 1936–1947," *Federal Reserve Bulletin,* May, 1948.

CHART I

ALL COMMERCIAL BANKING OFFICES IN THE UNITED STATES

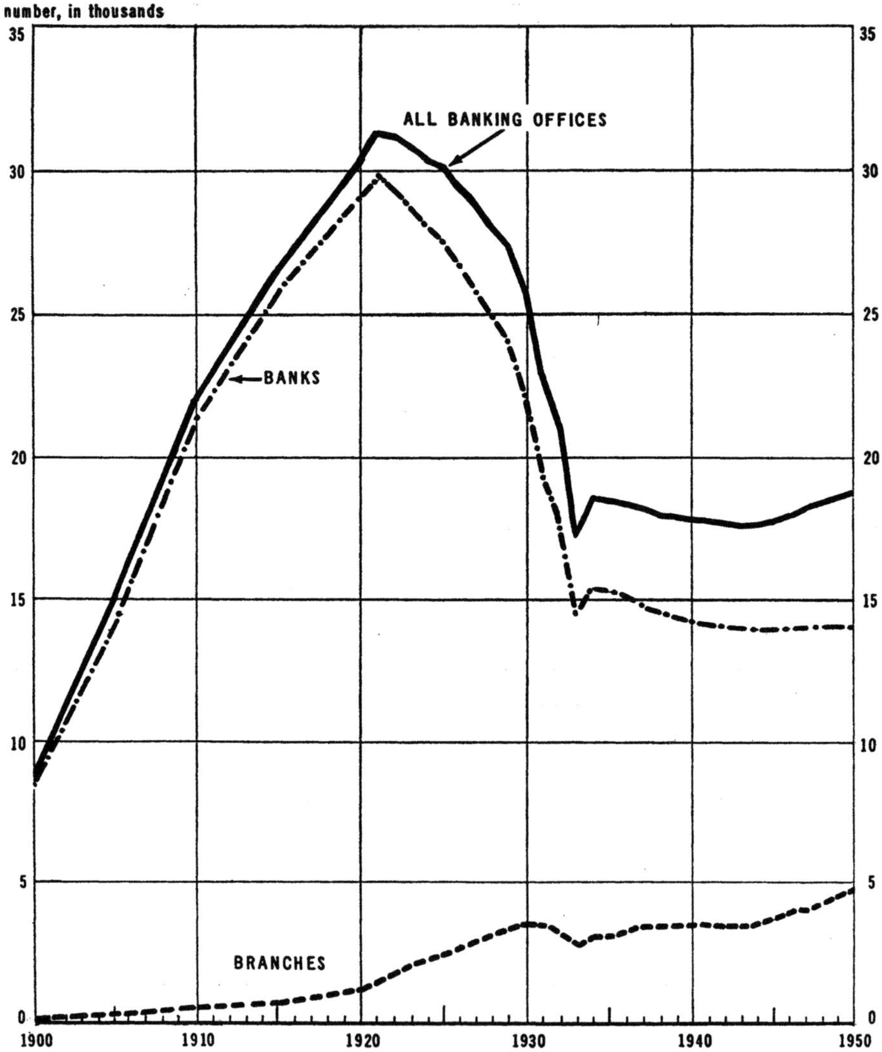

Source: Federal Reserve System, Board of Governors, *Monetary Policy and the Management of the Public Debt,* Part 1, p. 545.

in 1933–35, the number continued to decline until 1943, but at a relatively moderate rate of about 158 banks per year. Small increases occurred annually from 1945 through 1947, but after 1947 the number of banks declined further from 14,181 to 14,089 at the end of 1951.

By contrast, banking offices began to increase in 1944, for the first time since 1922, by reason of a fairly steady growth in new branches.

The turnover in the number of banks in 1945–51 is analyzed in Table 3.

TABLE 3
MAJOR STRUCTURAL CHANGES AFFECTING THE NUMBER OF COMMERCIAL BANKS, 1945–51

Year	*New Banks*	*Suspensions*	*Consolidations and Absorptions*	*Voluntary Liquidations*	*Number of Banks*
1945	118		79	18	14,011
1946	144		93	16	14,044
1947	111	1	84	11	14,181
1948	80		75	12	14,171
1949	72	4	77	12	14,156
1950	68	1	91	12	14,121
1951	62	3	82	11	14,089

Source: Board of Governors of the Federal Reserve System; see *Monetary Management and the Public Debt,* Part 1, Tables XVII and XIX, pp. 554 and 556.

Recently, consolidations and absorptions have exceeded the formation of new banks. While there has been a tendency since the end of World War II for mergers to increase, the annual rate of mergers is far less than in earlier decades, as Table 4 shows.

TABLE 4
MERGERS, CONSOLIDATIONS, AND ABSORPTIONS OF COMMERCIAL BANKS, 1924–51

Period	*Total*	*Average*
1924–33	5,257	526
1934–37	760	190
1938–51	1,228	88

Source: Board of Governors of the Federal Reserve System, Staff Report on *Concentration of Banking in the United States,* September 10, 1952.

In recent years mergers have been made for a variety of reasons: (1) to enable stockholders of absorbed banks to realize actual book values in cash, a preferred alternative to sale of their shares in the market at a discount; (2) to expand capital and increase legal lending limits in order to provide credits required by large business borrowers; (3) to reduce operating costs; (4) to expand branch facilities; (5) to gain prestige; (6) to acquire new personnel; and, (7) in the case of some small banks, as a result of retirement or death on the management level. Some observers say that the principal motives in recent mergers have been higher lending limits and cheaper operating costs.[11] Others have argued that the chief purposes of mergers have been to enable the stockholders of merged banks to withdraw their capital in cash at book value instead of depreciated market value and to increase earning power through expansion of facilities.[12] The fact that the shares of many New York banks sell at rates below their book value has given rise to the observation that banks are worth more dead than alive, a reflection of the low earning power of invested capital in an era of easy money, growing competition from other lending institutions, and adverse taxation. In contrast with the 1920s, when many mergers were "life saving jobs," the recent mergers have not been caused by the need to escape insolvency. While many recent mergers have involved the conversion of banks into branches, this factor has not been as important as it was in the early 1930s when branch banking laws were liberalized.

GOVERNMENT SUPERVISION

American commercial banking is often described as a dual system, referring to the fact that banks may be chartered by the states or by the Federal government. This is a reflection of the constitutional principle that the Federal government has only those powers specifically granted to it. Although the Federal government chartered the First Bank of the United States (1791–1811) and the Second Bank of the United States (1816–36), it was not until the National Bank Act (1863) that Congress provided a permanent arrangement for the chartering of national banks. The dual system was subsequently modified by the Federal Reserve Act in 1913 and by the Federal Deposit Insurance Corporation Act in 1933. Membership of national banks in the Federal Reserve System is mandatory, but membership of state-chartered banks is voluntary. Membership in the Federal Deposit Insurance Corporation is mandatory for all members of the Federal Reserve System, but is voluntary for state-chartered banks which have not joined the Federal Reserve System.

11 Staff Report of the Board of Governors of the Federal Reserve System submitted to the Subcommittee on Monopoly of the Select Committee on Small Business, 82d Cong., 2d Sess., *Concentration of Banking in the United States*, Sept. 10, 1952, p. 7.

12 A Staff Report to Subcommittee No. 5 of the Committee on the Judiciary, House of Representatives, 82d Cong., 2d Sess., *Bank Mergers and Concentration of Banking Facilities*, Sept. 17, 1952, pp. 20–22.

Table 5 classifies commercial banks according to their supervisory jurisdiction.

TABLE 5

CLASSIFICATION OF COMMERCIAL BANKS ACCORDING TO SUPERVISORY JURISDICTION, DECEMBER 31, 1951

(NUMBERS IN THOUSANDS; AMOUNTS IN MILLIONS OF DOLLARS)

Type of Bank	*Number of Banks*	*Amount of Deposits*
National charter	4,939	94
State charter		
Member of Federal Reserve	1,898	47
Nonmember, insured	6,618	22
Nonmember, noninsured	677	2
Total	14,132	165

It is apparent that the banks which belong to the Federal Reserve System represent only about half the number but 85 percent of the total deposits at all commercial banks. While state member banks represent only 20 percent of the number of all state commercial banks, they hold over 65 percent of the deposits in all state commercial banks. Only 677 uninsured banks lie entirely under state jurisdiction.

The overlapping authority of the Federal Reserve System, the Federal Deposit Insurance Corporation, the Comptroller of the Currency (national banks), and the 48 state supervisory agencies accounts for the complexity of American banking law and regulation. A national bank, for example, is under the jurisdiction in varying degrees of all three federal supervisory agencies, while a state member bank is under the jurisdiction of the Federal Reserve and the Federal Deposit Insurance Corporation in addition to its own state supervisory agency.

SUPERVISORY AGENCIES

A brief summary of the powers and functions of the federal supervisory agencies is given herewith.[13]

The office of Comptroller of the Currency was established under the National Banking Act of 1863 within the United States Treasury Department. As his title suggests, the Comptroller's original function was concerned with the issuance and retirement of national bank notes. At the present time the Comptroller is primarily responsible

13 See Board of Governors of the Federal Reserve System, *Annual Report*, 1938, pp. 1-18; R. F. Leonard, "Supervision of the Commercial Banking System" in *Banking Studies*, Board of Governors of the Federal Reserve System, 1941, pp. 189-210.

for the supervision of national banks. He receives, investigates, and issues or rejects applications for new charters; is required to examine each bank at least twice a year and to call for reports of condition; is responsible for liquidating insolvent national banks; and exercises various powers such as those over changes in capital structure and the establishment of branches.

The Board of Governors of the Federal Reserve System, created by the Federal Reserve Act of 1913, does not charter banks. However, it reviews applications by state-chartered banks for membership in the Reserve System and has broad powers to examine members including national banks. In practice, neither the Board nor the twelve Reserve banks examines national banks, since the Comptroller is directly responsible and the reports of his examinations are made available to the Federal Reserve authorities. The Board of Governors and the twelve Reserve banks are empowered to regulate various phases of banking operations (including the maintenance of reserves, the establishment of branches, the exercise of trust powers, the payment of interest on time and savings deposits) and to exercise various credit controls over the credit activities of member banks.

The Federal Deposit Insurance Corporation was established in 1933. Its primary function is to guarantee the deposits of insured banks, presently up to $10,000 per account. However, the Corporation is empowered to pass upon applications for admission to insurance by state-chartered banks which have not joined the Federal Reserve System. It is also empowered to examine insured banks, including national banks and state-chartered members of the Reserve System.[14] In practice, the Corporation regularly examines only state non-member insured banks. The Corporation is also empowered to institute proceedings for the termination of insurance and to act as a receiver in the liquidation of national banks whose insurance is terminated.

While there is obviously much overlapping of function among the various supervisory agencies, working arrangements have been evolved to define the responsibilities and areas of jurisdiction of the

[14] The Federal Deposit Insurance Act, Sec. 10(b) as approved Sept. 21, 1950, authorizes the Corporation to make special examinations of national banks and state member banks when such action is deemed advisable to determine insurance risk. Theretofore, examination by the FDIC of national and state member banks required the written consent of the Comptroller or the Federal Reserve.

respective agencies and to develop uniformity in regulatory policies and standards.[15]

CHARTERING OF NEW BANKS

American banking law, both state and federal, was based at an early date upon the principle of "free banking"—"the principle that banking should not be the privilege of a few but should be open to all." Beginning with the New York Free Banking Act in 1838, the special charter system was gradually abandoned and free banking laws enacted whereby any group of persons might enter the banking business by applying to a state official for a charter. Certain minimum requirements, such as minimum capital on organization, had to be satisfied. However, for many years these capital requirements were quite low. The principle of free banking was significantly modified by the Banking Act of 1935 which provided that, in addition to capital requirements, certain other factors needed to be considered if an overbanked condition was to be avoided. Consequently, the Act required the Comptroller of the Currency, before granting a newly organized national bank authority to commence business, the Federal Reserve System before admitting a non-insured state bank to membership, and the Federal Deposit Insurance Corporation before insuring a non-member state bank to consider: "the financial history and condition of the bank, the adequacy of its capital structure, its future earnings prospects, the general character of its management, the convenience and needs of the community to be served by the bank, and whether or not its corporate powers are consistent with the purposes of this section." [16] This requirement, of course, does not apply to the establishment of non-insured, non-member state banks. Similar requirements are considered in the establishment of branches.

The general policy of the federal supervising authorities in the granting of charters and in the admission of banks to membership in

15 See *Joint Statement of the Executive Committee of the National Association of Supervisors of State Banks, The Federal Deposit Insurance Corporation, the Comptroller of the Currency, and the Board of Governors of the Federal Reserve System,* mimeographed, agreed to July 3, 1952; also, the Federal Deposit Insurance Corporation, *Annual Report,* 1938, "Development of Uniform Examination Procedure among Federal and State Bank Supervisors," pp. 61–78; and Robert F. Leonard, "Supervision of the Commercial Banking System," in *Banking Studies,* Board of Governors of the Federal Reserve System, 1941, pp. 189–210.

16 U.S.C., title 12, Sec. 264(g), as added by Act of Aug. 23, 1935.

the Reserve System and in the Deposit Insurance Corporation has been to stress the need of a community for banking facilities. However, the practical determination of what constitutes need has not been precisely defined and, as would be expected, is based on the judgment of the supervisory officials. According to the Deposit Insurance Corporation "need can best be measured by the willingness of individuals to supply capital for new or additional banking facilities." [17] A similar viewpoint is expressed by the Comptroller of the Currency. "Our experience with banking conditions through the country over many decades has proved that a substantial lack of adequate and convenient banking facilities in communities large enough to support them almost invariably will give rise to an effective demand for such facilities, usually in the form of an application for a new bank charter, either State or national, or a branch thereof where permissible." [18] Although need presumably is reflected in the applications for charters or branches, the fact is that during the ten years 1941–50 "insufficient need" was cited 104 times as one of the reasons for the rejection of 114 applications for authority to organize new national banks. It was also the leading reason for the rejection of applications by national banks for branches.[19] This apparent contradiction of supervisory philosophy is explained by the fact that the authorities are fearful of excessive competition. Although the Comptroller of the Currency has stated that "one of the fundamental tenets of our views and actions on applications for charters and branches is the desirability of competition wherever possible," [20] this factor is not given much weight in communities with more than one bank where competition already exists, "for competition can result in such a weakening of existing banking institutions as to bring consequences so injurious to the welfare of the community as to outweigh any benefits to be anticipated from increasing the intensity of competition." [21]

A clearly defined policy with regard to entry into the banking business is yet to be evolved. There is a strong desire to preserve a unit banking system on the grounds that competition is desirable, yet the authorities appear loath to foster competition through the estab-

[17] *Monetary Policy and the Management of the Public Debt,* Part 2, p. 954.

[18] *Ibid.,* p. 926.

[19] In replies from 21 state bank supervisors the most frequently mentioned reason for refusal was lack of profit possibilities.

[20] *Ibid.,* p. 929.

[21] *Idem.*

lishment of new banks and branches. There is a traditional resistance to the development of branch banking except within limited areas. Mergers are regarded in some circles of government with suspicion based on the fear of concentration and monopoly.

BRANCH, GROUP, AND CHAIN BANKING

Although banking in the United States is carried on typically through unit banks, three types of multiple office banking are in existence: branch banking, group banking, and chain banking. Of these, branch banking is the most important, the other forms often being substitutes for branch banking in states where it is prohibited or severely restricted.[22]

The development of branch banking has been hampered by numerous restrictions under both federal and state laws. At the end of the year 1950, out of 14,121 banks, only 1,241 operated branches and most of these banks operated a relatively small number of offices. Of the 4,721 branches, 2,035 were located in the head office city, reflecting the limited geographical development.

Thirty-five states and the District of Columbia specifically authorize branch banking but thirteen other states prohibit it or have no permissive statutes. There is no uniformity among these permissive statutes. Generally speaking, branch banking is restricted territorially and by minimum capital requirements. However, California is one of eighteen states which permit statewide branch banking. The federal laws permit national banks (and state banks which are members of the Federal Reserve System) to establish branches only where permitted by the laws of the states in which the banks operate.

Branch banking played an important role in the United States before the Civil War. However, during the last hundred years the growth of American banking, except in certain periods, was characterized by the establishment of additional unit banks rather than the expansion of branch facilities. A number of factors have been cited to explain the failure of branch banking to develop after the Civil War. Banks in the South were destroyed during the Civil War. The passage of the National Bank Act in 1863, together with the attitude

22 See U.S. Congress, 82d Cong., 2d Sess., Joint Committee on the Economic Report, *Monetary Policy and the Management of the Public Debt,* Part 1, pp. 548–52; also, Board of Governors of the Federal Reserve System, *Banking Studies,* 1941, pp. 113–40; also "Branch Banking in the United States, 1939 and 1949," *Federal Reserve Bulletin,* July, 1950.

of the office of the Comptroller of the Currency, were instrumental in encouraging the conversion of state branch banks into unit national banks. The act did not specifically authorize branch banking by national banks, although branch banking was still permitted under some state laws. The low minimum capital requirements for the establishment of new banks also favored unit rather than branch banking; the capital requirement was lowered from $50,000 to $25,000 in 1900, and the $50,000 level was not restored until 1933.

It was not until California enacted a statewide branch banking law in 1909 that branch banking received any real impetus. Subsequently, the Consolidation Act of 1918 permitted national banks to operate branches obtained through consolidations. In 1923 the Comptroller of the Currency permitted national banks located in states where state banks were allowed to operate branches to maintain "letter window" offices to perform limited banking services. On February 25, 1927, the McFadden Act was approved permitting national banks to open branches, with the approval of the Comptroller, but only in the home city and only in states whose laws permitted branch banking. No branches could be established in places of small population. The Banking Act of 1933 liberalized the branch banking provisions by authorizing the establishment of branches, with the approval of the Comptroller, on the same conditions that governed state banks. However, until 1952 a national bank was prohibited from establishing branches outside the home city unless it had a capital of $500,000 (lesser capital was required in states having a population of less than one million persons). A similar capital restriction was imposed by regulation upon state banks which belonged to the Federal Reserve System. Because this requirement is more stringent than many state laws and has often precluded membership in the Federal Reserve System by banks with, or wishing to establish, out-of-town branches, it was eliminated on July 15, 1952. National and state member banks continue to be subject to the requirement that a bank must have aggregate capital stock equal to the amount which would be required for the establishment of a national bank in the place where its branches are situated.

The large decline in the number of unit banks during the 1920s through failures, bank mergers and voluntary liquidations left many communities without banking facilities and reacted in favor of the development of branch banking. Following the epidemic of bank failures from 1930 to 1933, state laws respecting branch banking were progressively liberalized. In 1927 states either prohibited branch banking entirely or limited the operation of branches to the home city and contiguous suburban areas; [23] in contrast, by 1939 only nine states prohibited branch banking while four had no permissive statutes and two prohibited branches outside the head office city.[24]

Although there has been a steady if not spectacular growth in the number of branches during the last several decades, it is quite obvious that American banking has not experienced the consolidation or amalgamation movement that has taken place in England and other countries resulting in the establishment of a few large banks with vast networks of branches.

The failure of branch banking to expand geographically can be attributed to the political strength and opposition to branch banking by many independent unit bankers, to the reluctance of the large city banks to promote branch banking for fear of offending their correspondent unit banks, and to the decentralization of bank supervision and lack of uniformity in the banking laws.

In recent years the federal supervisory agencies have taken a more friendly attitude toward branch banking and at times have even encouraged it. However, as recently as 1949 the Comptroller of the Currency stated that "it is appropriate to mention our general policy of encouraging independent local banking, rather than expansion of branch systems, whenever the former gives promise of operating soundly and to the satisfaction of the community." [25] A year later, in discussing the absorption of small banks as a result of inability to secure competent management upon the death of key personnel, the Comptroller observed that "in certain areas, particularly where State-wide branch banking is permitted, this is causing a steady reduction in the number of small unit banks and ever greater concentration of banking resources under the control of relatively few large institutions." [26] The attitude of the Federal Deposit Insurance Corporation is expressed as follows: "It is our belief that each State should retain the right to decide for itself whether or not the advantages to be gained from branch banking offset the disadvantages." [27] The Board

23 Steiner, W. H., and Eli Shapiro, *Money and Banking*, rev. ed., 1941, p. 483.

24 *Ibid.*, p. 483, and *Banking Studies*, p. 114. For a list of the number of branches by states and a summary of the status of the state laws on branch banking in 1920, 1930, 1940, and 1950, see *Monetary Policy and the Management of the Public Debt*, Part 2, p. 558.

25 *87th Annual Report of the Comptroller of the Currency*, 1949, p. viii.

26 *88th Annual Report of the Comptroller of the Currency*, 1950, p. 3.

27 *Monetary Policy and the Management of the Public Debt*, Part 2, p. 954.

of Governors of the Federal Reserve System in discussing remedies for inadequate banking facilities appears to favor some relaxation of "the specific and onerous dollar capital requirements for the establishment of branches by national banks and State member banks" so as to permit additional banking facilities in states where branch banking is permitted.

Chain banking differs from branch banking in respect to its legal form and control and is concentrated in states where branch banking is prohibited. Chain banking is defined as "a type of multiple office banking through which the operations or policies of a number of independently incorporated banks are controlled by one or more individuals," the control being exercised through stock ownership or common directors.[28] Only a small proportion of the banks and deposits of the country are represented in chains. It was estimated that there were 115 chain systems in the United States on December 31, 1945, involving 522 banks.[29] The great majority of chains consist of five or less banks built around a key bank. Most of the chains operate in a few states where branch banking is prohibited and are found in agricultural areas.

In contrast with chain banking, group banking denotes corporate as contrasted with personal control. Group banking is defined as "that form of multiple office banking in which independently incorporated banks are controlled directly or indirectly by a corporation, business trust, association or similar organization." [30] This is in reality "holding company" banking.

At the end of 1950 there were 28 of these holding company groups controlling 367 banks in 26 states and operating 1,019 branches. Deposits of these 367 banks represented 12 percent of the deposits of all commercial banks.[31] Groups vary widely in size and geographic distribution of offices. In some degree, group banking is a substitute for branch banking but it also coexists with branch banking. The largest group, or holding company affiliate, is the Transamerica Corporation, organized under the laws of the State of Delaware, but having its principal office in San Francisco, California. At the end of 1950 this company was reported to hold stock in 48 banks with 623 branches and to operate in five states (California, Oregon, Nevada, Arizona,

28 *Banking Studies*, p. 125.
29 *Monetary Policy and the Management of the Public Debt*, Part 1, p. 552.
30 *Banking Studies*, p. 130.
31 *American Banker*, April 23, 1952, p. 1.

and Washington). The largest of the banks in the Transamerica group was the Bank of America National Trust and Savings Association, San Francisco, with more than 500 branches in the State of California.[32]

The development of group banking commenced in the middle 1920s in response to a variety of factors including: (1) the desire for profits; (2) the restrictions against branch banking; (3) the failure of a number of chains; (4) the desire for more centralized control; and (5) the realization of operating economies. Like other forms of multiple office banking, group banking provides more economical operation than unit banking. However, in some cases it led to speculation in bank stocks and increased the difficulties of bank supervision and regulation. Since it is less economical than branch banking, some students regard group banking as "a temporary scheme, of which the owned banks will gradually be absorbed by branch banks as laws are gradually modified to permit a wider extension of branches." [33]

The further development of either chain or group banking will probably be arrested also by the antipathy in the United States toward holding companies and other forms of intercorporate control carrying a suspicion of monopoly. Repeated efforts have been made by the federal supervisory authorities to strengthen control over group banking. Following a study in 1930 of group, chain, and branch banking, the Banking Act of 1933 brought group banking under federal supervision in any case in which a member of the Federal Reserve System was involved as a constituent bank. The provisions of the Banking Act of 1933 require holding company affiliates (holding companies which control banks that are members of the Federal Reserve System) to obtain voting permits before voting the stock of member banks under their control. This provision does not apply to the voting stock of subsidiary banks which are not members of the Federal Reserve System. The holding company affiliates were also made subject to examination by the Federal Reserve authorities, as were constituent banks, and were required to make regular reports of condition. Certain other provisions established limits and collateral requirements for member bank loans to affiliates. The Federal Reserve authorities have repeatedly requested Congress to curtail group banking. In 1938 a bank holding company bill, designed to force the dissolution of group

32 Transamerica has since disposed of its holdings in the Bank of America.
33 John M. Chapman and Ray B. Westerfield, *Branch Banking*, 1942, p. 17.

bank systems over a three-year period was introduced in Congress but was not acted upon. Since then the Board of Governors has repeatedly urged the enactment of legislation to prevent the further expansion of bank holding companies or the creation of new holding companies.[34] Existing laws are deemed by the Board to be unsatisfactory in the following respects: (1) inadequate statutory definition of a holding company; (2) the regulation of holding companies is effective only as an incident to the obtaining of a voting permit; (3) insufficient penalties for violations.

The request for new legislation is based on the contention that in exceptional cases the holding company device has not been used simply as a mechanism for the efficient operation of the controlled banks but as a means of: (1) engaging in extraneous businesses such as owning and operating industrial enterprises; (2) escaping supervisory powers; (3) engaging in monopolistic practices; and (4) profiting through trading in bank stocks.

The primary objection of the federal authorities to holding company banking is undoubtedly their fear of monopolies. On June 24, 1948, the Board of Governors of the Federal Reserve System issued a complaint against Transamerica Corporation and subsequently held hearings to determine whether or not an order should be entered requiring Transamerica to cease and desist from violating Section 7 of the Clayton Antitrust Act.[35] The proceedings evoked widespread interest since the Act vests specifically in the Board the responsibility for enforcement with respect to banks. The Transamerica proceeding represented the first such action to be undertaken. On March 27, 1952, the Board reported its findings and conclusions and by a split vote ordered Transamerica to divest itself fully and completely of all capital stock in 47 banks.[36] Transamerica was to be permitted to retain ownership of the largest of its banks, the Bank of America National Trust and Savings Association although Transamerica had sometime earlier started to dispose of its holdings in this bank. The argument presented by the Board was based largely upon the fact that Transa-

[34] See especially Board of Governors of the Federal Reserve System, *Annual Report*, 1943, pp. 34–37. For a summary of the provisions of various bills to regulate bank holding companies, 1941–52, see "Bank Mergers and Concentration of Bank Facilities," pp. 67–71.

[35] "An Act to supplement existing laws against unlawful restraints and monopolies, and for other purposes," approved October 14, 1914 (38 Stat. 731, 15 U.S.C. 18).

[36] The Board's findings, conclusions, and order appear in the *Federal Reserve Bulletin*, April, 1952, pp. 368–98.

merica controls 40 percent of the banking offices and 39 percent of the deposits in five states.[37] The Board's order was set aside by the United State Court of Appeals for the Third Circuit on July 16, 1953. The court held that the Board "failed to find the facts as to lessening of competition and tendency to monopoly in the areas of effective competition actually involved." On appeal the United States Supreme Court refused on November 30, 1953, to review the lower court's decision.

INTEGRATION

The limited development of multiple office banking in the United States has brought about the invention of a variety of arrangements by which the commercial banking structure is integrated and the movement of funds between banks is facilitated. The oldest of these arrangements is that by which banks act as correspondent for one another. Another is found in the local and regional clearinghouse associations. Finally, the Federal Reserve banks constitute a unifying force by the performance of certain functions and through the provision of various facilities including the collection and clearance of checks for both member and non-member banks.

Banks in outlying places have found it necessary to maintain balances in the financial and commercial centers as a form of cash reserve and as a means of facilitating domestic and foreign exchange operations.[38] The lack of an important discount market before the First World War was also a factor in correspondent transactions for the adjustment of reserve positions. The note brokers, or "commercial paper" dealers, did supply a certain amount of trade paper arising outside of the community but there was no liquid and well-developed money market. With increasing use of checks during the last half of the nineteenth century, the correspondent relationship became increasingly important. The basis of this relationship was an agreement by the depositary bank to collect and remit checks in return for the deposit of a minimum balance. This relationship was given a statutory basis under the National Bank Act and under various state laws which permitted both national and state banks outside certain designated cities to count, as a portion of their legal reserves, the balances which

37 See dissenting statement of Gov. Oliver S. Powell, *Federal Reserve Bulletin*, April, 1952, p. 395.

38 B. H. Beckhart and J. G. Smith, "Sources and Movement of Funds," *The New York Money Market*, II, 195.

they kept on deposit with the city correspondents. The permission to count interbank balances as legal reserves still characterizes the legal reserve requirements governing non-member state banks. However, since the establishment of the Federal Reserve System national and state member banks are required to maintain legal reserve balances with their Federal Reserve banks, and such balances are the only form of reserve eligible to satisfy the legal requirement. In spite of this change the correspondent system has survived and today meets a variety of needs. An unknown but substantially large amount of out-of-town checks of both member and non-member banks are still collected through correspondent banks rather than through the Federal Reserve banks.[39] Moreover, correspondent banks are employed to collect non-cash items since the Reserve banks do not handle them. City correspondents provide a variety of services including safekeeping facilities and the clipping and collection of maturing coupons; they furnish investment counsel and credit information, and also provide exchange for making out-of-town payments both domestic and foreign. Interbank loans represent an important feature of correspondent banking. Member as well as non-member banks borrow for temporary purposes from city correspondents. Non-member banks are not ordinarily eligible to borrow from Federal Reserve banks and, moreover, borrowing from Federal Reserve banks may be accomplished only in certain legally defined ways and may be less convenient or subject to greater secrecy than borrowing from a correspondent bank.[40]

The relative importance of interbank deposits is evident from Table 6.

New York City is probably still just as important a point of concentration of bankers' balances relative to other centers as it was before the Federal Reserve System, although bankers' balances relative to total deposits is less important than it was before the Federal Reserve System.[41] Since the First World War two important factors have tended to decrease the use of interbank balances for check clearing and collection. These are the establishment and development of the Federal Reserve System and the extension of branch banking.[42] City

39 B. H. Beckhart and James G. Smith, "Sources and Movements of Funds," *The New York Money Market,* II, 234–37.

40 *Ibid.*, pp. 238–39.

41 *Ibid.*, p. 231.

42 George Garvy, *The Development of Bank Debits and Clearings and Their Use in Economic Analysis,* Board of Governors of the Federal Reserve System, January, 1952, p. 57

TABLE 6
RATIO OF INTERBANK DEMAND DEPOSITS TO TOTAL DEMAND DEPOSITS OF MEMBER BANKS, DECEMBER 31, 1929, 1939, AND 1946–51
(IN PERCENT)

Year	*All Member Banks*	*New York*	*Chicago*	*Reserve City*	*Country*
1929	16.4	18.8	23.0	20.7	6.3
1939	24.7	30.7	31.3	27.4	7.3
1946	13.2	18.2	22.7	16.5	3.7
1947	13.1	18.7	22.2	16.1	3.5
1948	12.5	18.7	20.1	15.6	3.1
1949	12.6	18.4	20.8	15.8	3.2
1950	12.7	18.5	20.4	16.1	3.3
1951	12.7	18.2	20.9	16.4	3.5

Source: calculated from *Member Bank Call Reports,* Board of Governors of the Federal Reserve System. Interbank deposits include demand deposits due to banks in the United States and banks in foreign countries. Deposits of member banks due to banks in the United States on December 31, 1951, amounted to $12,634,017,000 and deposits due to banks in foreign countries were $1,368,777,000, of which $1,128,347,000 was held by banks in New York City.

correspondents usually collect local items through local clearing houses, but forward many or all out-of-town items to the district Federal Reserve bank, its branches, or to other Federal Reserve banks. Consequently, checks sent by country banks to their city correspondents often ultimately pass through the Reserve banks.[43]

THE FEDERAL RESERVE SYSTEM

The establishment of the Federal Reserve System in 1914 made little or no alteration in the commercial banking structure. As will be explained at a later point, it was set up to exercise various central banking powers and functions, and its form of organization was designed to suit the peculiarities of a unit banking system. In addition to its supervisory and credit control functions, the System serves member as well as non-member banks in a variety of ways.

Perhaps the most important operating function of the Federal Reserve banks is the nationwide system for the collection and clearance of checks and other cash items on out-of-town banks. Each of the twelve Federal Reserve banks is in fact required by the Board of Governors of the System to act as a clearinghouse for its members. Non-members may use these facilities under certain conditions. While the Federal Reserve banks do not ordinarily handle local checks, in

[43] *Ibid.,* p. 57.

most cities having a Federal Reserve bank or branch, settlement of local clearinghouse balances are made on the books of the Federal Reserve bank by debit or credit to the accounts of the participating banks.

Several features of this collection system deserve mention. First it is a voluntary system. Member banks are not compelled to use the Federal Reserve collection facilities and, indeed, only about half of the member banks regularly send their out-of-town items to the Reserve banks for collection.[44] Secondly, the collection system is a par remittance system. The Reserve banks are not allowed to receive checks for collection which cannot be collected at par. All clearing banks must agree to remit at par, that is, without the deduction of exchange from the face amount of checks. At the end of 1950 there were 1,853 banks not on the par list. Thirdly, non-member banks have been admitted to clearing privileges since 1917, provided they agree to remit at par all checks sent to them by the Reserve banks and provided they maintain with the Reserve bank of the district a balance sufficient to offset items in transit. Finally, the Reserve banks give immediate credit, or credit within one or two days, for checks received. Federal Reserve "float,"—that is, the difference between the amount of checks in process of collection by the Reserve banks and the amount of checks for which credit has been deferred—averages about one-half billion dollars, a measure of the free credit given in advance of actual collection.

In addition to the operation of the nationwide system for the collection and clearance of out-of-town checks, the Reserve banks also supply currency and coin in response to the needs of the public. As noted *infra,* the Reserve banks issue the principal form of paper currency in use, the Federal Reserve note, and they also are the agency through which various kinds of United States Treasury paper currency and coin are put into circulation. Member banks obtain currency from the Reserve banks and have it charged to their accounts in much the same way that individual depositors obtain currency from their commercial banks. The cost of printing and the expenses for shipping currency to out-of-town member banks are borne by the Reserve banks.

Finally, the Reserve banks provide domestic exchange. Member

[44] Edward L. Smead, "Operations of the Reserve Banks," *Banking Studies,* Board of Governors of the Federal Reserve System, p. 251.

banks are permitted to draw on them, in amounts up to $50,000, exchange drafts which are receivable for immediate availability at par at any Reserve bank. In effect, a member bank has exchange facilities equivalent to those it would enjoy if it carried accounts with each of the other eleven Reserve banks and their branches.[45] Also, member bank balances can be transferred in round amounts for member bank account free of charge over leased wires. Transfers for member banks for the accounts of others are made over commercial wires at the cost of the telegram.

CLEARINGHOUSES

Local and regional clearinghouses are another means by which the banks have been unified. In September, 1951, there were about 233 city clearinghouses located in the 48 states and the District of Columbia. In addition, there were perhaps roughly 300 regional clearinghouse associations. These do not clear checks; their concern is with public relations, the solution of common banking problems, uniformity in financial statements, and standardization of banking practices.

Clearinghouses are private voluntary associations founded for the primary purpose of exchanging checks and facilitating prompt collection. The oldest in the United States is the New York Clearing House Association, founded in 1853.[46] At the present time it is comprised of 18 members and 5 clearing non-members.[47] The Federal Reserve Bank of New York and the Clearing House City Collection Department also make exchanges at the Clearing House.

Clearinghouses have assumed a variety of non-clearing functions. For mutual protection, clearinghouses at an early date kept informed of the condition of each of the members. Beginning in Chicago in 1906 some clearinghouses have maintained an examining force to determine the solvency of members, but in recent years this practice has been largely discontinued. The New York Clearing House dispensed with special examinations of its members in November, 1939, in view of the adequacy of the examinations by the supervisory authorities and because of a desire to economize. Other clearinghouse functions have included the issuance of certificates to members in

[45] W. H. Steiner and Eli Shapiro, *Money and Banking*, 1941, pp. 539–40.

[46] New York Clearing House Association, "Information Regarding the Operation of The New York Clearing House," rev., December, 1939.

[47] New York Clearing House Association, "Extracts from Managers Annual Report for 1951."

periods of crisis in exchange for promissory notes and other obligations, the maintenance of central credit files for the use of the associated banks, the standardization of routine banking practices (hours of banking, schedules of service charges, and so on), and the solution of common problems.

FINANCIAL STRUCTURE

The financial structure of the commercial banks is characterized at the present time by relatively large holdings of cash reserves and investments in securities. Only about one third of the total assets of the commercial banks is loans and discounts, while about two fifths is represented by investments in securities and one quarter by cash reserves. Of the total resources only about 7 percent has been supplied from invested capital and retained earnings and about 70 percent by demand deposits and 22 percent by time deposits.

The principal assets, liabilities, and capital accounts of the commercial banks are given in absolute amounts in Table 7 and in percent in Table 8. Since the end of the war a large rise in loans has been accompanied by a large decline in investments in government securities. The ratio of loans to total assets has risen from 16 percent at the end of the Second World War to 33 percent at the end of 1951, the highest proportion since the mid-1930s. Nevertheless, the current proportion remains well below the figure of nearly 60 percent which was reached in the 1920s.

CASH RESERVES

The various types of cash reserves held by the commercial banks are shown in Table 9. Part of these are reserves required by law and part are funds needed for operating purposes.

In contrast with many foreign countries, American banking laws have for a long time imposed legal reserve requirements upon commercial banks. These requirements were conceived originally as a means of protecting the note holder and later the depositor. In recent years they have served, like the conventional ratio in the United Kingdom, as a fulcrum for the exercise of general credit controls involving changes in the supply of available reserves.

The details of the legal reserve formulae are quite complicated.

TABLE 7
ASSETS AND LIABILITIES OF ALL COMMERCIAL BANKS IN THE UNITED STATES AND POSSESSIONS, DECEMBER 31, 1945–51
(AMOUNTS IN MILLIONS OF DOLLARS)

Assets	*1945*	*1946*	*1947*	*1948*	*1949*	*1950*	*1951*
Cash and funds due from banks	34,975	34,366	37,674	38,758	35,803	40,439	44,830
United States Government obligations	91,149	75,253	69,659	62,987	67,326	62,320	61,776
Obligations of states and political subdivisions	3,974	4,411	5,297	5,683	6,571	8,161	9,246
Other securities	3,366	3,707	3,745	3,555	3,717	4,314	4,166
Loans, discounts, and overdrafts	26,193	31,283	38,287	42,767	43,250	52,574	58,139
Miscellaneous assets	1,525	1,532	1,648	1,852	1,883	2,047	2,266
Total	161,182	150,552	156,310	155,602	158,550	169,856	180,424
Liabilities and Capital Accounts							
Deposits							
Demand	n.a. [a]	n.a.	108,974	107,071	108,956	118,773	126,654
Time	n.a.	n.a.	35,992	36,565	36,995	37,316	39,035
Total	151,089	139,883	144,966	143,637	145,951	156,089	165,688
Miscellaneous liabilities	1,160	1,108	1,236	1,411	1,556	2,098	2,436
Total capital accounts	8,933	9,561	10,108	10,555	11,044	11,669	12,299
Total	161,182	150,552	156,310	155,602	158,550	169,856	180,424
Number of banks included [b]	14,079	14,114	14,222	14,129	14,205	14,164	14,132

Source: Annual Reports of the Federal Deposit Insurance Corporation.
[a] Not available.
[b] Noninsured nondeposit trust companies are not included in the figures for 1945–1946.

Member banks are all subject to the requirements of the Federal Reserve Act while non-member banks are governed by their respective state laws; these state laws are not uniform.[48]

In the case of member banks, the amount of required reserve must be held entirely in the form of a balance with the Federal Reserve Bank of the district. Neither vault cash nor balances due from other banks will satisfy the requirement. In contrast, state laws ordinarily

[48] See Board of Governors of the Federal Reserve System, "Provisions of State Laws Relating to Bank Reserves as of December 31, 1944"; "The History of Reserve Requirements for Banks in the United States"; and *Monetary Policy and the Management of the Public Debt,* Part 1, pp. 463–74.

TABLE 8
ASSETS AND LIABILITIES OF ALL COMMERCIAL BANKS IN THE UNITED STATES AND POSSESSIONS, DECEMBER 31, 1945–51
(IN PERCENT)

Assets	*1945*	*1946*	*1947*	*1948*	*1949*	*1950*	*1951*
Cash and funds due from banks	21.7	22.8	24.1	24.9	22.6	23.8	24.8
United States Government obligations	56.5	50.0	44.6	40.5	42.5	36.7	34.2
Obligations of states and political subdivisions	2.5	2.9	3.4	3.6	4.1	4.8	5.1
Other securities	2.1	2.5	2.4	2.3	2.3	2.5	2.3
Loans, discounts, and overdrafts	16.3	20.8	24.5	27.5	27.3	31.0	32.2
Miscellaneous assets	0.9	1.0	1.0	1.2	1.2	1.2	1.3
Total	100.0	100.0	100.0	100.0	100.0	100.0	100.0
Liabilities and Capital Accounts							
Deposits							
Demand	n.a [a]	n.a.	69.7	68.8	68.7	69.9	70.1
Time	n.a	n.a.	23.0	23.5	23.3	22.0	21.6
Total	93.7	92.9	92.7	92.3	92.1	91.9	91.7
Miscellaneous liabilities	0.7	0.7	0.8	0.9	1.0	1.2	1.4
Total capital accounts	5.6	6.4	6.5	6.8	7.0	6.9	6.8
Total liabilities and capital	100.0	100.0	100.0	100.0	100.0	100.0	100.0

[a] Not available.

TABLE 9
CASH ASSETS OF ALL COMMERCIAL BANKS IN THE UNITED STATES, DECEMBER 31, 1945–51
(AMOUNTS IN MILLIONS OF DOLLARS)

	1945 [a]	*1946* [a]	*1947*	*1948*	*1949*	*1950*	*1951*
Currency and coin	1,832	2,015	2,288	2,039	2,076	2,233	2,766
Reserve with Federal Reserve banks (member banks)	15,810	16,013	17,796	20,404	16,428	17,458	19,911
Demand balances with banks in the United States	11,007	9,429	10,227	9,413	9,883	10,890	12,011
Other balances with banks in the United States	75	60	67	54	43	42	47
Balances with banks in foreign countries	24	57	31	40	51	159	54
Cash items in process of collection	5,556	6,130	7,265	6,808	7,324	9,657	10,042
Total	34,303	33,704	37,674	38,758	35,803	40,439	44,830

Source: Annual Reports of the Federal Deposit Insurance Corporation.

[a] Data for 1945 and 1946 cover insured commercial banks only.

permit the required reserve to be held partly in cash in vault and partly as a balance with correspondent banks in designated places. In some cases government securities may be counted as part of the legal reserve.

The formula by which the amount of required reserve of an individual member bank is calculated relates the amount of required reserve to the amount of its deposit liabilities. A larger amount is required against demand than against time deposits. Furthermore, the member banks are classified for reserve purposes in three groups: Central Reserve cities (New York and Chicago); the Reserve cities (35 cities where there is a Federal Reserve bank or branch and 18 other cities in which the amount of deposits due to banks is above a prescribed standard or through the preference of the banks in those cities for a Reserve city designation); and country.[49] Historically, the tripartite classification was carried over from the national bank requirements in the pre-Federal Reserve era when legal reserves could be redeposited in part with banks in designated reserve cities.

Net demand deposits for purposes of calculating reserve requirements are defined as gross deposits less cash items in process of collection and demand deposits due from banks. Time deposits are taken gross. The percentages are applicable to weekly periods in the case of Central Reserve and Reserve City banks and to semimonthly periods for country banks to permit flexibility.

The percentage requirements are subject to change by order of the Board of Governors within limits prescribed by the Federal Reserve Act. This discretionary authority was given by the Banking Act of 1935 and was first used to sterilize the large excess reserves which resulted from the gold inflow during the 1930s at a time when the portfolio of government securities held by the Federal Reserve banks was too small to permit sales of securities to offset gold imports.

The percentage requirements for member banks in force at the present time are given in Table 10.

At the end of June, 1952, the actual ratio of required reserves to total deposits (net demand deposits plus time deposits) was 15.8 percent. The corresponding average for Central Reserve city banks was 22.0 percent, for Reserve City banks 16.2 percent and for Country banks 11.2 percent.

[49] The formula used in classification is given in Board of Governors of the Federal Reserve System, *Annual Report*, 1947, pp. 85–87.

TABLE 10
LEGAL RESERVE REQUIREMENTS OF MEMBER BANKS
(IN PERCENT OF DEPOSITS)

	STATUTORY		Regulatory Requirement
	Maxima	*Minima*	*June, 1952*
Against net demand deposits			
Central Reserve city banks	26	13	24
Reserve city banks	20	10	20
Country banks	14	7	14
Against time deposits			
All classes of banks	6	3	6

Source: Board of Governors of the Federal Reserve System, *Regulation A*.

Although the legal requirements appear more onerous to city banks than to country banks, banks outside the reserve cities have to carry relatively larger cash reserves. As Table 11 shows, the amount of actual cash reserves of all kinds held by the banks in the three classifications is more evenly balanced in relation to total assets than the legal requirements suggest.

TABLE 11
CASH ASSETS OF MEMBER BANKS, DECEMBER 26, 1951
(IN PERCENT OF TOTAL ASSETS)

Type of Reserve	*New York*	*Chicago*	*Reserve Cities*	*Country*
Cash in vault	0.7	1.3	1.2	2.3
Due from Federal Reserve banks	17.8	17.7	13.3	10.1
Balances with other banks	0.3	1.3	3.4	7.8
Cash items in process of collection	7.1	6.3	6.4	1.8
Total cash reserves	25.9	26.6	24.3	22.2

Banks hold only enough cash in vault to take care of operating requirements. Demands by the public for additional currency can be met by obtaining currency from the Federal Reserve banks in exchange for legal reserve balances. The large proportion of cash reserves in the form of interbank deposits is explained by the use of these accounts in correspondent relationships and by the fact that non-member bank legal reserves are held largely in this form.

BANK LOANS

The commercial banks make a wide variety of loans as shown in Table 12. Although the classification employed in this table rests

TABLE 12

LOANS OF ALL COMMERCIAL BANKS IN THE UNITED STATES AND POSSESSIONS, DECEMBER 31, 1945–51

(IN TOTAL)

Type of Loan	*1945* [a]	*1946* [a]	*1947*	*1948* [b]	*1949* [b]	*1950* [b]	*1951* [b]
Commercial and industrial loans	9,462	14,019	18,264	19,014	17,161	22,038	26,013
Loans to farmers directly guaranteed by the Commodity Credit Corp.	304	102	68	915	1,004	382	290
Other loans to farmers (excluding loans on real estate)	1,010	1,256	1,610	1,977	2,070	2,543	3,139
Loans to brokers and dealers in securities	3,164	1,517	831	1,344	1,763	1,802	1,581
Other loans for carrying securities	3,606	1,609	1,243	985	893	1,078	1,002
Real estate loans							
On farm land	507	684	823	878	908	968	1,004
On residential properties	3,332	5,058	6,933	8,062	8,676	10,431	11,270
On other properties	840	1,365	1,691	1,957	2,060	2,264	2,458
Other loans to individuals (consumer loans)	3,361	4,032	5,745	6,905	8,095	10,156	10,508
Loans to banks	49	81	116	122	98	90	150
All other loans (including overdrafts)	1,133	1,017	964	1,019	1,072	1,498	1,541
Total loans and discounts, gross	n.a. [c]	n.a.	n.a.	43,177	43,800	53,250	58,955
Valuation reserves	n.a.	n.a.	n.a.	411	550	675	816
Total loans and discounts, net	25,769	30,740	38,287	42,767	43,250	52,574	58,139

Source: Annual Reports of the Federal Deposit Insurance Corporation.

[a] Data for 1945 and 1946 cover insured commercial banks only. Loans of insured banks represented more than 98 percent of the loans of all banks.

[b] Beginning 1948 various loan items are shown gross, i.e., before deduction of valuation reserves.

[c] Not available.

upon mixed criteria, it affords a general idea of the purposes for which loans are made. Table 13 shows that of the total loans outstanding December 31, 1951, about 44 percent was represented by loans to non-financial business borrowers (commercial and industrial), 6 percent by loans to finance agricultural operations, 5 percent by loans for the purpose of purchasing or carrying securities, 25 percent by loans for the purchase or construction of real estate, and 18 percent by direct loans for consumption and other personal uses. As explained further below a significant proportion of the commercial and industrial

TABLE 13
PERCENTAGE DISTRIBUTION OF LOANS OF ALL COMMERCIAL BANKS IN THE UNITED STATES AND POSSESSIONS, DECEMBER 31, 1945–51
(IN PERCENT)

	1945 [a]	*1946* [a]	*1947*	*1948* [b]	*1949* [b]	*1950* [b]	*1951*
Commercial and industrial loans	36.7	45.6	47.7	44.0	39.2	41.4	44.1
Loans to farmers directly guaranteed by the Commodity Credit Corp.	1.2	0.3	0.2	2.1	2.3	0.7	0.5
Other loans to farmers (excluding loans on real estate)	3.9	4.1	4.2	4.6	4.7	4.8	5.3
Loans to brokers and dealers in securities	12.3	4.9	2.2	3.1	4.0	3.4	2.7
Other loans for carrying securities	14.0	5.2	3.2	2.3	2.0	2.0	1.7
Real estate loans							
On farm land	2.0	2.2	2.1	2.0	2.1	1.8	1.7
On residential property	12.9	16.5	18.1	18.7	19.8	19.6	19.1
On other properties	3.3	4.4	4.4	4.5	4.7	4.3	4.2
Other loans to individuals	9.2	13.1	15.0	16.0	18.5	19.1	17.8
Loans to banks	0.2	0.3	0.3	0.3	0.2	0.2	0.3
All other loans (including overdrafts)	4.4	3.3	2.5	2.4	2.4	2.8	2.6
Total loans and discounts, gross total	n.a. [c]	n.a.	n.a.	100.0	100.0	100.0	100.0
Valuation reserves	n.a.	n.a.	n.a.				
Total loans and discounts, net total	100.0	100.0	100.0				

Source: Annual Reports of the Federal Deposit Insurance Corporation.

[a] Data for 1945 and 1946 cover insured commercial banks only. Loans of insured banks represented more than 98 percent of loans of all commercial banks.

[b] Beginning with 1948 various loan items are based on gross figures, i.e., before deduction of valuation reserves.

[c] Not available.

loans is represented by loans to sales finance companies, which in turn finance consumption.

COMMERCIAL AND INDUSTRIAL LOANS

This is the largest single category of loans made by the commercial banks. A special survey [50] of the business loans of member banks, November 20, 1946, revealed that manufacturing enterprises accounted for 42.8 percent of the amount borrowed, wholesale trade 18.3 percent, and retail trade 11.2 percent. The remainder was divided as follows: public utilities, 9.3 percent; services, 3.7 percent, construction,

[50] Albert R. Koch, "Business Loans of Member Banks," *Federal Reserve Bulletin*, March, 1947.

3.4 percent; sales finance companies, 5.9 percent; all others, 5.4 percent.

The indebtedness of business borrowers to banks is small in comparison with other liabilities. Table 14 indicates that for large companies notes payable to banks represented only about 16 percent of current liabilities at the end of 1939, 8 percent at the end of 1945, and 13 percent at the end of 1948. A very high proportion of the current liabilities of business firms is represented by trade credit. Although the total amount of short-term bank loans to business is small in comparison with trade credit outstanding, the turnover is high as compared with other sources of business funds. Considerable variation exists among types of industry.

TABLE 14
RATIO OF NOTES PAYABLE TO BANKS TO CURRENT LIABILITIES, AS OF DECEMBER 31
(IN PERCENT)

	1939	*1945*	*1948*
847 Manufacturing corporations	7.6	8.7	10.2
64 Extractive corporations	18.9	4.3	6.1
75 Railroads	10.7	1.0	0.3
34 Other transport corporations	3.3	4.0	15.3
57 Public utility systems	8.6	4.3	16.6
108 Trade corporations	7.2	8.0	5.9
37 Financial corporations (predominantly commercial credit and personal finance companies)	61.6	45.6	54.8
1275 Registered corporations [a]	16.1	7.8	13.2

Source: Calculated from data in "Working Capital of 1,275 Registered Corporations," Securities and Exchange Commission, June 14, 1949.

[a] Includes only those companies registered with the Securities and Exchange Commission which have since the end of 1943 been reporting comprehensive data on their current assets and liabilities. Smaller companies are not well represented. Includes 3 agriculture, 7 communications, 33 service, and 10 construction companies in addition to the 1,222 companies classified by industry.

Table 15 lists the types of manufacturing which rely upon bank credit to a relatively large extent in comparison with other means of current financing. In this table reliance upon bank credit is measured by the ratio of short-term bank loans to current liabilities and by the ratio of bank loans to total assets. It is noteworthy that food manufacturing shows a high ratio of bank loans to other sources of funds and also absorbs a high proportion of all short-term business credit extended by banks.

TABLE 15

RELATIVE USE OF BANK CREDIT IN MANUFACTURING, DECEMBER, 1950

(IN PERCENT)

Type of Manufacturing	*Distribution of Total Short-Term Bank Loans*	*Ratio of Short-Term Bank Loans to Current Liabilities*	*Ratio of Total Bank Loans to Total Assets*
Food	34.2	32.0	9.9
Tobacco	9.0	54.9	13.0
Textile mill products	11.0	21.5	6.2
Apparel and finished textiles	5.3	28.2	10.5
Furniture and fixtures	1.3	14.5	5.6
Printing and publishing	1.6	10.3	3.9
Chemicals and allied products	10.9	13.6	4.5
Leather and leather products	2.4	26.5	10.0
All other manufacturing	24.4	4.0	2.2
Total	100.0	10.9	3.9

Source: Calculated from *Quarterly Industrial Financial Report Series for All Manufacturing Corporations,* Federal Trade Commission and Securities and Exchange Commission.

The industries which rely habitually upon short-term bank accommodation are those with clearly established and pronounced seasonal characteristics in cash receipts or disbursements. The tobacco, food, textile, and leather industries all exhibit pronounced seasonals in inventories and sales with resultant cycles in cash requirements. Within manufacturing the large companies make relatively less use of bank credit than the smaller companies, as shown in Table 16.

TABLE 16

RATIO OF NOTES PAYABLE TO BANKS TO CURRENT LIABILITIES OF MANUFACTURING CORPORATIONS, DECEMBER, 1939–48

(IN PERCENT)

	1939	*1945*	*1948*
146 companies with assets under $5 million	14.3	20.8	18.6
585 companies with assets from $5 million to $100 million	15.4	12.5	13.9
116 companies with assets above $1,000 million	5.8	7.2	8.6

Source: Calculated from data in "Working Capital of 1,275 Registered Corporations," Securities and Exchange Commission, June 14, 1949.

In non-manufacturing the important users of short-term bank credit are trade and financial enterprises. The sales finance companies are particularly important. As shown earlier in Table 14, notes payable to banks of the sales finance companies at the end of 1948 were about 55 percent of their current liabilities. Railroads and public utility corporations use relatively little short-term bank credit. The large number of small enterprises and their relatively greater dependence upon bank credit explains the small size of the typical bank loan. The Federal Reserve Survey of December 20, 1946, indicated that borrowers with total assets of under $50,000 represented 65.4 percent of the number of loans but only 9.4 percent of the amount. Small borrowers predominate in retail trade and in the services. Koch found that "medium and small business units, defined as those with total assets of less than 5 million dollars each, accounted for the great bulk of the total number of loans and over half of the total amount."

LENDING TECHNIQUE

Bank credit in the United States is customarily extended in the form of advances against or discounts of promissory notes. The amount of overdrafts is insignificant. The ordinary practice is to credit the borrower's deposit account in exchange for a promissory note or discount of a customer's paper. The borrower draws against the credit thereby established. This practice is in contrast with the British practice of allowing overdrafts or debit balances to customers accounts. Consequently, the balance sheets of American banks report a larger total of loans and deposits than would be the case if the overdraft technique were a customary practice.

Overdrafts are regarded as an irregular and bad form of lending. The courts and the supervisory authorities have discouraged the practice. Overdrafts of national banks are required to be reported as such and not as loans. Moreover, it is unlawful for a member bank to certify a check drawn upon it unless the drawer has on deposit at the time not less than the specified amount. The supervisory authorities discourage overdrafts because ordinarily they do not represent prearranged accommodation. Overdrafts are usually unauthorized by a bank and occur without prior arrangement for pledge of security or repayment. In the past, they have resulted from slipshod banking, excessive competition, or from miscalculation on the part of the drawer.[51]

[51] Ray B. Westerfield, *Money, Credit and Banking,* rev. ed., 1947, pp. 220–21 and 300–301.

LINES OF CREDIT

The commercial banks habitually extend lines of credit to their better regular customers, an arrangement by which the bank agrees in advance of a customer's borrowing season to lend up to a stipulated maximum if the borrower's credit position remains substantially unchanged. Confirmed lines of credit are those confirmed to a customer in writing. However, these agreements establish a moral rather than a legal obligation of the bank. It is doubtful whether refusal to extend a loan, after the establishment of a line of credit, would afford a basis for a claim for damages because it would be difficult to prove that damages were the proximate result of refusal to make the loan.[52] Besides enabling the customer to plan his future operations, the line of credit device has arisen partly to protect bank directors who cannot legally delegate their responsibility for making loans and discounts.[53]

The banks often require or expect most customers borrowing on an unsecured basis to maintain a compensating deposit balance. The required balance may be from 10 percent to 25 percent of the maximum borrowing or credit line. The amount of balance required and the method of calculation vary greatly among banks and the requirement is more often enforced in periods of tight credit and in city banks than otherwise.[54]

LENDING RATES

The rates of interest charged by the commercial banks for business credit vary not only with credit worthiness but also with the size of loans. Also, there is considerable geographic variation as shown in Table 17.

The lack of geographical uniformity in bank lending rates on business loans is partly explained by the relative lack of mobility of funds in a unit type of banking system and by the absence of competition in some communities. Among the large banks in the financial centers there is strong competition and a high degree of uniformity in prevailing rates on business loans.

52 B. H. Beckhart, "An Analysis of the Business Loans of Commercial Banks in the United States, 1933–1951," a paper submitted to the International Credit Conference, Rome, Italy, Oct. 18, 1951.

53 W. H. Steiner and E. Shapiro, *Money and Banking*, rev. ed., 1941, p. 175.

54 Steiner and Shapiro, *op. cit.*, p. 175, and Roland I. Robinson, *The Management of Bank Funds*, 1951, p. 105.

TABLE 17
BANK RATES ON BUSINESS LOANS, DECEMBER, 1951
(IN PERCENT)

AREA	ALL LOANS	SIZE OF LOAN $1,000–$10,000	$10,000–$100,000	$100,000–$200,000	$200,000 and Over
New York City	3.01	4.37	3.91	3.34	2.87
7 Northern and Eastern cities	3.23	4.81	4.04	3.46	3.03
11 Southern and Western cities	3.67	4.95	4.5	3.62	3.35

Source: *Federal Reserve Bulletin;* for description of this statistical series see issue of March, 1949, pp. 228–37.

The basic short-term loan rate available to the highest grade borrowers is known as the "prime rate." This was 3 percent in November, 1952; it was 1.5 percent at the end of the Second World War—the level at which it had remained since 1935, owing to easy money conditions and an abundance of loanable funds. It has been estimated that "between one-third and one-half of the business loans made by the nation's largest banks is of sufficient quality to command a rate very close to the 'prime' level." [55] Rates on business loans of less than prime quality move with the prime rate but by a relatively less amount.

The nature of the prime rate is aptly described in the following passage:

> It is not a statistic that is definitely ascertained through scientific reporting methods. By and large, it is set by individual bank policy, with the information spread by word of mouth and being publicly recorded chiefly in the press.
>
> As an administered rate, there is no revelation of week-to-week fluctuations in the prime rate such as are common to its open market complement—market yields on short-term prime commercial paper. Nonetheless, from time to time loans to prime grade borrowers are made at rates different from the publicized "prime level" . . .
>
> The changeability of market conditions and the negotiated nature of large loans makes such occurrences inevitable. Competition for large loans among both bank and nonbank lenders is strong. Most corporations of any size have a choice of several alternative methods of obtaining funds, and in making that choice the borrowing cost is a consideration of consequence. A prime rate set too high—in relation to either the cost of borrowing nonbank money or the disadvantage of a firm's use of its own liquid assets—runs the risk of diverting some excellent corporate business.[56]

[55] Federal Reserve Bank of Chicago, *Business Conditions,* November, 1952, p. 14.
[56] *Ibid.*

TERM LOANS

One of the most significant changes which occurred in commercial bank lending practices during the last twenty years is the growth of term loans. Term loans have three principal characteristics. They are defined as business loans with an original maturity of more than one year, made for the purpose of financing intermediate capital needs of a borrower, and requiring periodic repayment of principal.

A survey of the loans of member banks near the end of 1946 indicated that term loans represented about 34 percent of total business loans, approximately the prewar ratio.[57] This survey also indicated that large banks have been more important as a source of term loans. However, smaller banks have become increasingly important in this field, especially since business loans to war veterans have been guaranteed by the Veterans' Administration.[58]

Term loans provide a significant source of funds for medium and small concerns as well as for large corporations. The Federal Reserve Survey indicated that near the end of 1946 about 30 percent of the bank loans outstanding to very small enterprises—those with total assets of under $50,000 each—was long-term.[59] This survey also showed that small business accounted for 81 percent of the number and 13 percent of the dollar amount of bank term loans outstanding at that time.[60]

The following are some of the specific purposes for which term loans were designed: to refund high-rate bonds or debentures; to purchase machinery and equipment; to replace short-term credit and thereby fix the interest rate for a given period; to avoid the costs of registration of public issues and of listing on organized securities exchanges; to eliminate mortgages and indenture restrictions; and to provide the convenience of dealing with a bank instead of numerous holders. Among the more important types of borrowers on a term loan basis are public utilities, oil, finance companies, transportation (including airlines), and various types of manufacturers, including metal and metal products, chemicals, coal and rubber.[61]

57 Albert R. Koch, "Business Loans of Member Banks," *Federal Reserve Bulletin,* March, 1947.

58 Roland I. Robinson, *The Management of Bank Funds,* 1951, p. 180.

59 Albert R. Koch, *op. cit.*

60 Cf. 82d Cong., 2d Sess., Joint Committee on the Economic Report, *Monetary Policy and the Management of the Public Debt,* Part 1, pp. 604 and 607.

61 B. H. Beckhart, "An Analysis of the Business Loans of the Commercial Banks in the United States, 1933–1951."

Term loans are more often unsecured than secured. However, the loan agreements include a number of restrictive convenants designed to protect the lending bank. Default of these covenants matures the loan and allows for a rearrangement of the credit. Among the more important covenants are the maintenance of a minimum working capital, a negative pledge to the effect that no security or collateral will subsequently be given to others, and a prohibition against the retirement of capital and the sale or pledge of assets, and sometimes a prohibition against incurring loans in excess of one year or other than in the course of normal business.

Repayment provisions of term loans usually require that the principal of the loan be repaid in installments. However, the repayment schedules are adapted to the needs of the case and, consequently, often do not require equal installments. Many term loans are "balloon" notes in which the last payments are large.

Another type of arrangement is the "revolving credit" or "standby credit" which became popular during the Second World War when future financial needs of borrowers were difficult to predict. When the borrower is unable to schedule his financial needs with any precision the lending bank or banks may negotiate a revolving credit under which borrowings may be made continuously or in part from time to time so long as the aggregate outstanding borrowing at any one time does not exceed the credit commitment.[62] The borrower executes individual promissory notes for the amounts borrowed. In some agreements the credit may be converted at the option of the borrower into a fixed serial payment term loan. Commitment fees varying from .25 to .5 percent per annum are levied on the unused portion of the credit.

Term loans are sometimes "syndicated," that is, shared by a number of banks or by a bank and a life insurance company. The amounts advanced, the repayments, and the losses are prorated among the participants. The principal bank may issue a so-called "participation certificate" to those sharing in the credit. The reasons for participations are various. A lending bank may be unable to supply the full amount because it exceeds its legal lending limit, or it may wish to diversify, or the bank may wish only the shorter term part of a credit, in which case the rest of the credit may be taken by a insurance

[62] See excerpts from an address by James L. Buchanan, Vice President of the First National Bank of Chicago, on "Term Loans" before the Summer School of Banking at the University of Wisconsin, June 9, 1947, reproduced in Herbert V. Prochnow, *Term Loans and Theories of Bank Liquidity*, 1949, pp. 24–26.

company. Another reason for participation is that the borrower may have accounts with several banks and, therefore, wish to strengthen his relationship with them. The banks themselves may see an advantage in strengthening their own mutual relationships.[63]

Rates of interest charged on term loans are moderately higher than rates on short-term loans and appear to be competitive with the rates on high-grade corporate bonds of maturity of 10 years or less. All of the large banks in New York City have used escalator clauses in some of their term loans, clauses which provide for an increase in the interest cost to the borrower commensurate with future increases in basic money rates. The reference rates employed are either the Federal Reserve discount rate or the bank's own prime rate. Not all term loans carry these escalators and the extent of the practice varies a good deal from bank to bank, ranging in March, 1952, from 5 percent to 41 percent of the amount of term loans outstanding. These proportions are sufficiently high to suggest that changes in the Federal Reserve discount rate are of more direct influence upon the cost of private credit than is sometimes assumed.

SECURED BUSINESS LOANS

Although a large proportion of the business loans of commercial banks is unsecured, being based upon an analysis and appraisal of the borrower's credit standing, many loans are secured by the pledge of assets of various kinds, including stocks, bonds, mortgages, receivables, warehouse receipts for merchandise, and trust receipts.

Within the last two or three decades the commercial banks have resorted increasingly to secured business loans and have developed new techniques by which accounts receivable and merchandise inventory are made bankable.

Financing of Accounts Receivable.—The assignment of accounts receivable as collateral for bank borrowing is to be distinguished from "factoring," that is, the guaranteeing of credit through the purchase of accounts receivable, from which it evolved.[64] In accounts receivable financing the borrower merely pledges certain accounts to

[63] Herbert V. Prochnow, *op. cit.*, pp. 40–41.

[64] This summary is based in part upon: Raymond W. Burman, "Practical Aspects of Inventory and Receivables Financing" in the symposium *Secured Commercial Financing*, "Law and Contemporary Problems," (School of Law, Duke University), III, No. 4, 1948; and Raymond J. Saulnier and Neil H. Jacoby, *Accounts Receivable Financing*, National Bureau of Economic Research, 1943.

the lending bank, which advances a predetermined percentage of the net value of the accounts. A normal figure may range from 70 percent to 90 percent but, regardless of the particular percentage, the lender has the option of rejecting individual invoices. Ordinarily, the borrower's customer is not notified of the assignment of his account to the bank and remits payment of his account to the vendor who, in turn, forwards it in its original form by endorsement to the lending bank. Furthermore, in these arrangements the lending bank ordinarily does not assume the losses on individual accounts which have been pledged but has recourse on the borrower. In contrast, the old line factor or commission agent purchases the receivables of a manufacturer or shipper, notifies the individual debtors, and collects payment directly from them.

When receivables are assigned as security for loans, the loan balance may be paid down immediately as collections are made, as noted above, or at intervals through withdrawals from a cash collateral account into which collections are paid as received.

The selection of receivables to be pledged involves an audit of the client's books. The receivables are classified according to such items as maturity, amount, collection, and experience. The lending bank sets a limit upon the total amount of receivables the lender is willing to hold as well as upon the amount of individual receivables it will hold. The bank also eliminates unacceptable assets.

The contractual basis of lending against accounts receivable varies with state laws and sometimes involves a purchase and sale agreement and, at other times, an assignment of collateral to secure a loan balance. For example, in the state of Ohio the lender's lien is perfected if an intention to take assignments of accounts receivable from a borrower has been recorded, whereas in Tennessee notification of each client is necessary to establish the lien.[65] In any event, whether trade debtors are notified or not, the ledger books must be stamped to indicate which accounts have been assigned.

The rates of interest on this type of loan are naturally high because of the cost of making such loans and because in many cases, but not always, borrowers are unable to obtain credit on an unsecured basis. The practice is to express rates as a percentage of gross receivables and they may vary between .02 percent and .04 percent per day, that is, between 9.7 percent and 19.5 percent per annum.

[65] Saulnier and Jacoby, *Accounts Receivable Financing*, pp. 27–28.

It is estimated that the volume of accounts receivable financed in 1946 exceeded $4,500 million, compared to $2,500 million in 1941, and that about one half is accounted for by commercial banks and one half by commercial credit companies.[66]

FINANCING INVENTORY IN FIELD WAREHOUSE RECEIPTS

Bank loans have been secured by warehouse receipts representing commodities deposited in a "terminal" or other public warehouse. Within the last two decades further refinements have been made in the lending technique through the establishment of "field" warehouses. The field warehouse is physically located on the premises of the borrower and exists only for the purpose of receiving deposits of commodities belonging to a single depositor. The depositor is enabled to make "bankable" his inventories of raw materials, semiprocessed and finished goods and avoids the inconvenience and cost of transplanting them to a warehouse in some other place as well as costs of storage. The lender obtains a field warehouse receipt as security which is said to be superior to that afforded by a chattel mortgage or a trust receipt.[67]

The types of business which borrow against field warehouse receipts are those with highly seasonal working capital requirements and slender equities. Generally speaking, this form of financing is suited to small and medium-sized enterprises. The types of merchandise stored in field warehouses include canned goods, miscellaneous groceries, lumber, building supplies, coal, and petroleum in tanks.

INSTALLMENT EQUIPMENT LOANS

Another form of longer term business credit extended by commercial banks is the installment equipment loan. The credit is used by the borrower for the specific purpose of acquiring income producing machinery or equipment. These loans, in contrast with ordinary term loans, are secured through the retention by the lender of title to or by a lien on the equipment. Like term loans, the debt is amortized.

Commercial banks extend such credit either indirectly, by pur-

[66] Raymond W. Burman, *op. cit.*, p. 556. See also Table 18.

[67] Chattel mortgages must be recorded to establish a lien and the commodities must be meticulously described. Trust receipts have certain disadvantages such as the fact that the lender can recover goods in bankruptcy only if they can be identified. Cf. Neil H. Jacoby and Raymond J. Saulnier, *Financing Inventory on Field Warehouse Receipts*, p. 11.

chasing or discounting the installment sales contracts held by manufacturers or distributors who sell the equipment or, directly, by means of installment loans to the concerns buying the equipment enabling them to pay cash to the manufacturers or distributors.

AGRICULTURAL LOANS

Country banks are the most important source of short-term credit to farmers and have also always been an important source of long-term mortgage credit. According to a special survey in the middle of 1947 the insured commercial banks held nearly 2,500,000 individual loans outstanding to farmers aggregating about $2,200 million. About nine tenths of the number and two thirds of the amount were extended to finance the planting, harvesting, and the purchase of equipment and livestock. The remaining tenth of the number and one third of the amount were based upon real estate mortgages and financed the purchase of land and other longer term needs.[68]

This survey showed that the production loans extended to farmers were typically for small amounts and for short periods of time. Only 4 percent of the number of loans and 6 percent of the amount had original maturities of more than one year. The two main purposes of such loans were to pay production and living costs and to purchase machinery and livestock. Other major purposes included the purchase and improvement of land or buildings and the repayment of debts. About two thirds of the number of farm production loans and more than two thirds of the amount of production loans were secured by pledge of specific assets or by endorsement, the remainder being unsecured.

Loans to farmers directly guaranteed by the Commodity Credit Corporation (see Table 13) represent loans made for the purpose of supporting the prices of agricultural products. The Corporation is wholly owned by the government. Its main function is to support the prices of agricultural commodities. This is accomplished in part through price support loans to the producers of a variety of agricultural commodities. These loans may be made by commercial banks in the first instance under an arrangement whereby the Corporation agrees to purchase the loans if tendered on or before a fixed date. The

68 See "Bank Loans to Farmers," a group of articles summarizing the findings of a survey conducted jointly by the Federal Reserve System and the Federal Deposit Insurance Corporation as of mid-1947, reprinted from the *Federal Reserve Bulletin* for October and December, 1947.

loans are secured by commodities or collateral under warehouse receipts or chattel mortgages. The Corporation places a fixed collateral value on the commodities pledged for the loans and waives recourse against the borrowers in case later sale of the collateral brings less than the amount of the loan. In effect, the producer sells the commodity to the Corporation but retains an option to repurchase upon payment of the note, carrying charges, and interest.[69]

LOANS TO FINANCE SECURITIES

Commercial banks in the financial centers make a wide variety of security loans. In Table 13 these loans are classified as "Loans to brokers and dealers in securities" and "Other loans for carrying securities."

Brokers and dealers borrow from banks in order to finance their customers' purchases of securities, their own positions in securities, their purchasing and carrying of new security issues pending sale to investors, and the delivery or clearance of securities traded.[70] The financing of new security issues represents an important part of loans to brokers and dealers. United States Treasury refundings as well as new borrowing are often an important cause of fluctuations in the amount of loans as are the public sale of the issues of private corporations. The length of the life of such loans depends on the ability of the market to absorb new issues.

Brokers borrow in order to finance their loans to customers buying securities on margin. Their demands for accommodation from banks arise when the credit demanded by their customers exceeds their own capital funds and free credit balances of customers. Generally, movements in the volume of brokers' borrowings correspond with movements in customers' debit balances.

Dealers in securities require certain special types of accommodation due to the practice of making full cash payment daily for security purchases (in contrast with the longer settlement periods in other countries). "Day loans," payable the same day, may be for a few hours only. They enable dealers to pay for securities they have contracted to purchase. Overnight loans provide funds with which to pay off day loans and to hold overnight securities which could not be de-

69 Cf. *Banking Studies*, p. 148.

70 Stanley L. Miller, "Financing Security Brokers and Dealers," *Money Market Essays*, Federal Reserve Bank of New York, March, 1952, pp. 27–28. See also George L. Leffler, *The Stock Market*, 1951, Ch. 17.

livered during the day. Day loans are secured by a lien on the securities in process of receipt but the lender does not have possession of the securities; overnight loans are secured by the securities awaiting delivery.

The bulk of the loans to brokers and dealers are demand loans. Time loans constitute only a small percentage of the whole. "Strict call loans" have diminished considerably in importance since the days when brokerage houses were not able to secure all the loan accommodation they required at their own banks and, in consequence, were forced to borrow from other banks. At the present time, brokers borrow mainly, if not entirely, from their own banks and, consequently, the lending banks classify these loans as between "strict call" and "other demand" depending upon the length of time the funds are likely to be required.

The demand or call loan takes the form of a general agreement, under which successive loans and repayments are made, substitution of collateral being freely permitted with due regard for quality of collateral and margin required. The indebtedness may be terminated at short notice either on demand of the lender or repayment by the borrower. Under conditions prevailing in recent years loans are seldom called and repayment is usually at the initiative of the borrower.

A factor of major importance in security loans are Regulations T and U of the Board of Governors of the Federal Reserve System under the Securities and Exchange Act of 1934, which were designed to limit the amount of credit used to finance speculative transactions by establishing maximum loan values for certain classes of securities. In governmental circles "margin requirements" are expressed as the difference between market value (100 percent) and loan value; but in the language of Wall Street the percentage of margin has always been considered as the ratio of excess collateral to the face of the loan or debit balance.

Regulation U applies to the "purpose" loans of banks, that is, loans made by banks on *any* stock for the purpose of purchasing or carrying *listed* stocks (bonds are exempt). Regulation T applies to extensions of credit by brokers and dealers to their customers for purchasing or carrying securities, both stocks and bonds. Federal Government, state, and municipal bonds are exempt from both regulations.

At the present time the maximum loan values are 25 percent—a required cash down payment equal to 75 percent of the purchase price of a security. From January 21, 1946, to January 31, 1947, a "no loan value" order was in effect which prevented the granting of "purpose" loans by banks.

REAL ESTATE LOANS

The real estate loans of the commercial banks consist mainly of first mortgages on residential properties but also include a lesser amount of mortgages on farm land and commercial properties.

At the end of 1951 the commercial banks held about 19 percent of the 1–4 family residential mortgage debt, about 16 percent of the farm mortgage debt, and 14 percent of the multifamily residential and commercial mortgage debt.[71]

While the state-chartered banks have long engaged in the financing of real estate, the national banks were prohibited from doing so from their inception in 1863 until the Federal Reserve Act was passed in 1913. Such loans were considered to be illiquid fixed capital loans. The Federal Reserve Act permitted the national banks to receive time deposits and also gave the banks outside the central reserve cities limited authority to lend on farm land. Since then the authority to make real estate loans has been greatly liberalized, although it is still surrounded by definite restrictions.

National banks are allowed to lend on first mortgage only on improved property. Such loans shall not exceed 50 percent of the "appraised value" of the real estate offered as security and no loans shall be made for a longer term than 5 years with certain exceptions. If the loan is amortized at a rate sufficient to amortize 40 percent of the principal within ten years, the loans may be made for 60 percent of appraised value and run for a term of as long as ten years. The foregoing restrictions do not apply to loans insured by the Federal Housing Administration and the Veterans' Administration. Finally, the aggregate amount of real estate loans is limited to the amount of a bank's capital and surplus or 60 percent of time and savings deposits, whichever is greater.

CONSUMER LOANS TO INDIVIDUALS

Commercial banks have always been an important source of credit to individual borrowers. However, it is only in the last three decades

[71] Based on *Survey of Current Business*, U.S. Department of Commerce, September, 1952, Table 6, p. 14.

that the commercial banks have engaged aggressively and systematically in direct lending to finance personal consumption. During the 1930s an increasing number of banks established personal loan departments and by the end of 1938 it was estimated that about 1,222 banks had such departments engaged in making of small loans to individual borrowers.[72] This development was influenced by the successful experience of the sales finance companies, personal loan companies, and other consumer credit agencies, by the inauguration of the Federal Housing Administration's program for insuring amortized loans for home repair and modernization, and by the need to improve bank earning power. After the war many of the large banks in New York City established consumer credit or personal loan departments, as an integral part of their branch operations.

Since the end of the war commercial banks appear to have acquired an increasing share of the consumer installment credit business evidenced not only by the expansion of their installment loans to consumers in competition with other lenders but also through the purchase of installment paper from retailers.

Of the "other loans to individuals" in Table 13 about 70 percent represents consumer credit and the remainder loans to individuals for other purposes. A large proportion of consumer credit was extended on an installment basis. At the end of 1951 consumer installment credits by the commercial banks to individuals amounted to $5,434 million which was about 40 percent of all consumer installment credit. In addition, single payment loans to individual for consumption probably amounted to about $1,500 million, or roughly one fifth of all non-installment consumer credit.

Of the $5,434 million of bank installment credit at the end of 1951, about $2,510 million represented cash installment loans and the remainder consisted of purchased paper. Table 18, as of September 30, 1950, compares the installment receivables of commercial banks with those of other financial businesses.

In appraising the importance of commercial banks as a source of consumer credit, it should be noted that commercial banks are an important source of accommodation to other consumer financing agencies, especially the sales finance companies and the personal loan companies. Loans to sales finance companies are classified in Table

[72] John M. Chapman and Associates, *Commercial Banks and Consumer Instalment Credit,* National Bureau of Economic Research, 1940, p. 27.

TABLE 18
INSTALLMENT RECEIVABLES OF COMMERCIAL BANKS,[a]
SEPTEMBER 30, 1950
(AMOUNTS IN MILLIONS OF DOLLARS)

	Loans Extended Directly	*Paper Purchased*	*Total Receivables of Commercial Banks*	*Total Receivables of All Financial Businesses*
Retail automobile loans	1,324	1,201	2,525	6,129
Other retail loans	173	1,215	1,388	2,574
Repair and modernization loans				
FHA insured	364	491	855	1,248
Other	45	93	138	
Personal loans	1,032	20	1,052	2,866
Total	2,939	3,020	5,958	12,819

Source: "Credit and Sales Reported by Regulation W Registrants." *Federal Reserve Bulletin,* October, 1951.
[a] 11,463 commercial banks and trust companies.

13 as "commercial and industrial loans" while loans to personal finance companies are classified as "all other loans."

INVESTMENTS

At the present time more than 40 percent of the total assets of the commercial banks consists of investments in marketable securities, including mainly direct obligations of the United States and relatively small amounts of obligations of states and municipalities and high grade corporate bonds.

American banking laws generally require that investments be confined to marketable securities of high quality representing indebtedness. The purchase of shares of stock is generally forbidden.

The purchase of investment securities by national banks is governed by Section 5136 of the Revised Statutes of the United States which also applies to state member banks. The principal statutory provisions are as follows:

1. A national bank may purchase for its own account investment securities under regulations prescribed by the Comptroller of the Currency.

2. The total amount of investment securities of any one obligor shall not exceed 10 percent of the bank's capital stock and surplus.

3. The purchase of shares is prohibited except that a bank may hold shares in a subsidiary for the purpose of carrying on a "safe-deposit" business. National banks are also required to purchase stock of the Federal Reserve bank to which they belong; and, in order to protect themselves against loss, they may acquire stock pledged as collateral against a loan.

4. The business of *dealing* in securities and stock shall be limited to purchasing and selling such securities without recourse and solely upon order, and for the account of customers. In other words, the national banks are not allowed to underwrite the sale of new issues of securities. This restriction does not apply to dealings in obligations of the United States or to obligations of any state or political subdivision.

The regulation of the Comptroller of the Currency states that all purchases of investment securities must be securities "in the form of bonds, notes, and /or debentures." [73]

It defines the term "investment securities" as meaning "a marketable obligation, i.e., it must be salable under ordinary circumstances with reasonable promptness at a fair value." [74] The regulation prohibits the purchase of "investment securities" which are distinctly or predominantly speculative, or of securities which are in default.

A major exception to the requirement of marketability permits the purchase of securities "issued by established commercial or industrial businesses or enterprises" which mature not later than ten years after date of issuance and which, by their terms, provide for amortization of the debt so that at least 75 percent of the principal will be extinguished by the maturity date by substantial periodic payments. This exception in effect exempts "term loans" from the requirement of marketability and the condition that a public distribution of the securities must have been provided.

The investment portfolio policies of banks vary widely. In general, the average life of their holdings is much shorter than those of savings banks, insurance companies, and other investors. For example, at the end of 1951 the average life of the government securities held by commercial banks was about 3 years as compared with 12 years for mutual savings banks and about 14 years for insurance companies. The per-

[73] *Investment Securities Regulation,* Treasury Department, Comptroller of the Currency, Washington, 1938.

[74] *Ibid.*

centage distribution of the holdings of the United States Government securities held by the insured commercial banks is given below in Table 19.

TABLE 19

UNITED STATES GOVERNMENT OBLIGATIONS HELD BY INSURED COMMERCIAL BANKS, DECEMBER 31, 1945–51

(IN PERCENT)

	1945	*1946*	*1947*	*1948*	*1949*	*1950*	*1951*
Bills	2.8	1.7	3.1	4.6	5.6	6.7	11.9
Certificates	21.5	16.7	11.1	16.4	19.0	3.2	12.4
Notes	18.0	9.2	8.7	5.5	8.8	27.5	18.6
Bonds maturing in:							
5 years or less	10.2	17.3	27.0	31.6	41.4	37.0	32.4
5 to 10 years	36.2	40.4	32.7	24.6	11.7	12.7	11.6
10–20 years	6.9	9.0	11.1	10.7	6.8	4.9	5.1
Over 20 years	3.1	4.1	3.9	3.4	3.6	4.2	3.9
Nonmarketable issues	1.3	1.6	2.4	3.2	3.1	3.8	4.1
Total	100.0	100.0	100.0	100.0	100.0	100.0	100.0

Source: *Annual Report of the Federal Deposit Insurance Corporation, 1951,* Table 23, p. 36.

The commercial banks are one of the most important groups of investors in Government securities. On June 30, 1952, they held about 23.6 percent of the total federal securities outstanding as compared with 31.3 percent when the debt reached its peak in February, 1946. About 33 percent of the increase in federal debt during the five war years ended June 30, 1945, was absorbed by the commercial banks.

Commercial bank investments in corporate securities are confined to those of the best quality. In practice, examiners do not question those which are rated in the first four grades by the manuals of the leading private rating agencies.

DEPOSITS

At the end of 1951 the gross deposit liabilities of the commercial banks amounted to about $166,000 million (Table 20). Table 21 shows that 82.5 percent of the gross were business and personal deposits, 8.3 percent deposits of governmental agencies, 8.8 percent interbank, and 1.1 percent foreign. Demand deposits amounted to $127,000 million; time deposits to $39,000 million.

Time deposits include several varieties of notice deposits. A "savings

TABLE 20

DEPOSITS OF ALL COMMERCIAL BANKS IN THE UNITED STATES AND POSSESSIONS, DECEMBER 31, 1945–51

(AMOUNTS IN MILLIONS OF DOLLARS)

Depositor	*1945*	*1946*	*1947*	*1948*	*1949*	*1950*	*1951*
Individuals, partnerships and corporations							
Demand	73,867	81,265	85,291	83,155	83,443	91,301	96,992
Time	29,917	33,432	34,710	34,970	35,146	35,200	36,592
Certified checks, etc.	2,613	2,395	2,598	2,149	2,367	2,934	3,184
Total	106,397	117,092	122,599	120,274	120,956	129,435	136,768
United States Government							
Demand	n.a.[a]	n.a.	n.a.	2,398	3,135	2,869	3,433
Time	n.a.	n.a.	n.a.	114	180	187	263
Total	24,767	3,161	1,531	2,512	3,315	3,056	3,696
States and political subdivisions							
Demand	n.a.	n.a.	n.a.	7,356	7,612	8,081	8,492
Time	n.a.	n.a.	n.a.	1,203	1,340	1,457	1,601
Total	5,784	6,893	7,786	8,559	8,952	9,538	10,093
Domestic interbank and postal savings							
Demand	n.a.	n.a.	n.a.	10,482	11,053	12,110	13,139
Time	n.a.	n.a.	n.a.	237	182	143	150
Total	n.a.	n.a.	n.a.	10,719	11,235	12,253	13,289
Banks in foreign countries							
Demand	n.a.	n.a.	n.a.	1,530	1,346	1,479	1,414
Time	n.a.	n.a.	n.a.	35	139	318	400
Total foreign banks	n.a.	n.a.	n.a.	1,568	1,485	1,797	1,814
Postal savings	n.a.	n.a.	n.a.	6	7	11	28
Total interbank and postal savings	14,141	12,737	13,050	12,291	12,728	14,060	15,131
Gross deposits	151,089	139,883	144,966	143,637	145,951	156,089	165,688

Source: Federal Deposit Insurance Corporation, *Annual Report*, 1948, Table 17, p. 34, and subsequent annual reports.

[a] Not available.

TABLE 21
DEPOSITS OF ALL COMMERCIAL BANKS IN THE UNITED STATES AND POSSESSIONS, DECEMBER 31, 1945–51
(IN PERCENT)

Depositor	*1945*	*1946*	*1947*	*1948*	*1949*	*1950*	*1951*
Individuals, partnerships, and corporations							
Demand	48.9	58.1	58.8	57.9	57.2	58.5	58.5
Time	19.8	23.9	23.9	24.3	24.1	22.6	22.1
Certified checks, etc.	1.7	1.7	1.8	1.5	1.6	1.9	1.9
Total	70.4	83.7	84.6	83.7	82.9	82.9	82.5
United States Government							
Demand	n.a.[a]	n.a.	n.a.	1.7	2.1	1.8	2.1
Time	n.a.	n.a.	n.a.	0.1	0.1	0.1	0.2
Total	16.4	2.3	1.1	1.7	2.3	2.0	2.2
State and political subdivisions							
Demand	n.a.	n.a.	n.a.	5.1	5.2	5.2	5.1
Time	n.a.	n.a.	n.a.	0.8	0.9	0.9	1.0
Total	3.8	4.9	5.4	6.0	6.1	6.1	6.1
Domestic interbank and postal savings							
Demand	n.a.	n.a.	n.a.	7.3	7.6	7.8	7.9
Time	n.a.	n.a.	n.a.	0.2	0.1	0.1	0.9
Total	n.a.	n.a.	n.a.	7.5	7.7	7.9	8.8
Banks in foreign countries							
Demand	n.a.	n.a.	n.a.	1.1	0.9	0.9	0.9
Time	n.a.	n.a.	n.a.	n.a.	0.1	0.2	0.2
Total foreign banks	n.a.	n.a.	n.a.	1.1	1.0	1.2	1.1
Postal savings	n.a.	n.a.	n.a.	n.a.	n.a.	n.a.	n.a.
Total interbank and postal savings	9.4	9.2	9.0	8.6	8.7	9.0	9.9
Gross deposits	100.0	100.0	100.0	100.0	100.0	100.0	100.0

Source: Federal Deposit Insurance Corporation, *Annual Report*, 1948, Table 17, p. 34, and subsequent annual reports.
[a] Not available.

deposit" is evidenced by a passbook, may be held only by individuals or non-profit organizations, and is subject to at least thirty days notice of withdrawal. "Time certificates" are payable thirty days after date of deposit on surrender of the certificate while "time deposits open account" are based on written contracts which provide that the funds may not be withdrawn prior to a maturity date at least 30 days after date of deposit.

The payment of interest on demand deposits was prohibited by the Banking Act of 1933. Rates of interest payable on time deposits held by member banks are limited by Regulation Q, which also applies to all insured banks. The regulation allows a higher rate to be paid on savings deposits than on other deposits.

Ordinarily, deposits are unsecured general creditors' claims. Furthermore, there is no segregation of assets in respect to demand and time deposits. However, federal and state governments require depositaries to secure their accounts by pledging United States bonds and other approved collateral. The deposits of the trust department of a bank with the banking department must also be secured. All types of preferred deposits probably do not ordinarily exceed 10 percent of total deposits.

Deposits in banks which have been admitted to insurance by the Federal Deposit Insurance Corporation are insured up to a maximum $10,000 per insurable account.[75] A special survey of information as of September 19, 1951, indicates that 98.4 percent of the *number* of deposit accounts in insured commercial banks, but only 50 percent of the *amount* were fully protected by the FDIC.[76] In certain of the large individual banks the amount of deposits protected by insurance is as low as 10 percent of their total deposits, a result of the fact that the balances of large business and financial depositors are far in excess of the protected maximum.

It should be noted that while the maximum insurable deposit is $10,000, the Corporation was authorized to make loans to or to purchase assets from a bank in financial difficulties when such action would facilitate a merger with another bank. Where this was done the depositors in the weak bank received 100 percent protection. Under the new law of September 21, 1950, the Corporation was given greater discretion and may make loans to or purchase assets from or make deposits in any insured bank in danger of closing, if continued operation is essential to provide adequate banking facilities.

The Federal Deposit Insurance Corporation, like a number of

[75] The maximum insurable deposit was increased from $5,000 to $10,000 by the Federal Deposit Insurance Act of 1950. The text of this law will be found in *Annual Report of the Federal Deposit Insurance Corporation,* 1950, pp. 105–132. A history of legislation for the insurance of deposits is given on pp. 63–101.

[76] Federal Deposit Insurance Corporation, *Annual Report,* 1951, pp. 59–77.

other federal agencies, actually has no capital stock outstanding. Originally, capital stock was issued to the United States and to the Federal Reserve banks. However, under laws approved August 5, 1947, and June 29, 1948, this stock has been retired. In the financial sense, the Corporation is a fund representing accumulated income from assessments against insured banks. The fund has increased from $289 million initial capital in 1934 to $1,282 million at the end of 1951. This fund represented a ratio to insured deposits of 1.33 percent and to total deposits of 0.72 percent. Assessments are levied against the insured banks at the rate of 1/12 of 1 percent of average deposits. Under the Act of September 21, 1950, the insured banks receive a credit against this assessment equal to three fifths of the Corporation's assessment income after losses on account of bank failures and operating expenses. Assuming deposit insurance losses remain low as they have been since 1934, the fund should continue to increase by about 6 percent per year as compared with 12 percent from 1936 to 1946.[77] In addition, the Corporation is authorized to borrow from the Treasury for insurance purposes not exceeding $3,000 million outstanding at any one time.

CAPITAL ACCOUNTS

The structure of the capital accounts of the commercial banks is set forth in Table 22. The composition of these accounts reflects certain peculiarities of American banking laws.

Beginning with the earliest special charters, banks have been required to obtain a certain absolute minimum of capital as a condition of organization. Today, national banks must have a stock capitalization of at least $50,000 in places where the population is 6,000 persons or less, $100,000 in places of population of more than 6,000 and not in excess of 50,000, and $200,000 if the population exceeds 50,000. In addition, before the commencement of business, a bank must have a paid-in surplus equal to 20 percent of common stock. Before the declaration of a dividend a national bank must retain 10 percent of its net earnings until surplus has been built up to 100 percent of capital stock. Before the Second World War, the laws of 18 states contained provisions which required that bank capital and surplus

[77] *Ibid.*, p. 6.

bear a certain ratio to deposits, typically 10 percent, although there is no fixed statutory rule for national banks. These statutory ratio rules have been amended or suspended as a result of the decline in capital ratios resulting from the wartime expansion in deposits.

Adequacy of capital structure is a factor which is considered by the Federal Reserve System and the Federal Deposit Insurance Corporation in admitting banks to membership. For this and other supervisory purposes capital ratios are employed as a "screening" standard.[78]

Before 1937 stock issued by national banks carried "double liability," that is, the stockholder was liable to assessment up to the par value of the stock in order to cover losses if assets were insufficient to satisfy the claims of creditors. This requirement was removed for a variety of reasons. In actual practice less than 50 percent of assessments were made good. The requirement was also considered less necessary

TABLE 22
CAPITAL ACCOUNTS OF ALL COMMERCIAL BANKS IN THE UNITED STATES AND POSSESSIONS, DECEMBER 31, 1945–51
(AMOUNTS IN MILLIONS OF DOLLARS)

	AMOUNTS					PERCENT OF TOTAL CAPITAL ACCOUNTS TO	
	Total Capital Accounts	*Common Stock*	*Preferred Stock, etc.*	*Surplus*	*Undivided Profits and Reserves*	*Total Assets*	*Assets Other than Cash and U.S. Govt. Obligations*
1945	8,933	2,903	227	3,873	1,930	5.5	25.5
1946	9,561	3,068	175	4,155	2,163	6.4	23.4
1947	10,107	3,192	145	4,450	2,320	6.5	20.6
1948	10,555	3,296	122	4,646	2,491	6.8	19.6
1949	11,044	3,431	113	4,948	2,552	7.0	19.9
1950	11,669	3,561	104	5,337	2,666	6.9	17.4
1951	12,299	3,749	91	5,636	2,824	6.8	16.7

Source: Federal Deposit Insurance Corporation, *Annual Reports*, 1949, 1950, and 1951.

for the protection of depositors after the introduction of deposit insurance and, moreover, was held to be an obstacle in the sale of new shares.[79]

Ordinarily national banks have only one class of stock outstanding. In March, 1933, national banks were authorized to issue preferred

[78] Comptroller of the Currency, *Annual Report*, 1948, p. 4.

[79] J. Brooke Willis, *The Functions of the Commercial Banking System*, pp. 187–88.

stock. This emergency action permitted the Reconstruction Finance Corporation, a government agency, to purchase about $1,000 million of preferred stock, notes, and debentures in over 6,000 banks. By the end of 1951 the amount held by the Reconstruction Finance Corporation had been reduced to $69 million. Although the sale of preferred stock to private investors is sometimes advocated as a means of improving the adequacy of bank capital, some of the supervisory authorities regard the authority to sell preferred stock as intended solely for emergency situations.[80]

The combined capital accounts represented at the end of 1951 only 6.7 percent of total assets for all commercial banks combined. The so-called "risk assets" ratio, or ratio of capital funds to total assets less cash and government securities, was 17.4 percent. The ratio of capital to total assets has been declining for a long time. The present ratio of 6.7 percent compares with 20 percent in 1920 and 14 percent in 1929. In view of this trend and, particularly in the light of the rapid growth in deposits before and during the Second World War, and the rapid rise in risk assets after the war, the supervisory authorities have placed great emphasis upon the accumulation of capital.[81]

A recent study of the changes in the capital structure of 130 member banks shows that retained earnings have provided about 95 percent of all new capital since 1939. Only 5 percent was provided by cash sales of new common stock. Of the new capital nearly one fourth was transferred into common stock accounts through stock dividends and an additional half was used to build up surplus, the final one fourth remaining as undivided profits.[82] Increases in the common stock and surplus accounts enlarge the legal lending limit upon loans to a single borrower of individual banks and may have certain advantages in connection with liability to pay the excess profits tax.

It is apparent that very little bank capital has been raised through the sale of new shares for cash. This is attributable to the relatively low earning power of the banks and the fact that for some years the shares of banks have been selling in the market below book value.[83]

80 Comptroller of the Currency, *Annual Report*, 1949, p. vii.

81 See Tynan Smith and Raymond E. Hengran, "Bank Capital: the Problem Restated," *Journal of Political Economy*, December, 1947; and Roland I. Robinson, "Bank Capital and Dividend Policies," *Harvard Business Review*, July, 1948.

82 Federal Reserve Bank of Chicago, *Business Conditions*, March, 1952, pp. 2–4.

83 A recent analysis of the adequacy of bank capital and of the impact of taxation on bank earnings and capital is Gaylord A. Freeman, Jr., *The Problems of Adequate Bank Capital*, an Analysis Prepared for the Illinois Bankers Association, May 23, 1952.

CENTRAL BANKING

It is beyond the scope of this chapter to present a detailed discussion of central banking in the United States.[84] Nevertheless, in order to complement the earlier discussion of commercial banking it is desirable to point out some of the more important as well as some of the unusual features of the Federal Reserve System.

STRUCTURE AND ORGANIZATION OF THE FEDERAL RESERVE SYSTEM

While the Federal Reserve System performs the same basic functions as central banks in other countries, its form of organization was designed to meet the peculiarities of the American unit banking tradition. Because of the wide expanse and diverse character of the country the Federal Reserve Act provided for a number of regional central banks. The country was divided into twelve districts in each one of which a Federal Reserve bank was established. In addition, there are twenty-four branches.

Although the Federal Reserve banks are public institutions, their stock is held by the member banks. A member bank is required as a condition of membership to purchase the stock of the Federal Reserve bank of its district in an amount equal to 6 percent of its own capital and surplus, one half paid in and the remainder subject to call. This stock entitles the member bank to vote in the election of six of nine members of the board of directors of a Federal Reserve bank and to receive dividends fixed by law at 6 percent cumulative on the paid-in stock. The Presidents of the Reserve banks are chosen by the directors but subject to approval of the Board of Governors of the Federal Reserve System; this is a seven-member board, appointed by the President of the United States and possessing extensive powers of

[84] The literature dealing with the Federal Reserve System is extensive. In addition to many textbooks, the following publications of the Board of Governors of the Federal Reserve System will be found useful: *The Federal Reserve System, Its Purposes and Functions*, 1947; *Banking Studies*, 1941; *The Federal Reserve Act as Amended to November 1, 1946*, and subsequent amendments; *Digest of Rulings to October 1, 1947; Banking and Monetary Statistics;* and *Regulations of the Board of Governors*, individual Regulations A to X. See also replies by the Chairman of the Board of Governors and by the twelve Presidents of the Federal Reserve Banks to questionnaires contained in *A Compendium of Materials on Monetary, Credit, and Fiscal Policies*, Joint Committee on the Economic Report, 81st Cong., 2d Sess., Senate Doc. No. 132, 1950, and in *Monetary Policy and the Management of the Public Debt*, Parts 1 and 2, Joint Committee on the Economic Report, 82d Cong., 2d Sess., Senate Doc. No. 123, 1952.

control over the twelve Federal Reserve banks and the member banks. The credit control function is shared in part with the twelve Federal Reserve banks and with another body, the Federal Open Market Committee, which consists of twelve members including the seven members of the Board of Governors and five representatives elected by the twelve Federal Reserve banks.

While the Federal Reserve System is a regional system, its credit control activities are now highly centralized and, in the conduct of monetary and credit policy, it operates virtually as a single central bank. Each of the twelve Federal Reserve banks is required by law to publish a balance sheet. However, their holdings of gold certificates and government securities are controlled as a single system account over which the individual Reserve banks have no independent discretionary authority. In contrast, in the extension of Federal Reserve credit through loans and discounts the district Reserve banks do operate regionally and independently of each other under the regulations of the Board of Governors.

Table 23 presents the consolidated balance sheet of the twelve Federal Reserve banks.

It will be noted from Table 23 that the Federal Reserve banks do not own at the present time any gold as such but instead hold gold certificates.[85] The emergency laws in 1933 and the Gold Reserve Act of 1934 required the delivery of all gold to the United States Treasury and provided for the substitution of gold certificates for actual gold as legal reserves of the twelve Reserve banks. By the Act of June 12, 1945, the amount of gold certificates required to be held by each Federal Reserve bank was reduced to 25 percent of its note and 35 percent of its deposit liabilities (formerly 40 percent in gold certificates against notes and 35 percent in gold certificates or lawful money against deposits). Actual holdings of gold certificates are now well in excess of this requirement; they were 46.4 percent of combined note and deposit at the end of 1951. Actual holdings of gold certificates exceeded the amount legally required by about $10,000 million and would have permitted a theoretical expansion in liabilities of nearly $40,000 million. Under present-day conditions the gold certificate requirement is merely a remote limitation upon the potential expansion of Federal Reserve bank credit.

85 Under certain circumstances they make loans on gold to foreign central banks; they also hold gold under earmark and government securities for foreign account.

TABLE 23
COMBINED STATEMENT OF CONDITION OF FEDERAL RESERVE BANKS, DECEMBER 31, 1945–51
(AMOUNTS IN MILLIONS OF DOLLARS)

Assets	*1945*	*1946*	*1947*	*1948*	*1949*	*1950*	*1951*
Gold certificate reserves	17,861	18,381	21,497	22,966	23,176	21,458	21,468
Other cash	236	268	273	292	258	267	323
Discounts and advances	248	163	85	223	78	67	19
United States Government securities	24,262	23,350	22,559	23,333	18,885	20,776	23,801
Uncollected cash items	2,198	2,600	2,985	2,860	2,967	4,270	3,905
All other assets	258	244	313	369	279	334	374
Total assets	45,063	45,006	47,712	50,043	45,643	47,172	49,890
Liabilities and Capital							
Federal Reserve notes	24,649	24,945	24,820	24,161	23,483	23,587	25,064
Deposits							
Member bank reserve accounts	15,915	16,139	17,899	20,479	16,568	17,681	20,056
United States Treasury, general account	977	393	870	1,123	821	668	247
Foreign	862	508	392	642	767	895	526
Other deposits	446	314	569	547	750	565	363
Total deposits	18,200	17,353	19,731	22,791	18,906	19,810	21,192
Deferred availability cash items	1,620	2,020	2,450	2,319	2,413	2,902	2,722
Other liabilities	7	10	15	11	9	5	13
Capital accounts	586	678	697	761	833	869	909
Total liabilities and capital	45,063	45,006	47,712	50,043	45,643	47,712	49,890
Ratio of total reserves to deposit and Federal Reserve note liabilities combined (percent)	41.7	43.5	48.3	48.9	54.7	49.4	46.4

The amount of gold certificates held by the Reserve banks is governed by the amount of gold bought or sold by the United States Treasury and "financed" by the deposit (or redemption) of gold certificates. As the Treasury accumulates gold it "monetizes" it by issuing gold certificate credits to those Reserve banks at which it wishes to increase its deposit balance. Gold certificates are shifted from one Reserve bank to another in the settlement participations in System account operations, for example in government securities.

Since domestic production of gold is quite small, the amount of gold certificate reserves held by the Reserve banks is influenced primarily, as was the amount of gold held before 1933, by purchases and sales from foreign central banks and governments. However, under the Gold Reserve Act of 1934 the Treasury was given certain discretionary powers with respect to the terms and conditions on which gold is bought and sold; it was authorized to buy and sell "at such rates and upon such terms and conditions" as was considered advantageous in the public interest (Section 8). However, the Act requires that "the amount of gold certificates issued and outstanding shall at no time exceed the value, at the legal standard, of the gold so held against gold certificates" (Section 14). The value of gold at the legal standard is $35 per ounce and the discretionary authority of the President to devalue this standard expired June 30, 1943. Consequently, if, for the sake of argument, the Treasury were to pay more than $35 for gold, the premium would have to be financed by borrowing or by taxation; it could not be "financed" through the deposit of gold certificates at the Federal Reserve banks. Of still greater moment is the obligation of the United States under the Articles of Agreement of the International Monetary Fund to maintain a par value of the dollar equivalent to $35 per ounce of gold. The par value of $35 which was communicated to the Fund cannot be changed unless Congress by law authorizes such action (Section 5 of the Bretton Woods Agreement Act of July 31, 1945).

DISCOUNTS AND ADVANCES

The Reserve banks are authorized to discount certain types of loan paper offered by member banks and to make advances to member banks against their promissory notes secured by government securities (and other approved collateral). For many years member bank borrowing has taken the form of advances secured by government securities, since this procedure is much simpler than discounting of customer loan paper. The amount of discounts and advances shown in Table 23 is smaller than is normally the case owing to window dressing by member banks at the year end. Since March, 1951, the Reserve System has been reluctant to extend Federal Reserve credit through open-market operations except around Treasury financing dates and member banks have resumed the use of the "discount window" with the result that the amount of discounts and advances has risen substantially, reaching about $1,800 million in the fall of 1952.

Unlike many foreign central banks the Reserve banks do not ordinarily lend to the general public or to non-member banks. Although the Reserve banks are authorized in exceptional circumstances to lend to business borrowers under Section 13b, the amount of such loans has been quite small.

U.S. Government securities constitute the largest single asset other than gold. These securities were acquired mainly during the Second World War when the System supported the Treasury market according to a fixed pattern of interest rates. While the System continued to support the government bond market at prices above 100 until March, 1951, the amount of government securities held by the Reserve banks has shown only a relatively small net change since the end of the war because of the ability of the System to offset purchases of one type of securities with sales of other types or by redemption of maturing issues.

The authority of the Reserve banks to acquire securities is covered in Section 14 and Section 12a of the Federal Reserve Act. In practice the securities held by the Reserve banks are confined to obligations of the United States, although formerly they held substantial amounts of bankers acceptances. Ordinarily, securities may be purchased only "in the open market" which means the purchase of government securities already outstanding from dealers rather than directly from banks or other investors. The principal exception is the authority to acquire and hold up to an aggregate of $5,000 million directly from the Treasury. This authority, which expires on June 30, 1954, has been used only as a temporary borrowing privilege to accommodate the Treasury in anticipation of tax receipts and to relieve it of the necessity of carrying large working balances and of drawing against deposits in commercial banks when to do so would disrupt the money market.

An undisclosed but small element in the reported total of government securities held by the Reserve banks are securities acquired under repurchase agreements with non-bank dealers in government securities whereby the Reserve banks purchase short-term government securities under an agreement that the dealers will repurchase the same securities from the Reserve banks within a prescribed time.[86] These operations are tantamount to loans and are made for the purpose of maintaining "orderly market conditions."

As noted above, purchases and sales of government securities are

86 Board of Governors of the Federal Reserve System, *Annual Report,* 1951, pp. 85–87.

for System account and are directed by the Federal Open Market Committee, the actual transactions being executed by the Federal Reserve Bank of New York as agent. This Committee has very broad discretion, its policy being guided only by the provision that open market operations "shall be governed with a view to accommodating commerce and business and with regard to their bearing upon the general credit situation of the country"—Section 12a(c). In contrast, in lending to member banks the Reserve banks must have regard for "the maintenance of sound credit conditions" and are directed by Section 4 of the Federal Reserve Act to refuse accommodation if undue use is being made of Federal Reserve credit for speculative purposes.

The principal liabilities of the Federal Reserve banks consist of Federal Reserve notes and deposits. Federal Reserve notes are the principal form of hand-to-hand currency in use. At the end of 1951 the $25,000 million of Federal Reserve notes in circulation amounted to 86 percent of total currency in circulation, the remainder consisting of various forms of Treasury currency, mainly silver certificates. Except for silver certificates and minor coin the note-issue function has been assumed by the central bank and the amount of Federal Reserve notes outstanding responds seasonally and cyclically to the demands of the public for currency. Note issues of the state-chartered commercial banks were taxed out of existence shortly after the provision of national bank currency in 1863, and in 1935 the issuance of additional national bank currency was precluded by the fact that government securities no longer carried the "circulation privilege," that is, were not eligible as collateral to secure the note issue of national banks.

The issuance of Federal Reserve notes is surrounded by a variety of highly technical and involved requirements which reflect the endeavor of the legislators to make the note holder a preferred creditor of banks and to protect him against overissue. These restrictions nowadays have little or no relevance to the over-all limitation of the money supply, since for all practical purposes the Federal Reserve note is readily expansible and freely interchangeable with Federal Reserve deposit liabilities. However, technically speaking, the Federal Reserve note is protected by a reserve of gold certificates of at least 25 percent, including a redemption fund of at least 5 percent deposited with the Treasurer of the United States, and is secured by

100 percent collateral consisting of the aforementioned gold certificates and the remaining 75 percent collateral in gold certificates, government securities, and "eligible" paper acquired under Section 13, in any combination.[87]

The deposit liabilities of the Federal Reserve banks, as shown in Table 23, consist mainly of the legal reserve balances of member banks. In addition, the Reserve banks serve as a depositary of the government. The deposit balance of the Treasurer of the United States is the government's working account from which virtually all disbursements are made by means of checks drawn on the Treasurer of the United States. In addition to serving as a depositary for foreign central banks and governments, the Reserve banks receive deposits from nonmember banks who are entitled to collect checks through the Reserve System in return for a balance adequate for clearing purposes.

SAVINGS INSTITUTIONS

The major portion of personal savings is held by savings institutions other than commercial banks as shown in Table 24.

TABLE 24
SELECTED TYPES OF LONG-TERM SAVINGS OF INDIVIDUALS, DECEMBER 31, 1945–51
(AMOUNTS IN MILLIONS OF DOLLARS)

	1945	*1946*	*1947*	*1948*	*1949*	*1950*	*1951p*
Commercial banks	29,929	33,447	34,694	34,970	35,145	35,200	36,592
Mutual savings banks	15,332	16,813	17,744	13,385	19,269	20,002	20,880
Savings and loan associations	7,365	8.548	9,753	10,964	12,471	13,978	16,079
Life insurance companies	37,509	40,713	43,820	47,139	50,231	53,630	57,000
Postal savings	3,013	3,279	3,523	3,442	3,302	3,035	2,808
United States savings bonds	42,900	44,200	46,200	47,800	49,300	49,600	49,000
Increase during year	19,722	11,052	8,634	6,966	7,018	5,727	6,914

Source: Home Loan Bank Board, *Savings and Home Financing Source Book*, 1952.
p = preliminary.

In addition to the institutions listed in Table 24, savings also flow through a variety of other institutional investors including fire and casualty companies, investment companies ("investment trusts"),

[87] For detailed information see Section 16 of the Federal Reserve Act and *Coins and Currency of the United States, June 30, 1947*, Office of the Secretary of the Treasury.

trust departments of commercial banks, philanthropic foundations, and educational institutions. However, information concerning the amount of savings held by these institutions is less adequate than for those listed in Table 24.[88]

At the end of 1951 there were approximately 529 mutual savings banks, 6,000 savings and loan associations, and 580 life insurance companies. Mutual savings banks function exclusively as depositaries of personal savings. Most of them are situated in the New England and Middle Atlantic states. All operate under state charters, investing their funds mainly in real estate mortgages, government securities, and approved high-grade corporate securities. Recently, a number of states have given them permission to make limited investments in common stocks.[89]

Savings and loan associations are mutual societies operating under either state or federal charter. They are sometimes called building and loan associations, cooperative banks, and homestead associations. Except for investing a small percentage of resources in government securities they are concerned almost exclusively with financing home purchase and construction. Strictly speaking, they do not use the deposit technique but instead issue shares, or "share accounts," of various descriptions which the issuing association will repurchase on notice at stated value. Their authority to make home mortgage loans is broader than is that of the mutual savings banks.[90]

Section 313 of the Revenue Act of 1951 removed the exemption of mutual savings banks and savings and loan associations from the payment of federal income tax but permits the deduction of amounts paid to depositors and shareholders and amounts placed in bad debt reserves until these reserves plus undivided profits and surplus equal 12 percent of total deposits or share accounts.

Life insurance companies operate under state laws. They are pri-

88 The postwar role of the savings banks, savings and loan associations and life insurance companies is described in Charles H. Schmidt, "Savings Institutions and the Capital Markets," *Federal Reserve Bulletin,* March, 1949.

89 The activities of mutual savings banks are described in the following: John Lintner, *Mutual Savings Banks in the Savings and Mortgage Markets,* Graduate School of Business Administration, Harvard University, 1948; Carl F. Distelhorst, "Savings and Loan Associations and Mutual Savings Banks," *American Financial Institutions* (Herbert V. Prochnow, ed.), 1951; and Weldon Welfling, *Savings Banking in New York State,* 1939.

90 The activities of these institutions are described in Morton Bodfish and A. D. Theobald, *Savings and Loan Principles,* 1940, and in *Annual Reports of the Housing and Home Finance Agency.*

marily engaged in assuring a predetermined income or lump sum payments to beneficiaries in the event of death or on maturity of an endowment or an annuity policy. However, because of their steady growth and the use of the level premium plan they attract annually a large proportion of current personal savings. About twelve of these companies have resources in excess of $1,000 million and represent three quarters of the entire industry's resources. Their lending and investing activities are well diversified and include: government and corporate securities; real estate mortgages on both farm and urban property; direct investments in residential, industrial, and commercial real estate; direct long-term loans to business borrowers; and policy loans. Limited investment in common stock equities is permitted. Because of the nature of their liabilities and their steady growth they have less need for liquidity than most other savings institutions.[91]

SPECIALIZED CREDIT SYSTEMS

While the commercial banks are an important source of credit for both housing and agriculture, specialized credit systems have been developed in these areas. The farm credit system is the older, dating from 1916. The Home Loan Bank System, established in 1932, was a creature of the great depression. Although both housing and agriculture are financed mainly by nongovernmentally owned institutions, government credit plays an important role either through subsidy or guaranty.

FARM CREDIT SYSTEM

The creation of specialized agricultural credit institutions was brought about by the demand for low cost credit, the inability of small individual farmers to tap the national credit supply, and by recurrent shortages in the available local supply of credit especially during periods of economic depression.

91 The savings and investing functions of these institutions are described in Lintner, *Mutual Savings Banks in the Savings and Mortgage Markets,* Ch. IV; Joseph M. Bell, Jr., "Investing for a Life Insurance Company," *Fundamentals of Investment Banking,* sponsored by the Investment Bankers Association of America, 1949; and, Erwin W. Boehmler, *et al., Financial Institutions,* 1951.

Most of the specialized agricultural credit institutions are under the supervision of the Farm Credit Administration.[92]

The Farm Credit Administration, headed by a governor appointed by the President of the United States, now supervises and coordinates the activities of four main classes of lending institutions created at various times. These are: the twelve Federal Land Banks and the 1,200 associated national farm loan associations; the twelve Production Credit Corporations and the 500 associated production credit associations; the twelve Federal Intermediate Credit Banks; and the thirteen Banks for Cooperatives (one central bank in Washington, D.C.).

The organization of the system is less complex than appears, since in each of the twelve Farm Credit districts the Land Bank, the Production Credit Corporation, the Intermediate Credit Bank, and the Bank for Cooperatives are all administered by the same board of directors—the district Farm Credit Board. Although each bank and corporation has its own officers, the officers and personnel may be joint officers or employees in more than one of the institutions.

The Land banks engage exclusively in farm-mortgage lending through the local stockholding national farm loan associations with funds obtained mainly from the sale to private investors of consolidated farm loan bonds. On January 1, 1952, they held nearly $1,000 million of mortgage loans, or about 15.8 percent of the outstanding farm mortgage debt.

The Production Credit Corporations charter and supervise the production credit associations and originally capitalized the local production credit associations. The local associations are engaged exclusively in financing the short-term production credit needs of farmers, in competition with commercial banks and other local lenders, with funds obtained largely by discounting the borrowers paper with the

[92] The literature is voluminous. Among the more useful publications are the following: Donald C. Horton, Harold C. Larsen, and Norman J. Wall, *Farm Mortgage Credit Facilities in the United States*, U.S. Department of Agriculture, Miscellaneous Publication No. 478, 1942; Annual Reports of the Farm Credit Administration, *Laws Administered by the Farm Credit Administration as Amended, January 1, 1949*, Farm Credit Administration Circular No. 20, revised; *Risk Problems of Production Credit Associations*, Farm Credit Administration, Bulletn CR-5, January, 1952; I. W. Duggan and Ralph V. Battles, *Financing the Farm Business*, 1950; *Agricultural Finance Review*, United States Department of Agriculture; and *Monetary Credit and Fiscal Policies*, a collection of statements, Joint Committee on the Economic Report, 81st Cong., 1st Sess., November, 1949, Ch. VIII, Reply by I. W. Duggan, Governor of the Farm Credit Administration.

Federal Intermediate Credit banks. On January 1, 1952, loans amounted to $561 million which was about 18 percent of the amount of non-real-estate loans to farmers held by the principal lending institutions, and about 8 percent of the total non-real-estate farm debt.

The Federal Intermediate Credit banks, whose stock is held by the United States, are not authorized to lend to individual borrowers. Their function is to discount agricultural and livestock paper (maturing up to three years) for local financing institutions and to make loans to them on the security of such paper. In practice, the production credit associations are the principal users of credit supplied by the Intermediate Credit Banks. During the year ended June 30, 1951, they obtained 81.6 percent of the total, the remainder going in part to the Banks for Cooperatives. The Intermediate Credit Banks, like the Land Banks, obtain funds by sale to private investors of consolidated collateral trust debentures.

The Banks for Cooperatives (12 district banks and one Central Bank for Cooperatives) were initially capitalized by the United States, but are now owned in part by their borrowers. They were established to lend to eligible cooperatives engaged in marketing agricultural products, purchasing farm supplies, and the like. They finance a full range of credit needs including commodity, operating capital, and physical facility loans. Loans amounted to $311 million on June 30, 1951. The greater part of their loanable funds is derived from their capital and retained earnings supplemented by discounts with the Intermediate Credit Banks and more recently by the sale of debentures to private investors.

The various agricultural credit systems have several financial features in common. They all have relied at one time or another upon the following devices for raising loanable funds: (1) a revolving capital fund supplied by borrowers through the purchase of stock in the amount of 5 percent of the loan; (2) partial or total contributions to capital by the United States; (3) the sale of bonds or debentures to private investors secured by the pledge of mortgages or other loan paper. In addition, the principle is followed that local lending rates should be related to the cost of borrowing money from private investors. In practice, loan rates are limited by a specified spread theoretically sufficient to cover costs of operation and losses. In general, the various farm credit agencies enjoy exemption from a variety of taxes. The Federal Land banks, national farm loan associations, and Federal Intermediate credit banks are exempt from federal and state taxation except upon real estate held by them. The Banks for Cooperatives, Production Credit Corporations, and production credit associations, while they have government capital, are exempt from federal and state taxation except upon their real and tangible property.[93] Tax exemption together with cost free capital contributed by government has been a cause for complaint by competing private lenders.

The over-all long-run loss experience of the farm credit agencies compares favorably with that of other lenders. However, the local cooperative associations, especially the national farm loan associations, have encountered serious difficulties arising from their inability to spread risks.[94] In 1943 more than half of these institutions had an impairment of capital. As a result, a long range rehabilitation program was undertaken. The number of associations has been reduced from about 5,000 to 1,200, and a system of allowances has been devised to provide a steadier source of income than the dividends received on the stock held in the Federal Land banks.

The production credit associations, established only since 1933, have had a satisfactory loss experience to date. However, they have not faced the test of a severe economic depression and there is some doubt whether their present net worth and accumulated reserves, considering the small size of the associations and the local concentration of loans, are adequate to cope with prolonged periods of agricultural distress without governmental help. The annual subsidy of the Production Credit System in 1943 was estimated to be about 1 percent of average loans outstanding.[95]

Alternative methods of risk-bearing have been suggested.[96] Among the alternatives are the use of a mutual loan insurance reserve, a group reserve for contingencies, the consolidation of the production credit associations with the Intermediate Credit Banks or possibly with an entirely new agency which would extend both long-term and short-term credit to farmers.

93 *Monetary, Credit, and Fiscal Policies,* Joint Committee on the Economic Report, pp. 274–75.

94 See Horton and others, *Farm Mortgage Credit Facilities in the United States,* Ch. XIV, "Problems of National Farm Loan Associations."

95 Earl L. Butz, *The Production Credit System for Farmers,* 1944.

96 See *Risk Problems of Production Credit Associations,* Farm Credit Administration, January, 1952.

HOUSING CREDIT SYSTEM

The specialized housing credit agencies have been organized under the Housing and Home Finance Agency which embraces a number of constituent elements.[97] The oldest of these, the Home Loan Bank System, was created in 1932, as a permanent central banking system for private home financing agencies.

The Home Loan Bank System is comprised of eleven district Federal Home Loan Banks, the management of which is vested in twelve directors, four of which are appointed by the Home Loan Bank Board and eight elected by member institutions. The membership is composed almost entirely of savings and loan associations. At the end of 1951 membership comprised 3,950 savings and loan associations, 25 savings banks, and 6 insurance companies with combined total assets of $18,415 million.

The Home Loan banks are authorized to lend to members. Short-term advances may be made on an unsecured basis and long-term advances, up to ten years, may be made against various classes of home mortgages at collateral values established by the Home Loan Banks under statutory maxima and at rates approved by the Home Loan Bank Board. At the end of December, 1951, the Home Loan Banks held advances of $806 million or about 4.4 percent of the assets of member institutions. The original purpose of the System was to provide liquidity for home financing institutions, the eleven Banks serving as a reservoir upon which members could draw in order to meet withdrawals. Since the end of the war the Home Loan banks have made an increasing amount of advances to members for business expansion purposes to enable them to meet loan commitments when their current inflow of new savings proved inadequate.

The Federal Home Loan banks are financed by their capital stock, which is partly held by members and partly by the United States (now being retired) through the sale of consolidated Federal Home Loan Bank debentures, and from deposits received from members. Consolidated debentures represent the principal and most flexible source of funds to the banks. These obligations are not guaranteed

97 For a more detailed description of activities of the various governmental or semi-governmental agencies see the following: Housing and Home Finance Agency, *Housing Statistics* (monthly) and *Annual Reports;* Federal Housing Administration, *Insured Mortgage Portfolio* (quarterly); Husband and Anderson, *Real Estate Analysis;* C. J. Devine and Company, Inc., "Local Housing Authority Bonds and Notes," April, 1949; Miles Colean, *The Impact of Government on Real Estate Finance in the United States,* 1950.

by the United States but the Treasury is authorized to purchase up to a total of $1,000 million.

The principal functions of the Home Loan Bank Board are to charter and supervise federal savings and loan asssociations, to fix required liquidity reserve (cash and United States Government securities) of members between 4 percent and 8 percent of share capital (currently 6 percent), to prescribe regulations governing borrowing by the eleven Home Loan banks, and to prescribe regulations governing the advances made by the banks to their members. The Home Loan Bank Board also administers the Federal Savings and Loan Insurance Corporation, which insures accounts in savings and loan associations up to $10,000 (analogous to insurance of deposits by the Federal Deposit Insurance Corporation).

The Federal Housing Administration's principal function is the insurance of mortgages and the improvement of housing standards and conditions. It does not make loans nor does it construct housing. FHA insures approved private lenders against loss on several types of loans. At the end of 1951 FHA had a net balance of insurance written of $14,500 million, most of it covering small home mortgages. Except for repair and modernization loans, the insurance of mortgages on homes and on rental projects covers the full value of the mortgage. In default the insured mortgagee is entitled to the benefits of insurance upon foreclosure and assignment to the FHA of all rights in the mortgage. In return, the FHA issues to the mortgagee FHA debentures equal to the value of the mortgage and a certificate of claim which will reimburse him for all or part of the costs incident to foreclosure. These debentures, which run for a period of roughly 3 years, are paid out of the various insurance funds in which the annual premiums (.5 percent of the loan) paid by mortgagors are pooled. The insurance funds are primarily liable for the payment of the debentures, which, in addition, are fully and unconditionally guaranteed as to principal and interest by the United States.

The Veterans' Administration guarantees home, farm, and business loans made by private lending institutions to veterans of World War II.[98] From the inception of the loan guaranty program late in 1944 through June, 1952, more than 2,729,054 loans were closed, amounting to about $16,000 million of which nearly $9,000 million was guaranteed by the Veterans' Administration. The maximum loan guaran-

98 See Annual Reports, Administrator of Veterans' Affairs.

tee was raised by the Housing Act of 1951 to 60 percent of the loan up to $7,500 (formerly 50 percent up to $4,000). In contrast with FHA insured loans, the VA guarantee provides for cash payment on default or foreclosure. The Veterans' Administration also has limited authority to lend directly to veterans for the purchase or construction of homes if private capital is not available and if the borrower is a satisfactory credit risk.

The Federal National Mortgage Association, a government-owned corporation popularly known as "Fanny May," was intended to provide a secondary mortgage market through the purchase and sale of insured or guaranteed home mortgages. With the expansion in the rental and veterans' housing programs in 1948, FNMA holdings of mortgages increased rapidly. By mid-1952 mortgages held by FNMA amounted to $2,000 million, undisbursed commitments $266 million and funds available $416 million. Beginning August, 1949, efforts were made to sell mortgages and to place operations on a revolving basis. However, mortgage holdings have continued to increase.

The Public Housing Administration is responsible for five separate housing programs including slum clearance and low-rent housing. The basic long-term program is the low-rent public housing program for low-income families, first authorized by the Housing Act of 1937 and greatly expanded by the Housing Act of 1949, which authorized the development of 810,000 new units of low-rent public housing in six annual increments of 135,000 each, beginning July 1, 1949. This program was temporarily interrupted by the defense program following the outbreak of war in Korea. The actual construction of housing is initiated by local housing authorities created by local governments. More than 1,100 of these bodies are in existence. In return for federal financial assistance, local housing authorities are required to enter into a cooperation agreement with the Public Housing Authority, which sets forth the arrangements for local contributions through tax exemption, payments in lieu of taxes by the local authority to the local governments, and the provision of public services to the housing projects. Federal financial assistance to local housing authorities may take two forms, annual contributions or subsidy payments and capital loans. The Federal Government's pledge of annual contributions sufficient to cover payment of principal and interest makes the obligations issued by the local housing authorities to finance the projects a prime investment for private capital. Exemption of these obligations from all federal taxation enables them to be marketed at favorable rates.[99]

AN APPRAISAL

The prerequisites of a well-ordered banking system include: (1) responsiveness of credit volume to monetary policy; (2) ability to withstand economic crisis; (3) equitable distribution of credit among borrowers; (4) mobility of funds; and (5) economical operation.[100]

There can be little doubt that these requirements would be better satisfied by the American banking system if it were more fully integrated and its constituent parts better coordinated and articulated. For a long time it has been evident that the structural organization of American banking leaves much to be desired. The more glaring weaknesses are the extraordinarily large number of small independent local banking units; the rudimentary nature of branch banking; the lack of uniformity in the banking laws, regulations and supervisory standards; and the prevalence of specialized lending institutions some of which are unseasoned and still dependent upon governmental support of one kind or another.

The very complexity of the institutional and legal structure weakens the responsiveness of its component units to monetary and credit control. However, the lack of cohesion in commercial banking is not as serious as would appear from the large number of banks, since fully 85 percent of the banking resources are under Federal Reserve control. In recent years the failure of credit volume to respond to credit policy has been most evident in the case of the special purpose agencies, particularly those concerned with agricultural and housing credit, whose policies are not determined by Federal Reserve authority.

The ability of the commercial banks and other credit agencies to withstand severe economic crisis has not really been tested since the Great Depression. A large body of opinion holds that the danger of a liquidity crisis has been greatly reduced by the insurance of bank deposits and the enlargement of the powers of the Federal Reserve

[99] The financing of the projects is described in the *Annual Report of the Housing and Home Finance Agency,* 1949, pp. 328–29.

[100] See Harold L. Reed, *Money Currency and Banking,* New York, 1942, Ch. XXXX; R. S. Sayers, *American Banking System, a Sketch,* London, 1948, Ch. VII; Eugene E. Agger, *Money and Banking Today,* New York, 1941, Ch. XXX.

System to expand the credit base. On the other hand, a declining ratio of capital funds to risk assets affords reason to doubt the ability of local unit banks, lacking adequate diversification of risks, to absorb losses in periods of economic distress. Commercial banks, mutual savings banks, savings and loan associations, production credit associations and the national farm loan associations are typically small local lenders exposed to the vicissitudes of their local economies. In the case of depositary institutions this weakness is compensated to some extent by their ability to borrow from central institutions to which they belong. Generally speaking, capital funds appear to be inadequate considering the lack of diversification of risks within individual units and the very limited extent to which risks are shared among groups of these units. The best solution of this problem is by consolidation of units and by the enlargement of their capital funds. Loan insurance has reduced the risk exposure of local lenders, but this development has been confined mainly to residential mortgage credit. Proposals to insure business credit, except for war or defense purposes, have not found much favor because of the danger of weakening the lender's incentive to make a careful selection of individual risks and because of an antipathy to governmental intervention in credit matters.

The inadequacy of commercial banking capital is basically the result of low earning power. Low earning power is partly attributable to high cash requirements imposed on commercial banks, to the need to hold a high proportion of assets in liquid form, and to competition. Banks face strong competition from other saving and credit institutions which have the advantage of tax exemption and in some cases of cost free capital supplied by Government.

American banking institutions serve a wide variety of credit needs and have shown remarkable ingenuity in designing new financing techniques for the effective use of credit. In the last three decades commercial banks have vastly broadened the range of their credit activities; for example, consumer credit, "term lending" to business borrowers and the financing of accounts receivable. To judge by political opinion the principal class of business borrowers that is not being adequately served is the so-called small business man. Attempts have been made to satisfy these demands by government loans through the Reconstruction Finance Corporation, the Federal Reserve banks, and more recently the Small Business Administration. However, the demand for new private institutions to furnish credit and venture capital to small businesses will undoubtedly persist.

Another area where new credit arrangements are said to be needed is in the financing of foreign trade and investment. American exporters are beginning to feel the effects of foreign competition with respect to credit terms and as a result increasing interest is being shown in proposals for export credit insurance.

The ever growing demand for credit in the American economy has been met in part by various supplementary financial institutions not fully equipped as depositaries and not responsible for the creation of circulating media. These institutions bring otherwise idle credit into effective use and serve needs which might be neglected. In some instances they also constitute a medium to which banks can extend credit with more safety than if their loans were made directly to ultimate borrowers.[101] The functions of many of these institutions are still in process of development and change. The most appropriate allocation of functions between commercial banks and other financial agencies, with which they are in many respects competitive, is still the subject of heated debate.

The mobility of short-term loanable funds among commercial banks is quite high in spite of unit banking organization. This feature of banking operation was radically improved by the establishment of the Federal Reserve System in 1914 and subsequently by the development of a liquid short-term money market. Similarly, the creation of the Federal Land Bank System in 1916, the Federal Intermediate Credit Banks in 1923, and the Federal Home Loan Bank System in 1932 have improved the availability and the mobility of funds to meet particular credit needs. Perhaps the main area where local shortages of funds still occur is residential real estate credit. The need for a secondary mortgage market in guaranteed real estate mortgages has been debated for some time. This problem will probably be solved by the creation of a new privately financed institution to buy and sell mortgage loan paper. At the same time, lending institutions will be given increased authority to finance real estate outside their immediate localities.

Professor Sayers has observed that "the cost of running American banking is probably rather high, as it is impossible to get the economies of large-scale organization." [102] Undoubtedly operating econo-

[101] Harold L. Reed, *op. cit.*, pp. 478–79.

[102] R. S. Sayers, *op. cit.*, p. 115.

mies would be realized from the consolidation of banks and the expansion of branch banking even though at some sacrifice of personalized service at the customer level. However, the efficiency of the check-payments system is probably much greater than a foreign observer would expect to find in a unit banking system. The widespread use of the check-deposit system in America reflects its low cost in relation to the advantages derived by the public. On the other hand the unit banking system does explain the relatively high and rigid costs of lending in some localities removed from the financial centers.

In the past, reforms in banking have too often depended for their impetus on financial or economic crises. The adaptation of the banking laws to the changing needs of the economy has been piecemeal. If banking is to keep pace with the future needs of a dynamic economy, its structure and functions need to be modernized and the role of commercial banks and those of the savings institutions more clearly defined. Eventually it is to be hoped that the banking laws will be simplified and unified and that provision will be made for periodic review.

REFERENCES

OFFICIAL PUBLICATIONS

Agriculture, Department of. *Agricultural Finance Review.*

—— Farm Credit Administration. Annual Reports.

—— Risk Problems of Production Credit Associations, Bulletin CR-5, January, 1952.

Commission on Organization of the Executive Branch of the Government, Task Force. Report on Activities and Organization of Lending Agencies of the Government. January, 1949.

Comptroller of the Currency. Digest of Opinions of the Office of the Comptroller of the Currency Relating to Operations and Powers of National Banks, August, 1948, and supplements.

—— Federal Laws Affecting National Banks, January 1, 1950.

—— Instructions of the Comptroller of the Currency Relative to the Organization and Powers of National Banks, Washington, 1928.

Congress of the United States. Joint Committee on the Economic Report, 80th Cong., 2d Sess., Credit Policies, Hearings, Washington, D.C., April, 1948.

—— Joint Committee on the Economic Report, 82d Cong., 2d Sess., Monetary Policy and the Management of the Public Debt: Replies to Questions, Parts 1 and 2; Senate Document No. 123, February, 1952; Hearings before the Subcommittee on General Credit Control and Debt Management, March, 1952; Report of the Subcommittee on General Credit Control and Debt Management, Senate Document No. 163, July, 1952.

—— House of Representatives. Committee on Banking and Currency, The Banking Act of 1935, Hearings, 74th Cong., 1st Sess., and House Report No. 742, Washington, D.C., 1935.

—— House of Representatives, Committee on Banking and Currency, 80th Cong., 1st Sess., on H. R. 2233, Direct Purchases of Government Securities by the Federal Reserve Banks, Washington, D.C., March, 1947.

—— House of Representatives, Committee on the Judiciary, Subcommittee No. 5, 82d Cong., 2d Sess., Bank Mergers and Concentration of Banking Facilities, September, 1952.

—— Senate, Committee on Banking and Currency. The Banking Act of 1935, Hearings, 74th Cong., 1st Sess., and Senate Report No. 1007, Washington, D.C., 1935.

—— Senate, Consolidation of National Banking Associations, Hearings before a Subcommittee of the Committee on Banking and Currency, 69th Cong., 1st Sess., February 16, 17, 18 and 24, 1926.

—— Subcommittee of the Committee on Banking and Currency, Operation of the National and Federal Reserve Banking Systems, Hearings, 71st Cong., 3d Sess., pursuant to S. Res. 71, 1931.

Federal Deposit Insurance Corporation. Annual Reports.

Federal Housing Administration, Mortgagees Handbook, Rev. 1952.

Federal Reserve Bank of New York. Bank Reserves, Some Major Factors Affecting Them. 1951.

—— Money Market Essays. 1952.

Federal Reserve Banks. Monthly reviews.

Federal Reserve System, Washington, D.C. Board of Governors Annual Reports.

—— Banking and Monetary Statistics. 1943.

—— Banking Studies. 1941.

—— Digest of Rulings to October 1, 1947.

—— The Federal Reserve Act as Amended.

—— The Purposes and Functions of the Federal Reserve System. 1947.

—— "Commercial and Industrial Loans at Member Banks, April 16–May 15, 1942." Three articles summarizing data received in a survey of the period April 16–May 15, 1942, reprinted from *Federal Reserve Bulletin* for August, September, and November, 1942.

—— "Commercial Bank Loans to Farmers." A group of articles summarizing the findings of a survey conducted jointly by the Federal Reserve System and the Federal Deposit Insurance Corporation as of mid-1947, reprinted from *Federal Reserve Bulletin,* October and December, 1947.

—— Concentration of Banking in the United States. Staff Report, September, 1952.

——Federal Reserve Policy. Postwar Economic Studies No. 8, November, 1947.

—— "The History of Reserve Requirements for Banks in the United States." *Federal Reserve Bulletin,* November, 1938.

Financial Statements of Certain Government Agencies. Letter from The Secretary of the Treasury, Transmitting in Further Response to Sen. Res. 150, Certain Information, 76th Cong., 3d Sess., Senate Doc. No. 172, Parts 1 and 2, Washington, D.C., 1940.

Housing and Home Financing Agency. Annual Reports. Washington, D.C.

—— Home Loan Bank Board. Savings and Home Financing Source Book. Washington, D.C., 1952.

Treasury Department. "Coins and Currency of the United States, June 30, 1947." Office of the Secretary of the Treasury, Washington, D.C.

BOOKS AND ARTICLES

Agger, Eugene E. Money and Banking Today. New York, 1941.

American Bankers Association, Bank Management Commission. Regional Clearinghouse Association Organization Manual. New York, 1940.

American Institute of Banking. Fundamentals of Banking. New York, 1951.

—— Utilizing the Weekly Federal Reserve Statement. New York, 1938.

Beckhart, B. H. "An Analysis of the Business Loans of Commercial Banks in the United States, 1933–1951." International Credit Conference, Rome, 1951.

—— The Discount Policy of the Federal Reserve System, New York, 1924.

Beckhart, B. H., and others. The New York Money Market. 4 vols. New York, 1932.

Benner, Claude L. The Federal Intermediate Credit System. New York, 1926.

Bodfish, Morton, and A. D. Theobald. Savings and Loan Principles. New York, 1940.

Boehmler, Erwin W., ed. Financial Institutions. Chicago, 1951.

Bradford, Frederick A. The Legal Status of Branch Banking in the United States. New York, 1940.

Burgess, W. Randolph. The Reserve Banks and the Money Market. Rev. ed. New York, 1946.

Burman, Raymond W. "Practical Aspects of Inventory and Receivables Financing." *Law and Contemporary Problems* (School of Law, Duke University), III, No. 4, 1948.

Butz, Earl L., The Production Credit System for Farmers. Washington, D.C., 1944.

Cagle, Caroline H., and Raymond C. Kolb, "New Commercial Banking Offices, 1936–1947." *Federal Reserve Bulletin,* May, 1948.

Cagle, C. E. "Branch, Chain, and Group Banking," Banking Studies. Board of Governors of the Federal Reserve System, 1941, pp. 113–40.

Chandler, Lester V. The Economics of Money and Banking. New York, 1948.

Chapman, John M. Bibliography on Branch Banking. New York, 1939.

Chapman, John M., and Associates. Commercial Banks and Consumer Instalment Credit. New York, 1940.

Chapman, John M., and Ray B. Westerfield. Branch Banking. New York, 1942.

Duggan, I. W., and Ralph U. Battles. Financing the Farm Business. New York, 1950.

Dunkman, William E. A Study of Savings and Savings Facilities in New York State, 1941 and 1951. Prepared for the Branch Policy Committee of the New York State Bankers Association. New York, 1952.

Freeman, Gaylord A., Jr. The Problem of Adequate Bank Capital. Illinois Bankers Association, May 23, 1952.

Garvy, George. The Development of Bank Debits and Clearings and Their Use in Economic Analysis. Washington, D.C., 1952.

Goldenweiser, E. A. American Monetary Policy. New York, 1951.

Greef, Albert O. The Commercial Paper House in the United States. Cambridge, Mass., 1938.

Hardy, Charles O. Credit Policies of the Federal Reserve System. Washington, D.C., 1932.

Harr, Luther, and W. Carlton Harris. Banking Theory and Practice. New York, 1936.

Horton, Donald C., and others. Farm Mortgage Credit Facilities in the United States. U.S. Department of Agriculture, Misc. Pub. No. 478, 1942.

Investment Bankers Association of America. Fundamentals of Investment Banking. New York, 1949.

Jacoby, Neil H., and Raymond J. Saulnier. Business Finance and Banking. National Bureau of Economic Research, New York, 1947.

—— Financing Inventory on Field Warehouse Receipts. National Bureau of Economic Research, 1942.

—— Term Lending to Business. National Bureau of Economic Research, 1942.

James, F. Cyril. The Economics of Money Credit and Banking. 3d ed. rev. New York, 1940.

Kemmerer, Edwin Walter, and Donald L. Kemmerer. The ABC of the Federal Reserve System. 12th ed. New York, 1950.

Kent, Raymond P. Money and Banking. New York, 1947.

Leffler, George L. The Stock Market. New York, 1951.

Lintner, John. Mutual Savings Banks in the Savings and Mortgage Markets. Cambridge, Mass., 1948.

Moulton, Harold G. Financial Organization and the Economic System. New York, 1938.

Myers, Margaret G. "The Peculiarity of the Commercial Banking System in the United States." International Credit Conference, Rome, 1951.

O'Hara, Jay L. Money and Banking. New York, 1948.
Petersen, J. Marvin, and D. R. Cawthorne. Money and Banking. New York, 1949.
Prather, Charles L. Money and Banking. 3d ed. Chicago, 1946.
Prochnow, Herbert V. Term Loans and Theories of Bank Liquidity. New York, 1949.
Prochnow, Herbert V., and Roy A. Foulke. Practical Bank Credit. 2d ed. rev. New York, 1950.
Prochnow, Herbert V., ed. American Financial Institutions. New York, 1951.
Reed, Harold L. Money, Currency and Banking. New York, 1942.
Ritter, Lawrence S. Money and Economic Activity, a Selection of Readings. New York, 1952.
Robinson, Roland I. "Bank Capital and Dividend Policies." *Harvard Business Review,* July, 1948.
—— The Management of Bank Funds. New York, 1951.
Rodkey, Robert G. Sound Policies for Bank Management. New York, 1944.
Saulnier, Raymond J., and Neil H. Jacoby. Financing Equipment for Commercial and Industrial Enterprise. National Bureau of Economic Research, 1944.
Sayers, R. S. American Banking System, a Sketch. London, 1948.
Schwartz, Carl Herbert. Financial Study of the Joint Stock Land Banks. Washington, D.C., 1938.
"Secured Commercial Financing." A symposium, in *Law and Contemporary Problems* (School of Law, Duke University), Vol. XIII, No. 4, Autumn, 1948.
Smith, Paul F. "Branch Banking in the United States, 1939 and 1949." *Federal Reserve Bulletin,* July, 1950.
Smith, Tynan, and Raymond E. Hengren. "Bank Capital: The Problem Restated." *Journal of Political Economy,* December, 1947.
Southworth, Shirley Donald, and John M. Chapman. Banking Facilities for Bankless Towns. New York, 1941.
Steiner, William Howard, and Eli Shapiro. Money and Banking. Rev. ed. New York, 1941.
Stockwell, Eleanor J. "Financing of Large Corporations in 1950." *Federal Reserve Bulletin,* August, 1951.
Thomas, Rollin G. Our Modern Banking and Monetary System. Rev. ed. New York, 1950.
Twentieth Century Fund, Inc. The Security Markets. New York, 1935.
Watkins, Leonard L. Commercial Banking Reform in the United States. Ann Arbor, Michigan, 1938. Michigan Business Studies, Vol. VIII, No. 5.
Welfling, Weldon. Savings Banking in New York State. Durham, N.C., 1939.
Westerfield, Ray B. Historical Survey of Branch Banking in the United States. New York, 1939.

Westerfield, Ray B. Money, Credit and Banking. Rev. ed. New York, 1947.
—— Selected Bibliography of Money, Credit, Banking and Business Finance. Cambridge, Mass., 1940.
Willis, H. Parker. The Federal Reserve System. New York, 1923.
—— The Theory and Practice of Central Banking. New York, 1936.
Willis, H. Parker, and J. I. Bogen. Investment Banking. Rev. New York, 1936.
Willis, H. Parker, and William H. Steiner. Federal Reserve Banking Practice. New York, 1926.
Willis, J. Brooke. The Functions of Commercial Banks. New York, 1942.
Willis, Parker B. The Federal Reserve Bank of San Francisco. New York, 1937.

INDEX

INDEX

Bei Fragen zur Produktsicherheit wenden Sie sich bitte an:
If you have any questions regarding product safety,
please contact:

Walter de Gruyter GmbH
Genthiner Straße 13
10785 Berlin
productsafety@degruyterbrill.com